Lecture Notes in Computer Science 9952

Commenced Publication in 1973
Founding and Former Series Editors:
Gerhard Goos, Juris Hartmanis, and Jan van Leeuwen

More information about this series at http://www.springer.com/series/7407

Tiziana Margaria · Bernhard Steffen (Eds.)

Leveraging Applications of Formal Methods, Verification and Validation

Foundational Techniques

7th International Symposium, ISoLA 2016
Imperial, Corfu, Greece, October 10–14, 2016
Proceedings, Part I

 Springer

Editors
Tiziana Margaria
Lero
Limerick
Ireland

Bernhard Steffen
TU Dortmund
Dortmund
Germany

ISSN 0302-9743 ISSN 1611-3349 (electronic)
Lecture Notes in Computer Science
ISBN 978-3-319-47165-5 ISBN 978-3-319-47166-2 (eBook)
DOI 10.1007/978-3-319-47166-2

Library of Congress Control Number: 2016953300

LNCS Sublibrary: SL1 – Theoretical Computer Science and General Issues

Printed on acid-free paper

This Springer imprint is published by Springer Nature
The registered company is Springer International Publishing AG
The registered company address is: Gewerbestrasse 11, 6330 Cham, Switzerland

Preface

Welcome to ISoLA 2016, the 7th International Symposium on Leveraging Applications of Formal Methods, Verification and Validation, that was held in Corfu, Greece during October 10–14, 2016, endorsed by EASST, the European Association of Software Science and Technology.

This year's event followed the tradition of its forerunners held 2004 and 2006 in Cyprus, 2008 in Chalkidiki, 2010 and 2012 in Crete, and 2014 in Corfu, and the series of ISoLA Workshops in Greenbelt (USA) in 2005, Poitiers (France) in 2007, Potsdam (Germany) in 2009, in Vienna (Austria) in 2011, and 2013 in Palo Alto (USA).

As in the previous editions, ISoLA 2016 provided a forum for developers, users, and researchers to discuss issues related to the *adoption and use of rigorous tools and methods* for the specification, analysis, verification, certification, construction, test, and maintenance of systems from the point of view of their different application domains. Thus, since 2004 the ISoLA series of events serves the purpose of bridging the gap between designers and developers of rigorous tools, on one hand, and users in engineering and in other disciplines on the other hand. It fosters and exploits synergetic relationships among scientists, engineers, software developers, decision makers, and other critical thinkers in companies and organizations. By providing a specific, dialogue-oriented venue for the discussion of common problems, requirements, algorithms, methodologies, and practices, ISoLA aims in particular at supporting researchers in their quest to improve the usefulness, reliability, flexibility, and efficiency of tools for building systems and users in their search for adequate solutions to their problems.

The program of the symposium consisted of a collection of *special tracks* devoted to the following hot and emerging topics:

- Correctness-by-Construction and Post-Hoc Verification: Friends or Foes?
  (Organizers: Maurice ter Beek, Reiner Haehnle, Ina Schaefer)
- Static and Runtime Verification: Competitors or Friends?
  (Organizers: Dilian Gurov, Klaus Havelund, Marieke Huisman, Rosemary Monahan)
- Testing the Internet of Things
  (Organizers: Michael Felderer, Ina Schieferdecker)
- Rigorous Engineering of Collective Adaptive Systems
  (Organizers: Stefan Jähnichen, Martin Wirsing)
- RVE: Runtime Verification and Enforcement, the (Industrial) Application Perspective
  (Organizers: Ezio Bartocci, Ylies Falcone)
- ModSyn-PP: Modular Synthesis of Programs and Processes
  (Organizers: Boris Düdder, George Heineman, Jakob Rehof)
- Variability Modelling for Scalable Software Evolution
  (Organizers: Ferruccio Damiani, Christoph Seidl, Ingrid Chieh Yu)
- Statistical Model Checking
  (Organizers: Kim Larsen, Axel Legay)

- Detecting and Understanding Software Doping
  (Organizers: Christel Baier, Holger Hermanns)
- Formal Methods and Safety Certification: Challenges in the Railways Domain
  (Organizers: Alessandro Fantechi, Stefania Gnesi)
- Semantic Heterogeneity in the Formal Development of Complex Systems
  (Organizers: Idir Ait Sadoune, Paul Gibson, Marc Pantel)
- Privacy and Security Issues in Information Systems
  (Organizers: Axel Legay, Fabrizio Biondi)
- Evaluation and Reproducibility of Program Analysis and Verification
  (Organizers: Markus Schordan, Dirk Beyer, Jonas Lundberg)
- Towards a Unified View of Modeling and Programming
  (Organizers: Manfred Broy, Klaus Havelund, Rahul Kumar, Bernhard Steffen)
- Learning Systems: Machine-Learning in Software Products and Learning-Based
  Analysis of Software Systems
  (Organizers: Falk Howar, Andreas Rausch, Karl Meinke)

The following embedded events were also hosted:

- RERS: Challenge on Rigorous Examination of Reactive Systems (Falk Howar,
  Markus Schordan, Bernhard Steffen, Jaco van de Pol)
- Doctoral Symposium and Poster Session (Anna-Lena Lamprecht)
- Tutorial: Automata Learning in Practice (Falk Howar, Karl Meinke)
- Industrial Day (Axel Hessenkämper)

Co-located with the ISoLA Symposium was:

- STRESS 2016 – 4th International School on Tool-Based Rigorous Engineering of
  Software Systems (J. Hatcliff, T. Margaria, Robby, B. Steffen)

In addition to the contributions of the main conference, the proceedings also comprise contributions of the four embedded events and tutorial papers for STRESS. We thank the track organizers, the members of the Program Committee and their reviewers for their effort in selecting the papers to be presented, the local organization chair, Petros Stratis, and the EasyConferences team for their continuous precious support during the week as well as during the entire two-year period preceding the events, and Springer for being, as usual, a very reliable partner for the publication of the proceedings. Finally, we are grateful to Kyriakos Georgiades for his continuous support for the website and the program, and to Markus Frohme, Johannes Neubauer, and Julia Rehder for their help with the online conference service (OCS).

Special thanks are due to the following organizations for their endorsement: EASST (European Association of Software Science and Technology) and Lero – The Irish Software Research Centre, and our own institutions – the TU Dortmund and the University of Limerick.

October 2016   Tiziana Margaria
                                                           Bernhard Steffen

Organization

Symposium Chair

Tiziana Margaria   Lero, Ireland

Program Chair

Bernhard Steffen   TU Dortmund, Germany

Program Committee

Yamine Ait Ameur	IRIT-ENSEEIHT, France
Idir Ait-Sadoune	SUPELEC, France
Christel Baier	TU Dresden, Germany
Ezio Bartocci	TU Wien, Austria
Dirk Beyer	LMU Munich, Germany
Fabrizio Biondi	Inria, France
Manfred Broy	TUM, Germany
Ferruccio Damiani	University of Turin, Italy
Boris Duedder	TU Dortmund, Germany
Ylies Falcone	University of Grenoble, France
Alessandro Fantechi	Università di Firenze, Italy
Michael Felderer	University of Innsbruck, Austria
Paul Gibson	Telecom Sud Paris, France
Stefania Gnesi	CNR, Italy
Kim Guldstrand Larsen	Aalborg University, Denmark
Dilian Gurov	KTH Royal Institute of Technology, Sweden
Klaus Havelund	Jet Propulsion Laboratory, USA
George Heineman	WPI, USA
Holger Hermanns	Saarland University, Germany
Axel Hessenkämper	Hottinger Baldwin Messtechnik GmbH, Germany
Falk Howar	Clausthal University of Technology, Germany
Marieke Huisman	University of Twente, The Netherlands
Reiner Hähnle	TU Darmstadt, Germany
Stefan Jaehnichen	TU Berlin, Germany
Jens Knoop	TU Wien, Austria
Anna-Lena Lamprecht	University of Limerick, Ireland
Axel Legay	Inria, France
Martin Leucker	University of Lübeck, Germany
Jonas Lundberg	Linneaus University, Sweden
Tiziana Margaria	Lero, Ireland

Karl Meinke	KTH Royal Institute of Technology, Sweden
Rosemary Monahan	NUI Maynooth, Ireland
Marc Pantel	Université de Toulouse, France
Jakob Rehof	TU Dortmund, Germany
Ina Schaefer	TU Braunschweig, Germany
Ina Schieferdecker	Fraunhofer FOKUS/TU Berlin, Germany
Markus Schordan	Lawrence Livermore National Laboratory, USA
Christoph Seidl	TU Braunschweig, Germany
Bernhard Steffen	TU Dortmund, Germany
Maurice ter Beek	ISTI-CNR, Italy
Martin Wirsing	LMU, Germany
Ingrid Chieh Yu	University of Oslo, Norway

Additional Reviewers

Vahdat Abdelzad	University of Ottawa, Canada
Michał Antkiewicz	University of Waterloo, Canada
Davide Basile	ISTI-CNR Pisa, Italy
Bernhard Beckert	Karlsruhe Institute of Technology, Germany
Lenz Belzner	LMU, Germany
Saddek Bensalem	Verimag, France
Gérard Berry	Collège de France, France
Marius Bozga	Verimag, France
Tomas Bures	Charles University Prag, Czech Republic
Laura Carnevali	STLAB, Italy
Sofia Cassel	Uppsala University, Sweden
Vincenzo Ciancia	ISTI-CNR, Italy
Loek Cleophas	TU Eindhoven, The Netherlands
Francesco Luca De Angelis	University Geneva, Switzerland
Rocco De Nicola	IMT Lucca, Italy
Julien Delange	CMU-SEI, USA
Giovanna Di Marzo Serugendo	CUI, Switzerland
Maged Elaasar	Modelware Solutions, USA
Hilding Elmqvist	Mogram AB, Sweden
Uli Fahrenberg	Inria, France
Alessio Ferrari	CNR, Italy
John Fitzgerald	Newcastle University, UK
Thomas Given-Wilson	Inria, France
Sorren Hanvey	University of Limerick, Ireland
Anne E. Haxthausen	Technical University of Denmark, Denmark
Robert Heinrichs	TU Berlin, Germany
Rolf Hennicker	LMU, Germany
Phillip James	Swansea University, UK
Einar Broch Johnsen	University of Oslo, Norway
Gabor Karsai	Vanderbilt University, USA

Contents – Part I

Statistical Model Checking

Statistical Model Checking: Past, Present, and Future   3
  Kim G. Larsen and Axel Legay

Hypothesis Testing for Rare-Event Simulation: Limitations and Possibilities . . .   16
  Daniël Reijsbergen, Pieter-Tjerk de Boer, and Werner Scheinhardt

Survey of Statistical Verification of Linear Unbounded Properties:
Model Checking and Distances   27
  Jan Křetínský

Feedback Control for Statistical Model Checking of Cyber-Physical
Systems   46
  K. Kalajdzic, C. Jegourel, A. Lukina, E. Bartocci, A. Legay,
  S.A. Smolka, and R. Grosu

Probabilistic Model Checking of Incomplete Models   62
  Shiraj Arora and M.V. Panduranga Rao

Plasma Lab: A Modular Statistical Model Checking Platform   77
  Axel Legay, Sean Sedwards, and Louis-Marie Traonouez

Synthesizing Energy-Optimal Controllers for Multiprocessor Dataflow
Applications with UPPAAL STRATEGO   94
  Waheed Ahmad and Jaco van de Pol

Statistical Model Checking for Product Lines   114
  Maurice H. ter Beek, Axel Legay, Alberto Lluch Lafuente,
  and Andrea Vandin

Towards Adaptive Scheduling of Maintenance for Cyber-Physical Systems. . . .   134
  Alexis Linard and Marcos L.P. Bueno

Better Railway Engineering Through Statistical Model Checking   151
  Enno Ruijters and Mariëlle Stoelinga

On Creation and Analysis of Reliability Models by Means of Stochastic
Timed Automata and Statistical Model Checking: Principle   166
  Josef Strnadel

Automatic Synthesis of Code Using Genetic Programming   182
  Doron Peled

Evaluation and Reproducibility of Program Analysis and Verification

Evaluation and Reproducibility of Program Analysis and Verification
(Track Introduction)   191
   Markus Schordan, Dirk Beyer, and Jonas Lundberg

Symbolic Execution with CEGAR.   195
   Dirk Beyer and Thomas Lemberger

Multi-core Model Checking of Large-Scale Reactive Systems
Using Different State Representations   212
   Marc Jasper and Markus Schordan

Sparse Analysis of Variable Path Predicates Based upon SSA-Form   227
   Thomas S. Heinze and Wolfram Amme

A Model Interpreter for Timed Automata.   243
   M. Usman Iftikhar, Jonas Lundberg, and Danny Weyns

ModSyn-PP: Modular Synthesis of Programs and Processes

ModSyn-PP: Modular Synthesis of Programs and Processes Track
Introduction   261
   Boris Düdder, George T. Heineman, and Jakob Rehof

Combinatory Process Synthesis.   266
   Jan Bessai, Andrej Dudenhefner, Boris Düdder, Moritz Martens,
   and Jakob Rehof

Synthesis from a Practical Perspective   282
   Sven Jörges, Anna-Lena Lamprecht, Tiziana Margaria, Stefan Naujokat,
   and Bernhard Steffen

A Long and Winding Road Towards Modular Synthesis   303
   George T. Heineman, Jan Bessai, Boris Düdder, and Jakob Rehof

Semantic Heterogeneity in the Formal Development of Complex Systems

Semantic Heterogeneity in the Formal Development of Complex Systems:
An Introduction   321
   J. Paul Gibson, Idir Aït-Sadoune, and Marc Pantel

On the Use of Domain and System Knowledge Modeling in Goal-Based
Event-B Specifications.   325
   Amel Mammar and Régine Laleau

Strengthening MDE and Formal Design Models by References to Domain
Ontologies. A Model Annotation Based Approach.   340
   Kahina Hacid and Yamine Ait-Ameur

Towards Functional Requirements Analytics.   358
  Zouhir Djilani, Nabila Berkani, and Ladjel Bellatreche

Heterogeneous Semantics and Unifying Theories   374
  Jim Woodcock, Simon Foster, and Andrew Butterfield

Static and Runtime Verification: Competitors or Friends?

Static and Runtime Verification, Competitors or Friends? (Track Summary) . . .   397
  Dilian Gurov, Klaus Havelund, Marieke Huisman,
  and Rosemary Monahan

StaRVOOrS — Episode II: Strengthen and Distribute the Force   402
  Wolfgang Ahrendt, Gordon J. Pace, and Gerardo Schneider

A Model-Based Approach to Combining Static and Dynamic
Verification Techniques   416
  Shaun Azzopardi, Christian Colombo, and Gordon Pace

Information Flow Analysis for Go.   431
  Eric Bodden, Ka I. Pun, Martin Steffen, Volker Stolz,
  and Anna-Katharina Wickert

Challenges in High-Assurance Runtime Verification   446
  Alwyn Goodloe

Static versus Dynamic Verification in Why3, Frama-C and SPARK 2014 . . .   461
  Nikolai Kosmatov, Claude Marché, Yannick Moy, and Julien Signoles

Considering Typestate Verification for Quantified Event Automata   479
  Giles Reger

Combining Static and Runtime Methods to Achieve Safe Standing-Up
for Humanoid Robots   496
  Francesco Leofante, Simone Vuotto, Erika Ábrahám,
  Armando Tacchella, and Nils Jansen

On Combinations of Static and Dynamic Analysis – Panel Introduction   515
  Martin Leucker

Safer Refactorings.   517
  Anna Maria Eilertsen, Anya Helene Bagge, and Volker Stolz

Rigorous Engineering of Collective Adaptive Systems

Rigorous Engineering of Collective Adaptive Systems Track Introduction . . .   535
  Stefan Jähnichen and Martin Wirsing

Programming of CAS Systems by Relying on Attribute-Based
Communication.   539
   Yehia Abd Alrahman, Rocco De Nicola, and Michele Loreti

Towards Static Analysis of Policy-Based Self-adaptive Computing Systems . . .   554
   Andrea Margheri, Hanne Riis Nielson, Flemming Nielson,
   and Rosario Pugliese

A Calculus for Open Ensembles and Their Composition   570
   Rolf Hennicker

Logic Fragments: Coordinating Entities with Logic Programs.   589
   Francesco Luca De Angelis and Giovanna Di Marzo Serugendo

Mixed-Critical Systems Design with Coarse-Grained Multi-core
Interference   605
   Peter Poplavko, Rany Kahil, Dario Socci, Saddek Bensalem,
   and Marius Bozga

A Library and Scripting Language for Tool Independent Simulation
Descriptions.   622
   Alexandra Mehlhase, Stefan Jähnichen, Amir Czwink,
   and Robert Heinrichs

Adaptation to the Unforeseen: Do we Master our Autonomous Systems?
Questions to the Panel – Panel Introduction   639
   Stefan Jähnichen and Martin Wirsing

Smart Coordination of Autonomic Component Ensembles in the Context
of Ad-Hoc Communication   642
   Tomas Bures, Petr Hnetynka, Filip Krijt, Vladimir Matena,
   and Frantisek Plasil

A Tool-Chain for Statistical Spatio-Temporal Model Checking
of Bike Sharing Systems   657
   Vincenzo Ciancia, Diego Latella, Mieke Massink, Rytis Paškauskas,
   and Andrea Vandin

Rigorous Graphical Modelling of Movement in Collective Adaptive
Systems.   674
   N. Zoń, S. Gilmore, and J. Hillston

Integration and Promotion of Autonomy with the ARE Framework   689
   Emil Vassev and Mike Hinchey

Safe Artificial Intelligence and Formal Methods (Position Paper)   704
   Emil Vassev

Engineering Adaptivity, Universal Autonomous Systems Ethics and
Compliance Issues: ISOLA'2016 - Panel Discussion Position Paper.   714
   Giovanna Di Marzo Serugendo

Correctness-by-Construction and Post-hoc Verification: Friends or Foes?

Correctness-by-Construction and Post-hoc Verification: Friends or Foes?   723
   Maurice H. ter Beek, Reiner Hähnle, and Ina Schaefer

Correctness-by-Construction and Post-hoc Verification: A Marriage
of Convenience?.   730
   Bruce W. Watson, Derrick G. Kourie, Ina Schaefer, and Loek Cleophas

Deductive Verification of Legacy Code   749
   Bernhard Beckert, Thorsten Bormer, and Daniel Grahl

Correctness-by-Construction ∧ Taxonomies ⇒ Deep Comprehension
of Algorithm Families   766
   Loek Cleophas, Derrick G. Kourie, Vreda Pieterse, Ina Schaefer,
   and Bruce W. Watson

Conditions for Compatibility of Components: The Case of Masters
and Slaves   784
   Maurice H. ter Beek, Josep Carmona, and Jetty Kleijn

A Logic for the Statistical Model Checking of Dynamic Software
Architectures   806
   Jean Quilbeuf, Everton Cavalcante, Louis-Marie Traonouez,
   Flavio Oquendo, Thais Batista, and Axel Legay

On Two Friends for Getting Correct Programs: Automatically Translating
Event B Specifications to Recursive Algorithms in RODIN   821
   Zheng Cheng, Dominique Méry, and Rosemary Monahan

Proof-Carrying Apps: Contract-Based Deployment-Time Verification   839
   Sönke Holthusen, Michael Nieke, Thomas Thüm, and Ina Schaefer

Supervisory Controller Synthesis for Product Lines Using CIF 3.   856
   Maurice H. ter Beek, Michel A. Reniers, and Erik P. de Vink

Partial Verification and Intermediate Results as a Solution to Combine
Automatic and Interactive Verification Techniques   874
   Dirk Beyer

Privacy and Security Issues in Information Systems

Security and Privacy of Protocols and Software with Formal Methods.   883
   Fabrizio Biondi and Axel Legay

A Model-Based Approach to Secure Multiparty Distributed Systems   893
  Najah Ben Said, Takoua Abdellatif, Saddek Bensalem,
  and Marius Bozga

Information Leakage Analysis of Complex C Code and Its application
to OpenSSL   909
  Pasquale Malacaria, Michael Tautchning, and Dino DiStefano

Integrated Modeling Workflow for Security Assurance   926
  Min-Young Nam, Julien Delange, and Peter Feiler

A Privacy-Aware Conceptual Model for Handling Personal Data   942
  Thibaud Antignac, Riccardo Scandariato, and Gerardo Schneider

Guaranteeing Privacy-Observing Data Exchange   958
  Christian W. Probst

Erratum to: Leveraging Applications of Formal Methods, Verification
and Validation (Part I) E1
  Tiziana Margaria and Bernhard Steffen

Author Index   971

Contents – Part II

Towards a Unified View of Modeling and Programming

Towards a Unified View of Modeling and Programming (Track Summary)   3
   Manfred Broy, Klaus Havelund, Rahul Kumar, and Bernhard Steffen

Programming $\subset$ Modeling $\subset$ Engineering   11
   Bran Selić

On a Unified View of Modeling and Programming Position Paper   27
   Ed Seidewitz

On the Feasibility of a Unified Modelling and Programming Paradigm   32
   Anne E. Haxthausen and Jan Peleska

Modeling Meets Programming: A Comparative Study in Model Driven
Engineering Action Languages   50
   Maged Elaasar and Omar Badreddin

Abstractions for Modeling Complex Systems   68
   Zsolt Lattmann, Tamás Kecskés, Patrik Meijer, Gábor Karsai,
   Péter Völgyesi, and Ákos Lédeczi

Specifying and Verifying Advanced Control Features   80
   Gary T. Leavens, David Naumann, Hridesh Rajan, and Tomoyuki Aotani

Simplifying OMG MOF-Based Metamodeling   97
   Nicolas F. Rouquette

Modelling and Testing of Real Systems   119
   Andreas Prinz, Birger Møller-Pedersen, and Joachim Fischer

Unifying Modelling and Programming: A Systems Biology Perspective   131
   Hillel Kugler

Formally Unifying Modeling and Design for Embedded Systems -
A Personal View.   134
   G. Berry

Interactive Model-Based Compilation Continued – Incremental Hardware
Synthesis for SCCharts   150
   Francesca Rybicki, Steven Smyth, Christian Motika,
   Alexander Schulz-Rosengarten, and Reinhard von Hanxleden

Towards Semantically Integrated Models and Tools for Cyber-Physical
Systems Design 171
   Peter Gorm Larsen, John Fitzgerald, Jim Woodcock, René Nilsson,
   Carl Gamble, and Simon Foster

Merging Modeling and Programming Using Umple.................... 187
   Timothy C. Lethbridge, Vahdat Abdelzad, Mahmoud Husseini Orabi,
   Ahmed Husseini Orabi, and Opeyemi Adesina

Systems Modeling and Programming in a Unified Environment Based on
Julia 198
   Hilding Elmqvist, Toivo Henningsson, and Martin Otter

Meta-Level Reuse for Mastering Domain Specialization............... 218
   Stefan Naujokat, Johannes Neubauer, Tiziana Margaria,
   and Bernhard Steffen

Towards a Unified View of Modeling and Programming 238
   Manfred Broy, Klaus Havelund, and Rahul Kumar

**Formal Methods and Safety Certification: Challenges in the
Railways Domain**

Formal Methods and Safety Certification: Challenges in the Railways
Domain 261
   Alessandro Fantechi, Alessio Ferrari, and Stefania Gnesi

On the Use of Static Checking in the Verification of Interlocking Systems... 266
   Anne E. Haxthausen and Peter H. Østergaard

Compositional Verification of Multi-station Interlocking Systems 279
   Hugo D. Macedo, Alessandro Fantechi, and Anne E. Haxthausen

OnTrack: The Railway Verification Toolset: Extended Abstract 294
   Phillip James, Faron Moller, Hoang Nga Nguyen, Markus Roggenbach,
   Helen Treharne, and Xu Wang

Experiments in Formal Modelling of a Deadlock Avoidance Algorithm
for a CBTC System...................................... 297
   Franco Mazzanti, Alessio Ferrari, and Giorgio O. Spagnolo

Tuning Energy Consumption Strategies in the Railway Domain:
A Model-Based Approach 315
   Davide Basile, Felicita Di Giandomenico, and Stefania Gnesi

RVE: Runtime Verification and Enforcement, the (Industrial) Application Perspective

Runtime Verification and Enforcement, the (Industrial) Application
Perspective (Track Introduction) 333
   Ezio Bartocci and Ylies Falcone

What Is a Trace? A Runtime Verification Perspective 339
   Giles Reger and Klaus Havelund

Execution Trace Analysis Using LTL-FO$^+$ 356
   Raphaël Khoury, Sylvain Hallé, and Omar Waldmann

Challenges in Fault-Tolerant Distributed Runtime Verification 363
   Borzoo Bonakdarpour, Pierre Fraigniaud, Sergio Rajsbaum,
   and Corentin Travers

The HARMONIA Project: Hardware Monitoring for Automotive
Systems-of-Systems. 371
   Thang Nguyen, Ezio Bartocci, Dejan Ničković, Radu Grosu,
   Stefan Jaksic, and Konstantin Selyunin

Runtime Verification for Interconnected Medical Devices. 380
   Martin Leucker, Malte Schmitz, and Danilo à Tellinghusen

Dynamic Analysis of Regression Problems in Industrial Systems:
Challenges and Solutions 388
   Fabrizio Pastore and Leonardo Mariani

Towards a Logic for Inferring Properties of Event Streams. 394
   Sean Kauffman, Rajeev Joshi, and Klaus Havelund

Runtime Verification for Stream Processing Applications 400
   Christian Colombo, Gordon J. Pace, Luke Camilleri, Claire Dimech,
   Reuben Farrugia, Jean Paul Grech, Alessio Magro, Andrew C. Sammut,
   and Kristian Zarb Adami

On the Runtime Enforcement of Evolving Privacy Policies in Online Social
Networks 407
   Gordon J. Pace, Raúl Pardo, and Gerardo Schneider

On the Specification and Enforcement of Privacy-Preserving Contractual
Agreements 413
   Gerardo Schneider

Variability Modeling for Scalable Software Evolution

Introduction to the Track on Variability Modeling for Scalable Software
Evolution   423
   Ferruccio Damiani, Christoph Seidl, and Ingrid Chieh Yu

Towards Incremental Validation of Railway Systems   433
   Reiner Hähnle and Radu Muschevici

Modeling and Optimizing Automotive Electric/Electronic (E/E)
Architectures: Towards Making Clafer Accessible to Practitioners   447
   Eldar Khalilov, Jordan Ross, Michał Antkiewicz, Markus Völter,
   and Krzysztof Czarnecki

Variability-Based Design of Services for Smart Transportation Systems   465
   Maurice H. ter Beek, Alessandro Fantechi, Stefania Gnesi,
   and Laura Semini

Comparing AWS Deployments Using Model-Based Predictions   482
   Einar Broch Johnsen, Jia-Chun Lin, and Ingrid Chieh Yu

A Toolchain for Delta-Oriented Modeling of Software Product Lines   497
   Cristina Chesta, Ferruccio Damiani, Liudmila Dobriakova,
   Marco Guernieri, Simone Martini, Michael Nieke, Vítor Rodrigues,
   and Sven Schuster

A Technology-Neutral Role-Based Collaboration Model for Software
Ecosystems   512
   Ştefan Stănciulescu, Daniela Rabiser, and Christoph Seidl

Adaptable Runtime Monitoring for the Java Virtual Machine   531
   Andrea Rosà, Yudi Zheng, Haiyang Sun, Omar Javed,
   and Walter Binder

Identifying Variability in Object-Oriented Code Using Model-Based Code
Mining   547
   David Wille, Michael Tiede, Sandro Schulze, Christoph Seidl,
   and Ina Schaefer

User Profiles for Context-Aware Reconfiguration in Software Product Lines . . .   563
   Michael Nieke, Jacopo Mauro, Christoph Seidl, and Ingrid Chieh Yu

Refactoring Delta-Oriented Product Lines to Enforce Guidelines
for Efficient Type-Checking   579
   Ferruccio Damiani and Michael Lienhardt

Detecting and Understanding Software Doping

Detecting and Understanding Software Doping — Track Introduction   598
  Christel Baier and Holger Hermanns

Facets of Software Doping   601
  *Gilles Barthe, Pedro R. D'Argenio, Bernd Finkbeiner,
  and Holger Hermanns*

Software that Meets Its Intent   609
  *Marieke Huisman, Herbert Bos, Sjaak Brinkkemper, Arie van Deursen,
  Jan Friso Groote, Patricia Lago, Jaco van de Pol, and Eelco Visser*

Compliance, Functional Safety and Fault Detection by Formal Methods   626
  Christof Fetzer, Christoph Weidenbach, and Patrick Wischnewski

What the Hack Is Wrong with Software Doping?   633
  Kevin Baum

Learning Systems: Machine-Learning in Software Products and Learning-Based Analysis of Software Systems

Learning Systems: Machine-Learning in Software Products and
Learning-Based Analysis of Software Systems: Special Track at ISoLA
2016   651
  Falk Howar, Karl Meinke, and Andreas Rausch

ALEX: Mixed-Mode Learning of Web Applications at Ease   655
  *Alexander Bainczyk, Alexander Schieweck, Malte Isberner,
  Tiziana Margaria, Johannes Neubauer, and Bernhard Steffen*

Assuring the Safety of Advanced Driver Assistance Systems Through a
Combination of Simulation and Runtime Monitoring   672
  Malte Mauritz, Falk Howar, and Andreas Rausch

Enhancement of an Adaptive HEV Operating Strategy Using Machine
Learning Algorithms   688
  *Mark Schudeleit, Meng Zhang, Xiaofei Qi, Ferit Küçükay,
  and Andreas Rausch*

Testing the Internet of Things

Testing the Internet of Things   704
  Michael Felderer and Ina Schieferdecker

Data Science Challenges to Improve Quality Assurance of Internet of
Things Applications.   707
   Harald Foidl and Michael Felderer

Model-Based Testing as a Service for IoT Platforms   727
   *Abbas Ahmad, Fabrice Bouquet, Elizabeta Fourneret, Franck Le Gall,
   and Bruno Legeard*

Doctoral Symposium

ISoLA Doctoral Symposium.   744
   Anna-Lena Lamprecht

Handling Domain Knowledge in Formal Design Models: An Ontology
Based Approach   747
   Kahina Hacid

Industrial Track

A Retrospective of the Past Four Years with Industry 4.0   754
   Axel Hessenkämper

Effective and Efficient Customization Through Lean Trans-Departmental
Configuration   757
   Barbara Steffen, Steve Boßelmann, and Axel Hessenkämper

A Fully Model-Based Approach to Software Development for Industrial
Centrifuges.   774
   Nils Wortmann, Malte Michel, and Stefan Naujokat

RERS Challenge

RERS 2016: Parallel and Sequential Benchmarks with Focus on LTL
Verification   787
   *Maren Geske, Marc Jasper, Bernhard Steffen, Falk Howar,
   Markus Schordan, and Jaco van de Pol*

STRESS

Introduction   806

DIME: A Programming-Less Modeling Environment for Web Applications . . .   809
   *Steve Boßelmann, Markus Frohme, Dawid Kopetzki, Michael Lybecait,
   Stefan Naujokat, Johannes Neubauer, Dominic Wirkner,
   Philip Zweihoff, and Bernhard Steffen*

Verification Techniques for Hybrid Systems.   833
    Pavithra Prabhakar, Miriam Garcia Soto, and Ratan Lal

On the Power of Statistical Model Checking.   843
    Kim G. Larsen and Axel Legay

Erratum to: Verification Techniques for Hybrid Systems E1
    Pavithra Prabhakar, Miriam Garcia Soto, and Ratan Lal

Author Index   863

Statistical Model Checking

Statistical Model Checking

Statistical Model Checking:
Past, Present, and Future

Kim G. Larsen and Axel Legay[(✉)]

Aalborg University Inria, Aalborg, Denmark
axel.legay@inria.fr

Abstract. Statistical Model Checking (SMC) is a compromise between verification and testing where executions of the systems are monitored until an algorithm from statistics can produce an estimate for the system to satisfy a given property.

The objective of this introduction is to summarizes SMC as well as a series of challenges for which contributors at Isola propose a solution.

Contributions include new SMC toolsets, new flexible SMC algorithms for larger classes of systems, and new applications.

1 Introduction

Computers play a central role in modern life and their errors can have dramatic consequences. For example, such mistakes could jeopardize the banking system of a country or, more dramatically, endanger human life through the failure of some safety systems. It is therefore not surprising that proving the correctness of computer systems is a highly relevant problem.

The most common method to ensure the correctness of a system is *testing* (see [BJK+05] for a survey). After the computer system is constructed, it is tested using a number of *test cases* with predicted outcomes. Testing techniques have shown effectiveness in bug hunting in many industrial problems. Unfortunately, testing is not a panacea. Indeed, since there is, in general, no way for a finite set of test cases to cover all possible scenarios, errors may remain undetected.

There are also methods that can ensure the full correctness of a system. Those methods, also called *formal methods*, use mathematical techniques to check whether the system will behave correctly for all possible scenarios. There are several mathematical representations for a system. In this thesis, we will consider (extensions of) *Transition Systems*. The behaviors of a transition system can be represented by (possibly infinite) sequences of state changes and time stamps, which we call *executions*. The relation between successive states being obtained by a so-called *transition relation*. This relation may not be finite; it may also be implicit.

There is a long history of formal methods, going from logical proofs and invariants to model checking [BK08]. In this thesis, we focus on the second approach. It consists in checking that each behavior of the system satisfies a given requirement by exploring its state-space. In early work on the subject,

© Springer International Publishing AG 2016
T. Margaria and B. Steffen (Eds.): ISoLA 2016, Part I, LNCS 9952, pp. 3–15, 2016.
DOI: 10.1007/978-3-319-47166-2_1

requirements are often expressed in some temporal logic such as Linear Temporal Logic [Pnu77], or computational Tree Logic [CE81]. Those logics extend classical Boolean logics with (quantification of) temporal operators that allows us to reason on the temporal dimension of a given execution.

It can be shown that solving the model checking problem boils down to compute a (repeated) set of reachable states [CGP99]. A simple state-space exploration technique starts the exploration from the set of initial states and then adds new reachable states by applying the reachability relation. If the number of states is finite, repeating this operation will eventually produce a stable set, that is the set of reachable states of the system. However, even for simple systems, finite-state spaces can be much too large to be computed and represented with realistic amounts of computer resources. For several decades now, researchers have been looking at ways to reduce the computational burden associated with these state space exploration based techniques.

A first family of strategies developed for coping with large state spaces is to exploit similarities and repetitive information. Among such techniques, one finds the so-called partial reduction [WG93,FG05]. This approach avoids the exploration of sequences of states by showing that their effect is already captured by another sequence. Another technique is called bisimulation reduction [DPP04]. It exploits equivalence classes of bisimilar states (i.e., states that generate the same behaviors) to reduce the state space. Predicate abstraction techniques [BMR05] extend bisimulation reduction by abstracting sets with a given predicate that subsumes their behaviors. The difficulty being to find the predicate that do not blow up the set of behaviors artificially. Predicate abstraction based techniques can be combined with CounterExample approaches used to calibrate the precision of the abstraction [CV03].

In addition to compute state-space, one of the major difficulties in model checking is to represent sets of state in an efficient way. One of the very first family of strategies developed for coping with large state spaces is based on symbolic methods which use symbolic representation to manipulate set of states implicitly rather than explicitly. Symbolic methods have managed to broaden the applicability of simple analysis methods, such as state space exploration, to systems with impressively large sets of states. One of the most used symbolic representation is known as Binary Decision Diagrams (BDD in short) [Bry92]. In BDDs, the states of the system are encoded with fixed-length bit vectors. In such a context, a finite set of states can be viewed as the set of solutions of a Boolean formula for which a BDD provides a representation that is often more compact than conjunctive or disjunctive normal form. This representation, algorithmically easy to handle, allows to efficiently represent the regular structure that often appears in the set of reachable states of finite state-transition systems. The BDD-based approach has been used to verify systems with more than 10^{20} reachable states [BCM+92], and it is now well-admitted that Boolean formal verification of large-size systems can be performed. Over the last decade, BDD have been replaced (or combined with) logical representation. Those consists in representing the sequence of states via formulas, and then use a sat-solvers to check for a reachable state [BCCZ99,GPS02].

For two decades, logics and formal models did not exploit and model informations such as real-time or probabilities. This is however needed to reason large class of systems such as Embedded systems, Cyber physical systems, or systems biology. There, one is more interested in computing the level of energy needed to stay above a certain threshold, or the time needed to reach a given state. Motivated by this observation, the research community extended transitions systems with the ability to handle quantitative features. This includes, e.g., the formalism of timed automata [A.99] that exploits real-time informations to guide the executions, stochastic systems that can capture uncertainty in the executions, or weighted automata which permits to quantify the weight of a set of transitions [DG07]. In a similar fashion, LTL/CTL were extended with timed and quantitative informations. Those formalisms have been largely discussed in the literature, and have extended to other classes such as energy automata, or hybrid systems. It has been observed that reasoning on quantities amplifies the state-space explosion problem. However, tools such as UPPAAL or PRISM provided efficient approaches to partly overcome those problems. In this work, we focus on the stochastic aspects.

1.1 The Stochastic World: Towards SMC

Among the prominent extensions of transitions sytems, one finds quantitative sytems whose transitions are equipped with a probability distribution. This category includes, e.g., both discrete and continuous timed Markov Chains[1]. Our main interest will be in computing the probability to satisfy a given property of a stochastic system. This quantification replaces the Boolean world and permits us to quantify the impact of changes made on a given system.

Like classical transition systems, quantitative properties of stochastic systems are usually specified in linear temporal logics that allow one to compare the measure of executions satisfying certain temporal properties with thresholds. The model checking problem for stochastic systems with respect to such logics is typically solved by a numerical approach that, like state-space exploration, iteratively computes (or approximates) the exact measure of paths satisfying relevant subformulas. The algorithm for computing such measures depends on the class of stochastic systems being considered as well as the logics used for specifying the correctness properties. Model checking algorithms for a variety of contexts have been discovered [BHHK03,CY95,CG04] and there are mature tools (see e.g. [KNP04,CB06]) that have been used to analyze a variety of systems in practice.

Despite the great strides made by numerical model checking algorithms, there are many challenges. Numerical algorithms work only for special systems that have certain structural properties. Further the algorithms require a lot of time and space, and thus scaling to large systems is a challenge. In addition, the logics for which model checking algorithms exist are extensions of classical temporal

---

[1] As we shall see later, stochastic systems may deal with additional quantities such as real-time.

logics, which are often not the most popular among engineers. Finally, those numerical techniques do not allows us to consider extended stochastic models whose semantics also depends on other quantities such as real-time, or energy.

Another approach to verify quantitative properties of stochastic systems is to *simulate* the system for finitely many runs, and use techniques coming from the area of statistics to infer whether the samples provide a *statistical* evidence for the satisfaction or violation of the specification [YS02]. The crux of this approach is that since sample runs of a stochastic system are drawn according to the distribution defined by the system, they can be used to get estimates of the probability measure on executions. Those techniques are known under the name of Statistical Model Checking (SMC).

The SMC approach enjoys many advantages. First, these algorithms only require that the system be simulatable (or rather, sample executions be drawn according to the measure space defined by the system). Thus, it can be applied to larger class of systems than numerical model checking algorithms including black-box systems and infinite state systems. Second the approach can be generalized to a larger class of properties, including Fourier transform based logics. Finally, the algorithm is easily parallelizable, which can help scale to large systems. In case the problem is undecidable or too complex, SMC is often the only viable solution. SMC algorithms have been implemented in a series of tools such as Ymer [You05a], PRISM [KNP11], or UPPAAL [DLL+11]. Recently, we have implemented a series of SMC techniques in a flexible and modular toolset called Plasma Lab [BCLS13]. In the next section, we introduce the basic SMC algorithm and the major challenges that will be tackled at Isola.

2   Statistical Model Checking: A Brief Technical Introduction

Model of Computation. We consider a set of states S and a time domain $T \subseteq \mathbb{R}$. We first introduce the general definition of stochastic systems.

Definition 1 (Stochastic system). *A stochastic system over S and T is a family of random variables $\mathcal{X} = \{X_t \mid t \in T\}$, each random variable X_t having range S.*

The definition of a stochastic system as a family of random variables is quite general and includes systems with both continuous and discrete dynamics. In this thesis, we will focus our attention on a limited, but important, class of stochastic system: stochastic discrete event systems, which we note $\mathcal{S} = (S, T)$. This class includes any stochastic system that can be thought of as occupying a single state for a duration of time before an event causes an instantaneous state transition to occur. An *execution* for a stochastic system is any sequence of observations $\{x_t \in S \mid t \in T\}$ of the random variables $X_t \in \mathcal{X}$. It can be represented as a sequence $\omega = (s_0, t_0), (s_1, t_1), \ldots, (s_n, t_n) \ldots$, such that $s_i \in S$ and $t_i \in T$, with time stamps monotonically increasing, e.g. $t_i < t_{i+1}$. Let $0 \le i \le n$, we denote $\omega^i = (s_i, t_i), \ldots, (s_n, t_n)$ the suffix of ω starting at position i. Let $\bar{s} \in S$, we denote $Path(\bar{s})$ the set of executions of $\mathcal{X}$ that starts in state $(\bar{s}, 0)$ (also called initial state) and $Path^n(\bar{s})$ the set of executions of length n.

In [You05a], Youness showed that the executions set of a stochastic system is a measurable space, which defines a probability measure μ over $Path(\bar{s})$. The precise definition of μ depends on the specific probability structure of the stochastic system being studied.

Requirements. In this thesis, except if explicitly mentioned, Properties over traces of Sys are defined via the so-called Bounded Linear Temporal Logic (BLTL). BLTL restricts Linear Temporal Logic by bounding the scope of the temporal operators. The syntax of BLTL is defined as follows:

$$\phi = \phi \vee \phi \mid \phi \wedge \phi \mid \neg \phi \mid F^{\leq t}\phi \mid G^{\leq t}\phi \mid \phi U^{\leq t}\phi \mid X\phi \mid \alpha$$

$\vee, \wedge$ and $\neg$ are the standard logical connectives and α is a Boolean constant or an atomic proposition constructed from numerical constants, state variables and relational operators. X is the *next* temporal operator: $X\phi$ means that ϕ will be true on the next step. F, G and U are temporal operators bounded by time interval $[0, t]$, relative to the time interval of any enclosing formula. We refer to this as a *relative interval*. F is the *finally* or *eventually* operator: $F^{\leq t}\phi$ means that ϕ will be true at least once in the relative interval $[0, t]$. G is the *globally* or *always* operator: $G^{\leq t}\phi$ means that ϕ will be true at all times in the relative interval $[0, t]$. U is the *until* operator: $\psi U_{\leq t}\phi$ means that in the relative interval $[0, t]$, either ϕ is initially true or ψ will be true until ϕ is true. Combining these temporal operators creates complex properties with interleaved notions of *eventually* (F), *always* (G) and *one thing after another* (U).

Verifying BLTL Properties: A Simulation Approach. Consider a stochastic system (S, T) and a property ϕ. *Statistical model checking* refers to a series of simulation-based techniques that can be used to answer two questions: (1) **Qualitative:** Is the probability that (S, T) satisfies ϕ greater or equal to a certain threshold? and (2) **Quantitative:** What is the probability that (S, T) satisfies ϕ? Contrary to numerical approaches, the answer is given up to some correctness precision. As we shall see latter, SMC solves those problems with two different approaches, while classical numerical approaches only solve the second problem, which implies the first one, but is harder.

In the rest of the section, we overview several statistical model checking techniques. Let B_i be a discrete random variable with a Bernoulli distribution of parameter p. Such a variable can only take 2 values 0 and 1 with $Pr[B_i = 1] = p$ and $Pr[B_i = 0] = 1 - p$. In our context, each variable B_i is associated with one simulation of the system. The outcome for B_i, denoted b_i, is 1 if the simulation satisfies ϕ and 0 otherwise. The latter is decided with the help of a monitoring[2] procedure [HR02]. The objective of an SMC algorithm is to generate simulations and exploit the Bernouili outcomes to extract a global confidence on the system.

---

[2] This thesis is not concerned with the definition of efficient monitoring procedures.

In the next subsections, we present three algorithms used in history work on SMC to solve both the quantitative and the qualitative problems. Extension of those algorithms to unbounded temporal operators [SVA05,HCZ11] and to nested probabilistic operators exist [You05b]. As shown in [JKO+07] those extensions or debatable and often slower than their. Consequently, we will not discuss them.

2.1   Qualitative Answer Using Statistical Model Checking

The main approaches [You05a,SVA04] proposed to answer the qualitative question are based on *hypothesis testing*. Let $p = Pr(\phi)$, to determine whether $p \geq \theta$, we can test $H : p \geq \theta$ against $K : p < \theta$. A test-based solution does not guarantee a correct result but it is possible to bound the probability of making an error. The *strength* (α, β) of a test is determined by two parameters, α and β, such that the probability of accepting K (respectively, H) when H (respectively, K) holds, called a Type-I error (respectively, a Type-II error), is less or equal to α (respectively, β).

A test has *ideal performance* if the probability of the Type-I error (respectively, Type-II error) is exactly α (respectively, β). However, these requirements make it impossible to ensure a low probability for both types of errors simultaneously (see [You05a] for details). A solution to this problem is to relax the test by working with an *indifference region* (p_1, p_0) with $p_0 \geq p_1$ ($p_0 - p_1$ is the *size of the region*). In this context, we test the hypothesis $H_0 : p \geq p_0$ against $H_1 : p \leq p_1$ instead of H against K. If the value of p is between p_1 and p_0 (the indifference region), then we say that the probability is sufficiently close to θ so that we are indifferent with respect to which of the two hypotheses K or H is accepted. The thresholds p_0 and p_1 are generally defined in terms of the single threshold θ, e.g., $p_1 = \theta - \delta$ and $p_0 = \theta + \delta$. We now need to provide a test procedure that satisfies the requirements above. In the next two subsections, we recall two solutions proposed by Younes in [You05a,You06].

Single Sampling Plan. This algorithm is more for history than for direct usage. However, it is still exploited in subsequent algorithms. To test H_0 against H_1, we specify a constant c. If $\sum_{i=1}^{n} b_i$ is larger than c, then H_0 is accepted, else H_1 is accepted. The difficult part in this approach is to find values for the pair (n, c), called a *single sampling plan (SSP in short)*, such that the two error bounds α and β are respected. In practice, one tries to work with the smallest value of n possible so as to minimize the number of simulations performed. Clearly, this number has to be greater if α and β are smaller but also if the size of the indifference region is smaller. This results in an optimization problem, which generally does not have a closed-form solution except for a few special cases [You05a]. In his thesis [You05a], Younes proposes a binary search based algorithm that, given p_0, p_1, α, β, computes an approximation of the minimal value for c and n.

Sequential Probability Ratio Test (SPRT). The sample size for a single sampling plan is fixed in advance and independent of the observations that are made.

However, taking those observations into account can increase the performance of the test. As an example, if we use a single plan (n, c) and the $m > c$ first simulations satisfy the property, then we could (depending on the error bounds) accept H_0 without observing the $n-m$ other simulations. To overcome this problem, one can use the *sequential probability ratio test (SPRT in short)* proposed by Wald [Wal45]. The approach is briefly described below.

In SPRT, one has to choose two values A and B $(A > B)$ that ensure that the strength of the test is respected. Let m be the number of observations that have been made so far. The test is based on the following quotient:

$$\frac{p_{1m}}{p_{0m}} = \prod_{i=1}^{m} \frac{Pr(B_i = b_i | p = p_1)}{Pr(B_i = b_i | p = p_0)} = \frac{p_1^{d_m}(1-p_1)^{m-d_m}}{p_0^{d_m}(1-p_0)^{m-d_m}}, \tag{1}$$

where $d_m = \sum_{i=1}^{m} b_i$. The idea behind the test is to accept H_0 if $\frac{p_{1m}}{p_{0m}} \geq A$, and H_1 if $\frac{p_{1m}}{p_{0m}} \leq B$. The SPRT algorithm computes $\frac{p_{1m}}{p_{0m}}$ for successive values of m until either H_0 or H_1 is satisfied; the algorithm terminates with probability 1[Wal45]. This has the advantage of minimizing the number of simulations. In his thesis [You05a], Younes proposed a logarithmic based algorithm SPRT that given p_0, p_1, α and β implements the sequential ratio testing procedure.

SPRT has been largely used in the formal methods area. In this thesis, we shall show that the approach extends to a much larger class of problems that the one originally foreseen.

2.2 Quantitative Answer Using Statistical Model Checking and Estimation

In the case of estimation, existing SMC algorithms rely on classical Monte Carlo estimation. More precisely, they calculate a priori the required number of simulations according to a Chernoff bound [Oka59] that allows the user to specify an error ε and a probability δ that the estimate $\hat{p}$ will not lie outside the true value $\pm\varepsilon$. Given that a system has true probability p of satisfying a property, the Chernoff bound ensures $P(|\hat{p} - p| \geq \varepsilon) \leq \delta$. Parameter δ is related to the number of simulations N by $\delta = 2e^{-2N\varepsilon^2}$ [Oka59], giving

$$N = \left\lceil (\ln 2 - \ln \delta)/(2\varepsilon^2) \right\rceil. \tag{2}$$

2.3 On Expected Number of Simulations

The efficiency of the above algorithms is characterized by the number of simulations needed to obtain an answer. This number may change from executions to executions and can only be estimated (see [You05a] for an explanation). However, some generalities are known. For the qualitative case, it is known that, except for some situations, SPRT is always faster than SSP. When $\theta = 1$ (resp. $\theta = 0$) SPRT degenerates to SSP; this is not problematic since SSP is known to be optimal for such values. Monte Carlo can also be used to solve the qualitative problem, but it is always slower than SSP [You05a]. If θ is unknown, then a good strategy is to estimate it using Monte Carlo with a low confidence and then validate the result with SPRT and a strong confidence.

2.4   Challenges

Unfortunately, the SMC approach we introduced above is not a panacea and many important classes of systems and properties are still out of its scope. This includes, e.g., unbounded properties. Moreover, In addition, SMC still indirectly suffers from an explosion linked to the number of simulations needed to converge when estimating small probabilities, a.k.a rare events. Finally,the approach has not yet been lifted to a professional toolset directly usable by industry people. Consequently, it remains unclear whether the approach can handle applications that are beyond the academic world.

This session proposes solutions to those challenges.

3   Contribution to the Track

This tracks contains several contributions to improve the weakness of SMC pointed in the previous section. Those are divided into three main categories, that are 1. imrpoving SMC algorithm in terms of speeds or models that can be handled, 2. improving tooling, and 3. applying SMC to new categories. A summary is given here after.

3.1   On Extension of SMC Algorithms

– Statistical model checking avoids the exponential growth of states associated with probabilistic model checking by estimating probabilities from multiple executions of a system and by giving results within confidence bounds. Rare properties are often important but pose a particular challenge for simulation-based approaches, hence a key objective for SMC is to reduce the number and length of simulations necessary to produce a result with a given level of confidence. In the literature, one finds two techniques to cope with rare events: *Importance Sampling* (IS) and *importance Splitting* (IP). One of the majors problems with IS simulation is that it does not yield 0/1-outcomes, as assumed by the existing hypothesis tests, but likelihood ratios that are typically close to zero, but may also take large values. In [RdBS], the authors consider two possible ways of combining IS and SMC. One involves an easily applicable IS-scheme that yields likelihood ratios with bounded support when applied to a certain (nontrivial) class of models. The other involves a particular hypothesis testing scheme that does not require a-priori knowledge about the samples, only that their variance is estimated well.
– One of the major limitations of SMC is that it is limited to bounded properties, i.e., properties that can be evaluated on finite traces. A series of recent work shows that this situation can be improved for several classes of systems/property. In [Kre], the author survey statistical verification techniques aiming at linear properties with unbounded or infinite horizon, as opposed to properties of runs of fixed length. Moreover, the author also discusses when it is possible to statistically estimate linear distances between Markov chains.

- One of the major difficulties of stochastic model checking is to obtain a model on which SMC can be applied. In [JLL+], the authors introduce feedback-control statistical system checking (FCSSC), a new approach to statistical model checking that exploits principles of feedback-control for the analysis of cyber-physical systems (CPS). FC-SSC uses stochastic system identification to learn a CPS model, importance sampling to estimate the CPS state, and importance splitting to control the CPS so that the probability that the CPS satisfies a given property can be efficiently inferred. They show the applicability of the approach on concrete applications.
- It is crucial for accurate model checking that the model be a complete and faithful representation of the system. Unfortunately, this is not always possible, mainly because of two reasons: (i) the model is still under development and (ii) the correctness of implementation of some modules is not established. In [AM], the author examinates circumstances, is it still possible to get correct answers for some model checking queries in the case of PCTL and Markov Chains.

3.2 On Tools

1. In [LST], the authors present an overview of Plasma Lab, a modular statistical model checking (SMC) platform that facilitates multiple SMC algorithms, multiple modelling and query languages and has multiple modes of use. Plasma Lab may be used as a stand-alone tool with a graphical development environment or invoked from the command line for high performance scripting applications. Plasma Lab is written in Java for maximum cross-platform compatibility, but it may interface with tools and libraries written in arbitrary programming languages. Plasma Lab's API also allows it to be incorporated as a library within other tools.
2. Streaming applications for mobile platforms impose high demands on a system's throughput and energy consumption. Dynamic system-level techniques have been introduced, to reduce power consumption at the expense of performance. We consider DPM (Dynamic Power Management) and DVFS (Dynamic Voltage and Frequency Scaling). The complex programming task now includes mapping and scheduling every task onto a heterogeneous multiprocessor hardware platform. Moreover, DPM and DVFS parameters must be controlled, to meet all throughput constraints while minimizing the energy consumption. In [AvdP], the authors experiment with an alternative approach, based on stochastic hybrid games. Their main contribution is to compare simulation-based tools applied to this problematic.

3.3 On New Applications

- In [tBLVL], the authors examine the problem of applying SMC to systems with variability. They mostly focus on product lines paradigm. They report on the suitability of statistical model checking for the analysis of quantitative properties of product line models by an extended treatment of earlier work by the authors. The type of analysis that can be performed includes the likelihood of specific product behaviour, the expected average cost of products (in terms of the attributes of the products' features) and the probability of features to be (un)installed at runtime. They illustrate the feasibility of their framework by applying it to a case study of a product line of bikes.

- Scheduling and control of Cyber-Physical Systems (CPS) are becoming increasingly complex, requiring the development of new techniques that can effectively lead to their advancement. This is also the case for failure detection and scheduling component replacements. In [LdPB], the authors propose a technique that not only relies on machine learning classification models in order to classify component failure cases vs. non-failure cases, but also on real-time updating of the maintenance policy of the sub-system in question. The technique is implemented in UPPAAL.

- In [RS], the authors present a framework, fault maintenance trees (FMTs), integrating maintenance into the industry-standard formalism of fault trees. By translating FMTs to priced timed automata and applying statistical model checking, we can obtain system dependability metrics such as system reliability and mean time to failure, as well as costs of maintenance and failures over time, for different maintenance policies. The approach is applied on two case studies from the railway industry: electrically insulated joints, and pneumatic compressors.

- Finally, the work in [Str] presents a panacea of applications for Statistical Model Checking on timed stochastic systems.

4   Conclusion

In this track, the authors have presented major advances for Statistical Model Checking. However, a lot remains to do. This include, e.g., better strategies to handle non determinism, more applications to real-life systems, or combining SMC with other approaches such as machine learning or testing.

References

[A.99]   Alur, R.: Timed automata. In: Halbwachs, N., Peled, D. (eds.) CAV 1999. LNCS, vol. 1633, pp. 8–22. Springer, Heidelberg (1999). doi:10.1007/3-540-48683-6_3

[AM]   Arora, S.: Panduranga Rao, M.V.: Probabilistic model checking of incomplete models. In: Margaria, T., Steffen, B. (eds.) ISoLA 2016, Part I. LNCS, vol. 9952, pp. 62–76. Springer, Cham (2016)

[AvdP]   Ahmad, W., van de Pol, J.: Synthesizing energy-optimal controllers for multi-processor dataflow applications with uppaal. In: Margaria, T., Steffen, B. (eds.) ISoLA 2016, Part I. LNCS, vol. 9952, pp. 94–113. Springer, Cham (2016)

[BCCZ99] Biere, A., Cimatti, A., Clarke, E., Zhu, Y.: Symbolic model checking without BDDs. In: Cleaveland, W.R. (ed.) TACAS 1999. LNCS, vol. 1579, pp. 193–207. Springer, Heidelberg (1999). doi:10.1007/3-540-49059-0_14

[BCLS13] Boyer, B., Corre, K., Legay, A., Sedwards, S.: PLASMA-lab: a flexible, distributable statistical model checking library. In: Joshi, K., Siegle, M., Stoelinga, M., D'Argenio, P.R. (eds.) QEST 2013. LNCS, vol. 8054, pp. 160–164. Springer, Heidelberg (2013). doi:10.1007/978-3-642-40196-1_12

[BCM+92] Burch, J.R., Clarke, E.M., McMillan, K.L., Dill, D.L., Hwang, L.J.: Symbolic model checking: 10^{20} states and beyond. Inf. Comp. **98**(2), 142–170 (1992)

[BHHK03] Baier, C., Haverkort, B.R., Hermanns, H., Katoen, J.-P.: Model-checking algorithms for continuous-time markov chains. IEEE Trans. Software Eng. **29**(6), 524–541 (2003)

[BJK+05] Broy, M., Jonsson, B., Katoen, J.-P., Leucker, M., Pretschner, A. (eds.): Model-Based Testing of Reactive Systems. LNCS, vol. 3472. Springer, Heidelberg (2005)

[BK08] Baier, C., Katoen, J.-P.: Principles of Model Checking (Representation and Mind Series). The MIT Press, Cambridge (2008)

[BMR05] Ball, T., Millstein, T.D., Rajamani, S.K.: Polymorphic predicate abstraction. ACM Trans. Program. Lang. Syst. **27**(2) (2005)

[Bry92] Bryant, R.: Symbolic boolean manipulation with ordered binary-decision diagrams. ACM Comput. Surv. **24**(3), 293–318 (1992)

[CB06] Ciesinski, F., Baier, C.: Liquor: a tool for qualitative and quantitative linear time analysis of reactive systems. In: Proceedings of 3rd International Conference on the Quantitative Evaluation of Systems (QEST), pp. 131–132. IEEE (2006)

[CE81] Clarke, E.M., Emerson, E.A.: Design and synthesis of synchronization skeletons using branching time temporal logic. In: Kozen, D. (ed.) Logic of Programs 1981. LNCS, vol. 131, pp. 52–71. Springer, Heidelberg (1982). doi:10.1007/BFb0025774

[CG04] Ciesinski, F., Größer, M.: On probabilistic computation tree logic. In: Baier, C., Haverkort, B.R., Hermanns, H., Katoen, J.-P., Siegle, M. (eds.) Validation of Stochastic Systems. LNCS, vol. 2925, pp. 147–188. Springer, Heidelberg (2004). doi:10.1007/978-3-540-24611-4_5

[CGP99] Clarke, E., Grumberg, O., Peled, D.: Model Checking. MIT Press, Cambridge (1999)

[CV03] Clarke, E., Veith, H.: Counterexamples revisited: principles, algorithms, applications. In: Dershowitz, N. (ed.) Verification: Theory and Practice. LNCS, vol. 2772, pp. 208–224. Springer, Heidelberg (2003). doi:10.1007/978-3-540-39910-0_9

[CY95] Courcoubetis, C., Yannakakis, M.: The complexity of probabilistic verification. J. ACM **42**(4), 857–907 (1995)

[DG07] Droste, M., Gastin, P.: Weighted automata and weighted logics. Theor. Comput. Sci. **380**(1–2), 69–86 (2007)

[DLL+11] David, A., Larsen, K.G., Legay, A., Mikučionis, M., Wang, Z.: Time for statistical model checking of real-time systems. In: Gopalakrishnan, G., Qadeer, S. (eds.) CAV 2011. LNCS, vol. 6806, pp. 349–355. Springer, Heidelberg (2011). doi:10.1007/978-3-642-22110-1_27

[DPP04] Dovier, A., Piazza, C., Policriti, A.: An efficient algorithm for computing bisimulation equivalence. Theoret. Comput. Sci. **311**(1–3), 221–256 (2004)

[FG05] Flanagan, C., Godefroid, P.: Dynamic partial-order reduction for model checking software. In: POPL, pp. 110–121. ACM (2005)

[GPS02] Cabodi, G., Camurati, P., Quer, S.: Can BDDs compete with sat solvers on bounded model checking? In: Proceedings of 39th Design Automation Conference (DAC), pp. 117–122. ACM (2002)

[HCZ11] Younes, H.L.S., Clarke, E.M., Zuliani, P.: Statistical verification of probabilistic properties with unbounded until. In: Davies, J., Silva, L., Simao, A. (eds.) SBMF 2010. LNCS, vol. 6527, pp. 144–160. Springer, Heidelberg (2011). doi:10.1007/978-3-642-19829-8_10

[HR02] Havelund, K., Roşu, G.: Synthesizing monitors for safety properties. In: Katoen, J.-P., Stevens, P. (eds.) TACAS 2002. LNCS, vol. 2280, pp. 342–356. Springer, Heidelberg (2002). doi:10.1007/3-540-46002-0_24

[JKO+07] Jansen, D.N., Katoen, J.-P., Oldenkamp, M., Stoelinga, M., Zapreev, I.: How fast and fat is your probabilistic model checker? an experimental performance comparison. In: Yorav, K. (ed.) HVC 2007. LNCS, vol. 4899, pp. 69–85. Springer, Heidelberg (2008). doi:10.1007/978-3-540-77966-7_9

[JLL+] Jegourel, C., Lukina, A., Legay, A., Smolka, S., Grosu, R., Bartocci, E.: Feedback control for statistical model checking of cyber-physical systems. In: Margaria, T., Steffen, B. (eds.) ISoLA 2016, Part I. LNCS, vol. 9952, pp. 46–61. Springer, Cham (2016)

[KNP04] Kwiatkowska, M.Z., Norman, G., Parker, D.: Prism 2.0: a tool for probabilistic model checking. In: QEST, pp. 322–323. IEEE (2004)

[KNP11] Kwiatkowska, M., Norman, G., Parker, D.: PRISM 4.0: verification of probabilistic real-time systems. In: Gopalakrishnan, G., Qadeer, S. (eds.) CAV 2011. LNCS, vol. 6806, pp. 585–591. Springer, Heidelberg (2011). doi:10.1007/978-3-642-22110-1_47

[Kre] Kretinsky, J.: Survey of statistical verification of linear unbounded properties: model checking and distances. In: Margaria, T., Steffen, B. (eds.) ISoLA 2016, Part I. LNCS, vol. 9952, pp. 27–45. Springer, Cham (2016)

[LdPB] Linard, A., de Paula Bueno, M.L.: Towards adaptive scheduling of maintenance for cyber-physical systems. In: Margaria, T., Steffen, B. (eds.) ISoLA 2016, Part I. LNCS, vol. 9952, pp. 134–150. Springer, Cham (2016)

[LST] Legay, A., Sedwards, S., Traonouez, L.-M.: Plasma lab: a modular statistical model checking platform. In: Margaria, T., Steffen, B. (eds.) ISoLA 2016, Part I. LNCS, vol. 9952, pp. 77–93. Springer, Cham (2016)

[Oka59] Okamoto, M.: Some inequalities relating to the partial sum of binomial probabilities. Ann. Inst. Stat. Math. **10**, 29–35 (1959)

[Pnu77] Pnueli, A.: The temporal logic of programs. In: Proceedings of 18th Annual Symposium on Foundations of Computer Science (FOCS), pp. 46–57 (1977)

[RdBS] Reijsbergen, D., de Boer, P.-T., Scheinhardt, W.: Hypothesis testing for rare-event simulation: limitations and possibilities. In: Margaria, T., Steffen, B. (eds.) ISoLA 2016, Part I. LNCS, vol. 9952, pp. 16–26. Springer, Cham (2016)

[RS] Ruijters, E., Stoelinga, M.: Better railway engineering through statistical model checking. In: Margaria, T., Steffen, B. (eds.) ISoLA 2016, Part I. LNCS, vol. 9952, pp. 151–165. Springer, Cham (2016)

[Str] Strnadel, J.: On creation, analysis of reliability models by means of stochastic timed automata, statistical model checking: principle. In: Margaria, T., Steffen, B. (eds.) ISoLA 2016, Part I. LNCS, vol. 9952, pp. 166–181. Springer, Cham (2016)

[SVA04] Sen, K., Viswanathan, M., Agha, G.: Statistical model checking of black-box probabilistic systems. In: Alur, R., Peled, D.A. (eds.) CAV 2004. LNCS, vol. 3114, pp. 202–215. Springer, Heidelberg (2004). doi:10.1007/978-3-540-27813-9_16

[SVA05] Sen, K., Viswanathan, M., Agha, G.: On statistical model checking of stochastic systems. In: CAV, pp. 266–280 (2005)

[tBLVL] ter Beek, M., Legay, A., Vandin, A., Lafuente, A.L.: Statistical model checking for product lines. In: Margaria, T., Steffen, B. (eds.) ISoLA 2016, Part I. LNCS, vol. 9952, pp. 114–133. Springer, Cham (2016)

[Wal45] Wald, A.: Sequential tests of statistical hypotheses. Ann. Math. Stat. **16**(2), 117–186 (1945)

[WG93] Wolper, P., Godefroid, P.: Partial-order methods for temporal verification. In: Best, E. (ed.) CONCUR 1993. LNCS, vol. 715, pp. 233–246. Springer, Heidelberg (1993). doi:10.1007/3-540-57208-2_17

[You05a] Younes, H.L.S.: Verification and planning for stochastic processes with asynchronous events. Ph.D. thesis, Carnegie Mellon (2005)

[You05b] Younes, H.L.S.: Verification and planning for stochastic processes with asynchronous events. Ph.D. thesis, Carnegie Mellon University (2005)

[You06] Younes, H.L.S.: Error control for probabilistic model checking. In: Emerson, E.A., Namjoshi, K.S. (eds.) VMCAI 2006. LNCS, vol. 3855, pp. 142–156. Springer, Heidelberg (2005). doi:10.1007/11609773_10

[YS02] Younes, H.L.S., Simmons, R.G.: Probabilistic verification of discrete event systems using acceptance sampling. In: Brinksma, E., Larsen, K.G. (eds.) CAV 2002. LNCS, vol. 2404, pp. 223–235. Springer, Heidelberg (2002). doi:10.1007/3-540-45657-0_17

Hypothesis Testing for Rare-Event Simulation: Limitations and Possibilities

Daniël Reijsbergen[1], Pieter-Tjerk de Boer[2(✉)], and Werner Scheinhardt[2]

[1] University of Edinburgh, Edinburgh, Scotland, UK
dreijsbe@inf.ed.ac.uk
[2] University of Twente, Enschede, The Netherlands
{p.t.deboer,w.r.w.scheinhardt}@utwente.nl

Abstract. One of the main applications of probabilistic model checking is to decide whether the probability of a property of interest is above or below a threshold. Using statistical model checking (SMC), this is done using a combination of stochastic simulation and statistical hypothesis testing. When the probability of interest is very small, one may need to resort to rare-event simulation techniques, in particular importance sampling (IS). However, IS simulation does not yield 0/1-outcomes, as assumed by the hypothesis tests commonly used in SMC, but likelihood ratios that are typically close to zero, but which may also take large values.

In this paper we consider two possible ways of combining IS and SMC. One involves a classical IS-scheme from the rare-event simulation literature that yields likelihood ratios with bounded support when applied to a certain (nontrivial) class of models. The other involves a particular hypothesis testing scheme that does not require a-priori knowledge about the samples, only that their variance is estimated well.

1 Introduction

One of the main applications of statistical model checking (SMC) [13,19] is the use of computer simulation and hypothesis testing to determine whether some probability p in a model is larger or smaller than a given probability threshold p_0. Thus, several suitable hypothesis tests have been developed by various authors to test the hypothesis $p > p_0$ against $p < p_0$, and they are implemented in different tools; for an overview see [16]. These can be combined easily with simulation experiments in which each sample yields a Bernoulli random variable (representing whether the event of interest was observed or not).

In the rare-event context, where the probability p is extremely small, standard simulation is not efficient since observing the target event would require an excessively large number of samples. Techniques to estimate such small probabilities include importance sampling and splitting/restart, both going back to the early days of computing [11]. Recently there has been much interest in applying such techniques in the statistical model checking context, as witnessed by various PhD theses [3,10,14] and associated publications. These techniques have in com-

© Springer International Publishing AG 2016
T. Margaria and B. Steffen (Eds.): ISoLA 2016, Part I, LNCS 9952, pp. 16–26, 2016.
DOI: 10.1007/978-3-319-47166-2_2

mon[1] that the simulation samples no longer yield Bernoulli random variables, i.e., the outcomes are no longer restricted to $\{0,1\}$; in fact their distribution may be highly asymmetric. It is a challenging goal to combine rare-event simulation techniques with hypothesis testing schemes in such a way that sound statistical conclusions can be obtained within reasonable simulation time.

In this short paper, we explore the options of extending hypothesis tests to importance sampling. In Sect. 2, we investigate existing tests and the assumptions they make on the samples. Based on that, we consider two options: upper-bounding the likelihood ratio in Sect. 3, and using the normal approximation in Sect. 4. We provide a numerical illustration in Sect. 5, and brief conclusions in Sect. 6.

2   Generalizability of Existing Hypothesis Tests

Almost all existing hypothesis tests for statistical model checking fit in a relatively simple framework, cf. [16]. Independent samples $X_i \in \{0,1\}$ are generated for $i = 1, 2, \ldots$. The test statistic after N samples is $Z_N = \sum_{i=1}^{N} X_i - N p_0$. The test draws a conclusion when (N, Z_N) leaves the so-called critical area; then $Z_N > 0$ is evidence for the hypothesis H_1, which asserts that $p > p_0$. Conversely, $Z_N < 0$ is evidence for the hypothesis H_{-1}, which asserts that $p < p_0$. The shape of the boundaries of the critical area varies from test to test, and is chosen such that confidence levels are upheld; i.e., the probability of errors of the first [2] kind (accepting the wrong hypothesis) and the second kind (finishing undecided, as some tests can do) are upper-bounded by, e.g. 5 % for a 95 % confidence level. Some tests decide after a fixed number N samples have been drawn (fixed sample size tests, often related to confidence interval calculation), whereas others are sequential, meaning that after every new sample the test decides whether a conclusion can be drawn or more samples are needed. Another difference between tests is how they behave if p is closer to p_0 than some indifference level: class-I tests no longer live up to their confidence guarantee, class-II will tend to terminate undecided, while class-III will insist on drawing more and more samples until a confident conclusion can be drawn. For an overview of tests, and much more detail about their properties, see [16, 20].

So far it was assumed that X_i is an indicator: in each simulation replication the event of interest either does or does not occur, and we are interested in its probability. In case the target event is rare, $X_i = 0$ for all or almost all samples, leading to an unusable estimator. One popular solution for this is importance

---

[1] For importance sampling this is obvious. For splitting, one common implementation (e.g., [7]) produces each independent sample as the sum of the weights of all target-reaching offspring of an initial particle, so clearly these samples are no longer Bernoulli. Other variants exist which do this differently, with their own complications for hypothesis testing. However, this is outside the scope of this short paper.

[2] Note that "first" and "second" kind are a bit different here than in most hypothesis testing literature, since we have *two* hypotheses to be tested ($p > p_0$ and $p < p_0$), besides the null hypothesis ($p = p_0$). See Sect. 2.2 in [16].

sampling (see e.g. [11]), where the probability distributions in the model are modified to make the target event more likely, while keeping track of a so-called likelihood ratio by which the events need to be weighed. Effectively then, X_i takes on either the value 0 or the likelihood ratio value, so it is no longer restricted to $\{0, 1\}$. The X_i will typically be very small (representing the rarity of the event), but may take any non-negative real number. Their mean is still p, the probability of interest; however, their variance, which was $p(1 - p)$ in the Bernoulli case, may be totally different. Thus, we need to reconsider whether the hypothesis tests are still valid when the X_i are no longer Bernoulli. Table 1 provides an overview. (A similar comparison, but for confidence intervals rather than hypothesis tests, is found in Chap. 2 of [3].)

The table's third column lists conditions on the samples X_i that are used in the derivation or correctness proof of the respective test. As we see, about half of the tests explicitly assume that X_i is an indicator function, which is no longer the case when importance sampling is used. For some of these tests (SPRT and Darling-Robbins), it is crucial that there are indeed only two possible outcomes; for some others, the proof can be generalized to any X_i as long as they are bounded. This is the first option we will explore. In [4], one approach for bounding likelihood ratios was discussed, but it required rather complicated and model-dependent proofs. In Sect. 3, we show bounded likelihood ratio for a more general class of models and a well-known importance sampling scheme. In fact, our method and model class is similar to [2], where also an upper bound for the likelihood ratios is guaranteed; however, their upper bound is 1, which would lead to very conservative (and thus inefficient) hypothesis tests.

The other tests have normality listed in the third column. This means that these tests rely on the Central Limit Theorem: for sufficiently large N, Z_N becomes approximately normally distributed, so the normal distribution can be used to set decision thresholds such that confidence levels are upheld. This holds for any distribution of the X_i with finite variance, but suffers from the problem of needing to know when N is large enough. The lack of restrictions on X_i makes these tests attractive for use with importance sampling, and we explore this in Sect. 4, where we will find that only Chow-Robbins can be used.

3   Bounded Likelihood Ratios in Multicomponent Systems

As discussed in the previous section, several hypothesis tests can still be applied if the likelihood ratios returned by the IS scheme can be bounded from above. Although it is difficult to construct such bounds in general, there are restricted modelling classes in which this is more straightforward. In this section we discuss the modelling class of multicomponent systems, with a particular focus on the Distributed Database System (DDS). We consider the probability that, after the first component has failed, such a system reaches a system failure state before all components are repaired. This probability is interesting because it appears in expressions for other performance measures such as the system unreliability, unavailability and mean time to failure — in those expressions it is the only quantity that is difficult to estimate. We focus on the specific IS scheme of Balanced Failure Biasing (BFB), a classic IS scheme [18] for highly reliable Markovian systems, although the result of Eq. (1) holds in more general cases.

The general set-up of a multicomponent system is as follows. The system consists of d component types; let $\mathcal{D} = \{1, \ldots, d\}$. Let $\boldsymbol{x}$ be the state of the Markov chain, where the i-th entry x_i (with $i \in \mathcal{D}$) is the number of failed components of type i. Here, x_i takes values in $0, \ldots, n_i$, where n_i is the number of components of type i needed to trigger system failure. The initial state is given by $\boldsymbol{x}_0$, which is a d-dimensional zero-valued vector. The failure rate of components of type i is denoted by $\lambda_i(\boldsymbol{x})$, and their repair rate is $\mu_i(\boldsymbol{x}) \ \forall i \in \mathcal{D}, \boldsymbol{x} \in \mathbb{N}^d$. Note that these rates are state-dependent — e.g., in the DDS example, the failure rate of components of type i depends on how many components of type i are still operational. The *exit rate* of a state $\boldsymbol{x} \in \mathbb{N}^d$ is given by

$$\eta(\boldsymbol{x}) = \sum_{j \in \mathcal{D}} (\lambda_j(\boldsymbol{x}) + \mu_j(\boldsymbol{x})).$$

Let e_i, $i \in \mathcal{D}$, be a vector of length d filled with $d - 1$ zeros and a 1 at position i, and $\boldsymbol{x}_0$ the initial state. The probability of a 'straight' path (see [15]) leading to

Table 1. Overview of existing hypothesis tests for SMC (from [16]) and their requirements w.r.t. the samples X_i

Test	Class	Conditions on X_i	Generalisable to non-Bernoulli?
SPRT	I	$X_i \in \{0, 1\}$	No: assumes hypotheses describe entire outcome distribution.
Gauss-SSP	I	Sum of many X_i is approximately normally distributed	No: sample variance under $p = p_0 \pm \delta$ is needed.
Gauss-CI	II	Sum of many X_i is approximately normally distributed	No: sample variance under $p = p_0$ is needed.
Chow-Robbins	II	Sum of many X_i is approximately normally distributed	Yes: only variance under the true p is needed, which can be estimated during the simulation.
Chernoff-Hoeffding[a]-CI	II	$X_i \in \{0, 1\}$	Yes: to any bounded X_i.
Azuma	III	$X_i \in \{0, 1\}$	Yes: to any bounded X_i.
Darling-Robbins	III	$X_i \in \{0, 1\}$	No: D-R theorem is about entire distributions, not expectations.

[a]The actual bound on which this is based, is due to Hoeffding [9], but since literature and tools frequently refers to this as Chernoff's, we choose to mention both names here.

failure of component type $i \in \mathcal{D}$:

$$\prod_{j=0}^{n_i-1} \frac{\lambda_i(\boldsymbol{x}_0 + je_i)}{\eta(\boldsymbol{x}_0 + je_i)}.$$

Using IS, we simulate under different failure rates $\lambda_i^*(\boldsymbol{x})$ and repair rates $\mu_i^*(\boldsymbol{x})$. Assume (without loss of generality) that the rates are normalized such that the exit rates are the same under the new measure. Then the likelihood ratio of a straight path leading to failure of component type $i \in \mathcal{D}$ is given by

$$\prod_{j=0}^{n_i-1} \frac{\lambda_i(\boldsymbol{x}_0 + je_i)}{\lambda_i^*(\boldsymbol{x}_0 + je_i)}.$$

We define $L^{\max}$ as the largest of these likelihood ratios:

$$L^{\max} = \max_{i \in \mathcal{D}} \prod_{j=0}^{n_i-1} \frac{\lambda_i(\boldsymbol{x}_0 + je_i)}{\lambda_i^*(\boldsymbol{x}_0 + je_i)}.$$

To avoid the rare-event problem, $\lambda_i^*(\boldsymbol{x}_0 + je_i) > \lambda_i(\boldsymbol{x}_0 + je_i)$, so $L^{\max}$ is typically smaller than 1. However, since the exit rates are the same, it must hold that $\mu_i^*(\boldsymbol{x}_0 + je_i) < \mu_i(\boldsymbol{x}_0 + je_i)$, so if a μ-transition takes place the likelihood ratio increases. However, for every μ-transition there must be an accompanying λ-transition that took place earlier, since we started in the state where all components were operational. Let $\iota \in \mathcal{D}$ be the component type in which there's a failure — for every time the μ_ι-transition there has to be a λ_ι-transition to compensate, or else the system cannot end up in a failure state. Also, for the component types i for which the system doesn't fail, the μ_i-transition can only be fired if a spurious (i.e., not contributing to the rare event) λ_i-transition has been fired.

This leads to the following proposition, which is trivial to prove using the above line of reasoning. Let $\boldsymbol{X}'$ be the set of states reachable from the initial state $\boldsymbol{x}_0$. If

$$\frac{\max_{\boldsymbol{x} \in \boldsymbol{X}'} \lambda_i(\boldsymbol{x})}{\min_{\boldsymbol{x} \in \boldsymbol{X}'} \lambda_i^*(\boldsymbol{x})} \frac{\max_{\boldsymbol{x} \in \boldsymbol{X}'} \mu_i(\boldsymbol{x})}{\min_{\boldsymbol{x} \in \boldsymbol{X}'} \mu_i^*(\boldsymbol{x})} \leq 1 \tag{1}$$

then the values of the likelihood ratios are bounded from above by $L^{\max}$.

We will now consider what this means specifically for the application of BFB to the DDS. First, BFB is defined $\forall i \in \mathcal{D}$ as

$$\frac{\lambda_i^*(\boldsymbol{x})}{\eta(\boldsymbol{x})} = \begin{cases} 1/n_f(\boldsymbol{x}) & \text{if } n_r(\boldsymbol{x}) = 0, \\ 0 & \text{if } n_f(\boldsymbol{x}) = 0, \\ (2n_f(\boldsymbol{x}))^{-1} & \text{if failure and } n_r(\boldsymbol{x}) > 0, \end{cases}$$

for failure transitions and

$$\frac{\mu_i^*(\boldsymbol{x})}{\eta(\boldsymbol{x})} = \begin{cases} 0 & \text{if } n_r(\boldsymbol{x}) = 0, \\ 1/n_r(\boldsymbol{x}) & \text{if } n_f(\boldsymbol{x}) = 0, \\ (2n_r(\boldsymbol{x}))^{-1} & \text{if repair and } n_f(\boldsymbol{x}) > 0. \end{cases}$$

for repair transitions. Here, $n_f(\boldsymbol{x})$ is the amount of failures enabled in state $\boldsymbol{x}$, $n_r(\boldsymbol{x})$ is the number of repairs.

The benchmark parameters of the DDS, as used for example in [17], are as follows. There are $d = 9$ component types — one set of processors, two sets of disk controllers and 6 sets of disks. We have $n_i = 2$ for all $i \in \mathcal{D}$. Let $\lambda = 1/6000$, and x_i the number of operational components of type i. Then the failure rate for type i is $3(2 - x_i)\lambda$ if type i consists of processors or disk controllers, and $(4 - x_i)\lambda$ if type i consists of disks. The repair rate μ_i is 1 if $x_i > 0$. We are interested in the rare event that after the first component has failed, we reach the system failure state before returning to x_0.

The quantities involved in (1) are as follows:

- $\max_{x \in X'} \lambda_i(x) = 6 \cdot \frac{1}{6000}$, namely the failure rates of processors and disk controllers if they all are operational;
- $\max_{x \in X'} \mu_i(x) = 1$, in fact $\mu_i(x)$ for all component types and all $x \in X'$;
- $\min_{x \in X'} \lambda_i^*(x) \geq \frac{1}{2d} \min_{x \in X'} \eta_i(x) \geq \frac{1}{2d}$, because in all states in X' at least one repair is enabled, meaning that the exit rate must be at least 1;
- $\min_{x \in X'} \mu_i^*(x) \geq \frac{1}{2d} \min_{x \in X'} \eta_i(x) \geq \frac{1}{2d}$ for similar reasons.

Hence, the expression on the left in (1) evaluates to $4d^2/1000 = 0.364 < 1$, so BFB has bounded likelihood ratios in the DDS. Note that this is the maximum contribution of *a single cycle*, not the likelihood ratio on a complete path.

As a side note: if x_0 were a valid state, then $\min_{x \in X'} \lambda_i^*(x)$ would be very small as $\eta(x_0)$ is very small. However, since we are interested in reaching failure before full repair, we have no so-called high-probability cycles [8].

Regarding $L^{\max}$, this is achieved on the 'straight' paths involving failure of processors or disk controllers. In particular, straightforward computations show that $L^{\max} = \frac{6}{671} \cdot \frac{9}{7} \approx 0.0114967$. Using the approach underlying the Chernoff-Hoeffding bound, we obtain the expression $\alpha = 2e^{-2w^2 N^2/(L^{\max})^2}$, for the confidence interval half-width w and confidence level α after having drawn N samples, which leads to:

$$w = \sqrt{\log\left(\frac{2}{\alpha}\right) \cdot \frac{(L^{\max})^2}{2N}}.$$

We will compare this confidence interval to the one obtained using the Central Limit Theorem in Sect. 5.

4 CLT-Based Tests for Importance Sampling

Before we discuss the use of CLT-based tests for importance sampling, we will first spend a few words on the validity of the normality assumption in an Importance Sampling context.

4.1 Correctness of CLT-Based Tests

All hypothesis tests based on the central limit theorem rely on the assumption that the number of samples N is large enough to warrant the use of the CLT;

i.e., that the distribution of Z_N is sufficiently close to normal. This does not just hold for hypothesis tests, but also for establishing confidence intervals around a point estimate. However, in general there is no way of knowing when N is sufficiently large.

The fact that there is no way of being sure that N is large enough, has caused many practitioners to prefer other, more rigorous tests. Indeed, in the Bernoulli case, there are good alternatives as noted earlier. Then again, precisely in the Bernoulli case, one may be able to make slight adjustments to the CLT interval to make it conservative (e.g. [1,5]).

However, in many cases using the CLT is the only option, and generally accepted as such by practitioners. One such case is using standard (i.e., not importance sampling) simulation to estimate the mean of a non-Bernoulli, and in general not a-priori bounded, random variable, such as a waiting time in a queueing model. At any finite N, one has no assurance that there cannot still later come a very rare, very large X_i that will significantly change the estimate of the mean and variance. The practitioner simply trusts this will not happen, based on his/her understanding of the model.

When using importance sampling with a good change of measure, the distribution of the likelihood ratios will not have a long tail, and the CLT can give a good estimate of the mean and a confidence interval around it. However, a bad change of measure may lead to a distribution of likelihood ratios which does have a long tail, having very large values occurring very rarely, requiring very large N. Among importance sampling practitioners, it is customary to do one's best to make a good change of measure (e.g., one with such nice properties as asymptotic efficiency or bounded normal approximation, cf. [12]), and then apply the CLT to obtain a confidence interval.

We argue that using a CLT-based hypothesis test with importance sampling simulation is not fundamentally different or more "dangerous" than using the CLT to obtain a confidence interval. In either case, one makes a statement about being e.g. 95 % sure that the true value is in some interval. So if obtaining confidence intervals from the CLT is deemed reliable in some importance sampling simulation, then hypothesis tests based on the CLT should also be considered reliable.

4.2   Suitability of CLT-Based Tests for Importance Sampling

As listed in Table 1, there are several hypothesis tests based on the CLT. Unfortunately, some of those require knowledge of the estimator variance as a function of the probability p of interest. This is used to compute *in advance* how many samples N will be enough to draw the right conclusion with the prescribed confidence level even in the worst (most difficult) case, which typically occurs when p is at or near p_0. In the Bernoulli case, the estimator variance can indeed be computed for any given p. But in the importance sampling case, this is generally impossible. In fact, the question in that case is meaningless, since for a given p (without further information) there can be many different distributions for X_i, with different variances.

The only test from the table which does not require knowing variance as a function of p, is the Chow-Robbins test. This test is based on a theorem by Chow and Robbins [6] which says that if one wants a confidence interval of predetermined width, one can just keep adding samples and increase N until the CLT indicates that this width has been reached, based on the observed sample variance. This is made into a hypothesis test by simulating long enough so that the half-width of the confidence interval on Z_N is less than ζN, where ζ is an indifference level: if $|p - p_0| < \zeta$, one is willing to accept that the test's probability of terminating conclusively may be less than the specified confidence level (e.g., 95 %).

4.3   Extension of the Chow-Robbins Test to Class I and III

The Chow-Robbins test as discussed above is a class-II test: it risks terminating inconclusively if p is near p_0. However, the same principle can be used to form a class-I or class-III test, as described briefly below.

For a class-I test, the requirement is that the probability of accepting the wrong hypothesis is less than α if $|p - p_0| \geq \delta$, where $1 - \alpha$ is the confidence level of the test and δ the indifference level. This can be achieved by choosing the confidence interval halfwidth of Z_N to be δN and its level to be $1 - 2\alpha$. One easily verifies that then if $|p - p_0| = \delta$ (the hardest case) the probability of accepting the wrong hypothesis is at most α.

A crude class-III test can be constructed by concatenating class-II tests as follows. The ith (for $i = 1, 2, \ldots$) class-II test is given probability of error of first kind $\alpha_i = \alpha/2^i$, indifference level $\zeta_i = \zeta/2^i$, and probability of error of second kind (i.e., taking no decision) $\beta_i = \beta$; here α is the desired probability of wrong conclusion of the resulting class-III test, and β and ζ are parameters to be chosen. Then apply the first test ($i = 1$). If it draws a conclusion, that is the final conclusion. If it finishes undecided, apply test 2, with *new* samples, and so on, until a conclusion is drawn. Clearly, the total probability of drawing a wrong conclusion is upperbounded by $\sum_{i=1}^{N} \alpha_i = \alpha$, as required, and the fact that $\zeta_i \to 0$ makes sure a conclusion is eventually reached.

5   Numerical Results

In this section we present numerical results to illustrate the results of Sect. 3. Since all tests that we are still considering are based on confidence intervals, we show results on confidence interval coverage levels here, rather than results on hypothesis test decision correctness (which would be equivalent).

In particular we present two tables. Table 2 displays sample 95 % confidence intervals created using both the CLT and the Chernoff-Hoeffding bound using both standard Monte Carlo and Balanced Failure Biasing. Table 3 displays coverage statistics, i.e., simulation estimates of the probability that the confidence interval contains the true probability (this should at least be equal to the confidence level). We compare BFB to similar results for standard Monte Carlo (MC) simulation, which is based on Bernoulli samples.

Table 2. Sample 95 % confidence intervals generated using both the Gaussian approximation and the Chernoff-Hoeffding bound for several values of N. This is done for both standard Monte Carlo (MC) simulation and Balanced Failure Biasing (BFB). The confidence intervals are for estimates for p in the benchmark DDS. For both methods, the results in each row are based on the same sample, but results in the lower columns are not continuations of the previous samples. The Gaussian confidence intervals are asymptotically narrower, but for small values they are prone to being incorrect. The true probability equals 5.0285E-4.

N	MC-Gauss	MC-Ch.-Hffd.	BFB-Gauss	BFB-Ch.-Hffd.
10	—	[−4.295E-1, 4.295E-1]	[−3.295E-6, 3.080E-5]	[−4.924E-3, 4.951E-3]
30	—	[−2.480E-1, 2.480E-1]	[−1.406E-6, 4.479E-6]	[−2.849E-3, 2.852E-3]
100	—	[−1.358E-1, 1.358E-1]	[6.295E-5, 7.950E-4]	[−1.132E-3, 1.990E-3]
300	—	[−7.841E-2, 7.841E-2]	[4.278E-4, 9.915E-4]	[−1.918E-4, 1.611E-3]
1000	—	[−4.295E-2, 4.295E-2]	[3.315E-4, 5.787E-4]	[−3.867E-5, 9.488E-4]
3000	[2.754E-5, 2.639E-3]	[−2.346E-2, 2.613E-2]	[4.396E-4, 5.925E-4]	[2.309E-4, 8.011E-4]
10000	[6.184E-5, 9.382E-4]	[−1.308E-2, 1.408E-2]	[4.858E-4, 5.701E-4]	[3.718E-4, 6.841E-4]
30000	[5.068E-4, 1.160E-3]	[−7.008E-3, 8.674E-3]	[4.850E-4, 5.328E-4]	[4.187E-4, 5.990E-4]
100000	[3.357E-4, 6.043E-4]	[−3.825E-3, 4.765E-3]	[4.943E-4, 5.203E-4]	[4.579E-4, 5.567E-4]

As we can see in Table 2, both standard MC simulation and BFB produce confidence intervals for small values for N that are unreliable (either because they are completely uninformative or wrong), but for high values of N the BFB-Gauss confidence intervals are narrower than for those based on the Chernoff-Hoeffding bound. For MC, if no likelihood ratios had the value 1 then we cannot construct a meaningful confidence interval. However, this is possible using the Chernoff-Hoeffding bound. Note that for MC better methods for constructing confidence intervals exist such as the Agresti-Coull interval and the exact binomial (Clopper-Pearson) confidence interval. For BFB with small samples sizes, it is reasonably likely that only very small likelihood ratios are observed, leading to confidence intervals that do not contain the true probability using the CLT. However, if we use the Chernoff-Hoeffding bound the confidence intervals are sufficiently conservative.

In Table 3, we display coverage statistics. In particular, we conduct N_1 simulation experiments, where in each experiment we use N_2 samples to create a confidence interval and then check whether this interval contains the true probability. For the case of MC Gauss, two ways of treating the (rather likely) case where all simulation runs result in 0: it can be counted as giving a confidence interval of $[-\infty, \infty]$ and thus indeed containing the true value, but since $[-\infty, \infty]$ is totally uninformative, from a practical point of view it makes more sense to not count it as a correct confidence interval. Only for very large values of N_2 will the coverage of MC Gauss approach 95 %. BFB Gauss's coverage approaches 95 % much earlier. As we can see, the Chernoff-Hoeffding-based results are much more reliable than the Gauss-based results.

Note that the good performance of the methods based on the CLT for high N_2 justified their use as discussed in Sect. 4. Of course, it depends on the application

Table 3. Coverage results for the DDS benchmark setting. $N_1 = 10000$. In MC Gauss 1, a sample with only zeroes is counted as producing an incorrect interval, while in MC Gauss 2, it is counted as producing a correct (but non-informative) interval of $[-\infty, \infty]$.

N_2	MC Gauss 1	MC Gauss 2	MC Ch.-Hffd.	BFB Gauss	BFB Ch.-Hffd.
10	0.0043 ± 0.0013	1.0000 ± 0.0000	1.0000 ± 0.0000	0.4298 ± 0.0097	1.0000 ± 0.0000
30	0.0116 ± 0.0021	1.0000 ± 0.0000	1.0000 ± 0.0000	0.8153 ± 0.0076	1.0000 ± 0.0000
100	0.0463 ± 0.0041	1.0000 ± 0.0000	1.0000 ± 0.0000	0.8907 ± 0.0061	1.0000 ± 0.0000
300	0.1384 ± 0.0068	1.0000 ± 0.0000	1.0000 ± 0.0000	0.9341 ± 0.0049	1.0000 ± 0.0000
1000	0.3886 ± 0.0096	0.9998 ± 0.0003	1.0000 ± 0.0000	0.9458 ± 0.0044	1.0000 ± 0.0000
3000	0.7830 ± 0.0081	0.9991 ± 0.0006	1.0000 ± 0.0000	0.9502 ± 0.0043	1.0000 ± 0.0000
10000	0.8742 ± 0.0065	0.8777 ± 0.0064	1.0000 ± 0.0000	0.9470 ± 0.0044	1.0000 ± 0.0000

when N_2 is high 'enough', whereas the Chernoff-Hoeffding-based methods are safe regardless of the choice of N_2. On the other hand, the Chernoff-Hoeffding-based methods clearly are rather conservative and thus such a test would take more simulation effort than strictly needed to come to a conclusion with the requisite confidence level.

6   Conclusions

In this short paper we have considered the options for hypothesis tests for importance sampling in statistical model checking with rare events. Two approaches seem promising: tests which work if the likelihood ratio is upper bounded, and tests based on the Chow-Robbins theorem if the normal approximation is known to be applicable (i.e., the number of samples high enough). For the former we have shown that for a particular class of models the well-known BFB heuristic indeed has an upper bound on the likelihood ratio. Two obvious lines for future work are (i) finding more general ways of constructing changes of measure with provably bounded likelihood ratio, and (ii) finding ways of establishing whether the normal approximation is indeed applicable.

Acknowledgments. This work is partially supported by the EU projects SENSATION, 318490, and QUANTICOL, 600708.

References

1. Agresti, A., Coull, B.A.: Approximate is better than "exact" for interval estimation of binomial proportions. Am. Stat. **52**(2), 119–126 (1998)
2. Alexopoulos, C., Shultes, B.C.: Estimating reliability measures for highly-dependable markov systems, using balanced likelihood ratios. IEEE Trans. Reliab. **50**(3), 265–280 (2001)
3. Barbot, B.: Acceleration for statistical model checking. Ph.D thesis, École normale supérieure de Cachan (2014)

4. Barbot, B., Haddad, S., Picaronny, C.: Coupling and importance sampling for statistical model checking. In: Flanagan, C., König, B. (eds.) TACAS 2012. LNCS, vol. 7214, pp. 331–346. Springer, Heidelberg (2012). doi:10.1007/978-3-642-28756-5_23
5. Brown, L.D., Cai, T., DasGupta, A.: Interval estimation for a binomial proportion. Stat. Sci. **16**(2), 101–117 (2001)
6. Chow, Y.S., Robbins, H.: On the asymptotic theory of fixed-width sequential confidence intervals for the mean. Ann. Math. Stat. **36**(2), 457–462 (1965)
7. Dean, T., Dupuis, P.: Splitting for rare event simulation: a large deviation approach to design and analysis. Stochast. Process. Appl. **119**, 562–587 (2009)
8. Goyal, A., Shahabuddin, P., Heidelberger, P., Nicola, V.F., Glynn, P.W.: A unified framework for simulating Markovian models of highly dependable systems. IEEE Trans. Comput. **41**(1), 36–51 (1992)
9. Hoeffding, W.: Probability inequalities for sums of bounded random variables. J. Am. Stat. Assoc. **58**, 13–30 (1963)
10. Jegourel, C.: Rare event simulation for statistical model checking. Ph.D thesis, Université de Rennes 1 (2014)
11. Kahn, H., Harris, T.E.: Estimation of particle transmission by random sampling. In: Monte Carlo Method; Proceedings of a Symposium held June 29, 30, and July 1, 1949. Nat. Bur. Standards Appl. Math. Series, vol. 12, pp. 27–30 (1951)
12. L'Ecuyer, P., Blanchet, J., Tuffin, B., Glynn, P.: Asymptotic robustness of estimators in rare-event simulation. ACM Trans. Model. Comput. Simul. (TOMACS) **20**(1), 6 (2010)
13. Legay, A., Delahaye, B., Bensalem, S.: Statistical model checking: an overview. In: Barringer, H., et al. (eds.) RV 2010. LNCS, vol. 6418, pp. 122–135. Springer, Heidelberg (2010). doi:10.1007/978-3-642-16612-9_11
14. Reijsbergen, D.P.: Efficient simulation techniques for stochastic model checking. Ph.D thesis, University of Twente, Enschede, December 2013
15. Reijsbergen, D.P., de Boer, P.T., Scheinhardt, W., Haverkort, B.R.: Fast simulation for slow paths in Markov models. Proc. RESIM **2012**, 36–38 (2012)
16. Reijsbergen, D.P., de Boer, P.T., Scheinhardt, W.R.W., Haverkort, B.R.: On hypothesis testing for statistical model checking. Int. J. Softw. Tools Technol. Transfer **17**(4), 377–395 (2015)
17. Sanders, W.H., Malhis, L.M.: Dependability evaluation using composed SAN-based reward models. J. Parallel Distrib. Comput. **15**(3), 238–254 (1992)
18. Shahabuddin, P.: Importance sampling for the simulation of highly reliable Markovian systems. Manage. Sci. **40**(3), 333–352 (1994)
19. Younes, H.L.S.: Error control for probabilistic model checking. In: Emerson, E.A., Namjoshi, K.S. (eds.) VMCAI 2006. LNCS, vol. 3855, pp. 142–156. Springer, Heidelberg (2005). doi:10.1007/11609773_10
20. Companion website to our paper [16]. http://wwwhome.ewi.utwente.nl/~ptdeboer/hyptest-for-smc/

Survey of Statistical Verification of Linear Unbounded Properties: Model Checking and Distances

Jan Křetínský[(✉)]

Technische Universität München, Munich, Germany
jan.kretinsky@tum.de

Abstract. We survey statistical verification techniques aiming at linear properties with unbounded or infinite horizon, as opposed to properties of runs of fixed length. We discuss statistical model checking of Markov chains and Markov decision processes against reachability, unbounded-until, LTL and mean-payoff properties. Moreover, the respective strategies can be represented efficiently using statistical techniques. Further, we also discuss when it is possible to statistically estimate linear distances between Markov chains.

1 Introduction

Verification of stochastic systems such as Markov chains (MC) and Markov decision processes (MDP) traditionally relies on numeric approaches. However, numeric analysis of the whole system is often inapplicable in practice: (i) when the system is too large due to state space explosion or (ii) when the exact transitions are unknown (black-box systems). In such cases, *statistical* approaches and simulation form a powerful alternative. They have been successfully applied to various biological [JCL+09, PGL+13], hybrid [ZPC10, DDL+12, EGF12, Lar12] or cyber-physical [BBB+10, CZ11, DDL+13] systems to name just a few and there is a substantial tool support available [JLS12, BDL+12, BCLS13, BHH12]. The statistical approach typically consists in

1. observing (finitely many finitely long) simulation runs,
2. analysis of each run,
3. inferring properties of the system from statistics on the results of the analysis.

The traditional properties we want to infer are given (i) logically as satisfaction of a given temporal property, verified by *model checking* and (ii) behaviourally as conformance to another system, verified by *equivalence checking*. Both classes of properties can be considered in two flavours, in (i) *linear* and (ii) *branching* understanding. For classical systems, this gives rise to property

This research was partially supported by the Czech Science Foundation under grant agreement P202/12/G061.

T. Margaria and B. Steffen (Eds.): ISoLA 2016, Part I, LNCS 9952, pp. 27–45, 2016.
DOI: 10.1007/978-3-319-47166-2_3

Table 1. Typical examples of properties of non-deterministic systems, depending on the description mechanism and the notion of time.

	Logic: model checking	Behaviour: equivalence checking
Linear	LTL	Trace equivalence
Branching	CTL	Bisimulation

Table 2. Qualitative properties of probabilistic systems. Here qLTL denotes qualitative satisfaction of LTL formulae (with probability 0 or 1) in the sense of [CY95] and qPCTL [LS83] is the qualitative fragment of PCTL [HJ94]

	Logic: model checking	Behaviour: equivalence checking
Linear	qLTL	Probabilistic trace equivalence
Branching	qPCTL	Probabilistic bisimulation

classes exemplified by the popular instances in Table 1. The extension to probabilistic systems is depicted in Table 2.

However, for probabilistic systems, the Boolean notions of satisfaction and equivalence are not satisfactory. For instance, even a highly safety-critical systems such as nuclear plants, with each hardware component failing with certain probability, do not satisfy the safety properties, but with some (preferably high) probability. Computing this probability is the task of *quantitative* probabilistic verification. Similarly, the probabilities of failures of the components are only empirically estimated and the slightest imprecision in the estimate may result in system being or not being equivalent. The task of measuring how much they differ can be captured by the quantitative notion of *distance*. This gives rise to property classes summarized in Table 3.

Table 3. Quantitative properties of probabilistic systems. Here pLTL is LTL with a single proabilistic threshold operator in front [Var85].

	Logic: model checking	Behaviour: equivalence checking
Linear	pLTL	Probabilistic trace distance
Branching	PCTL	Probabilistic bisimulation distance

Furthermore, for MDPs, which combine probabilistic behaviour and non-determinism, we have to consider the way the non-determinism is resolved. Typically, the best and worst case are of interest. Either way, we are interested in *computing* and *representing* the witnessing *strategy* (policy, scheduler, controller).

This paper surveys recent development of statistical techniques for these tasks, focusing mostly on the *linear* setting, which is naturally closer to methods based on simulation runs. Several descriptions are based on presentation in our previous work [DHKP16a, DHKP16b, BCC+14, BCC+15]

2 Models

In this section we briefly recall the models of interest and discuss the black-box setting. We consider a finite set Ap of atomic propositions and denote $\Sigma = 2^{Ap}$.

Definition 1 (Markov chain). *A* Markov chain (MC) *is a tuple* $\mathcal{M} = (S, \mu, \mathbf{P}, L)$, *where*

- S *is a set of* states,
- μ *is an* initial *probability distribution over* S,
- $\mathbf{P} : S \times S \to [0,1]$ *is a* transition *probability matrix, such that for every* $s \in S$ *it holds* $\sum_{s' \in S} \mathbf{P}(s, s') = 1$,
- $L : S \to \Sigma$ *is a* labelling *function.*

A *run* of $\mathcal{M}$ is an infinite sequence $\rho = s_1 s_2 \cdots$ of states, such that $\mu(s_1) > 0$ and $\mathbf{P}(s_i, s_{i+1}) > 0$ for all $i \geq 1$; we let $\rho[i]$ denote the state s_i. A *path* in $\mathcal{M}$ is a finite prefix of a run of $\mathcal{M}$. Each path π in $\mathcal{M}$ determines the set of runs $\mathsf{Cone}(\pi)$ consisting of all runs that start with π. To $\mathcal{M}$ we assign the probability space $\mathcal{P}^{\mathcal{M}} = (\mathsf{Runs}, \mathcal{F}, \mathbb{P}^{\mathcal{M}})$, where Runs is the set of all runs in $\mathcal{M}$, $\mathcal{F}$ is the σ-algebra generated by all $\mathsf{Cone}(\pi)$, and $\mathbb{P}^{\mathcal{M}}$ is the unique probability measure such that $\mathbb{P}^{\mathcal{M}}(\mathsf{Cone}(s_1 \cdots s_n)) = \mu(s_1) \cdot \prod_{i=1}^{n-1} \mathbf{P}(s_i, s_{i+1})$, where the empty product equals 1. We will omit the superscript in $\mathbb{P}^{\mathcal{M}}$ if the Markov chain is clear from the context. Further, we write $\mathbb{P}_s^{\mathcal{M}}$ for the probability measure, where $\mu(s) = 1$ and $\mu(s') = 0$ for $s' \neq s$.

An *ω-word* is an infinite sequence $a_1 a_2 \cdots \in \Sigma^{\omega}$ of symbols from Σ; a *word* is a finite prefix $w \in \Sigma^*$ of an ω-word. We extend the labelling notation so that for a path (or run) π, the projected sequence $L(\pi)$ is the word (or ω-word) w, where $w[i] = L(\pi[i])$ for all i. Besides, the inverse map is $L^{-1}(w) = \{\pi \mid L(\pi) = w\}$. Furthermore, we overload the notation and for a path π we write $\mathbb{P}(\pi)$ meaning $\mathbb{P}(\mathsf{Cone}(\pi))$, and for a (ω)-word w, we write $\mathbb{P}(w)$ meaning $\mathbb{P}(L^{-1}(w))$.

A *bottom strongly connected component (BSCC)* is a set $S' \subseteq S$ such that (1) if $\mathbf{P}(s, s') > 0$ for some $s \in S'$ then $s' \in S'$, and (2) for all $s, s' \in S'$ there is a path $\omega = s_0 \cdots s_n$.

Definition 2 (Markov decision process). *A* Markov decision process (MDP) *is a tuple* $\mathcal{M} = (S, \mu, A, E, (\mathbf{P}_a)_{a \in A}, L)$, *where*

- S *is a finite set of* states,
- $\mu \in S$ *is an* initial state,
- A *is a finite set of* actions,
- $E : S \to 2^A$ *assigns non-empty sets of* enabled *actions to all states,*

– *for each $a \in A$, $\mathbf{P}_a : S{\times}S \to [0,1]$ is a (partial)* probabilistic transition
  function *defined for all (s,s') where $a \in E(s)$,*
– $L : S \to \Sigma$ *is a* labelling *function.*

A *run* of an MDP $\mathcal{M}$ is an infinite sequence $\omega = s_1 a_1 s_2 a_2 \ldots$ such that
$a_i \in E(s_i)$ and $\mathbf{P}_{a_i}(s_i, s_{i+1}) > 0$ for every $i \in \mathbb{N}$. A *finite path* is a finite
prefix of an infinite path ending in a state. A *strategy* maps a finite path to a
distribution over action enabled in the last state of the path. Intuitively, the
strategy resolves the choices of actions in each finite path by choosing (possibly
at random) an action enabled in the current state. In standard fashion [KSK76],
a strategy σ induces a Markov chain $\mathcal{M}^\sigma$ and the respective probability measure
$\mathbb{P}^{\mathcal{M},\sigma} := \mathbb{P}^{\mathcal{M}^\sigma}$ over the infinite paths of $\mathcal{M}$.

An *end component* (EC) of $\mathcal{M}$ is a pair (S', A') where $S' \subseteq S$ and $A' \subseteq$
$\bigcup_{s \in S'} E(s)$ such that: (1) if $\mathbf{P}_a(s, s') > 0$ for some $s \in S'$ and $a \in A'$, then
$s' \in S'$, and (2) for all $s, s' \in S'$ there is a path $\omega = s_1 a_1 \ldots s_n$ such that $s_1 = s$,
$s_n = s'$. A *maximal end component* (MEC) is an EC that is maximal with respect
to the point-wise subset ordering.

A state s is *terminal* if all actions $a \in E(s)$ satisfy $\mathbf{P}_a(s,s) = 1$.

2.1 Black-Box Systems

A black-box system is MC or MDP where we know neither the set of states S
nor the transition probability matrix $\mathbf{P}$ (matrices $(\mathbf{P}_a)_{a \in A}$). We can only sample
runs of the system: we can sample the initial state and for the current state we
know the enabled actions and can pick any of them (in case of MDP), and can
sample a successor or terminate the run. This definition confroms to black-box
systems in the sense of [SVA04], slightly different from e.g. [YS02] or [RP09],
where simulations can be run from any desired state.

Additionally, since unbounded properties cannot be analyzed without further
information, various approaches additionally assume knowledge of some further
quantities, such as

– an upper bound on the size $|S|$ of the state space,
– a lower bound on the minimum (non-zero) transition probability p_{min},
– the second largest eigenvalue λ of the MC,
– or even the topology of the system, not knowing the exact transition probabilities, but knowing which are positive.

On the one hand, assuming the knowledge of the topology is bordering with
white-box analysis where the complete system is known. Further, obtaining a
bound on λ is typically as hard as the white-box analysis itself. On the other
hand, finding p_{min} is a light assumption in many realistic scenarios [DHKP16a]
and often does not depend on the size of the chain. For instance, bounds on the
rates for reaction kinetics in chemical reaction systems are typically known; for
models in the Prism language, the bounds can be easily inferred without con-
structing the respective state space. Furthermore, $|S|$ can in principle be bounded
using p_{min} and sufficiently many simulations using methods of [DHKP16a].

3   Linear Temporal Properties

3.1   Bounded and Unbounded Properties

Most of the previous efforts in SMC has focused on the analysis of properties with bounded horizon [YS02, SVA04, YKNP06, JCL+09, JLS12, BDL+12]. For bounded properties (e.g. state r is reached with probability at most 0.5 in the first 1000 steps), statistical guarantees can be obtained in a completely black-box setting, where execution runs of the system can be observed, but no other information is available. Unbounded properties (e.g. state r is reached with probability at most 0.5 in any number of steps) are significantly more difficult, as a stopping criterion is needed when generating a potentially infinite execution run, and some information about the system is necessary for providing statistical guarantees. Table 4 presents and overview of the assumptions for the statistical analysis of unbounded properties.

Table 4. Statistical approaches organised by (i) the class of verifiable linear properties, and (ii) by the required information about the Markov chain, where p_{min} is the minimal transition probability, $|S|$ is the number of states, and λ is the second largest eigenvalue of the chain.

	No info	p_{min}	$|S|, p_{min}$	λ	Topology
Bounded	e.g. [YS02, SVA04]				
$\Diamond$, U	×	[DHKP16a]	[BCC+14]	[YCZ10]	[YCZ10, HJB+10]
LTL, mean payoff	×	[DHKP16a]	[BCC+14]		

3.2   Statistical Model Checking for MCs

Statistical model checking (SMC) [YS02] of Markov chains refers to algorithms with the following specification:

Specification of Markov chains statistical model checking

Input:
- a finite black-box MC $\mathcal{M}$ (i.e., access to any desired finite number of sampled simulation paths of any desired finite lengths)
- a linear property φ
- a threshold probability p
- an indifference region $\varepsilon > 0$
- two error bounds $\alpha, \beta > 0$
- possibly some characteristics of $\mathcal{M}$ from Table 4

Output: if $\mathbb{P}[\mathcal{M} \models \varphi] \geq p + \varepsilon$, return YES with probability at least $1 - \alpha$, and if $\mathbb{P}[\mathcal{M} \models \varphi] \leq p - \varepsilon$, return NO with probability at least $1 - \beta$

SMC of unbounded properties, usually "unbounded until" properties, was first considered in [HLMP04] and the first approach was proposed in [SVA05], but observed incorrect in [HJB+10]. Notably, in [YCZ10] two approaches are described. The *first approach* proposes to terminate sampled paths at every step with some probability p_{term} and re-weight the result accordingly. In order to guarantee the asymptotic convergence of this method, the second eigenvalue λ of the chain must be computed, which is as hard as the verification problem itself. It should be noted that the method provides only asymptotic guarantees as the width of the confidence interval converges to zero. The correctness of [LP08] relies on the knowledge of the second eigenvalue λ, too. The *second approach* of [YCZ10] requires the knowledge of the chain's topology, which is used to transform the chain so that all potentially infinite paths are eliminated. In [HJB+10], a similar transformation is performed, again requiring knowledge of the topology. The (pre)processing of the state space required by the topology-aware methods, as well as by traditional numerical methods for Markov chain analysis, is a major practical hurdle for large (or unknown) state spaces. Another approach, limited to ergodic Markov chains, is taken in [RP09], based on coupling methods. There are also extensions of SMC to timed systems [DLL+15].

Finally, a class of algorithms that do not require much knowledge of the system is based on detecting that a simulation run reached a bottom strongly connected component. Then and only then we can deduce what the rest of the infinite run will be like and can thus terminate the run. Moreover, this also implies that such algorithms can be applied not only to reachability and unbounded-until properties, but can also be extended to LTL or mean payoff. In [BCC+14] a priori bounds for the length of execution runs are calculated from the minimum transition probability p_{min} and the number of states $|S|$ only. After a long enough trace, we can deduce we are in a BSCC. The length of the trace can be bounded (for a given confidence) by $|S|$ and p_{min}. Indeed, if there is a way out of the BSCC it is sufficient to take a path of length S, which has probability at least p_{min}^S. However, without taking execution information into account, these bounds are exponential in the number of states and highly impractical, as illustrated in Example 1.

[DHKP16a] improves on this idea and declares that we have reached a BSCC if the same states are repeated for long enough time. As it looks at the states visited, it does not need the size of the state space $|S|$ as a bound, but only p_{min}. The main idea is to *monitor each execution run on the fly in order to build statistical hypotheses about the structure of the Markov chain.* In particular, if from observing the current prefix of an execution run we can stipulate that with high probability a bottom strongly connected component (BSCC) of the chain has been entered, then we can terminate the current execution run. This is the first SMC algorithm that uses information obtained from execution prefixes.

Example 1. Consider the property of reaching state r in the Markov chain depicted in Fig. 1. While the execution runs reaching r satisfy the property and can be stopped without ever entering any v_i, the finite execution paths without r, such as *stuttutuut*, are inconclusive. In other words, observing this path does not rule out the existence of a transition from, e.g., u to r, which, if existing, would eventually be taken with probability 1. This transition could have arbitrarily low probability, rendering its detection arbitrarily unlikely, yet its presence would change the probability of satisfying the property from 0.5 to 1. However, knowing that if there exists such a transition leaving the set, its transition probability is at least $p_{\min} = 0.01$, we can estimate the probability that the system is stuck in the set $\{t, u\}$ of states. Indeed, if existing, the exit transition was missed at least four times during the execution above, no matter whether it exits t or u. Consequently, the probability that there is no such transition and $\{t, u\}$ is a BSCC is at least $1 - (1 - p_{\min})^4$.

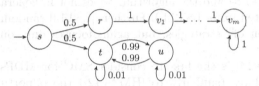

Fig. 1. A Markov chain.

This means that in the approach of [DHKP16a], in order to get 99 % confidence that $\{t, u\}$ is a BSCC, we only need to see both t and u around 500 times on a run, since $1 - (1 - p_{\min})^{500} = 1 - 0.99^{500} \approx 0.993$. This is in stark contrast to a priori bounds that provide the same level of confidence, such as the $(1/p_{\min})^{|S|} = 100^{\mathcal{O}(m)}$ runs required by [BCC+14], which is infeasible for large m of our example. In contrast, the performance of the method [DHKP16a] is independent of m. $\qquad\qquad \triangle$

Experimental results show that for many chains arising in practice, such as the concurrent probabilistic protocols from the PRISM benchmark suite, the BSCCs are reached quickly and, even more importantly, can be small even for very large systems. Consequently, many execution runs can be stopped quickly. Moreover, since the number of execution runs necessary for a required confidence level is independent of the size of the state space, it is not very large even for highly confident results (think of opinion polls). It is therefore not surprising that, experimentally, in most cases from the benchmark suite, this method outperforms previous methods (often even the numerical methods) despite requiring much less knowledge of the Markov chain, and despite providing strong guarantees in the form of confidence bounds.

3.3   Statistical Model Checking for MDPs

The development of statistical model checking techniques for probabilistic models with *nondeterminism*, such as MDPs, is an important topic, treated in several recent papers.

In [BFHH11], unbounded properties are analysed for MDPs with spurious nondeterminism, where the way it is resolved does not affect the desired property. In the case with general non-determinism, one approach is to give the nondeterminism a probabilistic semantics, e.g., using a uniform distribution instead, as for timed automata in [DLL+11a, DLL+11b, Lar13]. Others [LP12, HMZ+12, BCC+14] aim to quantify over all strategies and produce an ϵ-optimal strategy. The work in [LP12] and [HMZ+12] deals with the problem in the setting of discounted (and for the purposes of approximation thus bounded) or bounded properties, respectively. In the latter work, candidates for optimal strategies are generated and gradually improved, but "at any given point we cannot quantify how close to optimal the candidate scheduler is" (cited from [HMZ+12]) and the algorithm "does not in general converge to the true optimum" (cited from [LST14]). Further, [LST14] randomly samples (compact representation of) strategies, but again focuses only on (time-)bounded properties.

Finally, [BCC+14] is the first to consider SMC for MDPs and unbounded properties. It explores (similarly to [HMZ+12]) the opportunities offered by learning-based methods, as used in fields such as planning or reinforcement learning [SB98]. The algorithm assumes information limited to $|S|$ and $p_{\min}$ and is based on *delayed Q-learning* (DQL) [SLW+06]. Throughout the algorithm both lower and upper bounds on the result are gradually improved. These bounds are guaranteed to be *probably approximately correct (PAC)*, i.e., there is a non-zero probability that the bounds are incorrect, but they are correct with probability that can be set arbitrarily close to 1.

The crucial steps of [BCC+14] are (1) modifying the DQL algorithm with PAC guarantees of [SLW+06] from the discounted setting to the undiscounted setting, but where terminating states are reached almost surely, and (2) lifting this to general MDPs with MECs, where terminating states may not be reached.

The idea of step (1) is to simulate the system using a continuously updated strategy, implicitly defined by choosing the action that currently yields the highest upper bound. Intuitively, we pick actions that seem most promising, offering the highest gain, and if they turn out not to stand up to our expectation, we lower their upper bound and thus implicitly cause to choose a different action next time. The updates of the values are happening based on the average of the recent samples and thus simulate value iteration using experimental data (since transition probabilities are not available).

The idea of step (2) is to detect end components on the fly. After a long enough trace, we can deduce we are stuck in an EC. The length of the trace can be bounded (for a given confidence) by $|S|$ and $p_{\min}$. Indeed, similarly to the case with MCs, if there is a way out of the EC it is sufficient to take a path of length $|S|$, which has probability at least $p_{\min}^{|S|}$.

This technique extends easily to all LTL objectives and thus also to both maximum and minimum probabilities.

3.4 Strategy Representation

Representing the resulting strategy compactly is important since either (i) it needs to be implemented as a controller and must be simple enough, or (ii) it is a counterexample when trying to prove a property for all strategies and then the corresponding bug needs to be understood and fixed. There are several different classes of data structures and algorithms to represent strategies.

Firstly, in artificial intelligence, compact (factored) representations of MDP structure have been developed using dynamic Bayesian networks [BDG95, KK99], probabilistic STRIPS [KHW94], algebraic decision diagrams [HSaHB99], and also decision trees [BDG95]. Formalisms used to represent MDPs can, in principle, be used to represent values and strategies as well. In particular, variants of decision trees are probably the most used [BDG95, CK91, KP99]. For a detailed survey of compact representations see [BDH99].

Secondly, in the context of verification, MDPs are often represented using variants of (MT)BDDs [dAKN+00, HKN+03, MP04], and strategies by BDDs [WBB+10].

Thirdly, [AL09] uses a directed on-the-fly search to compute sets of most probable diagnostic paths. The notion of paths encoded as AND/OR trees has also been studied in [LL13] to represent probabilistic counter-examples visually as fault trees, and then derive causal (the cause and effect) relationship between events. [WJV+13, DJW+14] compute a smallest set of guarded commands (of a PRISM-like language) that induce a critical subsystem, but, unlike other methods, does not provide a compact representation of actual decisions needed to reach an erroneous state; moreover, there is not always a command based counterexample.

Finally, *decision trees* have been used in connection with real-time dynamic programming and reinforcement learning to represent the learned approximation of the value function [BD96, Pye03]. Learning a compact decision tree representation of a strategy has been investigated in [SLT10] for the case of body sensor networks with discounted objectives. In [BCC+15], three steps are proposed to obtain the desired strategy representation. Each of them has a positive effect on the resulting size.

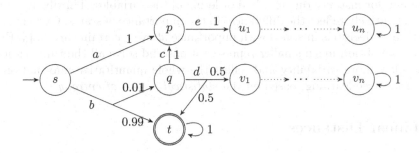

Fig. 2. An MDP M with reachability objective t

1. *Obtaining a (possibly partially defined and liberal) ε-optimal strategy.* The ε-optimal strategies produced by standard methods, such as value iteration of PRISM [KP13], may be too large to compute and overly specific. Firstly, as argued in [BCC+14], typically only a small fraction of the system needs to be explored in order to find an ε-optimal strategy, whereas most states are reached with only a very small probability. Without much loss, the strategy may not be defined there. For example, in the MDP M depicted in Fig. 2, the decision in q (and v_i's) is almost irrelevant for the overall probability of reaching t from s. Such a partially defined strategy can be obtained using *statistical* methods [BCC+14].

2. *Identifying important parts of the strategy.* A concept of *importance* of a state s w.r.t. a strategy for reaching *goal* is defined by $\mathbb{P}[\Diamond s \mid \Diamond goal]$. Let us shed some light on this definition. Observe that only a fraction of states can be reached while following the strategy, and thus have positive importance. On the unreachable states, with zero importance, the definition of the strategy is useless. For instance, in M, both states p and q must have been explored when constructing the strategy in order to find out whether it is better to take action a or b. However, if the resulting strategy is to use b and d, the information what to do in u_i's is useless. In addition, we consider v_i's to be of zero importance, too, since they are never reached on the way to target. Furthermore, apart from ignoring states with zero importance, it is desirable to partially ignore decisions that are unlikely to be made (in less important states such as q), and in contrast, stress more the decisions in important states likely to be visited (such as s). The crucial notion of importance is obviously not computed, but only estimated *statistically by simulating* the system under the given strategy.

3. *Data structures for compact representation of strategies.* The explicit representation of a strategy by a table of pairs (state, action to play) results in a huge amount of data since the systems often have millions of states. Therefore, a symbolic representation by binary decision diagrams (BDD) looks as a reasonable option. However, there are several drawbacks of using BDDs. Firstly, due to the bit-level representation of the state-action pairs, the resulting BDD is not very readable. Secondly, it is often still too large to be understood by human, for instance due to a bad ordering of the variables. Thirdly, it cannot quantitatively reflect the differences in the importance of states. Of course, we can store decisions in states with importance above a certain threshold. However, we obtain much smaller representations and solve all the three issues if we allow more variability and reflect the whole quantitative information by decision-tree learning, based on the *statistical notion of entropy.*

4   Linear Distances

The distance between processes s and t is typically formalized as $\sup_{p \in \mathcal{C}} |p(s) - p(t)|$ where $\mathcal{C}$ is a class of properties of interest and $p(s)$ is a quantitative value of the property p in process s [DGJP99]. This notion has been introduced in [DGJP99] for Markov chains and further developed in various settings, such as Markov decision processes [FPP04], quantitative transition systems [dAMRS07], or concurrent games [dAFS04].

Several kinds of distances have been investigated for Markov chains. On the one hand, [Aba13, DGJP99, vBW06, vBSW07, BBLM13c, BBLM13b, BBLM13a, GP11], lift the equivalence given by the probabilistic bisimulation of Larsen and Skou [LS89] into *branching distances*. On the other hand, there are *linear distances*, in particular total variation distance [CK14, BBLM15b] and trace distances [JMLM14, BBLM15a]. Linear distances are particularly appropriate when (i) we are interested in linear-time properties, and/or (ii) we want to estimate the distance based only on simulation runs of the system, i.e. in a black-box setting. (Recall that for branching distances, the underlying probabilistic bisimulation corresponds to testing equivalence where not only runs from the initial state can be observed, but also the current state of the system can be dumped at any moment and system copies restarted from that state [LS89].)

In contrast, a simple framework for linear distances between Markov chains can be defined (as in [DHKP16b]) by the formula above, where $p(s)$ is the probability of satisfying p when starting a simulation run in state s (when p is seen as a language it is the probability to generate a trace belonging to p).

There are two main linear distances traditionally considered for Markov chains: total variation distance and trace distance. Algorithms have been proposed for both of them in the case when the Markov chains are known (*white-box setting*).

Firstly, for the *total variation distance* in the white-box setting, [CK14] shows that deciding whether it is 1 can be done in polynomial time, but computing it is NP-hard and not known to be decidable, however, it can be approximated; [BBLM15b] considers this distance more generally for semi-Markov processes, provides a different approximation algorithm, and shows it coincides with distances based on (i) metric temporal logic, and (ii) timed automata languages.

Secondly, *trace distance* is based on the notion of trace equivalence, which can be decided in polynomial time [DHR08] (however, trace refinement on Markov decision processes is already undecidable [FKS16]). Variants of trace distance are considered in [JMLM14] where it is taken as a limit of finite-trace distances, possibly using discounting or averaging. In [BBLM15a] the finite-trace distance is shown to coincide with distances based on (i) LTL and (ii) LTL without U-operator, i.e., only using X-operator and Boolean connectives; it is also shown NP-hard and not known to be decidable, similarly to the total variation distance; finally, an approximation algorithm is shown (again in the white-box setting), where the over-approximants are branching-time distances, showing a nice connection between the branching and linear distances.

Estimating distances only from simulating the systems (*black-box setting*) is considered in [DHKP16b]. One of the main difficulties is that the class C typically includes properties with arbitrarily long horizon or even infinite-horizon properties, whereas every simulation run is necessarily finite. Note that we do not want employ here any simplifications such as imposed fixed horizon or discounting, typically used for obtaining efficient algorithms, e.g., [DGJP99,vBW06,BBLM13b], and the undiscounted setting is fundamentally more complex [vBSW07]. Since even simpler tasks are impossible for unbounded horizon in the black-box setting without any further knowledge, it is assumed we know an upper bound on the size of the state space $|S|$ and a lower bound on the minimum transition probability $p_{\min}$. We now survey the results of [DHKP16b] in more detail.

4.1 Language-Based Framework and Statistical Estimation of Distances

For $i \in \{1, 2\}$, let $\mathcal{M}_i = (S, \mathbf{P}_i, \mu_i, L)$ denote a Markov chain and $(\mathsf{Runs}, \mathcal{F}, \mathbb{P}_i)$ the induced probability space. Since single runs of Markov chains typically have measure 0, the linear distances are introduced in [DHKP16b] using measurable sets of runs:

Definition 3 ($\mathcal{L}$-distance). *For a class $\mathcal{L} \subseteq \mathcal{F}$ of measurable ω-languages[1], the $\mathcal{L}$-distance $\mathsf{D}_{\mathcal{L}}$ is defined by*

$$\mathsf{D}_{\mathcal{L}}(\mathcal{M}_1, \mathcal{M}_2) = \sup_{X \in \mathcal{L}} |\mathbb{P}_1(X) - \mathbb{P}_2(X)| .$$

Note that every $\mathsf{D}_{\mathcal{L}}$ is a pseudo-metric, i.e. it is symmetric, it satisfies the triangle inequality, and the distance between identical MCs is 0. However, two different MCs can have distance 0, for instance, when they induce the same probability space. We now discuss several particularly interesting instantiations:

Example 2 (Total variation). One extreme choice is to consider all measurable languages, resulting in the *total variation distance* $\mathsf{D}_{\mathsf{TV}}(\mathcal{M}_1, \mathcal{M}_2) = \sup_{X \in \mathcal{F}(\Sigma)} |\mathbb{P}_1(X) - \mathbb{P}_2(X)|$.

Example 3 (Trace distances). The other extreme choices are to consider (1) only the generators of $\mathcal{F}(\Sigma)$, i.e. the cones $\{w\Sigma^{\omega} \mid w \in \Sigma^*\}$, resulting in the *finite-trace distance* $\mathsf{D}_{\mathsf{FT}}(\mathcal{M}_1, \mathcal{M}_2) = \sup_{w \in \Sigma^+} |\mathbb{P}_1(w) - \mathbb{P}_2(w)|$; or (2) only the elementary events, i.e. Σ^{ω}, resulting in the *infinite-trace distance* $\mathsf{D}_{\mathsf{IT}}(\mathcal{M}_1, \mathcal{M}_2) = \sup_{w \in \Sigma^{\omega}} |\mathbb{P}_1(w) - \mathbb{P}_2(w)|$.

Example 4 (Topological distances). There are many possible choices for $\mathcal{L}$ between the two extremes above, such as *clopen sets* Δ_1, which are finite unions of cones (being both closed and open), *open sets* Σ_1, which are infinite unions of cones, *closed sets* Π_1, or classes higher in the *Borel hierarchy* such as the class of ω-*regular* languages (within Δ_3), or languages given by thresholds for *mean payoff* (within Σ_3).

---

[1] Formally, the measurable space of ω-languages is given by the set Σ^{ω} equipped with a σ-algebra $\mathcal{F}(\Sigma)$ generated by the set of cones $\{w\Sigma^{\omega} \mid w \in \Sigma^*\}$. This ensures, for every measurable ω-language X, that $L^{-1}(X)$ is measurable in every MC.

Example 5 (Automata distances). The class $\mathcal{L}$ can be given by a class $\mathcal{A}$ of automata as $\{L(A) \mid A \in \mathcal{A}\}$. For instance, deterministic Rabin automata generate the class of ω-regular languages.

Example 6 (Logical distances). The class $\mathcal{L}$ can be given by a set of formulae $\mathfrak{L}$ of a linear-time logic inducing the languages of models $\mathcal{L} = \{L(\varphi) \mid \varphi \in \mathfrak{L}\}$. For instance, the class of ω-regular languages can also be given by the monadic second-order logic. Further useful choices include the *linear temporal logic* (LTL), or its fragments.

The introduced distances can also be considered in the discrete understanding, resulting in various notions of equivalence. For instance, the *finite-trace equivalence* E_{FT} can be derived from the finite-trace distance by the following discretization:

$$
\mathsf{E}_{\mathsf{FT}}(\mathcal{M}_1, \mathcal{M}_2) = \begin{cases} 0 & \text{if } \mathsf{D}_{\mathsf{FT}}(\mathcal{M}_1, \mathcal{M}_2) = 0 \\ 1 & \text{otherwise, i.e., } \mathsf{D}_{\mathsf{FT}}(\mathcal{M}_1, \mathcal{M}_2) > 0. \end{cases}
$$

We can now use statistics on finite simulation runs to (i) deduce information on the whole infinite runs and (ii) estimate the distance of the systems. For a particular distance function $\mathsf{D}_{\mathcal{L}}$, the goal is to construct an algorithm with the following specification:

Specification of $\mathcal{L}$-distance estimation

Input:
- two finite black-box MCs $\mathcal{M}_1, \mathcal{M}_2$ (i.e., access to any desired finite number of sampled simulation paths of any desired finite lengths)
- confidence $\alpha \in (0,1)$
- interval width $\delta \in (0,1)$

Output: interval I such that $|I| \leq \delta$ and $\Pr[\mathsf{D}_{\mathcal{L}}(\mathcal{M}_1, \mathcal{M}_2) \in I] \geq 1 - \alpha$

The method of [DHKP16b] assumes that $|S|$ and p_{min} (or the respective bounds) are known. Moreover, $|S|$ can be bounded using p_{min} and sufficiently many simulations; consequently, only p_{min} must be known. It is shown that the total variation distance cannot be estimated by simulating the systems, and that the finite-trace distance can be estimated. The former result is further exploited to show that the inestimability result holds also already for clopen sets, Rabin automata, and LTL (even without the Until-operator). However, it is also shown that infinite-trace distance and distances for some fragments of LTL are estimable. Moreover, restricting the size of automata also yields estimability. Furthermore, assuming finite precision of transition probabilities, e.g. they are given by at most two decimal digits, even the total variation distance can be estimated, exploiting the white-box algorithms. Under this assumption, *trace equivalence* can also be decided correctly with arbitrarily high probability.

5   Conclusion

We have surveyed statistical methods for model checking systems and estimating their distances for various classes of linear properties. While SMC for MCs is already a practical approach even for unbounded properties, SMC for MDPs and distance estimation for MCs can be applied in principle, but the current algorithms are not expected to scale and the search for efficient algorithms has just started. Some problems, such as distance estimation of MDPs cannot be done precisely even in the white-box setting. However, approximations and heuristics could still be considered and the statistical approach could be a viable option to achieve some positive results.

References

[Aba13] Abate, A.: Approximation metrics based on probabilistic bisimulations for general state-space Markov processes: a survey. Electr. Notes Theor. Comput. Sci. **297**, 3–25 (2013)

[AL09] Aljazzar, H., Leue, S.: Generation of counterexamples for model checking of markov decision processes. In: QEST, pp. 197–206. IEEE Computer Society (2009)

[BBB+10] Basu, A., Bensalem, S., Bozga, M., Caillaud, B., Delahaye, B., Legay, A.: Statistical abstraction and model-checking of large heterogeneous systems. In: Hatcliff, J., Zucca, E. (eds.) FMOODS/FORTE-2010. LNCS, vol. 6117, pp. 32–46. Springer, Heidelberg (2010). doi:10.1007/978-3-642-13464-7_4

[BBLM13a] Bacci, G., Bacci, G., Larsen, K.G., Mardare, R.: The BisimDist, library: efficient computation of bisimilarity distances for Markovian models. In: QEST, pp. 278–281 (2013)

[BBLM13b] Bacci, G., Bacci, G., Larsen, K.G., Mardare, R.: Computing behavioral distances, compositionally. In: Chatterjee, K., Sgall, J. (eds.) MFCS 2013. LNCS, vol. 8087, pp. 74–85. Springer, Heidelberg (2013). doi:10.1007/978-3-642-40313-2_9

[BBLM13c] Bacci, G., Bacci, G., Larsen, K.G., Mardare, R.: On-the-fly exact computation of bisimilarity distances. In: Piterman, N., Smolka, S.A. (eds.) TACAS 2013. LNCS, vol. 7795, pp. 1–15. Springer, Heidelberg (2013). doi:10.1007/978-3-642-36742-7_1

[BBLM15a] Bacci, G., Bacci, G., Larsen, K.G., Mardare, R: Converging from branching to linear metrics on Markov chains. In: ICTAC, pp. 349–367 (2015)

[BBLM15b] Bacci, G., Bacci, G., Larsen, K.G., Mardare, R.: On the total variation distance of Semi-Markov chains. In: Pitts, A. (ed.) FoSSaCS 2015. LNCS, vol. 9034, pp. 185–199. Springer, Heidelberg (2015). doi:10.1007/978-3-662-46678-0_12

[BCC+14] Brázdil, T., Chatterjee, K., Chmelík, M., Forejt, V., Křetínský, J., Kwiatkowska, M., Parker, D., Ujma, M.: Verification of Markov decision processes using learning algorithms. In: Cassez, F., Raskin, J.-F. (eds.) ATVA 2014. LNCS, vol. 8837, pp. 98–114. Springer, Heidelberg (2014). doi:10.1007/978-3-319-11936-6_8

[BCC+15] Brázdil, T., Chatterjee, K., Chmelík, M., Fellner, A., Křetínský, J.: Counterexample explanation by learning small strategies in markov decision processes. In: Kroening, D., Păsăreanu, C.S. (eds.) CAV 2015. LNCS, vol. 9206, pp. 158–177. Springer, Heidelberg (2015). doi:10.1007/978-3-319-21690-4_10

[BCLS13] Boyer, B., Corre, K., Legay, A., Sedwards, S.: PLASMA-lab: a flexible, distributable statistical model checking library. In: QEST, pp. 160–164 (2013)

[BD96] Boutilier, C., Dearden, R.: Approximating value trees in structured dynamic programming. In: Proceedings of the Thirteenth International Conference on Machine Learning, pp. 54–62 (1996)

[BDG95] Boutilier, C., Dearden, R., Goldszmidt, M.: Exploiting structure in policy construction. In: IJCAI-95, pp. 1104–1111 (1995)

[BDH99] Boutilier, C., Dean, T., Hanks, S.: Decision-theoretic planning: structural assumptions and computational leverage. JAIR 11, 1–94 (1999)

[BDL+12] Bulychev, P.E., David, A., Larsen, K.G., Mikucionis, M., Poulsen, D.B., Legay, A., Wang, Z.: UPPAAL-SMC: statistical model checking for priced timed automata. In: QAPL (2012)

[BFHH11] Bogdoll, J., Ferrer Fioriti, L.M., Hartmanns, A., Hermanns, H.: Partial order methods for statistical model checking and simulation. In: Bruni, R., Dingel, J. (eds.) FMOODS/FORTE -2011. LNCS, vol. 6722, pp. 59–74. Springer, Heidelberg (2011). doi:10.1007/978-3-642-21461-5_4

[BHH12] Bogdoll, J., Hartmanns, A., Hermanns, H.: Simulation and statistical model checking for modestly nondeterministic models. In: MMB/DFT, pp. 249–252 (2012)

[CK91] Chapman, D., Kaelbling, L.P.: Input generalization in delayed reinforcement learning: an algorithm and performance comparisons. Morgan Kaufmann (1991)

[CK14] Chen, T., Kiefer, S., On the total variation distance of labelled Markov chains. In: CSL-LICS, pp. 33:1–33:10 (2014)

[CY95] Courcoubetis, C., Yannakakis, M.: The complexity of probabilistic verification. J. ACM 42(4), 857–907 (1995)

[CZ11] Clarke, E.M., Zuliani, P.: Statistical model checking for cyber-physical systems. In: Bultan, T., Hsiung, P.-A. (eds.) ATVA 2011. LNCS, vol. 6996, pp. 1–12. Springer, Heidelberg (2011). doi:10.1007/978-3-642-24372-1_1

[dAFS04] Alfaro, L., Faella, M., Stoelinga, M.: Linear and branching metrics for quantitative transition systems. In: Díaz, J., Karhumäki, J., Lepistö, A., Sannella, D. (eds.) ICALP 2004. LNCS, vol. 3142, pp. 97–109. Springer, Heidelberg (2004). doi:10.1007/978-3-540-27836-8_11

[dAKN+00] Alfaro, L., Kwiatkowska, M., Norman, G., Parker, D., Segala, R.: Symbolic model checking of probabilistic processes using MTBDDs and the kronecker representation. In: Graf, S., Schwartzbach, M. (eds.) TACAS 2000. LNCS, vol. 1785, pp. 395–410. Springer, Heidelberg (2000). doi:10.1007/3-540-46419-0_27

[dAMRS07] de Alfaro, L., Majumdar, R., Raman, V., Stoelinga, M.: Game relations and metrics. In: LICS, pp. 99–108 (2007)

[DDL+12] David, A., Du, D., Larsen, K.G., Legay, A., Mikucionis, M., Poulsen, D.B., Sedwards, S.: Statistical model checking for stochastic hybrid systems. In: HSB, pp. 122–136 (2012)

[DDL+13] David, A., Du, D., Larsen, K.G., Legay, A., Mikucionis, M.: Optimizing control strategy using statistical model checking. In: NASA Formal Methods, pp. 352–367 (2013)

[DGJP99] Desharnais, J., Gupta, V., Jagadeesan, R., Panangaden, P.: Metrics for labeled Markov systems. In: Baeten, J.C.M., Mauw, S. (eds.) CONCUR 1999. LNCS, vol. 1664, pp. 258–273. Springer, Heidelberg (1999). doi:10. 1007/3-540-48320-9_19

[DHKP16a] Daca, P., Henzinger, T.A., Křetínský, J., Petrov, T.: Faster statistical model checking for unbounded temporal properties. In: Chechik, M., Raskin, J.-F. (eds.) TACAS 2016. LNCS, vol. 9636, pp. 112–129. Springer, Heidelberg (2016). doi:10.1007/978-3-662-49674-9_7

[DHKP16b] Daca, P., Henzinger, T.A., Křetínský, J., Petrov, T.: Linear distances between Markov chains. In: CONCUR (2016)

[DHR08] Doyen, L., Henzinger, T.A., Raskin, J.-F.: Equivalence of labeled Markov chains. Int. J. Found. Comput. Sci. 19(3), 549–563 (2008)

[DJW+14] Dehnert, C., Jansen, N., Wimmer, R., Ábrahám, E., Katoen, J.-P.: Fast debugging of PRISM models. In: Cassez, F., Raskin, J.-F. (eds.) ATVA 2014. LNCS, vol. 8837, pp. 146–162. Springer, Heidelberg (2014). doi:10. 1007/978-3-319-11936-6_11

[DLL+11a] David, A., Larsen, K.G., Legay, A., Mikučionis, M., Poulsen, D.B., Vliet, J., Wang, Z.: Statistical model checking for networks of priced timed automata. In: Fahrenberg, U., Tripakis, S. (eds.) FORMATS 2011. LNCS, vol. 6919, pp. 80–96. Springer, Heidelberg (2011). doi:10.1007/ 978-3-642-24310-3_7

[DLL+11b] David, A., Larsen, K.G., Legay, A., Mikučionis, M., Wang, Z.: Time for statistical model checking of real-time systems. In: Gopalakrishnan, G., Qadeer, S. (eds.) CAV 2011. LNCS, vol. 6806, pp. 349–355. Springer, Heidelberg (2011). doi:10.1007/978-3-642-22110-1_27

[DLL+15] David, A., Larsen, K.G., Legay, A., Mikucionis, M., Poulsen, D.B.: Uppaal SMC tutorial. STTT 17(4), 397–415 (2015)

[EGF12] Ellen, C., Gerwinn, S., Fränzle, M.: Confidence bounds for statistical model checking of probabilistic hybrid systems. In: Jurdziński, M., Ničković, D. (eds.) FORMATS 2012. LNCS, vol. 7595, pp. 123–138. Springer, Heidelberg (2012). doi:10.1007/978-3-642-33365-1_10

[FKS16] Fijalkow, N., Kiefer, S., Shirmohammadi, M.: Trace refinement in labelled Markov decision processes. In: FOSSACS, pp. 303–318 (2016)

[FPP04] Ferns, N., Panangaden, P., Precup, D.: Metrics for finite Markov decision processes. In: IAAI, pp. 950–951 (2004)

[GP11] Girard, A., Pappas, G.J.: Approximate bisimulation: a bridge between computer science and control theory. Eur. J. Control 17(5–6), 568–578 (2011)

[HJ94] Hansson, H., Jonsson, B.: A logic for reasoning about time and reliability. Formal Asp. Comput. 6(5), 512–535 (1994)

[HJB+10] He, R., Jennings, P., Basu, S., Ghosh, A.P., Wu, H.: A bounded statistical approach for model checking of unbounded until properties. In: ASE, pp. 225–234 (2010)

[HKN+03] Hermanns, H., Kwiatkowska, M., Norman, G., Parker, D., Siegle, M.: On the use of MTBDDs for performability analysis and verification of stochastic systems. J. Logic Algebraic Program. 56(1–2), 23–67 (2003)

[HLMP04] Hérault, T., Lassaigne, R., Magniette, F., Peyronnet, S.: Approximate probabilistic model checking. In: Steffen, B., Levi, G. (eds.) VMCAI 2004. LNCS, vol. 2937, pp. 73–84. Springer, Heidelberg (2004). doi:10.1007/978-3-540-24622-0_8

[HMZ+12] Henriques, D., Martins, J., Zuliani, P., Platzer, A., Clarke, E.M.: Statistical model checking for Markov decision processes. In: QEST, pp. 84–93 (2012)

[HSaHB99] Hoey, J., St-aubin, R., Hu, A., Boutilier, C.: Spudd: stochastic planning using decision diagrams. In: Proceedings of the Fifteenth Conference on Uncertainty in Artificial Intelligence, pp. 279–288. Morgan Kaufmann (1999)

[JCL+09] Jha, S.K., Clarke, E.M., Langmead, C.J., Legay, A., Platzer, A., Zuliani, P.: A Bayesian approach to model checking biological systems. In: Degano, P., Gorrieri, R. (eds.) CMSB 2009. LNCS, vol. 5688, pp. 218–234. Springer, Heidelberg (2009). doi:10.1007/978-3-642-03845-7_15

[JLS12] Jégourel, C., Legay, A., Sedwards, S.: A platform for high performance statistical model checking - PLASMA. In: TACAS, pp. 498–503 (2012)

[JMLM14] Jaeger, M., Mao, H., Guldstrand Larsen, K., Mardare, R.: Continuity properties of distances for Markov processes. In: Norman, G., Sanders, W. (eds.) QEST 2014. LNCS, vol. 8657, pp. 297–312. Springer, Heidelberg (2014). doi:10.1007/978-3-319-10696-0_24

[KHW94] Kushmerick, N., Hanks, S., Weld, D.: An algorithm for probabilistic least-commitment planning. In: Proceedings of AAAI-94, pp. 1073–1078 (1994)

[KK99] Kearns, M., Koller, D.: Efficient reinforcement learning in factored MDPs. In: IJCAI, pp. 740–747. Morgan Kaufmann Publishers Inc., San Francisco (1999)

[KP99] Koller, D., Parr, R.: Computing factored value functions for policies in structured MDPs. In: Proceedings of the Sixteenth International Joint Conference on Artificial Intelligence, pp. 1332–1339. Morgan Kaufmann (1999)

[KP13] Kwiatkowska, M., Parker, D.: Automated verification and strategy synthesis for probabilistic systems. In: Hung, D., Ogawa, M. (eds.) ATVA 2013. LNCS, vol. 8172, pp. 5–22. Springer, Heidelberg (2013). doi:10.1007/978-3-319-02444-8_2

[KSK76] Kemeny, J., Snell, J., Knapp, A.: Denumerable Markov Chains. Springer, New York (1976)

[Lar12] Larsen, K.G.: Statistical model checking, refinement checking, optimization, ..for stochastic hybrid systems. In: Jurdziński, M., Ničković, D. (eds.) FORMATS 2012. LNCS, vol. 7595, pp. 7–10. Springer, Heidelberg (2012). doi:10.1007/978-3-642-33365-1_2

[Lar13] Guldstrand Larsen, K.: Priced timed automata and statistical model checking. In: Johnsen, E.B., Petre, L. (eds.) IFM 2013. LNCS, vol. 7940, pp. 154–161. Springer, Heidelberg (2013). doi:10.1007/978-3-642-38613-8_11

[LL13] Leitner-Fischer, F., Leue, S.: Probabilistic fault tree synthesis using causality computation. IJCCBS 4(2), 119–143 (2013)

[LP08] Lassaigne, R., Peyronnet, S.: Probabilistic verification and approximation. Ann. Pure Appl. Logic 152(1–3), 122–131 (2008)

[LP12] Lassaigne, R., Peyronnet, S.: Approximate planning and verification for large Markov decision processes. In: SAC, pp. 1314–1319 (2012)

[LS83] Lehmann, D., Shelah, S.: Reasoning with time and chance. In: Diaz, J. (ed.) ICALP 1983. LNCS, vol. 154, pp. 445–457. Springer, Heidelberg (1983). doi:10.1007/BFb0036928

[LS89] Larsen, K.G., Skou, A: Bisimulation through probabilistic testing. In: POPL, pp. 344–352 (1989)

[LST14] Legay, A., Sedwards, S., Traonouez, L.-M.: Scalable verification of Markov decision processes. In: Canal, C., Idani, A. (eds.) SEFM 2014. LNCS, vol. 8938, pp. 350–362. Springer, Heidelberg (2015). doi:10.1007/978-3-319-15201-1_23

[MP04] Miner, A., Parker, D.: Symbolic representations and analysis of large probabilistic systems. In: Baier, C., Haverkort, B.R., Hermanns, H., Katoen, J.-P., Siegle, M. (eds.) Validation of Stochastic Systems. LNCS, vol. 2925, pp. 296–338. Springer, Heidelberg (2004). doi:10.1007/978-3-540-24611-4_9

[PGL+13] Palaniappan, S.K., Gyori, B.M., Liu, B., Hsu, D., Thiagarajan, P.S.: Statistical model checking based calibration and analysis of bio-pathway models. In: Gupta, A., Henzinger, T.A. (eds.) CMSB 2013. LNCS, vol. 8130, pp. 120–134. Springer, Heidelberg (2013). doi:10.1007/978-3-642-40708-6_10

[Pye03] Pyeatt, L.D.: Reinforcement learning with decision trees. In: The 21st IASTED International Multi-Conference on Applied Informatics (AI 2003), February 10–13, 2003, Innsbruck, Austria, pp. 26–31 (2003)

[RP09] Rabih, D., Pekergin, N.: Statistical model checking using perfect simulation. In: Liu, Z., Ravn, A.P. (eds.) ATVA 2009. LNCS, vol. 5799, pp. 120–134. Springer, Heidelberg (2009). doi:10.1007/978-3-642-04761-9_11

[SB98] Sutton, R., Barto, A., Learning, R.: An Introduction. MIT Press, Cambridge (1998)

[SLT10] Raghavendra, C.S., Liu, S., Panangadan, A., Talukder, A.: Compact representation of coordinated sampling policies for body sensor networks. In: Proceedings of Workshop on Advances in Communication and Networks (Smart Homes for Tele-Health), pp. 6–10. IEEE (2010)

[SLW+06] Strehl, A.L., Li, L., Wiewiora, E., Langford, J., Littman, M.L.: PAC model-free reinforcement learning. In: ICML, pp. 881–888 (2006)

[SVA04] Sen, K., Viswanathan, M., Agha, G.: Statistical model checking of black-box probabilistic systems. In: Alur, R., Peled, D.A. (eds.) CAV 2004. LNCS, vol. 3114, pp. 202–215. Springer, Heidelberg (2004). doi:10.1007/978-3-540-27813-9_16

[SVA05] Sen, K., Viswanathan, M., Agha, G.: On statistical model checking of stochastic systems. In: Etessami, K., Rajamani, S.K. (eds.) CAV 2005. LNCS, vol. 3576, pp. 266–280. Springer, Heidelberg (2005). doi:10.1007/11513988_26

[Var85] Vardi, M.Y.: Automatic verification of probabilistic concurrent finite-state programs. In: FOCS, pp. 327–338 (1985)

[vBSW07] van Breugel, F., Sharma, B., Worrell, J.: Approximating a behavioural pseudometric without discount for probabilistic systems. In: FOSSACS, pp. 123–137 (2007)

[vBW06] van Breugel, F., Worrell, J.: Approximating and computing behavioural distances in probabilistic transition systems. Theor. Comput. Sci. 360(1–3), 373–385 (2006)

[WBB+10] Wimmer, R., Braitling, B., Becker, B., Hahn, E.M., Crouzen, P., Hermanns, H., Dhama, A., Theel, O.: Symblicit calculation of long-run averages for concurrent probabilistic systems. In: QEST, pp. 27–36, Washington, DC, USA. IEEE Computer Society (2010)

[WJV+13] Wimmer, R., Jansen, N., Vorpahl, A., Ábrahám, E., Katoen, J.-P., Becker, B.: High-level counterexamples for probabilistic automata. In: Joshi, K., Siegle, M., Stoelinga, M., D'Argenio, P.R. (eds.) QEST 2013. LNCS, vol. 8054, pp. 39–54. Springer, Heidelberg (2013). doi:10.1007/978-3-642-40196-1_4

[YCZ10] Younes, H.L.S., Clarke, E.M., Zuliani, P.: Statistical verification of probabilistic properties with unbounded until. In: Davies, J., Silva, L., Simao, A. (eds.) SBMF 2010. LNCS, vol. 6527, pp. 144–160. Springer, Heidelberg (2011). doi:10.1007/978-3-642-19829-8_10

[YKNP06] Younes, H.L.S., Kwiatkowska, M.Z., Norman, G., Parker, D.: Numerical vs. statistical probabilistic model checking. STTT 8(3), 216–228 (2006)

[YS02] Younes, H.L.S., Simmons, R.G.: Probabilistic verification of discrete event systems using acceptance sampling. In: Brinksma, E., Larsen, K.G. (eds.) CAV 2002. LNCS, vol. 2404, pp. 223–235. Springer, Heidelberg (2002). doi:10.1007/3-540-45657-0_17

[ZPC10] Zuliani, P., Platzer, A., Clarke, E.M. Bayesian statistical model checking with application to simulink/stateflow verification. In: HSCC, pp. 243–252 (2010)

Feedback Control for Statistical Model Checking of Cyber-Physical Systems

K. Kalajdzic[1], C. Jegourel[4], A. Lukina[1(✉)], E. Bartocci[1], A. Legay[2],
S.A. Smolka[3], and R. Grosu[1]

[1] Vienna University of Technology, Vienna, Austria
anna.lukina@tuwien.ac.at
[2] INRIA Rennes, Bretagne Atlantique, Rennes, France
[3] Stony Brook University, New York, NY, USA
[4] National University of Singapore, Singapore, Singapore

Abstract. We introduce *feedback-control statistical system checking (FC-SSC)*, a new approach to statistical model checking that exploits principles of feedback-control for the analysis of cyber-physical systems (CPS). FC-SSC uses stochastic system identification to learn a CPS model, importance sampling to estimate the CPS state, and importance splitting to control the CPS so that the probability that the CPS satisfies a given property can be efficiently inferred. We illustrate the utility of FC-SSC on two example applications, each of which is simple enough to be easily understood, yet complex enough to exhibit all of FC-SCC's features. To the best of our knowledge, FC-SSC is the first statistical system checker to efficiently estimate the probability of rare events in realistic CPS applications or in any complex probabilistic program whose model is either not available, or is infeasible to derive through static-analysis techniques.

1 Introduction

Modern distributed systems, and *cyber-physical systems* (CPSs) in particular, embed sensing, computation, actuation, and communication within the physical substratum, resulting in open, probabilistic, systems of systems. CPS examples include smart factories, transportation systems, and health-care systems [4].

Openness, uncertainty, and distribution, however, render the problem of *accurate prediction* of the (emergent) behavior of CPSs extremely challenging. Because of (exponential) state explosion, model-based approaches to this problem that rely on *exhaustive state-space exploration* such as classical model checking (MC) [5], are ineffective. *Approximate prediction* techniques, such as *statistical model checking* (SMC), have therefore recently become increasingly popular [6,10,22]. The key idea behind SMC is to sample the model's execution behavior through simulation, and to use statistical measures to predict, with a desired confidence and error margin, whether the system satisfies a given property. An important advantage of SMC is that the sampling can be parallelized, thus benefiting from recent advances in *multi-core* and *GPU* technologies [2].

© Springer International Publishing AG 2016
T. Margaria and B. Steffen (Eds.): ISoLA 2016, Part I, LNCS 9952, pp. 46–61, 2016.
DOI: 10.1007/978-3-319-47166-2_4

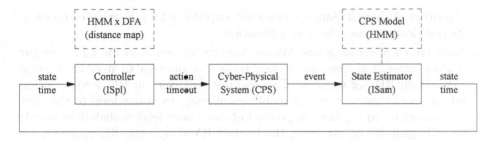

Fig. 1. FC-SSC as a feedback controller exploiting ISam and ISpl.

A serious obstacle in the application of SMC techniques is their poor performance in predicting the satisfaction of properties holding with very low probability, so-called *rare events* (REs). In such cases, the number of samples required to attain a high confidence ratio and a low error margin explodes [10,23]. Two sequential Monte-Carlo techniques, *importance sampling (ISam)* [7] and *importance splitting (ISpl)* [9], originally developed for statistical physics, promise to overcome this obstacle. These techniques have recently been adopted by the robotics [19,21] and SMC communities [11,12,15,20,23].

ISpl and ISam have individually demonstrated their utility on a number of models. We are still, however, *a long way from the statistical checking (SC) of CPSs*. In particular, the following three challenges have not yet been addressed:

1. *The CPS model is generally not known*, as either the basic laws of the substratum, or the control program, are only partially available. Consequently, a finite-model abstraction through static analysis is infeasible.
2. *The CPS state is generally not known*, as either the output represents only a small fraction of the set of state variables, or the output represents an arbitrary function defined on a subset of the state variables.
3. *The CPS steering policy towards REs is generally not known*, as the system model is not available in advance, and consequently, the relationship between the RE property and the CPS behavior is not known as well.

In this paper, we attack these three challenges by proposing a novel *feedback-control framework for the SC of CPSs (FC-SSC)*; see Fig. 1. To the best of our knowledge, this is the first attempt to define SC as control and to completely automate RE estimation in CPSs. In FC-SSC, we automatically:

1. *Learn the CPS model.* We assume that we *can observe the CPS outputs*, which are either measurements of the physical part or values output by the cyber part. Using a (learning) set of observation sequences and statistical system-identification (machine-learning) techniques [18], we automatically *learn a hidden Markov Model* (HMM) of the CPS under investigation.
2. *Infer the CPS state.* Having access to the current observation sequence and the learned HMM, we employ statistical inference techniques to determine the hidden state [18]. To scale up the inference, we use ISam as an approximation

algorithm. Although ISam was originally introduced for rare-event estimation, its practical success is in state estimation.

3. *Infer the CPS control policy.* We assume that we *can start the CPS, run for a given amount of time, pause, and resume it.* In order to steer the system towards an RE, we use ISpl. This requires, however, an RE decomposition into a set of *levels*, s.t. the probabilities of going from one level to the next are essentially equal, and the product of these inter-level probabilities equals the RE probability. By using the learned HMM and the RE property, we automatically derive an optimal RE decomposition into levels.

In FC-SSC, ISam estimates the current CPS state and the current level, and ISpl controls the execution of the CPS based on this information. Both techniques depend on the HMM identified during a preliminary, learning stage. FC-SSC may be applied to the approximate analysis of any complex probabilistic program whose: (1) Monitoring is feasible through appropriate instrumentation, but whose (2) Model derivation is infeasible through static analysis techniques (due to e.g. sheer size, complicated pointer manipulation).

The rest of the paper is organized as follows. In Sect. 2, we introduce two running examples, simple enough to illustrate the main concepts, while still capturing the essential features of complex CPSs. In Sect. 3, we introduce our learning algorithm, based on expectation maximization [18]. In Sect. 4, we present our ISam-based state-estimation algorithm, while in Sect. 5, we present our ISpl-based control algorithm. In Sect. 7, we discuss the results we obtained for the two example systems. Finally, in Sect. 8, we offer our concluding remarks and discuss future work.

2   Running Examples

In order to illustrate the techniques employed in FC-SSC, we use as running examples two simple (but not too simple) probabilistic programs: Dining Philosophers and Success Runs.

Dining Philosophers. This example was chosen because its model is very well known, its complexity nicely scales up, and its rare events are very intuitive. Moreover, the multi-threaded program we use to implement Dining Philosophers illustrates the difficulties encountered when trying to model check real programs, such as their interaction with the operating system and their large state vector. In classic model checking, the former would require checking the associated operating-system functions, and the latter would require some cone-of-influence program slicing. Both are hard to achieve in practice.

For monitoring purposes however, all that one needs to do is to instrument the entities of interest (variables, assignments, procedure calls, etc.) and to run the program. Extending monitoring to SSC requires however an HMM, a way of estimating the hidden states, and a way to control the program. Our code is based on the variant of randomized Dining Philosophers problem without fairness assumption, introduced in [8]. To minimize the interference of instrumentation

```
void *philosopher(int this) { while (true) {
  do_some_work();
  switch (phil_state[this]) {
  case 0: /* cannot stay thinking so move to trying */
    phil_state[this] = 1; break;
  case 1: /* draw randomly */
    if (flip_coin() == COIN_HEADS) phil_state[this] = 2;
    else phil_state[this] = 3; break;
  case 2: /* try to pick up left fork */
    emit_symbol(SYM_TRY); pthread_mutex_lock(&fork[this]);
    if (fork_state[this] == FORK_FREE)
      phil_state[this] = 4; fork_state[this] = FORK_TAKEN;
    pthread_mutex_unlock(&fork[this]); break;
  case 3: /* try to pick up right fork */
    emit_symbol(SYM_TRY); pthread_mutex_lock(&fork[(this + 1) % n_phil]);
    if (fork_state[(this + 1) % n_phil] == FORK_FREE)
      phil_state[this] = 5; fork_state[(this + 1) % n_phil] = FORK_TAKEN;
    pthread_mutex_unlock(&fork[(this + 1) % n_phil]); break;
  ...
  case 9: /* eat */
    emit_symbol(SYM_EAT);
    if (flip_coin() == COIN_HEADS) {
      pthread_mutex_lock(&fork[this]); phil_state[this] = 10;
      fork_state[this] = FORK_FREE; pthread_mutex_unlock(&fork[this]);}
    else {
      pthread_mutex_lock(&fork[(this + 1) % n_phil]); phil_state[this] = 11;
      fork_state[(this + 1) % n_phil] = FORK_FREE;
      pthread_mutex_unlock(&fork[(this + 1) % n_phil]);} break;
  case 11: /* drop left fork */
    emit_symbol(SYM_DROP_FORKS); pthread_mutex_lock(&fork[this]);
    phil_state[this] = 0; fork_state[this] = FORK_FREE;
    pthread_mutex_unlock(&fork[this]); break;
  default: fatal_error("incorrect philosopher state"); }}}
```

Fig. 2. C code snippet of the main loop in the Dining Philosophers

with the program execution, we instrument only one thread. To account for the unknown and possibly distinct executions of the uninstrumented part of the program, we add loops (do_some_work) whose execution time is distributed, for simplicity, according to a uniform probability distribution.

For space reasons, we show in Fig. 2 only a snippet of the C-code of the main loop of a philosopher. The full code is available from [1]. As it is well known, each philosopher undergoes a sequence of modes, from thinking, to picking one fork, then the other, eating and then dropping the forks. It may drop the single fork it holds also when it cannot pick up the other fork. Given, say, 100 philosophers, the RE in this case is the property that a particular philosopher k succeeds to eat within a given interval of time.

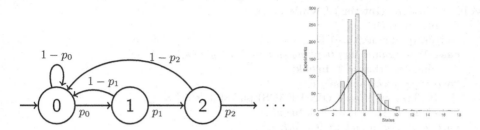

Fig. 3. Success Runs: the state-transition graph (left) and distribution of maximal reached states for $N = 1000$ experiments with $p_i = 0.5$ $\forall i = 0{:}n$ (right)

Success Runs. This model is a sequence of independent Bernoulli trials. An event in each state i of the discrete-time Markov chain below results in a success with probability p_i, or a failure with probability $1 - p_i$, where $0 < p_i < 1$. The example is straightforward and, at the same time flexible enough, to illustrate the steps of the core statistical approach of FC-SSC.

A simulation of even a simple case, when the chances of success and failure are equal, for $T > 7$ time units without resetting back to zero is already a challenge. Thus, as a RE we consider reaching a state n within $T = n - 1$ steps, i.e. without any failures or delay. In an automotive industry this event corresponds to the number of time units without stochastic freezing or restarting of an on-board computer.

3   System Identification

We assume that the CPS models are finite state. This captures the influence of the cyber part on the CPS. For simplicity, we also assume that the models have only one state variable, that is, they are *Hidden Markov Models* (HMMs) [19]. Note, however, that all the techniques introduced in this and the following sections work as well for continuous-state linear Gaussian models [18].

An HMM defines two sequences, $X_1, X_2, \ldots, X_t$ and $Y_1, Y_2, \ldots, Y_t$, over time, where X_t and Y_t are the random state and output variable at time t, respectively. The values x_t of X_t and y_t of Y_t range over the finite sets Σ and Υ, respectively. Since in an HMM X_{t+1} only depends on X_t, and Y_t only depends on X_t, the HMM can be concisely represented by three probability distributions (PDs):

- $\pi = P(X_1)$, the prior *initial state* PD,
- $A = P(X_{t+1}|X_t)$, the conditional *next state* PD,
- $C = P(Y_t|X_t)$, the conditional *output* PD.

Equivalently, an HMM consists of a triple $H = (\pi, A, C)$, where π is a probability vector of dimension $N = |\Sigma|$ having an entry for each $P(X_1 = x_1)$, and A and C are probability matrices of dimensions $N \times N$ and $N \times |\Upsilon|$, respectively. Given N, Υ, and observation sequence $\overline{y} = y_1 y_2 \ldots y_T$, the goal of *system identification* is to learn the HMM $H = (\pi, A, C)$, maximizing the expectation that an execution sequence $\overline{x} = x_1 \ldots x_T$ of H produces output $\overline{y}$.

The algorithm is therefore known as the *expectation-maximization (EM)*, or *Baum-Welch (BW)* (after its authors) algorithm [17,18]. Maximizing the expectation as a function of H is equivalent to maximizing:

$$\mathcal{L}(H) = \log P(\overline{y}|H) = \log \sum_x P(x, \overline{y}|H) = \log \sum_x Q(x)(P(x, \overline{y}|H)/Q(x))$$

where $Q(x)$ is an arbitrary distribution over the state variable. Using Jensen's inequality and expanding the division within the logarithm one obtains:

$$\mathcal{L}(H) \geq \sum_x Q(x) \log P(x, \overline{y}|H) - \sum_x Q(x) \log Q(x) = \mathcal{F}(H, Q)$$

The EM algorithm now alternates between two maximization steps:

$$\text{E-step} : Q_{k+1} = \text{argmax}_Q \ \mathcal{F}(H_k, Q) \quad \text{M-step} : H_{k+1} = \text{argmax}_H \ \mathcal{F}(H, Q_k)$$

The E-step is maximized when $Q_{k+1}(x) = P(X = x \mid \overline{y}, H_k)$, in which case likelihood $\mathcal{L}(H_k) = \mathcal{F}(H_k, Q_{k+1})$. The M-step is maximized by maximizing the first term in $\mathcal{F}(H, Q)$, as the second (the entropy of Q) is independent of H [18]. Computing $P(X = x \mid \overline{y}, H)$ is called *filtering*, which for HMMs, takes the form of the *forward-backward* algorithm. Maximizing the M-step also takes advantage of filtering, as shown in algorithm Learn below. Let:

$$\alpha_i(t) = P(\overline{y}_{1:t}, X_t = x_i \mid H) \qquad \beta_i(t) = P(\overline{y}_{t+1:T} \mid X_t = x_i, H)$$
$$\gamma_i(t) = P(X_t = x_i \mid \overline{y}, H) \qquad \xi_{ij}(t) = P(X_t = x_i, X_{t+1} = x_j \mid \overline{y}, H)$$

Then the system-identification algorithm Learn is defined as in Algorithm 1.

Algorithm 1. HMM Learn ($\overline{y}$, N, Υ, ϵ)

---

initialize $H^* = (A, C, \pi)$ randomly
repeat
$\quad H = H^*$;
$\quad$(* E-Step *)
$\quad \alpha_i(1) = \pi_i c_i(y_1)$; $\quad \alpha_i(t) = c_i(y_t) \sum_{j=1}^N \alpha_j(t-1) a_{ji}$; $\quad \forall i=1{:}N, t=2{:}T$ //Fwd
$\quad \beta_i(T) = 1$; $\quad \beta_i(t) = \sum_{j=1}^N \beta_j(t+1) a_{ij} c_j(y_{t+1})$; $\quad \forall i=1{:}N, t=1{:}T-1$ //Bwd
$\quad \gamma_i(t) = \alpha_i(t)\beta_i(t)/\sum_{j=1}^N \alpha_j(t)\beta_j(t)$; $\quad \forall i=1{:}N, t=1{:}T$ $\qquad$ //Fwd-Bwd
$\quad \xi_{ij}(t) = \alpha_i(t)a_{ij}\beta_j(t+1)c_j(y_{t+1})/\sum_{k=1}^N \alpha_k(t)\beta_k(t)$; $\quad \forall i,j=1{:}N, t=1{:}T$

$\quad$(* M-Step *)
$\quad \pi_i^* = \gamma_i(1)$; $\quad \forall i=1{:}N$
$\quad a_{ij}^* = \sum_{t=1}^{T-1} \xi_{ij}(t)/\sum_{t=1}^{T-1} \gamma_i(t)$; $\quad \forall i,j=1{:}N$
$\quad c_{iy}^* = \sum_{t=1}^T 1_{y_t = y}\gamma_i(t)/\sum_{t=1}^T \gamma_i(t)$; $\quad \forall i=1{:}N, y \in \Upsilon$

until ($\mathcal{L}(H^*) - \mathcal{L}(H) \leq \epsilon$);
return (H^*)

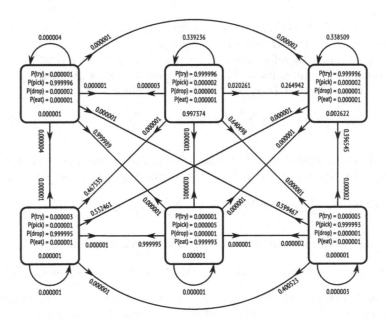

Fig. 4. HMM modelling a single thread of the Dining Philosophers program.

Table 1. HMM modelling with a uniform transition matrix for a Success Runs automaton with 4 states and 4 observations

Initial C	1	2	3	4	Learned C	1	2	3	4
$x_1 = 1$	0.5	0.5	0	0	$x_1 = 1$	0.6	0.4	0	0
$x_2 = 2$	0	0.5	0.5	0	$x_2 = 2$	0	0	1.0	0
$x_3 = 3$	0	0	0.5	0.5	$x_3 = 3$	0	0	0	1.0
$x_4 = 4$	0.5	0	0	0.5	$x_4 = 4$	0	0	0	1.0

For the Dining Philosophers, we have collected a number of long traces emitted by a single thread and used them to learn a 6-state HMM shown in Fig. 4.

For the Success Runs example, the traces were produced by simulating the automaton with 4 states starting from $x_1 = 1$. Deterministic behaviour guarantees that every state generates its number as an output. Hence, the resulting trace consists of $\{1, 2, 3, 4\}$. The transition matrix A was initialized as uniform: $a_{ij} = 0.25 \ \forall i, j$. The experiments with observation matrix C in Table 1 show that the closer our assumption about the system to reality the more accurate our learning results are. Since the Baum-Welch algorithm used for training an HMM is a local iterative hill-climbing method, initial choice of observation matrix is crucial.

4   State Estimation

Algorithm 1 uses the entire observation sequence $\bar{y}$ to *a posteriori* compute the probability $P(X_t = x_i \,|\, \bar{y}, H)$. If, however, one has the observation $\bar{y}$ only up to time $T = t$, this becomes a *forward state-estimation* algorithm:

$$P(X_t = x_i \,|\, \bar{y}, H) = \alpha_i(t) / \sum_{j=1}^{N} \alpha_j(t) \quad \forall i = 1{:}N$$

In practice, this algorithm may be inefficient, and an approximate version of it based on *importance sampling* (ISam) is preferred. The key idea is as follows. Each sample, also called a *particle*, takes a random transition from its current state $X_t = x_i$ to a next state $X_{t+1} = x_j$ according to a_{ij}. Its importance (weight) $c_j(y_{t+1})$ is thereafter used in a resampling phase which discards particles that poorly predicted y_{t+1}. ISam is therefore a *particle filtering* algorithm.

Initially distributing the K particles according to π confers on ISam two salient properties: (1) The K particles are always distributed among the most promising states; and (2) When K approaches infinity, the probability $P(X_t = x_i \,|\, \bar{y}, H)$ is accurately estimated by the average number of particles in state x_i.

In addition to the HMM H identified as discussed in Sect. 3, we also assume that the RE property of interest is given as a *deterministic finite automaton (DFA)* $D = (s_0, B, F)$ where $s_0 \in S$ is the *initial state*, B is the *transition function* from $S \times \Upsilon \to S$, and $F \subseteq S$ is the set of *accepting states*.

The DFA D accepts the output of the HMM H as its input, and it is run as a consequence in conjunction with H. Formally, this corresponds to the parallel composition of H and D as shown in Algorithm 2. This composition is used by ISpl to determine the levels used by the control algorithm.

Algorithm 2. Estimate (K, H, D)

$x_i = \text{sample}(\pi); \quad s_i = s_0; \quad w_i = 1; \quad \forall i = 1{:}K$
    while (true) **do**
        $\llcorner$ **on** y **do** $(\bar{x}, \bar{s}, \bar{w}) = \text{nextEstimate}(K, y, \bar{x}, \bar{s}, \bar{w}, A, B, C);$

The input to Estimate is the number of particles K, the HMM H, and the DFA D. Its local state is a configuration of particles $(\bar{x}, \bar{s}, \bar{w})$, containing for each particle i, the state x_i in the HMM, the state s_i in the DFA, and a weight w_i. The initial state $\bar{x}$ is distributed according to π, the initial state $\bar{s}$ is equal to s_0, and the initial weight $\bar{w}$ is equal to 1. On every output y thrown by the CPS, Estimate calls nextEstimate to get the next particle configuration.

NextEstimate works as described at the beginning of this section. For each particle i, it samples the next state x_i from $A(x_i)$, computes the next state s_i as $B(s_i, y)$, and computes the next weight w_i. To improve accuracy, this weight is multiplied with its previous value. NextEstimate then normalizes $\bar{w}$ and resamples the particles if necessary. It returns the new particle configuration PC.

Algorithm 3. PC nextEstimate $(K, y, \overline{x}, \overline{s}, \overline{w}, A, B, C)$

$x_i = \text{sample}(A(x_i));\quad s_i = B(s_i, y);\quad w_i = w_i\, C(x_i, y);\quad \forall i = 1{:}K$
normalize($\overline{w}$);
if $(1/\sum_{i=1}^{K} w_i^2 \ll K)$ **then** $(\overline{x}, \overline{s}, \overline{w}) = \text{resample}(\overline{x}, \overline{s}, \overline{w})$
return $(\overline{x}, \overline{s}, \overline{w})$

---

5   Feedback Control

Given a system model H and a safety property $\varphi = \mathbf{F}^T \psi$, where ϕ holds true if and only if, within time T, ψ is true, a statistical model checker aims at estimating the probability $P(\varphi \mid H)$ of H satisfying φ. The property ψ is an atomic expression over the variables of H and can be evaluated using the observations of system.

If φ is a *rare event* (RE), i.e. its satisfaction probability in H is very low, the *importance splitting algorithm* (ISpl) [9,12,14] seeks to decompose φ into a set of M formulas $\varphi_1, \ldots, \varphi_M$, with $\varphi_0 \equiv \top$, also called *levels*, such that:

$$P(\varphi \mid H) = P(\varphi_M \mid \varphi_{M-1}, H) \cdot P(\varphi_{M-1} \mid \varphi_{M-2}, H) \cdot \ldots \cdot P(\varphi_1 \mid \varphi_0, H),$$

where $\forall k = 1{:}M\ \ \varphi_k = \varphi_{k-1} \wedge \mathbf{F}^{T_k}\psi_k = \bigwedge_{\ell=1}^{k} \mathbf{F}^{T_\ell}\psi_\ell$. Time bounded properties are defined based on the system simulation trace. Thus, $T_k = \sum_{j=1}^{k} t_j$ and $T = \sum_{i=1}^{n} t_i$, meaning the system spent time t_i in state x_i before transitioning to state x_{i+1}. By construction, $T = T_M \leqslant \ldots \leqslant T_2 \leqslant T_1$ and $\psi_{1 \leqslant k \leqslant M}$ is defined as a set of increasing atomic properties. For $k = 1{:}M\ P(\varphi_k \mid \varphi_{k-1}, H)$ are considerably larger and essentially equal. If $\Omega = \{\omega_j\}_{j=1}^{N}$ is a set of simulation traces then from $\varphi = \varphi_M \Rightarrow \varphi_{M-1} \Rightarrow \ldots \Rightarrow \varphi_0 \equiv \top$ we can induce a set of strictly nested paths: $\Omega_M \subset \Omega_{M-1} \subset \ldots \subset \Omega_0 \equiv \Omega$, $\omega \models \varphi_0\ \forall \omega \in \Omega$, where $\Omega_k = \{\omega \in \Omega : \omega \models \varphi_k\}$. Effectiveness of the importance splitting largely depends on the choice of levels. The resulting estimated probability being a product of the estimates at each level minimizes the cumulative variance of the estimation[1]:

$$\gamma = \prod_{k=1}^{M} P\left(\omega \models \varphi_k \mid \omega \models \varphi_{k-1}\right).$$

The intractable problem of model checking $P(\varphi \mid H)$ is thus reduced to a set of more tractable estimation problems $P(\varphi_k \mid \varphi_{k-1}, H)$, computation of which may still be hard. ISpl, like ISam, is therefore using an approximate particle-filtering technique. Like ISam, it starts N particles of H from level φ_{k-1}, runs

---

[1] Importance splitting has been first used in [14] to estimate the probability that neutrons would pass through certain shielding materials. The distance traveled in the shield can then be used to define a set of increasing levels $0 = \ell_1 < \ell_2 < \cdots < \ell_n = \tau$ that may be reached by the paths of neutrons, with the property that reaching a given level implies having reached all the lower levels.

Algorithm 4. AdaptiveLevels $(MC, N, N_k, t, S(\omega))$

Let $\tau_\varphi = \min \{S(\omega) \mid \omega \models \varphi\}$ be the minimum score of paths that satisfy φ
and N_k be the minimum number of particles retained at each step
$k = 1; \quad s_0 = 0; \quad \forall i = 1{:}N \; \omega_j^k = \text{simulate}(MC, s_0, T);$
repeat
$\quad Q = \{S(\omega_j^k), \forall j \in \{1, \ldots, N\}\}; \; Q^* = \text{sort}(Q, \text{ascend})$
$\quad$ Find minimum $\tau_k \in Q^* : |\{\tau \in Q^* : \tau \geqslant \tau_k\}| \geqslant N_k; \; \tau_k = \min(\tau_k, \tau_\varphi);$
$\quad I_k = \{j \in \{1, \ldots, N\} : S(\omega_j^k) \geqslant \tau_k\};$
$\quad \tilde{\gamma}_k = |I_k|/N;$
$\quad \forall j \in I_k, \, \omega_j^{k+1} = \omega_j^k;$
$\quad$ **for** $j \notin I_k$ **do**
$\quad\quad$ Choose uniformly randomly $\ell \in I_k;$
$\quad\quad \tilde{\omega}_j^{k+1} = \min_{|\omega|} \{\omega \in \text{pref}(\omega_\ell^k) : S(\omega) = \tau_{k-1}\};$
$\quad\quad \hat{\omega}_j^{k+1} = \text{simulate}(MC, \tau_k, T - |\tilde{\omega}_j^{k+1}|) \text{ with prefix } \tilde{\omega}_j^{k+1};$
$\quad M = k; \, k = k + 1;$
until $\tau_k \geqslant \tau_\varphi;$
$\tilde{\gamma} = \prod_{k=1}^M \tilde{\gamma}_k$

---

them for at most $T - |\omega_j^{k-1}|$ time for $j = 1{:}N$, and computes their scores $S(\omega_j^k)$
for $j = 1{:}N$, according to how close their traces ω_j^k are to satisfying φ_k.

The number of particles satisfying φ_k divided by N approximates the
probability $P(\varphi_k \mid \varphi_{k-1}, H)$. Moreover, the particles with the lowest scores
get discarded and cloned starting from the current level. The estimation of
$P(\varphi_{k+1} \mid \varphi_k, H)$ is then initiated with the resulting sample of the particles. The
process continues up to φ_M.

Like ISam, ISpl always directs the particles towards the most promising parts
in H, and when N tends to infinity, the estimate it computes becomes exact.
ISpl thus closely resembles ISam, except for the way it computes the particle
weights (which have a different meaning) and for the idea of decomposing φ.

While various decomposition ideas were presented, for example in [9,12], the
automatic derivation of $\varphi_1, \ldots, \varphi_M$, however, has so far proved elusive. Moreover, this becomes a *grand challenge* if one is given a real CPS, say R, instead
of a model H. The only thing one can typically do with R is to start it from a
(most often opaque) state, run it for some time T, observe during this time its
output $\bar{y}$, and possibly store its last (again opaque) state for later reuse.

Fortunately, as we have seen in Sect. 3, this is enough for identifying an HMM
H of CPS R, whose dimension N is chosen such that: (1) It best reproduces $\bar{y}$;
and (2) A dimension of $N{+}1$, does not significantly improve its predictions.

As seen in Sect. 4, the product of the HMM H with the DFA D encoding the
safety property φ is a Markov chain MC, whose states are marked as accepting
according to D. The use of D instead of φ is with no loss of generality, as φ is
a safety property, and its satisfying traces are the accepting words of D.

The states of MC are computed by ISam and they can be used to compute
the levels φ_k. For this purpose, we apply offline the statistical model checker of

the PRISM model-checking suite (prismmodelchecker.org) to H. This is feasible since the size of H is small. In a simple and intuitive way, the level of a state s is computed as the minimum distance to an accepting state. In a more refined version, the level of s is computed as the probability of reaching an accepting state from s. Section 6 describe our scoring (leveling) algorithm in more detail.

6   Scoring

The process of computing levels for ISpl begins by an offline reachability analysis first proposed in [3]. With this approach, we first compose the system HMM H with the property DFA D to obtain a Discrete-Time Markov Chain (DTMC) MC. We then formulate the problem of reaching an accepting state of the DFA as a reward-based reachability query, and finally execute the PRISM model checker to compute the expected number of steps (distance) required to reach an accepting state from any compound state (i,j) of MC.

Through this reward-based bounded-reachability analysis, for each DTMC state $(i,j), i \in \{1, 2, \ldots, N_h\}, j \in \{1, 2, \ldots, N_d\}$, we calculate the distance $\delta_{i,j}$ from an accepting state. We subsequently normalize all the distances by dividing them with $max(\delta_{i,j})$ and subtract the normalized distances from 1. The result is a numerical measure of the "closeness" of every state (i,j) to the satisfaction of the property. We will call this measure a *level* and denote it as $L_{i,j}$ such that:

$$L_{i,j} = 1 - \frac{\delta_{i,j}}{max(\delta_{i,j})}$$

In a state farthest from the satisfaction of the property, $L = 0$, whereas in an accepting state, $L = 1$. Having defined the level of all the states, we can order them numerically. In the specific case of our Dining Philosophers example, after performing the PRISM reachability analysis, we obtain the ordering of states shown in Fig. 5.

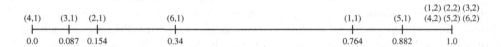

Fig. 5. Compound states (i,j) of the parallel composition $H \times D$, ordered on a scale from 0 to 1 based on their potential for satisfying the property.

The levels $L_{i,j}$ are computed in advance of executing FC-SSC, and, in some cases, they might be too coarse for a good estimation of the RE probability by ISpl. To help refine the estimation process, we use Algorithm 4, proposed by [13], which adaptively derives the levels in a way which seeks to minimize the variance of the final estimate. In the context of this algorithm, a level is the value of the score function $S(\omega)$, whose purpose is to help discriminate good execution paths from bad ones with respect to a given property.

Intuitively, the score is a weighted average of precalculated levels $L_{i,j}$, whereby the value of each level is weighted with the probability that, at time t, the system has reached that particular level.

7   Experimental Results

To investigate the behavior of FC-SSC for the case of Dining Philosophers, we performed multiple experiments on a PC computer with a dual-core Intel® Pentium® G2030 CPU running at 3.0 GHz with 4 GB of RAM, running Linux. In the preparatory phase, we first executed the program for an extended period of time, collecting the traces of emitted symbols. These traces were subsequently used with UMDHMM [16] to learn an HMM for the program. This HMM is shown in Fig. 4. The Success Runs Markov chain was simulated in Matlab R2015a. Then we used Matlab HMM Toolbox, employing Baum-Welsh algorithm, to build the learning curve and analyze learned transition and observation matrices. We further implemented Algorithm 4 in Matlab and executed it on the collected traces of the Success Runs automaton.

7.1   Dining Philosophers

We have executed the program with 100 threads in order to find, within a short time T, the probability that a particular one of them satisfies the property

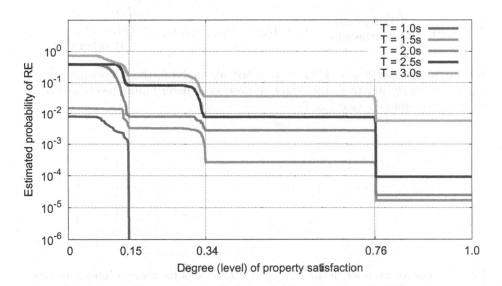

Fig. 6. FC-SSC in action. Shown is the process of estimating the probability of RE expressed by the temporal property $\varphi = \mathbf{F}^T eat$ for different values of T in the Dining Philosophers program with $N = 100$ threads. ISpl was run with 1000 traces and ISam used 280 particles for state estimation.

$\varphi = \mathbf{F}^T eat$. We repeated the experiment for different values of T, varying from 1 to 3 s. The results are summarized in Fig. 6.

In Fig. 6, we can observe that in the case of the $T = 1s$, even with a fairly number of sample ISpl was not able to cross the first level boundary. This is not a failing of the ISpl process, rather, it can be attributed to the fact that the startup time of the Dining Philosophers program takes a big fraction of this 1 s. Thus, it is difficult to observe any events at all from the program in such a short time, no matter how many samples are used. A rigorous timing analysis may find that observing the *eat* event from any philosopher within the first second is impossible.

7.2 Success Runs

If s is a system state then the property of interest is $\varphi = \mathbf{F}^T(x = M)$. Similar to the Dining Philosophers example it is essential to first decompose the property into a sequence of nested subproperties: $\varphi = \varphi_M \Rightarrow \varphi_{M-1} \Rightarrow \ldots \Rightarrow \varphi_0 \equiv \top$, where $\forall k = 1{:}M$ $\varphi_k = \mathbf{F}^{k-2}(x = k - 1) \wedge \mathbf{F}^1(x = 1) = \bigwedge_{\ell=1}^{k} \mathbf{F}^\ell(x = \ell)$. For the Success Runs the levels will coincide with the states of the automaton. Therefore, we can denote a level-based score function the following way:

$$S(\omega) = \max_{k=1{:}M} \{k : \omega \models \varphi_k\},$$

It satisfies the properties of a general score function:

$$S(\omega \in \Omega_1) = \begin{cases} 1, \omega \models \varphi_1, \\ 0, \text{otherwise}, \end{cases} S(\omega \in \Omega_2) = \mathbb{I}_{\omega \models \varphi_1} + \mathbb{I}_{\omega \models \varphi_2} = \begin{cases} 2, \omega \models \varphi_2, \\ 1, \omega \models \varphi_1 \wedge \neg \varphi_2, \\ 0, \text{otherwise}, \ldots \end{cases}$$

Although a property $\varphi = \mathbf{F}^3(x = 4)$ is trivial, applying the Algorithm 4 on it allows to clearly illustrate the adaptive process of determining levels according to initial parameters (see Fig. 7).

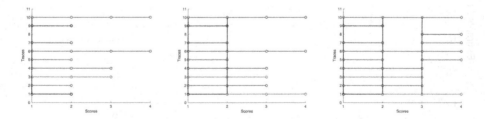

Fig. 7. Adaptive levels for the property $\varphi = \mathbf{F}^3(x = 4)$ of the Success Runs automaton 4×4 ($p = 0.5$, $N = 10$, $N_k = 1$) in 3 iterations of importance splitting: black bars are the levels, colorful lines are the paths to the maximum states reached by the particles within time bound. (Color figure online)

7.3 Discussion

It is interesting to note that there are several critical points in the ISpl process at which the probabilities fall significantly. Incidentally, these critical points correspond to the levels calculated by PRISM in the initial reachability analysis and shown in Fig. 5. Between these levels, the scoring function guides the ISpl process slowly forward, by discarding only the traces with the very lowest score. As such, the traces with the best potential (i.e. the highest scores) will be brought to the level boundary. If there is a critical mass of traces with scores greater than the level boundary, these will be multiplied through resampling and enable the ISpl process to continue towards its intended destination, which is the satisfaction of the property. If, on the other hand, only a small number of traces cross the level boundary, chances are that the ISpl process will be left with a degenerate set of traces all having the same score, in which case no further progress can be made.

Our results collectively show that FC-SSC typically provides a very good approximation of the actual probability and addresses the difficult CPS problem of steering a program along unlikely but successful paths with respect to an RE property. It also, as observed in the case of the Success Runs Markov chain, can be used to provide a lower bound $\tilde{\gamma}$ such that the system in question likely satisfies the qualitative property $P(\varphi \mid H) \geqslant \tilde{\gamma}$. However, the question arises about the sufficient rare event statistics for increasing the accuracy of the model checking algorithm. It seems reasonable to formulate the dependency between error estimate and initial data quality.

8 Conclusions

In this paper, we introduced *feedback-control statistical system checking*, or FC-SSC for short, a new approach to statistical model checking that exploits principles of feedback-control for the analysis of cyber-physical systems. To the best of our knowledge, FC-SSC is the first statistical system checker to efficiently estimate the probability of rare events in realistic CPS applications or in any complex probabilistic program whose model is either not available, or is infeasible to derive through static-analysis techniques.

FC-SSC is also a new and intuitive approach for combining importance sampling (ISam) and importance splitting (ISpl) as two distinct components of a feedback controller. ISam and ISpl were originally developed for the same purpose, viz. rare event (RE) estimation. With FC-SSC, we have shown how they can be synergistically combined.

A key component of our current approach is that we learn an HMM model of a representative process (or thread) of the system we are attempting to verify. We then compose this HMM with the DFA of the property under investigation to obtain an DTMC, which we then subject to level-set analysis. The benefit of this approach is that the representative process is small enough to render the HMM-learning process and subsequent analysis readily tractable, as we have carefully avoided the pitfalls of state explosion. The price to paid in doing so is that the level-set analysis is performed on a local process-level basis, possibly resulting in an increase in the number of particles that must be considered in the subsequent importance-sampling phase.

Due to the noise the result of particle filtering is a distribution of states. Current importance splitting algorithm starts from the state with the highest probability in the estimated distribution. *An optimal controller from the belief-states* could be designed using dynamic programming techniques. These lines of investigation will be a focus of our future work.

Acknowledgements. This work was partially supported by the Doctoral Program Logical Methods in Computer Science funded by the Austrian FWF, and the Austrian National Research Network (nr. S 11405-N23 and S 11412-N23) SHiNE funded by the Austrian Science Fund (FWF).

References

1. Code repository. https://ti.tuwien.ac.at/tacas2015/
2. Barbara, M., Frédéric, D., Gerhard, R., Alain, L., Frans, J., Thierry, P. (eds.): Parallel Computing: From Multicores and GPU's to Petascale. Advances in Parallel Computing, vol. 19. IOS Press, Amsterdam (2010). Proceedings of the Conference ParCo 2009, 1–4, September 2009, Lyon, France
3. Bartocci, E., Grosu, R., Karmarkar, A., Smolka, S.A., Stoller, S.D., Zadok, E., Seyster, J.: Adaptive runtime verification. In: Qadeer, S., Tasiran, S. (eds.) RV 2012. LNCS, vol. 7687, pp. 168–182. Springer, Heidelberg (2013). doi:10.1007/978-3-642-35632-2_18
4. Broy, M., Geisberger, E.: Cyber-physical Systems, Driving Force for Innovation in Mobility, Health, Energy and Production. The National Academy Of Science and Engineering, Acatech (2012)
5. Clarke, E., Grumberg, O., Peled, D.: Model Checking. MIT Press, Cambridge (1999)
6. Clarke, E.M., Zuliani, P.: Statistical model checking for cyber-physical systems. In: Bultan, T., Hsiung, P.-A. (eds.) ATVA 2011. LNCS, vol. 6996, pp. 1–12. Springer, Heidelberg (2011). doi:10.1007/978-3-642-24372-1_1
7. Doucet, A., de Freitas, N., Gordon, N.: Sequential Monte Carlo Methods in Practice. Springer, New York (2001)
8. Duflot, M., Fribourg, L., Picaronny, C.: Randomized dining philosophers without fairness assumption. Distrib. Comput. **17**(1), 65–76 (2004)
9. Glasserman, P., Heidelberger, P., Shahabuddin, P., Zajic, T.: Multilevel Splitting for Estimating Rare Event Probabilities. Oper. Res. **47**(4), 585–600 (1999)
10. Grosu, R., Smolka, S.A.: Monte Carlo model checking. In: Halbwachs, N., Zuck, L.D. (eds.) TACAS 2005. LNCS, vol. 3440, pp. 271–286. Springer, Heidelberg (2005). doi:10.1007/978-3-540-31980-1_18
11. Jegourel, C., Legay, A., Sedwards, S.: Cross-entropy optimisation of importance sampling parameters for statistical model checking. In: Madhusudan, P., Seshia, S.A. (eds.) CAV 2012. LNCS, vol. 7358, pp. 327–342. Springer, Heidelberg (2012). doi:10.1007/978-3-642-31424-7_26
12. Jegourel, C., Legay, A., Sedwards, S.: Importance splitting for statistical model checking rare properties. In: Sharygina, N., Veith, H. (eds.) CAV 2013. LNCS, vol. 8044, pp. 576–591. Springer, Heidelberg (2013). doi:10.1007/978-3-642-39799-8_38

13. Jegourel, C., Legay, A., Sedwards, S.: An effective heuristic for adaptive importance splitting in statistical model checking. In: Margaria, T., Steffen, B. (eds.) ISoLA 2014. LNCS, vol. 8803, pp. 143–159. Springer, Heidelberg (2014). doi:10.1007/ 978-3-662-45231-8_11
14. Kahn, H., Harris, T.E.: Estimation of particle transmission by random sampling. In: Applied Mathematics, vol. 5 of series 12. National Bureau of Standards (1951)
15. Kalajdzic, K., Bartocci, E., Smolka, S.A., Stoller, S.D., Grosu, R.: Runtime verification with particle filtering. In: Legay, A., Bensalem, S. (eds.) RV 2013. LNCS, vol. 8174, pp. 149–166. Springer, Heidelberg (2013). doi:10.1007/978-3-642-40787-1_9
16. Kanungo, T.: UMDHMM tool. http://www.kanungo.com/software/software.html
17. Rabiner, L.: A tutorial on hidden Markov models, selected applications in speech recognition. Proc. IEEE **77**(2), 257–286 (1989)
18. Roweis, S., Ghahramani, Z.: A unifying review of linear gaussian models. Neural Comput. **11**(2), 305–345 (1999)
19. Russell, S., Norvig, P., Intelligence, A.: A Modern Approach, 3rd edn. Prentice-Hall, Upper Saddle River (2010)
20. Stoller, S.D., Bartocci, E., Seyster, J., Grosu, R., Havelund, K., Smolka, S.A., Zadok, E.: Runtime verification with state estimation. In: Khurshid, S., Sen, K. (eds.) RV 2011. LNCS, vol. 7186, pp. 193–207. Springer, Heidelberg (2012). doi:10. 1007/978-3-642-29860-8_15
21. Verma, V., Gordon, G., Simmons, R., Thrun, S.: Real-time fault diagnosis [robot fault diagnosis]. IEEE Robot. Autom. Mag. **11**(2), 56–66 (2004)
22. Younes, H., Kwiatkowska, M., Norman, G., Parker, D.: Numerical vs. statistical probabilistic model checking. STTT **8**(3), 216–228 (2006)
23. Zuliani, P., Baier, C., Clarke, E.: Rare-event verification for stochastic hybrid systems. In: Proceedings of the 15th ACM International Conference on Hybrid Systems: Computation and Control, HSCC 2012, pp. 217–226. ACM (2012)

Probabilistic Model Checking
of Incomplete Models

Shiraj Arora and M. V. Panduranga Rao$^{(\boxtimes)}$

Indian Institute of Technology Hyderabad, Hyderabad, India
{cs14resch11010,mvp}@iith.ac.in

Abstract. It is crucial for accurate model checking that the model be a complete and faithful representation of the system. Unfortunately, this is not always possible, mainly because of two reasons: (i) the model is still under development and (ii) the correctness of implementation of some modules is not established. In such circumstances, is it still possible to get correct answers for some model checking queries?

This paper is a step towards answering this question. We formulate the problem for the Discrete Time Markov Chains (DTMC) modeling formalism and the Probabilistic Computation Tree Logic (PCTL) query language. We then propose a simple solution by modifying DTMC and PCTL to accommodate three valued logic. The technique builds on existing model checking algorithms and tools, obviating the need for new ones to account for three valued logic. Finally, we provide an experimental demonstration of our approach.

Keywords: Probabilistic models · Probabilistic model checking three-valued logic · Discrete time markov chain · Probabilistic computation tree logic

1 Introduction

Probabilistic model checking is an important technique in the analysis of stochastic systems. Given a formal description of the system in an appropriate modeling formalism and a requirement specification in an appropriate system of formal logic, the problem is to decide whether the system satisfies the requirement specification or not. Popular model checking techniques for such systems include numerical model checking which is expensive but accurate, and statistical model checking wherein accuracy can be traded off for speed [9,17,23].

Modeling formalisms for stochastic systems are usually variants of Markov Chains like Discrete and Continuous Time Markov Chains (DTMC and CTMC respectively) [2], Constrained Markov Chains [6] and Probabilistic Automata [10]. Specification requirement queries are typically formulated in logics like Probabilistic Computation Tree Logic (PCTL) [13] and Continuous Stochastic Language (CSL) [3].

© Springer International Publishing AG 2016
T. Margaria and B. Steffen (Eds.): ISoLA 2016, Part I, LNCS 9952, pp. 62–76, 2016.
DOI: 10.1007/978-3-319-47166-2_5

However, for more complex systems, it is convenient to use more powerful modeling techniques like Discrete Event Simulation (DES) and agent based simulation, and statistical model checking for analysis [24]. Indeed, statistical model checkers that can be coupled with discrete event simulators have been designed. A recent example is MultiVesta [21], which builds on the statistical model checker Vesta [22] and its parallel variant PVesta [1]. While substantial work has been done in the model checking domain, important practical problems can arise due to the quality of the simulation tool itself. For example, there could be stubs for unwritten modules in the simulation tool, or modules whose correctness is not yet established. It is not clear how good such a simulator is for the purpose of model checking. Is it, for example, impossible to verify the satisfaction of a given query on such an implementation? Or is it the case that in spite of lacunas in the implementation, some model checking queries can still be answered?

In this paper, we demonstrate a simple algorithm towards answering this question. The central idea originates from the observation that at an abstract level, the problem boils down to the inability of assigning truth values to atomic propositions in a state of the model. We demonstrate the approach using appropriately modified DTMC and PCTL. The proposed modifications are as follows: In the state of a DTMC, an atomic proposition can take the value $Unknown$ (abbreviated "?") in addition to the usual $True$ (T) or $False$ (F). The syntax and semantics of PCTL are modified so that a PCTL formula can also take the value "?".

Intuitively, the question that we ask is: Are there a sufficient number of paths in the DTMC that do not evaluate to "?"? If so, does the modified PCTL query evaluate to $True$ or to $False$ on this DTMC? Our algorithm answers these questions by invoking the model checking tool twice (PRISM [16] in our case) as a subroutine. This is a crucial advantage, as it means that the model checker itself need not be changed to account for three valued logic.

The paper is arranged as follows. The next section briefly discusses some preliminary notations and definitions, and relevant previous work done on model checking using three valued logics. Section 3 discusses our modifications in the definitions of DTMC and PCTL, the modified model checking algorithm, implementation details, and Sect. 4 concludes the paper with a brief discussion on future directions.

2   Preliminaries and Related Work

This section briefly discusses some basic definitions and terminology that will be used subsequently in the paper. For details, see [3].

2.1   Discrete Time Markov Chains (DTMC)

A Discrete Time Markov Chain(DTMC) is one in which transition from one state to another occurs in discrete time steps.

Definition 1. *A DTMC is a tuple $M = (S, \mathbb{P}, s_{init}, AP, L)$ where S is a non-empty set of states, $\mathbb{P} : S \times S \rightarrow [0, 1]$ is the transition probability function such that for all states $s \in S$:*

$$\sum_{s' \in S} \mathbb{P}(s, s') = 1$$

$s_{init} \in S$ is the initial state, AP is a set of atomic propositions, and $L : S \rightarrow 2^{AP}$ is a labeling function, which assigns to each state a subset of AP that are true in that state.

Definition 2. *A **path** π in a DTMC M is a sequence of states $s_0, s_1, s_2...$ such that for all $i = 0, 1, 2, ...$, $\mathbb{P}(s_i, s_{i+1}) > 0$. The $(i+1)^{th}$ state in a path π is written as $\pi[i]$. Path(s) denotes the set of all infinite paths which start from a state s in the model, M. Paths$_{fin}(s)$ is the set of all finite paths starting from state s.*

Definition 3. *A **cylinder set**, $C(\omega)$ is the set of infinite paths that have a common finite prefix ω of length n. Let $\Sigma_{Path(s)}$ be the smallest σ-algebra generated by $\{C(\omega) \mid \omega \in Paths_{fin}(s)\}$. Then, we can define μ on the measurable space $(Path(s), \Sigma_{Path(s)})$ as the unique probability measure such that:*

$$\mu(C(\omega)) = \prod_{i=0}^{n-1} \mathbb{P}(s_i, s_{i+1})$$

2.2 Probabilistic Computation Tree Logic (PCTL)

Probabilistic Computation Tree Logic (PCTL), an extension of Computation Tree Logic (CTL), was introduced by Hansson and Johnson [13] for analyzing discrete time probabilistic systems.

Syntax of PCTL:

$$\Phi ::= T \mid a \mid \Phi_1 \wedge \Phi_2 \mid \neg\Phi \mid \mathbb{P}_{\bowtie\theta}[\psi]$$

$$\psi ::= X\Phi \mid \Phi_1 U \ \Phi_2 \mid \Phi_1 U^{\leq k} \ \Phi_2$$

where Φ, Φ_1, and Φ_2 are state formulae, ψ is a path formula, a is an atomic proposition, $\theta \in [0, 1]$ is the probability constraint, $\bowtie \in \{ <, >, \leq, \geq \}$ represents the set of operators, and $k \in \mathbb{N}$ is the time bound. The X, U, and $U^{\leq k}$ operators are called *Next, Until* and *Bounded Until* respectively.

Semantics of PCTL: Let $M : (S, \mathbb{P}, s_{init}, AP, L)$ be a Discrete Time Markov Chain. Let $s \in S, a \in AP$, and Φ, Φ_1, Φ_2 be PCTL state formulae, and ψ be a PCTL path formula. Then, Φ is said to be satisfied in state s i.e. $(s, \Phi) = T$ if:

$$
\begin{aligned}
(s, T) &= T, \\
(s, a) &= T \quad \text{iff} & a &\in L(s) , \\
(s, \neg\Phi) &= T \quad \text{iff} & (s, \Phi) &= F , \\
(s, \Phi_1 \wedge \Phi_2) &= T \text{ iff} & (s, \Phi_1) = T \ &\wedge (s, \Phi_2) = T , \\
(s, \mathbb{P}_{\bowtie\ \theta}(\psi)) &= T \text{ iff} & \mu(\{\pi \in Path(s) \mid (\pi, \psi) = T\}) &\bowtie \theta
\end{aligned}
$$

If $\pi = s_0\ s_1\ s_2...$ is a path in $Path(s_0)$ then $\Pr((s, \psi) = T) = \mu\{\ \pi \in Path(s)\ |\ (\pi, \psi) = T\}$ i.e. the probability of the set of paths starting from s which satisfy the path formula ψ. The last satisfaction relation for a state formula thus states that the probability that ψ is true on paths starting at s satisfies $\bowtie \theta$. A path formula ψ is said to be satisfied for path π i.e. $(\pi, \psi) = T$ if:

$$(\pi, X\Phi) = T \quad \text{iff} \quad (\pi[1], \Phi) = T\ ,$$
$$(\pi, (\Phi_1\ U\ \Phi_2)) = T \quad \text{iff} \quad [\exists i \geq 0\ |\ (\pi[i], \Phi_2) = T]\ \wedge\ [\ \forall j < i, (\pi[j], \Phi_1) = T\ ]\ ,$$
$$(\pi, (\Phi_1\ U^{\leq k}\ \Phi_2)) = T \quad \text{iff} \quad [\exists\ i \leq k\ |\ (\pi[i], \Phi_2) = T]\ \wedge\ [\ \forall j < i, (\pi[j], \Phi_1) = T\ ].$$

Problem Statement for PCTL Model Checking: Given a DTMC M, decide whether a PCTL formula ϕ evaluates to T or F on M.

2.3   Three-Valued Logic and Model Checking

Multi-valued logics have been comprehensively investigated in the past few decades. In addition to having a rich theory, they have also found practical applications. Depending on the problem, classical binary language can be extended to additional truth values. For example, an additional truth value can be used to represent inconsistent and incomplete information. An application might also demand that we use two different values to denote inconsistent and incomplete information separately.

In this work, we will use three valued logic. We expand the logic associated with atomic propositions in the state of a DTMC to include *Unknown*, denoted by the question mark symbol "?". In what follows, we will use *Unknown* and ? interchangeably. A number of different truth tables have been designed for three valued logics [18–20]. The three valued logic used in this work has all the properties of a Quasi-Boolean lattice and the truth tables for logic operations are described in Tables 1, 2 and 3.

Indeed, three valued logic has been used in the past for model checking in non-probabilistic settings-for example, LTL [4,5,12] and CTL [7,8]. Chechik et al. [7,8] have used three valued logic for atomic propositions as well as for the transition functions. In case of transition functions, the *True* and *False* values denote the presence or absence of a transition between two states respectively. The third truth value represents the lack of information about the transition.

Three valued logic has also been used with numerical model checking of probabilistic systems, but with a different motivation and solution. To overcome the

Table 1. AND operator   **Table 2.** OR operator   **Table 3.** NOT operator

$\wedge$	T	?	F
T	T	?	F
?	?	?	F
F	F	F	F

$\vee$	T	?	F
T	T	T	T
?	T	?	?
F	T	?	F

$\neg$	
T	F
?	?
F	T

problem of state-space explosion in numerical model checking, two or more states of a model are combined, yielding an *abstract* Markov chain. However, over-abstraction often leads to a significant loss of information. Three valued logics have been associated with abstract probabilistic systems wherein an *Unknown* value represents loss of information, indicating that the level of abstraction should be decreased. Model checking of an abstract Markov chain is often done by reducing it to a Markov decision process and then using model checking techniques for Markov decision processes. For more details, please see [11,14,15].

3   Problem Statement and Solution

As mentioned earlier, the aim of this work is to study the effect of an unknown information in asserting whether a given property is satisfied in the model or not. To perform model checking on such three valued systems, both DTMC and PCTL need to be modified. While in case of DTMC the labeling function L is modified, the semantics are altered for PCTL. The modifications made in semantics of PCTL differ from the changes made by Fecher et al. in [11], for numerical model checking.

Intuitively, in our approach, the model checker aims to identify if there are too many paths in a model wherein it is not known whether a property will be satisfied or not. Thus, the model checker first evaluates whether the property is satisfied in the model and if not, it examines the reason behind the lack of satisfaction. In [11], on the other hand, unknown is used only when both the probability of a property being satisfied and the probability of a property being not satisfied, do not cross their respective thresholds.

In the coming subsections, we discuss the modifications in DTMC and PCTL, and the problem statement.

3.1   DTMC with Question Marks

A Discrete Time Markov Chain with question marks (qDTMC) is a tuple M : $(S, \mathbb{P}, s_{init}, AP, L)$ with a finite non-empty set of states S, a transition probability function $\mathbb{P} : S \times S \rightarrow [0, 1]$ such that for all states $s \in S : \sum_{s' \in S} \mathbb{P}(s, s') = 1$, the initial state $s_{init} \in S$, a set of atomic propositions AP and labeling function $L : S \times AP \rightarrow \{T, F, ?\}$.

3.2   PCTL with Question Marks

The syntax of PCTL in the context of three valued logic (hereafter referred to as qPCTL for convenience) remains the same. The operators ($\wedge$, $\vee$, $\neg$) and operands ($T, F, ?$) however, are as defined in Tables 1, 2 and 3 for three valued logic. Therefore, the structure of the queries remains unchanged.

However, the semantics need to be modified:

Semantics: Let $M : (S, \mathbb{P}, s_{init}, AP, L)$ be a qDTMC model. Let $s \in S$, $a \in AP$, Φ, Φ_1, Φ_2 be qPCTL state formulae, and ψ be a qPCTL path formula. Then, semantics for Φ are as stated below:

$$(s, T) = T,$$
$$(s, ?) = ?,$$
$$(s, F) = F.$$

$$(s, a) = \begin{cases} T \text{ iff } L(s, a) = T, \\ ? \text{ iff } L(s, a) = ?, \\ F \text{ iff } L(s, a) = F. \end{cases}$$

$$(s, \neg\Phi) = \begin{cases} T \text{ iff } (s, \Phi) = F, \\ ? \text{ iff } (s, \Phi) = ?, \\ F \text{ iff } (s, \Phi) = T. \end{cases}$$

$$(s, \Phi_1 \wedge \Phi_2) = \begin{cases} T \text{ iff } (s, \Phi_1) = T \wedge (s, \Phi_2) = T, \\ F \text{ iff } (s, \Phi_1) = F \vee (s, \Phi_2) = F, \\ ? \qquad otherwise. \end{cases}$$

The intuition behind the above definitions follows directly from three valued logic. The semantics of the probabilistic state formula are defined as follows:

$$(s, Pr_{\geq\theta}(\psi)) = \begin{cases} T \text{ if } \mu(\{\pi \in Path(s) : (\pi, \psi) = T\}) \geq \theta, \\ ? \text{ if } \mu(\{\pi \in Path(s) : (\pi, \psi) = ?\}) \geq 1 - \theta, \\ F \text{ otherwise.} \end{cases}$$

We first note that the formula must evaluate to one of T, F, or $?$. The above definition follows from the intuition that $(s, Pr_{\geq\theta}(\psi))$ evaluates to T if at least θ fraction of the paths evaluate ψ to T. Further, if $1 - \theta$ (or more) fraction of the paths evaluate to $?$, then there do not exist enough paths to decisively tell whether or not the property ψ holds for at least θ fraction of the sampled paths. Thus $(s, Pr_{\geq\theta}(\psi))$ evaluates to $?$. Otherwise, if the fraction of paths that evaluate to T is less than θ in spite of the number of $?$ paths being less ($< 1 - \theta$), it means that $(s, Pr_{\geq\theta}(\psi))$ must evaluate to F. We now turn to the semantics of the path formulae.

$$(\pi, X\phi) = \begin{cases} T \text{ if } (\pi[1], \phi) = T, \\ ? \text{ if } (\pi[1], \phi) = ?, \\ F \text{ if } (\pi[1], \phi) = F. \end{cases}$$

$$(\pi, \phi_1 U^{\leq k} \phi_2) = \begin{cases} T \text{ if } \exists i \leq k : (\pi[i], \phi_2) = T \wedge \forall i' < i : (\pi[i'], \phi_1) = T \\ F \text{ if } (\forall i \leq k : (\pi[i], \phi_2) = F) \vee (\exists i \leq k : (\pi[i], \phi_2) = T \wedge \\ \qquad\qquad\qquad\qquad\qquad \exists i' < i : (\pi[i'], \phi_1) = F), \\ ? \text{ otherwise.} \end{cases}$$

$$(\pi, \phi_1 U \phi_2) = \begin{cases} T \text{ if } \exists i : (\pi[i], \phi_2) = T \wedge \forall i' < i : (\pi[i'], \phi_1) = T \\ F \text{ if } (\forall i : (\pi[i], \phi_2) = F) \vee (\exists i : (\pi[i], \phi_2) = T \wedge \\ \qquad\qquad\qquad\qquad \exists i' < i : (\pi[i'], \phi_1) = F), \\ ? \text{ otherwise.} \end{cases}$$

First, we note that $(\pi, X\Phi)$ evaluates to T, F or ? depending on whether Φ is T, F or ? in $\pi[1]$ that is, in the next state. The *bounded until* formulae in qPCTL are a simple extension of the corresponding formulae in the standard PTCL. A *bounded until* formula $\phi_1 U^{\leq k} \phi_2$ evaluates to ? if one of the following happens:

- ϕ_2 is ? in at least one state and F for the rest of the states along the path up to k
- $\phi_2 = T$ for some $i \leq k$ but $\phi_1 =$? for some $j < i$, and $\phi_1 = T$ for all other states upto i.

Unbounded until can also be extended similarly for qPCTL. We are now in a position to formally define the problem.

Problem Statement: Given a qDTMC M, decide whether a qPCTL formula ϕ evaluates to T, F or ? on M.

3.3   The Algorithm

As mentioned earlier, our algorithm for model checking qDTMC using qPCTL uses classical binary model checkers as a subroutine. The algorithm involves modifying the input qDTMC suitably before subjecting it to binary model checking queries. The central idea behind the algorithm is to use these modifications to filter the three truth values successively, using only binary valued model checkers. In what follows, for ease of exposition, we denote the outcomes of the binary model checker by T' and F'. Algorithm qMC describes our approach.

Algorithm 1. qMC

INPUT: A qDTMC M and a qPCTL formula Φ.
Set ? to F in the original qDTMC to obtain binary DTMC M_1
if BINARY_MC(M_1, Φ) $= T'$ **then**
  return T
else
  Set F to T and ? to F in the original qDTMC to obtain binary DTMC M_2.
  if BINARY_MC(M_2, Φ) $= F'$ **then**
    return ?
  else
    return F
  end if
end if

Recall that the formulae to be evaluated in qPCTL are only state formulae. Therefore, technically, the formula in the conditionals of the algorithm have to be state formulae. However, in the process of evaluating state formulae, we need to compute the truth values of path formulae as well. Thus, in a slight abuse of convention, we use the same algorithm listing to argue for both state and path formulae.

Lemma 1. *For the path formulae* $X\phi$, $\phi_1 U^{\leq k}\phi_2$ *and* $\phi_1 U\phi_2$, *Algorithm qMC matches the semantics of qPCTL:*

- *qMC(M, Xϕ)=T (alt., F or ?) iff (s, Xϕ)=T (resp., F or ?)*
- *qMC(M, $\phi_1 U^{\leq k}\phi_2$)=T (alt., F or ?) iff (s, $\phi_1 U^{\leq k}\phi_2$)=T (resp., F or ?)*

Proof. The proof for *next* and *bounded until* operators are given below. The proof for *unbounded until* is a simple extension.

- $X\phi$: The correctness of *next* operator can be proved through the following claims:

Claim. In the first conditional of Algorithm qMC, $X\phi$ evaluates to T' in the binary DTMC M_1 if and only if it evaluates to T in the original qDTMC.

Proof. The mapping of the truth values while constructing the binary DTMC M_1 does not disturb T. Thus, ϕ evaluates to T in $\pi[1]$ the original qDTMC, if and only if it evaluates to T' in $\pi[1]$ in the binary DTMC.

Claim. In the second conditional of Algorithm qMC, the formula $X\phi$ evaluates to F' in the binary DTMC M_2 if and only if it evaluates to ? in the original qDTMC.

Proof. The second mapping of truth values maps both T and F to T. Thus, if ϕ is evaluated to T' in $\pi[1]$ of the binary DTMC M_2, it could be either because ϕ is T or F in the original qDTMC. The first conditional filtered out the possibility of ϕ to be T. Therefore, it must be F in the original qDTMC. Indeed, an output of T' by the binary model checker is correctly interpreted as F in the original qDTMC. On the other hand, if $\pi[1]$ is ? in the original qDTMC, it is mapped to F. Therefore, the binary model checker outputs F', which is then correctly interpreted as ?.
- $\phi_1 U^{\leq k}\phi_2$: The correctness of *bounded until* operator is similarly proved using two claims.

Claim. In the first conditional, $\phi_1 U^{\leq k}\phi_2$ evaluates to T' in the binary DTMC M_1 if and only if it evaluates to T in the original qDTMC.

Proof. Again, the truth value mapping during the construction of the binary DTMC M_1 does not alter T and F. Therefore, if ϕ_1 holds on a path until ϕ_2 becomes true, it will continue to remain that way in the binary DTMC M_1. Hence, if $\phi_1 U^{\leq k} \phi_2$ is T in the original qDTMC, it will continue to be T in the binary DTMC and the model checker will output T'. On the other hand, if $\phi_1 U^{\leq k} \phi_2$ is not T in the original qDTMC, it could be because either $\phi_1 U^{\leq k} \phi_2$ evaluates to F or ?. In either case, because of the truth value mapping, the classical model checker will output F' for the input binary DTMC M_1.

Claim. In the second conditional, the formula $\phi_1 U^{\leq k} \phi_2$ evaluates to F' in the binary DTMC M_2 if and only if it evaluates to ? in the original qDTMC.

Proof. In the original qDTMC, $\phi_1 U^{\leq k} \phi_2$ can evaluate to F if one of the following happens:

- ϕ_2 is F all along the path up to the kth state. In this case, the truth value mapping causes ϕ_2 to be evaluated to T everywhere. Further, any F for ϕ_1 also maps to T. Therefore, the binary model checker outputs T'. But T' is (correctly) interpreted as F by Algorithm qMC.
- ϕ_2 evaluates to T at some $i \leq k$ but ϕ_1 is F for some $j < i$ in the path. All ϕ_1 instances that evaluate to F on the path are assigned T by the truth value mapping in the binary DTMC M_2. Thus, $\phi_1 U^{\leq k} \phi_2$ is evaluated to T' by the binary model checker, which is then mapped to F.

After the second conditional, $\phi_1 U^{\leq k} \phi_2$ has to evaluate to either F or ?, as T has been already ruled out at the first conditional. Note that $\phi_1 U^{\leq k} \phi_2$ evaluates to ? if either (i) ϕ_2 is ? in at least one state and F for the rest of the states along the path up to k or (ii) ϕ_2 is T for some $i \leq k$ but ϕ_1 is ? for all $j < i$ other than when it is T. In both cases, it is clear that the binary model checker outputs F', because of the truth value mapping. This is then correctly interpreted as ?.

Lemma 2. *For all state formulae Algorithm qMC matches the semantics of the qPCTL. In particular, for probabilistic state formulae:*

$$qMC(M, Pr_{\geq \theta}(\psi)) = T \; (alt., \; F \; or \; ?) \; iff \; (s, Pr_{\geq \theta}(\psi)) = T \; (resp., \; F \; or \; ?)$$

Proof. The proof is straightforward for non-probabilistic state formulae. For formulae of the type $Pr_{\geq \theta}(\psi)$, we first prove the following claims.

Claim. At the first conditional in the qMC algorithm, $Pr_{\geq \theta}(\psi)$ evaluates to T in the original qDTMC if and only if it evaluates to T' in the binary DTMC M_1.

Proof. By the previous lemma, a path formula ψ is evaluated to T on a path in the qDTMC, if and only if it is evaluated to T' in the binary DTMC M_1. Therefore, in particular, at least θ fraction of the paths evaluate to T in the qDTMC, if and only if at least θ fraction of the paths evaluate to T' in the binary DTMC M_1.

Claim. At the second conditional in the qMC algorithm, $Pr_{\geq\theta}(\psi)$ evaluates to ? in the original qDTMC if and only if it evaluates to F' in the binary DTMC M_2.

Proof. If the binary model checker evaluates to F' in the first conditional, it could be either because there are too many paths evaluating to ?, or to F in the original qDTMC. Note that setting T and F to T does not change ψ from being *Unknown* to T or F on any path. Thus, if the binary model checker returns T' at the second conditional, then it means that a large fraction $(\geq \theta)$ of paths evaluate to a T or F in the original qDTMC. Since the first conditional eliminated the possibility that required quantity of paths evaluate to T in the original model, we conclude that $Pr_{\geq\theta}(\psi)$ must be F. In other words, there were sufficient number of conclusive (T or F) paths for $Pr_{\geq\theta}(\psi)$ to be T, but it is not. Therefore, $Pr_{\geq\theta}(\psi)$ is not ?, but F in the qDTMC. On the other hand, if the binary model checker returns F', it means that at least $1 - \theta$ fraction of the paths evaluate $Pr_{\geq\theta}(\psi)$ to ? in the qDTMC.

Lemmas 1 and 2 allow us to conclude that:

Theorem 1. *The algorithm qMC solves the model checking problem for qPCTL: for a model M and a qPCTL formula ϕ,*

– *qMC(M, ϕ)=T (alt., F or ?) iff (s, ϕ)=T (resp., F or ?)*

Remark 1. If the state formula occurs in negated form as $\neg\phi'$, then we use $\phi = \neg\phi'$ in the qMC algorithm, proceed as usual and negate the final answer as per the semantics of three valued logic.

Remark 2. If the probabilistic query is of the type $Pr_{<\theta}(\psi)$, we use the identity $Pr_{<\theta}(\psi) = \neg Pr_{\geq\theta}(\psi)$ and proceed as usual.

3.4   Implementation

We used PRISM [16] for the classical model checker subroutine in the implementation of the qMC algorithm. The algorithm works for both numerical and statistical model checking. The inputs to the model checker are the three valued probabilistic model and the property specification. The model checker then verifies the input property in the given model. If the input property contains nested probabilistic operators, then each inner probabilistic formula is considered as a separate property and verified first. The results of these sub-formulae are then replaced in the input property to remove nesting. However, the current version of PRISM does not support statistical model checking of nested properties.

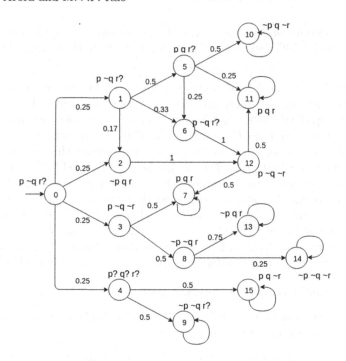

Fig. 1. An example input qDTMC model

3.5   Example Results

We report example results on two qDTMCs which have same set of states and transition function, but differ in the labelling functions. The two qDTMCs are used to observe the influence of $Unknown$ values in verifying an input property. While, the first model, given in Fig. 1, contains less number of $Unknown$ values; the second model, given in Fig. 2, has a large number of $Unknown$ values. In these models, p, q and r are three atomic propositions, each having exactly one truth value from the set $\{T, F, ?\}$. If a state, in the model, is annotated with p, then the atomic proposition is true in that state. Similarly, $\neg p$ denotes that p is F, and p? denotes p is $Unknown$ in the state. The two models are verified using the above algorithm, for two properties: $\Pr_{\geq \theta}[p \ U \ r]$ and $\Pr_{\geq \theta}[Xq]$.

As explained earlier, the algorithm qMC modifies the input qDTMC to two different binary models. For instance, the first model, given in Fig. 1, gets converted to models in Fig. 3(a) and (b) in the two steps respectively.

The models were verified for different values of θ for both the properties and the result is shown in the Tables 4 and 5. It is evident from the tables that when the probability threshold θ is increased, the model checker returns a ? value instead of T or F due to a lack of a sufficient number of paths to provide a "definitive" answer. From the tables, we can also see that when a model has large number of $Unknowns$, then a ? result could occur for lower values of θ as well.

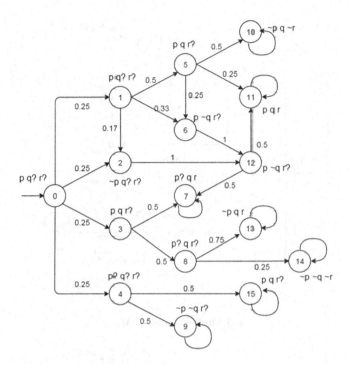

Fig. 2. Input qDTMC model containing more *Unknowns*

Table 4. Results for various values of θ for the model in Fig. 1

θ	0.1	0.2	0.3	0.4	0.5	0.6	0.7	0.8	0.9
$\Pr_{\geq\theta}[pUr]$	T	T	T	T	T	T	F	?	?
$\Pr_{\geq\theta}[Xq]$	T	T	F	F	F	?	?	?	?

Table 5. Results for various values of θ for the model in Fig. 2

θ	0.1	0.2	0.3	0.4	0.5	0.6	0.7	0.8	0.9
$\Pr_{\geq\theta}[pUr]$	T	T	F	F	F	?	?	?	?
$\Pr_{\geq\theta}[Xq]$	T	T	?	?	?	?	?	?	?

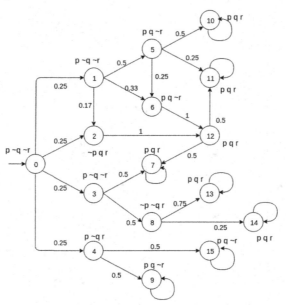

(a) Modified model–M_1

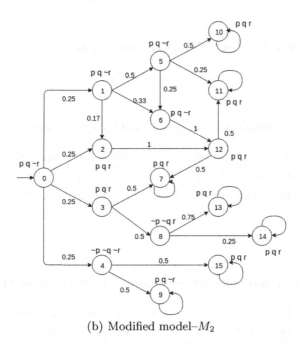

(b) Modified model–M_2

Fig. 3. The two step modification procedure of the model in Fig. 1

4   Conclusions and Future Directions

In this paper we presented a technique to determine the feasibility of model checking in the presence of uncertainty in the implementation of a stochastic model of the system.

While we reported results for DTMC, it would be of immense practical value if the method is applied to complex modeling formalisms like Discrete Event Simulators. It would then be possible to incrementally construct simulators, yielding model checking results for some queries in the interim; and also work with simulators that have some modules whose correctness is not established.

References

1. AlTurki, M., Meseguer, J.: PVeStA: a parallel statistical model checking and quantitative analysis tool. In: Corradini, A., Klin, B., Cîrstea, C. (eds.) CALCO 2011. LNCS, vol. 6859, pp. 386–392. Springer, Heidelberg (2011). doi:10.1007/978-3-642-22944-2_28
2. Baier, C., Haverkort, B., Hermanns, H., Katoen, J.P.: Model-checking algorithms for continuous-time markov chains. IEEE Trans. Software Eng. **29**(6), 524–541 (2003)
3. Baier, C., Katoen, J.P.: Principles of Model Checking (Representation and Mind Series). The MIT Press, Cambridge (2008)
4. Bruns, G., Godefroid, P.: Model checking partial state spaces with 3-valued temporal logics. In: Halbwachs, N., Peled, D. (eds.) CAV 1999. LNCS, vol. 1633, pp. 274–287. Springer, Heidelberg (1999). doi:10.1007/3-540-48683-6_25
5. Bruns, G., Godefroid, P.: Generalized model checking: reasoning about partial state spaces. In: Palamidessi, C. (ed.) CONCUR 2000. LNCS, vol. 1877, pp. 168–182. Springer, Heidelberg (2000). doi:10.1007/3-540-44618-4_14
6. Caillaud, B., Delahaye, B., Larsen, K.G., Legay, A., Pedersen, M.L., Wsowski, A.: Constraint markov chains. Theoret. Comput. Sci. **412**(34), 4373–4404 (2011). http://www.sciencedirect.com/science/article/pii/S0304397511003926
7. Chechik, M.: On interpreting results of model-checking with abstraction. University of Toronto, Technical report (2000)
8. Chechik, M., Easterbrook, S., Petrovykh, V.: Model-checking over multi-valued logics. In: Oliveira, J.N., Zave, P. (eds.) FME 2001. LNCS, vol. 2021, pp. 72–98. Springer, Heidelberg (2001). doi:10.1007/3-540-45251-6_5
9. Courcoubetis, C., Yannakakis, M.: Verifying temporal properties of finite-state probabilistic programs. In: 1988, 29th Annual Symposium on Foundations of Computer Science, pp. 338–345. IEEE (1988)
10. Delahaye, B., Katoen, J.P., Larsen, K.G., Legay, A., Pedersen, M.L., Sher, F., Wsowski, A.: Abstract probabilistic automata. Inf. Comput. **232**, 66–116 (2013). http://www.sciencedirect.com/science/article/pii/S0890540113001132
11. Fecher, H., Leucker, M., Wolf, V.: *Don't Know* in probabilistic systems. In: Valmari, A. (ed.) SPIN 2006. LNCS, vol. 3925, pp. 71–88. Springer, Heidelberg (2006). doi:10.1007/11691617_5
12. Godefroid, P., Piterman, N.: LTL generalized model checking revisited. Int. J. Softw. Tools Technol. Transfer **13**(6), 571–584 (2011)
13. Hansson, H., Jonsson, B.: A logic for reasoning about time and reliability. Formal Asp. Comput. **6**(5), 512–535 (1994). http://dx.doi.org/10.1007/BF01211866

14. Huth, M., Piterman, N., Wagner, D.: Three-valued abstractions of markov chains: completeness for a sizeable fragment of PCTL. In: Kutyłowski, M., Charatonik, W., Gębala, M. (eds.) FCT 2009. LNCS, vol. 5699, pp. 205–216. Springer, Heidelberg (2009). doi:10.1007/978-3-642-03409-1_19

15. Klink, D.: Three-Valued Abstraction for Stochastic Systems. Verlag Dr. Hut, Munich (2010)

16. Kwiatkowska, M., Norman, G., Parker, D.: PRISM 4.0: verification of probabilistic real-time systems. In: Gopalakrishnan, G., Qadeer, S. (eds.) CAV 2011. LNCS, vol. 6806, pp. 585–591. Springer, Heidelberg (2011). doi:10.1007/978-3-642-22110-1_47

17. Legay, A., Delahaye, B., Bensalem, S.: Statistical model checking: an overview. In: Barringer, H., Falcone, Y., Finkbeiner, B., Havelund, K., Lee, I., Pace, G., Roşu, G., Sokolsky, O., Tillmann, N. (eds.) RV 2010. LNCS, vol. 6418, pp. 122–135. Springer, Heidelberg (2010). doi:10.1007/978-3-642-16612-9_11

18. Malinowski, G.: Many-Valued Logics. Clarendon Press, Oxford (1993)

19. Putnam, H.: Three-valued logic. Philos. Stud. 8(5), 73–80 (1957)

20. Rescher, N.: Many-Valued Logic. Springer, Netherlands (1968)

21. Sebastio, S., Vandin, A.: Multivesta: statistical model checking for discrete event simulators. In: 7th International Conference on Performance Evaluation Methodologies and Tools, ValueTools 2013, Torino, Italy, December 10–12, 2013, pp. 310–315 (2013)

22. Sen, K., Viswanathan, M., Agha, G.A.: VESTA: a statistical model-checker and analyzer for probabilistic systems. In: Second International Conference on the Quantitative Evaluation of Systems (QEST 2005), 19–22, September 2005, Torino, Italy, pp. 251–252 (2005)

23. Younes, H.L.S., Kwiatkowska, M.Z., Norman, G., Parker, D.: Numerical vs. statistical probabilistic model checking: an empirical study. In: Tools and Algorithms for the Construction and Analysis of Systems, 10th International Conference on TACAS 2004, Held as Part of the Joint European Conference on Theory and Practice of Software, ETAPS 2004, Barcelona, Spain, 29 March–2 April, 2004, Proceedings, pp. 46–60 (2004)

24. Younes, H.L.S., Simmons, R.G.: Probabilistic verification of discrete event systems using acceptance sampling. In: Brinksma, E., Larsen, K.G. (eds.) CAV 2002. LNCS, vol. 2404, pp. 223–235. Springer, Heidelberg (2002). doi:10.1007/3-540-45657-0_17

Plasma Lab: A Modular Statistical Model Checking Platform

Axel Legay, Sean Sedwards, and Louis-Marie Traonouez[✉]

Inria Rennes – Bretagne Atlantique, Rennes, France
louis-marie.traonouez@inria.fr

Abstract. We present an overview of Plasma Lab, a modular statistical model checking (SMC) platform that facilitates multiple SMC algorithms, multiple modelling and query languages and has multiple modes of use. Plasma Lab may be used as a stand-alone tool with a graphical development environment or invoked from the command line for high performance scripting applications. Plasma Lab is written in Java for maximum cross-platform compatibility, but it may interface with tools and libraries written in arbitrary programming languages. Plasma Lab's API also allows it to be incorporated as a library within other tools.

We first describe the motivation and architecture of Plasma Lab, then proceed to describe some of its important algorithms, including those for rare events and nondeterminism. We conclude with a number of industrially-relevant case studies and applications.

1 Introduction

Statistical model checking (SMC) employs Monte Carlo methods to avoid the state explosion problem of probabilistic (numerical) model checking. To estimate probabilities or rewards, SMC typically uses a number of statistically independent stochastic simulation traces of a discrete event model. Being independent, the traces may be generated on different machines, so SMC can efficiently exploit parallel computation. Reachable states are generated on the fly and SMC tends to scale polynomially with respect to system description. Properties may be specified in bounded versions of the same temporal logics used in probabilistic model checking. Since SMC is applied to finite traces, it is also possible to use logics and functions that would be intractable or undecidable for numerical techniques. In recent times, dedicated SMC tools, such as YMER[1], VESPA, APMC[2] and COSMOS[3], have been joined by statistical extensions of established tools such as PRISM[4], UPPAAL[5] and MRMC[6]. In this work we describe

---

[1] www.tempastic.org/ymer/.
[2] http://archive.is/OKwMY.
[3] www.lsv.ens-cachan.fr/~barbot/cosmos/.
[4] www.prismmodelchecker.org.
[5] www.uppaal.org.
[6] www.mrmc-tool.org.

© Springer International Publishing AG 2016
T. Margaria and B. Steffen (Eds.): ISoLA 2016, Part I, LNCS 9952, pp. 77–93, 2016.
DOI: 10.1007/978-3-319-47166-2_6

Plasma Lab[7], a modular Platform for Learning and Advanced Statistical Model checking Algorithms [5].

SMC approximates the probabilistic model checking problem by estimating the parameter of a Bernoulli random variable, for which there are well defined confidence bounds (e.g., [21]). The general principle is to simulate the model or system in order to generate execution traces. These traces are checked with respect to a logic such as Bounded Linear Temporal Logic (BLTL) [4] and the results are combined with statistical techniques.

BLTL restricts the classical Linear Temporal Logic by bounding the scope of the temporal operators. Syntactically, we have

$$\varphi, \varphi' := \mathsf{true} \mid P \mid \varphi \wedge \varphi' \mid \neg\varphi \mid X_{\leq t} \mid \varphi \, U_{\leq t} \, \varphi',$$

where φ, φ' are BLTL formulas, $t \in \mathbb{Q}_{\geq 0}$, and P is an atomic proposition that is valid in some state. As usual, we define $F_{\leq t}\varphi \equiv \mathsf{true} \, U_{\leq t}\varphi$ and $G_{\leq t}\varphi \equiv \neg F_{\leq t}\neg\varphi$. The semantics of BLTL, presented in Table 1, is defined with respect to an execution trace $\omega = (s_0, t_0), (s_1, t_1), \ldots, (s_n, t_n)$ of the system, where each state (s_i, t_i) comprises a discrete state s_i and a time $t_i \in \mathbb{R}_{\geq 0}$. We denote by $\omega^i = (s_i, t_i), \ldots, (s_n, t_n)$ the suffix of ω starting at step i.

Table 1. Semantics of BLTL.

$\omega \models X_{\leq t} \, \varphi$ iff $\exists i, \, i = max\{j \mid t_0 \leq t_j \leq t_0 + t\}$ and $\omega^i \models \varphi$	
$\omega \models \varphi_1 \, U_{\leq t} \, \varphi_2$ iff $\exists i, \, t_0 \leq t_i \leq t_0 + t$ and $\omega^i \models \varphi_2$ and $\forall j, \, 0 \leq j < i, \, \omega^j \models \varphi_1$	
$\omega \models \varphi_1 \wedge \varphi_2$ iff $\omega \models \varphi_1$ and $\omega \models \varphi_2$	$\omega \models \neg\varphi$ iff $\omega \not\models \varphi$
$\omega \models P$ iff $s_i \models P$	$\omega \models \mathsf{true}$

Plasma Lab implements qualitative and quantitative SMC algorithms. Quantitative algorithms decide between two contrary hypotheses (e.g., is the probability to satisfy the requirement is above a given threshold), while quantitative techniques compute an estimation of a stochastic measure (e.g., the probability to satisfy a property).

The "crude" Monte Carlo algorithm is a quantitative technique that uses N simulation traces $\omega_i, \, i \in \{1, \ldots, N\}$, to calculate $\tilde{\gamma} = \sum_{i=1}^{N} \mathbf{1}(\omega_i \models \varphi)/N$, an estimate of the probability γ that the system satisfies a logical formula φ, where $\mathbf{1}(\cdot)$ is an indicator function that returns 1 if its argument is true and 0 otherwise. Using the Chernoff-Hoeffding bound [21], setting $N = \lceil (\ln 2 - \ln \delta)/(2\varepsilon^2) \rceil$ guarantees the probability of error is $\Pr(\mid \tilde{\gamma} - \gamma \mid \geq \varepsilon) \leq \delta$, where ϵ and δ are the precision and the confidence, respectively.

The sequential probability ratio test (SPRT) of Wald [23] evaluates hypotheses of the form $\Pr(\omega \models \varphi) \bowtie p$, where $\bowtie \in \{\leq, \geq\}$. The SPRT distinguishes between two hypotheses, $H_0 : \Pr(\omega \models \varphi) \geq p^0$ and $H_1 : \Pr(\omega \models \varphi) \leq p^1$, where $p^0 > p^1$ and the test cannot work if $p^0 = p^1$. Hence, the SPRT requires

---

[7] https://project.inria.fr/plasma-lab/.

a region of indecision (an 'indifference region' [24]) which may be specified by parameter ϵ, such that $p^0 = p + \epsilon$ and $p^1 = p - \epsilon$. The SPRT also requires parameters α and β, which specify the maximum acceptable probabilities of errors of the first and second kind, respectively. An error of the first kind is incorrectly rejecting a true H_0 (a false positive); an error of the second kind is incorrectly accepting a false H_0 (a false negative). To choose between H_0 and H_1, the SPRT defines the probability ratio

$$ratio = \prod_{i=1}^{N} \frac{(p^1)^{\mathbf{1}(\omega_i \models \varphi)}(1 - p^1)^{\mathbf{1}(\omega_i \not\models \varphi)}}{(p^0)^{\mathbf{1}(\omega_i \models \varphi)}(1 - p^0)^{\mathbf{1}(\omega_i \not\models \varphi)}},$$

where N is now the number of simulation traces generated *so far*. The test proceeds by performing a simulation and calculating *ratio* until one of two conditions is satisfied: H_1 is accepted if $ratio \geq (1 - \beta)/\alpha$ and H_0 is accepted if $ratio \leq \beta/(1 - \alpha)$. These thresholds are good approximations of the exact values that guarantee error probabilities α and β, improving as α and β approach zero [23].

2 Plasma Lab Architecture

One of the main differences between Plasma Lab and other SMC tools is that Plasma Lab proposes an API abstraction of the concepts of stochastic model simulator, property checker (monitoring) and SMC algorithm. In other words, the tool has been designed to be capable of using external simulators or input languages. This not only reduces the effort of integrating new algorithms, but also allows us to create direct plugin interfaces with standard modelling and simulation tools used by industry. The latter being done without using extra compilers.

The tool architecture is displayed in Fig. 1. The core of Plasma Lab is a lightweight controller that manages the experiments and the distribution mechanism. It implements an API that allows to control the experiments either through user interfaces or through external tools. It loads three types of plugins: 1. algorithms, 2. checkers, and 3. simulators. These plugins communicate with each other and with the controller through the API. Only a few classes must be implemented to extend the tool with custom plugins for adding new languages or checkers.

An SMC algorithm collects samples obtained from a checker component. The checker asks the simulator to initialize a new trace. Then, it controls the simulation by requesting new states, with a *state on demand* approach: new states are generated only when needed to decide the property. Depending on the property language, the checker either returns Boolean or numerical values. Finally, the algorithm notifies the progress and sends the results through the controller API.

Table 2 presents the list of simulator and checker plugins currently available with Plasma Lab. Plasma Lab has also been used to verify other types of models through a connection or an integration with other tools. Some of these case-studies are presented in Sect. 4.

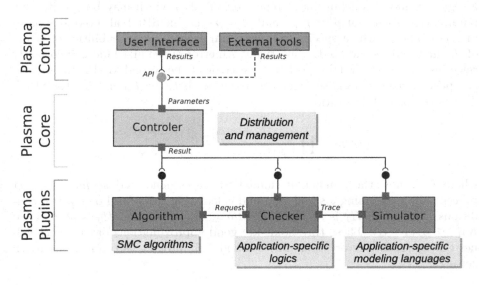

Fig. 1. Plasma Lab architecture.

Table 2. Plasma Lab plugins.

Simulators	
RML	Reactive Module Language: input language of the tool Prism for Markov chains models
RML adaptive	Extension of RML for adaptive systems
Bio	Biological language for writing chemical reactions
Matlab session	Allows to control the simulator of Matlab/Simulink
SystemC	Simulation of SystemC models. The plugin requires an external tool (MAG, https://project.inria.fr/pscv/) to instrument SystemC models and generate a C++ executable used by the plugin.
Checkers	
BLTL	Bounded Linear Temporal Logic
ALTL	Adaptive Linear Temporal Logic, and extension of BLTL with new operators for adaptive systems
GSCL	Goal and Contract Specification Language, a high level specification language for systems of systems
Nested	BLTL checker enhanced with nested probability operator
RML observer	A plugin that allows to write requirement as observers using a language similar to RML. It is used to write rare properties

Plasma Lab also includes several user interfaces capable of launching SMC experiments through the controller API, either as standalone applications or integrated with external tools:

- Plasma Lab Graphical User Interface (GUI). This is the main interface of Plasma Lab. It incorporates all the functionalities of Plasma Lab and allows to open and edit PLASMA project files.
- Plasma Lab Command Line. A terminal interface for Plasma Lab, with experiment and simulation functionalities, that allows to incorporate Plasma Lab algorithms into high performance scripting applications.
- Plasma Lab Service. A graphical or terminal interface for Plasma Lab distributed service. Its purpose is to be deployed on a remote computer to run distributed experiments, in connection with the Plasma Lab main interface.
- PLASMA2Simulink. This is a small "App" running from Matlab that allows to launch Plasma Lab SMC algorithms directly from Simulink.

2.1 Distributing SMC Experiments

Plasma Lab API provides generic methods to define distributed algorithms, which are a significant advantage of the SMC approach.

The distribution of the experiments is implemented with Restlet technology, using the architecture presented in Fig. 2. The main interface of Plasma Lab launches an SMC algorithm scheduler, while a series of services are launched on remote computers. Each service is loaded with a copy of the model simulator and a copy of the property checker. Then, the scheduler sends work orders to the services, via Restlet. These orders consist in performing

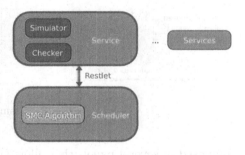

Fig. 2. Distributed architecture.

a certain number of simulations and checking them with the checker. When a service has finished its work it sends the result back to the scheduler. According to the SMC algorithm, the scheduler either displays the results via the interface or decides that more work is needed.

We have also implemented distributed SMC algorithms with Apache Spark. This alternative implementation allows to abstract even more the distribution mechanisms and facilitates the deployment of SMC experiments over large computing grids.

2.2 Tool Usage

We briefly present the usage of the tool. A more detailed description is provided on the website https://project.inria.fr/plasma-lab/documentation/. A generic usage of the tool GUI is presented in the flow diagram of Fig. 3. The GUI is

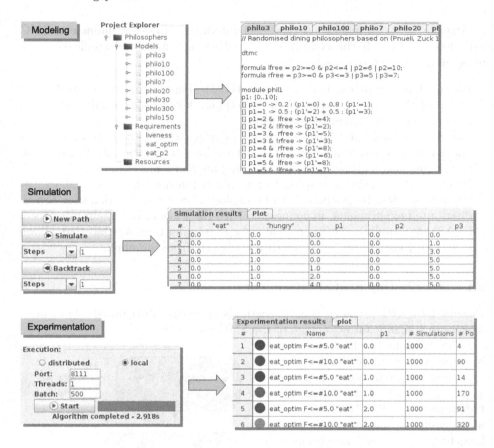

Fig. 3. Plasma Lab usage

composed of several panels that allow (*i*) to load, create and edit projects that comprise models and requirements, (*ii*) to perform simulations and debugging step-by-step, and (*iii*) to perform various forms of SMC experimentation and optimization, either locally or using distributed algorithms.

3   Plasma Lab SMC Algorithms

In addition to standard Monte Carlo and SPRT, Plasma Lab offers a number of advanced SMC algorithms for rare events simulation, nondeterminism optimisation and change detection.

3.1   SMC Algorithms for Nondeterminisitic Models

Markov decision processes (MDP) comprise probabilistic subsystems whose transitions depend on the states of the other subsystems. The order in which concurrently enabled transitions execute is nondeterministic and may radically affect the probability to satisfy a given property or the expected reward. Since it is useful to evaluate the upper and lower bounds of these quantities, we are interested in finding the optimal *schedulers* that do this.

Memoryless schedulers have the complexity of the state space, while history-dependent schedulers have the complexity of the trace space of an MDP. Using hash functions and pseudo-random number generators, Plasma Lab encodes both memoryless and history-dependent schedulers as *seeds*, using $\mathcal{O}(1)$ memory. Each seed induces a Markov chain from an MDP, enabling Plasma Lab to find optimal schedulers using randomised algorithms with minimal memory.

The core of Plasma Lab's nondeterminism engine is its "simple sampling" algorithms [16]: a number of scheduler seeds are chosen at random and each induced Markov chain is verified using standard qualitative and quantitative SMC algorithms. Since the result of each sampling experiment has some probability of being incorrect, Plasma Lab implements confidence bounds modified for multiple schedulers [16].

Simple sampling has the disadvantage of allocating equal budget to all schedulers, regardless of their merit. To maximise the probability of finding an optimal scheduler with finite budget, Plasma Lab implements "smart sampling" algorithms [10,17], comprising three stages:

1. An initial undirected sampling experiment to approximate the distribution of schedulers and discover the nature of the problem.
2. A targeted sampling experiment to generate a candidate set of schedulers with high probability of containing an optimal scheduler.
3. Iterative refinement of the candidate set of schedulers, to identify the best scheduler with specified confidence.

Note that smart hypothesis testing may quit at any stage if an individual scheduler is found to satisfy the hypothesis with required confidence or if individual schedulers do not satisfy the hypothesis with required confidence but the average of all schedulers satisfies the hypothesis.

Stages 1 and 2 are based on the following formula for the probability of seeing a "near optimal" scheduler with a budget of $M \times N$ simulations:

$$(1 - (1 - p_g)^M)(1 - (1 - p_{\bar{g}})^N) \tag{1}$$

M is the number of schedulers and N is the number of simulations per scheduler. The values of p_g, the probability of seeing a near optimal scheduler, and $p_{\bar{g}}$, the average probability of the property using a near optimal scheduler, are unknown. Hence, since (1) is symmetrical, M and N are set equal in Stage 1. The results of Stage 1 provide approximations of p_g and $p_{\bar{g}}$, allowing the values of M and N to be chosen to approximately maximise (1) in Stage 2. Stage 3 applies simple sampling to the candidate set of schedulers produced by Stage 2. At each iterative step, the per-iteration budget is divided between the current candidate schedulers, SMC is applied and the least good half of the candidates are discarded. This refinement may continue until there remains only a single scheduler, so the initial value of N must be greater than or equal to the minimum number of simulations required to ensure the confidence of a single estimate.

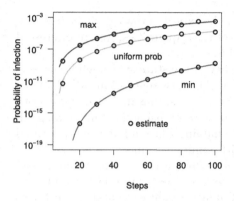
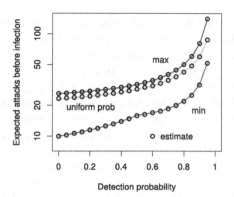

Fig. 4. Nondeterminism and rare events.

Fig. 5. Optimising rewards.

Figure 4 illustrates typical results for a virus infection model. The solid lines in Figs. 4 and 5 are the values calculated using numerical algorithms. The estimates of "uniform prob" confirm that our algorithms select uniformly from schedulers.

Costs or rewards may be assigned to the states and / or transitions of MDPs, so Plasma Lab also implements qualitative and quantitative smart reward estimation algorithms [17]. The algorithms consider *reachability rewards* (the expected cumulative reward over paths of a property with probability one), *cumulative rewards* (the expected cumulative reward of all path of a fixed length) and *instantaneous rewards* (the expected reward on a fixed step of all paths). Since in all cases no paths are rejected, $p_{\bar{g}}$ in (1) is effectively 1 and Stage 1 may be omitted, such that all the budget is directly assigned to M in Stage 2. Figure 5 illustrates typical results for a virus infection model.

3.2 Rare Event Simulation

Rare properties (i.e., with low probability) pose a problem for SMC because they are infrequently observes in simulations. Plasma Lab addresses this with the standard variance reduction techniques of importance sampling [11] and importance splitting [12–14].

Importance sampling works by weighting the probability distribution of the original system to favour the rare event. Since the weights are known, the correct result can be computed on the fly while simulating under the favourable importance sampling distribution. In addition to quantifying the probability of rare events in purely probabilistic systems, importance sampling can be useful when searching for optimal schedulers of nondeterministic systems whose optimal probability is low. E.g., importance sampling was used to generate the results shown in Fig. 4.

Importance splitting decomposes a property with low probability into a product of higher conditional probabilities that are easier to estimate. It proceeds by estimating the probability of passing from one *level* to another, defined in Plasma Lab with respect to the range of a *score function* that maps states of the system × property product automaton to values. The lowest level is the initial state. The highest level satisfies the property. The initial states of intermediate simulations are the terminal states of simulations reaching the previous level.

The best performance is generally achieved with many levels of equal probability, requiring suitable score functions. Plasma Lab includes a "wizard" to construct *observers* in a reactive modules-like syntax from BLTL properties. The score function is defined within the observer and has access to all the variables of the system [14].

Plasma Lab implements a fixed level algorithm and an adaptive level algorithm [13,14]. The fixed level algorithm requires the user to define a monotonically increasing sequence of score values whose last value corresponds to satisfying the property. The adaptive algorithm finds optimal levels automatically and requires only the maximum score to be specified. Both algorithms estimate the probability of passing from one level to the next by the proportion of a constant number of simulations that reach the upper level from the lower. New simulations to replace those that failed to reach the upper level are started from states chosen uniformly at random from the terminal states of successful simulations. The overall estimate is the product of the estimates of going from one level to the next.

Table 3. Importance splitting results.

		Adaptive	Single	Parallel
Leader	Std. dev.	4.8×10^{-8}	1.3×10^{-7}	5.2×10^{-8}
	Levels	20	6	6
	Budget	1000	1000	5×1000
	Time (MC)	7.3s (30h)	2.5s (4.4h)	5.8s (5.0h)
Philosophers	Std. dev.	4.2×10^{-7}	7.7×10^{-7}	2.8×10^{-7}
	Levels	109	5	5
	Budget	1000	1000	5×1000
	Time (MC)	5.4s (2.3h)	1.7s (41m)	3.7s (1.4h)
Counters	Std. dev.	2.1×10^{-7}	5.0×10^{-7}	2.3×10^{-7}
	Levels	3942	4	4
	Budget	500	500	5×500
	Time (MC)	15s (7.5h)	2.8s (1.2h)	4.8s (1.9h)

The adaptive algorithm maximises variance reduction by minimising the number of simulations that fail at each level. This optimises performance on a single machine, but makes parallelisation inefficient. To take advantage of distributed computing, Plasma Lab therefore implements a parallel importance splitting algorithm based on the fixed level algorithm. We give performance results for various algorithms and models in Table 3. The adaptive algorithm outperforms the fixed level algorithm on a single machine, but the fixed level algorithm outperforms the adaptive algorithm in time and variance reduction when parallelised. All algorithms significantly outperform crude Monte Carlo (MC) [14].

3.3 Change Detection with CUSUM

Statistical techniques can also be used to perform runtime monitoring. The change detection problem consists in determining the occurrence of an event during the execution of the system, by looking at the variation of a probability measure along the execution. The CUSUM algorithm [3,22] has been used in signal theory to solve this problem. It computes a cumulative sum during the execution that is compared to a sensitivity threshold. When this sum exceeds the stopping rule the algorithm determines that the expected event has occurred.

In Plasma Lab we have adapted this algorithm to SMC [19]. The idea is to observe the variation of the probability to satisfy a BLTL formula. In contrast to other SMC algorithms, the CUSUM algorithm only generates a single trace of the model. This trace is split in a set of samples taken at a regular time interval from the trace. Using this set of samples we can define the probability to satisfy a requirement at a certain time in the trace, by counting the number of samples that have satisfied the property. The CUSUM algorithm is then used to determine the time in the trace when this probability changes, which is the sign that an expected event has occurred.

Formally, we consider an execution $\omega = (s_0, t_0), (s_1, t_1), \ldots$ of the system and a BLTL property φ. We define a sequence of Bernoulli variables X_i such that X_i takes the value 1 iff $\omega^i \models \varphi$. We assume that we know the initial probability p_{init} of $\Pr(\omega \models \varphi)$. We want to observe a change of this probability such that $\Pr(\omega \models \varphi) > k$, with $k \in]0, 1[$. Like the SPRT, the CUSUM comparison is based on a likelihood-ratio test: it computes the cumulative sum S_n of the logarithm of the likelihood-ratios s_i over the sequence of samples $X_1, \ldots X_n$.

$$S_n = \sum_{i=1}^{n} s_i \qquad s_i = \begin{cases} \ln \frac{k}{p_{\text{init}}}, & \text{if } X_i = 1 \\ \ln \frac{1-k}{1-p_{\text{init}}}, & \text{otherwise} \end{cases}$$

The typical behaviour of the cumulative sum S_n is a global decreasing before the change, and a sharp increase after the change. Then the stopping rule's purpose is to detect when the positive drift is sufficiently relevant to detect the change. It consists in saving $m_n = \min_{1 \leq i \leq n} S_i$, the minimal value of CUSUM, and comparing it with the current value. If the distance is sufficiently great, the stopping decision is taken, i.e., an alarm is raised at time $t_a = \min\{t_n : S_n - m_n \geq \lambda\}$, where λ is a sensitivity threshold.

4   Case Studies and Applications

In this section we present the different models and simulators that have been plugged with Plasma Lab, and used in case studies.

4.1   Systems of Systems: The DANSE Case Study

The DANSE[8] (Designing for Adaptability and evolutioN in System of systems Engineering) European project focuses on the development of a new methodology for System of Systems (SoS).

SMC techniques and Plasma Lab have been used within the project to analyse large heterogeneous systems like SoS. Plasma Lab has been integrated in the toolchain presented in Fig. 6. The SoS model is designed in UPDM (Unified Profile

---

[8] http://danse-ip.eu/.

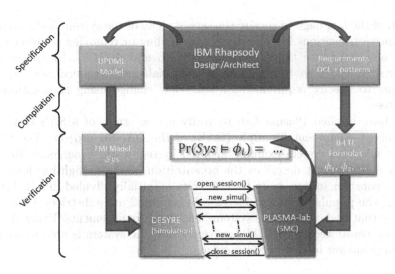

$$Pr(Sys \vDash \phi_i) = \; ...$$

Fig. 6. DANSE methodology and toolchain.

for DoDAF/MODAF) with the tool IBM Rhapsody. Requirements are written with the Goal and Contract Specification Language (GCSL) and translated to BLTL. Plasma Lab SMC algorithms are used in combination with the tool DESYRE, developed by Ales, that simulates UPDM model using the FMI/FMU interface.

Goal and Contract Specification Language (GCSL). The DANSE project has introduced GCSL [2], a text-pattern based specification language with a formal semantics given by a temporal logic. This bridges the gap between natural language requirements and formal requirements. It is a combination of the Object Constraint Language (OCL) and the Contract Specification Language (CSL) developed in the SPEEDS project. CSL patterns are used to give a high-level specification of real-time components. They have been introduced to enable the user to reason about event triggering, that are equivalently replaced in DANSE by property satisfaction. The properties handled by these patterns are about the state of a SoS and we use OCL to specify these state properties. This language allows to build behavioural properties that express temporal relations about facts or events of the system. It is sufficiently powerful to describe precisely a state of a SoS. GCSL contracts can be translated to BLTL. Plasma Lab GCSL plugin allows to write requirement directly in GCSL.

Adaptive Reactive Module Language. Within the DANSE project we have also proposed [6] an extension of the RML language to describe stochastic adaptive systems (SAS). These systems consists in a set of components, organized with a certain topology, which we call a view. The composition of the system and its topology can evolve by changing its view. Views are represented by a combination of Markov chains modelled in the RML language. We introduce an extension

A-RML of the language to specify the sets of views of the system and to stochastic adaptive transitions between them (e.g. adding or removing components).

We also introduce the extensions A-BLTL and A-GCSL to reason about sequences of views in SAS. These new formalisms introduce new temporal operators to specify requirements about view change using assumptions and guarantees.

We have applied Plasma Lab to verify a case study of a SAS taken from the Concept Alignment Example (CAE) of the DANSE project. The CAE is a fictive adaptive system example inspired by real-world Emergency Response data to a city fire. It describes the organization of the firefighting forces in a city. We consider in our study that the city is initially divided into 4 districts, and that the population might increase by adding 2 more districts. Using SMC we verify that each view of the systems satisfy the requirements. Using A-GCSL contracts, translated to A-BLTL, we verify that the system is able to adapt its emergency answer in case the city expands.

4.2   Dynamic Motion Planning in DALi and ACANTO Projects

Plasma Lab has been integrated with robotic devices for the DALi[9] FP7 and ACANTO[10] H2020 projects, in the context of motion planning for assisted living [7,8]. Both projects rely on a novel online motion planning application of SMC to help those with impaired ability to negotiate complex crowded environments, such as museums and shopping malls. While DALi is focused on helping a single user reach a number of specific locations, ACANTO is concerned with therapeutic activities of groups of users, where group cohesion, social interaction and exercise are the metrics of interest.

The basic system architecture of our motion planner is illustrated in Fig. 7. Sensors, such as fixed cameras and cameras on robotic devices, locate fixed and moving objects in the environment. From this information a predictive stochastic model of human motion (the "social force model", SFM) is constructed, which is then used to generate plausible future trajectories of all the detected moving agents, given initial deviations from their current trajectories. Motion planning proceeds by hypothesizing different initial directions, then using Plasma Lab to estimate the probability that future trajectories will satisfy global constraints and objectives expressed in temporal logic. The best deviation is suggested to the user.

The operation of our motion planner for a single user (rectangular agent) is illustrated in Fig. 8. The solid red line denotes the direct path to the user's next local waypoint (green dot). The position and velocity of other pedestrians (circles) are indicated by vectors. With no modification, Plasma Lab estimates that the pedestrians will collide with high probability (not illustrated), but by making a deviation to the user's trajectory that diminishes over time (dashed

---

[9] www.ict-dali.eu.
[10] www.ict-acanto.eu.

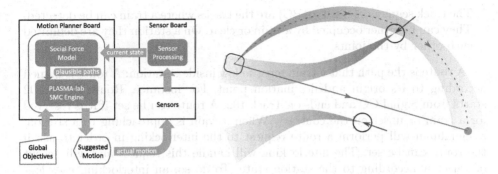

Fig. 7. Architecture of motion planner.

Fig. 8. Operation of motion planner.

red line), Plasma Lab predicts that the pedestrians will avoid each other with high probability (shaded areas).

To aid rapid development of a prototype algorithm, Plasma Lab was first integrated with MATLAB. The production algorithm was subsequently implemented on embedded hardware and finds the optimum trajectory in a fraction of a second.

4.3   Train Interlocking Systems

This case study has been analysed in collaboration with Université Catholique de Louvain and Alstom. We have analysed Braine l'Alleud station's interlocking system, a medium size railway station of the Belgian network. A representation of its track layout is shown on Fig. 9.

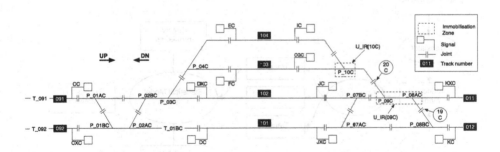

Fig. 9. Layout of Braine l'Alleud station.

Each station is composed of a set of physical components:

- The points (e.g. P_01BC) are the track components that guide the train from one track to another.
- The signals (e.g. CC) are the interface between the interlocking and the trains.

– The track segments (e.g. T_01BC) are the tracks where a train can be detected. They can be either occupied by a train or clear. On a station they are delimited each other by the joints.

A route is the path that a train must follow inside a station. A route is named according to its origin and destination point. For instance, Route R_CC_102 starts from Signal CC and ends on Track 102. A route can be set if it is reserved for a train or unset on the contrary. When a train is approaching to a station, a signalman will perform a route request to the interlocking in order to ask if the route can be set. The interlocking will handle this request and will accept or reject it according to the station state. To do so, an interlocking uses logical components like the subroutes or the immobilization zones, materializing the availability of some physical components. Such components are locked or released if they are not requested. Braine l'Alleud station is controlled by a unique interlocking composed of 32 routes, 12 signals, 13 track-circuits, and 12 points.

We verify two types of requirements: safety properties (e.g., avoid collisions of two trains on the same track), and availability properties (e.g., a route can always be eventually set). The verification process that we apply is described in Fig. 10. We use a simulator developed by Université Catholique de Louvain that is able to generate traces of the interlocking systems from a track layout and application data. This simulator is plug with Plasma Lab using a small interface developed with Plasma Lab's API. Then, the traces generated by the simulator are be used by Plasma Lab SMC algorithms to measure the correctness of the system. We have used Monte Carlo and importance splitting algorithms to verify this system.

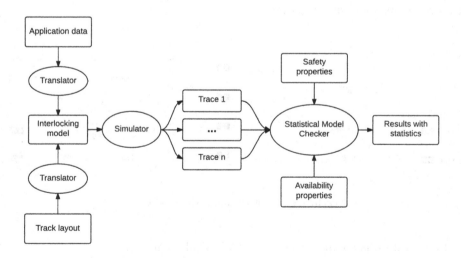

Fig. 10. Train interlocking verification steps.

4.4 Matlab/Simulink

Simulink models can be formally translated to hybrid automata [1] that inter-leave discrete state automata with complex dynamic behaviours described by differential equations. Model checking of these models is however undecidable. It is therefore interesting to use SMC to provide a formal analysis technique. Rather than translating Simulink models to a specific formal language, we have been able to directly interface Plasma Lab and Simulink [18]. We thus apply SMC algorithms by using the simulation engine provided by Simulink.

To achieve this we have developed a Mat-lab plugin for Plasma Lab, whose architecture is described in Fig. 11. It allows to control the Simulink simulator through the Matlab Control library[11]. It returns traces of observable vari-ables to Plasma Lab SMC algorithms through the controller's API. Besides this plugin we have developed PLASMA2Simulink, a Matlab APP that provides a user interface to launch SMC experiments directly from Matlab.

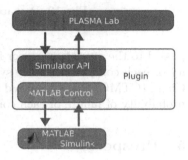

Fig. 11. Plasma Lab–Simulink interface.

We have used this plugin to analyse a Simulink model of a temperature controller of a pig shed. First, we use Monte Carlo techniques to verify that the controller maintains the temperature within comfortable lim-its, by activating fans and heaters. Second, by adding failures and wear to the system, we use the Plasma Lab CUSUM algorithm to determine the time when the controller becomes too inefficient – useful information that can be used to schedule maintenance of the system.

4.5 SystemC

SystemC is a high-level modelling language for specifying concurrent processes. It is implemented as a set of C++ classes that allow to perform event-driven simulation. Probabilistic behaviours can also be added.

We have implemented a SystemC plugin for Plasma Lab that is able to load a SystemC executable model and use it to generate simulations. Plasma Lab and the SystemC plugin is embedded in the toolchain of the Probabilistic SystemC Verifier (PSCV) tool [20]. The tool chain is presented in Fig. 12.

This toolchain has been used to analyse a SystemC model of an embedded control system, similar to [15], but with more components. The system consists of an input processor (I) connected to 50 groups of 3 sensors, an output processor (O), connected to 30 groups of 2 actuators, and a main processor (M), that com-municates with I and O through a bus. At every cycle, 1 min, the main processor polls data from the input processor that reads and processes data from the sen-sor groups. Based on this data, the main processor constructs commands to be

---

[11] https://code.google.com/p/matlabcontrol/.

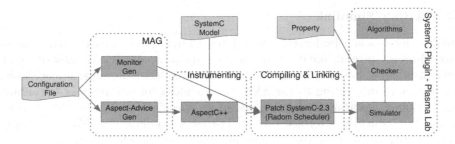

Fig. 12. Probabilistic SystemC Verifier toolchain.

passed to the output processor for controlling the actuator groups. The reliability of each component in the system is modeled as a Continuous-Time Markov Chain (CTMC) that is realized in SystemC. Using Plasma Lab we compute the probability of failure of each components.

5   Prospects

Our ongoing research is focused on the many interesting technical challenges arising from nondeterminism and continuous time [9]. In combination with our work on rare events, our longer term aim is to ensure Plasma Lab is able to address industrial scale verification problems in a way that is efficient and convenient for system engineers.

References

1. Agrawal, A., Simon, G., Karsai, G.: Semantic translation of Simulink/Stateflow models to hybrid automata using graph transformations. Electron. Notes Theor. Comput. Sci. **109**, 43–56 (2004)
2. Arnold, A., Boyer, B., Legay, A.: Contracts and behavioral patterns for sos: the EU IP DANSE approach. In: Proceedings of AiSoS. EPTCS, vol. 133, pp. 47–66 (2013)
3. Basseville, M., Nikiforov, I.V.: Detection of Abrupt Changes: Theory and Application. Prentice-Hall, Inc., Upper Saddle River (1993)
4. Biere, A., Heljanko, K., Junttila, T.A., Latvala, T., Schuppan, V.: Linear encodings of bounded LTL model checking. Logical Methods Comput. Sci. **2**(5) (2006). doi:10.2168/LMCS-2(5:5)2006
5. Boyer, B., Corre, K., Legay, A., Sedwards, S.: PLASMA-lab: a flexible, distributable statistical model checking library. In: Joshi, K., Siegle, M., Stoelinga, M., D'Argenio, P.R. (eds.) QEST 2013. LNCS, vol. 8054, pp. 160–164. Springer, Heidelberg (2013). doi:10.1007/978-3-642-40196-1_12
6. Boyer, B., Legay, A., Traonouez, L.-M.: A formalism for stochastic adaptive systems. In: Margaria, T., Steffen, B. (eds.) ISoLA 2014. LNCS, vol. 8803, pp. 160–176. Springer, Heidelberg (2014). doi:10.1007/978-3-662-45231-8_12

7. Colombo, A., Fontanelli, D., Legay, A., Palopoli, L., Sedwards, S.: Motion planning in crowds using statistical model checking to enhance the social force model. In: IEEE Conference on Decision and Control (CDC), pp. 3602–3608 (2013)

8. Colombo, A., Fontanelli, D., Legay, A., Palopoli, L., Sedwards, S.: Efficient customisable dynamic motion planning for assistive robots in complex human environments. J. Ambient Intell. Smart Environ. **7**, 617–633 (2015)

9. D'Argenio, P.R., Hartmanns, A., Legay, A., Sedwards, S.: Statistical approximation of optimal schedulers for probabilistic timed automata. In: Ábrahám, E., Huisman, M. (eds.) IFM 2016. LNCS, vol. 9681, pp. 99–114. Springer, Heidelberg (2016). doi:10.1007/978-3-319-33693-0_7

10. D'Argenio, P., Legay, A., Sedwards, S., Traonouez, L.: Smart sampling for lightweight verification of Markov decision processes. STTT **17**(4), 469–484 (2015)

11. Jegourel, C., Legay, A., Sedwards, S.: Cross-entropy optimisation of importance sampling parameters for statistical model checking. In: Madhusudan, P., Seshia, S.A. (eds.) CAV 2012. LNCS, vol. 7358, pp. 327–342. Springer, Heidelberg (2012). doi:10.1007/978-3-642-31424-7_26

12. Jegourel, C., Legay, A., Sedwards, S.: Importance splitting for statistical model checking rare properties. In: Sharygina, N., Veith, H. (eds.) CAV 2013. LNCS, vol. 8044, pp. 576–591. Springer, Heidelberg (2013). doi:10.1007/978-3-642-39799-8_38

13. Jegourel, C., Legay, A., Sedwards, S.: An effective heuristic for adaptive importance splitting in statistical model checking. In: Margaria, T., Steffen, B. (eds.) ISoLA 2014. LNCS, vol. 8803, pp. 143–159. Springer, Heidelberg (2014). doi:10.1007/978-3-662-45231-8_11

14. Jegourel, C., Legay, A., Sedwards, S., Traonouez, L.: Distributed verification of rare properties using importance splitting observers. In: ECEASST, vol. 72 (2015)

15. Kwiatkowska, M., Norman, G., Parker, D.: Controller dependability analysis by probabilistic model checking. Control Eng. Pract. **15**(11), 1427–1434 (2006)

16. Legay, A., Sedwards, S., Traonouez, L.-M.: Scalable verification of Markov decision processes. In: Canal, C., Idani, A. (eds.) SEFM 2014. LNCS, vol. 8938, pp. 350–362. Springer, Heidelberg (2015). doi:10.1007/978-3-319-15201-1_23

17. Legay, A., Sedwards, S., Traonouez, L.: Estimating rewards & rare events in nondeterministic systems. In: ECEASST, vol. 72 (2015)

18. Legay, A., Traonouez, L.-M.: Statistical model checking of Simulink models with Plasma Lab. In: Artho, C., Ölveczky, P.C. (eds.) FTSCS 2015. CCIS, vol. 596, pp. 259–264. Springer, Heidelberg (2016). doi:10.1007/978-3-319-29510-7_15

19. Legay, A., Traonouez, L.: Statistical model checking with change detection. In: FOMACS (2016, to appear)

20. Ngo, V.C., Legay, A., Joloboff, V.: PSCV: a runtime verification tool for probabilistic SystemC models. In: Chaudhuri, S., Farzan, A. (eds.) CAV 2016. LNCS, vol. 9779, pp. 84–91. Springer, Heidelberg (2016). doi:10.1007/978-3-319-41528-4_5

21. Okamoto, M.: Some inequalities relating to the partial sum of binomial probabilities. Ann. Inst. Stat. Math. **10**, 29–35 (1959)

22. Page, E.S.: Continuous inspection schemes. Biometrika **41**(1/2), 100–115 (1954)

23. Wald, A.: Sequential tests of statistical hypotheses. Ann. Math. Stat. **16**(2), 117–186 (1945)

24. Younes, H.L.S., Simmons, R.G.: Probabilistic verification of discrete event systems using acceptance sampling. In: Brinksma, E., Larsen, K.G. (eds.) CAV 2002. LNCS, vol. 2404, pp. 223–235. Springer, Heidelberg (2002). doi:10.1007/3-540-45657-0_17

Synthesizing Energy-Optimal Controllers for Multiprocessor Dataflow Applications with UPPAAL STRATEGO

Waheed Ahmad[(✉)] and Jaco van de Pol

University of Twente, Enschede, The Netherlands
{w.ahmad,j.c.vandepol}@utwente.nl

Abstract. Streaming applications for mobile platforms impose high demands on a system's throughput and energy consumption. Dynamic system-level techniques have been introduced, to reduce power consumption at the expense of performance. We consider DPM (Dynamic Power Management) and DVFS (Dynamic Voltage and Frequency Scaling). The complex programming task now includes mapping and scheduling every task onto a heterogeneous multi-processor hardware platform. Moreover, DPM and DVFS parameters must be controlled, to meet all throughput constraints while minimizing the energy consumption.

Previous work proposed to automate this process, by modeling streaming applications in SDF (Synchronous Data Flow), modeling the processor platform, translating both models to PTA (Priced Timed Automata, where prices model energy), and using UPPAAL CORA to compute energy-optimal schedules that adhere to the throughput constraints.

In this paper, we experiment with an alternative approach, based on stochastic hybrid games. We investigate the applicability of UPPAAL STRATEGO to first synthesize a permissive controller satisfying a throughput constraint, and then select a near-optimal strategy that additionally minimizes the energy consumption. Our goal is to compare the UPPAAL CORA and UPPAAL STRATEGO approaches in terms of modeling effort, results and computation times, and to reveal potential limitations.

1 Introduction

Power management. The power consumption of computing systems has increased exponentially [19]. Minimizing power consumption has become one of the most critical challenges for these systems. Therefore, over the past years, dynamic system-level power management has gained significant value and success [8,19, 32]. Two well-known techniques are DVFS (Dynamic Voltage and Frequency Scaling) and DPM (Dynamic Power Management). Power consumption of a processor scales linearly in frequency and quadratically in voltage. But, frequency and voltage also have a linear relation, therefore, when the clock frequency decreases, the voltage is also reduced, so the power is reduced cubically. Switching off idle processors saves on static power consumption.

This research is supported by the EU FP7 project SENSATION (318490).

© Springer International Publishing AG 2016
T. Margaria and B. Steffen (Eds.): ISoLA 2016, Part I, LNCS 9952, pp. 94–113, 2016.
DOI: 10.1007/978-3-319-47166-2_7

DVFS [28] lowers the dynamic power consumption of modern processors, by lowering the voltage and clock frequency, at the expense of the execution time of a task. DPM switches the processor to a low power state when it is not used, thus reducing static power consumption in idle mode. Besides the savings in dynamic and static power usage, one should also take into account the non-negligible costs of switching between power states [25]. DPM is widely used, for instance in modern processors by Intel and AMD. Global DVFS is employed in modern processors such as Intel Core i7 and NVIDIA Tegra 2 [15]. It has been shown [2,14] that optimal energy savings require a combination of DPM and DVFS.

DVFS can be applied globally, or locally per processor [23]. Clearly, local DVFS provides more flexibility in choosing clock frequencies and voltage, so it is potentially more energy-efficient. However, it requires complex logic to implement many clock domains. To balance energy efficiency with design complexity, the concept of *Voltage and Frequency Islands* (VFIs) has been put forward [18]. One VFI consists of a clustered group of processors, running on a common clock frequency/voltage domain. Recently, some modern multicore processors, such as IBM Power 7 series, have adopted VFIs [16].

Programming streaming applications. We consider streaming applications for multi-processor mobile systems, like cell phones and PDAs. These applications consist of a series of encoding/decoding, signal processing and other computational tasks. We assume that the task graph has been modeled in Synchronous Data Flow (SDF [21]). The hardware consists of multiple processors, partly to increase the performance (streaming applications demand an ever higher throughput), partly since some tasks require specialised hardware capabilities.

Programming streaming applications on heterogeneous multi-processor hardware is difficult. Besides programming the basic functionality, the programmer must also design a mapping of the computation tasks to appropriate processors, and schedule them in such a way that all throughput constraints are met. With the advent of flexible energy management techniques, this becomes even more complicated: also the DVFS and DPM parameters must be adapted dynamically to save energy. Typically, a task should run at the lowest possible frequency, while still meeting its deadline.

Previous work. In previous work, we proposed to automate this mapping and scheduling process. First [1], we complemented the SDF application model with a separate hardware platform model of the heterogeneous multi-processors. This model specifies on which processors each task can run (processor capabilities), together with an upper bound on the running time. We also provided a translation of the SDF graph and processor models to Timed Automata. We used UPPAAL [6] to compute a mapping/schedule with maximal throughput on a limited set of processors. This provides a tradeoff between throughput and the used number of processors, potentially saving energy.

Subsequently [2], the hardware platform model was extended with the DPM, DVFS and VFI energy management techniques. In particular, it now also describes the VFI partitioning, the available frequency levels, power usage, switching costs, and task durations per processor/frequency. That paper provides a mapping of SDF graphs and the extended platform to *Priced Timed Automata* (PTA). We used prices to model the energy usage in various power modes and frequency levels, and to model the power costs of switching between those modes. We proposed UPPAAL CORA [7] to synthesize safe energy schedules. In this way, we computed concrete mappings and schedules that always meet a given throughput constraint, while minimizing the energy consumption. The translation has been implemented as a model transformation between SDF metamodels and UPPAAL metamodels [4], and was applied to an industrial Face Detection and Recognition application [26].

Recently [3], we extended our work in [2] to systems with batteries. Once the batteries are out of charge, the processors cannot run anymore. This signifies the end of *system life time*. In this work, we considered the concise *Kinetic Battery Model* (KiBaM) [22]. We modeled the system as a hybrid automaton [17], and applied statistical model checking to evaluate its Quality of Service in terms of, (1) the achievable application performance limited by a given battery capacity; and (2) the minimum required battery capacity to achieve a required application performance.

However, all these approaches are pessimistic, since they consider that the actors require worst-case execution time (WCET). On the contrary, practical systems have variability in execution time requirements. This variability can be modeled with stochastic systems, and analysed with statistical model checking, as in UPPAAL SMC [10]. However, UPPAAL SMC does not feature non-deterministic scheduling decisions. Hence, we model our system as *Stochastic Hybrid Games*, which distinguish controllable and non-controllable actions, which allows us to consider stochastic execution times and synthesize efficient strategies.

Contribution. In this paper, we derive energy-optimal solutions with a novel approach, based on stochastic hybrid games. These feature clock variables (used to model task duration and throughput constraints), continuous variables (used to model power consumption), controllable choices (used to model mapping and scheduling decisions), and uncontrollable choices (used for environment actions, e.g. the exact finishing time of a task). Remaining choices are implicitly resolved by uniform or exponential distributions. Stochastic hybrid games can be analysed by the tool UPPAAL STRATEGO [12], which provides synthesis of safe and near-optimal strategies for stochastic hybrid games, using a combination of symbolic synthesis, statistical model checking, and reinforcement learning. Here, by near-optimal we mean strategies which are not optimal because they are computed using simulations (statistical model checking) instead of classical model checking. However, as these simulations are run multiple times, they are close to optimal strategies. Hence, we call them near-optimal.

The second purpose of this paper is to compare the approaches of UPPAAL CORA and UPPAAL STRATEGO. In particular, we are interested in the modeling effort for the transition. We also compared the computed results, since we only compute near-optimal strategies. We are interested in the potential performance gain provided by the use of statistical model checking. Finally, we wanted to reveal potential limitations. We try to answer these questions by repeating a case study, based on an MPEG-4 decoder, modeled in [27].

Paper organization. Section 2 recapitulates some important notions, in particular SDF graphs (2.1), our hardware platform model (2.2), and the analysis of stochastic hybrid games with UPPAAL STRATEGO (2.3). Section 3 offers a translation from an SDF graph plus hardware platform model to a stochastic hybrid game; we also describe the steps of our method to compute a safe and near-optimal scheduler using UPPAAL STRATEGO. Section 4 describes our experiment on an MPEG-4 decoder; we also compare the results with our previous approach using UPPAAL CORA. Finally, in Sect. 5 we discuss some related work and a research perspective.

2 Preliminaries

This section recapitulates *Synchronous Data Flow* (SDF) graphs to model task graphs of streaming applications, and *hardware platform models* including heterogeneous processors organized in VFIs, and featuring energy management techniques DVFS and DPM. We also recapitulate the analysis of *Stochastic Hybrid Games* with UPPAAL STRATEGO.

2.1 SDF Graphs

Typically, real-time streaming applications execute a set of periodic tasks, which consume and produce a fixed amount of data. Such applications are naturally modelled as SDF graph: directed graphs, in which nodes represent *actors* (tasks) and edges represent data buffers (communication streams). Individual data elements are represented by *tokens*, produced and consumed by actors, and stored in data buffers.

Definition 1. *An SDF graph is a tuple* $G = (A, D, \mathsf{Tok}_0)$ *where A is a finite set of actors, $D \subseteq A^2 \times \mathbb{N}^2$ is a finite set of dependency edges, and* $\mathsf{Tok}_0 : D \to \mathbb{N}$ *denotes the initial distribution of tokens per edge.*

Definition 2. *Given an SDF graph* $G = (A, D, \mathsf{Tok}_0)$, *the sets of input and output edges of an actor $a \in A$ are* $In(a) := \{(a', a, p, q) \in D \mid a' \in A, p, q \in \mathbb{N}\}$ *and* $Out(a) := \{(a, b, p, q) \in D \mid b \in A, p, q \in \mathbb{N}\}$, *respectively. The consumption and production rate of an edge $e = (a, b, p, q) \in D$ are defined as $CR(e) := q$ and $PR(e) := p$, respectively.*

The execution of an actor is known as an *actor firing*. Edges connect producers to consumers, and serve as token buffers. Actor a *can fire* if each input edge $(a', a, p, q) \in In(a)$ contains at least q tokens. If it fires, actor a removes q tokens from each input edge $(a', a, p, q) \in In(a)$ and produces p' tokens on each output edge $(a, b, p', q') \in Out(a)$.

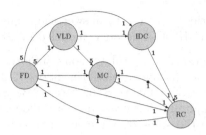

Fig. 1. MPEG-4 decoder

Example 1. Figure 1 shows the SDF graph of an MPEG-4 decoder [27]. It contains five actors $A = \{FD, VLD, IDC, RC, MC\}$, representing tasks performed in MPEG-4 decoding. For example, the frame detector (FD) determines the number of macro blocks to decode. By decoding a single frame, FD produces 5 macroblocks (in reality this is an arbitrary number between 0 and 99). The other modeled tasks are Variable Length Decoding (VLD), Inverse Discrete Cosine transformation (IDC), Motion Compensation (MC), and Reconstruction (RC) of the final video picture.

To avoid unbounded accumulation of tokens in a certain edge, we require SDF graphs to be *consistent*, i.e. an iteration can be defined that does not change the token distribution.

Definition 3. *A* repetition vector *of an SDF graph* $G = (A, D, \mathsf{Tok}_0)$ *is a function* $\gamma : A \rightarrow \mathbb{N}_{>0}$ *such that for every edge* $(a, b, p, q) \in D$, *the equation* $p.\gamma(a) = q.\gamma(b)$ *holds. An SDF graph is consistent if and only if it admits a repetition vector. In that case, an* iteration *of* G *is a multiset of actor firings, which contains exactly* $\gamma(a)$ *firings of each actor* $a \in A$.

2.2 Hardware Platform Model

The Hardware Platform Model (HPM) models the multi-processor platform on which the application (modelled as SDF graph) is mapped. Our HPM supports several features, including (1) heterogeneity: actors can only run on certain processors; (2) VFI: a partitioning of the processors in Voltage Frequency Islands; (3) DVFS: different frequency levels each processor can run on; (4) DPM: power consumption by a processor at a certain frequency, both when in use and when idle; (5) power-overhead required to switch between frequency levels; and (6) best- and worst-case computation times of tasks at a particular frequency level.

Definition 4. *A* Hardware Platform Model *(HPM) is a tuple* $\mathcal{P} = (\Pi, \zeta, F, P_{idle}, P_{occ}, P_{tr}, \tau_{worst}, \tau_{best})$, *consisting of*

- *a finite set of processors* Π. *We assume that* $\Pi = \{\pi_1, \ldots, \pi_n\}$ *is partitioned into disjoint blocks of voltage/frequency islands (VFIs);*
- *a function* $\zeta : \Pi \rightarrow 2^A$ *indicating which processors can handle which actors;*

– *a finite set of discrete frequency levels available to all processors denoted by* $F = \{f_1, \ldots, f_m\}$ *such that* $f_1 < f_2 < \ldots < f_m$;
– *functions* $P_{idle}, P_{occ} : \Pi \times F \to \mathbb{N}$ *denoting the static power consumption (in idle state) and static plus dynamic power consumption (in operating state) of a processor* $\pi \in \Pi$ *at a certain frequency level* $f \in F$,
– *a partial function* $P_{tr} : \Pi \times F^2 \nrightarrow \mathbb{N}$ *expressing the transition overhead between frequency levels* $f_1, f_2 \in F$ *for each processor* $\pi \in \Pi$, *and*
– *functions* $\tau_{best}, \tau_{worst} : A \times F \to \mathbb{N}_{\geq 1}$ *defining the best- and worst-case execution times for each actor* $a \in A$ *operating at frequency level* $f \in F$.

Note that it is straightforward to refine this model further, by explicitly introducing processor types, distinguishing frequency levels per processor type, and let execution times depend on processor types. By incorporating memory elements and buses, it would also be possible to model communication costs. Currently, we assume that communication times are included in the actor execution times.

Table 1. DVFS levels of Samsung Exynos 4210

Level	Voltage	Frequency
1	1.2	1400
2	1.15	1312.2
3	1.10	1221.8
4	1.05	1128.7
5	1.00	1032.7

Example 2. Exynos 4210 is a state-of-the-art processor used in high-end platforms such as Samsung Galaxy Note, SII etc. Table 1 shows its different DVFS levels, and corresponding CPU voltage (V) and clock frequency (MHz) [25].

2.3 Stochastic Hybrid Games and UPPAAL STRATEGO

We review Stochastic Hybrid Games and their analysis in UPPAAL STRATEGO. *Timed Automata* [5] have locations, transitions and clock variables. Residence time in states is constrained by invariants on clocks. Transitions are guarded by clock constraints as well and can reset a subset of the clock variables. For convenience, UPPAAL adds discrete variables (that can be used in guards, invariants and updates) and allows networks of timed automata that synchronize by means of handshake or broadcast channels. *Hybrid Automata* extend Timed Automata with continuous variables, governed by differential equations. They generalize *Priced Timed Automata*, where prices are hybrid variables that cannot be used in guards. In *Stochastic Automata*, choices and time delays are governed by stochastic distributions, like uniform and exponential distributions. *Timed Games* distinguish controllable actions (like scheduling choices by the system) and uncontrollable actions (like inputs or time delays that are determined by the environment). Finally, *Stochastic Hybrid Games* combine all features.

UPPAAL STRATEGO [12] supports strategy synthesis for Stochastic Hybrid Games. It integrates the symbolic algorithms for model checking Priced Timed Automata (from UPPAAL CORA [7]) and for synthesizing optimal strategies of Timed Games (from UPPAAL TIGA [9]) with the statistical model checking algorithms for Stochastic Timed Automata (UPPAAL SMC [13]). Moreover, it implements reinforcement learning to synthesize near-optimal strategies for Stochastic Hybrid Games [11]. UPPAAL STRATEGO comes with an extended query language, where strategies are first class objects that may be synthesized, compared, further optimized or restricted, and analyzed for correctness and performance. New symbolic or statistical model checking and synthesis queries on Stochastic Timed Games can be performed under the constraints of previously synthesized stragies.

We illustrate the features and queries of UPPAAL STRATEGO with a small example adapted from [29]. Figure 2 models a job with two phases. In the first phase, the scheduler must choose between two machines, indicated by the locations A and B. The slow machine A takes up to 100 time-units to finish (indicated by the invariant on clock variable x), but consumes less power (indicated by the differential equation $c' == 3$ (e.g. 3 kW/h). The alternative machine B is twice as fast, but consumes considerably more power. In the second phase, the scheduler must choose between the machines C and D. The choice of machine is in both phases controllable by the scheduler (indicated by the solid transitions), while the exact completion time within the specified upperbound is left to an uncontrollable environment (indicated by the dashed transitions). Implicitly, a uniform distribution of the actual computation time is assumed. Next, we are interested in synthesizing controllers for various objectives. We consider the following scenarios.

Scenario 1: Safe Strategy. The job in Fig. 2 must be completed before 175 time-units. To this end, we generate the most permissive (non-deterministic) strategy Safe, and compute its expected cost (based on 1000 simulation runs), using the following two queries. The expected cost (when the choice for the exact finishing time is resolved uniformly) appears to be 437.317.

> **strategy** Safe = **control** : A <> Job.End and **time** <= 175 .
> **E**[<= 175; 1000](**max** : c) **under** Safe .

Scenario 2: Optimal Strategy. Now we are interested in completing the job with minimal energy consumption. We compute a near-optimal strategy and visualize it with 10 random simulation runs with the following two queries.

> **strategy** Opt = **minE**(c) [<= 175] : <> Job.End .
> **simulate** 10 [<= 200]
> {Job.A, 2 + Job.B, 4 + Job.C, 6 + Job.D, 8 + Job.End} **under** Opt .

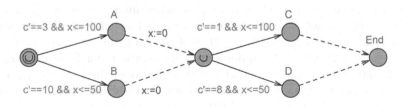

Fig. 2. A job with two phases

UPPAAL STRATEGO employs random simulation and reinforcement learning to select a strategy that minimizes the expected completion cost, which is estimated to be 276.661. The 10 random simulation runs are shown in Fig. 3(a). Clearly, in these runs only the cheaper machines (A and C) are chosen. However, strategy Opt does not always finish within 175 time-units.

Scenario 3: Optimal and Safe Strategy. To find a strategy that both finishes within 175 time units and minimizes the energy consumption, we query:

$$\text{strategy OptSafe} = \text{minE}(c)[<= 200] : <> \text{Job.End under Safe} .$$

This learns a new sub-strategy OptSafe under the constraints of the strategy Safe derived in Scenario 1. Figure 3(b) shows 10 random runs according to OptSafe. One sees that in this case sometimes machine D is used: If machine A finishes its job early, the slower but cheaper machine C can be utilized in the second phase. However, if the machine A takes longer, only the faster, more expensive machine D can be selected, or we would miss the deadline. The expected completion cost of OptSafe appears to be 316.738, which is higher than Opt, but better than Safe. Note that, opposed to Opt, the strategy OptSafe will always finishes within the deadline of 175 time-units, thus being guaranteed safe and near-optimal.

3   Energy-Optimal Schedules Under Throughput Constraints

3.1   Translating SDF Graphs to Stochastic Hybrid Games

In our framework [1,2], the input consists of separate models of an SDF task graph, the hardware platform model, and a throughput constraint. In this way, we split the problem statement of optimal energy management in terms of tasks and resources. In this section, we describe a systematic translation of an SDF graph along with a hardware platform model into a Stochastic Hybrid Game. Subsequently, we summarize our method of using UPPAAL STRATEGO for computing an energy-optimal strategy under the given throughput constraint.

Given an SDF graph $G = (A, D, \text{Tok}_0)$ mapped on a hardware platform model $(\Pi, \zeta, F, P_{idle}, P_{occ}, P_{tr}, \tau_{worst}, \tau_{best})$, we generate a parallel composition of stochastic hybrid games:

$$A_G \| Processor_1 \|, \ldots, \| Processor_n \| Scheduler .$$

Here A_G encodes the SDF task graph G, keeping track of the number of tokens in all buffers. $Processor_i$ models $\pi_i \in \Pi$, keeping track if it is idle or occupied, and of the current frequency level for DVFS. The task of the *Scheduler* is to synchronize frequency switches between all processors in the same voltage and frequency island (VFI).

Translating the SDF graph. The automaton A_G has a single location and no clocks. Figure 4 illustrates A_G for the MPEG decoder in Fig. 1. For each

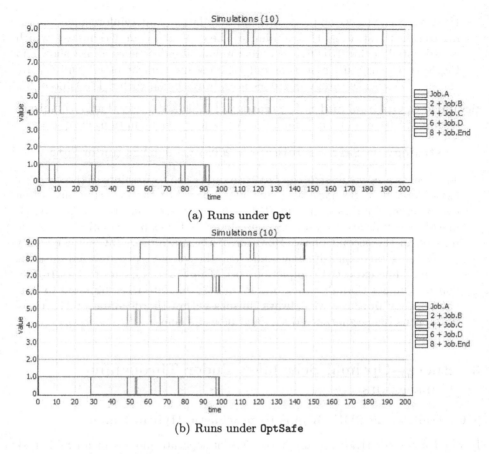

(a) Runs under Opt

(b) Runs under OptSafe

Fig. 3. UPPAAL STRATEGO simulations for Opt and OptSafe Controllers

edge (a, b, p, q), it contains an integer variable buff_a2b containing the number of buffered tokens in this edge. It also counts the number of times a has fired in a variable counter_a for later querying. Initially, counter_a $= 0$ and buff_a2b $= Tok_0(\mathsf{a}, \mathsf{b}, \mathsf{p}, \mathsf{q})$. Moreover, for each processor $\pi_i \in \Pi$, the automaton A_G reads a boolean variable Pbusy[i]. This variable ensures that the actors in the SDF graph G are only mapped on the processor $\pi_i \in \Pi$ when it is free. This extra administration is needed because UPPAAL STRATEGO only supports broadcast communication, but not blocking handshake communication. Furthermore, UPPAAL STRATEGO requires that each location must either be urgent, committed, have an exponential rate or carry an invariant. Therefore, we have 5 as a *Rate of Exponential* in location Initial.

There are two parametrized actions in A_G namely, fire![i][a] and end?[i][a] to communicate between A_G and *Processor*$_i$, representing the start and end of executing actor a on processor π_i. For each $a \in A$, we add two edges in A_G. The controllable transition labeled fire![i][a] consumes q tokens from buffer

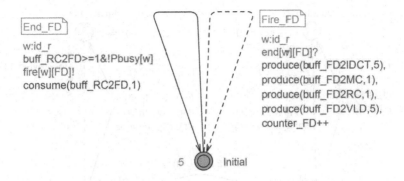

Fig. 4. UPPAAL STRATEGO model A_G for SDF graph G

buff_b2a, for each input edge (b, a, p, q) in G (specified by an auxiliary function consume(buff_b2a, q) not detailed here). The uncontrollable transition labeled end?[i][a] produces p tokens into buffer buff_a2b, for each output edge (a, b, p, q) in G (specified by auxiliary function produce(buff_a2b, p)).

Translating the hardware platform model. For each $\pi_i \in \Pi_y \subseteq \Pi$, we introduce an automaton *Processor$_i$*. See Fig. 5 for a part of this automaton. It maintains two variables, to properly synchronize with the *Scheduler* (only needed since UPPAAL STRATEGO doesn't support handshake synchronization). Variable freq_lev[y] counts the number of currently occupied processors in the VFI Π_y, and curr_freq[y] determines the current frequency level of all $\pi_i \in \Pi_y$. Initially, freq_lev[y] $= 0$ and curr_freq[y] $= m$, where $f_m = \max\{F\}$. The counter freq_lev[y] is incremented and decremented by one on each fire?[i][a] and end![i][a] transition.

Processor$_i$ has location Idle_f for each $f \in F$, and for each $a \in A$ an additional location InUse_a_f. The edges between these states both synchronize with A_G. The worst-case execution time $\tau_{worst}(a, f)$ is encoded in the invariant of InUse_a_f. The best-case execution time $\tau_{best}(a, f)$ is encoded as the guard. In this paper, we assume that the execution time of the actor is determined stochastically by the environment, uniformly in the interval $[\tau_{best}(a, f), \tau_{worst}(a, f)]$. The power consumption P_{idle} at each frequency $f \in F$ and P_{occ} for each actor $a \in A$ are encoded as a differential equation in the invariant in Idle_f and InUse_a_f, respectively, using the hybrid variable $cost_i'$. As required by UPPAAL STRATEGO, we have 5 as a *Rate of Exponential* in all locations Idle_f.

Encoding frequency switches. See Fig. 6 for the *Scheduler*. It triggers frequency switches from f_ℓ to f_k (for $k = \ell \pm 1$). It synchronizes with *Processor$_i$* for all $\pi_i \in \Pi_y$ that are in the same VFI y, through the parameterized broadcast action fjump_lk[y]. The automaton *Scheduler* checks whether all processors in the switched VFI y are in the idle location (this excludes switching frequencies in the middle of a task execution), and are running at the same frequency. This is done by testing the global counters freq_lev[y]=0 and curr_freq[y]=ℓ.

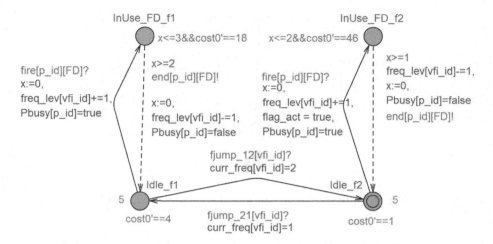

Fig. 5. UPPAAL STRATEGO model *Processor* for process p_id in VFI vfi_id (restricted to frequencies f_1, f_2 and transitions for actor FD)

To avoid traces with infinite switching between Idle locations (Zeno behavior), we needed some extra restrictions. We defined that each processor starts in the highest frequency (by setting the initial location in *Processor*). We further ensure that a processor can only switch frequencies after firing an actor (at the highest frequency, using flag_act). Furthermore, to switch frequencies, the scheduler must wait for 2 time units (denoted by $x >= 2$ where x is a local clock). We also have 5 a *Rate of Exponential* in location Initial.

3.2 Learning and Optimization Using UPPAAL STRATEGO

Recall the repetition vector γ, which captures the number of actor firings in a single iteration. Usually, one is interested in a periodic cycle, which consists of a number of iterations. In this paper, we restrict to the execution of one iteration. So for each actor $a \in A$, $\gamma(a)$ denotes the number of times a must fire. For example, the repetition vector γ of the example SDF graph given in Sect. 3 is $\gamma(\langle \text{FD}, \text{VLD}, \text{IDC}, \text{RC}, \text{MC} \rangle) = \langle 1, 5, 5, 1, 1 \rangle$. We capture the states after firing according to the repetition vector γ by predicate Q:

$$Q := \bigwedge_{a \in A} \{\text{counter\_a} = \gamma(a)\}$$

We now summarize our method to synthesize an energy-optimal controller from an SDF graph G and a HPM $\mathcal{P}$ with n processors that meets the throughput-constraint T using UPPAAL STRATEGO, by the following steps:

1. Generate stochastic hybrid games from G and $\mathcal{P}$ according to the translation in Sect. 3.1, resulting in $A_G \| Processor_1 \| \ldots \| Processor_n \| Scheduler$. This network of timed automata forms the input to UPPAAL STRATEGO.

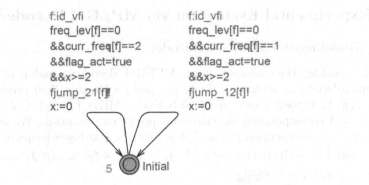

Fig. 6. UPPAAL STRATEGO model for the Scheduler

2. Synthesize the most permissive safe strategy that finishes one iteration within time T, by running the following query, where clock variable *time* is never reset, but just used to observe the overall time progress.

$$\textbf{strategy Safe} = \textbf{control} : \textbf{A} <> (\textbf{Q and time} <= \textbf{T})$$

3. Obtain a near-optimal strategy with respect to energy consumption that finishes within time T, by running the following query:

$$\textbf{strategy OptSafe} = \textbf{minE} : (\sum_{\pi_i \in \Pi} \text{cost}_i) \, [<= \text{T}] :<> (\textbf{Q}) \textbf{ under Safe}$$

4. To get an impression of the minimal energy needed when the throughput constraint would be ignored, one may optionally run the following query:

$$\textbf{strategy Opt} = \textbf{minE} : (\sum_{\pi_i \in \Pi} \text{cost}_i) \, [<= \text{T}] :<> (\textbf{Q})$$

5. For all strategies $S \in \{Safe, OptSafe, Opt\}$ one can compute the average energy consumption from a number of simulation runs (say 100) by the following query:

$$\textbf{E}[<= \text{T}; 100] \, (\textbf{max} : \sum_{\pi_i \in \Pi} \text{cost}_i) \textbf{ under S}$$

A number of 10 simulations for executing actor $a, b, ... \in A$ under the strategy S can be visualized with the query

$$\textbf{simulate 10} \, \{\text{counter\_a}, 2 + \text{counter\_b}, ...\} \textbf{ under S}$$

Table 2. Platform description

Voltage (V)	Frequency (MHz)	P_{idle} (W)	P_{occ} (W)
1.2	1400	0.1	4.6
1.00	1032.7	0.4	1.8

4   Experimental Evaluation via MPEG-4 Decoder

4.1   Modeling the MPEG-4 Decoder

Let us consider the example of an MPEG-4 decoder capable of processing five macroblocks as shown in Fig. 1, mapped on Exynos 4210 processors $\Pi = \{\pi_1, \ldots, \pi_n\}$. Table 2 shows two DVFS levels (MHz) $\{f_1, f_2\} \in F$ taken from Table 1 and corresponding experimental power consumption. We assume that the (best/worst) execution times of all actors $a \in A$ at lower frequency level, i.e., f_1 are rounded to the next integer. As $f_1 = 0.738 \times f_2$, $\tau_{best}(a, f_1) = \lceil \frac{\tau_{best}(a, f_2)}{0.738} \rceil$ and $\tau_{worst}(a, f_1) = \lceil \frac{\tau_{worst}(a, f_2)}{0.738} \rceil$.

The UPPAAL STRATEGO models of this example are shown in Figs. 4, 5 and 6. For easier understanding, the models are shown with respect to one actor only, i.e., FD $\in A$. Figure 4 shows the automaton A_G which models the actor FD, and its incoming $In(FD)$ and outgoing $Out(FD)$ edges. The automata $Processor_1, \ldots, Processor_n$ model the processors $\Pi = \{\pi_1, \ldots, \pi_n\}$, as shown in Fig. 5. Figure 6 presents the automaton of $Scheduler$. As clocks in UPPAAL STRATEGO can only take integer values, all power consumption values are multiplied by 10 in Fig. 5.

Initially, all processors $Processor_1, \ldots, Processor_n$ are in the idle location at the highest frequency level, Idle_f2. The idle power consumption $P_{idle}(\pi, f_2) = 0.4$ W is annotated as an invariant in the location Idle_f2.

Let us consider that the MPEG-4 Decoder in Fig. 1 is mapped on 4 Exynos 4210 Processors. For the constraint of finishing an iteration within 15 ms (67 frames per second (fps)), Fig. 7 shows 10 random runs for each controller, i.e., Safe, Opt, and OptSafe respectively. Figure 7a shows the strategies that achieve 67 fps without optimising energy consumption. Whereas, Fig. 7b shows the strategies having minimal energy consumption without any constraint on the throughput. In particular, Fig. 7c shows the strategies that after learning the strategy Safe, guarantee to be both energy-optimal and achieve 67 fps.

We also generated various strategies for the MPEG-4 decoder on a varying number of processors. For the constraint of 67 fps, the evaluation of the energy consumption under different controllers explained in Subsect. 3.2 are summarised in Table 3. If we analyse the OptSafe strategy in Table 3, we observe that achieving the same number of frames per second at fewer processors lowers the energy consumption. The reason is the high slack at the higher number of processors, and therefore the processors stay idle for most of the time. As a result, the static energy surpasses the dynamic energy. For instance, the energy consumption is decreased by 5.4 %, when moving from 5 to 4 processors. Since the strategy Opt is not guaranteed to finish within the deadline, we will not consider it in the rest of the paper.

4.2   Comparison with UPPAAL CORA

In this subsection, we compare the approach presented in this paper (stochastic hybrid games) with the priced timed automata based approach in [2]. The work in [2] like us, computes the energy-optimal schedules for SDF applications running on multiprocessor platforms. However, in comparison to our approach of using stochastic hybrid games, the problem of finding the schedules is encoded as a reachability property over priced timed-automata models. This is then checked by the model checker UPPAAL CORA [7]. For comparison, we take the example

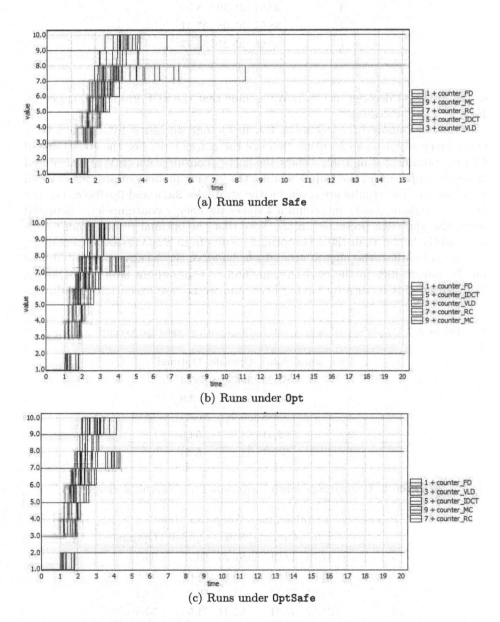

(a) Runs under Safe

(b) Runs under Opt

(c) Runs under OptSafe

Fig. 7. UPPAAL STRATEGO simulations for MPEG-4 decoder under Safe, Opt, and OptSafe Controllers

Table 3. Energy estimations with adaptive execution times

Processors	Safe	Opt	OptSafe
5	42.76	41.64	42.21
4	40.87	39.79	39.94
3	39.61	38.39	38.57
2	38.57	37.08	37.31
1	36.96	35.21	35.47

of the MPEG-4 decoder in Fig. 1. We assume that the SDF graph is mapped on Exynos 4210 processors.

First, we removed the stochastic features in our stochastic hybrid models by considering worst-case execution times of the actors only. For the constraint of 67 fps, columns 2–3 in Table 4 show the energy consumption (mWs), calculated using the approach of this paper, against the varying number of processors given in column 1. The results are given for the strategies Safe and OptSafe. For the same throughout constraint, column 4 shows the energy consumption calculated using the approach presented in [2]. Note that the optimal results from CORA are slightly better than the near-optimal results from STRATEGO.

As said earlier, the biggest strength of UPPAAL STRATEGO is the ability to handle uncertainty in the environment, and to compute an adaptive strategy. We utilized this feature by having best- and worst-case execution time in our

Table 4. Comparison of energy estimations with worst-case execution times

Processors	Safe	OptSafe	Optimal
5	67.26	59.7	55.4
4	66.9	58.01	53.8
3	63.83	56.2	53.4
2	62.41	54.5	54.5
1	64.07	63.4	63.4

Table 5. Comparing adaptive with worst-case execution times

Processors	Adaptive time		Worst-case time		
	Safe	OptSafe	Safe	OptSafe	Optimal
5	42.76	42.21	67.26	59.7	55.4
4	40.87	39.94	66.9	58.01	53.8
3	39.61	38.57	63.83	56.2	53.4
2	38.57	37.31	62.41	54.5	54.5
1	39.69	35.47	64.07	63.4	63.4

UPPAAL STRATEGO model. On the other hand, UPPAAL CORA considers worst-case execution times only. Table 5 compares this strength of UPPAAL STRATEGO with UPPAAL CORA, by combining Tables 3 and 4. In Table 5, columns 2–3 shows the energy consumption, when having best- and worst-case (adaptive) execution times. Columns 3–5 copy the results from Table 4, considering worst-case execution times only. Clearly, the adaptive strategy saves energy.

Table 6. Comparing time and memory consumption of the STRATEGO and CORA-tools

Processors	Safe		OptSafe		Optimal	
	Memory	Time	Memory	Time	Memory	Time
5	2622.06	50354.44	2660.15	75831.63	71.13	144.52
4	634.14	5911.04	695.42	8487.192	29.46	7.27
3	165.86	327.85	224.75	505.09	21.46	0.71
2	86.6	5.32	123.21	18.38	19.75	0.31
1	79.28	0.02	115.55	1.96	19.62	0.09

Table 6 compares the computation time (sec) and the memory consumption (MB), of both methods, when having worst-case execution times. As we can see, for our running example, UPPAAL CORA is more efficient in terms of memory and time, in particular when analysing systems with more cores.

5   Conclusion

5.1   Discussion

We set out an alternative method to map and schedule streaming applications specified in SDF onto heterogeneous multi-processor hardware. We conducted an experiment in UPPAAL STRATEGO, and compared it with a previous approach in UPAAL CORA. We will discuss some limitations and strengths of the approach with UPPAAL STRATEGO.

The most important issue is that UPPAAL CORA provides a concrete schedule (in the form of a timed trace), from which a concrete implementation can be derived. This is clearly not possible in UPPAAL STRATEGO, since it deals with stochastic systems. However, apart from the visualization, we have found no way to retrieve the computed strategy in a form that can be used to synthesize real controller code. In [1,2] we used the traces also to find out the number of iterations needed to get into the periodic phase of the schedule. This would be needed to really compute the long-term throughput of streaming applications like an MPEG-4 decoder.

Next, we found some limitations in the input language of UPPAAL STRATEGO. Some of them are inherent due to the use of statistical model checking engine.

In particular, the absence of handshake synchronization led us to add more and more global variables and guards, in order to keep the components synchronized despite using broadcast communication only. Another issue is that we could not add discrete jumps in costs on transitions. This means that we couldn't model the costs of switching between frequencies (as specified by P_{tr}), as we do in our original CORA models. Another consequence is that we had to modify the model to avoid Zeno-runs between infinitely switching frequencies in idle mode, which now happen "for free".

We also compared the results of CORA's optimal schedule, and STRATEGO's near-optimal strategies. The good news is that the estimated near-optimal results by STRATEGO are quite close to those computed by CORA (at most 10 % deviation). We also had hoped that STRATEGO would be faster, due to the use of statistical model checking and learning, but this was not the case. Actually, the computations in STRATEGO took considerably longer time than in CORA.

We want to stress that the several drawbacks that we encountered are inherent due to the stronger capabilities of STRATEGO. Using STRATEGO, we can handle uncertainty in the environment, and compute an adaptive strategy based on the actual behavior so far. We already exploited this by distinguishing the best- and worst-case execution time of the actors in the MPEG-4 decoder. STRATEGO assumes that the actual time is distributed uniformly in this interval.

This feature shows the distinguishing power of STRATEGO and it provides an enormous potential for energy savings compared to the traditional approach. The traditional approach will always take into account the worst-case execution time, even when this is not realistic at all. This could result in an over-dimensioning of the system, leading to idle-time intervals. This is energy-inefficient, because those intervals could have been used to lower the clock frequency in the busy intervals. A truly adaptive strategy would thus make more efficient use of the same resources.

5.2   Related Work

The state-of-the-art method of applying DVFS on SDF graphs is proposed in [24, 31]. These papers consider dynamic power usage, but they ignore static power usage, which is non-negligible in modern processors. The work in [24] requires the expensive transformation of SDF graphs to equivalent Homogeneous SDF (HSDF) graphs, which we avoid in our approach. Also, their work is not applicable to platforms with a limited number of processors. The approach in [31] considers that each task is executed as soon as it is enabled, unlike real-life applications where this is not possible due to limitations on the available number of processors. A recent stochastic approach [20] introduces exponential Scenario-Aware SDF models, which add mode switches and exponential delays to SDF graphs. They compute minimal and maximal expected values, but cannot derive concrete schedules. Another direction [29] takes into account strategies for battery schedules, in order to minimize battery wear and optimize for a system's life time. In [3], we integrated task scheduling on heterogeneous hardware with battery strategies, as an approach to energy-self-supporting systems. Finally, an interesting alternative is to use mean-payoff games to synthesize a controller for resource- and scenario-aware SDF graphs, which reacts to environment behavior [30]. They use policy iteration algorithms to optimize for throughput, in contrast to our approach, where the goal is to optimize for energy consumption.

5.3   Research Perspectives

In this paper, we have presented a method of synthesizing energy-optimal controllers for dataflow applications mapped on heterogeneous platforms using UPPAAL STRATEGO. We further have compared this approach with an approach with UPPAAL CORA, in terms of modeling effort, results and computation times. For deterministic systems, currently UPPAAL CORA provides a more expressive input language, faster algorithms, and ready to use results in the form of a concrete schedule, when compared to UPPAAL STRATEGO. However, UPPAAL CORA cannot handle environment uncertainty, which leads to assuming worst-case behavior everywhere, and potentially energy-wasteful schedulers. UPPAAL STRATEGO provides the means to compute adaptive schedules, optimizing for energy in an uncertain environment.

A future research direction is to carry on from the results achieved in this paper and explore the possibilities of battery-aware scheduling of SDF graphs. As real-life batteries are hybrid in nature, UPPAAL STRATEGO is a natural choice to model them. Then using the combination of symbolic synthesis, statistical model checking, and reinforcement learning, we can synthesize battery-aware controllers.

Acknowledgement. The authors are grateful to Jakob Haahr Taankvist and Peter Gjøl Jensen for their valuable help to understand UPPAAL STRATEGO. The authors would also like to thank the anonymous reviewers for their helpful and constructive comments that greatly contributed to improving the final version of the paper.

References

1. Ahmad, W., de Groote, R., Hölzenspies, P.K.F., Stoelinga, M., van de Pol, J.: Resource-constrained optimal scheduling of synchronous dataflow graphs via timed automata. In: Proceedings of 14th International Conference on Application of Concurrency to System Design, (ACSD), pp. 72–81 (2014)
2. Ahmad, W., Hölzenspies, P.K.F., Stoelinga, M., van de Pol, J.: Green computing: power optimisation of VFI-based real-time multiprocessor dataflow applications. In: Proceedings of 18th Euromicro Conference on Digital Systems Design (DSD), pp. 271–275 (2015)
3. Ahmad, W., Jongerden, M., Stoelinga, M., van de Pol, J.: Model checking and evaluating QoS of batteries in MPSoC dataflow applications via hybrid automata. In: Proceedings of 16th International Conference on Application of Concurrency to System Design (ACSD), pp. 114–123 (2016)
4. Ahmad, W., Yildiz, B.M., Rensink, A., Stoelinga, M.: Evaluating the tools on the face detection and recognition case study, Chap. 2, pp. 4–6. FP7 EU Project SENSATION, Deliverable D1.4 (2016)

5. Alur, R., Dill, D.L.: A theory of timed automata. Theoret. Comput. Sci. **126**, 183–235 (1994)
6. Behrmann, G., David, A., Larsen, K.G.: A tutorial on UPPAAL. In: Bernardo, M., Corradini, F. (eds.) SFM-RT 2004. LNCS, vol. 3185, pp. 200–236. Springer, Heidelberg (2004)
7. Behrmann, G., Larsen, K.G., Rasmussen, J.I.: Optimal scheduling using priced timed automata. SIGMETRICS Perform. Eval. Rev. **32**(4), 34–40 (2005)
8. Benini, L., Bogliolo, A., Micheli, G.D.: A survey of design techniques for system-level dynamic power management. IEEE Trans. Very Large Scale Integr. (VLSI) Syst. **8**(3), 299–316 (2000)
9. Cassez, F., David, A., Fleury, E., Larsen, K.G., Lime, D.: Efficient on-the-fly algorithms for the analysis of timed games. In: Abadi, M., Alfaro, L. (eds.) CONCUR 2005. LNCS, vol. 3653, pp. 66–80. Springer, Heidelberg (2005). doi:10.1007/11539452_9
10. David, A., Du, D., Larsen, K.G., Legay, A., Mikučionis, M., Bøgsted Poulsen, D., Sedwards, S.: Statistical model checking for stochastic hybrid systems. ArXiv e-prints (2012)
11. David, A., Jensen, P.G., Larsen, K.G., Legay, A., Lime, D., Sørensen, M.G., Taankvist, J.H.: On time with minimal expected cost!. In: Cassez, F., Raskin, J.-F. (eds.) ATVA 2014. LNCS, vol. 8837, pp. 129–145. Springer, Heidelberg (2014). doi:10.1007/978-3-319-11936-6_10
12. David, A., Jensen, P.G., Larsen, K.G., Mikučionis, M., Taankvist, J.H.: UPPAAL STRATEGO. In: Baier, C., Tinelli, C. (eds.) TACAS 2015. LNCS, vol. 9035, pp. 206–211. Springer, Heidelberg (2015). doi:10.1007/978-3-662-46681-0_16
13. David, A., Larsen, K.G., Legay, A., Mikučionis, M., Poulsen, D.B.: Uppaal SMC tutorial. Int. J. Softw. Tools Technol. Transf. **17**(4), 397–415 (2015)
14. Devadas, V., Aydin, H.: On the interplay of voltage/frequency scaling and device power management for frame-based real-time embedded applications. IEEE Trans. Comput. **61**(1), 31–44 (2012)
15. Gerards, M.E.T., Hurink, J.L., Kuper, J.: On the interplay between global DVFS and scheduling tasks with precedence constraints. IEEE Trans. Comput. **64**, 1742–1754 (2014)
16. Han, J.J., Wu, X., Zhu, D., Jin, H., Yang, L.T., Gaudiot, J.L.: Synchronization-aware energy management for VFI-based multicore real-time systems. IEEE Trans. Comput. **61**(12), 1682–1696 (2012)
17. Henzinger, T.: The theory of hybrid automata. In: Proceedings of Eleventh Annual IEEE Symposium on Logic in Computer Science (LICS), pp. 278–292 (1996)
18. Herbert, S., Marculescu, D.: Analysis of dynamic voltage/frequency scaling in chip-multiprocessors. In: Proceedings of ACM/IEEE International Symposium on Low Power Electronics and Design (ISLPED), pp. 38–43 (2007)
19. Irani, S., Pruhs, K.R.: Algorithmic problems in power management. ACM SIGACT News **36**(2), 63–76 (2005)
20. Katoen, J.-P., Wu, H., Exponentially timed SADF: compositional semantics, reductions, and analysis. In: Proceedings of 14th ACM/IEEE International Conference on Embedded Software (EMSOFT), pp. 1:1–1:10 (2014)
21. Lee, E.A., Messerschmitt, D.G.: Synchronous data flow. Proc. IEEE **75**(9), 1235–1245 (1987)
22. Manwell, J.F., McGowan, J.G.: Lead acid battery storage model for hybrid energy systems. Sol. Energy **50**(5), 399–405 (1993)

23. March, J.L., Sahuquillo, J., Hassan, H., Petit, S., Duato, J.: A new energy-aware dynamic task set partitioning algorithm for soft and hard embedded real-time systems. Comput. J. **54**(8), 1282–1294 (2011)
24. Nelson, A., Moreira, O., Molnos, A., Stuijk, S., Nguyen, B.T., Goossens, K.: Power minimisation for real-time dataflow applications. In: Proceedings of 14th Euromicro Conference on Digital System Design (DSD), pp. 117–124 (2011)
25. Park, S., Park, J., Shin, D., Wang, Y., Xie, Q., Pedram, M., Chang, N.: Accurate modeling of the delay and energy overhead of dynamic voltage and frequency scaling in modern microprocessors. IEEE Trans. Comput. Aided Des. Integr. Circ. Syst. **32**(5), 695–708 (2013)
26. ter Braak, T.D., Sunesen, K., Ahmad, W., Stoelinga, M., van de Pol, J., Katoen, J.-P., Wu, H.: Evaluating the tools on the face detection and recognition case study, Chap. 2, pp. 6–23. FP7 EU Project SENSATION, Deliverable D4.4 (2016)
27. Theelen, B., Geilen, M., Basten, T., Voeten, J., Gheorghita, S., Stuijk, S.: A scenario-aware data flow model for combined long-run average and worst-case performance analysis. In: Proceedings of 4th ACM/IEEE International Conference on Formal Methods and Models for Co-design (MEMOCODE), pp. 185–194 (2006)
28. Weiser, M., Welch, B., Demers, A., Shenker, S.: Scheduling for reduced CPU energy. In: Proceedings of 1st USENIX Conference on Operating Systems Design and Implementation (1994)
29. Wognsen, E.R., Haverkort, B.R., Jongerden, M., Hansen, R.R., Larsen, K.G.: A score function for optimizing the cycle-life of battery-powered embedded systems. In: Sankaranarayanan, S., Vicario, E. (eds.) FORMATS 2015. LNCS, vol. 9268, pp. 305–320. Springer, Heidelberg (2015). doi:10.1007/978-3-319-22975-1_20
30. Yang, Y., Geilen, M., Basten, T., Stuijk, S., Corporaal, H.: Playing games with scenario- and resource-aware SDF graphs through policy iteration. In: Proceedings of Design, Automation and Test in Europe (DATE), pp. 194–199 (2012)
31. Zhu, J., Sander, I., Jantsch, A.: Energy efficient streaming applications with guaranteed throughput on MPSoCs. In: Proceedings of 8th ACM/IEEE International Conference on Embedded Software (EMSOFT), pp. 119–128 (2008)
32. Zhuravlev, S., Saez, J.C., Blagodurov, S., Fedorova, A., Prieto, M.: Survey of energy-cognizant scheduling techniques. IEEE Trans. Parallel Distrib. Syst. **24**(7), 1447–1464 (2013)

Statistical Model Checking for Product Lines

Maurice H. ter Beek[1]([⊠]), Axel Legay[2], Alberto Lluch Lafuente[3],
and Andrea Vandin[4]

[1] ISTI–CNR, Pisa, Italy
maurice.terbeek@isti.cnr.it
[2] Inria Rennes, Rennes, France
[3] DTU, Lyngby, Denmark
[4] IMT Lucca, Lucca, Italy

Abstract. We report on the suitability of statistical model checking for the analysis of quantitative properties of product line models by an extended treatment of earlier work by the authors. The type of analysis that can be performed includes the likelihood of specific product behaviour, the expected average cost of products (in terms of the attributes of the products' features) and the probability of features to be (un)installed at runtime. The product lines must be modelled in QFLan, which extends the probabilistic feature-oriented language PFLan with novel quantitative constraints among features and on behaviour and with advanced feature installation options. QFLan is a rich process-algebraic specification language whose operational behaviour interacts with a store of constraints, neatly separating product configuration from product behaviour. The resulting probabilistic configurations and probabilistic behaviour converge in a discrete-time Markov chain semantics, enabling the analysis of quantitative properties. Technically, a Maude implementation of QFLan, integrated with Microsoft's SMT constraint solver Z3, is combined with the distributed statistical model checker MultiVeStA, developed by one of the authors. We illustrate the feasibility of our framework by applying it to a case study of a product line of bikes.

1   Introduction

Recently, much effort is put into making (process-algebraic) modelling languages and formal analysis techniques amenable to product lines [7,13,23,28,32,36,37]. The challenge is to handle their inherent variability, due to which the number of possible products to be analysed may be exponential in the number of features.

In [10], two of the authors introduced the feature-oriented language FLAN implemented in Maude [18], allowing analyses like consistency checking by SAT solving and model checking. In FLAN, a rich set of process-algebraic operators allows one to specify the configuration and the behaviour of a product line, while a constraint store allows one to specify all constraints from feature models as well as additional action constraints typical of feature-oriented programming. The execution of a process is constrained by the store (e.g. to avoid introducing

© Springer International Publishing AG 2016
T. Margaria and B. Steffen (Eds.): ISoLA 2016, Part I, LNCS 9952, pp. 114–133, 2016.
DOI: 10.1007/978-3-319-47166-2_8

inconsistencies), but a process can also query the store (e.g. to resolve configuration options) or update the store (e.g. to add new features, even at runtime).

In [8], we equipped FLAN with a means to specify probabilistic product line models, resulting in PFLAN. In PFLAN, each action (including those installing a feature, possibly at runtime) is equipped with a rate to represent uncertainty, failure rates, randomisation or preferences. An executable Maude implementation, together with the statistical model checker MultiVeStA [34], allows to estimate the likelihood of specific configurations or behaviour of product lines to measure non-functional aspects like quality of service, reliability or performance.

In [9], we enriched PFLAN with the possibility to uninstall or replace features at runtime and with advanced quantitative constraint modelling options based on the 'cost' of features, i.e. attributes related to non-functional aspects like reliability, weight or price. The result, QFLAN, offers three constraint modelling options:

1. Arithmetic relations among feature attributes (e.g. the total cost of a set of features must be less than a given threshold);
2. Propositions relating the absence or presence of a feature to a constraint of type 1 (e.g. if a certain feature is present, then the total cost of a set of features must be less than a given threshold);
3. Action constraints conditioning the runtime execution of an action by a constraint of type 1 (e.g. a certain action can be executed only if the total cost of the set of features constituting the product is less than a given threshold).

The uninstallation or replacement of features can be the result of malfunctioning or of the need to install a better version of the feature (e.g. a software update). We will illustrate this in a case study, together with examples of each of the above types of constraints. Note that these are significantly more complex constraints than the ones that are commonly associated with attributed feature models [12].

Feature attributes typically are not Boolean [19], meaning that the problem of deciding whether or not a product satisfies an attributed feature model with quantitative constraints requires more general satisfiability-checking techniques than mere SAT solving. This leads to the use of Satisfiability Modulo Theory (SMT) solvers like Microsoft's Z3 [20], which allow one to deal with richer notions of constraints, like arithmetic ones. In fact, an important contribution of [9] is the adoption of SMT solving by integrating Z3 in the Maude QFLAN interpreter.

In [9], we combined the Maude/Z3 QFLAN interpreter with MultiVeStA to be able to apply SMC to product lines. Formally, our SMC approach is to perform a sufficient number of probabilistic simulations of a QFLAN model of a product line to obtain statistical evidence (with a predefined level of statistical confidence) of the quantitative properties being verified. Such properties are formulated in MultiVeStA's property specification language MultiQuaTEx. SMC offers unique advantages over exhaustive (probabilistic) model checking. First, SMC does not need to generate entire state spaces and hence scales better without suffering from the combinatorial state-space explosion problem typical of model checking. In particular in the context of product lines, given their possibly exponential number of products, this outweighs the main disadvantage of having to give up on obtaining exact results (100 % confidence) with exact analysis techniques like (probabilistic) model checking. Second, SMC scales better with hardware resources since the set of simulations to be carried out can be trivially parallelised and distributed. MultiVeStA, indeed, can be run on multi-core machines, clusters or distributed computers with almost linear speedup. A unique selling point of MultiVeStA is that it can use the same set of simulations for checking numerous properties at once, thus offering further reductions of computing time. Details on (probabilistic) model checking can be found in [4] and on SMC in [26,27].

While we know of several, quite different, approaches that apply probabilistic model checking to product lines [16,21,22,24,29,38], to the best of our knowledge, we were the first to apply SMC to product lines in [8,9]. In this paper, however, we give more details of QFLAN and of the case study and report more analyses.

Outline. Section 2 presents QFLAN. A case study of a product line of bikes is modelled in QFLAN in Sect. 3. In Sect. 4, we show how to apply SMC to QFLAN models by analyses over the case study. Section 5 concludes the paper.

2   Modelling Product Lines with QFLan

The feature-oriented language QFLAN [9] is an evolution of PFLAN [8], a probabilistic process algebra that separates declarative configuration from procedural runtime aspects. The FLAN family (FLAN [10], PFLAN [8], QFLAN [9]) is inspired by the concurrent constraint programming paradigm of [31], its adoption in process calculi [15], and its stochastic extension [14]. A constraint store allows to specify all common constraints from feature models (and more) in a *declarative* manner, while a rich set of process-algebraic operators allows to specify the configuration and behaviour of product lines in a *procedural* manner. The semantics unifies *static* (configuration) and *dynamic* (runtime) feature selection.

QFLAN's core notions are *features*, *constraints*, *processes* and *fragments* (i.e. constrained processes), cf. its syntax in Fig. 1. More precisely, the syntactic categories F, S and P correspond to fragments, constraint stores (with constraints from K, using arithmetic expressions over feature attributes from E) and processes (with actions from A), respectively. The universe of (primitive) features is denoted by $\mathcal{F}$, that of actions by $\mathcal{A}$ and that of propostions by $\mathcal{P}$.

The declarative part of QFLAN is represented by a constraint store on features extracted from the product line requirements with additional information (e.g. about the context wherein the product will be operated). Two important notions of a constraint store S are the *consistency* of S, denoted by *consistent(S)* (which amounts to logical satisfiability of all constraints constituting S) and the *entailment* $S \vdash c$ of constraint c in S (which amounts to logical entailment).

A constraint store contains any term generated by S according to QFLAN's syntax. The basic constraint stores are $\top$ (true, i.e. no constraint at all), $\bot$ (false, i.e. an inconsistent constraint) and arbitrary Boolean constraints over propositions generated by K, exploiting the well-known fact that feature constraints can be expressed using Boolean propositions. Constraints can be combined by juxtaposition (its semantics amounts to logical conjunction) of basic constraints.

$$F ::= [S \mid P]$$
$$S,T ::= K \mid f \triangleright g \mid f \otimes g \mid S\,T \mid \top \mid \bot$$
$$P,Q ::= \emptyset \mid X \mid (A,r).P \mid P+Q \mid P;Q \mid P \parallel Q$$
$$A ::= a \mid \mathsf{install}(f) \mid \mathsf{uninstall}(f) \mid \mathsf{replace}(f,g) \mid \mathsf{ask}(K)$$
$$K ::= p \mid \neg K \mid K \vee K \mid E \bowtie E$$
$$E ::= r \mid \mathsf{attribute}(f) \mid E \pm E$$

Fig. 1. QFLAN syntax ($f,g \in \mathcal{F}$, $r \in \mathbb{R}^{+}$, $a \in \mathcal{A}$, $p \in \mathcal{P}$, $\bowtie \in \{\leq,<,=,\neq,>,\geq\}$, $\pm \in \{+,-,\times,\div\}$)

While Boolean encodings of feature constraints allow to handle all common constraints, we provide syntactic sugar for two common cross-tree constraints: $f \triangleright g$ expresses that feature f requires feature g, whereas $f \otimes g$ expresses that features f and g mutually exclude each other (i.e. they are alternative). We in fact use such logical encodings to reduce consistency checking and entailment to logical satisfiability (and hence exploit Z3's SAT/SMT solving capabilities).

We assume $\mathcal{P}$ to contain a Boolean predicate $has(f)$ to denote the presence of feature f in a product. Let $\mathcal{P}_{\mathcal{F}}$ denote a product of the product line. In our case study, $\neg has(g)$ then models $g \notin \mathcal{P}_{\mathcal{F}}$, i.e. a bike without an engine. A QFLAN novelty is that we also consider quantitative constraints based on arithmetic relations among feature attributes. In our case study, we could use a constraint $\neg has(g) \rightarrow \sum_{f \in \mathcal{P}_{\mathcal{F}}} weight(f) \leq 10$ to impose a weight bound on non-electric bikes.

QFLAN moreover admits a class of *action constraints*, reminiscent of featured transition systems (FTS) [17]. In an FTS, transitions are labelled with actions and with feature expressions, i.e. Boolean constraints over the set of features. We associate arbitrary constraints to actions rather than to transitions (and we also equip actions with rates, discussed below). In general, we assume that each action a may have a constraint $do(a) \rightarrow p$, where $p \in \mathcal{P}$ is a proposition. Such constraints act as a kind of guards to allow or forbid the execution of actions.

The procedural part of QFLAN is represented by *processes* which can be combined by non-deterministic choice, in sequence or in parallel, and which can consist of the empty process or of a single (rated) action followed by a process. We distinguish ordinary actions from $\mathcal{A}$ and special actions $\mathsf{install}(f)$ (dynamic installation of a feature f), $\mathsf{uninstall}(f)$ (dynamic uninstallation of a feature f), $\mathsf{replace}(f,g)$ (dynamic replacement of feature f by g) and $\mathsf{ask}(K)$ (query the store for the validity of constraint K). We will see below that each action type is treated differently in the operational semantics. As anticipated, each action moreover has an associated *rate*, which is used to determine the probability that this action is executed. As usual, the probability to execute an action in a certain state depends on the rates of all other actions enabled in the same state. These action rates, originating from PFLAN, allow one to specify probabilistic aspects of product line models (e.g. the behaviour of the user of a product, failure rates of the components of a product or the likelihood of installing a certain feature at a specific moment). We will illustrate all this in our example in Sect. 3.

Finally, a *fragment* F is a term $[S \mid P]$ composed of a constraint store S and a process P. These components may influence each other according to the concurrent constraint programming paradigm [31]: a process may update its store which, in turn, may condition the execution of the process' actions. For the sake of simplicity, initial fragments are such that S uniquely characterises a product of a product line (i.e. for each feature f, S contains either $has(f)$ or $\neg has(f)$).

The operational semantics of fragments is formalised in terms of the state transition relation $\rightarrow \subseteq \mathbb{N}^{\mathbb{F} \times \mathbb{R}^+ \times \mathbb{F}}$ defined in Fig. 2, where $\mathbb{F}$ denotes the set of all terms generated by F in the grammar of Fig. 1. Note that we use multisets of transitions to deal with the possibility of multiple instances of a transition $F \xrightarrow{r} G$. Technically, such a reduction relation is defined in structural operational semantics (SOS), i.e. by induction on the structure of the terms denoting a fragment, modulo the structural congruence relation $\equiv \subseteq \mathbb{F} \times \mathbb{F}$ defined in Fig. 3.

As usual, the reduction rules in Fig. 2 are expressed as a set of premises (above the line) and a conclusion (below the line). The reduction relation implicitly defines a labeled transition system (LTS), with rates as labels. It is straightforward to obtain a discrete-time Markov chain (DTMC) from such an LTS by normalising the rates into $[0..1]$ such that in each state, the sum of the rates of its outgoing transitions equals one. In the resulting DTMC, a transition label corresponds to the probability that the transition is taken from its source state. Recall that we advocate the use of SMC since it uses on-the-fly generated simulations of the DTMC, which in general is too large to be generated explicitly.

The rules INST, UNST, RPL and ACT are very similar, all allowing a process to execute an action if certain constraints are satisfied. Rules INST, UNST and RPL deal with the installation, removal and replacement of features, respectively, and are applicable as long as they do not introduce inconsistencies. Rule ACT forbids inconsistencies with respect to action constraints. A typical action constraint is $do(a) \rightarrow has(f)$, i.e. action a is subject to the presence of feature f.

$$(\text{INST}) \quad \frac{consistent(S\ has(f))}{[S\ \neg has(f) \mid (\mathsf{install}(f), r).P] \xrightarrow{r} [S\ has(f) \mid P]}$$

$$(\text{UNST}) \quad \frac{consistent(S\ \neg has(f))}{[S\ has(f) \mid (\mathsf{uninstall}(f), r).P] \xrightarrow{r} [S\ \neg has(f)\ \mid P]}$$

$$(\text{RPL}) \quad \frac{consistent(S\ \neg has(f)\ has(g))}{[S\ has(f)\ \neg has(g)\ \mid (\mathsf{replace}(f, g), r).P] \xrightarrow{r} [S\ \neg has(f)\ has(g) \mid P]}$$

$$(\text{ACT}) \quad \frac{S = (do(a) \rightarrow K) \qquad S \vdash K}{[S \mid (a, r).P] \xrightarrow{r} [S \mid P]} \qquad (\text{ASK}) \quad \frac{S \vdash K}{[S \mid (\mathsf{ask}(K), r).P] \xrightarrow{r} [S \mid P]}$$

$$(\text{OR}) \quad \frac{[S \mid P] \xrightarrow{r} [S' \mid P']}{[S \mid P + Q] \xrightarrow{r} [S' \mid P']} \qquad (\text{SEQ/PAR}) \quad \frac{[S \mid P] \xrightarrow{r} [S' \mid P']}{[S \mid P\,?\,Q] \xrightarrow{r} [S' \mid P'\,?\,Q]} \quad ? \in \{; , \|\}$$

Fig. 2. Reduction semantics of QFLAN

$$P + (Q + R) \equiv (P + Q) + R \qquad P + \emptyset \equiv P \qquad\qquad P + Q \equiv Q + P$$
$$P \parallel (Q \parallel R) \equiv (P \parallel Q) \parallel R \qquad P \parallel \emptyset \equiv P \qquad\qquad P \parallel Q \equiv Q \parallel P$$
$$P; (Q; R) \equiv (P; Q); R \qquad\quad P; \emptyset \equiv P \equiv \emptyset; P \qquad\quad P \equiv P[^Q\!/_X] \text{ if } X \doteq Q$$

Fig. 3. Structural congruence in QFLAN

Rule ASK formalises the ask($\cdot$) operation semantics from concurrent constraint programming [31], blocking a process until a proposition can be derived from the store. Rules OR, SEQ and PAR, finally, are standard, formalising non-deterministic choice, sequential composition and interleaving parallel composition, respectively. Note that non-determinism introduced by choice and parallel composition is probabilistically resolved in the aforementioned DTMC semantics.

We note three ways to include a feature f in a product configuration. First, an *explicit, declarative* way is to include the proposition $has(f)$ in the initial store; this is the way to include core features. Second, an *implicit, declarative* way is to derive f from other constraints; this is the way to include features that are not known as core features, but that turn out to be enforced by the constraints (e.g. if a store contains $g \triangleright f$ and $has(g)$, then f's presence follows). Third, a *procedural* way is to dynamically install f at runtime, possibly by replacement.

3   A Product Line of Bikes

In this section, we briefly describe a product line of bikes that we have used as a case study to validate our approach. It stems from an ongoing collaboration with PisaMo S.p.A., a public mobility company of the Municipality of Pisa, in the context of the European project QUANTICOL (www.quanticol.eu). PisaMo introduced the bike-sharing system *CicloPi* in the city of Pisa in 2013. It is supplied and maintained by Bicincittà S.r.l. (www.bicincitta.com).

We performed requirements elicitation on documents given to us by PisaMo and Bicincittà to distill a product line of bikes. We identified the common and variable features of the bikes they sell as part of their bike-sharing systems, including indicative prices, to which we added some features after consulting a number of documents on the technical characteristics and prices of bikes and their components as currently being sold by major bike vendors. The resulting model has thus more variability than typical in bike-sharing systems. Indeed, vendors of such systems traditionally allow little variation to their customers (e.g. most vendors only sell bikes with a so-called step-thru frame, a.k.a. open frame or low-step frame, typical of utility bikes instead of considering other kind of frames as we do). This is partly due to the difficulties of analysing systems with high variability to provide guarantees on the deployed products and services.

The resulting *attributed feature model* [12], depicted in Fig. 4, is an and/or-tree of features of a product line, regulating their presence in products: a trivial root feature is always present, *optional* features may be present provided their

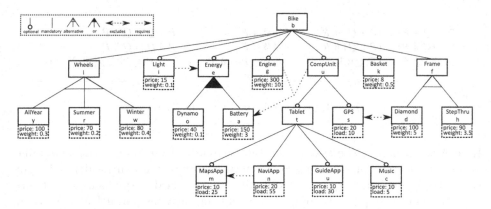

Fig. 4. Attributed feature model of bikes product line (shorthand names for features)

parent is, *mandatory* features must be present provided their parent is, exactly one *alternative* feature must be present provided their parent is and at least one *or* feature must be present whenever their parent is. A *cross-tree constraint* either *requires* the presence of another feature for a feature to be present or *excludes* two features to both be present. Ignoring the attributes, this model of 20 non-trivial features yields 1, 314 different products. This number can be reduced by quantitative constraints over feature attributes (e.g. limiting the price or weight of a bike) but not so much as to mitigate the inherent exponential explosion.

In Fig. 4, the primitive features (leaves of the tree) are equipped with non-functional attributes, like *price* and *weight* or *load*, which represent the specific feature's price in euros, weight in kilos and computational load, respectively.

Given the set $\mathcal{F}$ of all features, a product of the product line is identified by a non-empty subset $\mathcal{P}_{\mathcal{F}} \subseteq \mathcal{F}$ that moreover fulfills the additional quantitative constraints over features and attributes.[1] As we have seen in the Introduction, these can range from rather simple constraints (e.g. $price(u) \leq 20$, i.e. the price of the computational unit must be less than 20 euros) to quite more complex ones (e.g. $g \notin \mathcal{P}_{\mathcal{F}} \rightarrow \sum_{f \in \mathcal{P}_{\mathcal{F}}} weight(f) \leq 10$, i.e. a bike without engine cannot weigh more than 10 kilos). Without such constraints, deciding whether or not a product satisfies a feature model reduces to Boolean satisfiability (SAT), which can efficiently be computed with SAT solvers [6]. However, we specifically allow quantitative constraints, requiring the use of SMT solvers like Microsoft's Z3 [20]. In our case study, we consider the following constraints:

(C1) $\sum_{f \in \mathcal{P}_{\mathcal{F}}} price(f) \leq 600$: a bike may cost at most 600 euros;
(C2) $\sum_{f \in \mathcal{P}_{\mathcal{F}}} weight(f) \leq 15$: a bike may weigh up to 15 kilos;
(C3) $\sum_{f \in \mathcal{P}_{\mathcal{F}}} load(f) \leq 100\,\%$: a bike's computational load may not exceed 100 %.

---

[1] The attribute functions extend to non-primitive features and products in a straight-forward manner (e.g. the function $load\colon \mathcal{F} \rightarrow \mathbb{N}$, associated to the attribute *load*, extends to $load(\mathcal{P}_{\mathcal{F}}) = \sum \{\, load(f) \mid f \in \mathcal{P}_{\mathcal{F}} \,\}$.

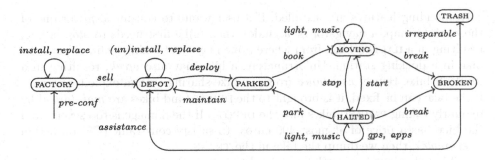

Fig. 5. Sketch of bike-sharing behaviour

Constraints (C1)–(C3) will be part of the constraint store of the QFLAN model of the case study presented below. As such, they prohibit the execution of any action (e.g. the runtime (un)installation or replacement of features) that would violate these constraints since its execution would make the store inconsistent. Furthermore, the store contains two constraints similar to (C1) as explicit constraints on actions, specifying the precise subset of actions affected by them. These constraints will be used in the behavioural part of the QFLAN model, presented below, to forbid selling bikes cheaper than 250 euros (C4) and to forbid dumping broken (irreparable) bikes that cost more than 400 euros (C5):

(C4) $do(sell) \rightarrow \sum_{f \in \mathcal{P}_\mathcal{F}} price(f) \geq 250;$
(C5) $do(irreparable) \rightarrow \sum_{f \in \mathcal{P}_\mathcal{F}} price(f) \leq 400.$

The behaviour of the bikes product line is based on a bike-sharing scenario that we abstracted from *CicloPi*, with some additional futuristic behaviour concerning still to be realised features such as the use of electric bikes and the possible runtime installation of apps. A rough sketch of it is depicted in Fig. 5.

Initially, we assume a *pre-conf*igured bike, containing precisely one of the alternative subfeatures from each of the core features Wheels (l) and Frame (f), to arrive in the (initial state) FACTORY (a process). In the QFLAN model of this product line, described below, we will assume an initial product to contain the features AllYear (y) and Diamond (d). Moreover, all actions that we will describe next actually have an associated rate (omitted in Fig. 5 to avoid clutter).

In FACTORY (e.g. of Bicincittà), further features may be *install*ed or *replace*d (e.g. different wheels or a different frame). At a certain point, one may *sell* the configured bike (as part of a bike-sharing system), but only if it costs at least 250 euro (to satisfy constraint (C4) on action *sell*), after which it arrives at the DEPOT (e.g. of PisaMo). It may then be ready to be *deploy*ed as part of the bike-sharing system run from the DEPOT, or it may first need to be further fine-tuned (i.e. (*un*)*install* or *replace* factory-installed features). Once *deploy*ed, it results PARKED in one of the docking stations of the bike-sharing system (e.g. *CicloPi*).

A user may *book* a PARKED bike and *start* biking (MOVING). While biking, a user may decide to listen to *music* or switch on the *light*, in case the corresponding features are installed. If a user wants to consult a *gps* or one of the *apps* (a map, a navigator or a guide), then (s)he first needs to *stop* biking, resulting in a HALTED bike, from where (s)he may *start* biking again or *park* the bike in a docking station. Unfortunately, a bike may also *break*, resulting in a BROKEN bike. Hence, *assistance* from the bike-sharing system exploiter arrives. If the bike can be fixed, it is brought to the DEPOT (and bikes are *maintain*ed by regularly taking PARKED bikes into the DEPOT). If the damage is too severe, and the bike has a price of at most 400 euros (to satisfy constraint (C5) on action *irreparable*), then we dump the bike in the TRASH.

This behaviour is probabilistic, in the sense that in case of several enabled actions some may occur with a higher likelihood than others. Such a probabilistic specification models the uncertainty of the behaviour of the bike, its components and its interacting environment (the users, the exploiters, road conditions, etc.).

The following are some typical properties of interest for the case study:

P_1 Average price, weight and load of a bike when it is first deployed, or as time progresses;

P_2 For each of the 15 primitive features, the probability to have it installed when a bike is first deployed, or as time progresses;

P_3 The probability for a bike to be disposed of;

P_4 The probability to uninstall a factory-installed feature of a bike during a given time interval after it was sold.

When analysed at the first deployment of a bike, P_1 and P_2 are useful for studying a sort of *initial scenario*, in order to estimate the required initial investments and infrastructures. For instance, bikes with a high price and a high load (i.e. with a high technological footprint) or equipped with a battery might require docking stations with specific characteristics or they might have to be collected for the night to be stored safely. Instead, analysing P_1 and P_2 as time progresses provides an indication of how those values evolve, e.g. to estimate the average value in euros of a deployed bike and the monetary consequences of its loss.

From a more general perspective, properties like P_2 measure how often (on average) a feature is actually installed in a product from a product line, which is important information for those responsible for the production or programming of a specific feature or software module. Property P_3 is similar to P_2, but it allows to estimate how often, on average, a bike is dumped in the trash.

Property P_4, finally, is useful for analysing the effect of the factory's pre-configuration choices, and to adapt them to better fit specific scenarios. It might be worthwhile, e.g., to reconsider the installation of a certain feature if there is a high probability of uninstalling it shortly after.

In the remainder of this section, we show how we can specify the case study in QFLAN, after which the rest of this paper is devoted to showing how to analyse the above properties with QFLAN's tool support.

In Fig. 6, we provide a QFLAN model of the bikes product line. Fragment *FR* is composed of a constraints store *S* and a process *F*. The former has five subsets:

DS Constraints from the feature diagram of Fig. 4, like $d \otimes h$, requiring precisely one feature among Diamond and StepThru to be installed, and $g \triangleright a$, requiring the Battery feature to be installed whenever the Engine feature is;

PS Predicates for the attributes of the concrete features in the feature diagram of Fig. 4, like $\mathsf{price}(y) = 100$ and $\mathsf{weight}(y) = 0.3$, indicating that the AllYear feature costs 100 euros and weighs 0.3 kilos;

QS Quantitative constraints affecting all actions, i.e. (C1)–(C3);

AS Action constraints discussed above, like (C4), (C5) or $do(c) \rightarrow has(c)$, requiring Music to be installed in order to play music;

IS The initially installed feature set $has(y)\ has(d)$, implying that the AllYear and Diamond features are pre-installed.

The process F specifies the behaviour of the bikes product line. In particular, it has one process for each node in Fig. 5. F corresponds to FACTORY, implemented as a choice, weighted by the rates, among three main activities:

(1) With rate 7 the bike is sold and sent to the depot (D corresponds to DEPOT). This action can only be executed if (C4) is respected;
(2) Install optional features and iterate on F. The installations are performed only if *FS* and *QS* are respected;
(3) Replace pre-installed mandatory exclusive features *IS*, i.e. Wheels or Frame. Again, *FS* and *QS* must be preserved.

Note that in (2) we assume that Music (c) is the feature installed with higher probability, followed by MapsApp (m), Dynamo (o) and Light (i). Recall that the semantics of QFLAN (Fig. 2) forbids the re-installation of installed features. In (3), we favour the replacement of Winter or Summer wheels by AllYear ones. A frame may be changed as well, but with lower probability. The actual probability to replace Winter or Summer wheels by AllYear ones is $\frac{10+10}{10+10+5+5+5+5+3+3} = 20/46$, whereas the probability to change a frame is $\frac{3+3}{46} = 6/46$. Ideally, the rates in an product line model are inferred from statistical analyses of its historical records.

D corresponds to DEPOT, and is similar to F. One obvious difference is the possibility to perform an action *deploy* leading to P (P corresponds to PARKED). In addition, features may be uninstalled in the depot to allow for customisation. Optional features can be installed and uninstalled with the same rates, except for Engine(g), Battery (a) and Dynamo (o), which can be uninstalled with a lower rate to penalise their occurrences. This modelling choice is justified by the fact that it is reasonable to assume that uninstalling such features might cost more than installing them. We further assume that the frame identifies the bike that was sold, and thus it cannot be modified in the depot. The final action that can occur in the depot is an interesting one: a Battery (a) can be replaced with a much cheaper Dynamo (o). According to the semantics of QFLAN, this action is performed only if no subfeatures of CompUnit nor the Engine are currently installed (cf. Fig. 4). This is useful to reduce costs and weight, in case some previously installed feature requiring the Battery has by now been uninstalled.

$FR \doteq [\,S \mid F\,]$

$\quad S \doteq DS \;\; PS \;\; QS \;\; AS \;\; IS$

$\quad DS \doteq y \otimes r \otimes w \quad d \otimes h \;\ldots\; g \rhd a \quad n \rhd m \;\ldots$

$\quad PS \doteq \mathsf{price}(y) = 100 \quad \mathsf{weight}(y) = 0.3 \;\ldots\; \mathsf{price}(c) = 100 \quad \mathsf{load}(c) = 5 \;\ldots$

$\quad QS \doteq \mathsf{price}(b) < 800 \quad \mathsf{weight}(b) < 20 \quad \mathsf{load}(b) < 100$

$\quad AS \doteq do(sell) \rightarrow (\mathsf{price}(b) > 250) \;\ldots\; do(c) \rightarrow \mathsf{has}(c) \;\ldots$

$\quad IS \doteq \mathsf{has}(y) \;\; \mathsf{has}(d)$

$\quad F \doteq (sell, 7).D$

         // Installing optional features

$\quad + (\mathsf{install}(s), 6).F + (\mathsf{install}(i), 10).F + (\mathsf{install}(n), 6).F + (\mathsf{install}(o), 10).F + (\mathsf{install}(c), 20).F$

$\quad + (\mathsf{install}(g), 4).F + (\mathsf{install}(a), 5).F + (\mathsf{install}(u), 3).F + (\mathsf{install}(m), 10).F + (\mathsf{install}(k), 8).F$

         // Replacing mandatory and exclusive features

$\quad + (\mathsf{replace}(y, r), 5).F + (\mathsf{replace}(y, w), 5).F + (\mathsf{replace}(r, y), 10).F + (\mathsf{replace}(r, w), 5).F$

$\quad + (\mathsf{replace}(w, y), 10).F + (\mathsf{replace}(w, r), 5).F + (\mathsf{replace}(d, h), 3).F + (\mathsf{replace}(h, d), 3).F$

$\quad D \doteq (deploy, 10).P$

         // Installing optional features; same as F

$\quad + (\mathsf{install}(s), 6).F + (\mathsf{install}(i), 10).F + (\mathsf{install}(n), 6).F + (\mathsf{install}(o), 10).F + (\mathsf{install}(c), 20).F$

$\quad + (\mathsf{install}(g), 4).F + (\mathsf{install}(a), 5).F + (\mathsf{install}(u), 3).F + (\mathsf{install}(m), 10).F + (\mathsf{install}(k), 8).F$

         // Uninstalling optional features; same features and rates as installing ...

$\quad + (\mathsf{uninstall}(s), 6).F + (\mathsf{uninstall}(i), 10).F + (\mathsf{uninstall}(n), 6).F + (\mathsf{uninstall}(c), 20).F$

$\quad + (\mathsf{uninstall}(u), 3).F + (\mathsf{uninstall}(m), 10).F + (\mathsf{uninstall}(k), 8).F$

$\quad + \ldots \textit{except for}$

$\quad + (\mathsf{uninstall}(g)), 1).D + (\mathsf{uninstall}(a), 2).D + (\mathsf{uninstall}(o), 3).D$

         // Replacing mandatory and exclusive features; like F, but Frame cannot be changed

$\quad + (\mathsf{replace}(y, r), 5).F + (\mathsf{replace}(y, w), 5).F + (\mathsf{replace}(r, y), 10).F + (\mathsf{replace}(r, w), 5).F$

$\quad + (\mathsf{replace}(w, y), 10).F + (\mathsf{replace}(w, r), 5).F$

         // Replacing battery by dynamo in case no features requiring a Battery are installed

$\quad + (\mathsf{replace}(a, o), 1).D$

$\quad P \doteq (book, 10).M + (maintain, 1).D$

$\quad M \doteq (stop, 5).H + (break, 1).B + (i, 20).M + (c, 20).M$

$\quad H \doteq (i, 10).H + (c, 20).H + (s, 10).H + (u, 10).H + (m, 10).H + (n, 10).H$

$\quad\quad + (park, 5).P + (start, 5).M + (break, 1).B$

$\quad B \doteq (assistance, 10).D + (irreparable, 1).T$

$\quad T \doteq (\mathsf{install}(trashed), 1).\mathbf{0}$

Fig. 6. QFLAN specification of bikes product line

The remaining processes P, M, H, B and T correspond to PARKED, MOVING, HALTED, BROKEN and TRASH, respectively. These processes are rather simple and are faithful to their description above. The process T installs a fictitious feature *trashed* to express the bike's disposal, after which it evolves into the idle process.

Note that F is a pure configuration process, while D is not. In fact, once parked a bike can be returned to D so features can be (un)installed or replaced at runtime. This is an example of a staged configuration process, in which some optional features are bound at runtime rather than at configuration time.

The interested reader can find the full specification of the case study at http://sysma.imtlucca.it/tools/multivesta/qflan/

4 Statistical Model Checking of QFLan Models

In this section, we first briefly explain MultiVeStA's SMC capabilities and then set some parameters for the analyses described in the second part of this section.

MultiVeStA [34] is a distributed statistical model checker co-developed and maintained by one of the authors. It extends statistical analysis tools VeStA [35] and PVeStA [2] with distributed statistical analysis capabilities. It allows easy integration with any existing discrete event simulator or formalism catering for probabilistic simulations. It has already been used successfully in the analysis of a broad variety of scenarios, including public transportation systems [25], volunteer clouds [33], crowd-steering [30], swarm robotics [11], opportunistic network protocols [3], contract-oriented middleware [5] and software product lines [8,9].

Below we will describe the tool's usage for obtaining statistical estimations of quantitative properties of QFLAN specifications, repeating and extending the analysis results reported in [9]. MultiVeStA provides such estimations by means of efficient distributed statistical analysis techniques known from statistical model checking (SMC) [26,27]. The integration of MultiVeStA and QFLAN is available at http://sysma.imtlucca.it/tools/multivesta/qflan/ together with all files necessary to reproduce the experiments discussed in this paper.

MultiVeStA's property specification language MultiQuaTEx is a highly flexible extension of QuaTEx [1] with the following features: real-valued observations on the system states (e.g. the total cost of installed features), arithmetic expressions and comparison operators, if-then-else statements, a one-step next operator (which triggers the execution of one step of a simulation) and recursion. Intuitively, we can use MultiQuaTEx to associate a value from $\mathbb{R}$ to each simulation and then use MultiVeStA to estimate the expected value of such number (in case this number is 0 or 1 upon the occurrence of a certain event, we thus estimate the probability of such an event to happen).

We can obtain probabilistic simulations of a QFLAN model by executing it step-by-step applying the rules of Fig. 2, each time selecting one of the computed one-step next-states according to the probability distribution resulting from normalising the rates of the generated transitions (cf. Sect. 2).

Classical SMC techniques allow one to perform analyses like "is the probability that a property holds greater than a given threshold?" or "what is the probability that a property is satisfied?". Next to performing such classical SMC analyses over products, MultiVeStA can estimate the expected values of properties that can take on any value from $\mathbb{R}$, like "what is the average cost, weight or load of products configured according to a product line specification?".

MultiVeStA estimations are computed as the mean value of n samples obtained from n independent simulations, with n large enough to grant that the size of the $(1 - \alpha) \times 100\%$ *confidence interval* is bounded by δ, i.e. if a

MultiQuaTEx expression is estimated as $\bar{x} \in \mathbb{R}$, then with probability $(1 - \alpha)$ its actual expected value belongs to the interval $[\bar{x} - \delta/2, \bar{x} + \delta/2]$. A confidence interval is thus specified in terms of two parameters: α and δ. For all the experiments discussed below, we fix $\alpha = 0.1$ and we set $\delta = 20.0$ for costs, $\delta = 1.0$ for weights, $\delta = 5.0$ for loads, $\delta = 1.0$ for steps and $\delta = 0.1$ for probabilities. The experiments were performed on a laptop equipped with a 2.4 GHz Intel Core i5 processor and 4 GB of RAM, distributing the simulations among its 4 cores.

We now apply MultiVeStA to analyse properties P_1–P_4 from Sect. 3 on the bikes product line case study. We start with P_1 and P_2, which we study both at a precise point in time (when a bike is first deployed) and as time progresses.

Listing 1.1 depicts a MultiQuaTEx expression for evaluating P_1 and P_2 at a bike's first deployment. Lines 1–4 define a parametric recursive temporal operator ObsAtFD which is evaluated against a simulation. It takes as input a string obs representing a *state observation* of interest. Then, if the bike has completed its first deployment (Line 1), the value in the current simulation state of the provided observation is returned (Line 2). Otherwise, the operator is recursively evaluated in the next simulation state (Line 3). Intuitively, # is the one-step temporal operator, while real-valued observations on the current state are evaluated resorting to the keyword s.rval. A number of predefined observations is supported. For instance, we can query whether a given feature is currently installed, obtaining 1 if it is installed and 0 otherwise. An example can be found in Line 1 for first-deploy, a fictitious feature installed when terminating the first phase of deployment (for ease of presentation, we did not show this in Sect. 3). In addition, we can query for price, weight and load of the current product, obtained by summing the corresponding values for all installed features. Finally, Lines 5–6 specify the properties to be studied: the expected price, weight and load of bikes (Line 5), as well as the probabilities of installing each of the 15 primitive features (Line 6), all measured at first deployment.

```
1   ObsAtFD(obs) = if {s.rval("first-deploy") == 1.0}
2   then s.rval(obs)
3   else #ObsAtFD(obs)
4   fi ;
5   eval E[ObsAtFD("price")]; eval E[ObsAtFD("weight")]; eval E[ObsAtFD("load")];
6   eval E[ObsAtFD("y")]; eval E[ObsAtFD("r")]; ... eval E[ObsAtFD("c")];
```

Listing 1.1. P_1 and P_2 at first deployment

Listing 1.1 shows how MultiQuaTEx allows one to express more properties at once (18 in this case) which are estimated by MultiVeStA reusing the same simulations. A procedure considering that each property might require a different number of simulations is adopted to satisfy the given confidence interval.

We evaluated the MultiQuaTEx expression of Listing 1.1 against the QFLAN model of Sect. 3. The results are shown in the first row of Table 1. Notably, the probability of installing an Engine (g) is very low, estimated at 0 (i.e. with probability 0.9 it belongs to $[0, 0.05]$, according to the given confidence interval). This is presumably due to constraints (C1) and (C2), imposing bikes to cost less than 600 euros, and weighing less than 15 kilos. In fact, the estimated average price and weight of bikes at first deployment is 391.91 euros and 7.8 kilos, respectively, while an Engine costs 300 euros and weighs 10 kilos. In order to confirm this hypothesis, we analysed the same property in a new model where (C1) and (C2) allow bikes to cost at most 800 euros and weigh at most 20 kilos. The results, shown in the second row of Table 1, confirm our hypothesis. This reveals that the constraints are sort of in disagreement with the quantitative attributes of the features. The estimation of the average price required $1,200$ simulations, as opposed to 120 in the aforementioned case. This is because the looser constraints of the latter analysis induce a higher variability of bike prices. In fact, the installation of an Engine, the most expensive among the considered features, results in a steep increase of bike prices.

Table 1. Properties P_1 and P_2 evaluated when a bike is first deployed

Attributes (P_1)				Features (P_2)													
C1	C2	price	weight	load	y	r	w	i	o	a	g	m	n	u	c	s	k	d	h
600	15	391.91	7.80	33.50	0.57	0.24	0.18	0.59	0.84	0.92	0.0	0.50	0.20	0.24	0.47	0.17	0.60	0.61	0.39
800	20	509.83	11.98	34.45	0.54	0.23	0.19	0.57	0.88	0.92	0.40	0.52	0.21	0.25	0.47	0.20	0.63	0.60	0.40

We now discuss the variants of P_1 and P_2 measured as time progresses, demonstrating how MultiVeStA can be used to analyse properties upon varying a parameter, in this case the number of performed simulation steps. Listing 1.2 shows how the MultiQuaTEx expression of Listing 1.1 can be made parametric with respect to a given set of simulation steps. First, the temporal operator was modified so that it is evaluated with respect to a specific step given as parameter (Lines 1–4). Second, it was necessary to specify a range of values for the parameter. Lines 5–7 specify that we are interested in measuring the properties for steps going from 0 to 500, with an increment of 2. Recall from Sect. 3 that dumping a bike is modelled by the installation of a fictitious feature *trash*. Hence, we can use the expression of Listing 1.2 to measure also P_3 (the probability of a bike being dumped) by simply adding E[ObsAtStep("trashed",st)] (Line 7).

```
1  ObsAtStep(obs,st) = if {s.rval("steps") == st}
2  then s.rval(obs)
3  else #ObsAtStep(obs,st)
4  fi;
5  eval parametric(E[ObsAtStep("price",st)], E[ObsAtStep("weight",st)],
6  E[ObsAtStep("load",st)], E[ObsAtStep("y",st)], E[ObsAtStep("r",st)], ...,
7  eval E[ObsAtStep("c",st)]; E[ObsAtStep("trashed",st)], st, 0, 2, 500);
```

Listing 1.2. P_1–P_3 for varying simulation steps

Next, we evaluated the parametric property of Listing 1.2 against the model. We report the results obtained for the model in which (C1) and (C2) bound the price and weight of the bike to 800 and 20, respectively. All such analyses (19×251 different properties) were evaluated using the same simulations. Overall, $1,200$ simulations were necessary. The results are presented in six plots in Fig. 7: one each for average prices (7a), weights (7c) and loads (7e), one for the probability of dumping a bike (7b), one for the probability of installing features (7d) and one for the probability of uninstalling pre-installed features (7f).

Figure 7a show that the average price (on the y-axis) of the intermediate bikes generated from the product line starts at 200 euros, in line with the initial configuration (*IS* in Fig. 6, i.e. with AllYear and Diamond installed). Then the price grows with respect to the number of performed simulation steps.

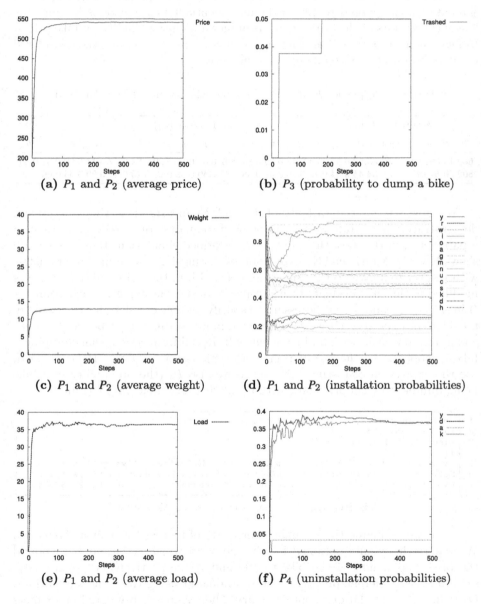

(a) P_1 and P_2 (average price)   (b) P_3 (probability to dump a bike)

(c) P_1 and P_2 (average weight)   (d) P_1 and P_2 (installation probabilities)

(e) P_1 and P_2 (average load)   (f) P_4 (uninstallation probabilities)

Fig. 7. Results of measuring P_1–P_4 with MultiVeStA

In particular, it is possible to see an initial fast growth until reaching an average price of about 510 euros, after which the growth slows down, reaching about 537 euros at step 100 and 542 at step 500. This is consistent with the QFLAN specification, which has a pre-configuration phase (FACTORY) during which a number of features can be installed, followed by a customisation phase (DEPOT), where features can be (un)installed and replaced. We recall that features cannot be uninstalled in the FACTORY and we note that uninstalling features in the DEPOT does not introduce decrements of the price, on average. A manual inspection of the data revealed that the phase of fast growth terminates after about 19 steps. This is consistent with the analysis described in the second row of Table 1, where the average number of steps to complete the first DEPOT phase is estimated as being close to 19 (not shown in the table). In addition, the average price at the end of such a phase is estimated to be around 510 euros, exactly as in Table 1. Note, finally, that the probability of a bike to return to the DEPOT after its first deployment is quite low, viz. $1/11$, based on a transition from PARKED with rate 10 towards MOVING and with rate 1 towards DEPOT (cf. Fig. 6). Thus, on average, the price of bikes is only slightly affected by (un)installations and replacements performed by successive phases spent in the DEPOT.

Figures 7c and e shows that the average weight and load, respectively, of a bike evolve similarly to its average price: an initial phase of fast growth of 19 steps is followed by one of slower growth.

Figure 7b shows that bikes are dumped with a very low probability. The reason is twofold. First, the transition from BROKEN to TRASH has a much lower rate than the one to DEPOT, i.e. often a bike is not *irreparable*, and likewise for those from MOVING and HALTED to BROKEN, i.e. bikes do not *break* all the time (cf. Figure 6). Second, the average price of a bike quickly exceeds 400 euros (cf. Fig. 7a) and action constraint (C5) prohibits dumping such bikes.

Figure 7d confirms that also the probabilities (on the y-axis) for each of the features to be installed evolve similarly to the average price, weight and load of the generated products, although, clearly, with different scales. Note that the pre-installed features AllYear (y) and Diamond (d) both have probability 1 of being installed at step 0, after which their probabilities decrease.

We conclude this section by considering P_4. This property was analysed against a slight variant of the behavioural scenario, viz. without the FACTORY phase but with the following set of four features pre-installed: AllYear (y), Diamond (d), Battery (a) and Basket (k). Subsequently, we studied how the probability of *not* having each of these features installed at a certain simulation step changes upon varying the considered simulation step. The corresponding MultiQuaTEx expression, adapted from Listing 1.2, is given in Listing 1.3.

```
1  ObsAtStep(obs,st) = if {s.rval("steps") == st}
2  then 1 - s.rval(obs)
3  else #ObsAtStep(obs,st)
4  fi;
5  eval parametric(E[ObsAtStep("y",st)], E[ObsAtStep("d",st)],
6  E[ObsAtStep("a",st)], E[ObsAtStep("k",st)], st, 0, 2, 500);
```

Listing 1.3. P_4 for varying simulation steps

We again focus on the case in which (C1) and (C2) bound the cost and weight of bikes to 800 and 20, respectively. The analysis required 380 simulations. The results are presented in Fig. 7f, where we can once more appreciate the two distinct phases of faster and slower growth. A manual inspection of the data revealed that the turning point of these two phases again lies around step 19. Diamond (d) has 0 probability of being uninstalled. This is coherent with the QFLAN model, as the Frame can be replaced only during the FACTORY phase, which was however removed for this particular experiment. As regards the three remaining features, Fig. 7f highlights the effect of constraints on the behaviour of QFLAN specifications. In fact, we can clearly see that the feature set can be partitioned in two, based on the probability of being uninstalled: Battery (a) has almost no probability of being uninstalled, while AllYear (y) and Basket (k) have a higher probability to be uninstalled. The lower uninstall probability manifested by Battery (a) is justified by the fact that it is required by the Engine as well as by all subfeatures of CompUnit, thus the presence of even one of these features in the store (i.e. installed on the bike) blocks the uninstallation of Battery (a). Finally, the remaining two features, AllYear (y) and Basket (k), uninstalled with higher probability, produce a similar graph. This is consistent with process D for DEPOT given in Fig. 6, as AllYear (y) can be replaced with rate 10 (due to the two replace actions) and Basket (k) can be uninstalled with rate 8.

5   Conclusions and Future Work

We have presented the probabilistic feature-oriented language QFLAN and its tool support: a prototypical Maude interpreter integrated with Z3 and Multi-VeStA, originally introduced in a short paper at SPLC'15 [9]. In this paper, we provide more explanations of QFLAN, more details of the case study and more analyses. The bikes product line case study was developed from interactions with companies we work with in the context of the European project QUANTICOL.

Our analyses have revealed a number of interesting properties of the product line specification, such as the existence of an apparent disagreement between the constraints imposed on the total price and weight of bikes with respect to the price and weight of some of its features, as well as the high probability of replacing certain features that tend to appear in initial factory configurations, which suggest to prioritise their installation in the earliest stages of configuration.

To improve the performance of our analyses, which currently take minutes, we developed a Java implementation of QFLAN integrated with Z3 and Multi-VeStA, reducing analysis time to seconds. We now work on completing this tool with a user-friendly interface for the specification and SMC of QFLAN models.

Acknowledgements. Maurice ter Beek and Andrea Vandin are supported by the EU project QUANTICOL, 600708. We thank Bicincittà and M. Bertini of PisaMo for the case study and D. Lucanu, G. Rosu, A. Stefanescu and A. Arusoaie for sharing their Maude/Z3 integration, which we adapted for our purposes.

References

1. Agha, G.A., Meseguer, J., Sen, K.: PMaude: rewrite-based specification language for probabilistic object systems. ENTCS **153**, 213–239 (2005)
2. AlTurki, M., Meseguer, J.: PVESTA: a parallel statistical model checking and quantitative analysis tool. In: Corradini, A., Klin, B., Cîrstea, C. (eds.) CALCO 2011. LNCS, vol. 6859, pp. 386–392. Springer, Heidelberg (2011). doi:10.1007/978-3-642-22944-2_28
3. Arora, S., Rathor, A., Rao, M.V.P.: Statistical model checking of opportunistic network protocols. In: Proceedings 11th Asian Internet Engineering Conference (AINTEC 2015), pp. 62–68. ACM (2015)
4. Baier, C., Katoen, J.: Principles of Model Checking. The MIT Press, Cambridge (2008)
5. Bartoletti, M., Cimoli, T., Murgia, M., Podda, A.S., Pompianu, L.: A contract-oriented middleware. In: Braga, C., Ölveczky, P.C. (eds.) FACS 2015. LNCS, vol. 9539, pp. 86–104. Springer, Heidelberg (2016). doi:10.1007/978-3-319-28934-2_5
6. Batory, D.: Feature models, grammars, and propositional formulas. In: Obbink, H., Pohl, K. (eds.) SPLC 2005. LNCS, vol. 3714, pp. 7–20. Springer, Heidelberg (2005). doi:10.1007/11554844_3
7. ter Beek, M.H., Clarke, D., Schaefer, I.: Special issue on formal methods in software product line engineering. J. Log. Algebr. Meth. Program. **85**(1), 123–124 (2016)
8. ter Beek, M.H., Legay, A., Lluch Lafuente, A., Vandin, A.: Quantitative analysis of probabilistic models of software product lines with statistical model checking. EPTCS **182**, 56–70 (2015)
9. ter Beek, M.H., Legay, A., Lluch Lafuente, A., Vandin, A.: Statistical analysis of probabilistic models of software product lines with quantitative constraints. In: Proceedings 19th International Software Product Line Conference (SPLC 2015), pp. 11–15. ACM (2015)
10. ter Beek, M.H., Lluch Lafuente, A., Petrocchi, M.: Combining declarative and procedural views in the specification and analysis of product families. In: Proceedings 17th International Software Product Line Conference (SPLC 2013), vol. 2, pp. 10–17. ACM (2013)
11. Belzner, L., De Nicola, R., Vandin, A., Wirsing, M.: Reasoning (on) service component ensembles in rewriting logic. In: Iida, S., Meseguer, J., Ogata, K. (eds.) Specification, Algebra, and Software. LNCS, vol. 8373, pp. 188–211. Springer, Heidelberg (2014). doi:10.1007/978-3-642-54624-2_10
12. Benavides, D., Segura, S., Ruiz-Cortés, A.: Automated analysis of feature models 20 years later: a literature review. Inf. Syst. **35**(6), 615–636 (2010)
13. Borba, P., Cohen, M.B., Legay, A., Wąsowski, A.: Analysis, test and verification in the presence of variability. Dagstuhl Rep. **3**(2), 144–170 (2013)
14. Bortolussi, L.: Stochastic concurrent constraint programming. ENTCS **164**, 65–80 (2006)
15. Buscemi, M.G., Montanari, U.: CC-Pi: a constraint-based language for specifying service level agreements. In: Nicola, R. (ed.) ESOP 2007. LNCS, vol. 4421, pp. 18–32. Springer, Heidelberg (2007). doi:10.1007/978-3-540-71316-6_3
16. Chrszon, P., Dubslaff, C., Klüppelholz, S., Baier, C.: Family-based modeling and analysis for probabilistic systems – featuring ProFeat. In: Stevens, P., Wasowski, A. (eds.) FASE 2016. LNCS, vol. 9633, pp. 287–304. Springer, Heidelberg (2016). doi:10.1007/978-3-662-49665-7_17

17. Classen, A., Cordy, M., Schobbens, P., Heymans, P., Legay, A., Raskin, J.: Featured transition systems: foundations for verifying variability-intensive systems and their application to LTL model checking. IEEE Trans. Softw. Eng. **39**(8), 1069–1089 (2013)
18. Clavel, M. (ed.): All About Maude. LNCS, vol. 4350. Springer, Heidelberg (2007). doi:10.1007/978-3-540-71999-1
19. Cordy, M., Schobbens, P., Heymans, P., Legay, A.: Beyond Boolean product-line model checking: dealing with feature attributes and multi-features. In: Proceedings 35th International Conference on Software Engineering (ICSE 2013), pp. 472–481. IEEE (2013)
20. de Moura, L., Bjørner, N.S.: Z3: an efficient SMT solver. In: Ramakrishnan, C.R., Rehof, J. (eds.) TACAS 2008. LNCS, vol. 4963, pp. 337–340. Springer, Heidelberg (2008). doi:10.1007/978-3-540-78800-3_24
21. Dubslaff, C., Baier, C., Klüppelholz, S.: Probabilistic model checking for feature-oriented systems. In: Chiba, S., Tanter, É., Ernst, E., Hirschfeld, R. (eds.) Transactions on AOSD XII. LNCS, vol. 8989, pp. 180–220. Springer, Heidelberg (2015). doi:10.1007/978-3-662-46734-3_5
22. Dubslaff, C., Klüppelholz, S., Baier, C.: Probabilistic model checking for energy analysis in software product lines. In: Proceedings 13th International Conference on Modularity (MODULARITY 2014), pp. 169–180. ACM (2014)
23. Erwig, M., Walkingshaw, E.: The choice calculus: a representation for software variation. ACM Trans. Softw. Eng. Methodol. **21**(1), 6 (2011)
24. Ghezzi, C., Sharifloo, A.: Model-based verification of quantitative non-functional properties for software product lines. Inform. Softw. Technol. **55**(3), 508–524 (2013)
25. Gilmore, S., Tribastone, M., Vandin, A.: An analysis pathway for the quantitative evaluation of public transport systems. In: Albert, E., Sekerinski, E. (eds.) IFM 2014. LNCS, vol. 8739, pp. 71–86. Springer, Heidelberg (2014). doi:10.1007/978-3-319-10181-1_5
26. Larsen, K.G., Legay, A.: Statistical model checking: past, present, and future. In: Margaria, T., Steffen, B. (eds.) ISoLA 2014. LNCS, vol. 8802, pp. 135–142. Springer, Heidelberg (2014). doi:10.1007/978-3-662-45231-8_10
27. Legay, A., Delahaye, B., Bensalem, S.: Statistical model checking: an overview. In: Barringer, H., et al. (eds.) RV 2010. LNCS, vol. 6418, pp. 122–135. Springer, Heidelberg (2010). doi:10.1007/978-3-642-16612-9_11
28. Lochau, M., Mennicke, S., Baller, H., Ribbeck, L.: DeltaCCS: a core calculus for behavioral change. In: Margaria, T., Steffen, B. (eds.) ISoLA 2014, Part I. LNCS, vol. 8802, pp. 320–335. Springer, Heidelberg (2014). doi:10.1007/978-3-662-45234-9_23
29. Rodrigues, G.N., et al.: Modeling and verification for probabilistic properties in software product lines. In: Proceedings 16th International Symposium on High Assurance Systems Engineering (HASE 2015), pp. 173–180. IEEE (2015)
30. Pianini, D., Sebastio, S., Vandin, A.: Distributed statistical analysis of complex systems modeled through a chemical metaphor. In: Proceedings International Conference on High Performance Computing and Simulation (HPCS 2014), pp. 416–423. IEEE (2014)
31. Saraswat, V., Rinard, M.: Concurrent constraint programming. In: Conference Record 17th Annual Symposium on Principles of Programming Languages (POPL 1990), pp. 232–245. ACM (1990)
32. Schaefer, I., Hähnle, R.: Formal methods in software product line engineering. IEEE Comput. **44**(2), 82–85 (2011)

33. Sebastio, S., Amoretti, M., Lluch Lafuente, A.: A computational field framework for collaborative task execution in volunteer clouds. In: Proceedings 9th International Symposium on Software Engineering for Adaptive and Self-managing Systems (SEAMS 2014), pp. 105–114. ACM (2014)
34. Sebastio, S., Vandin, A.: MultiVeStA: statistical model checking for discrete event simulators. In: Proceedings 7th International Conference on Performance Evaluation Methodologies and Tools (ValueTools 2013), pp. 310–315. ACM (2013)
35. Sen, K., Viswanathan, M., Agha, G.A., VESTA: a statistical model-checker and analyzer for probabilistic systems. In: Proceedings 2nd International Conference on Quantitative Evaluation of Systems (QEST 2005), pp. 251–252. IEEE (2005)
36. Thüm, T., Apel, S., Kästner, C., Schaefer, I., Saake, G.: A classification and survey of analysis strategies for software product lines. ACM Comput. Surv. **47**(1), 6 (2014)
37. Tribastone, M.: Behavioral relations in a process algebra for variants. In: Proceedings 18th International Software Product Line Conference (SPLC 2014), pp. 82–91. ACM (2014)
38. Varshosaz, M., Khosravi, R.: Families, discrete time Markov chain: modeling and verification of probabilistic software product lines. In: Proceedings 17th International Software Product Line Conference (SPLC 2013), vol. 2, pp. 34–41. ACM (2013)

Towards Adaptive Scheduling of Maintenance for Cyber-Physical Systems

Alexis Linard$^{(\boxtimes)}$ and Marcos L.P. Bueno$^{(\boxtimes)}$

Institute for Computing and Information Sciences, Radboud University Nijmegen,
P.O. Box 9010, 6500 GL Nijmegen, The Netherlands
{A.Linard,M.Bueno}@cs.ru.nl

Abstract. Scheduling and control of Cyber-Physical Systems (CPS) are becoming increasingly complex, requiring the development of new techniques that can effectively lead to their advancement. This is also the case for failure detection and scheduling component replacements. The large number of factors that influence how failures occur during operation of a CPS may result in maintenance policies that are time-monitoring based, which can lead to suboptimal scheduling of maintenance. This paper investigates how to improve maintenance scheduling of such complex embedded systems, by means of monitoring in real-time the critical components and dynamically adjusting the optimal time between maintenance actions. The proposed technique relies on machine learning classification models in order to classify component failure cases vs. non-failure cases, and on real-time updating of the maintenance policy of the sub-system in question. The results obtained from the domain of printers show that a model that is responsive to the environmental changes can enable consumable savings, while keeping the same product quality, and thus be relevant for industrial purposes.

Keywords: Model-based scheduling · Predictive maintenance · Machine learning · Cyber-physical systems

1 Introduction

Due to the growing complexity of Cyber-Physical Systems [11,19], many techniques have been proposed to improve failure detection and scheduling component replacement [17,21]. Indeed, new needs in terms of reliability and safety have appeared with the new applications of such systems. That is the reason why leading-edge technology manufacturers seek to design more robust and reliable systems [12]. Currently, a major issue in many industrial settings is how to correlate failure occurrences and the maintenance actions performed in order to prevent breakdowns. Modeling the failure behavior of many components in advance is an intricate task. Indeed, we claim that maintenance actions are frequently scheduled with fixed intervals that are suboptimal and implemented to the detriment of productivity and efficiency.

© Springer International Publishing AG 2016
T. Margaria and B. Steffen (Eds.): ISoLA 2016, Part I, LNCS 9952, pp. 134–150, 2016.
DOI: 10.1007/978-3-319-47166-2_9

Exclusively relying on experts to build models that can describe the behavior of machines has been recently recognized as a limiting feature [14,23]. Therefore, the use of machine learning techniques to construct such models has been investigated [3,10,16,18]. However, using such techniques in order to update the maintenance scheduling of a CPS in real time has so far not been explored. The main difficulties in this case relate to finding an appropriate predictive model, and then defining a procedure for updating the timing conditions. Predictive models can be used instead of costly sensors intended to provide information about the state of the machine at any moment, which is an additional reason why we introduce machine learning techniques to maintenance scheduling. The ultimate goal would be to develop embedded systems capable of dynamically scheduling their own maintenance. To that end, we aim to define a procedure for updating in real time when maintenance should be performed. Our work is based on an experiment carried out in partnership with industry, specifically in the domain of printers. In addition, we consider the scope of *automatic* maintenance, where the intervention of human beings is no longer needed.

In this study, we investigate to what extent machine learning can help to improve fixed maintenance scheduling of complex embedded systems. The contributions of this paper are as follows. First, we propose using machine learning techniques, in which the embedded system learns to distinguish between failure vs. non-failure cases using data related to critical components of the CPS. This can be done by monitoring critical components in real time. Next, we propose an algorithm to dynamically adjust the timing of maintenance actions. This algorithm uses timed automata [2], which is the formalism used to model the maintenance policy. Indeed, timed automata can provide an intuitive representation of the maintenance policy and its real-time update is proceeded by using information on the overall printer at any moment. Thus, our main contributions are (a) the use of decisions from a data-driven model to dynamically schedule maintenance, and (b) the use of timed automata to formally describe and analyze the proposed algorithm. Naturally, we only select relevant features to determine if the printer is working properly – that is to say, if we can schedule the maintenance actions later – or not. To that end, we consider a set of realistic, industry-based scenarios and simulations to provide evidence that a reduced amount of maintenance can be done while achieving similar product quality [8,9]. The considered scenarios have been implemented in *Uppaal* [4], which is another relevant practical-oriented contribution of this paper.

The remainder of this paper is organized as follows. In Sect. 2 we present the industrial problem that motivated our approach. In Sect. 3, we define the key concepts associated with model-based scheduling and classification techniques used to separate the failure from the non-failure cases of a Cyber-Physical System, as well as discuss the related literature. In Sect. 4 we explain our approach to updating when to trigger maintenance and the experiments done, using a model-checking tool and data about large-scale printers. Finally, we discuss the results.

2   Case Study

Large-scale printers are cyber-physical systems made of a large number of complex components, the interaction of which is often challenging to understand. Among their main components are the printheads, which are composed of thousands of printing nozzles. These are designed to jet ink on paper according to specifications concerning, for example, jetting velocity and direction. During the operation of these industrial printers, nozzles can behave inadequately with respect to the demanded task, e.g. by jetting incorrect amounts of ink or jetting in an incorrect direction. If that is the case, a nozzle is considered to be failing.

Failing nozzles can be repaired by performing one or more maintenance actions, including for example different types of cleaning actions. The maintenance actions are executed automatically, e.g. the printer cleans its own nozzles. In this context, determining the appropriate moment to execute each nozzle-related maintenance action is crucial to achieving a proper balance of conflicting objectives, such as productivity, machine lifetime, and final product quality. However, the number of individual nozzles, their physical architecture, the substantial number of variables that can potentially be correlated to them and the definition of printing quality, make particularly difficult to manually construct models that express all the potentially relevant correlations among these variables and nozzles. Ultimately, this creates a challenge when designing maintenance policies, since they are intended to be either too conservative or tolerant, otherwise one or more of the mentioned requirements could be seriously degraded.

A solution that is sometimes used to construct a policy consists of performing a large set of tests involving different usages of the CPS, aiming to derive time-based maintenance policies. These policies are based on monitoring, hence they do not suffer so much from the drawbacks of fixed-time-based strategies [17]. However, these policies rely on time counters that are not directly related to the state of machine parts, e.g. the time elapsed since the last finished printing task and the period that the printer stands idle. This implies that the only failure behaviors that can be explicitly captured by these rules are those that were previously seen during the tests, usually only accounting for a fraction of all possible machine statuses. Hence, unseen failure behavior cannot be handled properly by such maintenance strategies, which is likely since these machines can be used with a wide range of parameter combinations. In other words, such policies are prone to perform blindly on at least some situations, which can lead to too many or too few maintenance actions.

Nowadays, industrial printers record large amounts of data about the state of their components over time, so a data-driven approach seems feasible. A data-driven approach can provide evidence that helps to decide on whether the current time parameters are adequate or not, given the current state of the CPS. In order to represent time parameters and system states, a state machine appears to be an appropriate formalism. In this study we show how to dynamically update the parameters of a maintenance scheduler, which is based on timed state machines. This formalism is used in order to capture the intuition that the CPS moves between different states during its operation, in a time-dependent manner. A significant advantage of combining a statistical approach and state machines is that the real-time updating of timed parameters requires no human intervention, since correlations between potentially relevant variables can be learned algorithmically. In addition, the involvement of a failure behavior model is substantiated in our case, since there is no sensor available to directly provide, at any moment, information on the state of the nozzles. That is the reason why such a model could provide the desired outcome whenever required.

3 Background

In this section, we present the different concepts on which our definition of an adaptive scheduler is based. First, we describe how to model and verify maintenance schedulers. Then, we discuss the machine learning techniques used in our paper and to what extent the need for them is relevant for real-time updating of scheduling. Finally, we discuss related literature.

3.1 Modeling Maintenance Strategies

State machines are abstract machines with a wide range of applications such as in process modeling, software checking and pattern matching. They are composed of a set of states and transitions between states. They can be used in our industrial case study, that is to say modeling maintenance actions schedules of CPS, since it is possible to gather as many states as different maintenance actions plus one or more states representing when no maintenance action (MA) is being performed in the CPS. Transitions between the states would take place when a given maintenance is started and completed [1]. As shown in Fig. 1, the maintenance policy of a system can be represented intuitively by means of a specific type of state machine: a timed automaton (TA).

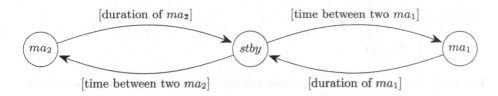

Fig. 1. Maintenance policy of a component represented by a simplified TA.

A timed automaton [2] is a finite-state machine extended with a finite set of real-valued clocks constraints. During the execution of a timed automaton, clock values increase at the same speed. A timed automaton has also clock guards, that enable or disable transitions and constrain the possible behaviors of the automaton. Furthermore, when a transition occurs, clocks can be reset.

The particular TA presented in Fig. 1 is a way of modeling a given maintenance strategy. In our case, we assume that maintenance actions are executed
sequentially. In order to establish that the derived maintenance strategy achieves
an optimal trade-off, many techniques exist, including model-checking of real-
time systems [9]. We used the tool *Uppaal* [4] to evaluate time-monitoring-based
maintenance strategies. More details about how this tool was used are presented
in Sect. 4.2.

3.2   Classification Techniques

This study relies on the use of classification techniques [13], also known as supervised learning, belonging to the field of Machine Learning. These techniques
consist of learning models from data. They are designed to classify instances
into a set of possible classes, according to the values of the attributes of each
instance. To that end, we used Weka [29], a suite of implemented learning algorithms. Among the possible classifiers that can be used for the classification task,
we considered in particular: bayesian networks, naives Bayes classifiers, decision
trees, random forests and neural networks.

The main reason for the choice of the classifiers listed above is related to our
case of study. Indeed, most of them can be considered as *white box* classifiers, in
the sense that it is easy to interpret their provided outcomes. This is particularly
important in the context of industrial cases, because such a readable model can
be more insightful than a *black box* oracle.

In order to learn a classifier from log data, labeled data from each possible class is needed. In the case of learning the failure behavior of the CPS of
interest (i.e. nozzles of large-scale printers), we assume that nozzles are either
failing or not failing. Thus, each instance is composed of a number of features
corresponding to relevant machine components and the class feature indicating
the occurrence of a failure or not.

actual→ predicted↓	f	!f
f	A	B
!f	C	D

$$P_f = \frac{A}{A+C} \quad R_f = \frac{A}{A+B} \quad P_{!f} = \frac{B}{B+D} \quad R_{!f} = \frac{B}{C+D}$$

Fig. 2. Confusion matrix and evaluation criteria for the classes *failure* (denoted by f)
and *non-failure* (denoted by !f).

In machine learning, an important goal when learning classifiers is that of
properly generalizing to new data. To meet this goal, overfitted models should be
detected, since they tend to perform very well on the data used during learning.
This issue is often dealt by using the n fold cross-validation evaluation. Cross-
validation with n folds consists of first dividing the dataset into n disjoint sets,
then learning the model on the $n-1$ first folds and evaluating the learned model

on the last fold. Then, learning is done on folds 2 to n and evaluation is done on fold 1, and so on. The part of the data used to learn a model is usually called training data, while the part used to evaluate it is usually called test data. On each fold, a classifier is typically evaluated by comparing the predicted class provided by the classifier and the original class, as seen on each instance from the test set. The results are placed in the confusion matrix shown in Fig. 2, and from this matrix the metrics precision P and recall R are computed. After processing all the folds, the mean of precision and recall is taken, corresponding to the final result of cross-validation.

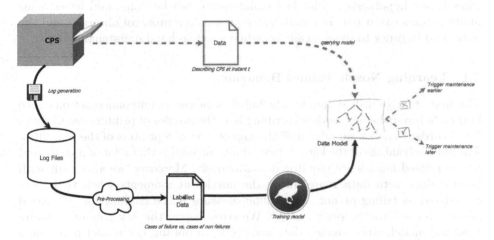

Fig. 3. The process of collecting log data for a CPS component, learning classifier models, and using the outcomes as input to reschedule maintenance.

Once a classifier has been trained, it is possible to use it in order to classify new unlabeled instances. The process is as follows: in real-time, new data about the same features used to train the model are recorded and represent the state of the CPS at instant t. Such state of the system corresponds to an instance to be classified by the model. Once the outcome is provided, a decision is taken by the real-time updating method controlling the schedule of maintenance actions. The overall process of learning and using the classifier in our case is described in Fig. 3.

3.3   Related Work

Extensive research has been done in the field of timed automata [2], including algorithmic and computability aspects [5,7] and model-checking oriented research [9]. To a lesser extent, research has been developed in the context of passive learning of TA from data [28], and learning sub-classes of TA known as event recording automata [15]. In the context of CPS, real-time online learning of TA has been investigated [22], however not related to predictive maintenance.

With regard to predictive maintenance, timed automata were applied to model the operating modes in the case of duration of tasks in manufacture scenario [27]. Statistical approaches to model the failure behavior of CPS have already been considered [20,24], but none of them combined the use of TA to model maintenance actions together with machine learning models.

4   Proposed Method and Experiments

In this section, we describe our method and the results of our experiments. Indeed, our hypothesis is that less maintenance can be done, and fewer or as many failures can occur. Hereinafter, we present the protocol observed and the data used in order to dynamically schedule nozzle-related maintenance[1].

4.1   Learning Nozzle Failure Behavior

The first step towards dynamic scheduling of nozzle maintenance actions is to build a failure behavior model describing how the nozzles of printers are likely to fail. In order to do so, we rely on all the logs of a set of 8 printers of the year 2015. The main advantage of the logs we have at our disposal is that a lot of metrics and nozzle-related factors are monitored continuously. Moreover, we also dealt with labeled data with data representing the nozzles at moments when they were considered as failing or not. The failing measure is the conjunction of several metrics related to the print quality. We stress again the key role of a failure behavior model, since labeled data are costly to obtain: the model reproduces the outcome provided by printing *test pages*, a process that inevitably leads to a loss of productivity on the overall printer. We thus trained the corresponding model by selecting relevant features. To this end, we benefited from the expertise of engineers related to the field, who indicated to us the possible relevant features.

In Table 1, we present the results achieved for failure detection (f). We state the results in terms of precision and recall. Precision (P) represents the proportion of failure cases as correctly classified. Recall (R) reflects the proportion of caught failure cases among the cases of failures and non failures. We also present the results achieved for the other class (non-failure − !f). Both results are important since both outcomes are used by our scheduler i.e. to advance or postpone maintenance. The classifiers have been trained with 117k instances to classify, the same features, and evaluated with a cross-validation of 10 folds. The set was divided into 10 % of instances belonging to the *failure* class and 90 % to the *non-failure* class.

In our experiments, we consider the results above as good enough to be considered as reliable. Moreover, we trained several classifiers (among others, decision trees, naive Bayes classifiers, neural networks, etc.), and the decision tree always performed the best. A decision tree is an interesting way of modeling the failure behavior of a component thanks to its high understandability. As a

---

[1] Experimental data available upon request.

Table 1. Quality of the best classification models trained with the data.

Classification algorithm	f		!f	
	P	R	P	R
Decision tree	0.788	0.631	0.951	0.977
Random forest	0.626	0.579	0.943	0.953
Bayesian network	0.683	0.809	0.973	0.949
Naive Bayes	0.329	0.424	0.918	0.882
Multilayer perceptron	0.652	0.224	0.903	0.984

consequence, we consider that we can safely schedule nozzle-related maintenance actions using the outcomes of the built Decision Tree.

In this case, we have used the J48 implementation of the C4.5 algorithm to learn it [25]. This algorithm builds a model from the training set using information entropy. It iteratively builds nodes choosing the attribute that best splits the current sample into subsets, using information gain. The attribute having the greatest information gain is chosen to make the decision, that is to say to be used as the next decision node. Of course, once a subset is only composed of instances belonging to the same class, no further node is created, but a leaf instead, standing for the final class of all the instances belonging to the subset.

The fact that a decision tree can be implemented easily by a succession of *if* conditions is another reason to consider it as premium model for industrial purposes. The lower quality of the results for the class *failure* is due to the low number of instances belonging to this class.

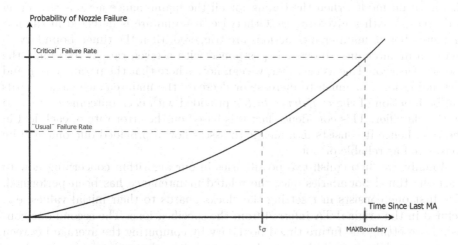

Fig. 4. Nozzle failure rate in function of the time since last MA.

4.2   Scheduling Nozzle-Related Maintenance Actions

The idea of dynamic scheduling of maintenance actions is to rely on the outcome of a predictor (component failure behavior model that classifies the system at instant t into two classes, failure or not failure) to put forward or backward the moment when to trigger it.

Algorithm 1. Dynamic Scheduling of a Maintenance Action

- q : query made periodically
- y : the reducing factor for the timing of the MA
- z : the increasing factor for the timing of the MA
- t_σ : the timing where the MA is usually triggered
- $currentBoundary$: the current timing when the MA will be triggered
- $MAXBoundary$: the maximum acceptable time to wait until triggering the MA

1: **for** each q **do**
2:     $prediction \leftarrow failureBehaviorModelQuery()$
3:     **if** prediction = failure **then**   ▷ Advance the MA schedule
4:         $currentBoundary \leftarrow currentBoundary \times y\%$
5:     **else**   ▷ Postpone the MA schedule
6:         $currentBoundary \leftarrow currentBoundary \times z\%$
7:     **if** currentBoundary is reached **then**
8:         $triggerMaintenance()$
9:         $currentBoundary \leftarrow t_\sigma$ **OR** $(currentBoundary + t_\sigma)/2$

As presented in Algorithm 1, we first of all consider the actual maintenance policy of the printer. Our idea is to query the classification model built previously in order to get the outcome desired. In case a failure is detected by our classification model, then the timing for all the maintenance actions triggering is decreased with a given rate y. Otherwise, if no failure is detected in the few moments before maintenance actions are triggered, then the timed boundary to enable a maintenance to occur is postponed with a given rate z. Assuming the use of a Decision Tree as classifier, we can notice here that the parameters y and z standing for how much to increase or decrease the maintenance clock guards can be function of the *confidence factor* provided with each outcome performed by the classifier. This confidence factor is based on the error rate of each leaf in the tree, hence it consists in a metric to assess how a provided outcome can be considered as reliable or not.

Finally, we distinguish two possibilities in our algorithm concerning how to reset the timed boundaries once the related maintenance has been performed. The first one consists in resetting the clocks guards to their initial values, e.g. defined in the original TA inferred from the specifications. The second one consists in resetting the future timed boundary by computing the average between the last used limit and the actual moment when the maintenance has been launched. In such a way, we assume that after several runs of the algorithm, the value computed will tend to the ideal time to wait between two maintenance actions. Both options are presented in Sect. 4.3 and the benefits between those two variants are compared.

4.3 Simulations Using Uppaal-SMC

In order to make simulations and evaluate the benefits of our dynamic scheduler, we used the *Uppaal-SMC* [8] modeling tool. *Uppaal* is a toolbox for verification of real-time systems represented by one or more timed automata extended with integer variables, data types and channel synchronization. The relevance of using *Uppaal-SMC* in our case lies in the possibility of running simulations of the system specified as a set of probabilistic timed automata.

One of the challenges of this work and its practical case study is to validate the failure behavior model built using machine learning techniques, and to use it in order to schedule maintenance actions. Of course, we had to find a way of integrating such a model in a tool like *Uppaal*, in order to benefit from the integration of the representation of the maintenance strategy (gathered from specifications of the component, and using TA), the decision tree providing insight on the failure behavior of the nozzles (learned prior to its implementation in *Uppaal* following description in Sect. 4.1), and the function that dynamically updates the triggering of maintenance (presented in Sect. 4.2).

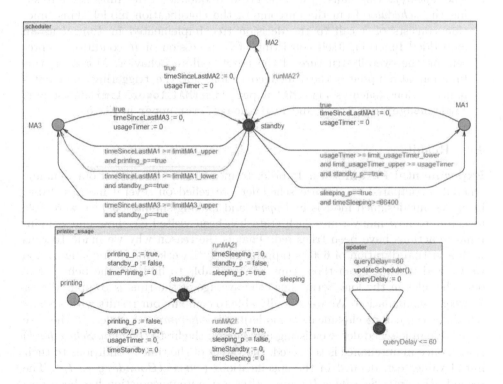

Fig. 5. Designing components by state-machines in *Uppaal*.

As shown in Fig. 5, the whole system is composed of 3 components, all of them modeled using state-machines:

1. The *printer usage*: this models how the printer is currently being used. It is composed of 3 states, printing, standby (e.g. waiting for a print job) and sleeping (for long periods out of use). It is important to model the printer usage since the way maintenance actions are scheduled depends on the usage of the printer. Indeed, print jobs will never be interrupted to perform maintenance. It is similar when the printer is in sleeping mode, since less maintenance is required when the printer is not in use.
2. The *scheduler*: this models the maintenance actions and under what conditions they are performed. In our case, we focuses especially on 3 nozzle-related maintenance actions. Inside the specifications of the scheduler, an inner function is defined reproducing the outcome of the decision tree as well as the values set to the refreshed timed conditions (see Algorithm 1). The *scheduler* reflects the specifications of the nozzles under which maintenance is supposed to be performed.
3. The *updater*: this calls – with a given frequency – the function refreshing the *scheduler* from the outcome of the classification model. This function consists of a call to the decision tree implemented in *Uppaal* as an embedded function, itself consisting of a succession of *if* conditions representing the overall structure of the nozzle failure behavior. Moreover, this function also updates the timed conditions for the triggering of maintenance actions (such as `limitMA1_upper`, `limitMA1_lower`, `limitMA3_upper`, `limit_usageTimer_lower` and `limit_usageTimer_upper` in Fig. 5).

4.4   Results

Experimental Parameters. In order to measure the benefits of our dynamic scheduler compared to a static scheduler, we relied on several metrics. First, by using our designed models in *Uppaal* and making simulations, we were able to compute how many times each state has been visited e.g. how many maintenance actions have been triggered. That is the reason why we made 10 runs with a virtual duration of 600 ks (approximately 1 week) for each configuration we wanted to test. From those runs, we were able to find out the behavior of our scheduler in the long term, since the average of the runs is computed over 10 weeks of simulation. We were finally able to compare our results with a *static* scheduler (no call to classification model) and a *dynamic* scheduler. In the case of the dynamic scheduler, we distinguish 3 cases: the first (*Dynamic Scheduler I*) resets, once maintenance is triggered, the values of the timed conditions to their initial values e.g. defined in the specifications ($currentBoundary \leftarrow t_\sigma$). The second (*Dynamic Scheduler II*) aims, after a maintenance action has been performed, to average the timed conditions between the past boundary and when the MA has really been done ($currentBoundary \leftarrow (currentBoundary + t_\sigma)/2$). The last one (*Dynamic Scheduler III*) computes the parameters y and z as a function of the confidence factor provided by the classification model.

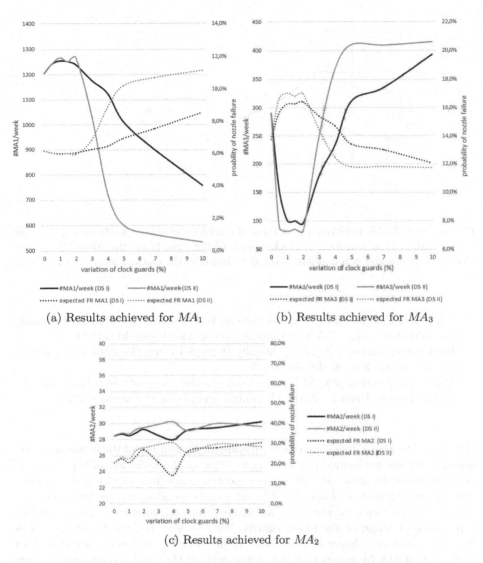

(a) Results achieved for MA_1 (b) Results achieved for MA_3

(c) Results achieved for MA_2

Fig. 6. Results concerning *Dynamic Scheduler I* and *II*. The value corresponding to a variation of clock guards of 0 % stands for the *Static Scheduler*.

In order to run experiments with *Uppaal*, several parameters have been set, such as the refreshing frequency (60 s), the variation of how much to postpone or advance maintenance actions (from 0.5 % to 10 %), the usage of the printer (the printer goes to sleeping mode every 8 hours and during at least 2 hours; after being printing during more than 2 min, then, the printer can stop printing and go into standby mode; after being without printing during more than 1 min, then, the printer can start printing again) and the nozzle behavior (a nozzle is likely to fail every 20 min). We can also mention maintenance-related additional information and settings:

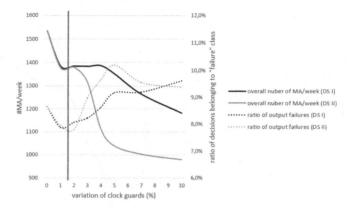

Fig. 7. Overall MA performed and ratio of decisions classified as *failure*. The value corresponding to a variation of clock guards of 0 % stands for the *Static Scheduler*. The vertical line shows a possible optimal variation of the clocks guards. (Color figure online)

- Maintenance action #1 (MA_1): according to the usage of the printer, usually triggered every 40 s – 3.5 h. Maximum acceptable threshold set: 5 h.
- Maintenance action #2 (MA_2): usually triggered when the system is going to and coming back from sleeping mode.
- Maintenance action #3 (MA_3): according to the usage of the printer, usually triggered every 15 min – 3.5 h. Maximum acceptable threshold set: 5 h.

Results. We give a graphical representation of the number of the achieved maintenance actions performed per week in function of the variation of the degree of clock increase/decrease, as well as the expected nozzle failure rate in Fig. 6a to c (for *Dynamic Scheduler I* and *II*). The value corresponding to a variation of clock guards of 0 % stands for the static scheduler, since parameters y and z equaling 0 means no change of the clock guards. We also give the results of the *Static Scheduler* and the *Dynamic Scheduler III* in Table 2. The results are stated for each type of MA by number of MA performed ($\#MA$) and the expected failure rate when the maintenance is performed (FR_{MA}). The expected failure rate is computed from the distribution shown in Fig. 4, since the information providing the nozzle failure rate as a function of the time since last maintenance has been computed from the logs. We also present for each scheduler the proportion of cases classified as failures by our failure behavior model (C_f in Table 2 and ratio of output failures in Fig. 7).

Discussion. From the results achieved, we can see that in some settings, the number of maintenance actions performed can decrease. Nonetheless, while the number of maintenance actions is decreasing, the *expected* nozzle failure rate slightly increases, yet still within acceptable values. We can refer to the first

Table 2. Number of maintenance actions triggered using *Dynamic Scheduler III*.

Scheduler	$\#MA_1$	FR_{MA_1}	$\#MA_2$	FR_{MA_2}	$\#MA_3$	FR_{MA_3}	C_f
Static	1205.6	6.1 %	28.5	20.5 %	290.3	13.8 %	8.7 %
Dynamic III	806.6	8.2 %	29.1	25.6 %	378.1	12.3 %	9.5 %

dynamic scheduler and to MA_3 with an optimal decrease of three times as few maintenance actions performed. The counterpart is an increase of the expected failure rate by 2 points. We can also see that in some cases, especially MA_2, our scheduler has no influence on the triggering of this specific type of maintenance. Indeed, MA_2 is an example of usage-based maintenance, whereas our method only modifies timed-based maintenance. According to the results achieved by the *Dynamic Scheduler III* e.g. advancing or postponing the clock guards using the confidence factor of the Decision Tree, we can see that less MA_1 is performed but the expected failure rate when MA_1 is triggered is increased by 2 points, whereas MA_3 is done more often. Furthermore, according to the number of cases detected as failure cases by our classifier as well as the number of actions performed (whatever the type), we can see that in some cases, less maintenance is done and fewer failures are detected by our model, in particular when using a variation of how much to postpone or advance maintenance actions of 1 or 2 %. This is shown in Fig. 7 by a red line. This result proves our assumption stating that we can at the same time save maintenance and improve the print quality. Finally, for some settings and independently of the scheduler, our dynamic schedulers perform more actions than a static scheduler.

5   Conclusion

In this paper, we describe a new method for dynamic maintenance scheduling. We expect that our method can be generalized to other domains. The major novelty we bring, to the best of our knowledge, is a method involving machine learning techniques by using the decision of a classifier in order to put forward or postpone when maintenance should be triggered, i.e. how to update scheduling of automatic periodic maintenance defined by a TA.

According to our results, we can conclude that our dynamic scheduler reduces the number of actions performed in different settings. We also note that the price to pay in order to do less maintenance is a slight increase of the expected failure rate. Thus, depending on how critical the component is, our technique can reduce maintenance costs for a negligible increase in the risk of breakdown. In our case, it entailed an insignificant loss of print quality. Moreover, in some settings, we could reduce the failure rate as well as the number of maintenance performed. We also believe that our technique can be particularly interesting in the case of the unavailability of sensors that provide direct information about component failures. The strength of an embedded decision model is its availability at any time. Furthermore, we expect that, applied to other real systems, our technique could achieve similar results to those found in our simulation.

With regard to further work, we think that within the scope of our case study, we can extend the current experiment not only to nozzles but also to other related components, or at least components that share related maintenance actions. Furthermore, in future, we will look into the use of fault trees [26]. Indeed, we believe that a fault tree pattern can be used to model interactions between several components, and how a failure can propagate from one component to others. We also hope that extending such a technique to the use of real-time automata can enhance the schedulability and control of CPS. We can also enhance the scheduler by taking into account the timing occurrences of anomalies [21]. Finally, we could orientate the choice of the machine learning techniques used towards stream mining tools and algorithms [6], which would additionally offer the possibility of updating the failure behavior model the more new labeled data are available. Then, it could be possible to deal with unseen events or combination of parameters, and keep an accurate model throughout the life of the CPS.

Acknowledgments. Thanks to Lou Somers and Patrick Vestjens for providing industrial datasets as well as required expertise related to the case of study. This research is supported by the Dutch Technology Foundation STW under the Robust CPS program (project 12693).

References

1. Abdeddaïm, Y., Asarin, E., Maler, O.: Scheduling with timed automata. Theor. Comput. Sci. **354**(2), 272–300 (2006)
2. Alur, R., Dill, D.L.: A theory of timed automata. Theor. Comput. Sci. **126**(2), 183–235 (1994)
3. Arab, A., Ismail, N., Lee, L.S.: Maintenance scheduling incorporating dynamics of production system and real-time information from workstations. J. Intell. Manuf. **24**(4), 695–705 (2013)
4. Bengtsson, J., Larsen, K., Larsson, F., Pettersson, P., Yi, W.: UPPAAL - a tool suite for automatic verification of real-time systems. In: Alur, R., Henzinger, T.A., Sontag, E.D. (eds.) Hybrid Systems III: Verification and Control. LNCS, vol. 1066, pp. 232–243. Springer, Heidelberg (1996)
5. Bengtsson, J.E., Yi, W.: Timed automata: semantics, algorithms and tools. In: Desel, J., Reisig, W., Rozenberg, G. (eds.) Lectures on Concurrency and Petri Nets. LNCS, vol. 3098, pp. 87–124. Springer, Heidelberg (2004)
6. Bifet, A., Holmes, G., Kirkby, R., Pfahringer, B.: MOA: massive online analysis. J. Mach. Learn. Res. **11**, 1601–1604 (2010)
7. Bouyer, P., Brihaye, T., Markey, N.: Improved undecidability results on weighted timed automata. Inf. Process. Lett. **98**(5), 188–194 (2006)
8. Bulychev, P., David, A., Larsen, K.G., Mikučionis, M., Poulsen, D.B., Legay, A., Wang, Z.: UPPAAL-SMC: statistical model checking for priced timed automata. arXiv preprint arXiv:1207.1272 (2012)
9. Burns, A.: How to verify a safe real-time system: the application of model checking and timed automata to the production cell case study. Real-Time Syst. **24**(2), 135–151 (2003)

10. Butler, K.L.: An expert system based framework for an incipient failure detection and predictive maintenance system. In: Proceeding of the International Conference on Intelligent Systems Applications to Power Systems, Orlando, Florida, USA, pp. 321–326 (1996)

11. Cardenas, A.A., Amin, S., Sastry, S.: Secure control: towards survivable cyber-physical systems. In: 2013 IEEE 33rd International Conference on Distributed Computing Systems Workshops, pp. 495–500 (2008)

12. Derler, P., Lee, E.A., Vincentelli, A.S.: Modeling cyber-physical systems. Proc. IEEE **100**(1), 13–28 (2012)

13. Flach, P.: Machine Learning: The Art and Science of Algorithms that Make Sense of Data. Cambridge University Press, Cambridge (2012)

14. Fumeo, E., Oneto, L., Anguita, D.: Condition based maintenance in railway transportation systems based on big data streaming analysis. Procedia Comput. Sci. **53**, 437–446 (2015)

15. Grinchtein, O., Jonsson, B., Leucker, M.: Learning of event-recording automata. In: Lakhnech, Y., Yovine, S. (eds.) FORMATS 2004 and FTRTFT 2004. LNCS, vol. 3253, pp. 379–395. Springer, Heidelberg (2004)

16. Gross, P., Boulanger, A., Arias, M., Waltz, D.L., Long, P.M., Lawson, C., Anderson, R., Koenig, M., Mastrocinque, M., Fairechio, W., et al.: Predicting electricity distribution feeder failures using machine learning susceptibility analysis. In: Proceedings of the 21st National Conference on Artificial Intelligence, Boston, Massachusetts, USA, vol. 21, pp. 1705–1711 (2006)

17. Hashemian, H.M., Bean, W.C.: State-of-the-art predictive maintenance techniques. IEEE Trans. Instrum. Meas. **60**(10), 3480–3492 (2011)

18. Kaiser, K.A., Gebraeel, N.Z.: Predictive maintenance management using sensor-based degradation models. IEEE Trans. Syst. Man Cybern. Part A: Syst. Hum. **39**(4), 840–849 (2009)

19. Lee, E.A.: Cyber physical systems: design challenges. In: Proceedings of the 11th IEEE International Symposium on Object Oriented Real-Time Distributed Computing, Orlando, Florida, USA, pp. 363–369 (2008)

20. Li, H., Parikh, D., He, Q., Qian, B., Li, Z., Fang, D., Hampapur, A.: Improving rail network velocity: a machine learning approach to predictive maintenance. Transp. Res. Part C: Emerg. Technol. **45**, 17–26 (2014)

21. Maier, A., Niggemann, O., Eickmeyer, J.: On the learning of timing behavior for anomaly detection in cyber-physical production systems. In: Proceedings of the 26th International Workshop on Principles of Diagnosis, Paris, France, pp. 217–224 (2015)

22. Maier, A.: Online passive learning of timed automata for cyber-physical production systems. In: Proceedings of the 12th IEEE International Conference on Industrial Informatics, Porto Alegre, Brazil, pp. 60–66 (2014)

23. Niggemann, O., Biswas, G., Kinnebrew, J.S., Khorasgani, H., Volgmann, S., Bunte, A.: Data-driven monitoring of cyber-physical systems leveraging on big data and the internet-of-things for diagnosis and control. In: Proceedings of the 26th International Workshop on Principles of Diagnosis, Paris, France, pp. 185–192 (2015)

24. Nowaczyk, S., Prytz, R., Rögnvaldsson, T., Byttner, S.: Towards a machine learning algorithm for predicting truck compressor failures using logged vehicle data. In: Proceedings of the 12th Scandinavian Conference on Artificial Intelligence, Aalborg, Denmark, pp. 205–214 (2013)

25. Quinlan, J.R.: C4.5: Programs for Machine Learning. Elsevier, Amsterdam (2014)

26. Ruijters, E., Stoelinga, M.: Fault tree analysis: a survey of the state-of-the-art in modeling, analysis and tools. Comput. Sci. Rev. **15**, 29–62 (2015)

27. Simeu-Abazi, Z., Bouredji, Z.: Monitoring and predictive maintenance: modeling and analyse of fault latency. Comput. Ind. **57**(6), 504–515 (2006)
28. Verwer, S., Weerdt, M., Witteveen, C.: Efficiently identifying deterministic real-time automata from labeled data. Mach. Learn. **86**(3), 295–333 (2011)
29. Witten, I.H., Frank, E., Trigg, L.E., Hall, M.A., Holmes, G., Cunningham, S.J.: Weka: practical machine learning tools and techniques with Java implementations (1999)

Better Railway Engineering Through Statistical Model Checking

Enno Ruijters[(✉)] and Mariëlle Stoelinga

University of Twente, EWI-FMT, P.O. Box 217,
7500 AE Enschede, The Netherlands
{e.j.j.ruijters,m.i.a.stoelinga}@utwente.nl

Abstract. Maintenance is essential to ensuring the dependability of a technical system. Periodic inspections, repairs, and renewals can prevent failures and extend a system's lifespan. At the same time, maintenance incurs cost and planned downtime. It is therefore important to find a maintenance policy that balances cost and dependability.

This paper presents a framework, fault maintenance trees (FMTs), integrating maintenance into the industry-standard formalism of fault trees. By translating FMTs to priced timed automata and applying statistical model checking, we can obtain system dependability metrics such as system reliability and mean time to failure, as well as costs of maintenance and failures over time, for different maintenance policies.

Our framework is flexible and can be extended to include effects specific to the system being analysed. We demonstrate that our framework can be used in practice using two case studies from the railway industry: electrically insulated joints, and pneumatic compressors.

1 Introduction

In today's world, safety-critical systems are all around us. Complex systems like nuclear power plants, pacemakers, and trains have become essential to the operation of society, and failure of these systems can have disastrous consequentes. It is therefore important to analyse such systems to ensure that they meet dependability requirements.

In addition to safe design, proper maintenance is essential to keeping technological systems functioning. Few systems can remain operational for decades without any maintenance or repairs, and so this must be included in the safety analysis. Traditionally, this has been examined separately from the system design: First components manufacturers specify what maintenance is required, and what the reliability properties are if this maintenance is performed. Then, these properties are used to analyze whole-system dependability, thus assuming this maintenance is performed as specified.

A recent trend in asset management is towards reliability-centerd, a.k.a. risk based, maintenance [10]. This involves focussing maintenance efforts on the more critical components, while performing less maintenance on less important parts.

T. Margaria and B. Steffen (Eds.): ISoLA 2016, Part I, LNCS 9952, pp. 151–165, 2016.
DOI: 10.1007/978-3-319-47166-2_10

Thus, better dependability can be achieved at lower cost. Planning such maintenance, however, requires knowledge of how maintenance at the component level affects whole-system dependability. We have developed a framework called *fault maintenance trees* [12] combining maintenance and system design, which can be analysed using statistical model checking to obtain quantitative information about system dependability under different maintenance policies. This can then be used to find cost-optimal maintenance plans without compromising on safety.

Concretely, we combine the industry-standard for dependability analysis, fault trees, with maintenance models. The combined models are translated into timed automata, which can be analysed using the UPPAAL-SMC [6] model checking tool. We can obtain key performance indicators such as system reliability, expected number of failures over time, and expected costs. Our case studies for the railway industry show that this framework is suitable to maintenance policies found in practise, and yields the information necessary to optimize maintenance policies.

This paper first explains key information about maintenance and maintenance policies in Sect. 2. Next, Sect. 3 explains our framework of fault maintenance trees. Section 4 describes two case studies, and we conclude in Sect. 5.

1.1   Related Work

The automata used in this work are based on the Input/Output Interactive Markov Chains used by the DFTCalc tool [2], which uses stochastic model checking to analyse dynamic fault trees without maintenance.

For an overview of a large number of analysis techniques and extensions for fault trees, we refer the reader to [14]. We mention some of the most closely related works here.

Bucci et al. [4] extend tradition fault trees with non-Markovian failure distributions and present a tool to analyse such FTs. This tool can be used to analyze components that wear out over time, but does not consider maintenance to undo this wear.

Buchacker [5] presents an alternative extension called Extended fault trees, to model systems where the failure rates of some components depend on the status of other components. This formalism does not include repairs or non-exponentially-distributed failure times, nor maintenance decisions based on the state of an entire subtree.

Aside from fault trees, numerous methods have been developed for the analysis and optimization of maintenance strategies. As this field is very broad, we refer the reader to surveys such as [1] for techniques based on simulation or [15] on o.a. analytic approximations and Bayesian reasoning.

One technique that is particularly close to our work is by Carnevali et al. [7] and examines the effect of maintenance in phased systems. Here resources are used by several tasks in a sequence, and in-between these tasks faults can be detected and repaired.

2   Maintenance

Most long-lived systems require some form of maintenance to avoid premature failures. From simple procedures like inflating your tires, to large overhauls of entire power plants, certain operations must be performed to keep a system in working order. This section explains how maintenance is typically performed in the railway industry.

2.1   Types of Maintenance

Maintenance actions can be broadly divided into two categories: *preventive* and *corrective* maintenance. Preventive maintenance is performed before a system or component experiences a failure, where failure means that the system or component is no longer able to performs one of its intended functions. Corrective maintenance is performed after a failure has occurred, and is intended to restore the system or component to a functioning state.

Note that we consider component failures separate from system failures, as not all components are always necessary for the entire system to operate. For example, a datacenter with a redundant power supply can experience a failure of one power source while the datacenter as a whole remains fully functional. Section 3 explains fault trees, which are a formalism to describe how component failure combine to cause system failures.

An important aspect to preventive maintenance is the notion of *degradation* of components. Due to time and use, components typically degrade over time until they reach a point where a failure occurs. For example, the treads on a car's tires gradually decreases with use, until the tread is too worn to perform a necessary function of the tires, namely retain grip on the road when wet.

The choice of which type of maintenance depends on several factors, including the different costs of maintenance and failures, and the practical applicability of preventive maintenance. In systems where failures are much more expensive than maintenance, such as a nuclear power plant, preventive maintenance is almost always cost-beneficial. Conversely, when failures not more expensive than the planned downtime for maintenance, such as for your home lightbulbs, corrective maintenance is the better options. Some types of failures, such as lightning strikes, cannot be prevented by periodic maintenance.

2.2   Planning of Maintenance

Besides what maintenance needs to be performed, it is important to decide when to do this maintenance. In general, we can distinguish three types of planning: *use-based*, *condition-based*, and *failure-based* maintenance [9].

Use-based maintenance is the simplest type of maintenance plan for preventive maintenance: It performs certain activities after some specified amount of use of the system, in whatever units of use are relevant. For example, changing the oil in a car can be performed after a given number of miles have been driven, or after a given length of time has elapsed.

Condition-based maintenance is more elaborate, as it specified the future maintenance plan given the current condition of the system. A simple example of such a plan is replacing the battery in your smoke-detector when it starts emitting low-battery beeps. Most condition-based maintenance plans also involve some use-based component, such as inspections at fixed times, since most systems do not measure their own condition well enough to completely on for maintenance.

Finally, failure-based maintenance is mostly used for corrective maintenance, where action is only taken when a failure occurs. This type of plan is not necessarily the same as only performing corrective maintenance, as it may involve repairing or replacing still-functional parts of a system as preventive maintenance against future failures.

3   Fault Maintenance Trees

One of the industry-standard methods for reliability analysis is fault tree analysis. A fault tree describes how failures at a component level interact to cause system failures. Our framework of *fault maintenance trees* extends fault trees by including maintenance. This section gives a brief overview of fault trees and fault maintenance trees.

3.1   Fault Trees

Fault trees are directed acyclic graphs describing the combinations of component failures that lead to a system failures. The leaves of a fault tree, called *basic events* (BEs), denote the component failures. The internal nodes of the graph, called *gates* or *intermediate events*, describe the different ways that failures can interact to cause (sub)system failures. The root node of the graph is called the *top level event* (TE), and denotes the failure of the entire system.

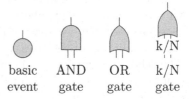

Fig. 1. Images of the elements in a standard fault tree

The gates in a fault tree can be of several types, shown in Fig. 1, describing the various forms of interactions between failures. The AND-gate fails when all of its children fail, the OR-gate when any of its children fail, and the k/N-gate when at least k out of its N children fail.

These fault trees, also called *standard* or *static* fault trees, do not capture all possible interactions that can occur in practical systems, and many extensions have been developed to model more complex behaviours. An overview of such extensions can be found in [14].

To analyse the dependability of a system modeled using a fault tree and obtain quantitative values, the basic events must be decorated with numeric attributes describing their failure behaviour. The most common approach is to a attach probabilities or *failure rate* to each basic event. Fault trees decorated with probabilities abstract away the evolution over time, while failure rates provides the parameters of exponential distributions governing the times when the events fail.

3.2 Metrics

Given an FT with failure information, several metrics of the system can be computed:

Reliability denotes the probability of the system failing within a given time window. Formally, if we describe the behaviour of the system described by a fault tree F using $X_F(t) = 1$ when this system has failed at time t, and 0 if it has not, the reliability is defined as $Re_F(t) = \mathbb{P}(X_F(t) = 0)$. Conversely, we use the term *unreliability* for the probability that the system has failed. For fault trees with only probabilities, the reliability is constant over time.

Availability denotes the expected fraction of time in a given time window that the system is functioning. Formally, we say $A_F(t) = \mathbb{E}(\frac{1}{t}\int_0^t X_F(x)\mathrm{d}x)$.

Mean time to failure denotes the expected time before a failure occurs. Formally, $MTTF(F) = \mathbb{E}(\operatorname{argmin}_t X_F(t) = 1)$.

Expected cost denotes the expected cost incurred within a given time frame. Although not very useful for FTs without maintenance, costs are very useful when comparing different maintenance strategies. Typically costs are incurred either on a per-event basis, e.g. a fixed cost to replace a broken component, or per unit time, e.g. lost productivity while a system is down. Formally, we write $C(t)$ for the cumulative cost incurred up to time t, hence the expected cost is either $\mathbb{E}(C(t))$ for a fixed time window, or $\frac{1}{t}\mathbb{E}(C(t))$ for the average cost per unit time.

3.3 Fault Maintenance Trees

The industry-standard approach to including repairs in a fault tree is to equip basic events with a *repair rate* as well as a failure rate [16]. This repair rate gives the parameter of an exponential distribution governing the time taken to repair the component after it has failed.

More complicated repair policies can be modeled using *repair boxes* described in [3,8]. While this approach supports complex policies for repairs after component failures, is does not allow for preventive maintenance, nor does it support the modeling of components with non-exponentially-distributed failure times.

We propose the formalism of *fault maintenance trees*, which supports complex preventive and corrective repair policies as well as components with arbitrary distributions of failure times. This formalism extends basic events by introducing *degraded states* (similar to those in extended fault trees [5]) in which the component is still functional but has worn to some extent. The tree structure is also augmented with *repair modules* and *inspection modules*, which act on the extended basic events by returning them to a less degraded state, or initiating a repair depending on the current state.

We further introduce a new gate type, the *rate dependency* or RDEP, depicted in Fig. 2. This gate describes a situation where the failure of one component (called the *trigger* causes the accelerated degradation one or more other components (called the *dependent children*. For example, if one pump in a redundant setup fails, the other pump is sufficient to keep the system functioning but the increased load results in faster wear of the functional pump. When the trigger is subsequently repaired, the dependent children return to the normal wear rate, but do not return to their original state of degradation.

3.4   Analysis Through Priced Timed Automata

To compute quantitative metrics of FMTs, such as reliability and availability, we translate the FMT into a network of priced timed automata (PTA), which we then analyze using the UPPAAL-SMC [6] model-checking tool.

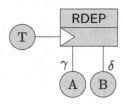

Fig. 2. RDEP gate where the failure of BE T leads to accelerated wear of BE A with a factor γ, and of BE B with factor δ.

A priced time automaton is a model consisting of locations and transitions between these locations. The locations represent states of the system, and transitions describe situations when the system may move from one state to another. Constraints on the edges and invariants on locations may be used to block or force certain transitions at certain times. These constraints and invariants are specified in terms of clocks, which increase linearly over time but may be reset when a transition is taken. Multiple PTAs can be combined using synchronisation on transitions, where some edges waiting for a signal *sig?* can only be taken simultaneous with a transition in another PTA emitting the corresponding signal *sig!*.

An example of a PTA can be seen in Fig. 4, describing an inspection module (IM). The initial location is the one on the left. Here, the clock x denotes the time since the previous inspection, and increases until it is reset when an inspection is performed. The invariant on the initial location prevents the PTA from remaining in this state when the time to perform an inspection has been reached. Before this time, the guard on the self-looping transition prevents a premature inspection. When the clock x is equal to the time *interval*, the self-loop is taken and the clock is reset. The edge to the location on the right is a synchronization transition on the channel *thres*, and is taken when a component has degraded enough to take the corresponding transition its PTA. After this, the IM still waits for the inspection time, but the transition back to the initial location now also synchronizes with the repair module to begin a repair. Finally, both transitions corresponding to performing an inspection add a fixed amount *cost* to a global counter.

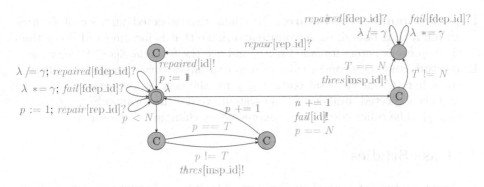

Fig. 3. PTA of a basic event with a failure time governed by a (N, λ)-Erlang distribution, with a threshold for the inspection at phase T. The counter p denotes the current phase, and is incremented according to exit rate of the initial state. If the current phase is equal to the threshold phase, a signal $thres$[insp_id] is send to the listening IM. When the current phase equals the number of phases N in the distribution, the PTA emits a signal $fail$[id] to all listening gates, possibly emits the threshold signal, and waits for a signal $repair$[red_id] from the RM. When this repair signal is received, the PTA emits a signal $repaired$[id] to any listening gates, reset the current phase to 1, and returns to the initial state. The signal $fail$[fdep_id] triggers an acceleration of the degradation due the the failure of an FDEP trigger, and $repaired$[fdep_id] return the rate to normal.

An addition to PTA for statistical model checking is the option to attach an *exit rate* to a location, which specifies an exponential distribution for the time that a transition is taken, unless an invariant forces a transition before this time.

To analyze an entire FMT, we convert each element (i.e. basic event, gate, IM, and RM) into a PTA, with appropriate synchronization depending on the structure of the FMT. Each element is assigned a unique ID to coordinate the signals for synchronization. The PTA for the basic event, IM, RM, and AND-gate are shown in Figs. 3, 4, 5, and 6 respectively. The other gates are constructed analogously to the AND gate.

After converting an FMT into a network of PTA, the model-checking tool UPPAAL-SMC is used to compute quantitative metrics of the model. The different metrics described in Sect. 3.2 can be expressed in the tCTL-like logic of UPPAAL as follows, where x denotes a clock counting global time:

Reliability: For convenience we describe only the unreliability, which is the probability of experiencing a failure within time t. If we denote the failed state of the top event as $T.Failed$, the unreliability corresponds to the formula $\mathbb{P}[x \leq t]\{\Diamond T.Failed\}$.

Availability: To compute the expected fraction of time the system is up, we introduce an auxiliary clock a that is stopped, but not reset, while the top event is in the failed state. The availability within time t can then be expressed as $\mathbb{E}[x \leq t]\{\max : a/t\}$.

Expected number of failures: To count the expected number of failures within a time bound, we introduce a variable that is incremented every time the top event enters its failed state, and use the formula $\mathbb{E}[x \leq t]\{\max : n\}$.

Expected cost: Our model tracks several variables corresponding to different costs (e.g. C_{total} for total costs, C_{insp} for the cost of inspections, etc.). To find the expected total cost of the system, we use the formula $\mathbb{E}[x \leq t]\{\max : C_{total}\}$. The other costs can be expressed by changing the counter.

4   Case Studies

To demonstrate the practical applicability of fault maintenance trees and SMC in practice, we have applied this method to two cases from the railway industry: The electrically insulated railway joint (EI-Joint) [13], and a trainbound pneumatic compressor [11].

4.1   EI-joint

The electrically insulated joint is a component used to physically connect two railroad tracks while maintaining electrical separation between them. This is necessary since many train detection systems use electrical signals to determine whether a train is present, and such systems can only detect which isolated section of track the train is occupying. Failures of these joints are a major contributor to disruptions of train service.

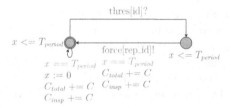

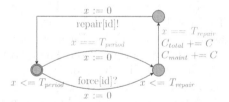

Fig. 4. PTA for an inspection module. The PTA begins in the leftmost state, and waits until either the time until the inspection interval (T_{period}) elapses, or until a threshold signal (thres[id]) is received from a BE. If the time elapses before a signal is received, then the inspection cost is incurred and the timer resets. If a threshold signal is received, the module waits for the scheduled inspection time, then signals its associated repair module to begin a repair (force[rep_id]), and then resets the timer.

Fig. 5. PTA for a repair module. The PTA begins in the leftmost state with clock x initially zero. It waits until either the waiting time for a periodic repair (T_{period}) elapses, or a repair request signal (*force[id]*) is received. In either case, the module waits some time T_{repair}, incurs the C for a repair, sends a signal (*repair[id]*) to any BEs repaired by this module, and resets the timer.

A fault tree of the EI-joint can be seen in Fig. 7, the exact failure modes are listed in Table 1. In broad terms, failures of the joints can be divided into mechanical failures where the physical connection between the rails is broken, and electrical failures where an electrical connection is made between the rails.

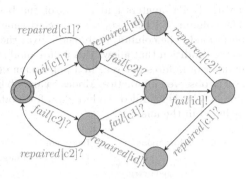

Aside from the distribution of the failure time, all failure modes have an associated 'condition' which is required for the failure to occur. For example, a joint can be short-circuited by metal shavings when the wheels of a train scrape against the track, which only occurs in joints installed where the track curves. We model this by a probability in each basic event, corresponding to the fraction of all joints that are susceptible to the particular failure mode.

Fig. 6. PTA of an AND gate with two children with IDs c1 and c2. The gate listens for the failure signals of its children, and emits its own failure signal when both children have failed. Likewise, it listens for the signals that its children have been repaired, and emits its own repaired signal if either child is repaired after the gate emits its failure signal.

The maintenance policy for the joints is fairly straightforward: Periodic visual inspections are performed, and any problems found are corrected shortly after. Some failures, such as when a conductive path is formed by iron shavings, can be easily corrected, e.g. by sweeping away the shavings. Mechanical defects and faults internal to the joint can only be repaired by replacing the entire joint. We leave out exact details of the current policy for reasons of confidentiality.

The goal of this case study was to improve the current maintenance policy with respect to cost. We consider three categories of costs: (1) costs of inspections, (2) costs of maintenance (preventive and corrective), and (3) costs of failures. These costs were provided by ProRail, as an average over all the joints they maintain (as the actual costs vary, e.g. a failure in a high-traffic rail is more expensive than in some rarely-used sidetrack). The costs of failure include both monetary cost, and a model of the social costs of unavailability based on passenger delays.

Results. We have analyzed the model of the EI-joint, both under the current maintenance policy and under several possible improvements. In general, we find that our results for the current policy closely match historical records of failures, indicating that the model is a good representation of the actual system. We find that the current policy is close to optimal, and that this optimum is fairly insensitive to small variations in inspection frequency.

The results shown in this section are computed using 40,000 simulation runs, resulting in a 95 % confidence interval with a width less than 1 % of the indicated values. When comparing to historical records, we consider the entire population of 50,000 EI-joints in the Netherlands.

Table 1. Parameters and results of the basic events of the FMT for the EI-joint. The column 'ETTF' lists the expected time to failure, assuming no maintenance is performed. The column 'prob. cnd.' gives the probability that a given joint is subject to the condition that allows this failure mode to occur. The last three columns give the number of failures per year in a population of 50,000 joints as predicted by the model and as observed in practice. Modes 5a and 5b have a fixed probability of occurring every time a joint is installed. Failure data for mode 15 was not available, and therefore not included in the analysis.

BE nr	Failure mode	Parameters			Failure rates		
		ETTF (yrs)	Phases	Prob. cnd	Predicted	Actual	Difference
1	Poor geometry	5	4	10 %	110	48	62
2	Broken fishplate	8	4	33 %	129	83	46
3	Broken bolts	15	4	33 %	2.3	2.1	0.2
4	Rail head broken out	10	4	33 %	68	30	38
5	Glue connection broken	10	4	33 %	70	37	33
5a	Manufacturing defect	–	-	0.25 %			
5b	Installation error	–	-	0.25 %			
6	Battered head	20	4	5 %	3.4	5.5	2.1
7	Arc damage	5	3	0.2 %	7	3.4	3.6
8	End post broken out	7	3	33 %	12	9.4	2.6
9	Joint bypassed: overhang	5	4	100 %	212	200	12
10a	Joint shorted: shavings (normal)	1	4	12 %			
10b	Joint shorted: shavings (coated)	10	4	3 %			
10	Joint shorted: sharings (total)				156	150	6
11	Joint shorted: splinters	200	1	100 %	254	261	7
12	Joint shorted: foreign object	250	1	100 %	199	200	1
13	Joint shorted: shavings (grinding)	5000	1	100 %	10	10	0
14	Sleeper shifted	5000	1	100 %	19	18	1
15	Internal insulation failure	5000	1	100 %			

In detail, Table 1 also shows the predicted and actual number of occurrences of the various failure modes. We observe that most failure modes occur about as frequently as predicted. Furthermore, we consider the total number of failures each year, which the model predicts at 3680 replacements per year, while historical records indicate approx. 3000 joints are purchased. We expect that this difference is due to some failure modes being modeled as needing a complete joint replacement, but which can be repaired by minor maintenance if the degradation has not progressed very far.

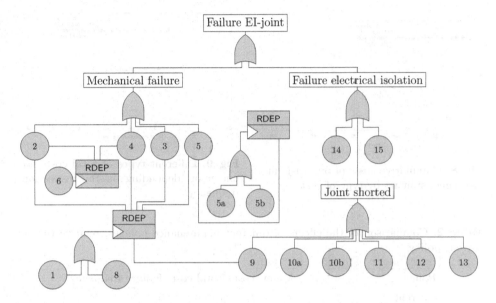

Fig. 7. Fault tree of the electrically insulated railway joint. The numbers in the basic events correspond to those in Table 1.

Figure 8 shows a breakdown of the costs of a joint over a 50-year timespan. We note that the costs increase almost linearly, and thus we do not need to consider a specific time bound when evaluating the annual cost of a maintenance policy.

We now consider alternative maintenance policies where we vary the inspection frequency. The results of this analysis are shown in Fig. 9. As expected, the cost of inspections increases linearly with frequency and the cost of failures decreases but with diminishing returns. The cost for maintenance is nearly constant, as the inspection will only determine whether a repair action is performed before or after failure, but does not change the number of needed repairs.

We find that the optimal inspection frequency is approx. four inspections per year, but the total cost is nearly constant between two and six inspections per year. The current policy lies within this range, so it is as optimal as our model can predict.

Next, we examine several qualitative changes to the maintenance policy. The three changes are: (1) always replacing the entire joint rather than correcting single defects, (2) reducing the threshold for when corrective action is taken after an inspection, and (3) periodically replace the entire joint after a given time rather than waiting for its condition to deteriorate. The results of these policies are shown in Table 2.

We observe that periodic replacements have only a small impact on the failure frequency but incur significant costs, and are thus not useful. Replacing whenever a defect is found is more productive, but still prohibitively expensive. Finally, the reduced threshold cuts the number of failures nearly in half for only a small

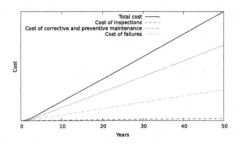

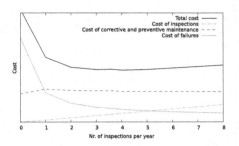

Fig. 8. Cumulative costs of one EI-joint over time, split up by type of cost.

Fig. 9. Different types of total costs for one joint, depending on the inspection frequency.

Table 2. Comparison of the effects of different maintenance policies, relative to the current policy.

Policy	Maint. cost	Total cost	Failure frequency
Current	1	1	1
Replace instead of repair	2.20	1.65	0.76
Reduce threshold by $\frac{1}{3}$	1.49	1.16	0.48
Replace every 5 yrs	2.49	1.85	0.88
Replace every 10 yrs	1.59	1.34	0.96
Replace every 20 yrs	1.30	1.17	0.97

increase in total cost. Nonetheless, since the total cost includes the social costs of the failures, we do not expect this policy to be an improvement overall.

4.2 Pneumatic Compressor

Our second case study concerns the pneumatic compressor used in a Dutch trains of the VIRM type. Each train has one such compressor, which provides compressed air for the operation of the brakes, automatic doors, etc. The systems that operate on this compressed air are designed to be fail-safe (e.g. the brakes are automatically applied when air pressure drops), but a failure of the compressor leaves the train stranded resulting in delays for the passengers.

The model of this compressor was developed in cooperation with NedTrain, the company responsible for maintenance of Dutch trains, among others. For reasons of confidentiality, all times in this section (e.g. failure rates, inspection intervals, etc.) are scaled by a constant factor.

Figure 10 shows the fault tree for the compressor, and the exact failure modes are listed in Table 3.

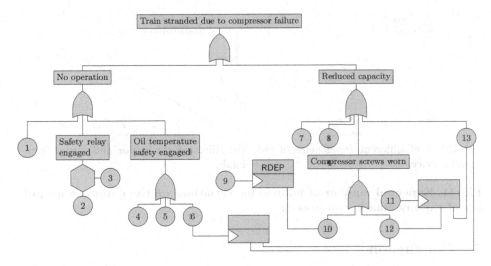

Fig. 10. Fault tree of the pneumatic compressor. The numbers in the basic events correspond to the failure modes in Table 3.

The compressor has a more complex maintenance policy than the EI-joint, with different kinds of inspections and repairs. The policy consists of (1) inspections and minor corrective repairs every two days, (2) more involved check-ups and preventine maintenance every three months, (3) a minor overhaul every three years, and (4) a major overhaul every six years after which the compressor is considered as good as new.

Table 3. Parameters of the failure modes of the compressor. The values have been scaled for anonymity.

Nr.	Failure mode	Nr. of phases	ETTF
1	Motor does not start when asked	3	16.6
2	De-aeration valve defective	3	200
3	Two starts in short time	2	0.001
4	Radiator obstructed	4	5.5
5	Oil thermostat defective	3	16.6
6	Low oil level	4	5.5
7	Pressure valve leakage	3	3.3
8	Air filter obstructed	2	500
9	Degraded air filter	4	5
10	Particle-induced rupture	4	120
11	Oil pollution	4	5.5
12	Lubrication-induced wear	4	120
13	Motor/bearings degraded	4	120

Results. We again consider various alternative maintenance policies, the results of which are shown in Fig. 11. We notice that removing the overhauls has very little effect on the failure rate, which leads us to question their cost-effectiveness (with the caveat that degradation behaviour past the 6-year overhaul time is not known, so nonlinear effects such as metal fatigue may cause a large increase in failure rate). Changing the service interval does have a substantial effect, indicating that this is an important parameter when deciding the policy. Unfortunately, since we do not have information on costs, we cannot show what frequency would be optimal.

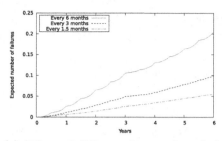
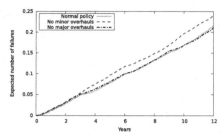

(a) Effect of different frequencies of the small service.

(b) Effect of the minor and major overhauls.

Fig. 11. Expected number of failures for variations on the maintenance policy of the pneumatic compressor.

5   Conclusion

This paper presents the framework of fault maintenance trees, integrating maintenance into fault trees to analyze the dependability of systems under different maintenance regimes.

We have shown how these fault maintenance trees can be analyzed by converting them into priced timed automata and applying statistical model checking. This analysis yields quantitative metrics such as system reliability and expected cost, which can be used to find optimal maintenance strategies.

Two case studies from the railway industry demonstrate that this framework is applicable in practice, and yields results that can be used in decision-making to reduce expenses and improve system dependability.

Acknowledgements. This work has been supported by the STW-ProRail partnership program ExploRail under the project ArRangeer (122238) with participation by Movares.

References

1. Alrabghi, A., Tiwari, A.: State of the art in simulation-based optimisation for maintenance systems. Comput. Ind. Eng. **82**, 167–182 (2015)
2. Arnold, F., Belinfante, A., Van der Berg, F., Guck, D., Stoelinga, M.: DFTCALC: a tool for efficient fault tree analysis. In: Bitsch, F., Guiochet, J., Kaâniche, M. (eds.) SAFECOMP. LNCS, vol. 8153, pp. 293–301. Springer, Heidelberg (2013)
3. Bobbio, A., Codetta-Raiteri, D.: Parametric fault trees with dynamic gates and repair boxes. In: Proceedings Reliability and Maintainability Symposium, pp. 459–465 (2004)
4. Bucci, G., Carnevali, L., Vicario, E.: A tool supporting evaluation of non-Markovian fault trees. In: Proceedings of the 5th International Conference on Quantitative Evaluation of Systems (QEST), pp. 115–116, September 2008
5. Buchacker, K.: Modeling with extended fault trees. In: Proceedings of the 5th IEEE International Symposium on High Assurance Systems Engineering (HASE), pp. 238–246 (2000)

6. Bulychev, P., David, A., Larsen, K.G., M. Mikučionis, D. B. Poulsen, A. Legay, Z. Wang.: UPPAAL-SMC: statistical model checking for priced timed automata. In: Proceedings of the 10th workshop on Quantitative Aspects of Programming Languages (QAPL 2012) (2012)
7. Carnevali, L., Paolieri, M., Tadano, K., Vicario, E.: Towards the quantitative evaluation of phased maintenance procedures using non-Markovian regenerative analysis. In: Balsamo, M.S., Knottenbelt, W.J., Marin, A. (eds.) EPEW 2013. LNCS, vol. 8168, pp. 176–190. Springer, Heidelberg (2013)
8. Codetta-Raiteri, D., Franceschinis, G., Iacono, M., Vittorini, V.: Repairable fault tree for the automatic evaluation of repair policies. In: Proceedings of the International Conference on Dependable Systems and Networks (DSN), pp. 659–668. IEEE (2004)
9. Gits, C.W.: Design of maintenance conceps. Int. J. Prod. Econ. **24**(3), 217–226 (1992)
10. Moubray, J.: Reliability Centered Maintenance. Industrial Press, South Norwalk (1997)
11. Ruijters, E., Guck, D., Drolenga, P., Peters, M., Stoelinga, M.: Maintenance analysis and optimization via statistical model checking: evaluating a train pneumatic compressor. In: Agha, G., Van Houdt, B. (eds.) QEST 2016. LNCS, vol. 9826, pp. 331–347. Springer, Heidelberg (2016). doi:10.1007/978-3-319-43425-4_22
12. Ruijters, E., Guck, D., Drolenga, P., Stoelinga, M.: Fault maintenance trees: reliability centered maintenance via statistical model checking. In: Proceedings Reliability and Maintainability Symposium, January 2016
13. Ruijters, E., Guck, D., van Noort, M., Stoelinga, M.: Reliability-centered maintenance of the electrically insulated railway joint via fault tree analysis: a practical experience report. In: Proceedings of the International Symposium on Dependable Systems and Networks (DSN), pp. 662–669 (2016)
14. Ruijters, E., Stoelinga, M.: Fault tree analysis: a survey of the state-of-the-art in modeling, analysis and tools. Comput. Sci. Rev. **15–16**, 29–62 (2015)
15. Sharma, A., Yadava, G.S., Deshmukh, S.G.: A literature review and future perspectives on maintenance optimization. J. Qual. Maint. Eng. **17**(1), 5–25 (2011)
16. Vesely, W.E., Goldberg, F.F., Roberts, N.H., Haasl, D.F.: Fault Tree Handbook. Office of Nuclear Regulatory Reasearch, U.S. Nuclear Regulatory Commision, North Bethesda (1981)

On Creation and Analysis of Reliability Models by Means of Stochastic Timed Automata and Statistical Model Checking: Principle

Josef Strnadel[✉]

Faculty of Information Technology, Centre of Excellence IT4Innovations,
Brno University of Technology, Bozetechova 2, 612 66 Brno, Czech Republic
strnadel@fit.vutbr.cz
http://www.fit.vutbr.cz/~strnadel

Abstract. The paper presents a method for creation and analysis of reliability models by means of stochastic timed automata and statistical model checking approach available in the UPPAAL SMC tool; its application is expected in, but not limited to, the area of electronic systems. The method can be seen as an alternative to classical analytic approaches based on instruments such as fault-tree or Markov reliability models of the above-specified systems. By the means of the method, reliability analysis of systems can be facilitated even for adverse conditions such as inconstant failure (hazard) rate of system components, various fault scenarios or dependencies among components and/or faults. Moreover, the method is applicable to dynamic, evolvable/reconfigurable systems able to add, remove their components and/or change their parameters at run-time; last but not least, it can be utilized to analyze and study reliability in the context of further system parameters such as liveness, safety and/or timing, power and other, application-specific, constraints. A solution to the related problems is far beyond the scope of recent methods.

Keywords: Reliability · Model · Analysis · Fault tolerant · Stochastic timed automata · Statistical model checking · UPPAAL SMC · Fault · Hazard · Rate

1 Introduction

Technological, parametrical and other progress related to electronic systems has resulted into the rapid expansion of such systems into many application areas, including safety, time and/or mission critical ones such as anti-lock braking or airbag control in cars, avionics, medical devices such as a pacemaker, automated control of an industrial heavy payload robot or a nuclear plant operation. It is a

J. Strnadel—This work was supported by The Ministry of Education, Youth and Sports of the Czech Republic from the National Programme of Sustainability (NPU II); project IT4Innovations excellence in science - LQ1602.

© Springer International Publishing AG 2016
T. Margaria and B. Steffen (Eds.): ISoLA 2016, Part I, LNCS 9952, pp. 166–181, 2016.
DOI: 10.1007/978-3-319-47166-2_11

common practice that a critical system must be designed, constructed, realized and especially analyzed in such a way that, within a given degree of confidence interval or probability interval, its predetermined properties being significant from the criticality point of view (such as a deadlock-free operation or high availability of provided services) are guaranteed during the system operation yet before the system starts to operate in real operating conditions.

For critical systems, it holds that they are constructed for apriori known and well-defined (*fault* and *load*) hypotheses used to specify conditions under which a system must still be able to operate to provide its services as expected. It is typical that such systems are constructed for the *guaranteed* rather than for the *best-effort* response. Thus, the probability of the failure of a perfect system with guaranteed response is reduced to probability (so-called *assumption coverage*) that the assumptions about the peak load and number and types of faults do not hold in reality [1]. Since those systems require careful planning and extensive analysis during the design phase, this paper is limited in this way (i.e., to the design-time modeling and analysis); moreover, it further reduces this complex problem just to reliability of electronic systems, although the proposed concept is general enough to cope with further systems as well.

This paper is organized as follows. Section 2.1 outlines basic terms and principles related to fault tolerance, completed by several illustrations to reliability models of basic fault-tolerant systems. Section 2.2 outlines main attributes of various model checking techniques and in Sect. 2.3, basic ideas related to the timed-automata based modeling in the UPPAAL SMC tool are summarized. Section 3 outlines our method while Sect. 4 presents some results achieved by the method. Finally, Sect. 5 concludes the paper and gives an idea about prospective future research directions based on this paper.

2 Preliminary

Any physical system is a subject to faults (such as aging, stress, radiation, manufacturing defects, poor maintenance etc.). The design of a *reliable* system – such a system can be informally defined as a system able to guarantee continuity of its services – must start with a precise specification of the *fault hypothesis* (utilized to characterize faults that must not affect the services it provides). To guarantee serviceability, the following means can be incorporated into the original, typically non-reliable, design to make the system (more) reliable: *fault avoidance*, with *prevention*, *removal* and *forecast* sub-classes, and *fault tolerance* [2]. Since each of the means is able to affect reliability in a different way, they must be combined to maximize the overall reliability. To save its space, the paper focuses – without any loss of generality – just to the fault tolerance in the next.

2.1 Fault Tolerance

Fault tolerance (*FT*) presumes that a fault can occur rather than it can be avoided before. Basically, FT is carried out by processing and/or treatment of an *error*, i.e. an effect of the associated fault. The *error processing* is based on the *error detection*, followed by the consecutive *recovery*, e.g. by *masking* the presence of a fault by voting over replicated components. The *fault treatment* is able to *passivate* a fault, i.e. prevent it to occur (be activated) again [17]; this can be done e.g. by disabling or reconfiguration of a faulty component or its replacement by a, non-faulty, spare. FT is typically based on some form of redundancy utilized to extend reliability by extra resources; the *redundancy* may be in a hardware, software, information, time, or combinations thereof. For the hardware and software – let us stay just by those in the next –, the following types of redundancy can be distinguished: *static* (sometimes called *passive*), *dynamic* (sometimes called *active*), and *hybrid* [16].

The *static redundancy* masks a fault e.g. by taking a majority of the results being produced by three replicas of the same module (*Triple Modular Redundancy, TMR*). For TMR, it is typical that the replicas are operational (active) and the majority is processed by a *voter*. The voter is a *single point of a failure (SPF)*, i.e. if it does not operate correctly then its output may be incorrect despite of the fault-free operation of the replicas. An illustration to the Markov (reliability) model of TMR can be seen in the left part of Fig. 1a. It is assumed here that the modules operate independently and a module can fail with probability given by, typically constant, *failure rate* (λ). Initially (state 1), the system is fault-free, i.e. its all three modules operate correctly. If one of them fails, probability of which equals to 3λ then the model transits to its state 2. If one of the remaining fault-free modules fails while the model is in the state 2 (this may happen with probability equal to 2λ) then the model transits to the state 3 in which an error cannot be detected since just one module is fault-free. In this state a fault cannot be tolerated, which may result into a failure (a state potentially resulting into a failure is visualized using a bold-lined circle). The model aims to enumerate probability of a failure, i.e. probability of entering into the bold-lined state. The right part of Fig. 1a models an SPF in the state 1; an SPF, such as a fault (e.g., a short) in the power distribution in one of the modules, may lead to a failure although the remaining two modules are fault-free.

a) TMR w.o. resp. with SPF on the left (TMR$_{NSF}$) resp. right (TMR$_{1SF}$)

b) Triplex with successive degradation (TSD)

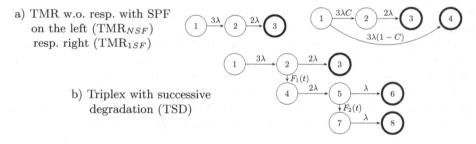

Fig. 1. Markov (reliability) models of selected FT systems based on the static redundancy (a) and the dynamic reconfiguration by degradation (b). λ is the permanent-failure rate, $F_1(t)$, $F_2(t)$ are used to model the removal of a permanent fault, C is the ratio of non-SPF faults and t is the actual time instant; for more see [18]

For the *dynamic redundancy*, it is typical that on top of the operational, *primary* module, one or more of its *spare* (*backup*) modules stays in the *active* (*hot*), *warm* (*standby*) or *cold* mode until the primary module fails. For that purpose, each module must be associated with the corresponding error-detection circuitry able to signalize whether the module is faulty or not. The signal is processed by a component called *switch* that is able to (locally) isolate the fault to avoid propagation of its effects. After finishing the isolation phase, the switch replaces the faulty module by one of its spares and consequently, remaining system assets are reconfigured to operate with the spare. For example, let us suppose that the model in Fig. 1b is in state 2, in which one of the two scenarios may happen: (i) a fault may occur with probability 2λ, resulting into a failure being represented by the state 3, (ii) before such a fault occurs, the faulty module is replaced by a spare, probability of which is given by $F_1(t)$ and the model enters the state 4. Alike, the second spare can be utilized in the state 5 to replace the second faulty module (state 7). If the second spare is not operational before the third module fails, a failure may occur (state 6). Finally, the state 8 is entered when the primary module or one of the two spares fails. *Hybrid redundancy* combines both static and dynamic redundancy so that any disagreement among replicas leads to replacement of the faulty replica(s) by spare(s) from the common pool of spares, as long as the pool is not exhausted.

2.2   Model Checking

Various techniques can be utilized to check whether particular properties (such as probability of a failure) are guaranteed under a given model of a system; in this paper it is supposed that so-called *model checking* (MC) technique [3] is utilized for that purpose. Contrary to testing, MC can identify all potential bugs in a system; this allows a designer to deal with the bugs yet in early phases of the system's life cycle. MC has been implemented in powerful tools such as SPIN [4] or SMV [5] being successfully applied in practice. Classical MC techniques are binary, i.e. they check whether a system satisfies a property or not, and exhaustive, i.e. they analyze the state space exhaustively to check the satisfaction. Indeed, in many situations it is not enough to know whether something could or could not happen; rather, one needs to have a precise estimate of the time when some situation could arise. This motivated the creation of a number of new, so-called timed MC techniques. However, even though various optimizations and/or heuristics exist (partial order, symbolic approach etc.) they cannot prevent MC techniques from the state-space explosion in general due to problems they solve. To avoid the exhaustive exploration of the state-space of a model, so-called *statistical model checking* (SMC) has been proposed. Simply, SMC is design to monitor some simulations of a system and to process them statistically (e.g., using the sequential hypothesis testing or Monte Carlo simulation) in order to estimate the satisfaction probability of a specified property under some degree of confidence. SMC is implemented in tools such as PRISM [6] or UPPAAL SMC [7] as a compromise between the testing and classical MC techniques; it is known to be far less memory/time intensive than the classical MC, and is oftentimes the only option to approximate undecidable problems. SMC has been applied to problems that are far beyond the scope of classical MC and it has been widely accepted in areas such as biology [7], software engineering [8,9], aerospace applications [10,11] or system analysis [6,12–15].

2.3   Concepts of Modeling in UPPAAL and UPPAAL SMC

UPPAAL [19] is a toolbox primarily designed for the formal verification of *real-time* (RT) systems modeled by (a network of) *Timed Automata* (TA) extended with instruments such as typed variables and channel synchronization. SMC extension of UPPAAL, denoted as UPPAAL SMC, has been proposed [20] to avoid the state-space explosion w.r.t. checking properties of RT systems. The modeling formalism of UPPAAL SMC is based on a stochastic extension of the original TA formalism. On basis of the extension, called *Stochastic Timed Automata* (STA), one can validate properties of a given deterministic or stochastic system in the given stochastic environment or conditions such as radiation or aging. In the next, concepts of (S)TA-based modeling are informally outlined.

First of all, it should be noted that a TA [21] is formed of at least the start state, represented by two concentric circles (e.g. the state a in Fig. 2); a state of a TA is called a *location* too. A transition between two locations (e.g. from a to b, denoted by $a \rightarrow b$) is represented by an oriented edge from a to b. While the transition in Fig. 2a can be made anytime (but the concrete time is unknown), the transition in Fig. 2b, being conditioned by so-called *guard* (where x is a variable of the clock type), can be made if x is 5 or later, but again – no upper bound is specified for x. In Fig. 2c, the maximum time of staying in a is limited by so-called *invariant*, i.e., an upper-bound condition, over a variable of the clock type, defined for a location. In Fig. 2d, a guard/invariant combination is utilized to model a transition that can be made if $x \geq 5$, but must be made if $x \leq 7$, i.e., can be made if $5 \leq x \leq 7$. Description of further TA instruments related to communication via channels, location types etc. is omitted herein because of the limited scope of this paper and no meaning for the planned illustrative examples.

Fig. 2. Illustration to the basic TA terms: place, transition, guard, invariant

The above-mentioned principles as well as the non-deterministic behavior of TAs (e.g. a choice among multiple transitions between two locations) are refined in STAs by stochastic ones, being briefly illustrated in the next. For example, the annotations on STA locations are extended to describe the time of staying in a location by means of a probability distribution; in Fig. 3a, the time of staying in a (i.e., entering b) is given by the exponential distribution with the rate (λ) set to $\frac{1}{2}$. In Fig. 3b, the probabilistic uniform-distribution choice between $a \rightarrow b$ (with probability $\frac{1}{5}$) and $a \rightarrow c$ (with probability $\frac{4}{5}$) is modeled. Figure 3c illustrates the following (so-called *stopwatch*) concept able to determine the exact time that has elapsed. During $a \rightarrow b$, the clock x is reset along with setting a value, produced by a user-defined function f, to the *delay* variable of the clock type. Staying in b cannot take longer than *delay* units of time, whereas the time is measured using x while *delay* is stopped by $delay' == 0$. Thus, $b \rightarrow c$ is possible just if x matches *delay*.

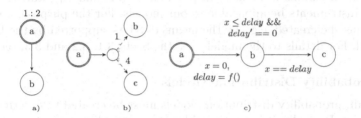

Fig. 3. Illustration to the basic STA instruments

Properties of an STA-based model can be checked using special queries a user can post in the UPPAAL SMC tool w.r.t. model [20]; among others, queries in the following basic forms are supported: (i) *probability estimation* in the form $Pr[bound](\phi)$ for getting probability that something (ϕ) – such as entering a state/place – happens under the specified *bound*, (ii) *hypothesis testing* in the form $Pr[bound](\phi) \geq p$ for checking whether probability of something (ϕ) is greater or equal to a certain probability threshold (p) under the specified *bound*, (iii) *probability comparison* in the form $Pr[bound_1](\phi_1) \geq Pr[boun-d_2](\phi_2)$ for checking whether probability of ϕ_1 is greater or equal to ϕ_2 under the specified $bound_1$, $bound_2$, where *bound*, $bound_1$, $bound_2$ define how to bound, e.g. the number of, simulation runs, ϕ, ϕ_1, ϕ_2 are assertions to check and p is a real-number value. E.g., for Fig. 3a one can post the Pr[<=3000](<> STA.b) query to get probability of eventual entering the state b within 3000 units of the simulation time. A possible (probabilistic) result of the query is visualized in Fig. 4.

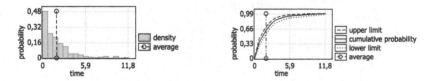

Fig. 4. Illustration to probability of entering b (left) and cumulative probability with confidence intervals (right) of that for the STA model from Fig. 3a

3   Proposed Method

The method presented in this paper has been initially inspired by [22] giving an idea of creating a model of basic components for constructing FT systems to verify their properties by means of the formal verification in classical UPPAAL. However, the approach was based on a timed, but deterministic, model and exhaustive verification with binary decisions about the satisfaction of the properties. We have decided to utilize a completely different approach, allowing (i) creation of probabilistic models, inspired by Fig. 1, and (ii) statistical model checking instruments be applicable to our models. For the purpose, a couple of models must be created, e.g., by the means of STAs supported by the UPPAAL SMC tool. For details to the models, see the Sects. 3.1, 3.2 and 3.3, please.

3.1   Probability Distribution Models

First of all, probability distribution models must be created to describe various failure rates. Basically, it is not a problem to create almost any time-dependent failure rate function; but, due to the limited space in this paper, just a simplified model of the typical *bathtub* curve (see Fig. 5a) is discussed since to model such a shape is a problem in itself [23]. The curve consists of several regions [2, 16] – such as *early (infant mortality), constant, aging, wear out, break in* –, each defining how the rate evolves in particular parts of a system's life cycle. For example, it is typical that probability of a failure decreases exponentially in the early region, while it does not change much in the constant region (the life time of a product is typically situated into that region since the rate is well-bounded and the product can be constructed for that); finally, in the wear-out region, probability of a failure increases exponentially. The problem is that most of the actual reliability-analysis methods are constructed so that they are practically applicable just to the constant region.

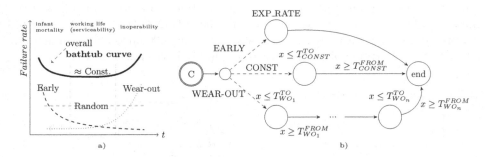

Fig. 5. Bathtub: (a) its shape and key regions, (b) idea of composing the probability distribution model by means of STAs

The skeleton of our STA-based model of the bathtub can be seen in Fig. 5b, where x is the clock-type variable, EARLY, CONST and WEAR-OUT are probability weights corresponding to the associated regions, EXP_RATE is the rate of the exponential distribution of probability and T^{FROM}_{CONST}, T^{TO}_{CONST}, $T^{FROM}_{WO_i}$, $T^{TO}_{WO_i}$, $i = 1, \ldots, n$, are constants specific to the particular bathtub's region. In principle, a separate branch exists in the model for each region; from its initial state, the STA can transit into one of the three consecutive states, starting the associated branch. Each of the states is enabled with different probability – typically, low probability is utilized for the early and wear out regions, while high probability is utilized for the constant region. The time interval in which a fault can appear is limited later in the particular branch.

For example, a failure from the early region occurs rarely and in short time – this is guaranteed by the low ($EARLY$) probability weight, and with the exponential distribution of probability defined by EXP_RATE. Alike, a failure from the constant region occurs more often, being achieved by the high value of ($CONST$), rate of which is uniformly distributed in the $<T^{FROM}_{CONST}, T^{TO}_{CONST}>$ interval, with a lower resp. upper bound defined by a guard resp. invariant (Fig. 2d). In the same sense, the shape for the wear-out region is formed using a chain of consequent uniform distributions of probability.

3.2 Fault Generation Models

In the next step, it is necessary to create models of fault generators. A fault generator is utilized to produce a fault at the desired rate, i.e. in time instants given by a probability distribution model (such as from 3.1) that corresponds to the rate. When the time comes for the occurrence of a fault, the fault is introduced so that an instance of the STA, representing the behavioral model of the fault, is dynamically created (see Sect. 3.3). To create a fault dynamically, the *spawn* keyword must be utilized in STA. This kind of modeling is very close to the reality: after a fault is introduced into a system, it can remain there for a predetermined time and then disappear and do not show again for some time (a *transient fault*) or occur/disappear repeatedly (an *intermittent fault*) or, a fault may last until it is removed (a *permanent fault*), timing of which may vary across faults of the same type [2,16]. In Fig. 6, an example to the dynamic creation of faults with the rates described using (a) exponential resp. (b) constant, i.e. uniform, distributions of probabilities of their arrivals is given.

Fig. 6. Illustration to dynamic creation of faults with their rates described using the (a) exponential resp. (b) constant distribution of probability. `factive[gid]` is utilized as a counter of the number of active faults dynamically created by the generator identified by *gid*. For better readability, `fid[gid]` is substituted by N

For the bathtub case, the *spawn* construction will be applied to the *end* state of the STA from Fig. 5. Let it be noted there that a fault can be characterized by an extendable set of parameters such as its type or probabilistic attributes related to the time of occurrence/disappearance of a fault; such an information is stored in the t_sFault structure (Listing 1.1).

Listing 1.1. Basic parameters/attributes of a fault

```
1   typedef struct {     // fault:
2       t_ftype ft;      // - type: 0-permanent, 1-transient, 2-intermittent
3       t_ttf ttf;       // - time to (occurrence of a) fault: 0, 1, ...
4       t_pdist pttf;    // - probab. distr.: 0-uni., 1-exp.,
5       //                                 2-norm., 3-bathtub, 4-early, ...
6       t_ttd ttd;       // - time to disappear: 0, 1, ...
7       t_pdist pttd;    // - probab. distr.: 0-uni., 1-exp., ...
8   } t_sFault;
```

On basis of the structure, particular templates of faults can be described using the fdef[] array (Listing 1.2) to define a set of faults utilizable in further parts of a model.

Listing 1.2. Definition of the fault templates

```
1   const t_sFault fdef[t_nfault] = {
2   //   ft      ttf      pttf      ttd     pttd    array-index
3        {1,     100,       0,      100,       0},     // 0
4        {0,     500,       0,      500,       0},     // 1
5        {1,       1,       1,        1,       1},     // 2
6        {1,       5,       1,        5,       1}      // 3
7   };
```

Particularly, the templates can be utilized to choose instances of faults to be introduced into the simulation model (Listing 1.3). For that purpose, the mapping represented by the fid[] array is utilized to make a relation between (the generator of) a fault and its template. Using fid[], a fault of the corresponding template can be introduced into the simulation model, whereas one template might be reused to introduce multiple fault-instances of the same template.

Listing 1.3. Mapping the index of a fault generator (gid) onto the index to fdef[]

```
1   // generator indexes (gid): 0  1  2 ...
2   t_nfault fid[t_ngen] =    { 0, 1, 1 };  // indexes to fdef[]
```

Let a realization of such a mapping be illustrated using Listing 1.3 – by means of fid[], each of the three fault generators (indexed by 0, 1, 2) is mapped to a fault it is associated to, i.e. fid[0]=0 means that the generator indexed by 0 is associated to the fault defined by fdef[0], i.e. 3rd row of Listing 1.2, whereas fid[1]=1 and fid[2]=1 mean that the generators indexed by 1 and 2 are associated with the fault defined by fdef[1], i.e. 4th row of Listing 1.2.

3.3   Fault Behavior Models

After a fault is introduced (by the generator identified by gid), it behaves in a way that can be expressed in the form of an STA. In Fig. 7, a skeleton of the behavioral model for intermittent, permanent and transient faults is illustrated, focusing to the branch for transient faults. Attributes of a fault, stored in t_sFault, are accessed using fdef[fid[gid]]. On basis of ft, stored in the attributes, a transition from the initial state is enabled for a particular value of ft, i.e. the type of a fault ($F_{PERM} == 0$, $F_{TRAN} == 1$ or $F_{INTER} == 2$). In the next state, a branch for modeling the fault's lifetime is chosen on basis of pttd (P_{UNI} resp. P_{EXP} for uniform resp. exponential probability distribution specified by ttd, using the STA design patterns from Fig. 2d resp. Fig. 3a).

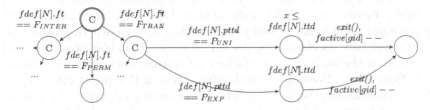

Fig. 7. Illustration to the behavioral, STA-based model of a fault. After its duration is over, a dynamically created transient fault removes itself from a system by calling exit() and decreasing the number (factive[gid]) of active faults introduced by the corresponding generator. For better readability, fid[gid] is substituted by N

Before reliability models (inspired by Fig. 1) can be created on basis of the above-mentioned modeling techniques, an instrument able to signalize the occurrence of a fault is needed to make the construction of reliability models as straightforward as possible. In our approach, we have based the signalization mechanism on the STA from Fig. 8.

The mechanism (see Fig. 8) relies on continuous sending a message via the array fail[] of broadcast channels, each of being reserved for a particular generator identified by gid. The idea is as follows: a fault, produced by the generator with gid, sends a signal via the fault[gid] channel until the fault disappears (i.e., while it is active). If ! resp. ? follows the channel name (i.e., fail[gid]! resp. fail[gid]? is associated with a transition) then a message is sent resp. expected via the fail[gid] channel reserved for the generator with gid.

$$x \leq 1$$

$$factive[gid] \leq 0 \qquad\qquad factive[gid] > 0$$
$$x = 0 \qquad\qquad\qquad fail[gid]!, x = 0$$

Fig. 8. Illustration to the mechanism utilized to signalize a fault

3.4   Reliability Models

In the next, a method for construction of reliability models by means of the above-mentioned modeling techniques is described. To create a reliability model, definitions of considered faults must be prepared (such as in Listing 1.2) first in fdef[]. Then, a decision about the number of fault generators – each able to produce a fault of a given definition – must be made and stored into fid[]. Let it be noted that it is possible to create multiple generators for the same fault definition; for example, in Listing 1.3 three generators are utilized, where generator identified by gid=0 is associated with the fault definition fdef[gid] = (1, 0, 100), i.e. a transient fault with probability of its ocurence uniformly distributed over 100 units of time while generators identified by gid=1 and gid=2 are associated with fdef[gid] = (0, 0, 500), i.e. a permanent fault with uniform probability distribution over 500 units of time. Once STA-based models for the fault generator, fault behavior and fault signalization are created, process of creation of a reliability model can be started. In the next, an idea of such a process is discussed in the form of a straightforward transformation from the classical models from Fig. 1. Because of the limited space in this paper and simplicity of the transformation, the resulting STA-based models are omitted herein. Key principle w.r.t. our model relies on replacing λ – or similar probabilistic quantity such as $F_1(t)$, $F_2(t)$, from Fig. 1 – in a Markov model by waiting for a message on the fail[N] channel (Fig. 9).

Fig. 9. Principle of converting a Markov model (a) to an STA model (b). N identifies a generator producing a fault the edge is sensitive to

With no impact to the generality, all important design patterns w.r.t reliability models can be presented over a simple TMR model from Fig. 1a. Basically, a separate fault generator is needed for each of independent faults (TMR_{NSF} from Figs. 1a and 10a) – in such a case, separate fault signalization mechanisms are available. On the contrary, signalization of the same fault can be utilized e.g. to model a SPF (TMR_{1SF} from Fig. 1a, Fig. 10b). STA-based versions of the TMR are depicted in Fig. 10. In (a), the $1 \rightarrow 2$ transition is utilized to wait for a reception of a signal over three channels, i.e., fail[i], $i = 1, 2, 3$, each belonging to one of the three replicas in the TMR system. If a fail signal is received on a particular channel then the corresponding value of i is stored into $failed$ to identify the failed replica. The consecutive $2 \rightarrow 3$ is sensitive just to a failure in replicas identified by $i = 1, 2, 3$, $i \neq failed$, i.e., it is sensitive just to a failure of the remaining two replicas.

The same principle is applied in the case (b), extended to model a SPF by means of a probabilistic choice made at the end of the transition outgoing from 1, i.e., after one of the three replicas fails; then, TMR can either operate in a two-replica mode (if it transits to 2; here, it operates in the same way as in the (a) case) or it can be a subject to a SPF and fail (if it goes to 4).

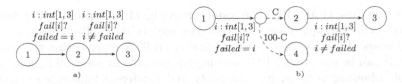

Fig. 10. STA-based realization of the TMR models from Fig. 1: (a) TMR_{NSF}, (b) TMR_{1SF}. C is probability that a fault is not SPF

4   Evaluation

To show practical applicability of our above-mentioned modeling techniques and its benefits, we have decided to present few results produced on basis of our

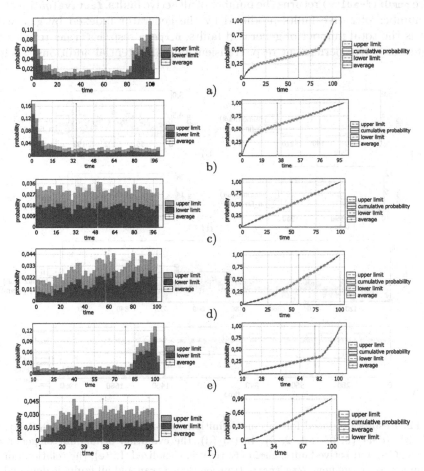

Fig. 11. Illustration to probability (left) and cumulative probability (right) with confidence intervals for selected failure rates models realized by means of UPPAAL SMC: (a) bathtub, (b) early (infant mortality), (c) constant, (d) aging, (e) wear out, (f) break-in

models (see Figs. 11 and 12). The results from Fig. 11 were produced on basis of the model-checking query Pr[<=100](<> sta.end) being applied consequently to special cases of the Fig. 5; *sta* is the name of an STA representing the bathtub model. It can be seen that STA-based models are able to cover all regions of the bathtub, allowing us to analyze reliability under different fault rate scenarios.

The results from Fig. 12 have been achieved on basis of several queries, details of which follows; in all cases, one simulation run has been performed, which is denoted by simulate 1 at the beginning of the queries. For (a) – (d), the query simulate 1 [<=N] {numOf(fault), n_fin/K} has been utilized with $N = 200$ resp. $N = 2000$ for (a), (b) resp. (c), (d) and $K = 1, 50, 100, 200$ for (a), (b), (c), (d). For 12e) resp. (f), simulate 1 [<=1000] {numOf(fault), 2*n_fperm, n_ftrans} resp. simulate 1 [<=2000] {factive[0], 10+factive[1], 20+factive[2], 30+factiv-e[3], 40+factive[4], 50+factive[5]} queries have been utilized, where numOf(f-aults) returns the number of all active faults, factive[*gid*] returns the number of active faults produced by the generator indexed by gid, n_fin returns the total number of generated faults, n_fperm resp. n_ftrans returns the number of active permanent resp. transient faults. Potential additions (such as

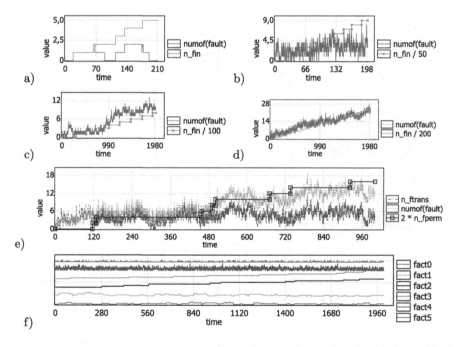

Fig. 12. Results produced for various definitions of fid[]: (a) {0}, (b) {0, 2, 3}, (c) {0, 1, 3}, (d–f) {0, 0, 1, 1, 2, 3}. In (a)–(d), the evolution of amount of generated faults, n_fin, and active faults, numOf(fault), is visualized. In (e), the relation among the number of permanent, 2*n_fperm, transient 2*n_ftran and all faults is depicted. In (f), the evolution of amount of active faults (fact*i*) produced by the particular fault generator, indexed by $i = 0, 1, \ldots, 5$, is visualized

`10+factive[1]`) or multiplications (such as `2*n_fperm`) are utilized to define an offset for particular curves in order to make the corresponding charts more expressive.

Benefits of utilizing modeling instruments proposed in this paper can be summarized as follows. First, our models are scalable and our solution is open to additions – proposed models can be easily extended to further types of fault rates, behavior types etc. Moreover, our approach can be utilized to analyze properties of systems (i) with variable failure rates described e.g. by means of the complete bathtub curve(s) rather than just by their isolated portions, (ii) formed of dependent components or prone to dependent faults, (iii) dynamic, evolvable/reconfigurable systems able to add, remove their components and/or change their parameters at run-time, (iv) in the context of further parameters such as liveliness, safety and/or timing, power and other constraints. Second, model checking engine in the UPPAAL SMC tool can be utilized to simply check key properties (such as probability that something, like a failure, may happen) w.r.t. a system being modeled. Third, transformation of existing reliability models (such as widely-utilized Markov models) is straightforward and there is no need to solve any system of equation by your own. It can be concluded that the benefits represent a very good prerequisite for rapid prototyping and reliability analysis of FT systems under various fault scenarios and applied FT techniques.

5   Conclusion

In the paper, a method of creation and analysis of reliability models by means of the STAs and SMC approach supported by the UPPAAL SMC tool has been presented. The method allows more precise and close-to-reality modeling comparing to classical approaches such as Markov reliability models. Further activity w.r.t. topic of the paper can be seen especially in

- designing a model of a general, parameterizable shape of the bathtub curve by means of UPPAAL SMC,
- applying the proposed method to complex, practical FT systems, systems with dynamic redundancy and hybrid (i.e., discrete/continuous) systems,
- reliability analysis through multiple bathtub regions and of particular system classes such as memories, CPU cores or operating system kernels,
- analyzing an impact of multiple faults of same/different type to reliability of an FT system equipped by particular FT techniques.

References

1. Kopetz, H.: Real-Time Systems - Design Principles for Distributed Embedded Applications. Real-Time Systems. Springer, New York (2011). doi:10.1007/978-1-4419-8237-7
2. Geffroy, J.C., Motet, G.: Design of Dependable Computing Systems. Springer, Dordrecht (2002). doi:10.1007/978-94-015-9884-2
3. Baier, C., Katoen, J.-P.: Principles of Model Checking. MIT Press, Cambridge (2008)

180   J. Strnadel

4. Holzmann, G.J.: The model checker SPIN. IEEE Trans. Softw. Eng. **23**(5), 279–295 (1997). doi:10.1109/32.588521
5. McMillan, K.L.: Symbolic model checking: an approach to the state explosion problem. Ph.D. thesis, Carnegie Mellon University (1992)
6. Kwiatkowska, M., Norman, G., Parker, D.: PRISM: probabilistic model checking for performance and reliability analysis. SIGMETRICS Perform. Eval. Rev. **36**(4), 40–45 (2009). doi:10.1145/1530873.1530882
7. David, A., Larsen, K.G., Legay, A., Mikucionis, M., Poulsen, D.B., Sedwards, S.: Statistical model checking for biological systems. Int. J. Softw. Tools Technol. Transf. **17**(3), 351–367 (2015). doi:10.1007/s10009-014-0323-4
8. Dubslaff, C., Klüppelholz, S., Baier, C.: Probabilistic model checking for energy analysis in software product lines. In: 13th International Conference on Modularity, pp. 169–180. ACM, New York (2014). doi:10.1145/2577080.2577095
9. Calinescu, R., Ghezzi, C., Johnson, K., Pezze, M., Rafiq, Y., Tamburrelli, G.: Formal verification with confidence intervals to establish quality of service properties of software systems. IEEE Trans. Reliab. **65**(1), 107–125 (2015). doi:10.1109/TR.2015.2452931
10. Hoque, K.A., Mohamed, O.A., Savaria, Y., Thibeault, C.: Early analysis of soft error effects for aerospace applications using probabilistic model checking. In: Artho, C., Ölveczky, P.C. (eds.) FTSCS 2013. CCIS, vol. 419, pp. 54–70. Springer, Heidelberg (2014). doi:10.1007/978-3-319-05416-2_5
11. Lu, Y., Peng, Z., Miller, A.A., Zhao, T., Johnson, C.W.: How reliable is satellite navigation for aviation? Checking availability properties with probabilistic verification. Reliab. Eng. Syst. Saf. **144**, 95–116 (2015). doi:10.1016/j.ress.2015.07.020
12. Benes, N., Buhnova, B., Cerna, I., Oslejsek, R.: Reliability analysis in component-based development via probabilistic model checking. In: 15th ACM SIGSOFT Symposium on Component Based Software Engineering, pp. 83–92. ACM, New York (2012). doi:10.1145/2304736.2304752
13. Basu, A., Bensalem, S., Bozga, M., Delahaye, B., Legay, A.: Statistical abstraction and model-checking of large heterogeneous systems. Int. J. Softw. Tools Technol. Transf. **14**(1), 53–72 (2012). doi:10.1007/s10009-011-0201-2
14. Peng, Z., Lu, Y., Miller, A., Johnson, C., Zhao, T.: A probabilistic model checking approach to analysing reliability, availability, and maintainability of a single satellite system. In: European Modelling Symposium, pp. 611–616. IEEE (2013). doi:10.1109/EMS.2013.102
15. Swain, P., Bhaduri, P., Nandi, S.: Probabilistic model checking of IEEE 802.11 IBSS power save mode. Int. J. Wirel. Mob. Comput. **7**(5), 465–474 (2014). doi:10.1504/IJWMC.2014.064818
16. Koren, I., Krishna, C.M.: Fault-Tolerant Systems. Morgan Kaufmann Publishers, San Francisco (2007)
17. Laprie, J.-C.: Dependable computing: concepts, limits, challenges. In: 25th International Conference on Fault-Tolerant Computing, pp. 42–54. IEEE Computer Society, Washington (1995)
18. Butler, R.W., Johnson, S.C.: Techniques for modeling the reliability of fault-tolerant systems with the Markov state-space approach. NASA Reference Publication 1348 (1995). http://shemesh.larc.nasa.gov/fm/papers/Butler-RP-1348-Techniques-Model_Rel-FT.pdf
19. Behrmann, G., David, A., Larsen, K.G.: A tutorial on UPPAAL. In: Bernardo, M., Corradini, F. (eds.) SFM-RT 2004. LNCS, vol. 3185, pp. 200–236. Springer, Heidelberg (2004)

20. David, A., Larsen, K., Legay, A., Mikuionis, M., Poulsen, D.: Uppaal SMC tutorial. Int. J. Softw. Tools Technol. Transf. **17**(4), 397–415 (2015). doi:10.1007/s10009-014-0361-y
21. Alur, R., Dill, D.L.: A theory of timed automata. Theor. Comput. Sci. **126**(2), 183–235 (1994). doi:10.1016/0304-3975(94)90010-8
22. Zhang, M., Liu, Z., Morisset, C., Ravn, A.P.: Design and verification of fault-tolerant components. In: Butler, M., Jones, C., Romanovsky, A., Troubitsyna, E. (eds.) Methods, Models and Tools for Fault Tolerance. LNCS, vol. 5454, pp. 57–84. Springer, Heidelberg (2009). doi:10.1007/978-3-642-00867-2_4
23. Zhang, T., Dwight, R., El-Akruti, K.: On a Weibull related distribution model with decreasing, increasing and upside-down bathtub-shaped failure rate. In: Reliability and Maintainability Symposium, pp. 1–6. IEEE Computer Society, Orlando (2013). doi:10.1109/RAMS.2013.6517749

Automatic Synthesis of Code Using Genetic Programming

Doron Peled$^{(\boxtimes)}$

Department of Computer Science, Bar Ilan University, 52900 Ramat Gan, Israel
doron.peled@gmail.com

Abstract. Correct-by-design automatic system construction can relieve both programmers and quality engineers from part of their tasks. Classical program synthesis involves a series of transformations, starting with the given formal specification. However, this approach is often prohibitively intractable, and in some cases undecidable. Model-checking-based genetic programming provides a method for software synthesis; it uses randomization, together with model checking, to heuristically search for code that satisfies the given specification. We present model checking based genetic programming as an alternative to classical transformational synthesis and study its weakness and strengths.

1 Introduction

Automatic synthesis of correct-by-design code is a very appealing approach. It can assist programmers in producing the hard-to-code parts of systems. Further, the code is already correct with respect to the specification. We are still quite far from achieving this situation. For one, it is not always clear that writing correct and complete specification is easier than programming. Moreover, classical approaches for software synthesis is proved to be doubly exponential for interactive systems [16], and undecidable for concurrent systems [17].

Genetic programming (GP) [12] is a search based software engineering approach [4], i.e., an evolutionary based heuristic search methodology for finding computer programs that perform user defined tasks. In GP, programs are generated and evolved by applying biologically inspired ideas, such as reproduction, mutations, and natural selection. GP uses a fitness function that measures the quality of the candidate solutions generated during the search. GP can also be used to improve programs, e.g., to speeding up the performance of systems [13] or correct erroneous programs [10].

Model-checking based genetic programming (MCGP) [6–10], is basically a search technique that uses model checking as its fitness function (heuristic measure). In [1], model checking was used within a generate-and-test feedback loop in order to construct correct-by-design solutions for the mutual exclusion problem. It exhaustively passes throughout the possible candidates (given some limit on

D. Peled—The research was supported in part by ISF grant 126/12 "Efficient Synthesis Method of Control for Concurrent Systems".

© Springer International Publishing AG 2016
T. Margaria and B. Steffen (Eds.): ISoLA 2016, Part I, LNCS 9952, pp. 182–187, 2016.
DOI: 10.1007/978-3-319-47166-2_12

the resources), revealing the correct solutions. MCGP offers a heuristic, rather than exhaustive, search through candidates. It utilizes randomness in initially generating the candidates and in progressing between them.

One of the main obstacles in using MCGP is that the fitness function of GP requires a good separation between different candidates. The fitness function provides a measure for how far the candidate program is from completely satisfying the complete specification, and needs to separate between stronger and weaker candidates. However, it is hard to attain this goal based on model checking, as there are often a very limited number of specification properties. This makes the landscape of the fitness function discrete rather than smooth. We discuss how this problem can be alleviated.

The traditional use of a large test suite can provide a smother fitness function. The test suite can use standard manual testing techniques to generate a test suite that captures a large set of expected problems. However, it does not guarantee the correctness of the constructed code, and the set of test cases may prove itself to be biased.

In contrast, in transformational synthesis of reactive systems [16], even a single specification property is sufficient. This consists of translating the specification(s) into an automaton determinizing it, finding a game strategy such that the system will be able to make good choices in response to the choices of the environment.

2   Preliminaries

Model Checking of Temporal Properties

Model checking [2] is an automatic method for verifying the correctness of a finite state software or hardware system against its formal specification. It is often used to verify models of concurrent algorithms, protocols and reactive systems. Such models usually have many possible executions, due to concurrency and nondeterministic choices made by scheduling or interacting with the environment.

A finite state system can be modeled by an automaton. Each *state* of the automaton corresponds to an evaluation of the variables, programs counters, communication buffers of the system. An *execution* is then a maximal sequence of *states*, starting from some *initial* state; *transitions* between subsequent states represent the effect of atomic actions of the system. Propositions are used to represent properties of states, e.g., p may hold in states where $x > 0$ and q in states where the program is at the beginning of its first loop. The specification can be written as a set of properties in a logic such as *Linear Temporal Logic* (LTL), which combines propositional variables and logic operators with temporal operators. For example, $\Box p$ stands for 'p holds in every state' (in the execution) and $\Diamond q$ stands for 'q holds in some future state'.

A standard model checking procedure checks whether a system M satisfies a specification φ. The specification φ is often converted into automata A_φ over infinite words [3]. The simplest kind of such automata is called Büchi automata [19];

an infinite word (representing in our context an execution) is *accepted* if in a run
of the automaton over that word, at least one of a set of states that are distinguished as *accepting* occurs infinitely many times. For some LTL specifications
such as $\Diamond\Box p$ ('*p* holds for some state forever'), the translation necessarily results
in a nondeterministic Büchi automaton [19]. In transformational synthesis, this
nondeterminism needs to be removed by a further transformation into another
kind of automata [18].

The specification automaton represents all of the executions (abstracted
as sequences of propositional values) *allowed* by the specification properties.
The model checking algorithm then checks whether the language of the model
automaton is *contained* in the language of the specification automaton. If this
holds, then the checked property is satisfied by the model. Otherwise, there are
executions of the model that violate the specification.

Genetic Programming

During the 1970s, Holland established the field known as *Genetic Algorithms* [5].
According to this methodology, individual candidate solutions are represented
as fixed length strings of bits, and are manipulated mainly by the *crossover*
and *mutation* genetic operations. The *crossover* operation takes parts of strings
from two parent solutions; it combines them into a new solution, which potentially inherit useful attributes from his parents, and become fitter. The *mutation*
operation randomly alters the content of small number of bits in the string, thus
allowing the insertion of new building blocks (or genes) into the population.

Genetic programming [12] is a direct successor of genetic algorithms. In GP,
each individual "organism" represents a computer program. Thus, instead of
fixed length strings, programs are represented by variable length structures, such
as trees, linear lists or graphs. Each individual solution is built from a set of
functions and terminals, and corresponds to a program or an expression in a
programming language that can be executed. In tree-based genetic programming,
crossover is performed by selecting type compatible subtrees on each of the
parents, and then swapping between them. Mutation can be carried out by
choosing a subtree and replacing it by another randomly generated subtree of the
same type. The fitness is calculated by directly running the generated programs
on a large set of test cases and evaluating the results.

3   Software Synthesis Using Genetic Programming Based on Model Checking

In [7–10], we present a framework combining genetic programming and model
checking that allows to automatically synthesize software code for given problems. The user provides the formal specification of the problem, as well as additional constraints on the structure of the desired solutions.

The synthesis process generally goes through the following steps:

1. The user provides a *configuration*, which is a set of structural constraints on
   the programs that are allowed to be generated (thus, defining the space of
   candidate programs).

2. The user provides a formal specification for the problem. This can be a set of LTL properties, as well as additional requirements on the program behavior.
3. The GP engine randomly generates an initial population of programs based on the configuration.
4. The model checking based verifier analyzes the behavior of the generated programs against the specification properties, and provides fitness measures based on the amount of satisfaction.
5. Based on the verification results, the GP engine then creates new programs by applying genetic operations of crossover and mutation. The next iteration contains the newly generated candidates, and also some of the old candidates that were chosen using a random selection: the probability to remain in the next iteration is based on the relative fitness value. The number of candidate solutions remains invariant between the different iterations.

   Steps 4 and 5 are repeated until either a perfect program is found (fully satisfying the specification), or until the maximal number of iterations is reached.
6. The results are sent back to the user. This includes a program that satisfies all the specification properties, or a failure report.

4 Fitness Functions Based on Model Checking

The shortcomings of transformational synthesis and of testing based GP motivates the MCGP approach. However, in order to make MCGP practical, we need a way of smoothening the fitness function. The result of model checking is binary: yes or no (providing also a counterexample in the latter case). Naively counting the number of properties that are satisfied does not provide a good fitness function, and it will often fail to stir the genetic process towards convergence. It is also not clear that e.g., satisfying the first two properties is better than satisfying the third one. In many cases in fact, the number of properties given is rather small. We present several possibilities to provide more meaningful fitness values for MCGP.

Quantitative levels. The fitness function is made proportional also to the fraction of executions that are correct. For properties based on finite executions or their approximations, one can generate many levels by applying statistical model checking [14]. This approach also helps alleviating the intractability of model checking.

Qualitative levels. One can define meaningful levels of satisfaction of properties that can be verified using variants of model checking. One such level represent the fact that *some* (but not *all*) executions satisfy some property. Another level confines the bad executions to those that are highly improbable, e.g., where the same nondeterministic choices made all the time.

Co-evolution. We can develop test cases along with the genetic process. The fitness of a test case can grow up with the number of candidates that it manages to fail.

5 Experience and Further Work

We discussed MCGP approach. This has been implemented as a prototype tool [11]. In particular, it was used successfully in different cases:

- Finding existing and new solutions for mutual exclusion.
- Finding a solution to the leader election problem in a ring.
- Correcting the α-core algorithm [15].

Implementing MCGP is a comprehensive effort: it consists of the following components:

- Translation between code and syntax tree representation.
- Implementation of model checking and its derivatives (probabilistic model checking, statistical model checking).
- The search engine, including the fitness calculation and the genetic operations of mutation and crossover.

Because the synthesis problem is in general undecidable (in particular, for concurrent systems with LTL specifications), MCGP cannot always guarantee to terminate successfully. Often, after a number of iterations, the user would stop the running of the tool and would restart it either with a new random seed, or by changing parameters. The latter can involve giving different weights for the different properties when calculating the fitness functions. Indeed, while the success cases reported here would for in a few minutes using the tool, tuning the parameters until this has started to happen often took days or weeks.

In [10] a broad approach to co-evolution is presented. There, the goal is to use MCGP to correct a large, parametric, communication protocol [15]. While model checking is undecidable for parametric (e.g., in the communication architecture) programs, it can be seen as a generalization of testing: each particular communication architecture forms an instance of model checking; hence model checking is exhaustive against the *particular chosen architectures*. The different architectures are also generated using the genetic programming techniques (e.g., using mutation). The more useful architectures (based on causing candidate programs to fail) are kept from generation to generation for checking against further candidates.

References

1. Bar-David, Y., Taubenfeld, G.: Automatic discovery of mutual exclusion algorithms. In PODC, p. 305 (2003)
2. Clarke, E.M., Grumberg, O., Peled, D.A.: Model Checking. The MIT Press, Cambridge (2000)
3. Gerth, R., Peled, D., Vardi, M.Y., Wolper, P.: Simple on-the-fly automatic verification of linear temporal logic. In: Dembiński, P., Średniawa, M. (eds.) IFIP WG6.1. IFIP, pp. 3–18. Springer, Heidelberg (1995)
4. Harman, M., Jones, B.F.: Software engineering using metaheuristic innovative algorithms: workshop report. Inf. Softw. Technol. 43(14), 905–907 (2001)

5. Holland, J.H.: Adaptation in Natural and Artificial Systems: An Introductory Analysis with Applications to Biology, Control and Artificial Intelligence. MIT Press, Cambridge (1992)
6. Johnson, C.G.: Genetic programming with fitness based on model checking. In: Ebner, M., O'Neill, M., Ekárt, A., Vanneschi, L., Esparcia-Alcázar, A.I. (eds.) EuroGP 2007. LNCS, vol. 4445, pp. 114–124. Springer, Heidelberg (2007)
7. Katz, G., Peled, D.A.: Genetic Programming and model checking: synthesizing new mutual exclusion algorithms. In: Cha, S.S., Choi, J.-Y., Kim, M., Lee, I., Viswanathan, M. (eds.) ATVA 2008. LNCS, vol. 5311, pp. 33–47. Springer, Heidelberg (2008)
8. Katz, G., Peled, D.: Model checking-based genetic programming with an application to mutual exclusion. In: Ramakrishnan, C.R., Rehof, J. (eds.) TACAS 2008. LNCS, vol. 4963, pp. 141–156. Springer, Heidelberg (2008). doi:10.1007/978-3-540-78800-3_11
9. Katz, G., Peled, D.: Synthesizing solutions to the leader election problem using model checking and genetic programming. In: Namjoshi, K., Zeller, A., Ziv, A. (eds.) HVC 2009. LNCS, vol. 6405, pp. 117–132. Springer, Heidelberg (2011). doi:10.1007/978-3-642-19237-1_13
10. Katz, G., Peled, D.: Code mutation in verification and automatic code correction. In: Esparza, J., Majumdar, R. (eds.) TACAS 2010. LNCS, vol. 6015, pp. 435–450. Springer, Heidelberg (2010). doi:10.1007/978-3-642-12002-2_36
11. Katz, G., Peled, D.: MCGP: a software synthesis tool based on model checking and genetic programming. In: Bouajjani, A., Chin, W.-N. (eds.) ATVA 2010. LNCS, vol. 6252, pp. 359–364. Springer, Heidelberg (2010)
12. Koza, J.R.: Genetic Programming: On the Programming of Computers by Means of Natural Selection. MIT Press, Cambridge (1992)
13. Langdon, W.B., Harman, M.: Optimizing existing software with genetic programming. IEEE Trans. Evol. Comput. 19(1), 118–135 (2015)
14. Legay, A., Delahaye, B., Bensalem, S.: Statistical model checking: an overview. In: Falcone, Y., Finkbeiner, B., Havelund, K., Lee, I., Pace, G., Roşu, G., Sokolsky, O., Tillmann, N., Barringer, H. (eds.) RV 2010. LNCS, vol. 6418, pp. 122–135. Springer, Heidelberg (2010)
15. Perez, J.A., Corchuelo, R., Toro, M.: An order-based algorithm for implementing multiparty synchronization. Concurr. Pract. Exp. 16(12), 1173–1206 (2004)
16. Pnueli, A., Rosner, R.: On the synthesis of a reactive module. In: POPL, pp. 179–190 (1989)
17. Pnueli, A., Rosner, R.: Distributed reactive systems are hard to synthesize. In: FOCS, pp. 746–757 (1990)
18. Safra, S.: On the complexity of omega-automata. In: 29th Annual Symposium on Foundations of Computer Science, White Plains, New York, USA, 24-26 October 1988, pp. 319–327 (1988)
19. Thomas, W.: Automata on infinite objects. In: Handbook of Theoretical Computer Science, Volume B: Formal Models and Sematics (B), pp. 133–192 (1990)

Evaluation and Reproducibility
of Program Analysis and Verification

Evaluation and Reproducibility of Program Analysis and Verification (Track Introduction)

Markus Schordan[1], Dirk Beyer[2], and Jonas Lundberg[3]

[1] Lawrence Livermore National Laboratory, Livermore, CA, USA
[2] LMU Munich, Munich, Germany
[3] Linnaeus University, Växjö, Sweden

1 Overview

Manual inspection of complex software is costly and error prone. Techniques and tools that do not require manual inspection are in dire need as our software systems grow at a rapid rate. This track is concerned with the methods of comparative evaluation of program analyses and the tools that implement them. It also addresses the question how program properties that have been verified can be represented such that they remain reproducible and reusable as intermediate results for other analyses and verification phases. In particular, it is of interest how different tools can be combined to achieve better results than with only one of those tools alone.

We therefore focus on how analysis results can be specified and how to allow an exact re-computation of the analysis results irrespective of a chosen (internal) intermediate representation. Therefore we address specification languages for program properties and program analysis results, their representation in existing analysis infrastructures, compilers, and tools, along with meta-models. This track also addresses the reuse of verification results, the combination of multiple verifiers using conditional model checking [4], and how to overcome obstacles in combining tools that implement different approaches (e.g., model checking and data-flow analysis). In summary the topics of interest are

- Specification languages for program properties and program-analysis results
- Representation and specification of program-analysis results in existing program analysis infrastructures, compilers, and tools along with meta-models and evolution of these representations
- Generation and checking of verification witnesses
- Reuse of verification results and combination of multiple verifiers using conditional model checking
- Analysis benchmarking and experimental evaluation of analysis accuracy
- Parallel verification by using parallel algorithms on multi-core systems with shared-memory, GPUs, and/or distributed systems
- Identification of undefined behavior in programs (e.g. C and C++)

© Springer International Publishing AG 2016
T. Margaria and B. Steffen (Eds.): ISoLA 2016, Part I, LNCS 9952, pp. 191–194, 2016.
DOI: 10.1007/978-3-319-47166-2_13

2   Contributions with Published Papers in the Track

Heinze and Amme present a novel sparse data-flow analysis [10] based on static-single assignment (SSA) form [9] for deriving a predicate-based characterization of the values of a program's variables. The analysis benefits from the SSA representation because relevant parts of the program state can be easily identified for each variable following the def-use chains that are implicitly given in the SSA form. It also allows to interpret instructions and branching conditions as first-order predicates when substituting the assignment operator with the equality operator. The presented analysis has been implemented in a system for the generation of more precise low-level models that are used for model checking distributed business processes [11] and the analysis evaluation shows promising run times.

Beyer and Lemberger present a new approach [6] to address the path-explosion problem in symbolic execution. They apply abstraction to symbolic execution, and refine the abstraction using counterexample-guided abstraction refinement (CEGAR) [8]. The abstraction is applied lazily [12], which allows to use a precision as weak as possible for managing the state space, and as strong as necessary to prove a program safe or to detect a bug. The technique is implemented in the open-source software verification framework CPACHECKER [5]. The approach is lazy in the way that it ignores loop conditions if they are not necessary to verify a given property or to satisfy a coverage criterion. A novel aspect of this approach is that it weakens the *precision* of the symbolic execution.

Jasper and Schordan present a detailed evaluation [15] of a parallel verification technique for reachability properties and behavioral properties specified in linear temporal logic (LTL) using benchmarks from the RERS Challenges 2012–2014 [13]. The presented approach to the verification of large-scale software systems aims at a trade-off between the quality of verification results (i.e., number of verified/falsified properties) and the execution time required to produce them. It uses two distinct analysis phases based on the concepts of bounded model checking (BMC) and model checking of abstract models, respectively. A benchmark's state space is analyzed systematically by computing up to a certain depth of the state space by number of iterations of the main loop in a benchmark. Additionally, results are presented showing the number of traces to distinct reachable error labels and counterexamples for violated LTL properties. This indicates how "difficult" the reachable error labels are to find and LTLs are to falsify. These results are presented for a set of benchmarks that is also used in SV-COMP [1].

Iftikhar, Lundberg, and Weyns present an approach [14] to model interpretation. Being able to execute the model directly, without any intermediate model-to-code translation, has a number of advantages: the model is always up-to-date and run-time updates of the model are possible. The model is defined in a domain-specific modeling language. The presented technique also allows to address features like simultaneous execution, system wide signals, and time constraints. It focuses on timed automata, which is a widely used formalism to model real-time systems and the aforementioned features. Formal properties of models described by timed automata can be verified by the tool UPPAAL. What makes this approach unique is that it uses a model representation that is both verifiable and executable.

3   Selected Discussion Topics in the Track

- Reliable and replicable benchmarking with BENCHEXEC: The benchmarking framework BENCHEXEC [7] supports precise and reliable performance evaluation of CPU-intensive tools, such as verifiers and solvers. It provides means to control and measure computing resources (e.g., CPU time and memory). The ability to limit resource usage (e.g., memory consumption) of a tool during benchmarking is a hard requirement for replicable and comparable results. BENCHEXEC allows to enforce an agreed resource limit in order to accurately guaranteeing a fair comparison w.r.t. these resource constraints.
- Reusing counterexamples from model checking: Model checkers produce counterexamples when a property violation is found or produce a correctness proof. What can be done with the counterexamples? Is the error reproducible? Can the error report later be re-used for bug fixing [2] or regression testing? The advent of exchangeable witnesses [3] is a paradigm shift in verification that goes from boolean answers indicating whether a property is violated or not, to a more valuable information about the cause of the property violation.
- Utilizing parallel architectures for efficient verification: One of the key factors in verification is to account for resource limits, in particular the run time of an analysis. As software verification tools become more integrated in large-scale projects, the scalability of a verification tool and its run time become crucial factors to determine its applicability at different stages of development.
- Combining several model checkers within given resource constraints: Can we utilize different model checkers to achieve better results than with only one of the tools and can results of one verification tool be reused by a different tool? What are the requirements to an exchange format for information exchange via conditional model checking [4]. How can verification tools adapt to given resource constraints (e.g., different state-space search strategies)?

4   Conclusion

The combination of various areas of program analysis that are presented in this track, predicate-based sparse data-flow analysis, symbolic execution, CEGAR, the combination of BMC and verification with state abstractions separated in distinct verification phases, and model-execution for model-driven development with time constraints, forms a rich basis for the discussion of aspects of evaluation and reproducibility. Together, these contributions provide an overview of the comprehensive response of the research community to the increasing importance of analysis and verification in the design and development of evolving software.

References

1. Beyer, D.: Software verification and verifiable witnesses. In: Baier, C., Tinelli, C. (eds.) TACAS 2015. LNCS, vol. 9035, pp. 401–416. Springer, Heidelberg (2015)
2. Beyer, D., Dangl, M.: Verification-aided debugging: An interactive web-service for exploring error witnesses. In: Chaudhuri, S., Farzan, A. (eds.) CAV 2016. LNCS, vol. 9780, pp. 502–509. Springer, Heidelberg (2016)
3. Beyer, D., Dangl, M., Dietsch, D., Heizmann, M., Stahlbauer, A.: Witness validation and stepwise testification across software verifiers. In: FSE 2015, pp. 721–733. ACM (2015)
4. Beyer, D., Henzinger, T.A., Keremoglu, M.E., Wendler, P.: Conditional model checking: a technique to pass information between verifiers. In: FSE 2012. ACM (2012)
5. Beyer, D., Keremoglu, M.E.: CPACHECKER: A tool for configurable software verification. In: Gopalakrishnan, G., Qadeer, S. (eds.) CAV 2011. LNCS, vol. 6806, pp. 184–190. Springer, Heidelberg (2011)
6. Beyer, D., Lemberger, T.: Symbolic execution with CEGAR. In: Margaria, T., Steffen, B. (eds.) ISoLA 2016. LNCS, vol. 9952, pp. 195–211. Springer, Heidelberg (2016)
7. Beyer, D., Löwe, S., Wendler, P.: Benchmarking and resource measurement. In: Fischer, B., Geldenhuys, J. (eds.) SPIN 2015. LNCS, vol. 9232, pp. 160–178. Springer, Heidelberg (2015)
8. Clarke, E., Grumberg, O., Jha, S., Lu, Y., Veith, H.: Counterexample-guided abstraction refinement for symbolic model checking. J. ACM 50(5), 752–794 (2003)
9. Cytron, R., Ferrante, J., Rosen, B.K., Wegman, M.N., Zadeck, F.K.: Efficiently computing static single assignment form and the control dependence graph. ACM Trans. Program. Lang. Syst. 13(4), 451–490 (1991)
10. Heinze, T., Amme, W.: Sparse analysis of variable predicates based upon SSA-form. In: Margaria, T., Steffen, B. (eds.) ISoLA 2016. LNCS, vol. 9952, pp. 227–242. Springer, Heidelberg (2016)
11. Heinze, T.S., Amme, W., Moser, S.: Compiling more precise Petri net models for an improved verification of service implementations. In: SOCA 2014, pp. 25–32. IEEE (2014)
12. Henzinger, T.A., Jhala, R., Majumdar, R., Sutre, G.: Lazy abstraction. In: POPL 2002, pp. 58–70. ACM (2002)
13. Howar, F., Isberner, M., Merten, M., Steffen, B., Beyer, D., Păsăreanu, C.S.: Rigorous examination of reactive systems. Int. J. Softw. Tools Technol. Transf. 16(5), 457–464 (2014)
14. Iftikhar, M.U., Lundberg, J., Weyns, D.: A model interpreter for timed automata. In: Margaria, T., Steffen, B. (eds.) ISoLA 2016. LNCS, vol. 9952, pp. 243–258. Springer, Heidelberg (2016)
15. Jasper, M., Schordan, M.: Multi-core model checking of large-scale reactive systems using different state representations. In: Margaria, T., Steffen, B. (eds.) ISoLA 2016. LNCS, vol. 9952, pp. 212–226. Springer, Heidelberg (2016)

Symbolic Execution with CEGAR

Dirk Beyer[1] and Thomas Lemberger[2]

[1] LMU Munich, Munich, Germany
[2] University of Passau, Passau, Germany

Abstract. Symbolic execution, a standard technique in program analysis, is a particularly successful and popular component in systems for test-case generation. One of the open research problems is that the approach suffers from the path-explosion problem. We apply abstraction to symbolic execution, and refine the abstract model using counterexample-guided abstraction refinement (CEGAR), a standard technique from model checking. We also use refinement selection with existing and new heuristics to influence the behavior and further improve the performance of our refinement procedure. We implemented our new technique in the open-source software-verification framework CPACHECKER. Our experimental results show that the implementation is highly competitive.

1 Introduction

Symbolic execution was introduced in 1976 for program testing and verification [27]. By extending the interpreter of a programming language to handle symbolic values without changing the program syntax, programs can be executed in such interpreter using symbolic values as input. If a fork in the program's control flow occurs, e.g., due to a branching statement for which both branches are possible, the execution splits into two separate executions, recording the particular branching condition. Each such execution represents the execution of the program for a *set* of concrete input values, which can be derived based on all recorded branching conditions of an execution. This way, a lot fewer *symbolic* executions are necessary for reaching a certain test coverage in comparison to executions with concrete input values. The main problem of symbolic execution is that the number of separate executions is exponential in the number of branching statements in the program. Because every visit of a loop head can be seen as a branching statement, the number of separate executions for a single program may easily exceed feasible amounts. This is known as the *path-explosion problem*. Figure 1 demonstrates this via a simple example program. It uses a function ? that returns a non-deterministic, arbitrary value at every call. In a real-world application this could be, for example, a system call or user input. The program counts a program variable a from 0 to 100 in a non-deterministic number of loop iterations (caused by the non-deterministic assumption in the loop body). After that, it checks whether the non-deterministic, but unchanged value stored in b is still smaller than its increment stored in c. This is always true. Although the number of iterations through the loop has no influence on this property, an eager

© Springer International Publishing AG 2016
T. Margaria and B. Steffen (Eds.): ISoLA 2016, Part I, LNCS 9952, pp. 195–211, 2016.
DOI: 10.1007/978-3-319-47166-2_14

```
1   a  :=  0;
2   b  :=  ?;
3   c  :=  b + 1;
4   while  a < 100  do
5     if  ?  do
6        a++;
7   if  c <= b  do
8      error ;
```

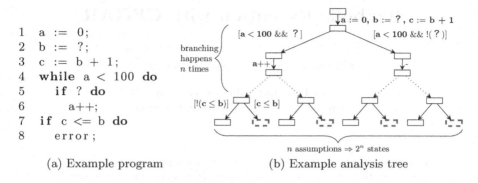

(a) Example program   (b) Example analysis tree

Fig. 1. A simple program demonstrating the path-explosion problem

approach like symbolic execution will explore the complete state-space before proving the property violation (symbolized by the dashed nodes) as infeasible. We propose a lazy approach that, in this example, ignores the loop conditions if they are not necessary to verify a given property or to satisfy a given coverage criterion. Different approaches exist to mitigate the path-explosion problem, but none of them tries to weaken the *precision* of the symbolic execution. In formal software verification, abstraction is a widely-used technique to reduce the state-space, with counterexample-guided abstraction refinement (CEGAR) [18] being a popular and successful approach for computing an abstract model.

We present SYMEX$^+$, a combination of symbolic execution with abstraction, which automatically refines the abstract model using CEGAR [18] in a lazy manner [22]. The automatic precision adjustment [7] with lazy CEGAR allows us to use a precision as weak as possible (to manage the state-space) and as strong as necessary (to prove a program safe or find a bug). Considering the example above, an analysis using CEGAR will not track the value of program variable a, because it is not necessary for proving that the error is not reachable. This idea makes it possible to prove the property after only one iteration of CEGAR and without unrolling the loop (and thus keeping the state-space significantly smaller).

Further, we are able to benefit from improvements to CEGAR. As a first improvement, we apply *refinement selection* [11] to our precision adjustment to have control over the choice of precision from multiple candidate precisions, and using this method, we can better control the overall symbolic-execution process.

Since symbolic execution is the composition of two abstract domains, namely (1) tracking explicit and symbolic values of variables and (2) tracking constraints over symbolic values, we apply CEGAR to two abstract domains at once instead of only to one abstract domain, as in previous work. We extend CEGAR to refining several abstract domains simultaneously by using a composite strongest-post operator of the configurable program analysis (CPA) [6]. This special case of using CEGAR can be generalized to any composition of abstract domains, allowing novel applications. Until now, CEGAR was applied to only one single abstract domain independently for one error path, even in composite setups [7].

Availability. We implemented symbolic execution with CEGAR in the open software-verification framework CPACHECKER [8]. All experimental results are available on our supplementary web page[1].

Structure. After clarifying the preliminaries in Sect. 2, we formalize the application of CEGAR and interpolation to symbolic execution in Sect. 3. In Sect. 4, we perform a thorough evaluation to show the applicability and high competitiveness of our approach to reachability analysis in software verification. The results show a major speed-up compared to traditional symbolic execution for most verification tasks.

Related Work. There are four major ways to address the path-explosion problem of symbolic execution: (1) search heuristics for achieving a high level of branch or path coverage as fast as possible, (2) compositional execution, creating summaries of functions or paths, and reuse them instead of recomputing already explored states, (3) handling of unbounded loops, and (4) using interpolants for tracking reasons why a certain path is infeasible. While many concepts are presented in the context of testing, they can be applied to verification as well.

Search Heuristics. Burnim and Sen [14] propose three different heuristics for reaching a target region or uncovered branches faster in state-space exploration, in contrast to the standard depth-first search. KLEE [15] is a tool for automatic test-case generation that runs one symbolic execution for each branch separately. The implementation uses two different heuristics to decide at a certain program location which execution to continue first. While heuristics can assist in speeding up the process of finding an error, they do not mitigate the problem of path-explosion for proving that a program is error-free.

Compositional Execution. Compositional symbolic execution [20] tests functions in isolation in order to create summaries of the functions for reuse. It is implemented in SMART, an extension of the symbolic-execution-based testing tool DART [21]. Demand-driven compositional symbolic execution extends compositional symbolic execution by *lazy* and *relevant exploration* [1].

Handling of Unbounded Loops. Lazy Annotation [29] tackles potentially infinite analyses that are caused by loops, by computing inductive invariants for loops. A major downside of this approach is that it will only terminate if such invariants can be found. Based on this insight, loop invariants can be computed inductively, in order to speed up computation by using speculative loop invariants [25]. Strongest possible invariants are used to keep the analysis as eager as possible, while keeping the analysis tree finite. If invariants are too coarse to prove the infeasibility of an inconclusive counterexample, a refinement procedure similar to CEGAR (restricted to loop headers) is used. This is a compromise between performing eager symbolic execution and lazy CEGAR when encountering unbounded loops. Compact symbolic execution [30] analyzes cyclic paths in the control-flow automaton (CFA) and computes a so called *template* for each one, describing all possible program states that may leave the cycle after any number of iterations.

---

[1] http://www.sosy-lab.org/~dbeyer/cpa-symexec/

This mitigates the path-explosion problem considerably, because no more loops exist in the execution. However, due to quantifiers in formulas, the complexity of formulas that have to be solved is increased significantly. The experimental evaluation shows that despite this trade-off, the analysis performance is still considerably improved compared to the previous approaches.

Using CEGAR with symbolic execution, as proposed in this work, may also avoid the problem of path-explosion in the presence of unbounded loops, because information altered by loops is not always necessary for reasoning about programs. Since we implemented symbolic execution in the verification framework CPACHECKER, we are able to make use of the possibility to combine several different analyses that are implemented in the framework. For handling unbounded loops, an analysis that is specialized on this could be used in parallel.

Interpolation. The technique of interpolation [19, 28] is often used to identify reasons for path infeasibility. If a path is found to be infeasible, an interpolant is computed for each program location on the path and stored as "precision" of the analysis. If such a program location is re-visited on a different path, it is checked whether the interpolant is implied by the current abstract state. If it is, execution on this path may halt, if it is known that the path is infeasible based on the interpolant. This concept was used in the context of the constraint-logic programming scheme [23, 26]. There were experiments on using weakest pre-conditions instead of strongest post-conditions for the computation of weaker interpolants [25], on various search heuristics [24], and on adding the notion of *laziness* to symbolic execution [17]. Instead of computing interpolants immediately after a path is determined as infeasible, the symbolic execution might continue on this path ignoring the infeasibility, in order to be able to learn better interpolants.

Lazy Annotation [29] uses interpolants to store conditions for nodes and edges on the CFA under which no target region is reachable from this node or using this edge. Instead of annotating all edges on an infeasible path with interpolants in a separate procedure, interpolants are computed bottom-up during state-space exploration.

A main difference that persists between symbolic execution with CEGAR and symbolic execution using interpolants is the amount of information stored. CEGAR is lazy, starting with a coarse precision and refining it, while traditional symbolic execution is eager, tracking all information and computing interpolants for subsuming new states only. Using CEGAR, refinements to compute the needed level of abstraction and iterative analysis replace unnecessary state-space exploration. This pays off if only few program variables or constraints have to be tracked, or only few possible error paths exist.

2   Background

Control-Flow Automaton, State, Path, Semantics, and Precision. For presentation, all theoretical concepts are based on a simplified programming language where all operations are either variable assignments or assumptions.[2] All values in this language are integers of arbitrary range. We represent a program by a *control-flow automaton* (CFA) [13]. A CFA $A = (L, l_0, G)$ is a directed graph whose nodes L represent the program locations of the program, the initial node $l_0 \in L$ represents the program entry, and the set $G \subseteq L \times Ops \times L$ represents all edges of the graph. An edge $g \in G$ exists between two nodes if a program statement exists that transfers control between the program locations represented by the nodes. Each edge is labeled with the operation that transfers the control. The set X is the set of all program variables occurring in the program. A *concrete state* (l, c) consists of a program location $l \in L$ and a concrete variable assignment $c : X \to \mathbb{Z}$, which assigns to a program variable $x \in X$ an integer value from $\mathbb{Z}$ (the set of integer numbers). The set of all concrete states of a program is C. A set $r \subseteq C$ is called a *region*. The region of concrete states that violate a given specification is called *target region* r^t. For a partial function $f : M \nrightarrow N$ for two sets M and N, we denote the *definition range* as $\mathbf{def}(f) = \{x \mid \exists y : (x, y) \in f\}$ and the *restriction* to a new definition range M' as $f_{|M'} = f \cap (M' \times N)$. An abstract state $s \in \mathbb{A}$ is an element of an arbitrary type $\mathbb{A}$ that depends on the analysis. Abstract state s represents the region $[\![s]\!]$ of concrete variable assignments. The special value $\bot$ with $[\![\bot]\!] = \varnothing$ is part of every abstract-state type. An abstract variable assignment $v : X \nrightarrow \mathbb{V}$ is a partial function that assigns to a program variable from X a value from the set $\mathbb{V}$, which consists of arbitrary values. The strongest-post operator $\mathrm{SP}_{op} : \mathbb{A} \to \mathbb{A}$ defines the semantics of an operation $op \in Ops$, i.e., $\mathrm{SP}_{op}(a) = a'$ expresses that abstract state a' represents the set of concrete variable assignments that are reachable by executing op from concrete variable assignments represented by abstract state a.

A *path* σ is a sequence $\langle (op_1, l_1), \ldots, (op_n, l_n) \rangle$ of operations and their corresponding target program locations. A path σ is a *program path* if σ represents a syntactic walk through the CFA, that is, for every $1 \le i \le n$, a CFA edge $g = (l_{i-1}, op_i, l_i)$ exists and l_0 is the initial program location. Every path $\sigma = \langle (op_1, l_1), \ldots, (op_n, l_n) \rangle$ defines a *constraint sequence* $\gamma_\sigma = \langle op_1, \ldots, op_n \rangle$ [9]. The *conjunction* of two constraint sequences $\gamma = \langle op_1, \ldots, op_n \rangle$ and $\gamma' = \langle op'_1, \ldots, op'_n \rangle$ is defined as their concatenation: $\gamma \wedge \gamma' = \langle op_1, \ldots, op_n, op'_1, \ldots, op'_n \rangle$.

The *semantics of a path* $\sigma = \langle (op_1, l_1), \ldots, (op_n, l_n) \rangle$ is defined as the successive application of the strongest-post operator to each operation of the corresponding constraint sequence γ_σ, that is, $\mathrm{SP}_{\gamma_\sigma}(a) = \mathrm{SP}_{op_n}(\ldots \mathrm{SP}_{op_1}(a))$. A program path σ is *feasible* if $\mathrm{SP}_{\gamma_\sigma}(\varnothing)$ is not contradicting, that is, $\mathrm{SP}_{\gamma_\sigma}(\varnothing) \ne \bot$. Otherwise, it is *infeasible*. An *error path* is a path $\sigma = \langle (op_1, l_1), \ldots, (op_n, l_n) \rangle$ for which $\mathrm{SP}_{\gamma_\sigma}(\varnothing)$ represents at least one concrete variable assignment c_{γ_σ} for which (l_n, c_{γ_σ}) is part of the target region r^t. A program is *safe* if no feasible error path exists. The *precision* $\pi : L \to 2^\Pi$ assigns to each program location some information that defines the level of abstraction of the analysis. The information type Π depends on the abstract domain of the analysis. For an explicit-value domain for example, the set Π is a set X of program variables, and the precision defines the program variables that should be tracked at the respective location.

---

[2] Our implementation in CPACHECKER is based on the language C.

Algorithm 1. $CEGAR(\mathbb{D}, e_0, \pi_0)$, adapted from [7]

Input: a CPA $\mathbb{D}$ with dynamic precision adjustment, an initial abstract state $e_0 \in E$
    with precision $\pi_0 \in \Pi$
Output: the verification result TRUE or FALSE
Variables: the sets `reached` and `waitlist` of elements of $E \times \Pi$, an error path σ
 1: `reached` $:= \{(e_0, \pi_0)\}$
 2: `waitlist` $:= \{(e_0, \pi_0)\}$
 3: $\pi := \pi_0$
 4: **while** true **do**
 5:    (`reached`, `waitlist`) $:= CPA(\mathbb{D}, \text{reached}, \text{waitlist})$
 6:    **if** `waitlist` $= \varnothing$ **then**
 7:      **return** TRUE
 8:    **else**
 9:      $\sigma := $ `extractErrorPath(reached)`
10:      **if** `isFeasible`(σ) **then**
11:        **return** FALSE
12:      **else**
13:        $\pi := \pi \cup \text{refine}(\sigma)$
14:        `reached` $:= \{(e_0, \pi)\}$
15:        `waitlist` $:= \{(e_0, \pi)\}$

Counterexample-guided Abstraction Refinement (CEGAR). CEGAR [18] is a technique to construct an abstract model that contains as few information as possible while retaining enough information to prove or disprove the correctness of a program. The technique starts the analysis with a coarse abstraction and refines it based on infeasible error paths. An error path is a witness of a property violation. If no error path is found by the analysis, it terminates and reports that no property violation exists. If an error path is found, it is checked whether the path is feasible, e.g., by repeating the analysis with full precision $\pi(l) = \Pi$ for all $l \in L$. If the path is feasible, the analysis terminates and reports the found property violation. If the error path is infeasible, then it was due to a too coarse abstract model (too low precision). To eliminate this infeasible error path from future state-space explorations, the precision is increased (which refines the abstract model) using information extracted from the infeasible error path. Afterwards, the analysis starts again, using the new precision. Algorithm 1 uses a configurable program analysis (CPA) with dynamic precision adjustment $\mathbb{D}$ [7] and an initial state e_0 with initial precision π_0 (usually $\pi_0(l) = \varnothing$ for all $l \in L$) to perform the state-space exploration.

The CPA algorithm operates on a set of reached abstract states (`reached`) and a subset of this set that contains all reached abstract states that have not been handled yet (`waitlist`). If `waitlist` is empty, the CPA algorithm has handled all reachable states without encountering any target state. If this is the case, no property violation was found and the algorithm can return TRUE. Otherwise, an error path is extracted from the reached set. If the error path is reported as feasible, a property violation exists and the algorithm returns FALSE. If the error path is infeasible, the current precision is too coarse. The precision is refined based on the infeasible error path by using function $\texttt{refine} : \Sigma \rightarrow 2^{\Pi}$ with Σ being the type of all infeasible error paths. The function assigns to an infeasible error path a precision that is sufficient to prove the infeasibility of the error path and eliminate this infeasible path from future explorations. After this, the reached set and waitlist are reset to their initial values and the algorithm continues the analysis with the refined precision. It is important to note that the return type of $\texttt{refine}$ has to be equal to the precision type 2^{Π} used in D. Because of this, analyses are in general not exchangeable without changing the refinement component as well. Since the problem of finding the coarsest possible refinement for a given abstract model based on an infeasible error path is NP-hard [18], heuristics have to be used to find suitable refinements [11].

A boolean formula Γ is a Craig interpolant [19] for two boolean formulas γ^- (called prefix) and γ^+ (called suffix), if the following three conditions are fulfilled:

(a) The prefix implies Γ, that is, $\gamma^- \Rightarrow \Gamma$.
(b) Γ contradicts the suffix, that is, $\Gamma \wedge \gamma^+$ is contradicting.
(c) Γ only contains variables occurring in *both* prefix γ^- and suffix γ^+.

It is proven that such an interpolant always exists in the domain of abstract variable assignments [9] as well as in the theory of linear arithmetics [19]. A Craig interpolant describes information that is sufficient for proving a remaining path, i.e., the suffix, infeasible (contradicting). This information can be used to derive a new precision for abstraction refinement.

Refinement Selection. Usually, several different Craig interpolants exist for a single infeasible path. Each of them may represent a different reason for infeasibility. When using interpolants for abstraction refinement in CEGAR, the choice of interpolant for an infeasible path, and as such the tracked reason, may greatly influence the further course of the analysis. Traditional abstraction refinement does not account for the differences between these interpolants and just takes arbitrarily the interpolants that the interpolation engine returns (based on the heuristics inside the interpolation engine). In contrast, *refinement selection* [11] tries to select the interpolant that promises the best verification progress for a given infeasible path. It looks at various possible interpolants, e.g., by using sliced path prefixes [12], and chooses the most promising one based on a selected heuristic. Some heuristics proposed in other work [11] include:

- Selection of the shortest prefix (called *short*).
- Selection based on a score computed from the domain type [2] of program variables, with easy/small types like boolean and integer being preferred (called *domain good*).
- Selection of the interpolant with the most narrow width (called *width narrow*). The width of an interpolant is defined by the number of locations on an error path for which the interpolant is not *false* and not *true*, i.e., the number of locations at which additional information must be tracked.

Several heuristics may be applied sequentially, in case one heuristic alone is not able to choose a single best interpolant.

3   Symbolic Execution Using CEGAR and Interpolation

Abstract Domain and Abstract Semantics. Our new approach SYMEX$^+$
is the combination of traditional symbolic execution with CEGAR. An abstract
state (v, γ) in symbolic execution consists of an abstract variable assignment v
and a sequence $\gamma = \langle [\rho_1], \ldots, [\rho_n] \rangle \in \widehat{\$}$ of constraints $[\rho_i]$ over symbolic values
from $\$$. The abstract variable assignment $v : X \rightharpoonup V$ used in symbolic execution
assigns to a program variable from X either a concrete integer value from $\mathbb{Z}$, a
symbolic value from $\$$, or the special value $\bot$, which represents a contradicting
assignment, i.e., $V = \mathbb{Z} \cup \$ \cup \{\bot\}$. An abstract state (v, γ) represents the set
$[\![(v, \gamma)]\!]$ of concrete variable assignments, which is formally defined as follows:
$[\![\bot]\!] = \varnothing$ and

$$[\![(v, \gamma)]\!] = \{c \mid \forall x \in \mathtt{def}(v) : v(x) \in \mathbb{Z} \implies v(x) = c(x)$$
$$\wedge \ \exists s : \bigwedge_{[\rho] \in \gamma} \rho \wedge \forall x \in \mathtt{def}(v) : v(x) \in \$ \implies v(x) = s(v(x)) = c(x) \}$$

where $s : \$ \rightarrow \mathbb{Z}$ maps symbolic to concrete values. The strongest-post opera-
tor $\widehat{SP}_{op} : X \times \widehat{\$} \rightarrow X \times \widehat{\$}$ is defined as follows:

1. For an assignment operation $x := exp$ we have

$$\widehat{SP}_{x:=exp}((v, \gamma)) = \left(v_{|X \setminus \{x\}} \cup \{(x, y)\}, \ \gamma \right)$$

with

$$y = \begin{cases} d & \text{if } d \in \mathbb{Z} \cup \$ \text{ is the evaluation of arithmetic expression } exp_{/v} \\ e & \text{if } exp_{/v} \text{ can not be evaluated and } e \text{ is a new symbolic value } e \in \$ \end{cases}$$

and $exp_{/v}$ is the interpretation of expression exp for the abstract variable
assignment v. If exp contains a program variable of X that is not in the
definition range $\mathtt{def}(v)$, then $exp_{/v}$ can not be evaluated. If $exp_{/v}$ contains a
symbolic value of $\$$, the evaluation of $exp_{/v}$ equals $exp_{/v}$ and $exp_{/v} \in \$$.

2. For an assume operation $[p]$ we have

$$\widehat{SP}_{[p]}((v, \gamma)) = \begin{cases} \bot & \text{if } p_{/(v, \gamma)} \text{ is unsatisfiable} \\ (v \cup v_p, \ \gamma \wedge \langle [p_{/(v \cup v_p)}] \rangle) & \text{otherwise} \end{cases}$$

with new abstract variable assignments

$$v_p = \{(x, e) \in (X \setminus \mathtt{def}(v) \times \$) \mid x \text{ occurs in } p \text{ and}$$
$$e \text{ is a new symbolic value } e \in \$\}$$

that assign a new symbolic value to every unknown program variable occurring in p, the interpretation $p_{/(v \cup v_p)}$ of p for the abstract variable assignment
$v \cup v_p$ and

$$p_{/(v, \gamma)} = p \wedge \bigwedge_{x \in \mathtt{def}(v)} x = v(x) \wedge \bigwedge_{[\rho] \in \gamma} \rho \ .$$

If $p_{/(v,\gamma)}$ is satisfiable, an assignment to a new symbolic value is added to the abstract variable assignment for every unknown program variable occurring in p and the assume operation $[p_{/(v \cup v_p)}]$ is appended to the existing constraints sequence.

Using these operations, the conditions ρ of the assume operations $[\rho] \in \gamma$ contain symbolic values from $\$$, but no program variables from X.

Precision and Interpolation. For our symbolic-execution domain, the set Π (for defining a precision) is a composition of the set X of program variables and the set $\widehat{\$}$ of constraint sequences, i.e., $\Pi = X \times \widehat{\$}$. The precision defines the program variables and the constraints that should be tracked at each location.

We base our refinement procedure for the precision of symbolic execution on the refinement procedure for the precision of abstract variable assignments [9], using Craig interpolants to derive the precision. Algorithm 2 shows our computation of interpolants for a prefix γ^- and a suffix γ^+. Since we want to create an interpolant Γ that contains all information necessary for proving that $\widehat{\mathsf{SP}}_{\Gamma \wedge \gamma^+}$ is contradicting, we have to consider not only abstract variable assignments but also constraints. First, the algorithm computes the strongest-post condition (v, γ) for the prefix γ^- based on the initial abstract state $(\varnothing, \varnothing)$. We then eliminate all constraints from γ that are not necessary for proving that γ^+ is contradicting. Next, we remove every mapping of a program variable to a value from v that is not required. This way we try to get the weakest interpolant possible. We then build the interpolant from all constraints left in γ and all assignments left in v.

Refinement of Abstract Model. Algorithm 3 defines the complete refinement procedure used in the CEGAR algorithm. It starts with an initial, empty interpolant Γ and empty precision π with $\pi(l) = (\varnothing, \varnothing)$ for all $l \in L$. For each location (l_i, op_i) on the infeasible error path, the suffix γ^+ for this location is set and the interpolant is computed from the previous interpolant in conjunction with the current operation (i.e., $\Gamma \wedge \langle op_i \rangle$) and the suffix (line 5). The full prefix $\langle op_1, \ldots, op_i \rangle$ must not be used for interpolation, because multiple reasons for the infeasibility of a path may exist; if the full prefix is available for interpolation, then different reasons for infeasibility might be used for consecutive interpolants on a path, resulting in a precision that is not able to prove the path infeasible in further analysis iterations. Because of this, inductive interpolants that are derived from the same reason for the infeasibility of the given infeasible error path must be computed by reusing the previous interpolant as part of the prefix.

In the next step, a precision for the current program location is extracted from the interpolant using `extractPrecision`. The extracted precision for symbolic execution is an object of type $X \times \widehat{\$}$; such a pair consists of the set of all program variables that occur in an assignment operation in the interpolant and all assume operations that occur in the interpolant, formally:

$$\texttt{extractPrecision}(\Gamma) = (\texttt{def}(v),\ \gamma)\ ,$$

where $\widehat{\mathsf{SP}}_\Gamma(\varnothing, \varnothing) = (v, \gamma)$.

Algorithm 2. interpolate(γ^-, γ^+)

Input: two constraint sequences γ^- and γ^+, with $\gamma^- \wedge \gamma^+$ contradicting
Output: a constraint sequence Γ, which is an interpolant for γ^- and γ^+
Variables: an abstract variable assignment v and a constraints sequence γ
1: $(v, \gamma) := \widehat{SP}_{\gamma^-}((\varnothing, \varnothing))$
2: **for each** $[p] \in \gamma$ **do**
3:     **if** $\widehat{SP}_{\gamma^+}((v, \gamma \setminus [p]))$ is contradicting **then**
4:         $\gamma := \gamma \setminus [p]$
5: **for each** $x \in \text{def}(v)$ **do**
6:     **if** $\widehat{SP}_{\gamma^+}((v_{|\text{def}(v) \setminus \{x\}}, \gamma))$ is contradicting **then**
7:         $v := v_{|\text{def}(v) \setminus \{x\}}$
8: $\Gamma := \gamma$
9: **for each** $x \in \text{def}(v)$ **do**
10:     $\Gamma := \Gamma \wedge \langle x := v(x) \rangle$
11: **return** Γ

Algorithm 3. refine(σ)

Input: infeasible error path $\sigma = \langle (op_1, l_1), \ldots, (op_n, l_n) \rangle$
Output: precision $\pi : L \to X \times \widehat{\$}$
Variables: interpolant constraint sequence Γ
1: $\Gamma := \langle \rangle$
2: $\pi(l) := (\varnothing, \varnothing)$ for all program locations l
3: **for** $i := 1$ to $n - 1$ **do**
4:     $\gamma^+ := \langle op_{i+1}, \ldots, op_n \rangle$
5:     $\Gamma := \text{interpolate}(\Gamma \wedge \langle op_i \rangle, \gamma^+)$
6:     $\pi(l_i) := \text{extractPrecision}(\Gamma)$
7: **return** π

Refinement Selection. We apply refinement selection based on sliced path prefixes analogously to the application for the domain of abstract variable assignments [11,12]. In addition to the existing heuristics, we define heuristics that select an interpolant based on the amount of assumptions in it. We call the heuristic selecting the interpolant with most assumptions *assumptions – most*.

Refinement for Compositions of Abstract Domains. In the same way as demonstrated above, a composite precision of any composition of analyses can be refined and used with CEGAR. While CEGAR has been used with a composition of analyses before (c.f. [9]), the precision of only one analysis was refined in each step, first refining a less expensive analysis' precision, and only if not avoidable refining a more expensive analysis' precision. Due to the nature of the previous method, only analyses without an interdependency can be refined and no information exchanged between analysis is considered. In contrast, using our new approach, any composition of analyses of arbitrary number and possibly information exchange between them can be used to extract a composite precision.

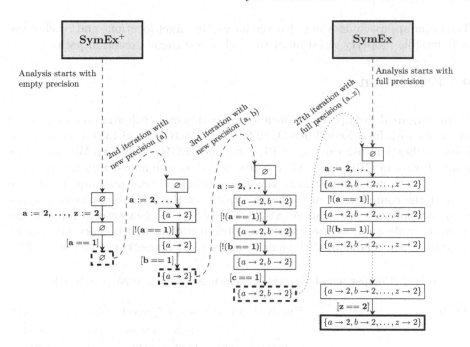

Fig. 2. An example for which the lazy analysis of SYMEX$^+$ performs worse than the traditional eager analysis of SYMEX. Highlighted nodes represent error locations. Every dashed rectangle represents an error location that is infeasible when using full precision.

Discussion. Using CEGAR, we change the symbolic execution from being eager to being lazy, while keeping its potential expressiveness. For an arbitrary verification task, it is difficult to say upfront whether the lazy or the eager approach is better suited. While a lazy approach may keep the state-space potentially smaller if only little information is necessary (many operations can be abstracted away), its refinement iterations can be time-consuming if the abstraction is not effective enough. On the other hand, an eager approach suffers from the path-explosion problem, but may stop the analysis at unreachable branches and avoid unnecessary computation. Figure 2 shows the analysis of such a program for both lazy symbolic execution with CEGAR (SYMEX$^+$) and traditional eager symbolic execution (called SYMEX). The highlighted nodes are error locations. The program first initializes the program variables **a** to **z** with value 2. Afterwards, it checks whether program variables **a** to **y** are initialized with a value different from 1 and whether **z** is initialized with a value different from 2. If one of these conditions is wrong, an error location is reached. Since all program variables are initialized with value 2 at the beginning of the program, only the last error location can be reached. Despite this, the CEGAR algorithm visits one error location after the other, always refining the precision to track only one additional variable and then restarting from the beginning of the program with the adjusted precision. This lazy approach performs many computations that are unnecessary.

The eager approach does not visit the infeasible target locations and reaches the only feasible property violation at the end in one single execution path.

4 Evaluation

Experimental Setup. We perform our experimental evaluation on a cluster of machines with Intel Xeon E5-2650 v2 CPUs at 2.60 GHz and 135 GB of memory. Each verification task can use 2 CPU cores and 15 GB of memory. We use a time limit of 900 s of CPU time. After 1000 s, a task is terminated if it has not shut down yet. To get a statistically significant result, we run our implementation against the complete set of verification tasks[3] of the 5th International Competition on Software Verification (SV-COMP'16) [5]. To guarantee a reliable and accurate evaluation, we use BENCHEXEC [10] to run our benchmarks. Our implementation is available in CPACHECKER under tag `cpachecker-1.6-isola16`.[4]

Table 1. Comparison of different refinement-selection heuristics in SYMEX$^+$

Verdict	Unsolved	Solved	Correct TRUE	Correct FALSE	Incorrect TRUE	Incorrect FALSE
No preference	4341	2336	1737	443	0	**156**
Domain good – width narrow	4444	2233	1702	531	0	171
Domain good – short	3906	**2771**	**2042**	567	0	162
Assumptions most – short	4028	2491	1892	**599**	0	158

Refinement Selection. We compare different heuristics for refinement selection to find the one suited best for our approach. Table 1 shows three selected heuristics, *domain good* combined with *width narrow*, *domain good* combined with *short*, and *assumptions most* combined with *short*. The best heuristic for proving tasks safe is *domain good – short*, raising the number of tasks that can be proven safe by 305 (which equals an increase by almost 18 %). The best heuristic for finding errors is *assumptions most – short*, which allows us to raise the number of tasks correctly found erroneous by 156 (which equals an increase by 35 %). Using one of the two heuristics performs significantly better for both proving tasks safe and finding errors, compared to using no refinement selection (*no preference*). The combination *domain good – width narrow* performs worse for proving tasks safe and better for finding errors than the use of no refinement selection.

This is especially notable since for two other analyses, predicate analysis and explicit value analysis, the combination *domain good – width narrow* yields the best results compared to other heuristics [11]. This shows that the best choice of a heuristic not only depends on the task, but also on the analysis that is used.

---

[3] https://github.com/sosy-lab/sv-benchmarks/tree/svcomp16
[4] https://svn.sosy-lab.org/software/cpachecker/tags/

Table 2. Comparison of classical symbolic execution (SYMEX) to SYMEX$^+$ (both implemented in CPACHECKER) and SYMBIOTIC (an external tool)

Verdict	Unsolved	Solved	Correct TRUE	Correct FALSE	Incorrect TRUE	Incorrect FALSE
SYMEX	5756	921	171	**634**	1	115
SYMEX$^+$	3906	**2771**	**2042**	567	0	162
SYMBIOTIC 1	5388	1289	769	503	2	**15**

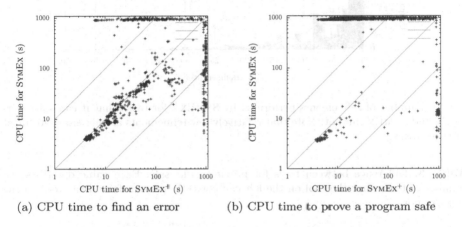

(a) CPU time to find an error   (b) CPU time to prove a program safe

Fig. 3. Runtime performance of SYMEX$^+$ and SYMEX in comparison

Comparison to Other Tools. We compare our implementation to the implementation of symbolic execution in CPACHECKER that does not use CEGAR (SYMEX) and to the mature symbolic-execution tool SYMBIOTIC 3 [16] in version 3.0.1 (SYMBIOTIC participated in SV-COMP in 2013, 2014 and 2016 [3–5]). For this evaluation, we use SYMEX$^+$ with refinement selection, using the heuristics *domain good – short*. Our benchmarks show the competitiveness of SYMEX$^+$ (Table 2). Figure 3a underlines the already mentioned contrast between eager SYMEX and lazy SYMEX$^+$. It shows the CPU time required for both approaches to find a (possibly non-existent) error. For a significant amount of tasks in our task set, only one of SYMEX and SYMEX$^+$ is able to find an error within 900 s. These cases are represented by the points at the right border (SYMEX$^+$ reaches the time limit) and upper border (SYMEX reaches the time limit) of the plot. For proving the safety of a program, SYMEX$^+$ performs significantly better, showing bad performance for only few programs, due to its laziness (Fig. 3b). The high precision of eager symbolic execution is often unnecessary to correctly decide whether a program is safe or unsafe. This is underlined by the number of refinements that are necessary for SYMEX$^+$ to analyze a task. For most tasks for which

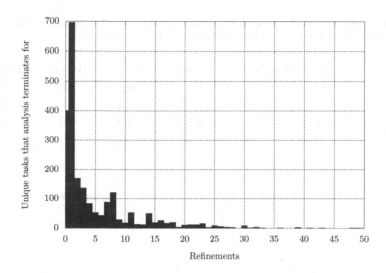

Fig. 4. Number of refinements performed by SYMEX$^+$ for tasks that it can solve correctly and SYMEX can not. Note that relatively few refinements are necessary for most of these tasks.

Table 3. Difference between tools for proving tasks safe. Each value describes the number of tasks that the tool on the left can correctly prove safe and the tool on the top can not.

	¬ SYMEX	¬ SYMEX$^+$	¬ SYMBIOTIC		correct TRUE
SYMEX	-	83	62	of	171
SYMEX$^+$	1954	-	1444	of	2042
SYMBIOTIC	660	171	-	of	769

SYMEX$^+$ is able to compute a result for, and for which SYMEX is not able to, a small number of refinements are necessary (Fig. 4). For an unsafe program, this implies that no or only few infeasible error paths have to be explored before a feasible error path is found (which eager analysis could not explore in the time limit at all). For a safe program, this implies that only few information must be tracked to prove all error paths infeasible.

Tables 3 and 4 show the number of tasks that one tool can solve while another can not. As already shown, the higher performance of SYMEX$^+$ for many tasks in comparison to SYMEX results in more tasks that can be successfully solved within the time limit. But due to the existing limitations of our analysis (e.g., pointer arithmetic), some of these are bound to be wrong, resulting in more tasks that are incorrectly declared as FALSE. Compared to SYMBIOTIC, the difference in solved tasks is even higher than compared to SYMEX, which can be accounted to

Table 4. Difference between tools for finding errors in tasks. Each value describes the number of tasks that the tool on the left correctly finds unsafe and the tool on the top does not.

	¬ SYMEX	¬ SYMEX⁺	¬ SYMBIOTIC		correct FALSE
SYMEX	-	213	318	of	634
SYMEX⁺	146	-	302	of	567
SYMBIOTIC	187	238	-	of	503

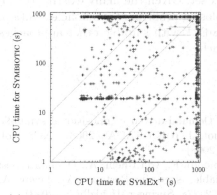

(a) CPU time to analyze a task

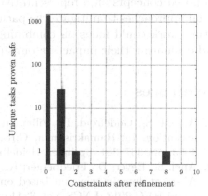

(b) Number of constraints necessary to prove tasks that SYMBIOTIC can not prove

Fig. 5. Comparison of SYMEX⁺ and SYMBIOTIC

its different optimizations and its implementation outside of CPACHECKER. It is obvious that the strengths of both analyses are different, as they follow a lazy and an eager approach. Figure 5a illustrates this. It displays the CPU time that each analysis takes for every task of our task set. It can be seen that both SYMBIOTIC and SYMEX⁺ have significantly different behavior for the same tasks. Because of its laziness, SYMEX⁺ is still able to correctly prove a significant amount of more tasks safe and declare a few more tasks unsafe in the given environment. For most of the safe tasks, no constraints on symbolic values have to be tracked at all (Fig. 5b). Thanks to CEGAR, SYMEX⁺ ignores these unnecessary constraints and keeps the state-space small.

5   Conclusion

By transferring the lazy approach of CEGAR to the domain of symbolic execution, we were able to mitigate the path-explosion problem of symbolic execution considerably. We implemented our proposed concepts in the open-source verification framework CPACHECKER and created a generic refinement procedure based on Craig interpolants which allows compositional refinement of precisions that is independent from the analyses' domain. In addition, we applied refinement selection based on sliced path prefixes and implemented new heuristics for it. Our evaluation shows the significant improvement that can be gained by using CEGAR with refinement selection and the impact that different heuristics can have on the analysis. By comparing our implementation with an implementation of the classical approach within the same tool, and with the external symbolic execution tool SYMBIOTIC, we were able to illustrate the differences between eager and lazy approaches. Our experimental study shows the competitiveness of our proposed concepts on a representative task set. Given the many existing orthogonal approaches to mitigate the path-explosion problem of symbolic execution, future work could focus on combining SYMEX$^+$ with suitable other approaches and evaluating their impact on our approach.

References

1. Anand, S., Godefroid, P., Tillmann, N.: Demand-driven compositional symbolic execution. In: Ramakrishnan, C.R., Rehof, J. (eds.) TACAS 2008. LNCS, vol. 4963, pp. 367–381. Springer, Heidelberg (2008)
2. Apel, S., Beyer, D., Friedberger, K., Raimondi, F., von Rhein, A.: Domain types: Abstract-domain selection based on variable usage. In: Bertacco, V., Legay, A. (eds.) HVC 2013. LNCS, vol. 8244, pp. 262–278. Springer, Heidelberg (2013)
3. Beyer, D.: Second competition on software verification. In: Piterman, N., Smolka, S.A. (eds.) TACAS 2013. LNCS, vol. 7795, pp. 594–609. Springer, Heidelberg (2013)
4. Beyer, D.: Status report on software verification. In: Ábrahám, E., Havelund, K. (eds.) TACAS 2014. LNCS, vol. 8413, pp. 373–388. Springer, Heidelberg (2014)
5. Beyer, D.: Reliable and reproducible competition results with BENCHEXEC and witnesses (report on SV-COMP 2016). In: Chechik, M., Raskin, J.-F. (eds.) TACAS 2016. LNCS, vol. 9636, pp. 887–904. Springer, Heidelberg (2016)
6. Beyer, D., Henzinger, T.A., Théoduloz, G.: Configurable software verification: Concretizing the convergence of model checking and program analysis. In: Damm, W., Hermanns, H. (eds.) CAV 2007. LNCS, vol. 4590, pp. 504–518. Springer, Heidelberg (2007)
7. Beyer, D., Henzinger, T.A., Théoduloz, G.: Program analysis with dynamic precision adjustment. In: ASE 2008, pp. 29–38. IEEE (2008)
8. Beyer, D., Keremoglu, M.E.: CPACHECKER: A tool for configurable software verification. In: Gopalakrishnan, G., Qadeer, S. (eds.) CAV 2011. LNCS, vol. 6806, pp. 184–190. Springer, Heidelberg (2011)
9. Beyer, D., Löwe, S.: Explicit-state software model checking based on CEGAR and interpolation. In: Cortellessa, V., Varró, D. (eds.) FASE 2013. LNCS, vol. 7793, pp. 146–162. Springer, Heidelberg (2013)
10. Beyer, D., Löwe, S., Wendler, P.: Benchmarking and resource measurement. In: Fischer, B., Geldenhuys, J. (eds.) SPIN 2015. LNCS, vol. 9232, pp. 160–178. Springer, Heidelberg (2015)
11. Beyer, D., Löwe, S., Wendler, P.: Refinement selection. In: Fischer, B., Geldenhuys, J. (eds.) SPIN 2015. LNCS, vol. 9232, pp. 20–38. Springer, Heidelberg (2015)

12. Beyer, D., Löwe, S., Wendler, P.: Sliced path prefixes: An effective method to enable refinement selection. In: Graf, S., Viswanathan, M. (eds.) Formal Techniques for Distributed Objects, Components, and Systems. LNCS, vol. 9039, pp. 228–243. Springer, Heidelberg (2015)

13. Beyer, D., Wendler, P.: Algorithms for software model checking: Predicate abstraction vs. IMPACT. In: FMCAD 2012, pp. 106–113 (2012)

14. Burnim, J., Sen, K.: Heuristics for scalable dynamic test generation. In: ASE 2008, pp. 443–446. IEEE (2008)

15. Cadar, C., Dunbar, D., Engler, D.R.: KLEE: Unassisted and automatic generation of high-coverage tests for complex systems programs. In: USENIX 2008, vol. 8, pp. 209–224 (2008)

16. Chalupa, M., Jonáš, M., Slaby, J., Strejcek, J., Vitovská, M.: SYMBIOTIC 3: New slicer and error-witness generation. In: Chechik, M., Raskin, J.-F. (eds.) TACAS 2016. LNCS, vol. 9636, pp. 946–949. Springer, Heidelberg (2016)

17. Chu, D.-H., Jaffar, J., Murali, V.: Lazy symbolic execution for enhanced learning. In: Bonakdarpour, B., Smolka, S.A. (eds.) RV 2014. LNCS, vol. 8734, pp. 323–339. Springer, Heidelberg (2014)

18. Clarke, E.M., Grumberg, O., Jha, S., Lu, Y., Veith, H.: Counterexample-guided abstraction refinement for symbolic model checking. J. ACM 50(5), 752–794 (2003)

19. Craig, W.: Linear reasoning. a new form of the Herbrand-Gentzen theorem. J. Symb. Log. 22(3), 250–268 (1957)

20. Godefroid, P.: Compositional dynamic test generation. In: POPL 2007, pp. 47–54. ACM (2007)

21. Godefroid, P., Klarlund, N., Sen, K.: DART: Directed automated random testing. In: PLDI 2005, pp. 213–223. ACM (2005)

22. Henzinger, T.A., Jhala, R., Majumdar, R., Sutre, G.: Lazy abstraction. In: POPL 2002, pp. 58–70. ACM (2002)

23. Jaffar, J., Michaylov, S., Stuckey, P.J., Yap, R.H.C.: The CLP(R) language and system. ACM Trans. Program. Lang. Syst. 14(3), 339–395 (1992)

24. Jaffar, J., Murali, V., Navas, J.A.: Boosting concolic testing via interpolation. In: FSE 2013, pp. 48–58. ACM (2013)

25. Jaffar, J., Navas, J.A., Santosa, A.E.: Unbounded symbolic execution for program verification. In: Khurshid, S., Sen, K. (eds.) RV 2011. LNCS, vol. 7186, pp. 396–411. Springer, Heidelberg (2012)

26. Jaffar, J., Santosa, A.E., Voicu, R.: An interpolation method for CLP traversal. In: Gent, I.P. (ed.) CP 2009. LNCS, vol. 5732, pp. 454–469. Springer, Heidelberg (2009)

27. King, J.C.: Symbolic execution and program testing. Commun. ACM 19(7), 385–394 (1976)

28. McMillan, K.L.: Interpolation and SAT-based model checking. In: Hunt, W.A., Somenzi, F. (eds.) CAV 2003. LNCS, vol. 2725, pp. 1–13. Springer, Heidelberg (2003)

29. McMillan, K.L.: Lazy annotation for program testing and verification. In: Touili, T., Cook, B., Jackson, P. (eds.) CAV 2010. LNCS, vol. 6174, pp. 104–118. Springer, Heidelberg (2010)

30. Slaby, J., Strejcek, J., Trtík, M.: Compact symbolic execution. In: Hung, D., Ogawa, M. (eds.) ATVA 2013. LNCS, vol. 8172, pp. 193–207. Springer, Heidelberg (2013)

Multi-core Model Checking of Large-Scale Reactive Systems Using Different State Representations

Marc Jasper[1,2(✉)] and Markus Schordan[1]

[1] Lawrence Livermore National Laboratory, Livermore, CA 94551, USA
{jasper3,schordan1}@llnl.gov
[2] TU Dortmund University, Dortmund 44227, Germany
marc.jasper@cs.tu-dortmund.de

Abstract. Model checking software systems allows to formally verify that their behavior adheres to certain properties. The state explosion problem presents a major obstacle to model checking due to the implied large concrete state spaces. We present an approach to efficient model checking of large-scale reactive systems that aims at a trade-off between the number of verifiable and falsifiable properties and the required analysis time. Our two-phase approach is based on a parallel state space exploration with explicit states for falsifying linear temporal logic (LTL) properties, and an abstract phase reasoning on the entire state space for verifying LTL properties. This two-phase approach enabled us to win the Rigorous Examination of Reactive Systems Challenge (RERS) in 2014 and 2015. We present a detailed evaluation based on 30 different RERS benchmarks regarding both our verification results and the obtainable parallel speedup.

1 Introduction

Model checking serves as a formal method for verifying certain temporal properties of an analyzed system [9]. Its application to software systems allows to verify aspects of how an analyzed program should behave, instead of just increasing the confidence in such properties by testing the program. Despite many advances in the field of model checking, the state explosion problem frequently prevents analysis tools from assessing the correctness of desired properties [11,29]. In order to guarantee that a property holds on an analyzed system, all feasible execution paths need to be explored. However, every choice within a program due to input or non-determinism can entail branching behavior. These branches often lead to an exponential blow-up of the analyzed program's state space.

Within the past years, many approaches have made progress in overcoming the state explosion problem, for example by switching to symbolic state representations [7] or by applying (iteratively refinable) abstractions [10]. Even though these advances have helped to increase the usefulness of model checking to real-world problems, the underlying problem of large state spaces still remains.

© Springer International Publishing AG 2016
T. Margaria and B. Steffen (Eds.): ISoLA 2016, Part I, LNCS 9952, pp. 212–226, 2016.
DOI: 10.1007/978-3-319-47166-2_15

In this paper, we present our approach to the verification of large-scale software systems that aims at a trade-off between the quality of verification results and the execution time required to produce them. Verification tasks from challenges such as the Competition on Software Verification (SV-COMP) [4] or RERS [19] provide benchmarks that help to compare algorithmic approaches and the verification tools that implement them. Using our analysis tool Code-Thorn which is based on the ROSE Compiler Infrastructure [25], we were able to win the RERS challenge in both 2014 and 2015 with error-free submissions.

In order to achieve these results, we have designed two distinct analysis phases that utilize the concepts of bounded model checking (BMC) and model checking of abstractions respectively. During the BMC phase, we analyze the initial segment of a given program's state space up to a certain depth k. This allows us to find counterexamples of violated properties. During a second analysis phase, we over-approximate the possible behavior of an analyzed system by using a coarse abstraction. When considering each variable as a dimension of each state in the program, our abstraction projects the state space onto few remaining dimensions. Furthermore, a prefix of the concrete state space with a fixed bound k can be included in the abstract model in order to increase the precision of our abstraction. By model checking this over-approximated state space, we can verify some properties that hold on the analyzed system.

Our implementations of both analysis phases greatly benefit from multi-core architectures. Multiple threads can explore the analyzed program's (abstract) state space in parallel which helps to reduce the required execution time of our tool.

We present a thorough evaluation of our approach based on benchmarks from the RERS challenges. More specifically, we use benchmark problems 1 to 9 from 2012, problems 28 to 36 from 2013, and problems 1 to 12 from 2014. We focus on these benchmarks because their difficulty scales according to their enumeration and because their variety covers most aspects of RERS. Our evaluation includes detailed results for the verification tasks and an assessment of the parallel speedup of our analysis.

The utilized benchmarks follow the paradigm of event-condition-action (ECA) systems that is used for varying purposes such as database management systems [21]. ECA systems can be described as (infinite) loops with each iteration containing the steps reading input, evaluating the next program state, and producing related output. By exploring the state space systematically according to the ECA layout of these programs, we further highlight some of their structural properties. This evaluation can also help to characterize benchmarks from future verification challenges because the RERS 2012 programs are used as part of SV-COMP.

The following section discusses our approach in the context of related work. In Sect. 3, we introduce our analysis and its application to ECA systems. Section 4 evaluates our approach based on benchmarks from the RERS challenge, whereas Sect. 5 presents both a conclusion and future work.

2   Related Work

The RERS challenge provides ECA systems as program verification benchmarks [19]. ECA systems are frequently implemented for example in logic controllers due to their easily (re-)configurable reactive behavior [1]. The RERS C and Java programs are auto-generated to allow for convenient scalability of their complexity for example considering the number of lines of codes, used code features, and the size of the input and output alphabets. These programs cover many of the C language features but exclude heap allocation and recursive function calls. The benchmark generation guarantees that the results to all provided queries of reachability and LTL properties adhere to the designed solution. In contrast to the verification challenge SV-COMP that only covers reachability and termination properties [4], RERS benchmarks feature a more general mix of safety and liveness properties that have to be assessed by the participants [28].

The RERS'12 challenge covered 19 ECA benchmarks of varying categories[1]. 5 teams participated that year, applying different approaches such as symbolic bounded model checking [22]. All but one of the participants provided some wrong answers to the verification tasks, partly by choice if the confidence in their results was high [30]. The single error-free submission to RERS'12 could not produce any results for problems 8 and 9 while using an approach that employs binary decision diagrams [6]. In comparison, our current approach allows us to compute the entire state space for the initial 9 problems and therefore to assess all reachability and LTL properties correctly.

Since its 2014 iteration, SV-COMP incorporates slightly modified versions of the RERS'12 benchmarks[2]. Within SV-COMP, the LTL verification tasks of RERS are ignored and only the reachability of violated assertions has to be analyzed. Support for proving liveness properties was only recently added to symbolic model checkers [12,13], which is why many tools are restricted to analyzing safety properties [2,3,6,15].

Many symbolic model checkers are based on specializations and therefore prove properties separately [3]. This approach can be time consuming if multiple properties have to be checked on the same program. In contrast, our approach based on BMC and model checking of an abstraction allows to check several properties at once because our generated state transition system (STS) is not influenced by a specific analyzed property.

The initial phase of our analysis is conceptually an instance of BMC. Usual bounded model checkers rely on SAT or SMT solving to answer queries of whether or not a certain property holds [8]. Given a (model of) a program, a property, and an exploration depth k, BMC extracts a verification condition (VC) such that the property holds within k steps if and only if the VC is unsatisfiable. In order to have the same basic algorithm for both analysis phases, we choose to instead store the analyzed segment of the state space explicitly in an STS like in [24]. The STS can consist of concrete or abstract states.

---

[1] http://www.rers-challenge.org/2012/index.php?page=problems.
[2] http://sv-comp.sosy-lab.org/2014/benchmarks.php.

During the BMC phase, our goal is to efficiently compute a large portion of the analyzed program's state space. In this regard our approach is similar to tools that focus on exhaustively exploring the explicit concrete state space [16,31]. However, BMC is not sound as it never allows to exclude the possibility of an error after more than k steps. In order to verify properties, we therefore also model check an abstracted version of the analyzed program.

Model checking abstract models derived from programs has been investigated for over two decades. One of the earliest works described how several data-flow analysis problems could be viewed as model checking of an abstraction derived from the program [26]. Referring to this correlation, our abstraction can be described as an instance of property-oriented expansion (POE) [27] which aims to increase the precision of a data-flow analysis by refining a program model such as its control flow graph (CFG) (see Sect. 3). The relation between data-flow analyses and model checking was later clarified in [23].

Recent work has proposed conditional model checking as a way of extracting information gained from one model checking attempt in order to reuse this information in a subsequent run of the analysis [5]. The second analysis phase in our approach can reuse the STS generated during phase one, but no conditions are extracted that aid the model checking in phase two.

Although model checking has been an active research topic for more than 30 years, multi-core support has been introduced only recently into well-established tools such as SPIN [17,18]. The usual expectation when parallelizing the state space exploration using only shared memory is that such an approach does not scale well due to the required locks or semaphores. Multiple threads can compute successor states in parallel, but maintaining the resulting states and accessing the global worklist can severely reduce the achievable speedup. One possible solution is to apply a partition function along with local worklists and a load balancing scheme, an approach that is also applicable to distributed model checking [20]. Even though implementing advanced parallelization techniques could further improve the parallel speedup of our tool, we show in our evaluation that using the shared-memory approach together with a global worklist scales well when analyzing computation-intensive programs.

3 Parallel, Loop-Aware State Space Exploration

Within this section, we introduce our two-phase analysis approach to model checking programs with a finite state space. By dividing our analysis into two distinct phases, we can generate STS's for the efficient falsification and verification of large numbers of properties. We compute these STS's using a parallel and loop-aware state space exploration. The term loop-aware refers to the fact that we unroll the most outer loop in the analyzed program iteration by iteration.

We choose this loop-aware exploration instead of a breadth-first search because it allows to explore the state space of ECA systems more systematically. The additional synchronization after each loop iteration might reduce the parallel speedup slightly. During our measurements however, the loop-aware exploration was on average less than 13.98 % slower compared to a breadth-first search when analyzing the first 9 problems from RERS'12 using concrete states.

Table 1 shows the applied techniques, the implications for the computed STS, as well as the obtainable verification results for each analysis phase. A precise STS does not contain any spurious behavior whereas an over-approximated one might. An STS is sound if and only if all of the properties it allows to verify are also valid for the actual program.

The table further distinguishes between state space exploration and model checking. As a result of phase 1a, we retrieve a precise and bounded STS that allows to find reachable labels during its construction. Phase 2a generates an over-approximated and sound STS consisting of abstract states that is used to determine non-reachable labels after it has been computed. In order to check the validity of LTL properties (phases 1b and 2b), we transform the STS into a Buechi automaton and present an interface for traversing this automaton to the SPOT model checking library [14] (version 1.2.6).

Table 1. Overview of our two analysis phases and the obtainable results. Each phase is further divided into state space exploration (a) and model checking (b).

Phase	Technique	Computed model	Verification results
1a	Loop-bounded exploration (concrete/explicit states)	Precise & bounded STS	Reachable labels (failing assertions)
1b	Model checking the STS	-	Falsified LTL
2a	Exploration using an abstract interpretation	Over-approximated &sound STS	Non-reachable labels (correct assertions)
2b	Model checking the STS (abstract model)	-	Verified LTL

Our abstract interpretation of the analyzed program always preserves precise program locations. For both phases 1a and 2a, we use Algorithm 1 (PLSE) to explore the state space of the analyzed program and generate the STS. This algorithm explores the state space by unrolling the most outer loop of the program iteration by iteration. For the systems analyzed within this paper, this is equivalent to the ECA loop. PLSE uses two worklists W_c and W_n to store states from the current loop iteration and states from the next loop iteration respectively. Once the current iteration has been explored completely, the worklists either switch roles or the analysis terminates.

The loop-aware state space exploration in PLSE supports multiple threads. Our straight-forward parallelization uses shared data structures for both the STS and the worklist. The access to shared data has to be locked appropriately. Because multiple threads are working in parallel, the next loop iteration is only

---

Algorithm 1. Parallel, loop-aware state space exploration (PLSE)

Input: Inter-procedural control flow graph: ICFG
Input: number of loop iterations to explore: bound
Input: number of threads: n
Output: State transition system (STS): G
s_0 := init(ICFG);   ▷ the initial program state
S := $\{s_0\}$;   ▷ initialize set of program states (shared)
G := $\varnothing$;   ▷ (shared)
W_c := S_p;   ▷ worklist current loop iteration (shared)
W_n := $\varnothing$;   ▷ worklist next loop iteration (shared)
i := 0;   ▷ loop counter (shared)
busy[n] := [**false** for t in (1..n)];   ▷ thread activity vector (shared)
parallel loop
  t := get_thread_id();
  if all_false(busy) **then**
    if $W_n = \varnothing$ **or** $i =$ bound **then**
      | **return** G
    else
      | swap(W_c, W_n);
      | i++;
    end
  end
  if empty(W_c) **then**
    | busy[t] := **false**;
  else
    busy[t] := **true**;
    s := choose(W_c);
    S_n := successor_states(s);
    foreach $s_n \in S_n$ **do**
      G += $\{(s, s_n)\}$;
      if $s_n \notin S$ **then**
        if is_most_outer_loop_label(s_n) **then**
          | W_n += $\{s_n\}$;
        else
          | W_c += $\{s_n\}$;
        end
        S += $\{s_n\}$;
      end
    end
  end
end

---

explored once both the current worklist is empty and all threads are idle. This implies a synchronization at the end of each loop iteration.

An essential part of the presented algorithm is the function call "successor_states(s)". The implementation of this transfer function decides for example whether or not the STS contains concrete states or abstract ones. In addition, a sequence of states without any branching behavior can be evaluated using large-step semantics. We apply this technique during our evaluation (Sect. 4) in order to compute one state per ECA loop iteration. In the case of abstract states, function "successor_states(s)" can evaluate the next state based on the applied abstract interpretation.

We optimize the source code of the analyzed ECA programs in order to reduce the resource requirements of our analysis. For evaluating our tool based on the benchmarks from the RERS challenge (Sect. 4), we first transform the input and output calls of these program. In particular, the input is the only local variable within these programs and gets passed on from function to function. We transform the input to a global variable. In addition, we add a new global output variable that stores the most recent output value and also information about errors that have occurred. We check that encoding failing assertions in the output does not alter the program semantics by verifying that no instructions follow any of the assertions in the inter-procedural CFG. In addition to this transformation, we alter the code using function inlining, constant propagation and array-specific optimizations.

For the ECA systems analyzed within this paper, we choose a coarse abstraction based on the input and output variables of the transformed programs during phase 2 of the analysis. The state space is projected onto these two global variables, implying that all others are ignored within the state representation. We apply PLSE while using a version of the function call "successor_states(s)" according to our abstract interpretation. Whenever a condition is evaluated based on the value of a variable other than input and output, both possible branches are added to the set of successor states. The bound parameter of algorithm PLSE is set to infinity during analysis phase 2.

In general, it is not guaranteed that we are able to evaluate a subset of variables precisely while ignoring the remaining ones. This is however not a problem regarding the input of a program because we have to explore all possible valuations regardless. In the setting of the analyzed ECA systems, the output is always a number from a predefined set of constants and not computed based on the values of other variables. Instead, the chosen path in the inter-procedural CFG determines the output value. We therefore explore additional execution paths that are not feasible in the analyzed program, but the values of both input and output are always known precisely.

Because of the finite set of input and output symbols of the analyzed ECA systems, our analysis phase 2 always terminates. Given the domains of possible input symbols I, possible output symbols O, and program locations L, the maximum number of abstract states can be computed as $|S_{max}| = |I| \cdot |O| \cdot |L|$. Our evaluation (Sect. 4) shows that using this coarse abstraction only does not always yield favorable results. We therefore increase the precision by appending the STS from analysis phase 2 to an STS from phase 1 that was generated using a fixed bound.

Due to the finite nature of I and O and because of the fact that the output is never computed based on other variables, our abstract interpretation is an instance of POE. The equivalent description in terms of POE would be to expand the control flow graph based on the information stored within the domain $I \times O$. By using the presented projection onto input and output variables, we were able to obtain results that helped us to win the RERS challenges 2014 and 2015 (Sect. 4).

4   Evaluation

We evaluate our analysis approach (Sect. 3) using benchmarks from previous RERS challenges. During this evaluation, we use an extended naming scheme for these benchmarks that includes in which year they were released. `Problem1.c` from the RERS'12 challenge becomes "problem 1201", `Problem10.c` from the RERS'14 challenge "problem 1410" and so on. The listed number of variable states represents all encountered different valuations of program variables after we apply our transformations (Sect. 3). We do not consider different program locations when counting the number of states in order to better characterize the complexity of the underlying ECA structure.

4.1   Verification Results for RERS Benchmarks

Using our presented approach, we are able to compute the entire reachable state space for problems 1201 through 1209 as well as for problems 1328 and 1401. Table 2 summarizes some results for RERS benchmarks that are achievable using our approach presented within this paper. For each benchmark, we list the bound parameter of analysis phase 1 ("p1") and also the fixed bound of the concrete STS that the abstract model from phase 2 is appended to ("p2"). We choose to increase the precision of our abstract STS using a concrete STS prefix with loop bound 6 in order to improve our verification results. For the RERS'13 benchmarks, the increased precision does not yield additional verified properties. When analyzing the RERS'14 benchmarks however, including the bounded prefix increases the number of verified LTL properties during analysis phase 2 from 116 to 129.

In addition to detailed results for the verification tasks that comprise (un-)reachable failing assertions and LTL properties, we present the number of distinct variable states that are computed during phase 1 and the required execution time of each phase while using up to 36 threads. The entry "not required" indicates that the entire concrete state space could be computed during analysis phase 1.

For problems 1201 through 1209, 1328, and 1401, we can quickly compute the entire concrete state space. The presented results cover all of the reachable

Table 2. Results of our approach for various benchmarks of the RERS challenges. The loop bounds for phase 1 ("p1") and phase 2 ("p2") serve as parameters of our analysis. We list the number of verified ("yes") and falsified ("no") properties as well as additional analysis statistics.

Problem	Depth k p1/p2	Reachability yes/no/?	LTL yes/no/?	#states p1	Time p1	Time p2
1201	7/-	14/47/ 0	29/ 71/ 0	312	0.635	Not required
1202	4/-	8/53/ 0	33/ 67/ 0	181	0.600	Not required
1203	6/-	14/47/ 0	44/ 56/ 0	342	1.216	Not required
1204	21/-	25/36/ 0	26/ 74/ 0	1365	3.056	Not required
1205	8/-	25/36/ 0	23/ 77/ 0	1690	6.338	Not required
1206	7/-	26/35/ 0	30/ 70/ 0	1494	5.834	Not required
1207	8/-	25/36/ 0	46/ 54/ 0	19437	1:10.731	Not required
1208	11/-	25/36/ 0	47/ 53/ 0	22657	2:07.590	Not required
1209	25/-	25/36/ 0	28/ 72/ 0	13472	1:40.860	Not required
1328	16/-	28/32/ 0	28/ 72/ 0	1515	1.861	Not required
1329	13/6	26/ 9/25	35/ 59/ 6	10748915	1:35:49.325	12.093
1330	14/6	26/15/19	20/ 64/16	2684980	18:50.641	10.154
1331	12/6	29/ 8/23	40/ 58/ 2	7865244	2:14:47.644	30.682
1332	10/6	22/ 9/29	0/ 74/26	5305725	12:34.673	26.238
1333	9/6	27/ 9/24	0/ 85/15	1300986	6:25.937	54.857
1334	9/6	27/ 8/25	49/ 51/ 0	1189625	21:01.769	10:01.659
1335	9/6	0/10/50	20/ 69/11	1116354	12:54.104	20:32.995
1336	9/6	0/ 8/52	15/ 82/ 3	522763	21:38.828	55:29.747
1401	26/-	39/61/ 0	37/ 63/ 0	5567	3.463	not required
1402	14/6	23/ 8/69	43/ 52/ 5	7429	2.990	2.038
1403	14/6	16/41/43	10/ 47/43	2809	3.390	3.463
1404	14/6	35/11/54	9/ 79/12	1095312	3:58.770	29.729
1405	14/6	37/ 2/61	6/ 74/20	1468068	3:25.899	26.385
1406	14/6	5/10/85	25/ 62/13	1326093	10:43.076	1:55.930
1407	14/6	7/16/77	21/ 73/ 6	490102	1:42.492	14:07.099
1408	14/6	11/22/67	15/ 78/ 7	3923824	14:22.406	28:06.280
1409	14/6	51/ 5/44	4/ 73/23	539017	7:07.030	2:19:13.139
1410	9/-	23/ 0/77	0/ 67/33	97662	6:19.408	timeout(3h)
1411	9/-	32/ 0/68	0/ 55/45	97739	5:02.011	timeout(3h)
1412	9/-	30/ 0/70	0/ 67/33	125467	16:32.987	timeout(3h)

failing assertions except for problems 1332, 1335 and 1336. We have overall successfully discovered 92.03 % of the reachable failing assertions within these programs, in addition to many that we can verify as unreachable. Considering the LTL solutions, we found counterexamples for all violated LTL properties of all problems except for 1332, 1333, and 1409 through 1412. The discovered LTL counterexamples amount to 97.23 % of all violated LTL properties.

Using our loop-aware search that unrolls the most outer ECA loop iteration by iteration, we can further characterize the benchmarks of RERS. Due to space restrictions, we focus on analyzing some structural properties of the initial 9 RERS problems 1201 through 1209. In Table 3 we list up to which loop bound i these programs need to be explored in order to find what subsets of reachable

Table 3. Number of traces to distinct reachable errors (R) and counterexamples for violated LTL properties (L) that can be discovered up to a certain ECA iteration i. Statistics for problems 1201 through 1209. Empty entries indicate that the state space exploration terminates before the given number of iterations is reached.

i	1201 R/L	1202 R/L	1203 R/L	1204 R/L	1205 R/L	1206 R/L	1207 R/L	1208 R/L	1209 R/L
1	0/ 0	0/ 0	0/ 0	0/ 0	0/ 0	0/ 0	0/ 0	0/ 0	0/ 0
2	1/ 0	0/22	1/ 0	1/ 0	1/ 0	1/ 0	1/ 0	1/ 0	1/ 0
3	1/45	4/57	1/ 0	1/ 0	1/ 0	1/ 0	1/ 0	1/ 0	1/ 0
4	2/48	8/67	2/ 0	1/ 0	1/23	1/33	1/ 0	1/ 0	1/ 0
5	7/48		9/47	1/ 0	1/75	1/70	1/46	1/49	1/ 0
6	11/66		14/56	1/63	1/75	26/70	1/54	1/53	1/62
7	14/71			1/71	1/77	26/70	1/54	25/53	1/72
8				1/72	25/77		25/54	25/53	1/72
9				1/72				25/53	1/72
10				1/74				25/53	1/72
11				1/74				25/53	1/72
12				1/74					1/72
13				1/74					1/72
14				1/74					1/72
15				1/74					1/72
16				1/74					1/72
17				12/74					1/72
18				18/74					1/72
19				24/74					1/72
20				24/74					1/72
21				25/74					1/72
22									7/72
23									14/72
24									18/72
25									25/72

failing assertions and counterexamples for LTL properties. These statistics can help to better evaluate different results for these benchmarks, for example in future iterations of the SV-COMP challenge.

4.2 Performance Improvement Due to Parallel Speedup

This section assesses to what extend the straight-forward parallelization discussed in Sect. 3 decreases the execution time of our analysis.

First of all, we measure the time for each step in our sequential analysis (phase 1) in order to assess the impact of parallelizing the computation of the STS. Figure 1 shows the required execution time for each step when analyzing the medium-sized problem 1407 up to different ECA iterations. This stacked bar plot reveals an exponential increase of the STS when considering different loop bounds. When analyzing all of the first 14 iterations that where used for the results in Table 2, the computation of the STS amounts to 96 % of the required analysis time. Similar observations can be made for other RERS benchmarks.

The fact that computing the STS is by far the most time consuming part of our approach justifies that we only focus on parallelizing this step.

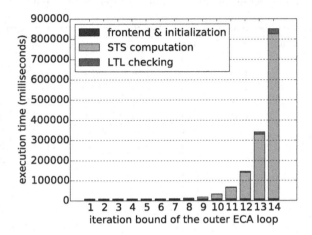

Fig. 1. Execution time in milliseconds for increasing ECA loop bounds while considering individual steps of our analysis (phase 1)

Figure 2 illustrates the parallel speedup of the STS computation for all RERS benchmarks analyzed in Table 2. The measurements were taken on a machine featuring two Intel Xeon E5-2699 v3 processors (18 physical CPU cores each at 2.3 GHz base frequency) combined with 128GB RAM. All of the sub-figures in Fig. 2 show that our straight-forward parallel STS computation scales well when analyzing computation-intensive ECA systems like problems 1207, 1208, and 1209. The sequential STS computation time for these problems falls in the range between 2 and 6 min, and this time decreases in an almost linear manner when using additional threads.

The speedup for RERS benchmarks with lower problem numbers per year does not scale as nicely, especially the very small problems (graphs using circular markers) suffer from comparably little performance increase when using additional threads. The following observations form the main reasons for this behavior.

First of all, the size of the generated STS is significantly smaller for some of these problems than for more complex problems (cf. Table 2). This can imply a certain idle time for some of the threads when there are not enough different states in the STS for which successors can be computed simultaneously. In addition, the transfer function has to evaluate fewer lines of code for the smaller problems. This leads to a faster calculation of the next ECA state and therefore entails more locking overhead when different threads are trying to access the STS or the global worklist at the same time. For the problems from RERS'14, the input alphabet size also increases after every three problems, potentially allowing for more parallelism when analyzing the larger programs. We noticed

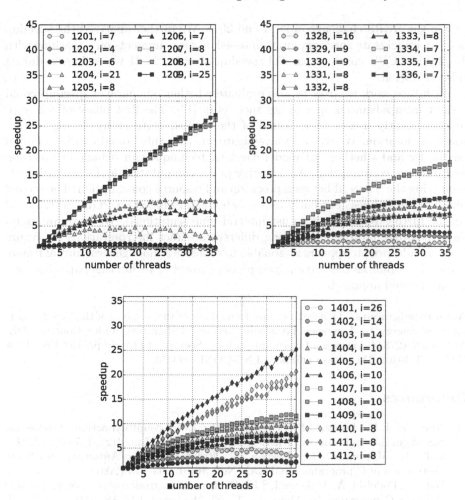

Fig. 2. Speedup values based on the number of threads used. The state space is explored up to a certain loop bound i (analysis phase 1). Function $f(x) = x$ defines a linear speedup when computing successor states individually.

that the parallel speedup usually increases with higher loop bounds i, meaning that the graphs in Fig. 2 might reach larger values when i is increased further.

5 Conclusion and Future Work

We presented our approach of a parallel state space exploration that aims to efficiently analyze a large number of safety and liveness properties. Two different analysis phases were introduced that allow to falsify and verify properties respectively. Our evaluation contains results for various RERS benchmarks from 2012 to 2014 and demonstrates the capabilities of this approach that helped us to win the RERS challenge in 2014 and 2015. We further analyzed the speedup of our parallel state space exploration based on measurements on a machine with 36 physical CPU cores. A parallel speedup of up to 27.21 was achieved during this evaluation.

In future work we plan to also evaluate whether our parallel speedup could benefit from advanced approaches such as in [17]. The first phase of our approach currently uses a fixed bound of the explicit state prefix during a state space exploration. We will also investigate whether this bound can be adapted on the fly and whether our model checking technique can benefit in precision and resource consumption. An adaptive prefix computation looks promising for improving the trade-off between precision and resource consumption. The second phase of our analysis currently uses an abstraction based on POE (Sect. 3) and can be further refined (e.g. to use interval representations). We leave an analysis of possible improvements using different abstract interpretations for future work. In addition, it appears reasonable to conceive a more general formal framework that combines the two analysis phases presented within this paper into one parameterized approach.

Acknowledgments. This work was performed under the auspices of the U.S. Department of Energy by Lawrence Livermore National Laboratory under Contract DE-AC52-07NA27344, Lawrence Livermore National Security, LLC, via project ProVESA KJ0401/KJ0402. IM release number LLNL-CONF-690843.

References

1. Almeida, E.E., Luntz, J.E., Tilbury, D.M.: Event-condition-action systems for reconfigurable logic control. IEEE Trans. Autom. Sci. Eng. **4**(2), 167–181 (2007)
2. Ball, T., Majumdar, R., Millstein, T., Rajamani, S.K.: Automatic predicate abstraction of C programs. SIGPLAN Not. **36**(5), 203–213 (2001)
3. Ball, T., Podelski, A., Rajamani, S.K.: Boolean and cartesian abstraction for model checking C programs. In: Margaria, T., Yi, W. (eds.) TACAS 2001. LNCS, vol. 2031, p. 268. Springer, Heidelberg (2001)
4. Beyer, D.: Software verification and verifiable witnesses. In: Baier, C., Tinelli, C. (eds.) TACAS 2015. LNCS, vol. 9035, pp. 401–416. Springer, Heidelberg (2015)
5. Beyer, D., Henzinger, T.A., Keremoglu, M.E., Wendler, P.: Conditional model checking: a technique to pass information between verifiers. In: Proceedings of the ACM SIGSOFT 20th International Symposium on the Foundations of Software Engineering, p. 57. ACM (2012)
6. Beyer, D., Stahlbauer, A.: BDD-based software verification. Applications to event-condition-action systems. Intl. J. Softw. Tools Technol. Transf. **16**(5), 507–518 (2014)
7. Burch, J.R., Clarke, E.M., McMillan, K.L., Dill, D.L., Hwang, L.-J.: Symbolic model checking: 10^{20} states and beyond. Inf. Comput. **98**(2), 142–170 (1992)
8. Clarke, E., Biere, A., Raimi, R., Zhu, Y.: Bounded model checking using satisfiability solving. Form. Methods Syst. Des. **19**(1), 7–34 (2001)
9. Clarke, E.M., Emerson, A.E.: Design and synthesis of synchronization skeletons using branching time temporal logic. In: Kozen, D. (ed.) Workshop on Logic of Programs. LNCS, vol. 131, pp. 52–71. Springer, Heidelberg (1981)

10. Clarke, E.M., Grumberg, O., Long, D.E.: Model checking and abstraction. ACM Trans. Program. Lang. Syst. (TOPLAS) **16**(5), 1512–1542 (1994)
11. Clarke, E.M., Klieber, W., Nováček, M., Zuliani, P.: Model checking and the state explosion problem. In: Meyer, B., Nordio, M. (eds.) LASER 2011. LNCS, vol. 7682, pp. 1–30. Springer, Heidelberg (2012)
12. Cook, B., Gotsman, A., Podelski, A., Rybalchenko, A., Vardi, M.Y.: Proving that programs eventually do something good. In: Proceedings of the 34th Annual ACM SIGPLAN-SIGACT Symposium on Principles of Programming Languages, POPL 2007, pp. 265–276. ACM, New York (2007)
13. Cook, B., Khlaaf, H., Piterman, N.: Fairness for infinite-state systems. In: Baier, C., Tinelli, C. (eds.) TACAS 2015. LNCS, vol. 9035, pp. 384–398. Springer, Heidelberg (2015)
14. Duret-Lutz, A., Poitrenaud, D.: SPOT: an extensible model checking library using transition-based generalized Büchi automata. In: The IEEE Computer Society's 12th Annual International Symposium on Modeling, Analysis, and Simulation of Computer and Telecommunications Systems, 2004 (MASCOTS 2004), pp. 76–83. IEEE (2004)
15. Henzinger, T.A., Jhala, R., Majumdar, R., Sutre, G.: Software verification with BLAST. In: Ball, T., Rajamani, S.K. (eds.) SPIN 2003. LNCS, vol. 2648, pp. 235–239. Springer, Heidelberg (2003)
16. Holzmann, G.: The SPIN Model Checker Primer and Reference Manual, 1st edn. Addison-Wesley Professional, Boston (2011)
17. Holzmann, G.J.: Parallelizing the spin model checker. In: Donaldson, A., Parker, D. (eds.) SPIN 2012. LNCS, vol. 7385, pp. 155–171. Springer, Heidelberg (2012)
18. Holzmann, G.J., Bosnacki, D.: Multi-core model checking with SPIN. In: Parallel and Distributed Processing Symposium, 2007. IPDPS 2007. IEEE International, pp. 1–8, March 2007
19. Howar, F., Isberner, M., Merten, M., Steffen, B., Beyer, D.: The RERS greybox challenge 2012: analysis of event-condition-action systems. In: Margaria, T., Steffen, B. (eds.) ISoLA 2012, Part I. LNCS, vol. 7609, pp. 608–614. Springer, Heidelberg (2012)
20. Kumar, R., Mercer, E.G.: Load balancing parallel explicit state model checking. Electron. Notes in Theor. Comput. Sci. **128**(3), 19–34 (2005)
21. McCarthy, D., Dayal, U.: The architecture of an active database management system. ACM Sigmod Rec. **18**(2), 215–224 (1989). ACM
22. Morse, J., Cordeiro, L., Nicole, D., Fischer, B.: Applying symbolic bounded model checking to the 2012 RERS greybox challenge. Intl. J. Softw. Tools Technol. Transf. **16**(5), 519–529 (2014)
23. Schmidt, D.A.: Data flow analysis is model checking of abstract interpretations. In: Proceedings of the 25th ACM SIGPLAN-SIGACT Symposium on Principles of Programming Languages, POPL 1998, pp. 38–48. ACM, New York (1998)
24. Schordan, M., Prantl, A.: Combining static analysis and state transition graphs for verification of event-condition-action systems in the RERS 2012 and 2013 challenges. Intl. J. Softw. Tools Technol. Transf. **16**(5), 493–505 (2014)
25. Schordan, M., Quinlan, D.: A source-to-source architecture for user-defined optimizations. In: Böszörményi, L., Schojer, P. (eds.) JMLC 2003. LNCS, vol. 2789, pp. 214–223. Springer, Heidelberg (2003). doi:10.1007/978-3-540-45213-3_27
26. Steffen, B.: Data flow analysis as model checking. In: Ito, T., Meyer, A.R. (eds.) TACS 1991. LNCS, vol. 526, pp. 346–364. Springer, Heidelberg (1991). doi:10.1007/3-540-54415-1_54

27. Steffen, B.: Property-oriented expansion. In: Cousot, R., Schmidt, D.A. (eds.) International Static Analysis Symposium. LNCS, vol. 1145, pp. 22–41. Springer, Heidelberg (1996)

28. Steffen, B., Isberner, M., Naujokat, S., Margaria, T., Geske, M.: Property-driven benchmark generation: synthesizing programs of realistic structure. Softw. Tools Technol. Transf. **16**(5), 465–479 (2014)

29. Valmari, A.: The state explosion problem. In: Reisig, W., Rozenberg, G. (eds.) APN 1998. LNCS, vol. 1491, pp. 429–528. Springer, Heidelberg (1998)

30. van de Pol, J., Ruys, T.C., te Brinke, S.: Thoughtful Brute-force attack of the RERS 2012 and 2013 challenges. Intl. J. Softw. Tools Technol. Transf. **16**(5), 481–491 (2014)

31. Visser, W., Mehlitz, P.: Model checking programs with Java pathfinder. In: Godefroid, P. (ed.) SPIN 2005. LNCS, vol. 3639, pp. 27–27. Springer, Heidelberg (2005). doi:10.1007/11537328_5

Sparse Analysis of Variable Path Predicates Based upon SSA-Form

Thomas S. Heinze$^{(\boxtimes)}$ and Wolfram Amme

Institute of Computer Science, Friedrich Schiller University Jena, Jena, Germany
{t.heinze,wolfram.amme}@uni-jena.de

Abstract. Static Single Assignment Form benefits data flow analysis by its static guarantees on the definitions and uses of variables. In this paper, we show how to exploit these guarantees to enable a sparse data flow analysis of variable predicates, for gaining a rich predicate-based and path-oriented characterization of the values of program variables.

1 Introduction

Static Single Assignment Form (SSA-form) [3] is now widely used as an intermediate format for supporting program analysis and optimization. Various analysis and optimization techniques have been defined for SSA-form, each exploiting the properties of SSA-form to enable a sparse analysis. In a *sparse data flow analysis* [9,17], instead of propagating abstract information about global program state along the program's control flow, as done in classical data flow analysis [14], information is propagated only from the information source to the points where the information is needed, in case of SSA-form therefore from variable definition to variable use. As a result, less information is stored at fewer program points.

In this paper, we enlarge the set of sparse analyses on SSA-form by a novel technique for deriving *variable predicates* as a predicate-based abstraction on a program's variables' values. We will in particular show how the static single assignment property of SSA-form naturally facilitates the analysis sparseness, in that it allows for the characterization of the values of variables by predicates collected along the chains of data dependences for the variables' defining instructions, instead of using global program state. Furthermore, it enables the incorporation and derivation of path information in terms of set-based predicate encodings, in order to distinguish variables' values among different control flow paths. As variable predicates in this way constitute a rich though finite model for a program's variables, methods for program verification and model checking can benefit from incorporating the information derived by our analysis.

The rest of the paper is structured as follows: Sect. 2 introduces foundations and main concepts, namely SSA-form, variable predicates and our sparse analysis for deriving them. In Sect. 3, we map the analysis to the notion of montone dataflow frameworks for proving its correctness. Afterwards, improvements are developed with respect to spurious data flow and unreachable code. Section 5 sketches the use of the analysis in a system for the generation of more precise

© Springer International Publishing AG 2016
T. Margaria and B. Steffen (Eds.): ISoLA 2016, Part I, LNCS 9952, pp. 227–242, 2016.
DOI: 10.1007/978-3-319-47166-2_16

Petri net models of WS-BPEL programs used for model checking. We summarize this paper and relate our approach to others' in Sects. 6 and 7, respectively.

2   Sparse Analysis of Variable Path Predicates

We are interested in deriving a predicate-based characterization of variables' values. In other words, a predicate for each program variable, describing the fraction of program state relevant for its value. In addition, the derived predicates shall distinguish among a variable's value on differing control flow paths. A natural match for the hereby defined analysis problem is *Static Single Assignment Form (SSA-form)* [3], as it provides for the predicates to describe program state due to its single assignment property, and at the same time separates the variable definitions of different control flow paths. Beyond that, SSA-form supports a sparse analysis, which enables a more scalable derivation of predicates. Therefore, we will first introduce SSA-form and preliminaries in the following section. After that, we formalize our concept of a predicate-based characterization of variables' values by so-called *variable (path) predicates*, which allows us then to define the derivation of a program's variable predicates using sparse data flow analysis.

2.1   Program Representation in SSA-Form

We represent a program in terms of a control flow graph, i.e., a directed graph $CFG = (N, E, s, e)$ with a set of nodes N, a set of edges $E \subseteq N \times N$, unique start node $s \in N$, and unique end node $e \in N$. Nodes are labeled by $i \in Instr$ or $c \in Cond$, where $Instr$ is the set of the program's instructions and $Cond$ the set of the program's branching conditions. Instructions and branching conditions are defined over the program's variables Var and form the set of atomic predicates $Pred$ (see Definition 1). Furthermore, let $\overline{Pred_x}$ denote those atomic predicates, i.e., instructions and branching conditions, where x is neither used nor defined.

Our analysis operates on *SSA-form* [3], which guarantees for each variable a statically unique definition. This way, variables behave like values, which also means that the relation (def-use chain) between the instruction defining variable x, denoted $def(x) \in Instr$, and the set of instructions where x is used, denoted $uses(x) \subseteq Instr$, is implicitly given. For convenience, let $var(i)$ denote the variable defined by $i \in Instr$ and $node$ denote the node $n \in N$ for $x \in Var$, where n's label links to $def(x)$. As usual, SSA-form is realized by introducing a new variable for each static definition and renaming uses accordingly. At join nodes of the control flow graph, i.e., nodes with multiple incoming edges, Φ-functions $x = \Phi(x_1, \ldots, x_n)$ are inserted to merge confluent definitions, such that the value of x equals x_j if the join node is reached via its j-th incoming edge.

A mechanism that we use for incorporating the effects of a branching condition into SSA-form in order to support the analysis is to insert assertions at the true and false branch. Without loss of generality, we assume branching conditions $y \; op \; c$, where y is a variable and c a constant. An assertion then looks like $x = assert(y \; op \; c)$, where $y \; op \; c$ is the branching predicate valid at the respective branch. Uses of y inside the branch are updated to the newly defined variable x, whose value equals y but is guaranteed to satisfy the branching predicate. For the presentation of our analysis, we will focus – without loss of generality – on scalar expressions and neglect, e.g., memory operations or composite data structures.

Example 1. As an example, consider the following program snippet (left), its SSA-form (middle), and its SSA-form with assertions added (right):

```
x = 1;
while (x % 2) {
    x = x + 2;
}
```

```
x₁ = 1;
x₂ = Φ(x₁,x₃);
while (x₂ % 2) {
    x₃ = x₂ + 2;
}
```

```
x₁ = 1;
x₂ = Φ(x₁,x₄);
while (x₂ % 2) {
    x₃ = assert(x₂ % 2);
    x₄ = x₃ + 2;
}
```

2.2 Variable Predicates

For the formal development, we now introduce *atomic predicates*, *variable path predicates*, and *all-paths variable predicates*. We can interpret instructions and branching conditions as first-order predicates, characterizing variables' values, when substituting the assignment with the equality operator. A program's instructions and branching conditions thus constitute the set of *atomic predicates*, augmented with additional simple equalities of form $x = y$, $x, y \in Var$:

Definition 1. *Let Instr, Cond, and Var denote the set of instructions, branching conditions, and variables of the given program, respectively. The set of atomic predicates is defined by* $Pred = Instr \cup Cond \cup \{x = y \mid x, y \in Var\}$.

Characterizing a variable's value for a single path is then done by a *variable path predicate*, i.e., a conjunction of instructions and branching conditions determining the variable's value on this path. We denote such a conjunction as a set of atomic predicates. Considering instructions x = 10; y = x * 2, we thus get $\{x = 10, y = x * 2\}$, representing the conjunction $x = 10 \land y = x * 2$ for describing y's value. Note that we, as usual, universally quantify over free variables. To reflect a variable's value for all paths, the variable path predicates for individual paths are disjunctively combined. The resulting formulæ, called *all-paths variable predicate* (or just *variable predicate*), is also denoted as a set:

Definition 2. *A variable path predicate is a set* $p \in \mathcal{P}(Pred)$ *interpreted as a conjunction of atomic predicates. An (all-paths) variable predicate is then a set* $f \in \mathcal{P}(\mathcal{P}(Pred))$ *interpreted as a disjunction of conjunctions of predicates.*

Assuming, e.g., if (a <0) x = 1; else x = 3; y = x, variable y's value can be characterized by $\{\{x = 1, y = x\}, \{x = 3, y = x\}\}$, such that y's path predicates for the branching's true and false branch are disjunctively combined by $(x = 1 \land y = x) \lor (x = 3 \land y = x)$. In addition, we define the empty set $\emptyset$ to denote the truth value *true*. This is justified by variable predicates acting as premises about variables' values, where *true* is the weakest, always safe premise.

2.3 Derivation of Variable Predicates

As mentioned before, a program's SSA-form allows for a sparse derivation of variable predicates. To this end, instead of propagating a set of predicates, denoting the program state for all variables, along all control flow paths, we derive variable predicates by analyzing each variables' definitions and uses. In principle, there are two reasons why this works: First, SSA-form guarantees that each variable is (statically) defined once and, with the exception of Φ-functions, every use is dominated by its definition. In consequence, a variable's value does not change along the paths from definition to use, such that the program state valid directly after the definition can be used to characterize the variable's value on all paths. Second, only part of the overall program state is relevant for a single variable, which can in particular be captured by following the variable's data dependences along the def-use chains implicitly encoded in SSA-form. Note that in this way, we may omit predicates affecting a variable's value through side effects or control dependences, which does however not invalidate the approach as it is always safe to infer a weaker variable predicate, i.e., p instead of $p \wedge q$.

Thus, we assign to each variable x its variable predicate $pred(x)$ based upon its defining instruction. For a constant assignment $x = c$, we can obviously set $pred(x) = \{\{x = c\}\}$. In case of a simple assignment $x = y$, the union over variable path predicates $p \in pred(y)$, each augmented by the equality predicate $x = y$, is used, in this way including derived information about y also in x's variable predicate. However, in order to prevent inconsistent predicates in case of cyclic data dependences, atomic predicates other than $x = y$ containing variable x are removed. The same principle applies to an assertion $x = assert(y\ op\ c)$, though the asserted predicate $x\ op\ c$ for variable x is added to each path predicate besides the equality predicate $x = y$. The variable predicate for a variable defined through assignment $x = y\ op\ z$ is derived by considering all pairs (p,q) of variable path predicates $p \in pred(y)$, $q \in pred(z)$ of the operand variables, flattening each into a single set $p \cup q$ and adding the assignment as predicate. Once more, existing atomic predicates containing variable x are removed to avoid inconsistencies. Remember that due to SSA-form, x's definition is dominated by the definitions of variables y and z, which means that predicates for y and z are also reasonable for describing the program state at the assignment. Consider, e.g., $x = y * z$ with $pred(y) = \{\{y = 10\}\}$, $pred(z) = \{\{z = v, v = -1\}, \{z = w, w = 1\}\}$, then $pred(x) = \{\{z = v, v = -1, y = 10, x = y * z\}, \{z = w, w = 1, y = 10, x = y * z\}\}$. Finally, in case of a Φ-function $x = \Phi(x_1, \ldots, x_n)$ merging confluent definitions x_j into a single value x, the variable predicate equals the union of the operands' path predicates, each augmented with an equality predicate $x = x_j$ for x and the respective operand x_j. Atomic predicates containing a variable simultaneously defined with x, i.e., within the same control flow graph node, are again removed. As an example, assuming $x = \Phi(x_1, x_2)$ with predicates $pred(x_1) = \{\{x_1 = 10\}\}$ and $pred(x_2) = \{\{x_2 = z + 3, z = 9\}\}$, then $pred(x) = \{\{x_1 = 10, x = x_1\}, \{x_2 = z + 3, z = 9, x = x_2\}\}$. The following definition summarizes these rules:

```
                                    function computePred(i) begin
                                      switch (i)
                                        case constant assignment i: x = c
worklist := {i ∈ Instr}                   return {{x = c}}
foreach i ∈ worklist do                 case simple assignment i: x = y
    pred(i) := ∅                            return {(p ∩ Pred̄ₓ) ∪ {x = y}
end for                                            | p ∈ pred(def(y))}
while worklist ≠ ∅ do                    case complex assignment i: x = y op z
    select an arbitrary i ∈ worklist        return {((p ∪ q) ∩ Pred̄ₓ) ∪ {x = y op z}
    worklist := worklist \ {i}                        | p ∈ pred(def(y)),
    new := computePred(i)                               q ∈ pred(def(z))}
    if pred(i) ≠ new then                 case assertion i: x = assert(y op c)
        pred(i) := new                        return {(p ∩ Pred̄ₓ) ∪ {x = y, x op c}
        foreach u ∈ uses(var(i)) do                   | p ∈ pred(def(y))}
            worklist := worklist ∪ {u}     case Φ-function i: x = Φ(x₁,...,xₙ)
        end for                               let V be all variables defined in node(x)
    end if                                    return  ⋃   {(p ∩  ⋂   Pred̄ᵥ) ∪ {x = xⱼ}
end while                                          1≤j≤n      v∈V
                                                              | p ∈ pred(def(xⱼ))}
                                      end switch
                                    end
```

Algorithm 1: Sparse analysis of variable predicates

Definition 3. *Variable predicates are defined for a given program in SSA-form by* $pred: Var \to \mathcal{P}(\mathcal{P}(Pred))$ *for each variable* $x \in Var$ *according to its defining instruction* $i \in Instr$ *based upon the following equations:*

– *constant assignment* $i: x = c$

$$pred(x) = \{\{x = c\}\}$$

– *simple assginment* $i: x = y$

$$pred(x) = \{(p \cap \overline{Pred_x}) \cup \{x = y\} \,|\, p \in pred(y)\}$$

– *complex assignment* $i: x = y \ op \ z$

$$pred(x) = \{((p \cup q) \cap \overline{Pred_x}) \cup \{x = y \ op \ z\} \,|\, p \in pred(y), q \in pred(z)\}$$

– *assertion* $i: x = assert(y \ op \ c)$

$$pred(x) = \{(p \cap \overline{Pred_x}) \cup \{x = y, x \ op \ c\} \,|\, p \in pred(y)\}$$

– Φ-*function* $i: x = \Phi(x_1,\ldots,x_n)$, *with* $V \subseteq Var$ *variables defined in* $node(x)$

$$pred(x) = \bigcup_{1 \le j \le n} \{(p \cap \bigcap_{v \in V} \overline{Pred_v}) \cup \{x = x_j\} \,|\, p \in pred(x_j)\}$$

For solving the equation system defined by Definition 3, we use Algorithm 1. Due to SSA-form's single assignment property, variables can be identified by their unique defining instructions, such that variable predicates *pred* are assigned to instructions instead of variables. Having initialized all variable predicates to the empty set and the worklist to comprise the program's instructions, the algorithm continuously takes an instruction i from the worklist and recomputes its variable predicate using *computePred*. Each time a change is observed, $pred(i)$ is updated accordingly and all use sites of the variable defined by i are again added to the worklist. If eventually a stable solution is reached, the algorithm terminates.

Reconsidering Example 1 and applying the algorithm, we get the solution:

$$pred(x_1) = \{\{x_1 = 1\}\}$$
$$pred(x_2) = \{\{x_1 = 1, x_2 = x_1\}, \{x_1 = 1, x_3 \% 2, x_4 = x_3 + 2, x_2 = x_4\}\}$$
$$pred(x_3) = \{\{x_1 = 1, x_2 = x_1, x_3 \% 2, x_3 = x_2\}, \{x_1 = 1, x_2 = x_4, x_3 \% 2, x_3 = x_2\}\}$$
$$pred(x_4) = \{\{x_1 = 1, x_2 = x_1, x_3 \% 2, x_3 = x_2, x_4 = x_3 + 2\},$$
$$\{x_1 = 1, x_3 \% 2, x_3 = x_2, x_4 = x_3 + 2\}\}$$

As can be seen, the derived predicate for variable x_2 consists of two path predicates, characterizing x_2's value before initially entering the loop and before reentering the loop, respectively. Note that, assuming C semantics such that $x \% 2$ equals $x \% 2 \neq 0$, x_2's predicate apparently determines the loop condition's value, i.e., $(x_1 = 1 \wedge x_2 = x_1) \vee (x_1 = 1 \wedge x_3 \% 2 \neq 0, x_4 = x_3 + 2, x_2 = x_4) \models x_2 \% 2 \neq 0$, as can be automatically inferred using a SMT solver for testing the implication.

3   Correctness of the Analysis Algorithm

In the previous section, we have developed a sparse analysis algorithm for the derivation of variable predicates. In this section, we will prove that the algorithm always terminates while yielding the correct set of predicates for characterizing variables' values. The algorithm can be seen as an optimized version of the general iterative algorithm for data flow problems [14], which is already proven to terminate with a safe solution for monotone problems. We will therefore first present the concept of a *monotone data flow framework* and afterwards show how our algorithm and conceptual universe can be mapped to a monotone data flow framework for proving the correctness of the sparse analysis algorithm.

The principle of data flow analysis is to gather information for each instruction by iteratively propagating locally computed data flow information through the control flow graph of a program. In general, each data flow problem can be modeled using a *data flow framework* $(L, \wedge, F)$, where L is the *data flow information set*, $\wedge$ is the *meet operator*, and F is the set of *semantic functions*. The data flow information set is a conceptual universe of objects upon which the analysis is working. A semantic function corresponds to an instruction and models the effect that an execution of the instruction has onto the incoming information. The meet operator implements the effect of joining control flow paths. A maximum fixpoint solution for a data flow framework can be computed, if and only if the semantic functions are monotone and $(L, \wedge)$ forms a bounded semi lattice with a one element 1 and a zero element 0 [14]. Data flow frameworks satisfying these requirements are called *monotone data flow frameworks (MDF)*.

There are multiple ways for constructing a MDF for deriving variable predicates. An obvious approach is to derive for each node n of a control flow graph a set of pairs (x, p), in which x stands for a variable and p for a set of predicates that characterize the value of x at node n. While a single pair (x, p) describes a path predicate of x, the union of all pairs represents x's all-paths variable predicate. The data flow framework for the calculation of variable predicates is defined by $MDF_{VP} = (L_{VP}, \wedge_{VP}, F_{VP})$, where $L_{VP} = \mathcal{P}(Var \times \mathcal{P}(Pred))$, $\wedge_{VP}: L_{VP} \rightarrow L_{VP}$ is the set-theoretic union operator such that $l \wedge_{VP} k = l \cup k$ for all $l, k \in L_{VP}$.

Lemma 1. $(L_{VP}, \wedge_{VP})$ *is a bounded semi lattice with zero element* $0 \in L_{VP}$ *and one element* $1 \in L_{VP}$ *such that* $\forall l \in L_{VP}: l \wedge_{VP} 1 = l$ *and* $l \wedge_{VP} 0 = 0$.

Proof. Since *Var* and *Instr* are finite sets for a given program, and thus is $\mathcal{P}(Var \times \mathcal{P}(Pred))$, the lemma follows immediately from the fact that for every finite set M, $(\mathcal{P}(M), \cup)$ is a bounded semi lattice with $1 = \emptyset$ and $0 = M$.   □

In the control flow graph used for the analysis, we can unambiguously assign a semantic function to each node. This semantic function is used to transform the set of variable path predicates when processing the node. Each semantic function models for a given node of the control flow graph the effect of executing the node, i.e., the node's attached instructions on the incoming data flow information.

Definition 4. *The semantic functions* F_{VP} *are defined according to* $i \in Instr$:

- Φ-*function* $i: x = \Phi(x_1, \ldots, x_n)$, *with* $V \subseteq Var$ *variables defined in* $node(x)$
  $VP_{out} = update_i(remove(VP_{in}, V))$
- *any other instruction* i *defining value* x
  $VP_{out} = update_i(remove(VP_{in}, \{x\}))$

where $remove: L_{VP} \times \mathcal{P}(Var) \rightarrow L_{VP}$ *is defined for* $k \in L_{VP}$ *and* $V \subseteq Var$ *by*

- $remove(k, V) = \{(y, p \cap \bigcap_{v \in V} \overline{Pred_v}) \mid (y, p) \in k \wedge y \notin V\}$

and $update_i: L_{VP} \rightarrow L_{VP}$ *is defined for* $l \in L_{VP}$ *according to* $i \in Instr$ *by:*

- *constant assignment* $i: x = c$
  $update_i(l) = l \cup \{(x, \{x = c\})\}$
- *simple assignment* $i: x = y$
  $update_i(l) = l \cup \{(x, p \cup \{x = y\}) \mid (y, p) \in l\}$
- *complex assignment* $i: x = y \ op \ z$
  $update_i(l) = l \cup \{(x, p \cup q \cup \{x = y \ op \ z\}) \mid (y, p), (z, q) \in l\}$
- *assertion* $i: x = assert(y \ op \ c)$
  $update_i(l) = l \cup \{(x, p \cup \{x = y, x \ op \ c\}) \mid (y, p) \in l\}$
- Φ-*function* $i: x = \Phi(x_1, \ldots, x_n)$
  $update_i(l) = l \cup \bigcup_{1 \leq j \leq n} \{(x, p \cup \{x = x_j\}) \mid (x_j, p) \in l\}$

Lemma 2. *The semantic functions* F_{VP} *defined in Definition 4 are monotone.*

Proof. To prove that the semantic functions $f \in F_{VP}$ are monotone, we have to show $l \leq_{VP} k \Rightarrow f(l) \leq_{VP} f(k)$ for every $l, k \in L_{VP}$. Since $l \leq_{VP} k$ iff $l = l \wedge_{VP} k$ and $\wedge_{VP} = \cup$, we can alternatively show that $f(l) \cup f(k) \subseteq f(l \cup k)$ holds. First, we prove $remove(l, V) \cup remove(k, V) = remove(l \cup k, V)$ for $l, k \in L_{VP}$:

– $remove(l, V) \cup remove(k, V)$

$$= \{(y, p \cap \bigcap_{v \in V} \overline{Pred_v} \mid (y, p) \in l \wedge y \notin V\} \cup \{(y, p \cap \bigcap_{v \in V} \overline{Pred_v} \mid (y, p) \in k \wedge y \notin V\}$$

$$= \{(y, p \cap \bigcap_{v \in V} \overline{Pred_v} \mid (y, p) \in l \cup k \wedge y \notin V\} = remove(l \cup k, V)$$

and thereafter that $update_i(l) \cup update_i(k) \subseteq update_i(l \cup k)$ for every $i \in Instr$:

– constant assignment $i\colon x = c$

$update_i(l) \cup update_i(k) = l \cup \{(x, \{x = c\})\} \cup k \cup \{(x, \{x = c\})\}$
$= l \cup k \cup \{(x, \{x = c\})\} = update_i(l \cup k)$

– simple assignment $i\colon x = y$

$update_i(l) \cup update_i(k) = l \cup \{(x, p \cup \{x = y\}) \mid (y, p) \in l\}$
$$\cup\, k \cup \{(x, p \cup \{x = y\}) \mid (y, p) \in k\}$$
$= l \cup k \cup \{(x, p \cup \{x = y\}) \mid (y, p) \in l \cup k\} = update_i(l \cup k)$

– complex assignment $i\colon x = y \ op \ z$

$update_i(l) \cup update_i(k) = l \cup \{(x, p \cup q \cup \{x = y \ op \ z\}) \mid (y, p), (z, q) \in l\}$
$$\cup\, k \cup \{(x, p \cup q \cup \{x = y \ op \ z\}) \mid (y, p), (z, q) \in k\}$$
$\subseteq l \cup k \cup \{(x, p \cup q \cup \{x = y \ op \ z\}) \mid (y, p), (z, q) \in l \cup k\} = update_i(l \cup k)$

– assertion $i\colon x = assert(y \ op \ c)$

$update_i(l) \cup update_i(k) = l \cup \{(x, p \cup \{x = y, x \ op \ c\}) \mid (y, p) \in l\}$
$$\cup\, k \cup \{(x, p \cup \{x = y, x \ op \ c\}) \mid (y, p) \in k\}$$
$= l \cup k \cup \{(x, p \cup \{x = y, x \ op \ c\}) \mid (y, p) \in l \cup k\} = update_i(l \cup k)$

– Φ-function $i\colon x = \Phi(x_1, \ldots, x_n)$

$$update_i(l) \cup update_i(k) = l \cup \bigcup_{1 \leq j \leq n} \{(x, p \cup \{x = x_j\}) \mid (x_j, p) \in l\}$$

$$\cup\, k \cup \bigcup_{1 \leq j \leq n} \{(x, p \cup \{x = x_j\}) \mid (x_j, p) \in k\}$$

$$= l \cup k \cup \bigcup_{1 \leq j \leq n} \{(x, p \cup \{x = x_j\}) \mid (x_j, p) \in l \cup k\} = update_i(l \cup k)$$

From the fact that the composition of the thus monotone functions *remove* (with respect to its first argument) and *update_i* is monotone, follows the lemma.   □

Theorem 1. *The general iterative algorithm terminates with the maximum fixpoint solution for each instance of the data flow framework MDF_VP.*

Proof. This is an immediate consequence of MDF_{VP} being a monotone data flow framework according to Lemmas 1 and 2.   □

In fact, the algorithm for sparse analysis of variable predicates we have presented in Sect. 2 can be seen as an optimized variant of the general iterative algorithm solving MDF_{VP}. In principle, the sparse analysis differs in that path predicates for all variables are not propagated along the control flow, as is done by the general iterative algorithm, but rather derived and stored directly at the control flow graph's variable-defining instructions in terms of variable predicates. Since each variable is statically defined once in SSA-form and MDF_{VP}'s meet operator is the set union, the sparse approach does not invalidate the correctness of the analysis, which allows us to state the following corollary:

Corollary 1. *A safe solution to the equation system pred defined in Definition 3 can be computed using Algorithm 1.*

4   Improvements of the Analysis

Due to the nature of sparse analysis, precision of our analysis of variable predicates is impeded by the omittance of program information which is not represented by the relations of variable definition and use. However, two reasons for imprecision, namely unreachable code and the local merging of data flow facts at join nodes, can be addressed by the analysis extensions described next.

4.1   Spurious Data Flow

Our analysis exploits the single assignment property of SSA-form and propagates data flow information, i.e., variable predicates, only along def-use chains. Precision is thus being lost at join nodes, since the analysis does not track the correlation of variables' values defined conjointly along converging control flow paths.

Example 2. Consider the program snippet below and its derived predicates:

```
if (...) {
    a1 = 2;
    b1 = 3;
} else {
    a2 = 3;
    b2 = 2;
}
a3 = Φ(a1,a2);
b3 = Φ(b1,b2);
c1 = a3 + b3;
```

$pred(a_1) = \{\{a_1 = 2\}\}$ $pred(b_1) = \{\{b_1 = 3\}\}$

$pred(a_2) = \{\{a_2 = 3\}\}$ $pred(b_2) = \{\{b_2 = 2\}\}$

$pred(a_3) = \{\{a_1 = 2, a_3 = a_1\}, \{a_2 = 3, a_3 = a_2\}\}$

$pred(b_3) = \{\{b_1 = 3, b_3 = b_1\}, \{b_2 = 2, b_3 = b_2\}\}$

$pred(c_1) = \{\{a_1 = 2, a_3 = a_1, b_1 = 3, b_3 = b_1, c_1 = a_3 + b_3\},$
$\{a_1 = 2, a_3 = a_1, b_2 = 2, b_3 = b_2, c_1 = a_3 + b_3\},$
$\{a_2 = 3, a_3 = a_2, b_1 = 3, b_3 = b_1, c_1 = a_3 + b_3\},$
$\{a_2 = 3, a_3 = a_2, b_2 = 2, b_3 = b_2, c_1 = a_3 + b_3\}\}$

Therein, the values of a_3 and b_3 are characterized with different path predicates, so that the values on the true and false branch are distinguished. Though after the join, when considering $c_1 = a_3 + b_3$, spurious combinations of path predicates arise, e.g., $\{a_1 = 2, a_3 = a_1, b_2 = 2, b_3 = b_2, c_1 = a_3 + b_3\}$, coming from mutually exclusive control flow paths. Therefore, c_1's derived variable predicate is imprecise in that it allows for values 4, 5, 6, while only 5 can occur at runtime.

In order to remove this imprecision but still support a sparse analysis, variable path predicate are attached information about the represented control flow paths. To this end, we introduce *path designators* for denoting a path based on the edges entering a control flow graph's join nodes throughout the path:

Definition 5. *A path designator $\delta \in \mathcal{P}(N \times \mathbb{N})$ is a definite relation, such that $\forall n \in N \colon (n, i) \in \delta \wedge (n, j) \in \delta \rightarrow i = j$, which determines for each node n of a subset of a control flow graph's join nodes a predecessor node using the predecessor's index. Overriding of a path designator δ by a path designator γ is defined as $\delta \oplus \gamma = \{(x, i) \mid (x, i) \in \delta \wedge \nexists (x, j) \in \gamma\} \cup \{(y, i) \mid (y, i) \in \gamma\}$.*

Apparently, two path designators δ and γ defining different predecessors $\delta(n) \neq \gamma(n)$ for the same node n characterize mutually exclusive control flow paths. Augmenting variable path predicates with path designators, we are able to rule out the spurious combinations of path predicates:

Definition 6. Variable predicates with path designators *are defined for a given program in SSA-form by* pred$\colon Instr \rightarrow \mathcal{P}(\mathcal{P}(N \times \mathbb{N}) \times \mathcal{P}(Pred))$ *for each variable $x \in Var$ according to its defining instruction $i \in Instr$ based upon equations:*

- *constant assignment $i\colon x = c$*

  $pred(x) = \{(\emptyset, \{x = c\})\}$

- *simple assginment $i\colon x = y$*

  $pred(x) = \{(\delta, (p \cap \overline{Pred_x}) \cup \{x = y\}) \mid (\delta, p) \in pred(y)\}$

- *assertion $i\colon x = assert(y \; op \; c)$*

  $pred(x) = \{(\delta, (p \cap \overline{Pred_x}) \cup \{x = y, x \; op \; c\}) \mid (\delta, p) \in pred(y)\}$

- *Φ-function $x\colon x = \Phi(x_1, \dots, x_n)$, with $V \subseteq Var$ variables defined in $node(x)$*

  $pred(x) = \bigcup_{1 \leq j \leq n} \{(\delta \oplus \{(node(x), j)\},$

  $$(p \cap \bigcap_{v \in V} \overline{Pred_v}) \cup \{x = x_j\}) \mid (\delta, p) \in pred(x_j)\}$$

- *complex assignment $i\colon x = y \; op \; z$*

  $pred(x) = \{(\delta \cup \gamma, ((p \cup q) \cap \overline{Pred_x}) \cup \{x = y \; op \; z\})$
  $\mid (\delta, p) \in pred(y), (\gamma, q) \in pred(z) \wedge (\delta \cup \gamma) \; is \; definite\}$

For constant assignments, we thus attach the empty set as path designator to derived path predicates. In case of simple assignments and assertions, path designators are merely propagated as there is just a single variable operand and line of control. For a Φ-function, path designators attached to the operands' path predicates are updated according to the operands' indices, determining the respective predecessors of the Φ-function's join node. In case of a complex assignment, the union of path designators is created for each combination of the operands' path predicates. If the union is not a definite relation, the path predicates come from mutually exclusive paths and their combination is skipped.

In order to solve the equation system of Definition 6, we can again use Algorithm 1. Reconsidering Example 2 and assuming a node *join* for the two Φ-functions $a_3 = \Phi(a_1, a_2)$ and $b_3 = \Phi(b_1, b_2)$, we now get:

$$pred(a_1) = \{(\emptyset, \{a_1 = 2\})\} \qquad\qquad pred(a_2) = \{(\emptyset, \{a_2 = 3\})\}$$
$$pred(b_1) = \{(\emptyset, \{b_1 = 3\})\} \qquad\qquad pred(b_2) = \{(\emptyset, \{b_2 = 2\})\}$$
$$pred(a_3) = \{(\{(join, 1)\}, \{a_1 = 2, a_3 = a_1\}), (\{(join, 2)\}, \{a_2 = 3, a_3 = a_2\})\}$$
$$pred(b_3) = \{(\{(join, 1)\}, \{b_1 = 3, b_3 = b_1\}), (\{(join, 2)\}, \{b_2 = 2, b_3 = b_2\})\}$$
$$pred(c_1) = \{(\{(join, 1)\}, \{a_1 = 2, a_3 = a_1, b_1 = 3, b_3 = b_1, c_1 = a_3 + b_3\}),$$
$$(\{(join, 2)\}, \{a_2 = 3, a_3 = a_2, b_2 = 2, b_3 = b_2, c_1 = a_3 + b_3\})\}$$

Therein, each path predicate has a conjoined path designator, determining the represented control flow path in terms of *join*'s predecessors. For instance, a_3's path predicates $\{a_1 = 2, a_3 = a_1\}$, $\{a_2 = 3, a_3 = a_2\}$ are assigned designators $\{(join, 1)\}$, $\{(join, 2)\}$, denoting the if and else branch, respectively. Spurious combinations of path predicates are thus ruled out for variable $c_1 = a_3 + b_3$ such that c_1's all-paths predicate allows for deriving its precise value 5.

4.2   Unreachable Code

Another source of imprecision is *unreachable code*, i.e., program statements that can never be executed due to unsatisfiable branching conditions. The analysis considers data dependences but ignores control dependences, assuming that each branching condition is satisfiable and therefore every branch can be executed.

Example 3. Consider the program snippet below and its derived predicates:

```
if (a1 > 10) {
    a2 = assert(a1 > 10);
    if (a2 > 5) {
        a3 = assert(a2 > 5);
        b1 = 1;
    } else {
        a4 = assert(a2 ≤ 5);
        b2 = -1;
    }
    b3 = Φ(b1,b2);
```

$pred(a_2) = \{\{\ldots, a_2 > 10, a_2 = a_1\}\}$

$pred(a_3) = \{\{\ldots, a_2 > 10, a_2 = a_1, a_3 > 5, a_3 = a_2\}\}$

$pred(b_1) = \{\{b_1 = 1\}\}$

$pred(a_4) = \{\{\ldots, a_2 > 10, a_2 = a_1, a_4 \leq 5, a_4 = a_2\}\}$

$pred(b_2) = \{\{b_2 = -1\}\}$

$pred(b_3) = \{\{b_1 = 1, b_3 = b_1\}, \{b_2 = -1, b_3 = b_2\}\}$

As can be seen, in spite of the fact that the condition of the inner branching is always satisfied and its false branch can therefore never be executed, the analysis considers variable b_2's value -1, defined inside the false branch, to flow into variable b_3. Thus, b_3's variable predicate is imprecise in that it contains the path predicate $\{b_2 = -1, b_3 = b_2\}$ and consequently allows for values 1 and -1.

Fortunately, we can resort to the approach of combining analyses to include a kind of *unreachable code elimination* [17]. The main principle of the combined analysis is to defer the propagation of data flow information through a node until the node is determined to be executable. Therefore, instructions' variable predicates are not computed in an arbitrary order but rather in conformance with the control flow relation. In addition, a branching instruction's condition is evaluated based upon derived variable predicates. If evaluation results in a definite value, the executed branch is statically known such that all other, unreachable branches can be ignored. Otherwise, if derived variable predicates do not allow for determining the branching result, all branches are considered instead.

Algorithm 2 implements the combined analysis, keeping track of executable nodes using bit map *executable*. As before (refer to Algorithm 1), instructions' variable predicates *pred* are continuously computed by *computePred* until a fixpoint has been found, though this time, only for instructions whose nodes are marked executable. The function *evaluateCond*, used in the algorithm for evaluating a branching condition, is generic in the applied solver, in that it allows for a SMT solver as well as for, e.g., a simpler constant evaluation. The solver is used to test whether the derived variable predicate for x implies the value of a condition expression x op c. Though, in order to allow for an overapproximation, *evaluateCond* does not test for condition d itself, but rather for its negation. Thus, if $\neg d$ is shown for $pred(x)$, the condition is determined unsatisfiable. We naturally assume for the solver to guarantee that if $\{p, q\} \models d$ (i.e., $p \vee q \models d$) is shown, $p \models d$ and $q \models d$ can be shown as well for $p, q \in \mathcal{P}(Pred)$.

Reconsidering Example 3 and applying the algorithm, we get the solution:

$$pred(a_2) = \{\{\ldots, a_2 > 10, a_2 = a_1\}\} \qquad pred(a_4) = \emptyset$$
$$pred(a_3) = \{\{\ldots, a_2 > 10, a_2 = a_1, a_3 > 5, a_3 = a_2\}\} \quad pred(b_2) = \emptyset$$
$$pred(b_1) = \{\{b_1 = 1\}\} \qquad pred(b_3) = \{\{b_1 = 1, b_3 = b_1\}\}$$

As can be seen, the inner branching's false branch has been identified unreachable, assuming that the used solver is able to show $\{\{\ldots, a_2 > 10, a_2 = a_1\}\} \models a_2 > 5$. As a result, the empty set is derived for variables defined in the false branch, so that b_3's variable predicate only comprises one path predicate for the reachable true branch and consequently only allows for deriving b_3's precise value 1.

We can obviously combine the improved analyses with path designators and unreachable code elimination and again state a correctness argument:

Corollary 2. *Algorithm 2 computes a safe solution to the equation system pred defined in Definition 6 while removing some effects of unreachable code.*[1]

5   Application to Model Checking

We have implemented the presented analysis in a system for the generation of more precise Petri net models used for model checking distributed business processes (see Fig. 1) [12]. The system expects a program of the *Web Services Business Process Execution Language (WS-BPEL)* [19]. A WS-BPEL program is first translated into our SSA-form intermediate format, where analyses and

---

[1] For the complete proofs, we refer the reader to [10].

```
let s ∈ Instr be the start instruction
executable(node(s)) := true
worklist := {s}
pred(s) := ∅
foreach i ∈ Instr \ {s} do
  executable(node(i)) := false
  pred(i) := ∅
end for
while worklist ≠ ∅ do
  select an arbitrary i ∈ worklist
  worklist := worklist \ {i}
  if executable(node(i)) then
    new := computePred(i)
    if pred(i) ≠ new then
      pred(i) := new
      foreach u ∈ uses(var(i)) do
        worklist := worklist ∪ {u}
      end for
    end if
    if i is a branch instruction then
      let t be i's successor in true branch
      let f be i's successor in false branch
      let d be i's branching condition
      if evaluateCond(d) = true then
        executable(node(t)) := true
        worklist := worklist ∪ {t}
      end if
      if evaluateCond(¬d) = true then
        executable(node(f)) := true
        worklist := worklist ∪ {f}
      end if
    else if i has successor s then
      executable(node(s)) := true
      worklist := worklist ∪ {s}
    end if
  end if
end while
```

```
function computePred(i) begin
  switch (i)
    case constant assignment i: x = c
      return {{x = c}}
    case simple assignment i: x = y
      return {(p ∩ Pred_x) ∪ {x = y}
             | p ∈ pred(def(y))}
    case complex assignment i: x = y op z
      return {((p ∪ q) ∩ Pred_x) ∪ {x = y op z}
             | p ∈ pred(def(y)),
               q ∈ pred(def(z))}
    case assertion i: x = assert(y op c)
      return {(p ∩ Pred_x) ∪ {x op c, x = y}
             | p ∈ pred(def(y))}
    case Φ-function i: x = Φ(x_1,...,x_n)
      let V be all variables defined in node(x)
      return  ⋃      {(p ∩   ⋂    Pred_v) ∪ {x = x_j}
             1≤j≤n        v∈V
              | p ∈ pred(def(x_j))}
              ∧ node(x)'s jth predecessor
                       is marked as executable}
  end switch
end
```

```
function evaluateCond(d) begin
  let d = x op c
  if pred(x) |≠ ¬d then
    return false
  else
    return true
  end if
end
```

Algorithm 2: Analysis of variable predicates with unreachable code elimination

optimizations are performed. The format is then transformed into Petri nets, the usual formalism in the area of business process verification, which are afterwards passed into the model checker *Fiona/LoLA*[2] for verifying soundness properties.

Program data is usually omitted when compiling Petri net models, which however impairs precision when using the models for verification. Integrating program data to regain precision requires some kind of data abstraction, i.e., a finite model for program data. We have thus used variable path predicates, as derived for a WS-BPEL program by our analysis, to encode program data into the Petri net models by means of a technique called *control flow unfolding* [11]. This technique in principle splits and duplicates control flow paths revealing distinct variable path predicates. In this way, a program's branching conditions can be evaluated and resolved along unfolded paths using a SMT solver on the variable path predicates. We were able to demonstrate the potential of this approach in a case study of WS-BPEL programs supplied by an industrial partner [12], where we provided precise Petri net models and thus enabled a safe verification

---

[2] http://service-technology.org/fiona/.

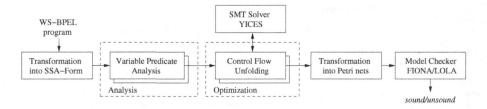

Fig. 1. System for the improved Petri-net-based verification of WS-BPEL programs

for half of the case study's programs using our system. Due to space constraints, we refer the reader to [10,12] for a detailed discussion and concrete numbers.

6   Related Work

In model checking, *predicate abstraction* [7] is used to exhaustively reason about infinitely many concrete program states in terms of a finite number of abstract states as determined by a predefined set of predicates. *Counterexample-guided abstraction refinement* [2] in addition iteratively refines the set of predicates such that an initially coarse abstraction is made more precise until an ideal abstraction is found. To this end, each abstract state that has been identified as counterexample is validated for the feasibility of its concrete states. If a counterexample is thus shown to be spurious, the abstraction is refined with new predicates to remove the counterexample. While generating predicates for describing the program's state in this way is accurate and precise, it is at the same time complex and expensive, as it requires multiple iterations and powerful decision procedures. Further, model checking in general is focussed on a specific program property, which determines the resulting abstraction and thus predicates.

A particular fraction of work considers the problem of infeasible paths as a cause of imprecision in data flow analysis. A common approach is to augment the analysis lattice with a set of fixed predicates or assertions on variable values, resulting in a so-called *qualified data flow problem* [13], which helps to avoid merging data flow values with contradicting assertions, e.g., infeasible paths. However, compared to the analysis described in this paper, the set of considered predicates is either limited to predicates appearing in branching conditions and which are only propagated as long as their value does not change [1,15] or predefined by a given set of predicates by means of a specification [4]. The more advanced techniques in [5,6] instead iteratively refine the set of considered predicates for ruling out both infeasible paths and imprecise merging of data flow facts, until a precise enough solution to the data flow problem is found.

Bodík et al. [1] apply demand-driven analysis for identifying infeasible paths by propagating branching predicates backwards until their value is determined. The used symbolic resolution mechanism is limited to constant assignments and condition predicates. In the same line of work falls [18], where predicates describing program state are derived in a backward fashion based on the weakest precondition calculus. While the formal framework allows for arbitrary predicates, its implementation again confines considered predicates to simple forms x op c, where x is a variable and c a constant, to regain analysis effectiveness.

Similar methods have been used to identify false positives for static analysis using backward symbolic execution [8,16]. These methods infer *path conditions*, i.e., predicates describing necessary requirements of program state for paths, which can be fed into constraint solvers. If insatisfiability is then shown, the paths and thus any associated program information are false positives.

To the knowledge of the authors, the presented analysis is the first data flow analysis for deriving predicates describing program state on a per variable basis. Furthermore, we are not aware of an analysis using the sparse analysis approach based on SSA-form [9,17] for deriving predicates describing program state.

7 Conclusion

In this paper, we have presented a novel data flow analysis based upon SSA-form for deriving variable predicates as predicate-based characterization of a program's variables' values. We have motivated how SSA-form benefits such an analysis by multiple means: First, exploiting the single assignment property allows us to use instructions and branching conditions as predicates for describing program state. Additionally, relevant parts of the program state can be easily identified for each variable following the def-use chains implicitly given in SSA-form, which facilitates a sparse analysis. Furthermore, Φ-functions depict variable definitions on confluent control flow paths and thus enable a natural derivation of path information. While the variable predicates derived by our analysis have currently only been used for generating Petri net models to more precisely model check WS-BPEL programs, we are confident on applying our analysis also to other programming languages and application domains in future work.

References

1. Bodík, R., Gupta, R., Soffa, M.L.: Refining data flow information using infeasible paths. In: ESEC-FSE 1997, Proceeding, pp. 361–377. ACM (1997)
2. Clarke, E., Grumberg, O., Jha, S., Lu, Y., Veith, M.: Counterexample-guided abstraction refinement. In: Emerson, E.A., Sistla, A.P. (eds.) CAV 2000. LNCS, vol. 1855, pp. 154–169. Springer, Heidelberg (2000)
3. Cytron, R., Ferrante, J., Rosen, B.K., Wegman, M.N.: Efficiently computing static single assignment form and the control dependence graph. ACM TOPLAS 13(4), 451–490 (1991)
4. Das, M., Lerner, S., Seigle, M.: ESP: path-sensitive program verification in polynomial time. In: PLDI 2002, Proceeding, pp. 57–68. ACM (2002)
5. Dhurjati, D., Das, M., Yang, Y.: Path-sensitive dataflow analysis with iterative refinement. In: Yi, K. (ed.) SAS 2006. LNCS, vol. 4134, pp. 425–442. Springer, Heidelberg (2006)
6. Fischer, J., Jhala, R., Majumdar, R.: Joining dataflow with predicates. In: ESEC-FSE 2005, Proceeding, pp. 227–236. ACM (2005)

7. Graf, S., Saidi, H.: Construction of abstract state graphs with PVS. In: Grumberg, O. (ed.) CAV1997. LNCS, vol. 1254, pp. 72–83. Springer, Heidelberg (1997)
8. Hammer, C., Schaade, R., Snelting, G.: Static path conditions for Java. In: PLAS 2008, Proceeding, pp. 57–66. ACM (2008)
9. Hardekopf, B., Lin, C.: Semi-sparse flow-sensitive pointer analysis. In: POPL 2009, Proceeding, pp. 226–238. ACM (2009)
10. Heinze, T.S., Amme, W.: Sparse analysis of variable path predicates (2016). http://swt.informatik.uni-jena.de/swt_multimedia/SWT/PDFs/heinze16.pdf
11. Heinze, T.S., Amme, W., Moser, S.: A restructuring method for WS-BPEL business processes based on extended workflow graphs. In: Dayal, U., Eder, J., Koehler, J., Reijers, H.A. (eds.) BPM 2009. LNCS, vol. 5701, pp. 211–228. Springer, Heidelberg (2009)
12. Heinze, T.S., Amme, W., Moser, S.: Compiling more precise petri net models for an improved verification of service implementations. In: SOCA 2014, Proceeding, pp. 25–32. IEEE (2014)
13. Holley, L.H., Rosen, B.K.: Qualified data flow problems. In: POPL 1980, Proceeding, pp. 68–82. ACM (1980)
14. Kam, J.B., Ullman, J.D.: Monotone data flow analysis frameworks. Acta Inf. **7**(3), 305–317 (1977)
15. Murphy, B.R.: Frameworks for precise program analysis. Ph.D. thesis, Stanford University (2001)
16. Snelting, G.: Combining slicing and constraint solving for validation of measurement software. In: Cousot, R., Schmidt, D.A. (eds.) SAS 1996. LNCS, vol. 1145, pp. 332–348. Springer, Heidelberg (1996)
17. Wegman, M.N., Zadeck, F.K.: Constant propagation with conditional branches. ACM TOPLAS **13**(2), 181–210 (1991)
18. Winter, K., Zhang, C., Hayes, I.J., Keynes, N., Cifuentes, C., Li, L.: Path-sensitive data flow analysis simplified. In: Groves, L., Sun, J. (eds.) ICFEM 2013. LNCS, vol. 8144, pp. 415–430. Springer, Heidelberg (2013)
19. Web Services Business Process Execution Language Version 2.0. OASIS Standard (2007). http://docs.oasis-open.org/wsbpel/2.0/wsbpel-v2.0.html

A Model Interpreter for Timed Automata

M. Usman Iftikhar[1]([⊠]), Jonas Lundberg[1], and Danny Weyns[2,3]

[1] Institute of Computer Science, Linnaeus University,
351 95 Växjö, Sweden
{usman.iftikhar,jonas.lundberg}@lnu.se
[2] Katholieke Universiteit Leuven, Leuven, Belgium
danny.weyns@kuleuven.be
[3] Linnaeus University, Växjö, Sweden

Abstract. In the model-centric approach to model-driven development, the models used are sufficiently detailed to be executed. Being able to execute the model directly, without any intermediate model-to-code translation, has a number of advantages. The model is always up-to-date and runtime updates of the model are possible. This paper presents a model interpreter for timed automata, a formalism often used for modeling and verification of real-time systems. The model interpreter supports real-time system features like simultaneous execution, system wide signals, a ticking clock, and time constraints. Many existing formal representations can be verified, and many existing DSMLs can be executed. It is the combination of being both verifiable and executable that makes our approach rather unique.

Keywords: Model-driven development · Model interpretation · Timed automata · Virtual machine

1 Introduction

Model-driven development (MDD) is a software development methodology focusing on creating and exploiting domain models [17]. A domain model is an abstraction that describes selected aspects of a specific domain. An important part of MDD is the use of domain-specific modeling languages (DSML) [6]. Developers use DSMLs to efficiently build application models using elements of the domain and often express design intent declaratively rather than imperatively.

In a model-centric approach, models of the system are established in sufficient detail that the model can be executed, or used to generate executable code [17]. To achieve this, the models defined in a DSML might include, for example, representations of persistent and non-persistent data, business logic, and presentation elements. Integration to legacy data and services might require that the interfaces to those models are also modeled.

There are two common approaches to model execution. In the code-generation approach a DSML specified model can be translated to a program in a language like Java that can later be executed using the standard Java virtual machine.

T. Margaria and B. Steffen (Eds.): ISoLA 2016, Part I, LNCS 9952, pp. 243–258, 2016.
DOI: 10.1007/978-3-319-47166-2_17

This approach works fine when the DSML is (roughly) a more abstract, richer version of an ordinary programming language. However, code-generation runs into trouble when the model has more declarative features like *simultaneous execution*, *system wide signals*, and *time constraints*, that is, model features that have no simple counterpart in the target language into which it should be translated. Furthermore, model updates at runtime are basically impossible and any manual change in the generated code will ruin the connection to the model.

An alternative to code-generation is model interpretation that relies on the existence of a virtual machine able to directly read and run the model. The major advantage of this approach is that model updates at runtime are possible (see Sect. 5) and, as we will see in Sects. 3 and 4, the domain specific interpreter can provide support for model specific declarative features like the ones presented above. Having the model available at runtime also simplifies runtime verification of model dependent system goals (see Sect. 5).

The goal of this paper is to present a model interpreter for timed automata [2], first presented in [10]. Timed automata are an often used formalism to model real-time systems and it supports features like simultaneous execution, system wide signals, and time constraints[1]. Timed automata has a graphical representation suitable for humans and a corresponding XML based DSML suitable for machine processing. Formal properties (system goals) of models described by timed automata can be verified by a tool called UPPAAL [4]. In addition to handling real-time features, it is the use of a domain specific model being verifiable, executable in a real world scenario, and allowing model updates at runtime that makes our approach rather unique. See related work in Sect. 6 for more details.

Timed automata will be presented in Sect. 2. The model interpretation is done in two steps: (1) The DSML defining the model is translated into an internal task graph based executable model (Sect. 3), and (2) A virtual machine, specifically designed for timed automata, interprets the executable model (Sect. 4). Step (1) is not novel since standard techniques from compiler design are used. The virtual machine on the other hand has novel features extending the functionality of a standard stack machine to handle a wide set of timed automata specific features. Additional features of our approach (e.g. support for runtime model updates and runtime verification) are discussed in Sect. 5. In Sect. 6 we present related work, and in Sect. 7 we present summary and conclusions.

2   Timed Automata

A timed automaton [2] is a finite automaton extended with a finite set of real-valued clocks. During a run of a timed automaton, all clock values increase with the same speed. The clock values can be compared to integers and these comparisons form guards that may enable or disable transitions and therefore constrain the automaton's behavior.

---

[1] See the uppaal.org website for a list of industrial projects using timed automata and the UPPAAL verification tool.

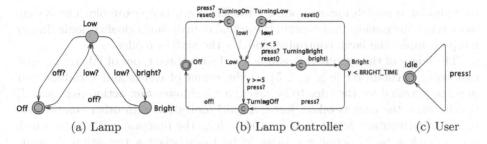

(a) Lamp   (b) Lamp Controller   (c) User

Fig. 1. The simple lamp example.

UPPAAL [5] is an integrated tool environment for modeling, validation and verification of real-time systems modeled as networks of timed automata. UPPAAL comes with an XML based description language in which systems of timed automata can be defined, which is our DSML. UPPAAL also includes a number of tools for visualizing the automata, simulation, and model verification. The aim of this section is to provide a brief introduction to timed automata as defined by the UPPAAL DSML. It can be considered as a brief (and informal) summary of the official UPPAAL tutorial [4], inspired by [8], with a focus on modeling and interpretation of timed automata. To simplify the presentation we use standard automata terminology (e.g. state, transition) rather than the standard timed automata terminology (e.g. location, fire an edge).

2.1   Networks of Timed Automata

A timed automaton is a finite-state machine extended with clock variables. All clocks progress synchronously. In UPPAAL, a system is modelled as a network of several such timed automata in parallel. The model is further extended with ordinary variables and the state of the system is defined by the state of all automata, the clock values, and the values of the variables. An automata may make a state transition separately or due to synchronization with another automata through channels. For example, for a channel x, a sender $x!$ can synchronize with a receiver $x?$ through a signal.

Figure 1 shows three automata modelling a simple system with a lamp, a lamp controller, and a button to be pressed by a user. At start, when both the lamp and the controller are in state *Off*, if the user presses a button a signal *press!* is sent and the controller moves to state *TurningOn* due to synchronization *press?* followed by *LowLight* (sending a signal *low!*), and the lamp is turned on (due to *low?*). If the user presses the button again, the lamp is turned off. However, if the user is fast and within 5 time units presses the button twice, the lamp is turned on and becomes bright. The clock y of the lamp controller is used to detect if the user was fast ($y < 5$) or slow ($y >= 5$). The lamp stays bright for a certain period of time *BRIGHT_TIME* and then returns to *Low* state again.

We divide the models into two categories: *environment models* and *system models*. Environment models are used for simulation and enables offline verification of the system by providing input and getting output. For example, the user and lamp models are environment models in our lamp example. The system models are the models that contain the actual domain functionality/logic. In our lamp example, the lamp controller model is the system model.

The edges of the automata are annotated with three types of labels: a *guard*, expressing a condition (e.g. $y < 5$) on the values of clocks and variables that must be satisfied for the edge to be taken; a *synchronization* action (e.g. *press!*) which, when the edge is taken, forces a synchronization with other components on a complementary action, and an *update* (e.g. the function call *reset()* which resets clock y to 0) defining actions to be taken when a transition is made. All three types of labels are optional: absence of a guard is interpreted as the condition *true*, and absence of a synchronization action indicates an internal (non-synchronizing) edge (e.g. *BrightLight* → *TurningLow* in the controller).

Only one state per automaton, called *control* or *active* state, is active at a time. States can also be annotated with *invariants* expressing constraints on the clock values for control to remain in a particular state. For example, the system can only remain in *BrightLight* as long as the value of y is less than *BRIGHT_TIME*.

UPPAAL defines two types of transitions between states: *action transition* and *delayed transition*. Action transitions can be further divided into *synchronization transition* and *internal transition*. If two complementary labeled edges (e.g. *press!* and *press?*) in two different automata are enabled then they can synchronize and a simultaneous *synchronization transition* is activated. In a delayed transition only the clock ticks and no actual state transition is made (e.g. *Bright* remains active in the controller while $y < BRIGHT\_TIME$ and as long as no-one is pushing the button). Further progress in time might lead to an invariant violation ($y \geq BRIGHT\_TIME$) and an *internal transition* (*Bright* → *TurningLow*).

Finally, to enable modeling of atomicity of transition sequences in a given automaton (i.e. multiple transitions with no time delay) states may be marked as *committed* (indicated by a *c* in the circle). Commited states (e.g. *TurningOn* in the controller) make it possible to receive a signal (*press?* in *Off* → *TurningOn*) and send a signal (*low!* in *TurningOn* → *LowLight*) without any time delay.

2.2 The Timed Automata Modeling Language

The timed automata DSML is a straight forward XML markup of the transition graphs described previously. States (locations in UPPAAL) are nodes with a number of attributes (`id`, `name`, `commited`, `invariant`, etc.) and transitions are edges connecting source and target states (identified by their `id`s) with attributes (`guard`, `synchronization`, `assignment`) describing the transition conditions.

Figure 2 shows an excerpt of the DSML for our lamp example. It starts with a section of global declarations `<declaration>` with variables and signals that are accessible anywhere in the system. In our lamp example, the global declaration section consists only of signal declarations, i.e., *press*, *off*, *low*, and *bright*.

The declaration section is followed by one or more template definitions describing a single automaton. Templates have a name (element `<name>`), a set of local variables and clocks (`<declaration>`), a set of states (`<location>`), an initial state (element `<init>`), and a set of transitions (`<transition>`).

```
<?xml version="1.0" encoding="utf-8"?>
<nta>
    <declaration>chan press, off, low, bright;</declaration>
    <template>
        <name>LampController</name>
        <declaration>const int BRIGHT_TIME = 10;
            clock y;
            void reset(){ y = 0;}
        </declaration>
        <location id="id0">
            <name>TurningLow</name>
            <committed/>
        </location>
        <location id="id1">
            <name>Bright</name>
            <label kind="invariant">y &lt; BRIGHT_TIME</label>
        </location>
        <location id="id2">
            <name>Off</name>
        </location>
        <init ref="id2"/>
        <transition>
            <source ref="id1"/>
            <target ref="id0"/>
            <label kind="synchronisation">low!</label>
            <label kind="assignment">reset()</label>
        </transition>
        <!-- missing transitions -->
    </template>
    <!-- missing templates for Lamp and User-->
    <system> system Lamp, LampController, User;</system>
</nta>
```

Fig. 2. Excerpt of the XML based DSML for the lamp example.

The final DSML section, the *system declaration*, lists the *automata instances* planned to be used in the system. The system section is a description of how the system is going to be initialized. In our lamp example, we have one instance of each of the *User*, *Lamp* and *LampController* automata. In general however, a system might contain multiple instances (e.g. multiple users) of a single automation.

3 Executable Model Generation

A network of timed automata as described in Sect. 2 is a system model with sufficient detail to be interpreted. The model interpretation can be divided into two steps: (1) Executable Model Generation, and (2) Model Execution. Both are handled in sequence each time a model is executed. In this section we present the model generation and in Sect. 4 we present the model execution.

An overview of the executable model generation is presented in Fig. 3. The input is an XML based DSML describing the system (Model.xml), the final result (State Transition Graphs, Task Graphs) is an internal representation

Fig. 3. Overview of the executable model generation.

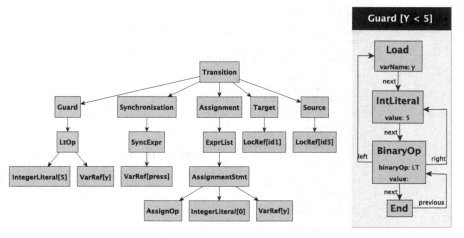

Fig. 4. AST for transition *Low* to *TurningBright*.

Fig. 5. Task graph for guard y < 5

of the system that later will be executed by our virtual machine. The executable model generation is divided into two steps: (1) A *compiler frontend* that parses the input XML file and creates a single abstract syntax tree (AST) and a symbol table. (2) An *executable model generator* that traverses the AST to generate the final executable model representation.

The compiler frontend uses standard compiler techniques and will not be described in detail. In short, UPPAAL DSML is defined as a context-free grammar that can easily be used to generate a parser using the Antlr [16] parser generator tool. The resulting AST is then traversed once more to construct a symbol table, a mapping from scopes to variable declarations. A scope in the UPPAAL DSML can be a global declaration, system declaration, template declaration, or a function.

Figure 4 shows a subtree of the AST representing the transition *Low* to *Turning Bright* in LampController. Apart from source and target information of the transition (**Source**, **Target** subtrees) it also includes three labels: **Guard** $(y < 5)$, **Synchronization** (*press?*), and **Assignment** $(y = 0)$.

The executable model representation later to be executed by a virtual machine consists of two parts: (1) *State transition graphs*, one for each automata, and (2) a number of *Task graphs*. The state transition graphs are just an internal graph representation of the system's timed automata as described in Sect. 2. There exists one graph for each automaton. The states are nodes and the transitions are edges. Both nodes and edges are annotated with references to task graphs. Each transition label (guard, synchronization, update) is represented by a separate task graph, and each node attribute (invariant) is also represented as a task graph.

A task graph defines the control flow of a task graph evaluation. It consists of a collection of task nodes that are connected with *next* and *previous* attributes.

Each task node has a task type attribute defining the role of that node. Examples of task types are: *DECL* declares a variable, *LITERAL* defines a integer literal, *BINARY_OP* for binary operations, *STORE/LOAD* store/load a variable value from/to the heap, *END* signals the termination of a task graph evaluation, etc. Depending upon task type a node can have additional attributes, e.g. the task node for binary operators have *left* and *right* attributes pointing to left and right expression nodes.

Figure 5 shows the task graph for the guard $y < 5$ of the *Low* to *TurningBright* transition in Lamp Controller. The execution order is defined by the *next* edges (non-essential *previous* edges are omitted for simplicity) and the less-then operator is represented as a binary operation (tagged with LT) with two node type specific edges (*left* and *right*) referencing the values to be used in the operator. The *previous* edge in the *END* node points to the final result of the task graph evaluation.

In addition to task graphs generated due to various state and transition attributes we also generate task graphs for all declarations of global variables and signals defined in the <declaration> part of the AST, and for all clock and variable declarations local to a certain automaton. These additional task graphs are not directly referenced by any transition graph, they will be used in the initialization phase of the virtual machine before the execution starts.

Task and transition graphs are generated in a single AST traversal. Due to space limitations the actually used algorithm will not be presented here.

4   Model Execution

The model interpretation starts with an initialization phase (Sect. 4.1) where global and template variables are declared and initialized, the real-time time unit is set, and connections to environment models are established. Then the actual execution can start (Sect. 4.2).

The core of the model interpreter is the *timed automata virtual machine* (TAVM). Apart from heap and stack management the TAVM has two parts that together are responsible for the actual execution. The *state transition machine* (STM) is responsible for the state transitions, and the *task graph interpreter* (TGI) is (on requests from the STM) evaluating task graphs. Several of the design decisions for the TAVM are inspired by UPPAAL Tron [9], a model based testing tool from UPPAAL.

4.1   Virtual Machine Setup

Declarations: The first step is to execute global and system declarations by the task graph interpreter in order to initialize all variable and clock declarations used by the system. For example, it declares what channels are going to be used. The system declarations provide a list of automata instances that are to be executed by the virtual machine. Finally, for each instantiated automaton, all local declarations are executed and a list of initial active states is created.

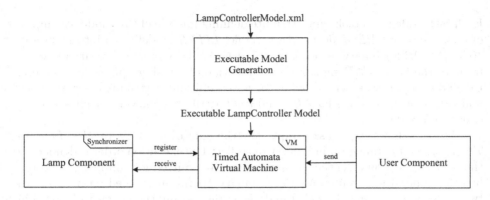

Fig. 6. Overview of the lamp example interpretation.

Model time unit: In timed automata, a time tick is an abstract entity that can be assigned to any real time unit, e.g. milliseconds, seconds, minutes, etc. In order to correctly behave as real-time clocks, the TAVM must know the real time unit of a tick. It therefore provides a method $setRealTimeUnit(milliseconds)$ to set the time unit in milliseconds. How clocks progress is discussed in more detail at Sect. 4.2.

Environment connection: As mentioned in Sect. 2.2, the entire model is divided into two categories: Environment models representing external components that interact with the running system, and system models that are to be executed in the TAVM. The TAVM connects with the environment through signals defined in the automata model.

Figure 6 shows an overview of the Lamp example interpretation. The input is an XML based system specification (LampControllerModel.xml) that is used to generate an executable model which is then fed to the TAVM for execution. At runtime, TAVM must be connected to a real lamp and a real button. To realize this in our approach, we replace the models of the environment with an actual environment represented by the Lamp and User components in Fig. 6, and the TAVM executes only the Lamp Controller model. A component in this case is a piece of software which handles the communication with external devices.

The TAVM assigns a unique identifier to each channel. This identifier can be used to send and receive signals from the TAVM. TAVM has a public interface (named VM) providing a method $getChannelId("channel")$ that can be used to get channel identifiers. To send a signal, the VM interface provides a $send(channelId)$ method that can be used to send a signal from the environment to the virtual machine. Data can also be sent using the $send$ method as a string expression like "$a = 2$". These expressions are converted to task graphs on-the-fly and evaluated by the task graph interpreter when a signal is consumed. More details about how signals are consumed are provided in the next section.

The TAVM provides an abstract class *Synchronizer*, that should be extended by components interested in receiving signals from the TAVM. A component registers itself for a certain channel by, first, getting the channel identifier using the *getChannelId* method, and then call the *register* method provided by the VM interface. The *register* method take three parameters: (1) a channel identifier identifying which type of signal we are interested in, (2) an instantiation of the *Synchronizer* class, that will receive the signals, (3) and a array of variable names specifying what variable values we are interested in. The *Synchronizer* class defines one abstract method *receive* that has two parameters: (1) a channel identifier that can be used to determine which signal is received, (2) the data that comes with the signal.

4.2   Virtual Machine Execution

The TAVM provides a *start* method which starts the actual execution once the setup is completed. Once started, the virtual machine is idle until triggered either by input from the environment, or by a time tick. The heart of the TAVM is the State Transition Machine (STM). The STM keeps track of all active nodes and decides what and when transitions are triggered. The STM is using another component, the Task Graph Interpreter (TGI), whenever a task graphs needs to be evaluated. In what follows we first present the STM and then the TGI.

The State Transition Machine. The STM maintains a set of all active nodes N and a set S, representing the current state, containing N and the values of all the variables and clocks. From now on "state" refers to the global state S and we refer to individual timed automata states/locations as nodes. Upon start, the STM checks all instantiated models and execute those that are in a committed state. To do that, the STM checks (one by one) all the active nodes in N, if a node is in a committed state, then STM randomly selects one outgoing transition from that node and tries to execute it. If that transition cannot be taken (e.g. a guard evaluates to false), STM tries another one. This process is repeated until all committed nodes are handled, and will also be repeated after each taken transition ending up in a committed state. The STM supports non-determinism by randomly selecting nodes and transitions if multiple available.

Algorithm 1 shows the pseudo code for executing one transition which does not interact with the environment. That is, it can only handle signals sent and received within the system model. The handling of signals involving external components is discussed later on.

In what follows, S' is a temporary state that can be rolled back to S, or S can become S', and if there is no guard on a transition (or invariant on a node), then the evaluation of the guard (invariant) expression returns true. Evaluation calls (e.g. *evaluateGuard(transition, S)*) are calls to the task graph interpreter requesting a task graph guard (*transition*) to be evaluated in a given state (S).

Algorithm 1 starts by making sure that a transition can only be taken when the guard of the transition is true (line 2). If guard is true, and the transition involves synchronization (line 3), then it makes sure that the guard of the receiving transition is also true (line 6). After these preliminary checks we have

A1. Algorithm for executing a transition

Input N set of all active nodes
Input S current state including N and the value of all variables and clocks
Input *transition* to be taken and it's source *node*
Return *true* if transition accepted, otherwise *false*

1. $recvTransition \leftarrow NULL$
2. **if** $evaluateGuard(transition, S) ==$ **true then**
3.   **if** $transition.synch \;! = null$ **and** $transition.synch.type == SEND$ **then**
4. $channelId = evaluateSynchronization(transition, S)$
5. $recvTransition = findReceivingTransition(channelId, N, S)$
6.   **if** $evaluateGuard(recvTransition) \;! =$ **true then**
7.   **return false**
8.   **end if**
9.   **end if**
10. $S' \leftarrow S$
11. $evaluateUpdate(transition, S')$
12.   **if** $recvTransition! = null$ **then**
13. $evaluateUpdate(recvTransition, S')$
14.   **end if**
15.   **if** $checkAllInvariants(N, S') ==$ **true then**
16. $S \leftarrow S'$
17. $N.remove(node)$
18. $N.add(transition.targetNode)$
19.   **if** $recvTransition \;! = null$ **then**
20. $N.remove(recvTransition.srcNode)$
21. $N.add(transition.targetNode)$
22.   **end if**
23.   **return true**
24.   **else**
25. $discard(S')$
26.   **return false**
27.   **end if**
28. **end if**
29. **return false**

---

a potential transition to a new state and we clone the current state ($S' \leftarrow S$, line 10) to make sure that we can roll back to S if future steps fails. Then we start to evaluate the update task graphs (line 11, 13), and verify that all invariants still holds (line 15). These steps might update S' and still fail. If they succeed we decide to make the transition and update the current state $S \leftarrow S'$ (line 16) and update N by adding and removing the old and new active node (also for the signal receiving transition), lines 17–22.

In order to communicate with the environment, we must modify our algorithm at a few places. For sending a signal to the environment, and after getting *channelId* of the sender, we must look at the list of registered synchronizers. If any synchronizer is found registered for the same channel, we take the transition after executing update task graph and evaluating all the invariants. Then we call the *receive* method of the associated instance of the *Synchronizer* class with the requested data.

When a signal is received from the environment, the STM finds the receiving transition through *channelId*, and execute the *guard* and *update* task graphs. It can happen that the system models in the STM and the environment models are not synchronized, and there is no transition at the moment who could receive the signal. STM then takes a flexible approach, and if the signal is not consumed, that signal is moved to a queue. Then the queue of signals is checked repeatedly whenever the clock ticks or a new signal arrives to consume the pending signals.

The STM maintains an internal timer, whose time period can be configured as discussed in Sect. 4.1. The STM keeps an internal data structure for all the clocks in the model. When the timer ticks, the STM temporarily increases the time of all the clock variables modelled in the automata, i.e., S' and checks the invariants of all enabled nodes. If all the invariants hold, the STM increases time for all the clock variables permanently $S \leftarrow S'$ and the timer goes to wait state. If the invariants of any active nodes are violated by the temporary increment of the timer, the STM reverts the time increment S and executes those nodes first, whose invariants are violated, by evaluating their transitions as discussed in the Algorithm 1. If a node can not take a transition, then the system ends in a timelock (this points to a design flaw in the model). The STM will then stop execution and throw a *TimelockException*.

If the selected time tick unit is very small we might end up in a situation where the TAVM can not manage all the required computations (or transitions) before the next tick. In addition to the general STM overhead this might occur when waiting for an external signal or due to certain time consuming TGI computations to check if a transition is possible or not. Our implementation handles this situation by buffering the time ticks and then executes them as soon as possible. This is (of course) problematic since it might cause a delay in the signals sent to the real world components. Thus, for each application, the real time unit to be used should be chosen carefully to make sure that the TAVM always manage to do all the required work before the next tick.

The Task Graph Interpreter. The task graph interpreter (TGI) evaluates task graphs on request from the STM. On initialization of the model, the STM requires the TGI to evaluate the initialization expressions for all the declared variables. Later on the TGI evaluates the *guard* and other transition and state attributes to take transitions as described previously in Algorithm 1. The TGI keeps track of a heap which stores all the global, system and template declarations, and a stack to store the state of local variables and function parameters when a call occur. Algorithm 2 shows an excerpt of the algorithm used by the TGI. With each evaluation request the STM also provides the *processId* that is needed to know which variables belongs to which instantiated model. For evaluating global and system declarations, the STM uses 0, and −1 respectively as *processId*. The CT (Current Task) always points to the current task. Upon receiving a request for evaluation, the TGI checks the task type (line 3, 6, 10)

A2. Algorithm for task graph interpretation

Input *taskGraph* to be executed and the model instance identifier *processId*
Return Result of the task graph evaluation

1. $CT \leftarrow taskGraph.getFirst()$
2. **while** $CT \notin END$ **do**
3.   **if** $CT \in LOAD$ **then**
4. $varName \leftarrow CT.getVarName()$
5. $CT.value = heap.get(processId).get(varName)$
6.   **else if** $CT \in STORE$ **then**
7. $varName \leftarrow CT.getVarName()$
8. $value \leftarrow CT.getPrev().getvalue()$
9. $heap.get(processId).get(varName).setValue(value)$
10.   **else if** $CT \in BINARY\_OP$ **then**
11. $op \leftarrow CT.getOp()$
12.   **if** $op \in LT$ **then**
13. $CT.value = CT.getLeft().getValue < CT.getRight().getValue()$
14.   **else**
15.   ... more operators here
16.   **end if**
17.   **else**
18.   ... more tasks here
19.   **end if**
20. $CT \leftarrow CT.getNext()$
21. **end while**
22. **return** $CT.getPrev().getvalue()$

---

and takes the appropriate action. Once a task is evaluated, CT moves to the next task (line 20). This process is repeated until CT reaches the END task, which stops the task graph evaluation and the result of the evaluation is returned.

4.3   Validation

Apart from extensive in-house testing, our model interpreter has been evaluated in various adaptive systems. The original idea was presented in [10] where the adaptation logic of a robotic system is formally verified and executed by the model interpreter. Later on the model interpreter was evaluated in several case studies, including a smart house system, a security system, and two vehicular traffic systems [11]. Other applications where we applied the model interpreter are a digital story telling application and an e-health system [18]. See the project website [1] for more details about these case studies.

5   Additional Features and Future Work

Direct access to the model at runtime provides many additional advantages. Some of these features are already implemented and tested (Sect. 5.1) whereas others can be considered as future work (Sect. 5.2). See [10] for more details.

5.1   Additional Features

System Model Updates. The model interpreter supports online updates of the system models, which is crucial to deal with bugs, or adding new functionality to the running system. Our approach follows the classical process of runtime updates based on quiescence states [12]. The model interpreter provides a method *changeModel(model)* which receives an updated model description (DSML). After that, the interpreter waits until each automaton of the current model reaches a quiescence state (i.e., no ongoing input or time triggered transactions) and interrupts the execution. The state of the current model is then saved and any new external inputs received while the update takes place are stored in a buffer. The interpreter then generates a new executable model (Sect. 3) and initialize that model (Sect. 4.1). Next, the interpreter restores the saved state of the previous model to the updated model and initializes new variables if applicable. Finally, the TAVM restarts the execution using the updated model.

Goal Verification. The model interpreter provides basic support for runtime verification of system goals. The *goal manager* component in the interpreter provides a function *addGoal(goal, client)* that register goals to be monitored. A goal is a boolean expression involving clocks and variables (e.g. $y \leq 10$). The client is an implementation of the *GoalClient* interface registering to receive updates of the goal status. When a goal is registered the interpreter converts it to a task graph and start to notify the client every time a goal status is changed. Using this approach an interested component can track state changes and check whether the system goals hold or are violated. This feature was used in [10] to verify the correctness when updating the feedback loop models to deal with a new set of adaptation goals in a self-adaptive system.

Model Visualization. The model interpreter also comes with a graphical user interface allowing a user to inspect the running model, its ongoing execution, and to monitor variable values. This is useful for debugging the running system. The model interpreter provides a probe for interested components to get updates of the running model. The goal manager used in the goal verification uses the probe to listen to the updates and notifies the graphical user interface which display the current status of the model, see, e.g., Fig. 13, 14 and 15 in [10].

5.2   Future Features

The goal manager currently used for both goal verification and model visualization has certain limitations. For example, goal types are limited to only boolean expressions. In the future we plan to provide an interface offering plug and play facilities for arbitrary external components, and this new interface should give access to the complete model of the system (including the environment models) and allow every type of expression that can be represented as a task graph to be evaluated. This new machine interface opens up the possibility for a wide range of components to be attached to the virtual machine.

Our primary candidate for such plugin component is *online verification*. UPPAAL is foremost an offline verification tool. Given a model and a set of TCTL properties, the tool can prove that these properties are never invalidated. However, due to the so-called state explosion problem, incomplete knowledge about environment and memory constraints, offline verification may not be achieved. The interpreter on the other hand has runtime access to the complete model and can after each transition verify that the provided TCTL properties, converted to task graphs, are still valid. It is not a formal verification, it is however a pragmatic approach to verify that the running system behaves correctly. We are currently implementing an online verification component providing support for a subset of the timed computation tree logic (TCTL) properties, like constraints, safety and liveness properties.

Another possible approach to model checking problem is to delegate that work to other model checking tools. For example, using the plugin mechanism the model interpreter should be able to incorporate other trusted external modules (e.g., runtime model checking engines to support continuous verification at runtime).

6   Related Work

Ever since D.C. Schmidt's seminal paper on Model-Driven Software Engineering in 2006 [17] the interest for various aspects of model-driven design has flourished. In our approach we take the model-centric approach one step further and consider the model not only as a vehicle for code-generation, but also as a design specification suitable for verification. The number of existing models (DSMLs) that can be verified, executed in a real world environment, and that allows runtime model updates are rather few.

The Foundational Subset of Executable UML (fUML) defines the semantics for a subset of UML that can be executed by the fUML execution engine [15]. The fUML execution engine executes an in-memory representation of fUML models. Progress in the verification of these models has recently been achieved [14] but, to the best of our knowledge, no progress has been made yet for runtime model updates.

Ghezzi et al. [7] introduce adaptive model-driven execution to mitigate non-functional uncertainties. Using UML interaction diagrams a Markov decision model of the system is generated. The model is augmented with probability distribution of different execution paths of the system. The model is then executed by an ad-hoc interpreter that drives the execution of the system according to specified probabilities to guarantee the highest utility for a set of quality properties. In their model each state is associated with an implementation of an abstract functionality of the system, and the interpreter invokes the implementations while state-by-state traversing the automaton, whereas we model and execute the actual implementation of the system. Markov decision models are well-known to allow probabilistic model checking and verification tools are available [13].

Anlauf et al. [3] presents an interpretable language XASM (Extensible Abstract State Machine). XASM uses a notion of external functions as defined in ASMs to realize a component-based modularization. The support environment of XASM consists of the XASM-compiler translating XASM programs to C source code, the runtime system, and the graphical debugging and animation tool. This approach lacks support for runtime update of the model, and although computer-aided verification of ASM models is possible in theory, it is well-known to be difficult in practice [19].

7   Summary and Conclusions

In this paper, we presented a model interpreter for timed automata, a formalism often used for modeling and verification of real-time systems. In addition to handling real-time features, it is the use of a domain specific model being verifiable, executable in a real world scenario, and allowing model updates at runtime that makes our approach rather unique. Given a model of the system the interpreter converts it into an executable model that can be interpreted by a timed automata virtual machine. Contrary to traditional approaches, where models are converted to code, using a model interpreter provides a number of additional advantages: (1) models are executed directly without converting them to a source code; hence no model-based testing is required, (2) models can be replaced at runtime without stopping the system, e.g., to add new functionality, (3) models can be used to verify system properties at runtime, (4) and it is also possible to visualize the running models. Our virtual machine can handle real-time system features like simultaneous execution, system wide signals, a ticking clock, and time constraints, not usually handled by ordinary stack based virtual machines. We included a future work section pointing out the possibility to use a model of the entire system to perform online verification.

A byte code version of the model interpreter can be downloaded from the project website [1].

References

1. ActivFORMS: Active Formal Models for Self-Adaptation (2016). https://people. cs.kuleuven.be/~danny.weyns/software/ActivFORMS/
2. Alur, R., Dill, D.L.: A theory of timed automata. Theor. Comput. Sci. **126**(2), 183–235 (1994)
3. Anlauff, M.: XASM - an extensible, component-based abstract state machines language. In: Gurevich, Y., Kutter, P.W., Odersky, M., Thiele, L. (eds.) ASM 2000. LNCS, vol. 1912, pp. 69–90. Springer, Heidelberg (2000)
4. Behrmann, G., David, A., Larsen, K.G.: A tutorial on UPPAAL. In: Bernardo, M., Corradini, F. (eds.) SFM-RT 2004. LNCS, vol. 3185, pp. 200–236. Springer, Heidelberg (2004)
5. Bengtsson, J.E., Yi, W.: Timed automata: semantics, algorithms and tools. In: Desel, J., Reisig, W., Rozenberg, G. (eds.) Lectures on Concurrency and Petri Nets. LNCS, vol. 3098, pp. 87–124. Springer, Heidelberg (2004)

6. Fowler, M.: Domain-specific Languages. Pearson Education, Upper Saddle River (2010)
7. Ghezzi, C., Pinto, L.S., Spoletini, P., Tamburrelli, G.: Managing non-functional uncertainty via model-driven adaptivity. In: Proceedings of the International Conference on Software Engineering, ICSE 2013, pp. 33–42. IEEE Press, Piscataway (2013)
8. Havelund, K., Larsen, K.G., Skou, A.: Formal verification of a power controller using the real-time model checker UPPAAL. In: Katoen, J.-P. (ed.) AMAST-ARTS 1999, ARTS 1999, and AMAST-WS 1999. LNCS, vol. 1601, p. 277. Springer, Heidelberg (1999)
9. Hessel, A., Larsen, K.G., Mikucionis, M., Nielsen, B., Pettersson, P., Skou, A.: Testing real-time systems using UPPAAL. In: Hierons, R.M., Bowen, J.P., Harman, M. (eds.) FORTEST. LNCS, vol. 4949, pp. 77–117. Springer, Heidelberg (2008)
10. Iftikhar, M.U., Weyns, D.: ActivFORMS: active formal models for self-adaptation. In: Proceedings of the 9th International Symposium on Software Engineering for Adaptive and Self-managing Systems, SEAMS, pp. 125–134. ACM, New York (2014)
11. Iglesia, D., Weyns, D.: MAPE-K formal templates to rigorously design behaviors for self-adaptive systems. ACM Trans. Auton. Adapt. Syst. 10(3), 15:1–15:31 (2015)
12. Kramer, J., Magee, J.: The evolving philosophers problem: dynamic change management. IEEE Trans. Softw. Eng. 16(11), 1293–1306 (1990)
13. Kwiatkowska, M., Norman, G., Parker, D.: PRISM 4.0: verification of probabilistic real-time systems. In: Gopalakrishnan, G., Qadeer, S. (eds.) CAV 2011. LNCS, vol. 6806, pp. 585–591. Springer, Heidelberg (2011)
14. Laurent, Y., Bendraou, R., Baarir, S., Gervais, M.-P.: Formalization of fUML: an application to process verification. In: Jarke, M., Mylopoulos, J., Quix, C., Rolland, C., Manolopoulos, Y., Mouratidis, H., Horkoff, J. (eds.) CAiSE 2014. LNCS, vol. 8484, pp. 347–363. Springer, Heidelberg (2014)
15. Mellor, S.J., Balcer, M.: Executable UML: A Foundation for Model-Driven Architectures. Addison-Wesley Longman Publishing Co. Inc., Boston (2002)
16. Parr, T.J., Quong, R.W.: ANTLR: a predicated-LL(K) parser generator. Softw. Pract. Exper. 25(7), 789–810 (1995)
17. Schmidt, D.C.: Model-driven engineering. Comput.-IEEE Comput. Soc. 39(2), 25 (2006)
18. Shevtsov, S., Iftikhar, M.U., Weyns, D.: SimCA vs ActivFORMS: comparing control- and architecture-based adaptation on the TAS exemplar. In: Proceedings of the 1st International Workshop on Control Theory for Software Engineering, CTSE , pp. 1–8. ACM, New York (2015)
19. Spielmann, M., Machines, A.S.: Verification problems and complexity. PhD thesis, Bibliothek der RWTH Aachen (2000)

ModSyn-PP: Modular Synthesis of Programs and Processes

ModSyn-PP: Modular Synthesis of Programs and Processes Track Introduction

Boris Düdder[1]($\boxtimes$), George T. Heineman[2], and Jakob Rehof[1]

[1] Technical University Dortmund, Dortmund, Germany
{boris.duedder,jakob.rehof}@tu-dortmund.de
[2] Worcester Polytechnic Institute, Worcester, USA
heineman@cs.wpi.edu

1 Introduction

It is an old and beautiful dream of computer science to synthesize software applications from specifications. The beginning can be traced back to, at least, to 1957 (Summer Institute of Symbolic Logic, Cornell 1957) when Alonzo Church proposed to consider the problem of automatically constructing a finite-state procedure implementing a given input/output relation over infinite bitstreams specified as a logical formula. The problem, since then widely known as "Church's Problem", gave rise to a major branch of theoretical computer science which has been concerned with many different forms of synthesis.

We know today, after 60 years of research, that realizing this dream faces at least the three following fundamental challenges:

1. Synthesis problems typically have high computational complexity. Synthesis problems of interest tend to begin at PSPACE and many are known to be superexponential (synthesis is one of relatively few sources of natural problems with practical relevance where the class 2-EXPTIME is richly represented).
2. Perhaps a greater hurdle in practice, it is challenging to write correctly the complex specifications required by standard program logics traditionally used in synthesis.
3. It is still not clear how software engineers could apply these research results to solve practical problems they face every day.

Whereas synthesis has traditionally been conceived as the construction of a system "from scratch", work in component-oriented design has recently inspired the idea of component-based synthesis [11], where software is synthesized relative to a given collection of components. From the standpoint of component-based synthesis, components are fabricated building blocks providing higher-valued raw material for synthesis. Taking this concept one step further, we envision a wide range of modularity mechanisms being applied to reduce the essential complexity found in software product lines [14]. Since systems development in modern computational environments is increasingly based on the extended use of repositories of reusable components [7] (e.g., software framework libraries,

© Springer International Publishing AG 2016
T. Margaria and B. Steffen (Eds.): ISoLA 2016, Part I, LNCS 9952, pp. 261–265, 2016.
DOI: 10.1007/978-3-319-47166-2_18

web services, embedded software, and hardware components), modularity would appear to be an important pragmatic strategy for tailoring synthesis to practical circumstances. Here, components must be understood at a (variable) level of component abstraction allowing varying granularity of software components for synthesis, e.g. full hierarchical modeling, [12,15].

For practical purposes, tool support for designing, specifying, synthesizing, and analyzing synthesized software is a crucial enabler for broader (industrial) acceptance of modular synthesis. Software synthesis is in particular interesting in software families with high product variability, e.g. in software product lines. Therefore, software synthesis has been studied in this area very early, even before the term software product line was coined, and also with industrial acceptance leading to market-ready products, e.g. for telecommunication services by Steffen et al. in [17,19] as tool for a product line organized via a library of domain-specific components and adapted standard products to user specific requirements in [4]. A comprehensive overview of variability modelling from a constraint-oriented perspective can be found in [9]. A additional branch of early applications of software synthesis are mediator generators, that automatically resolve type conflicts between services and clients, e.g. using a taxonomy over types as a semantic component specification with linear temporal logic in [18].

2   Track

The accepted submissions cover various aspects of modular synthesis and also report on experiments conducted with synthesis tools. Since the scope of this track is not only on synthesis of algorithms/routines, e.g. sorting routines, but also processes that also contain concurrent control flows as well as data flows, a established and succinct way of representing such programs are process graphs. Process graphs explicitly model concurrent and distributed workflows with data dependencies. An example for such a workflow, is the product line of gene alignment workflows for biologists by Lamprecht et al. [10].

The track "ModSyn-PP: Modular Synthesis of Programs and Processes" is a follow-up of Dagstuhl Seminar 14232 "Design and Synthesis from Components" (June 1–6, 2014) [16] which brought together researchers from the component-oriented design community, researchers working on interface theories, and researchers working in synthesis, as well as of the workshop ModSyn-PL (Modular Synthesis of Product Lines), which was held in conjunction with the 19th International Software Product Line Conference (SPLC) July 20 2015, Nashville, Tennessee. This track consists of two sessions: *Modular Synthesis of Processes* and *Techniques and Design Methods for Modular Synthesis* as well as an invited talk given by Fritz Henglein (DIKU, Copenhagen).

Modular Synthesis of Processes. This session contains one paper proposing modular synthesis methods and experimental results with implemented tools.

In the paper "Combinatory Process Synthesis" [2] by Jan Bessai, Andrej Dudenhefner, Boris Düdder, Moritz Martens, and Jakob Rehof, a type-theoretic method for functional synthesis of processes from repositories of components

(CPS) is presented. The proposed method relies on an existing framework based on combinatory logic [6,15] and tool for composition synthesis called (CL)S [3]. Processes, here, are expressed as BPMN 2.0 workflows. BPMN 2.0 is a standardized workflow language with many available design and enactment tools. Types for specifying BPMN 2.0 components and a comprehensive taxonomy of domain specific concepts are used to assign types to BPMN 2.0 fragments, e.g. subprocesses, and functional fragment constructors. A novelty in this computational abstraction of workflows is the fact that constructors can be powerful higher-order functions transforming fragments or functions analog to [13]. Both serve as input for the automatic synthesis of semantically meaningful processes. The synthesis is staged into two distinct levels. The staging provides a separation of concerns between the task of extracting fragments from existing processes in a library and the more sophisticated task of deducing functional fragment transformations. The goal is to automatically synthesize a valid, specified goal workflow in BPMN 2.0. In the experimental section of the paper, the applicability of CPS is evaluated by synthesizing control processes for LEGO® Mindstorms® NXT robots. The automatically synthesized control processes are then deployed to and executed on the open-source BPMN 2.0 platform Activiti. Experimental results are analyzed with respect to various factors. Because BPMN 2.0 uses XML documents, there does not exist a predefined, general composition operation (functional composition) to compose BPMN 2.0 processes in a modular way. Therefore, the core contribution of this paper is a method for injecting functional applicative composition of BPMN 2.0 processes with certain guarantees into languages without pre-defined composition operations.

Techniques and Design Methods for Modular Synthesis. In this session, we have two papers focusing on design, analysis, and synthesis methods for constructing modules that are usable for modular synthesis.

The paper "Synthesis from a Practical Perspective" [8] by Sven Jörges, Anna-Lena Lamprecht, Tizian Margaria, Stefan Naujokat, and Bernhard Steffen presents a practical perspective of a more general approach to synthesis by the means of generation of programming artifacts from higher level specifications. The paper's scope includes various approaches for code generation, e.g. model synthesis from temporal logic specifications and also meta-mode-based tool generation. The approaches can be unified in the way that product parts are factored-out, similar to frameworks, and remain underspecified. These factored-out parts can later be augmented by implementations by designers or developers and result in a full end-user product. State-of-the-art synthesis techniques apply combinations of substitution and partial evaluation with local or global patterns. The paper presents over a decade experience with various synthesis approaches and corresponding design and synthesis tools. It also discusses the potential of combining tools, e.g. to reduce computational complexity of the underlying search space. The authors conclude that this way of synthesis achieves a fundamentally higher simplicity in IT system design.

The paper "A Long and Winding Road Towards Modular Synthesis" [1] by Jan Bessai, Boris Düdder, George T. Heineman, and Jakob Rehof reflects on a number of various approaches for constructing product lines. A product line for solitaire card games implemented in Java serves a study object [5]. A product line shares a common set of features developed from a common set of software artifacts. A feature is a unit of functionality within a system that is visible to an end-user. The ultimate research goal is to automatically assemble a product out of a product line by selecting a set of pre-designed modular units associated to features and developing new units as necessary for individual solitaire variations. A secondary goal was to develop a suitable tool chain that could be integrated with existing IDEs, e.g. Eclipse, to achieve widespread acceptance of the approach. The progress is compared against the routine by-hand development of different variations in the object-oriented paradigm. During this period a number of approaches are investigated by implementations and experiments from the research literature, including components, aspects, and layers. The end result is a description of a productive collaboration that demonstrates a practical tool chain supported by type theoretic methods.

Summary. Modular synthesis is a challenging but also very promising topic for next-generation development methods and tools. The papers of the track and the invited talk of Fritz Henglein have shown that many new ideas are emerging and the sessions delivered new insights and ideas on methods and related tools. Questions that have been discussed cover various topics: specification and algorithmic complexity, computation and logic, (combined) synthesis approaches and also design methods for modular composition and synthesis. Industrial acceptance and trust in such methods remains as a big challenge for the modular synthesis community. The acceptance depends on various factors, e.g. on the pay-off of synthesized versus routine by-hand developed programs as well as a synthesized program's correctness. More research will be needed to master the challenges of modular synthesis of programs and processes.

References

1. Bessai, J., Düdder, B., Heineman, G.T., Rehof, J.: A Long and Winding Road Towards Modular Synthesis. In: Margaria, T., Steffen, B. (eds.) ISoLA 2016, Part I. LNCS, vol. 9952, pp. 303–317. Springer, Heidelberg (2016)
2. Bessai, J., Dudenhefner, A., Düdder, B., Martens, M., Rehof, J.: Combinatory process synthesis. In: Margaria, T., Steffen, B. (eds.) ISoLA 2016, Part I. LNCS, vol. 9952, pp. 266–281. Springer, Heidelberg (2016)
3. Bessai, J., Dudenhefner, A., Düdder, B., Martens, M., Rehof, J.: Combinatory logic synthesizer. In: Margaria, T., Steffen, B. (eds.) ISoLA 2014, Part I. LNCS, vol. 8802, pp. 26–40. Springer, Heidelberg (2014)
4. Braun, V., Margaria, T., Steffen, B., Yoo, H., Rychly, T.: Safe service customization. In: Intelligent Network Workshop 1997, IN 1997, vol. 2, p. 4. IEEE, May 1997
5. Düdder, B., Heineman, G.T., Rehof, J.: Towards migrating object-oriented frameworks to enable synthesis of product line members. In: Proceedings of the 19th International Software Product Line Conference (SPLC 2015), pp. 56–60. ACM, New York (2015)

6. Düdder, B., Martens, M., Rehof, J.: Staged composition synthesis. In: Shao, Z. (ed.) ESOP 2014 (ETAPS). LNCS, vol. 8410, pp. 67–86. Springer, Heidelberg (2014)
7. Heineman, G.T., Councill, W.T.: Component-based Software Engineering: Putting the Pieces Together. Addison-Wesley Longman Publishing Co., Inc., Boston (2001)
8. Jörges, S., Lamprecht, A.L., Margaria, T., Naujokat, S., Steffen, B.: Synthesis from a practical perspective. In: Margaria, T., Steffen, B. (eds.) ISoLA 2016, Part I, LNCS, vol. 9952, pp. 282–302. Springer, Heidelberg (2016)
9. Jörges, S., Lamprecht, A.L., Margaria, T., Schaefer, I., Steffen, B.: A constraint-based variability modeling framework. Int. J. Softw. Tools Technol. Transf. (STTT) 14(5), 511–530 (2012)
10. Lamprecht, A.L., Naujokat, S., Margaria, T., Steffen, B.: Semantics-based composition of EMBOSS services. J. Biomed. Semant. 2(Suppl. 1), S5 (2011). http://www.jbiomedsem.com/content/2/S1/S5
11. Lustig, Y., Vardi, M.Y.: Synthesis from component libraries. In: de Alfaro, L. (ed.) FOSSACS 2009. LNCS, vol. 5504, pp. 395–409. Springer, Heidelberg (2009)
12. Margaria, T., Steffen, B., Reitenspiess, M.: Service-oriented design: the roots. In: Benatallah, B., Casati, F., Traverso, P. (eds.) ICSOC 2005. LNCS, vol. 3826, pp. 450–464. Springer, Heidelberg (2005)
13. Neubauer, J., Steffen, B., Margaria, T.: Higher-order process modeling: product-lining, variability modeling and beyond. Electron. Proc. Theoret. Comput. Sci. 129, 259–283 (2013)
14. Pohl, K., Böckle, G., van Der Linden, F.J.: Software Product Line Engineering - Foundations, Principles, and Techniques. Springer, Heidelberg (2005)
15. Rehof, J.: Towards combinatory logic synthesis. In: BEAT 2013, 1st International Workshop on Behavioural Types. ACM, 22 January 2013
16. Rehof, J., Vardi, M.Y.: Design and synthesis from components. In: Dagstuhl Seminar 14232. Dagstuhl Reports, vol. 7941 (2014). http://dx.doi.org/10.4230/DagRep.4.6.29
17. Steffen, B., Margaria, T., Braun, V., Kalt, N.: Hierarchical service definition. Ann. Rev. Commun. ACM 51, 847–856 (1997)
18. Steffen, B., Margaria, T., Braun, V.: The electronic tool integration platform: concepts and design. Int. J. Softw. Tools Technol. Transf. (STTT) 1(1–2), 9–30 (1997)
19. Steffen, B., Margaria, T., Claen, A., Braun, V., Reitenspie, M.: An environment for the creation of intelligent network services. In: Intelligent Networks: IN/AIN Technologies, Operations, Services and Applications - A Comprehensive Report, pp. 287–300. IEC: International Engineering Consortium (1996)

Combinatory Process Synthesis

Jan Bessai[⊠], Andrej Dudenhefner, Boris Düdder,
Moritz Martens, and Jakob Rehof

Technical University of Dortmund, Dortmund, Germany
{jan.bessai,andrej.dudenhefner,boris.duedder,
moritz.martens,jakob.rehof}@cs.tu-dortmund.de

Abstract. We report on a type-theoretic method for functional synthesis of processes from repositories of components. Our method relies on the existing framework for composition synthesis based on combinatory logic, (CL)S. Simple types for BPMN 2.0 components and a taxonomy of domain specific concepts are used to assign types to BPMN 2.0 fragments and functional fragment constructors. Both serve as input for the automatic creation of meaningful processes. Staging synthesis into two levels provides a separation of concerns between the easy task of extracting fragments from existing processes and the more sophisticated task of deducing functional fragment transformations.

We study the applicability of the described approach by synthesizing control processes for LEGO® Mindstorms® NXT robots deployed on the Activiti platform. We evaluate experimental results analyzing synthesized processes regarding correctness, variability and the time consumed for their creation by the (CL)S framework. Additionally, the steps necessary to target a different application domain are described.

1 Introduction

In this case study we introduce and explore the *Combinatory Process Synthesis* framework (CPS) to synthesize processes from a repository of components according to a synthesis goal. Our work is based on combinatory logic synthesis, where an algorithm solves the problem of inhabitation (provability) [4,12,13] using functional application of components according to rules imposed by type theory. More specifically, process synthesis uses the recently developed strategy of staged composition [12]. In a first stage, compositions of components retrieved from a repository are constructed exploiting taxonomical concepts. These compositions contain meta-computation code which, when executed in a second stage, generates code yielding a well-typed process, in our case study a BPMN 2.0 process. CPS is implemented making use of the Combinatory Logic Synthesizer (CL)S [4].

BPMN 2.0 (Business Process Model and Notation) is a graphical formalism for specifying business processes in diagrams similar to UML activity diagrams. BPMN 2.0 is interesting as target for process synthesis for at least two reasons. First, BPMN 2.0 is provided with an XML schema for persistence allowing to

© Springer International Publishing AG 2016
T. Margaria and B. Steffen (Eds.): ISoLA 2016, Part I, LNCS 9952, pp. 266–281, 2016.
DOI: 10.1007/978-3-319-47166-2_19

synthesize BPMN 2.0 processes as XML documents. Second, BPMN 2.0 execution is supported by a number of execution engines such as Activiti. A challenge for BPMN 2.0 synthesis is that such processes lack an operational semantics of (functional) composition. So far, there is no natural notion of combining separate BPMN 2.0 (sub-)processes. Composition needs further constructs, e.g. gateways or subprocesses, that function as a glue for these processes. Second-stage meta-computation allows to generate such gluing constructs and consequently inclusion of an operational semantics of (function) composition. The computational phase distinction in stages is enforced by separating programs for the different phases into two languages. The *implementation language* describes domain specific *process components*, such as BPMN 2.0 fragments. The *metalanguage* is used to define *complex components*, comprised of functional fragment constructors and application specific process fragment transformations. The distinction between implementation language and metalanguage in (CL)S, formally described in [12], is a universal approach to introduce a notion of composition, necessary for functional synthesis, to any domain of interest.

Contributions and Organization. This case study has two main contributions. First, the CPS Framework is developed (Sect. 2). It includes a type-theoretic formalization of a core subset BPMN 2.0 of process fragments. Second, in order to assess its usefulness, the framework is applied to synthesize processes for two different domains. The first domain (Sect. 3) are LEGO® Mindstorms® NXT robots. It is accompanied by a description of the experimental setup. Results for this domain are critically discussed wrt. encoded variability, synthesis time consumption and assessment of generated outputs. The second domain (Sect. 4) considers shipment processes in logistics. It shows which concepts are reusable and supports the claim that CPS is a generally applicable method.

1.1 Related Work

Software diversity, particularly in the context of software product lines [1,20] has been a field of active study for over a decade. Schaefer et al. present an overview survey classifying different approaches to software variability [22]. Within this classification (CL)S [4], as the underlying framework of CPS, is suited for describing emergent rather than planned variability. New variability points can be added to an existing system leaving the previous solution space intact. In the extreme, any preexisting system without variability points can be included as a single component, representing just the implementation of that system. The use of intersection types [12] allows to combine problem and solution spaces within the same type based description. This alleviates the burden of establishing a traceable mapping between the two spaces, which is studied in [3]. Due to the flexibility of (CL)S, it is possible to realize feature modeling [1] as well as decision modeling [23]. Feature modeling with (CL)S is covered in detail in [6]. CPS implicitly encompasses an enumerative decision model based on the usage of type variables with restricted substitutions. Any decision, e.g. which sensors should be used to perform a task, is captured by a corresponding type variable and propagated to the final product.

Compositional approaches are traditionally associated with positive variability, where features are designed in an opt-in fashion. A well-known example is aspect-oriented programming (e.g. employed in [18]). In (CL)S composition is achieved at the metalanguage level. Meta computations can add features, e.g. by using templates, similar to generative programming [9]. Moreover, complex components in CPS may perform a broad range of code transformations, e.g. moving BPMN nodes between contexts. This is characteristic of transformational approaches such as delta modeling [8]. In fact, (CL)S has been demonstrated to be powerful enough to perform mixin composition synthesis [5].

CPS pervades the layers of variability modeling, component specification, component implementation, automatic composition synthesis, and product generation in a uniform way using modal intersection types. Similarly to constraint-based variability modeling [17,24], CPS represents variability by individually classifying reusable artifacts wrt. a domain-specific taxonomy. Instead of using Boolean [14] or temporal logic [25] for classification, (CL)S relies on type information that is often already present as an API specification and is naturally related to the actual code of individual artifacts. In fact, type information is more expressive than a simple taxonomical or Boolean logic classification and is in itself a Turing complete logic programming language [13].

Previously studied approaches for automatic workflow construction vary from generation of executable workflows for given processes (e.g., [21]), over synthesis and adaptation of (existing) processes (e.g., [10,16]), completion of sketched processes (e.g., [18]), to synthesis of complete processes similar to CPS. Employed techniques are equally wide ranged, e.g., machine learning is used to iteratively refine processes heavily relying on human intelligence tasks [27], single tasks are aligned in a workflow according to ontology based coordination rules [7,16], or theorem provers are used in deductive approaches [26] closely related to CPS. Incremental planning [15] relies on a library of predefined simple and scenario-specific workflows from which complex workflows are generated to suit specific more complex scenarios. Model-based approaches for choreography realizability have also been studied [2]. Taxonomy supported process synthesis with semantic types was first introduced by Steffen et al. [25]. This development inspired the DyWA [19] framework and DIME (cf. article in the current volume), that allow state of the art semantic description oriented development of processes.

2   Combinatory Process Synthesis

In this section we develop the CPS Framework to create BPMN 2.0 processes. In practice, processes are built from existing entities. Therefore, it must be possible to extract components encoded in an underlying implementation language as constructs usable in CPS. We call such components process components (PCs).

Consider the PC "box stop$_{\text{Car}}$", shown in Fig. 1. It can be found in existing processes as a subprocess that stops a car robot with two motors. It is regarded

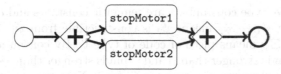

Fig. 1. A subprocess stopping an NXT robot with two motors

a black-box where the box-constructor acts as a quotation mechanism wrapping program text. We specify the intended function and semantics of PCs by ascribing types to them. For example, we may assign the type □subproc to the extracted code of a subprocess. Here, subproc is a native type describing a subprocess in the domain of BPMN 2.0 processes. The modal type constructor □ can be understood as a counterpart for "box" at the level of types. Intuitively, the type $\Box\psi$ represents "code in the implementation language of type ψ" [12].

The type □subproc describes solely the interface behavior with regard to native types (being a subprocess), however, does not display that the subprocess stops a car robot. For that matter, if only the native type, subproc, is considered, it could be any subprocess. This observation leads to the necessity to inspect the domain of NXT robots and further *semantically* specify this component, if we want to be able to compose it with others in a meaningful way. The domain of NXT robots contains different shapes of robots captured in the taxonomy in Fig. 2a. Each robot has different stop routines which can be extracted from existing processes. Similarly, a taxonomy for robot movement, presented in Fig. 2b, can be identified.

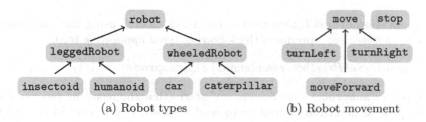

(a) Robot types   (b) Robot movement

Fig. 2. Taxonomies for robot shapes and robot movement

We extend the type of the PC "box stop$_{Car}$" using domain specific semantics:

$$\text{box stop}_{Car} : \Box(\text{subproc} \cap \text{car} \cap \text{stop})$$

The intersection type operator, $\cap$, is used to state that the PC is a code of a subprocess and also describes the stop routine for a car robot. Note the difference between subproc and car. The first is a native type, whereas the second is a semantic type representing an abstract concept which attaches additional information, namely describing a routine for a car robot. Formalizing these observations leads to the definition of modal intersection types [12]:

$$\psi ::= \text{a} \mid \text{b} \mid \alpha \mid \psi \to \psi \mid \psi \cap \psi \mid \Box\psi$$

where a are native type constants, b are semantic constants and α are type variables. Intuitively, $\psi_1 \to \psi_2$ means ψ_2 is constructible from ψ_1, $\psi_1 \cap \psi_2$ means ψ_1 and ψ_2, and $\Box\psi$ means piece of code of type ψ. By convention, $\to$ is right-associative, $\Box$ binds stronger than $\cap$ and $\cap$ binds stronger than $\to$. The subset of used BPMN 2.0 native types is found in Table 1. Note that from metalanguage perspective native types capture coherent structures in the implementation language, e.g. control flow operators or even whole processes, that are meaningful wrt. the defined notion of composition. In addition to PCs, we want to define complex components (CCs), written in a metalanguage, which may manipulate implementation code. At least, we need to define code templates into which code fragments (e.g. boxed PCs) can be substituted. For example, we consider the routine that converts a task to a subprocess by wrapping it into a subprocess with own start and end events (for a graphical representation see Sect. 3, Fig. 5). We represent this routine by the following *typed CC*:

$$taskToSubProc : \Box(\mathsf{task} \cap \alpha) \to \Box(\mathsf{subproc} \cap \alpha)$$

(Implementation language combinators are **green** and metalanguage combinators are black *cursive*.) From the native type perspective, *taskToSubProc* creates code of a subprocess given code of a task. From the semantic type perspective, the variable α is used to preserve domain specific semantics in the result. As an example, assume that a task that reads a sensor was extracted as the following typed PC:

$$\mathsf{box}\ \mathsf{readSensor} : \Box(\mathsf{task} \cap \mathrm{read} \cap \mathrm{sensor})$$

The application of *taskToSubProc* to "$\mathsf{box}\ \mathsf{readSensor}$" using the substitution "$\alpha \mapsto \mathrm{read} \cap \mathrm{sensor}$" produces the following *typed applicative term*:

$$taskToSubProc(\mathsf{box}\ \mathsf{readSensor}) : \Box(\mathsf{subproc} \cap \mathrm{read} \cap \mathrm{sensor})$$

The type "$\Box(\mathsf{subproc} \cap \mathrm{read} \cap \mathrm{sensor})$" states that the resulting piece of code is a subprocess describing a routine to read a sensor. Given a set of typed PCs and typed CCs, many meaningful applicative terms can be derived in which the semantics is specified by the corresponding type.

While PCs are plain BPMN 2.0 XML code fragments extracted from existing processes, CCs need to manipulate BPMN 2.0 XML code and are implemented in the programming language Scala. In the theoretic framework [11,12], the $\lambda_e^{\Box,\to}$-calculus extending the λ-calculus by box- and letbox-constructs is required to interact with boxed code. In practice, however, the $\lambda_e^{\Box,\to}$-calculus is too simplistic for large CCs. Therefore, Scala is used to specify CCs while retaining the functionality of the $\lambda_e^{\Box,\to}$-calculus and leveraging abstraction.

Recapturing our progress so far, we have identified the set $\mathcal{D}$ of typed PCs and typed CCs. This set forms a repository suitable as input for CPS. In order to synthesize meaningful compositions, we need to specify a synthesis goal. A natural way to do this is to interpret the type of such a composition as its goal specification. We formulate a synthesis question (abbreviated as $\mathcal{D} \vdash ? : \psi$):

Table 1. Subset of BPMN 2.0 native types

Native Type	Description	Examples
task	Denotes something that is done, e.g. read sensor data.	
event	Denotes something that happens, e.g. start or end of a process.	
gateway	Determines forking and merging of paths, e.g. by parallel and or exclusive or.	
expr	Expression that may be evaluated to either true of false.	
proc	Describes a BPMN 2.0 process.	
subproc	Contains additional levels of process detail with own start/end events.	

Given a type ψ as goal specification and a repository $\mathcal{D}$, does there exist an applicative term e of type ψ?

For example, with $\psi = \Box(\text{subproc}\cap \text{read} \cap \text{sensor})$ the synthesis question

$$\left\{ \begin{array}{l} \text{box } \textbf{readSensor} : \Box(\text{task} \cap \text{read} \cap \text{sensor}), \\ taskToSubProc : \Box(\text{task} \cap \alpha) \to \Box(\text{subproc} \cap \alpha) \end{array} \right\} \vdash ? : \psi$$

is positively answered by the synthesis result "$taskToSubProc(\text{box } \textbf{readSensor})$".

The above synthesis question is interpreted as a *type inhabitation problem*, following [12]. While the problem in general is undecidable, meaningful restrictions on variable substitutions (applicable in our case) result in decidability [13]. An algorithm, given in [12], can be used to automatically enumerate all solutions. Although the algorithm given in [12] has exponential complexity, practical problems usually do not trigger worst case runtime scenarios. We will substantiate this claim by timing information for the experiments described in Sect. 3. Expressions of type $\Box\psi$ evaluate, in the metalanguage, to values of the form box e where e is of type ψ in the implementation language (see [12]).

3   Experiments

We present a practical evaluation scenario, namely, control of LEGO NXT robots. This domain is useful for illustrating process synthesis because it is well structured and contains inherent variability. Inputs, including their XML schema definition, and results of CPS are available as an accompanying download[1].

---

[1] http://www-seal.cs.tu-dortmund.de/seal/downloads/research/ISoLA16.zip.

Setup. We want a robot to perform a specific job, namely to follow a line or a wall, using specific sensors until a stop condition is met. In Sect. 2 we identified different robot shapes in Fig. 2a and introduced semantic constants, e.g. `car`, to describe them. Similarly, we inspect each dimension of variability in the given setting and introduce semantic constants (cf. Table 2) to describe different possibilities.

Table 2. Semantic constants for different variability dimensions

Constants	Dimension
`car`, `caterpillar`, `humanoid`, `insectoid`	Robot shapes
`followsLine`, `followsWall`	Robot jobs
`oneLightSensor`, `twoLightSensors`, `twoUltrasoundSensors`	Sensor configuration
`stopsOnTouch`, `stopsOnLight`, `stopsOnSound`	Stop conditions

The dimensions of variability are robot shapes, robot jobs, sensor configurations and stop conditions. As an example, to describe a car robot that follows a line, uses two light sensors and stops on touch we require the corresponding constants `car`, `followsLine`, `twoLightSensors` and `stopsOnTouch`. In Sect. 2 we extracted the typed PC box $\text{stop}_{\text{Car}} : \Box(\textbf{subproc} \cap \text{car} \cap \text{stop})$. We continue by manually extracting other functions, such as box $\text{moveForward}_{\text{Car}} : \Box(\textbf{subproc} \cap \text{car} \cap \text{moveForward})$, to complete the set of movement related PCs for different robots. Similarly, we extract PCs to set and read sensors as well as interpret sensor data according to specific conditions. Whenever necessary, we capture domain semantics using semantic constants summarized in Table 3.

Table 3. Semantic constants in the domain of LEGO NXT robots

Constants	Description
`set`, `read`	Sensor functions
`abort`	Job abort condition
`turnLeft`, `turnRight`, `moveForward`, `stop`	Movement types

Extracting PCs from existing programs is a simple manual task of copying meaningful fragments and assigning types to them. However, to extract a CC for the example scenario, we need to analyze and abstract given robot programs. We observe a common structure shown in Fig. 3a. First, a robot sets all sensors, then executes a given job until it is done or aborted and finally stops. We define the following typed CC to capture the described common behavior:

$$createRobotProgram : \Box(\textbf{subproc} \cap \alpha \cap \beta \cap \text{set}) \rightarrow$$
$$\Box(\textbf{subproc} \cap \alpha \cap \beta \cap \gamma \cap \delta) \cap \text{jobProc} \rightarrow$$
$$\Box(\textbf{subproc} \cap \gamma \cap \text{stop}) \rightarrow$$
$$\Box(\textbf{proc} \cap \alpha \cap \beta \cap \gamma \cap \delta) \cap \text{robotProgram}$$

The semantic constant `robotProgram` indicates that the resulting piece of code is a deployable robot program. Similarly, `jobProc` is necessary to identify pieces of code that execute the main robot job. Subprocesses `setSensors`, `executeJob` and `stop` (cf. Fig. 3a) are the three necessary arguments to create a BPMN 2.0 process that is a robot program. To create a robot control program that makes a car robot follow a line while using two light sensors until the robot is touched, the synthesis algorithm carries out the following steps automatically. First, substitutions $\alpha \mapsto$ `twoLightSensors`, $\beta \mapsto$ `stopsOnTouch`, $\gamma \mapsto$ `car` and $\delta \mapsto$ `followsLine` are computed to match the example goal. Second, three arguments are synthesized recursively:

1. `setSensors'` : $\Box$(`subproc` $\cap$ `twoLightSensors` $\cap$ `stopsOnTouch` $\cap$ `set`) a subprocess to set the light and touch sensors.
2. `executeJob'` : $\Box$(`subproc` $\cap$ `twoLightSensors` $\cap$ `stopsOnTouch` $\cap$ `car` $\cap$ `followsLine`) $\cap$ `jobProc` a subprocess that makes the robot execute the job until aborted.
3. `stop'` : $\Box$(`subproc` $\cap$ `car` $\cap$ `stop`) a subprocess that makes a car robot stop.

Third, the robot program is created by applying *createRobotProgram* to the synthesized arguments. The result is the following typed applicative term that matches the required specification:

$$createRobotProgram(\textsf{setSensors}', \textsf{executeJob}', \textsf{stop}') : \textsf{robotProgram}$$
$$\cap \Box(\textsf{proc} \cap \textsf{twoLightSensors} \cap \textsf{stopsOnTouch} \cap \textsf{car} \cap \textsf{followsLine})$$

Analyzing existing robot programs, we identify additional typed CCs, presented in Table 4. We capture dimensions of variability using type variables by restricting substitutions of individual variables as follows:

- α is one of the strategies {`oneLightSensor`, `twoLightSensors`, `twoUltrasoundSensors`}
- β is a stop condition {`stopsOnLight`, `stopsOnSound`, `stopsOnTouch`}
- γ is a robot shape {`car`, `caterpillar`, `humanoid`, `insectoid`}
- δ is a job {`followsLine`, `followsWall`}

Inhabitation. Given the repository $\mathcal{D}$ of typed PCs and typed CCs, asking the inhabitation question $\mathcal{D} \vdash ?$: $\Box$(`proc` $\cap$ `car` $\cap$ `followsLine` $\cap$ `twoLightSensors` $\cap$ `stopsOnTouch`) $\cap$ `robotProgram` automatically synthesizes the following applicative term:

createRobotProgram(
  setSensors(box `set`$_{\text{TwoLightsSensors}}$, *taskToSubProc*(box `set`$_{\text{TouchSensor}}$)),
  executeJob(*taskToSubProc*(box `read`$_{\text{TouchSensor}}$),
    box `abortCondition`$_{\text{TouchSensor}}$, box `read`$_{\text{TwoLightSensors}}$,
    conditionalMove(box `turnLeftCondition`$_{\text{LineFollowerTwoLightSensors}}$,
      box `turnRightCondition`$_{\text{LineFollowerTwoLightSensors}}$),
      box `turnLeft`$_{\text{Car}}$, box `turnRight`$_{\text{Car}}$, box `moveForward`$_{\text{Car}}$)),
  box `stop`$_{\text{Car}}$)

Table 4. Robot domain specific typed CCs

Name	Type	Argument Name
createRobotProgram	$\square$(subproc $\cap$ α $\cap$ $\beta\cap$ set) $\rightarrow$	setSensors
	$\square$(subproc $\cap$ α $\cap$ β $\cap$ γ $\cap$ δ)$\cap$ jobProc $\rightarrow$	executeJob
	$\square$(subproc $\cap$ $\gamma\cap$ stop) $\rightarrow$	stop
	$\square$(proc $\cap$ α $\cap$ β $\cap$ γ $\cap$ δ)$\cap$ robotProgram	cf. Fig. 3a
setSensors	$\square$(subproc $\cap$ $\alpha\cap$ set) $\rightarrow$	setStrategySensors
	$\square$(subproc $\cap$ $\beta\cap$ set) $\rightarrow$	setStopSensor
	$\square$(subproc $\cap$ α $\cap$ $\beta\cap$ set)	cf. Fig. 3b
executeJob	$\square$(subproc $\cap$ $\beta\cap$ read) $\rightarrow$	readStopSensor
	$\square$(expr $\cap$ $\beta\cap$ abort) $\rightarrow$	abortCondition
	$\square$(subproc $\cap$ $\alpha\cap$ read) $\rightarrow$	readStrategySensors
	$\square$(subproc $\cap$ α $\cap$ γ $\cap$ δ)$\cap$ moveProc $\rightarrow$	conditionalMove
	$\square$(subproc $\cap$ α $\cap$ β $\cap$ γ $\cap$ δ)$\cap$ jobProc	cf. Fig. 3c
conditionalMove	$\square$(expr $\cap$ α $\cap$ $\delta\cap$ turnLeft) $\rightarrow$	turnLeftCondition
	$\square$(expr $\cap$ α $\cap$ $\delta\cap$ turnRight) $\rightarrow$	turnRightCondition
	$\square$(subproc $\cap$ $\gamma\cap$ turnLeft) $\rightarrow$	turnLeft
	$\square$(subproc $\cap$ $\gamma\cap$ turnRight) $\rightarrow$	turnRight
	$\square$(subproc $\cap$ $\gamma\cap$ moveForward) $\rightarrow$	moveForward
	$\square$(subproc $\cap$ α $\cap$ γ $\cap$ δ)$\cap$ moveProc	cf. Fig. 3d

In fact, this term constructs a BPMN 2.0 process (cf. Fig. 4) describing a car robot that follows a line using two light sensors and stops on touch. The resulting process is immediately deployable on the Activiti platform. Asking a different inhabitation question $\mathcal{D} \vdash ?$: $\square$(proc $\cap$ humanoid $\cap$ followsWall $\cap$ twoUltrasoundSensors $\cap$ stopsOnSound) $\cap$ robotProgram results in a different term that constructs a BPMN 2.0 process describing humanoid robot that follows a wall using two ultrasound sensors and stops on sound.

Execution. Prototypical tool support has been built to conduct the described experiments. To make use of these tools, we first describe our taxonomy, restrictions of type variable substitutions and typed PC implementations using XML. The encoding is self explaining and modern XML editors are, supplied with the provided schema information, capable of automatic validation and completion.

Before implementing CCs (cf. Fig. 3), we introduce several functional BPMN 2.0 constructors (cf. Fig. 5) reusable in domain specific CC implementations. For example, the constructor *forkWithGateway* connects two given subprocesses with a given gateway and is used to implement the CC *setSensors* (cf. Fig. 3b) with the first argument fixed to the constructor *parallelAnd*. Note that functional constructors may also be added as CCs, if their type is enriched to carry semantics. An example for such a CC is *taskToSubProc*. Mentioned functional constructors have been implemented in Scala as well typed functions mapping BPMN 2.0 XML nodes. Listings of their code are omitted for brevity.

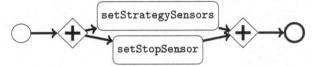

(a) A robot program performing a job and stopping

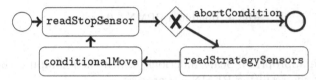

(b) A subprocess setting strategy- and stop-sensors

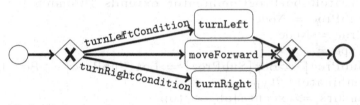

(c) A subprocess moving the robot until aborted

(d) A subprocess choosing a movement accodring to a condition

Fig. 3. BPMN 2.0 representations of robot domain specific CCs

Having prepared everything necessary, we can finally implement CCs in Scala. Listing 1.1 shows the implementation of *createRobotProgram* (cf. Fig. 3a). For each combinator we declare a Scala-trait extending `DCombinator`, which provides a common interface for CCs. We alias BPMN 2.0 types to Node, the Scala type for XML data. The modal box type constructor, □, is represented by the Scala type `Box` declared in a tool library outside of the trait. This makes the particular type used for boxes exchangeable, forbidding invalid assumptions about its structure in combinator implementations and allowing it to be instantiated according to the needs of library functions (e.g. to carry state information about used names). The combinator implementation, reachable via the method `combinator`, is just a lambda function that uses functional BPMN 2.0 constructors. The value `combinatorDefinition` holds the combinator name and type used during inhabitation. It is encoded using an embedded domain specific language (EDSL) closely resembling the mathematical notation.

The tool support was extended to automatically compile Scala combinator implementations and XML process fragments to repositories suitable as input for the webservice provided by the CL(S) framework [4]. Its reply is interpreted

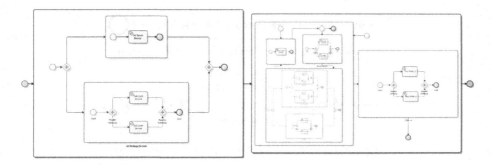

Fig. 4. Inhabited BPMN 2.0 process

as calls to the appropriate Scala functions, which then compute the XML representation of the resulting BPMN 2.0 process.

```scala
trait CreateRobotProgCombinator extends DCombinator {
  type SubProc = Node
  type Proc = Node
  type Type =
  Box[SubProc] =>Box[SubProc] =>Box[SubProc] =>Box[Proc]
  def combinator: Type =
  setSensors =>executeJob =>stop =>
    subProcToProc.combinator(
      createSequence.combinator
        (setSensors)
        (createSequence.combinator(executeJob)(stop)))

  val combinatorDefinition: DCombinatorType = ...
}
```

Listing 1.1. Scala implementation of the CC *createRobotProg*

Evaluation. Our approach has several benefits. First, we can represent the almost orthogonal dimensions of variability, namely job type, robot shape, strategy and stop condition. Second, extracting PCs from existing processes is an easy task of copying XML code and semantically ascribing it with a type. Since each PC belongs to a small subset of variability dimensions, the number of necessary PCs is much lower than the number of meaningful synthesized combinations. Third, CCs add an extra layer of abstraction while respecting variability and are easily built using functional BPMN 2.0 constructors. Fourth, despite the exponential worst case behavior of the inhabitation algorithm, the measurements below indicate its practical applicability to CPS.

The average time consumption over 500 measurements for answering the inhabitation question presented above and synthesizing the BPMN 2.0 process

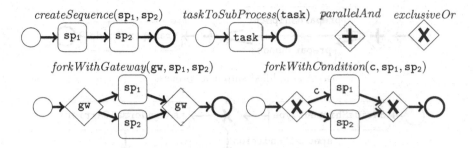

Fig. 5. Functional BPMN 2.0 fragment constructors

(cf. Fig. 4) was $2 s^2$. Synthesizing 50 processes for the inhabitation question $\mathcal{D} \vdash ? : \Box(\texttt{proc} \cap \texttt{humanoid}) \cap \texttt{robotProgram}$ took 590 s. The measurements include compiling the (CL)S webservice reply to a Scala program executing the combinators, which was the most time consuming part. The synthesized processes were deployed via the Activiti platform on LEGO® Mindstorms® NXT robots, that correctly executed the required task. The main difference between the results was the actual job that the robot performed, its sensor configuration and its stop condition. However, processes that initialized sensors twice were also produced. A topic in current and future work concerns assessing the "usefulness" of the synthesized programs. While all of them are guaranteed to be correct wrt. their type information, not all programs are useful or particularly smart in a real world setting. The inhabitant presented above is the first solution to its question and its correctness has been verified by deploying it with Activity to control a real robot. However, infinitely many solutions to the question are useless, because they contain cyclic applications of the CC *setSensors* to itself. Dealing with such issues may require extensions (including cycle detection, testing, or manual inspection) not described here.

The CCs and PCs we have identified so far all made use of a subset of the possibilities available in Combinatory Logic. Especially, there has not yet been the need to define a higher order CC, taking other CCs as argument. Also, polymorphic CCs have been represented using variables instead of subtyping. While our usecases do not need them, these features are supported by the implementation and add even greater flexibility to the overall approach.

4   Shipment Processes in Logistics

In this section we shift the domain of interest from robots to shipment of goods. In a simplistic scenario, one has to prepare the shipment along with the goods to be shipped and then transport the prepared goods (cf. Fig. 6a). To prepare a shipment, a carrier needs to be assigned depending on whether it is a special shipment or a normal shipment (cf. Fig. 6b). Adding variability, we distinguish

---

[2] Experiments conducted on a 2.7GHz Intel® Core™ i7-4800MQ CPU.

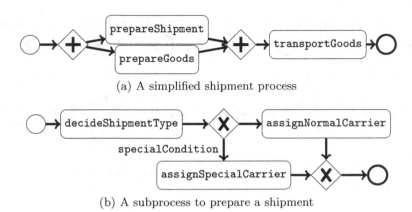

(a) A simplified shipment process

(b) A subprocess to prepare a shipment

Fig. 6. BPMN 2.0 representations of shipment process CCs

Table 5. Shipment domain specific typed PCs

Name	Type
box prepareGoods	□(subproc ∩ prepare ∩ goods)
box transportGoods$_{Train}$	□(subproc ∩ transport ∩ goods ∩ train)
box transportGoods$_{Truck}$	□(subproc ∩ transport ∩ goods ∩ truck)
box decideShipmentType	□(subproc ∩ decide ∩ shipment)
box specialCondition	□(expr ∩ special)
box assignSpecialCarrier$_{Train}$	□(subproc ∩ assign ∩ special ∩ train)
box assignSpecialCarrier$_{Truck}$	□(subproc ∩ assign ∩ special ∩ truck)
box assignNormalCarrier$_{Train}$	□(subproc ∩ assign ∩ normal ∩ train)
box assignNormalCarrier$_{Truck}$	□(subproc ∩ assign ∩ normal ∩ truck)

between shipment by train and shipment by truck, each with an individual carrier assignment and transport.

Since we change the domain of interest from robots to shipment of goods with its own domain specific concepts, we introduce new semantic constants. Therefore, we introduce train and truck for the different types of transport. To distinguish between a normal and a special shipment we introduce special and normal. The semantic constants prepare, transport, decide and assign describe possible actions while shipment and goods describe possible referenced objects. Finally, shipmentProcess describes a complete shipment process. We assume that typed PCs (cf. Table 5) are extracted from existing processes.

Figures 6a, b describe CCs that are typed in Table 6. The existing functional BPMN 2.0 fragment constructors (cf. Fig. 5) are reused for implementation:

Table 6. Shipment domain specific typed CCs

Name	Type	Argument Name
createShipmentProc	$\square$(subproc $\cap$ prepare $\cap$ shipment $\cap$ α) $\rightarrow$	prepareShipment
	$\square$(subproc $\cap$ prepare $\cap$ goods) $\rightarrow$	prepareGoods
	$\square$(subproc $\cap$ transport $\cap$ goods $\cap$ α) $\rightarrow$	transportGoods
	$\square$(proc $\cap$ α)$\cap$ shipmentProcess	cf. Fig. 6a
prepareShipment	$\square$(subproc $\cap$ decide $\cap$ shipment) $\rightarrow$	decideShipmentType
	$\square$(expr $\cap$ special) $\rightarrow$	specialCondition
	$\square$(subproc $\cap$ assign $\cap$ special $\cap\alpha$) $\rightarrow$	assignSpecialCarrier
	$\square$(subproc$\cap$ assign $\cap$ normal $\cap\alpha$) $\rightarrow$	assignNormalCarrier
	$\square$(subproc $\cap$ prepare $\cap$ shipment $\cap\alpha$)	cf. Fig. 6b

createShipmentProc(**prepareShipment**, **prepareGoods**, **transportGoods**) =
  createSequence(
    forkWithGateway(*parallelAnd*, **prepareShipment**, **prepareGoods**),
    transportGoods)
prepareShipment(**decideShipmentType**, **specialCondition**,
  assignSpecialCarrier, **assignNormalCarrier**) =
  createSequence(**decideShipmentType**,*forkWithCondition*(
specialCondition,
    assignSpecialCarrier, **assignNormalCarrier**))
Given the repository $\mathcal{D}$ of typed PCs and CCs, asking the inhabitation question
$\mathcal{D} \vdash ? : \square$(**proc** $\cap$ **train**) $\cap$ shipmentProcess synthesizes the applicative term:
createShipmentProc(*prepareShipment*(
    box **decideShipmentType**, box **specialCondition**,
    box **assignSpecialCarrier**$_{\text{Train}}$, box **assignNormalCarrier**$_{\text{Train}}$),
  box **prepareGoods**, box **transportGoods**$_{\text{Train}}$)
In fact, this term constructs a BPMN 2.0 process describing shipment by train.
Asking the question $\mathcal{D} \vdash ? : \square$(**proc**$\cap$ **truck**) $\cap$ shipmentProcess results in a
term that constructs a BPMN 2.0 process describing shipment by truck.

As a conclusion, switching the domain requires the definition of domain specific semantics, the extraction of typed PCs and the implementation of typed
CCs. This underlines the main benefits of the presented approach. Neither of
these tasks is particularly complex, assuming PCs can be extracted from existing
processes. New CCs are defined by compositions of presented functional BPMN
2.0 fragment constructors. More variability, e.g. shipment by ship or even by
a line following robot, is easily achieved by adding semantic constants ship or
robot and adding corresponding PCs. Other dimensions of variability such as
different packaging of goods can be explored orthogonally.

5   Conclusion and Future Work

We developed and studied an approach for BPMN 2.0 process synthesis, CPS, exploring an existing framework based on combinatory logic. CPS has proven useful to synthesize control processes from repositories of components, semantically ascribed according to conceptual specifications, allowing for additional abstraction and variability. The synthesized processes were executed on LEGO® Mindstorms® NXT robots deployed via the Activiti platform. Interaction with the existing synthesis framework presented neither any overhead from execution time perspective nor from specification perspective, given the described tool support. CPS benefits from inherent variability of a given domain. Additionally, orthogonality of variability dimensions reduces the required specification overhead. Furthermore, CPS allows to change the domain of interest naturally by providing the new domain specific fragments. Future work includes techniques for assessing "usefulness" of synthesized code. Changing the domain of native types and adding new fragment constructor functionality can allow CPS to be applied to modeling tools different from BPMN. DyWA [19] and DIME (cf. article in this volume) are currently investigated as new targets for CPS. They are particularly well suited, because they focus on semantic descriptions. Additionally, they offer code generation to allow more flexible deployments in comparison to the rigid process engine setting required by BPMN.

As a conclusion, the realization of an automated end-to-end chain from repositories of components to deployable processes via CPS is achievable, provided an intelligent repository design.

Acknowledgments. The authors would like to thank Anna Vasileva and Zani Sarkisyan for spending a lot of time building and experimenting with the NXTs.

References

1. Apel, S., Batory, D., Kästner, C., Saake, G.: Feature-Oriented Software Product Lines. Springer, Heidelberg (2013)
2. Autili, M., Di Ruscio, D., Di Salle, A., Inverardi, P., Tivoli, M.: A model-based synthesis process for choreography realizability enforcement. In: Cortellessa, V., Varró, D. (eds.) FASE 2013 (ETAPS 2013). LNCS, vol. 7793, pp. 37–52. Springer, Heidelberg (2013)
3. Berg, K., Bishop, J., Muthig, D.: Tracing software product line variability: from problem to solution space. In: SAICSIT 2005, pp. 182–191 (2005)
4. Bessai, J., Dudenhefner, A., Düdder, B., Martens, M., Rehof, J.: Combinatory logic synthesizer. In: Margaria, T., Steffen, B. (eds.) ISoLA 2014, Part I. LNCS, vol. 8802, pp. 26–40. Springer, Heidelberg (2014)
5. Bessai, J., Dudenhefner, A., Duedder, B., De'Liguoro, U., Chen, T.C., Rehof, J.: Mixin composition synthesis based on intersection types. In: TLCA 2015, vol. 38, pp. 76–91 (2015)
6. Bessai, J., Düdder, B., Heineman, G.T. Rehof, J.: Combinatory synthesis of classes using feature grammars. In: FACS 2015, pp. 123–140 (2016)

7. Chun, S.A., Atluri, V., Adam, N.R.: Domain knowledge-based automatic workflow generation. In: Hameurlain, A., Cicchetti, R., Traunmüller, R. (eds.) DEXA 2002. LNCS, vol. 2453, pp. 81–92. Springer, Heidelberg (2002)

8. Clarke, D., Helvensteijn, M., Schaefer, I.: Abstract delta modeling. In: GPCE 2010, pp. 13–22 (2010)

9. Czarnecki, K., Ulrich, E.: Generative Programming: Methods, Tools, and Applications. Addison-Wesley, Reading (2000)

10. Dadam, P., Manfred, R.: The ADEPT project: a decade of research and development for robust and flexible process support – challenges and achievements. Comput. Sci.- R&D **23**(2), 81–97 (2009)

11. Davies, R., Pfenning, F.: A modal analysis of staged computation. J. ACM **48**(3), 555–604 (2001)

12. Düdder, B., Martens, M., Rehof, J.: Staged composition synthesis. In: Shao, Z. (ed.) ESOP 2014 (ETAPS). LNCS, vol. 8410, pp. 67–86. Springer, Heidelberg (2014)

13. Düdder, B., Martens, M., Rehof, J., Urzyczyn, P.: Bounded combinatory logic. In: CSL 2012. LIPIcs, vol. 16, pp. 243–258 (2012)

14. Eichberg, M., Klose, K., Mitschke, R., Mezini, M.: Component composition using feature models. In: Grunske, L., Reussner, R., Plasil, F. (eds.) CBSE 2010. LNCS, vol. 6092, pp. 200–215. Springer, Heidelberg (2010)

15. Fernandes, A., Ciarlini, A.E.M., Furtado, A.L., Hinchey, M.G., Casanova, M.A., Breitman, K.K.: Adding flexibility to workflows through incremental planning. ISSE **3**(4), 291–302 (2007)

16. Grambow, G., Oberhauser, R., Reichert, M.: Semantically-driven workflow generation using declarative modeling for processes in software engineering. In: EDOCW 2011, pp. 164–173 (2011)

17. Jörges, S., Lamprecht, A.L., Margaria, T., Schaefer, I., Steffen, B.: A constraint-based variability modeling framework. STTT **14**(5), 511–530 (2012)

18. Lamprecht, A., Naujokat, S., Margaria, T., Steffen, B.: Synthesis-based loose programming. In: QUATIC 2010, pp. 262–267 (2010)

19. Neubauer, J., Frohme, M., Steffen, B., Margaria, T.: Prototype-driven development of web applications with DyWA. In: Margaria, T., Steffen, B. (eds.) ISoLA 2014, Part I. LNCS, vol. 8802, pp. 56–72. Springer, Heidelberg (2014)

20. Pohl, K., Böckle, G., van Der Linden, F.J.: Software Product Line Engineering - Foundations, Principles, and Techniques. Springer, Heidelberg (2005)

21. Roser, S., Lautenbacher, F., Bauer, B.: Generation of workflow code from DSMs. In: OOPSLA 2007 (2007)

22. Schaefer, I., Rabiser, R., Clarke, D., Bettini, L., Benavides, D., Botterweck, G., Pathak, A., Trujillo, S., Villela, K.: Software diversity: state of the art and perspectives. STTT **14**(5), 477–495 (2012)

23. Schmid, K., Rabiser, R., Grünbacher, P.: A comparison of decision modeling approaches in product lines. In: VaMoS 2011, pp. 119–126 (2011)

24. Steffen, B., Lamprecht, A., Margaria, T.: User-level synthesis: treating product lines as systems of constraints. In: SPLC 2015, pp. 427–431 (2015)

25. Steffen, B., Margaria, T., von der Beeck, M.: Automatic synthesis of linear process models from temporal constraints: an incremental approach. In: AAS 1997 (1997)

26. Yang, B., Bundy, A., Smaill, A., Dixon, L.: Deductive synthesis of workflows for e-Science. In: CCGrid 2005, pp. 168–175 (2005)

27. Zhang, H., Horvitz, E., Parkes, D.C.: Automated workflow synthesis. In: AI 2013 (2013)

Synthesis from a Practical Perspective

Sven Jörges[1], Anna-Lena Lamprecht[2], Tiziana Margaria[2,3],
Stefan Naujokat[1(✉)], and Bernhard Steffen[1]

[1] Chair for Programming Systems, TU Dortmund University, Dortmund, Germany
{sven.joerges,stefan.naujokat,bernhard.steffen}@tu-dortmund.de
[2] Lero - The Irish Software Research Centre, University of Limerick,
Limerick, Ireland
{anna-lena.lamprecht,tiziana.margaria}@lero.ie
[3] Chair of Software Systems,University of Limerick, Limerick, Ireland

Abstract. Based on a very liberal understanding of synthesis as a
generic term for techniques that generate programming artifacts from
higher-level specifications, the paper discusses several corresponding
facets from a practical perspective. The synthesis examples we consider
comprise variations of code generation, model synthesis from temporal logic descriptions, and metamodel-based tool generation. Although
very different, they can all be regarded as means to "factor out" predefined aspects of the envisioned product or the production environment
so that developers/designers can simply focus on the remaining issues.
This "factoring out" of what is pre-agreed or predefined is a primary
goal of domain-specific languages design, and it is applicable to both
modeling and programming languages. Leading synthesis techniques ele-
gantly achieve this factoring by combining forms of substitution/partial
evaluation to those steps that can be determined *locally*, as is typically
the case for most parts of code generation, with (heuristic) search for
those parts where more *global* patterns need to be matched, as is the
case, e.g., for temporal- logic synthesis. The paper presents our experience with a variety of synthesis approaches and corresponding design and
synthesis tools. It also discusses the synergetic potential of their combination, e.g., to control the computational complexity by reducing the
underlying search space. This is, in our opinion, a viable path to achieve
a fundamentally higher simplicity in IT system design.

Keywords: Code generation · Linear-time synthesis · Metamodeling ·
Domain-specific languages

1 Introduction

Synthesis, here very liberally meant to comprise all techniques to generate programming artifacts from higher-level specifications, has multiple facets, depending on the kind of specification formalism, the chosen algorithmic foundation, and
the target language or platform. Different forms of synthesis as transformation
include classical techniques like parsing of textual input, hardware synthesis from

© Springer International Publishing AG 2016
T. Margaria and B. Steffen (Eds.): ISoLA 2016, Part I, LNCS 9952, pp. 282–302, 2016.
DOI: 10.1007/978-3-319-47166-2_20

high-level descriptions (see e.g. [10,11,38]), and compilers that translate higher level programs into machine code (see e.g. [4]). But also the synthesis of models, processes or programs from logical specifications (see e.g. [6,7,13,19,46]) is successful. More recently, we have witnessed also the generation and deployment of entire domain-specific modeling tools from (meta-level) domain specifications, and the generation of running instances of complex (embedded) systems from a corresponding set of descriptions that comprise the desired functionality, the hardware architecture, GUI aspects, real time constraints, and the like.

From a bird's eye view, all these variants of generation share their intention and their means:

Intention: These synthesis methods all aim at bridging a WHAT/HOW gap in order to drive an abstract (more declarative) description into the direction of a more concrete and specialized (technical) realization. The goal is to free developers/designers from dealing with aspects that are pre-defined in the considered domain, and to let them focus on the remaining, orthogonal issues. This *factoring out design complexity*, which allows one to treat common aspects once and for all upfront, provides a very powerful and elegant form of reuse. It is the conceptual foundation for the successful design of domain-specific languages.

Means: Leading synthesis techniques combine *substitution/partial evaluation* [22] for steps that can be determined *locally*, as is typically the case for most parts of code generation, and *(heuristic) search* [14] for parts where more *global* patterns need to be matched, as is case for, e.g., temporal logic synthesis. The main difference between the different synthesis problems lies in their underlying structural knowledge, which can have a dramatic impact on the complexity of the required algorithms, which ranges from linear time to undecidability. This wide range explains the importance of well-chosen restrictions and powerful heuristics. For example, in classical parsing, the agreed-upon underlying context-free structure is key to allowing cubic algorithms to construct syntax trees. Nevertheless, for practical solutions a lot of effort has been put into adequate restrictions of context-free languages to allow deterministic parsing in linear time. Similarly, the synthesis of, e.g., models from monadic second order formulas, which is known to have a non-elementary worst case complexity, has strongly profited from BDD-based heuristics: they do not improve upper complexity bounds, but often work surprisingly well in practical situations [26,32,37].

In general, key to efficiency is here the reduction of the problem complexity, typically by reducing the underlying search space, ideally to the point where target entities can be uniquely determined. It should be noted, however, that there are typically multiple (incomparable) realizations, and the practical impact of synthesis solutions strongly depends on powerful heuristics, defaults, ways for informed user interaction and/or specialization to a restricted target domain.

This paper reviews a selection of synthesis approaches and corresponding tools from our personal experience, essentially covering all the aspects mentioned above. Our discussion is organized according to the specification formats for the different synthesis steps, namely (behavioral) models, Semantic Linear-Time Temporal Logic, and metamodels:

(Behavioral) Models are useful to model the control flow of applications like business processes and (scientific) workflows in terms of component libraries that are specified using taxonomies/ontologies. The original approach to just generate code for individual behavioral models [23] has recently been extended to comprise also other model types, like data models and GUI specifications, in order to generate, e.g., entire web applications [8].

Semantic Linear-time Temporal Logic (SLTL) was originally designed as a specification language for workflows or process chains. It is interpreted over the set of all *finite* paths. Our corresponding synthesis tools have been applied for:

- Synthesis of linear program structures. Our main application here comprised tool chaining/ tool pipelines [55] and scientific workflows [5, 28].
- A heuristic for branching-time generalization. To overcome the restriction to linear program structures, the jABC process modeling framework [57] was extended to allow for models with'loose' branches, i.e., edges which are not concretely given, but are placeholders only constrained via temporal logic constraints. The resulting *loose models/programs* are then automatically expanded to concrete ones via our synthesis algorithm [29, 39].
- A branching-time view of linear temporal logics. If one is only interested in deterministic program structures, linear time logic can also be used to specify graph structures, namely the smallest corresponding deterministic automaton, that for SLTL is unique. This view is the basis for the model adaptation technique described in [9, 52] and the generation principle for the benchmarks [53] used for the RERS challenge.

Metamodels are used to specify domain-specific (graphical) languages. In the context of our work, we have used metamodels for:

- Generation of domain-specific building blocks. Once a domain language is specified with, e.g., the Ecore metamodeling language of the Eclipse Modeling Framework (EMF) [58] it is possible to generate most of the building blocks required to analyze or transform the elements of that domain language. Essentially, this capability turns the jABC into a domain-specific tool for writing such code generators [23].
- Generation of *Domain-Specific Modeling* (DSM) tools. The approach sketched above can be pushed further to generate entire DSM tools just from meta-level specifications [40]. This goes even to the extent that even highly specialized DSM tools – which are tailored to their domain much more than conventional approaches – become feasible.

The goal of the discussion in this paper is to illustrate how the various synthesis technologies start converging towards a common conceptual core [41] and how this conceptual commonality can be exploited to, e.g., establish a powerful technology of reuse. There, agreed-upon functionality and structure is factored out not only at development time, but already during the design of the underlying domain-specific modeling language and tools.

The paper is structured according to the three specification formats described above. Section 2 sketches our code generation approach for behavioral models. Section 3 then describes our linear-time temporal logic synthesis as well as two approaches to address branching. Subsequently, Section 4 presents the generation of process building blocks, as well as of entire domain-specific modeling tools from meta-level specifications, and Sect. 5 gives our conclusions and perspectives.

2   Code Generation from Models

From its inception the jABC focused on executability, both via interpretation and code generation. Cornerstone of this executability is the code generation framework Genesys, a specific instance of the jABC itself which supports high-level modeling of code generators (cf. Sect. 2.2). This approach has been generalized to the generation/synthesis of entire running web application as sketched in Sect. 2.3.

2.1   The jABC Modeling Framework

jABC [57] is a framework for model-driven and service-oriented development. The modeling notation employed in jABC is called *Service Logic Graphs (SLGs)*, which are directed graphs that represent the dynamic flow of actions in an application.

SLGs are built from a library of basic building blocks called *Service Independent Building Blocks (SIBs)* [36]. Following the ideas of service orientation, a SIB represents an atomic, reusable and configurable service, that provides a single functionality of arbitrary granularity. Accordingly, a SIB's behavior may, e.g., range from low-level tasks like string concatenation or displaying a message, to ready-made web services or even the interaction with highly complex systems, such as *Enterprise Resource Planning* (ERP) software. Consequently, as SLGs are assembled from such fully functional building blocks, SLGs are *executable*.

Furthermore, SLGs are *hierarchical* constructs [54], i.e., SLGs can be embedded as building blocks in other SLGs. Such embedded SLGs are called *macros* and represent reusable application aspects, such as error handling or security management. Those aspects are modeled once – afterwards, they are part of the modeling repertoire and can be reused across applications and domains.

jABC provides a tool for graphically modeling SLGs. The functional range of the tool can be extended by plugins, which support development phases such as debugging, monitoring, verification and testing [57].

2.2   Code Generation with Genesys

Genesys [23] is a framework for the model-driven development of code generators based on jABC. With Genesys, the code generators are themselves modeled as SLGs on the basis of a model and service library that is specifically tailored to the domain of code generation.

The provided services offer typical functionality required for most code generators, such as type conversion, identifier generation, model transformations and code formatting. Those services are available as SIBs, so that they can be used as atomic building blocks for code generators built with jABC. The models contained in Genesys' library realize further typical functionality and aspects, such as loading and traversing input models. Just like the atomic services, those models can be directly reused as macros when building a new code generator.

Furthermore, all code generators that have been created with Genesys are included in the library. The rationale behind this is that each new code generator contributes to the library, so that the available repertoire and the potential for reuse is growing continuously. In particular, this facilitates the construction of entire code generator families by deriving new generators from existing ones [23].

An example for such a code generator family is given by the *jABC code generators* [24]. Code generators in this family support SLGs as their source language, and translate SLGs to desired target platforms. Effectively, the purpose of this code generator family is to provide code generation capabilities for jABC. In sum, this family contains 17 code generators, covering a wide range of target platforms, such as Java-based platforms (e.g., plain Java classes, Servlets, JUnit tests), embedded systems (e.g., iOS, the leJOS API for Lego's Mindstorms, Java Micro Edition) and further languages and platforms like Ruby, Perl or C#.

Most code generators built with Genesys use templating, which is a widely-used standard approach in code generation [12]. Templates are textual skeletons that contain placeholders which are filled with dynamic content during code generation. The latter task is typically performed by a *template engine*. Genesys supports several template engines such as StringTemplate [44], Velocity, and FreeMarker, which are available as corresponding SIBs.

2.3   Full Generation of Web Applications

Based on code generation with the Genesys framework, jABC constitutes the cornerstone of the *One-Thing Approach* (OTA) [35]. Its focus has always been on modeling the business logic (i.e., workflows and processes in the form of SLGs). The DyWA Integrated Modeling Environment (DIME) [8] is based on the concepts of jABC, but is distinctive in two regards:

1. The whole application is modeled, comprising also data types and user interfaces, and not only the processes.
2. The modeling and runtime environment is specialized to the domain of complex web applications.

With DIME, the framework evolved to a true OTA experience where multiple models of different types, specialized to certain areas of development, are interdependently connected. The connection is to the extent that they can be one-click-generated to a running web application by means of multiple model-to-code transformations. DIME utilizes the domain specialization of the CINCO meta tooling suite (cf. Sect. 4.2) and thus provides dedicated model types focused on individual aspects of specification.

DIME puts application experts (potential non-programmers) in the center of the development process, providing them with an early prototype of an up-and-running web application right from the beginning. The target of DIME's product generation is the DyWA framework [42] that fosters prototype-driven development of web applications throughout the whole application life-cycle in a service-oriented manner [36]. In short, modeling and code generation is done in DIME whereas DyWA supports the product deployment phase, constitutes the actual runtime environment, and manages data persistence. As front-end running in the user's browser, a single-page application basing on Angular [2] and Dart [1] is generated that communicates with the DyWA via REST services [15] and JSON [3,20].

In DIME three (top-level) types of models define aspects of the web application[1]:

1. **Data models** define the basic domain model of the application. Their structure is based on common data modeling concepts in terms of types with inheritance, attributes, and relations (i.e. unidirectional and bidirectional associations) between them. Visually, they resemble UML class diagrams [49], as they are widespread and usually quite well understood.
2. **Process models** define the business logic in DIME. They are conceptually based on the *Service Logic Graphs* (SLGs) already used in jABC4 [43] and its predecessors [57], but provide different – more specialized yet similarly structured and handled – types for dedicated aspects of the application:
   - **Basic processes** characterize the smallest parts of the application's business logic. They can be included as subprocesses in other processes and are usually used to model *CRUD* (create, read, update, and delete) and data processing operations on entities.
   - **Interaction processes** are executed client-side within the user's web browser. They define the immediate interaction between user and application and can be regarded as a sitemap.
   - **Interactable processes** are slightly restricted basic processes that are provided as REST services and can thus be included in interaction processes.
   - **Long running processes** describe the entire life-cycle of entities. They integrate interactions with one or multiple users as well as business logic in form of interactable and basic processes.

---

[1] For a more detailed introduction to the available model types please refer to [8] and DIME's web site: http://dime.scce.info.

- **Security processes** realize access control based on the currently logged in user and his associations to other entities in the system.
3. **GUI models** allow the definition of the target web application's user interfaces. They reflect the structure of the individual web pages and can either be included within the sitemap processes as an interaction point for the user, or within other GUI models to reuse already modeled parts.

In combination, those model types specify the complete application. However, a model is not generated into a single target artifact. Rather, a many-to-many relation is the usual case, i.e., a model is generated to multiple target source code files, but a single such file can also be influenced by multiple models. This management completely happens within the code generator and the running application without any need for the modeling user, i.e. the application expert who develops the system, to actually know this structure.

3   Temporal Logic Synthesis

Distinctive feature of the jABC is its modeling support via temporal logic synthesis. Modelers were freed from dealing with type mismatches or technically required intermediate process steps by automated mediator synthesis and the synthesis of tool chains and (scientific) workflows (cf. Sect. 3.1). This approach was heuristically generalized to deal with process branching as described in Sect. 3.2. Finally, Sect. 3.3 illustrates how linear-time temporal logic can be regarded as a branching time specification for deterministic structures.

3.1   SLTL Synthesis

Generally, the term *process synthesis* is used to refer to techniques that construct workflows from sets of services according to logical specifications [17,31]. SLTL synthesis is our approach to automatically compose sequences of services according an abstract specification. It is based on the modal logic SLTL (*Semantic Linear Time Logic*) that combines relative time with descriptions and taxonomic classifications of types and services [16,56]. It takes two aspects into account: On the one hand, the workflow must ensure a valid execution regarding type correctness, on the other hand, the constraints specified by the workflow designer must be met.

The following paragraphs sketch the basic ideas of the approach (for further details the reader is referred to [56]) and looks at some applications. Concretely, we describe how the *synthesis universe* (which constitutes the search space in which the synthesis algorithm looks for solutions to the synthesis problem) is built from the provided domain model, how SLTL is used for the abstract workflow *specification formula*, and what the *synthesis algorithm* does with it, before we describe applications of SLTL synthesis in the field of scientific workflows.

Domain Modeling and the Synthesis Universe. The synthesis method relies on behavioral service interface descriptions, that is, services are regarded as transformations that perform particular actions on the available data. Concretely, each service interface description must characterize the service by means of four subsets of the set of all data types:

- *USE* are the types that must be available before execution of the service (i.e. the input types of the service),
- *FORBID* describes a set of types that must not be available before execution of the service,
- *GEN* is the set of types that are created by the execution of the services (i.e. the output types of the service),
- *KILL* defines those types that are destroyed and therefore removed from the set of types that were available prior to execution of the service.

The synthesis algorithm then combines service descriptions in terms of these sets into the synthesis universe, that is, an abstract representation of all possible solutions that contains all service sequences that are valid (type-correct) executions, without taking into account any problem-specific information. The synthesis universe is in essence an implicitly defined automaton that connects states with edges according to available services. While each state represents a subset of all types, the connecting edges perform the transition on those types, according to the service interface descriptions. Every path in this automaton constitutes an executable service sequence.

Furthermore, the SLTL synthesis also uses *taxonomies* to define semantic classifications of types and services. Taxonomies are simple ontologies that relate entities in terms of *is-a* relations and thus allow for the hierarchical structuring of the involved types and services. The actually available services and types are named *concrete*, whereas semantic classifications are named *abstract*. The taxonomies are considered by the synthesis algorithm when constructing the synthesis universe and when evaluating type and service constraints.

Specification Formula and the Synthesis Algorithm. The specification formula describes all sequences of services that meet the individual workflow specification, but without taking care of actual executability concerns. It is given declaratively as a formula in SLTL, a semantically enriched version of the well known propositional linear-time logic (PLTL) that is focused on finite paths. The syntax of SLTL is defined by the following BNF, where t_c and s_c express type and service constraints, respectively:

$$\phi ::= true \mid t_c \mid \neg\phi \mid \phi \wedge \phi \mid \langle s_c \rangle \phi \mid G\phi \mid \phi U \phi$$

Thus, SLTL combines static, dynamic, and temporal constraints. The static constraints are the taxonomic expressions (boolean connectives) over the types or classes of the type taxonomy. Analogously, the dynamic constraints are the taxonomic expressions over the services or classes of the service taxonomy. The temporal constraints are covered by the modal structure of the logic, suitable to express ordering constraints.

- $\langle s_c \rangle \phi$ states that ϕ must hold in the successor state, and that it must be reachable with service constraint s_c.
- G expresses that ϕ must hold generally.
- U specifies that ϕ_1 has to be valid until ϕ_2 finally holds.

A complete definition of the semantics of SLTL can be found, for instance, in [29, 55]. The distinctive feature of SLTL formulae is that they cover two dimensions:

1. The *horizontal* dimension, covered by the modalities that describe aspects of relative time, addresses the workflow model, including its loosely specified parts, and deals with the actual service sequences.
2. The *vertical* dimension evaluates taxonomic expressions over types and services, allowing for the usage of abstract type and service descriptions within the specifications.

Both kinds of constraints can deliberately be combined in order to express more complex intents about the workflows. This allows for a very flexible fine-tuning of the workflow specifications. The specification formula that is finally used as input for the synthesis algorithm is simply a conjunction of all available SLTL constraints, comprising the definition of the start condition(s) of the workflow (i.e., the set of data types that is available at the beginning), the definition of its end condition(s) (i.e., the set of data types that must be available at the end of the synthesised workflow), and the set of available workflow constraints.

The synthesis algorithm then interprets the SLTL formula that specifies the synthesis problem over paths of the synthesis universe, that is, it searches the synthesis universe for paths that satisfy the given formula and thus computes all service compositions that satisfy the given specification. Note that as the synthesis universe is usually very large, it is not immediately generated from the domain definition, but incrementally during the synthesis process.

Currently there are two different implementations of the algorithm available: A tableau-based approach that works by forward proof construction [56], and a version making use of monadic second-order logic on strings for synthesis by compositional automata construction [34].

Application to Scientific Workflows. The SLTL synthesis method has been available for several years, and it has been used in different application contexts, for example in the scope of the *Semantic Web Services Challenge* [45] for synthesizing mediators between different message formats [33]. One of its major application domains in recent years was the field of scientific workflows. In fact, scientific workflows are often pipelines that process a given input and return a specific output, so the possibility of synthesizing linear sequences of services is sufficient in most cases. Furthermore, many researchers know their input data and what they want to get from it, but they are not familiar with the tools required to get them there, and with their data formats and dependencies. Thus, having these workflows automatically composed is a big simplification.

For our case studies in the bioinformatics domain, we greatly benefited from the development of the *EMBRACE Data and Methods Ontology* (EDAM) [21], which provides a controlled vocabulary for the description of bioinformatics types, formats, and operations. The taxonomies for the domain model could directly be derived from EDAM, and tool collections like the *European Molecular Biology Open Software Suite* (EMBOSS) [47], that was one of the first to be completely annotated with EDAM terms, provided excellent playgrounds and benchmarks [28, Chapter 3]. Ontologies and annotations are, however, not available for all domains, so for applications in metabolic flux analysis [28, Chapter 5], microarray data analysis [28, Chapter 6], and recently in climate impact analysis [5], we had to go through the crucial (but by no means trivial) task of designing the taxonomies and annotating the tools ourselves, before the synthesis framework could be applied.

Figure 1 illustrates the use of synthesis for the automatic composition of scientific workflows. It shows a small example from a case study on *Microarray Data Analysis* pipelines [28, Chapter 6]. The domain model describes the available services in terms of the service and data type terminology defined by the respective taxonomies. It also comprises a set of so-called domain constraints, which capture general properties of the targeted workflows. Synthesis can then be applied to derive possible concretizations from loosely specified workflows. A very simple, yet common, example of a workflow specification is shown at the lower left of the figure: It starts with the loading of an available data set, and ends with a display of results, this way using the synthesis for a comprehensive exploration of the many possible analysis processes. Two possible synthesis outcomes are shown in the figure. If no further constraints are applied, the workflow at the upper right would be a default shortest possible solution. If the five textually described constraints are applied in addition, one of the shortest solutions in this case is the sequence shown below. The rounded rectangles around the SIBs in the workflow show which of the constraints were involved for their inclusion in the solution. Note that the constraints that are formulated in natural languages here and the workflow specification are based on according patterns that directly translate into SLTL formulas used as input for the synthesis algorithm.

3.2   Loose Programming: A Heuristics for Branching

Loose programming [29] is a pragmatic approach to making synthesis functionality available to users that are not trained in formal methods and for whom it would be hard or impossible to formulate formal workflow specifications. The loose programming paradigm promotes a form of semantically assisted and model-based graphical software development specifically tailored to enabling application experts to design their purpose-specific processes and workflows in an intuitive fashion. In particular, loose programming introduces underspecified complex processes to be used in combination with SLTL synthesis. This enables users to specify their intentions about a workflow in a very sparse way, by just giving intuitive high-level specifications that refer to concepts and activities from the domain-specific vocabulary, because it offers a mechanism that automatically translates such requests into syntactically correct and executable running workflows.

Domain model:

service and type
taxonomies

services

domain constraints

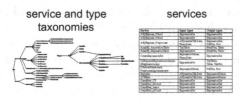

Enforce the use of *Data Loading*
Enforce the use of *Preprocessing*
Enforce the use of *Statistical Analysis*
Do not use *Benchmark Data Loading* more than once.
Do not use *Preprocessing* more than once.
Do not use *Statistical Analysis* more than once.
Use *File Writing* as last service in the solution.
If *Statistical Analysis* is used, do not use *Filtering* subsequently.
At most one of **LoadDilutionBenchmarkData** and
DifferentialExpressionAnalysis4ReplicateArrays may exist.

Synthesis problem:

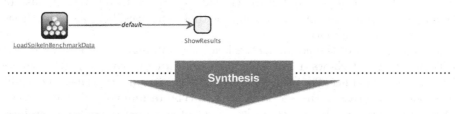

Possible synthesis results:

with no further constraints (only constraints from the domain model):

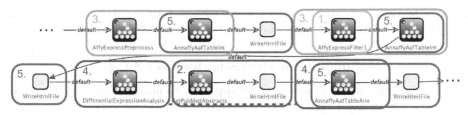

with additional constraints:

1. Enforce the use of *Filtering*
2. Enforce the use of `GetPubMedAbstracts`.
3. If *Preprocess* or *Filter* is used, *Annotation* has to be used next.
4. If *Statistical Analysis* is used, *Annotation* has to be used subsequently.
5. If Annotation is used, WriteHtmlFile has to be used next.

Fig. 1. Example: synthesis of scientific workflows.

Figure 2 illustrates the idea: Instead of implementing a complex workflow completely, the user can leave parts of the workflow underspecified (the dashed edges in the model), indicating that he does not know how or does not want to model the respective parts. SLTL synthesis will be applied to all loosely specified branches, making use of the information from the domain model. As shown in the example, this may lead to the replacement of the loose specification by a single building block, the synthesis may determine that actually nothing

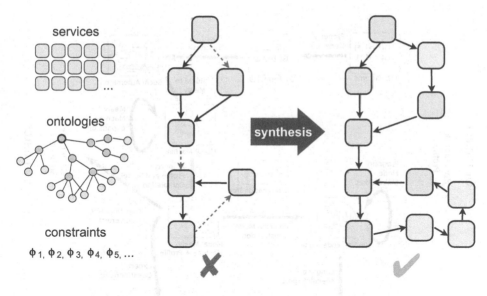

services

ontologies

constraints

$\phi_1, \phi_2, \phi_3, \phi_4, \phi_5, \ldots$

synthesis

Fig. 2. Loose programming.

needs to be done, or insert a sequence of services. Note that in addition to simplifying the specification of synthesis problems for the user, this approach has also a performance advantage in contrast to synthesizing the complete complex structure from scratch, as the structure given by the user directly partitions the overall problem into small and quickly solvable chunks.

The PROPHETS[2] plugin [39] to the jABC framework [57] is the current reference implementation of the loose programming paradigm. With the introduction of PROPHETS, the SLTL synthesis method described above has become conveniently accessible also for "normal" users: Background knowledge about the underlying method is not required for using the plugin, since all formal specifications that the synthesis algorithm needs are derived automatically from the intuitive, graphical specification mechanisms that PROPHETS provides. The user does not need to do the entire workflow design manually anymore, but can just sketch the most salient elements and let PROPHETS complete it into a compatible and executable service composition.

3.3   A Branching-Time View of LTL

Classically, a model of an LTL formula is a trace or a path, and automata are only used to specify sets of such models. If one is only interested in deterministic program structures, linear-time logic can also be used to specify graph structures, namely (for SLTL unique) minimal corresponding deterministic automata. This

---

[2] PROPHETS = Process Realization and Optimization Platform using Human-readable Expression of Temporal-logic Synthesis.

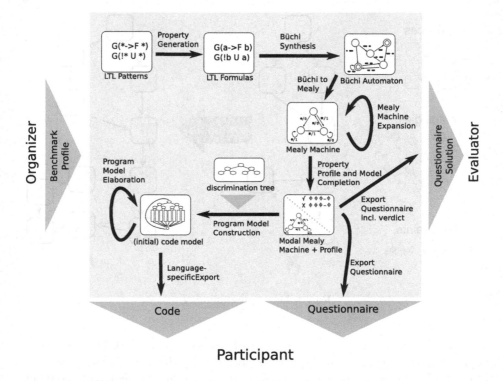

Fig. 3. Overview of the RERS benchmark generation process.

view is the basis for the model adaptation technique described in [9,52] and the generation principle for the benchmarks [53] used for the RERS challenge.

Figure 3 provides an overview of the RERS generation process, which is characterized by first synthesizing an equivalent Büchi automaton for the conjunction of the LTL formulas that the generated benchmark program should satisfy, followed by a sequence of property-preserving transformations that transform the generated Büchi automaton stepwise into C, C++ or Java Code. Algorithmic bottleneck of the construction is the synthesis of the Büchi automaton, which is therefore only done for the conjunction of around 10 temporal formulas. In order to obtain the required 100 properties for the RERS benchmarks, the 10 formulas are complemented by around 90 randomly generated and then model-checked formulas. This combination of model synthesis and model checking turned out to work well for our benchmark generation. Such pragmatic approaches are typical, as one often has to find compromises to deal with the high inherent complexity of LTL synthesis.

4   Meta-Level Language Generation

Aiming at domain-specific languages and tools comprises the so-called "design for-" paradigm, with instances like *design for testability*, *design for verifiability*, and here *design for synthesizability*. The following two subsections will illustrate that metamodeling languages are *designed for component synthesis* as well as *designed for DSM tool synthesis*.

4.1   Generating Domain-Specific SIBs

As outlined in Sect. 2.2, Genesys is shipped with a basic repertoire of SIBs that can be used for modeling code generators. This SIB library is entirely "hand-crafted", i.e., these SIBs were built on-demand and based on experience gained with the practical application of Genesys. Typically, in order to be reusable for a wide range of potential code generators and target platforms, such SIBs tended to be generic and highly configurable.

In [25], we described an approach for automatically generating code generator SIBs from domain knowledge. The rationale behind this is to enable the generator developer to resort to the specific concepts and terminology of the source language when constructing a code generator. For representing the domain knowledge, we employed the *Eclipse Modeling Framework (EMF)* [58], which allows metamodeling based on its meta-metamodel *Ecore*. With respect to their basic structure, metamodels specified with Ecore are very similar to UML class diagrams.

Our approach is depicted in Fig. 4. Initially, a metamodel is created with Ecore. This metamodel establishes relevant concepts and notions for corresponding models of the desired domain. In the next step, we use a special code generator, the *EMF SIB Generator*, to automatically generate SIBs based on the given metamodel. The EMF SIB Generator itself was also built and generated with Genesys. The resulting SIBs are able to process any model that conforms to the metamodel, and thus can be considered on a par with a domain-specific "model API" for those models. Subsequently, the generated SIBs serve as a basis

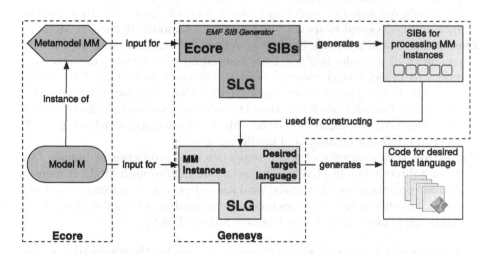

Fig. 4. Approach for constructing code generators for EMF with Genesys

for constructing further Genesys code generators, that translate any instances of the metamodel into a desired target language (bottom part of Fig. 4). This way, a generator developer profits from the advantages of Genesys without having to give up EMF's strengths in domain-specificity.

4.2 Generating Domain-Specific Modeling Tools

The CINCO SCCE Meta Tooling Suite [40] builds on the ideas of the Genesys' EMF SIB Generator. However, it does not just generate the SIBs used to model code generators for models conforming to a given Ecore metamodel: the whole tool, including a dedicated graphical editor required to produce models of that type, is generated as well. Such tools, called "CINCO Products", provide a complete solution for domain-specific model-driven development. This big generative lever is primarily achieved by CINCO's focus on graph model structures. Overall, the formalisms used by CINCO to fully specify and automatically generate the modeling tool can be regarded under four orthogonal aspects:

Metamodels of a CINCO Product are defined in the *Meta Graph Language* (MGL), a textual meta-level DSL specializing on the definition of graph structures built from *nodes, edges*, and *containers* (special nodes that can contain other nodes). While *cardinality constraints* define which types of nodes and how many of them can be included in containers, *incoming constraints* and *outgoing constraints* on edges define how nodes can be interconnected with these edges. The actual Ecore metamodel of each modeling language in a CINCO Product is generated from an own MGL specification. For example, three MGL models (for data, processes, and GUI) are defined in DIME (cf. Sect. 2.3).

The visual appearance of nodes and edges is defined with a *Meta Style Language* (MSL) model, which is also a CINCO-specific textual DSL. It allows for the simple definition of rendering styles in form of shapes and their appearance and is designed to specifically support metamodels defined in MGL.

The semantics in a CINCO Product is defined in a translational way, i.e. the semantics of a model is given by a translation (i.e. a code generator or a model to model transformation), and the inherent semantics of the target structure. Code generators are modeled with Genesys using SIBs generated from the metamodel definition. Model transformations work similarly, but use the "TransEM" extension [30] to the EMF SIB Generator, which additionally generates SIBs for creating and modifying models.

Validation covers aspects of static semantics, i.e., properties of models that can not directly be reflected by the metamodel defined with MGL. It requires similar constructs as the translational semantics, e.g., regarding model traversal, but checks for properties instead of generating a target artifact. Thus, validation is also realized with Genesys SIBs and SLGs.

The core of CINCO is a code generator that generates the complete modeling tool from these specifications. As MGL and MSL are themselves based on Ecore,

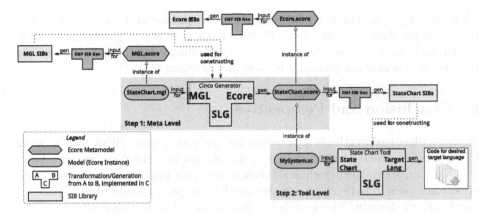

Fig. 5. In CINCO, modeling of code generators with Genesys and its EMF SIB generator happens on two levels: on the meta level within CINCO itself, and on the tool level within the generated CINCO Product.

we were able to develop the whole CINCO Generator with Genesys. Figure 5 visualizes this relation, focusing on the aspects of metamodels[3]. MGL.ecore is the metamodel of our MGL language. Giving this into Genesys' EMF SIB Generator results in the "MGL SIBs", a library of building blocks with which generator SLGs can be modeled that take MGL instances as input. As the CINCO Generator not only generates Java code but also the CINCO Product's Ecore metamodel, it needs a second SIB library to process Ecore metamodels. For this we use the EMF SIB Generator on the metamodel of Ecore itself. As Ecore is a reflexive metamodeling language, i.e., it is used to describe itself, the according metamodel is Ecore.ecore, which is part of EMF. The generated Ecore and MGL SIBs are then used for constructing the CINCO Generator SLGs.

As an example, we assume that we wish to build a CINCO Product for modeling state charts [18] and for their generation into executable code. On the one hand, the developer of this state chart tool provides the StateChart.mgl. This is used as input for the CINCO Generator to produce the corresponding StateChart.ecore metamodel (cf. step 1 in Fig. 5). On the other hand, the developer needs to provide the translational semantics for state charts modeled with the tool[4]. This semantics is again modeled with SLGs, so the EMF SIB Generator needs to be applied to the tool's metamodel for state charts (the generated StateChart.ecore) to produce the required 'StateChart SIBs' library. Finally, a system modeled by some user of the state chart tool, here depicted as MySystem.sc, is generated to executable code by these SLGs (cf. step 2 in Fig. 5). A particularly intriguing aspect is the double role of the StateChart.ecore:

---

[3] Of course, not only the Ecore metamodel is generated from MGL and MSL, but also a lot of Java source code for the actual editor and other supporting code. However, including all those aspects into Fig. 5 would considerably lower its comprehensibility.

[4] The previously introduced aspects of visual appearance and validation are not discussed here, and follow very similar concepts.

while in step 1 it was regarded as an Ecore instance and thus created and processed by SIBs generated from `Ecore.ecore`, it is now regarded as a meta-model itself used to generate an according SIB library for the definition of the translational semantics (executable code in this example).

5 Conclusion and Perspective

We have discussed synthesis as a means for bridging a WHAT/HOW gap in order to drive an abstract (more declarative) description into the direction of a more concrete and specialized (technical) realization, This way, we wish to free developers/designers from dealing with aspects that are pre-defined in the considered (application) domain. The goal is to "factor out" design complexity by treating common aspects once and for all upfront. This factoring provides a very powerful and elegant form of reuse, and it is the conceptual foundation for the successful design of domain-specific languages. Examples for synthesis that we have discussed in their traits comprise variations of code generation, model synthesis from temporal logic descriptions, and metamodel-based tool generation. They all achieve this "factoring out" by combining forms of substitution/partial evaluation to those steps that can be determined *locally*, and (heuristic) search for those parts where more *global* patterns need to be matched to bridge the translation gap.

In order to control the overall computational complexity, which can be extremely high for global matching problems, it is a good strategy to establish ways to localize global problems. The example of parsing mentioned in the introduction, where the restriction to special grammatical patterns leads to linear-time algorithms, is striking in this regard. In our industrial experience, "service oriented abstraction", i.e., considering complex functions or data structures as abstract entities with an ontological description, is an extremely powerful reduction technique. It establishes a simplified higher level of abstraction where, e.g., temporal logic synthesis can be applied. (Scientific) workflow synthesis, loose programming, the RERS benchmark generation, as well as many of the domain constraints used in CINCO are based on this abstraction.

In fact, even the `gen/kill` abstraction of statements underlying most bit vector analyses in data-flow analysis frameworks can be regarded retrospectively as a special form of this service-oriented abstraction. This has been first exploited in [50] for reducing data-flow analysis to a model checking problem, this way drastically simplifying the correctness and optimality proofs. This simplificaiton led to today's standard algorithm for partial redundancy elimination [27] and bore long term effects: it was the basis for solving three corresponding open problems: the optimal reduction of register pressure [27], the optimal treatment of complex expression [48], and the elimination of all partial redundancies via *Property-Oriented Expansion* (POE) [51]. Actually POE is quite similar to SLTL synthesis, it has exponential worst case complexity, and achieves practicality only because of the underlying service-oriented abstraction.

All the described methods and tools are part of a continuously growing common conceptual core, which can be regarded as a foundation for a powerful technology of reuse where agreed-upon functionality and structure is factored out at various levels, resulting in highly efficient domain-specific modeling/development environments [41]. CINCO is designed with the aim to fully leverage this potential and to provide a continuously evolving platform for the development of such modeling tools in a bootstrapping fashion. A first step in this evolution, which we sketch in [41], will be to use CINCO to develop a successor of the Genesys framework. On the one hand, this will free the CINCO ecosystem from jABC's legacy technology, so that a new CINCO-version of Genesys can replace jABC in both the definition of the semantics for CINCO Products and in the CINCO Generator itself. On the other hand, this new Genesys can be tailored more specifically to the task of modeling code generators, transformations, and validation checks. Actually, such functionalities may themselves be the starting point for a product line of even more specialized Genesys variants, focusing on each task individually.

A second way to extend the CINCO framework is by providing so-called *meta plug-ins*: plug-ins for the CINCO Generator itself, conceptually distinct from "normal" plug-ins on the level of CINCO Products. Meta plug-ins are used to introduce generative solutions for additional complex concepts in CINCO, making them easily available for any CINCO Product. We envision meta plug-ins for, e.g., "executability" or "loose programming", "data-flow analysis", "model checking", and "model synthesis", which directly facilitate product lines of, e.g., new variants of Genesys or PROPHETS, addressing various domain-specific scenarios of code generation and/or synthesis.

Acknowledgments. This work was supported, in part, by Science Foundation Ireland grant 13/RC/2094 and co-funded under the European Regional Development Fund through the Southern & Eastern Regional Operational Programme to Lero - the Irish Software Research Centre (www.lero.ie).

References

1. Dart programming language. https://www.dartlang.org/. Accessed 26 July 2016
2. One framework. - Angular 2. https://angular.io/. Accessed 05 Aug 2016
3. Standard ECMA-404. The JSON Data Interchange Format (2013). http://www.ecma-international.org/publications/standards/Ecma-404.htm
4. Aho, A.V., Lam, M.S., Sethi, R., Ullman, J.D.: Compilers: Principles, Techniques, and Tools, 2nd edn. Addison Wesley, Boston (2007)
5. Al-Areqi, S., Lamprecht, A.-L., Margaria, T.: Constraints-driven automatic geospatial service composition: workflows for the analysis of sea-level rise impacts. In: Gervasi, O., et al. (eds.) ICCSA 2016. LNCS, vol. 9788, pp. 134–150. Springer, Heidelberg (2016). doi:10.1007/978-3-319-42111-7_12
6. Bessai, J., Dudenhefner, A., Duedder, B., Martens, M., Rehof, J.: Combinatory process synthesis. In: Proceedings of the 7th International Symposyum on Leveraging Applications of Formal Methods, Verification and Validation (ISoLA 2016) (2016)

7. Bodik, R., Jobstmann, B.: Algorithmic program synthesis: introduction. Int. J. Softw. Tools Technol. Transf. **15**(5), 397–411 (2013)

8. Boßelmann, S., Frohme, M., Kopetzki, D., Lybecait, M., Naujokat, S., Neubauer, J., Wirkner, D., Zweihoff, P., Steffen, B.: DIME: a programming-less modeling environment for web applications. In: Proceedings of the 7th International Symposium on Leveraging Applications of Formal Methods, Verification and Validation (ISoLA 2016) (2016)

9. Braun, V., Margaria, T., Steffen, B., Yoo, H., Rychly, T.: Safe service customization. In: Intelligent Network Workshop, IN 1997, vol. 2, p. 4. IEEE, May 1997

10. Coussy, P., Gajski, D.D., Meredith, M., Takach, A.: An introduction to high-level synthesis. IEEE Des. Test Comput. **26**(4), 8–17 (2009)

11. Coussy, P., Morawiec, A.: High-Level Synthesis: from Algorithm to Digital Circuit. Springer, Heidelberg (2010)

12. Czarnecki, K., Helsen, S.: Feature-based survey of model transformation approaches. IBM Syst. J. **45**, 621–645 (2006)

13. Düdder, B., Martens, M., Rehof, J.: Staged composition synthesis. In: Shao, Z. (ed.) ESOP 2014 (ETAPS). LNCS, vol. 8410, pp. 67–86. Springer, Heidelberg (2014)

14. Edelkamp, S., Schroedl, S., Koenig, S.: Heuristic Search: Theory and Applications. Morgan Kaufmann Publishers Inc., San Francisco (2010)

15. Fielding, R.T.: Architectural styles and the design of network-based software architectures. Ph.D. thesis, University of California, Irvine (2000)

16. Freitag, B., Margaria, T., Steffen, B.: A pragmatic approach to software synthesis. SIGPLAN Not. **29**(8), 46–58 (1994). doi:10.1145/185087.185102

17. Campbell, Grady H., J., Faulk, S.R., Weiss, D.M.: Introduction to synthesis. Technical report, Software Productivity Consortium, June 1990

18. Harel, D.: Statecharts: a visual formalism for complex systems. Sci. Comput. Program. **8**(3), 231–274 (1987)

19. Heineman, G., Bessai, J., Duedder, B., Rehof, J.: A long and winding road towards modular synthesis. In: Proceedings of the 7th International Symposium on Leveraging Applications of Formal Methods, Verification and Validation (ISoLA 2016) (2016)

20. Internet Engineering Task Force (IETF): The JavaScript Object Notation (JSON) Data Interchange Format (2014). https://tools.ietf.org/html/rfc7159

21. Ison, J., Kalaš, M., Jonassen, I., Bolser, D., Uludag, M., McWilliam, H., Malone, J., Lopez, R., Pettifer, S., Rice, P.: EDAM: an ontology of bioinformatics operations, types of data and identifiers, topics and formats. Bioinformatics **29**, 1325–1332 (2013)

22. Jones, N.D., Gomard, C.K., Sestoft, P.: Partial Evaluation and Automatic Program Generation. Prentice-Hall Inc., Upper Saddle River (1993)

23. Jörges, S.: Construction and Evolution of Code Generators - A Model-Driven and Service-Oriented Approach. LNCS, vol. 7747. Springer, Heidelberg (2013)

24. Jörges, S., Lamprecht, A.L., Margaria, T., Schaefer, I., Steffen, B.: A constraint-based variability modeling framework. Int. J. Softw. Tools Technol. Transf. (STTT) **14**(5), 511–530 (2012)

25. Jörges, S., Steffen, B.: Exploiting ecore's reflexivity for bootstrapping domain-specific code-generators. In: Proceedings of 35th Software Engineering Workshop (SEW 2012), pp. 72–81. IEEE (2012)

26. Gsottberger, C., Margaria, T., Mendler, M., Gsottberger, S.: MOSEL: A flexible toolset for monadic second-order logic. In: Grumberg, O. (ed.) CAV 1997. LNCS, vol. 1254, pp. 1–20. Springer, Heidelberg (1997)

27. Knoop, J., Rüthing, O., Steffen, B.: Optimal code motion: theory and practice. ACM Trans. Program. Lang. Syst. **16**(4), 1117–1155 (1994)
28. Lamprecht, A.L.: User-Level Workflow Design - A Bioinformatics Perspective, vol. 8311. Springer, Heidelberg (2013)
29. Lamprecht, A.L., Naujokat, S., Margaria, T., Steffen, B.: Synthesis-based loose programming. In: Proceedings of the 7th International Conference on the Quality of Information and Communications Technology (QUATIC 2010), pp. 262–267. IEEE, Porto, Portugal, September 2010
30. Lybecait, M.: Entwicklung und Implementierung eines Frameworks zur grafischen Modellierung von Modelltransformationen auf Basis von EMF-Metamodellen und Genesys. Diploma thesis, TU Dortmund (2012)
31. Manna, Z., Wolper, P.: Synthesis of communicating processes from temporal logic specifications. ACM Trans. Program. Lang. Syst. **6**(1), 68–93 (1984)
32. Margaria, T.: Fully automatic verification and error detection for parameterized iterative sequential circuits. In: Margaria, T., Steffen, B. (eds.) TACAS 1996. LNCS, vol. 1055. Springer, Heidelberg (1996)
33. Margaria, T., Bakera, M., Kubczak, C., Naujokat, S., Steffen, B.: Automatic generation of the SWS-challenge mediator with jABC/ABC. In: Petrie, C., Margaria, T., Zaremba, M., Lausen, H. (eds.) Semantic Web Services Challenge: Results from the First Year, pp. 119–138. Springer, New York (2008)
34. Margaria, T., Meyer, D., Kubczak, C., Isberner, M., Steffen, B.: Synthesizing semantic web service compositions with jMosel and Golog. In: Bernstein, A., et al. (eds.) ISWC 2009. LNCS, vol. 5823, pp. 392–407. Springer, Heidelberg (2009)
35. Margaria, T., Steffen, B.: Business process modelling in the jABC: the one-thing-approach. In: Cardoso, J., van der Aalst, W. (eds.) Handbook of Research on Business Process Modeling. IGI Global, Hershey (2009)
36. Margaria, T., Steffen, B., Reitenspiess, M.: Service-oriented design: the roots. In: Benatallah, B., Casati, F., Traverso, P. (eds.) ICSOC 2005. LNCS, vol. 3826, pp. 450–464. Springer, Heidelberg (2005)
37. Margaria, T., Steffen, B., Topnik, C.: Second-order value numbering. Electron. Commun. EASST (ECEASST) **30**, 1–15 (2010)
38. Martin, G., Smith, G.: High-level synthesis: past, present, and future. IEEE Des. Test Comput. **26**(4), 18–25 (2009)
39. Naujokat, S., Lamprecht, A.-L., Steffen, B.: Loose programming with PROPHETS. In: de Lara, J., Zisman, A. (eds.) Fundamental Approaches to Software Engineering. LNCS, vol. 7212, pp. 94–98. Springer, Heidelberg (2012)
40. Naujokat, S., Lybecait, M., Kopetzki, D., Steffen, B.: CINCO: a simplicity-driven approach to full generation of domain-specific graphical modeling tools (2016, to appear)
41. Naujokat, S., Neubauer, J., Margaria, T., Steffen, B.: Meta-level reuse for mastering domain specialization. In: Proceedings of the 7th International Symposium on Leveraging Applications of Formal Methods, Verification and Validation (ISoLA 2016) (2016)
42. Neubauer, J., Frohme, M., Steffen, B., Margaria, T.: Prototype-driven development of web applications with DyWA. In: Margaria, T., Steffen, B. (eds.) ISoLA 2014, Part I. LNCS, vol. 8802, pp. 56–72. Springer, Heidelberg (2014)
43. Neubauer, J., Steffen, B., Margaria, T.: Higher-order process modeling: product-lining, variability modeling and beyond. Electron. Proc. Theoret. Comput. Sci. **129**, 259–283 (2013)

44. Parr, T.: Enforcing strict model-view separation in template engines. In: Proceedings of the 13th International Conference on World Wide Web (WWW 2004), pp. 224–233. ACM, New York (2004)

45. Petrie, C., Margaria, T., Lausen, H., Zaremba, M.: Semantic Web Services Challenge: Results from the First Year. Semantic Web and Beyond, vol. 8. Springer, New York (2009)

46. Rehof, J., Vardi, M.Y.: Design and synthesis from components (Dagstuhl seminar 14232). Dagstuhl Rep. 4(6), 29–47 (2014)

47. Rice, P., Longden, I., Bleasby, A.: EMBOSS: the European molecular biology open software suite. Trends Genet. 16(6), 276–277 (2000)

48. Rüthing, O., Knoop, J., Steffen, B.: Sparse code motion. In: Proceedings of the 27th ACM SIGPLAN-SIGACT Symposium on Principles of Programming Languages (POpPL 2000), pp. 170–183. ACM (2000)

49. Rumbaugh, J., Jacobsen, I., Booch, G.: The Unified Modeling Language Reference Manual. The Addison-Wesley Object Technology Series. Addison-Wesley Professional, Boston (2004)

50. Steffen, B.: Generating data flow analysis algorithms from modal specifications. Sci. Comput. Program. 21(2), 115–139 (1993)

51. Steffen, B.: Property-oriented expansion. In: Cousot, R., Schmidt, D.A. (eds.) SAS 1996. LNCS, vol. 1145. Springer, Heidelberg (1996)

52. Steffen, B.: Method for incremental synthesis of a discrete technical system (1998)

53. Steffen, B., Isberner, M., Naujokat, S., Margaria, T., Geske, M.: Property-driven benchmark generation synthesizing programs of realistic structure. Softw. Tools Technol. Transf. 16(5), 465–479 (2014)

54. Steffen, B., Margaria, T., Braun, V., Kalt, N.: Hierarchical service definition. Ann. Rev. Commun. ACM 51, 847–856 (1997)

55. Steffen, B., Margaria, T., Braun, V.: The electronic tool integration platform: concepts and design. Int. J. Softw. Tools Technol. Transf. (STTT) 1(1–2), 9–30 (1997)

56. Steffen, B., Margaria, T., Freitag, B.: Module configuration by minimal model construction. Technical report, Fakultät für Mathematik und Informatik, Universität Passau (1993)

57. Steffen, B., Margaria, T., Nagel, R., Jörges, S., Kubczak, C.: Model-driven development with the jABC. In: Bin, E., Ziv, A., Ur, S. (eds.) HVC 2006. LNCS, vol. 4383, pp. 92–108. Springer, Heidelberg (2007)

58. Steinberg, D., Budinsky, F., Paternostro, M., Merks, E.: EMF: Eclipse Modeling Framework, 2nd edn. Addison-Wesley, Boston (2008)

A Long and Winding Road Towards Modular Synthesis

George T. Heineman[(⊠)], Jan Bessai, Boris Düdder, and Jakob Rehof

Worcester Polytechnic Institute, Technical University of Dortmund,
Dortmund, Germany
heineman@cs.wpi.edu,
{jan.bessai,boris.duedder,jakob.rehof}@tu-dortmund.de

Abstract. This paper offers a personal reflection on a number of
attempts over the past decade to apply a variety of approaches to construct a product line for solitaire card games implemented in Java. A
product line shares a common set of features developed from a common
set of software artifacts. A *feature* is a unit of functionality within a
system that is visible to an end-user and can be used to differentiate
members of the product line. The ultimate research goal is to assemble a
product line by selecting a configuration of a set of pre-designed *modular units* and developing new units as necessary for individual members;
in short, incorporating configuration into routine development. A secondary goal was to develop a suitable tool chain that could be integrated
with existing IDEs to achieve widespread acceptance of the approach.
We compare progress against by-hand development in Java. During this
period we investigated a number of approaches from the research literature, including components, aspects, and layers; these efforts led to a
productive collaboration supported by type theory.

1   Introduction

A product line shares a common set of features developed from a common set
of software artifacts [4]. A feature is a unit of functionality within a system
that is visible to an end-user and can be used to differentiate members of the
product line. One can specify (at the requirements level) that a member of the
product line should support a set of features; however, the engineering of the
resulting system is complicated because one cannot cleanly encapsulate features
as *modular units* to be simply linked together, as one can do with code libraries.
In realizing software product lines, one of the best practices is to use an *object-
oriented framework*, which can be briefly described as a concrete implementation
of a semi-complete architecture [3]. Successfully developing an OO framework
requires that software engineers become experts in a specific application domain
and then faithfully translate that domain into a software system that supports
a range of extensions. The result of this effort is often a complicated codebase
that is cognitively hard to use because programmers must fully comprehend the
usage patterns of the framework to even begin to write the simplest of extensions.
Fayad and Schmidt summarize the challenges in both developing and using OO

© Springer International Publishing AG 2016
T. Margaria and B. Steffen (Eds.): ISoLA 2016, Part I, LNCS 9952, pp. 303–317, 2016.
DOI: 10.1007/978-3-319-47166-2_21

Table 1. Reusability comparison

	#Classes (#reused)	#Layers (#reused)
Idiot	6 (0)	13 (10) 77 %
Narcotic	7 (0)	14 (10) 71%
GrandFatherClock	6 (0)	13 (11) 85%
Klondike	11 (0)	21 (15) 71%

Stack	Abstract representation of cards in sequence from bottom to top
BuildablePile	Pile of cards face down on top of which a column can be built
Card	Single card
Column	Stack of cards that reveals cards lower in the column
Deck	Deck of playing cards
MutableInteger	Integer that can change during play (such as the score)
Pile	Stack whose topmost card is visible

Fig. 1. Classes within KS model hierarchy

frameworks [7]. They argue there is a significant learning curve to using OO frameworks, and often developers need hands-on mentoring or training courses to succeed. The essential problem is that deep knowledge about the framework is locked in the heads of expert developers [7] and programmers cant easily get this knowledge. There is thus a gap between an OO framework and its extenders.

Our work was initially motivated by a course project for use in undergraduate and graduate classes in Software Engineering at WPI. Heineman developed Kombat Solitaire (KS), a Java application that enables users to download and retrieve solitaire variations as plugins to be played in head-to-head competition. To enable the rapid development of solitaire plugins, a rich set of model elements are provided, as shown in Table 1. Each model element shown (except for abstract Stack) has a corresponding view element that depicts the model element within the solitaire playing field.

Each KS plugin is responsible for constructing a model of the game, which may include a deck, columns where cards are stacked, a running score, and waste piles. The plugin then defines the views for these model elements over a 2-dimensional playing field such that no two views intersect each other. Finally, a controller is registered with each view to manage mouse events (such as press, release, click) and perform moves as allowed by the solitaire variation. The collection of controller classes enforces the rules of a specific solitaire variation (Fig. 1).

The initial success of the KS framework was based on following best practices of Object-Oriented design, and in particular the Model/View/Controller paradigm [8] and related design patterns, such as *Observer*. Hundreds of students have completed solitaire variations, yet one concern has always been that students had to complete each variation from scratch with only a tutorial to help understand how to proceed. What was missing, we felt, was some way to describe a solitaire variation with respect to a common set of *features*; to find some way to encode partial fragments of solitaire games as modular units that could be combined together.

1.1 Review Alternate Frameworks

Our initial question was whether there might have been a better way to model the solution in an object-oriented way; one which supported the composition of variations from pre-defined units. We found a comparable open-source project, PySol [14], written in Python, an interpreted object-oriented programming language. PySol has an extensible solitaire engine and supports features such as multi-level undo/redo, loading stored games, and storing statistics.

In PySol, each solitaire Game has a *talon* that holds the initial deck, a waste pile of cards dealt from the talon, a set of foundation piles where cards are placed for the final solution, a set of row piles to hold intermediate storage as allowed by the solitaire variation, a set of additional reserve piles for holding cards, and a set of internal piles that are invisible during game play and are used to simplify the coding of a particular variation. The Game class thus provides a rich set of primitive objects that the PySol designers expected would be in any variation.

The definition of Klondike as an extension to the base Game class is shown in Fig. 4. The behavior for the Klondike variation is encoded in several ways: (a) By fixing the class for an object to determine allowable moves (i.e., in Klondike the foundation piles are Same Suit (SS) piles of increasing card rank, and the row piles must be Alternating Color (AC) and start with a King if empty). The definitions of SS_FoundationStack and KingAC_RowStack are provided by the PySol infrastructure, and are themselves extensions of abstract base classes.

```
1   class Klondike(Game):
2     Layout_Method = Layout.klondikeLayout
3     Talon_Class = WasteTalonStack
4     Foundation_Class = SS_FoundationStack
5     RowStack_Class = KingAC_RowStack
6     Hint_Class = KlondikeType_Hint
7
8     def createGame(self, max_rounds=-1, num_deal=1, **layout):
9       # create layout
10      l, s = Layout(self), self.s
11      kwdefault(layout, rows=7, waste=1, texts=1, playcards=16)
12      apply(self.Layout_Method, (l,), layout)
13      self.setSize(l.size[0], l.size[1])
14
15      # create stacks
16      s.talon = self.Talon_Class(l.s.talon.x, l.s.talon.y, self,
17                  max_rounds=max_rounds, num_deal=num_deal)
18      if l.s.waste:
19        s.waste = WasteStack(l.s.waste.x, l.s.waste.y, self)
20      for r in l.s.foundations:
21        s.foundations.append(
22          self.Foundation_Class(r.x, r.y, self, suit=r.suit))
```

```
23      for r in l.s.rows:
24        s.rows.append(self.RowStack_Class(r.x, r.y, self))
25      l.defaultAll()
26      return l
```

Listing 1.1. Klondike PySol Implementation

Once the Klondike game has been instantiated, there are two methods for controlling its behavior, `startGame` and `shallHighlightMatch`.

```
1     def startGame(self, flip=0, reverse=1):
2       for i in range(1, len(self.s.rows)):
3         self.s.talon.dealRow
4           (rows=self.s.rows[i:], flip=flip,
5             frames=0, reverse=reverse)
6       self.startDealSample()
7       self.s.talon.dealRow(reverse=reverse)
8
9       # deal first card to WasteStack
10      if self.s.waste:
11        self.s.talon.dealCards()
12
13    def shallHighlightMatch(self, stack1, card1, stack2, card2):
14      return (card1.color != card2.color and
15               (card1.rank+1 == card2.rank or
16                card2.rank+1 == card1.rank))
```

Listing 1.2. Klondike PySol Implementation cont...

It is clear that PySol satisfies its main objective of providing an extensible engine for solitaire games (with over 200 variations). Yet the design has flaws:

- In PySol, there is no separation of Model, View, and Controller. In fact, it supports a "pseudo MVC scheme" by creating three class variables – `model`, `view`, and `controller` – that are all set to `self`, the python version of this! The `Stack` class has 23 methods that access/update the model, 15 that access/update the view, and 31 methods that access/update a controller. *Observation: the design is complex.*
- If a new variation requires a specialized layout, the `Layout` class must be modified to include a method written for the new variation. For example, the `freeCellLayout` method in `Layout` exists only for use by the FreeCell variation. *Observation: core classes become unnecessarily complicated when they are changed to support an individual variation.*
- Often logic for a variation is spread throughout multiple Python modules. In PySol, one can use an integer seed to select a random game. If the same seed is used, the deck will be shuffled identically. Because FreeCell is so popular, the base `Game` class in PySol has a sub-case (used only by FreeCell) that will shuffle the deck to appear exactly as it would have if played on Windows. *Observation: It is hard to understand the logic of individual classes when specific functionality for a variation is intermingled with generic functionality needed for all variations.*

- Much of the logic is embedded within the objects themselves. In Klondike in Listing 1.1, for example, the `WasteTalonStack` knows that the cards dealt from the talon end up in the waste pile. *Observation: should separate model from view.*

In reviewing PySol, we find three classes, `FreeCell_AC_RowStack`, `Spider_AC_RowStack`, `Yukon_AC_RowStack`; all ensure that cards are in alternating colors/decreasing rank, but additional variation-specific logic is woven together. Also PySol designers have "fixed in concrete" the possible variation points through parameters.

It is inappropriate to localize variation-specific logic in `Klondike` that could potentially be (re)used by different variations, but it is equally incorrect to "pollute" `Game` or `Layout` with arbitrary logic that appears only within a few (or even one) variations.

1.2 Review Alternate Approaches

The initial idea, back in 2005, was to identify promising approaches above-and-beyond programming, that would properly model a solitaire variation and enable it to be used for constructing a working plugin. During this early stage, Heineman began to investigate using two different languages – one to represent the logic of the solitaire variation, and a "higher-level" language to represent the way the variation was composed. This approach was inspired by the use of the ACME Architectural Description Interchange Language [9]. ACME was used to model structural relationships in a Software Architecture, while special-purpose extensions were written in different languages.

The solitaire application domain is rich with details about numerous variations, so we considered developing a *Domain Specific Language* to capture the essence of a variation, which would then be translated into Java. This alternative was quickly discarded because:

- Using a DSL does not solve the composition problem, namely, assembling variation from predefined modular units. In fact, it might even further complicate the situation. *Observation: it is challenging to identify the proper granularity of these units.*
- Using a DSL leads to an *ad hoc* approach to composing code fragments together, based on the syntax and semantics of the DSL. *Observation: algebraic or functional compositional approaches would be cleaner and easier to understand and explain.*
- Code snippets appear in the listing: any attempt to write the logic for a variation invariably leads to writing actual code fragments. *Observation: often it is simpler and more accurate to use a native programming language to describe logic.*

1.3   Component-Based Software Engineering

One of the most common ways championed by Software Engineering is to modularize a software system using *software components*. There are countless approaches to developing a software component and there are surprisingly few agreements on the nature of a software component. We use the following definition [11].

> A software component is a software element that conforms to a **component model** and can be independently deployed and composed without modification according to a composition standard. A component model defines specific interaction and composition standards.

This definition identifies the centrality of composition when using software components. Most component models rely on a binary or black-box form of composition, where components are connected to other components by means of well-defined interfaces. Nearly all component models require that the components themselves are not modified during composition. While the final solitaire variation would become a meaningful software component (i.e., a plugin to be executed within a solitaire-playing game engine) it is challenging to identify meaningful fine-grained component units that could be assembled to create the variation. This was exactly the research issue we identified in evolving system features into fine-grained components [13]. Ultimately we discarded this approach from consideration due to the perceived overhead of making this work with existing Java-based component models:

- Components are coarse-grained entities best identified by their functional interfaces. *Observation: we need fine-grained mechanisms to specify the variation as found in the solitaire application domain.*
- Treating modular units in a black-box fashion significantly limits the composition of units to be strictly assembling connections between interfaces. *Observation: we need invasive access to modular units to support composition.*

1.4   Model View Controller

The investigations of the past ten years were motivated by observing how challenging it was to reuse code within a Model/View/Controller (MVC) paradigm. MVC is a pervasive technique that separates responsibilities in software to avoid overly restrictive coupling that otherwise might occur [8]. While MVC has most commonly been associated with GUI programming, it can also be applied to separately manage the input, processing, and output of software systems. The primary benefit of MVC is the resulting extensibility and ease of change, but it also offers the possibility of increasing the use (and reuse) of code.

The philosophical motivation is that using MVC naturally leads to the inability to reuse controllers. Domain experts have considerable expertise in using inheritance to capture the rich information to be stored in a model. HCI experts show how to build user interfaces that decouple the model from the view presented to the users. But the complex logic found in controllers can quickly be unmanageable because of the inherent limitations of the basic extension constructs in OO programming languages. Since business logic is encapsulated within controllers, MVC may actually be an impediment to the proper reuse or extension of business logic. Rather quickly one sees the limitations of using inheritance (a typing mechanism) as a means of capturing the way that one (complex) behavior is related to, or extends, another; this is especially true when one requires multiple sets of simultaneous extensions. To manage the multiple tailoring of several components within a product line, we must provide a more rigorous foundation.

In the rest of this paper, we delve into the different approaches chronologically, presenting snippets of modular units as well as code fragments. We feel this unusual approach best explains how we ended up in the direction we are heading.

2   Design

After reviewing a number of possible approaches, we settled on the following desired criteria to identify how to move forward.

- *Modular units must be stored in a hierarchical repository* – most programming languages depend on having namespaces (C++), package hierarchies (Java), or nested directory structures (Python) to store code artifacts.
- *Support algebraic composition* – the AHEAD approach pioneered by Batory [1] was especially persuasive in clarifying this requirement. Using algebraic notations and principles leads to a clean approach to composition.
- *Assembly by configuration* – selecting the desired modular units would lead immediately to the construction of an assembly.
- *Fine-grained structure of the modular units* – Early indications suggested that these modular units could not be "black box" units (as with components) but rather would have to contain perhaps multiple source code files.
- *Industrial-quality tool support* – No solution would be widely accepted without having a proper tool chain to support the overall approach.

We started with Batory's AHEAD tool suite [1] and developed the *AHEAD Component Development Kit* [10] to satisfy the above criteria.

2.1   AHEAD Component Development Kit

AHEAD (Algebraic Hierarchical Equations for Application Design) is an architectural model for feature oriented programming (FOP) and a basis for large-scale compositional programming [1]. In AHEAD, one defines a collection of *layers*, where each layer L_i contains potentially a number of artifacts, a_1, a_2,

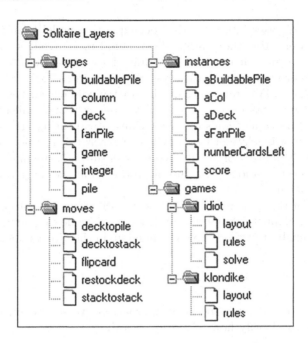

Fig. 2. Repository of AHEAD layers for solitaire variation in ACDK.

..., a_n; for our purpose, we focused on creating *Jak* artifacts which are composed together to produce a collection of Java classes. Each artifact a_i either defines a new Java class, or is a refinement to an existing Java class. To specify a composition, one writes an equation that lists an ordered composition of layers. For example, assume you have two layers with a total of four Jak artifacts:

1. **h** (a_1, a_3)
2. **j** (a_2, a_3)

The equation **h** • **j** will result in the composition of three artifacts and the order of the layers in the equation shows that design artifact a_3 in **h** refines the existing design artifact a_3 in **j**. Three Java files will be composed and created from the Jak files, however if you were to read the source files themselves, they would clearly show signs that they were generated. The AHEAD tool suite generates "towers" of abstract classes embedded within the individual class files. We started by developing a collection of layers suitable for capturing the various elements found in Solitaire games. Figure 2 shows a partial snapshot of the overall repository of nearly fifty layers designed to compose solitaire variations in ACDK.

Let's review the details of one of these layers, namely *rules* which is one of the layers in the *FreeCell* solitaire variation implementation. This layer contains seven Jak files and determines the valid rules for the game, such as when it is valid to move a card from a BuildablePile to a Pile. The `BuildablePileToPile.jak` file refines the *BuildablePileToPile* class by overriding its *valid* method to validate the move in the context of the *FreeCell* variation.

```
1   /** Deal with Moves between BuildablePile and Pile objects. */
2   refines class BuildablePileToPile {
3    public boolean valid (Solitaire theGame) {
4     // not ours to handle
5     if (draggedStack == null) {
6      return Super(Solitaire). valid(theGame);
7     }
8
9     // DENY if stack contains more than one card
10    if (draggedStack. count() != 1) {
11     return false;
12    }
13
14    // Find out if HOME cell or a FREE cell
15    boolean isHome=getPileManager().isHome(to);
16    boolean isFree=getPileManager().isFree(to);
17
18    if (isHome) {
19     if (to.empty()) {
20      return (draggedStack.rank() == Card.ACE);
21     } else {
22      return ((draggedStack.suit()==to.suit()) &&
23             (draggedStack.rank()==to.rank()+1));
24     }
25    } else if (isFree) {
26     return to.empty();
27    } else {
28     // not ours to handle!
29     return Super(Solitaire). valid(theGame);
30    }
31   }
32  }
```

Listing 1.3. Jak artifact to validate move

A Jak file is defined using Java syntax with just two exceptions. First, when a Jak file refines an existing class, the syntax includes the keyword *refines* just before the class definition in the Jak file. Second, when a Jak file wishes to delegate a method call back to the original artifact being refined, then it uses the *Super().method* construct, which is based on the **super** keyword in Java. This simple mechanism enables a layer to revert to the "default" behavior previously defined by an earlier layer in the equation. Observe how most of the code in these Jak fragments are nothing more than Java classes with just a bit of "syntactic sugar" to explain how these fragments are to be composed with other Jak artifacts. Also observe that this Jak extension can only be understood in context, with all the other Jak layers that it extends. Ultimately, the only reason this Jak layer works properly is because its designer fully understands the collection of layers that form the repository; this inability to compartmentalize information and dependencies was a noticeable limitation of the ACDK approach.

We now describe the set of layers that can be assembled to form solitaire variation plugins. The **game** layer describes the empty solitaire plugin; it is analogous to an abstract base class. The equation describing the simplest legal variation is: **score • numLeft • integer • game**. In other words, each solitaire variation needs to show both a score and the number of cards left in the face-down deck. Since both of these values depend on the **integer** concept, we need to include that layer as well. Naturally, this generated game has no behavior. We chose four variations and developed a collection of layers to use; some became generic and were used by all variations, while others were specialized to different variations. Here are the equations representing these variations:

- *Idiot* – **stacktostack • layout • solve • rules • decktostacks • aCol • column • Deck • deck • numCardsLeft • score • integer • game**
- *Narcotic* – **solve • rules • stacktostack • reassembleDeck • layout • decktostacks • aPile • pile • aDeck • deck • numCardsLeft • score • integer • game**
- *GrandfatherClock* – **layout • aDeck • rules • stacktostack • aPile • aCol • numCardsLeft • score • deck • pile • column • integer • game**
- *Klondike* – **rules • buildablePileMoves • pileMoves • restockDeck • flipCard • stacktostack • deckMoves • deal • klondikeLayout • aFan-Pile • fanpile • aPile • pile • aBuildablePile • buildablepile • aDeck • deck • numCardsLeft • score • integer • game**

The ACDK solutions showed increased reuse when compared directly to their OO implementation counterparts. While we use Batory's AHEAD tool suite "as is", we made three novel contributions.

- The AHEAD tool *jak2java* composed layers "in place", which made it hard to reuse layers. ACDK transparently manages layers in an equation by reference;
- ACDK provides a GUI to rapidly construct layers and supports arbitrary search through all layers (both Jak files and composed Java files);
- We developed an instance-oriented layered style of design which partnered MVC with layers. Layers can introduce new "types" which are like object factories; as "instance" layers are composed downstream, refining the type layer, objects of that type are constructed. Each layer performs its task, and then invokes the appropriate logic on the upstream layer (similar to the way subclasses should invoke **super()** in constructors).

Ultimately these impressive results led to a "dead-end" in terms of productive research, primarily because individual layers had to be designed to perfectly fit within the larger whole, yet there was no way to specify accurately inter-layer dependencies. In some ways, the experience was very much like switching from a typed language, such as Java, to an untyped language, such as Javascript.

To provide a simple explanation for the weakness of the ACDK approach, consider that there is no formal way to use ACDK to produce type information about the resulting generated code. To explain why this matters, consider the trivial example in Fig. 3 containing three AHEAD layers, each containing a single C.jak file:

Valid compositions specified using AHEAD equations include: **Base, Layer1 • Base, Layer2 • Base, Layer1 • Layer2 • Base** and **Layer2 • Layer1 •**

Base	Layer1	Layer2
class C {	refines class C {	refines class C {
void f() {	void f() {	void f() {
out("here");	Super().f();	out("before");
}	out("after");	Super().f();
}	}	}
	}	}

Fig. 3. Small AHEAD example

Base. Each of these results in different output arrangements which guarantees that the "here" string never appears before the "before" string or after the "after" string. The composition tool detects that **Layer1 • Layer2** is invalid through its typing mechanism which detects that there is no base class to refine. However it is only the proper ordering of method invocations in the refinements that ensures the above guarantee, and there is no way to specify this semantically in AHEAD.

The authors of this current paper met at a Dagstuhl Seminar on Design and Synthesis from Components [15] and realized that they could apply Combinatory Logic Synthesis (CLS) to address this problem. In particular, using CLS it is possible to introduce a second language suitable for capturing fundamental abstractions needed to properly represent the semantic composition of modular units, in this case, defined as *combinators*.

3   LaunchPad

Combinatory logic synthesis [2,6] is a type-based approach to component-oriented synthesis using types as interface specifications. The basic idea of CLS is to automate the composition of components from a repository using combinatory logic [5]. Here we use the term "component" in a general sense to denote a combinator. Upon discovering this formalism, we set out to develop a full repository of combinators to synthesize a solitaire variation. This process took several months and in time a partial repository of combinators was produced to synthesize two different solitaire variations. Starting from the original KS tutorial, we iteratively identified the core abstractions in the OO framework and mapped them to combinators at different levels of granularity. Several sample combinators for a FreeCell variation are shown in Fig. 4.

The **HomePileRule** combinator maps the concept number of home card piles (i.e., where the Aces are placed) to the integer value 4. By encoding this concept into a single combinator, the designer has separated concerns which can be reused in other combinators. The **WinRule** combinator produces a Java code fragment that determines whether the game has been won by checking whether all home card piles are full. This combinator depends on having the **Home-PileRule** combinator so it can generate code using the appropriate number of

```
NameRule_type: (freeCell ∩ namerule)
NameRule_term: { box["FreeCell"] }

HomePileRule_type: (freeCell ∩ pilerule ∩ homePile)
HomePileRule_term: { box["4"] }

WinRule_type:        (freeCell ∩ pilerule ∩ homePile) →
                     (freeCell ∩ winrule)

WinRule_term: {
  λ piles. {letbox NumPiles = {piles} in {

    box["
    boolean won = true;
    for (int i = 0; i < " NumPiles "; i++) {
      if (fieldHomePiles[i].count() != 13) {
        won = false;
      }
    }

    if (won) { return true; }
    "]
  }}}
```

Fig. 4. Sample combinators for FreeCell variation

piles. The code resulting from **WinRule** is synthesized from the Java code fragment by replacing the meta-variable *NumPiles* with the Java code fragment, 4. Finally, the **NameRule** combinator maps to a string constant which refers to the name of the top-level class of the plugin implementation.

The power of this approach comes from its ability to assign type information to intermediate code fragments synthesized from combinators. The inhabitation uses this goal query to drive the generation of code resources as required by the FreeCell solitaire variation.

LaunchPad [12] is an Eclipse plugin that extends the FeatureIDE open-source framework for feature-oriented software development (FOSD) [16]. FeatureIDE successfully integrates a number of composition tools (including AHEAD) through a well-documented extensible interface. We wanted to integrate the CLS inhabitation tool and make it easy for developers to use and write their own combinators. First we designed a text-based representation for combinators that would be easier for programmers to use by eliminating the λ syntax that appears in the standard representations of combinators; Fig. 5 shows a sample. In the implementation of the **WinRule** combinator note how the embedded Java code has "<NumPiles>" which will ultimately be replaced by the Java code associated with the meta-variable *NumPiles*. These files are edited within a LaunchPad editor that properly formats the L1-embedded Java code, making it easier for programmers to read. These combinators appear in files that are associated with the individual features. Each intersection type A ∩ B is written textually as [A, B]. A combinator is defined by its type and its implementation.

```
define {
  [freeCell, namerule] NameRule -> FreeCell;
}
define {
  [freeCell, pilerule, homePile] HomePileRule -> 4;
}
type WinRule {
  NumPiles    [alpha.gameType, pilerule, homePile];
              [alpha.gameType, winrule];
}
implementation WinRule {
  boolean won = true;
  for (int i = 0; i < <NumPiles>; i++) {
    if (fieldHomePiles[i].count() != 13) {
      won = false; break;
    }
  }
  if (won) { return true; }
}
```

Fig. 5. Equivalent LaunchPad combinator syntax

One can design an abstract combinator by only defining its type specification in a combinator file; alternatively, it is possible to override the implementation of an existing combinator by providing an implementation of an existing combinator.

Each valid product line member is defined by a configuration which represents a valid subset of the features defined in the feature model, based upon the semantics of the diagram. Table 1 lists three variations - *FreeCell*, *FourteenOut*, and *Narcotic* - and the features that are included in their respective configurations. Upon selecting a configuration file in FeatureIDE, the LaunchPad plugin composes the associated combinator files and constructs the necessary λ combinator specification files which it passes to the CLS tool to synthesize the final code. The code is generated within the src/ source folder in an Eclipse project, which allows programmers to easily include the generated code into their own projects by simply linking to the FeatureIDE project in which the generated code exists.

The journey presented here is far from over. We continue to develop these ideas by eliminating a number of limitations of the approach (Fig. 6):

- The LaunchPad language does not support error/warning detection while being edited. One of the most important contributions of modern IDEs is their ability to parse the code as it is entered into the editor, to detect syntactic as well as semantic errors. *Requirement: To achieve our goal of an industrial-quality tool chain, we will have to ensure the fragments are supported by a syntax-directed editor.*

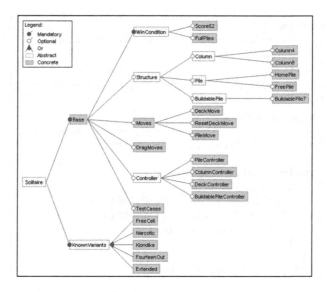

Fig. 6. Solitaire feature model in FeatureIDE

- The embedded Java fragments within the combinators are not reviewed using the same syntax-directed editor provided by Eclipse. While LaunchPad does provide syntax-directed highlighting of keywords, this is not the same thing as detecting errors in the Java fragments. *Requirement: We need type-check capabilities of the underlying embedded Java fragments within the combinators.*
- Compositional patterns within LaunchPad are limited to String concatenation. Ultimately the goal is to embrace a functional language for specifying combinators to enable more advanced processing of embedded code fragments. *Requirement: We need to manipulate object-oriented code fragments using functional capabilities as drawn from a language such as F# or Scala.*

4   Conclusion

This paper offers a personal reflection on successive attempts to develop an approach to construct a product line for solitaire card games. In writing the paper using this chronological structure, it is not possible to properly present related work for each of the iterative attempts. After all, the idea was to document insights learned from applying different approaches to the *exact same application domain* over time. Now that the overall trajectory of this research has stabilized, we can find other researchers with similar aims and approaches. We hope to encourage researchers to reproduce each others' case studies to better be able to compare different approaches.

We are pursuing a research program in which we consider automatically composing prefabricated units of composition from given software repositories, and, rather than specifying synthesis goals from scratch in a universal program logic, we use type structure to capture high-level semantic intentions of the designer.

The greatest impact of this project is it enables designers to encode abstractions and formally define how the abstractions can be composed together. Today designers often rely on a common technique for describing and documenting abstractions, namely, Design Patterns [8]. However, design patterns by themselves can only educate designers in how to structure a specific solution to a problem addressed by that design pattern; they cannot be used as is to synthesize code that applies the design pattern to a given code base. The L2-combinators described in this project go further by giving designers the ability to synthesize software that conforms to the abstractions encoded in the type specifications. This multilingual technique enables software engineers to program using abstractions and synthesize efficient and correct code using an automated process.

References

1. Batory, D., Sarvela, J., Rauschmayer, A.: Scaling stepwise refinement, May 2003
2. Bessai, J., Dudenhefner, A., Düdder, B., Martens, M., Rehof, J.: Combinatory logic synthesizer. In: Margaria, T., Steffen, B. (eds.) ISoLA 2014, Part I. LNCS, vol. 8802, pp. 26–40. Springer, Heidelberg (2014)
3. Butler, G.: Object-Oriented Frameworks Tutorial. In: 18th European Conference on Object-Oriented Programming (ECOOP) (2002)
4. Clements, P., Northrop, L., Lines, S.P.: Practices and Patterns. Addison Wesley, Boston (2002)
5. Hindley, J.R.: Intersection types for combinatory logic. Theoret. Comput. Sci. **100**(2), 303–324 (1992)
6. Düdder, B., Martens, M., Rehof, J.: Staged composition synthesis. In: Shao, Z. (ed.) ESOP 2014 (ETAPS). LNCS, vol. 8410, pp. 67–86. Springer, Heidelberg (2014)
7. Fayad, M., Schmidt, D.: Object-oriented application frameworks. Commun. ACM **40**(10), 32–38 (1997)
8. Gamma, E., Helm, R., Johnson, R., Vlissides, J.: Design Patterns: Elements of Reusable Object-oriented Software. Addison-Wesley, Boston (1995)
9. Garlan, D., Monroe, R., Wile, D.: ACME: an architecture description interchange language. In: Proceedings of CASCON, pp. 169–183. IBM Press (1997)
10. Heineman, G.: An instance-oriented approach to constructing product lines from layers. Technical report, WPI-CS-TR-05-06, Department of CS, WPI, April 2005
11. Heineman, G.T.: Component-based Software Engineering: Putting the Pieces Together. Addison-Wesley Longman Publishing Co., Inc., Boston (2001)
12. Heineman, G.T., Hoxha, A., Düdder, B., Rehof, J.: Towards migrating object-oriented frameworks to enable synthesis of product line members. In: Proceedings of SPLC 2015, pp. 56–60 (2015)
13. Mehta, A., Heineman, G.T.: Evolving legacy system features into fine-grained components. In: Proceedings of the 24th International Conference on Software Engineering, ICSE 2002, pp. 417–427. ACM, New York (2002)
14. Oberhumer, M.: Python Solitaire (2003)
15. Rehof, J., Vardi, M.Y.: Design and Synthesis from Components (Dagstuhl Seminar 14232) (2014)
16. Thüm, T., Kästner, C., Benduhn, F., Meinicke, J., Saake, G., Leich, T.: FeatureIDE: an extensible framework for feature-oriented software development. Sci. Comput. Program. **79**, 70–85 (2014)

Semantic Heterogeneity in the Formal Development of Complex Systems

Semantic Heterogeneity in the Formal Development of Complex Systems: An Introduction

J. Paul Gibson[1](✉), Idir Aït-Sadoune[2], and Marc Pantel[3]

[1] SAMOVAR, Télécom Sud Paris, CNRS, Université Paris Saclay,
9 rue Charles Fourier, 91011 Evry Cedex, Paris, France
paul.gibson@telecom-sudparis.eu
[2] LRI - CentraleSupelec - Université Paris Saclay, Gif sur Yvette, France
idir.aitsadoune@centralesupelec.fr
[3] Institut de Recherche en Informatique de Toulouse, Toulouse, France
marc.pantel@enseeiht.fr

Abstract. Nowadays, the formal development of complex systems (including hardware and/or software) implies the writing, synthesis and analysis of many kind of models on which properties are expressed and then formally verified. These models first provide separation of concerns, but also the appropriate level of abstraction to ease the formal verification. However, the building of such heterogeneous models can introduce gaps and information loss between the various models as elements that are explicit in the whole integrated models are only explicit in some concerns and implicit in others. The whole correct development should thus only be conducted on the whole integrated model whereas separate development is mandatory for scalability of system development. More precisely, parts of these systems can be defined within contexts, imported and/or instantiated. Such contexts usually represent the implicit elements and associated semantics for these systems. Several relevant properties are defined on these implicit parts according to the formal technique being used. When considering these properties in their context with the associated explicit semantics, these properties may be not provable or even can be satisfiable in the limited explicit semantics whereas they would be unsatisfiable in the whole semantics including the implicit part. Therefore, the development activities need to be revisited in order to facilitate handling of both the explicit and implicit semantics.

Keywords: Verification · Contexts · Domains · Implicit · Explicit

The semantic heterogeneity in the formal development of complex systems has many different, yet related forms, e.g.:

- Abstraction — as our models move from the abstract to the concrete — from the *what* to the *how* — there is usually a need for a mix of non-operational and operational semantics [1].

This work was supported by grant ANR-13-INSE-0001 (The IMPEX Project http://impex.gforge.inria.fr) from the Agence Nationale de la Recherche (ANR).

T. Margaria and B. Steffen (Eds.): ISoLA 2016, Part I, LNCS 9952, pp. 321–324, 2016.
DOI: 10.1007/978-3-319-47166-2_22

- Composition — systems are composed with other systems, and such compositions cannot reasonably be expected to be done within a single homogeneous semantic framework. As the number of possible ways in which we may wish to compose different types of systems is increasing, so too increases the importance of being able to model and manage the heterogeneity [2].
- Separation of concerns — complex systems involve many different aspects (data, behavior, safety, performance, security, etc.) which are usually handled in a separated timely manner to provide scalability according to their size and complexity. This leads to heterogeneous models where some parts are explicit and other implicit according the related concern. This can be related to composition where each model does not correspond to a part of the system but to a concern in the system development.
- Reasoning — the language in which one models a system is not usually the same language in which one reasons about the relationship between models, and the correctness of one model with respect to another [3].
- Implicit versus explicit — in every model, the semantics of the language used to establish the meaning of the model are implicit. In order to understand the meaning of any model one must implicitly understand the semantics of the language in which it is expressed. Similarly, in order to validate the model one needs to establish a relationship between the model and the implicit semantics of the real-world domain in which the model has relevance. Each of these 2 implicit semantics must be made explicit and combined in order to achieve a coherent integration. However, each of these implicit semantics has a very different nature. This type of heterogeneity is a major challenge [4].

A previous thematic track — addressing the same issues — introduced some of the first research results concerned with techniques that can be used to manage the heterogeneous nature of formal modeling [5]. In *Modeling and Verifying an Evolving Distributed Control System Using an Event-based Approach* [6] the techniques were concerned with component-based system engineering where it is necessary to be able to compose components whose behavior was expressed using different modeling languages. In *Requirements driven Data Warehouse Design: We can go further* [7] the techniques were based on the use of ontological reasoning mechanisms can used to automatically construct a set of requirements that are coherent and non-conflictual, even when expressed in a variety of modeling languages. Finally, the paper *On Implicit and Explicit Semantics: Integration issues in proof-based development of systems* [8], the techniques were founded on the principle that re-usable domain knowledge should be modelled explicitly using formal ontologies.

In this year's thematic track, we emphasis the heterogeneous nature of complex systems engineering and the need for automated tool support for supporting the techniques that manage the heterogeneity in a formal way. We note that the accepted papers are concerned with theoretical advances, together with pragmatic application of these advances in real-world industrial case studies.

In *On the Use of Domain and System Knowledge Modeling in Goal-Based Event-B Specifications* [9], we see an example of semantic heterogeneity due to the application of several different formalisms in a single system development. The paper combines Goal Oriented Requirement Engineering [10] and the refinement-based Event-B formal method [11] in order to improve the handling of requirements in a formal development. The authors rely on an ontology in order to model part of the requirements usually expressed in natural language [12]. Then the content of the ontology is translated to Event B contexts. The proposal is illustrated with the Landing Gear case study proposed in the ABZ 2014 conference [13].

In *Strengthening MDE and Formal Design Models by references to Domain Ontologies. A Model Annotation Based Approach* [14], we see how we can enrich design models involved in critical systems development in order to integrate heterogeneous domain constraints. The paper proposes to integrate these domain constraints by enhancing design models with references to domain knowledge. The domain knowledge is modelled by means of ontologies and references are built by annotation mechanism linking design models to domains constraints. The key to the technique is the methodological combination of an MDE approach [15] using Eclipse together with a refinement and proof formal process using Event-B [11].

In *Towards Functional Requirements Analytics* [16], the authors present the design of warehouses for Functional Requirements [17]. The authors advocate the use of a pivot model as there can be a huge heterogeneity between the Functional Requirements stakeholders. Then, they apply the usual warehouse methods based on ETL (Extract, Transform, Load) [18]. The proposal relies on the implementation of a proof of concept based on the Oracle RDBMS using SparQL and the QB4OLAP W3C proposal. This proof of concept is based upon the common Course Management System example provided by the Van Der Bilt university.

In *Heterogeneous Semantics and Unifying Theories* [19], the paper illustrates the use of the Unifying Theory of Programming [20] to combine heterogeneous semantics. The paper reports on two core use cases: the introduction of references in the action part of Hoare logic based on separation logic [21]; and the introduction of the theory of design in CSP [22].

References

1. Hazzan, O., Kramer, J.: The role of abstraction in software engineering. In: Companion of the 30th International Conference on Software Engineering, ICSE Companion 2008, pp. 1045–1046. ACM, New York (2008)
2. Baldwin, W.C., Sauser, B.: Modeling the characteristics of system of systems. In: IEEE International Conference on System of Systems Engineering, SoSE 2009, pp. 1–6. IEEE (2009)
3. Adrion, W.R., Branstad, M.A., Cherniavsky, J.C.: Validation, verification, and testing of computer software. ACM Comput. Surv. (CSUR) 14(2), 159–192 (1982)
4. Ait-Ameur, Y., Méry, D.: Making explicit domain knowledge in formal system development. Sci. Comput. Program. 121, 100–127 (2016)

5. Gibson, J.P., Ait-Sadoune, I.: Semantic heterogeneity in the formal development of complex systems: an introduction. In: Margaria, T., Steffen, B. (eds.) ISoLA 2014, Part II. LNCS, vol. 8803, pp. 570–572. Springer, Heidelberg (2014)
6. Attiogbé, C.: Modelling and verifying an evolving distributed control system using an event-based approach. In: Margaria, T., Steffen, B. (eds.) ISoLA 2014, Part II. LNCS, vol. 8803, pp. 573–587. Springer, Heidelberg (2014)
7. Khouri, S., Bellatreche, L., Jean, S., Ait-Ameur, Y.: Requirements driven data warehouse design: we can go further. In: Margaria, T., Steffen, B. (eds.) ISoLA 2014, Part II. LNCS, vol. 8803, pp. 588–603. Springer, Heidelberg (2014)
8. Ait-Ameur, Y., Gibson, J.P., Méry, D.: On implicit and explicit semantics: integration issues in proof-based development of systems. In: Margaria, T., Steffen, B. (eds.) ISoLA 2014, Part II. LNCS, vol. 8803, pp. 604–618. Springer, Heidelberg (2014)
9. Mammar, A., Laleau, R.: On the use of domain and system knowledge modeling in goal-based event-B specifications. In: Margaria, T., Steffen, B. (eds.) ISoLA 2016, Part I, LNCS, vol. 9952, pp. 325–339. Springer, Heidelberg (2016)
10. Van Lamsweerde, A.: Goal-oriented requirements engineering: a guided tour. In: Fifth IEEE International Symposium on Requirements Engineering, Proceedings, pp. 249–262. IEEE (2001)
11. Abrial, J.R.: Modeling in Event-B: System and Software Engineering. Cambridge University Press, Cambridge (2010)
12. Jureta, I., Mylopoulos, J., Faulkner, S.: Revisiting the core ontology and problem in requirements engineering. In: 2008 16th IEEE International Requirements Engineering Conference, pp. 71–80. IEEE (2008)
13. Mammar, A., Laleau, R.: Modeling a landing gear system in event-B. In: Wiels, V., Ait Ameur, Y., Schewe, K.-D., Boniol, F. (eds.) ABZ 2014. CCIS, vol. 433, pp. 80–94. Springer, Heidelberg (2014)
14. Hacid, K., Ait-Ameur, Y.: Strengthening mde and formal design models by references to domain ontologies. A model annotation based approach. In: Margaria, T., Steffen, B. (eds.) ISoLA 2016, Part I, LNCS, vol. 9952, pp. 340–357. Springer, Heidelberg (2016)
15. France, R., Rumpe, B.: Model-driven development of complex software: a research roadmap. In: 2007 Future of Software Engineering, pp. 37–54. IEEE Computer Society (2007)
16. Djilania, Z., Berkani, N., Bellatreche, L.: Towards functional requirements analytics. In: Margaria, T., Steffen, B. (eds.) ISoLA 2016, Part I, LNCS, vol. 9952, pp. 358–373. Springer, Heidelberg (2016)
17. McGinnis, L.: An object oriented and axiomatic theory of warehouse design. In: 12th International Material Handling Research Colloquium, pp. 328–346 (2012)
18. Vassiliadis, P.: A survey of extract-transform-load technology. Int. J. Data Warehous. Min. (IJDWM) 5(3), 1–27 (2009)
19. Woodcock, J., Foster, S.: Heterogeneous semantics and unifying theories. In: Margaria, T., Steffen, B. (eds.) ISoLA 2016, Part I, LNCS, vol. 9952, pp. 374–394. Springer, Heidelberg (2016)
20. Hoare, C.A.R., Jifeng, H.: Unifying Theories of Programming, vol. 14. Prentice Hall, Englewood Cliffs (1998)
21. Reynolds, J.C.: Separation logic: a logic for shared mutable data structures. In: 17th Annual IEEE Symposium on Logic in Computer Science, Proceedings, pp. 55–74. IEEE (2002)
22. Hoare, C.A.R., et al.: Communicating Sequential Processes, vol. 178. Prentice-Hall, Englewood Cliffs (1985)

On the Use of Domain and System Knowledge Modeling in Goal-Based Event-B Specifications

Amel Mammar[1](✉) and Régine Laleau[2]

[1] SAMOVAR, Télécom SudParis CNRS, Université Paris-Saclay, France
amel.mammar@telecom-sudparis.eu
[2] Université Paris-Est, LACL UPEC, IUT Sénart Fontainebleau,
Créteil, France
laleau@u-pec.fr

Abstract. When using formal methods, one of the main difficulties is
to elaborate the initial formal specification from informal descriptions
obtained during the requirements analysis phase. For that purpose, we
propose a goal-based approach in which the building of an initial formal
model (in Event-B) is driven by a goal-oriented requirements engineering
model (SysML/KAOS). In a previous work, we have defined a set of rules to
derive a partial Event-B specification from a goal model. In this paper, we
propose to enhance the goal model in order to obtain a more complete formal specification. First, we advocate the specification of a domain ontology in order to share common understanding of the structure of the different applications of the underlying domain. This is particularly useful
for complex systems to explicit and make clearer the domain knowledge.
For a specific system, a class and an object diagrams are then specified
to detail its components and their relationships. Finally, we describe how
the ontology and the structural model are translated into Event-B. The
proposed approach is illustrated through a landing gear system.

1 Introduction

It is well-known that requirements engineering (RE) is critical in software
and system design. Indeed, a major part of the cost of software and system
development is known to be traceable to the understanding of the application
domain and requirements. Today current industrial practices and tools are not
sufficiently efficient [10]. Furthermore, in the domain of RE for complex embedded systems, a study conducted in industry [21] highlights the main needs
expressed by the practitioners. Among them, we can cite: the need of taking
into account the high complexity of such systems, the need of a better integration of RE with verification and validation techniques to ensure a better quality
of requirements, the need of incorporating domain-specific models in current RE
approaches. In the framework of a research project, called FORMOSE [9], we
address these three challenges by elaborating a formally-grounded, model-based
requirements engineering method for critical complex systems. Indeed, formal
methods have shown their ability to produce such systems for large industrial

© Springer International Publishing AG 2016
T. Margaria and B. Steffen (Eds.): ISoLA 2016, Part I, LNCS 9952, pp. 325–339, 2016.
DOI: 10.1007/978-3-319-47166-2_23

problems [15] and, recently, certification authorities have taken into account (DO178B level C for commercial aeronautics software) the use of formal methods in the new development processes for high critical systems.

However, a serious problem with formal methods is the difficulty of using them. In fact, even if the formal development chain from abstraction via refinement to implementation is well mastered, the major remaining weakness in this chain is that there is no well-defined process to assist designers in the building of the initial formal specification. Most of the time, this initial model is built 'intuitively' from the informal, or sometimes semi-formal, description obtained by the requirements analysis and it requires a high level of competence and a lot of practice. Therefore, it will be difficult to fully understand the correspondence between requirements and initial formal specifications, and the validation of these specifications is very difficult mainly due to: (i) the inability for stakeholders to understand formal models; (ii) the inability for designers to link them with the initial requirements. It can result that an initial formal model may not be a correct realization of the requirements.

In FORMOSE, we explore how to cope with this problem using Goal Oriented Requirements Engineering (GORE) approach [18], and more precisely the SysML/KAOS approach [11], and the Event-B formal method [2]. The main objective is that this combination helps system designers elaborate pertinent abstract Event-B specifications. The proposed approach aims to build abstract Event-B models from GORE goal models.

The first step, described in [17], consists in elaborating a SysML/KAOS goal model representing the functional requirements of a system and then deriving an abstract Event-B specification. Each SysML/KAOS functional goal gives an Event-B event and the structure of the goal model gives the architecture of the Event-B specification. However, there is not enough information provided by the goal model to precisely describe this formal specification. In particular, the description of the structural part of the system that represents its current state is missing. In this paper we present our approach to handle this issue.

Some RE methods, such as KAOS [14] or i* [8], use an object model to describe the structural part of a system. We think that it is also necessary to model domain knowledge, as advocated by [6,7], also called explicit knowledge by [3]. For a long time, it is well-known in RE that domain knowledge is one of the crucial factors to perform high quality requirements elicitation [13]. We suggest to use it also in the requirements specification step. Thus, in our approach, a goal model is enhanced by: (i) *a domain model* to capture domain knowledge. We chose ontologies, more preciseley OWL [12], to model domain knowledge, as they are very commonly used in RE for this purpose [13]. Moreover, ontologies have precise semantics allowing reasoning and are supported by tools. (ii) *a structural model* to describe the current state of the system. We use class diagrams, possibly coupled with object diagrams, that shall conform to the domain model. Finally, the Event-B translation of these models allows to complete the Event-B specification obtained from the goal model.

To illustrate the presented approach, we use the case study proposed by the ABZ'14 conference [5]. It deals with the landing gear system of an aircraft whose objective is to permit a safe extension/retraction of the gear when the aircraft is going to land/fly. Each gear is placed in a landing-gear set equipped with a door that must be open when a gear is extending/retracting and closed when it becomes completely extended/retracted. To make that possible, the aircraft is equipped with a handle that is put *up* (resp. *down*) to make the gear retract (resp. extend).

The remainder of this paper is organized as follows. Section 2 overviews Event-B and SysML/KAOS that are employed in the proposed approach. Sections 3 and 4 detail the approach by illustrating it on the case study. Section 3 concerns domain knowledge modeling with ontology and Event-B and Sect. 4 deals with the modeling of the system structure. We conclude the paper in Sect. 5 with an outline of future work.

2   Background

This section briefly presents the modeling and specification languages used in our approach, that are: Event-B and SysML/KAOS languages.

2.1   Event-B Method

Event-B is the successor of the B method [1] enabling modeling discrete systems using mathematical notations. The complexity of a system is mastered thanks to the refinement concept that allows to gradually introduce the different parts that constitute the system starting from an abstract model to a more concrete one. In this paper, we use a particular variant of the Event-B, called the B system, because our development is achieved under the AtelierB. We use the AtelierB tool since it is the environment chosen by the different partners of the FORMOSE project in which the current work is achieved. A B system specification is made of a set of system and refinement components. In this paper, some components that we call *contexts* permit to describe the static part of the studied system; it consists of constants (user-defined types) together with their properties. These contexts can be seen by other components that model the dynamic part by variables V and a set of events E. The possible values that the variables hold are restricted using an invariant written using a first-order predicate on the state variables. In this paper, we only consider event of the following form: (**SELECT G THEN** *Act* **END**). This event can be executed if it is enabled, i.e. all the conditions G, named guards, prior to its execution hold. Among all enabled events, only one is executed. In this case, substitutions *Act*, called actions, are applied over variables. In this paper, we restrict ourselves to the *becomes equal* substitution, denoted by $(x := e)$. Proof obligations are generated to verify that the execution of each event maintains the invariant.

Refinement is a process of enriching or modifying a model in order to augment the functionality being modeled, or/and explain how some purposes are achieved.

A refinement consists in adding new variables and/or replacing existing variables by new ones. New events can also be introduced to implicitly refine a **skip** event. To be correct, the refinement of an event has to verify the following properties:

- *guard refinement*: the guard of the refined event should be stronger than the guard of the abstract one
- *Simulation*: the effect of the refined action should be stronger than the effect of the abstract one

In the rest of the paper, we use indifferently the terms of "Event-B specification" and "B system specification".

2.2   SysML/KAOS

The SysML/KAOS language is an extension of the SysML requirements language [19] with the most relevant concepts of the KAOS goal model [14]. Several models exist to represent goal oriented requirements such as i* [8], Goal-Based Requirements Analysis Method (GBRAM) [4]. The choice of KAOS is motivated by the following reasons. Firstly, it permits the expression of several models (goal, agent, object, behavioral models) and relationships between them. Secondly, KAOS provides a powerful and extensive set of concepts to specify goal models. This facilitates the design of goal hierarchies with a high level of expressiveness that can be considered at different levels of abstraction. As SysML is an extension of UML, it provides concepts to represent requirements and to relate them to model elements, allowing the definition of traceability links between requirements and system models. However the set of SysML concepts for requirements modeling is not as extensive as in goal models. The objective of the SysML/KAOS language is to take advantage of both models while considering functional and non functional requirements from the earlier development phase. In this paper we focus on functional requirements (For non functional requirements concepts, see [11]).

In SysML/KAOS, a functional goal prescribes intended behaviors where some target condition must sooner or later hold whenever some other condition holds in the current system state (this state is an arbitrary current one). It is denoted as follows: *[TargetCondition From CurrentCondition]*. This notation has the following informal temporal pattern where *CurrentCondition* prefix is optional (said otherwise, it can be true):

[if CurrentCondition then] sooner-or-later TargetCondition.

A goal model is an AND/OR graph where higher-level goals can be refined into lower-level sub-goals, and then, recursively, into low-level sub-goals that lead to the satisfaction of requirements of the system-to-be:

- the goals G_1 and G_2 is a AND-refinement of a goal G, then both goals, $G1$ and $G2$, should be satisfied in order to satisfy the goal G,
- the goals G_1 and G_2 is a OR-refinement of a goal G, then the satisfaction of one of these goals, $G1$ or $G2$, is sufficient to satisfy the goal G.

Figure 1 describes a part of the goal model of the case study, which corresponds to the retraction of the landing gear system. The root goal, called **makeLGRetracted**, is defined as follows:

Functional Goal **makeLGRetracted**
InformalDef: The landing gear system must be retracted.

This goal is AND refined into two sub-goals **putHandleUp** and **makeLSRetracted** defined as follows:

Functional Goal **putHandleUp**
InformalDef: The handle is put Up

Functional Goal **makeLSRetracted**
InformalDef: If the handle is put Up then the landing gear set must be retracted.

2.3   Combining SysML/KAOS and Event-B

The complete approach of mapping a SysML/KAOS model into an Event-B specification is described in [17], including a justification of the choices. To summarize, the transformation consists in expressing each SysML/KAOS goal as an Event-B event, where: (i) the ***CurrentCondition*** of this goal is considered as the guard; (ii) the action part encapsulates the ***TargetCondition*** of this goal.

Let us consider Goal **makeLGRetracted** in Fig. 1. Figure 2 is its Event-B specification. As we can see, with the information existing in the goal model, we can obtain just a partial Event-B specification. Up to now, the variables and their types, the invariants and the initialization part are manually completed by the designer. The purpose of the next sections is to show how it is possible to obtain them more systematically. Furthermore, once these parts completed, it is possible to formally specify the content of the events (guard and actions).

Then, we use the Event-B refinement relation and additional custombuilt proof obligations to derive all the subgoals of the system by means

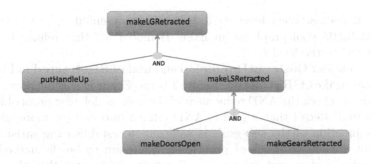

Fig. 1. The goal model of the landing gear system

```
SYSTEM
    LandingGear

VARIABLES

INVARIANT

INITIALISATION

EVENTS
MakeLGRetracted=
BEGIN
    //The landing gear system must be retracted
END
END
```

Fig. 2. Translation of the root goal

```
REFINEMENT
    LandingGearSet
REFINES
    LandingGear

ABSTRACT_VARIABLES

INVARIANT

INITIALISATION

EVENTS
    putHandleUp=
    BEGIN
        // The handle is put Up
    END;

    makeLSRetracted=
    SELECT
        // The handle is put Up
    THEN
        // The landing gear set must be retracted
    END
END
```

Fig. 3. First refinement

of Event-B events. Each level $i(i \in [1..n])$ is represented in the hierarchy of the SysML/KAOS goal graph as an Event-B model M_i that refines the model M_{i-1} related to the level $i - 1$.

Let us consider Goals **putHandleUp** and **makeLSRetracted** in Fig. 1 that refine Goal **makeLGRetracted**. Figure 3 is the Event-B specification.

In order to check the AND refinement of the goal model, new proof obligations are generated. Recall that a goal is AND refined into two (or more) sub-goals if the conjunction of the sub-goals is sufficient to establish the satisfaction of the parent goal. Two kinds of proof obligations are to be discharged: guard strengthening and correct refinement. The first one ensures that the concrete guard of each sub-goal is stronger than the abstract guard of the parent goal. The second kind ensures that the interleaving of the concrete events transforms the concrete variables in a way which does not contradict the abstract event. A formal argumentation of the identified proof obligations is detailed in [16]. Illustrating this on the case study gives the following proof obligations:

$$putHandleUp\text{-}Guard \Rightarrow makeLGRetracted\text{-}Guard$$
$$makeLSRetracted\text{-}Guard \Rightarrow makeLGRetracted\text{-}Guard$$
$$putHandleUp\text{-}PostCondition \land makeLSRetracted\text{-}PostCondition$$
$$\Rightarrow makeLGRetracted\text{-}PostCondition$$

3   Domain Knowledge Modeling

3.1   Modeling with ontology

As stated before, an ontology is used to model the main concepts manipulated in a specific domain and their relationships. Building an ontology is based on the expert knowledge of the domain who are capable of selecting the right concepts that are relevant to the actual systems of the domain. In fact, the domain can be very large with a huge number of entities where some of them, even if named differently, represent the same concepts (called synonyms), or also some entities can be subset of others, etc.

Regarding the case study, the following concepts have been selected:

1. *Gear*: it represents the main concept of the system we are studying. A gear can be extended or retracted.
2. *Door*: it is used to maintain a gear in a given position (extended/retracted). A door can be open or closed.
3. *Landing set*: it represents each couple of a gear and its associated door. A landing set can be extended or retracted
4. *Handle*: it is the device manipulated by the pilot to make the gears retract/extend. A handle can be up or down
5. *Landing gear*: it represents any number of landing sets. A landing gear can be extended or retracted

Figure 4 depicts the OWL ontology that captures the domain knowledge of landing gear systems where:

1. classes are represented by rectangles tagged with circles: *LandingGear, LandingSet, Door, Gear, HandleStates*, etc.
2. data types are represented by classes with individuals denoting the possible values of an object of this class: : *up* and *down* for *HandleStates*, etc.
3. arrows between classes, called *object properties*, denote the relations that exist between their respective individuals. These properties are named and can have multiplicities. Nevertheless, such information cannot be displayed on the graphical representation of the ontology.

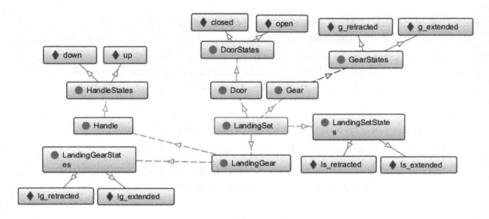

Fig. 4. The landing gear ontology

Let us remark that at this stage no constraints is put on the object properties relating two given classes. In fact, we want our ontology be as general as possible in order to be reused for several system types. For instance, the same ontology can be used for landing gear system with any number of landing sets and/or handle, etc. Such specific constraints will be fixed in a next step.

3.2   Event-B Representation of an Ontology

In this section, we illustrate how an OWL ontology is mapped into an Event-B system specification. As an ontology can be seen as defining the different data types of a domain, we suggest to translate it as a *context* component containing the following elements:

1. each class Cl is mapped into an abstract set S_{Cl} that represents the set of all possible instances of the class.
2. each class Cl with individuals is mapped into an enumerated set containing these individuals.
3. each object property, relating two classes Cl_1 and Cl_2, is modeled as a constant. This constant is defined as a relation between the abstract sets S_{Cl1} and S_{Cl2}. The domain and the range of this relation are conform to the direction of the corresponding arrow.

Figure 5 depicts the Event-B specification we generate from the ontology of Fig. 4. We can remark that this approach is close to the work presented in [3] where the authors advocated the use of ontologies with formal models for capturing domain knowledge during the design of complex systems. It consists in deriving specific types from domain ontologies to enrich Event-B formal specifications. However, it is only presented through an example and no guidelines or rules are defined to facilitate its use.

```
SYSTEM
    LGOntology
SETS
    LandingGear; LandingSet; Handle; Door; Gear;
    DoorStates={open,closed};
    GearStates={g_extended,g_retracted};
    HandleStates={up, down};
    LandingGearStates={lg_extended, lg_retracted};
    LandingSetStates={ls_extended, ls_retracted}
CONSTANTS
    doorState, gearState, handleState, doorOfLS,
    gearOfLS, handelOfLG, landingGearOfLS,
    landingGearState,landingSetState
PROPERTIES
  doorOfLS= LandingSet ↔ Door ∧
  gearOfLS=LandingSet ↔ Gear ∧
  doorState= Door ↔ DoorStates ∧
  gearState= Gear ↔ GearStates ∧
  handleState= Handle ↔ HandleStates ∧
  handelOfLG= LandingGear ↔ Handle ∧
  landingGearOfLS=LandingSet ↔ LandingGear  ∧
  landingGearState=LandingGear ↔ LandingGearStates ∧
  landingSetState=LandingSet ↔ LandingSetStates
END
```

Fig. 5. Event-B translation of an ontology

4   Modeling a Specific System

Once the ontology of a domain is specified, the next step consists in modeling a specific system of the domain by fixing the multiplicities of the relations and naming the different elements that model the current state of the system to be built. This is achieved through a class and an object diagrams.

4.1   Class and Object Diagrams

A class diagram is designed to make more specific the different relationships in terms of multiplicity, fixed/variables elements. As noticed before, an ontology does not specify how much instances of a given class may be attached to an other instance. Indeed, the use of a logical formula would make the mapping into Event-B more difficult. Moreover, we have to know which characteristics of an instance should be considered as variable/fixed, etc. This is why, we suggest to use a UML class diagram for that purpose. Figure 6 is the class diagram associated with the ontology of Fig. 4. This class diagram must conform to the ontology in the following way:

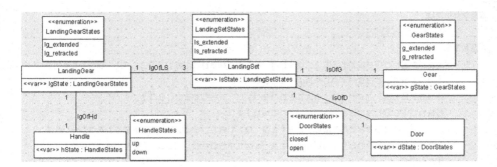

Fig. 6. The class diagram of the landing gear

- both diagrams contain the same classes where the classes with individuals are represented by enumeration since they denote data types. For instance, an enumeration class *LandingGearStates* is defined with two possible values *lg_extended* and *lg_retracted*.
- the link between a class *A* and a data type *B* is modeled by an attribute, of type *B*, defined in class *A*. For instance, the attribute *lgState*, of type *LandingGearStates*, is defined in the class *LandingGear*.
- the link between two classes are modeled by associations for which multiplicities are specified. For the landing gear system that we consider:
  - each landing gear is composed of 3 landing sets; each landing set belongs to a single landing gear;
  - each landing gear is composed of a single handle; each handle belongs to a single landing gear;
  - each landing set is composed of a single gear (resp. door); each gear (resp. door) belongs to a single landing set.
- a stereotype <<*var*>> may be attached to an element (an attribute, a class or an association) to specify that its value is variable. According to Fig. 6, the state of a door is variable, thus an event may change its value.

When the components of the studied system are fixed and can be enumerated, they can be represented in an object diagram which should conform to the constraints of the associated class diagram. Figure 7 depicts the structure of the specific landing gear system composed of three landing sets, a single handle, etc. The initial values of the attributes of each object are specified.

4.2 Completing the Event-B Specification with Elements from Class and Object Diagrams

The generation of a B specification from the class and the object diagrams is driven by the structure of the goal model. In fact, we gradually translate class and object diagrams according to the objects used by each decomposition level of the goal model. Thus, a first step, prior to the Event-B translation, consists in specifying for each goal which objects are required. Figure 8 shows the results

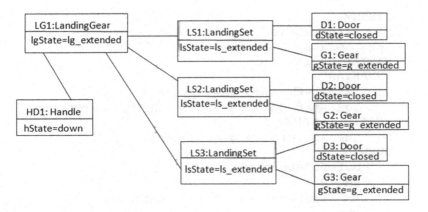

Fig. 7. The object diagram of the landing gear

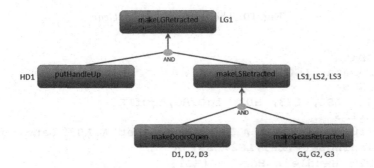

Fig. 8. Annotating the goal model with the relevant objects

```
SYSTEM
    LGData
SEES LGOntology
CONSTANTS LG1
PROPERTIES
    LG1∈ LandingGear ∧ LandingGear={LG1}
END
```

Fig. 9. The context *LGData*

of this step on the goal model and the object diagram of the running case study
where, for instance, the high level goal **makeLGRetracted** refers to the single
object *LG1*, whereas the goals **makeLSRetracted** and **putHandleUp** refer to
the objects *HD1, LS1, LS2, LS3*.

Recall that the Event-B specification generated in Sect. 2.3 is not complete
but only gives the structure of the Event-B components. The goal of this section
is to complete it by generating the variables, the invariant and the initializa-

```
SYSTEM
    LandingGear
SEES LGData, LGOntology
VARIABLES lgState
INVARIANT
    lgState∈ landingGearState ∧
    lgState∈ LandingGear → LandingGearStates
INITIALISATION
    lgState:={LG1↦lg_extended}
EVENTS
    makeLGRetracted=
    BEGIN
        lgState:={LG1↦lg_retracted}
    END
END
```

Fig. 10. The machine *LandingGear*

```
SYSTEM
    LSData
SEES LGData, LGOntology
CONSTANTS
    LS1, LS2, LS3, HD1, lgOfHd,lgOfLS
PROPERTIES
    LS1∈ LandingSet ∧ LS2∈LandingSet ∧ LS3∈LandingSet ∧
    LandingSet={LS1,LS2,LS3} ∧
    HD1∈ Handle ∧ Handle={HD1} ∧
    lgOfHd ∈ handelOfLG ∧
    lgOfHd ∈ LandingGear ↠ Handle ∧
    lgOfHd = {LG1 ↦HD1} ∧
    lgOfLS∈ landingGearOfLS ∧
    lgOfLS∈LandingSet→LandingGear ∧
    ∀lg.(lg∈ LandingGear ⇒ card(lgOfLS⁻¹[{lg}])=3)
END
```

Fig. 11. The context *LSData*

tion. We start by the high level goal **makeLGRetracted** and its associated component **LandingGear**:

– a new context system is created to declare, as constants, objects used by the goal **makeLGRetracted** ($LG1$) but also the invariable part of the class diagram related to these objects. This context sees the context $LGOntology$ (See Fig. 9).
– the clause *Variables* of the machine *LandingGear* contains the variable parts of the class diagram related to the object $LG1$, that is the attribute $lgState$ that is initialized to $lg\_extended$ (See Fig. 10). Each variable is concerned with two invariants: the first one expresses that the variable belongs to a given type,

```
ABSTRACT_VARIABLES
    lgState, hState, lsState
INVARIANT
    hState∈ handleState ∧
    hState∈ Handle → HandleStates ∧
    lsState∈ landingSetState ∧
    lsState∈ LandingSet → LandingSetStates
INITIALISATION
    lgState := { LG1 ↦ lg_extended }  ||
    hState:= {HD1↦down} ||
    lsState:={LS1↦ls_extended, LS2↦ls_extended,
                                    LS3↦ls_extended}
EVENTS
    putHandleUp=
    BEGIN
        hState:= {HD1↦up}
    END;
    makeLSRetracted=
    SELECT (hState(lgOfHd(LG1))=up) THEN
        lsState:=lsState ◁ (lgOfLS⁻¹[{LG1}]*{ls_retracted})
    END
END
```

Fig. 12. The refinement component *LandingGearSet*

the second translates the multiplicity constraints. In fact, each attribute is monovalued.
– the body of the event, corresponding to each goal, is completed by hand (See Fig. 10).

The first refinement level defines two goals **putHandleUp** and **makeLSRetracted** that refer to the objects *HD1, LS1, LS2* and *LS3*. Thus we complete the specification of the refinement component *LandingGearSet* as follows:

– a new context system is created to declare, as constants, objects used by the goals **putHandleUp** and **makeLSRetracted** (*HD1, LS1, LS2* and *LS3*) but also the invariable part of the class diagram related to these objects (*lgOfLS* association). This context sees both contexts *LGOntology* and *LGData* (See Fig. 11). Generated automatically, this context translates all the multiplicity constraints of the class diagram as a property.
– As before, the clause *Variables* of the refinement *LandingGearSet* is completed with the variable parts of the class diagram related to the objects *HD1, LS1, LS2* and *LS3*, that are the attributes *hState* and *lsState* initialized to *down* and *ls_extended* respectively (See Fig. 12). The bodies of the sub goals **putHandleUp** and **makeLSRetracted** are completed by hand.

5 Conclusion

This paper presents an approach for the formal development of complex systems by combining the goal-oriented requirements engineering language (SysML/KAOS) and the Event-B formal language. The paper particularly answers the problem of building an initial formal specification (Event-B in that case) by driving it from a `SysML/KAOS` model augmented by an ontology to explicit and share common understanding of the domain knowledge but also a class and an object diagrams to detail the structure of a specific application of such a domain. Basically, the approach consists of a set of rules to translate these different models into an Event-B specification.

A work in progress consists in integrating the work presented here under the `Openflexo` [20] framework. This open source and generic collaborative platform is based on the *model federation* approach that provides the means to integrate heterogeneous models conforming to different paradigms. This is particularly useful to ensure traceability between these models and is a meaningful support for system maintenance and evolution. Future work also includes the formal verification of some useful properties like equivalence, expressed on ontologies, using the provers associated to Event-B.

Acknowledgment. The work in this paper is supported by the FORMOSE project ANR-14-CE28-0009 funded by the French ANR (National Research Agency).

References

1. Abrial, J.-R.: The B-Book, Assigning Programs to Meanings. Cambridge University Press, Cambridge (2005)
2. Abrial, J.R.: Modeling in Event-B: System and Software Engineering. Cambridge University Press, Cambridge (2010)
3. Aït Ameur, Y., Méry, D.: Making explicit domain knowledge in formal system development. Sci. Comput. Program. **121**, 100–127 (2016)
4. Anton, A.I.: Goal-based requirements analysis. In: Proceedings of International Conference on Requirements Engineering (1996)
5. Boniol, F., Wiels, V.: The landing gear system case study. In: Boniol, F., Wiels, V., Ait Ameur, Y., Schewe, K.-D. (eds.) ABZ 2014. CCIS, vol. 433, pp. 1–18. Springer, Heidelberg (2014)
6. Bjørner, D.: Software Engineering 3 - Domains, Requirements, and Software Design. Texts in Theoretical Computer Science. An EATCS Series. Springer, Heidelberg (2006)
7. Broy, M.: Domain modeling and domain engineering : key tasks in requirements engineering. In: Munch, J., Schmid, K. (eds.) Perspectives on the Future of Software Engineering, pp. 15–30. Springer, Heidelberg (2013)
8. Chung, L., Nixon, B., Yu, E., Mylopoulos, J.: Non-functional Requirements in Software Engineering. Kluwer Academic, Boston (2000)
9. FORMOSE Project: ANR-14-CE28-0009. http://formose.lacl.fr/
10. Fricker, S., Grau, R., Zwingli, A.: Requirements engineering: best practice. In: Fricker, S., Thummler, C., Gavras, A. (eds.) Requirements Engineering for Digital Health. Springer, Heidelberg (2014)
11. Gnaho, C., Semmak, F., Laleau, R.: Modeling the impact of non-functional requirements on functional requirements. In: Parsons, J., Chiu, D. (eds.) ER Workshops 2013. LNCS, vol. 8697, pp. 59–67. Springer, Heidelberg (2014)

12. Hitzler, P., Krotzsch, M., Parsia, B., Patel-Schneider, P.F., Rudolph, S. (eds.): OWL 2 Web Ontology Language: Primer, W3C Recommendation (2009). http:// www.w3.org/TR/owl2-primer
13. Kaiya, H., Saeki, M.: Using domain ontology as domain knowledge for requirements elicitation. In: 14th IEEE International Conference on Requirements Engineering (2006)
14. van Lamsweerde, A.: Requirements Engineering: From System Goals to UML Models to Software Specifications. Wiley, Hoboken (2009)
15. Lecomte, T.: Applying a formal method in industry: a 15-year trajectory. In: Alpuente, M., Cook, B., Joubert, C. (eds.) FMICS 2009. LNCS, vol. 5825, pp. 26–34. Springer, Heidelberg (2009)
16. Matoussi, A., Gervais, F., Laleau, R.: An Event-B formalization of KAOS goal refinement patterns. LACL, University of Paris-Est, Technical report TRLACL-2010-1 (2010). http://lacl.univ-paris12.fr/Rapports/TR/TR-LACL-2010-1.pdf
17. Matoussi, A., Gervais, F., Laleau, R.: A goal-based approach to guide the design of an abstract Event-B specification. In: 16th IEEE International Conference on Engineering of Complex Computer Systems (2011)
18. Nuseibeh, B., Easterbrook, S.: Requirements engineering: a roadmapp. In: 22nd ACM International Conference on Software Engineering. The Future of Software Engineering (2000)
19. OMG. SysML Specification. v1.3, 12 June 2012. http://www.sysml.org/docs/specs/OMGSysML-v1.3-12-06-02.pdf
20. Openflexo project. http://www.openflexo.org
21. Sikora, E., Tenbergen, B., Pohl, K.: Industry needs and research directions in requirements engineering for embedded systems. Requir. Eng. 17(1), 57–78 (2012)

Strengthening MDE and Formal Design Models by References to Domain Ontologies. A Model Annotation Based Approach

Kahina Hacid[(✉)] and Yamine Ait-Ameur

Université de Toulouse, INP, IRIT Institut de Recherche
en Informatique de Toulouse, Toulouse, France
{kahina.hacid,yamine}@enseeiht.fr

Abstract. Critical systems are running in heterogeneous domains. This heterogeneity is rarely considered explicitly when describing and validating processes. Handling explicitly such domain knowledge increases design models robustness due to the expression and validation of new properties mined from the domain models. This paper proposes a stepwise approach to enrich design models describing complex information systems with domain knowledge. We use ontologies to model such domain knowledge. Design models are annotated by references to domain ontologies. The resulting annotated models are checked. It becomes possible to verify domain-related properties and obtain strengthened models. The approach is deployed for two design model development approaches: a Model Driven Engineering (MDE) approach and a correct by construction formal modeling one based on refinement and proof using Event-B method. A case study illustrates both approaches (This work is partially supported by the French ANR-IMPEX project.).

Keywords: Domain ontologies · Model annotation · Property verification · MDE · Proof and refinement · Event-B

1 Introduction

As part of the system engineering and complex system design, the models designed by engineers are placed at the center of the development process of the understudied system. Engineers use them to describe, reason, analyse and verify systems operating in different environments, domains and contexts. In addition, these models correspond to partial views of the studied system (e.g. functional, real-time, energy, mechanics, reliability, architecture, etc.). This leads to the production of several heterogeneous models corresponding to the same system which we qualify as *"design models"*.

In this context, the most important heterogeneity factors, in addition to the modeling languages, are those related to information, knowledge and assumptions of the underlying studied domain (environment and context of implementation and execution of designed systems). Domain knowledge information is usually not explicitly handled and therefore not included in the models associated to the

© Springer International Publishing AG 2016
T. Margaria and B. Steffen (Eds.): ISoLA 2016, Part I, LNCS 9952, pp. 340–357, 2016.
DOI: 10.1007/978-3-319-47166-2_24

systems under design that may be critical systems. In fact, although these models are developed in accordance with the standards and good practices, some knowledge, required for model interpretation and validation, remain implicit. As a consequence, a system may be considered as correct with respect to the initial requirements but, it can miss some of its relevant properties if the information related to its application domain are not black handled by the modeling activity. Therefore, the verification and validation activities are partially covered since domain requirements and constraints are themselves partially included in the designed models. Handling domain knowledge and properties requires the availability of (1) models for such knowledge and properties and (2) of a relationship to link both design models and domain knowledge models. Ontologies are good candidates for describing such domain knowledge. In particular, they are well suited for the characterization of engineering domains.

In order to handle domain knowledge in design models, our approach advocates (1) the use of conceptual ontologies to model and make explicit the domain knowledge and properties. These ontologies are designed from domain concepts. They represent the basic concepts of a domain together with their relationships and properties. Then, (2) we propose a reasoned, based on model annotation, approach to integrate knowledge mined from the studied application domain to the design models.

The objective of this paper is to increase the quality of engineering models by handling new hypotheses and properties entailed by making explicit the engineering knowledge.

Our proposal consists in annotating models by explicit references to ontologies. We propose a four-steps methodology. First, ontologies are used to clarify and formalize domain knowledge concepts, relationships and constraints. Then, the specific defined design models produced from given requirements and specifications are annotated by references to ontologies. These annotations link design models concepts with the corresponding ontology concepts. These ontology concepts offer an explicit semantics to the design model concepts. As a consequence, new design models overloaded by explicit references to ontologies are obtained. It becomes possible to express and verify new domain related properties on the obtained annotated design models.

This paper is structured as follows. Section 2 presents a didactic case study illustrating our approach. Section 3 gives a global definition of domain ontologies. Our approach for strengthening models through an annotation based method is presented in Sect. 4. Sections 5 and 6 give details of the implementation within MDE and a correct-by-construction approaches. Section 7 overviews different approaches promoted for annotation and semantic enrichment of models. A conclusion ends this paper and identifies some research directions.

2   A Case Study

In order to illustrate our proposal, we have chosen a didactic case study describing a simple information system. This information system results from requirements and is described through a set of concepts, actions and constraints as it is the case for applications in the engineering domain. The defined case study deals with the management of students diplomas and registration in the European higher education system. This system offers two kinds of curricula: first the Bachelor (Licence), Master and Phd, LMD for short, and second the Engineer curriculum. Each diploma of the LMD curricula corresponds to a given level: Bachelor/ Licence (high school degree + 6 semesters/180 ECTS credits), Master (Bachelor + 4 semesters/120 credits) and PhD (Master + 180 credits). Engineer curricula offers the engineer diploma five years after high school degree. Both Master and Engineer diplomas are obtained five years after high school degree.

2.1   Additional Requirements for Students Registration

In the studied information system, students register to prepare their next expected diploma. This registration action takes into account the last hold academic degree (or last diploma) as a pre-requisite to register for the next diploma. Constraints on the registration action require that the information system does not allow a student to register for a new diploma if he/she does not have the necessary qualifications. Therefore, the designed information system must check the logical sequence of obtained diplomas before allowing a student to register. For example, Phd degree registration is authorized only if the last obtained degree corresponds to a Master degree. The studied information system **prescribes** the necessary conditions for registering students for preparing diplomas.

2.2   The Domain Knowledge for Diplomas

Diplomas and their characteristics represent a central knowledge for the previously defined case study (but also for other possible applications). A knowledge model to **describe** the diploma knowledge through diplomas characteristics, rules and constraints can be defined as an ontology. This ontology shall model the whole concepts, properties and constraints associated to the **description** of diplomas. It shall cover the diplomas descriptions beyond their usage in the previously described information system, independently of any context of use. Several candidate ontologies are possible. We shall use a consensual ontology for this purpose. Reaching consensual agreements is out of scope of this paper. This activity is usually carried out by standards or users communities.

3   Domain Ontologies as Models for Domain Knowledge

Gruber defines an ontology as *an explicit specification of a conceptualization* [1]. In our work, a domain ontology is considered as a *formal and consensual dictionary of categories and properties of entities of a domain and the relationships that hold among them* [2]. In this definition, entity represents any concept belonging to the studied domain. The term dictionary emphasizes that any entity and any kind of domain relationship described in the domain ontology may be referenced directly by a symbol (URI i.e. unique resource identifier). This referencing mechanism is the ground model for the annotation process. An ontology modeling language is required to describe such ontologies. Several ontology modeling languages have been developed so far. OWL[1] [3], PLIB [4,5], RDFS [6] are some examples of such languages. They describe ontology entities using different modeling artifacts like class hierarchies, properties, relationships, instances and individuals, constraints, etc. According to [2], a domain ontology is a domain conceptualization that shall obey to the three fundamental criteria: being formal, consensual and offering references capabilities.

1. Formal. An ontology is a conceptualization based on a formal theory which allows to check consistency properties and to perform some automatic reasoning over the ontology-defined concepts and individuals.

2. Consensual. An ontology is a conceptualization agreed upon by a community larger than the members involved in one particular application development (one design model). Ontology standards are good supports for such agreements.

3. Capability to be Referenced. Each ontological concept is associated with an identifier or URI. References to this concept becomes possible, using this identifier, from any environment, independently of the particular ontology where this concept was defined.

One other important characteristic is related to the design process. In the case of the engineering domain, ontologies are built from canonical (primitive) concepts, then non canonical (derived) concepts are defined from canonical ones by composition of derivation operators (restriction, union, intersection, algebraic operators, etc.) available in the ontology modeling language. Note that terms are associated to each concept. In this paper, we do not address the ontology design process, we suppose that ontologies already exist.

This section is voluntarily made concise. The literature related to ontology engineering is full of definitions, approaches, work, tools, applications etc. In this section we just reviewed some basic definitions and characteristics of ontologies that are relevant to set up our proposal described in the remaining sections.

4 Strengthening Design Models Using Domain Models: An Annotation Based Approach

The work presented in this paper addresses the case of design models described in an engineering context, where structured models are designed within specific design languages being either semi-formal or formal modeling languages. By strengthening design models, we mean enriching these models with relevant properties mined from domain knowledge models expressed by ontologies. Annotation based techniques are set up in order to link design models to ontologies. A four-steps methodology is proposed for this purpose.

4.1 A Stepwise Methodology

Our approach advocates the exploitation of domain knowledge, carried out by conceptual ontologies, in design models. This approach is stepwise, it is made of different steps. Figure 1 shows the overall schema of the approach.

---

[1] http://www.w3.org/2001/sw/wiki/OWL.

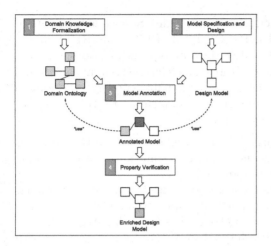

Fig. 1. A four steps methodology for handling domain knowledge in models.

1. Domain Knowledge Formalization. This step consists in making explicit the domain knowledge with a formalized knowledge model. So, information of the domain (concepts, links between these concepts, properties or these concepts and rules and constraints) are explicitly described in a knowledge model.

Formal ontologies are used for this purpose. The choice of this modelling language depends on the kind of reasoning to be performed. Note that this ontology shall be described independently of any context of use. It may also be built from existing ontologies (e.g. standard ontologies).

2. Model Specification and Design. Specific design models corresponding to a given specification are defined. They are formalized within a specific modelling language supporting different analysis, classically performed at the design modelling level.

3. Model Annotation. In this step, the relationships between design model entities and the corresponding knowledge concepts are made explicit. They correspond to model annotation and these relationships are themselves described with a modelling language.

4. Properties Verification. The annotated model obtained at the previous step is enriched by domain properties borrowed from the ontology. The annotated model is analysed to determine whether, on the one hand, the properties and/or the constraints expressed on the annotated model are still valid and, on the other, new properties entailed by the annotation are valid.

Finally, a new design model enriched with new domain information is obtained. Verification and validation of this model (step 4) are required to check if the former properties and/or domain ones, resulting from annotation still hold.

4.2   Some Remarks

The languages used to model ontologies, design models and annotation relationships may differ, semantic alignment between these modeling languages may be required. This topic is out of the scope of this paper, we consider that these languages have the same ground semantics. A single and shared modeling language for the description of both ontologies, design models and annotations is used in this work. Furthermore, the engineering application domain uses modeling languages with classical semantics using closed world assumption (CWA) [7].

The annotation step (step 3) described above requires the definition of annotation mechanisms. Different kinds of annotation mechanisms can be set up (inheritance, partial inheritance and algebraic relationships) [8,9]. The details and choice of the right mechanism are also out of the scope of this paper.

Next two sections show the deployment of this methodology on two different modeling techniques. The first one is based on model driven approaches where constraint checking is performed and the second one is based on a refinement and proof formal modeling technique with the Event-B method.

5   First Deployment: Integration in a Model Based Development

We show below how the proposed stepwise methodology can be deployed in an MDE setting.

5.1   Model Driven Engineering (MDE) Based Developments

MDE brought several significant improvements to the development cycle of complex systems allowing system developers to focus on more abstract levels than classical programming level. MDE is a form of generative engineering [10] in which all or part of an information system is generated from models. A system can be described by several models corresponding to several views or abstraction levels. These models are often described using either graphical or textual notations supported by semi-formal modeling languages. These languages support the description and representation of both structural, descriptive and behavioral aspects of a system. The capability to define constraints that limit the interpretation domain of models is offered using constraints definition languages. In this context, UML [11], the MOF [12] and OCL [13] play the role of standard, they are widely and commonly used by the MDE community.

Moreover, MDE handles models at different development stages of a system development life-cycle. MDE offers several techniques to automate different development steps. Indeed, model operationalization for code generation, documentation and testing, validation, verification, implementation, model analysis are available. These techniques use the capability to transform source models either to other target models in order to get benefits from the available analysis techniques offered by the target modeling technique or to source code in a given language. Transformations are defined by means of transformation rules describing the correspondence between the entities in the source model and those of the target model. This transformation process is automated as much as possible by means of processing programs, which are in most cases developed in general purpose languages (e.g. Java) or in dedicated transformation modeling languages (e.g. ATL[2], Kermeta[3], QVT [14]). In this work, MDE techniques are set up. Meta-models of each manipulated models (ontologies, design models and annotations) are defined in order to build an annotation model in an uniform setting, and ease the prototyping. We have implemented this approach using model

---

[2] ATLAS Transformation Language: http://www.eclipse.org/atl/.

[3] Kermeta: http://www.kermeta.org/.

driven engineering techniques with the Eclipse modeling Framework (EMF)[4]. The Ecore meta-model being the modeling language.

5.2 Step 1. Domain Knowledge Formalization

The deployment of our methodology requires, in its first step, the availability of an ontology formalizing the domain knowledge. The model of the ontology is designed to integrate all the relevant properties of the domain, including its constraints.

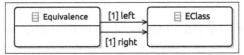

Fig. 2. The *Equivalence* Relationship.

Concepts and properties are modeled as classes and attributes of the ontology and the ontological constraints are added as OCL constraints. The whole ontological relationships like Equivalence, restriction, etc. are also expressed. As illustration, Fig. 2 gives the definition of the equivalence relationship as a class at the meta-modeling level.

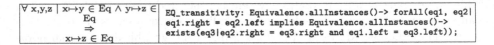

Fig. 3. Equivalence relationship: transitivity property expressed OCL.

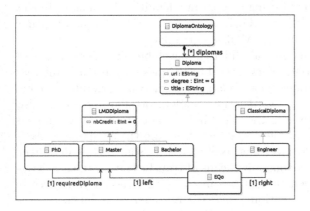

Fig. 4. The *Diplomas* ontology.

The properties related to *symmetry, reflexivity and transitivity* of the equivalence relationship are formalized as OCL constraints. For example, the formalization of transitivity property is given in Fig. 3.

The defined ontology for diplomas is depicted on Fig. 4. Diplomas and their characteristics represent a central knowledge for the previously defined case study (but for other possible applications as well). A model to *describe* the diploma knowledge through diplomas characteristics, rules and constraints defines an ontology. It represents a shared knowledge model that can be used beyond the described application. The defined ontology contains a set of inter-related classes and relevant properties as follows.

---

[4] Eclipse modeling framework: https://www.eclipse.org/modeling/emf/.

- A subsumption relationship (represented by the *is_a* relationship on Fig. 4) is used to define hierarchies between categories of diplomas. *LMDDiploma* and *ClassicalDiploma* describe respectively the *Bachelor, Master* and *PhD* diplomas and other diplomas (e.g. *Engineer*).

- Several descriptive properties, like *title, degree, uri* of the *Diploma* class describe the name, the uri and the level of a given diploma and *nbCredit* defines the credit number required for each diploma.

- An ontological constraint on the model states that *Master* is equivalent to *Engineer*. It is written in the ontology modeling language as *EQ_o(Master, Engineer)* where *EQ_o* is an instance of the *Equivalent_Class* of the ontology meta-model.

In the ontology, this constraint is represented by an *equivalent* class linking the *left: Master* and *right: Engineer* classes of the same ontology. Another constraint defined as *thesisRequirement* carried by the *requiredDiploma* relationship *requiredDiplom_i* property) is added to assert that any master (or any equivalent diploma) is required to prepare a PhD.

5.3   Step 2. Model Specification and Design

The design models are defined by the designer according to a given specification. Several design models corresponding to particular designs for a problem requirement may be produced. The designed models include specific design constraints expressed using OCL [13].

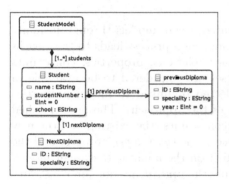

Fig. 5. Engineering student model.

Figure 5 depicts one possible UML class diagram describing a part of the information system related to the management of students. Obviously, other models can be defined as a solution for the problem requirements. In this model, a student holds a diploma (degree) represented by the last graduation diploma he obtained (*previousDiploma* relationship). A student, modeled by the *Student* class with the properties *name, studentNumber* and *school*, representing his name, his student number and his school. The *PreviousDiploma* class describes the last diploma hold by a student, with *speciality, year* and *iD* properties for the chosen speciality, a year of graduation and the type of diploma (*m, e, p* and *b* for master, engineer, Phd and Bachelor respectively). Last, the *NextDiploma* class describes the next diploma a student intends to prepare. Moreover, a constraint named *phdInscription* on the student *nextDiploma* is defined. It asserts that a student registering for a PhD diploma needs to hold a master diploma to be allowed to register for a PhD. It represents a model invariant and it is defined by the OCL constraint of Fig. 6.

Student.nextDiploma.iD = "p" ⇒ Student.previousDiploma.iD = "m"	phdInscritpion: self.NextDiploma.iD = 'p' implies self.PreviousDiploma.iD = 'm'

Fig. 6. Formalization of *phdInscritpion* constraint.

5.4   Step 3. Model Annotation

In step 3, relations, defining the defined annotation model, are set up between the design model entities and the ontology concepts. Figure 7 shows how the *PreviousDiploma* class of the students design model is annotated by the *Master* class of the Diplomas ontology.

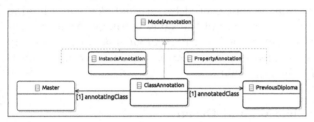

Fig. 7. Annotation of Student model.

Similarly, *NextDiploma* is annotated by *PhD* of the Diplomas ontology. The non-structural property *Equivalent_Class* and the *thesisRequirement* constraint can now be accessed and exploited. So, the equivalence between Master and Engineer classes is expressed and made explicit within the design model.

5.5   Step 4. Properties Verification

The last step analyses the obtained annotated design models through formally established links with the ontology. This annotation process leads to the enrichment of the original design model with new relations, properties, constraints and rules. Ontological properties and classes are considered to be available in the enriched model if they have been selected or linked to model properties during the annotation process (third step of the approach). The new enriched model is validated by (re-)checking all the constraints (the existing and the new added ones) on the model and all its instances. The *equivalence* property and the *thesisRequirement* constraint are now explicit on the annotated student model. The verification process ends with integrating the *equivalence* domain constraint into the enriched design model since all the properties it is relating to are available. At this level, it becomes possible to conclude that a student can apply for preparing a Phd thesis if he holds an engineer diploma. Thus, the *phdInscritpion* constraint is modified to integrate the result of annotation. Its formalization is given in Fig. 8. This property became explicit after handling domain knowledge (by annotation) expressed in the ontology.

Student.nextDiploma.iD="P" $\Rightarrow$ annotation(Student.previousDiploma) $\in$ eq(Master)	phdInscritpion: self.nextDiploma.iD = 'p' implies let c: ecore::EClass = ClassAnnotation.allInstances()-> select(inst|inst.annotatedClass = self.previousDiploma)-> at(0).annotatingClass in Equivalence.allInstances()-> exists(eq| eq.left.uri = 'Master_uri' and eq.right = c);

Fig. 8. The OCL constraint *phdInscritpion* after annotation.

6 Second Deployment: Integration in the Event-B Formal Method

In this section, we show how the proposed stepwise methodology can be deployed in the case of formal modeling. The refinement and proof Event-B[5][15] formal method has been chosen for this purpose. It applies the four defined steps (see Sect. 4) and gives the root Event-B models for the case study.

6.1 Event-B: A Refinement and Proof Based Formal Method

The Event-B method [15] is a stepwise formal correct-by-construction development method. It is based on the refinement of an initial model, a machine by gradually adding design decisions. A set of proof obligations (PO), based on the weakest precondition calculus [16], is associated to each machine. Development correctness is guaranteed by proving these PO.

An Event-B model [15] (see Fig. 9(a)) is defined by a*MACHINE*. It encodes a state transitions system which consists of: the variables declared in the

```
CONTEXT        MACHINE
  ctxt_id_2      machine_id_2
EXTENDS        REFINES
  ctxt_id_1      machine_id_1
SETS           SEES
  s              ctxt_id_2
CONSTANTS      VARIABLES
  c              v
AXIOMS         INVARIANTS
  A(s,c)         I(s,cv)
THEOREMS       THEOREMS
  Tc(s,c)        Tm(s,c,v)
END            VARIANT
                 V(s,c,v)
               EVENTS
                 Event evt =
                   any  x
                   where  G(s,c,v,x)
                   then
                     v : |BA(s,c,v,x,v')
                   end
               END
```

(a) Contexts and machines.

Theorems	$A(s,c) \Rightarrow T_c(s,c)$ $A(s,c) \wedge I(s,c,v) \Rightarrow T_m(s,c,v)$
Invariant preservation	$A(s,c) \wedge I(s,c,v) \wedge G(s,c,v,x)$ $\wedge BA(s,c,v,x,v') \Rightarrow I(s,c,v')$
Event feasibility	$A(s,c) \wedge I(s,c,v) \wedge G(s,c,v,x)$ $\Rightarrow \exists v'.BA(s,c,v,x,v')$
Variant progress	$A(s,c) \wedge I(s,c,v)$ $\wedge G(s,c,v,x) \wedge BA(s,c,v,x,v')$ $\Rightarrow V(s,c,v') < V(s,c,v)$

(b) Generated proof obligations for a model.

Fig. 9. Basic definitions: contexts, machines and proof obligations.

---

[5] http://www.event-b.org/.

VARIABLES clause to represent the state; and the events declared in the *EVENTS* clause to represent the transitions (defined by a Before-After predicate BA) from one state to another.

The model holds also *INVARIANTS* and *THEOREMS* to represent relevant properties of the defined model. Then a decreasing *VARIANT* may introduce convergence properties when needed. An Event-B machine is related, through the *SEES* clause to a *CONTEXT* which contains the relevant sets, constants axioms, andtheorems needed for defining an Event-B model. The refinement capability [17], introduced by the *REFINES* clause, decomposes a model (thus a transition system) into another transition system with more design decisions while moving from an abstract level to a less abstract one. New variables and new events may be introduced at the refinement level. In a refinement, the invariants shall link the variables of the refined machine with the ones of the refining machine. A gluing invariant is introduced for this purpose. It preserves the proved properties and supports the definition of new ones.

Once an Event-B machine is defined, a set of proof obligations is generated. They are submitted to the embedded prover in the RODIN [15] platform. Here the prime notation is used to denote the value of a variable after an event is triggered. More details on the Event-B method can be found in [15].

6.2   Step 1. Domain Knowledge Formalization

The different concepts describing the main features of an ontology language are defined in an Event-B context. All the basic ontological concepts and relationships are formally described within a general Event-B context. This context can be extended to be specialized for a specific ontology. Listing 1.1 is an extract of the Event-B *Ontology_Relations* context defining relevant finite sets for CLASS, PROPERTIES and INSTANCES. It also defines the basic ontological relationship EQUIVALENCE that may exist between two classes. Other concepts, relations and properties are defined to cover more ontological concepts. They are not given in this paper for space reasons. Note that this context can be extended to be specialized for a specific ontology. The context *Ontology_Relations* (Listing 1.1) is extended by *Diplomas_Ontology* (Listing 1.2). Diplomas are defined as Classes. The equivalences between the different classes are explicitly formalized using the specific equivalence relation *EQo* belonging to the set *EQUIVALENCE* of equivalence relationships.

Listing 1.1. Ontological relationship formalization context.

```
Context Ontology_Relations Sets CLASS, PROPERTIES,
INSATANCES Constants EQUIVALENCE Axioms
  axm1: EQUIVALENCE = { Eq| Eq ∈ CLASS ↔ CLASS ∧
    (∀ x· (x ∈ CLASS ⇒ x↦ x ∈ Eq)) ∧
    (∀ x, y· (x ∈ CLASS ∧ y ∈ CLASS ∧ x↦ y ∈ Eq ⇒ y↦ x ∈ Eq)) ∧
    (∀ x, y, z· (x ∈ CLASS ∧ y ∈ CLASS ∧ z ∈ CLASS ∧ x↦ y ∈ Eq ∧ y ↦ z ∈ Eq ⇒ x↦ z ∈ Eq)) }
    ...
End
```

The equivalences between the different classes are explicitly formalized using the specific equivalence relation *EQo* belonging to the set *EQUIVALENCE* of equivalence relationships. The correct definition of *EQo* relationship is guaranteed by proving the theorem in *thm3*. This proof requirement entailed by the use of formal methods guarantees that used specification relationships like *EQo* formally fulfill the equivalence relationship properties.

Listing 1.2. Diplomas ontology.

```
Context Diplomas_Ontology
Constants Master, Engineer, Bachelor, PhD
Axioms
axm1: partition(CLASS, {Master}, {PhD}, {Bachelor}, {Engineer})
axm2: EQo = {Bachelor↦Bachelor, Engineer↦Engineer, PhD↦PhD,
            Master↦Master, Master↦Engineer, Engineer↦Master}
thm3: EQo ∈ EQUIVALENCE    Theorem
End
```

In addition, the *Diplomas_Ontology* context describes the set *Master, Bachelor, PhD, Engineer* as specific diplomas. It also states that an *Engineer* diploma is equivalent to a *Master* diploma.

6.3   Step 2. Model Specification and Design

Design models are formalized within Event-B using contexts and machines. Static part (constants, types and data) of the design models is defined within contexts and the dynamic part is referred to as a machine which *sees* the defined contexts (static part). Listing 1.3 depicts a generic context defining the relevant set *CONCEPT* characterizing the concepts involved in the definition of a design model. This context is extended to define specific applicative contexts. The static part associated to the case study is given in the *student_Model* context (Listing 1.4). DIPLOMS and STUDENTS concepts are introduced.

Listing 1.3. Generic design model context.

```
Context Design_Model
  Set CONCEPT
End
```

Listing 1.4. Student design model context.

```
Context Student_Model Extends Design_Model
  Constants m, p, e, b, titi, toto, DIPLOMS, STUDENTS
  //Master, PhD, Engineer and Bachelor diplomas
  Axioms
    axm1 : CONCEPT = DIPLOMS ∪ STUDENTS
    axm2 : DIPLOMS ∩ STUDENT = ∅
    axm3 : partition(DIPLOMS, {e},{m},{p},{b})
    axm4 : partition(STUDENTS, {toto},{titi})
    axm5 : finite(CONCEPT)
End
```

Finally, once the different concepts are described, it becomes possible to describe the behavioral part of the model. Indeed, the model considers the case of a student willing to register for a PhD. For the case study, the dynamic part (Listing 1.5) defines the *Register* event within a machine. An invariant *inv1* ensures that a student can register for a *PhD* only if he/she holds a master degree.

Listing 1.5. Student design model machine.

```
Machine Student_Register
Invriants
inv1 : ∀ x (x ∈ STUDENTS ∧ x↦ p ∈ phd_register ⇒ previousDiplom[{x}] ⊆ {m})
Events
  Phd_Register ≜ Any Dip
              Where    grd1: dip ∈ {m}
                       grd2: previousDiplom[{student}]={dip}
              Then     act1: phd_register = phd_resgite ∪ {student ↦ p}
End
```

6.4 Step 3. Model annotation

An annotation model is defined within a general context as a generic relationship *ANNOTATION_CLASS* linking design models to ontologies (see Listing 1.6).

Listing 1.6. Annotation relationship formalization context.

```
Context Annotation_Relationship
Extends Ontology_Relations, Student_Model
Axioms
  axm1: ANNOTATION_CLASS =
                CLASS ↔ CONCEPT
End
```

Listing 1.7. Annotation model context.

```
Context Annotation_Model
Extends Annotation_Relationship
Axioms
  axm1: annotation ∈ ANNOTATION_CLASS
  axm2: annotation = {Master↦m, Engineer↦e}
End
```

Other annotation relationships can be defined, for example to link properties, relationships or constraints etc. Moreover, additional properties may be defined for the annotation. They have not been given in this paper due to space limitations. Listing 1.7 defines annotations for the m and e concepts manipulated at the design model level. The defined annotation states that m and e are annotated by the *Master* and *Engineer* ontological concepts respectively. It becomes possible to reason on the equivalence of these concepts (or any other ontological relationship that may exist between *Master* and *Engineer* concepts).

Once the annotations are achieved, they can be integrated into the design model and enrich it. Annotations are exploited to access to the ontological concepts and properties in design models. When the annotation relation is established on the design model (Listing 1.5) the annotated student design model is obtained. Listing 1.8 depicts the *Student_Register* machine after the annotation process. The invariant *inv1* is rewritten to integrate the annotations. Indeed, it states that any student holding a previous diploma that is equivalent to the inverse annotation of m can be registered for preparing a *PhD*. Thus, the equivalence ontological relationship can now be exploited to enrich the model.

Listing 1.8. Annotated Student_Register machine.

```
Machine Student_Register
Invariants    inv1 : ∀ x (x ∈ STUDENTS ∧ x↦ p ∈ phd_register ⇒ ((previousDiplom[{x}] ⊆ {m})
∨ (previousDiplom[{x}] ⊆ annotation[EQo[annotation⁻¹[{m}]]]) ))
Events
  Phd_Register ≜ Any Dip
              Where    grd1: dip ∈ {m,e}
                       grd2: previousDiplom[{student}]={dip}
              Then     act1: phd_register = phd_resgite ∪ {student ↦ p}
End
```

6.5   Step 4. Properties Verification

The property verification step is achieved trough discharging all the PO. The capability to annotate design models concepts independently of their usage in design models allows developers to express new properties acting on ontology concepts just by annotating the design models with new properties. The new definition of invariant *inv*1 of Listing 1.8 uses *explicitly* the defined annotation relationship. As a result, the design models can be questioned, verified or checked with regards to new properties exploiting annotations that borrow ontology concepts and properties to the design models. Invariants similar to *inv*1 are defined using the annotation relationship. For our case study, the correctness of the new enriched model is proven. The new POs generated by the annotation are discharged by proving that invariant *inv1* still holds after the *Phd_Register* event is triggered. All the POs associated to the *Student_Register* machine have been proved for all values of *dip* that are equivalent to *Master*.

7   Related Work

Semantic enrichment of models has drawn the attention of several research communities. Different methods and techniques emerged with the aim to enrich the semantics of models using annotation mechanisms. We distinguish three main categories of semantic annotations.

In [18–21], the authors use ontologies for raw data annotation in an informal context. Web pages and documents are annotated with semantic information formalized within linguistic ontologies. Once annotations achieved, formal reasoning is performed. This category of annotation is out of the scope of this paper.

In the second category of approaches ontologies are used for the semantic enrichment of models in a semi-formal context. [22] propose a fully automated technique for integrating heterogeneous data sources called "ontology-based database". This approach assumes the existence of a shared ontology and guarantees the autonomy of each source by extending the shared ontology to define its local ontology. In [23–27] annotations are made in an interoperable context and aim to improve the reading, common understanding and re-usability of the models and thus enabling unambiguous exchange of models. In [28], a reasoning phase is performed based on the output of the annotation phase. The reasoning rules produce inference results: (1) Suggestion of semantic annotation, (2) Detection of inconsistencies between semantic annotations and (3) Conflict identification between annotated objects. These approaches addressing interoperability issues focused on improving the common understanding of models. They do not deal with the formal correctness of models with respect to domain properties and constraints.

The third category of approaches is related to the semantic enrichment of design models related to an application domain using formal annotations. Annotations are directly set up inside the models. Examples of such approaches are the classical pre and post-conditions of Hoare pre-conditions [29] or program annotation tools like Why3 [30]. In [31], the authors introduce real-world types to document the programs with relevant characteristics and constraints of the real-world entities. Real-world types are connected to entities of the programs (variables, functions, etc.). The reasoning and checking of the correctness of programs in regards to real-world types becomes possible by type checking. These approaches seem close to ours, but, to the best of our knowledge, they do not use explicitly modeled ontologies.

Always in the context of formal methods, other approaches use annotations with expressions that make explicit references to ontologies. Indeed, in [32–34], the authors argue that many problems in the development of correct systems could be better addressed through the separation of concerns. [32,33] advocate the re-definition of design models correctness as a ternary relation linking the requirements, the system and application domains. Domain concepts are then explicitly modeled as first-class objects as we did in our approach. Furthermore, similarly to our approach, they propose the formalization of ontologies by Event-B contexts. The formalized information can then be integrated incrementally and directly in the behavioral requirements using refinements. In [34] a DSL abstract syntax and references to domain ontologies are axiomatized into logic theories. These two models are related using a third logical theory. The authors use the Alloy formal method to check the consistency of the unified theory.

Compared to our approach, the approaches cited above use, through annotations, domain information and knowledge directly (i.e. as built in concepts) in the design model. Our approach improves these approaches. It suggests to first separate the ontology and the design model and second to make the annotation explicit using an annotation model. In this way, models are separated from the domain model and thus ontologies and models can evolve asynchronously.

8   Conclusion and Future Work

The integration of domain knowledge and information during the system specification and design phases allows the developers to handle axioms, hypotheses, theorems or properties mined from the application domain. This requirement is a major concern in system engineering where different standards provide system designers with relevant domain knowledge information not explicitly handled by the design models.

In this paper, we have proposed a stepwise methodology allowing system designers to explicitly handle domain knowledge in their design models. Ontologies have been chosen to express the knowledge models describing explicitly the domain knowledge. Depending on the chosen modelling language, these ontologies modelled through concepts, relationships between concepts and associated constraints on the one hand and domain axioms and theorems on the other hand. We have shown that both ontologies and design models can be integrated in a single modelling language. The interest of such integration is semantic alignment where both ontologies, annotations and design models are described in a common shared modelling language.

We have shown, using a toy case study, the deployment of this approach in the case of model driven engineering techniques and formal methods based on refinement and proof using the Event-B method. We have used the Eclipse modelling framework and the Rodin platform to operationalize our proposal. In both cases, the approach proved powerful enough to enrich design models with knowledge domain properties. We have noticed that when used in design models, by annotation, ontologies strengthen with axioms and theorems that were not explicitly defined in the design models. In our case, thanks to the enrichment provided by the annotation mechanisms we have been able to enrich the design models with an equivalence property attached to concepts of the design models.

The proposed approach has been developed as part of the IMPEX-ANR project [35] and has been applied to several case studies in the engineering domain. Indeed, experiments with MDE based techniques have been conducted on the oilfield engineering models [8,36] and avionic systems [37,38]. Formal methods have been applied in the case of human computer interaction models [39], avionic systems [32] and in system engineering [33,40,41].

The work presented in this paper opened several new research directions. The whole coverage of available ontology languages like OWL or Plib and the associated annotation mechanisms is currently under study. We are designing meta-models in the MDE setting and generic contexts in the Event-B setting. Then, the case of semantic mismatch, where ontologies and design models are not described in the same modeling language, needs to be addressed. Semantic alignment shall be studied. Finally, the integration of more than one design model addressing different aspects or view of a single system sharing a common ontology needs to be handled as well. Indeed, our idea is to offer to the designer the capability to use validated properties of a given model as hypotheses and axioms as hypotheses in another design model.

References

1. Gruber, T.R.: A translation approach to portable ontology specifications. Knowl. Acquis. 5(2), 199–220 (1993)
2. Jean, S., Pierra, G., Aït Ameur, Y.: Domain ontologies: a database-oriented analysis. In: Filipe, J., Cordeiro, J., Pedrosa, V. (eds.) WEBIST 2006. LNBIP, pp. 238–254. Springer, Heidelberg (2006)
3. Bechhofer, S., Van Harmelen, F., Hendler, J., Horrocks, I., McGuinness, D., Patel-Schneider, P., Stein, L., et al.: Owl web ontology language reference. W3C Recommendation 10 (2004)
4. ISO: Industrial automation systems and integration - parts library - part42: description methodology: methodology for structuring parts families. ISO ISO13584-42, Geneva, Switzerland (1998)
5. ISO: Industrial automation systems and integration - parts library - part25: logical resource: logical model of supplier library with aggregate valuesand explicit content. ISO ISO13584-25, Geneva, Switzerland (2004)
6. Brickley, D., Guha, R.V.: RDF vocabulary description language 1.0: RDF schema. W3C Recommendation, W3C, February 2004

7. Aït Ameur, Y., Méry, D.: Making explicit domain knowledge in formal system development. Sci. Comput. Program. (2015, to appear)
8. Silveira Mastella, L., Aït-Ameur, Y., Jean, S., Perrin, M., Rainaud, J.-F.: Semantic exploitation of engineering models: an application to oilfield models. In: Sexton, A.P. (ed.) BNCOD 26. LNCS, vol. 5588, pp. 203–207. Springer, Heidelberg (2009)
9. Belaid, N., Jean, S., Aït Ameur, Y., Rainaud, J.F.: An ontology and indexation based management of services and workflows application to geological modeling. IJEBM **9**(4), 296–309 (2011)
10. Schmidt, D.C.: Model-driven engineering. IEEE Comput. Soc. **39**(2), 25 (2006)
11. OMG: OMG Unified Modeling Language (OMG UML), Superstructure, Version2.4.1 (2011)
12. OMG: Meta Object Facility (MOF) Core Specification Version 2.0 (2006)
13. OMG: OMG Object Constraint Language (OCL), Version 2.3.1, January 2012
14. OMG: Meta Object Facility (MOF) 2.0 Query/View/TransformationSpecification, Version 1.1, January 2011
15. Abrial, J.R.: Modeling in Event-B - System and Software Engineering. Cambridge University Press, Cambridge (2010)
16. Dijkstra, E.W.: A Discipline of Programming. Prentice Hall PTR, Upper Saddle River (1977)
17. Abrial, J.R., Hallerstede, S.: Refinement, decomposition, and instantiation of discrete models: application to event-b. Fundam. Inf. **77**(1–2), 1–28 (2007)
18. Bontcheva, K., Tablan, V., Maynard, D., Cunningham, H.: Evolving gate to meet new challenges in language engineering. NLE **10**(3–4), 349–373 (2004)
19. Cunningham, H., Maynard, D., Bontcheva, K.: Text Processing with Gate. Gateway Press, Murphys (2011)
20. Despres, S., Szulman, S.: TERMINAE method and integration process for legal ontology building. In: Ali, M., Dapoigny, R. (eds.) IEA/AIE 2006. LNCS (LNAI), vol. 4031, pp. 1014–1023. Springer, Heidelberg (2006)
21. Handschuh, S., Volz, R., Staab, S.: Annotation for the deep web. IEEE (5) (2003)
22. Bellatreche, L., Pierra, G., Xuan, D.N., Hondjack, D., Ameur, Y.A.: An a priori approach for automatic integration of heterogeneous and autonomous databases. In: Galindo, F., Takizawa, M., Traunmüller, R. (eds.) DEXA 2004. LNCS, vol. 3180, pp. 475–485. Springer, Heidelberg (2004)
23. Boudjlida, N., Panetto, H.: Annotation of enterprise models for interoperability purposes. In: CAISE, April 2008
24. Wang, Y., Li, H.: Adding semantic annotation to UML class diagram. In: ICCASM (2010)
25. Lin, Y., Strasunskas, D.: Ontology-based semantic annotation of process templates for reuse. In: Proceedings of the CAiSE, vol. 5. Citeseer (2005)
26. Lin, Y., Strasunskas, D., Hakkarainen, S.E., Krogstie, J., Solvberg, A.: Semantic annotation framework to manage semantic heterogeneity of process models. In: Martinez, F.H., Pohl, K. (eds.) CAiSE 2006. LNCS, vol. 4001, pp. 433–446. Springer, Heidelberg (2006)
27. Zouggar, N., Vallespir, B., Chen, D.: Semantic enrichment of enterprise models by ontologies-based semantic annotations. In: EDOC. IEEE (2008)
28. Liao, Y., Lezoche, M., Panetto, H., Boudjlida, N., Loures, E.R.: Formal semantic annotations for models interoperability in a PLM environment. arXiv (2014)
29. Hoare, C.A.R.: An axiomatic basis for computer programming. Commun. ACM **12**, 576–580 (1969)
30. Filliâtre, J.C., Paskevich, A.: Why3 – where programs meet provers. In: ESOP

31. Knight, J., Xiang, J., Sullivan, K.: A rigorous definition of cyber physical systems. In: Trustworthy Cyber Physical Systems Engineering (2016, to appear)
32. Ait-Ameur, Y., Gibson, J.P., Méry, D.: On implicit and explicit semantics: integration issues in proof-based development of systems. In: Margaria, T., Steffen, B. (eds.) ISoLA 2014, Part II. LNCS, vol. 8803, pp. 604–618. Springer, Heidelberg (2014)
33. Méry, D., Sawant, R., Tarasyuk, A.: Integrating domain-based features into event-b: a nose gear velocity case study. In: Bellatreche, L., Manolopoulos, Y., Zielinski, B., Liu, R. (eds.) MEDI 2015. LNCS, vol. 9344, pp. 89–102. Springer, Heidelberg (2015). doi:10.1007/978-3-319-23781-7_8
34. de Carvalho, V.A., Almeida, J.P.A., Guizzardi, G.: Using reference domain ontologies to define the real-world semantics of domain-specific languages. In: Jarke, M., Mylopoulos, J., Quix, C., Rolland, C., Manolopoulos, Y., Mouratidis, H., Horkoff, J. (eds.) CAiSE 2014. LNCS, vol. 8484, pp. 488–502. Springer, Heidelberg (2014)
35. IMPEX Consortium. Formal models for ontologies. Technical report (2015)
36. Mastella, L.S.: Semantic exploitation of engineering models: application to petroleum reservoir models. Ph.D. thesis, ENSMP (2010)
37. Aït Ameur, Y., Hacid, K.: Report ame corac-panda project. Technical report, Institut de Recherche en Informatique de Toulouse, Toulouse university (2015)
38. Hacid, K.: Explicit definition of prperties by model annotation. Technical report, Institut de Recherche en Informatique de Toulouse, Toulouse university (2014)
39. Chebieb, A., Aït Ameur, Y.: Formal verification of plastic user interfaces exploiting domain ontologies. In: TASE (2015)
40. Simon-Zayas, D.: A framework for the management of heterogeneous models in Systems Engineering. Theses, ISAE-ENSMA - Poitiers, June 2012
41. Zayas, D.S., Monceaux, A., Aït Ameur, Y.: Knowledge models to reduce the gap between heterogeneous models: application to aircraft systems engineering. In: ICECCS (2010)

Towards Functional Requirements Analytics

Zouhir Djilani[1], Nabila Berkani[2], and Ladjel Bellatreche[1(✉)]

[1] LIAS/ISAE-ENSMA - Poitiers University, Futuroscope, France
{zouhir.djilani,bellatreche}@ensma.fr
[2] National High School for Computer Science (ESI),Algiers, Algeria
n_berkani@esi.dz

Abstract. In the Era of sharing, several efforts have been launched to construct repositories (referential/warehouses) storing entities used in projects for enterprises (e.g., data, processes, models, APIs, etc.). These repositories augment the business value of the enterprises in terms of reuse, sharing, traceability and analysis. By exploring the literature, we figure out the absence of *appropriate warehouses* dedicated to functional requirements ($\mathcal{FR}$) for the analytical purpose. In a large scale software in the context of global enterprises, involving numerous partners, $\mathcal{FR}$ may be very heterogeneous in terms of the used vocabularies and formalisms to model them. Other aspects that have to be handled, when constructing a $\mathcal{FR}$ warehouse are: **(a)** the management of interdependencies that may exist among $\mathcal{FR}$ and **(b)** their scheduling. These aspects complicate the construction of such warehouse. In this paper, we first propose a complete and comprehensive semantic-driven methodology, to design $\mathcal{FR}$ warehouses. Secondly, all steps of our approach leveraged from the traditional warehouse design are highlighted: **(i)** the definition of the multidimensional model, **(ii)** adapting the existing operators of ETL (Extract, Transform, Load) to deal with $\mathcal{FR}$. ETL uses reasoning capabilities to eliminate the conflictual requirements. **(iii)** Translating the multidimensional model to its corresponding logical model and **(iv)** evaluating the performance of the final warehouse. Finally, a proof of concept for our proposal is presented using Oracle DBMS and the vocabulary *QB4OLAP* proposed by the W3C Government Linked Data Working Group to facilitate the manipulation of semantic warehouses.

1 Introduction

Global companies/enterprises in business areas such as Aerospace, Telecommunication, Automobile, etc. are launching products (systems and software) to respond to numerous *Functional Requirements* ($\mathcal{FR}$) (e.g., 8 000 requirements for in the domain of Aerospace, 6 000 in Telecommunication [6]). Collecting, eliciting and analysing $\mathcal{FR}$ of a large scale project in the context of a global enterprise are considered as a *precondition* for its success [7]. Over 41 % of the Information Technology (IT) development budget for software, staff and external professional services is consumed by poor requirements at the average company[1].

---

[1] http://www.techrepublic.com/blog/tech-decision-maker/
study-68-percent-of-it-projects-fail/.

© Springer International Publishing AG 2016
T. Margaria and B. Steffen (Eds.): ISoLA 2016, Part I, LNCS 9952, pp. 358–373, 2016.
DOI: 10.1007/978-3-319-47166-2_25

Recall that a $\mathcal{FR}$ describes the functionalities, the functioning, and the usage of the software and its components. They are specifying a behavioural input/output system such as calculation, data manipulation and processing, etc.

Generally speaking, in the business areas, enterprises store and maintain any manipulated entity from their projects (e.g., business data, experimental data, processes, workflows, APIs, etc.) for different usages such as *visualization, evolution, traceability, sharing* and *reuse* [3]. Each research and industrial community proposes repositories/referential of the manipulated entity. For instance, Walmark, the biggest retailer in the world builds its warehouse persisting data of the sales activities for analytical purposes [25]. Recently, the computational science community spent a lot of efforts in building repositories of data issued from their experiments and simulations for analysis, reuse and reproduction purposes. The *cTuning* repository[2] is an example of these initiatives. It is an open-source, customizable Collective Knowledge Repository for physics domain. Similar efforts have been conducted by the process community. *APROMORE* (*Advanced Process Model Repository*) is an example of these initiatives [21]. [23] proposes a repository for *APIs* (Application programming interface) to facilitate the development of new advanced applications. Unfortunately, these repositories are not designed for analytical purposes.

Some attempts have been proposed by the Requirement Engineering Community to propose repositories dedicated to $\mathcal{FR}$. We can cite the example of the referential model proposed in [6] for the requirement traceability purpose. Industrials propose tools to facilitate the management of requirements. The authors in [17] recommend the construction of repositories for large enterprises to facilitate their management (conflict detection) using linguistic techniques. The system *DOORS* of IBM considered as a dashboard, offers *visualization* and *tracing* capabilities of requirements[3]. These solutions focus mainly on traceability, visualisation, and reuse. In [11], a preliminary debate around the building of a $\mathcal{FR}$ warehouse. This work suffers from two main drawbacks: (1) the absence of the ETL phase considered as a keystone on which depends the success of OLAP projects[4]. (2) It is built for storing issue and not for analytical purposes (*the absence of the actors and the time when the requirements are elicited*). Note that *data analytics* emerges as a tool for business. It is usually associated to the data warehousing technology. It is defined as *"a subject-oriented, integrated, time-variant and non-volatile collection of data in support of management's decision making process"* [9]. This technology offers the following characteristics: (a) it is constructed from various heterogeneous sources, (b) it is designed specifically to enable data analysis across business, (c) it is designed specifically to help identify trends and previously unknown relationships in business processes. This technology offers several advantages: (i) analysing the stored data, (ii) reducing cost to access historical data, (iii) standardizing data across the organization,

---

[2] http://ctuning.org/index.html.

[3] http://www-03.ibm.com/software/products/fr/ratidoor.

[4] http://www.ewsolutions.com/resource-center/rwds_folder/rwds-archives/ rwds-2003-04/etl-data-migration-projects-failures.

a "single version of the truth" [5], (iv) sharing data and allowing others to easily access data, (v) tracing the data.

A $\mathcal{FR}$ warehouse perfectly fits in the context of global enterprises, such as AIRBUS[6], in which many distributed partners have to deal with heterogeneous $\mathcal{FR}$, where each partner expresses its requirements in a local *Requirement Document* with her/his own *vocabulary* corresponding to an universe of discourse and *formalism* (modelling language) (UML Use Cases, Goal Oriented Formalisms [24], B Method [1], etc.). *To the best of our knowledge, this paper is the first that proposes an appropriate warehousing technology for functional requirements.* To do so, we fix the following objectives: **(i)** the unification of vocabularies and formalisms, **(ii)** leverage the traditional ETL (Extract, Transform, Load) tool to deal with $\mathcal{FR}$, **(iii)** the definition of logical schema of the target warehouse, **(iv)** the deployment of the warehouse in a given platform and **(v)** the exploration of the obtained warehouse in *the easiest way* using a simple *vocabulary*. This paper develops a complete and comprehensive semantic-based methodology to achieve these objectives.

This paper is composed of five sections. Section 2 gives an overview related to our context. Section 3 explains in details the main phases of our semantic methodology for requirement warehouse. Section 4 presents proof of concept for our approach. Section 5 concludes the paper and sketches some perspectives.

2   Related Work

In this section, we review the main studies related to the four issues when constructing a $\mathcal{FR}$ warehouse: **(i)** the reduction of heterogeneity of the sources, related to the conceptual phase, **(ii)** the integration of $\mathcal{FR}$ ($\in$ ETL), **(iii)** the $\mathcal{FR}$ analysis ($\in$ ETL), and **(iv)** the $\mathcal{FR}$ persisting ($\in$ ETL).

The Reduction of Heterogeneity. $\mathcal{FR}$ in a global enterprise may be heterogeneous. This heterogeneity concerns mainly the vocabularies and the formalisms used by each partner. Recently, ontologies were proposed to eliminate semantic and syntactic or lexical conflicts [2,10,13]. To unify and interoperate the various used formalisms, several research efforts have proposed pivot models accompanied by Model Driven Engineering methods [2,8,15]. Each local formalism is mapped to the pivot model.

The Integration and Analysis of $\mathcal{FR}$**.** Usually, integrating requirements is associated to their analysis in order to detect conflictual requirements. To do so, reasoning techniques are used to identify relationships between $\mathcal{FR}$ and to check their consistency. Three main automatic categories of studies exist to analyse $\mathcal{FR}$: (i) meta-modelling driven approaches [8] in which languages like OCL (Object Constraint Language) are defined on the meta models of the semi formal formalisms of $\mathcal{FR}$ [18], (ii) formal method driven approaches (such as B

Method [1]) usually used when formal formalisms are used to model $\mathcal{FR}$, and (iii) ontology-based approaches that exploit the reasoning capabilities offered by ontologies [8,11].

The Persistence of $\mathcal{FR}$. Recent studies motivate the interests of persisting user requirements. The particularity of the work in [11] concerns the persisting of user requirements of a given application into ontology-based databases. These requirements can be requested by semantic query languages like SPARQL[7].

3   Background

In this section, we present definitions and concepts related to requirements, ontologies, pivot model to facilitate the understanding of our approach.

3.1   Conceptual and Linguistic Ontologies

As we said before, our methodology is based on ontologies to reduce the syntactic and semantic heterogeneities of requirement sources.

Note that two main types of ontologies exist [19]: *conceptual domain ontologies* ($\mathcal{CDO}$) and *linguistic ontologies* ($\mathcal{LO}$). A $\mathcal{CDO}$ represents the categories of objects and object properties that are used to apprehend some part of the world. Formally, it can be defined as follows [12]:
$\mathcal{CDO}: < \mathcal{C}, \mathcal{R}, \mathcal{R}ef(\mathcal{C}), \mathcal{R}ef(\mathcal{R}), \mathcal{F}ormalism >$, such as:

- $\mathcal{C}$: represents the concepts of the $\mathcal{CDO}$.
- $\mathcal{R}$: represents the roles of the $\mathcal{CDO}$.
- $\mathcal{R}ef(\mathcal{C})$: $\mathcal{C} \rightarrow (\mathcal{O}\text{perator}, \mathcal{E}\text{xp}(\mathcal{C},\mathcal{R}))$, where: $\mathcal{R}ef(C)$ is a function defining classes of the $\mathcal{DL}$ $\mathcal{T}$BOX, Operators can be inclusion ($\subseteq$) or equality ($\equiv$), $\mathcal{E}\text{xp}(\mathcal{C},\mathcal{R})$ is an expression composed of *concepts* and *roles* of the $\mathcal{DO}$.
- $\mathcal{R}ef(\mathcal{R})$: $\mathcal{R} \rightarrow (\mathcal{O}\text{perator}, \mathcal{E}\text{xp}(\mathcal{C},\mathcal{R}))$, where: $\mathcal{R}ef(\mathcal{R})$ is a function that defines *roles* in $\mathcal{DL}$ $\mathcal{T}$BOX, Operator can be inclusion ($\subseteq$) or equality ($\equiv$) and $\mathcal{E}\text{xp}(\mathcal{C},\mathcal{R})$ is an expression over *concepts* and *roles* of the $\mathcal{DO}$.
- $\mathcal{F}$ormalism: the ontology formalism model like $\mathcal{RDF}$, $\mathcal{OWL}$ $\mathcal{PLIB}$, etc.

$\mathcal{CDO}$ plays the role of the universe of discourse including the concepts and the properties of the business area. As a consequence, the enterprise imposes the use of such a domain ontology when expressing requirements.

On the other hand, a $\mathcal{LO}$ represents the meaning of the words used in a particular universe of discourse in a particular language. *Wordnet* is an example of these ontologies [16]. Since natural languages contain a number of different words for reflecting identical or similar meanings, $\mathcal{LO}$ are large in nature. They include a number of conservative definitions, i.e., defined items that only introduce terminology and do not add any knowledge about the world [19]. They are language-specific and they use a number of linguistic relationships such that

---

[7] https://www.w3.org/TR/rdf-sparql-query/.

synonym, hyponym, overlap, covering, disjoint to capture the meaning relations [19]. Formally, $\mathcal{LO}$ may be defined as follows: $\mathcal{LO} :< T\mathcal{R}, Rel(T\mathcal{R}), Refc(\mathcal{C}) >$, such as:

- $T\mathcal{R}$: represents the set of terms used in the $\mathcal{LO}$.
- $Rel(T\mathcal{R})$: $T\mathcal{R} \rightarrow (\mathcal{R}\ elation, 2^{TR})$: is a function that represents linguistic relationships between terms (*synonym, antonym*, etc.).
- $Refc(\mathcal{C})$: $C \rightarrow 2^{TR}$: represents the correspondence between terms and their ontological concept.

$\mathcal{LO}$ may contribute on managing the used words when documenting and validating requirements [5].

3.2 Heterogeneity of $\mathcal{FR}$ Formalisms: A Pivot Model as a Solution

In a global enterprise, each designer uses her/his favourite formalism to model requirements. Three main categories of formalisms exist [14]: (i) informal formalisms, (ii) semi formal formalisms (e.g., UML use case, *Goal oriented* [24] and *Treatment Conceptual Model* of the *MERISE* method [20]) and (iii) formal formalisms (e.g. B method). To interoperate these formalisms and to offer partners a great autonomy, we propose a pivot model in the context of semi formal category. Its development has been discussed in [2]. Generally speaking, a $\mathcal{FR}$ is composed of an ordered set of tasks, where each task may be defined by the following triple: $< subject, action, object >$ [4]. This fine-grained decomposition allows a comprehensive analysis of requirements and a detailed identification of requirements relationships.

Example 1. Let us consider the $\mathcal{FR}$ (R_{17},$R_{17'}$) of the course management system (CMS) requirements document[8].
R_{17}: The <u>system</u> shall <u>allow</u> <u>students</u> to <u>create</u> <u>teams</u>.
$R_{17'}$: The <u>system</u> shall <u>allow</u> <u>students</u> to <u>delete</u> <u>teams</u>.
Two ordered tasks, T_1^{17} and T_2^{17} compose R_{17}, T_1^{17} and T_2^{17} compose R_{17}:
$T_1^{17} :< System, Allow, Students >$ and $T_2^{17} :< Students, Create, Teams >$.
Two ordered tasks $T_1^{17'}$ and $T_2^{17'}$ compose the requirement $R_{17'}$:
$T_1^{17'} :< System, Allow, Students >$ and $T_2^{17'} :< Students, delete, Teams >$.

Note that each $\mathcal{FR}$ is issued by an actor that may represent a designer. Another important characteristic of $\mathcal{FR}$ concerns their interdependence meaning that there exist relationships between them (e.g. *Equal, Contain, Refine, Require, Conflicts_with, partially Refine*). Based on these notions, our pivot model is defined as: $EPivot_{model} :< Actor, Requirement, Relationships >$.
The source of $\mathcal{FR}$ can have it's own scheduling of tasks and requirements, as shown from R_{17} and $R_{17'}$ defined in above that *Student* can not delete *Teams* if they are not created. Based on the relationships of the pivot model, tasks and requirements can be scheduled as shown in Fig. 1.

---

[8] https://cft.vanderbilt.edu/guides-sub-pages/course-management-systems/.

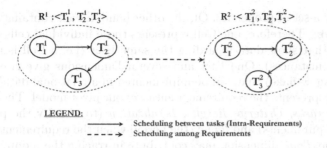

LEGEND:

⟶ Scheduling between tasks (Intra-Requirements)
---⟶ Scheduling among Requirements

Fig. 1. Scheduling of Tasks and $\mathcal{FR}$

4   Design of a Requirement Warehouse

Our methodology considers some hypothesis: (i) the existence of a shared domain ontology ($\mathcal{DO}$) that defines the domain of interest and a Multilingual Ontology ($\mathcal{LO}$), which consensually defines all terms used by requirements.

Figure 2 illustrates the different components of our solution. First of all, the multidimensional conceptual model of the warehouse has to be constructed. Then, the sources are transformed, analysed and loaded into our warehouse.

4.1   Multidimensional Requirement Schema

The multidimensional phase of the life cycle design of our warehouse has to identify facts (subject of analysis) and dimensions (analysis perspectives). Recall that a dimension may be a hierarchy of Levels representing different granularities ($year \longrightarrow semester \longrightarrow month \longrightarrow day$) to analyze data. Each dimension is

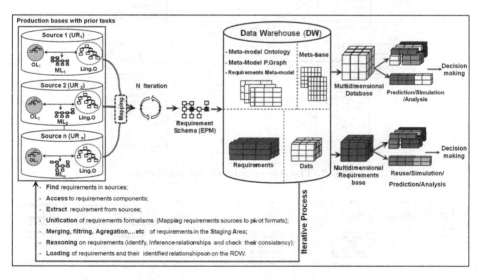

Fig. 2. The architecture of the requirement warehouse

described by a set of properties. On the other hand, a Fact contains *Cells* which have *Measures*. Therefore, one Cell represents those individual cells of the same granularity that show data regarding the same Fact (i.e. a Cell is a Class and cells are its instances). One Fact and several Dimensions give rises to a Star schema (or snow-flake) that can be implemented in a relational database. In our case, a fact represents the requirement entity of our pivot model. The dimensions are *Actors, Tasks, Criteria, Results, Localization* (to identify the partner that issues the requirements) and *Time* (the period when the requirements have been defined). The *Time* dimension may contribute in tracing the requirements. The star schema corresponding to our multidimensional model is given in Fig. 3.

4.2   The $\mathcal{ETL}$ Process

In this section, we describe in details the ETL phase of our design. ETL flows cover the following steps (Fig. 3): (i) including sources (*InputREQ*) participating in the construction of the warehouse in the ETL process, (ii) performing either unary or binary operations on requirements (*ReqOp*), (iii) identifying of relations between requirements (*REQRelation*) and (iv) loading requirement results (*REQResult*) into the warehouse.

[22] have defined ten ($\underline{10}$) brute generic conceptual $\mathcal{ETL}$ operators typically encountered in an $\mathcal{ETL}$ process dealing with data. In our context, we have four groups of operators: (i) basic operators, (ii) operators for $\mathcal{FR}$, (iii) inference operators and (iv) management operators.

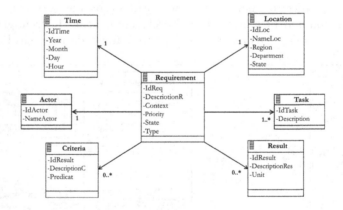

Fig. 3. The star schema of our warehouse

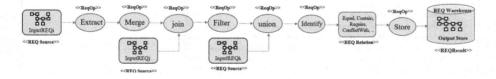

Fig. 4. ETL for requirements

The Basic Operators.

- $Retrieve(S_i, MF_i, R_j, C_j, TR_j)$: retrieves from a source S_i, the requirement R_j modelled by the formalism MF_i using the conceptual ontology classes C_j and the linguistic ontology terms TR_j.
- $Extract(S_i, MF_i, R_j, A_j, CS_j)$: enables selection and extraction of requirements R_j from source S_i having formalism MF_i using the conceptual ontology classes C_j and the linguistic ontology terms TR_j. Constraints CS_j are defined on classes level using axioms.
- $DD(R_j, R_k)$: detects duplicated requirements R_j and R_k deletes one of them.
- $Store(\mathcal{FRW}, R_j)$: enables loading requirement R_j into the target warehouse $\mathcal{FRW}$.

Operators Dedicated to Requirements.

- $Merge(S, R_i, A_i, R_j, A_j, \mathcal{PG})$: merges two requirements R_i and R_j into a third one R_k based on some constraints CS according to the precedence graph $(\mathcal{PG})$. Note that R_i and R_j should share at least one task argument.
- $Convert(S_i, MF_i, R_j, MF_T)$: converts R_j from source formalism MF_i and their elements to the target one MF_T (the converted requirement element *creation date* attribute format from $yyyy/mm/dd$ to $dd/mm/yyyy$).
- $Filter(S_i, R_j, A_j, CS)$: filters the requirement R_j (of the source S_i) based on its argument (A_j) keeping only the part satisfying constraint CS.
- $Join(S_i, R_j, R_k, rule)$: joins requirements R_j and R_k based on defined *rule*. It detects requirements relationships (*Equal, Contain,* ..., etc.).
- $Aggregate(\mathcal{FRW}, R_j, Res_j, C_j, Op_j)$: aggregates requirements R_j having result Res_j and criterion C_j based on functions Op_j. Note that aggregation is done on criterion that quantify satisfaction of requirements result and result realized by the system.

Example 2. Let us consider three requirements having the following values of criterion: $(R_1 : age < 20; R_2 : age > 55; R_3 : age < 40)$. Aggregation is done according to the predicate: $age < 40$ that aggregates R_1 and R_3.

Inference Operators.

- $Identification(\mathcal{FRW}, R_i, R_j, IdentRule)$: identifies complex relations between two requirements R_i and R_j such as *Equal, Contain, Refine,* etc. It is done via reasoning based on the identification rules.
- $Inference(\mathcal{FRW}, R_i, R_j, InfRule)$: enables inferring new complex relations between two requirements R_i and R_j. It is done via reasoning on inference rules and existing requirements relationships (*Equal, Contain,* ..., etc.) defined by the designer. Suppose that R_1 *Equal* R_2 and R_2 *Contains* R_3. By the presence of the inference rule: "$(R_i$ *Equal* $R_j)$ and $(R_j$ *Contains* $R_k)$ then $(R_i$ *Contains* $R_k)$", we can deduce that R_1 *Contains* R_3.
- $CheckConsistency(S, R_i, R_j, Rule)$: checks consistency of relations between requirements R_i and R_j, using reasoners, on the basis of defined *Consistency Checking rules* in order to verify existing complex relationships. If we have

R_1 *Equal* R_2 and R_1 *Conflict_With* R_2, and the rule *Consistency Check rule* saying that: if (R_i *Equal* R_j) and (R_i *Conflict_With* R_j) then (R_i *inconsistency_With* R_j) which is the case of R_1 and R_2.

Management Operators. Some primitives have been added to manage arguments of requirement such as: *AddSurrogateKey, AddTask, UpdateTask, DeleteTask, AddOrdering*.

- *AddSurrogatekey*($\mathcal{FRW}, R_j, T_i^j$): allows an automatic generation of sequence numbers (unique surrogate keys) for each requirement R_j and related tasks T_i^j in the warehouse.
- *AddTask*($\mathcal{FRW}, R_j, T_i^j$): adds the task T_i^j to the requirement R_j in the target $\mathcal{FRW}$, needed during union and merging of requirements.
- *UpdateTask*($\mathcal{FRW}, R_j, T_i^j$): updates the task T_i^j of the $\mathcal{FR}$ R_j in the target $\mathcal{FRW}$, during transformations operations.
- *DeleteTask*($\mathcal{FRW}, R_j, T_i^j$): deletes the task T_i^j from the requirement R_j, used for duplicated tasks.
- *AddOrdering*(DW_T, R_i, R_j, Ord): adds an ordering sequence Ord between two requirements R_i and R_j. It uses *identification* primitive to identify relations and reasoner to order tasks.

The following algorithm summarizes the different steps of our ETL process.

4.3 The Physical Phase

The logical model is translated into a physical one. This translation has to take into account the storage layout of the target DBMS. We distinguish three main types of storage: horizontal, vertical, hybrid models [12]. We choose to deploy our $\mathcal{RDW}$ using vertical representation of Oracle DBMS. Oracle is based on Semantic RDF[9] that supports SPARQL Semantic Query language and enhanced reasoning mechanism. On this basis, we translated the $\mathcal{RDW}$ schema into vertical model and we generated an N-Triple file loaded using Oracle's Bulk. Then, we apply the ETL algorithm to populate the target schema. For that, we translate each $\mathcal{ETL}$ operator according to the logical level of the target DBMS. Here an example of the translation of the filter operator in SPARQL:

```
PREFIX req:<http://www.owl-ontologies.com/OntoReqUnivWordnet.owl\#>
PREFIX rdf:      <http://www.w3.org/1999/02/22-rdf-syntax-ns\#>
RETREIVE: Retrieves incoming requirement sets.
Select ?instanceREQ where {{?InstanceREQ rdf:type req:Requirement }}
```

The following example shows the code that identifies thhe relationships between requirements:

```
Create or replace TRIGGER REQUIREMENT\_RELATION\_IDENTIFICATION
BEFORE INSERT OR DELETE OR UPDATE ON university\_rdf\_data
BEGIN    //Rulebase creation for relationships identification
   EXECUTE SEM\_APIS.CREATE\_RULEBASE('identif\_rb');
   //Index to associate the rulebase to ontology model
```

---

[9] https://www.w3.org/RDF/.

```
EXECUTE SEM\_APIS.CREATE\_RULES\_INDEX('rdfs\_rix\_university',
SEM\_Models('university'),SEM\_Rulebases('OWLPRIME','identify\_rb'));
//Insertion of the user defined rule
INSERT INTO mdsys.semr\_identif\_rb VALUES('rule','(?R1 :ComposedOfTask ?T1) (?R2
:ComposedOfTask ?T2) (?T1 :TaskComposedOfAction ?A1) (?T2 :TaskComposedOfAction ?A2)
(?A1 :Antonym ?A2)', NULL, '(?R1 :conflictwith ?R2)', SEM\_ALIASES(SEM\_ALIAS('',
 'http://www.owl-ontologies.com/OntoReqUnivWordnet1.owl\#')));
Commit;
//Generation of relationship by the rules
EXECUTE SEM\_APIS.CREATE\_ENTAILMENT('rdfs\_rix\_university',
SEM\_MODELS('university'),SEM\_RULEBASES('OWLPRIME','identify\_rb'));
END;
```

4.4   Exploration of the Requirement Cube

Our approach allows decision makers of the project performing analysis on the obtained warehouse using OLAP (On-Line Analytical Processing) queries. Usually, these queries are implemented using SQL. Our requirement warehouse is implemented using semantic solutions. As a consequence, any exploration has to be performed via SPARQL endpoints queries. Since the requirement designers and decision makers are not so familiar with warehousing technology, we propose the use of the Data Cube vocabulary (QB) to implement the cube queries. *QB4OLAP*[10] is a proposal by the W3C for RDF data. Its vocabulary is an extension to the Data Cube vocabulary that allows representing OLAP cubes in RDF, and also implementing OLAP operators (such as Roll-up, Slice, and Dice) as SPARQL queries on the RDF representation. *QB4OLAP* allows querying multidimensional data by considering their hierarchies and relations between levels and their members. In Oracle RDBMS, the implementation of translator package is required. The *QB4OLAP* query statement that defines the cube of requirements is defined as follows:

```
prefix req: <http://www.owl-ontologies.com/OntoReqUnivWordnet.owl\#>
PREFIX  qb:  <http://purl.org/linked-data/cube\#>
PREFIX qb4o:  <http://purl.org/olap\#>
//Define requirement structure and dimensions
  req:RequirementCube  a  qb:DataStructureDefinition;
  rdfs:label  "Requirement" ;
  rdf:type  req:Requirement.
//Dimensions
  qb:component  qb:dimension  req:Location.
  qb:component  qb:dimension  req:Time.
  qb:component  qb:dimension  req:Actor.
  qb:component  qb:dimension  req:Task.
  qb:component  qb:dimension  req:Criterion.
  qb:component  qb:dimension  req:Result.
  qb:component  qb:measure  req:context.
//Definition  of  measures
  qb:component qb:measure req:RquirementCount; qb4o:AggregateFuction
  qb4o:Count; rdf:predicate req:IDreq;
  qb:component qb:measure req:ResultReqAvg; qb4o:AggregateFuction
  qb4o:avg ; rdf:predicate req:IdResult;
//Attributes
  qb:component  qb:attribute  req:DescriptionReq.
  qb:component  qb:attribute  req:PriorityReq.
```

---

[10] http://publishing-multidimensional-data.googlecode.com/git-history/
6db60dff91cf4571432f6bf0b31b339579d63795/index.html.

```
qb:component  qb:attribute  req:Status.
qb:component  qb:attribute  req:TypeR.
qb:component  qb:attribute  req:context.
PREFIX req:<http://www.owl-ontologies.com/OntoReqUnivWordnet.owl\#>
PREFIX rdf:<http://www.w3.org/1999/02/22-rdf-syntax-ns\#>
RETREIVE: Retrieves incoming requirement sets.
Select ?instanceREQ where {
                    {?InstanceREQ rdf:type req:Requirement }}
```

Algorithm 1. $\mathcal{R}$equirement $\mathcal{ETL}$ Algorithm

---

begin

    1. **Inputs:** $\mathcal{FRW}$ schema, $\mathcal{S}_i$: Requirements sources ($InputREQ$).
    2. **Output:** $\mathcal{FRW}$ (schema + instances) containing $OutputREQ$.

    $R_{dw} := \emptyset;\ T_{dw} := \emptyset;\ F_{dw} := Formalism$
    $R_{Si} := \emptyset;\ T_{Si} := \emptyset;\ A_{Si} := \emptyset;$
    for *Each* $\mathcal{R}$*equirement Source* $\mathcal{S}_i$ **do**
        for *Each* $(R_j \in \mathcal{S}_i) \wedge (R_j\ isConcept)$ **do**
            $R_j := \text{Extract}(\mathcal{S}_i, R_j, A_i^j, \mathcal{CS});$
            $\text{Convert}(\mathcal{S}_i, R_j, F_i^j, F_{dw})$
            if $(R_j\ contains \equiv \mathcal{R}equirements \vee tasks)$ **then**
                $\text{UpdateTask}(R_{FRW}, T_k^{dw}, R_j, T_i^j)$
                $\text{Merge}(\mathcal{S}_i, R_i, A_k^i, R_j, A_l^j, \mathcal{PG});$
                $\text{Union}(\mathcal{FRW}, R_{dw}, A_k^{dw}, R_j, A_l^j, \mathcal{PG});$
            end
            else if $(R_j\ contains \subseteq/\supseteq \mathcal{R}equirements \vee tasks)$ **then**
                if R_j *has reflexive Object-Property* **then**
                    $\text{Join}(\mathcal{FFW}, R_{dw}, R_j, rule);$
                end
                else if $Res_i^j \neq \emptyset \vee C_l^j \neq \emptyset$ **then**
                    $\text{Aggregate}(\mathcal{FRW}, R_j, Res_i^j, C_l^j, Op);$
                end
            end
            if *(exists* $R_{FRW}.duplicate)$ **then**
                $\text{Filter}(R_{FDW}, DD(T_i^j));$
            end
            $\text{AddSurrogatekey}(\mathcal{FRW}, R_{dw})$
            $\text{Store}(\mathcal{FRW}, R_{FRW})$
        end
        for *Each* $\mathcal{R}$*equirement* R_{dw} **do**
            $\text{CheckConsistency}(\mathcal{FRW}, R_{FRW}, rule);$
            $\text{identification}(\mathcal{DW}, R_{FRW}, IdentRule);$
            $\text{Inference}(\mathcal{FRW}, R_{FRW}, InfRules);$
        end
    end

end

The *Facts* that correspond to a given data structure are called observations. Each observation represents a point in the multidimensional space formed by dimensions. For each point, a set of measure values is recorded. Since OLAP cubes are represented as RDF graphs, and the result of any OLAP query must be also a cube, OLAP queries have to be implemented as SPARQL queries.

Example 3. Let us assume that a designer wants to compute the number of requirements per country. The SPARQL query corresponding to this need is:

```
PREFIX qb: <http://purl.org/linked-data/cube\#>
PREFIX req: <http://req.org/schemas/>
SELECT  ?req ?loc ?time (COUNT(?REQ) AS ?requirementcount)
WHERE {
         { ?li a qb:Observation;
                qb:dataSet <http://req.org/data/dataset-aggview2>;
                req:Location ?loc ; req:Time ?time ; req:revenue ?REQ.}
         FILTER(?Loc \= 'PARIS')}
GROUP BY ?loc ?time
ORDER BY ?time DESC(?requirementcount)
```

Its corresponding *QB4OLAP* query is given by:

```
<http://www.owl-ontologies.com/OntoReqUnivWordnet1.owl\#R1>  a  qb:Observation;
qb:dataSet  req:RequirementDataWarehouse;
req:RequirementCount  36;
req:Country  <http://www.owl-ontologies.com/OntoReqUnivWordnet1.owl\#21> .
req:CountryName  "Paris".
```

5   Experimentation

To demonstrate the effectiveness and efficiency of our proposal, we conduct a set of experiments to evaluate three criteria: (i) the complexity of the proposed $\mathcal{ETL}$ requirement algorithm, (ii) the inference performance and (iii) the query answering to some requirements.

To do so, we have generated three data sets of requirements defined in three different formalisms ($\mathcal{G}$oal, $\mathcal{U}$ses Case and $\mathcal{T}$reatment), containing respectively 40, 30 and 40 requirements using $\mathcal{LUBM}$ ontology benchmark and the courses' management system ($\mathcal{CMS}$). *Wordnet* is used as a linguistic ontology. Oracle DBMS is used to deploy the sources and the target warehouse. Oracle offers different formats for data loading such as: RDF/XML, N-TRIPLES, N-QUADS, TriG and Turtle. We choose N-Triple format (.nt) to load instances using *Oracle Bulk*. Oracle integrates a reasoner engine defined based on *TrOWL* and *Pellet*. The following examples show user defined rules:

1. **Identification rules**: identify direct *conflicts* relationships: Rule1: (?R1 :ComposedOfTask ?T1) ∧ (?R2 :ComposedOfTask ?T2) ∧ (?T1 TaskComposedOfAction ?A1) ∧ (?T2 :TaskComposedOfAction ?A2) ∧ (?A1 :Antonym ?A2) → (?R1 :conflictwith ?R2)

   In Oracle, this leads to implement a user defined rule *identify-rb* and to insert it in the Oracle warehouse:

```
INSERT INTO mdsys.semr_identif_rb VALUES('1_ruleSC','(?R1 :ComposedOfTask ?T1)
          (?R2 :ComposedOfTask ?T2) (?T1 :TaskComposedOfAction ?A1)
          (?T2 :TaskComposedOfAction ?A2) (?A1 :Antonym ?A2)', NULL,
          '(?R1 :conflictwith ?R2)', SEM_ALIASES(SEM_ALIAS('',
          'http://www.owl-ontologies.com/OntoReqUnivWordnet1.owl\#')));
```

2. **Inference rules:** infers the indirect *Refine* requirement relation.

Rule2: refines(?R1, ?R2) ∧ refines(?R2, ?R3) → refines(?R1, ?R3)

In Oracle, this leads to implement a user defined rule *infer-rb* and insert it in the Oracle schema:

```
INSERT INTO mdsys.semr_infer_rb VALUES('1_ruleS','(?R1 :refines ?R2)
        (?R2 :refines ?R3)', NULL, '(?R1 :refines ?R3)', SEM_ALIASES(
        SEM_ALIAS('','http://www.owl-ontologies.com/OntoReqUnivWordnet1.owl\#')));
```

3. **Consistency checking rule:** checks the consistency of the detected relations. Rule3: (?R1 :equal ?R2) ∧ (?R1 :contains ?R2) → (?R1 :conflictwith ?R2)

In Oracle, this leads to implement a user defined rule *consist-rb* and to insert it in the Oracle schema:

```
INSERT INTO mdsys.semr_consist_rb VALUES('1_ruleSC','(?R1 :equal ?R2)
        (?R1 :contain ?R2)', NULL, '(?R1 :inconsistencywith ?R2)', SEM_ALIASES(
        SEM_ALIAS('','http://www.owl-ontologies.com/OntoReqUnivWordnet1.owl\#')));
```

Our evaluations were performed on a laptop computer (HP Elite-Book 840 G2) with an Intel(R) CoreTM i5-5200U CPU 2.20 GHZ and 8 GB of RAM and a 500 GB hard disk. We use Windows10 64 bits. We use *Oracle Database 12c release 1* that offers RDF Semantic features.

The experiment consists in integrating the three requirements sources into $\mathcal{FR}$ warehouse. The following results are obtained for each experiment:

Requirement ETL Algorithm Complexity. The algorithm is implemented based on requirement concepts and terms. We examine the number of iterations of our algorithm to populate the $\mathcal{RDW}$. The algorithm is based on searched concepts and not instances. The time complexity is $O(n)$, where n represents the number of involved concepts (which means conceptual ontology concepts and terms of the linguistic ontology). Figure 5 gives the number of iterations for concepts involved in $\mathcal{MD}$ schema. It indicates a polynomial time of the execution.

Reasoning Performance. We evaluate the inference mechanism using $\mathcal{OWLP}$rime, $\mathcal{RDF}$, $\mathcal{RDFS}$ fragments and user defined rules in order to: (i) Identify requirement relationships such as: *require, contain*; (ii) *infer* new relationships and (iii) check the consistency of detected relations. First, we define a new model that stores requirement instances integrated from the sources. Then, we use a reasoner to infer requirement instances using Oracle fragments and user

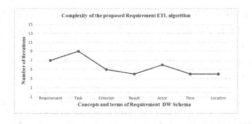

Fig. 5. Complexity of the proposed $\mathcal{R}$equirement $\mathcal{ETL}$ algorithm

Table 1. Inference performance: time and number of triples.

Criteria	Inferred instances	$\mathcal{FRW}$ requirements	Time (s)
RDF fragment	47	43118	3,75
RDFS fragment	18583	61701	8,62
OWLprime fragment	400	62101	5,11
Identify rules	1019	63120	4,4
Consistency rules	312	63432	2,28
Inferring rules	3062	66494	8,90

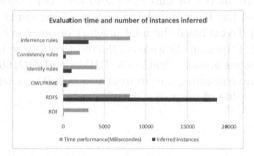

Fig. 6. Evaluation time and number of inferred instances.

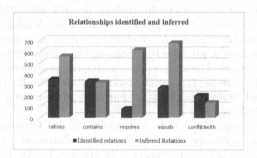

Fig. 7. Detected relations.

defined rules. Table 1 gives the obtained results. It clearly demonstrates that the number of inferred relationships is important. It includes also the number of the corrected relations which means that the target $\mathcal{FRW}$ contains more consistent requirements relationships which represents a added value for designer. Figure 6 shows the number of instances inferred and the response time.

Relationships Identified, Inferred and Corrected. The integration of $\mathcal{FR}$ in the $\mathcal{FRW}$ allows identifying and inferring relationships between requirements such as: *refines, requires, contains*, ..., etc. Defined rules are created and the reasoner mechanism is applied to identify the corrected and inferred relations. Figure 7 indicates the number of identified and inferred relationships.

6   Conclusion

In this paper, we present a comprehensive and a complete methodology to design requirement warehouses. It uses linguistic and conceptual domain ontologies. All the phases of the warehouse design are defined: (**a**) conceptual model build based on our pivot model used to inter-operate the different used formalisms to define user requirements. This model has been enriched by Location and the Period when the requirements are expressed to augment the traceability and evolution of the requirements. (**b**) The traditional operators of ETL have been leveraged to consider the requirements. The cleaning phase of ETL has been elaborated inference mechanism offered by ontologies and precedence graph. (**c**) The multidimensional model has been translated to logical one using defined rules into Oracle DBMS. (**d**) To evaluate the final product of our methodology, we stress our physical model. Experiments were conducted to evaluate the effectiveness of efficiency of our proposal using Oracle 12c DBMS and *QB4OLAP*.

Currently, we are extending our approach to include knowledge base such as Yago to give more value of our target warehouse.

References

1. Abrial, J.: The B tool (abstract). In: VDM, pp. 86–87 (1988)
2. Boukhari, I., Bellatreche, L., Jean, S.: An ontological pivot model to interoperate heterogeneous user requirements. In: ISOLA, pp. 344–358 (2012)
3. Dahlstedt, Å.G., Persson, A.: Requirements interdependencies: state of the art and future challenges. In: Aurum, A., Wohlin, C. (eds.) Engineering and Managing Software Requirements, pp. 95–116. Springer, Heidelberg (2005)
4. Djilani, Z., Khouri, S.: Understanding user requirements iceberg: semantic based approach. In: Bellatreche, L., Manolopoulos, Y., Zielinski, B., Liu, R. (eds.) MEDI 2015. LNCS, vol. 9344, pp. 297–310. Springer, Heidelberg (2015). doi:10.1007/978-3-319-23781-7_24
5. Farfeleder, S., Moser, T., Krall, A., Ståalhane, T., Omoronyia, I., Zojer, H.: Ontology-driven guidance for requirements elicitation. In: Antoniou, G., Grobelnik, M., Simperl, E., Parsia, B., Plexousakis, D., De Leenheer, P., Pan, J. (eds.) ESWC 2011, Part II. LNCS, vol. 6644, pp. 212–226. Springer, Heidelberg (2011)
6. Ramesh, M.: Toward reference models for requirements traceability. IEEE Trans. Softw. Eng. **27**(1), 58–93 (2001)
7. Giorgini, P., Rizzi, S., Garzetti, M.: Goal-oriented requirement analysis for data warehouse design. In: ACM DOLAP, pp. 47–56. ACM (2005)
8. Goknil, A., Kurtev, I., Berg, K., Veldhuis, J.-W.: Semantics of trace relations in requirements models for consistency checking and inferencing. Softw. Syst. Model. **10**(1), 31–54 (2011)
9. Inmon, W.H.: Data Warehousing: Using the Wal-Mart Model. Wiley, Hoboken (2005)
10. Kaiya, H., Saeki, M.: Ontology based requirements analysis: lightweight semantic processing approach. In: QSIC, pp. 223–230 (2005)
11. Khouri, S., Bellatreche, L., Jean, S., Ameur, Y.A.: Requirements driven data warehouse design: we can go further. In: ISOLA, pp. 588–603 (2014)

12. Khouri, S., Semassel, K., Bellatreche, L.: Managing data warehouse traceability: a life-cycle driven approach. In: CAISE, pp. 199–213 (2015)
13. Körner, S.J., Brumm, T.: Natural language specification improvement with ontologies. Int. J. Semant. Comput. 3(04), 445–470 (2009)
14. Laplante, P.: Requirements Engineering for Software and Systems, 2nd edn. CRC Press, Boca Raton (2003)
15. López, O., Laguna, M.A., Peñalvo, F.J.G.: Metamodeling for requirements reuse. In: ER, pp. 76–90 (2002)
16. Miller, G.A.: Wordnet: a lexical database for english. Commun. ACM 38(11), 39–41 (1995)
17. och Dag, J.N., Gervasi, V., Brinkkemper, S., Regnell, B.: A linguistic-engineering approach to large-scale requirements management. IEEE Softw. 22(1), 32–39 (2005)
18. Perrouin, G., Brottier, E., Baudry, B., Le Traon, Y.: Composing models for detecting inconsistencies: a requirements engineering perspective. In: Glinz, M., Heymans, P. (eds.) REFSQ 2009 Amsterdam. LNCS, vol. 5512, pp. 89–103. Springer, Heidelberg (2009)
19. Pierra, G.: Context representation in domain ontologies and its use for semantic integration of data. In: Spaccapietra, S. (ed.) Journal on Data Semantics X. LNCS, vol. 4900, pp. 174–211. Springer, Heidelberg (2008)
20. Rochfeld, A.: Merise, an information system design and development methodology, tutorial. In: ER, pp. 489–528 (1986)
21. Rosa, M.L., Reijers, H.A., Aalst, W.M.P., Dijkman, R.M., Mendling, J., Dumas, M., García-Bañuelos, L.: APROMORE: an advanced process model repository. Expert Syst. Appl. 38(6), 7029–7040 (2011)
22. Skoutas, D., Simitsis, A.: Designing ETL processes using semantic web technologies. In: ACM DOLAP, pp. 67–74 (2006)
23. Sun, Y.J., Barukh, M.C., Benatallah, B., Beheshti, S.: Scalable saas-basedprocess customization with casewalls. In: ICSOC, pp. 218–233 (2015)
24. Van Lamsweerde, A.: Goal-oriented requirements enginering: a roundtrip from research to practice [enginering read engineering]. In: Requirements Engineering Conference, pp. 4–7. IEEE (2004)
25. Westerman, P.: Data Warehousing: Using the Wal-Mart Model. Morgan Kaufmann, Burlington (2001)

Heterogeneous Semantics and Unifying Theories

Jim Woodcock[1(✉)], Simon Foster[1], and Andrew Butterfield[2]

[1] Department of Computer Science, University of York, York YO10 5GH, UK
{jim.woodcock,simon.foster}@york.ac.uk
[2] School of Computer Science and Statistics,
Trinity College, University of Dublin, Dublin 2, Ireland
Andrew.Butterfield@scss.tcd.ie

Abstract. Model-driven development is being used increasingly in the development of modern computer-based systems. In the case of cyber-physical systems (including robotics and autonomous systems) no single modelling solution is adequate to cover all aspects of a system, such as discrete control, continuous dynamics, and communication networking. Instead, a heterogeneous modelling solution must be adopted. We propose a theory engineering technique involving Isabelle/HOL and Hoare & He's Unifying Theories of Programming. We illustrate this approach with mechanised theories for building a contractual theory of sequential programming, a theory of pointer-based programs, and the reactive theory underpinning CSP's process algebra. Galois connections provide the mechanism for linking these theories.

1 Introduction

Modern complex computer-based systems are often designed using model-based design techniques, checking models against specified requirements. Many diverse models may be needed to achieve this, encompassing software control, communication networking, and physical dynamics, all of which must contribute to the correct functioning of the system. This multi-paradigm approach involves different modelling languages and tools, including a wide range of analysis and simulation techniques. At present, there is neither a universal modelling language nor a universal tool for managing this diversity. Instead, modelling languages and tools must be used together cooperatively; a solution that seems most appropriate for handling complexity, anyway.

In this paper, we consider one approach to understanding heterogeneity in modelling and analysis, and how links can be made between different languages and their tools. We advocate mechanised theory engineering: the computer-supported development of definitions, axioms, and theorems encapsulating a particular concept. Theory engineering is the study of a concept in isolation, as well as exploring relationships between different concepts. The theory engineer builds coherent theory libraries, giving guidelines for building and adding new theories in order to support open semantic heterogeneity. We use Isabelle for this task, mechanising Unifying Theories of Programming (UTP), our chosen formalism for modelling language semantics [25].

© Springer International Publishing AG 2016
T. Margaria and B. Steffen (Eds.): ISoLA 2016, Part I, LNCS 9952, pp. 374–394, 2016.
DOI: 10.1007/978-3-319-47166-2_26

Isabelle is an LCF-style interactive theorem prover: it has a special abstract type thm for theorems; the inference rules of the logical system are the constructors of the abstract type; it is implemented in a strongly typed high-level language. Logical correctness is enforced in the implementation language: everything of type thm has really been proved. The embedding in a full programming language allows the user to implement more sophisticated derived rules that decompose to the primitives without compromising soundness, allowing proof engineering at a much higher level than a simple proof checker.

Our embedding of UTP in Isabelle currently has three foundational theories: relations, designs, and reactive processes; further theories are under construction, including the hybrid relations. This allows us to build models of nondeterministic sequential programs, networks of reactive processes, and hybrid systems, including robotic and cyber-physical systems. These theories are accompanied by formalised and mechanised proofs of relevant properties. The theories themselves are structured as lattices linked by Galois connections, allowing for models to be translated between or embedded in different modelling paradigms.

In Sect. 2, we give an overview of UTP, and in Sect. 3, we give a detailed practical example of a UTP theory of separation logic. In Sect. 4, we consider the use of UTP in dealing with semantic heterogeneity by embedding the theory of designs in the theory of CSP processes. We show how this leads to a natural contract language for all constructs in all theories, including nonterminating reactive processes. In Sect. 5, we discuss related work and in Sect. 6, we draw some conclusions.

2 Unifying Theories of Programming

Unifying Theories of Programming (UTP) [33] is a long-term research agenda that records the relationship between different programming paradigms, both practical and theoretical. UTP has been widely used: Hoare & He formalise theories of sequential programming, with assertions; correct compilation; concurrent computation with reactive processes and communications; higher-order logic programming; and theories that link denotational, algebraic, and operational semantics [33]. More recent contributions include: angelic nondeterminism [16,22,43,44]; aspect orientation [21]; event-driven programs [67]; model checking [1]; object orientation [15,47,51,65]; references and pointers [12,27]; probabilistic programs [6,32,69]; real-time programs [28,31,48,49,55]; reversible computation [52,53]; synchronicity [9]; timed reactive programs [50,58]; and transaction processing [29,30]. Programming language semantics in UTP include: the hardware description languages Handel-C [40,41] and Verilog [68]; the multi-paradigm languages *Circus* [37,38,62] and CML [59,63]; Safety-Critical Java [17, 19,20,39]; and Simulink [14]. A wide variety of programming theories have been formalised in UTP, including theories of confidentiality [4,5], testing [10,11,56], interrupts [34], and undefinedness [3,61]. UTP has been embedded in a variety of theorem provers, notably in ProofPower Z and Isabelle [8,24,36,64]. This allows a theory engineer to mechanically construct UTP theories, experiment, prove properties, and eventually deploy them for use in program verification. In this paper, we focus on Isabelle/UTP [24].

UTP gives three principal ways to study the relationships between different programming paradigms. UTP classifies languages according to their computational model (structured, object-oriented, functional, logical, etc.). Common concepts are identified and variations treated separately. A different categorisation is by level of abstraction within a particular paradigm. This might range from platform-specific implementation technology at the bottom, and very high-level description of overall requirements at the top end. Between these, there are descriptions of components and their architectures. Each level has contractual interfaces, and UTP gives ways of mapping between these levels based on a formal notion of refinement that provides guarantees of correctness all the way from requirements to code. The final classification is by the method chosen to present a language definition. Three widely used scientific methods are: (i) *Denotational*, in which each syntactic phrase is given a single mathematical meaning, a specification is just a set of denotations, and refinement is a simple correctness criterion of inclusion: every program behaviour is also a specification behaviour. (ii) *Algebraic*, where no direct meaning is given to the language, but instead equalities relate different programs with the same meaning. (iii) *Operational*, where programs are defined by how they execute on an idealised abstract mathematical machine, giving a useful guide for compilation, debugging, and testing. As Hoare & He point out [33], a comprehensive account of a programming theory needs all three kinds of presentation, and the UTP technique allows us to study differences and mutual embeddings, and to derive each from the others by mathematical definition, calculation, and proof.

The UTP research agenda has as its ultimate goal to cover all the interesting paradigms of computing, including both declarative and procedural, hardware and software. It presents a theoretical foundation for understanding software and systems engineering, and has been already been exploited in areas such as hardware [41,70], hardware/software co-design [7] and component-based systems [66]. But it also presents an opportunity when constructing new languages, especially ones with heterogeneous paradigms and techniques.

Having studied the variety of existing programming languages and identified the major components of programming languages and theories, we can select theories for new, perhaps special-purpose languages. The analogy here is of a theory supermarket, where you shop for exactly those features you need while being confident that the theories plug-and-play together nicely.

UTP uses an alphabetised version of Tarski's relational calculus, presented in a predicative style. Each programming construct is formalised as a relation between an initial and an intermediate or final observation. The collection of these relations forms a *theory* of the paradigm being studied, and it contains three essential parts: an alphabet, a signature, and healthiness conditions. *The alphabet* is a set of variable names that gives the vocabulary for the theory being studied. Names are chosen for any relevant external observations of behaviour.

For instance, a program with variables x, y, and z would contain these names in its alphabet. Theories for particular programming paradigms require the observation of extra information; some examples are: a flag that says whether the program has started (ok); the current time ($clock$); the number of available resources (res); a trace of the events in the life of the program (tr); a set of refused events (ref); or a flag that says whether the program is waiting for interaction with its environment ($wait$).

The signature gives the rules for the syntax for denoting objects of the theory. For instance, in a theory of imperative programming this would include operators like sequential composition, assignment, if-then-else, and iteration. *Healthiness conditions* identify properties that characterise the predicates of the theory. Each healthiness condition embodies an important fact about the computational model for the programs being studied.

Example 1 (Boyle's Law). Consider a simple theory to model the behaviour of a gas with regard to varying temperature and pressure. The physical phenomenon of the behaviour of the gas is subject to Boyle's Law: "For a fixed amount of an ideal gas kept at a fixed temperature k, p (pressure) and V (volume) are inversely proportional (while one doubles, the other halves)". The alphabet of our theory contains the three mathematical variables described in Boyle's Law: k, p, and V. The model's observations correspond to real-world observations in what we might term *the model-based agenda*: the variables k, p, and V are *shared* with the real world. We now need to describe the syntax used to denote objects of the theory. There is a requirement that temperature remains constant, so, to use our model to simulate the effects of Boyle's law, we need just two operations, one to change the pressure and one change the volume. We know the observations we can make of our theory and the two operations we can use to change these observations. We now need to define some *healthiness conditions* as a way of determining membership of the theory. We are interested only in gases that obey Boyle's law, which states that $p * V = k$ must be *invariant*. Healthiness conditions determine the correct states of the system, and here we need both static and dynamic invariants:

- The equation $p * V = k$ is a *static* invariant: it applies to a *state*.
- We also require k to be constant. If we start in the state (k, p, V), where $p * V = k$, then transit to the state (k', p', V'), where $p' * V' = k'$, then we must have that $k' = k$. This is a *dynamic* invariant: it applies to a *relation*.

Suppose we have $\alpha(\phi) = \{p, V, k\}$; then define $\boldsymbol{B}(\phi) = (\exists k \bullet \phi) \wedge (k = p * V)$. Now, regardless of whether ϕ is healthy or not, $\boldsymbol{B}(\phi)$ certainly is. For example:

$$\phi = (p = 10) \wedge (V = 5) \wedge (k = 100)$$
$$\boldsymbol{B}(\phi) = (\exists k \bullet \phi) \wedge (k = p * V) = (p = 10) \wedge (V = 5) \wedge (k = 50)$$

Notice that $\boldsymbol{B}(\boldsymbol{B}(\phi)) = \boldsymbol{B}(\phi)$. This is known as *idempotence*: taking the medicine twice leaves you healthy, no more and no less so than taking the medicine only once. This give us a simple test for healthiness: ϕ is already healthy if applying $\boldsymbol{B}$ leaves it unchanged. That is, if it satisfies the equation $\phi = \boldsymbol{B}(\phi)$. In this sense, ϕ is a fixed point of the idempotent function $\boldsymbol{B}$.

Consider another observation, that the pressure is between 10 and 20Pa:

$$\psi = (p \in 10\,..\,20) \wedge (V = 5)$$

Clearly, $\phi \Rightarrow \psi$. If we make both ϕ and ψ healthy, we discover another fact; namely, that: $\boldsymbol{B}(\phi) \Rightarrow \boldsymbol{B}(\psi)$. In fact, $\boldsymbol{B}$ is *monotonic* in the sense that

$$\forall \phi, \psi \bullet (\phi \Rightarrow \psi) \Rightarrow (\boldsymbol{B}(\phi) \Rightarrow \boldsymbol{B}(\psi))$$

The most useful healthiness conditions are *monotonic idempotent functions*, which leads to some very important mathematical properties concerning complete lattices and Galois connections. □

Example 2 (Nondeterministic sequential programming language). The signature for designs consists of assignment $(x := e)$, sequential composition $(P;\ Q)$, conditional choice $(P \lhd b \rhd Q)$, nondeterministic choice $(P \sqcap Q)$, and recursion $(P = F(P))$. The only observations that can be made are of the program variables. There are no healthiness conditions for this simple programming language. The program operators are given the following meanings:

Command	Semantics	Alphabet
$x := e$	$(x' = e) \wedge (v' = v)$	$\{x, v, x', v'\}$
$P\,;\,Q$	$\exists v_0 \bullet P[v_0/v'] \wedge Q[v_0/v]$	$in\alpha P \cup out\alpha Q$
$P \sqcap Q$	$P \vee Q$	$\alpha P \cup \alpha Q$
$P \lhd b \rhd Q$	$(P \wedge b) \vee (Q \wedge \neg\, b)$	$\alpha P = \alpha Q \supseteq \alpha b$
$P = F(P)$	νF (the strongest fixed point of F)	αP

In this table, the alphabetised predicate P has the alphabet αP, which is partitioned into the disjoint sets $\in \alpha P$ (containing input variables, like x) and $out\alpha P$ (containing output variables, like x').

Example 3 (Hoare logic). Hoare logic is a set of axioms and inference rules for reasoning formally about the correctness of programs. The central feature of Hoare logic is the Hoare triple, which describes how the execution of a piece of code changes the state of the computation. A Hoare triple is of the form $\{p\}\ Q\ \{r\}$, where p and r are predicates on the program state (the precondition and the postcondition respectively) and Q is a command build from the signature of our programming language. Standard Hoare logic provides a way of reasoning about partial correctness; termination needs to be proved separately. The next definition defines the denotation of a Hoare triple.

Definition 4 (Hoare triple [33]).

$$\{p\}\ Q\ \{r\} \ \widehat{=}\ [\,Q \Rightarrow (p \Rightarrow r')\,] \qquad = \qquad (p \Rightarrow r') \sqsubseteq Q$$

In this definition, the notation $[A]$ is used to denote the universal closure of A over its alphabet. The notation $A \sqsubseteq B$ asserts that the predicate A is refined by the predicate B, which is defined as $[B \Rightarrow A]$ (as shown in the equivalence).

The axioms and inference rules are proved as theorems in UTP, providing the first link in this paper between different semantics: axiomatic and denotational.

Definition 5 (Hoare logic).

L1 *if* $\{p\}\,Q\,\{r\}$ *and* $\{p\}\,Q\,\{s\}$ *then* $\{p\}\,Q\,\{r \wedge s\}$
L2 *if* $\{p\}\,Q\,\{r\}$ *and* $\{q\}\,Q\,\{r\}$ *then* $\{p \vee q\}\,Q\,\{r\}$
L3 *if* $\{p\}\,Q\,\{r\}$ *then* $\{p \wedge q\}\,Q\,\{r \vee s\}$

L4 $\{r[e/x]\}\,x := e\,\{r\}$
L5 *if* $\{p \wedge b\}\,Q_1\,\{r\}$ *and* $\{p \wedge \neg\, b\}\,Q_2\,\{r\}$
    then $\{p\}\,Q_1 \lhd b \rhd Q_2\,\{r\}$
L6 *if* $\{p\}\,Q_1\,\{s\}$ *and* $\{s\}\,Q_2\,\{r\}$ *then* $\{p\}\,Q_1\,;\,Q_2\,\{r\}$

L7 *if* $\{p\}\,Q_1\,\{r\}$ *and* $\{p\}\,Q_2\,\{r\}$ *then* $\{p\}\,Q_1 \sqcap Q_2\,\{r\}$
L8 *if* $\{b \wedge c\}\,Q\,\{c\}$
    then $\{c\}\,\nu X \bullet (Q\,;\,X) \lhd b \rhd \amalg\,\{\neg\, b \wedge c\}$
L9 $\{false\}\,Q\,\{r\}$
L10 $\{p\}\,Q\,\{true\}$
L11 $\{p\}\,false\,\{false\}$
L12 $\{p\}\,\amalg\,\{p\}$

Note that the program $\amalg$ ("skip") is the relational identity and iteration is given a strongest fixed-point semantics (as defined in the table on p. 5).

Predicate transformers, and in particular the weakest precondition calculus, are closely related to Hoare Logic. We see this link in the next example, where we take an extreme solution to the Hoare triple, fixes two parameters (the command and the postcondition), and finding the weakest solution for the precondition.

Example 6 (Weakest preconditions [33]*).* The weakest precondition can be extracted by applying some simple manipulations in the predicate calculus to the definition of the Hoare triple. To keep track of before, after, and intermediate variables, we have parametrised the precondition, command, and postcondition.

$$\{p(v)\}\,Q(v,v')\,\{r(v)\}$$
$$= [\,Q(v,v') \Rightarrow (p(v) \Rightarrow r(v'))\,]$$
$$= [\,p(v) \Rightarrow (\,Q(v,v') \Rightarrow r(v'))\,]$$
$$= [\,p(v) \Rightarrow (\forall v' \bullet Q(v,v') \Rightarrow r(v'))\,]$$
$$= [\,p(v) \Rightarrow \neg\,(\exists v' \bullet Q(v,v') \wedge \neg\, r(v'))\,]$$
$$= [\,p(v) \Rightarrow \neg\,(\exists v_0 \bullet Q(v,v_0) \wedge \neg\, r(v_0))\,]$$
$$= [\,p(v) \Rightarrow \neg\,(\,Q(v,v')\,;\,\neg\, r(v))\,]$$

We have calculated the weakest solution for Q to guarantee r:

if $\mathcal{W} = \neg\,(\,Q\,;\,\neg\, r)$ **then** $\{\mathcal{W}\}\,Q\,\{r\}$

Definition 7 (Weakest precondition).

$$Q \; \textbf{wp} \; r \; \mathrel{\widehat{=}} \; \neg \, (Q \; ; \neg \, r)$$

Example 8 (Designs). The relational theory is adequate for describing partial correctness; termination requires a more expressive semantics. The signature of the programming language introduced in Example 2 is extended with the syntax of a design, $P \vdash Q$, with precondition P and postcondition Q [57]. The alphabet contains two boolean variables: ok, which is the observation that the program has started; and ok', which is the observation that the program has terminated. Each of these variables has a corresponding healthiness condition.

$$\textbf{H1}(P) \; \mathrel{\widehat{=}} \; ok \Rightarrow P$$
$$\textbf{H2}(P) \; \mathrel{\widehat{=}} \; P \; ; \; J \quad \text{where } J = (ok \Rightarrow ok') \wedge (v' = v), \alpha P = \{v, v', ok, ok'\}$$

H1 ensures that no observation may be made of P's behaviour until after the program has started. **H2** says that P is monotonic with respect to the ok' variable: one of the behaviours of an aborting program is unexpectedly to terminate. Both healthiness conditions are monotonic idenpotents. We define $\textbf{H} = \textbf{H1} \circ \textbf{H2}$. Finally, we define the design $P \vdash Q$ as the single relation $ok \wedge P \Rightarrow ok' \wedge Q$.

In advance of our discussion of separation logic, the following example shows the use of the assignment axiom from Hoare logic.

Example 9 (Programming with assertions). Consider the following outline of a Java class that keeps track of a bank account where overdrafts are not permitted (and, for the sake of simplcitiy in an example, arithmetic does not overflow):

```
1   class BankAccount {
2       private int balance;
3       { invariant : balance >= 0 }
4       ...
5       deposit(int x){
6           { precondition : x > 0 }
7           // is the invariant preserved?
8           // is balance >= 0?
9           ...
10      }
11  }
```

We need to prove that `deposit` preserves the class invariant $balance \geq 0$. The assignment axiom tells us that the precondition for this is that or rather $balance + x \geq 0$. This weaker precondition follows from a stronger one that involves the class invariant before executing `deposit` and the precondition stated for the method: $balance \geq 0 \wedge x > 0$ (**L3** in Defnition 5). Both are valid assumptions.

$$(balance \geq 0)[balance + x / balance]$$

3   Example Theory: Separation Logic

In this section, we present our basic theory for separation logic [46]. We start with a motivating example.

Example 10 (Hoare logic is unsound wrt aliasing). Consider the assignment axiom from Hoare Logic: $\{[E/x]P\}$ x := e $\{P\}$, which represents the fact that the value of a variable x after executing an assignment command x := E equals the value of the expression E in the state before executing it. Formally, if P is to be true after the assignment, then the statement obtained by substituting E for x in P must be true before executing it. Now consider the following program:

```
1   x := (new Cell(3,nil));80
2   y := x;
3   y.head := 4
```

Perversely, let's prove that the program makes the variables x and y distinct. Here, we need the assignment axiom and the proof rules for sequential composition and consequence (read the proof outline from the bottom to the top):

$$\{true\}$$
$$\{4 > 3\}$$
$$\{4 > (new\ Cell(3, nil)).head\}$$
x := new **Cell(3, nil)**
$$\{4 > x.head\}$$
y:=x
$$\{4 > x.head\}$$
y.head := 4
$$\{y.head > x.head\}$$

So, the program always has the postcondition $y.head > x.head$, even though x and y point to the same Cell object! We can tell that something is wrong here, since this doesn't match the expected semantics. It turns out that it's the assignment axiom that's at fault: it's unsound in the presence of aliasing.

Example 10 illustrates a classical problem in Computer Science: *the aliasing problem*. This comes about from using standard programming features: call-by-reference parameters and pointer variables. To overcome the soundness problem, we need more discrimination in our semantic model and inference rules. The frame problem is familiar elsewhere. In AI, it is the challenge of representing the effects of action in logic without having to represent explicitly a large number of intuitively obvious non-effects. More generally, it is about modular reasoning.

Separation logic is one of a number of approaches that solve this problem of unsoundness. It was developed by Reynolds and O'Hearn, based on some early work by Burstall. It helps a programmer to reason about programs that manipulate pointer data structures. More generally, it helps with modular reasoning about ownership of resources and virtual separation between concurrent processes. Our theory of separation logic (utp_seplog) is mechanised in Isabelle/UTP and builds upon the theories of utp_designs and utp_invariants.

We introduce three uninterpreted datatypes: *Var*, the set of program variables names (ranged over by x and y); *Loc*, the set of heap addresses (ranged over by l); and *Val*, the set of values manipulated by a program. As well as program variables, the following observations are made of a program.

1. $fp : \mathbb{F}\,Loc$ The footprint of the program, a finite set of heap addresses accessed by the program.
2. $st :: Var \nrightarrow Val \cup Loc$ The store: the denotations for variables, a finite function from variable names to values or heap addresses.
3. $hp :: Loc \nrightarrow Val \cup Loc$ The heap: the contents of the heap addresses, a finite function from heap addresses to values or further heap addresses.

(The notation $\mathbb{F}\,S$ describes the set of all the finite subsets of S, while $A \nrightarrow B$ describes the set of finite functions from A to B.)

3.1   Healthiness Conditions

Predicates in the theory of separation logic satisfy four healthiness conditions. (i) Nothing changes outside the footprint. (ii) The footprint contains only heap addresses. (iii) A program is independent of the heap outside its footprint. (iv) Every address used in the store or on the heap is itself a heap address (no dangling pointers). These conditions are formalised in the following definition.

Definition 11.

$$\textbf{SL1}(P) \;\widehat{=}\; \textbf{OIH}((fp' \lhd hp' = fp' \lhd hp))(P)$$

$$\textbf{SL2}(P) \;\widehat{=}\; \textbf{OSH}(fp \subseteq \operatorname{dom} hp)(P)$$

$$\textbf{SL3}(P) \;\widehat{=}\; \bigsqcap hp_0 \mid hp_0 \subseteq hp \wedge \operatorname{dom} hp_0 \cap fp' = \varnothing \bullet$$
$$hp :=_D hp \setminus hp_0 \; ; \; P \; ; \; hp :=_D hp \cup hp_0$$

$$\textbf{SL4}(P) \;\widehat{=}\; \textbf{OSH}(\forall l \mid l \in \operatorname{ran}(st) \cup \operatorname{ran} hp \bullet l \in \operatorname{dom} hp)(P)$$

$$\textit{where}\;\; \textbf{OIH}(I)(P) = P \wedge (ok \wedge \neg\, P^f \Rightarrow I)$$
$$\textbf{OSH}(q)(P) = P \wedge (ok \wedge \neg\, P^f \wedge q \Rightarrow q')$$

OIH *imposes an operation invariant and* **OSH** *output-state healthiness [17]. Note the use of the nondeterministic choice operator in* **SL3**, *a generalisation of that presented in the table on p.5 and the use of assignment from the theory of designs. The syntax of the generalised choice operator* $(\bigsqcap \cdots \mid \cdots \bullet \cdots)$ *is inspired by the syntax of Z [60]. The notation* P^f *is a shorthand for* $P[false/ok']$, *so that* $\neg\, P^f$ *in the definitions of invariants denotes the precondition of the design* P.

Theorem 12. *SL1–4 are monotonic idempotents that mutually commute.*

The next theorem is important in reasoning about heap predicates. First, an enabling lemma.

Lemma 13. (Contraction). *For* $\operatorname{dom} hp \cap \operatorname{dom} hp_0$ *and* *that* $\operatorname{dom} hp_0 \cap fp' = \varnothing$.

$$hp :=_D hp \setminus hp_0 \; ; \; P \; ; \; = \; hp :=_D hp \cup hp_0$$

New heap addresses added by P lie in $fp' \setminus fp$*, and the* hp_0*'s contribution is*

$$(fp' \setminus fp) \cap \operatorname{dom} hp_0$$

which is empty, since $\operatorname{dom} hp_0 \cap fp'$ *is empty by assumption. Disposed heap addresses lie in the set* $fp \setminus fp'$*. So, the new heap addresses* $(\operatorname{dom} hp')$ *are*

$$((\operatorname{dom} hp) \setminus (fp \setminus fp')) \cup (fp' \setminus fp)$$

which is clearly disjoint from $\operatorname{dom} hp_0$*, since* $(\operatorname{dom} hp) \setminus (fp \setminus fp') \subseteq \operatorname{dom} hp$*, which is disjoint from* $\operatorname{dom} hp_0$ *by assumption.* **SL3***'s following assignment is*

$(P_1 \vdash P2) \; ; \; hp :=_D hp \cup hp_0$

$= \{$ *definition: design assignment* $\}$

$(P_1 \vdash P2) \; ; \; (\textbf{true} \vdash hp := hp \cup hp_0)$

$= \{$ *design composition, simplification* $\}$

$(P_1 \vdash P2 \; ; \; hp := hp \cup hp_0)$

$= \{$ *relational assignment* $\}$

$(P_1 \vdash P2 \; ; \; (hp' = hp \cup hp_0) \wedge (st' = st) \wedge (fp' = fp))$

$= \{$ *from above,* $\operatorname{dom} hp \cap \operatorname{dom} hp_0 = \varnothing$ $\}$

$(P_1 \vdash P2 \; ; \; (hp = hp' \setminus hp_0) \wedge (st' = st) \wedge (fp' = fp))$

$= \{$ *relational calculus* $\}$

$(P_1 \vdash P2[hp' \setminus hp_0 / hp'])$

$= \{$ *assumption:* hp' *not free in* P_1*, substitution shorthand* $\}$

$P^{hp' \setminus hp_0}$

Now consider the leading assignment too:

$hp :=_D hp \setminus hp_0 \; ; \; P^{hp' \setminus hp_0}$

$= \{$ *design calculus: leading assignment* $\}$

$P^{hp' \setminus hp_0}_{hp \setminus hp_0}$

Theorem 14 (Contraction). *If P is* **SL3***-healthy, then for all* hp_0*, such that* $hp_0 \subseteq hp \wedge \operatorname{dom} hp_0 \cap fp' = \varnothing$

$$P \sqsubseteq P^{hp' \setminus hp_0}_{hp \setminus hp_0}$$

Proof. **SL3**(P) *is a greatest lower-bound and Lemma 13.*

3.2   Signature

We add five atomic heap assignment commands to the signature of the nondeterministic sequential programming language introduced in Example 2.

$$\mathcal{C} ::= x := y \mid [x] := v \mid [x] := y \mid x := [y] \mid x := \mathsf{ref}\ y$$

The following definitions explain the semantics of each of these assignments.

Definition 15 (vv-assign). *The variable-variable assignment $x :=_s y$ assigns to the variable x the denotation of y, namely $st(y)$, which must be well defined.*

$$\begin{array}{l} \_ :=_s \_ : Var \leftrightarrow Var \\ \hline x :=_s y \ = \ y \in \mathrm{dom}(st) \vdash st := st \cup \{x \mapsto st(y)\} \end{array}$$

Definition 16 (pc-assign). *The pointer-constant assignment $[x]_c :=_s v$ updates the heap location pointed to by the denotation of x, namely $st(x)$, to hold the value v. This command's footprint is exactly the location $st(x)$. The denotation $st(x)$ must be well defined and its valuation $st(x)$ must be current.*

$$\begin{array}{l} [\_]_c :=_s \_ : Var \leftrightarrow Val \cup Loc \\ \hline [x]_c :=_s v \ = \ \left(\begin{array}{c} x \in \mathrm{dom}(st) \wedge st(x) \in \mathrm{dom}\, hp \\ \vdash \\ hp, fp := hp \cup \{st(x) \mapsto v\}, fp \cup \{st(x)\} \end{array} \right) \end{array}$$

Definition 17 (pv-assign). *The pointer-variable assignment $[x] :=_s y$ updates the heap location pointed to by the denotation of x, namely $st(x)$, to hold the value denoted by the variable y, namely $st(y)$. The footprint is exactly $st(x)$. Both $st(x)$ and $st(y)$ must be well defined and $st(x)$ must be a heap address.*

$$\begin{array}{l} [\_] :=_s \_ :: Var \leftrightarrow Var \\ \hline [x] :=_s y \ = \ \left(\begin{array}{c} x \in \mathrm{dom}(st) \wedge y \in \mathrm{dom}(st) \wedge st(x) \in \mathrm{dom}\, hp \\ \vdash \\ hp, fp := hp \cup \{st(x) \mapsto st(y)\}, fp \cup \{st(x)\} \end{array} \right) \end{array}$$

Definition 18 (vp-assign). *The variable-pointer assignment $x :=_s [y]$ assigns to the variable x the denotation of the location of y. The footprint of this command is exactly $st(y)$, which must be well defined and be a heap address.*

$$\begin{array}{l} \_ :=_s [\_] :: Var \leftrightarrow Var \\ \hline x :=_s [y] \ = \ \left(\begin{array}{c} y \in \mathrm{dom}(st) \wedge st(y) \in \mathrm{dom}\, hp \\ \vdash \\ st, fp := st \cup \{x \mapsto hp(st(y))\}, fp \cup \{st(y)\} \end{array} \right) \end{array}$$

Definition 19 (vr-assign). *The variable-reference assignment $x :=_s \mathbf{ref}\ y$ assigns to x a fresh reference on the heap pointing to the denotation of y. Freshness means that the new reference is not on the current heap. The denotation $st(y)$ must be well defined. The footprint is exactly the new reference.*

$$\_ :=_s \mathit{ref}\_ :: \mathit{Var} \leftrightarrow \mathit{Var}$$

$$x :=_s \mathbf{ref}\ y\ =\ \exists\, l \bullet \left(\begin{array}{c} y \in \mathrm{dom}(st) \\ \vdash \\ l \notin \mathrm{dom}\, hp \\ \begin{pmatrix} st \\ hp \\ fp \end{pmatrix} := \begin{pmatrix} st \cup \{x \mapsto l\} \\ hp \cup \{l \mapsto st(y)\} \\ fp \cup \{l\} \end{pmatrix} \end{array} \right)$$

The vv-assignment command is healthy.

Theorem 20 $(x :=_s y\_is\_\mathbf{SL\_}healthy)$.

$(x :=_s y)$ *is* $\mathbf{SL1} \circ \mathbf{SL2} \circ \mathbf{SL3} \circ \mathbf{SL4}$

We prove the third part of the theorem.

Lemma 21 $(x :=_s y\_is\_\mathbf{SL3})$.

$(x :=_s y)$ *is* $\mathbf{SL3}$

Proof.

    $\mathbf{SL3}(x :=_s y)$

$= \{\, x :=_s y\_def,\ \mathbf{SL3}\_def\,\}$

$\bigsqcap hp_0 \mid hp_0 \subseteq hp \wedge \mathrm{dom}\, hp_0 \cap fp' = \varnothing \bullet$

    $hp :=_D hp \setminus hp_0\ ;\ (y \in \mathrm{dom}(st) \vdash st := st \cup \{x \mapsto st(y)\})\ ;\ hp :=_D hp \cup hp_0$

$= \{\, \text{leading, following assignment} \,\}$

$\bigsqcap hp_0 \mid hp_0 \subseteq hp \wedge \mathrm{dom}\, hp_0 \cap fp' = \varnothing \bullet$

    $(y \in \mathrm{dom}(st) \vdash (st := st \cup \{x \mapsto st(y)\})[hp \setminus hp_0/hp]\ ;\ hp := hp \cup hp_0)$

$= \{\, \text{substitution} \,\}$

$\bigsqcap hp_0 \mid hp_0 \subseteq hp \wedge \mathrm{dom}\, hp_0 \cap fp' = \varnothing \bullet$

    $(y \in \mathrm{dom}(st) \vdash st, hp := st \cup \{x \mapsto st(y)\}, hp \setminus hp_0\ ;\ hp := hp \cup hp_0)$

$= \{\, \text{assignment composition: } x := e\ ;\ x := f(x)\ =\ x := f(e) \,\}$

$\bigsqcap hp_0 \mid hp_0 \subseteq hp \wedge \mathrm{dom}\, hp_0 \cap fp' = \varnothing \bullet$

    $(y \in \mathrm{dom}(st) \vdash st, hp := st \cup \{x \mapsto st(y)\}, (hp \setminus hp_0) \cup hp_0)$

$= \{\, \text{lemma: } hp_0 \subseteq hp \Rightarrow (hp \setminus hp_0) \cup hp_0 = hp \,\}$

$\bigsqcap hp_0 \mid hp_0 \subseteq hp \wedge \mathrm{dom}\, hp_0 \cap fp' = \varnothing \bullet (y \in \mathrm{dom}(st) \vdash st := st \cup \{x \mapsto st(y)\})$

$= \{\, \text{lemma: } (\bigsqcap x \mid P \bullet Q) \doteq Q, \text{ providing } \exists x \bullet P \text{ and } x \text{ not free in } Q \,\}$

$y \in \mathrm{dom}(st) \vdash st := st \cup \{x \mapsto st(y)\}$

$= \{\, x :=_s y\_def \,\}$

$x :=_s y$

The vr-assignment is healthy.

Theorem 22 $(x :=_s \mathbf{ref}\ y\_is\_\mathbf{SL\_}healthy)$.

$(x :=_s \mathbf{ref}\ y)$ *is* $\mathbf{SL1} \circ \mathbf{SL2} \circ \mathbf{SL3} \circ \mathbf{SL4}$

Again, we prove the third part of the theorem.

Lemma 23 Proof.

$\textbf{SL3}(x :=_s \textbf{ref } y)$

$= \{\ vr\_assign\ \}$

$\bigsqcap hp_0 \mid hp_0 \subseteq hp \wedge \text{dom } hp_0 \cap fp' = \varnothing \bullet$

$\qquad hp :=_D hp \setminus hp_0 \ ;$

$$\exists l \bullet \left(\begin{array}{c} y \in \text{dom}(st) \\ \vdash \\ l \notin \text{dom } hp \\ \begin{pmatrix} st \\ hp \\ fp \end{pmatrix} := \begin{pmatrix} st \cup \{x \mapsto l\} \\ hp \cup \{l \mapsto st(y)\} \\ fp \cup \{l\} \end{pmatrix} \end{array} \right) ;$$

$\qquad hp :=_D hp \cup hp_0$

$= \left\{ \begin{array}{l} lemma: x :=_D e \ ; (q_1 \vdash Q_2) \ = \ (q_1[e/x] \vdash Q_2[e/x]), \\ lemma: (p_1 \vdash P2) \ ; x :=_D f \ = \ (p_1 \vdash P_2 \ ; x := f) \end{array} \right\}$

$\bigsqcap hp_0 \mid hp_0 \subseteq hp \wedge \text{dom } hp_0 \cap fp' = \varnothing \bullet$

$$\exists l \bullet \left(\begin{array}{c} y \in \text{dom}(st) \\ \vdash \\ l \notin \text{dom } (hp \setminus hp_0) \\ \begin{pmatrix} st \\ hp \\ fp \end{pmatrix} := \begin{pmatrix} st \cup \{x \mapsto l\} \\ (hp \setminus hp_0) \cup \{l \mapsto st(y)\} \\ fp \cup \{l\} \end{pmatrix} \ ; hp := hp \cup hp_0 \end{array} \right)$$

$= \{\ assignment\ composition\ \}$

$\bigsqcap hp_0 \mid hp_0 \subseteq hp \wedge \text{dom } hp_0 \cap fp' = \varnothing \bullet$

$$\exists l \bullet \left(\begin{array}{c} y \in \text{dom}(st) \\ \vdash \\ l \notin \text{dom } (hp \setminus hp_0) \\ \begin{pmatrix} st \\ hp \\ fp \end{pmatrix} := \begin{pmatrix} st \cup \{x \mapsto l\} \\ (hp \setminus hp_0) \cup \{l \mapsto st(y)\} \cup hp_0 \\ fp \cup \{l\} \end{pmatrix} \end{array} \right)$$

$= \{\ lemma: hp_0 \subseteq hp \Rightarrow (hp \setminus hp_0) \cup hp_0 = hp\ and\ commutativity\ of\ \cup\ \}$

$\bigsqcap hp_0 \mid hp_0 \subseteq hp \wedge \text{dom } hp_0 \cap fp' = \varnothing \bullet$

$$\exists l \bullet \left(\begin{array}{c} y \in \text{dom}(st) \\ \vdash \\ l \notin \text{dom } (hp \setminus hp_0) \\ (st, hp, fp) := (st \cup \{x \mapsto l\}, hp \cup \{l \mapsto st(y)\}, fp \cup \{l\}) \end{array} \right)$$

$= \{\ l \in fp' \wedge \text{dom } hp_0 \cap fp' = \varnothing \Rightarrow l \notin \text{dom } hp_0\ \}$

$\bigsqcap hp_0 \mid hp_0 \subseteq hp \wedge \text{dom } hp_0 \cap fp' = \varnothing \bullet$

$$\exists l \bullet \left(\begin{array}{c} y \in \text{dom}(st) \\ \vdash \\ l \notin \text{dom } hp \\ (st, hp, fp) := (st \cup \{x \mapsto l\}, hp \cup \{l \mapsto st(y)\}, fp \cup \{l\}) \end{array} \right)$$

$= \{\ lemma: (\bigsqcap x \mid P \bullet Q) = Q,\ providing \exists x \bullet P\ and\ x\ not\ free\ in\ Q\ \}$

$$\exists\, l \bullet \left(\begin{array}{c} y \in \mathrm{dom}(st) \\ \vdash \\ l \notin \mathrm{dom}\, hp \wedge (st, hp, f\!p) := (st \cup \{x \mapsto l\}, hp \cup \{l \mapsto st(y)\}, f\!p \cup \{l\}) \end{array} \right)$$

$$= \{\, vr\_assign\,\}$$

$$x :=_s \textbf{ref } y$$

SL-healthy predicates support sound modular reasoning about pointer programs. Next, we describe the essential part of separation logic that achieves this.

3.3   Separating Conjunction

Two disjoint heaplets can be joined compatibly:

Definition 24 (Compatible join).

$$st \circledast (s_1, s_2) \;\hat{=}\; \mathrm{dom}\, s_1 \cap \mathrm{dom}\, s_2 = \varnothing \wedge st = s_1 \cup s_2$$

The binary operator $*$ (pronounced "star" or "separating conjunction") asserts that the heap can be split into two disjoint parts where its two arguments hold.

Definition 25 (Separating conjunction).

$$p * q \;\hat{=}\; \exists\, h_1, h_2 \bullet hp \circledast (h_1, h_2) \wedge p_{h_1} \wedge q_{h_2}$$

In order to be able to give a meaning to exceptional faulting states, our theory of separation logic will be a subset embedding of our theory of designs. This means that we must revise our notion of Hoare logic for total correctness.

Definition 26 (Hoare triple revisited).

$$\{p\}\; Q\; \{r\} \;=\; (p \Rightarrow r') \sqsubseteq Q \qquad\qquad\qquad [\, p \Rightarrow \mathsf{fv}(Q) \subseteq \mathrm{dom}\, st\,]$$

The proviso formulation is due to Reynolds: p ensures Q cannot abort due to dangling pointers. Essentially

$$[\, p \Rightarrow \mathsf{fv}(Q) \subseteq \mathrm{dom}\, st \wedge (Q \Rightarrow r')\,]$$

Now we augment Hoare logic with separation logic's Frame Rule. This states that if Q can execute safely in a local state satisfying p, then it can also execute in any larger state satisfying $p * s$. This idea will be familiar from the semantics that we have presented so far. The footprint for an **SL**=healthy predicate P is an observation that describes a sufficiently large heap for P to execute satisfactorily. The minimal footprint adds necessity, but any larger heap will do. In what follows, we use the following shorthands $p_e = p[e/hp]$ $Q_e^f = Q[e, f/hp, hp']$.

Theorem 27 (Frame Rule). *Suppose that Q is* **SL** *and that Q's use of the store is no wider that of the precondition p. This inference rule is valid:*

$$\frac{\{p\}\; Q\; \{r\}}{\{p * s\}\; Q\; \{r * s\}} \;[\, \mathsf{use}(Q) \cap \mathsf{use}(s) = \varnothing\,]$$

Proof.

$\{\,p\,\}\ Q\ \{\,r\,\} \Rightarrow \{\,p*s\,\}\ Q\ \{\,r*s\,\}$

$= \{$ Definition 4 (Hoare triple) $\}$

$\{\,p\,\}\ Q\ \{\,r\,\} \Rightarrow [\,p*s \wedge Q \Rightarrow (r*s)_{hp'}\,]$

$\Leftarrow \{$ predicate calculus: $\forall$-I, arbitrary hp and hp' $\}$

$\{\,p\,\}\ Q\ \{\,r\,\} \wedge (p*s) \wedge Q \Rightarrow (r*s)_{hp'}$

$= \{$ Definition 25(separating conjunction) $\}$

$\{\,p\,\}\ Q\ \{\,r\,\} \wedge (\exists\, hp_1, hp_2 \bullet hp \circledast (hp_1, hp_2) \wedge p_{hp_1} \wedge s_{hp_2}) \wedge Q \Rightarrow (r*s)_{hp'}$

$\Leftarrow \{$ predicate calculus: $\exists$-E, arbitrary hp_1 and hp_2 $\}$

$\{\,p\,\}\ Q\ \{\,r\,\} \wedge hp \circledast (hp_1, hp_2) \wedge p_{hp_1} \wedge s_{hp_2} \wedge Q \Rightarrow (r*s)_{hp'}$

$\Leftarrow \{\ Q$ is **SL3**, Theorem 14 (Contraction) $\}$

$\{\,p\,\}\ Q\ \{\,r\,\} \wedge hp \circledast (hp_1, hp_2) \wedge p_{hp_1} \wedge s_{hp_2} \wedge Q^{hp'\backslash hp_2}_{hp\backslash hp_2} \Rightarrow (r*s)_{hp'}$

$= \{$ Defnition 4 (Hoare triple) $\}$

$[\,p \wedge Q \Rightarrow r_{hp'}\,] \wedge hp \circledast (hp_1, hp_2) \wedge p_{hp_1} \wedge s_{hp_2} \wedge Q^{hp'\backslash hp_2}_{hp\backslash hp_2} \Rightarrow (r*s)_{hp'}$

$\Leftarrow \{$ predicate calculus: $\forall$-E, $hp \backslash hp_2, hp' \backslash hp_2/hp, hp'$ $\}$

$(p_{hp\backslash hp_2} \wedge Q^{hp'\backslash hp_2}_{hp\backslash hp_2} \Rightarrow r_{hp'\backslash hp_2}) \wedge p_{hp_1} \wedge s_{hp_2} \wedge hp \circledast (hp_1, hp_2) \wedge Q^{hp'\backslash hp_2}_{hp\backslash hp_2}$
$\qquad \Rightarrow (r*s)_{hp'}$

$\Leftarrow \{$ lemma: $hp \circledast (hp_1, hp_2) \Rightarrow hp_1 = hp \backslash hp_2$ $\}$

$(p_{hp\backslash hp_2} \wedge Q^{hp'\backslash hp_2}_{hp\backslash hp_2} \Rightarrow r_{hp'\backslash hp_2}) \wedge p_{hp\backslash hp_2} \wedge s_{hp_2} \wedge Q^{hp'\backslash hp_2}_{hp\backslash hp_2} \Rightarrow (r*s)_{hp'}$

$\Leftarrow \{$ propositional calculus: $\wedge$-E $\}$

$r_{hp'\backslash hp_2} \wedge s_{hp_2} \Rightarrow (r*s)_{hp'}$

$= \{$ Definition 25 (separating conjunction) $\}$

$r_{hp'\backslash hp_2} \wedge s_{hp_2} \Rightarrow \exists\, hp'_1, hp'_2 \bullet hp' \circledast (hp'_1, hp'_2) \wedge r_{hp'_1} \wedge s_{hp'_2}$

$\Leftarrow \{$ predicate calculus: $\exists$-I, $(hp' \backslash hp_2), hp2/hp'_1, hp'_2$ $\}$

$r_{hp'\backslash hp_2} \wedge s_{hp_2} \Rightarrow hp' \circledast (hp' \backslash hp_2, hp_2) \wedge r_{hp'\backslash hp_2} \wedge s_{hp_2}$

$= \{$ lemma: $hp' \circledast (hp' \backslash hp_2, hp_2)$ $\}$

$r_{hp'\backslash hp_2} \wedge s_{hp_2} \Rightarrow r_{hp'\backslash hp_2} \wedge s_{hp_2}$

$= \{$ propositional calculus: tautology $\}$

true

This proof is the longest in this paper. The key step is Theorem 14 (Contraction).

4   Heterogeneous Semantics

In this section, we describe the mechanism that we use to connect heterogeneous semantics coherently: the Galois connection.

Definition 28 (Galois connection). (L, R) *is a Galois connection between lattices S and T iff the following three conditions hold:*

1. *L and R are both monotonic.*
2. *$L \circ R \sqsupseteq id_T$ (strengthening).*
3. *$id_S \sqsupseteq R \circ L$ (weakening).*

If $L \circ R = id_T$ (or L is surjective or R is injective), then (L, R) is a retract. If $R \circ L = id_S$ (or R is surjective or L is injective), then (L, R) is a co-retract.

To illustrate the use of Galois connections in heterogeneous semantics, consider the UTP theory of CSP processes [18]. We start with the theory of reactive processes.

Definition 29 (Reactive processes). *A reactive process has the following observations: (i) A trace tr of events that have occurred up to the moment of observation. (ii) A boolean flag wait that signals when the process is stable and waiting for interaction with its environment. (iii) A set ref of events that the process is refusing during its wait state. There are three healthiness conditions on these observations, but we concentrate on just one:*

$$\mathbf{R1}(P) \ \widehat{=} \ P \wedge tr \leq tr'$$

This monotonic idempotent function requires the history to be unchanged.

Definition 30 (CSP processes). *CSP processes are reactive processes with two additional healthiness conditions that mirror those for designs; but note the significant difference in the first condition.*

$$\mathbf{CSP1}(P) \ \widehat{=} \ \mathbf{R1}(\neg\, ok) \vee P$$
$$\mathbf{CSP2}(P) \ \widehat{=} \ P\,;J$$

Theorem 31 (CSP-design co-retraction). $(\mathbf{H}, \mathbf{CSP} \circ \mathbf{R1})$ *is a co-retract.*

Proof. We begin by proving that $\mathbf{CSP} \circ \mathbf{R1} \circ \mathbf{H}(P) = P$, for a CSP process P:

$\mathbf{CSP} \circ \mathbf{R1} \circ \mathbf{H}(P)$
$= \{\,\text{definition: } \mathbf{H}\,\}$
$\mathbf{CSP} \circ \mathbf{R1} \circ \mathbf{H1} \circ \mathbf{H2}(P)$
$= \{\,\text{lemma: } (P = \mathbf{R1}(P)) \Rightarrow \mathbf{CSP1}(P) = \mathbf{R1} \circ \mathbf{H1}(P)\,\}$
$\mathbf{CSP} \circ \mathbf{CSP1} \circ \mathbf{H2}(P)$
$= \{\,\text{definition: } \mathbf{CSP2}\,\}$
$\mathbf{CSP} \circ \mathbf{CSP1} \circ \mathbf{CSP2}(P)$
$= \{\,\text{assumption: } P \text{ is } \mathbf{CSP}\text{-healthy}\,\}$
P

Next, we prove that $\mathbf{H} \circ \mathbf{CSP} \circ \mathbf{R1}(D) \sqsupseteq D$:

$\mathbf{H} \circ \mathbf{CSP} \circ \mathbf{R1}(D)$

$= \{$ definition: **CSP1** $\}$

H2 ∘ **H1** ∘ **CSP1** ∘ **CSP2** ∘ **R1**(D)

$= \{$ lemma: **H1** ∘ **CSP1**$(P) =$ **H1**(P) $\}$

H2 ∘ **H1** ∘ **CSP2** ∘ **R1**(D)

$= \{$ lemma: **H1–H2** commute $\}$

H1 ∘ **H2** ∘ **CSP2** ∘ **R1**(D)

$= \{$ lemma: **H2** ∘ **CSP2**$(P) =$ **H2**(P) $\}$

H1 ∘ **H2** ∘ **R1**(D)

$\sqsupseteq \{$ lemma: **H** monotonic $\}$

H1 ∘ **H2**(D)

$= \{$ assumption: D is **H**-healthy $\}$

D

5   Related Work

Goguen and Burstall created the idea of an institution in the late 1970s to cope with what they saw as a population explosion among the logical systems used in computer science. The key notion captures the essence of the concept of a logical system [1]. Their research programme set out to develop concepts of specification languages, such as structuring mechanisms, parametrisation, implementation, refinement, proof calculi, and their tools independently from any foundational logical system. Categorical morphisms play the role of Galois connections in UTP, relating and translating logical systems. Important applications of this are borrowing (re-use of logical structure), heterogeneous specification, and combination of logics.

Gutman [26] gives an algebraic model for UTP designs based on modal semirings, a significant generalisation of UTP's foundational relational model. This is intended to expose the algebraic structure behind UTP and the general properties of designs, program and specification operators, and refinement. They show that designs form a Kleene algebra, and from this they calculate closed expressions for the waqekest and strongest fixed-point semantics for while loops that are simpler than the ones obtained from standard UTP theory and previous algebraic approaches.

6   Conclusions

We have shown how UTP can be used to construct semantic theories for particular programming paradigms. The main example that we presented, designs, is a contractual theory of total correctness for a nondeterministic sequential programming language with an embedded subtheory underpinning separation logic. In Sect. 4, we introduced two further theories for reactive processes and for CSP processes, and showed that CSP is a co-retraction of the theory of designs.

The benefit that arises from this embedding of designs in the CSP world is that it imports the assertional reasoning technique from sequential programming into concurrent programming in CSP. Every CSP process can be expressed as a reactively healthy design $R(P \vdash Q)$. Hoare logic can now be defined in reactive theories as $\{p\}\ Q\ \{r\} = R(p \vdash r') \sqsubseteq Q$. The standard rules of Hoare logic, augmented perhaps by those for separatin logic, can now be extended to all elements of the signature of the theory of CSP. This includes rules for reasoning about concurrency, nonterminating recursive processes, renaming, hiding, prefixing, input, output, etc.

Acknowledgements. The work reported in this paper is partially supported by the European Commission INTO-CPS project (Horizon 2020, 664047). The authors are grateful to the anonymous referees for their careful reading of the paper and helpful suggestions.

References

1. Anderson, H., Ciobanu, G., Freitas, L.: UTP and temporal logic model checking. In: [13], pp. 22–41 (2008)
2. Julliand, J., Kouchnarenko, O. (eds.): B 2007: Formal Specification and Development in B, Proceedings 7th International Conference of B Users, Besancon, France, 17–19 , LNCS, 4355 Springer, 2006., January 2007
3. Bandur, V., Woodcock, J.: Unifying theories of logic and specification. In: [47], pp. 18–33 (2013)
4. Banks, M.J., Jacob, J.L.: Unifying theories of confidentiality. In: [44], pp. 120–136 (2010)
5. Banks, M.J., Jacob, J.L.: On modelling user observations in the UTP. In: [44], pp. 101–119 (2010)
6. Bresciani, R., Butterfield, A.: A probabilistic theory of designs based on distributions. In: [56], pp. 105–123 (2012)
7. Butterfield, A.: Saoithín: a theorem prover for UTP. In: [44], pp. 137–156 (2010)
8. Butterfield, A.: The Logic of U·(TP)^2. In: [56], pp. 124–143 (2012)
9. Butterfield, A., Sherif, A., Woodcock, J.: Slotted-Circus. In: Davies, J., Gibbons, J. (eds.) IFM 2007. LNCS, vol. 4591, pp. 75–97. Springer, Heidelberg (2007)
10. Cavalcanti, A., Gaudel, M.-C.: A note on traces refinement and the *conf* relation in the unifying theories of programming. In: [13], pp. 42–61 (2008)
11. Cavalcanti, A., Gaudel, M.-C.: Specification coverage for testing in Circus. In: [44], 1–45 (2010)
12. Cavalcanti, A., Harwood, W., Woodcock, J.: Pointers and records in the Unifying Theories of Programming. In: [24], pp. 200–216 (2006)
13. Butterfield, A. (ed.): UTP 2008. LNCS, vol. 5713. Springer, Heidelberg (2010)
14. Cavalcanti, A., Mota, A., Woodcock, J.: Simulink timed models for program verification. In: Liu, Z., Woodcock, J., Zhu, H. (eds.) Theories of Programming and Formal Methods. LNCS, vol. 8051, pp. 82–99. Springer, Heidelberg (2013)
15. Cavalcanti, A., Sampaio, A., Woodcock, J.: Unifying classes and processes. Softw. Syst. Model. **4**(3), 277–296 (2005)
16. Cavalcanti, A., Woodcock, J., Dunne, S.: Angelic nondeterminism in the Unifying Theories of Programming. Formal Asp. Comput. **18**(3), 288–307 (2006)

17. Cavalcanti, A., Wellings, A.J., Woodcock, J.: The Safety-critical Java memory model formalised. Formal Asp. Comput. **25**(1), 37–57 (2013)
18. Cavalcanti, A., Woodcock, J.: A tutorial introduction to CSP in *Unifying Theories of Programming*. In: Cavalcanti, A., Sampaio, A., Woodcock, J. (eds.) PSSE 2004. LNCS, vol. 3167, pp. 220–268. Springer, Heidelberg (2006)
19. Cavalcanti, A., Wellings, A.J., Woodcock, J., Wei, K., Zeyda, F.: Safety-critical Java in Circus. In: Wellings, A.J., Ravn, A.P. (eds) ACM 9th International Workshop on Java Technologies for Real-time and Embedded Systems, JTRES 2011, York, 26–28 September 2011, pp. 20–29 (2011)
20. Cavalcanti, A., Zeyda, F., Wellings, A.J., Woodcock, J., Wei, K.: Safety-critical Java programs from Circus models. Real-Time Syst. **49**(5), 614–667 (2013)
21. Chen, X., Ye, N., Ding, W.: A formal approach to analyzing interference problems in aspect-oriented designs. In: [44], pp. 157–171 (2010)
22. Dunne, S., Chorus Angelorum. In: [2], pp. 19–33 (2007)
23. Dunne, S., Stoddart, B. (eds.): UTP 2006. LNCS, vol. 4010. Springer, Heidelbreg (2006)
24. Foster, S., Woodcock, J.: Unifying theories of programming in Isabelle. In: Liu, Z., Woodcock, J., Zhu, H. (eds.) Unifying Theories of Programming and Formal Engineering Methods. LNCS, vol. 8050, pp. 109–155. Springer, Heidelberg (2013)
25. Foster, S., Zeyda, F., Woodcock, J.: Isabelle/UTP: a mechanised theory engineering framework. In: [37], pp. 21–41 (2014)
26. Goguen, J.A., Burstall, R.M.: Introducing Institutions. In: Clarke, E.M., Kozen, D. (eds.) Logics of Programs. LNCS, vol. 164, pp. 221–256. Springer, Heidelberg (1984)
27. Harwood, W.T., Cavalcanti, A., Woodcock, J.: A theory of pointers for the UTP. In: Fitzgerald, J.S., Haxthausen, A.E., Yenigun, H. (eds.) ICTAC 2008. LNCS, vol. 5160, pp. 141–155. Springer, Heidelberg (2008)
28. Hayes, I.J.: Termination of real-time programs: definitely, definitely not, or maybe. In: [24], pp. 141–154 (2006)
29. He, J.: Transaction Calculus. In: [13], pp. 2–21 (2008)
30. He, J.: A probabilistic BPEL-like language. In: [44], pp. 74–100 (2010)
31. He, J., Qin, S., Sherif, A.: Constructing property-oriented models for verification. In: [24], pp. 85–100 (2006)
32. He, J., Sanders, J.W.: Unifying Probability. In: [24], pp. 173–199 (2006)
33. Hoare, C.A.R., Jifeng, H.: Unifying Theories of Programming. Prentice Hall, Upper Saddle River (1998)
34. McEwan, A.A., Woodcock, J.: Unifying Theories of Interrupts. In: [13], pp. 122–141 (2008)
35. Naumann, D. (ed.): UTP 2014. LNCS, vol. 8963. Springer, Heidelberg (2015)
36. Oliveira, M., Cavalcanti, A., Woodcock, J.: Unifying Theories in ProofPower-Z. In: [24], pp. 123–140 (2006)
37. Oliveira, M., Cavalcanti, A., Woodcock, J.: A denotational semantics for circus. Electr. Notes Theor. Comput. Sci **187**, 107–123 (2007)
38. Oliveira, M., Cavalcanti, A., Woodcock, J.: A UTP semantics for Circus. Formal Asp. Comput. **21**(1–2), 3–32 (2009)
39. Oliveira, M., Cavalcanti, A., Woodcock, J.: Unifying theories in ProofPower-Z. Formal Asp. Comput. **25**(1), 133–158 (2013)
40. Perna, J.I., Woodcock, J.: A denotational semantics for Handel-C hardware compilation. In: Butler, M., Hinchey, M.G., Larrondo-Petrie, M.M. (eds.) ICFEM 2007. LNCS, vol. 4789, pp. 266–285. Springer, Heidelberg (2007)

41. Perna, J.I., Woodcock, J.: UTP semantics for Handel-C. In: [13], pp. 142–160 (2008)
42. Qin, S. (ed.): UTP 2010. LNCS, vol. 6445. Springer, Heidelberg (2010)
43. Ribeiro, P., Cavalcanti, A.: Designs with angelic nondeterminism. In: Seventh IEEE International Symposium on Theoretical Aspects of Software Engineering, TASE 2013, 1–3 July 2013, Birmingham, pp. 71–78 (2013)
44. Ribeiro, P., Cavalcanti, A.: Angelicism in the theory of reactive processes. In: [37], pp. 42–61 (2014)
45. Iyoda, J., de Moura, L. (eds.): Formal Methods: Foundations and Applications. LNCS, vol. 8195. Springer, Heidelberg (2013)
46. Reynolds, J.C.: Separation logic: a logic for shared mutable data structures. In: 17th IEEE Symposium on Logic in Computer Science, LICS 2002, 22–25 July 2002, Copenhagen, Denmark, pp. 55–74 (2002)
47. Santos, Thiago L. V. L Cavalcanti, A., Sampaio, A.: Object-orientation in the UTP. In: [24], pp. 18–37 (2006)
48. Sherif, A., Cavalcanti, A., He, J., Sampaio, A.: A process algebraic framework for specification and validation of real-time systems. Formal Asp. Comput. 22(2), 153–191 (2010)
49. Sherif, A., Kleinberg, R.D.: Towards a time model for *Circus*. In: George, C.W., Miao, H. (eds.) ICFEM 2002. LNCS, vol. 2495, pp. 613–624. Springer, Heidelberg (2002)
50. Sherif, A., Jifeng, H., Cavalcanti, A., Sampaio, A.: A framework for specification and validation of real-time systems using Circus actions. In: Liu, Z., Araki, K. (eds.) ICTAC 2004. LNCS, vol. 3407, pp. 478–493. Springer, Heidelberg (2005)
51. Smith, M.A., Gibbons, J.: Unifying Theories of Locations. In: [13], pp. 161–180 (2008)
52. Stoddart, B., Bell, P.: Probabilistic choice, reversibility, loops, and miracles. In: [44], pp. 253–270 (2010)
53. Stoddart, B., Zeyda, F., Lynas, R.: A design-based model of reversible computation. In: [24], pp. 63–83 (2006
54. Wolff, B., Gaudel, M.-C., Feliachi, A. (eds.): UTP 2012. LNCS, vol. 7681. Springer, Heidelberg (2013)
55. Wei, K., Woodcock, J., Cavalcanti, A.: Circus time with reactive designs. In: [56], pp. 68–87 (2012)
56. Weiglhofer, M., Aichernig, B.K.: Unifying input output conformance. In: [13], pp. 181–201 (2008)
57. Woodcock, J., Cavalcanti, A.: A tutorial introduction to designs in Unifying Theories of Programming. In: Boiten, E.A., Derrick, J., Smith, G.P. (eds.) IFM 2004. LNCS, vol. 2999, pp. 40–66. Springer, Heidelberg (2004)
58. Woodcock, J.: The miracle of reactive programming. In: [13], pp. 202–217 (2008)
59. Woodcock, J.: Engineering UToPiA. In: Jones, C., Pihlajasaari, P., Sun, J. (eds.) FM 2014. LNCS, vol. 8442, pp. 22–41. Springer, Heidelberg (2014)
60. Woodcock, J., Davies, J.: Using Z-Specification, Refinement, and Proof. Prentice Hall, Upper Saddle River (1996)
61. Woodcock, J., Bandur, V.: Unifying theories of undefinedness in UTP. In: [56], pp. 1–22 (2012)
62. Woodcock, J., Cavalcanti, A.: A concurrent language for refinement. Butterfield, A., Strong, G., Pahl, C. (eds) 5th Irish Workshop on Formal Methods, IWFM 2001, Dublin, Ireland, 16–17, BCS Workshops in Computing, July 2001 (2001)

63. Woodcock, J., Cavalcanti, A., Fitzgerald, J.S., Larsen, P.G., Miyazawa, A., Perry, S.: Features of CML: a formal modelling language for systems of systems. In: 7th IEEE International Conference on System of Systems Engineering, SoSE 2012, Genova, pp. 445–450, 16–19 July 2012 (2012)

64. Zeyda, F., Cavalcanti, A.: Encoding Circus programs in ProofpowerZ. In: [13], pp. 218–237 (2008)

65. Zeyda, F., Cavalcanti, A.: Higher-order UTP for a theory of methods. In: [56], pp. 204–223 (2012)

66. Zhan, N., Kang, E.-Y., Liu, Z.: Component publications and compositions. In: [13], pp. 238–257 (2008)

67. Zhu, H., He, J., Peng, X., Jin, N.: Denotational approach to an event-driven system-level language. In: [13], pp. 258–278 (2008)

68. Zhu, H., Liu, P., He, J., Qin, S.: Mechanical approach to linking operational semantics and algebraic semantics for verilog using Maude. In: [56], pp. 164–185 (2012)

69. Zhu, H., Sanders, J.W., He, J., Qin, S.: Denotational semantics for a probabilistic timed shared-variable language. In: [56], pp. 224–247 (2012)

70. Zhu, H., Yang, F., He, J.: Generating denotational semantics from algebraic semantics for event-driven system-level language. In: [44], pp. 286–308 (2010)

Static and Runtime Verification: Competitors or Friends?

Static and Runtime Verification, Competitors or Friends? (Track Summary)

Dilian Gurov[1], Klaus Havelund[2(✉)], Marieke Huisman[3], and Rosemary Monahan[4]

[1] KTH Royal Institute of Technology, Stockholm, Sweden
dilian@kth.se
[2] Jet Propulsion Laboratory, Pasadena, USA
klaus.havelund@jpl.nasa.gov
[3] University of Twente, Enschede, The Netherlands
m.huisman@utwente.nl
[4] Maynooth University, Maynooth, Ireland
Rosemary.Monahan@nuim.ie

1 Motivation and Goals

Over the last years, significant progress has been made both on static and runtime program verification techniques, focusing on increasing the quality of software. Within this track, we would like to investigate how we can leverage these techniques by combining them. Questions that will be addressed are for example: what can static verification bring to runtime verification to reduce impact on execution time and memory use, and what can runtime verification bring to static verification to take over where static verification fails to either scale or provide precise results? One can to some extent consider these two views (static verification supporting runtime verification, and runtime verification supporting static verification) as fundamentally representing the same scenario: prove what can be proved statically, and dynamically analyze the rest.

The session will consist of several presentations, some on the individual techniques, and some on experiences combining the two techniques. When preparing this session, we aimed at finding a balance between static and runtime verification backgrounds of the presenters. This is also reflected by the papers associated to this track. There are several papers describing systems that first attempt to verify as much as possible by static verification, and then use runtime verification for the properties that cannot be verified statically. There is another group of papers that use static program information to generate appropriate runtime checks. Finally, a last group of papers discuss program specification techniques for static verification, and how they can be made suitable for runtime verification, or the other way round.

K. Havelund—The research performed by this author was carried out at Jet Propulsion Laboratory, California Institute of Technology, under a contract with the National Aeronautics and Space Administration.

T. Margaria and B. Steffen (Eds.): ISoLA 2016, Part I, LNCS 9952, pp. 397–401, 2016.
DOI: 10.1007/978-3-319-47166-2_27

During the conference, three panel discussions on this topic are planned. The first panel focuses on static verification. What are the challenges, and how can it benefit from runtime verification? The second panel focuses on the opposite question: what are the challenges in runtime verification, and how can it benefit from static verification? The last panel discusses future research directions in this area, and what are the most promising ideas for combining static and runtime verification. Concrete topics that will be discussed include the limitations and benefits of each approach, how we can combine efforts to benefit verification, what are the overheads/benefits of combining efforts, industrial application in each area, industrial needs, etc.

2   Contributions

The paper contributions in cbelow. The papers are ordered according to the three sessions of the track: (1) how can static verification benefit from runtime verification? (2) how can runtime verification benefit from static verification? and (3) how can we bridge the gap? (more generally). The papers are ordered alphabetically according to authors within each session.

2.1   How Can Static Verification Benefit from Runtime Verification?

Ahrendt et al. [1] (*StaRVOOrS Episode II, Strengthen and Distribute the Force*) build on StaRVOOrS as presented at ISoLA 2012, which aims at a unifying framework for static and runtime verification of object-oriented software. Advances on a unified specification language for data and control oriented properties, a tool for combined static and runtime verification, and experiments are presented. Future research concern (i) the use of static verification techniques to further optimize the runtime monitor, and (ii) extending the framework to the distributed case. A roadmap for addressing these challenges is presented.

Azzopardi et al. [2] (*A Model-Based Approach to Combining Static and Dynamic Verification Techniques*) present how static and runtime verification can be used to ensure safety of systems that are to be used in an unknown context. The system developer has to provide a model of the system. This model then is used to find the appropriate context for the system to work in, and an attempt is made to statically verify the desired properties of the composed system. Any property (or part of a property) that cannot be verified statically will be verified dynamically. Moreover, it will also be verified dynamically whether the concrete implementation of the system respects the model. In some cases, knowledge about the properties that will be monitored can be used to reduce the model. The paper discusses a concrete example of this approach for an online payment ecosystem.

Bodden et al. [3] (*Information Flow Analysis for Go*) present parts of the theory and implementation of an information flow analysis of Go programs. The purpose is to detect the flow of so-called tainted values, from untrusted sources (such as reading from input) to so-called sinks, which represent locations where such untrusted data should not end up. Go allows for concurrent programming via channels, requiring special techniques. Discussions include how dynamic analysis can be applied, to monitor execution paths, that cannot be determined safe due to the conservative static analysis. An option is to stop the execution of the program when a tainted datum is about to reach a sink. A dynamic coverage tool can also provide information as to how many of these potentially unsafe paths have been executed and verified.

2.2 How Can Runtime Verification Benefit from Static Verification?

Goodloe [5] (*Challenges in High-Assurance Runtime Verification*) first presents an overview of the Copilot RV framework, followed by several challenges that are barriers to realizing high-assurance runtime verification. More specifically, these challenges relate specification, observability of data, traceability from requirements, fault tolerance, composition of runtime verification and the system under observation, monitor specification and monitor correctness. While the challenges are formulated generally, Goodloe addresses them concretely in the context of the Copilot RV framework. Additional challenges to be addressed in future work, as well as challenges regarding the use of automated verification tools for high-assurance runtime verification, are also discussed.

Kosmatov et al. [6] (*Static versus Dynamic Verification in Why3, Frama-C and SPARK 2014*) describe the Why3 system, and two tools that use the Why3 system as a backend, namely Frama-C and SPARK. As these systems focus on different kinds of verification techniques (SPARK concentrates on runtime verification, while Frama-C and Why3 favor static verification) and properties of interest, there are differences in the specification languages, in the treatment of ghost code, and in the treatment of proof failures. The paper provides an in-depth discussion of these differences.

Reger [9] (*Considering Typestate Verification for Quantified Event Automata*) sketches how static verification techniques for type states can be used on a commonly used specification framework for runtime verification, namely quantified event automata. He gives an overview of type states and quantified event automata, and then sketches how type state techniques can be used, using some example properties specified as quantified event automata.

2.3 How Can We Bridge the Gap?

Leofante et al. [7] (*Combining Static and Runtime Methods to Achieve Safe Standing-Up for Humanoid Robots*) address how to improve a scripted stand up strategy for robots, making it safe and stable, using a combination of runtime verification and static verification. This paper describes a novel approach to achieve safe standing-up for humanoid robots. It proposes a combination of three methods. The first is reinforcement learning that uses Q-learning based on a robot simulator to construct a standing-up strategy. The second method is greedy model repair that uses efficient probabilistic model checkers to repair the strategy to avoid given unsafe states with a given probabilistic threshold. These two methods result in an initial strategy that is deployed on the robot. As the strategy has been obtained on an idealized model of the real robot and environment, it may still not be adequate. Therefore, the third method is runtime verification with a feedback loop to observe the real-time behavior of the robot and adapt the strategy on the go. The implementation of the presented theory is ongoing, but already some experimental results for (model free) reinforcement learning strategies are presented.

Leucker [8] (*On Combinations of Static and Dynamic Analysis*) elaborates in his presentation on the similarities and differences of model checking and runtime verification, and how they can benefit from each other. In particular, if model checking an abstract version of the system fails, how can runtime verification be used to investigate the unsuccessful run? The presentation also discusses ideas for how to use information obtained by static verification to improve runtime verification results.

Eilertsen et al. [4] (*Safer Refactorings*) present a method to avoid refactorings changing the behavior of a program. Refactorings are a way to restructure a program's code. If a refactoring is wrongly applied, this might actually change the behavior of the program, which should be avoided. Eilertsen et al. propose a technique to identify when the program's behavior is actually changed. For two concrete refactorings (extract local variable, and extract and move method) they describe how this is done. Essentially, together with the refactoring they generate an assertion which will fail if the refactoring changed the program behavior. To validate their approach, they automatically apply these refactorings on a large code base, and use unit tests to identify how many assertions actually fail.

References

1. Ahrendt, W., Pace, G.J., Schneider, G.: StaRVOOrS episode II, strengthen and distribute the force. In: Margaria, T., Steffen, B. (eds.) ISoLA 2016, Part I, LNCS, vol. 9952, pp. 402–415. Springer, Heidelberg (2016)
2. Azzopardi, S., Colombo, C., Pace, G.: A model-based approach to combining static and dynamic verification techniques. In: Margaria, T., Steffen, B. (eds.) ISoLA 2016, Part I, LNCS, vol. 995, pp. 416–430. Springer, Heidelberg (2016)
3. Bodden, E., Pun, K.I., Steffen, M., Stolz, V., Wickert, A.-K.: Information flow analysis for go. In: Margaria, T., Steffen, B. (eds.) ISoLA 2016, Part I, LNCS, vol. 9952, pp. 431–445. Springer, Heidelberg (2016)
4. Eilertsen, A.M., Bagge, A.H., Stolz, V.: Safer refactorings. In: Margaria, T., Steffen, B. (eds.) ISoLA 2016, Part I, LNCS, vol. 9952, pp. 517–531. Springer, Heidelberg (2016)
5. Goodloe, A.: Challenges in high-assurance runtime verification. In: Margaria, T., Steffen, B. (eds.) ISoLA 2016, Part I, LNCS, vol. 9952, pp. 446–460. Springer, Heidelberg (2016)
6. Kosmatov, N., Marché, C., Moy, Y., Signoles, J.: Static versus dynamic verification in Why3, Frama-C and SPARK. In: Margaria, T., Steffen, B. (eds.) ISoLA 2016, Part I, LNCS, vol. 9952, pp. 461–478. Springer, Heidelberg (2014)

7. Leofante, F., Vuotto, S., Ábrahám, E., Tacchella, A., Jansen, N.: Combining static and runtime methods to achieve safe standing-up for humanoid robots. In: Margaria, T., Steffen, B. (eds.) ISoLA 2016, Part I, LNCS, vol. 9952, pp. 496–514. Springer, Heidelberg (2016)
8. Leucker, M.: On combinations of static and dynamic analysis. In: Margaria, T., Steffen, B. (eds.) ISoLA 2016, Part I, LNCS, vol. 9952, pp. 515–516. Springer, Heidelberg (2016)
9. Reger, G.: Considering typestate verification for quantified event automata. In: Margaria, T., Steffen, B. (eds.) ISoLA 2016, Part I, LNCS, vol. 9952, pp. 479–495. Springer, Heidelberg (2016)

StaRVOOrS — Episode II

Strengthen and Distribute the Force

Wolfgang Ahrendt[1]([✉]), Gordon J. Pace[2], and Gerardo Schneider[3]

[1] Chalmers University of Technology, Gothenburg, Sweden
ahrendt@chalmers.se
[2] University of Malta, Msida, Malta
gordon.pace@um.edu.mt
[3] University of Gothenburg, Gothenburg, Sweden
gerardo@cse.gu.se

Abstract. Static and runtime techniques for the verification of programs are complementary. They both have their advantages and disadvantages, and a natural question is whether they may be combined in such a way as to get the advantages of both without inheriting too much from their disadvantages. In a previous contribution to ISoLA'12, we have proposed StaRVOOrS ('Static and Runtime Verification of Object-Oriented Software'), a unified framework for combining static and runtime verification in order to check data- and control-oriented properties. Returning to ISoLA here, we briefly report on advances since then: a unified specification language for data- and control-oriented properties, a tool for combined static and runtime verification, and experiments. On that basis, we discuss two future research directions to strengthen the power, and broaden the scope, of combined static and runtime verification: (i) to use static analysis techniques to further optimise the runtime monitor, and (ii) to extend the framework to the distributed case.

1 Introduction

The development of *lightweight* verification techniques in what concerns ease of use and automation is considered to be one of the major challenges being addressed by the verification community.

Runtime verification is one such technique: a monitor is usually automatically extracted from a property written in a formal language, and an executable program automatically synthesised. The monitor is then run in parallel with the monitored program, checking at runtime that its underlying property is being satisfied by the *current* run, and flagging a violation if this is the case. Though the overheads induced by runtime verification are small when compared to the computational effort required by most static analysis and verification techniques, these can still be a problem in certain settings.

Static verification has the advantage of being used pre-deployment, coming with strong guarantees in what concerns correctness for *all* possible runs. This generality is, however, hard to achieve (if not impossible) automatically,

© Springer International Publishing AG 2016
T. Margaria and B. Steffen (Eds.): ISoLA 2016, Part I, LNCS 9952, pp. 402–415, 2016.
DOI: 10.1007/978-3-319-47166-2_28

in particular when verifying data-oriented properties. Among other things, *loop invariants* typically need to be provided by a human user. Verification systems therefore rely on code annotations, or interactive proof construction. With that, they can achieve a lot, however introducing the additional constraint of needing highly trained experts.

Another dimension, somewhat orthogonal to the above, are complementary issues with checking *data-oriented* and *control-oriented* properties. Data-oriented properties (e.g. *all the numbers stored in the array are positive*) are typically very costly to monitor fully at runtime. Control-oriented properties (e.g. *files can be read only between a login and a logout*), on the other hand, typically require (often manual, sometimes unsafe) abstractions before they can be efficiently verified statically.

In 2012 we introduced StaRVOOrS to the ISoLA community [3], a promise of a unified framework for the specification and verification of data- and control-oriented properties combining static and runtime verification techniques. Though the approach was sketched as tool- and language-independent, had discussed a possible implementation targeting Java programs based on the runtime verifier LARVA [10] and the static verifier KeY [5] .

That promise started to materialise in recent years in the form of two published papers. In [1] we introduced the automata-based formalism *ppDATE* which may be seen as an extension of *DATE* [9] (the underlying specification language of LARVA), extended with pre/post-conditions. We gave a high-level description of the algorithm to translate *ppDATE* into *DATE*. In [8] we presented the tool StaRVOOrS, a full implementation of this framework.

In this paper we report on our achievements concerning StaRVOOrS (Sect. 2), and we discuss two interesting extensions and research directions: (i) the use of static analysis techniques to further optimise our runtime monitors, in particular by using control-flow approaches (Sect. 3), and (ii) the extension of the framework to the distributed case (Sect. 4).

2   StaRVOOrS — Episode I

StaRVOOrS (STAtic and Runtime Verification of Object-ORiented Software) [3] is a framework for the specification of data- and control-oriented properties, and their verification using static and dynamic techniques. It combines the use of the deductive source code verifier KeY [5] with that of the runtime monitoring tool LARVA [10] to analyse and monitor systems with respect to a specification written in a formalism called *ppDATE*.

KeY is a deductive verification system for data-centric *functional correctness* properties of Java source code that generates proof obligations from a Java program enriched with annotations written in JML (Java Modeling Language) [21]. These proof obligations are written in *dynamic logic*, a modal logic tailored to reason about programs.

LARVA (*Logical Automata for Runtime Verification and Analysis*) [10] is an automata-based tool for the runtime verification of Java programs. It automatically generates a runtime monitor from a property written in the automata-based specification formalism *DATE* (*Dynamic Automata with Timers and Events*). LARVA transforms the specification into monitoring code together with AspectJ code which links the system with the monitors.

In order to combine, and get advantage of, these two verification approaches, we have defined a specification language able to represent both data- and control-oriented properties. For the control-oriented part we rely on *DATEs*, which to a certain extent also allows for the specification of data. We extend *DATE* with pre/post-conditions (or more precisely, with *Hoare triples*) in order to get more elaborated ways to specify the data-oriented part.

In the rest of this section we briefly present the StaRVOOrS workflow, we describe *ppDATE* through an example, and we give an overview of the tool and some preliminary experiments.

The StaRVOOrS Workflow. The abstract workflow of the use of StaRVOOrS is given in Fig. 1. Given a Java program *P* and specification *S* of the properties to be verified, these are transformed into suitable input for the *Deductive Verifier* module (i.e. KeY) which attempts to statically prove the properties related to pre- and post-conditions. If any part of the specification is not fully verified by KeY, it will be left, in a specialised form, in the specification to be verified at runtime. The approach uses the *partial* proofs generated by KeY, which are used to generate conditions for execution paths not statically verified. The *Partial Specification Evaluator* module then rewrites the original specification *S* into *S'*, refining the original pre-conditions with the path conditions resulting from partial proofs, thus covering only executions that are not closed in the static verification step. The *Specification Translation* then converts the *ppDATE* specification *S'* into an equivalent specification in *DATE* format (*D*) which can be used by the runtime verifier LARVA. The *DATE* specification language does not support pre/post-conditions which thus have to be translated to use notions native to the LARVA input language. This also requires a number of changes to the system (through the *Code Instrumentation* module), in order to be able to distinguish different executions of the same code unit and adding methods which operationalise pre/post-condition evaluation. The instrumented program *P'* and the *DATE* specification *D* are then used by the *Runtime Verifier* LARVA, which

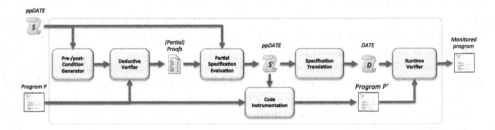

Fig. 1. High-level description of the StaRVOOrS framework workflow

generates a monitor M using aspect-oriented programming techniques capturing relevant system events and linking P' to M.

The monitor and the program are executed together after deployment, running P' in parallel with M. The instrumented system identifies violations at runtime, reporting error traces to be analysed.

The Specification Language *ppDATE*. *ppDATE* [1] is a formalism for specifying both control- and data-oriented properties. *ppDATE*s are automata with transitions labelled by a trigger (tr), a condition (c) and an action (a). Together, the label is written $tr \mid c \mapsto a$. Transitions are *enabled* whenever their triggers are active and the conditions guarding them hold. Triggers are activated by the occurrence of either a visible system event, such as the calling or termination of a method execution[1], or a *ppDATE* internal event generated by specific actions executed when a transition *fires* (that is, the transition is taken). The conditions may depend on the values of *system variables* (i.e., variables of the program to be monitored) and the values of *ppDATE variables* (i.e., variables which belong to the *ppDATE*). The latter can be modified via actions in the transitions. States in *ppDATE*s are decorated with Hoare triples of the form {pre} method-name(·) {post}, where pre and post are predicates in first-order logic describing what is to hold after the method method-name(·) is called (post), provided that pre holds before making the call.

We will not present *ppDATE*s formally in this paper, but rather illustrate the formalism through an example. Let us consider a *coffee machine* in which the filters needs to be cleaned after a certain amount of coffee cups are brewed. After this maximum number of brewed cups is reached the machine should stop brewing more cups until the filters are cleaned. The brewing process cannot be interrupted: no new coffee cup can be brewed nor the filters be cleaned until the brewing is done.

Figure 2 illustrates a *ppDATE* describing part of the behaviour of the coffee machine. Among other things, the *ppDATE* specifies the property that *it is not*

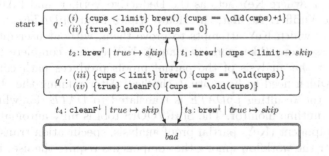

Fig. 2. A *ppDATE* controlling the brew of coffee

---

[1] $\sigma^{\downarrow}$ means that method σ has been called and $\sigma^{\uparrow}$ means that method σ has terminated its execution.

*possible to brew one more coffee cup or to clean the filters until the brewing
process is done.* That is, whenever the coffee machine is not active (i.e. is not
brewing) and the method `brew` starts the coffee brewing process, it is not possible
to execute this method again or to execute the method `cleanF`, which initialises
the task of cleaning the filter, until the brewing terminates.[2]

The *ppDATE* may be interpreted as follows: initially being in state q, whenever method `brew` is invoked, if it is possible to brew a cup of coffee (i.e. the
machine is not active and the limit of coffee cups was not reached yet), then
transition t_1 shifts the automaton from state q to state q'. While in q', if either
method `brew` or method `cleanF` are invoked, then transitions t_3 or transition t_4
shifts to state *bad*, respectively, in which case the property is violated. On the
other hand, if method `brew` terminates its execution, then transition t_2 is fired
going from state q' to state q.[3] The Hoare triples in state q specify the following:
(i) if the amount of brewed coffee cups has not reached its limit yet, then a coffee cup is brewed; (ii) cleaning the filters sets the amount of brewed coffee cups
to 0. The Hoare triple in state q' ensures that: (iii) no coffee cups are brewed;
(iv) filters are not cleaned. Note that the Hoare triples make reference to the
state of the coffee machine, i.e. there is no information on whether the machine
is active or not. This is because the machine's status is implicitly defined by
the *ppDATE*'s states. If the *ppDATE* is in state q, the coffee machine is not
active, and active if in state q': *ppDATEs* are *context dependent*. This allows
us to describe Hoare triples with the same precondition but with different postconditions, getting a different meaning depending in which state of the *ppDATE*
they are defined. To clarify the semantics of *ppDATEs*, consider, for instance, if
we are in state q and method `cleanF` is called, thus triggering the Hoare triple
requiring the number of cups to be zero upon exiting from the method. This
postcondition check is enforced even if, by the time method `cleanF` exits the
ppDATE has changed state to q'.

Tool and Experiments. We have implemented the StaRVOOrS tool [8], supporting the specification language *ppDATE*. The tool implements the workflow
given in Fig. 1, where KeY acts as the Deductive Verifier, and LARVA acts as
the Runtime Verifier. At first, the Hoare triples from *ppDATE* are translated
to JML, after which KeY attempts to prove them, without user interaction or
additional assertions (like loop invariants). KeY cannot complete most proofs
this way, but the analysis of the partial proofs produces path conditions for
those calls which need to be runtime checked. After refining the Hoare triples
accordingly, the resulting *ppDATE* is translated to *DATE*, for which LARVA
generates a runtime monitor. The StaRVOOrS tool is fully automatic, i.e., neither any component (KeY, partial proof analysis, specification transformations,
LARVA), nor the workflow among the components require the user to interfere.

---

[2] In what follows when we talk about a *method* we refer to the corresponding method
name of a Java implementation of the coffee machine controller.

[3] The names used on the transitions, e.g. t_1, are not part of the language; they are
included only to simplified the description of how the *ppDATE* works.

We have applied the tool to Mondex, an electronic purse application which has been used as a benchmark problem within the Verified Software Grand Challenge context [30]. Our variant is strongly inspired by a JML formalisation given in [29]. However, using *ppDATE*, we could more naturally represent the major 'status' of an observer as automata states, rather than in additional data. In that scenario, the combined approach makes monitoring up to 800 times faster than just using runtime verification [8].

3   Episode II, Trailer 'Control-Flow Optimisation'

Till now, in our framework we have emphasised the control-flow vs. data-flow dichotomy, arguing that although runtime verification can deal with control-flow properties in an effective manner, the approach can result in large overheads when dealing with data-flow. With this in mind, we have adopted static analysis techniques effective for data-flow properties in order to resolve expensive runtime analysis pre-deployment. This is the rationale behind the *ppDATEs* specification language — enabling specification of combined data- and control-flow properties.

Through the use of KeY, in StaRVOOrS we compositionally analyse the *ppDATE* specification without any control-flow information. The analysis looks at individual Hoare triples, either discarding them if a full proof is achieved, or refining their pre-conditions (such that they apply less often) if only a partial proof can be managed. Since *ppDATEs* deal with control-flow through the graph structure of the automaton, and the data-flow through the Hoare triples in the states, the static analysis leaves the *ppDATE* structure unchanged for runtime analysis. However, control-flow of the system might guarantee that parts of the *ppDATE* are not reachable, and thus, the Hoare triples for those states are unnecessary. The approach adopted in StaRVOOrS thus poses two challenges:

(i) Although static analysis is performed only once, pre-deployment, it can be an expensive process, and large specifications might require substantial resources to verify. However, the Hoare triples in the parts of the *ppDATEs* that are unreachable due to the system behaviour, need not be analysed.

(ii) The unreachable triples will result in additional code which dynamically verifies the system behaviour. Although unreachable, this will induce overheads in terms of the instrumented system's memory footprint and also result in additional checks when deciding which pre/post-conditions are applicable due to which *ppDATE* state the system resides in.

One solution is to adopt control-flow static analysis to reduce *ppDATEs* from a control structure perspective. A straightforward solution is to use the control flow graph of the system being analysed. For instance, reconsider the coffee-machine example given in Fig. 2. The information we extract from the system under scrutiny can be used to prune (i) transitions which can never be taken; (ii) states which are unreachable; and (iii) Hoare triples which can never

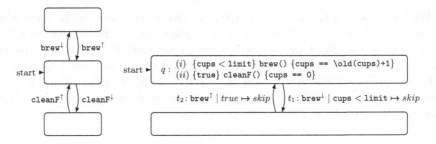

Fig. 3. (left) The control-flow graph of the system under scrutiny; and (right) an optimised 4 specification of brewing of coffee leaving out unnecessary checks

be triggered in a particular state. Consider a sequential controller of the coffee-machine, which will never attempt to start cleaning the filter or brewing halfway during a coffee brewing or a filter cleaning, respectively. The control-flow graph extracted from the system would correspond to the graph given in Fig. 3(left). Such a graph can be automatically extracted from the system using standard techniques, which would guarantee that the language of traces described by the graph is an over-approximation of traces that the system can produce[4].

By simply composing the original *ppDATE* specification (Fig. 2) using a *quasi-synchronous composition*[5] with the control-flow graph (Fig. 3(left)), we can obtain a leaner specification (Fig. 3(right)). Further, albeit more sophisticated, analysis can also enable us to discard the bottom state.

The soundness of the optimisation rests on (i) the fact that the control-flow graph provides an over-approximation of possible system behaviour; (ii) taking a quasi-synchronous composition of a *ppDATE* with a control-flow graph effectively results in a *ppDATE* which represents the conjunction of the original property and the property that the system's behaviour remains within the control-flow graph; and (iii) if we know that a system satisfies a property C (the control-flow graph), then verifying a property π is equivalent to verifying $\pi \wedge C$.

This approach is closely related to the optimisations used in Clara [6,7], and we could introduce control-flow optimisation before the data-based static analysis is applied, as depicted in Fig. 4.

---

[4] Note that, any event not appearing on any outgoing transition from a state is taken to mean that while in that state, that event is guaranteed not to occur. This visual notation contrasts with *ppDATEs*, in which, the semantics entail event not triggering any outgoing transition may occur, and leave the *ppDATE* in the same state.

[5] By quasi-synchronous composition, we mean the restriction of a *ppDATE* with an automaton, such that a *ppDATE* transition triggered by event e synchronises with a transition labelled e on the automaton, no matter what the condition and action are. Furthermore, the synchronisation is unidirectional, in that we limit the behaviour of the *ppDATE*, obtaining a *ppDATE* which is necessarily smaller, rather than the Cartesian product of the states of the *ppDATE* and the automaton.

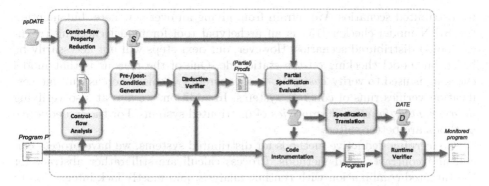

Fig. 4. High-level description of the StaRVOOrS framework workflow enriched with control-flow analysis

4 Episode II, Trailer 'Distributed StaRVOOrS'

The days of stand-alone software applications are largely over. Cloud solutions and mobile applications are perhaps the most prominent instances of a development towards ever more distributed computing. But this trend is equally dominant in areas less visible to end users. For instance, instead of singular embedded systems interacting largely with their physical environment, modern vehicles carry internal networks of interacting programmed units. Distributed software is ubiquitous. The overwhelming combinatorial complexity of possible interactions and interleavings makes distributed software systems particularly prone to unforeseen, unintended behaviour of multiple criticality. This makes system analysis and verification efforts even more important than in the stand-alone case. At the same time, distributed computational scenarios pose enormous challenges to static analysis and verification. There exist many approaches in the literature, partly supported by tools. But in general, sufficiently powerful methods tend to be heavy from a developer's perspective. We believe that the key to significantly advancing the state-of-the-art lies in a carefully designed interplay of static and runtime techniques both on the local and the global level of the distributed system. On either level, properties which are a bottleneck for static verification shall be addressed by runtime verification. On the other hand, properties which require too much overhead for runtime checking shall be addressed by static verification. This way, we can increase both the scope and the feasibility of verification in the realm of distributed systems. To achieve this, we will exploit the potential of *compositional assume-guarantee* (AG) reasoning [18,23,26], so far only used in the realm of static verification, in the context of combined static and runtime verification.

4.1 Static Verification of Distributed Software

The two main schools of static software verification are model checking and deductive verification. Of those, model checking has been extensively applied to distributed scenarios. We refrain from giving an overview here, but mention the SPIN model checker [15] as an archetypal tool for model checking (asynchronous) distributed scenarios. However, our next steps will not necessarily be based on model checking on the static side. One of the reasons is that model checking is used to verify *abstractions* of concrete systems, whereas runtime verification verifies runs of concrete systems. In addition, we aim at also verifying *data-oriented, functional properties* of distributed systems. For those, deductive methods are better suited.

Concerning deductive methods for distributed systems, we have process calculi and contract based methods. Process calculi are still rather abstract for the targeted combination with runtime analysis, and mostly lack integration to real world paradigms (like object-orientation). Highly relevant, however, for our project are contract based deductive methods for distributed systems, in particular the *compositional 'assume-guarantee'* (AG) approach to verification of distributed systems, first introduced by Misra and Chandy [23]. Compositionality means that the implementation of each component in the distributed system can be verified independent of the implementation of other components, against local contracts which state *assumptions* on the environment and *guarantees* of the component itself. This technique builds on principles of Hoare logic, and thereby can be instantiated for many concrete programming language of interest. The difference is that the contracts do not (only) talk about pre/post-states of some code, but also about the in- and outgoing communication *during* the execution of a component's implementation. Verifying each component's local compliance with its own contract, while assuming the other component's contracts (but not their implementation), proves correctness of the entire system.

More concretely, given a system which is composed by components communicating via (some form of) message passing, the implementation of each component can be specified by, and verified against, a local contract which states: (a) assumptions about the messages and data sent from the environment, and (b) guarantees about messages and data sent to the environment. Some variants of AG, including the work in [2], do not distinguish between assumption resp. guarantee formulas, but represent both in one invariant over the communication history. Intuitively, a component has to guarantee that outgoing messages maintain the invariant, given that incoming messages do so. In the case of object-oriented distributed systems, messages are method calls (with parameters) and method returns (with return values). Assumptions talk about incoming messages, i.e., method calls from callers of `this` object, and method returns from callees of `this` object. Similarly, guarantees talk about outgoing messages, i.e., method calls to callees of `this` object, and returns to callers of `this` object. This is true for both synchronous and asynchronous method execution.

When this principle is applied to modern software artefacts, it has to also cope with information hiding, by refining conditions on the communication to conditions on the internal (object) state. For instance, a positive account balance can be expressed externally in terms of summing up parameters of deposit resp. withdrawal messages, without reference to the internal state. An internal invariant can then refine the status of the event history to the internal state representation. For a comprehensive account on assume-guarantee style reasoning, see [11].

Among the recent contribution to integrating assume-guarantee style (static) verification of distributed software into contemporary verification technology are extensions [2,13] of the KeY verifier to the asynchronous distributed languages Creol [17] and ABS [16].

4.2 Runtime Verification of Distributed Software

Concerning runtime verification of distributed systems, some of the issues discussed in the literature are: (i) characteristics of properties and systems such that the former are *monitorable* on the latter [22]; (ii) dedicated formalisms tailored for distributed runtime monitoring, [27,28]; (iii) the choice of location of the runtime monitors [14].

Concerning formalisms for writing properties about distributed systems, a reference is *past-time Distributed Temporal Logic* (ptDTL) introduced by Sen et al. [28], and the more recent logic DTL [27]. DTL combines the three-valued linear temporal logic (LTL$_3$ [4]) with ptDTL, and is able to express more properties than ptDTL, like Boolean combinations of safety properties.

The choice of locations of the monitors is quite an important issue because communication across locations is usually expensive and information-sensitive. A good discussion about this choice is presented in [14], where a theoretical framework is presented for comparing those choices. Studying this aspect is not an exclusivity from the runtime verification community; it has been studied in other communities before, as for instance in security. The papers [20,25] provide a clear survey of those techniques for usage control.

From the practical side, a taxonomy of software-fault runtime verification tools is presented in [12], including some targeting distributed and parallel systems. Among those, it is worth mentioning the Java Runtime Timing-constraint Monitor (JRTM) [24]. JRTM monitors timing properties (written in Real Time Logic —RTL) of distributed, real-time systems written in Java. Zhou et al. [31] presents DMaC, a distributed monitoring and checking platform built upon: (i) the Monitoring and Checking (MaC) framework (providing means to monitor and check running systems against formal requirements), and (ii) a declarative domain-specific approach for specifying and implementing distributed network protocols. DMaC uses a formal specification language called MEDL, similar to past-time LTL, in which it is possible to specify safety properties of a distributed system.

4.3 Combined Static and Runtime Verification of Distributed Software

Our work on combining static and runtime verification of distributed software will be based on the following existing approaches, methods, and tools:

- The assume-guarantee paradigm for (static) distributed systems verification in general [11,23,26], and for (static) distributed *objects* verification in particular [2].
- Approaches to the scope and placement of runtime monitors in a distributed system [14].
- The results of our StaRVOOrS (Episode I) project for combined static and runtime verification of *sequential* object-oriented programs [1,8]. In particular, we will extend to the distributed case:
  - The general principle of using complete *and incomplete* static proofs, analysing the latter to refine the original specs by path conditions which prevent runtime verification of statically verified cases [3];
  - The language *ppDATE*, combining automata-style control-flow oriented specification with data-oriented specification in form of (state-dependent) Hoare triples [1];
  - Experience gained in implementing and using the StaRVOOrS tool [8].

We are convinced that compositional assume-guarantee (AG) specification and reasoning, so far only used in the realm of static verification, has enormous potential in the context of combined static and runtime verification. We will exploit this potential in a number of ways. AG was conceived and used solely as a means for *static* verification. One bottleneck of AG is that the reduction of properties of the outer communication to properties of the inner state can require smart proof engineering. In our future work, however, we will refer sub-properties which are difficult to establish statically to runtime verification. Another, very severe bottleneck for practical applicability of AG is that it requires full access to the implementation of all components. Even if the implementation of individual components can be verified without knowledge of the other components' implementation (after all, the method is compositional by design), still the implementation of all components must be verified to establish the correctness of the overall system. But in real distributed scenarios, we often only know the internals of certain components, not of others. (Those may be legacy systems, binaries, or remote proprietary services.) We can, however, formalise the documented external behaviour of such closed components with AG contracts. Actual compliance of closed components with such contracts can then be checked by *runtime verification*. At the same time, these contracts can be *used*, as assumptions, in the verification of open components interacting with the closed ones. The latter can be done statically, or at runtime, or with a combination.

5   Conclusions

In this paper we have reported on our previous results concerning StaRVOOrS, a framework for the combination of static and runtime techniques for the verification of data- and control-oriented properties. We have also identified two main research directions: (i) optimisation of our framework by using static analysis techniques to reduce runtime overheads, and (ii) extending StaRVOOrS to a distributed setting. We briefly present here a roadmap for achieving this endeavour.

Optimisation Using Control-Flow Static Analysis. As described in Sect. 3, the runtime monitor may be further optimised by considering additional constraints of the program being analysed. In particular, we will use standard techniques to get an automata based on the control-flow of the program and apply quasi-synchronisation to compose it with the *ppDATE*. We will explore the connection, and eventual combination, with techniques like the one used in Clara [6].

Control- and Data-Oriented Property Language for Distributed Components. Any formalism for stating assumptions/guarantees/invariants has to be capable of expressing conditions on the history of communication events, including the carried data. The formalisms typically used are either of too limited expressiveness or too difficult to use for formalisation and reasoning. We will extend and adapt the control- and data-oriented property language *ppDATE* [1] to the distributed setting. The native support for properties of data *and* events will be even more profitable in the distributed setting than it already is in the sequential setting, because typical AG contracts require characterisation of *event* histories together with the carried *data*.

Identify and Adapt Static Verification Methods and Tools. Neither the method nor the tool will be developed from scratch (one starting point can be [2]), but serious adaptions need to be made.

Identify and Adapt a Runtime Verification Method and Tool. Neither the method nor the tool will be developed from scratch. The prime candidate is LARVA [10] (which employs aspect-oriented programming), but extended to the distributed setting. Among the issues will be strategies for placing (or even moving) runtime monitors within the distributed system, see [14].

Integrating Static and Runtime Verification of Distributed Components. Develop a methodology and corresponding tool support which identifies sub-properties where static verification will be tried, analyses the result, and deploys the system for runtime monitoring of sub-properties which are not statically verified.

Tune the Balance of Static vs. Runtime Verification of Distributed Behaviour. The 'effort level' for static verification can be guided by the mixed criticality levels of components and their services in the distributed system. And it can be guided by limits in time, budget, and education in the software ecosystem using our method. Note that, in particular, we will support the effort level 'full automation', resulting in many unfinished proofs. Still, our current results show that even that can limit the runtime overhead by a factor of up to 800 [8] (through automated analysis of unfinished proofs).

Investigate Synchronous vs. Asynchronous Communication. Crosscutting the above concerns, we aim to investigate both synchronous and asynchronous communication. The choice has implications for all of the above. In terms of target languages/architectures, we will use Java-RMI (remote method invocation) for the synchronous case, and ABS [16] (an extension of Creol) or Active Objects [19] for the asynchronous case.

Case Studies. Will also have running case studies, to experiment with, and evaluate. When more machinery is in place, we will use a bigger, realistic scenario to evaluate the overall approach. A possible candidate is from the automotive domain in connection with a big car manufacturer.

Acknowledgments. This research has been partially supported by the Swedish Research Council *(Vetenskapsrådet)* under the project *StaRVOOrS: Unified Static and Runtime Verification of Object-Oriented Software,* no. 2012-4499. We would like to thank Jesús Mauricio Chimento, for his substantial contributions to the work we recapitulate in Sect. 2 (StaRVOOrS — Episode I), in particular the StaRVOOrS tool implementation and the experiments.

References

1. Ahrendt, W., Chimento, J.M., Pace, G.J., Schneider, G.: A specification language for static and runtime verification of data and control properties. In: Bjørner, N., Boer, F. (eds.) FM 2015. LNCS, vol. 9109, pp. 108–125. Springer, Heidelberg (2015)
2. Ahrendt, W., Dylla, M.: A system for compositional verification of asynchronous objects. Sci. Comput. Program. (2012). http://dx.doi.org/10.1016/j.scico.2010.08.003
3. Ahrendt, W., Pace, G.J., Schneider, G.: A unified approach for static and runtime verification: framework and applications. In: Steffen, B., Margaria, T. (eds.) ISoLA 2012, Part I. LNCS, vol. 7609, pp. 312–326. Springer, Heidelberg (2012)
4. Bauer, A., Leucker, M., Schallhart, C.: Runtime verification for LTL and TLTL. ACM Trans. Softw. Eng. Methodol. **20**(4), 14 (2011)
5. Beckert, B., Hähnle, R., Schmitt, P.H. (eds.): Verification of Object-Oriented Software: The KeY Approach. LNCS, vol. 4334. Springer, Heidelberg (2007)
6. Bodden, E., Lam, P.: Clara: partially evaluating runtime monitors at compile time. In: Barringer, H., et al. (eds.) RV 2010. LNCS, vol. 6418, pp. 74–88. Springer, Heidelberg (2010)
7. Bodden, E., Lam, P., Hendren, L.: Clara: a framework for partially evaluating finite-state runtime monitors ahead of time. In: Barringer, H., et al. (eds.) RV 2010. LNCS, vol. 6418, pp. 183–197. Springer, Heidelberg (2010)
8. Chimento, J.M., Ahrendt, W., Pace, G.J., Schneider, G.: StaRVOOrS: a tool for combined static and runtime verification of Java. In: Bartocci, E., Majumdar, R. (eds.) RV 2015. LNCS, vol. 9333, pp. 297–305. Springer, Heidelberg (2015). doi:10.1007/978-3-319-23820-3_21
9. Colombo, C., Pace, G.J., Schneider, G.: Dynamic event-based runtime monitoring of real-time and contextual properties. In: Cofer, D., Fantechi, A. (eds.) FMICS 2008. LNCS, vol. 5596, pp. 135–149. Springer, Heidelberg (2009)
10. Colombo, C., Pace, G.J., Schneider, G.: LARVA - a tool for runtime monitoring of Java programs. In: SEFM 2009, pp. 33–37. IEEE Computer Society (2009)
11. de Roever, W.-P., de Boer, F., Hannemann, U., Hooman, J., Lakhnech, Y., Poel, M., Zwiers, J., Verification, C.: Introduction to compositional and noncompositional methods. In: Number 54 in Cambridge Tracts in Theoretical Computer Science. Cambridge University Press, Cambridge, November 2001
12. Delgado, N., Gates, A.Q., Roach, S.: A taxonomy and catalog of runtime software-fault monitoring tools. IEEE Trans. Softw. Eng. **30**(12), 859–872 (2004)

13. Din, C.C., Tapia Tarifa, S.L., Hähnle, R., Johnsen, E.B.: History-based specification and verification of scalable concurrent and distributed systems. In: Butler, M., Conchon, S., Zaïdi, F. (eds.) ICFEM 2015. LNCS, vol. 9407, pp. 217–233. Springer, Heidelberg (2015). doi:10.1007/978-3-319-25423-4_14
14. Francalanza, A., Gauci, A., Pace, G.J.: Distributed system contract monitoring. J. Logic Algebraic Programm. 82(57), 186–215 (2013). Formal Languages and Analysis of Contract-Oriented Software (FLACOS 2011)
15. Holzmann, G.J.: The model checker SPIN. Softw. Eng. 23(5), 279–295 (1997)
16. Johnsen, E.B., Hähnle, R., Schäfer, J., Schlatte, R., Steffen, M.: ABS: a core language for abstract behavioral specification. In: Aichernig, B.K., Boer, F.S., Bonsangue, M.M. (eds.) Formal Methods for Components and Objects. LNCS, vol. 6957, pp. 142–164. Springer, Heidelberg (2011)
17. Johnsen, E.B., Owe, O.: An asynchronous communication model for distributed concurrent objects. Softw. Syst. Model. 6(1), 35–58 (2007)
18. Jones, C.B.: Development methods for computer programs including a notion of interference. Ph.D. thesis, Oxford University, UK (1981)
19. Lavender, R.G., Schmidt, D.C.: Active object: an object behavioral pattern for concurrent programming. In: Vlissides, J.M., Coplien, J.O., Kerth, N.L. (eds.) Pattern Languages of Program Design 2. Addison-Wesley Longman Publishing Co., Inc., Boston (1996)
20. Lazouski, A., Martinelli, F., Mori, P.: Usage control in computer security: a survey. Comput. Sci. Rev. 4(2), 81–99 (2010)
21. Leavens, G.T., Poll, E., Clifton, C., Cheon, Y., Ruby, C., Cok, D., Müller, P., Kiniry, J., Chalin, P., Zimmerman, D.M., Dietl, W.: JML reference manual. Draft 2344 (2013). http://www.eecs.ucf.edu/~leavens/JML/documentation.shtml
22. Malakuti Khah Olun Abadi, S., Akşit, M., Bockisch, C.M.: Runtime verification in distributed computing. J. Convergence 2(1), 1–10 (2011)
23. Misra, J., Chandy, K.: Proofs of networks and processes. IEEE Trans. Softw. Eng. 7(7), 417–426 (1981)
24. Mok, A.K., Liu, G.: Efficient run-time monitoring of timing constraints. In: RTAS 1997, pp. 252–262. IEEE Computer Society (1997)
25. Nyre, Å.A.: Usage control enforcement - a survey. In: Tjoa, A.M., Quirchmayr, G., You, I., Xu, L. (eds.) ARES 2011. LNCS, vol. 6908, pp. 38–49. Springer, Heidelberg (2011)
26. Pnueli, A.: In transition from global to modular temporal reasoning about programs. In: Apt, K.R. (ed.) Logics and Models of Concurrent Systems. Springer, Heidelberg (1985)
27. Scheffel, T., Schmitz, M.: Three-valued asynchronous distributed runtime verification. In: 2014 Twelfth ACM/IEEE International Conference on Formal Methods and Models for Codesign (MEMOCODE), pp. 52–61, October 2014
28. Sen, K., Vardhan, A., Agha, G., Rosu, G.: Efficient decentralized monitoring of safety in distributed systems. In: 26th International Conference on Software Engineering (ICSE 2004), 23–28 May 2004, Edinburgh, United Kingdom, pp. 418–427 (2004)
29. Tonin, I.: Verifying the mondex case study. The key approach. Technical report 2007–4, Universität Karlsruhe (2007)
30. Woodcock, J.: First steps in the verified software grand challenge. In: SEW 2006, pp. 203–206. IEEE Computer Society (2006)
31. Zhou, W., Sokolsky, O., Loo, B.T., Lee, I.: *DMaC*: distributed monitoring and checking. In: Peled, D.A., Bensalem, S. (eds.) RV 2009. LNCS, vol. 5779, pp. 184–201. Springer, Heidelberg (2009)

A Model-Based Approach to Combining Static and Dynamic Verification Techniques

Shaun Azzopardi, Christian Colombo, and Gordon Pace[(✉)]

University of Malta, Msida, Malta
gordon.pace@um.edu.mt

Abstract. Given the complementary nature of static and dynamic analysis, there has been much work on identifying means of combining the two. In particular, the use of static analysis as a means of alleviating the overheads induced by dynamic analysis, typically by trying to prove parts of the properties, which would then not need to be verified at runtime. In this paper, we propose a novel framework which combines static with dynamic verification using a model-based approach. The approach allows the support of applications running on untrusted devices whilst using centralised sensitive services whose use is to be tightly regulated. In particular, we discuss how this approach is being adopted in the context of the Open Payments Ecosystem (OPE) — an ecosystem meant to support the development of payment and financial transaction applications with strong compliance verification to enable adoption by payment institutions.

1 Introduction

Analysis of the dynamic behaviour of systems has long been used to ensure the correct behaviour of software. By adding monitors, for instance in the form of assertions, throughout the system, one can react accordingly whenever unexpected behaviour occurs. One issue with this is that of monitoring overheads. Monitors impose a temporal burden on the system, and in the case of properties which go beyond the well-formedness of the system state at a particular point in time (an example of such a property would be 'File access can only occur between a login and a logout'), such checks also require additional space overheads to store the state of the monitor. One prevalent approach in addressing these overheads has been that of applying static analysis techniques, typically in an attempt to prove parts of the specification which would not need to be checked at runtime.

Dynamic verification also fails to address certain verification scenarios. Consider a situation in which a service would need to be matched with an appropriate co-service. For example, an online sales application providing its services via an e-commerce portal may need to be paired with a postal service provider and

---

The Open Payments Ecosystem has received funding from the European Union's Horizon 2020 research and innovation programme under grant number 666363.

T. Margaria and B. Steffen (Eds.): ISoLA 2016, Part I, LNCS 9952, pp. 416–430, 2016.
DOI: 10.1007/978-3-319-47166-2_29

a payment institution to perform payment transactions. However, some postal service providers may only provide their services to e-commerce applications whose customers are from a particular geographic region, and certain payment institutions may only allow applications which store certain information about customers and have a guaranteed minimum payment throughput. Since the allocation of postal and payment service providers has to take place before the application is deployed, dynamic verification provides such information too late. In such a situation, static analysis can be used to address the issue of matching appropriate service providers with the application. However, one would typically expect such applications to run on the user's machine, making it hard to ensure that the analysed application is the one actually deployed.

Model-based approaches for the analysis of computer systems have long been adopted in various settings. In these settings, the notion of what constitutes a model is rather fluid, but is typically taken to be a description of the system such that: (i) it behaves in a manner which is faithful (with respect to certain features) to the system itself; but (ii) it abstracts away other unnecessary detail, hence making it more amenable to analysis. Typically, whether it is used for simulation, testing or model checking, the approach allows the analysis of the model prior to deployment. The underlying degree of trust that the model is similar to the actual system means that conclusions can be carried over from the model to the actual system. However, models do not always carry the same degree of trust — while a model deduced from a system using a verified-correct algorithm (e.g., extracting the control-flow graph of a system) can be guaranteed to be correct with respect to the information retained, other models (e.g., a UML model based on which a system is developed in an *ad hoc* manner) may not be faithful to the actual system.

In this paper, we present a model-based framework for the verification of systems which require analysis before deployment. An example of such a scenario is when one is required to match a system with compatible co-services (henceforth referred to as *service providers*) based on a model of the system as given by the developer (and thus not verified). To ensure behavioural correctness one thus also needs to runtime verify compliance of the actual application behaviour against the model.

This need for such an approach arose in the context of a platform for the deployment of financial systems which require services provided by financial institutions such as banks [3]. This brings in various constraints from the service providers: (i) capabilities e.g., which credit cards they can handle; (ii) legislation in countries they operate in e.g., anti-money laundering legislation places limits on individual spending depending on how much knowledge about the customer the financial institution has acquired (usually referred to as *customer due diligence*); and (iii) what risks they are willing to take (*risk appetite*). Applications submitted by registered developers to the payments platform would thus need to be analysed *prior to deployment* to ensure they are paired up with an appropriate service provider and also checked for regulatory compliance. However, an additional challenge is that developers are not constrained to a particular technology, and applications access the financial platform through a generic API, meaning that analysis and verification techniques cannot be technology-specific. The solution adopted is to have developers submit a model of their application's use of API calls which (i) is analysed to allow pairing up the application with a service provider; (ii) is used to (usually partially) verify the application against regulatory compliance. However, since the implementation cannot be trusted, the application behaviour is verified at runtime to ensure that it adheres to the model the developer submitted.

The solution we present in this paper uses a model-based approach to achieve various goals. Firstly, we ensure technology independence — by using the model for static verification instead of the actual system itself. Secondly, we also use the model to attempt to verify compliance properties statically, and although the model is typically too weak to ensure full compliance, it can serve to prove parts of them, reducing overheads induced due to runtime verification of these properties. Finally, since the system might not be a correct refinement of the model, we also verify the model at runtime.

The paper is organised as follows. We start by presenting static and dynamic analysis approaches in Sect. 2. Next, Sect. 3 provides an overview of our proposed solution, while Sect. 4 delves into an instantiation of our framework as a case study. Finally, we frame our work in the context of the OPE project in Sect. 5, and conclude in the last section.

2   Combining Static and Dynamic Verification Techniques

Much of the literature combining static and dynamic verification decomposes the specification π of a system P in such a way that part of the specification is statically verified at compile time, leaving the rest to be verified at runtime. At a most basic level, one takes conjuncts and sees which of these can be verified statically e.g., [2,4], leaving the rest to be verified at runtime:

$$\text{SA}(\,P,\pi_1)\ \dfrac{}{P \vdash \pi_1}\ \ \text{RV}\ \dfrac{}{P \vdash \pi_2}$$
$$\overline{P \vdash \pi_1 \wedge \pi_2}$$

In the pseudo-rule above, we abuse notation and use a family of static-analysis pseudo-axioms $\text{SA}(P, \pi)$ which asserts that by using a static analysis technique to check whether program P satisfies property π, we manage to automatically prove the entailment of the proof rule[1]. Similarly, we use the pseudo-axiom RV to indicate that the entailment will be verified at runtime.

The approach is thus to separate the conjuncts of the property which are verifiable statically (property π_1) from those which are not, and thus have to be verified at runtime (property π_2). In most cases, monitoring the structurally smaller formula π_2 induces less overheads than $\pi_1 \wedge \pi_2$, which is desirable. Note

---

[1] We show P and π as parameters to specify exactly what the verification question posed to the static analysis tool is.

that there are cases where this is not necessarily true. For instance, monitoring a predicate $P \implies Q$ might be more costly than monitoring $(P \implies Q) \wedge \neg P$ which a pre-processor might simplify to $\neg P$.

In fact, what is required to be monitored can be weakened to take into account that there may lie an overlap between the conjuncts. As we will show, if we know that π_1 is satisfied by the system, and we want to ensure that $\pi_1 \wedge \pi_2$ holds, it suffices to monitor any predicate α which satisfies (i) $\pi_1 \wedge \pi_2 \implies \alpha$; and (ii) $\alpha \implies \neg \pi_1 \vee \pi_2$. Trivial solutions for α include $\pi_1 \wedge \pi_2$ and π_2, but other solutions might be better suited for dynamic verification.

This view of the combination of static and dynamic analysis can be somewhat generalised so as not to be limited to static analysis, which can prove a sub-conjunct of the specification. In this case, if when trying to verify a specification π, the static verifier manages to prove property π', the runtime verification tool will have to verify what remains of the original specification modulo what was proved. This can be expressed using the notion of property quotients.

Definition 1. *Given predicates α and β, a predicate γ is said to be a* quotient *of α with respect to β, written as $\gamma \in \alpha \div \beta$, if $\beta \implies (\alpha \iff \gamma)$.*

Quotients are defined in such a way that if $\gamma \in \alpha \div \beta$, then to prove α when knowing β, it suffices to prove γ. Furthermore, knowing γ is necessary for α to hold (under β). For instance, if $\gamma \in P \wedge Q \div R \vee Q$ would mean that γ satisfies $(R \vee Q) \implies ((P \wedge Q) \iff \gamma)$ — with $P \wedge Q$ and $P \wedge (R \implies Q)$ being two possible solutions for γ.

The following proposition gives us two inequalities (implications) specifying the possible values, which the quotient of a specification with respect to a known property can take.

Proposition 1. *Given a specification S and known property π, if $\pi' \in S \div \pi$, then it follows that: (i) $S \wedge \pi \implies \pi'$; and (ii) $\pi' \implies S \vee \neg \pi$. Furthermore, for these implications to hold, it is necessary that π' is a quotient of S with respect to π.*

Proof. *Since π' is a quotient of S with respect to π, we know that: $\pi \implies (S \iff \pi')$. From this, it is straightforward to prove that $S \wedge \pi \implies \pi'$. The second implication $\pi' \implies S \vee \neg \pi$ also holds by case analysis on π'.*

For the second part of the proof, assume that these two implications hold. If π holds, from the first we obtain that $S \implies \pi'$, and from the second we get $\pi' \implies S$, from which we conclude that $S \iff \pi'$. □

We can use quotients to extend the verification rule to take into account whatever the static verification analysis managed to prove. When checking for a specification S, if a property π_1 is known (can be proved statically), we can dynamically check any property which is (under the effect of π_1) equivalent to S — in other words, any quotient of S with respect to π_1:

$$\frac{\text{SA}(\,P,\pi)\ \overline{\ P \vdash \pi_1\ }\ \ \text{RV}\ \overline{\ P \vdash \pi_2\ }}{P \vdash \pi}\ \pi_2 \in \pi \div \pi_1$$

Note that throughout this section, we have not committed ourselves to any particular specification logic, as long as it has conjunction and negation operators, and forms a Boolean algebra.

2.1 Related Work

StaRVOOrs [1,2,5] is a tool that reflects most closely the framework presented. In this framework, the static analysis tool KeY attempts to prove parts of specification by theorem proving pre-/post-conditions. The result of this analysis is to either (i) completely discharge conjuncts of the specification (similar to the initial approach we described in this section); or (ii) discharge parts of the specification along particular branches of execution (which corresponds to a quotient as defined above).

A residual specification is not always explicit, for example in the Clara framework [4], static analysis for finite-state properties are used to disable AspectJ monitors at program locations that have been proven to be safe. This is thus aimed at leveraging several static analyses to reduce monitoring overheads.

[8] illustrates the logic behind such an approach, wherein static analysis is leveraged to specify regions of a program that are safe, i.e., within which instrumentation can be avoided. If a certain method call is always present in such a safe region, then it is also removed from the specification, leaving a residual specification to be instrumented within the potentially unsafe regions of the program.

Another approach allows avoiding monitoring overheads completely by simply replacing these execution points by halt statements instead of weaving monitors at potentially unsafe locations [12]. This allows for the creation of a modified program that is safe, and that has no added overheads during runtime, although some (potentially unsafe) execution traces will simply halt the execution.

3 A Model-Based Approach

Under certain circumstances, it may be impractical if not impossible to have access to the actual system to analyse statically. For instance, consider an application accessing a sensitive central resource or service, which would itself be deployed on an untrusted device. Since there is no guarantee that the code executed is not tampered with, analysing the given code would be a futile exercise. Another consideration is that one might want to allow an application to be implemented using any of a wide range of technologies, accessing the sensitive resource through an API. Developing static analysis for any source technology would be prohibitively expensive and impractical. In both these examples, it is interesting to note that the use of the sensitive resource through a centralised server ensures that, provided that the properties are limited to the actual resource usage, dynamic analysis is still feasible, even if pre-deployment static analysis is not, thus precluding the use of techniques such as the ones described in the previous section.

One way of addressing this challenge is the use of models. By having access to a model of the system — an abstract description of how the system will behave with respect to the central resource — one can perform static analysis of the properties using the model rather than the system itself. However, if the property is verified statically against the model, we would still have no guarantee that the system actually behaves as promised by the model, a guarantee which for the reasons expounded earlier, we can only check dynamically at runtime.

We can extend the approaches presented in the previous section to enable the use of a model M (of which system P is supposed to be a refinement, written as $P \sqsubseteq M$). If the model is sufficient to prove property π, at runtime it suffices to verify that the system is a refinement of the model:

$$\mathrm{SA}(\,M,\pi)\ \frac{}{M \vdash \pi}\quad \mathrm{RV}\ \frac{}{P \sqsubseteq M}$$
$$\frac{}{P \vdash \pi}$$

In this approach, the model acts as both a description of the system (during the static analysis) and the property (for the dynamic analysis).

This approach poses a number of challenges. The first challenge is the obvious question of why we should put any weight on the promise of the model. After all, nothing stops the developer from submitting a 'perfect' model and then deploying an application which behaves in a completely different manner. Although we would realise the misbehaviour at runtime, and stop the application from proceeding once it diverges from what the model promised, what use was the static analysis? Wouldn't the alternative approach of just monitoring the property have been equally effective? In practice, however, the justification of the use of the model is twofold:

(i) In some scenarios, we would like to perform some pre-deployment static analysis to match the application with an appropriate service provider. Consider matching an application performing financial transactions, which would need to be matched with a service provider able to handle transactions of the size and volume that the application will produce, from the geographical locations supported by the application, providing the right financial instruments required by the application, etc. Unless we have a model of the application based on which an appropriate service provider can be found, we would not be able to proceed any further. Moreover, the fact that some service providers are not willing to engage with an application which does not promise to behave correctly, ensures that the developer is willing to provide such a model.

(ii) If an application fails to behave according to the model, appropriate action can be immediately taken, stopping or rectifying the problem. However, such misbehaviour can also be tagged; potentially leading, for instance, to a service provider refusing to supply a service to applications by the same developer in the future. This encourages developers to ensure that their applications conform to submitted models.

Providing models of applications, would thus be feasible in a service-oriented ecosystem. Another challenge is that the model abstracts detail without which certain properties are impossible to verify completely. In such situations, we would have to resort to techniques such as those described in the previous section to runtime verify residual parts of the properties. Whereas before, parts of the properties might have been unprovable due to limitations of the static analysis techniques, in this case, unprovable properties may be the result of a weak model.

Using a more formal syntax, given a specification π which is not completely provable from model M, we will use the quotient of π with respect to the property π_1 which the static analyser manages to prove:

$$\cfrac{\text{SA}(M,\pi) \; \cfrac{}{M \vdash \pi_1} \quad \text{RV} \; \cfrac{}{P \sqsubseteq M} \quad \text{RV} \; \cfrac{}{P \vdash \pi_2}}{P \vdash \pi} \quad \pi_2 \in \pi \div \pi_1$$

The architecture of this approach, when the system is potentially executed on an external address space is shown in Fig. 1(a), in which the system is runtime verified against the model and the residual specification by instrumenting the server to arbitrate the system's interaction with the central system.

Furthermore, since we are checking that the quotient (π_2) holds, parts of the model M might be discarded since they are being verified by checking for π_2. If the model has a semantics which is comparable to the property language (e.g., for a model M and property π, the formulae $M \wedge \pi$ and $M \implies \pi$ can be computed in the form of a model), we can express this in terms of the quotient operator:

$$\cfrac{\text{SA}(M,\pi) \; \cfrac{}{M \vdash \pi_1} \quad \text{RV} \; \cfrac{}{P \sqsubseteq M'} \quad \text{RV} \; \cfrac{}{P \vdash \pi_2}}{P \vdash \pi} \quad \pi_2 \in \pi \div \pi_1, \; M' \in M \div \pi_2$$

Such approaches have already been explored in other contexts such as [7].

The architecture of the resulting framework is shown in Fig. 1(b).

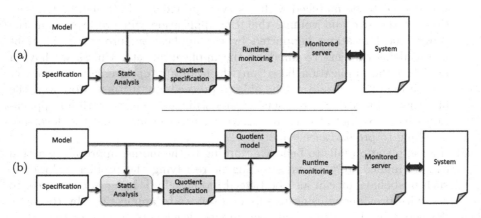

Fig. 1. (a) Architectures for model-based hybrid verification (top); (b) Extended architecture (bottom)

An example of this in action is [11], where model checking technology is extended to allow the partitioning of a model into two parts, a part free of errors and the rest. This allows for analyses to focus on the second part, further refining it. In effect this can be seen as an implementation of a model quotient with respect to the parts of the specification that the static analysis is able to prove.

4   A Control-Flow-Based Use Case

We will now look at instances of the model-based approach described in the previous section. In this section, we will be using automaton-based formalisms for both the model and the property. We will model the system using a control-flow graph of an application, while we will use a formalism based on the specification language used by the runtime verification tool Larva to write the properties. Despite the fact that both formalisms are given in terms of an automaton, it is important to note that they have different semantics. Let us start by presenting the formalism used to specify the model:

Definition 2. *A simple control-flow model M is a quadruple $\langle \Sigma, Q, Q_0, \rightarrow \rangle$, with initial states $Q_0 \subseteq Q$ and transition relation $\rightarrow \subseteq Q \times \Sigma \times Q$, and is interpreted as a labelled transition system. We will write the reflexive transitive closure of $\rightarrow$ as $\overset{w}{\Rightarrow}$ (with $w \in \Sigma^*$). The set of traces accepted by M, written $traces_M(M)$ is defined to be $\{w : \Sigma^* \mid \exists q_0 \in Q_0, q \in Q \cdot q_0 \overset{w}{\Rightarrow} q\}$.*

Model refinement is defined in terms of trace semantics: $M \sqsubseteq M' \overset{df}{=} traces_M(M) \subseteq traces_M(M')$.

For instance, the simple control-flow model, referred to in the rest of this section as M given in Fig. 2, models the control-flow behaviour of the system e.g. that the system will not write just after an anonymous login occurs, and will not perform two consecutive logouts, etc. We will now discuss how various properties can be checked for a system modelled by M.

Our properties in this section will be expressed using a simplified form of dynamic automata with timers and events (DATEs) as used in the runtime verification tool Larva [6]. These automata (which can be dynamically replicated) will have a number of bad states (marked by a cross). Transitions are labelled

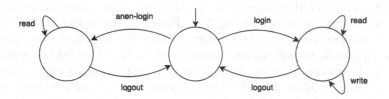

Fig. 2. Model M of the system showing no writes will be allowed during an anonymous login.

by triples: (i) a system event which triggers the transition; (ii) a condition which is checked whenever the event is triggered — if the condition holds, then the transition is enabled, otherwise it is not; and (iii) an action which is executed just before the transition is taken. The semantics of such properties are taken to be the set of traces which do not lead to a bad (crossed) state.

The full semantics of DATEs can be found in [6], but for the sake of this example, we will use a semantics over traces of pairs of events and system state snapshots (the latter, accessed through the use of aspect-oriented programming techniques, are required in order to be able to reason about conditions and actions which may refer to the state of the system), with the trace semantics of a DATE property π being written as $\text{traces}_D(\pi)$.

To avoid busy diagrams, we implicitly include reflexive transitions such that if an action happens while in a state in which the action does not appear on any outgoing transition from that state, the automaton allows it and remains in the same state. Consider property π_1 which states that 'a login may only happen while logged out' which is described using the DATE in Fig. 3(a).

A straightforward way of statically model checking whether a simple-control flow model satisfies a DATE property is by first (i) abstracting the DATE by discarding conditions and actions, thus ending up with an over-approximation of the property, and then (ii) taking the synchronous product of the property automaton and the model (M) to statically verify that no paths in the language of traces generated by the model lead to a bad state. This static analysis approach algorithm can be shown to be sound, though obviously not complete.

This static analysis suffices to show that π_1 is satisfied by M, which will allow us to discard completely the monitoring of the property.

Let us consider a more complex property π_2 which limits the total amount of data transferred while anonymously logged in, as shown in Fig. 3(b). Clearly, the model is not sufficient to guarantee the property. However, the model guarantees that no writing will ever take place while anonymously logged in.

Consider the restriction of a DATE property π with respect to a simple-control flow model M which works by discarding infeasible transitions through the semi-synchronous composition of π with M, akin to the approach used in [9,10]. This can be shown to yield a quotient of M with respect to π.

We can thus use this quotient of the property with respect to what can be proved based on the model. One solution allowed by our framework is to discard the property transitions tagged by write as shown in Fig. 4(a), an optimisation which can have a substantial impact in reducing monitoring overheads.

Finally, consider the property π_3 which states that 'Anonymous logins are not to be allowed' as shown in Fig. 3(c). Based on the model, which does not rule out anonymous logins, the property cannot be simplified using the static analysis approach shown earlier. However, given that the DATE contains no conditions or actions, it is possible to apply the restriction algorithm mentioned earlier to restrict M to π_3 (which will anyhow be dynamically verified). The resulting model, shown in Fig. 4(b), ignores anonymous logins since these would be detected as violations of the property anyway. At runtime, it still remains to

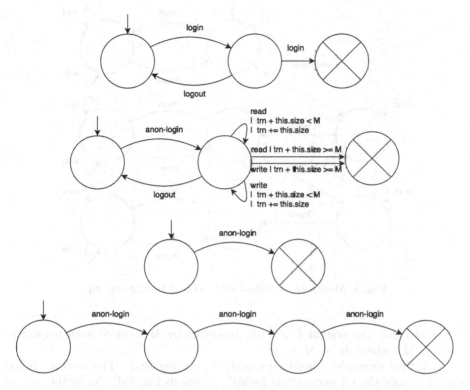

Fig. 3. (a) $\pi_1 =$ A login may not happen when already logged in; (b) $\pi_2 =$ No more than X bytes may be transferred while anonymously logged in; (c) $\pi_3 =$ Only logins with full credentials are allowed; (d) $\pi_4 =$ The system should allow no more than 2 anonymous logins.

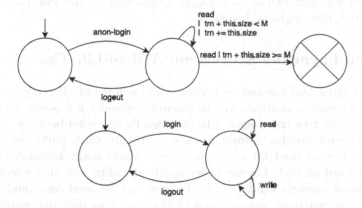

Fig. 4. (a) Property π_2 simplified with respect to model M; (b) Model M simplified with respect to property π_3.

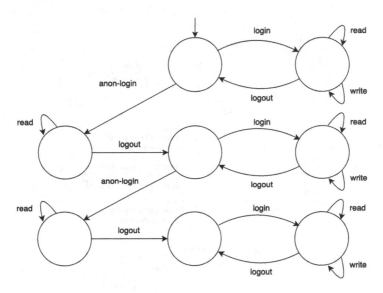

Fig. 5. Model M simplified with respect to property π_4.

be verified that the system P is really modelled by M reduced with respect to π_3: $P \sqsubseteq M'$, where $M' \in M \div \pi_3$.

As a final example, consider property π_4 stating that "The system should allow no more than 2 anonymous logins", shown in Fig. 3(d). As in the case of π_3, no part of the property can be verified with respect to the model. However, when computing the quotient model as done before, we can calculate a number of possible quotients — from the trivial solution of keeping M to expanding the model to keep count of transitions, obtaining a model as shown in Fig. 5. Although the model is larger, it can permit switching off monitors for anonymous logins after the first two of such logins. Depending on the way monitoring is implemented, this might be beneficial.

5   Open Payments Ecosystem: A Real-Life Case Study

Businesses often find themselves needing diverse ways of affecting or enabling payments in various contexts. As an example, consider a business providing a payment service to a travel agency to purchase flights, hotel bookings, etc. Having several such purchases from a single corporate card, particularly if that same card is also used for other purchases, would make reconciliation non-straightforward at best. On the other hand, providing one shot cards for use by the travel agency, which are cards that can be used once and disabled after the first purchase, makes reconciliation easier as only one purchase will be associated with any given card. However, for a business to set up such a payment programme is quite complex (implement cards processes for provisioning, reconciliation, dispute management, as well as creating a compliant application) and the costs may be prohibitive.

Open Payments Ecosystem (OPE) aims at building an infrastructure to address this need by building an *execution environment* for financial transactions where the process of deploying custom payment applications is simplified. OPE, thus brings together a number of players: (i) *developers* who create the payment applications; (ii) *service providers* (typically banks) which affect the underlying financial transactions; (iii) *corporate customers* (the travel agent in our example) who in turn provide the payment applications to their customers; and (iv) *program managers* who take responsibility of putting programs together — combining applications to service providers — and provide them to corporate customers.

In order to support developers, OPE provides a *development environment* with the necessary APIs for application development and service provider integration. The OPE itself does not hold funds (which legally, can only be held by a regulated institution). Therefore, applications developed are submitted to the OPE, and can be adopted by programme managers who rely on an automated *compliance check* to pair the adopted application with an integrated service provider to enable its execution on the OPE platform. We note that ultimately, service providers carry the financial and regulatory liability for the services offered, and therefore having a reliable automated compliance process goes a long way in enabling service providers to operate with more peace of mind.

The compliance subsystem at the core of OPE has multiple roles: (i) it is used to support programme managers when matchmaking an application and a service provider; (ii) it ensures that a programme does not violate national legislation and regulations based on the location where it is planned to be deployed; and (iii) provides runtime monitoring on the running programme to continually check whether the monitored constraints are violated.

Since the OPE architecture envisages that the payment application is executed outside the platform (typically on the end user's device or a web server), only accessing the OPE platform through API calls, it is possible that the application submitted for validation and matched with an appropriate service provider is compromised or tampered with. Furthermore, providing compliance algorithms which support different programming languages and technologies, which developers may adopt, is not scalable in the long run.

In this context, the approach presented earlier in the paper becomes useful: developers are expected to submit a sufficiently detailed model of the application behaviour, enabling matching with the service providers and preliminary checking of compliance to applicable legislation. The *Payment Application Modelling Language* (PAML) is a domain-specific language developed specifically to enable the description of a model of a payments application — its components, their attributes, and how the components can interact together.

Example 1 (Model). As a running example, consider a simple model of an application allowing customers to have managed cards, with a total maximum transactional value not exceeding £2,000 per month, with the possibility of depositing and redeeming[2] of funds.

This model is then subjected to the first round of checking, i.e., static analysis, of two types of constraints: that it adheres to the applicable legislation and that it is acceptable to the service provider who will run the application.

Example 2 (Static analysis). In the example model, according to legislation, the customer should always have the possibility of redeeming the money remaining in his or her account after closure. Using the model, we can statically check that this possibility is in fact supported. At this point, we note that regulations also state that money redemption should occur *at par value* and *without delay*. However, it is not possible to statically verify that these hold as the model does not contain this level of detail.

Once the application goes through the static analysis phase and is deployed, we runtime verify that the implementation is indeed a refinement of the model, and that it adheres to the regulations which could not be checked statically.

Example 3 (Runtime verification). Ensuring that the model is a true representation of the implementation in this example entails checking that the application does not exceed the £2,000 monthly limit on the user's transactions.

From the legal side, as noted earlier, we have to ensure that redemption takes place at par value, i.e., the customer receives the right amount, and without delay. These checks are both delegated to be carried out through runtime monitoring.

These are the types of checks we have mostly encountered in the context of OPE. We are currently looking into ways of enriching static analysis to be able to check parts of properties which involve summing and counting values. While the analysis techniques presented in the running example sound simple, we believe that their extension can be effective in lowering the overheads in dynamic verification, while still ensuring safe matching of applications with service providers.

6   Conclusions

The synergy afforded by the combination of static and dynamic analysis has been well studied under the assumption that the implementation is available during the static phase. As motivated by the OPE case study, this is not always the case, particularly when the code is run by an untrusted third party. Even when the analysis of the implementation is feasible, it might not be desirable to support the analysis of a plethora of different technologies.

By statically checking a model of the implementation rather than the implementation itself, we bypass the issues of untrusted and technology-varied code,

---

[2] Redeeming funds refers to the withdrawal of electronic money by the customer following the closure of his or her account.

requiring, however, the runtime checking of the adherence of the implementation to the model. Using the interplay of static and dynamic analysis once more to our advantage, we have shown how the checking of the model can also be simplified by exploiting the residual checks which will anyway be checked at runtime.

To illustrate the proposed approach, we have provided an instantiation based on control-flow models and properties, as well as how the theory is being used in practise in the context of the OPE.

The presented work leaves a number of venues for future exploration, not least how to calculate an efficiently monitorable residual both for checking the compliance to the model and the checks which could not be statically verified on the model. We also plan to implement the complete framework as part of the OPE project, possibly integrating existing tools in the process.

References

1. Ahrendt, W., Chimento, J.M., Pace, G.J., Schneider, G.: A specification language for static and runtime verification of data and control properties. In: Bjørner, N., de Boer, F. (eds.) FM 2015. LNCS, vol. 9109, pp. 108–125. Springer, Heidelberg (2015). doi:10.1007/978-3-319-19249-9_8
2. Ahrendt, W., Pace, G.J., Schneider, G.: A unified approach for static and runtime verification: framework and applications. In: Margaria, T., Steffen, B. (eds.) ISoLA 2012, Part I. LNCS, vol. 7609, pp. 312–326. Springer, Heidelberg (2012)
3. Azzopardi, S., Colombo, C., Pace, G.J., Vella, B.: Open payments ecosystem. In: Computer Science Annual Workshop 2015 (CSAW 2015). University of Malta, November 2015
4. Bodden, E., Lam, P., Hendren, L.: Clara: a framework for partially evaluating finite-state runtime monitors ahead of time. In: Barringer, H., et al. (eds.) RV 2010. LNCS, vol. 6418, pp. 183–197. Springer, Heidelberg (2010)
5. Chimento, J.M., Ahrendt, W., Pace, G.J., Schneider, G.: StarVOOrS: a tool for combined static and runtime verification of Java. In: Bartocci, E., Majumdar, R. (eds.) RV 2015. LNCS, vol. 9333, pp. 297–305. Springer, Heidelberg (2015)
6. Colombo, C., Pace, G.J., Schneider, G.: Dynamic event-based runtime monitoring of real-time and contextual properties. In: Cofer, D., Fantechi, A. (eds.) FMICS 2008. LNCS, vol. 5596, pp. 135–149. Springer, Heidelberg (2009)
7. Denis, F., Lemay, A., Terlutte, A.: Residual finite state automata. Fundam. Inform. 51(4), 339–368 (2002)
8. Dwyer, M.B., Purandare, R.: Residual dynamic typestate analysis exploiting static analysis: results to reformulate and reduce the cost of dynamic analysis. In: Proceedings of the Twenty-Second IEEE/ACM International Conference on Automated Software Engineering, ASE 2007, pp. 124–133, New York, NY, USA. ACM (2007)
9. Graf, S., Steffen, B.: Compositional minimization of finite state systems. In: Clarke, E.M., Kurshan, R.P. (eds.) CAV 1990. LNCS, vol. 531, pp. 186–196. Springer, Heidelberg (1991)
10. Krimm, J.-P., Mounier, L.: Compositional state space generation from LOTOS programs. In: Brinksma, E. (ed.) TACAS 1997. LNCS, vol. 1217, pp. 239–258. Springer, Heidelberg (1997)

11. Lal, A., Kidd, N., Reps, T., Touili, T.: Abstract error projection. In: Riis Nielson, H., Filé, G. (eds.) SAS 2007. LNCS, vol. 4634, pp. 200–217. Springer, Heidelberg (2007)
12. Wonisch, D., Schremmer, A., Wehrheim, H.: Zero overhead runtime monitoring. In: Hierons, R.M., Merayo, M.G., Bravetti, M. (eds.) SEFM 2013. LNCS, vol. 8137, pp. 244–258. Springer, Heidelberg (2013)

Information Flow Analysis for Go

Eric Bodden[1,2], Ka I. Pun[3], Martin Steffen[3], Volker Stolz[3,4(✉)],
and Anna-Katharina Wickert[1]

[1] Technical University of Darmstadt, Darmstadt, Germany
[2] University of Paderborn, Paderborn, Germany
[3] University of Oslo, Oslo, Norway
stolz@ifi.uio.no
[4] Bergen University College, Bergen, Norway

Abstract. We present the current state of the art of information flow
analyses for Go applications. Based on our findings, we discuss future
directions of where static analysis information can be used at runtime
to for example achieve higher precision, or optimise runtime checks. We
focus specifically on outstanding language features such as closures and
message-based communication via channels.

1 Introduction

The Go language [7,8,25] is a relative newcomer to the programming language
stage. Nonetheless, it has been quickly taken up for application development
by big players, most notably, Docker. There, it is used as a language for their
popular software container framework. Backed by Google, it is also speculated
to be the future language for Android development, and recently the mobile
development kit was published.

Like any other software, Go programs are frequently exposed to "hostile"
environments, whether it is on a web-facing server, or soon on a mobile phone.
Both are constant targets for attacks by hackers and malicious applications,
which try to break into the system through malicious input or specially crafted
interactions. To prevent the violations of program executions induced by malicious data, one effective way is to *statically* analyse the flows of such data within
programs.

We present here our information flow analysis of Go programs, where we
focus on the more interesting features of the Go language, such as channel-based
communication and deferred execution. This analysis is the foundation for a
monitoring framework to thwart such attacks, by identifying the flow of potential
malicious (tainted) data from a set of pre-defined sources to a set of sinks that
this data must not reach unprocessed. Based on our findings on the precision

The work was partially supported by the Norwegian-German bilateral PPP project
GoRETech (GoRuntime Enforcement Techniques), the EU COST Action IC1402
"ARVI—Runtime Verification Beyond Monitoring" and the EU project FP7-610582
ENVISAGE: Engineering Virtualized Services.

T. Margaria and B. Steffen (Eds.): ISoLA 2016, Part I, LNCS 9952, pp. 431–445, 2016.
DOI: 10.1007/978-3-319-47166-2_30

of our analysis, we give recommendations how monitoring can complement the inevitable gaps in a static analysis.

Related Work. Static analysis for information flows has been widely studied: Denning and Denning [5,6] present a mechanism in terms of a lattice model to guarantee secure information flows for sequential statements. Such a construct is the foundation of many static analysis frameworks, e.g., the Monotone Framework [18], which is also the starting point for our approach. Andrews and Reitman [1] propose an axiomatic approach to certifying flows in both sequential and parallel programs. Type systems are also a common approach to ensure noninterference for well-typed programs, e.g., Volpano et al. [27] formulate Denning's work in the form of a type system for a core imperative language; Pottier and Simone [21] propose a type-based analysis for a call-by-value λ-calculus.

Apart from guaranteeing program security by tracking the flow of sensitive data, our approach identifies potential tainted data flows within programs at compile time, which helps in detecting bugs as well as avoiding attacks by malicious applications. A number of work has been done to analyse flow information of tainted data using similar idea: Arzt et al. [2] propose a static taint analysis for Android applications. Livshits and Lam propose a variant of SSA to discover bugs in C programs [15], and use a context-sensitive pointer alias analysis to detect security violations in Java applications [14]. Pistoia et al. [20] present a control- and data-flow framework to find tainted variables in Java bytecode. Information flow analyses have also been applied for languages like PHP [13] and JFlow [17], which is an extension to the Java language. While Go shares some of the general features with those imperative languages, we also take a look at some of its novel constructs, which are mostly related to concurrency.

Paper Overview. Section 2 provides the background of the Go language and information flow analysis; Sect. 3 presents the abstract syntax of the language and the analysis for Go programs; Sect. 4 illustrates our implementations with examples, Sect. 5 discusses the potential for monitoring for Go programs, and finally Sect. 6 concludes the paper.

2   Preliminaries

2.1   The Go Language

Go, a language backed by Google, has gained a certain amount of traction after its inception. Its advertised design principles as being simple and concise together with its surface syntax make the language identifiable in the tradition of C. At its core, Go is a lexically scoped, concurrent, imperative language with higher-order functions, supporting object-oriented design (while notable not supporting classes nor inheritance). Concerning concurrency, Go's primary feature is *asynchronous* function calls (resp. asynchronous method calls), called *goroutines* (basically a lightweight form of threads with low overhead and lacking known thread synchronisation mechanisms such as wait and signal). The second core concurrency construct is (typed) *channel* communication, in the tradition of languages like CSP [9,10] or Occam. Since (references to) channels can be sent over channels, Go allows "mobile channel" flexibility for communication as known from the π-calculus [16].

Thus, despite the "simple" surface syntax in the tradition of C, Go combines features which are challenging from a program analysis perspective: Reference-data, imperative features, arrays, and slices require point-to analyses. Control-flow analyses are needed to obtain data-flow analyses of acceptable precision in the presence of higher-order functions. The Go compiler (at least in a developer branch) supports a static-single assignment intermediate format to facilitate flow analyses. Shared variable concurrency is featured by Go but frowned upon. The more dignified and recommended way of concurrent programming via message passing, using either synchronous or buffered channels of finite capacity. The static analysis of such channel communication has similarities to pointer analysis, as channels are a referenced shared data where channel pointers themselves can be communicated via channels (or stored and handed over to procedures as other references, as well). The analysis of data flow in the context of channel communication is challenging in itself, but at least avoids unprotected concurrent access to shared mutable data and shields the programmer from the subtleties of Go's weak memory model. In this work, we do *not* consider shared variable concurrency.

2.2 Information Flow Analysis

We discuss here in particular the challenges of information flow analysis when applied to Go. Information flow analysis [1,5] attempts to determine whether a given program can leak sensitive information, either directly or through indirect channels, for instance when secret values influence timing behaviour or power consumption, so-called indirect information flows. Dynamic information flow analysis attempts to detect such leaks by monitoring an application's execution. Such dynamic analyses are generally to detect direct information flows only, i.e., such flows that occur through direct memory copies. This is due to the fact that indirect flows occur through control-flow dependencies on secret values, and in particular because a program can leak information as it does *not* execute a certain behaviour at runtime. Since behaviour that does not execute cannot be monitored, this precludes the detection of certain indirect flows.

Static code analysis, however, can analyse all of a program's possible executions, detecting control-flow dependencies and also such "missing behaviour". It is for that reason that static analysis can detect not only direct but also indirect information flows. Recent research has shown that a static pre-analysis can assist a subsequent dynamic analysis by finding control-flow dependencies that can leak secret information and defining a special instrumentation scheme at runtime that signals when the respective branches are taken. Depending on some properties of the monitored programming language, and depending on the scope of the static pre-analysis this can allow the dynamic analysis to even monitor all possible information leaks at runtime. Indirect information flows, however, have the tendency to cause so-called "overtainting", where an analysis ends up tracking many—typically too many—information flows, the majority of which is to the security analyst often irrelevant. The underlying problem is a deeply semantic one: an indirect information flow signals not that a program leaks data but it signals that a program leaks *information about* data. But how much information will allow for a practical attack? This question is extremely hard to decide in terms of a program's structure. Recent work has thus focused on making the analysis of indirect information flows more precise, for instance by also regarding so-called *declassification*, i.e., the intentional disclosure of information about secret data. Since such declassification is intentional, a program analysis should avoid signalling it as leak of secret information. Declassification is generally quite essential. Without declassification, for instance, a password dialog may not even signal to the user whether or not the password was entered correctly, as this would signal some information about the secret password, even though this information is essential to reveal.

When conducting information-flow analysis for programs with pointers, it is essential to pair it with a pointer analysis, as otherwise the analysis would fail to resolve aliasing relationships. Consider the code sequence `a.f = secret();` `print(b.f);`. In this code, to determine whether the program may `print` the `secret`, an analysis must know whether `a` and `b` alias, i.e., point to the same object. Pointer analysis is generally expensive to compute, and to yield appropriate precision must share certain design properties with the alias analysis it seeks to support. Generally, a high-precision analysis should be context sensitive and flow sensitive, for instance. If the accompanying alias analysis does not share the same level of context and flow sensitivity, then this can cause imprecision to creep into the information-flow analysis, ultimately resulting in false warnings that threaten to distract the security analyst from the important true warnings.

3   Analysis

In this section, we present our information flow analysis for Go programs, and illustrate its use with some examples in the next section. The analysis is based on a suitable subset of the full language which is easy to formalise yet covers the most important features.

Information flow describes a dynamic property: in our setting, it is any value that originates from a particular API call (as denoted by a list of *sources*), and is used within the execution of the program. If the execution reaches a call to any of our denoted *sinks*, and the value is passed as a parameter, we would like to report an error or a warning. Of course, such tracking of data flow can happen at runtime, but naturally we are interested in whether we can give certain guarantees for a program *before* it is run. We thus need to reformulate this problem in the terms of a static analysis that can be defined in terms of the program *source code*.

To simplify the discussion, we assume in the paper a simplified representation of (Go) source code, assuming for example that each statement contains at most a single function call, with only variables or constants as arguments. Also, we stipulate that all variables must be initialised when declared.

In the following, we will handle expressions representatively build up by using primitive types, structs, channels and function types. We elide the other useful, built-in datatypes in Go, such as slices (arrays) and key/value maps, and appeal to the reader's intuition that common approaches to over-approximation of reference types as in the case of structs and channels can be applied.

The abstract syntax is given by Table 1. We shall concern ourselves with statements that are assignments to locally declared variables or struct members, conditionals, finalizers (defer), or initiators of concurrent execution (go). In addition, we have the channel operations read and write, return from function, and of course sequential composition of statements.

Table 1. Abstract syntax

$$s ::= x := e \mid x.f := e \mid \text{if } v \text{ then } s \text{ else } s \mid \text{defer}((\lambda x.s)\ v) \qquad \text{statements}$$
$$\quad \mid\ \text{go } s \mid x \leftarrow y \mid x \rightarrow y \mid \text{return } v \mid s; s$$
$$e ::= v \mid v\ v \mid \text{makeChan} \qquad\qquad\qquad\qquad\qquad \text{expressions}$$
$$v ::= x \mid x.f \mid ()\ \mid \text{true} \mid \text{false} \mid \lambda x.s \qquad\qquad\quad \text{values}$$

Expressions may be variables or values of the aforementioned supported types, functions calls (written as application here), or channel initialisation. Go's multiple return values from function calls would require a minor extension of the syntax which would not add much for our discussion, as would slice- and map manipulation. Function definitions straightforwardly have typed formal parameters, and bodies composed of statements.

We can then restate the problem as follows: we would like to report a warning, if the return value of a function call labelled as source is assigned to a variable, and the value *may* be propagated through assignments and function calls to a variable which is used as an actual parameter in a function call to a sink.

Furthermore, our analysis must take *channels* into account in a sound way: if a sensitive (tainted) value is written into a channel, as an over approximation, we assume that a read from that channel may return the tainted value. As static analysis of channel-based communication has been studied extensively for example in [11], we do not go into the details here and leave specialising this part of our analysis towards a more precise solution using those techniques for future (implementation) work.

3.1 Lattice

Our intended analysis can easily be expressed with the well-known concept of Monotone Framework [18]. For our taint analysis, we define a simple lattice where a value in a variable (attribute) is initially marked as "undefined" ($\bot$), and based on custom black-/whitelist of API calls, marked as either "tainted" (1), "untainted" (0), or "both" ($\top$). We define the least upper bound ($\cup$) of two taint values in a straight-forward manner:

∪	⊥	1	0	⊤
⊥	⊥	1	0	⊤
1	1	1	⊤	⊤
0	0	⊤	0	⊤
⊤	⊤	⊤	⊤	⊤

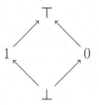

3.2 Aliasing and Channels

The Go language has several reference types, most prominently: structs, slices (arrays), and maps. Again, we do not model the required tracking of aliasing explicitly, but assume availability through a sound, context-insensitive over-approximation. Thus we make use of the following function[1], which, given a variable at a particular statement, over-approximates the set of allocation sites of objects and the variable they have been assigned to:

$$\textsc{pta} : \textsc{Var} \times \textsc{Lab} \to \mathcal{P}(\textsc{Loc}).$$

We use this function to additionally maintain the function

$$aliases : \textsc{Lab} \times \textsc{Var} \to \mathcal{P}(\textsc{Lab} \times \textsc{Var}),$$

which we require to identify potential aliases created through field-use in `structs`.

Another example of a reference type are of course Go's (typed) channels. Our rules for assignments, which are defined later in the section, track correctly the taint information associated with a channel when aliasing (e.g., `ch := makeChan; ch':= ch`) because of the points-to analysis described above. Additional processing that does not follow the control flow is now required when writing a tainted value into the alias `ch'`. A very coarse and obvious solution to achieve the required dataflow is to add dependencies between a write to a channel to all reads from it. A related analysis built on top of that allows a sound over-approximation of the *peers* of a channel referenced by a variable in a particular location, that is, all uses of the same channel reference in read or write statements.

3.3 Taint Analysis via the Control-Flow Graph

For the *intraprocedural* part of our analysis, we can set up the Monotone Framework with the help of the control-flow graph (CFG). As ultimately our analysis should warn on particular statements (function calls to sinks with tainted actual parameters), we decide on a *single-instruction graph*, i.e., each node in the control-flow graph represents a single, normalised (as per our grammar)

---

[1] https://godoc.org/golang.org/x/tools/go/pointer.

instruction. Conditionals result in branches in the control-flow graph, and loops lead to (additional) back-edges to nodes earlier in the graph. We do not describe how to obtain the graph, but rather refer to [18] and recapitulate the essential ingredients. We assume that the function NODES returns a set of labeled statements $[s]^l$ of a program. Furthermore, the flow-function

$$\text{FLOW} : \text{LAB} \to \mathcal{P}(\text{LAB} \times \text{LAB})$$

returns the edges in the CFG for a uniquely labeled statement $[s]^l$, and its extensions FLOW*, yielding the CFG for the entire program. Calls to go-routines can be handled through an additional control flow-edge from the caller to the body, as control does not return, and we only permit channel-based communication. Full Go also supports—but discourages—locks and shared variables.

To effectively be able to emit a warning, our analysis framework must yield the following information: is any of the actual parameters in a function call to a sink marked as possibly tainted on the entry to the statement? Information by our taint analysis is thus given for each node (statement) in the CFG by the partial TA function of type: LAB $\to$ (VAR $\to \mathcal{L}$), which yields the taint information associated with variables in scope at the particular node:

$$\text{TA}(l) = \Phi(S, N^l)$$
$$\text{where } S = \bigcup \{\text{TA}(l') \mid (l', l) \in \text{FLOW}^*(P)\} \text{ and } N^l \in \text{NODES}(P).$$

Note that we collect all the taint information flowing to the statement labelled with l in the set S. The function $\Phi(S, N^l)$ defined in Table 2 derives the equations for the standard programming constructs. In essence, the analysis resembles the well-known analyses of Def-Use chains or Reaching Definitions, extended by the required notions of transitivity and aliasing. A standard worklist algorithm can be used to generate the smallest solution to our dataflow problem, which we can then query for all actual parameters, at each statement that is marked as a sink.

One way to propagate taint information in our core language is to assign an expression to either a variable $x := e$ or to a struct member $x.f := e$. We use in Table 2 a function ϕ to derive the taint information of the expression on the right-hand side of an assignment. The expressions, including creating new channels makeChan, unit, boolean values and function definitions, do not taint any variable, and therefore the variable x (or struct member $x.f$) on the left-hand side is marked as *untainted* $(x \mapsto 0)$. In the case where the expression is a variable y, the function ϕ updates the analysis result of x with the one of y at the current state. For assigning a struct member $y.f$, we have to collect the taint information from all the aliases of the reference y with the help of the *aliases* function described above. For function calls $v_1 v_2$, in case the called function v_1 is a *source*, the assigned variable x is marked as *tainted* $(x \mapsto 1)$. Otherwise, we derive the taint information of the called function with *interprocedural analysis*.

Interprocedural Analysis. The function $\Phi_{exit}^{v_1}$ is integrated with the worklist algorithm as developed by Padhye and Khedker [19], which we have implemented to achieve a flow- and context-sensitive analysis. The idea of the authors is to

Table 2. Taint analysis

$$\Phi(S, [x := e]^l) = \phi(S, x, e, l)$$
$$\Phi(S, [x.f := e]^l) = \phi(S, x.f, e, l)$$
$$\Phi(S, [\mathbf{defer}((\lambda x.s)v)]^l) = id(S)$$
$$\Phi(S, [\mathbf{go}\ s]^l) = id(S)$$
$$\Phi(S, [x \rightarrow ch]^l) = S[ch \mapsto S(x)]$$
$$\Phi(S, [x \leftarrow ch]^l) = S[x \mapsto \bigcup\{\mathsf{TA}(l')_{\downarrow ch'} | \ [x' \rightarrow ch']^{l'} \ \text{f.a.}\ (l' : ch') \in aliases(l : ch)\}]$$
$$\Phi(S, [\mathbf{return}\ v]^l) = id(S)$$

$$\phi(S, x, y, l) = S[x \mapsto S(y)]$$
$$\phi(S, x, y.f, l) = S[x \mapsto \bigcup\{\mathsf{TA}(l')_{\downarrow y'} | \ [y' := e]^{l'} \vee [y' \leftarrow ch]^{l'}$$
$$\text{f.a.}\ (l' : y') \in aliases(l : y)\}]$$
$$\phi(S, x.f, y, l) = S[x.f \mapsto S(y)]$$
$$\phi(S, x.f, y.f', l) = S[x.f \mapsto \bigcup\{\mathsf{TA}(l')_{\downarrow y'} | \ [y' := e]^{l'} \vee [y' \leftarrow ch]^{l'}$$
$$\text{f.a.}\ (l' : y') \in aliases(l : y)\}]$$
$$\phi(S, x, (), l) = S[x \mapsto 0]$$
$$\phi(S, x, \mathbf{true}, l) = S[x \mapsto 0]$$
$$\phi(S, x, \mathbf{false}, l) = S[x \mapsto 0]$$
$$\phi(S, x, \lambda x.s, l) = S[x \mapsto 0]$$
$$\phi(S, x, v_1 v_2, l) = \begin{cases} S[x \mapsto 1] & \text{if } v_1 \text{ is a } source \\ S[x \mapsto \Phi_{exit}^{v_1}] & \text{otherwise} \end{cases}$$
$$\phi(S, x, \mathbf{makeChan}, l) = S[x \mapsto 0]$$

differ between calls and to save the data flow values for every context. Therefore, the algorithm can avoid that a function with identical input parameters is analysed multiple times. This is built upon the assumption that equivalent input parameters of a function will yield the same data flow values at the exit node of the function. Their approach increases precision over the trivial approach, where every exit-value from a return-statement flows back to *all* call sites, not just the actual caller. The algorithm uses an additional calling context $X := (S, actual\ param)$, which guarantees that identical contexts produce identical results. We will later describe the actual working on an example.

Another way to pass on taint data is to through channel communications. Sending values or variables to a channel $x \rightarrow ch$ will propagate the taint information of x to ch. To read from a channel $x \leftarrow ch$, we have to gather the knowledge of all the possible aliases of the channel to which tainted data may be sent. The statements, including finalizers (**defer**) and initiators of concurrent execution (**go**), do not affect the taint information.

Soundness. Here we elide formal claims and proofs with regard to the soundness of the analysis. The small-step operational semantics by Steffen [23] could serve as a starting point for such a formalisation, and the corresponding properties.

4   Implementation

Our information flow analysis relies partly on existing technologies and libraries: although our above analysis is formulated in terms of the single-instruction control-flow graph, our prototype implementation uses existing libraries from the Go compiler tool-chain and tools that go beyond this simplistic view. With the help of those libraries, we obtain the static single assignment-form (SSA)[2] [4], interprocedural call-graph[3], and the necessary points-to information. We shortly describe the APIs available to us.

The SSA library consists primarily of four interfaces. Firstly, the `Member` interface holds the member of a Go package being functions, types, global variables and constants. Secondly, the `Node` interface describes a node from the SSA graph. Valid values for the `Node` interface are types fitting either to the `Value` or `Instruction` interface. An expression which leads to a value is of type `Value`. A statement using a value and computes are part of the `Instruction` interface.

Through the fact that we consider the distinction between calling contexts, we need to differ whether a node is a call or not. For this aim, we use the `CallInstruction` interface allowing us to distinguish between a function call and Go specific calls being a goroutine and a defer statement. To define the desired behaviour, we need two additional inputs for our analysis: a blacklist of API calls that produce tainted values, and a whitelist of calls that either produce untainted values, or turn tainted ones into untainted.

A common property that is investigated with a taint analysis is whether unsanitized user input can e.g. reach SQL queries, where it could lead to SQL injection attacks. In that case, any user input, that is, console input, or e.g. data submitted through an HTML form, is marked as tainted. Correspondingly, we add those calls to our blacklist and call them *sources*. Our analysis shall report a warning if a tainted value reaches a *sink*. Sinks are again specified separately, just like sources.

4.1   Example

In this section, we explain our current taint analysis approach with the program in Fig. 1, which primarily reads a file and prints the file content to the standard output. The program consists of a main function and two additional functions h and g. The function h reads the first eight bytes of a file and returns the bytes as a string c and the status r. The function g copies the input string to another variable b and returns the variable. The main function calls the function g with a constant string value a and once with eight bytes from a file s. The last input parameter for g is obtained with the help of function h. `os.File.Read` is a *source*, and `fmt.Print` a *sink*.

To get the results, we use the functions and the lattice described in Sect. 3. The entry point of our analysis is the main function within a Go program, where

---

[2] https://godoc.org/golang.org/x/tools/go/ssa.

[3] https://godoc.org/golang.org/x/tools/go/callgraph.

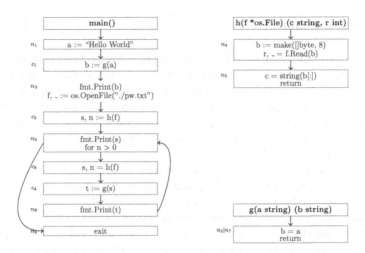

Fig. 1. A simplified control flow graph with different contexts

nothing is initialised. Thus the lattice at this point is empty and the worklist contains n_1, c_1, n_3, c_2, n_6, c_3, c_4, n_{10} and n_{11}. At the beginning a context X_0 is created. The entry value is the empty lattice and the exit lattice is currently not set because the execution is not yet finished.

The first element n_1 is removed from the worklist and then processed. It receives **untainted** for the variable a from the transfer function defined in Table 2. Through the next removal c_1 is obtained, being the first call in the example. A new context X_1 having an untainted value as input is created and a new transition from X_0 to X_1 is added. After the context is created, all nodes of the function are added to the worklist. In the following step n_2 is removed to be processed, and the exit lattice of X_1 is set to a^0, b^0 because n_2 contains a return statement.

As a subsequent step, the algorithm selects node n_3 for processing and creates a lattice with the **tainted** variable f. Afterwards c_2 is collected and produces a new value context X_2. The transfer function of the call passes a tainted parameter. Therefore, the entry lattice of the new context contains the tainted parameter. In the context X_2, n_4 is processed first. The transfer function returns for the variables b and r the **tainted** value and updates the lattice for the node. The next node n_5 is then selected, and the transfer function computes that the variable c is also **tainted**. The exit lattice for X_2 is updated such that b, r and c are **tainted**.

Back in context X_0, the algorithm picks node n_6 for processing and detects that a **tainted** value reaches a sink. Afterwards, c_3 with a **tainted** value as a parameter is handled as context X_3. The algorithm checks whether a call to function h with a **tainted** parameter already exists, finds X_2 and adds the transition from $\langle X_3, c_3 \rangle$ to X_2. For the succeeding call c_4 the value context currently does not exist, so a new context X_4 is created and the nodes of g are added to the worklist. In the ensuing step, the algorithm processes n_7, which leads to variable b becoming `tainted`. The next node from the worklist is n_8, which also reports a warning. Since all contexts with a fitting entry parameter already exist, the remaining nodes do not lead to the creation of new contexts, but only the transitions are added.

4.2   Concurrency in Go

A language specific characteristics of Go is that it supports concurrent programming by design [8]. The idea is that only one goroutine is allowed to access a value. Hence, Go encourages use of channels for message passing instead of concurrent access to shared variables. The channels are first-class values in Go.

As channels are an essential part of concurrent Go programs, our analysis must be able to handle channels correctly. The challenge is that channels are used for concurrency and therefore multiple different execution paths are possible. Our current idea is to add additional information in case of writing values to a channel. Every goroutine which uses the channel should get an entry node with the identity function. This allows the analysis to build the least upper bound of all incoming edges.

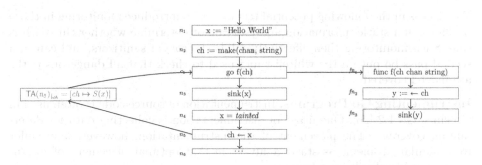

Fig. 2. An example which explains the challenges of channels for our analysis.

The program in Fig. 2 is a simple example which uses channels. First a variable x and a channel ch are created. The channel is used in a goroutine which calls function f. The function f reads a value from the channel. The value reaches a sink at node fn_3. The red node indicates the sub-equation for the flow-function that we use to propagate the taint-state of the channels back to (after) its declaration site, by dropping all other information from the exit of the `readChan` through this exit-branch.

While in this example, due to the unbuffered nature of synchronised channels, the value read from ch will always be tainted, in a larger program, non-deterministic execution orders may yield tainted or untainted results from read-statements, which the static analysis over-approximates to $\top$. In other words, a sink in a goroutine that consumes data from a channel, may only be reached by a tainted value in some cases. This illustrates the need for a runtime component, or sanitizers that takes care of those false positives.

In addition to the problem described above, the example illustrates a challenge for a precise solution of our analysis. We assume that x is untainted when it reaches the sink at node n_3 and is tainted at node n_4. Through the fact that the channel ch gets x as a value, we should assume that *every* read to ch could possibly produce a tainted value. As a conclusion the node fn_3 is reached by a tainted value.

Consequently, our analysis must know which goroutines uses ch. This can be achieved by a backward analysis. The challenge is to update only the channel with the taint information and not the tainted value x. Such an imprecision would yield to a report at node n_3, which is obviously a false positive.

A correct statically implementation of the analysis should therefore only report a potential flow at node fn_3. The precision of the analysis could be increased through a dynamic observation of the potential dangerous paths of concurrent execution. Then fn_3 should only be reported if fn_3 is executed after node n_5. This would make the analysis more precise, but will in general not be possible to deduce statically.

5   Potential for Monitoring

We discuss in the following potential techniques to introduce monitoring in those paths when a static information analysis cannot determine whether this path is safe. Such monitoring then effectively fulfils the role of sanitizers, and can in a second pass be put on the whitelist and used to check that all dangerous paths are indeed covered.

Instrumenting Go Programs. Instrumentation of source code is often used in Go since Go 1.2 [26]. One usage of instrumentation is collecting data for determining coverage. The placement of the instrumentation, however, may suffer from similar problems as static analysis, in that optimal placement of instrumentation is difficult to determine.

Such test coverage instrumentation tools can give us hints for our instrumentation to monitor flow as to whether paths we are interested in are executed or not. A further step is to instrument the source code with the required functionality for our taint analysis. Being interested in preventing tainted data from reaching a sink, an obvious instrumentation is to stop the execution of the program when the additional data recorded by the instrumentation reports that we are about to reach a sink.

A traditional approach to instrumentation, especially for object-oriented languages, is aspect-oriented programming. This declarative technique has been used with success e.g. for Java [24], but relies on extensive infrastructure. Although developers are experimenting with developing similar frameworks for Go, the prototypes are far from the necessary flexibility and convenient syntax, as offered for example by AspectJ [12].

Also object-oriented design techniques can be helpful in instrumenting either source code or code on the level of shared libraries: for example, as the sources and sinks in a taint analysis will mainly be API calls, it may be easy to generate wrappers for them, and recompile an application using those proxies.

What to Monitor. Another question is of course which other properties could be interesting to monitor in Go programs. Here, we have focused on a taint analysis that is useful for services processing sensitive data.

Currently we think that two different things could be interesting to monitor: First, it can be used to add sanitizers and secondly to monitor and influence the concurrent behaviour of a program run.

The first idea is to dynamically add *sanitizers*. A typical taint analysis can only add a taint status and does not remove it. The latter is important to avoid too many false positives because the taint status spreads during the program execution. An example which produces false positives is where the program logic should enforce sanitisation. This could be achieved e.g. by a password which is entered and then send via a hash function to a server. Classically, the taint analysis will report the flow described above because the taint status of the password is propagated to the send function [22].

The second idea is to actively influence scheduling to avoid tainted paths. If we assume the example from Fig. 2, the potential leak will only be reported if n_5 is reached before fn_3 is executed. In a more complicated setting, where there are more consumers to a channel, and some of them will not pass on data to any sink, we could develop a scheduler which routes tainted data along safe paths only. Of course this requires a more advanced analysis of the communication behaviour to be able to enable processes which have the capacity to consume a tainted item without becoming blocked. This problem is closely related to deadlock avoidance in schedulers [3].

6   Conclusion

In this paper we presented our attempt at implementing an information flow analysis for the Go language. The combination of object-based language constructs such as structs and arrays, and message-passing through typed channels, requires a combination of various techniques.

In one dimension, we have static analysis components that combine intra- and context-sensitive interprocedural techniques with reference-based analyses to capture aliasing effects. In the other dimension, we need dynamic checks that compensate for the over-approximation of the taint-analysis in the case where either tainted or untainted flows come from a source to a sink can occur.

Currently, our analysis only implements the static analysis part, and we are actively investigating the alternatives for monitoring the running application, for example through instrumentation. *The code for the analysis and examples area available from the project website.*[4]

Future Work. A very interesting approach that does not require instrumentation would be to integrate tighter with the Go runtime system: the Go runtime

---

[4] See http://www.mn.uio.no/ifi/english/research/projects/goretech/.

already contains a sophisticated, tuned framework for tracking data races in concurrent programs. Although due to its invasiveness it incurs a noticeably performance penalty, it could reasonably be extended to taint-tracking. The runtime would only need to be informed of sources and sinks. That could be achieved by introducing annotations, as an alternative to a global (runtime-wide) list.

Since our current prototype analysis is a combination of the worklist-based analysis for intra- and interprocedural data flow, yet we rely on existing Go analyses for aliasing, the program may be effectively traversed multiple times, for each analysis separately. If the different analyses could be integrated into a single framework, we may benefit from some synergy.

Also, we do not cover all language features yet. It is unclear how higher-order functions (and their application) could be analysed successfully statically, so runtime monitoring may prove as an effective solution there.

An alternative approach to providing warnings, or termination, when reaching a sink with tainted data, could be to fail as early as possible, that is, as soon as it becomes clear that a policy will be inevitable in the future. Here, static analysis would be the main contributor to identify the best places to insert such checks, once more illustrating the need for a combined approach, with static and dynamic aspects playing together to achieve a common goal.

References

1. Andrews, G.R., Reitman, R.P.: An axiomatic approach to information flow in programs. ACM Trans. Program. Lang. Syst. **2**(1), 56–76 (1980)
2. Arzt, S., et al.: FlowDroid: precise context, flow, field, object-sensitive and lifecycle-aware taint analysis for Androidapps. In: ACM SIGPLAN Conference on Programming Language Design and Implementation (2014)
3. Coffman Jr., E.G., Elphick, M., Shoshani, A.: System deadlocks. Comput. Surv. **3**(2), 67–78 (1971)
4. Cytron, R., et al.: Efficiently computing static single assignment form and the control dependence graph. ACM Trans. Program. Lang. Syst. **13**(4), 451–490 (1991)
5. Denning, D.E.: A lattice model of secure information flow. Commun. ACM **19**(5), 236–243 (1976)
6. Denning, D.E., Denning, P.J.: Certification of programs for secure information flow. Commun. ACM **20**(7), 504–513 (1977)
7. Donovan, A.A.A., Kernighan, B.W.: The Go Programming Language (2015)
8. Effective Go - The Go Programming Language. https://golang.org/doc/effective_go.html#concurrency. Accessed 29 Apr 2016
9. Hoare, C.A.R.: Communicating Sequential Processes. Prentice-Hall, Upper Saddle River (1985)
10. Hoare, C.A.R.: Communicating sequential processes. Commun. ACM **21**(8), 666–677 (1978)
11. Kobayashi, N.: Type-based information flow analysis for the π-calculus. Acta Informatica **42**(4), 291–347 (2005)
12. Laddad, R.: AspectJ in Action: Practical Aspect-Oriented Programming. Manning Publications Co., Greenwich (2003)

13. Livshits, B., Chong, S.: Towards fully automatic placement of security sanitizers and declassifiers. In: The 40th Annual ACMSIGPLAN-SIGACT Symposium on Principles of Programming Languages, pp. 385–398. ACM (2013)
14. Livshits, V.B., Lam, M.S.: Finding security vulnerabilities in Java applications with static analysis. In: Proceedings of the 14th Conference on USENIX Security Symposium. SSYM 2005. USENIX Association (2005)
15. Livshits, V.B., Lam, M.S.: Tracking pointers with path and context sensitivity for bug detection in C programs. In: Proceedings of the 9th European Software Engineering Conference. ESEC/FSE-11, pp. 317–326. ACM (2003)
16. Milner, R., Parrow, J., Walker, D.: A calculus of mobile processes, Part I/II. Inf. Comput. 100, 1–77 (1992)
17. Myers, A.C.: JFlow: practical mostly-static information flow control. In: Proceedings of the 26th ACM Symposium on Principles of Programming Languages, pp. 228–241 (1999)
18. Nielson, F., Nielson, H.-R., Hankin, C.L.: Principles of Program Analysis. Springer, Heidelberg (1999)
19. Padhye, R., Khedker, U.P.: Interprocedural data flow analysis in SOOT using value contexts. In: Proceedings of the 2nd ACM SIGPLAN International Workshop on State of the Art in Java Program Analysis. ACM (2013)
20. Pistoia, M., Flynn, R.J., Koved, L., Sreedhar, V.C.: Interprocedural analysis for privileged code placement and tainted variable detection. In: Gao, X.-X. (ed.) ECOOP 2005. LNCS, vol. 3586, pp. 362–386. Springer, Heidelberg (2005)
21. Pottier, F., Simonet, V.: Information flow inference for ML. ACM Trans. Program. Lang. Syst. 25(1), 117–158 (2003)
22. Schwartz, E.J., Avgerinos, T., Brumley, D.: All you ever wanted to know about dynamic taint analysis and forward symbolic execution (but might have been afraid to ask). In: 2010 IEEE Symposium on Security and Privacy (SP), pp. 317–331. IEEE (2010)
23. Steffen, M.: A small-step semantics of a concurrent calculus with goroutines and deferred functions. In: Abraham, E., Bonsangue, M., Johnsen, E.B. (eds.) Theory and Practice of Formal Methods: Essays Dedicated to Frank de Boer on the Occasion of His 60th Birthday. LNCS, vol. 9660, pp. 393–406. Springer, Heidelberg (2016)
24. Stolz, V., Bodden, E.: Temporal assertions using AspectJ. Electron. Notes Theor. Comput. Sci. 144(4), 109–124 (2006)
25. Summerfield, M.: Programming in Go (2012)
26. The cover story - The Go Blog. https://blog.golang.org/cover. Accessed 29 Apr 2016
27. Volpano, D., Irvine, C., Smith, G.: A sound type system for secure flow analysis. J. Comput. Secur. 4(2–3), 167–187 (1996)

Challenges in High-Assurance Runtime Verification

Alwyn Goodloe$^{(\boxtimes)}$

NASA Langley Research Center, Hampton, VA, USA
a.goodloe@nasa.gov

Abstract. Safety-critical systems are growing more complex and becoming increasingly autonomous. Runtime Verification (RV) has the potential to provide protections when a system cannot be assured by conventional means, but only if the RV itself can be trusted. In this paper, we present a number of challenges to realizing high-assurance RV and illustrate how we have addressed them in our research. We argue that high-assurance RV provides a rich target for automated verification tools in hope of fostering closer collaboration among the communities.

1 Introduction

Safety-critical systems, such as aircraft, automobiles, and medical devices are those systems whose failure could result in loss of life, significant property damage, or damage to the environment [23]. The grave consequences of failure have compelled industry and regulatory authorities to adopt conservative design approaches and exhaustive verification and validation (V&V) procedures to prevent mishaps. In addition, strict licensing requirements are often placed on human operators of many safety-critical systems. In practice, the verification and validation of avionics and other safety-critical software systems relies heavily on system predictability; and existing regulatory guidance, such as DO-178C [30], do not have provisions to assure safety-critical systems that do not exhibit predictable behavior at certification. Yet technological advances are enabling the development of increasingly autonomous (IA) cyber-physical systems (CPS) that modify their behavior in response to the external environment and learn from their experience. While unmanned aircraft systems (UAS) and self-driving cars have the potential of transforming society in many beneficial ways, they also pose new dangers to public safety. The algorithmic methods such as machine learning that enable autonomy lack the salient feature of predictability since the system's behavior depends on what it has learned. Consequently, the problem of assuring safety-critical IA CPS is both a barrier to industrial use and a significant research challenge [10].

Runtime verification (RV) [15], where monitors detect and respond to property violations at runtime, has the potential to enable the safe operation of safety-critical systems that are too complex to formally verify or fully test. Technically speaking, a RV monitor takes a logical specification ϕ and execution trace τ of

T. Margaria and B. Steffen (Eds.): ISoLA 2016, Part I, LNCS 9952, pp. 446–460, 2016.
DOI: 10.1007/978-3-319-47166-2_31

state information of the system under observation (SUO) and decides whether τ satisfies ϕ. The *Simplex Architecture* [33] provides a model architectural pattern for RV, where a monitor checks that the executing SUO satisfies a specification and, if the property is violated, the RV system will switch control to a more conservative component that can be assured using conventional means that *steers* the system into a safe state. *High-assurance* RV provides an assured level of safety even when the SUO itself cannot be verified by conventional means.

Contributions: During the course of our research we have been guided by the question "what issues must be addressed in a convincing argument that high-assurance RV can safeguard a system that cannot be otherwise assured?" In this paper, we chronicle a number of challenges we have identified that must be thoroughly addressed in order to actualize high-assurance RV. We hope that this helps inform other researchers that wish to apply RV to safety-critical systems. We examine how these issues have been addressed in our work on the Copilot RV framework [26,28]. A theme of our research has been the application of lightweight formal methods to achieve high-assurance and we identify opportunities for closer collaboration between the RV and tool communities.

2   Copilot

Copilot is an RV framework targeted at safety-critical hard real-time systems, which has served as an experimental platform enabling a research program in high-assurance RV. Copilot is a domain specific language embedded (EDSL) in

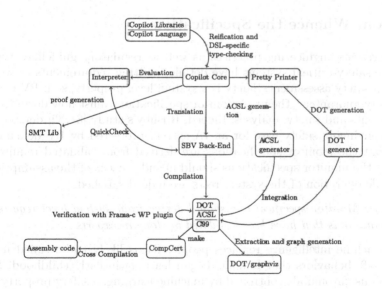

Fig. 1. The Copilot toolchain.

the functional programming language Haskell tailored to programming monitors for hard real-time, reactive systems.[1]

Copilot is a *stream* based language where a stream is an infinite sequence of values that must conform to the same type. All transformations of data in Copilot must be propagated through streams. Copilot guarantees that specifications compile to constant-time and constant-space implementations. Copilot streams mimic both the syntax and semantics of Haskell lazy lists with the exception that operators are automatically promoted point-wise to the list level.

Two types of temporal operators are provided in Copilot, one for delaying streams and one for looking into the future of streams:

```
(++) :: [a] → Stream a → Stream a
drop :: Int → Stream a → Stream a
```

Here `xs ++ s` prepends the list `xs` at the front of the stream `s`. The expression `drop k s` skips the first `k` values of the stream `s`, returning the remainder of the stream.

Copilot's toolchain is depicted in Fig. 1. A Copilot program is reified (i.e., transformed from a recursive structure into explicit graphs) and then some domain-specific type-checking is done. At this point, we have transformed the program into the "core" language, an intermediate representation. The core package contains an interpreter that can be viewed as an operational semantics for the language. The back-end translates a Copilot core program into the language of another Haskell-hosted EDSL, Symbolic Bit Vectors (SBV)[2], which we use to generate C monitors.

3   From Whence the Specification

Sound systems engineering practices as well as regulatory guidelines typically mandate safety-critical systems have detailed written requirements as well as a thorough safety assessment. Safety is a system level property, so if RV is to provide safety guarantees, then the monitor specifications must flow down from the requirements and safety analyses. Indeed, Rushby's study [31,32] demonstrated that a convincing safety case for an IA system protected by RV demands evidence that the monitor specifications are derived from validated requirements and that the monitor specifications should include checks of the assumptions on which safe operation of the system rests are indeed satisfied.

Challenge: Monitor specifications should derive from system level requirements and assumptions that have been validated by domain experts.

As machine intelligence replaces people, RV is likely to be called upon to enforce safe behaviors that humans began learning in early childhood. For an autonomous automobile controlled by machine learning, a safety property might

---

[1] https://github.com/Copilot-Language.

[2] http://hackage.haskell.org/package/sbv, BSD3 license.

be "do not hit a pedestrian" or "do not behave erratically", but what do these statements mean precisely? A more precise statement such as "maintain five meters distance from any object in the vehicle path" may be more formal, but is that what the expert wanted? Phrases like "erratic behavior" may seem reasonable to a mature adult, but formalizing such statements can be an open ended problem.

Challenge: Precisely formalize safety properties in a logic.

Copilot Approach: We are conducting case studies informed by collaborations with colleagues who are developing new concepts that will enable aircraft to perform autonomous flight by self-optimizing their four-dimensional trajectories while conforming to constraints such as required times of arrival generated by air-traffic service providers on the ground. Many of the proposed algorithms [21] do not behave with the predictability of conventional systems. Consequently, it is not possible to provide the required level of assurance that the newly computed trajectories preserve safe aircraft separation. The separation requirement for two aircraft is specified by a minimum horizontal separation D (typically, 5 nautical miles). Fortuitously, colleagues at NASA have discovered analytical formula, called *criteria* [25], that characterize resolution maneuvers that both ensure safe separation when one aircraft maneuvers and ensures separation when two conflicting aircraft both maneuver. The criteria have been extensively validated by domain experts who conducted sophisticated simulations as well as performing formal mathematical proofs using the Prototype Verification System (PVS) theorem prover. We have encoded these conditions as Copilot specifications. The criteria for horizontal separation for two aircraft is given as follows:

$$\texttt{horiz\_criteria}(\mathbf{s}, \epsilon, \mathbf{v}) \equiv \mathbf{s} \cdot \mathbf{v} \geq \epsilon \frac{\sqrt{\mathbf{s} \cdot \mathbf{s} - D^2}}{D} \det(\mathbf{s}, \mathbf{v})$$
$$\wedge \ \epsilon \ \det(\mathbf{s}, \mathbf{v}) \leq 0$$

where $\mathbf{s}$ is the relative position vector for the two aircraft, ϵ is 1 or -1, and $\mathbf{v}$ is the relative velocity vector after a planned maneuver. The position is assumed to be given in Earth Centered Earth Fixed (ECEF) coordinates. This is easily encoded in Copilot's EDSL as:

```
hor_rr :: Stream Double → Stream Double → Stream Double
hor_rr sx sy= (sqrt $ (normsq2dim sx sy) -
                    (minHorSep * minHorSep)) / (minHorSep)

horizontalCriterionForConflictResolution :: Stream Double →
        Stream Double → Stream Double → Stream Double →
        Stream Double → Stream Bool
horizontalCriterionForConflictResolution sx sy e vx vy =
        ((scalar2dim sx sy vx vy) ≥
              (e * (hor_rr sx sy) * (det2dim sx sy vx vy)))
        && (((det2dim sx sy vx vy) *e)  ≤ 0.0)
```

Formalizing the assumptions about the reliability of communicating aircraft position data is ongoing work. A case study formalizing what it means for a UAS to behave erratically is planned as future work.

4 Observability

Guaranteeing that all the data required by the specification is actually *observable* is one of the principal engineering challenges of RV. In embedded systems, the RV specification often involves data from a number of different types of data sources, including state data of executing programs, sensor data, as well as data that is communicated from other systems. The safety properties of cyber-physical systems are often formulated by aerospace and automobile engineers that are domain experts, but can have varying degrees of understanding of the computing systems, so the RV engineer needs to be very proactive in addressing the observability issue. In embedded systems, the closed nature of the hardware platforms and proprietary issues can make it impossible to observe the information required in the specification. Additional sensors may be needed or communication data formats changed. At times it is necessary to change the specification so that it only depends on observable data. The observability issue may seem like an "engineering detail", but based on our experience, it is often a significant obstacle resulting in delays, frustration, and sometimes preventing progress altogether.

Challenge: Determining observability of the state and environment variables in the specification.

Copilot Approach: How a RV framework obtains state data impacts the properties that can be monitored. Many RV frameworks such as MAC [22] and MOP [8] instrument the software and hardware of the SUO so that it emits events of interest to the monitor. While attractive from the viewpoint of maximizing state observability, the additional overhead may affect worst case execution times and consequently the scheduling; regulatory guidelines may also require recertification of that system. Copilot and several other RV frameworks [6,13,20] opt to sacrifice complete observability by sampling events. Copilot monitors run as dedicated threads and sample program variables and state information via shared memory. Currently, we rely on scheduling analysis and experimentation to ensure that we sample values at a sufficient rate that specification violations are detected. This has been very successful when the implementation platform is running a real-time operating system (RTOS) with deterministic scheduling guarantees, but we cannot make strong assertions of efficacy running on less specialized systems.

A critical lesson learned in the course of conducting many case studies is to ask questions about observability early and often. If monitoring the state of an executing program, is it possible that the monitor fails to detect a state change?

It is often necessary to read sensor data to obtain the required state data (e.g. aircraft pitch and vehicle position) or environmental data (e.g. temperature). If it is raw sensor data, do we apply filters before feeding the data into the monitors? Is the data available in the same coordinate systems demanded of the specification? Can we ensure the integrity and provenance of the data being observed?

The aircraft safe separation criteria specification introduced in Sect. 3 requires the monitor to observe state data for both the aircraft the monitor is executing on as well as the "intruder" aircraft. Hence, the monitors must sample data from executing programs (planned maneuver), onboard positioning sensors, and data broadcast from other vehicles.

5   Traceability

To ensure that the requirements and safety analyses performed early in systems development are reflected throughout the lifecycle, many guidelines for safety-critical software, such as DO-178C, require documentation of traceability from requirements to object code. Consequently, to promote the acceptance of high-assurance RV, the monitor generation frameworks should produce documentation that supports traceability from specification to monitor code.

Challenge: Support traceability from the requirements and system level analysis to the actual monitor code.

Copilot Approach: Using SBV to generate C monitors may create many small files and it can be quite difficult to relate this to the specification. The code generation module has recently been revised to generate documentation that improves traceability. The user can insert labels in their specifications that flow down to the documentation. The translation process creates C header files with documentation formatted to be processed by the plain text graph description language processor DOT [1]. Each C function has accompanying auto-generated graphical documentation.

In the case of the following example:

```
hor_rr sx sy  = (label "?hor_rr_dividend" $ sqrt $
                (normsq2dim sx sy) - (minHorSep * minHorSep))
                / (label "?hor_rr_divisor" $ minHorSep)
```

the SBV translation breaks this relatively simple expression into numerous small C functions and function parameters get instantiated with the variables being monitored. The auto-generated documentation for one of these files appears similar to Fig. 2, where the labels have the names of the program variables being monitored.

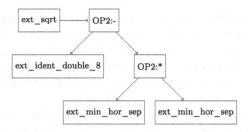

Fig. 2. Autogenerated documentation

6   Fault-Tolerant RV

Safety engineers employ a range of established methods to identify hazards and failure modes [3]. The level of desired reliability determines what faults the system must be designed to tolerate. If RV is to be the guarantor of safety, then it must at least meet the level of reliability demanded of the system as a whole. Thus, high-assurance RV should be designed to be *fault-tolerant* [7], meaning it continues to provide its required functionality in the presence of faults. A fault-tolerant system must not contain a *single point of failure*.

Ideally, the RV and the SUO should not be subject to common modes of failure. For instance, software errors in the SUO such as numerical overflows and memory leaks that can render a system inoperable should not affect the RV. A fault-tolerant system must also be robust in the presence of hardware faults such as sensor failures and voltage spikes. A *fault-containment region* (FCR) is a region in a system designed to ensure faults do not propagate to other regions. The easiest way to ensure this is to physically isolate one FCR from another. However, FCRs may need to communicate, hence they share channels. An FCR containing a monitor may need to share a channel with the SUO. Care must be taken to ensure faults cannot propagate over these channels. In the case of ultra-reliable systems, the only way to achieve the level of fault tolerance demanded of the system is by hardware replication that demands complex hardware redundancy management software.

Challenge: Isolating failures so that RV should not be rendered inoperable by the same failure conditions that impact the SUO.

Copilot Approach: Fault-tolerant RV has been an ongoing topic of investigation for the Copilot research group. The avionics industry has been migrating away from federated systems toward the use of integrated modular avionics that provide fault tolerance as a service. The Aeronautical Radio, Incorporated (ARINC) 653 [4] compliant RTOS provides temporal and spatial partitioning guarantees so applications can safely share resources. The Copilot group has been investigating design patterns for implementing fault-tolerant RV on such platforms [11]. Monitors are run on the same nodes as the software being monitored, but in separate partitions. Monitoring tasks executing in a separate partition observe the state of the executing program through very restricted channels that preserve the isolation guarantees. The spacial and temporal protections provided by ARINC 653 keep the monitors safe from other programs running on the same system.

Systems that need to be ultrareliable typically must employ redundancy to tolerate the most pernicious faults such as a *Byzantine fault* (i.e., a fault in which different nodes interpret a single broadcast message differently). There have been documented incidents in critical avionics where sensors failed in a Byzantine fashion with the potential to affect a vehicle's safety. The aircraft horizontal separation criteria in Sect. 3 depend on reliably sensing the position and velocity of both systems. In earlier work [28], we have addressed this issue in a case study where a system had redundant sensors and Copilot monitors performed Byzantine exchange and majority voting to create a system that could tolerate a single Byzantine fault. Fault injection testing was performed along with flight tests. The hardware used in these experiments were commodity microprocessors, but we have recently bought Mil-Spec hardened processors that are more reliable when operating under varying environmental conditions.

7   Do No Harm

The RV components must be composed with the SUO so that they are executing in parallel with the SUO. Care must be taken that the RV system itself does not compromise the correct functioning of the SUO. For instance executing monitors may impact timing and scheduling. Care must also be taken that any instrumentation of the SUO does not affect the functional correctness. In large systems, there are likely to be many monitors running; each monitor might trigger different steering procedures. A common pattern when things go wrong in complex safety-critical systems is that many alerts are sounded simultaneously often placing a burden on a human operator to sort things out. One can easily envision an analogous situation where several monitors detect violations, triggering their respective steering procedures. Hence it is necessary to verify that these different steering procedures do not interact with each other in ways that could compromise safety. In summary, high-assurance RV must uphold the Hippocratic oath "to do no harm". Ideally, we would formulate a noninterference theorem and the RV framework would produce a proof certificate that the composed system satisfies the property.

Challenge: Assured RV must safely compose with the SUO.

Copilot Approach: The Copilot research group has yet to develop a general theory of RV noninterference, but we have made a number of design decisions with this in mind. For instance, the choice of monitoring system state through sampling was a deliberate attempt to minimize interference with the SUO. Running monitors in separate partitions on an ARINC 653 compliant RTOS as discussed in Sect. 6 ensures that any fault in the RV will not negatively affect the executing SUO. The RTOS scheduler also provides guarantees that a missed deadline in the RV does not affect the SUO.

8 Monitor Specification Correctness

As RV is applied to guarantee sophisticated properties, the monitor specifications themselves will grow in complexity and may become prone to error. Our experience with a number of case studies involving complex monitor properties is that we were able to discover many simple theorems that should hold for a correct specification. Hence, applying formal proof tools to the monitors to ensure they are correct can safeguard that the last line of defense is actually effective. Ideally, specification verification capabilities should be integrated into the RV framework so engineers could write specifications, verify their correctness, and generate monitors in a seamless fashion.

Challenge: Assure the correctness of the monitor specification.

Copilot Approach: Copilot supports automated proofs of specification properties through its `Copilot.Theorem` module. Applying a "synchronous observer" approach [17], properties *about* Copilot programs are specified *within* Copilot itself. In particular, properties are encoded with standard Boolean streams and Copilot streams are sufficient to encode past-time linear temporal logic [18].

A proposition is a Copilot value of type `Prop Existential` or `Prop Universal`, which can be introduced using `exists` and `forall`, respectively. These are functions taking as an argument a normal Copilot stream of type `Stream Bool`. Propositions can be added to a specification using the `prop` and `theorem` functions, where `theorem` must also be passed a tactic for automatically proving the proposition. Currently, proof engines based on Satisfiability Modulo Theories (SMT) are used to discharge proofs. The Copilot prover was first introduced in [16], where its utility was demonstrated in assuring notoriously subtle voting algorithms.

In the course of the analysis of the separation criteria, a team of domain experts used the PVS interactive prover to prove theorems that characterize the correctness of the criteria. We were able to apply the Copilot prover using Z3 [12] to prove many of these theorems within the Copilot framework. Among the properties proven about the horizontal separation criteria are:

$$\mathtt{horiz\_criteria}(sx, sy, \epsilon, vx, vy) \iff \mathtt{horiz\_criteria}(-sx, -sy, \epsilon, -vx, -vy)$$

$$(\mathtt{horiz\_criteria}(sx, sy, \epsilon, vx, vy) \wedge$$
$$\mathtt{horiz\_criteria}(sx, sy, \epsilon, wx, wy)) \implies \mathtt{horiz\_criteria}(sx, sy, \epsilon, vx, vy)$$

$$(\mathtt{horiz\_criteria}(sx, sy, \epsilon, vx, vy) \wedge$$
$$\mathtt{horiz\_criteria}(sx, sy, \epsilon', vx, vy)) \implies \epsilon = \epsilon'$$

A few of the properties proven in PVS involve continuous mathematics that remains beyond the capabilities of fully automated tools, but combined with testing, we have a convincing argument that the specification is correct.

9   Correct Monitors

RV frameworks apply sophisticated algorithms to synthesize monitors from specifications. In safety-critical systems, subtle errors in the translation process can have potentially catastrophic consequences and consequently, a safety case for assured RV must include evidence of the correctness of the translation process.

Challenge: There should be assurance arguments with evidence that executable monitors correctly implement the specification. The monitor implementation should not be susceptible to unsafe or undefined behaviors such as buffer and floating point overflows.

Copilot Approach: The small Copilot interpreter can be seen as providing an executable operational semantics for the Copilot language. As reported in [27], our first efforts in monitor synthesis assurance were to support regression tests for the semantics of the EDSL using Haskell's QuickCheck [9] property testing engine. Type-correct Copilot programs get randomly generated and output from the interpreter is compared against the actual monitor. QuickCheck testing uncovered a number of bugs during early development of the monitor synthesis software. Among those bugs caught were forgotten witnesses needed by the code generation tools. The testing also highlighted differences in how GCC and Haskell implemented floating point numbers, without either violating the IEEE floating point standard.

Recent work leverages light-weight verification tools for monitor synthesis assurance. The process of translating a specification into a monitor transforms an abstract syntax tree (AST) of the "core" language representation into a SBV AST. SBV's C code generation capabilities are used to generate executable C code. To facilitate monitor verification, Copilot produces Hoare-logic style contracts directly from the Copilot core representation independent of the monitor generation process. The contracts are written in the ANSI C Specification Language (ACSL) [5], an assertion language for specifying behavioral properties of C programs in first-order logic. Each file has a contract with an ACSL postcondition specifying the subexpression of the core AST representation that the function should implement. Frama-C's [14] WP deductive verification engine is employed to prove that the code does indeed satisfy the contract. Deductive verification tools have evolved quite a bit recently, but scalability is still an issue. However, the verification is tractable because the translation process creates separate C functions for subexpressions of a large expression.

An example of an annotated monitor C function follows:

```
/*@
 assigns \ nothing;
 ensures \ result == (((ext_ident_double_8) -
                      (((ext_minimal_horizontal_separation) *
                      (ext_minimal_horizontal_separation)))));
*/
 SDouble ext_sqrt_9_arg0(const SDouble ext_ident_double_8,
     const SDouble ext_ownship_position_x,
     const SDouble ext_intruder_position_x,
     const SDouble ext_ownship_position_y,
     const SDouble ext_intruder_position_y,
     const SDouble ext_minimal_horizontal_separation)
{    const SDouble s0 = ext_ident_double_8;
     const SDouble s5 = ext_minimal_horizontal_separation;
     const SDouble s6 = s5 * s5;
     const SDouble s7 = s0 - s6;
     return s7;   }
```

Frama-C's WP plugin easily proves that the function satisfies the contract.

While this analysis demonstrates a faithful translation from core language to C code, it elides the issues that arise performing floating point arithmetic. We applied both the RV-Match tool [2] and Frama-C's abstract interpretation value analysis plugin to detect when floating point arithmetic produces infinite values or not a number (NaN). The RV-Match C undefinedness checker found a divide-by-zero error due to our initializing a variable to zero. The abstract interpreter produced warnings for every floating point operation. In the case of the ext_sqrt_9_arg0 function, the value analysis produces the following warnings:

```
\ext_sqrt_9_arg0.c:41:[kernel] warning: non-finite double value
([-1.79769313486e+308 .. 1.79769313486e+308]): assert
\is_finite((double)(s5*s5)); ext_sqrt_9_arg0.c:42:[kernel] warning:
non-finite double value ([-1.79769313486e+308
.. 1.79769313486e+308]): assert \is_finite((double)(s0-s6));
ext_sqrt_9_arg0.c:30:[value] Function ext_sqrt_9_arg0: postcondition
got status unknown.
```

Applying domain specific knowledge about the bounds on the velocity and state vectors eliminated this warning. At present, we must add these bounds to the contracts by hand, but intend to generate such information during monitor generation.

Assurance All the Way Down: Having assured that the C code implementing the monitor is correct, how can we guarantee that the executable binary code correctly implements the C program? For Copilot, we have experimented with using the verified Compcert compiler [24] to generate binaries. Unfortunately, Compcert does not yet target many of the processors used in our experiments limiting its utility.

10   Additional Challenges

The presentation so far has examined challenges in assured RV that have been addressed in our research. In this section, we will raise three of the key additional challenges that we have identified as critical to address in future work.

Safe Steering: The problem of what to do when a specification has been violated is one of the most thorny problems in high-assurance RV and almost completely application dependent. The simplest action is to log the violation for further analysis or raise an alarm for humans to intervene, but in many cases, the RV system must take proactive steps to preserve safety. For an autonomous robot, putting the system into a quiescent state may be a safe default operation depending on the operating environment. In the case of an adaptive control system, the RV framework may switch to a conventional controller, but whether this re-establishes safety depends on many factors. In many domains, the challenge in constructing an assured safe steering algorithm may be as difficult as constructing the adaptive autonomous algorithm itself.

Challenge: Verify the correctness and safety of the steering performed from any viable system state once a specification violation is detected.

Predictive Monitors: Applying RV to application domains that have strict timing constraints, such as an adaptive control system, raises many technical challenges. It is imperative that the monitor detects that the adaptive controller is about to lose stability in time to switch to a safe controller. In the case of our running example, the RV system needs to detect that two aircraft are about to lose separation in time for them to take corrective action. Assured predictive monitors are needed, but much work remains to be done. Johnson et al. [19] is a promising approach to predictive monitoring for controllers, but the general problem is very domain specific. Assured predictive monitoring remains a research challenge for the RV community.

Challenge: The monitor should detect impending violations of the specification and invoke the safety controller in time to preserve safe operation.

Secured RV: Adding more software or hardware to a system has the potential to introduce vulnerabilities that can be exploited by an attacker. Copilot and many other RV frameworks generate monitors that have constant time and constant space execution footprints and while this eliminates some common attacks, it does not provide general protection. Every sensor and unauthenticated message may contribute to the attack surface. If an attacker can trick the systems into a monitor specification violation, the triggered steering behavior may itself constitute a denial-of-service attack. Future research is needed in identifying attack surfaces and suitable techniques to thwart adversaries from turning the RV meant to protect a system into a liability that exposes the system to attack.

Challenge: Assured RV should not introduce security vulnerabilities into a system.

11   Better Together

High-assurance RV will only become practical if there is accompanying integrated tool support for verification and validation. From the perspective of a researcher in high-assurance RV, engaging with the communities building static analysis tools and proof engines seems obvious, especially in light of the fact that regulatory bodies that govern many safety-critical systems are increasingly willing to accept the analysis produced from such tools as evidence that can be applied to certification [29]. Similarly, there are many features of RV that make it a great target for the tool builder. For instance, there are formal specifications to work with and monitor code is generally small and conforms to coding practices that are friendly to static analysis.

Several of the challenges we have raised for high-assurance RV are really at the system level. Tools that can assist domain experts in validating safety properties are sorely needed. As in our case study, the safety properties of cyber-physical systems involve continuous mathematics. While advances in SMT solvers have been impressive, it is still necessary to often resort to using an interactive theorem prover. There are many opportunities to design domain specific decision procedures that would increase the utility of automated proof tools.

The problem of RV observability provides a rich source of problems for tool builders. If the RV approach involves instrumenting code, then static analysis can both assist in the instrumentation and prove that the instrumentation did not affect the correctness of the code. If sampling, static analysis has the potential to inform when to sample.

Floating point arithmetic is a source of problems that is readily amenable to static analysis and proof. In our work, we applied abstract interpretation to monitor source code, but analysis could be done at the specification level with proof obligations flowing down to the monitor code.

Applying tools to verify monitor correctness makes so much sense that it should be de rigueur. In Copilot, we applied deductive verification to verify the correctness of the translation from specification to monitor code. Monitors have many characteristics that make automatic proofs tractable, but the monitor synthesis must generate code suitable for the tool being used.

12   Conclusion

High-assurance RV has the potential of becoming the avenue to assuring otherwise unassurable IA safety-critical systems. We have presented a number of challenges that we have identified as barriers to actualizing high-assurance RV and surveyed how we have addressed these challenges in the course of our research using the Copilot framework. We hope this list will be useful to RV researchers as they apply their own work to safety-critical systems. In addition, we believe we have demonstrated the efficacy of applying light-weight formal methods tools to address many of these challenges. Progress on these issues is likely to come faster if a multidisciplinary approach is taken with domain specialists, safety engineers and verification tool builders collaborating with RV researchers. Much work remains and the list of challenges is likely to grow even as researchers solve many of the issues raised.

Acknowledgments. The Copilot project has been conducted in collaboration with Dr. Lee Pike (Galois). Jonathan Laurent (ENS Paris) and Chris Hathhorn (University of Missouri) did most of the coding of the Copilot.Theorem. Georges-Axel Jaloyan (ENS Paris) recently added the monitor verification capabilities.

References

1. The DOT language. http://www.graphviz.org/content/dot-language
2. RV-Match. http://runtimeverification.com/match/
3. SAE ARP4761 Guidelines and Methods for Conducting the Safety Assessment Process on Civil Airborne Systems and Equipment (1996)
4. Incorporated (ARINC) Aeronautical Radio. Avionics application software standard interface: Part I - required services (arinc specification 653-2) (2015)
5. Baudin, P., Cuoq, P., Filliâtre, J.-C., Marché, C., Monate, B., Moy, Y., Virgile Prevosto, A.: ANSI/ISO C Specification Language, version 1.10 (2015)
6. Bonakdarpour, B., Navabpour, S., Fischmeister, S.: Sampling-based runtime verification. In: 17th InternationalSymposium on Formal Methods (FM) (2011)
7. Butler, R.W.: A primer on architectural level fault tolerance. Technical report NASA/TM-2008-215108, NASA Langley Research Center (2008)
8. Chen, F., Roşu, G.: Java-MOP: a monitoring oriented programming environment for Java. In: Halbwachs, N., Zuck, L.D. (eds.) TACAS 2005. LNCS, vol. 3440, pp. 546–550. Springer, Heidelberg (2005)
9. Claessen, K., Hughes, J.: QuickCheck: a lightweight tool for random testing of Haskell programs. ACM SIGPLAN Not. **35**, 268–279 (2000). ACM
10. National Research Council. Autonomy Research for Civil Aviation: Toward a New Era of Flight. The National Academies Press (2014)
11. Darafsheh, K.: Runtime monitoring on hard real-time operating systems. Master's thesis, East Carolina University (2015)
12. de Moura, L., Bjørner, N.S.: Z3: an efficient SMT solver. In: Ramakrishnan, C.R., Rehof, J. (eds.) TACAS 2008. LNCS, vol. 4963, pp. 337–340. Springer, Heidelberg (2008)
13. Fischmeister, S., Ba, Y.: Sampling-based program execution monitoring. In: ACM International Conference on Languages, Compilers, and Tools for Embedded Systems (LCTES), pp. 133–142 (2010)
14. Frama-C. http://frama-c.com/index.html. Accessed Mar 2016
15. Goodloe, A., Pike, L.: Monitoring distributed real-time systems: a survey and future directions. Technical report NASA/CR-2010-216724, NASA Langley Research Center, July 2010
16. Laurent, J., Goodloe, A., Pike, L.: Assuring the guardians. In: Bartocci, E., et al. (eds.) RV 2015. LNCS, vol. 9333, pp. 87–101. Springer, Heidelberg (2015). doi:10.1007/978-3-319-23820-3_6
17. Halbwachs, N., Lagnier, F., Raymond, P.: Synchronous observers and the verification of reactive systems. In: Nivat, M., Rattray, C., Rus, T., Scollo, G., et al. (eds.) AMAST 1993. Workshops in Computing, pp. 83–96. Springer, Heidelberg (1994)

18. Havelund, K., Roşu, G.: Efficient monitoring of safety properties. Int. J. Softw. Tools Technol. Transf. **6**(2), 158–173 (2004)
19. Johnson, T.T., Bak, S., Caccamo, M., Sha, L.: Real-time reachability for verified simplex design. ACM Transactions on Embedded Computing Systems, September 2015
20. Kane, A.: Runtime monitoring for safety-critical embedded systems. Ph.D. thesis, Carnegie Mellon University (2015)
21. Karr, D.A., Vivona, R.A., Roscoe, D., DePascale, S.M., Consiglio, M.: Experimental performance of a genetic algorithm for airborne strategic conflict resolution. In: Proceedings of AIAA Guidance, Navigation and Control Conference (2008)
22. Kim, M., Lee, I., Kannan, S., Sokolsky, O.: Java-MaC: a run-time assurance tool for Java. Formal Methods Syst. Des. **24**(1), 129–155 (2004)
23. Knight, J.C.: Safety critical systems: challenges and directions. In: Proceedings of the 24th International Conference on SoftwareEngineering, ICSE 2002, pp. 547–550. ACM (2002)
24. Leroy, X.: Formal verification of a realistic compiler. Commun. ACM **52**, 107–115 (2009)
25. Narkawicz, A., Muñoz, C.: State-based implicit coordination and applications. Technical Publication NASA/TP-2011-217067, NASA, Langley Research Center, Hampton, VA 23681-2199, USA, March 2011
26. Pike, L., Goodloe, A., Morisset, R., Niller, S.: Copilot: a hard real-time runtime monitor. In: Falcone, Y., Finkbeiner, B., Havelund, K., Lee, I., Pace, G., Roşu, G., Sokolsky, O., Tillmann, N., Barringer, H. (eds.) RV 2010. LNCS, vol. 6418, pp. 345–359. Springer, Heidelberg (2010)
27. Pike, L., Wegmann, N., Niller, S., Goodloe, A.: Experience report: a do-it-yourself high-assurance compiler. In: Proceedings of the International Conference on Functional Programming (ICFP). ACM, September 2012
28. Pike, L., Wegmann, N., Niller, S., Goodloe, A.: Copilot: monitoring embedded systems. Innov. Syst. Softw. Eng. **9**(4), 235–255 (2013)
29. Formal methods supplement to do-178c and do-278a. RTCA Inc. (2011). RCTA/DO333
30. RTCA. Software considerations in airborne systems and equipment certification. RTCA Inc. (2011). RCTA/DO-178C
31. Rushby, J.: Runtime certification. In: Leucker, M. (ed.) RV 2008. LNCS, vol. 5289, pp. 21–35. Springer, Heidelberg (2008)
32. Rushby, J.: A safety-case approach for certifying adaptive systems. In: AIAA Infotech (2009)
33. Sha, L.: Using simplicity to control complexity. IEEE Softw. **18**, 20–28 (2001)

Static versus Dynamic Verification in Why3, Frama-C and SPARK 2014

Nikolai Kosmatov[1], Claude Marché[2,3]([✉]),
Yannick Moy[4], and Julien Signoles[1]

[1] CEA, LIST, Software Reliability Laboratory,
PC 174, 91191 Gif-sur-yvette, France
[2] Inria, Université Paris-Saclay, 91893 Palaiseau, France
Claude.Marche@inria.fr
[3] LRI, CNRS and University of Paris-Sud, 91405 Orsay, France
[4] AdaCore, 75009 Paris, France

Abstract. Why3 is an environment for static verification, generic in the
sense that it is used as an intermediate tool by different front-ends for
the verification of Java, C or Ada programs. Yet, the choices made when
designing the specification languages provided by those front-ends differ
significantly, in particular with respect to the executability of specifications. We review these differences and the issues that result from these
choices. We emphasize the specific feature of *ghost code* which turns out
to be extremely useful for both static and dynamic verification. We also
present techniques, combining static and dynamic features, that help
users understand why static verification fails.

1 Introduction

Why3 (http://why3.lri.fr) is an environment for deductive program verification,
providing a rich language for specification and programming, called WhyML.
The specification part of WhyML serves as a common format for theorem proving problems, suitable for multiple provers. The Why3 tool generates proof obligations from purely logic lemmas and from programs annotated with specifications, then dispatches them to multiple provers, including SMT solvers Alt-Ergo,
CVC4, Z3; TPTP first-order provers E, SPASS, Vampire; interactive theorem
provers Coq, Isabelle and PVS.

Frama-C (http://frama-c.com) is an extensible platform for source-code
analysis of C software. It features a plug-in architecture [42]: the Frama-C kernel
performs syntactic analysis and typing of C code, and then allows the user to
continue with different kinds of analyses, both static ones, e.g. based on theorem
proving or abstract interpretation, or dynamic ones. The Frama-C kernel provides the formal specification language ACSL [3,4] for specifying contracts on

Work partly supported by the Joint Laboratory ProofInUse (ANR-13-LAB3-0007,
http://www.spark-2014.org/proofinuse) of the French national research organization.

© Springer International Publishing AG 2016
T. Margaria and B. Steffen (Eds.): ISoLA 2016, Part I, LNCS 9952, pp. 461–478, 2016.
DOI: 10.1007/978-3-319-47166-2_32

C functions. Contracts can be written by users, or generated by plug-ins. Two plug-ins (Jessie and WP) permit deductive verification, that is, they can check that a given C function respects its ACSL specification, using theorem proving. Both plug-ins make use of Why3 as intermediate tool.

The SPARK language is a subset of Ada dedicated to real-time embedded software that requires a high level of safety, security, and reliability. It has been applied for many years in on-board aircraft systems, control systems, cryptographic systems, and rail systems [9]. Ada 2012 is the latest version of the Ada language [1], adding new features for specifying the behavior of programs, such as subprogram contracts and type invariants. SPARK2014 (http://www.spark-2014.org/) is the last major version of SPARK, designed to interpret Ada 2012 contracts [39]. To formally prove a SPARK program correct, the SPARK2014 toolset also uses WhyML as an intermediate language, and relies on Why3's interface to provers to discharge proof obligations.

Although deductive verification with both SPARK2014 and Frama-C proceeds through Why3, the design of their specification languages differ significantly, and they are also different from Why3's own specification language. One of the reasons is that specification languages in Frama-C or SPARK aim at being used for other purposes than purely deductive verification, in particular they can be used for *dynamic* verification. *Run-time assertion checking* is the dynamic verification approach originating from the concept of design-by-contract, as it was implemented first in the Eiffel language [40] and later in the Java Modeling Language (JML) [35]. In those settings, annotations or contracts are clauses (pre- and postconditions, loop invariants, assertions) associated with boolean expressions. The run-time assertion checker inserts some extra code into the regular program code, that will throw an exception if any of these clauses is violated during execution. Statically checking the validity of contracts came a bit later in particular with the ESC-Java [5] tool, and later tools like Spec# [2], Dafny [37], OpenJML [14]. The issues that arise when trying to combine static and dynamic verification are quite well known [35] (mainly, how to make them agree on a common semantics), and studied, in particular regarding the impact on end-users of formal methods [7,8].

In Sect. 2, we review the different choices made in the design of the specification languages of Why3, Frama-C and SPARK2014, and investigate the consequences and issues arising for the various kinds of analyses. One specific feature that is present in all of SPARK2014, ACSL and WhyML is the notion of *ghost variables* and *ghost code*. Ghost code is a versatile way for the user to instrument code, and to exploit this instrumentation both for static and dynamic verification. Yet, ghost code features in the three languages above also differ significantly, and we investigate these differences in Sect. 3. In the activity of deductive verification, a major issue is to understand why a proof fails. Frama-C and SPARK2014 implement different techniques to provide the user with hints about such a failure, using static or dynamic analysis in various ways. This aspect is reviewed in Sect. 4.

2 Design Choices in Specification Languages for Why3 and Its Front-Ends

Why3 is a versatile environment for deductive program verification. The WhyML language dedicated for specification and programming is mostly a purely functional programming language augmented with a notion of mutable variables [23]. Non-aliasing of mutable data is mandatory and is checked statically. Programs in WhyML are formally specified by contracts (mainly pre- and postconditions) written in an extended first-order logic partly detailed below. Verification proceeds by generating Verification Conditions (VCs) with a weakest precondition calculus. Why3 relies on external provers, both automated and interactive, in order to discharge these VCs. WhyML is used as an intermediate language for verification of SPARK programs as well as C and Java programs [22] (see Fig. 1), and can also be used as a primary programming language (it can be compiled to OCaml).

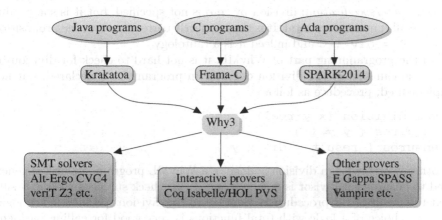

Fig. 1. Why3 front-ends and back-ends

2.1 Why3's Specification Language

Why3's core logic is a typed first-order logic with equality and built-in integer and real arithmetic. The user can enrich the logical context of a program's specification by designing extra theories defining new types, function symbols and predicates. New types can be defined e.g. by algebraic data type specification, while function and predicate symbols can be defined, possibly recursively, using pattern-matching on algebraic arguments. Types and logic symbols can also be declared axiomatically by giving symbol signatures and arbitrary axioms. Why3's core logic also provides extended features such as type polymorphism, inductive predicates and some form of higher-order functions [11]. Why3 comes which a pretty rich standard library of theories.

A Logic of Total Functions. The choice of basing Why3's logic on standard first-order logic implies that it is a 2-valued logic with only total functions. When new function symbols are defined recursively, Why3's kernel statically checks that this recursion is well-founded, so as to be sure that a total function is defined. However, this raises issues when a function is defined axiomatically. Consider for example the typical case of division on real numbers, axiomatized by:

```
function div real real : real
axiom div_spec: forall x y:real. y ≠ 0 → y * div x y = x
```

Notice first that if we omit the premise $y \neq 0$ then the axiomatization would be inconsistent: 0 * div 1 0 = 1 hence 0 = 1. A first issue is thus that nothing prevents the user from writing inconsistent axioms. A mean to avoid such issues is to ask a prover to try to derive `false` from the specification: if it succeeds then for sure there is an inconsistency, but this cannot be a complete check because of undecidability of first-order logic. Such a *smoke detection* check can be done on demand in Why3 similarly to other tools like Dafny. The second issue is *underspecification*: division by zero is not specified, but it is some value because all functions are total. It is thus perfectly correct to state the proposition div 1 0 = div 1 0 and indeed it is a tautology.

In the programming part of WhyML, it is not hard to check for division by zero: one can specify the division operator in programs as a declared, but not implemented, procedure as follows:

```
val division (x y:real) : real
requires { y ≠ 0 }              (* precondition *)
ensures { result = div x y }    (* postcondition *)
```

In other words, when a division is done in a WhyML program, a check is generated to ensure that divisor is not null, and if this check succeeds then it is sure that the result of the procedure is identical to the division specified in the logic.

This choice of a logic with total functions is very good for calling back-end provers such as SMT solvers or first-order provers, because they implement the very same choice. However, the issues discussed above are traps that a user more used to executable semantics of programs can fall into. These issues are extensively discussed by Chalin [7] based on experimental studies with practitioners. *Executable Features of Why3.* Why3's primary goal is static verification of contracts on WhyML procedures. Why3 also offers two features for executing programs: it implements a basic interpreter, and a compiler to OCaml. In both cases, the specifications are just discarded: there is no way to perform run-time assertion checking in Why3. As a consequence, the non-executability of logic specifications is not an issue. We discuss future work related to executability in Sect. 5.

```
/*@ predicate Swap{L1,L2}(int a[],              /*@ predicate Sorted{L}(int a[],
  @                 integer i, integer j) =       @              integer l, integer h) =
  @   \at(a[i],L1) == \at(a[j],L2) &&             @   \forall integer i j;
  @   \at(a[j],L1) == \at(a[i],L2) &&             @   l <= i <= j < h ==>
  @   \forall integer k; k != i && k != j ==>     @     \at(a[i] <= a[j],L) ;
  @     \at(a[k],L1) == \at(a[k],L2);             @*/
  @*/
                                                  /*@ requires t != null &&
/*@ inductive Permut{L1,L2}(int a[],              @   0 <= i < t.length &&
  @                  integer l, integer h) {      @   0 <= j < t.length;
  @ case Permut_refl{L}:                          @ assigns t[i],t[j];
  @   \forall int a[], integer l h;               @ ensures Swap{Old,Here}(t,i,j);
  @   Permut{L,L}(a, l, h) ;                       @*/
  @ case Permut_sym{L1,L2}:                       void swap(int t[], int i, int j) {
  @   \forall int a[], integer l h;                 int tmp = t[i]; t[i] = t[j]; t[j] = tmp;
  @   Permut{L1,L2}(a, l, h) ==>                  }
  @     Permut{L2,L1}(a, l, h) ;
  @ case Permut_trans{L1,L2,L3}:                  /*@ requires t != null;
  @   \forall int a[], integer l h;                @ assigns t[..];
  @   Permut{L1,L2}(a, l, h) &&                    @ behavior sorted:
  @   Permut{L2,L3}(a, l, h) ==>                   @   ensures Sorted{Here}(t,0,t.length);
  @     Permut{L1,L3}(a, l, h);                    @ behavior permutation:
  @ case Permut_swap{L1,L2}:                       @   ensures
  @   \forall int a[], integer l h i j;            @   Permut{Old,Here}(t,0,t.length);
  @   l <= i < h && l <= j < h &&                  @*/
  @   Swap{L1,L2}(a, i, j) ==>                     void selection_sort(int t[]) {
  @     Permut{L1,L2}(a, l, h) ;                     ...
  @ }                                             }
  @*/
```

Fig. 2. Krakatoa annotation language: illustration of hybrid symbols

2.2   The Krakatoa Specification Language

Krakatoa was historically the first front-end added to Why3 (actually to Why [22], the ancestor of Why3). It was designed in the context of the Verifi-Card European project, aiming to statically check properties of JavaCard source code [27]. The initial goal was to interpret contracts, added to the Java source code and written in JML [5].

A major feature of JML is that an existing Java method can be called in the clauses of a contract, provided it has no side-effects. This feature allows the user to design specific Java code for specifying the rest of the code, and indeed JML comes with a library of side-effect free Java classes implementing general-purpose structures like sets. This design choice implies that the specifications are exe-cutable, which is natural since JML was initially designed for run-time assertion checking. The primary tool for static checking of JML annotations was ESC-Java [5] now superseded by OpenJML [14]. A consequence of the choice of using pure Java methods in specifications is that ESC-Java must automatically turn them into logic symbols, which is a highly non-trivial task. Indeed, if such a Java method has itself a precondition, when should it be checked? Should the code or the contract of this method be used for specification? What if the method is not guaranteed to terminate? When should class invariants be checked? Leavens *et al.* [35] extensively discuss static versus dynamic verification for JML.

To avoid the issues of turning Java methods into logic symbols, it was decided in Krakatoa to forbid the use of Java method calls in specifications and provide access to Why's core logic instead [38]. This decision facilitates static verification, but removes the ability to execute specifications. It is to be noted however that when designing Krakatoa's specification language, we introduced the notion of so-called *hybrid* logic symbols: these are symbols whose definitions are not purely in the logic world but depend on the memory heap. Indeed they can even depend on several memory states, and this facility is made available to users using labels and JML's \at construct to refer to labels. This is exemplified by the annotated code for sorting an array of integers shown in Fig. 2. The type integer denotes unbounded mathematical integers. The predicate Permut is defined inductively by four clauses introduced by the keyword case, and depends on two memory states: Permut{L1,L2}(a,l,h) means that the elements of array a in memory states L1 and L2 can differ between indices l and h, by a permutation of elements, and are the same elsewhere. In the postconditions of the contracts, Old is used for L1 to refer to the pre-state of the method while Here is used for L2 to denote the post-state. Although the specifications seem quite involved, such a code is statically checked automatically using SMT solvers.

2.3   ACSL: The ANSI C Specification Language

Historically, the first C front-end of Why came quickly after the Java front-end and was implemented in the Caduceus tool [21]. There was no largely adopted specification language for C like JML, so a home-made specification language was designed. It is mostly reusing the same design choice as Krakatoa's variation on JML: specifications may use pure function symbols and not the C functions themselves.

The design of the Frama-C framework [30] started in 2006, aiming at analysis of C source code using various techniques. An open plug-in architecture was designed so that a user can choose among different kinds of analyses. Originally, plug-ins were provided for deductive verification and static verification using abstract interpretation. The language ACSL [3,4] was designed for attaching formal contracts to C functions. This language is also a way for plug-ins to communicate information.

Since the main initial objective of Frama-C was static verification, the ACSL language was largely inspired by Caduceus and Krakatoa. In particular, the same choice of using a first-order logic with total functions was made, the use of unbounded integer arithmetic was encouraged, and the notion of hybrid predicates showed up too.

Later on, the number of plug-ins available in Frama-C increased a lot, aiming at many different kinds of analyses and not just static verification (http://frama-c.com/plugins.html). With the increasing use of Frama-C in industrial applications [30], the need for dynamic verification approaches showed up. In the following we detail the design of the E-ACSL variation of ACSL, aiming at run-time verification.

2.4   E-ACSL: Run-Time Verification of ACSL Specifications

The E-ACSL plug-in [33] automatically translates a C program with ACSL annotations into another C program that reports a failure whenever an annotation
is violated at run time. If no annotation is violated, the functional behavior of
the new program is exactly the same as that of the original one. This plug-in
thus provides a run-time assertion checker in the same vein as the one for JML.
As such, it provides to the Frama-C environment the possibility to detect wrong
annotations using concrete execution of the program, that is one way to "debug"
specifications. Moreover, an executable specification makes it possible to check
assertions that cannot be verified statically, and thus to establish a link between
monitoring tools and static analysis tools [34]. An additional benefit of this plug-
in is that it helps in combining some Frama-C analyzers with other ones that do
not natively understand the ACSL specification language.

A major issue is that the initial design of ACSL did not take into account
the possibility of executing specifications. This is why the E-ACSL plug-in only
supports a subset of ACSL called E-ACSL [16,33]. The main features that are
excluded are: unbounded quantifications, that is quantification on sets that cannot be statically seen as finite; and logic symbols that are axiomatized. Support
of some ACSL clauses is not yet implemented (namely assigns clauses for
frame properties and decreases clauses for termination properties). However,
a significant effort was made to support the following important features.

Unbounded Mathematical Integers. These are compiled into C code, using GNU
Multi-Precision library [25] if needed. Moreover, a careful static analysis is performed to avoid use of GMP's unbounded integers in many cases, for instance
when the result of an arithmetical operation can still be represented by a machine
integer (of the same, or a longer C type). It was noted that in practice only few
uses of GMP integers are needed in the resulting code [16,28], meaning that
supporting unbounded integers does not induce a significant overhead.

Support for Memory-Related ACSL Constructs. ACSL provides built-in predicates that allow the user to express properties about the memory, for example
that a pointer refers to a valid memory location [3,4]. This is supported in
E-ACSL thanks to a custom C memory monitoring library, that tracks memory-
related C constructs (malloc and free functions, initialization of variables,
etc.) so that the generated instrumented code calls the monitoring library primitives to store validity and initialization information (whenever a memory location is allocated, deallocated and assigned), and to extract this information when
evaluating memory-related ACSL constructs. To optimize the performance of
the resulting code and avoid monitoring of irrelevant variables, a preliminary
backward dataflow analysis has been implemented to determine a correct over-
approximation of the set of memory locations that have to be monitored for a
given annotated program [28,32].

Coping with Underspecified Logic Functions. An annotation may contain underspecified functions (division by zero, but also access to an invalid pointer, etc.).
A design choice is not to model this kind of undefined behavior, but to report

an error instead. Technically, this is done by relying on the pre-existing Frama-C plug-in RTE dedicated to generate assertions from potential run-time errors. E-ACSL then translates the generated assertions as well. In practice, it means that an assertion such as

```
//@ assert (*p == *p);
```

although valid in any case in ACSL, will be reported as an error by E-ACSL when p is not valid, because RTE generates an assertion

```
//@ assert \valid(p);
```

This choice to have a different semantics in ACSL and E-ACSL with respect to underspecified functions follows the general observation by Chalin [7] that an end-user who writes ACSL annotations typically expects that an error is reported when dereferencing an invalid pointer in specifications.

2.5 SPARK2014: Static Verification of Ada 2012 Contracts

Historically, the SPARK toolset, up to version 2005, was using its own specification language, for static verification only. The new version of Ada in 2012 added a notion of contracts in the Ada language itself, in a similar fashion as Eiffel contracts: they can be checked dynamically, as the compiler turns these contracts into executable code. Then the new version SPARK2014 was redesigned, in order to use Ada2012 contracts as specification language, and a new static verification tool GNATprove was designed using Why3 as intermediate tool for VC generation.

The path followed by SPARK2014 is thus similar to JML, and the reverse of the path from ACSL to E-ACSL: a language initially designed for run-time checking had to be used in static verification. A major objective was to guarantee that the semantics of the contracts must be the same for both run-time checking and static checking. The main issues to achieve this objective are as follows.

Capture Undefinedness in Assertions. Any expression in contracts that may generate an error at run time (e.g. division by zero) should induce the generation of a verification condition that proves it is defined. This means that the GNATprove tool must analyze each expression to collect all possible run-time errors, and generate additional assertions for them. It is somehow very similar to the RTE plug-in of Frama-C.

Promote Program Procedures into Logic Functions. This is the same issue ESC-Java had to solve in order to handle Java methods in specifications. The solution adopted by SPARK is to completely forbid side-effects in functions used in specifications. Such a check is quite easy to perform in the context of SPARK because there are strict coding rules for an Ada program to be in the SPARK fragment: pointers are forbidden, aliasing is forbidden, and a dataflow analysis is performed to collect read and write effects. Also, Ada 2012 has the notion of expression-functions, whose translation into logic is immediate. In fact, the work on SPARK2014 was influential in getting expression-functions into Ada 2012, so that they can be used in static verification.

Providing Access to Non-executable Datatypes. It turns out that for complex specifications it is important to provide extra datatypes. Datatypes that are often needed are collections. In SPARK, there is a library of collections that are specifically designed for simultaneous use in dynamic and static verification [17]. The user can even design her own library of non-executable datatypes, using the so-called *external axiomatizations*, for example to support unbounded integers in proof. Partial support for unbounded integers is also available by selecting a compilation switch, which ensures that intermediate computations are performed in arbitrary precision: in SPARK, there is a library for unbounded arithmetic that is used for this purpose. When the switch is selected, contracts with arithmetic computations can be both dynamically checked with this library and also interpreted as mathematical integers in static verification.

Type Invariants. In Ada, dynamic verification of type invariants is partial, for efficiency reason. It is only done at exit of public procedures of a package, and only for types that are defined in the same package. The JML run-time assertion checker has similar restrictions when checking class invariants. In the SPARK subset of Ada, appropriate restrictions on the expressions used in invariants were chosen so that verification of invariants can be done statically. It is important to notice that non-aliasing restrictions of SPARK are crucial to be able to check invariants in a sound way. Why3 has a similar notion of type invariants, and their sound static verification is also possible thanks to non-aliasing restrictions. On the contrary, there is no Frama-C plug-in today that can statically check ACSL's type invariants because of the potential aliasing in C data structures.

2.6   Mixed Static-Dynamic Verification in Frama-C and SPARK2014

As seen above, both Frama-C and SPARK2014 have different techniques and tools to check specifications either statically or dynamically. A natural question that arises is whether it is safe to mix these various kinds of verification techniques on the same program. Both Frama-C and SPARK2014 have tool support to ensure consistency of verification activities.

The Frama-C kernel is the central core that communicates with all the plug-ins. When a given plug-in is able to verify that some annotation is valid, it is usually under the assumption that some other annotations are valid. For example, when a static verification plug-in can prove that a postcondition for a procedure is valid, it is under the hypothesis that the pre-condition holds. To ensure consistency, the Frama-C kernel attaches to each annotation some information status: it tells which plug-in validates it, together with the set of other annotations that are assumed by this plug-in [15]. The graph of dependencies between annotations that are assumed or proved can be displayed graphically, and it is checked automatically whether every specification has been proved by at least one plug-in.

Combining static and dynamic verification in SPARK is possible and indeed expected, including when the program also contains non-SPARK Ada code. SPARK reconciles the logic semantics and executable semantics of contracts, so users can execute contracts, debug them like code, and test them when formal verification is too difficult to achieve. Furthermore, by keeping the annotation language the same as the programming language, users don't have to learn another language. Like Ada has been designed to integrate smoothly with parts of the application written in C, SPARK has been designed to integrate smoothly with parts of the application written in Ada outside of the SPARK subset. Hence, a SPARK application may consist of functions in SPARK, Ada and C being linked together. While formal verification can be applied to the SPARK part of the application, this is not the case for the Ada part or (unless the user also uses Frama-C) the C part. Those parts should be verified using traditional verification techniques based on testing and reviews. The overall verification argument may be composed from individual verification arguments on the SPARK subprograms (using formal verification) and Ada or C subprograms (using other techniques), based on the subprogram contracts used in formal verification. Indeed, the assumptions made during formal verification of a subprogram can be verified during testing of another function called by or calling the first one: preconditions and postconditions can be executed with the very same semantics that they have in proofs. SPARK2014 offers a similar mechanism as Frama-C [29] to check what is proved, by which technique, under which assumptions.

3   Ghost Variables and Ghost Code

A *ghost variable* is a variable that is added to a given program only for the purpose of formal specification. This notion is reminiscent from the notion of auxiliary variables in Hoare logic. These variables typically need to be assigned, during the normal execution of the program: this is done by adding *ghost code*.

As an illustrative example, consider Euclide's algorithm to compute the greatest common divisor d of two integers x and y. One may want to state as a postcondition the Bézout property: there exist integers a and b such that $d = ax + by$. A postcondition with an existential quantification is typically hard to prove by automatic provers. Moreover, in this particular example, the property itself is a non-trivial mathematical one. It is a typical example where ghost code can help: in that example, the values of a and b can be computed during execution of the algorithm itself. A program in C annotated in ACSL is shown in Fig. 3. The ghost variables a, b, c and d store coefficients, modified in the ghost code of the loop body, so that they keep satisfying Bézout-like properties as described by the loop invariants.

Another example of ghost code is an alternative way to specify the permutation property of a sorting algorithm: instead of an inductive predicate as in Fig. 2, a sorting algorithm may return a ghost array, mapping the interval of indexes $[0 \ldots n-1]$ to itself in a bijective way, expressing the permutation of elements before and after sorting. The content of this ghost array can be updated

```
/*@ requires x >= 0 && y >= 0;
  @ ensures \exists integer a,b; a*x+b*y == \result;
  @*/
int gcd(int x, int y) {
  //@ ghost integer a = 1, b = 0, c = 0, d = 1;
  /*@ loop invariant x >= 0 && y >= 0 ;
    @ loop invariant a*\at(x,Pre)+b*\at(y,Pre) == x ;
    @ loop invariant c*\at(x,Pre)+d*\at(y,Pre) == y ;
    @ loop variant y;
    @*/
  while (y > 0) {
    int r = x % y;
    //@ ghost integer q = x / y;
    x = y; y = r;
    //@ ghost integer ta = a, tb = b;
    //@ ghost a = c, b = d, c = ta - c * q, d = tb - d * q;
  }
  return x;
}
```

Fig. 3. Ghost code for computing Bézout coefficients

with ghost code during the sorting algorithm, so that it keeps representing the permutation of elements from the initial array to its current state.

3.1   Ghost Code in Why3

The ability to set a ghost attribute to variable declarations and to arbitrary code is natively part of the WhyML language. The Why3 type system ensures that ghost code must not interfere with regular code, in the sense that it can be erased without observable difference in the program outcome. In particular, ghost data is forbidden to participate in regular computations and ghost code can neither mutate regular data nor diverge [20]. There are numerous and various examples of code that naturally need ghost code for their formal specification and their proof (http://toccata.lri.fr/gallery/ghost.en.html).

Lemma Functions. Beyond instrumenting the regular code, ghost code is an effective way to guide the automatic provers in static verification. Ghost code can be used to prove properties: if one writes a ghost function with a contract of the form

let $f(x_1 : \tau_1, \ldots, x_n : \tau_n) : \tau$
   requires *Pre*
   variant *var*
   ensures *Post*

and if this function has no side-effect and is proved terminating (with the decreasing measure *var* given by the `variant` clause), then it is a constructive proof of

$$\forall x_1, \ldots, x_n, \exists result, Pre \Rightarrow Post$$

In particular, if f is defined recursively, it simulates a proof by induction: the VC generator effectively generates the cases of an induction scheme. This technique of using programs to make proofs is nowadays called "auto-active verification" and is available in several other verification environments [36,44].

Lemma functions are often used in complex programs proved in Why3, for example to deal with recursive data structures [11] or to reason on semantics [12]. The most complex case study of static verification using Why3 up to now, a verified first-order prover [13], makes extensive use of ghost code and lemma functions.

3.2   Static and Dynamic Verification of Ghost Code

Ghost code is not only useful for static verification. It may be executed under some conditions, and thus is equally helpful for run-time verification: it can monitor properties dynamically. Environments like JML and Spec# have ghost variables and ghost code, primarily for run-time execution. Dafny also has a notion of lemma functions.

Ghost Code in Frama-C. In Frama-C, ghost code is just regular C code located in ACSL comments. As such, it is naturally possible to use it for static verification [6], and to execute it with E-ACSL. However, Frama-C has currently some limitations with respect to ghost code: unlike what is specified in the ACSL design [3,4], the current implementation of Frama-C only allows ghost variables to have a C type, not a logic type like unbounded integers. This, of course, simplifies execution of ghost code, but limits the ghost capabilities for static verification. As such, the example of Fig. 3 is not accepted because the ghost variables are declared as `integer` (unbounded mathematical integers of ACSL), so to statically check this code one currently needs to turn them into `int` and ignore overflow checks. Another current limitation is that the kernel does not check that ghost code does not interfere with regular code like in Why3. Statically checking this property is much more difficult in C than in Why3, because C allows arbitrary aliasing whereas Why3 controls aliasing statically [20].

Ghost Code in SPARK2014. In SPARK, ghost code is declared using an Ada aspect `Ghost` on the declaration. In the design of ghost code in SPARK, it was mandatory to be able to check non-interference of ghost code with regular code. In particular the compiler must be able to eliminate ghost code if the user wants to compile a program without ghost. Unlike the case of Frama-C, SPARK2014 can statically check, like Why3, the non-interference of ghost code. This is because SPARK code must follow strong non-aliasing properties (checked by data-flow analysis) and coding rules (http://docs.adacore.com/spark2014-docs/html/lrm/subprograms.html#ghost-entities).

As in other systems, ghost variables in SPARK are typically used for keeping intermediate values, keeping memory of previous states, or logging previous events (http://docs.adacore.com/spark2014-docs/html/ug/spark_2014.html#ghost-code). Various uses of ghost are presented in examples of the

SPARK manual (http://www.spark-2014.org/entries/detail/manual-proof-in-spark-2014): ghost code can be used to encode a state machine (functional properties of the Tetris game http://blog.adacore.com/tetris-in-spark-on-on-arm-cortex-m4) or to model a file system (proving standard Ada Get_Line function http://blog.adacore.com/formal-verification-of-legacy-code). Ghost code was extensively used in high-level specifications of memory allocators [18].

A limitation with respect to ghost code, similar to Frama-C, is the executability of ghost code in case of use of external axiomatizations: in that case the compiler would refuse to compile ghost code into run-time checks.

4 Understanding Proof Failures

In static verification, a major issue is understanding the reason why some proof fails. There are various reasons why it may fail:

1. The property to prove is indeed invalid: the code is not correct with respect to the given specification.
2. The property is in fact valid, but is not proved, for two possible reasons:
   a. The prover is not able to obtain a proof (in the given time and memory limits): this is the incompleteness of the proof search;
   b. The proof may need extra (or stronger) intermediate annotations, such as loop invariants, or more complete contracts of the subprograms.

For the user to be able to fix the code or the specification of her program, it is essential to understand into which of the above cases any undischarged VC falls. A general solution is to generate *counterexamples* in order to illustrate the issue on concrete values. This capability exists in different forms in Why3, SPARK2014 and Frama-C.

4.1 Counterexamples from SMT Models

A first solution is to exploit the SMT solvers' capability of generating *models*. Indeed, to discharge a given VC, the SMT solver is given the hypotheses and the negation of the goal, and it is asked to prove unsatisfiability. In case of failure, the SMT solver provides a model that can be turned into a counterexample for the initial program. This is how it is implemented in Why3 and SPARK2014 [26]. In Frama-C, the Counter-Example plug-in implements the very same idea [30], but it is still a not-yet-released research prototype which only supports a few constructs.

There are actually some issues with this approach, which limit its applicability. A first issue is related to the *incompleteness* of the solver: in presence of non-linear integer arithmetic, or arbitrary quantification, the logic is not decidable so the solver may time out. Second, when a model is generated, it can only lead to a *potential* counterexample, and the user still has to understand what should be fixed if it is not a true one. That is due to the solver's vision of the program, in which the code of a called function and the body of a loop are replaced by the corresponding *subcontracts*: the contract of the callee and the loop invariant, respectively. Thus, such a counterexample can illustrate either Reason 1 above (non-compliance between the code and the specification) or Reason 2b above (the code is in fact compliant to the specification, but the contracts of some callees or loops are too weak to complete the proof). Run-time checking of the program for such a counterexample candidate can be used to distinguish these cases.

4.2 Counterexamples from Testing

In Frama-C, the StaDy plug-in has been designed to generate counterexamples [41]. Unlike above, the technique does not rely on a counter-model generated by the prover, it is based on test generation instead. The annotations of the input program are first transformed into C code similarly to the E-ACSL plug-in. The instrumented code is then passed to a Dynamic Symbolic Execution (DSE) testing tool that tries to find tests producing annotation failures. An interesting aspect is that with this approach it is possible (using two different instrumentation techniques) to distinguish between a non-compliance (Reason 1 above) and a subcontract weakness (Reason 2b above). Other potential benefits come from the capacity of DSE to focus on one path at a time, and to use concrete values when the constraints are too complex for a solver. The main limitation of this approach is related to the combinatorial explosion of the path space to be explored by the test generation tool. Other related approaches have been reported in the context of Eiffel [43] and Dafny [10].

All these techniques being relatively recent, more research is required to better evaluate and understand their benefits and limitations in practice.

| | Why3 | Krakatoa | Frama-C | | SPARK |
			ACSL	E-ACSL	
Executable contracts	no	no	no	yes	yes
Only total functions in logic	yes	yes	yes	no[1]	no[2]
Unbounded integers in logic	yes	yes	yes	yes	no[3]
Unbounded quantification	yes	yes	yes	no	no
Ghost code	yes	partial[4]	partial[5]	partial[5]	yes
Counterexamples from solvers	yes	no	partial[6]	partial[6]	yes
Counterexamples from testing	no	no	no	yes[7]	no

[1] Run-time checks for well-definedness are generated.
[2] Run-time checks and VCs for well-definedness are generated.
[3] See discussion in Section 2.5.
[4] Non-interference with regular code is not checked.
[5] Only executable C code, and non-interference with regular code is not checked.
[6] The dedicated plug-in Counter-Example is not yet publicly available.
[7] The test generation tool PathCrawler, underlying StaDy, is currently not publicly available.

Fig. 4. Comparison of features supported by specification languages

5 Conclusions and Future Work

We have surveyed, in the context of Why3, Frama-C and SPARK2014, various cases where dynamic verification supplement static verification. The first one is related to verification by testing those parts of the program that are too complex to prove formally, and a safe combination of tests and proofs. We have also discussed the use of ghost code, essential for formally specifying complex functional behaviors and exploitable by both static and dynamic approaches. The third case — understanding the reason why a proof fails — can rely again either on a static method (exploiting the counter-model returned by an SMT solver) or a dynamic one (applying test generation on a code instrumented with executable annotations). Figure 4 summarizes the various aspects supported or not by the considered tools.

We emphasized the role of non-aliasing restrictions in Why3 and SPARK2014, which permits to check type invariants in a sound way, and also to statically check the non-interference of ghost code with regular code. We conclude with a few issues that are worth investigating further.

Need for Executability of Pure Logic Types. We have seen that using unbounded mathematical integers in specifications is natural in static verification, and can be supported in dynamic verification thanks to the use of libraries implementing unbounded integers. There are many other logic theories used in static verification (as present e.g. in Why3's standard library) and each of them should come with an executable counterpart to be able to use it dynamically. It should be done in a systematic way, that is, by synthesizing executable code from axiomatization [31]. A particular hard case is that of real numbers: it is a theory that is quite well supported in automatic provers, but there is no obvious solution how to provide an executable version of real numbers. Some authors propose approximation methods for that purpose [19,24].

Need for Unbounded Quantification. To be executable, quantification in formulas must necessarily range over finite sets. However, there are examples where specification requires quantification over infinitely many data, for instance, the solution of "patience game" from the VScomp competition in 2014 (http://toccata.lri.fr/gallery/patience.en.html) needs quantification over infinitely many sequences. JML and SPARK languages syntactically impose finite ranges of quantification so that the specification of this example can simply not be written. On that specific matter, there is still a gap between static and dynamic verification that needs to be filled.

References

1. Barnes, J.: Programming in Ada 2012. Cambridge University Press, Cambridge (2014)
2. Barnett, M., Leino, K.R.M., Schulte, W.: The Spec# programming system: an overview. In: Barthe, G., Burdy, L., Huisman, M., Lanet, J.-L., Muntean, T. (eds.) CASSIS 2004. LNCS, vol. 3362, pp. 49–69. Springer, Heidelberg (2005). doi:10.1007/978-3-540-30569-9_3

3. Baudin, P., Filliâtre, J.C., Marché, C., Monate, B., Moy, Y., Prevosto, V.: ACSL: ANSI/ISO C Specification Language, Version 1.10 (2013). http://frama-c.cea.fr/acsl.html

4. Bulwahn, L.: The new quickcheck for Isabelle. In: Hawblitzel, C., Miller, D. (eds.) CPP 2012. LNCS, vol. 7679, pp. 92–108. Springer, Heidelberg (2012)

5. Burdy, L., Cheon, Y., Cok, D.R., Ernst, M.D., Kiniry, J.R., Leavens, G.T., Leino, K.R.M., Poll, E.: An overview of JML tools and applications. Intl. J. Softw. Tools Technol. Transf. **7**(3), 212–232 (2005)

6. Burghardt, J., Gerlach, J., Lapawczyk, T., Carben, A., Gu, L., Hartig, K., Pohl, H., Soto, J., Völlinger, K.: ACSL by example, towards a verified C standard library. Version 11.11 for Frama-C Sodium. Technical report, Fraunhofer FOKUS (2015). http://publica.fraunhofer.de/dokumente/N-364387.html

7. Chalin, P.: Logical foundations of program assertions: what do practitioners want? In: SEFM, pp. 383–393. IEEE Computer Society (2005)

8. Chalin, P.: Reassessing JML's logical foundation. In: Proceedings of the 7th Workshop on Formal Techniques for Java-like Programs (FTfJP 2005), Glasgow, Scotland (2005)

9. Chapman, R., Schanda, F.: Are we there yet? 20 years of industrial theorem proving with SPARK. In: Klein, G., Gamboa, R. (eds.) ITP 2014. LNCS, vol. 8558, pp. 17–26. Springer, Heidelberg (2014). doi:10.1007/978-3-319-08970-6_2

10. Christakis, M., Leino, K.R.M., Müller, P., Wüstholz, V.: Integrated environment for diagnosing verification errors. In: Chechik, M., Raskin, J.-F. (eds.) TACAS 2016. LNCS, vol. 9636, pp. 424–441. Springer, Heidelberg (2016). doi:10.1007/978-3-662-49674-9_25

11. Clochard, M.: Automatically verified implementation of data structures based on AVL trees. In: Giannakopoulou, D., Kroening, D. (eds.) VSTTE 2014. LNCS, vol. 8471, pp. 167–180. Springer, Heidelberg (2014)

12. Clochard, M., Filliâtre, J.-C., Marché, C., Paskevich, A.: Formalizing semantics with an automatic program verifier. In: Giannakopoulou, D., Kroening, D. (eds.) VSTTE 2014. LNCS, vol. 8471, pp. 37–51. Springer, Heidelberg (2014). doi:10.1007/978-3-319-12154-3_3

13. Clochard, M., Marché, C., Paskevich, A.: Verified programs with binders. In: Programming Languages meets Program Verification (PLPV). ACM Press (2014)

14. Cok, D.R.: OpenJML: software verification for Java 7 using JML, OpenJDK, and Eclipse. In: F-IDE 2014. EPTCS 149, pp. 79–92 (2014)

15. Correnson, L., Signoles, J.: Combining analyses for C program verification. In: Stoelinga, M., Pinger, R. (eds.) FMICS 2012. LNCS, vol. 7437, pp. 108–130. Springer, Heidelberg (2012). doi:10.1007/978-3-642-32469-7_8

16. Delahaye, M., Kosmatov, N., Signoles, J.: Common specification language for static and dynamic analysis of C programs. In: SAC, pp. 1230–1235. ACM (2013)

17. Dross, C., Filliâtre, J.-C., Moy, Y.: Correct code containing containers. In: Gogolla, M., Wolff, B. (eds.) TAP 2011. LNCS, vol. 6706, pp. 102–118. Springer, Heidelberg (2011). doi:10.1007/978-3-642-21768-5_9

18. Dross, C., Moy, Y.: Abstract software specifications and automatic proof of refinement. In: RSSR (2016). http://www.spark-2014.org/entries/detail/spark-prez-at-new-conference-on-railway-systems

19. Dufour, J.L.: B extended to floating-point numbers: is it sufficient for proving avionics software? In: Formal Methods Applied to Complex Systems. Wiley (2014)

20. Filliâtre, J.C., Gondelman, L., Paskevich, A.: The spirit of ghost code. In: Formal Methods in System Design (2016, to appear)

21. Filliâtre, J.-C., Marché, C.: Multi-prover verification of C programs. In: Davies, J., Schulte, W., Barnett, M. (eds.) ICFEM 2004. LNCS, vol. 3308, pp. 15–29. Springer, Heidelberg (2004). doi:10.1007/978-3-540-30482-1_10
22. Filliâtre, J.-C., Marché, C.: The why/krakatoa/caduceus platform for deductive program verification. In: Damm, W., Hermanns, H. (eds.) CAV 2007. LNCS, vol. 4590, pp. 173–177. Springer, Heidelberg (2007). doi:10.1007/978-3-540-73368-3_21
23. Filliâtre, J.-C., Paskevich, A.: Why3 — where programs meet provers. In: Felleisen, M., Gardner, P. (eds.) ESOP 2013. LNCS, vol. 7792, pp. 125–128. Springer, Heidelberg (2013)
24. Gao, S., Avigad, J., Clarke, E.M.: Delta-complete decision procedures for satisfiability over the reals. CoRR abs/1204.3513 (2012). http://arxiv.org/abs/1204.3513
25. GMP: GNU multiple precision arithmetic library. https://gmplib.org/
26. Hauzar, D., Marché, C., Moy, Y.: Counter examples from proof failures in SPARK. In: De Nicola, R., Kühn, E. (eds.) SEFM 2016. LNCS, vol. 9763, pp. 215–233. Springer, Heidelberg (2016). doi:10.1007/978-3-319-41591-8_15
27. Jacobs, B., Marché, C., Rauch, N.: Formal verification of a commercial smart card applet with multiple tools. In: Rattray, C., Maharaj, S., Shankland, C. (eds.) AMAST 2004. LNCS, vol. 3116, pp. 241–257. Springer, Heidelberg (2004). doi:10.1007/978-3-540-27815-3_21
28. Jakobsson, A., Kosmatov, N., Signoles, J.: Rester statique pour devenir plus rapide, plus précis et plus mince. In: JFLA (2015)
29. Kanig, J., Chapman, R., Comar, C., Guitton, J., Moy, Y., Rees, E.: Explicit assumptions - a prenup for marrying static and dynamic program verification. In: Seidl, M., Tillmann, N. (eds.) TAP 2014. LNCS, vol. 8570, pp. 142–157. Springer, Heidelberg (2014). doi:10.1007/978-3-319-09099-3_11
30. Kirchner, F., Kosmatov, N., Prevosto, V., Signoles, J., Yakobowski, B.: Frama-C: a software analysis perspective. Formal Aspects of Computing, pp. 1–37 (2015)
31. Kneuss, E., Kuraj, I., Kuncak, V., Suter, P.: Synthesis modulo recursive functions. In: OOPSLA, pp. 407–426. ACM (2013)
32. Kosmatov, N., Petiot, G., Signoles, J.: An optimized memory monitoring for runtime assertion checking of C programs. In: Legay, A., Bensalem, S. (eds.) RV 2013. LNCS, vol. 8174, pp. 167–182. Springer, Heidelberg (2013). doi:10.1007/978-3-642-40787-1_10
33. Kosmatov, N., Signoles, J.: A lesson on runtime assertion checking with Frama-C. In: Legay, A., Bensalem, S. (eds.) RV 2013. LNCS, vol. 8174, pp. 386–399. Springer, Heidelberg (2013). doi:10.1007/978-3-642-40787-1_29
34. Kosmatov, N., Signoles, J.: Runtime assertion checking and its combinations with static and dynamic analyses. In: Seidl, M., Tillmann, N. (eds.) TAP 2014. LNCS, vol. 8570, pp. 165–168. Springer, Heidelberg (2014). doi:10.1007/978-3-319-09099-3_13
35. Leavens, G.T., Cheon, Y., Clifton, C., Ruby, C., Cok, D.R.: How the design of JML accomodates both runtime assertion checking and formal verification. Technical report 03-04, Iowa State University (2003)
36. Leino, K.R.M.: Automating induction with an SMT solver. In: Kuncak, V., Rybalchenko, A. (eds.) VMCAI 2012. LNCS, vol. 7148, pp. 315–331. Springer, Heidelberg (2012). doi:10.1007/978-3-642-27940-9_21
37. Leino, K.R.M., Wüstholz, V.: The Dafny integrated development environment. In: F-IDE. Electronic Proceedings in Theoretical Computer Science, vol. 149, pp. 3–15 (2014)

38. Marché, C., Paulin-Mohring, C., Urbain, X.: The KRAKATOA tool for certification of JAVA/JAVACARD programs annotated in JML. J. Logic Algebraic Program. **58**(1–2), 89–106 (2004)
39. McCormick, J.W., Chapin, P.C.: Building High Integrity Applications with SPARK. Cambridge University Press, Cambridge (2015)
40. Meyer, B.: Object-Oriented Software Construction, 1st edn. Prentice-Hall Inc., Upper Saddle River (1988)
41. Petiot, G., Kosmatov, N., Botella, B., Giorgetti, A., Julliand, J.: Your proof fails? Testing helps to find the reason. In: Aichernig, B.K.K., Furia, C.A.A. (eds.) TAP 2016. LNCS, vol. 9762, pp. 130–150. Springer, Heidelberg (2016). doi:10.1007/978-3-319-41135-4_8
42. Signoles, J.: Software architecture of code analysis frameworks matters: the Frama-C example. In: F-IDE, pp. 86–96 (2015)
43. Tschannen, J., Furia, C.A., Nordio, M., Meyer, B.: Program checking with less hassle. In: Cohen, E., Rybalchenko, A. (eds.) VSTTE 2013. LNCS, vol. 8164, pp. 149–169. Springer, Heidelberg (2014). doi:10.1007/978-3-642-54108-7_8
44. Tschannen, J., Furia, C.A., Nordio, M., Polikarpova, N.: AutoProof: auto-active functional verification of object-oriented programs. In: Baier, C., Tinelli, C. (eds.) TACAS 2015. LNCS, vol. 9035, pp. 566–580. Springer, Heidelberg (2015). doi:10.1007/978-3-662-46681-0_53

Considering Typestate Verification
for Quantified Event Automata

Giles Reger[✉]

University of Manchester, Manchester, UK
giles.reger@manchester.ac.uk

Abstract. This paper discusses how the existing static analyses developed for typestate properties may be extended to a more expressive class of properties expressible by a specification formalism originally developed for runtime verification. The notion of typestate was introduced as a refinement of the notion of type and captures the allowed operations in certain contexts (states) as a subset of those operations allowed on the type. Typestates therefore represent per-object safety properties. There exist effective static analysis techniques for checking typestate properties and this has been an area of research since typestates were first introduced in 1986. It has already been observed that common properties monitored in runtime verification activities take the form of typestate properties. Additionally, the notion of typestate has been extended to reflect the more expressive properties seen in this area and additional static and dynamic analyses have been introduced. This paper considers a highly expressive specification language for runtime verification, quantified event automata, and discusses how these could be viewed as typestate properties and if/how the static analysis techniques could be updated accordingly. The details have not been worked out yet and are not presented, this is intended for later work.

1 Introduction

This paper describes preliminary work considering the relationship between the typestate verification static analysis technique and a specification language for dynamic analysis (runtime verification). There are two main motivations behind this work:

1. Such static analyses can be used to reduce the amount of work required at runtime by partially evaluating properties (as shown in previous work [8,27]); and
2. The considered specification language (originally for runtime verification) can express properties not currently considered for static analysis and extending these analyses could strengthen such techniques.

Typestate properties [34] typically take the form of finite state machines attached to single types. This is also a common form of specification in runtime verification [14] and the relationship between the two has been explored previously [1,8].

© Springer International Publishing AG 2016
T. Margaria and B. Steffen (Eds.): ISoLA 2016, Part I, LNCS 9952, pp. 479–495, 2016.
DOI: 10.1007/978-3-319-47166-2_33

However, runtime verification typically considers more expressive properties such as non-safety properties, quantification over multiple objects, arbitrary state and existential quantification. The extension to multi-object typestates is must common in runtime verification (e.g. in the JavaMOP work [26]) and has already been explored [8,27] in the context of typestate analysis. In this work I consider the expressive specification language of quantified event automata (QEA) [4] that captures all of the above mentioned extensions. This is based on the parametric trace slicing [11] approach but introduces additional language features taking it far beyond what has currently been considered in typestate analysis.

This paper considers how QEA can be related to typestate and how the related static analysis techniques from typestate verification could be extended to support these more expressive properties.

Scope. I restrict my attention to typestate verification and review the relevant related topics in the next section. Notably I have not yet looked at *dependent types* [9] which seem heavily related (this relation is touched on in [13,25]). Although gradual typing is discussed briefly. I have also (so far) omitted extensions of JML with temporal constraints [20,22,35]. It seems likely that including these topics, and other automata-based verification techniques (e.g. [15]), will shed further light on possible ways to combine static and dynamic analysis for quantified event automata.

Structure. I begin by reviewing typestate verification (Sect. 2) and the quantified event automata specification language (Sect. 3). I then discuss the extensions of typestate required to support QEA and the possible static analysis extensions to support this (Sect. 4). I conclude with a discussion of plans for the future (Sect. 5).

2   A Review of Typestate Verification

Typestate properties [34] were introduced as a programming language concept. Whilst the initial work did not consider a language with objects, the notion has become associated with allowable operations on objects. In general, whilst types restrict the operations that can be performed on an object of that type, there may be different contexts in which only a subset of those operations should be allowed. Types are extended with a notion of state where only certain operations are allowed in each state. Each object of a type has a typestate with some operations updating the state i.e. a typestate property describes a finite state machine.

For example, the following typestate for a File type only allows **open** operations in the CLOSED state and allows **read** and **close** operations in the OPEN state with the **open** and **close** operations changing the state.

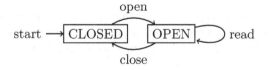

Typestate properties are safety properties i.e. they define behaviour that should always happen and can be violated by a finite trace. Importantly, the language described be a typestate property is *prefix closed*. A consequence of this is that a violation has a single witness in the code i.e. an instruction that causes failure.

At this point it is probably worth pointing out that there are two approaches to typestate verification in the literature:

1. The largest body of work focuses on developing new type systems and programming language concepts
2. Other work focusses on existing languages and programs and considers adding typestate support to these

Whilst more work has been done in the first area I am more interested in the second.

2.1 Typestate Verification

Verification of typestate properties is straightforward in the sense that one only needs to construct the *control-flow graph* (CFG) of the program and track each instance of an object. Here an instance of an object is introduced wherever an object is created in the code and that instance is identified by the variable it was assigned to. For certain classes of typestate properties and programs there exist polynomial time algorithms for verification [16]. For example, if a program is shallow (pointers are single-level i.e. allocated objects may not contain pointers) and the property is omission-closed (omitting an event from a valid trace gives a valid trace) then the problem can be reduced to a reachability problem over a graph of polynomial size (as in the IFDS framework [31]).

However, this process becomes non-trivial in the presence of *aliasing* and in the case of single-object typestates (see below for an alternative) most of the effort is concerned with the aliasing issue. The issue is that when objects can be aliased it is not possible to track a single typestate per object any more. Instead it is necessary to track an *abstract object* referring to possible objects and their possible states. The soundness of such techniques depends on the precision of the approach used to disambiguate pointer references. Note that (in general) typestate verification is undecidable in the presence of recursive data structures [23,28]; a further motivation for combination with dynamic techniques.

There are two general approaches to pointer analysis: *alias analysis* [3] and *points-to* analysis [2,33]. Alias analysis computes a set of pairs of variables that may or must point to the same location. Similarly, points-to analysis computes, for each pointer, the (points-to) set of variables that p may or must point to. Clearly these are similar techniques. To be useful, approaches generally take the form of *whole-program analysis* (i.e. interprocedural analysis) which requires the complete source code. Precision then depends on whether it is *context* and *flow* sensitive i.e. if it considers call-points or instruction order. Fink et al. utilise a context and flow sensitive analysis for typestate verification [17]. Requiring the full source code can be restrictive and whole-program analysis can be expensive. An alternative, modular, approach is to restrict or annotate aliasing to provide the analysis with enough information to reason about aliased objects effectively. For example, Bierhoff and Aldrich add a notion of *access permissions* [7] to typestates.

An additional concern is *subtyping* i.e. if a type has an associated typestate what should we require of its subtypes. This is dealt with by the notion of behavioural subtyping [24] which dictates the allowed behaviours of subtypes. This is most easily dealt with in the case where typestates are built-in to the programming language and there have been various type systems developed to deal with such cases within the context of typestate verification [6,13]. I am not aware of any work that deals with this issue without introducing a new type system.

2.2   Multi-object Typestates

Whilst the most common application of typestates remains the augmentation of an object type with a notion of state, it has been observed that it can be useful to define and check *multi-object* typestates. The above property on files only considered objects of File type and was therefore *single-object*. If we want to capture properties of the relationship between objects then necessarily we must refer to multiple objects. For example, the property that before reading from a FileReader object associated with a File we must first check that we have read access to the File. Here there are two objects related by the fact that the FileReader is associated with a particular File. Checking this property not only requires us to track the aliasing of each single object but also the relationships between objects. We will see further examples of these *multi-object* typestates later. There are two approaches to handling multi-object typestates.

The first approach is to keep the single-object view and include predicates on related (referenced) objects. In [7] the concept of *access permissions* are added to typestate to additionally indicate (i) how a reference is allowed to modify the referenced object, and (ii) how the object may be accessed through other references. This concept is, therefore, tightly related to aliasing. Figure 1 gives such a typestate property for the well known *UnsafeIterator* property that states that an iterator created from a collection should not be used after the collection is updated. Here this is achieved by line 20 which says (roughly) that whilst the collection is read-only (immutable) then the iterator is accessible (only) by the given reference (unique). Therefore, if the collection is updated then the iterator loses its access permission (cannot be used) thus preventing concurrent modification (the above property). This relates the collection (*this*) and the iterator (*result*) by placing a restriction on the iterator dependent on some property of the collection. Note the two states available and end on Iterator to indicate when it is safe to call next (see lines 5, 6 and 8). Clearly this property captures more than the traditional *UnsafeIterator* property i.e. it restricts usage of the iterator object further.

```
 1  interface Iterator<C : Collection , k : Fract> {
 2    states available, end refine alive
 3
 4    boolean hasNext() :
 5      pure(this) —o <(result = true ⊗ pure(this) in available)
 6                   ⊗ (result = false ⊗ pure(this) in end))
 7    Object next():
 8      full(this) in available —o full(this)
 9
10    void finalize ():
11      unique(this) —o immutable(c,k)
12  }
13
14  interface Collection {
15    void add(Object o) : full(this) —o full(this)
16    int size() : pure(this) —o result ≥ 0 ⊗ pure(this)
17    // remove(), contains() etc similar
18
19    Iterator<this,k> iterator ():
20      immutable(this,k) —o unique(result)
21  }
```

Fig. 1. Example of a typestate property with access permissions taken from [7].

The second approach is to specify multi-object typestates as separate entities. The only existing formalism for this seems to be that of tracematches [1]. These were first introduced as an extension of the AspectJ AOP system to temporal pointcuts i.e. instead of matching single points in the code a regular expression was given to match sequences of points. The semantics is based on slicing (as described later) and is suffix-matching. Figure 2 gives a tracematch property for the *UnsafeIterator* property described above. Lines 2–7 relate abstract events to specific points in the code and line 9 gives a (suffix-matching) regular expression that captures violation of the property. This is defined separately from the code, with the matching parts of the code used to identify events, following the AOP style. Then the tracematches are *weaved* into the code in a separate compilation step that adds additional instrumentation and inserts the specified code fragment wherever a match occurs.

```
 1  tracematch(Iterator i, DataSource ds){
 2    sym create_iter after returning (i):
 3      call(Iterator DataSource.iterator()) && target (ds);
 4    sym call_next before:
 5      call(Object Iterator.next()) && target(i);
 6    sym update_source after:
 7      call (* DataSource.update (..)) && target(ds);
 8
 9    create_iter call_next* update_source+ call_next
10    {
11      throw new ConcurrentModificationException ();
12    }
13  }
```

Fig. 2. A tracematch property for the *UnsafeIterator* property from [1].

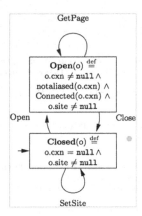

Fig. 3. Illustration of typestate with state invariants labelling states taken from [13].

The two main pieces of work in this second area both consider a setting where a tracematch property will be dynamically checked and static analysis is employed to remove instrumentation points in the code i.e. the property is partially evaluated statically. The Clara [8] work implements a number of increasingly precise analyses for partial evaluation. The most effective analysis is a flow-insensitive analysis that computes the may-point-to sets of variables in each transition statement and removes transition sequences without overlapping sets, as these would not relate to consistent bindings. Naeem and Lhotak [27] introduce an updated (operational) semantics for tracematches making them more suitable for static analysis. They then use this to introduce a technique for alias analysis to allow flow-sensitive tracking of individual objects along control flow paths. The final analysis conceptually tracks tracematch states for combinations of relevant objects (e.g. each pair of distinguishable collection and iterator objects). This is then refined to track pairs of over and under-approximations per object for efficiency reasons.

2.3   State Invariants and Pre/Post Conditions

There is a relationship between the notion of typestate and the usage of invariants, although the original work on typestates did not consider this. It is well known that a combination of object invariants and method pre and post conditions can be used to specify and verify certain kinds of program behaviour. Clearly a method precondition captures information about the required state of the object before the method call and the postcondition captures information about the state of the object after the method call. This highlights the relationship between a concrete notion of 'states' an object can be in and the abstract notion of state in a typestate property; however, it is not clear to this author that there can always be a direct mapping.

In [13] typestates and object invariants are combined in an *object typestate*, a language feature where a typestate is defined in terms of what properties hold of an object's concrete state. A similar approach is taken in [7] where typestates are mapped to predicates on fields. In both pieces of work they note the need for *intermediate states* that exist in the typestate property but do not relate to an existing state invariant i.e. states that should be passed through within a method body.

Figure 3 shows an illustration from [13] where they discuss how typestates of a web page fetcher can be defined in terms of invariants on the fields of that object. Note that they include aliasing information in this invariant.

The example from [7] in Fig. 1 shows how they combine logical expressions in their invariants in the following excerpt:

```
boolean hasNext()  :
pure(this)  ─◦ ((result = true ⊗ pure(this) in available)
⊗ (result = false ⊗ pure(this) in end))
```

It is not clear how such statements are checked in the analysis.

Additionally, the notion of combining runtime verification of state-based properties with static analysis code annotations has been explored in [12]. Here the temporal behaviour is checked dynamically whilst the code annotations are checked statically, representing an alternative combination.

2.4 Gradual Typing

There is an area of type theory that deals directly with the notion of mixing static and dynamic analysis: *gradual typing* [32] is the idea that some parts of the program can be statically type-checked whilst other parts are left to be type-checked dynamically (at runtime). This concept has been applied to typestate and there exists a body of work that has now been formulated as *typestate-oriented programming* [18,36] which describes a Gradual Featherweight Typestate system.

3 Quantified Event Automata

Quantified event automata (QEA) [4] (see also [21,29]) is a highly expressive specification language with an efficient runtime verification tool MARQ [30] (developed by the author). I refer the reader to previous publications for the technical details. Additionally I will not review the topic of runtime verification and refer the reader to relevant publications (e.g. [14]). In this section I review the fundamental concepts necessary for this paper in an example-led fashion.

3.1 The Structures

A QEA consists of an *event automata* and a list of *quantifications*. Event automata are an extended form (i.e. with variables) of finite state machine over *data words*. The alphabet of an event automaton consists of *events* built from event names and parameters that are either variables or constants. Additionally, the transitions of an event automaton can include guards (predicates on bindings of variables) and assignments (update functions on bindings of variables). An event automaton is therefore over zero of more variables and the quantifier list may quantify zero or more of these variables.

3.2 Examples

Let us consider some examples which will be used later to describe the semantics of QEA and discuss their role as typestate properties. We will present QEAs graphically and in this notation shaded states are accepting states, square states have a failing completion (if no transition can be taken an error occurs) and circular states have a skipping completion (if no transition can be taken then the event is skipped).

We will use the following properties (illustrated in Fig. 4):

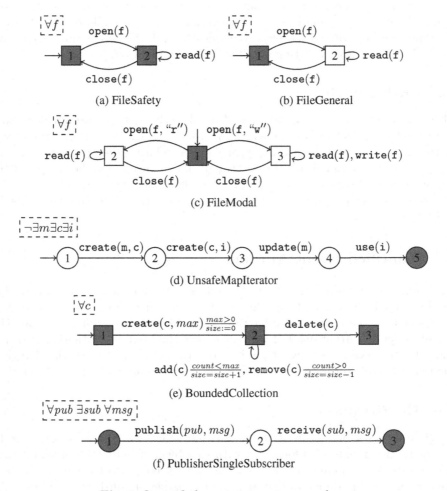

Fig. 4. Quantified event automata examples.

(a) *FileSafety*. This is a QEA for the property previously used to introduce typestate properties on page 2. A file f can be in two states, open or closed, if closed it can only be opened and if open it can be read or closed.

(b) *FileGeneral*. This adds a non-safety element to the previous property. A file that has been opened must eventually be closed.

(c) *FileModal*. This extends the previous file example further; a file can be opened in one of two modes, read or write, and in read mode it cannot be written to.

(d) *UnsafeMapIterator*. This concerns unsafe iteration over collections constructed from maps. If a collection c is created from a map m and an iterator i is created from c then if map m is updated the iterator i should no longer be used. This is related to, but not the same as, the previously discussed *UnsafeIterator* property.

(e) *BoundedCollection*. On creation a collection has a maximum size max and can contain at most max objects. Additionally, it should not be used after deletion.

(f) *PublisherSingleSubscriber*. Every publisher has at least one subscriber that reads all messages published by that publisher.

3.3   Quantification via Parametric Trace Slicing

Quantification is handled via *parametric trace slicing*, a quantification $\forall f$ means that for every value in the domain of f one should consider the (minimal) subtrace mentioning that value, called a *trace slice*. That is, given a binding $[f \mapsto v]$ we ask if the subtrace mentioning only v is accepted by the automaton where f is replaced by v. For multiple quantified variables one should consider the slice for each *combination* of values for the respective variables.

I illustrate this approach using the above *FileSafety* property. Consider the trace

$$\texttt{open(A).open(B).read(A).close(A).open(C).read(B).close(B).open(C)}$$

there are three possible values for f (A, B, and C) and therefore three trace slices

$$
\begin{array}{ll}
f \mapsto A & \texttt{open(A).read(A).close(A)} \\
f \mapsto B & \texttt{open(B)read(B).close(B)} \\
f \mapsto C & \texttt{open(C).open(C)}
\end{array}
$$

each trace slice is evaluated on the automaton where f is replaced by the appropriate value. In this case we can see that the slice for $f \mapsto C$ is not accepted by the automaton and therefore the whole trace is not accepted (as the quantification was $\forall$).

In the case of existential quantification (as in the *PublisherSingleSubscriber* property) the semantics is the obvious one; *at least one* trace slice needs to be accepting.

3.4   Event Automata Are Extended Finite State Machines

The parametric trace slicing approach can be parameterised by any mechanism for evaluating trace slices. In QEA this mechanism is event automata, which can use variables, guards and assignments to capture highly expressive properties. This is demonstrated in the previous formulation of the *BoundedCollection* property. Two *free* variables are introduced: max to store the maximum size and $size$ to track the current size of the collection. The syntax $\frac{guard}{assignment}$ is used to introduce basic arithmetic predicates and functions. The only non-obvious part of the semantics for these variables is that they are updated whenever they match a value in the trace. For example, when $\texttt{create}(\texttt{c}, max)$ matches with the concrete event $\texttt{create}(\texttt{c}, 5)$ the value 5 is bound to max.

In MARQ (the runtime verification tool for QEA) arbitrary code can be introduced as guards and assignments. This obviously extends expressiveness costing us analysability. Here we stick to basic arithmetic guards and assignments. The extension for more expressive theories is a separate research effort.

3.5   A Finite Trace Semantics with Four Values

Finally, QEA are defined over *finite traces*, which leads to a decision about what to do at the end of the trace (a topic that has received attention previously e.g. [5]). The choice taken here is to use a four-valued semantics. Consider the *FileGeneral* property on the two traces

$$\texttt{read(A).open(A)} \qquad and \qquad \texttt{open(A).read(A)}$$

neither trace is correct but they fail for different reasons and we would like to separate these failures. The first trace breaks the safety requirements whilst the second trace does not satisfy the reachability requirement. Notice that the second trace can be *extended* to a good trace but the first cannot. The four possible verdicts are

- *Success*. This trace and all extensions will be accepted
- *Failure*. This trace and all extensions will be rejected
- *Weak Success*. This trace is accepted but some extension may be rejected
- *Weak Failure*. This trace is rejected but some extension may be accepted

Clearly safety properties can only have *Failure* or *Weak Success* verdicts as once violated all extensions will also be violating.

4   Towards Typestate-Like Verification for QEA

In this section I reflect on how the quantified event automata introduced in the previous section could be handled (partially in some cases) statically using techniques from typestate verification. As previously discussed, a large amount of work on typestate analysis considers the introduction of new programming language concepts. However, I am interested in the other approach which considers existing programs and programming languages. I make an exception for extensions via additional annotations (e.g. JML) as they do not alter the behaviour of the underlying program.

In the following I discuss possible directions for typestate-like verification for QEA motivated by the examples presented in the previous section.

4.1 Single Object Properties

Clearly the *FileSafety* property is a standard typestate property. However, the QEA does not contain enough information to perform typestate analysis as there is no link between the abstract QEA property and the concrete program. Traditionally, typestates annotate programs like types. But a QEA is a separate object. This is also the case in tracematches, but in that instance the link to the program is built-in i.e. events are specified as pointcuts. However, in QEA the assumption is that some separate instrumentation will create the link between concrete program event and abstract specification event.

There are two alternatives here. One could provide pointcut instrumentation (as in tracematches) and this seems the most natural approach. However, it would also be possible to add annotations to the code that indicate what the event is. This would allow for more fine-grained associations as the AspectJ approach requires events to relate to method calls.

Once this has been sorted then the previously discussed techniques could be used to statically (partially) evaluate a QEA. The partial part is, of course, due to the possibly imprecise nature of reference disambiguation. In a setting where the starting point is dynamic analysis, any imprecision should be dealt with at runtime i.e. if a violation is detected due to an over or under approximation then the runtime checks must be preserved.

4.2 Non-safety Properties

In the *FileGeneral* property there is a non-safety element. When the typestate is in the open state there are two problematic behaviours to consider:

- The program can be shown to possibly terminate
- The program can be shown to possibly diverge

In either case the bad state is not left and this constitutes a violation. Note that this relates to the finite trace semantics discussed earlier. In QEA it is assumed that a trace is finite, however during static analysis one can consider the possibility of divergence. I discuss the two cases separately.

Early Termination. To detect such errors statically one would need to detect the possibility of (ordinary[1]) termination. As a rather trivial example consider the following piece of code.

---

[1] One cannot reason about abnormal termination such as the machine being switched off!.

```
public void writeSetToFile(Set<Integer> set, String name){
  File file = new File(name);
  file.open();
  for(Integer i : set){
    if(i==0){
      System.out.println(''Error'');
      System.exit(0);
    }
    file.write(i);
  }
  file.close();
}
```

There is a path leading to termination between **open** and **close** and therefore the property is (statically) violated. In the analysis one should label exit points of the program and consider their reachability. The issue is then whether certain paths in the control-flow graph are realisable by real executions. As before, the level of precision achieved will depend on whether the analysis is interprocedural and if it is context-sensitive.

This notion of termination is perhaps strange when considering the standard runtime verification approach. In the runtime verification literature it is (generally) assumed that we detect program termination without knowing which part of the monitored system this termination originates from. Or it is detected by monitoring the exit point of the main method/functional block. Therefore, there is no discussion of using static analysis to remove instrumentation points, as (usually) none are added. In this analysis it may be that the violation occurs in a part of the code that would not be instrumented.

Note that there may be different kinds of termination, for example we may wish to allow exceptional termination. This could be achieved by (automatically) extending the automaton as in Fig. 5. Now one must search for paths to termination that do not contain a **close** or **fileException** event.

Divergence. To show that it is possible that the program may never reach the next state transition it would be necessary to establish divergence. For example, via a possibly non-terminating loop. Clearly this is undecidable in general. However, there exists a lot of work [10,19] on showing that a particular program either always terminates or may possibly never terminate. This particular analysis appears more complex than the previous one and, perhaps, less fruitful.

4.3   Multi Object Properties

The *UnsafeMapIterator* property is a standard case of a multi-object typestate which has been dealt with in previous work. As previously discussed, there are currently two existing approaches [8,27] to multi-object typestate verification. As discussed in [27], the analyses are complementary. A starting point for multi-object typestate verification for QEA would be to extend either approach, possibly also combining them. As [27] is flow-sensitive and the later discussions demand such an analysis, it would seem that starting with this work would be sensible.

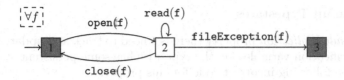

Fig. 5. Adding exceptional termination to *FileGeneral* property.

4.4 Guarded Transitions

In the *FileModal* property there is a check on the value of a method call with different values leading to different states. At this point we note that the variables present in the QEA are not necessarily in correspondence with variables in the program (a common misconception) and it might be that the value expected in the QEA would need to be extracted during instrumentation (for example via a method call). In general, it may be necessary to rewrite the program to make such values explicit.

To understand how to statically analyse this property let us consider the following piece of code that satisfies the property.

```
Set values = getValues();
boolean output = values.size() > 0;
File file = output ? new File(name,''w'') : new File(name,''r'');
String line = null;
Set seen = new Set();
while((line = file.readLine()) != null){
  seen.add(line);
}
for(String value : values){
  if(!seen.contains(value)){ file.write(value); }
}
```

Every path containing **write** necessarily starts with **new File(name,''w'')** as if the **values** set has no elements then the iterator containing the **write** will not execute. To check this statically one could carry predicates on program state with the object abstraction i.e. in this case at the point a file is created there are two abstractions that **file** could refer to: a file in state *read-only* with predicate *output = false* and a file in state *read/write* with a predicate *output = false*. These predicates can be used to determine which paths the abstract object may take, in this case the abstraction where *output = false* would not enter the final **for** loop. In other words, we could perform some form of symbolic computation. In more complex scenarios (e.g. numeric guards) some form of abstraction would be required.

Where the guard differentiates between valid and invalid behaviour the guard could be added as a precondition or assertion to be checked by standard methods (e.g. deductive verification). But in the general case where future behaviours are determined by the guard, or the property is non-safety, this would not be sufficient.

4.5   Statefull Typestates

In the *BoundedCollection* property there is a need to track and update the values
of two specification variables i.e. the typestate has some persistent state. Let us
consider the following incorrect code for this property.

```
Collection fill(int value){
  Collection c = new Collection(value);
  for(int i=0;i<=value;i++){
    c.add(i);
  }
  return c;
}
```

There is an out-by-one error in the loop. To check this property we should
add the information held by the specification into the code. This could simply
be achieved by adding *ghost* variables to track the values in the specification.
For example:

```
Collection fill(int value){
  Collection c = new Collection(value);

  //added code
  int max = value;
  int size = 0;

  for(int i=0;i<=value;i++){
    c.add(i);

    //added code
    assert(size+1 < max);
    size++;
  }
  return c;
}
```

Here single variables are added, but in general these would need to exist per
object (or collection of objects) i.e. if there were two collections here there would
need to be two copies. This could become complicated in the presence of aliasing.

Once these variables are added then the symbolic computation of the previous
step could check the guard (added explicitly here).

This example indicates a further complexity of the analysis, often met in static analysis, that of loops. Here, to establish that a violation occurs it would be
necessary to establish (automatically) the relationship between the loop counter
and the `size` variable and to conclude that `size=max` and `size+1 <max` is inconsistent.

4.6   Existential Quantification

In the *PublisherSingleSubscriber* property we have alternating quantification. Previously, it was necessary for all abstract objects (or collections of objects in the multi-object case) to satisfy the given property. This changes with existential quantification and alternation.

For a single existential quantifier there needs to be a single object across the whole program that satisfies the property. However, this object does not need to satisfy the property on all control paths as each path represents a different execution trace and the requirement is just that there exists an object per execution. Therefore, one object might satisfy it in one control-flow and another in a different one. With multiple quantifiers there is now a relation between the objects and it may be necessary to find an object of one type per an object of another, as in the *PublisherSingleSubscriber* example.

It would seem that some of this could be handled by post-processing of detected violations i.e. analysing which paths contain violations and whether there exists an object with the necessary non-violating paths. But in general it is not clear how to effectively deal with this feature.

5   Conclusion

In this paper I have reviewed typestate verification and the QEA specification language and discussed how the former could be applied to the later. My next step will be to attempt to do this concretely.

As mentioned previously, a starting point will be to take the existing work on multi-object typestate analysis [8,27] and see if this can be extended. The source code for Clara [8] is available online and there is already support for extending the framework to new tools, and the original authors already did this for JavaMOP. I have obtained the source code for [27] from the authors.

An alternative approach would be to take a tool for (single-object) typestate verification and extend this to add the notions of symbolic computation discussed in the previous section. This is not something I have fully explored yet.

References

1. Allan, C., Avgustinov, P., Christensen, A.S., Hendren, L., Kuzins, S., Lhoták, O., de Moor, O., Sereni, D., Sittampalam, G., Tibble, J.: Adding trace matching with free variables to AspectJ. SIGPLAN Not. **40**, 345–364 (2005)
2. Andersen, L.O.: Program analysis and specialization for the C programming language. Technical report (1994)
3. Appel, A.W., Palsberg, J.: Modern Compiler Implementation in Java, 2nd edn. Cambridge University Press, New York (2003)
4. Barringer, H., Falcone, Y., Havelund, K., Reger, G., Rydeheard, D.E.: Quantified event automata: towards expressive and efficient runtime monitors. In: FM, pp. 68–84 (2012)

494   G. Reger

5. Bauer, A., Leucker, M., Schallhart, C.: The good, the bad, and the ugly, but how ugly is ugly? In: Sokolsky, O., Taşıran, S. (eds.) RV 2007. LNCS, vol. 4839, pp. 126–138. Springer, Heidelberg (2007)
6. Bierhoff, K., Aldrich, J.: Lightweight object specification with typestates. SIG-SOFT Softw. Eng. Notes **30**(5), 217–226 (2005)
7. Bierhoff, K., Aldrich, J.: Modular typestate checking of aliased objects. In: Proceedings of the 22nd Annual ACM SIGPLAN Conference on Object-Oriented Programming Systems and Applications, OOPSLA 2007, pp. 301–320. ACM, New York (2007)
8. Bodden, E., Lam, P., Hendren, L.: Clara: a framework for partially evaluating finite-state runtime monitors ahead of time. In: Barringer, H., Falcone, Y., Finkbeiner, B., Havelund, K., Lee, I., Pace, G., Roşu, G., Sokolsky, O., Tillmann, N. (eds.) RV 2010. LNCS, vol. 6418, pp. 183–197. Springer, Heidelberg (2010)
9. Bove, A., Dybjer, P.: Dependent types at work. In: Bove, A., Barbosa, L.S., Pardo, A., Pinto, J.S. (eds.) Language Engineering and Rigorous Software Development, pp. 57–99. Springer, Heidelberg (2009)
10. Brockschmidt, M., Cook, B., Ishtiaq, S., Khlaaf, H., Piterman, N.: T2: temporal property verification. In: Chechik, M., Raskin, J.-F. (eds.) ETAPS 2016. LNCS, vol. 9636, pp. 387–393. Springer, Heidelberg (2016)
11. Chen, F., Roşu, G.: Parametric trace slicing and monitoring. In: Kowalewski, S., Philippou, A. (eds.) TACAS 2009. LNCS, vol. 5505, pp. 246–261. Springer, Heidelberg (2009)
12. Chimento, J.M., Ahrendt, W., Pace, G.J., Schneider, G.: STARVOORS: a tool for combined static and runtime verification of Java. In: Bartocci, E., et al. (eds.) RV 2015. LNCS, vol. 9333, pp. 297–305. Springer, Heidelberg (2015). doi:10.1007/978-3-319-23820-3_21
13. DeLine, R., Fähndrich, M.: Typestates for objects. In: Odersky, M. (ed.) ECOOP 2004. LNCS, vol. 3086, pp. 465–490. Springer, Heidelberg (2004)
14. Falcone, Y., Havelund, K., Reger, G.: A tutorial on runtime verification. In: Broy, M., Peled, D. (eds.) Summer School Marktoberdorf 2012 - Engineering Dependable Software Systems. IOS Press (2013, to appear)
15. Farzan, A., Heizmann, M., Hoenicke, J., Kincaid, Z., Podelski, A.: Automated program verification. In: Dediu, A.-H., Formenti, E., Martín-Vide, C., Truthe, B. (eds.) LATA 2015. LNCS, vol. 8977, pp. 25–46. Springer, Heidelberg (2015)
16. Field, J., Goyal, D., Ramalingam, G., Yahav, E.: Typestate verification: abstraction techniques and complexity results. In: Field, J., Goyal, D., Ramalingam, G., Yahav, E. (eds.) SAS 2003, vol. 2694, pp. 439–462. Springer, Heidelberg (2003)
17. Fink, S.J., Yahav, E., Dor, N., Ramalingam, G., Geay, E.: Effective typestate verification in the presence of aliasing. ACM Trans. Softw. Eng. Methodol. **17**(2), 9:1–9:34 (2008)
18. Garcia, R., Tanter, É., Wolff, R., Aldrich, J.: Foundations of typestateoriented programming. ACM Trans. Program. Lang. Syst. **36**(4), 1–44 (2014)
19. Giesl, J., Mesnard, F., Rubio, A., Thiemann, R., Waldmann, J., Deduction, A.: Termination competition (term- COMP 2015). In: Felty, A.P., Middeldorp, A. (eds.) CADE. LNAI, vol. 9195, pp. 105–108. Springer, Heidelberg (2015)
20. Giorgetti, A., Groslambert, J.: JAG: JML annotation generation for verifying temporal properties. In: Baresi, L., Heckel, R. (eds.) FASE 2006. LNCS, vol. 3922, pp. 373–376. Springer, Heidelberg (2006)

21. Havelund, K., Reger, G.: Specification of parametric monitors - quantified event automata versus rule systems. In: Drechsler, R., Kühne, U. (eds.) Formal Modeling and Verification of Cyber-Physical Systems, pp. 151–189. Springer, Wiesbaden (2015)
22. Hussain, F., Leavens, G.T.: temporaljmlc: a JML runtime assertion checker extension for specification and checking of temporal properties. In: 2010 8th IEEE International Conference on Software Engineering and Formal Methods, pp. 63–72 (2010)
23. Landi, W.: Undecidability of static analysis. ACM Lett. Program. Lang. Syst. 1(4), 323–337 (1992)
24. Liskov, B.H., Wing, J.M.: A behavioral notion of subtyping. ACM Trans. Program. Lang. Syst. 16(6), 1811–1841 (1994)
25. McGinniss, I.: Theoretical and practical aspects of typestate. Ph.D. thesis, University of Glasgow (2014)
26. Meredith, P., Jin, D., Griffith, D., Chen, F., Roşu, G.: An overview of the mop runtime verification framework. J. Softw. Tools Technol. Transf. 14(3), 249–289 (2012)
27. Naeem, N.A., Lhotak, O.: Typestate-like analysis of multiple interacting objects. In: Proceedings of the 23rd ACM SIGPLAN Conference on Object-Oriented Programming Systems Languages and Applications, OOPSLA 2008, pp. 347–366. ACM, New York (2008)
28. Ramalingam, G.: The undecidability of aliasing. ACM Trans. Program. Lang. Syst. 16(5), 1467–1471 (1994)
29. Reger, G.: Automata based monitoring and mining of execution traces. Ph.D. thesis, University of Manchester (2014)
30. Reger, G., Cruz, H.C., Rydeheard, D.: MarQ: monitoring at runtime with QEA. In: Proceedings of the 21st International Conference on Tools and Algorithms for the Construction and Analysis of Systems (TACAS 2015) (2015)
31. Reps, T., Horwitz, S., Sagiv, M.: Precise interprocedural dataflow analysis via graph reachability. In: Proceedings of the 22nd ACM SIGPLAN-SIGACT Symposium on Principles of Programming Languages, POPL 1995, pp. 49–61. ACM, New York (1995)
32. Siek, J.G., Taha, W.: Gradual typing for objects. In: Ernst, E. (ed.) ECOOP 2007. LNCS, vol. 4609, pp. 2–27. Springer, Heidelberg (2007)
33. Sridharan, M., Bodík, R.: Refinement-based context-sensitive points-to analysis for Java. SIGPLAN Not. 41(6), 387–400 (2006)
34. Strom, R.E., Yemini, S.: Typestate: a programming language concept for enhancing software reliability. IEEE Trans. Softw. Eng. 12(1), 157–171 (1986)
35. Trentelman, K., Huisman, M.: Extending JML specifications with temporal logic. In: Kirchner, H., Ringeissen, C. (eds.) AMAST 2002. LNCS, vol. 2422, p. 334. Springer, Heidelberg (2002)
36. Wolff, R., Garcia, R., Tanter, É., Aldrich, J.: Gradual typestate. In: Mezini, M. (ed.) ECOOP 2011. LNCS, vol. 6813, pp. 459–483. Springer, Heidelberg (2011)

Combining Static and Runtime Methods to Achieve Safe Standing-Up for Humanoid Robots

Francesco Leofante[1], Simone Vuotto[1,2], Erika Ábrahám[2],
Armando Tacchella[1(✉)], and Nils Jansen[3]

[1] University of Genoa, Genoa, Italy
armando.tacchella@unige.it
[2] RWTH Aachen University, Aachen, Germany
[3] University of Texas at Austin, Austin, USA

Abstract. Due to its complexity, the standing-up task for robots is highly challenging, and often implemented by scripting the strategy that the robot should execute per hand. In this paper we aim at improving the approach of a scripted stand-up strategy by making it more stable and safe. To achieve this aim, we apply both static and runtime methods by integrating reinforcement learning, static analysis and runtime monitoring techniques.

1 Introduction

Bipedal locomotion is a challenging task for a humanoid robot. In particular, in the case of a fall, it is essential for the overall robustness to have reliable recovery procedures, *i.e.*, the robot must be able to get back into an upright posture. However it is not trivial to come up with reliable *standing-up routines*. This is because standing-up requires that the robot's center of mass (COM) projection to the ground leaves the convex hull spanned by the feet contact points. Therefore, knees, elbows, hands, and the backside of the robot should be used to provide additional support. As mentioned, *e.g.*, in [1], this results in whole-body motions with sequences of support points. The many degrees of freedom of humanoid robots and the changing contact points make it difficult to apply conventional motion-planning techniques.

Given the intrinsic difficulties of the standing-up task, observation of the human example may well serve as inspiration for the development of adequate motion sequences. However, compared to humans, humanoid robots often lack essential degrees of freedom, *e.g.*, in the trunk. Furthermore, the robot joints are often restricted to a limited range of motion and can only provide limited torques. The authors of [1] developed standing-up routines using a physics-based simulation and implemented such routines on two small humanoid robots. The approach however lacks flexibility as the routines are *scripted*, *i.e.*, predetermined command sequences are fed to the motors in an open-loop fashion. Scripted routines are based on certain assumptions about the robot and its environment. If something

T. Margaria and B. Steffen (Eds.): ISoLA 2016, Part I, LNCS 9952, pp. 496–514, 2016.
DOI: 10.1007/978-3-319-47166-2_34

changes in the environment or in the robot, the assumptions may get violated and the routine may fail. To improve reliability, different solutions have been proposed in which a robot *learns* how to stand up (see, *e.g.*, [2–4]). However, these works consider rather simple scenarios, and none of them considers a full humanoid as a case study.

In this paper we propose an approach to improve scripted strategies by integrating static and runtime techniques.

Contribution 1. One drawback of scripted strategies is that the result of executing a certain robot action is not unique, for several reasons (*e.g.*, due to imprecise sensors and actuators, or uncertainties in the environment). In order to improve the stability of scripted standing-up strategies under consideration of those uncertainties, we apply (model-free) *reinforcement learning* [5], *i.e.*, the robot learns how to get up on its feet by interacting with the environment, observing the effects of its actions, and trying to come up with a strategy that maximises the probability to reach the desired final state. To avoid damage on the robot, we use a *simulator* in this learning process.

Contribution 2. Reinforcement learning gives us a stable strategy, determining actions the robot should execute for standing up. There are possibilities to drive the learning towards avoiding certain *unsafe* states (*e.g.*, with critical joint values or unstable poses). However, using reinforcement learning we cannot assure that the resulting strategy will avoid such unsafe states with a given probability. In [6], we proposed a *greedy model repair* approach, based on static analysis, which can be used to repair probabilistic strategies on Markov models such that the resulting repaired strategy assures certain probabilistic safety properties. Here we apply this approach to repair the strategy computed by reinforcement learning, such that the reachability of certain unsafe states is kept below a required threshold while still achieving the desired task of standing-up.

Contribution 3. As reinforcement learning uses simulation and because our repair is model-based, the repaired strategy assures safety for the model, but this safety property does not necessarily transfer to the real system. To maintain safety during operation, we propose the additional integration of *runtime monitoring* to observe the real-time behaviour. If the difference between the observed real-time behaviour and the model behaviour is too large, we use a feedback loop to the static methods to adapt the model and the strategy.

The rest of the paper is structured as follows: In Sect. 2 we recall some preliminaries. In Sect. 3 we introduce the standing-up task. We explain our approach to solve this task and present experimental results in Sect. 4. We conclude the paper in Sect. 5.

2   Preliminaries

Probabilistic Models. Here we introduce discrete-time Markov models we use as basic modeling formalism for probabilistic systems.

Definition 1 (DTMC). *A discrete-time Markov chain (DTMC) is a tuple* $\mathcal{D} = (S, s^{init}, P)$ *of a finite non-empty set* S *of states, an initial state* $s^{init} \in S$, *and a transition probability function* $P \colon S \times S \to \mathbb{R}$, *such that* $\sum_{s' \in S} P(s, s') = 1$ *for all* $s \in S$.

A *path* of a DTMC $\mathcal{D}$ is a non-empty (finite or infinite) sequence $s_0 s_1 \ldots$ of states $s_i \in S$ such that $P(s_i, s_{i+1}) > 0$ for all i. A unique probability measure $Pr^{\mathcal{D}}$ on sets of paths is defined via the usual cylinder set construction, see [7]. Notably, the cylinder set of a finite path $s_0 \ldots s_n$ (*i.e.*, the set of all infinite paths with prefix $s_0 \ldots s_n$) has the total probability $Pr^{\mathcal{D}}(s_0 \ldots s_n) = \Pi_{i=0}^{n-1} P(s_i, s_{i+1})$. We use $Pr_s^{\mathcal{D}}(\Diamond B)$ to denote the total probability of all paths of $\mathcal{D}$ that start in s and visit at least one state from a target set $B \subseteq S$.

Sometimes it is advantageous to use *parametric* DTMC models, where the parameters can represent, *e.g.*, design parameters, whose values should be fixed later. Let $Var = \{x_1, \ldots, x_n\}$ be a finite set of real-valued *parameters* x_i with parameter domains $\mathbb{D}_i \subseteq \mathbb{R}$, and let $Val \subseteq \{v : Var \to \cup_{i=1}^{n} \mathbb{D}_i\}$ be the set of all *valuations* v for Var that assign to each $x_i \in Var$ a value from its domain $v(x_i) \in \mathbb{D}_i$. Let furthermore Exp_{Var} be a set of arithmetic expressions over Var, such that each $e \in Exp_{Var}$ can be evaluated to a real value $v(e) \in \mathbb{R}$ in the context of a valuation $v \in Val_{Var}$; in this work we use linear arithmetic expressions, but in general one could also consider non-linear expressions or rational functions [8,9]. For $e \in Exp_{Var}$ we define $Var(e) \subseteq Var$ to be the set of all parameters that occur in e. We write $e \equiv 0$ if $v(e) = 0$ for each valuation $v \in Val$, and $e \not\equiv 0$ otherwise (*e.g.*, $x - x \equiv 0$ but $x - y \not\equiv 0$). Sometimes we skip the index Var if it is clear from the context.

Definition 2 (pDTMC). *A parametric discrete-time Markov chain (pDTMC) is a tuple* $\mathcal{P} = (S, s^{init}, Var, P)$ *of a finite non-empty set* S *of states, an initial state* $s^{init} \in S$, *a finite set* Var *of parameters, and a (parametric) transition probability function* $P \colon S \times S \to Exp_{Var}$. *A valuation* $v \in Val_{Var}$ *is realisable for* $\mathcal{P}$ *if* $\sum_{s' \in S} v(P(s, s')) = 1$ *for all* $s \in S$. *A pDTMC is called realisable if it has at least one realisable valuation.*

Note that each realisable valuation v of a pDTMC $\mathcal{P} = (S, s^{init}, Var, P)$ *induces* a DTMC $\mathcal{D} = (S, s^{init}, P_v)$ with $P_v(s, s') = v(P(s, s'))$ for all $s, s' \in S$. In the following we consider only realisable pDTMCs, and require that each variable is used to specify successor probabilities for at most one state:

$$\forall s_1, s_2, s_1', s_2' \in S. \; Var(P(s_1, s_2)) \cap Var(P(s_1', s_2')) \neq \emptyset \to s_1 = s_1'. \tag{1}$$

Probabilistic systems with non-deterministic behaviour can be modelled by Markov decision processes.

Definition 3 (MDP). *A Markov decision process (MDP) is a tuple* $\mathcal{M} = (S, s^{init}, Act, P)$ *of a finite non-empty set* S *of states, an initial state* $s^{init} \in S$, *a finite non-empty set* Act *of actions, and a transition probability function* $P \colon S \times Act \times S \to [0, 1]$ *such that* $\sum_{s' \in S} P(s, a, s') \in \{0, 1\}$ *for all* $(s, a) \in S \times Act$, *and for all* $s \in S$ *there exists at least one* $a \in Act$ *with* $\sum_{s' \in S} P(s, a, s') = 1$.

For a given $s \in S$ let Act_s denote the set $\{a \in Act \mid \sum_{s' \in S} P(s, a, s') = 1\}$ of actions that are *enabled* in s. Semantically, in each state, first an enabled action is determined non-deterministically and then a successor state is selected probabilistically. Thus a *path* of the MDP $\mathcal{M} = (S, s^{init}, Act, P)$ is a non-empty (finite or infinite) sequence $s_0 a_0 s_1 a_1 \ldots$ of states $s_i \in S$ and actions $a_i \in Act_{s_i}$ such that $P(s_i, a_i, s_{i+1}) > 0$ for all i.

We use *memoryless strategies* (also referred to as *schedulers* or *policies*) to resolve the non-determinism by defining for each state $s \in S$ a probability distribution over its enabled actions, *i.e.* a function $\sigma \colon S \times Act \to [0,1]$ such that $\sum_{a \in Act_s} \sigma(s, a) = 1$ and $\sigma(s, a) = 0$ for all $a \in Act \setminus Act_s$. If the strategy assigns in each state probability one to a single action, it is called *deterministic*. Each strategy σ for an MDP $\mathcal{M} = (S, s^{init}, Act, P)$ induces an DTMC $\mathcal{D}_\sigma = (S, s^{init}, P_\sigma)$ with $P_\sigma(s, s') = \sum_{a \in Act} \sigma(s, a) \cdot P(s, a, s')$ for all $s, s' \in S$.

We also need the notion of *rewards*, which can be used to model, *e.g.*, the costs of executing certain actions. A *reward function* is given by $R \colon S \times Act \times S \to \mathbb{R}$. For MDP $\mathcal{M}$, reward function R, and strategy σ, the *expected discounted total reward* in state s is the expected value of $\sum_{i=0}^{\infty} \gamma^i \cdot R(s_i, a_i, s_{i+1})$ along paths $s_0 a_0 s_1 a_1 \ldots$ starting in $s = s_0$ under the strategy σ, where $\gamma \in \mathbb{R}$, $0 < \gamma < 1$ is the *discount factor*. An optimal strategy σ^* maximising the expected discounted total reward can be computed by solving the equation system

$$\forall s \in S. \ \forall a \in Act. \ Q_{s,a}^* = \sum_{s' \in S} P(s, a, s') \left(R(s, a, s') + \gamma \cdot \max_{a' \in Act_{s'}} Q_{s',a'}^* \right) \quad (2)$$

and choosing in each state $s \in S$ the action $a_s^* = \operatorname{argmax}_{a \in Act_s} Q_{s,a}^*$ with probability $\sigma^*(s, a_s^*) = 1$, and defining $\sigma^*(s, a) = 0$ for all other actions $a \in Act \setminus \{a_s^*\}$. Intuitively, $Q_{s,a}^*$ is the expected discounted total reward of paths starting in s, executing a first, and following an optimal policy afterwards.

Reinforcement Learning. A general class of algorithms from machine learning called *reinforcement learning* [10] lets an agent learn such an optimal strategy σ^* for a non-deterministic probabilistic system. We consider a reinforcement learning algorithm called *Q-learning* [10]. This approach takes as input a set S of states and a set Act_s of actions for each state $s \in S$. Furthermore, it needs to observe (based on a simulator or the execution of a real system) the successor state and the reward achieved when executing an action $a \in Act$ in a state $s \in S$. Based on iterative observations, Q-learning maintains a *quantity-matrix* (*Q-matrix*) of dimension $|S| \times |Act|$, with the goal to approximate the values $Q_{s,a}^*$ by the entries $Q(s, a)$ (see Eq. 2).

Starting with an arbitrarily initialised Q-matrix, each *episode* observes a path of the system: starting from the initial state $s^{init} = s_0$, it selects some enabled action $a_0 \in Act_{s_0}$, and observes the successor state s_1 and the reward $r_0 = R(s_0, a_0, s_1)$ for this execution; we write (s_0, a_0, s_1, r_0) for this observation. This is continued iteratively until some condition becomes true (*e.g.*, some final state is reached); in this case a new episode starts. For each observation (s_i, a_i, s_{i+1}, r_i) in each episode, the Q-matrix-value $Q(s_i, a_i)$ is updated according to

$$Q_{k+1}(s_i, a_i) := (1 - \alpha)Q_k(s_i, a_i) + \alpha \left(r_i + \gamma \max_{a \in Act_{s_{i+1}}} Q_k(s_{i+1}, a) \right) \quad (3)$$

where $0 < \alpha < 1$ is the *learning rate* (which might dependent on k, s_i, and a_i).

We say that Q-learning is an *off-policy* algorithm, meaning that it learns an optimal strategy no matter what the agent does, as long as it explores enough. If the algorithm terminates, after a sufficiently large number of episodes, a strategy can be derived from the Q-matrix by specifying either a deterministic strategy taking in each state s the action a_s with the highest expected discounted total reward with probability 1 (*i.e.*, $\sigma(s, a_s) = 1$ for $a_s = argmax_{a \in Act_s} Q(s, a)$ and $\sigma(s, a) = 0$ for all other actions $a \in Act \setminus \{a_s\}$), or a strategy that defines a distribution over a set $Act'_s \subseteq Act_s$ of actions with the highest estimated rewards, *e.g.*, $\sigma(s, a) = e^{Q(s,a)/c^{temp}} / \sum_{a' \in Act'_s} e^{Q(s,a')/c^{temp}}$ for all $s \in S$ and $a \in Act'_s$ and $\sigma(s, a) = 0$ otherwise, where c^{temp} is the *temperature* parameter which moves the selection strategy from purely random (high c^{temp}) to fully greedy (low c^{temp}).

Model Repair. We will also make use of the following approach to adapt schedulers to satisfy certain safety requirements. Assume a parametric DTMC model with fixed variable domains, an initial (realisable) parameter valuation v_0 inducing a DTMC $\mathcal{D}_0$, a set B of unsafe states, and an upper bound $\lambda \in [0,1]$ on the probability $Pr^{\mathcal{D}_0}_{s^{init}}(\Diamond B)$ to reach unsafe states from the initial state s^{init} in $\mathcal{D}_0$. Assume furthermore that $Pr^{\mathcal{D}_0}_{s^{init}}(\Diamond B) > \lambda$. Our goal is to modify the initial valuation such that the resulting valuation satisfies the probability bound.

Some available approaches for this task are based on non-linear programming [11] or on approximative methods [12]. Statistical model checking combined with reinforcement learning was used in [13] for a related problem on robustness. In this work we use a *greedy model repair* approach [6]. This approach considers the DTMC $\mathcal{D}_0$ induced by the initial parameter valuation v_0 and uses efficient probabilistic model checkers like PRISM [9] or MRMC [14] to compute for each state s the probability $Pr^{\mathcal{D}_0}_s(\Diamond B)$ of reaching unsafe states from s. If this probability for the initial state is above the allowed bound, we heuristically select states and try to repair their probability distributions by changing the parameter values within their domains. These *local repair steps* successively reduce the probability of reaching an unsafe state from s^{init} until its value becomes lower than the required threshold λ.

The basic idea is illustrated in Fig. 1. Assume a valuation v_k and a DTMC $\mathcal{D}_k$ induced by it. Using model checking we know for each state s the probability $Pr^{\mathcal{D}_k}_s(\Diamond B)$ to reach unsafe states from s in $\mathcal{D}_k$. The higher this probability, the more "dangerous" it is to visit this state.

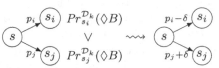

Fig. 1. The idea of greedy model repair

To repair the model, we iteratively consider single probability distributions in isolation, and modify the parameter values such that we decrease the probability to move to more "dangerous" successor states. Our approach is *sound and complete* for the considered model class: each local repair step improves the reachability probability towards a desired bound for a repairable pDTMC, and under the condition stated in Eq. 1, the repair algorithm always terminates with a satisfying solution (if one exists).

3   The Standing-Up Task

Our study is based on the humanoid robot Bioloid by ROBOTIS [15]. The robot provides all the features needed to make the standing-up task and the associated learning problem non-trivial. In particular, Bioloid has 18 degrees of freedom (DOF) and can stand up without exploiting dynamics from both prone and supine posture due to its powerful Dynamixel AX-12A actuators [16].

In our work we use a simulated model of such a robot [17]. We use the robot simulator V-REP [18] (see Fig. 2), which allows the creation of fully customisable simulations which can be controlled through an API. To study real-world physics and object interaction, V-REP includes four different physics engines which may give slightly different results and have different performances. Cur-

Fig. 2. The simulated Bioloid robot

rently, our experiments are carried out using Open Dynamics Engine (http://www.ode.org).

In Sect. 4.1 below we describe how we model the robot in its environment by a Markov model with rewards, where the transition probability function is not known a priori (but observable via experiments). We refer to the robot's states as *poses*. To solve the *standing-up task*, we seek for an optimal strategy maximising the expected discounted total reward in the Markov model. Due to our definition of the reward function, the solution is a strategy which leads to the stand-up pose (optimally with probability 1) and minimises the expected number of falls, self-collisions and the expected number of actions required to achieve the stand-up pose. We also define a variant, the *safe standing-up task*, wherein the probability of falls and self-collisions (in the model) should be *provably* below some upper bound. It should be noted that solving the standing-up task does not necessarily require explicit knowledge about the transition probability function, whereas solving the safe standing-up task requires it to be made explicit.

4   A Novel Approach for Solving the Standing-Up Task

First we discuss the global structure of our approach, illustrated in Fig. 3, to solve the standing-up task in a stable and safe way. We assume that the robot initially lies on the ground in pose s^{init}, and it should be brought to the stand-up pose s^{goal}. We assume furthermore that the robot can observe its state, and that it has a safe restart strategy available that brings it to its initial pose in a safe way. Finally, as input we assume a scripted action sequence $A = (a_0, \ldots, a_k)$

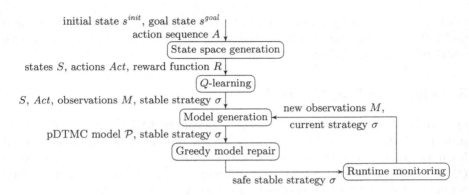

initial state s^{init}, goal state s^{goal}
action sequence A

State space generation

states S, actions Act, reward function R

Q-learning

S, Act, observations M, stable strategy σ

Model generation ← new observations M,
current strategy σ

pDTMC model $\mathcal{P}$, stable strategy σ

Greedy model repair

Runtime monitoring

safe stable strategy σ

Fig. 3. The framework of our approach to solve the standing-up task

that is expected to bring the robot from its initial state s^{init} to the stand-up pose s^{goal} via the execution of the actions $a_0, \ldots, a_k$ (see, *e.g.*, [1] on how to generate such a path).

Based on the scripted input path, the first module *"State space generation"* in our approach determines a portion of the state space and a finite subset of all possible actions; the following modules will restrict their search to these state and action sets. Additionally, this module encodes the goal of standing-up by a reward function.

These specifications serve as input for the second component *"Q − learning"*, which applies reinforcement learning to compute a *stable* strategy σ for standing-up: the strategy σ leads to the standing-up pose not only via the scripted path A, but it offers further alternatives such that the robot will be able to stand up even if due to some changes in the robot or in the environment A does not lead to the goal any more.

Based on observations M made about the robot's behaviour during $Q − learning$, the module *"Model generation"* builds a formal pDTMC model $\mathcal{P}$ of the robot's behaviour.

Reinforcement learning aimed at standing-up via a minimal (expected) number of actions and a minimal (expected) number of falls and self-collisions. However, as falling and self-colliding can break the robot, we want the probability of falling or self-colliding to be below a certain pre-defined threshold. The *"Greedy model repair"* component adapts the previously learnt strategy to be provably *safe*, regarding the above safety requirement (on the model).

The resulting safe stable strategy can now be applied on the real robot. To account for behavioural differences between the real robot and its model, the last component, *"Runtime monitoring"*, observes the robot's behaviour during execution, and adds a feedback loop to adapt the model and the strategy if remarkable differences between the model and the real robot are observed.

Our approach combines the strengths of static approximative methods, static formal verification and runtime monitoring to achieve a stable and safe solution for the standing-up task: (1) Reinforcement learning proved its value for the model-free computation of stable strategies, however, it cannot give any formal guarantees. (2) Greedy model repair, based on probabilistic model checking, adapts the output of reinforcement learning if needed to satisfy certain probabilistic safety requirements. (3) Finally, runtime monitoring provides feedback to bridge differences between the model and reality. In the following we describe each of the components in more detail.

4.1 Component 1: State Space Generation

Our modelling is based on the following assumptions:

Discrete Time. Starting from a known initial state, the interaction between the robot and the environment is represented as a discrete sequence of alternating (i) choice of an action and its execution, and (ii) observation of the next state and other feedback signals from the environment. It is assumed that the actions are fully accomplished before observing the next state, *i.e.*, the observation occurs once transient dynamics are over.

Time-Invariance. The properties of the environment and of the robot do not vary over time. Variations intervening at a later time can be accommodated by the feedback loop in our method (see Sect. 4.5).

Probabilistic effects. Actions have probabilistic effects, *i.e.*, given a state s and an action a, a probability distribution $P(s, a, \cdot)$ governs the set of potential next states. We assume that $P(s, a, \cdot)$ is not known, *i.e.*, no model describing the effects of actions is given.

Markov Property. The effect of an action depends only on the action and the state in which it is executed, but not on past executions.

Next we describe how we compute the action space, the state space and the reward function, which will be used by the other modules.

Action Space. An action of the robot can change all of its 18 joint angles within their physical limits. To achieve a manageable, but for our purposes still sufficient action space, we apply the following reductions. Firstly, some joints are assumed to be inhibited, *i.e.*, they cannot be used to stand up. This is the case of, *e.g.*, the ankle joints that make feet roll. Secondly, joints are always operated symmetrically, *i.e.*, if the left hip joint is moved so is the right one. This gives us a six-dimensional action space, three dimensions corresponding to pairs of joints in the arms, and three dimensions corresponding to pairs of joints in the legs. Thirdly, we make the action space discrete by allowing actions to either increment (1) or decrement (-1) each of the joint angles by a fixed amount Δ^{act}, or leave them unchanged (0), resulting in the action space $Act = \{-1, 0, 1\}^6 \cup \{a^{restart}\}$, where $a^{restart}$ indicates safe restart, leading back to the initial state. We will use the notation a^{skip} for the "do nothing" action $(0, 0, 0, 0, 0, 0)$, causing no state change. We assume that every action is enabled in each state (if the execution of an action is physically not possible, it will be reflected in the successor states), and that Δ^{act} is chosen such that each action in A can be realised by a sequence

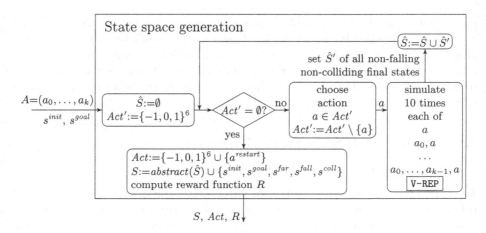

Fig. 4. The state space generation framework

of actions from Act. For simplicity, in the following we consider A to be refined accordingly, *i.e.*, we assume that the actions in A are in Act.

State Space. The state of the Bioloid, *i.e.*, its pose in the three-dimensional space, can be specified by a vector

$$\mathbf{s} = (x, y, z, q_0, q_1, q_2, q_3, \rho_1, \ldots, \rho_{18}) \in \mathbb{R}^{25} \ ,$$

where (x, y, z) are the COM coordinates and (q_0, q_1, q_2, q_3) are the quaternions defining the orientation of the torso according to the absolute coordinate system of the simulator; $(\rho_1, \ldots, \rho_{18})$ are the 18 joint angles corresponding to the 18 DOFs of the robot.

Due to physical constraints, the state space is bounded but infinite. To enable learning and the application of formal methods, we need to restrict ourselves to a finite subset S of the states. Standard grid-based discretisation is not applicable in our case as it would result in a finite but extremely large state set: if we would consider just two discrete points in each dimension, we would end up with 2^{25} states. Instead, we base our discretisation on the input action sequence $A = (a_0, \ldots, a_k)$ that leads the robot from its initial state s^{init} to its *stand-up pose* s^{goal} via a sequence of statically stable poses. Our aim is to keep the state space at a manageable size, but to cover not only the states reachable from s^{init} along A but include also a "tube" around those paths to be able to represent also further standing-up paths that have similarities with A but which are not identical to it.

The state space generation is illustrated in Fig. 4. Using V-REP and s^{init} as initial pose, for each action $a \in Act \setminus \{a^{restart}\}$ we simulate 10 times each action sequence of the form $a_0, \ldots, a_i, a$, where $a_0, \ldots, a_i$ is a (possibly empty) prefix of A, and collect in the set $\hat{S}$ the non-falling and non-colliding final states of all simulations. Next we build an abstraction of the state set $\hat{S}$ by determining the smallest box containing all states in $\hat{S}$, putting a grid on it, and picking the midpoints of all grid elements that contain at least one point from $\hat{S}$. We extend the resulting abstracted state set S with the initial state s^{init}, the goal state s^{goal}, and the special state s^{far} representing the not included grid elements, *i.e.*, poses that are "too far" away from the poses of interest. We also add two auxiliary states s^{fall} and s^{coll} to represent falling or self-collision of the robot. In order to keep the notion of distance between poses, states are stored in k-d trees [19].

Reward Function. To locally assess the quality of an action in terms of safety and effectiveness, we quantify the immediate reward (or penalty) associated to performing a given action in a given state by a reward function $R\colon S \times A \times S \to [-c, c]$ for some $c \in \mathbb{R}$ as follows, based on some fixed $c^{goal}, c^{fall}, c^{coll}, c^{far}, c^{exec} \in \mathbb{R}^+$:

1. if a collision is detected, either with the floor (fall) or with the robot itself (self-collision), then the robot is penalised by $R(s, a, s^{fall}) = -c^{fall}$ respectively $R(s, a, s^{coll}) = -c^{coll}$;
2. the robot is rewarded by $R(s, a, s^{goal}) = c^{goal}$ when an action leads (close) to the goal state;
3. when the robot ends up in the special state s^{far} we give it a large negative reward $R(s, a, s^{far}) = -c^{far}$;
4. in all other cases, a small negative reward $R(s, a, s') = -c^{exec}$ accounts for energy consumption to perform the action.

Above we assumed that collision detection is somehow made possible in the (simulated) robot, *e.g.*, by detecting abnormal accelerations of the COM in case of a fall, or by sensing abnormal forces or torques at the limbs or the joints upon the execution of an action which cannot be fully accomplished because of a self-collision. Note furthermore that, since the reward values are bounded, the expected discounted total reward is always finite.

Experimental Results. We used an input trace A of 13 actions, where each action changes the joint angles by -30, 0 or $+30$ degrees (*i.e.*, $\Delta^{act} = 30$). The action set $Act = \{-1, 0, 1\}^6 \cup \{a^{restart}\}$ contains $729 + 1$ actions.

For the state space generation we executed $13 \cdot 729 \cdot 10 = 94770$ simulations. From these simulations, $|\hat{S}| = 60272$ led to non-falling non-colliding final states.

For the state space abstraction we divided the box spawn by those final states into grids, where the grid structure was based on $n_1 = 50$ equidistant points in each COM dimension, $n_2 = 20$ points for the torso angles, and $n_3 = 12$ for the joint angles (for the joint dimensions this corresponds to a grid distance of $\Delta^{act} = 30$ degrees). Selecting those grid elements that contained at least one of the 60272 final states and adding the special states for falling etc. gave us a state set with $|S| = 17614$ states.

To improve precision, in the future we plan to experiment with larger state spaces by simulating each path several times (instead of once), and considering extensions of prefixes of the scripted path by two actions (instead of one).

For the reward function, we use the constants $c^{goal} = 1000$, $c^{fall} = 100$, $c^{coll} = 100$, $c^{far} = 100$ and $c^{exec} = 1$.

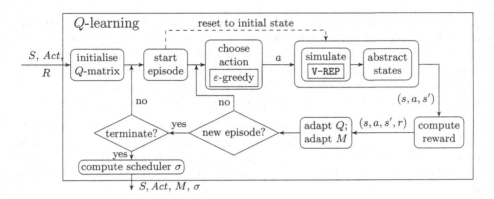

Fig. 5. The Q-learning framework

4.2 Component 2: Reinforcement Learning

In order to perform learning, we use the Q-learning [10] algorithm implemented in the **Pybrain** library [20].

The framework of our Q-learning application is illustrated in Fig. 5. We select the actions to be performed during the episodes with the $\varepsilon - greedy$ exploration strategy: based on some predefined value $\varepsilon \in \mathbb{R}^+$, the learner takes its current best action $a = \text{argmax}_{a \in Act \setminus \{a^{restart}, a^{skip}\}} Q(s, a)$ with probability $(1 - \varepsilon)$ and a randomly selected different action (according to a homogeneous distribution) from $Act \setminus \{a, a^{restart}, a^{skip}\}$ with probability ε. The value of ε decreases smoothly with each episode, in order to put stronger weight on exploration at the beginning of learning, and shift it on exploitation later [21].

We use the **V-REP** simulator for making observations $(\hat{s}, a, \hat{s}')$ about the execution of action a in state $\hat{s} \in \mathbb{R}^{25}$. The observed successor state $\hat{s}' \in \mathbb{R}^{25}$ is first abstracted to a state in $abs(\hat{s}') = s' \in S$ as follows. If we observe fall or self-collision, we map $\hat{s}'$ to s^{fall} respectively s^{coll}; otherwise, if $\hat{s}'$ lies "sufficiently near" to one of the considered states, we represent it by the "closest" state; otherwise, if it is "too far" from the defined poses of interest, we represent it by the special state s^{far}. Formally, we define a mapping $abs : \mathbb{R}^{25} \to S$ as

1. $abs(\hat{s}') = s^{fall}$ in case of falling, else
2. $abs(\hat{s}') = s^{coll}$ in case of self-collision, else
3. $abs(\hat{s}') = s^{goal}$ if $\| \hat{s}' - s^{goal} \| < d^{goal}$, else
4. $abs(\hat{s}') = s^*$ if $d^* \leq d^{far}$, and
5. $abs(\hat{s}') = s^{far}$ otherwise.

where $\| \cdot \|$ is the standard Euclidean norm, $d^{far} = \frac{1}{2} \min_{s_1, s_2 \in S} \| s_1 - s_2 \|$, $d^* = \min_{s \in S} \| \hat{s}' - s \|$, and $s^* = \text{argmin}_{s \in S} \| \hat{s}' - s \|$. Note that this mapping is efficient thanks to the k-d tree data structure we use.

Next the reward $r = R(s, a, s')$ is computed and the extended observation (s, a, s', r) is used to update the Q-matrix according to Eq. 3. Additionally, we remember that we observed (s, a, s') in a function M, which will be needed for an approximation of the probabilistic transition function (see Sect. 4.4).

More precisely, we use a function $M : S \times Act \times S \rightarrow \mathbb{N}$ with initial values $M(s, a, s') = 0$ for all $s, s' \in S$ and $a \in Act$ to represent this information; in the implementation, only entries with positive function values are stored. Each time s' was observed as the successor state of s when executing action a, we increase the value of $M(s, a, s')$ by 1.

An episode ends when the abstraction s' of the observed successor state $\hat{s}'$ is one of s^{goal}, s^{far}, s^{fall} or s^{coll}; in these cases, if a predefined termination condition of the learning algorithm is not yet satisfied, a new episode starts in the initial state. Otherwise, a next iteration starts from the successor state $\hat{s}'$.

In our implementation, the learning algorithm terminates after a fixed number of episodes; this number is experimentally determined to be sufficient for near-optimal strategies. Note that each episode terminates with probability 1.

After termination, for each state $s \in S \setminus \{s^{goal}, s^{far}, s^{fall}, s^{coll}\}$ we select a set $Act'_s \subseteq Act_s$ of actions with the highest $Q(s, \cdot)$-values. Q-learning outputs the strategy $\sigma : S \times Act \rightarrow [0, 1]$ defined by $\sigma(s^{goal}, a^{skip}) = \sigma(s^{far}, a^{restart}) = \sigma(s^{fall}, a^{restart}) = \sigma(s^{coll}, a^{restart}) = 1$,

$$\sigma(s, a) = \exp(Q(s, a)/c^{temp}) / \sum_{a' \in Act'_s} \exp(Q(s, a')/c^{temp}) \qquad (4)$$

for each $s \in S \setminus \{s^{goal}, s^{far}, s^{fall}, s^{coll}\}$ and $a \in Act'_s$, and $\sigma(s, a) = 0$ else.

Experimental Results. In our experiments we used for the ε-greedy strategy the value $\varepsilon = 0.15$, and for the generation of the scheduler the temperature value $c^{temp} = 10$. We initialised all entries in the Q-matrix by the value 10. To speed up learning, we use the scripted action sequence A in the first 50 episodes. The fact that 26 different states were visited during these first 50 episodes, all simulating the same sequence of 13 actions, shows that the robot exhibits random behaviour. From the 51st episode on, we used the ε-greedy strategy.

Though we defined a relatively small state set, after some first experiments we recognised that the learning converges very slowly, the main bottleneck being the simulation (taking about half a second per action). To speed up learning, we first implemented a batch approach [22], where several episode simulations are run in parallel on multiple cores and the Q-matrix is updated only when all simulations in the batch (400 in our case) terminate. In this setting the ε value for the ε-greedy strategy was initialized to 0.15 and decremented at the end of each batch with a decay factor 0.999 until it reached 0.1 and then left fixed to this value. Also α was initialized to 0.5 and decremented with the same decay factor. γ was instead left unchanged to the initial value of 0.9.

This improvement speeded up the learning, however we observed that even when executing over 100000 episodes, most of the exploration was still done close to the initial state and relatively few exploration happened close to the goal state. To give an intuition, in 105753 episodes, the following table lists for $i = 0, \ldots, 12$ the total number of simulation steps executed in states reachable via a prefix $(a_0, \ldots, a_{i-1})$ of length i of the input trace $A = (a_0, \ldots, a_{12})$ (first row, $i = 0$ stays for the empty prefix, i.e., executions in s^{init}), and splits this number into simulation steps that used the successor action a_i in A (second row) and simulation steps that used a different action (third row):

i	0	1	2	3	4	5	6	7	8	9	10	11	12
Total	105753	69210	55543	43399	36191	31181	24635	21383	17875	15285	13174	11765	9318
a_i	52697	44481	34556	31754	29195	24397	20974	17843	15250	13036	11381	9332	8213
not a_i	53056	24729	20987	11645	6996	6784	3661	3540	2625	2249	1793	2433	1105

Therefore, we introduced a new approach that starts episodes not only in the initial state, but randomly in any state reachable by executing a (possibly empty) prefix of our input trace A. The starting state is determined by a probability distribution choosing the prefix of length i with probability $p_i = \frac{2(|A|-i)}{|A|(|A|+1)}$ for $i = 0, \ldots, k$ (where $|A| = k + 1$). Thus the probability decreases with the prefix length as follows (numbers rounded, $|A| = 13$):

p_0	p_1	p_2	p_3	p_4	p_5	p_6	p_7	p_8	p_9	p_{10}	p_{11}	p_{12}
0.14	0.13	0.12	0.10	0.09	0.08	0.07	0.06	0.05	0.04	0.03	0.02	0.01

This approach speeded up learning remarkably by distributing the exploration. The following table is analogous to the previous one but is based on the new approach and 166147 episodes:

i	0	1	2	3	4	5	6	7	8	9	10	11	12
Total	23697	42862	59236	74388	81859	83676	84651	86884	83910	80263	85465	68568	61246
a_i	20731	37359	49761	60250	67399	71125	73265	73346	72485	69983	64605	59344	53778
not a_i	2966	5503	9475	14138	14460	12551	11386	13538	11425	10280	20860	9224	7468

4.3 Component 3: Model Generation

Q-learning does not rely on a concrete model but on an estimation obtained implicitly during the learning process, whereas verification requires an explicit model. In order to enable formal methods, we define a *parametric* DTMC model of the robot in its environment, where the parameters represent the scheduler choices, as follows.

We use parameters $p_{s,a}$ to represent the probabilities with which the strategy chooses action a in state s. When we instantiate the parameters to $p_{s,a} = \sigma(s, a)$, we get a DTMC model of the robot that chooses actions according to the strategy σ received from Q-learning. Exceptions are the unsafe states s^{fall}, s^{coll} and s^{far}, for which we choose the restart action $a^{restart}$ with probability 1 to bring the robot back to its initial state. Furthermore, we make the goal state s^{goal}

absorbing by taking a self-transitions (using the action a^{skip}) back to it with probability 1. Formally, we introduce a set

$$Var = \{p_{s,a} \mid s \in S \setminus \{s^{far}, s^{fall}, s^{coll}, s^{goal}\} \wedge a \in Act_s \wedge \sigma(s,a) > 0\}$$

of parameters and define an initial valuation $v_0 : Var \to (0,1]$, $v_0(p_{s,a}) = \sigma(s,a)$ according to the strategy σ determined by Q-learning. As we want to keep the graph structure of the DTMC, we define the domains of the parameters as $(0,1]$; choosing smaller domains could be used to put stronger restrictions on how far the modification may change the original scheduler.

We use the observations M to define for each state s and action a the probability distribution $\mu_{s,a} : S \to [0,1]$ which characterises the successor states when executing a in s. We define $\mu_{s,a}(s') = M(s,a,s')/M(s,a)$ with $M(s,a) = \sum_{s'' \in S} M(s,a,s'')$ if $M(s,a) > 0$. Otherwise, if $M(s,a) = 0$ then no observations were made for action a in state s, therefore we cannot predict the successors; in this case we define the far state s^{far} to be the successor with probability 1 by setting $\mu_{s,a}(s^{far}) = 1$ and $\mu_{s,a}(s') = 0$ for $s' \in S \setminus \{s^{far}\}$.

Now we can formalise the parametric DTMC model $\mathcal{P} = (S, s^{init}, Var, P)$ of the robot, where for $(s,s') \in S \times S$ we set $P(s,s')$ to

- 1   for $(s,s') \in \{(s^{goal}, s^{goal}), (s^{far}, s^{init}), (s^{coll}, s^{init}), (s^{fall}, s^{init})\}$;
- 0   for $(s = s^{goal} \wedge s' \neq s^{goal}) \vee (s \in \{s^{far}, s^{coll}, s^{fall}\} \wedge s' \neq s^{init})$;
- $\displaystyle\sum_{a \in Act_s, \sigma(s,a) > 0} p_{s,a} \cdot \mu_{s,a}(s')$ for $s \notin \{s^{far}, s^{fall}, s^{coll}, s^{goal}\}$.

Experimental Results. We generated the parametric DTMC as described above and instantiated it with the scheduler σ from Q-learning. To test validity, we applied model checking to compute the probabilities of reaching the unsafe states s^{fall}, s^{coll} or s^{far} from the initial state in the model, and compared these probabilities to statistical observations gained by simulation (using the same scheduler σ for 300 simulations). It is worth mentioning that the probability to reach the goal state in the model is 1, *i.e.*, the goal state is the only bottom strongly connected component in the model's graph. Especially it means also that the probability to reach the goal state without visiting unsafe states is 1 minus the probability to reach an unsafe state. The results in the following table show that the behaviour of our parametric model is close to reality under σ:

	s^{fall}	s^{coll}	s^{far}
Probability to reach in model	0.001	0.005	0.048
Probability to reach in simulation	0	0.003	0.046

For model checking we employed the StoRM tool[1]. Is is of course also possible to use other probabilistic model checkers like PRISM [9], however, the flexible API met our needs best in terms of incrementality.

---

[1] Yet unpublished, developed by Christian Dehnert, RWTH Aachen University, Germany.

Using graph analysis methods, the generated model also allowed us to gain some information about the action sequences that the underlying scheduler might choose to bring the robot in the stand-up pose. We observed that the model contained at least 15 such traces (we did not perform a complete search) of length at most $|A| = 13$, and even some *shorter* traces of length 12.

4.4   Component 4: Greedy Model Repair

Reinforcement learning gives us a scheduler to achieve the standing-up task, however, it does not assure any upper bounds on the probabilities of reaching unsafe states. To achieve not only stability but also safety, we instantiate the parametric DTMC with the initial valuation v_0 (corresponding to the scheduler σ received from Q-learning) and check the resulting DTMC model for safety. If yes, the induced strategy can be applied. Otherwise, we will *automatically repair* the strategy to become safe by modifying the parameter values using the greedy model repair approach [6], introduced in Sect. 2. For the kind of models we have in our application the model repair is complete, *i.e.*, it will always yield a repaired model that satisfies the safety constraints, if there exists any (Fig. 6).

More formally, given $\lambda \in (0,1) \subseteq \mathbb{Q}$, our aim is to modify the initial parameter valuation v_0 to a valuation v such that the probability to reach unsafe states s^{fall}, s^{coll} or s^{far} from s^{init} in the DTMC $\mathcal{D}(\mathcal{P}, v)$ induced by v is at most λ. For each state s and action a, the repair potentially changes the scheduler probabilities $\sigma(s,a)$, while the support $\{a \in Act_s \,|\, \sigma(s,a) > 0\}$ remains unchanged, *i.e.*, it neither introduces new actions nor assigns possible actions probability. Furthermore, to keep the strategy near-optimal, we are interested in a solution "close" to the initial scheduler, *i.e.*, we want to change the distributions smoothly.

Different heuristics can be used to select the state whose distribution should be repaired or affected by the repair and to decide how strong the modifications might be. We use the following ones: Assume a current parameter valuation v.

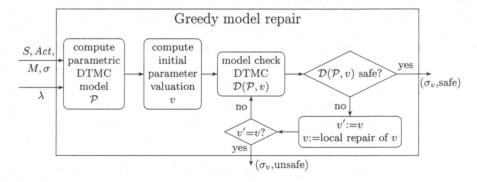

Fig. 6. The greedy model repair framework

From the model checking result we know for each state $s \in S$ the probability p_s^{unsafe} to reach one of the unsafe states from s in $\mathcal{D}(\mathcal{P}, v)$. Remember that for each state $s \in S \setminus \{s^{far}, s^{fall}, s^{coll}, s^{goal}\}$, the probability to reach a successor state s' is $P(s, s') = \sum_{a \in Act_s, \sigma(s,a)>0} v(p_{s,a}) \cdot \mu_{s,a}(s')$. For each such state s, we first determine the "safest" action $a_s^{safe} \in Act_s$, $\sigma(s, a_s^{safe}) > 0$ that minimises the probability $\sum_{s' \in S} \mu_{s,a}(s') \cdot p_{s'}^{unsafe}$ to reach unsafe states, and for each action $a \in Act_s \setminus \{a_s^{safe}\}$ with $v(p_{s,a}) > \delta$ we increase $v(p_{s,a_s^{safe}})$ by δ and decrease $v(p_{s,a})$ by δ. After we have repaired each repairable distribution, we iterate model checking and repair until the probability to reach an unsafe state from the initial state s^{init} in $\mathcal{D}(\mathcal{P}, v)$ is below $\lambda = 0.001$ (i.e., below 0.1 %). To speed up the repairing process, we first select a relatively large δ and decrement it when no further repair is possible (and the safety threshold is not yet reached). In our experiments we use $\delta \in \{0.2, 0.1, 0.05, 0.01\}$ in a decreasing order.

The algorithm returns a scheduler σ_v computed from the final valuation v by setting $\sigma(s, a) = v(p_{s,a})$.

Experimental Results. We performed model repair on the model generated in the previous section, following the heuristics described above. The model repair was fast and performed well without further adaptations. After the termination of the repair process, we used 300 simulations to validate the repaired model. The results are summarised in the following table:

	s^{fall}	s^{coll}	s^{far}
Probability to reach in *repaired* model	0.0001	0.0002	0.0012
Probability to reach in simulation	0.063	0.113	0.747

The above results demonstrate that the repaired model is not valid any more. After a thorough analysis we have found out that the model was invalidated by the repair because the repair increased the probabilities of actions for which relatively few observations were available, and therefore come with high uncertainties. To solve this problem, we modified the definition of the parametric DTMC by defining higher probabilities to get to unsafe successor states if fewer observations per successor state were available. More precisely, for a state s and an action a let $\nu_{s,a} = \exp(-\frac{M(s,a)}{50 \cdot |\{s' \in S \mid M(s,a,s')>0\}|}) \cdot 100$. For each state-action pair (s, a) with $M(s, a) > 0$, instead of specifying $\mu_{s,a}(s') = M(s, a, s')/M(s, a)$, we set $\mu_{s,a}(s') = M(s, a, s')/(M(s, a) + \nu_{s,a})$ for each $s' \neq s^{far}$ and define $\mu_{s,a}(s^{far}) = (M(s, a, s^{far}) + \nu_{s,a})/(M(s, a) + \nu_{s,a})$.

This adaptation gave us the following results, which suggest that, under the above consideration of uncertainties in the model generation, the repair leads to a valid model (we used 500 simulations):

	s^{fall}	s^{coll}	s^{far}
Probability to reach in *repaired* model	0.0003	$6.8 \cdot 10^{-6}$	0.02
Probability to reach in simulation	0	0	0

4.5   Component 5: Runtime Monitoring

Once a strategy is learnt and repaired, it can be deployed on the robot. If the model is valid and neither the robot nor the environment undergo changes, the robot is safe. However, if one of these conditions is violated, the previously safe and stable strategy might fail. To account for those cases, we integrate a feedback loop via runtime monitoring to the model generation and repair stages. During deployment, we collect observations like previously done in the M matrix, and from time to time we re-compute the model according to the new observations, and repair the current scheduler (if necessary) based on the adapted model. This process helps to improve the validity of the model in case there are no changes in the robot nor its environment.

However, if either the robot or its environment changes, due to large M-matrix entries it might take very long till observations of a modified setting will have a visible effect on the computed probability distributions in the model. To account also for such cases, after each model computation, we may scale down entries of M in such a way that new observations will lead to faster adaptations.

Experimental Results. To check the adaptiveness of our approach, after completed scheduler generation, we modified the simulations such that one of the actions in the input trace A leads to self-collision. In this way we modeled that a part of the robot is broken, such that the input trace did not lead from the initial to the goal state any more. We simulated 300 episodes; only 2 of them reached the goal, 297 collided, none has fallen, and 1 episode ended in a far state.

We used the observations from these 300 episodes, adapted the model and repaired the scheduler. The repair changed the scheduler towards alternative traces to the stand-up pose: from further 300 episodes (using the repaired scheduler), 197 reached the goal (without visiting unsafe states), 83 collided, 1 has fallen and 19 ended in a far state. These results hint to a potential improvement brought by monitoring, but further experiments with more episodes will be needed for a more precise evaluation of the monitoring feedback loop.

5   Lessons Learnt

We proposed an integrated approach, combining reinforcement learning, static analysis and runtime monitoring techniques to develop a stable and safe strategy for a robot to stand-up. First experimental results gave interesting insights into both the challenges as well as the potentials of such an application. In general, we can conclude with the following observations:

- Even for highly complex systems it is possible to find a manageable subset of the state space still representing sufficient information to solve relevant problems.
- In our application, formal methods were employable without any major obstacle. The main bottleneck was the time-consuming simulation.
- The combination of reinforcement learning and static methods allowed to derive new and even shorter paths, different from the original scripted one.
- Runtime monitoring can be successfully combined with formal methods to adapt systems to changing (internal or environmental) conditions.

To witness applicability, our next steps will focus on more detailed models and learning phases. Especially, we will consider (1) the generation of larger state spaces, allowing more alternatives for the standing-up procedure, (2) further adaptations of reinforcement learning to speed up its convergence, (3) improve the repair heuristics, and (4) further increase the adaptation speed to changing conditions by improving the feedback loop via runtime monitoring.

References

1. Stückler, J., Schwenk, J., Behnke, S.: Getting back on two feet: reliable standing-up routines for a humanoid robot. In: Proceedings of the IAS-9, pp. 676–685. IOS Press (2006)
2. Morimoto, J., Doya, K.: Acquisition of stand-up behavior by a real robot using hierarchical reinforcement learning. Robot. Auton. Syst. **36**(1), 37–51 (2001)
3. Morimoto, J., Doya, K.: Reinforcement learning of dynamic motor sequence: learning to stand up. In: Proceedings of the 1998 IEEE/RSJ International Conference on Intelligent Robots and Systems, vol. 3, pp. 1721–1726 (1998)
4. Schuitema, E., Wisse, M., Ramakers, T., Jonker, P.: The design of LEO: a 2D bipedal walking robot for online autonomous reinforcement learning. In: Proceedings of the IROS 2010, pp. 3238–3243 (2010)
5. Sutton, R.S., Barto, A.G.: Introduction to Reinforcement Learning. MIT Press, Cambridge (1998)
6. Pathak, S., Ábrahám, E., Jansen, N., Tacchella, A., Katoen, J.-P.: A greedy approach for the efficient repair of stochastic models. In: Havelund, K., Holzmann, G., Joshi, R. (eds.) NFM 2015. LNCS, vol. 9058, pp. 295–309. Springer, Heidelberg (2015). doi:10.1007/978-3-319-17524-9_21
7. Baier, C., Katoen, J.P.: Principles of Model Checking. The MIT Press, Cambridge (2008)
8. Hahn, E.M., Hermanns, H., Zhang, L.: Probabilistic reachability for parametric Markov models. Softw. Tools Technol. Transf. **13**(1), 3–19 (2010)
9. Kwiatkowska, M., Norman, G., Parker, D.: PRISM 4.0: verification of probabilistic real-time systems. In: Gopalakrishnan, G., Qadeer, S. (eds.) CAV 2011. LNCS, vol. 6806, pp. 585–591. Springer, Heidelberg (2011). doi:10.1007/978-3-642-22110-1_47
10. van Otterlo, M., Wiering, M.: Reinforcement learning and Markov decision processes. In: Wiering, M., van Otterlo, M. (eds.) Reinforcement Learning, vol. 12, pp. 3–42. Springer, Heidelberg (2012)
11. Bartocci, E., Grosu, R., Katsaros, P., Ramakrishnan, C.R., Smolka, S.A.: Model repair for probabilistic systems. In: Abdulla, P.A., Leino, K.R.M. (eds.) TACAS 2011. LNCS, vol. 6605, pp. 326–340. Springer, Heidelberg (2011). doi:10.1007/978-3-642-19835-9_30

12. Chen, T., Hahn, E.M., Han, T., Kwiatkowska, M., Qu, H., Zhang, L.: Model repair for Markov decision processes. In: Proceedings of the TASE 2013, pp. 85–92. IEEE (2013)
13. Bartocci, E., Bortolussi, L., Nenzi, L., Sanguinetti, G.: On the robustness of temporal properties for stochastic models. In: Proceedings of the HSB 2013. EPTCS, vol. 125, pp. 3–19 (2013)
14. Katoen, J.P., Zapreev, I.S., Hahn, E.M., Hermanns, H., Jansen, D.N.: The ins and outs of the probabilistic model checker MRMC. Perform. Eval. **68**(2), 90–104 (2011)
15. Bioloid premium kit. http://en.robotis.com/index/product.php?cate_code= 121010. Accessed 3 July 2016
16. Dynamixel actuators. http://en.robotis.com/index/product.php?cate_code= 101010. Accessed 3 July 2016
17. Bioloid URDF model. https://github.com/dxydas/ros-bioloid. Accessed 3 July 2016
18. Rohmer, E., Singh, S.P.N., Freese, M.: V-REP: a versatile and scalable robot simulation framework. In: Proceedings of the IROS 2013, pp. 1321–1326 (2013)
19. Bentley, J.L.: Multidimensional binary search trees used for associative searching. Commun. ACM **18**(9), 509–517 (1975)
20. Schaul, T., Bayer, J., Wierstra, D., Sun, Y., Felder, M., Sehnke, F., Rückstieß, T., Schmidhuber, J.: PyBrain. J. Mach. Learn. Res. **11**, 743–746 (2010)
21. Defazio, A., Graepel, T.: A comparison of learning algorithms on the arcade learning environment. arXiv preprint arXiv:1410.8620 (2014)
22. Lange, S., Gabel, T., Riedmiller, M.: Batch reinforcement learning. In: Wiering, M., van Otterlo, M. (eds.) Reinforcement Learning, pp. 45–73. Springer, Heidelberg (2012)

On Combinations of Static and Dynamic Analysis – Panel Introduction

Martin Leucker[✉]

Institute for Software Engineering and Programming Languages,
Universtity of Lübeck, Lübeck, Germany
leucker@isp.uni-luebeck.de

– Extended Abstract –

Model checking [1] deals with the problem of deciding whether all runs of a system under scrutiny satisfy a given specification. As typically infinite runs of the system are of interest, a dynamic analysis of complete runs is not possible. Hence, model checking is necessarily a static analysis technique. Runtime verification [2] on the other hand concentrates on prefixes of runs of the system as it typically considers the actual, necessarily finite run of the system. So while both model checking and runtime verification focus on runs of the system under scrutiny they have a different focus and are applied on a different level of abstraction. In this presentation we elaborate on the similarities and differences of model checking and runtime verification, yet, we mainly introduce question but questions to be studied in the future. We recall the work pointed out in [3] putting runtime verification and (LTL-based) model checking into the same formal framework.

Finite runs are also considered in model checking in the setting of bounded model checking [4]. Again bounded model checking is used statically and considers all runs up-to a given length while runtime verification considers a single run. In this presentation, we also describe the formal similarities and differences of bounded model checking with typical runtime verification semantics.

One of the core ideas for making model checking scalable to large systems is *abstraction*. Here systems which are smaller but have more behavior are examined. If the system with more behavior is shown to be correct, also the underlying system is correct. If on the other hand a counter-example is found it is checked whether it is spurious, i.e. it only exists in the abstraction but not in the real system, or whether it is a real counter-example. In the first case the abstraction is refined to eliminate the spurious counter-example. For finite state systems this procedure, known as CEGAR [5], is terminating with an exact result – at least theoretically. Practically, however, also CEGAR-based model checking does not terminate for many real examples. In the presentation, it is discussed in which way combinations of model checking and runtime verification could be built to make use of the partial information obtained in an unsuccessful model checking approach. In other words we explain what could be done when a model checking run is terminated due to a time-out and in which way runtime verification can profit from the so far explored state space. Likewise we explain how static

T. Margaria and B. Steffen (Eds.): ISoLA 2016, Part I, LNCS 9952, pp. 515–516, 2016.
DOI: 10.1007/978-3-319-47166-2_35

analysis as a method for obtaining partial information about the underlying system can be used to improve the runtime verification approach.

Altogether we sketch ideas for the combination of static and dynamic analysis. Yet we mostly point out directions for future research rather than giving satisfying answers.

References

1. Baier, C., Katoen, J.: Principles of Model Checking. MIT Press, Cambridge (2008)
2. Leucker, M., Schallhart, C.: A brief account of runtime verification. J. Log. Algebr. Program. **78**(5), 293–303 (2009)
3. Leucker, M.: Sliding between model checking and runtime verification. In: Qadeer, S., Tasiran, S. (eds.) RV 2012. LNCS, vol. 7687, pp. 82–87. Springer, Heidelberg (2013). doi:10.1007/978-3-642-35632-2_10
4. Biere, A., Cimatti, A., Clarke, E., Zhu, Y.: Symbolic model checking without BDDs. In: Cleaveland, W.R. (ed.) TACAS 1999. LNCS, vol. 1579, pp. 193–207. Springer, Heidelberg (1999). doi:10.1007/3-540-49059-0_14
5. Clarke, E.M., Grumberg, O., Jha, S., Lu, Y., Veith, H.: Counterexample-guided abstraction refinement. In: Emerson, E.A., Sistla, A.P. (eds.) CAV 2000. LNCS, vol. 1855, pp. 154–169. Springer, Heidelberg (2000)

Safer Refactorings

Anna Maria Eilertsen[1], Anya Helene Bagge[1], and Volker Stolz[2](✉)

[1] Institute for Informatikk, Universitetet i Bergen, Bergen, Norway
anna.eilertsen@student.uib.no, anya@ii.uib.no
[2] Institute for Data- og Realfag, Høgskolen i Bergen, Bergen, Norway
volker.stolz@hib.no

Abstract. Refactorings often require semantic correctness conditions that amount to software model checking. However, IDEs such as Eclipse's Java Development Tools implement far simpler checks on the structure of the code. This leads to the phenomenon that a seemingly innocuous refactoring can change the behaviour of the program. In this paper we demonstrate our technique of introducing runtime checks for two particular refactorings for the Java programming language: Extract And Move Method, and Extract Local Variable. These checks can, in combination with unit tests, detect changed behaviour and allow identification of which specific refactoring step introduced the deviant behaviour.

1 Introduction

Programmers refactor their code frequently [13]. According to Fowler, a *refactoring* is *"a change made to the internal structure of software to make it easier to understand and cheaper to modify without changing its observable behavior"* [5]. Refactoring is traditionally done on the source code, and can modify the structure on various levels.

For example, we may increase reuse or readability in almost all programming languages by splitting a large method or function into several or replacing a reoccurring expression with a local variable. Two of the refactorings we will discuss, a variant of Extract Method and Extract Local Variable, are frequently used in many languages.

In object-oriented programs, manipulation of the class hierarchy can also be a refactoring: examples of this are introducing a subclass, or collapsing a subclass into a superclass by repeatedly applying the Pull-up Method/Field refactoring. The other refactoring discussed in this work is the Move Method refactoring. It moves a method, not within the class hierarchy, but rather "side-ways" into a different class. Many of these refactoring steps correlate with software quality metrics, such as number of lines, and number of methods. The Move Method refactoring, for example, can affect coupling between classes.

Refactorings have traditionally been described in the form of patterns. For object-oriented languages these patterns usually consist of a structural

This article is based upon work from COST Action ARVI IC1402, supported by COST (European Cooperation in Science and Technology).

© Springer International Publishing AG 2016
T. Margaria and B. Steffen (Eds.): ISoLA 2016, Part I, LNCS 9952, pp. 517–531, 2016.
DOI: 10.1007/978-3-319-47166-2_36

match, and a description of the behaviour of the code. Informal natural language descriptions of behaviour have also been used to "specify" design patterns [6]: ideally programmers match their mental model of the code they are going to write against the available patterns. Various attempts have been made to formalise refactorings, see for example Opdyke's work [14], and Schäfer and de Moor [16], or design patterns, as in Cinnéide [2].

Describing the behaviour of refactorings, either formally or informally, pose various challenges. Natural language may impose ambiguities in the descriptions, while formal specifications are hard to communicate. Firstly, while the required static structure of software can be described concisely, through e.g. a class diagram, there is no agreed-on, commonly used notation for behaviour. Secondly, even though refactorings can be formalised for ideal subsets of programming languages (like Featherweight Java [8]), the resulting specification is not easily generalised to the full language. Currently, implementations in industrial-grade refactoring tools must be ad-hoc, and may consequently introduce subtle semantic changes. This is the case in e.g. Eclipse and NetBeans. In fact, an inspection of the Eclipse bug tracker reveals numerous cases of refactorings producing code that no longer compiles correctly.

As we will soon see in an example, an ad-hoc refactoring may accidentally change the behaviour of a program. According to Fowler's commonly used definition of refactorings above, this must be interpreted as a bug, and the "refactoring" should not have been applied in the first place. While it is relatively straightforward to check for structural issues, such as overriding a method, there can also be more subtle changes in the heap at run time. The behaviour might in fact change without any compiler warning, and the developer must rely on having suitable unit tests to uncover the newly introduced undesired behaviour.

Consider the fragment of code in Listing 1. Since the code in class C uses the public field x to call methods repeatedly, and since the field is not declared final, at runtime the value of x changes between the two method invocations.

```
1  public class C {                    public class X {
2    public X x = new X();               public void m(C c) {
3                                            c.x = new X();
4    public void f() {                       // If m is called from
5      x.m(this);                            // c, then c.x no longer
6      // Not the same x.                    // equals 'this'.
7      x.n();                              }
8    }                                     public void n() {...}
9  }                                     }
```

Listing 1: Source and destination for Extract- and Move-Method refactoring, before refactoring.

From informal observations we conclude that developers do not expect such intermittent reassigments as in our example, but work on the assumption that attribute values in syntactic proximity do not change. They expect the simpler behaviour of calling the methods on the same object for adjacent lines of code. Our example is certainly simplistic, but in a large code base such behaviour may not be evident. The pattern in our example can be generalised to longer (not necessarily contiguous) sequences of statements, using navigation path expressions with varying prefixes.

APIs frequently require sequences of invocations, and best practices of programming require to avoid repetition: as a programmer is invoking methods on the same variable, she may decide to refactor this sequence into a new method in the target class (assuming that the source code for the target is under her control, and not e.g. in a library). In case this variable is a local variable already, extracting and moving the statements is safe, as long as the local variable is not reassigned. If it is a non-final attribute though, as we have seen, the refactoring will produce valid code, but with changed behaviour: whereas the calls before have been on distinct objects, they are now on a single object, obviously giving the program a different meaning.

As this problem in general cannot be detected statically at the time the refactoring is applied, we combine the refactoring with the generation of an assertion that will report at runtime if the refactoring had been incorrectly applied. Applying the refactoring with the generated assertion on the above example, we obtain the following:

```
————— Refactored source —————          ————— New method h —————
1  public class C {                     public class X {
2     public X x = new X();                public void h(C arg) {
3                                             m(arg);
4     public void f() {                       /* generated by our approach: */
5        x.h(this);                           assert arg.x == this;
6     }                                        n();
7  }                                        }
                                          }
```

Listing 2: Changed code after refactoring.

We claim that it is easy for developers to make this mistake in practice: the illustrated refactoring step can easily be applied in e.g. Eclipse or IntelliJ through the Move Method refactoring, possibly preceded by the Extract Method refactoring. There are no checks that will warn the programmer about the changed behaviour. We note that a similar effect can be observed when extracting to a local variable: should any side-effect manipulate the value of the extracted sub-expression, the original code will execute subsequent method calls on different objects, and the refactored code on a single object. Both patterns are very similar, and we will see that our approach covers both.

Proposed Solution. The changed behaviour can be easily detected at runtime, if we *encode the necessary assumptions into assertions.* For the above example, it is straightforward to first store the target of the method call in a new variable, passing it along, and checking for object equality in the newly introduced method body, see again Listing 2.

We present the following contributions: (1) our technique of generating assertions for the Extract-Local and Move-Method refactorings, (2) a drop-in replacement for the Extract-Local refactoring with assertion generation for the Eclipse JDT, and assertion generation for the Extract-And-Move-Method refactoring plugin we developed in earlier work [10].

2   The Refactorings

In this section, we describe the two refactorings, how our assertions capture the semantic requirements, and the underlying theory.

Fowler's "observable behaviour" is open to interpretation up to a certain degree, even the notion that a refactored program should show the same input/output behaviour as the original code: are differences in intermediate output tolerated, e.g. when restructured control flow leads to different debugging output? In the absence of method specifications, does this notion apply to method output (results), or only for the cases covered by unit tests?

Here, we take the position that for an object-oriented program, the observable behaviour can also be understood as a *sequence of method invocations on particular objects* during the execution of a program. Note that this opens the possibility that we consider the refactoring as incorrect (different sequence), even though the output is unchanged. It is easy to see that the Extract-And-Move refactoring above produces different execution histories, as will the Extract-Local refactoring. Without going into the depth of the argument, we also observe that some refactorings require a notion of *history refinement*: the Extract Method refactoring preserves existing calls in the history, but adds intermediate calls to the newly created method. Extract Local Variable can collapse multiple calls to the same method into a single one. Other structural manipulations such as Pull-Up Method that modify the inheritance hierarchy, may, if incorrectly applied, preserve the objects in the history, but lead to calling different virtual methods with the same name.

2.1   Extract Local

Extract Local Variable (also called Extract Variable, or Introduce Explaining Variable [5, p. 124]) is a pattern for replacing a repeating expression with a reference to a local variable initialised to said expression.

Extract Local Variable takes as input an expression e and a consecutive selection of statements S. It declares a variable v and initialises it to the value of e. Then all occurrences of e in S are substituted with a reference to v.

The problem with respect to behaviour-preservation appears if e evaluates to different values throughout the selection, i.e. we are making a substitution where the introduced variable does not have the same value at that point as the original expression. The problem appears because v will be fixed to the value e evaluates to at that line, regardless of whether the expression e would evaluate to different values in the original expression where it has been replaced by v.

The underlying problem is essentially the requirement for a precise *points-to analysis* [15, 17] : we need to know that for all statements in the selected range, the target expression e evaluates always exactly to the same object.

Optimizing compilers or JVMs that would like to minimise redundant loads of fields, i.e. heap accesses where the value cannot have changed in between, use this analysis and suffer from the same limitations. The optimization in the compiler is known as Common Subexpression Elimination, and done statically and conservatively. On the JVM-level this has been tackled under the name "Hot Field-analysis" by Wimmer and Mössenböck [19] through an aggressive, dynamic technique that efficiently switches back to the unoptimized and correct behaviour, in case it detects that the relevant heap has been modified.

Thus, to ensure correctness of Extract Local Variable we check at every substitution that the introduced variable evaluates to the same value as the replaced expression, i.e. `assert v == e`. In some cases we can guarantee correctness without asserts under any of the following conditions:

- e is only referred to once in the program
- e is a local variable and it is not assigned to in S
- all segments of e are field references with the `final` modifier

The expression argument could also contain method calls, which introduces yet another problem concerning side-effects: if a method has side effects, it matters how many times it is called. In our work we assume e (but not S) to be free of side effects, and we do not pursue this problem further.

```
——— Before Extract Local Variable ———     After Safer Extract Local Variable

1                                          public void f() {
2                                            X temp = a.b.c.d;
3     public void f() {                      temp.m();
4       a.b.c.d.m();                         assert temp == a.b.c.d;
5       a.b.c.d.n();                         temp.n();
6       a.b.foo(a.b.c.d);                    assert temp == a.b.c.d;
7       a.b.bar();                           a.b.foo(temp);
8       a.b.c.d.m();                         a.b.bar();
9     }                                      assert temp == a.b.c.d;
                                             temp.m();
                                           }
```

Listing 3: Safer Extract Local Variable

Our Safer Extract Local Variable includes the following algorithm for inserting asserts, to be performed after the original refactoring is finished:

Let e be the expression argument, S a contiguous selection of statements, and v be the newly introduced variable:

for each statement s in S:

if s contains an expression with subexpression v

insert the following statement in S, before s: `assert v == e;`

We illustrate this with the example in Listing 3.

The Extract-Local refactoring can be applied to expressions of any non-void type, whether it is an object, or a primitive value. In the following, we will take this refactoring as the starting point for a more complex, object-oriented refactoring, where we will be only interested in object references.

2.2   Extract and Move

Generalising from the example in Listings 1 and 2, it is easy to see why a developer would want to Extract and Move such a fragment: from a software-quality metrics perspective, the so-called coupling between the two involved classes can be decreased. However, as our example illustrates, the resulting behaviour is not as clear-cut as it may seem at the first glance.

While the extraction of code fragments into a new temporary method (with a fresh name) is unproblematic, the origin of the problem lies in the updates to the navigations paths upon moving the temporary method into the new type. In fact, the Move Method-refactoring demonstrated here, as implemented for example by the Eclipse refactoring tools for Java, is not the only interpretation of what said refactoring should do.

```
————— Opdyke's original idea ————        ————————— Our idea —————————
1   class X {                             class X {
2     public void h(C c) {                  public void h(C c) {
3       c.x.m();                              m();
4       // Not necessarily the same x.        assert c.x == this;
5       c.x.n();                              n();
6   } }                                   } }
```

Listing 4: Result of Opdyke's refactoring (left) compared to ours (right)

Alternative characterizations of Move Method-refactorings (and a formalization) for C++ programs was given by Opdyke in his seminal PhD thesis [14, Sects.8.5 and 8.6]. He offers two alternatives, one where a reference back to the original object is passed as a parameter, and another where those references are handled through an additional field in the destination class. The snippets in Listing 4 contrasts the outcome of Opdyke's refactoring that uses parameters with our refactoring. The method is assumed to have been moved into the declared type for the field $c.x$. We observe that Opdyke's solution with parameters is more general, as it also preserves behaviour in the case of heap-manipulation, since it preserves all field accesses from the original code. The alternative solution with a field access requires a program flow analysis in the precondition. Both of his solutions yield more complex navigation paths and increased coupling, whereas in our case, coupling can be reduced.

Our approach requires passing additional data that is used in the equality check in the assertions. It serves the purpose of a *ghost variable* (see [7] for a discussion of their usefulness and a critique), and should be understood as existing on the level of a specification: after discharging the assertion (and thus proving correctness of the refactoring step), the variable could be removed.

While in the case of Extract Local, this is only an additional local variable, in the case of Extract And Move Method, this results in an additional parameter that gets passed into the newly extract method. Care must be taken in the subsequent development steps that no other dependencies are introduced on this variable, so that when the assertions eventually get removed/discharged, the unused parameter can also be removed, and thus avoiding increased coupling between classes. Nonetheless, other subexpressions used in the extracted method may also need to be passed as additional parameters, and increase coupling—but these are the responsibility of the refactorer.

```
––––––––––– Original code –––––––––––        ––––––– Extract Local w/assert –––––––
1  class C{                                  class C{
2    public void f() {                         public void f() {
3      x.m(this);                                X temp = x;
4      x.n();                                    temp.m(this);
5  } }                                           assert temp == x;
                                                 temp.n();
                                             } }
```

```
––––––––––– Extract Method –––––––––––        ––––––––––– Move Method –––––––––––
1  class C{                                  class C{
2    public void f() {                         public void f() {
3      X temp = x;                               X temp = x;
4      h(temp);                                  temp.h(this);
5    }                                         } }
6    public void h(X temp){                  class X{
7      temp.m(this);                           public void h(C c){
8      assert temp == x;                         this.m(c);
9      temp.n();                                 assert this == c.x;
10 } }                                           this.n();
                                             } }
```

Listing 5: Our Extract And Move Method with asserts starts with applying Extract Local Variable, which also introduces the asserts. Next, we extract the method, and use the extracted variable as the target for Move Method. Finally, the extracted variable temp can be safely inlined again (not shown).

Conceptually, Extract And Move Method is composed by Extract Method and Move Method. In our safer version we also need to introduce assertions to check that the value of the target expression does not change throughout the selection, i.e. method call. These are the same assertions as for Extract Local Variable, where we check that the value of the extracted variable does not change throughout the selection. Thus, we perform Extract And Move Method by composing Extract Local Variable, with Extract Method, followed by Move Method. A final Inline Variable removes the extra variable introduced by Extract Local Variable. This is illustrated in Listing 5. Extract Method and Move Method are defined as follows.

Extract Method [5, p. 110] takes as input a consecutive selection of statements S occurring in a class C. It introduces a new method m in C, with S as the method body. All occurrences of S in C are replaced with a call to m. Arguments are restricted in that they must form a syntactically correct method body with one return type or void. If S refers to local variables declared before S, these are passed as arguments to the method. If one local variable, v, that is assigned to in S is used in subsequent code, then the assigned value will be the return value of m, and v will be assigned the result of the method call. If two or more local variables assigned to in S are used in subsequent code, then S is not a legal selection. We will call a selection fulfilling these properties *well-formed.*

Move Method [5, p. 142] takes as input a method m in a class C and an expression e. The expression argument can only contain one or more segments of field lookups or local variables and cannot contain any method calls or other operators than the dot-operator. It declares a new method n in the type of e. If S refers to members of C, n will have an extra parameter c of type C. The method body of n is S with all occurrences of `this` replaced with c and all occurrences of e replaced with `this`. m is then removed from the original class, and all calls to m are replaced with a similar call to n. The argument given to c is `this`.

The safer Extract And Move Method takes two arguments: the expression argument e, corresponding to the target of Move Method, and the selection of statements S, corresponding to the selection argument to Extract Method. These are passed to Extract Local Variable, resulting in a local variable v. Then S is extracted to a new method m, taking at least one parameter corresponding to v. We then move m to the target type of e; a new parameter c is introduced, and all references to the v-parameter is replaced by the `this`-keyword. Obsolete parameters are removed. Remaining references to members in C is now referenced through c. Finally, in the original class, we inline all occurrences of v.

3   Experiment

In the previous section, we have described in detail and applied in examples our refactoring, and have shown that a violating example can be created easily. To validate our idea, that this semantic change could happen in the wild, and that our asserts would capture it, we did a case study. Our *case* is a large code base, representative for object oriented code. We decided to use the Java programming language. Since the asserts are runtime checks, we needed the code to actually run. Thus we focused on finding a code base with a well-covering test suite. We would run our refactoring on the code, then run the tests, and see:

1. do the tests trigger any of the generated assertions in the refactored code?
2. are the triggered asserts *sound*, i.e. do they tell us about actual behaviour changes resulting from the refactorings?
3. are the triggered asserts *complete*, i.e. are there behaviour changes that are not captured by them (but by the tests)?

To do this we needed an implementation of our refactorings that could be automatically applied to a large code base, which required finding sensible arguments for the refactorings: where to apply, and which target expression to use.

We developed a tool for automatically applying both refactorings in appropriate places across an entire Java code base. Our tool contains a heuristic for where a developer would think to apply the refactorings, and executes both refactorings with generated asserts. The heuristic for Extract and Move Method was partially developed in earlier works [10] with the intention of reducing coupling between classes. We have adapted the Extract And Move heuristic as described below, and developed a similar heuristic for Extract Local Variable. The heuristic finds suitable arguments for each refactoring, including the "target" type for Extract And Move Method. What we have previously referred to as the expression argument of the refactorings, is picked from a set of possible arguments called *prefixes*. A prefix is a qualifier, field access, local variable or this keyword, and the heuristic enumerates the set of possible prefixes. For Extract Local Variable we extend the notion of prefix to include single-line getters: a method whose name starts with "get" and whose method body contains a single return statement. This is the only method call we allow as expression. In general we cannot know which method is called at runtime, so we look up the method in the static type of its qualifier. For Extract And Move Method we did not include getters, or any other kind of methods. The heuristic excludes prefixes where the selection contains a statement assigning a new value to the prefix, a variable declared in the selection, local type, unmodifiable type, etc. [9, 2.7].

We extended both heuristics to exclude cases where we knew the asserts would hold, or where we knew the code would break, as explained below. For Extract Local Variable almost all prefixes are allowed, but if the expression has only one segment *and* only occurs once, then there is no need to extract it into a local variable. For Extract And Move Method there are more exlusions:

- If e has only one segment *and* occurs only once, by the same reasoning we exclude it from our prefixes.
- If e is a local variable, it cannot be changed by a method call, and the refactoring will not contribute to our findings.
- If e is a field, it has to be visible from the resulting method n, otherwise we cannot generate syntactically correct assertions. This can be remedied by generating getters, but we did not pursue this idea yet.
- If e's type has generic type arguments, we exclude it, as it is not trivial to move a method into such a class.
- If e is a member of an anonymous type we will not be able to access n, and we exclude such prefixes.
- If e is a static class that will make n static, which is usually undesirable, and we exclude such prefixes.

After pruning the set of prefixes, we rank the remaining expressions after number of occurrences and number of segments. The top ranked expression will be considered the best candidate to the refactoring. The best selection argument will be the selection containing the best candidate.

In the following, we report on our results of combining the two ideas: automated, search-based refactoring and assertion generation.

Firstly, for a case study, we identify a convincingly large, non-trivial Java project that is amenable to our analysis and transformation. Secondly, this project has to have a reasonable amount of existing unit tests that we can run after the transformation to see whether assertions are triggered.

We chose the Eclipse JDT UI project. We believe that it is a good representative of professionally written Java source code with many contributors over the years. It comprises over 300.000 lines of code (excluding blanks and comments), with more than 25.000 methods, and comes with an extensive set of unit tests.

Experiment Implementation

We implemented our refactorings in a plugin for Eclipse. Our plugin supports an interactive and an automated search-based version of both refactorings. They can be invoked either on a method or a project. The interactive Extract Local refactoring can also be invoked directly on a well-formed selection of statements. Invoking a search-based refactoring on a method causes our heuristic to analyze the method to find suitable arguments for the refactoring. Next, our program will execute the refactoring on the candidate provided by the heuristics or the user. Here we are heavily supported by Eclipse's implementation of the refactorings Extract Local Variable, Extract Method and Move Method.

In an Eclipse-instance with our plugin, we imported the Eclipse JDT UI code for version 4.5 (with all dependencies) and the corresponding tests. Before the refactorings were invoked on the code, we ran the Automated Test Suite, where all unit tests passed. The test code was not refactored. We invoked the Extract Local Variable refactoring on the whole project, and ran the tests on the resulting code. We then invoked the Extract And Move Method refactoring on the original code, and ran the tests on the resulting code. We did not refactor already refactored code.

Invoking the *Search-Based Extract Local Variable* refactoring on the full Eclipse project resulted in 4.538 single refactorings and 7.665 assertions. The results are summarised in Table 1. The refactoring introduced no compile errors. We then ran the Eclipse JDT UI Automated Test suite on the refactored code. The test suite finished with 4 failures and 11 errors. The difference between a failure and error in this case, is whether the test expected an exception or error, or not. The 4 failures originated from violation of our generated asserts. The 11 errors were due to build issues, where the build file required an old version of

Table 1. These are the results of our experiment

	Extract and move method	Extract local variable
Executed refactorings	755	4538
Generated asserts	610	7665
Resulting compile errors	14	0
Tests failing before	0	0
Tests errors	84	11
Tests failures	161	4
Asserts triggered in tests	0	2
Instances of asserts triggered	0	137

Java that did not handle our generated asserts, and consequently one file did not finish building. Changing the target Java version in the build file resolved the build problem and removed these 11 errors. In addition, we had 133 violations of the generated asserts that were reported in the console output from the tests, but did not seem to affect the test results. Running the test suite without asserts produced no failures and no errors (after modifying said build file).

The reported assertion violations originated from two specific asserts. In both cases the extracted expression was a get-method. In one case it seemed to be a factory-method. In the other case the assert was triggered by a method returning a fresh string, where the string object is created in the getter instead of accessing a field or otherwise stored reference. Calling such a method twice will produce objects that may be object-equal (depending on the `equal`-function), but will not be reference-equal (as checked with ==).

We invoked the *Search-Based Extract And Move Method* refactoring on the full (unrefactored) Eclipse project, resulting in 755 applied refactorings and 610 assertions. This produced 14 compilation errors. Initially we had 180 compile errors, and we incrementally improved our heuristic to exclude targets that would introduce the different types of errors, as previously explained. 3 of the 14 compile errors were due to project specific settings (e.g. an error on unused import). Most compile errors were due to references to enclosing instance, reference to non-visible or unaccessible members, and missing imports. Running the Automated Test suite on the resulting code (with compile errors) produced 84 errors (test not completed due to compilation errors) and 161 failures (unit test not having the expected result). No asserts were found violated. Manually correcting all compile errors (as good as we could) and rerunning the tests produced no errors or failures, and still no assertion violations. Thus, we did not sift through the original test errors and failures with the intention of cataloguing their source.

We should point out that for Extract And Move Method we still had some refactorings that were executed but without generated asserts. Our tool aborted the insertion of asserts if it was clear (usually due to visibility issues) that the asserts would produce a syntactically incorrect program. We did not keep a history of the method-level changes in the refactoring, and did not undo the ones where the algorithm found it impossible to generate asserts. This means that we are only applying the runtime check at a fraction of our Extract And Move Method refactorings. In future work, we would like to introduce special get-methods for these cases. Another approach would be to increase visibility of fields, but this would require yet another check of correctness.

Threats to validity. The following issues have to be kept in mind when considering the experimental results:

- The number of identified instances where the Extract Method refactoring can be applied depends on the quality of the code base. A "perfectly refactored" project, or a project using less object-orientation, will have a lower number of possible instances.
- As described above, we had applications of Extract And Move Method where we could not generate assertions due to issues of field-visibility. This lowers

the potential for assertions to be triggered (although changed results could still be uncovered by failing unit tests).
- Our evaluation uses unit tests to detect changed behaviour. Our results depend on the coverage of the test suite.
- The total number of executed Extract And Move Method refactorings with generated asserts is rather low. We may need a much higher number of applied refactorings to find a violating instance.

We conclude that our experiment was suited for finding the results we needed, and we would like to repeat it with an improved version of the refactoring tool for more code bases. The implementation of the assert generation is not yet ideal, as these results tell us. Nonetheless, the results are promising and there are many improvements that can be done.

4   Conclusion and Future Work

Our research is motivated by the observation that common refactorings can easily, and accidentally, change a program's behaviour. We have presented our idea of improved refactorings, where their semantic correctness conditions are encoded as assertions. As these conditions are impossible, or at least difficult, to check statically, we think that runtime checks present a suitable tradeoff. The generated assertions also serve the additional purpose of documenting which refactoring has been applied and what its semantic *risks* are.

The assertions capture the necessary conditions on the heap for the Extract Local and the Extract And Move Method refactoring. While the former is a standard refactoring, we have implemented the latter as a combination of existing refactorings based on earlier work. We have evaluated our approach by refactoring a code base in the same way as we anticipate developers would do. We execute existing unit tests and observe if the generated assertions are triggered, which would indicate that the refactoring indeed changed the behaviour.

Our findings show a limited success, in that some assertions are violated. This means that a developer *may* accidentally apply the refactoring incorrectly. However, our experimental setup yields a low number of applied refactorings and generated assertions. In Future Work below, we discuss how we could collect more empirical evidence as to the usefulness of our assertions.

Related work. Opdyke already gave refactorings a formal treatment and considered behaviour preservation essential [14]. In his variations of the "Moving Members into a Component" refactorings, he carefully gives formal preconditions which make sure that the refactorings are structurally sound. He is aware that behaviour will not be preserved upon intermediate reassignments to members: "[...] all references to each moving member will point to the same location at all times. Program flow analysis would be needed to determine this." [14, p. 130]. This is the problem that we try to tackle dynamically here.

Schäfer and de Moor [16] give a concise, formal definition of some refactorings that they can translate easily into code for the JastAdd [4] attribute grammar framework for Java. For the refactorings they look at, they are mostly concerned with visibility and shadowing, and consequently make use of infrastructure that tracks such references and either keeps bindings consistent, or rejects a refactoring if the refactored program would have different bindings. They do not go as far as e.g. work on refinement, where it is even formally proved using graph transformations that (consistent) renaming preserves the semantics [20]. Graph transformations have also been used to specify refactorings by Mens et al. [12]; however, in the particular case of the Move Method refactoring, they have opted to only deal with static methods/calls, even unlike Opdyke's original solution, where dependencies would at least be passed by additional parameters. Also Ó Cinnéide's "minitransformations" preserve behaviour due to a restriction to structural manipulation [2].

Soares et al. [18] have generated test cases when applying a refactoring to uncover non-behaviour preserving transformations. We see our approach as a more fine-grained attempt, that during testing (e.g. through unit tests a la Soares), can inspect the object graph in much more detail than just observing the output of the unit tests.

Future Work. While we have a proof-of-concept with hand-written examples, our larger case study in combination with automated refactorings [10] did not reveal many interesting instances of refactoring-induced problems. In future work, we would therefore like to extend our experiment to larger code bases, and identify deficiencies in other refactorings that could be addressed in a similar way. Additionally, in combination with repository mining, it would be interesting to identify where/when in a repository one of our supported refactorings has been applied, add our assertions, and see if we can discover any changed behaviour. Also, we could have a group of software developers use our refactoring, and observe their experience. As we lack the capacity for either set up, we have opted for a more automated solution.

The attentive reader may have noticed that it is not necessary to run the fully refactored code to detect if the Extract And Move Method refactoring changed the behaviour. It is sufficient to only generate the assertions, and then use e.g. a test suite to observe if the semantic preconditions hold. Only after all generated assertions have been covered by the execution without revealing a problem, we would actually apply the final step of the refactoring and move the method.

Accessibility and visibility of the prefix argument to the refactoring is a problem in assertion generation: the Extract And Moved Method refactoring may be applied in more situations than we can generate assertions for. We would like to solve this by generating additional getters to the required information that will only be used by our asserts (and hopefully discarded along with them following subsequent advances in proof support for object-oriented programs). This would increase the number of checks per applied refactoring.

An alternative to using Java's assertions is JML [11], which would have the advantage that the assertions would not pollute the source code, and the additional state-keeping would be confined to JML ghost variables. Also, a custom IDE that understands the notion of these variables and parameters, and could thus hide them and the generated assertions from the human eye, would most likely improve adoption among developers of our approach. Such an IDE could also take care of any other code modifications like the special getters above, that only need to be available intermittently for the purpose of runtime verification of the refactorings, but should not be visible—or accessible—to developers.

More ambitiously, it would also be possible to attempt to discharge the assertions, which would amount to a correctness proof of an instance of the refactoring (as opposed to proving the entire refactoring correct). We have experimented with the KeY theorem prover [1], which has been able to automatically discharge the vacuous assertions in the trivial example program. This could be attempted unattended in the background after applying the refactoring, or extended to involve a *proof engineer*, who, as support to the actual programmers, attempts to discharge the generated assertions.

The Git repository with our Eclipse-based Java refactorings to reproduce our experiment is available at git://git.uio.no/ifi-stolz-refaktor.git. Additional details are published in a Master thesis [3].

References

1. Ahrendt, W., Beckert, B., Hähnle, R., Schmitt, P.H.: KeY: a formal method for object-oriented systems. In: Bonsangue, M.M., Johnsen, E.B. (eds.) FMOODS 2007. LNCS, vol. 4468, pp. 32–43. Springer, Heidelberg (2007)
2. Cinnéide, M.Ó., Nixon, P.: A methodology for the automated introduction of design patterns. In: International Conference on Software Maintenance, ICSM 1999, pp. 463–472. IEEE Computer Society (1999)
3. Eilertsen, A.M.: Making software refactoring safer. Master's thesis, Department of Informatics, University of Bergen (2016)
4. Ekman, T., Hedin, G.: The JastAdd system - modular extensible compiler construction. Sci. Comput. Program. **69**(1–3), 14–26 (2007)
5. Fowler, M.: Refactoring: Improving the Design of Existing Code. Addison-Wesley, Boston (1999)
6. Gamma, E., Helm, R., Johnson, R., Vlissides, J.: Design Patterns: Elements of Reusable Object-Oriented Software. Addison-Wesley, Boston (1994)
7. Hofmann, M., Pavlova, M.: Elimination of ghost variables in program logics. In: Barthe, G., Fournet, C. (eds.) TGC 2007. LNCS, vol. 4912, pp. 1–20. Springer, Heidelberg (2008). doi:10.1007/978-3-540-78663-4_1
8. Igarashi, A., Pierce, B.C., Wadler, P.: Featherweight Java: a minimal core calculus for Java and GJ. ACM Trans. Program. Lang. Syst. (TOPLAS) **23**(3), 396–450 (2001)
9. Kristiansen, E.: Automated composition of refactorings. Master's thesis, Department of Informatics, University of Oslo (2014). http://www.mn.uio.no/ifi/english/research/groups/pma/completedmasters/2014/kristiansen/
10. Kristiansen, E., Stolz, V.: Search-based composed refactorings. In: 27th Norsk Informatikkonferanse, NIK. Bibsys Open Journal Systems, Norway (2014)
11. Leavens, G.T.: JML's rich, inherited specifications for behavioral subtypes. In: Liu, Z., Kleinberg, R.D. (eds.) ICFEM 2006. LNCS, vol. 4260, pp. 2–34. Springer, Heidelberg (2006)

12. Mens, T., Taentzer, G., Runge, O.: Analysing refactoring dependencies using graph transformation. Softw. Syst. Model. **6**(3), 269–285 (2007)
13. Murphy-Hill, E., Parnin, C., Black, A.P.: How we refactor, and how we know it. IEEE Trans. Softw. Eng. **38**(1), 5–18 (2012)
14. Opdyke, W.F.: Refactoring object-oriented frameworks. Ph.D. thesis, University of Illinois at Urbana-Champaign (1992). UMI Order No. GAX93-05645
15. Ryder, B.G.: Dimensions of precision in reference analysis of object-oriented programming languages. In: Hedin, G. (ed.) CC 2003. LNCS, vol. 2622, pp. 126–137. Springer, Heidelberg (2003). doi:10.1007/3-540-36579-6_10
16. Schäfer, M., de Moor, O.: Specifying, implementing refactorings. In: Cook, W.R., Clarke, S., Rinard, M.C. (eds.) Object Oriented Programming: Systems, Languages, and Applications (OOPSLA) 2010, pp. 286–301. ACM (2010)
17. Smaragdakis, Y., Balatsouras, G.: Pointer analysis. Found. Trends Program. Lang. **2**(1), 1–69 (2015)
18. Soares, G., Gheyi, R., Serey, D., Massoni, T.: Making program refactoring safer. IEEE Softw. **27**(4), 52–57 (2010)
19. Wimmer, C., Mössenböck, H.: Automatic feedback-directed object inlining in the Java HotSpot^tm virtual machine. In: Krintz, C., Hand, S., Tarditi, D. (eds.) 3rd International Conference on Virtual Execution Environments VEE, pp. 12–21. ACM (2007)
20. Zhao, L., Liu, X., Liu, Z., Qiu, Z.: Graph transformations for object-oriented refinement. Formal Asp. Comput. **21**(1–2), 103–131 (2009)

Rigorous Engineering of Collective Adaptive Systems

Rigorous Engineering of Collective Adaptive Systems Track Introduction

Stefan Jähnichen[1] and Martin Wirsing[2(✉)]

[1] Technische Universität Berlin, Berlin, Germany
stefan.jaehnichen@tu-berlin.de
[2] Ludwig-Maximilians-Universität München, Munich, Germany
wirsing@lmu.de

Today's software systems are becoming increasingly distributed and decentralized and it would be important to have them adapt autonomously to dynamically changing, open-ended environments. Often the nodes of such systems have their own individual properties and objectives; interactions with other nodes or with humans may lead to the emergence of unexpected phenomena. We call such systems collective adaptive systems. Examples for collective adaptive systems are robot swarms, smart cities, voluntary peer-to-peer clouds as well as sociotechnical systems and the internet of things.

The track "Rigorous Engineering of Collective Adaptive Systems" is a follow-up of the successful track on "Rigorous Engineering Autonomic Ensembles" at ISOLA 2014 and presents techniques and tools for modelling and analysing collective adaptive systems and for modelling, coordinating and programming such systems. The track was composed of three sessions and a panel discussion entitled "Adaptation to the unforeseen: Do we master our autonomic systems?"

Calculi for Modeling and Analyzing Collective Adaptive Systems. This session consists of three contributions on calculi for collective adaptive systems and how they can be used for runtime execution, for compositional design, and for regulating self-adaptive behaviour. In "Programming of CAS systems by relying on attribute-based communication" [1], Yehia Abd Alrahman, Rocco De Nicola, and Michele Loreti propose attribute-based communication in the so-called AbC calculus as a means for communicating with a dynamically changing group of partners in an anonymous way. They present a Java run-time environment for supporting the communication primitives of the AbC calculus and show how to use attribute-based communication by programming a smart conference system.

The PSCEL language for autonomic computing uses policies to regulate self-adaptive behaviour in a way similar to aspect-oriented programming. Because of the interplay between dynamic policy evaluation and process execution it is challenging to predict the overall system behavior. In "Towards Static Analysis of Policy-Based Self-Adaptive Computing Systems" [2] Andrea Margheri, Hanne Riis Nielson, Flemming Nielson, Rosario Pugliese propose a flow graph for statically approximating the policy evaluations at runtime and exploit this policy-flow graph to analyze the effects of policy evaluations on the progress of processes.

© Springer International Publishing AG 2016
T. Margaria and B. Steffen (Eds.): ISoLA 2016, Part I, LNCS 9952, pp. 535–538, 2016.
DOI: 10.1007/978-3-319-47166-2_37

The third paper "A Calculus for Open Ensembles and Their Composition" [3] by Rolf Hennicker studies open ensembles (of processes) and their composition. Based on a bisimulation relation for ensembles, a notion of equivalence between open ensembles is defined and it is shown that equivalence of ensemble specifications is preserved by ensemble composition. The main result is the compositionality of the ensemble semantics: the semantics of a (syntactically) composed ensemble specification can be obtained by (semantically) composing the semantic models of the single specifications.

Coordinating and Programming Collective Adaptive Systems. This session contains four papers proposing coordination models, mixed-critical design, and a scripting languge for simulation. In "Logic Fragments: coordinating entities with logic programs" [4] Francesco Luca De Angelis and Giovanna Di Marzo Serugendo study a coordination model called Logic Fragments Coordination Model. Agents communicate by injecting logic fragments into a shared tuple space; such fragments are active tuples and can change, add and remove other tuples. The paper defines a formal evaluation semantics of logic fragments and illustrates the creation of a new coordination law at run-time and the verification of emergent properties at design-time and at run-time.

Mixed-critical systems are embedded systems which contain safety-critical and non-safety critical parts. In the second paper of the session "Mixed-Critical Systems Design with Coarse-grained Multi-core Interference" [5], Peter Poplavko, Rany Kahil, Dario Socci, Saddek Bensalem, and Marius Bozga study resource management of multi-core mixed-critical systems that are time-critical and compute-intensive. The authors propose a design flow where an application is specified as a Fixed Priority Process Network with additional functional specifications. By automatically deriving a task-graph for offline scheduling from the network, the specification can be compiled into the BIP language which in turn is compiled into executable C++ code.

Simulating complex systems is often an error-prone process as it requires various parameter settings, the evaluation of the simulation results with measured data, and the use of different simulation tools. The paper "A Library and Scripting Language for Tool Independent Simulation Descriptions" [6] by Alexandra Mehlhase, Stefan Jähnichen, and Amir Czwink proposes an object-oriented, tool-independent, easy-to-use, domain-specific scripting language that allows to automate the simulation process and to describe simulations in an exchangeable and uniform manner. The language focusses on simulations which are based on differential-algebraic equations and is particularly suited for models in Modelica and Simulink.

The last paper of this session "Smart coordination of autonomic component ensembles in the context of ad-hoc communication" [7] by Tomas Bures, Petr Hnetynka, Filip Krijt, Vladimir Matena, and Frantisek Plasil presents a high-level architectural approach to the coordination of autonomic component ensembles. The approach is applied to smart cyber-physical systems where the devices forming the system are primarily connected by a Mobile Ad-Hoc Network.

Several experiments show that elevating data quality constraints to the architectural level enables application-specific utility optimization via network parameters.

Tool Support and Case Studies. The last session of the track consists of three contributions. The paper "A Tool-chain for Statistical Spatio-Temporal Model Checking of Bike Sharing Systems?" [8] by Vincenzo Ciancia, Diego Latella, Mieke Massink, Rytis Paskauskas, and Andrea Vandin proposes a novel modeling and analysis approach for collective adaptive systems. It is based on the idea that statistical spatio-temporal model checking is a form of statistical model checking applied to points of the space. A statistical model checking tool, a tool for spatio-temporal logics, and a simulation tool are combined into a tool chain and as a case study the approach is applied to a bike sharing system.

In "Rigorous graphical modelling of movement in Collective Adaptive Systems" [9] Natalia Zon, Stephen Gilmore, and Jane Hillston propose a graphical approach to modeling of Collective Adaptive Systems with constrained movements. The approach focusses on systems whose evolution can be described by Markov chains. The paper presents a graphical modelling tool which is implemented as an Eclipse IDE plug-in and which automatically translates the graphical model into the modeling language CARMA. The final paper of this session addresses the engineering of requirements of autonomic systems.

In "Integration and Promotion of Autonomy with the ARE Framework" [10] Emil Vassev and Mike Hinchey present an application of the ARE method of Autonomic Requirements Engineering. As a case study the BepiColombo mission of the European Space Agency is chosen and it is shown how specific autonomy requirements can be derived from more general objectives.

Adaptation to the Unforeseen: Do we Master our Autonomous Systems? The panel discussion was a main event of the track. Stefan Jähnichen as moderator and the panelists Saddek Bensalem, Rocco De Nicola, Giovanna di Marzo Serugendo, and Emil Vassev discussed this controversial topic along a list of questions described in the introduction to the panel [11]. This volume contains also the position papers of Giovanna Di Marzo Serugendo on "Engineering Adaptivity, Universal Autonomous Systems, Ethics and Compliance Issues" [12] and of Emil Vassev on "Safe Artificial Intelligence and Formal Methods" [13].

Summary. Adaptivity is probably the most challenging topic for further evolution of our current technologies. The papers of the track and the panel have discussed it very widely and have produced many valuable insights, e.g. how to deal with unforeseen events. Questions related to modelling, programming, and analysing collective adaptive systems as well as to tool support were covered and several case studies such as bike sharing systems and the "autonomous car" were used as examples of such systems. However, adaptivity is not only concerned with technical challenges and solutions but even more with questions of acceptance and trust as well as with liability and, in general, law. More research will be needed to master the rigorous engineering of collective adaptive systems.

References

1. Alrahman, Y.A., De Nicola, R., Loreti, M.: Programming of CAS systems by relying on attribute-based communication. In: Margaria, T., Steffen, B. (eds.) ISoLA 2016, Part I, LNCS, vol. 9952, pp. 539–553. Springer, Cham (2016)
2. Margheri, A., Nielson, H.R., Nielson, F., Pugliese, R.: Towards static analysis of policy-based self-adaptive computing systems. In: Margaria, T., Steffen, B. (eds.) ISoLA 2016, Part I, LNCS, vol. 9952, pp. 554–569. Springer, Cham (2016)
3. Hennicker, R.: A calculus for open ensembles and their composition. In: Margaria, T., Steffen, B. (eds.) ISoLA 2016, Part I, LNCS, vol. 9952, pp. 570–588. Springer, Cham (2016)
4. De Angelis, F.L., Di Marzo Serugendo, G.: Logic fragments: coordinating entities with logic programs. In: Margaria, T., Steffen, B. (eds.) ISoLA 2016, Part I, LNCS, vol. 9952, pp. 589–604. Springer, Cham (2016)
5. Poplavko, P., Kahil, R., Socci, D., Bensalem, S., Bozga, M.: Mixed-critical systems design with coarse-grained multi-core interference. In: Margaria, T., Steffen, B. (eds.) ISoLA 2016, Part I, LNCS, vol. 9952, pp. 605–621. Springer, Cham (2016)
6. Mehlhase, A., Jähnichen, S., Czwink, A.: A library and scripting language for tool independent simulation descriptions. In: Margaria, T., Steffen, B. (eds.) ISoLA 2016, Part I, LNCS, vol. 9952, pp. 622–638. Springer, Cham (2016)
7. Bures, T., Hnetynka, P., Krijt, F., Matena, V., Plasil, F.: Smart coordination of autonomic component ensembles in the context of ad-hoc communication. In: Margaria, T., Steffen, B. (eds.) ISoLA 2016, Part I, LNCS, vol. 9952, pp. 642–656. Springer, Cham (2016)
8. Ciancia, V., Latella, D., Massink, M., Paskauskas, R., Vandin, A.: A tool-chain for statistical spatio-temporal model checking of bike-sharing systems. In: Margaria, T., Steffen, B. (eds.) ISoLA 2016, Part I, LNCS, vol. 9952, pp. 657–673. Springer, Cham (2016)
9. Zoń, N., Gilmore, S., Hillston, J.: Rigorous graphical modelling of movement in collective adaptive systems. In: Margaria, T., Steffen, B. (eds.) ISoLA 2016, Part I, LNCS, vol. 9952, pp. 674–688. Springer, Cham (2016)
10. Vassev, E., Hinchey, M.: Integration and promotion of autonomy with the ARE framework. In: Margaria, T., Steffen, B. (eds.) ISoLA 2016, Part I, LNCS, vol. 9952, pp. 689–703. Springer, Cham (2016)
11. Jähnichen, S., Wirsing, M.: Adaptation to the unforeseen: do we master our autonomous systems? - Panel introduction. In: Margaria, T., Steffen, B. (eds.) ISoLA 2016, Part I, LNCS, vol. 9952, pp. 639–641. Springer, Cham (2016)
12. Di Marzo Serugendo, G.: Engineering adaptivity, universal autonomous systems, ethics and compliance Issues. In: Margaria, T., Steffen, B. (eds.) ISoLA 2016, Part I, LNCS, vol. 9952, pp. 714–719. Springer, Cham (2016)
13. Vassev, E.: Safe artificial intelligence and formal methods. In: Margaria, T., Steffen, B. (eds.) ISoLA 2016, Part I, LNCS, vol. 9952, pp. 704–713. Springer, Cham (2016)

Programming of CAS Systems by Relying on Attribute-Based Communication

Yehia Abd Alrahman[1]([✉]), Rocco De Nicola[1], and Michele Loreti[2]

[1] IMT School for Advanced Studies Lucca, Lucca, Italy
yehia.abdalrahman@imtlucca.it
[2] Università degli Studi di Firenze, Florence, Italy

Abstract. In most distributed systems, named connections (i.e., channels) are used as means for programming interaction between communicating partners. These kinds of connections are low level and usually totally independent of the knowledge, the status, the capabilities, ..., in one word, of the attributes of the interacting partners. We have recently introduced a calculus, called AbC, in which interactions among agents are dynamically established by taking into account "connection" as determined by predicates over agent attributes. In this paper, we present Ab^aCuS, a Java run-time environment that has been developed to support modeling and programming of collective adaptive systems by relying on the communication primitives of the AbC calculus. Systems are described as sets of parallel components, each component is equipped with a set of attributes and communications among components take place in an implicit multicast fashion. By means of a number of examples, we also show how opportunistic behaviors, achieved by run-time attribute updates, can be exploited to express different communication and interaction patterns and to program challenging case studies.

1 Introduction

Attribute-based communication is a novel communication paradigm that permits selecting groups of partners by considering the predicates over the attributes they expose. Thus communication takes place anonymously in an implicit multicast fashion without a prior agreement between the communicating partners. Because of the anonymity of the attribute-based interaction, scalability, dynamicity, and openness can be achieved at a higher degree in distributed settings. The semantics of output actions is non-blocking while input actions are blocking. This breaks the synchronization dependencies between interacting partners, and communicating partners can enter or leave the group at any time without any disruption of the overall system behavior.

This research has been partially supported by the European projects IP 257414 ASCENS and STReP 600708 QUANTICOL, and by the Italian project PRIN 2010LHT4KM CINA.

© Springer International Publishing AG 2016
T. Margaria and B. Steffen (Eds.): ISoLA 2016, Part I, LNCS 9952, pp. 539–553, 2016.
DOI: 10.1007/978-3-319-47166-2_38

Groups or collectives are dynamically formed at the time of interaction by means of available/interested receiving components that satisfy sender predicates. In this way run-time attribute updates introduce opportunistic interactions between components. Indeed, interaction predicates can be parametrized with respect to local attribute values and when these values change, the interaction groups or collectives do implicitly change. This makes modeling and programming adaptation quite natural.

Programming opportunistic behavior in classical communication paradigms like channel-based communication, e.g., $b\pi$-calculus [13], is challenging. Components should agree on specific names or channels to interact. Channels have no connection with the component attributes, characteristics or knowledge. They are specified as addresses where the exchange should happen. These names/channels are quite static and changing them locally at run-time requires explicit communication and intensive use of name restriction which affect program readability and compositionally.

As an example, consider the behavior of a component that inspects its sensor and based on the input message communicates with its peer components. This behavior can be modeled in $b\pi$-calculus as follows:

$$C \triangleq \nu b(\bar{b}a \mid b(c).\bar{c}d) \xrightarrow{\tau} \nu b\bar{a}d$$

where component C communicates with its sensor along a private channel "b" and uses the received channel "a" to communicate with its peers. Clearly, this intensive use of scoping and explicit communication for modeling a simple read operation hinders readability and compositionality of large models. In many cases, one is only interested in how components interact with each other and abstracts from local interactions. In this case we would like to define C as:

$$C \triangleq \overline{\mathcal{E}(c)}d$$

where $\mathcal{E}(c)$ is a function that returns a channel name based on the message received from the sensor. This would permit abstracting from local interactions and concentrating on components interactions while taking into account the environment/space in which they are operating. This intuition is captured by relying on attribute-based communication where we assume that components have local views of their own status and of their surrounding environment and their behaviors are parametrized with respect to these views. Formally a component is defined as $\Gamma : P$ where Γ is an abstraction of its local view and of its environment and P is its behavior. In fact, we generalize more and replace function $\mathcal{E}(\bullet)$ with a predicate that considers elements of Γ. Send and receive operations then rely on predicates, i.e., $(d)@\Pi$ rather than on names i.e., $\bar{c}d$.

The attribute-based system is more than just the parallel composition of interacting partners; it is also is parametric with respect to the shared environment or space where system components are executed. The shared environment has a great impact on how components behave. It introduces a new way of indirect communication, where components mutually influence each other unintentionally. For instance, in the ant foraging system [19], when an ant disposes pheromone in the shared space to keep track of her way back home, she influences other ants behavior as they are programmed to follow traces of pheromone with higher concentration. In this way, the ant unintentionally influences the behavior of the other ants by only modifying the shared space. This type of indirect communication cannot be easily modeled even by relying on asynchronous communication [18] where messages are placed with the intention that other addressed components will receive them at some point of time.

In this paper we present Ab^aCuS, a Java run-time environment for the AbC calculus. AbC is the first calculus that was designed to focus on a minimal set of primitives that permits attribute-based communication. AbC was first proposed in [6] and a new stable and refined version was released in [5]. The latest version is accompanied with a formal labeled semantics and a behavioral theory used to establish results about the relations with other existing approaches. Ab^aCuS was developed by building on the formal semantics of the latest version of AbC. Given the generality and flexibility of the interaction primitives of the AbC calculus, Ab^aCuS was developed for programming modern software systems where adaptation, reconfiguration and collaboration are key issues. We would like to use it to assess the practical impact of this new communication model on challenging case studies like the ones from the realm of collective-adaptive systems (CAS) [15] and to fully understand both its merits and limits.

The rest of the paper is organized as follows. In Sect. 2 we review the AbC calculus and its expressive power through a running example. In Sect. 3 we present Ab^aCuS, a run-time environment for the AbC calculus and in Sect. 4 we present a case study about a smart conference application that we have implemented in Ab^aCuS. In Sect. 5 we discuss related work and finally in Sect. 6 we draw some conclusions and sketch a plan for future work.

2   The AbC Calculus

In this section we briefly review the AbC calculus and its specific features and we illustrate how well-known interaction patterns can be naturally modeled in AbC. To help the reader appreciate AbC features, we proceed by a simple running example. We consider the classical stable marriage problem (SMP) [16], a problem of finding a stable matching between two equally sized sets of elements given an ordering of preferences for each element.

In our example, we consider n men and n women, where each person has ranked all members of the opposite sex in order of preferences, we have to engage the men and women together such that there are no two people of opposite sex who would both rather have each other than their current partners. When there are no such pairs of people, the set of marriages is deemed stable. For convenience we assume there are no ties; thus, if a person is indifferent between two or more possible partners he/she is nevertheless required to rank them in some order. We will use this example to gently introduce a subset of the AbC calculus and its informal semantics throughout this section. The presentation is intended to be intuitive and interested readers are referred to [5] for full details concerning the full AbC syntax and formal semantics.

The top-level entities of the AbC calculus are *components* (C), a component is either a process P associated with an *attribute environment* Γ (denoted by $\Gamma : P$) or the parallel composition $C_1 \| C_2$ of components. The *attribute environment* Γ is a partial map from attribute identifiers $a \in \mathcal{A}$ to values $v \in \mathcal{V}$. Values could be numbers, names (string), tuples, etc.

$$C :: = \Gamma : P \quad | \quad C_1 \| C_2 \quad | \quad \ldots$$

Example (step 1/3): The marriage scenario can be modeled in AbC as follows:

$$Man_1 \| \ldots \| Man_n \, \| \, Woman_1 \| \ldots \| Woman_n$$

Men and women interact in parallel and each is modeled as an AbC component, Man_i of the form $\Gamma_{m,i} : M$ and $Woman_i$ of the form $\Gamma_{w,i} : W$. The attribute environments of men and women, $\Gamma_{m,i}$ and $\Gamma_{w,i}$, contain the following attributes:

- *partner*: identifies the current partner identity; in case a person is not engaged yet, the value of its partner $= -1$;
- *preferences*: a ranking list of the person preferences, the top of this set is the person's first best;
- M_{id} for man and W_{id} for woman, identify their identities;
- *exPartner* for a woman, identifies her ex-fiancé.   □

The behavior of an AbC process can be generated by the following grammar:

$$P :: = 0 \quad | \quad \alpha.P \quad | \quad [\tilde{a} := \tilde{E}]P \quad | \quad \langle \Pi \rangle P \quad | \quad P_1 + P_2 \quad | \quad P_1 | P_2 \quad | \quad A(\tilde{x})$$

- 0 : denotes the inactive process;
- $\alpha.P$: denotes an action prefixed process, a process that executes action α and continues as P;
- $[\tilde{a} := \tilde{E}]P$: denotes an attribute update process, a process that behaves as P given that its attribute environment is updated by setting the value of each attribute in the sequence $\tilde{a}$ to the evaluation of the corresponding expression in the sequence $\tilde{E}$. The attribute updates and the first move of P are atomic;
- $\langle \Pi \rangle P$: denotes an awareness process, a process that tests awareness data about a component status or its environment by inspecting the local attribute environment where the process resides. It blocks the execution of process P until the predicate Π becomes true;
- the processes $P_1 + P_2$, $P_1 | P_2$, and $A(\tilde{x})$ are standard for nondeterminism, parallel composition, and parametrized process definition respectively. It should be noted that the parallel operator "|" does not allow communication between P_1 and P_2, they can only interleave while the parallel operator "$\|$" at the component level allows communication between components.

Example (step 2/3): The structures of process M, specifying the behavior of a man, and the process W, specifying the behavior of a woman, are defined as follows:

$$M \triangleq [\textbf{this}.partner := \text{Top}(\textbf{this}.preferences),$$
$$\textbf{this}.preferences := \ominus(\textbf{this}.preferences)] \, a.M'$$

$W \triangleq$ b. ($\langle \text{BOF}(\textbf{this}.partner, \ y)\rangle \ W_1 \ + \ \langle \neg\text{BOF}(\textbf{this}.partner, \ y)\rangle \ W_2$) | W

A man, M, picks his first best from the ranking list "$\textbf{this}.preferences$" and assumes it to be his partner. This element is removed from his preferences. In the same transition he proposes to this possible partner by executing action a (to be specified later) and then continues as M'. The prefix $\textbf{this}$ is a reference to the value assigned to the attribute identifier "$preferences$". Functions $\text{Top}(\textbf{arg})$ and $\ominus(\textbf{arg})$ both take a list as an argument. The former returns the first element of the list if the list is not empty and the empty string otherwise, while the latter returns the list resulting from the removal of its first element.

On the other hand, the behavior of a woman, W, is activated by receiving a proposal, i.e., executing action b (to be specified later). A woman either accepts this proposal from a "y" man if she will be better off with him and continues as W_1 or refuses it if she prefers her current fiancè and continues as W_2. The parallel composition with W ensures that the woman is always willing to consider new proposals. $\text{BOF}(arg_1, \ arg_2)$ is a boolean function that takes as arguments the current partner and the new man, respectively, and determines whether the woman will be better off with the new man or not, given her current fiancè and her preferences. If she is not engaged, this function will always return true.   □

The AbC communication actions can be generated by the following grammar:

$$\alpha ::= (\tilde{E})@\Pi \ \ | \ \ \Pi(\tilde{x})$$

- $(\tilde{E})@\Pi$: denotes an attribute-based output action, it evaluates the sequence of expressions $\tilde{E}$ under the local attribute environment Γ and then sends the result to the components whose attributes satisfy the predicate Π. If Π semantically equals to a logic "false", the message is not exposed and the action is used to represent a silent move;
- $\Pi(\tilde{x})$: denotes an attribute-based input action, it binds to sequence $\tilde{x}$ the corresponding received values from components whose *communicated attributes* or values satisfy the predicate Π.

Example (step 3/3): In the previous step, if we further specify the action "a" and the process M' in M, the action "b" and the processes W_1 and W_2 in W, the behavior of a man and a woman becomes:

$$M \triangleq [\textbf{this}.partner := \text{Top}(\textbf{this}.preferences),$$
$$\textbf{this}.preferences := \ominus(\textbf{this}.preferences)]$$
$$(propose, \ \textbf{this}.M_{id})@(W_{id} = \textbf{this}.partner).$$
$$(x = invalid)(x).M$$

$$W \triangleq (x = propose)(x,\ y).\ (\ \langle \text{BOF}(\text{this}.partner,\ y)\rangle$$
$$[\text{this}.exPartner := \text{this}.partner,\ \text{this}.partner := y]$$
$$(invalid)@(M_{id} = \text{this}.exPartner).0$$
$$+$$
$$\langle \neg \text{BOF}(\text{this}.partner,\ y)\rangle\ (invalid)@(M_{id} = y).0\ \ )\ |\ W$$

Obviously, action "a" is a proposal message to be sent to the selected partner. This message contains a label "*propose*" to indicate the type of the message and the sender identity M_{id}. The man stays engaged as long as he does not receive an invalidation message from the woman he proposed to. The invalidation message contains a label "*invalid*" to indicate the message type. If this message is received, the man starts all over again and picks his second best and so on.

On the other hand, action "b" is used to receive a proposal message from a "y" man. If the woman prefers "y", she will consider her current partner as her ex-partner, get engaged to "y", and send an invalidation message to her ex-fiancé so that he looks for another partner. This is also true for the case when she is not engaged, but in this case she will send an invalidation message with a predicate ($M_{id} = -1$) which will not be received by anyone. If she prefers her partner, she will send the invalidation message to "y".   □

Although the interaction in this specific scenario is based on partners identities, the interaction in AbC is usually more general and assumes anonymity between the interacting partners. Interaction relies on predicates over attributes that can be changed at anytime. This means that components interact without a prior agreement between each other.

Classical Interaction Patterns in AbC**.** In [5] we have shown how the classical group-based [4,11] and publish/subscribe-based [7,14] interaction patterns can be naturally translated into AbC. We have also shown how to translate channel-based communication like in $b\pi$-calculus [13] into AbC. The interested readers are referred to the website on [1]; in this website we discuss the direct implementation of these translations into AbC linguistic primitives. Below, we briefly introduce the basic idea behind such translations.

To select partners in *channel-based communication*, structured messages are used where the name of the channel is rendered as the first element in the message; receivers only accept messages with attached channels that match their receiving channels. Attributes do not play any role in such interaction so we assume components with empty environments i.e., $\Gamma = \emptyset$. Thus a pair of processes, one willing to receive on channel a and the other willing to send on the same channel, can be modeled as follows:

$$\emptyset : (x = a)(x, y).P \ \| \ \emptyset : (a, msg)@(\text{tt}).Q$$

Group names are rendered as attributes when translating *group-based interaction* as shown below:

$$\Gamma_1 : (msg)@(group = a).P \ \| \ \Gamma_2 : (\text{tt})(x).Q \quad \text{where} \quad \Gamma_2(group) = a$$

The operations for joining or leaving a given group are rendered as attribute updates.

The *publish and subscribe* paradigm can be seen as special cases of the attribute-based one; a natural modeling of the topic-based publish/subscribe model [14] into AbC can be obtained by allowing publishers to broadcast messages with "tt" predicates (i.e., satisfied by all) and making sure that only subscribers can check the compatibility of the exposed publishers attributes with their subscriptions:

$$\Gamma_1 : (msg, \text{this}.topic)@(\text{tt}).P \parallel \Gamma_2 : (y = \text{this}.subscription)(x, \ y).Q$$

The publisher broadcasts the message "msg" tagged with a specific topic for all possible subscribers (the predicate "tt" is satisfied by all), subscribers receive the message if the topic matches their subscription.

3 $Ab^{a}C$uS: A Run-time Environment for the AbC Calculus

In this section we present $Ab^{a}C$uS [1], a Java run-time environment for supporting the communication primitives of the AbC calculus. We also show how one can exploit these flexible primitives to provide a general programming framework that encompasses different communication frameworks and interaction patterns. Having a run-time environment allows us to assess the practical impact of this young communication paradigm in real applications. In fact, we plan to use the new programming framework to program challenging case studies, dealing with collective adaptive systems, from different application domains.

$Ab^{a}C$uS provides a Java API that allows programmers to use the linguistic primitives of the AbC calculus in Java programs. The implementation of $Ab^{a}C$uS fully relies on the formal semantics of the AbC calculus. There is a one-to-one correspondence between the AbC primitives and the programming constructs in $Ab^{a}C$uS. This close correspondence enhances the confidence on the behavior of $Ab^{a}C$uS programs after they have been analyzed via formal methods, which is made possible by relying on the operational semantics of the AbC calculus.

AbC's operational semantics abstracts from a specific communication infrastructure. An AbC model consists of a set of parallel components that cooperate in a highly dynamic environment where the underlying communication infrastructure can change dynamically. The current implementation $Ab^{a}C$uS is however a centralized one, in the sense that it relies on a message broker that mediates the interactions. In essence, the broker accepts messages from sending components, and delivers them to all registered components with the exception of the sending ones. This central component plays the role of a forwarder and does not contribute in any way to message filtering. The decision about accepting or ignoring a message is taken when the message is delivered to the receiving components.

We would like to stress that, although the current Ab^aCuS implementation is centralized, components interact anonymously and combine their behaviors to achieve the required goals. Components are unaware of the existence of each other, they only interact with the message broker. To facilitate interoperability with other tools and programming frameworks, Ab^aCuS relies on JSON [3], a standard data exchange technology that simplifies the interactions between heterogenous network components and provides the basis for allowing Ab^aCuS programs to cooperate with external services or devices.

The advantages of this programming framework can be summarized by saying that it provides a small set of programming constructs that naturally supports adaptation and guarantees a high degree of scalability in distributed settings by allowing anonymous interaction. The new programming framework also has a direct correspondence with an existing formal model with clear and understood semantics and with a sound foundational theory which lays the basis for formal reasoning and verification.

In what follows we summarize the main Ab^aCuS programming constructs, their implementation, and their relations with the AbC primitives. We consider the implementation of one of the *man* components introduced in the running example of the previous section.

Components. AbC components are implemented via the class `AbCComponent`. Instances of this class are executed in either virtual or physical machines that provide access to input/output devices and network connections. An instance of the class `AbCComponent` contains an attribute environment and a set of processes that represents the behavior of the component. Components interact via ports supporting either local communication, i.e., components run in the same application, or external communication, i.e., components run in different applications or different machines. The following Ab^aCuS code shows how to create a *man* component m_1, to assign the process `ManAgent()` to it, and finally to start its execution.

```
1    AbCComponent m1 = new AbCComponent("M_1");
2    m1.addProcess(new ManAgent());
3    m1.start();
```

Attribute Environments. AbC attribute environments are implemented via the class `AbCEnvironment`. An instance of the class `AbCEnvironment` contains a set of attribute identifiers, implemented via the class `Attribute`, and another set to store their values. The attribute environment maintains the attribute values by providing read and update operations via the methods `getValue(attribute)` and `setValue(attribute, value)` respectively. The class `Attribute` implements an AbC attribute and ensures type compatibility of the assigned values. The following Ab^aCuS code shows how to create an AbC attribute and to read and update its value.

```
1    Attribute<Integer> idAttribute = new Attribute<>("ID", Integer.class);
2    getValue(idAttribute);
3    setValue(idAttribute, 1);
```

Processes. The generic behavior of an *AbC* process is implemented via the abstract class AbCProcess. The *AbC* communication actions $(\tilde{E})@\Pi$ and $\Pi(\tilde{x})$ are implemented via the methods Send(predicate, values) and receive(msg− >Function(msg)) respectively. The receive operation accepts a message and passes it to a boolean function that checks if it satisfies the receiving predicate. The attribute updates are implemented via the method setValue(attribute, value) while the awareness operator and the process definition are implemented via the methods waitUntil(predicate) and call(process) respectively. The method exec(p) spawns a new process p and runs it in parallel with the executing process while the recursive call is implemented via a native Java while loop. The non-deterministic choice of several input actions possibly preceded by attribute updates and/or awareness operators is implemented in Ab^aCuS by overloading the receive method receive($in_1, \ldots, in_n$). This method takes a finite number of arguments of type InputAction, each of which has the following form $[\tilde{a} := \tilde{E}]\langle\Pi\rangle\Pi(\tilde{x})$. When a message arrives to the component this method only enables the correct branch or blocks the execution in case of unwanted messages. The non-deterministic choice between an input and output actions is not allowed because output actions are non-blocking. It should be noted that the method addProcess(p) for a component c has the same effect of running the process p in parallel with the already existing processes in component c. The generic behavior of a process is defined via the abstract method doRun() that is invoked when the process is executed. The programmer should implement this method to specify the behavior of the process. The following Ab^aCuS code implements a *man* behavior; the one-to-one correspondence with the *AbC* process M in Sect. 2 is evident.

```
1     public class ManAgent extends AbCProcess {
2       public ManAgent() {
3         super("ManAgent");
4       }
5       @Override
6       protected void doRun() throws Exception {
7         while ( !Definition.preferences.isEmpty() ) {
8           Integer partner = Definition.preferences.poll();
9           setValue(Definition.partnerAttribute, partner);
10          send( new HasValue("ID", partner) , new Tuple("PROPOSE" ,
                 getValue(Definition.idAttribute)) );
11          receive(o -> isAnInvalidationMessage(o) );
12        }
13      }
14    ...
```

Network Infrastructure. In Ab^aCuS each component is equipped with a set of ports for interacting with other components as mentioned above. A port is identified by an address that can be used to manage the interaction with a mediator or a message broker. It should be noted that these ports are not meant to be used by components to identify the addresses of the other components but rather as a way to communicate with the message broker. The components remain anonymous to each other and are not allowed to communicate directly; they only know the message broker. The latter can be seen as an access point which mediates the interaction between components. It serves as a forwarder that shepherds the interaction, but it has nothing to do with message filtering.

The abstract class `AbCPort` implements the generic behavior of a port. It provides the instruments to dispatch messages to components and implements the communication protocol used by AbC components to interact with each other. The send method in `AbCPort` is abstract to allow different concrete implementations for this method depending on the underlying network infrastructures (i.e., Internet, Wi-Fi, Ad-hoc networks, ...).

Currently, two concrete implementations are supported in Ab^aCuS: VirtualPort and AbCClient. The VirtualPort implements a port where interactions are performed via a buffer stored in the main memory. A VirtualPort is used to run components in a single application without relying on a specific network infrastructure. AbCClient instead assumes the presence of a server that mediates the interactions between components. The following Ab^aCuS code shows how to create an `AbCServer` and start its execution.

```
1    AbCServer server = new AbCServer();
2    server.start();
```

The following code shows how to create a client port, register it to an existing server, assign the port for the man component m_1, and finally starts its execution.

```
1    AbCClient client = new AbCClient(InetAddress.getLoopbackAddress(), 1234);
2    client.register( InetAddress.getLoopbackAddress() , DEFAULT_SUBSCRIBE_PORT );
3    m1.setPort(client);
4    client.start();
```

It should be noted that the AbC server and the client ports usually operate from different machines or networks.

Interested readers are referred to [1] for a detailed description of the implementation, source code, and also a few demos.

4   Case Study: A Smart Conference System

In this section we show how to use the programming constructs of the AbC calculus to program a smart conference system in an intuitive and easy way.

The idea is to exploit the mobile devices of the participants to guide them to their locations of interest. Each participant expresses his/her topic of interest and the conference venue is responsible for guiding each participant into the location that matches their interests. The conference venue is composed of a set of rooms where the conference sessions are to be held. We assume that the name of each room identifies its location. The conference program and room relocation can be dynamically adjusted at anytime to handle specific situations, i.e., a crowded session can be relocated into a larger room and this should be done seamlessly without disruption to the whole conference program. When relocation happens, the new updates should be communicated to the interested participants. A participant only receives updates about his/her topic of interest.

The conference venue is represented as a set of parallel AbC components, each of them representing a room $(Room_1 \| \ldots \| Room_n)$ and each room has the following form $\Gamma_i : R$. Participants instead have the following form $\Gamma_j : P$. We assume that each room has a unique name that identifies its location and each participant has a unique id. The overall system is represented as the parallel composition of the conference venue and the set of participants as shown below:

$$Room_1 \| \ldots \| Room_n \| Participant_1 \| \ldots \| Participant_m$$

When a participant arrives to the conference venue, he/she selects the topic of the talk of interest and updates his/her attribute $interest$ as shown in process P below:

$$P(x) \triangleq [\mathbf{this}.interest := x]Com$$

By doing so, a communication process Com, that is responsible for communicating the participant interests to the conference venue, is activated. Process Com sends a session request $Sreq$ to nearby providers (i.e., with a provider role); in our case, this is a room. The message also contains the participant topic of interest and its id. Once the message is emitted, the process blocks until a reply notification that matches his/her interest arrives. The notification contains the session name, an $interestRply$ label, and the name of the room where the session is to be held. By receiving this notification, the process updates the participant destination and activates process $Update$.

$$Com \triangleq (\mathbf{this}.interest,\ Sreq,\ \mathbf{this}.id)@(role = Provider).$$
$$(x = \mathbf{this}.interest \land y = interestRply)(x,\ y,\ z).$$
$$[\mathbf{this}.dest := z]()@\mathrm{ff}.Update$$

The process $Update$, defined below, blocks and waits for new updates or changes in schedule for the session of interest. Precisely, it blocks until it receives an $interestUpd$ notification about a session that matches the participant interest. The notification message contains the previous session that was supposed to be held in this room, the current session, an $interestUpd$ label, and the name of the room where the session of interest has been moved. Once a notification message is received, the process updates the destination to the new location and waits for future updates.

$$Update \triangleq (y = \mathbf{this}.interest \land z = interestUpd)(x,\ y,\ z,\ l).$$
$$[\mathbf{this}.dest := l]()@\mathrm{ff}.Update$$

On the other hand, the behavior of a room in the conference venue is modeled by process R which consists of three parallel processes:

$$R \triangleq Service\ |\ ReLoc\ |\ Swap$$

The room can provide a normal service, through the process $Service$ defined below, by replying to session requests from those participants who are interested in its current session. Once a session request $Sreq$ that matches the current room session is received from a participant, the room sends an *interestRply* to the requesting participant identifying them by their *id*. The reply contains the current session, an *interestRply* label, and the name of the room. The parallel composition with *Service* ensures that the room is always ready to handle concurrent requests from different participants.

$Service \triangleq (x = \text{this}.session \land y = Sreq)(x, y, z).$
$\quad ((\text{this}.session, interestRply, \text{this}.name)@(id = z).0 \mid Service)$

On the other hand, any room might experience a change in schedule unexpectedly at run-time. The process *ReLoc*, defined below, is responsible for handling this issue in a way such that interested participants in the new session and also other rooms where a swap of schedule should happen are notified.

$ReLoc \triangleq \langle\text{this}.relocate = \text{tt}\rangle[\text{this}.prevSession := \text{this}.session,$
$\quad\quad \text{this}.session := \text{this}.newSession, \text{this}.relocate := \text{ff}]$
$\quad\quad (\text{this}.prevSession, \text{this}.session, interestUpd, \text{this}.name)$
$\quad\quad\quad @(interest = \text{this}.session \lor session = \text{this}.session).ReLoc$

Relocation is triggered by setting the value of attribute *relocate* to true and assigning the attribute *newSession* with a new session name, the room updates its previous session to the current one and the current session to the new one. The relocation flag *relocate* is turned off by setting its value to false. The process continues by sending the updated previous and current sessions of the room accompanied with an *interestUpd* label and the room name to either participants who are waiting for updates about the updated session or to another room where a swap of schedule should happen.

Furthermore, a room can also receive update notifications from other rooms in case a swap of schedule is required, i.e., a small crowded room can switch its session with a larger one with few attendees. This message is exactly the same message that is received by the participants, the only difference is concerned with the receiving predicate. The room accept an *interestUpd* message only if the second value in the message matches its current session. By doing so, the room is made aware that a swap of sessions is required. So it performs the swap and then sends a message to interested participants to update their destination.

$Swap \triangleq (z = interestUpd \land y = \text{this}.session)(x, y, z, l).$
$\quad\quad [\text{this}.prevSession := \text{this}.session, \text{this}.session := x]$
$\quad\quad ((\text{this}.prevSession, \text{this}.session, interestUpd, \text{this}.name)$
$\quad\quad\quad @(interest = \text{this}.session \lor session = \text{this}.session).0$
$\quad\quad \mid Swap)$

The following $Ab^{a}CuS$ code corresponds to the participant process $P(x)$. The code is self-explanatory and has a one-to-one correspondence with the specifications in process $P(x)$.

```
1   public class ParticipantAgent extends AbCProcess {
2     private String selectedTopic;
3     public ParticipantAgent(String selectedTopic) {
4       super(name);
5       this.selectedTopic = selectedTopic;
6     }
7     @Override
8     protected void doRun() throws Exception {
9       setValue(Definition.interestAttribute, this.selectedTopic);
10      send(new HasValue(Definition.ROLE_ATTRIBUTE_NAME, Definition.PROVIDER),
11          new Tuple(getValue(Definition.interestAttribute),
12              Definition.REQUEST_STRING, getValue(Definition.idAttribute)
13          ));
14      Tuple value = (Tuple) receive(o -> isAnInterestReply(o));
15      setValue(Definition.destinationAttribute, (String) value.get(2));
16      while (true) {
17        value = (Tuple) receive(o -> isAnInterestUpdate(o));
18        setValue(Definition.destinationAttribute, (String) value.get(4));
19      }
20    }
21  ...
```

Due to space limitations we do not show the code for the whole system; interested readers are referred to [1] for a description of the full implementation, GUI demos, and source code.

5 Related Work

Attribute-based communication was used in the context of autonomic computing when the SCEL language [12] was designed. The interesting results of using attribute-based interactions to program in SCEL inspired the distillation of the AbC calculus [5]. There was a necessity to understand the full impact of attribute-based communication in distributed programming. SCEL was designed to support programming of autonomic computing systems. Compared with SCEL, the knowledge representation in AbC is abstract and is not designed for detailed reasoning during the model evolution. This reflects the different objectives of SCEL and AbC. While SCEL focuses on programming issues, AbC concentrates on a minimal set of primitives to study effectiveness of attribute-based communication. Further related work can be found in [8], where a specification language was designed based on the AbC primitives to support quantitive analysis of large systems.

jRESP [2] is a run-time environment for the SCEL language which provides an API to permit using SCEL linguistic constructs in Java programs. Ab^aCuS inherits from jRESP its large use of design patterns and integration capabilities. This is done by allowing abstract implementation of the underlying network infrastructure and by taking advantage of JSON date exchange technology [3] to facilitate the interaction with heterogenous network components.

Programming collective and/or adaptive behavior has been studied in different research communities like context-oriented programming and component-based approach. In Context-Oriented Programming (COP) [17], a set of linguistic constructs is used to define context-dependent behavioral variations.

These variations are expressed as partial definitions of modules that can be over-ridden at run-time to adapt to contextual information. They can be grouped via layers to be activated or deactivated together dynamically. These layers can be also composed according to some scoping constructs. Our approach is different in that components adapt their behavior by considering the run-time changes of the values of their attributes which might be triggered by either contextual conditions or by local interaction. Another approach that considers behavioral variations by building on the Helena framework is considered in [20].

The component-based approach, represented by FRACTAL [10] and its Java implementation, JULIA [9], is an architecture-based approach that achieves adaptation by defining systems that are able to adapt their configurations to the contextual conditions. System components are allowed to manipulate their internal structure by adding, removing, or modifying connectors. However, in this approach interaction is still based on explicit connectors. In Ab^aCuS prede-fined connections simply do not exist, we do not assume a specific architecture or containment relations between components. The connectivity is always sub-ject to change at any time by means of attribute updates. In our view, Ab^aCuS is definitely more adequate when highly dynamic environments have to be considered.

6   Concluding Remarks

We informally introduced the AbC calculus by considering a simple running example and we discussed the expressiveness of the calculus and compared it with different communication paradigms. We introduced Ab^aCuS, a Java run-time environment for supporting the communication mechanisms of the AbC calculus. We presented a case study about smart conference systems that repre-sents a typical application from the realm of collective adaptive systems. In the considered system, the conference venue collaborates with the mobile devices of the participants to guide them to the talks they are interested in. The sce-nario shows how, in case of session relocations, a change in the schedule for a room can be managed coherently with the allocation of other rooms and with the interest of the participants. The latter need to be kept updated about any schedule changes that impacts on the locations where the topics of their interest are presented.

To program component interactions Ab^aCuS relies on a mediator or a message broker. This represents a single point of failure which puts the communication reliability at risk. Our future efforts will be dedicated to providing an efficient distributed implementation of Ab^aCuS and to further investigating the practical impact of this programming framework with more realistic case studies. We are also interested in establishing a formal relationship between Ab^aCuS and AbC by providing a formal definition for a distributed abstract machine that is operationally complete with respect to AbC itself.

References

1. Ab^aCuS: A run-time environment for the AbC calculus. http://lazkany.github.io/AbC/. Accessed 08 Dec 2015
2. jRESP: Java runtime environment for scel. http://jresp.sourceforge.net
3. JSON: Javascript object notation. http://www.json.org
4. Agha, G., Callsen, C.J.: Actorspace: an open distributed programming paradigm, vol. 28. ACM (1993)
5. Abd Alrahman, Y., De Nicola, R., Loreti, M.: On the power of attribute-based communication. In: Albert, E., Lanese, I. (eds.) FORTE 2016. LNCS, vol. 9688, pp. 1–18. Springer, Heidelberg (2016). doi:10.1007/978-3-319-39570-8_1
6. Abd Alrahman, Y., De Nicola, R., Loreti, M., Tiezzi, F., Vigo, R.: A calculus for attribute-based communication. In: Proceedings of the 30th Annual ACM Symposium on Applied Computing, SAC 2015, pp. 1840–1845. ACM (2015)
7. Bass, M.A., Nguyen, F.T.: Unified publish and subscribe paradigm for local and remote publishing destinations, 11 June 2002. US Patent 6,405,266
8. Bortolussi, L., De Nicola, R., Galpin, V., Gilmore, S., Hillston, J., Latella, D., Loreti, M., Massink, M.: Carma: collective adaptive resource-sharing markovian agents. In: Workshop on Quantitative Aspects of Programming Languages and Systems, QAPL 2015, pp. 16–31 (2015)
9. Bruneton, E., Coupaye, T., Leclercq, M., Quéma, V., Stefani, J.-B.: The fractal component model, its support in Java. Softw. Pract. Experience $36(11-12)$, 1257–1284 (2006)
10. Bruneton, E., Coupaye, T., Stefani, J.-B.: The fractal component model. Draft Specif. Version 2(3) pp. 125–151(2004)
11. Chockler, G.V., Keidar, I., Vitenberg, R.: Group communication specifications: a comprehensive study. ACM Comput. (CSUR) $33(4)$, 427–469 (2001)
12. De Nicola, R., Loreti, M., Pugliese, R., Tiezzi, F.: A formal approach to autonomic systems programming: the SCEL language. ACM Trans. Auton. Adapt. Syst. $9(2)$, 1–29 (2014)
13. Ene, C., Muntean, T.: A broadcast-based calculus for communicating systems. In: Parallel and Distributed Processing Symposium, International, vol. 3, p. 30149b. IEEE Computer Society (2001)
14. Eugster, P.T., Felber, P.A., Guerraoui, R., Kermarrec, A.-M.: The many faces of publish/subscribe. ACM Comput. Surv. $35(2)$, 114–131 (2003)
15. Ferscha, A.: Collective adaptive systems. In: Proceedings of the 2015 ACM International Joint Conference on Pervasive and Ubiquitous Computing and Proceedings of the 2015 ACM International Symposium on Wearable Computers, pp. 893–895 (2015)
16. Gale, D., Shapley, L.S.: College admissions and the stability of marriage. Am. Math. Monthly $69(1)$, 9–15 (1962)
17. Hirschfeld, R., Costanza, P., Nierstrasz, O.: Context-oriented programming. J. Object Technol. $7(3)$, 125–151 (2008)
18. Honda, K., Tokoro, M.: An object calculus for asynchronous communication. In: America, P. (ed.) ECOOP 1991. LNCS, vol. 512, pp. 133–147. Springer, Heidelberg (1991)
19. Jackson, D.E., Ratnieks, F.L.W.: Communication in ants. Curr. Biol. $16(15)$, R570–R574 (2006)
20. Klarl, A.: Engineering self-adaptive systems with the role-based architecture of Helena. In: Infrastructure for Collaborative Enterprises, WETICE 2015, Larnaca, Cyprus, 15–17 June 2015, pp. 3–8 (2015)

Towards Static Analysis of Policy-Based Self-adaptive Computing Systems

Andrea Margheri[1,2(✉)], Hanne Riis Nielson[3],
Flemming Nielson[3], and Rosario Pugliese[1]

[1] Università di Firenze, Firenze, Italy
{andrea.margheri,rosario.pugliese}@unifi.it
[2] Università di Pisa, Pisa, Italy
margheri@di.unipi.it
[3] Technical University of Denmark, Kongens Lyngby, Denmark
{hrni,fnie}@dtu.dk

Abstract. For supporting the design of self-adaptive computing systems, the PSCEL language offers a principled approach that relies on declarative definitions of adaptation and authorisation policies enforced at runtime. Policies permit managing system components by regulating their interactions and by dynamically introducing new actions to accomplish task-oriented goals. However, the runtime evaluation of policies and their effects on system components make the prediction of system behaviour challenging. In this paper, we introduce the construction of a flow graph that statically points out the policy evaluations that can take place at runtime and exploit it to analyse the effects of policy evaluations on the progress of system components.

Keywords: Policy languages · Static analysis · Self-adaptive systems

1 Introduction

Modern computing systems are increasingly decentralised, pervade different administrative domains, include massive numbers of components featuring complex interactions, and operate in open-ended environments (see, e.g., [18]). To master their growing complexity, self-adaptation capabilities have been largely advocated, so that systems can autonomously adapt themselves to changing operating conditions. Various approaches for achieving self-adaptation have been recently introduced, among which Aspect Oriented Programming (AOP) [11] has proven to be effective enough to easily deal with multiple adaptation and behavioural strategies (see, e.g., [3,5]). The AOP approach relies on the idea that definite parts of a program, called join-points, trigger the execution of *before* and *after* actions, i.e. actions that will be performed before or after the join-point.

A principled development of self-adaptive computing systems can be achieved by employing the PSCEL language [14], which integrates the FACPL policy language [13] within SCEL [6], a formal language expressly devised for autonomic computing. In PSCEL, self-adaptive systems are made of many, possibly

T. Margaria and B. Steffen (Eds.): ISoLA 2016, Part I, LNCS 9952, pp. 554–569, 2016.
DOI: 10.1007/978-3-319-47166-2_39

distributed, components, each of them including an interface, a knowledge repository, a process and a policy. Processes define the computational behaviour of components, while policies regulate the actions performed by the processes and possibly adapt component behaviours by means of actions injected at runtime. There is thus a clear separation of concerns: the normal computational behaviour is defined through the processes, while the authorisation and adaptation logic is defined through the policies. The actions added by policies can be used for, e.g., reacting to changes of the operating conditions or achieving specific tasks. Interfaces expose different component features and contextual values that can be checked by the controls implemented within policies and used to dynamically establish the partners of an interaction, thus providing flexible and expressive communication mechanisms. Knowledge repositories store the component states and what is known to the component of its working environment.

By taking inspiration from AOP, PSCEL policies permit defining self-adaptation strategies based on before and after *obligations*, i.e. the PSCEL notion corresponding to the AOP actions. Obligations are dynamically injected into the controlled processes as result of policy evaluations and, like any process action, must be authorised before being executed.

The interplay between dynamic policy evaluation and process execution, however, makes the prediction of the overall behaviour of systems challenging. Indeed, it might happen that a policy generates an infinite sequence of evaluations, because the obligations injected due to an evaluation recursively trigger further evaluations, or that the progress of the controlled process is precluded, because the authorisation of some injected obligations is denied. It is then worthwhile to devise a static analysis approach supporting the development of PSCEL systems.

Therefore, in this paper we introduce the construction of a flow graph, called Policy-Flow graph, that points out the relationships among the different policy elements and the context dependencies that can take place during their evaluation. We show that the Policy-Flow graph statically approximates the policy evaluations that can occur and can be used for inspecting the effects of these evaluations on the progress of processes. Indeed, we demonstrate that the accomplishment of specific conditions on the structure of the flow graph guarantees that the anomalous system behaviours mentioned above cannot occur.

Outline. PSCEL and the motivations underlying its analysis are introduced through a Cloud case study in Sect. 2. The Policy-Flow graph is defined in Sect. 3, while Sect. 4 exploits the graph to address the verification of progress properties on systems. Section 5 outlines more strictly related and future work. The proofs of all results, and the detailed definitions, are reported in [14].

2 PSCEL at Work and Motivations

In this section, we first outline the PSCEL approach to build self-adaptive systems through the modelling of an Autonomic Cloud case study (Sect. 2.1), then we present the motivations of the analysis we propose (Sect. 2.2).

2.1   Specification of an Autonomic Cloud

An Autonomic Cloud [15] is a collection of distributed nodes, grouped according to the geographic locality where they are placed, that cooperate to offer computational services. Each group includes: (i) a *gateway* node managing communications intra and inter groups; (ii) a *server* node (or more, if needed) offering computational services; (iii) multiple *client* nodes creating tasks to execute.

In PSCEL, each node of the Autonomic Cloud is represented by a *component*, generally denoted as $\mathcal{I}[\mathcal{K}, \Pi, P]$, where

- the *interface* $\mathcal{I}$ publishes information on the component. It is a non empty list of *features*, i.e. pairs $n : e$ (n is a *name* and e is a *closed*, i.e. without variables, expression). The features of an interface can be dynamically modified, except for id that is the component name, and their names are pairwise distinct;
- the *knowledge repository* $\mathcal{K}$ stores information known to the component. It is a multiset of evaluated *items*, i.e. sequences of different elements where variables cannot occur, like, e.g., $\langle taskId, 5 \rangle$. Items are nondeterministically retrieved from knowledge repositories via pattern matching;
- the *process* P defines the component behaviour. It is specified through classical process algebraic operators. Basic process actions can manage, possibly remote, repositories by withdrawing/retrieving/adding items, restrict the scope of names, create new components, or act on interface features;
- the *policy* Π regulates and adapts the component behaviour. It is a structured collection of *rules* that are evaluated against *authorisation requests* dynamically generated to enable execution of process actions.

To get an intuition of the interplay between policies and processes, suppose that the process of a component named n^1 is willing to execute the action $\mathbf{put}(log, task)@n1$, for adding the item $\langle log, task \rangle$ to the knowledge repository of the component $n1$. To control action execution, the PSCEL semantics uses the function req to generate the corresponding authorisation request, that is

$$\mathsf{req}(\mathcal{I}, \mathbf{put}(log, task)@n1, \mathcal{J}) = \{(\mathsf{action/id}, \mathbf{put})\} \ \cup \ \{(\mathsf{action/arg}, (log, task))\}$$
$$\cup \ \{(\mathsf{subject/n}, e) \mid (n : e) \in \mathcal{I}\} \ \cup \ \{(\mathsf{object/n}, e) \mid (n : e) \in \mathcal{J}\}$$

A request is thus a set of pairs structured name^2-value representing the action to authorise and its evaluation context, i.e. the interfaces $\mathcal{I}$ and $\mathcal{J}$ of the components subject (i.e. executing) and object (i.e. destination) of the action, resp. The request is then evaluated by the policy in force at n that establishes if execution of the action can be authorised and if further actions must be injected.

For the sake of presentation we only consider a single group of nodes, placed at locality *UNIFI*. The group is rendered as the following PSCEL system

$$\mathcal{I}_1[\mathcal{K}, \Pi_S, P_S] \ \| \ \mathcal{I}_G[\mathcal{K}, \Pi_G, P_G] \ \| \ \mathcal{I}_{C_1}[\mathcal{K}_C, \Pi_C, P_C] \ \| \ \dots \ \| \ \mathcal{I}_{C_k}[\mathcal{K}_C, \Pi_C, P_C]$$

---

[1] We use n to denote a generic name and n to denote the name of a syntactic element.

[2] Structured names are composed by a category name, i.e. one among action, subject and object, and a name n. For example, action/id refers to the name of the action generating the request, while subject/label refers to the value of the interface feature label of the component subject of the action.

The component with interface $\mathcal{I}_1$ represents the *server* node, that with interface $\mathcal{I}_G$ represents the *gateway* node. The others represent *client* nodes. Each component interface $\mathcal{I}$ publishes the features: id, the name of the component; role, the type of the node, i.e. *server, client* or *gateway;* locality, the name of the node locality, i.e. *UNIFI;* level, the confidentiality level of the node, i.e. *1* (low) and *2* (high); load, the percentage of (overall) load of the hosting machine, i.e. an integer between 0 and 100. E.g., the server interface might be $\mathcal{I}_1 \triangleq (\mathsf{id}\!:\!s1, \mathsf{role}\!:\!server, \mathsf{level}\!:\!1, \mathsf{locality}\!:\!UNIFI, \mathsf{load}\!:\!70)$. To update the value of a feature, say load, the component process can execute the action **upd**(load, 75), while to assign its current value to variable x it can execute **read**($?\,x$, load).

We now explicitly describe the components above (except the gateway because, in our simplified setting, it only has the task of collecting logs from clients). The process P_S of the server component is defined as follows

$$P_S \triangleq \mathbf{get}(task, ?\underline{owner}, ?\underline{X}, ?\underline{taskId})@(\mathsf{locality}{=}UNIFI).$$
$$(\ X\ |\ \mathbf{get}(result, ?\underline{res})@\mathsf{self}.\mathbf{put}(result, \underline{taskId}, \underline{res})@\underline{owner}\,.\,P_S\ )$$

where the underlined names, e.g. $\underline{taskId}$, represent variables and, when preceded by ?, represent variable binders. The first action **get** is used to non-deterministically retrieve a task to compute from a component among those dynamically matching the destination predicate locality=*UNIFI*, i.e. a boolean expression on feature names dynamically checked to identify potential object components. A task is any process Q stored in an item of the form $\langle task, n, Q, i \rangle$ (n and i are a name and an integer, resp.), which is expected to terminate its execution by locally producing an item of the form $\langle result, v \rangle$. The retrieved task (bound to the process variable $\underline{X}$) is sent for execution by process P_S which then waits for the result via a local **get** (the reserved variable self refers to the name of the component subject of the action). The retrieved result is then sent to the task owner through a **put**, whereupon the process proceeds recursively.

The server policy $\varPi_S$, controlling execution of process P_S, is defined as follows

⟨ p-unless-d   rules:
  S1 (deny   target: equal(action/id,get) ∧ equal(subject/id,this)
              ∧ pattern-match(action/arg,$(task, \_, \_, \_)$)
              ∧ equal(subject/level,1) ∧ equal(object/level,2))
  S2 (deny   target: equal(action/id,get) ∧ equal(subject/id,this)
              ∧ pattern-match(action/arg,$(task, \_, \_, \_)$)
              ∧ greater-than(subject/load,90) $(\varPi_S)$
        obl : $[B$ **fresh**(n'). **new**$(\mathcal{I}_1[\mathsf{id} := n'], \mathcal{K}, \varPi_S, P_S).$**read**$(?\,\underline{load}, \mathsf{load})])$
  S3 (deny   target : equal(action/id, read) ∧ pattern-match(action/arg,$(\_, \mathsf{load})$))
              ∧ greater-than(subject/load,60)
  S4 (permit   target : equal(action/id, **put**) ∧ equal(subject/id, this)
        obl : $[B$ **put**$(log, \mathsf{action/arg})@\mathsf{self}])$ ⟩

The policy includes four rules (named S1, S2, S3 and S4) and uses the p-unless-d algorithm, thus it permits a request (i.e. returns the decision permit) unless at least an enclosed rule denies it (i.e. returns the decision deny). All the rules, but the last one, deny a request when it matches their target. The targets of S1 and S2 are matched by those requests such that (i) the corresponding action is a **get**, (ii) the subject component name is equal to the local one (which is retrieved through the reserved variable this), and (iii) the action argument matches the template $(task, \_, \_, \_)$ (_ is a wildcard matching any value). Due to the additional controls contained in the target, S1 applies only if the confidentiality level of the subject is low and that of the object is high. Similarly, S2 applies only if the local load is greater than 90. In this case, S2 enforces a self-adaptation strategy by means of the actions reported after the keyword obl, which are dynamically injected within process P_S immediately *Before* the action generating the matched request. This strategy consists in spawning a new server component, via the actions **fresh** and **new**, thus to guarantee availability of the computational service. The injected action **read** triggers application of rule S3 which blocks it (and the continuation process) until the load is higher than 60. Finally, rule S4 intercepts the action **put** of process P_S that sends the task result to the owner and injects an additional **put** to log this result in the local repository.

Let us now focus on the client components. Concerning their process P_C, we only assume that, besides some other actions, it performs actions of the form **put**$(task, loc\_res, Q)$@self that locally add items containing a new task Q to execute and a component name loc_res where the task evaluation result should be sent. Instead, the policy Π_C is defined as follows

⟨ p-unless-d   rules:
    C1 (permit target : equal(action/id, put) ∧ pattern-match(action/arg, $(task, \_, \_)$))
                  ∧ equal(subject/id,this)
          obl : $[A$ **get**$(taskId, ?\underline{num})$@self.**put**(action/arg, $\underline{num}$)@self .
                 put$(taskId, \underline{num} + 1)$@self $])$ (Π_C)
    C2 (permit target: equal(action/id,get) ∧ equal(subject/role,*server*)
          obl : $[A$ **put**$(log, task\ retrieved,$ subject/id$)$@$(role = gateway)])$
    C3 (deny target : equal(action/id, **put**) ∧ equal(object/id, this)
                  ∧ greater-than(object/load,90)) ⟩

The policy includes three rules and uses the p-unless-d algorithm. Rule C1 applies to the **put** actions adding a new task and accomplishes an incremental enumeration of tasks by means of three actions dynamically injected *After* the action generating the matched request: **get** retrieves the current task number, the first **put** locally adds the argument of the **put** to authorise (i.e., action/arg) extended with the retrieved task number, and the second **put** increments the task number. Rule C2 injects a **put** action informing the gateway about the retrieval of a task by a **get** action originated by a server, and C3 denies any **put** action with object the local component when the local load is higher than 90.

2.2   Dynamic Interplay Between Policies and Processes

The obligation actions injected in a process, like any other process action, need to be authorised before being executed. On the other hand, policy rules are initially designed to apply to certain process actions. Thus, if afterwards they also apply to injected actions, unforeseen interplays between policies and processes might arise that, e.g., could also prevent processes from actually proceed.

For example, let us consider process P_S and its controlling policy Π_S, and focus on the actions injected when rule S2 applies. Actions **fresh** and **new** are permitted due to the default decision of the algorithm (as no rule applies to them), while action **read** is permitted only when rule S3 does not apply, otherwise it is denied. In case of actions **put**, rule S4 also injects a new action **put** for logging purposes. As result of such an authorisation, the process becomes

$$\overline{\mathbf{put}(result, 12, 5)@n'} .\mathbf{put}(log, result, 12, 5)@\mathsf{self} . P_S$$

Indeed, the first **put** is overlined to denote that it has already been permitted and the bound variables occurring within in the process syntax have been replaced by realistic values (i.e., _owner_, _taskId_ and _res_ have been replaced by n', 12 and 5, respectively). The second **put** is instead the obligation action injected by the rule that has been fulfilled by replacing the structured name action/arg with the argument of the permitted **put**. Once the first **put** has been executed, the authorisation of the injected **put** modifies the process as follows

$$\overline{\mathbf{put}(log, result, 12, 5)@s1} .\mathbf{put}(log, log, result, 12, 5)@\mathsf{self} . P_S$$

Basically, rule S4 has applied again and injected an additional logging **put**! Clearly, this leads to an infinite introduction of actions and, hence, of policy evaluations, which prevents process P_S from proceeding further.

A different interplay may concern the authorisation decisions enforced by the rules since, when an action is permitted, the action itself or its continuation can be precluded from progressing due to an injected action that is denied. This interplay can occur between rules C1 and C3: when rule C1 permits an action **put**, the injected **put** action could be denied by rule C3, if the load of the object component is higher than 90.

3   Policy-Flow Graph

We now introduce an analysis approach that statically points out possible runtime interplays, like those just presented. It relies on a representation of policies that enables (automated) extensive checks on the applicability of policy rules to injected actions. Indeed, the injection of actions can trigger additional evaluations of rules, thus generating a sort of _flow_. Our approach over-approximates the potential flows that injected actions might generate at runtime.

We rely on the formal machinery of the PSCEL semantics (see [14] for a full account). Besides the function req already mentioned, we use the judgement $r, \rho \vdash d, s_B, s_A$ meaning that the rule r authorises the request ρ with decision d, i.e. permit or deny, and two (possibly empty) sequences s_B and s_A of before and after actions, resp. We also use the function $\mathcal{A}$ that evaluates action arguments with respect to a component name (i.e. the intended subject) and returns an action only containing values or variable binders. E.g., $\mathcal{A}(\mathbf{put}(1+2)@\mathsf{self}, n1)$ returns the evaluated action **put**(3)@$n1$, where the expression has been evaluated and the component name $n1$ has replaced the reserved variable self.

Due to the static nature of the approach, the injected actions a to consider are those produced by the syntax. Hence, they may contain *open terms*, i.e. terms where variables and structured names can occur. To make these actions evaluable through $\mathcal{A}$, we must apply to them a 'closing' *substitution*, denoted by ξ, i.e. a function mapping their variables and structured names to values.

As a matter of notation, we write Interf(S) to denote the set of component interfaces in the system S, $\mathcal{I}$.id to refer to the name of the component having interface $\mathcal{I}$, and $\Pi(S, m)$ to make it explicit that the policy Π is in force at the component named m in S. Hence, we set the following definition.

Definition 1 (Policy-Flow). *Given a system S with $\mathcal{I}, \mathcal{J} \in$ Interf(S), there is a flow from rule r_i to rule r_j in the policy $\Pi(S, \mathcal{I}.id)$ if, for any request ρ, it holds that*

$$r_i, \rho \vdash d, s_B, s_A \quad \text{and} \quad \exists\, a \in s_B.s_A \;,\; \xi \;:\; r_j, req(\mathcal{I}, \mathcal{A}(a\xi, \mathcal{I}.id), \mathcal{J}) \vdash d', s_B', s_A'$$

where $a \in s_B.s_A$ means that action a occurs in the sequence of actions $s_B.s_A$.

The flows in a policy can be statically determined by checking whether the authorisation requests corresponding to injected actions match rule targets. To automate this check, we represent targets in terms of constraints and authorisation requests in terms of assignments for constraints. Existence of a flow is thus equivalent to satisfiability of a constraint with an applied assignment.

In the following, first we introduce a constraint formalism (Sect. 3.1) and a translation procedure for targets (Sect. 3.2). Then, we present the construction of a flow graph, called *Policy-Flow graph*, collecting all the flows in a policy (Sect. 3.3) and its application to the case study (Sect. 3.4).

3.1 A Constraint Formalism

The constraint formalism we propose is defined by the following syntax

$$cstr ::= \text{true} \mid \neg\; cstr \mid cstr_1 \wedge cstr_2 \mid cstr_1 \vee cstr_2 \mid var = pv \mid var > pv$$
$$\mid var < pv \mid var \; \text{match} \; pv$$

A constraint can be either the value true, or a comparison between a variable *var* and a policy value *pv* through a relational operator, or a boolean combination of simpler constraints. Policy values are the values referred to by the attribute names of authorisation requests like, e.g., the action identifier **get** or an item argument of an action. Variables model the structured names *sn* occurring within rule targets and can either belong to the set A_Π or to the set F_S.

The set A_Π, given a policy $\Pi \triangleq \langle alg \; \text{rules} : r_1 \ldots r_k \rangle$, is defined as follows

$$A_\Pi \triangleq \{id\text{-}h, arg\text{-}h, sub\text{-}h, obj\text{-}h \mid h \in \{id(r_1) \ldots id(r_k)\}\}$$

where $id(r_j)$ stands for the name of the rule r_j. Variables in A_Π model: (i) action identifiers referred to by action/id; (ii) action arguments referred to by action/arg; (iii) the name of the subject (resp., object) component referred to by subject/id (resp., object/id).

The set F_S is formed by variables modelling the features of the components in the sytem S. Hence, given a system S, it is defined as follows

$$F_S \triangleq \{\text{z-}n \mid \exists\, \mathcal{I} \in \mathsf{Interf}(S) : \mathcal{I}.\mathsf{id} = n \wedge (\text{z} : e) \in \mathcal{I} \wedge \text{z} \neq \mathsf{id}\}$$

As features are associated to closed expressions, the variables in F_S are mapped to standard values.

To represent the authorisation requests corresponding to obligation actions, we use the function $\langle\!\langle \cdot \rangle\!\rangle_m^h$ which, given in input an obligation action, the name m of a component (i.e. the intended subject) and the name h of a policy rule, returns the assignments (induced by the obligation action) for the variables of A_Π corresponding to rule h. The function is smoothly defined by case analysis on the action syntax. As an example, we have $\langle\!\langle \mathbf{put}(taskId, \underline{num} + 1)@\mathsf{self}\,\rangle\!\rangle_m^h = [id\text{-}h := \mathbf{put}, arg\text{-}h := (taskId, \underline{num} + 1), sub\text{-}h := m, obj\text{-}h := m]$.

Since constraint variables are possibly mapped to elements containing open terms (as, e.g., the variable $\underline{num}$ in the previous example), checking the satisfiability of a constraint amounts to decide if there exists a closing substitution ξ such that the constraint evaluates to true. For instance, checking the satisfiability of a constraint with applied the previous assignment means identifying a substitution ξ for the variable $\underline{num}$ such that the constraint is satisfied. We write $\xi \models cstr\langle\!\langle a \rangle\!\rangle_m^h$ (resp., $\xi \not\models cstr\langle\!\langle a \rangle\!\rangle_m^h$) to mean that the constraint $cstr$, under the assignment $\langle\!\langle a \rangle\!\rangle_m^h$ induced by the obligation action a, is satisfiable (resp., not satisfiable) through the substitution ξ.

We conclude by stating that any obligation action possibly executed at runtime can be statically approximated starting from its syntactical definition.

Lemma 1. *For any obligation action a such that $\mathcal{A}(a\xi', m) = \mathbf{a}$ for some substitution ξ', it holds that*

$$\exists\, \xi \;:\; \langle\!\langle \mathbf{a} \rangle\!\rangle_m^h = [\![\, \langle\!\langle a \rangle\!\rangle_m^h \xi \,]\!]$$

where $[\![\, \langle\!\langle a \rangle\!\rangle_m^h \xi \,]\!]$ denotes the assignment obtained from $\langle\!\langle a \rangle\!\rangle_m^h \xi$ by evaluating all the expressions occurring within.

3.2 From Targets to Constraints

To represent targets in terms of constraints, we define a formal translation procedure which, intuitively, works in two steps. First, we approximate the potential subject and object components of those actions matching the target. Then, we exploit them to translate targets into their corresponding constraints.

Step (1/2): Potential Subject and Object Components. The components possibly involved in the actions matching the target of a rule can be over-approximated by inspecting the controls occurring in the rule target. In fact, controls concerning component names, i.e. subject/id and object/id, or features, e.g. subject/level, statically limit the components that can be represented by those authorisation requests that match the target. The sets of the potential subjects and objects of the actions matching the target, S and $\mathcal{O}$ resp., are determined by functions Sbj and Obj, resp. As Obj is specular to Sbj, we only briefly introduce the latter.

The function Sbj, inductively defined on the target syntax, takes in input a target τ and a system S, and returns a set of component names. Among its defining clauses, the most significant one is that for target functions controlling the identity of the subject component (i.e., subject/id); the clause is as follows

$$Sbj_S(f(\mathsf{subject/id}, pv)) = \begin{cases} \{n\} & \text{if } [\![pv]\!] = n \wedge f \in \{\mathsf{equal}, \mathsf{pattern\text{-}match}\} \\ \{\} & \text{otherwise} \end{cases}$$

If f is an equality function and pv evaluates to a name n, the resulting set S only contains such a name (otherwise, the function would not be satisfied through the name referred to by subject/id). The other clauses on target functions operate similarly, while those on target conjunction (resp., disjunction) correspond to the intersection (resp., union) of the sets calculated for the sub-targets.

Step (2/2): Generating the Constraint. The function $\mathcal{T}$ translating targets into constraints takes in input the sets S and $\mathcal{O}$ calculated from the target to translate and the name h of a policy rule. It is inductively defined on the target syntax. The most significant clause is that for target functions, which is as follows

$$\mathcal{T}\{\!| f(sn, pv) |\!\}_{S,\mathcal{O}}^h = \begin{cases} \bigvee_{n \in S} \mathsf{z\text{-}}n\ \mathsf{getOp}(f)\ pv & \text{if } sn = \mathsf{subject/z} \text{ and } z \neq \mathsf{id} \\ \bigvee_{n \in \mathcal{O}} \mathsf{z\text{-}}n\ \mathsf{getOp}(f)\ pv & \text{if } sn = \mathsf{object/z} \text{ and } z \neq \mathsf{id} \\ sub\text{-}h\ \mathsf{getOp}(f)\ pv & \text{if } sn = \mathsf{subject/id} \\ obj\text{-}h\ \mathsf{getOp}(f)\ pv & \text{if } sn = \mathsf{object/id} \\ id\text{-}h\ \mathsf{getOp}(f)\ pv & \text{if } sn = \mathsf{action/id} \\ arg\text{-}h\ \mathsf{getOp}(f)\ pv & \text{if } sn = \mathsf{action/arg} \end{cases}$$

Thus, if the structured name sn is a subject/object feature different from id, the generated constraint has as many variables $\mathsf{z\text{-}}n$ representing the feature as the component names n in the set $S/\mathcal{O}$. The disjunction ensures that the constraint addresses each possibly involved component. Instead, if the structured name represents the feature id or an attribute with category action, the generated constraint uses the variables referring to the rule named h. Notably, the function getOp maps the target function f to the corresponding constraint operator, e.g., the target function equal is mapped to the constraint operator $=$.

The following theorem states that satisfiability of the constraints representing targets under the assignments induced by (authorisation requests corresponding to) obligation actions correctly over-approximates the set of policy flows.

Theorem 1. *Given a system S with $\mathcal{I}, \mathcal{J} \in \mathsf{Interf}(S)$, for any rule r of the policy $\Pi(S, \mathcal{I}.id)$ with $id(r) = h$, and for any obligation action a such that $\mathcal{A}(a\xi', \mathcal{I}.id) = a$ for some substitution ξ', it holds that:*

$$r, req(\mathcal{I}, \mathbf{a}, \mathcal{J}) \vdash d', s_\mathsf{B}', s_\mathsf{A}' \quad \Rightarrow \quad \exists\, \xi\, :\, \xi \models \mathcal{T}\{\!| \tau |\!\}_{S,\mathcal{O}}^h \langle\!\langle a \rangle\!\rangle_m^h.$$

The converse of the previous theorem does not hold because, due to Lemma 1, the substitution ξ could map, e.g., some variables (modelling action arguments or features) to values that they cannot actually assume at run-time.

3.3   Policy-Flow Graph Construction

We now define the construction of a graph, called *Policy-Flow graph*, that, by relying on the previous constraint-based representation of rule targets and authorisation requests, graphically and compactly represents all the potential flows in a policy. Intuitively, the nodes of the graph represent policy rules, or its combining algorithm, while the directed edges represent the flows. Hence, the graph *paths* estimate the sequences of policy evaluations that might occur at runtime.

As policies can check conditions on the *context* (which is made of the component features), the edges are annotated with the contextual conditions holding when the corresponding flow takes place. For convenience, we re-organise the constraints representing targets so that the constraints involving variables from the set A_Π are separated from those involving variables from the set F_S[3]. In the following, we thus assume they are written in the form $act \wedge ctx$, where act is the constraint on the *action*, while ctx is that on the *context*. As a matter of notation, $r \rhd^{act \wedge ctx} s$ indicates the constraint representing the target of rule r and the sequence of obligation actions s generated when the rule r applies.

Definition 2. (Policy-Flow Graph). *The* Policy-Flow graph *of a policy* $\Pi \triangleq \langle alg\ rules{:}r_1 \ldots r_k \rangle$ *is a doubly labelled directed graph* (N, F, T, L) *where*

- N, *i.e. the set of* nodes, *is* $\{\mathrm{id}(r_1), \ldots, \mathrm{id}(r_k), alg\}$;
- F, *i.e. the set of* edge labels, *is* $\{ctx_j \mid r_j \rhd^{act_j \wedge ctx_j} s_j$ *with* $j = 1, \ldots, k\}$;
- $T \subseteq N \times F \times N$, *i.e. the set of labelled* directed edges, *contains the elements*

  - $(id(r_j), ctx_j, id(r_l))$ if $\exists\, a \in s_j$, ξ : $\xi \models (act_l \wedge ctx_l)\langle\!\langle a \rangle\!\rangle_m^l$
  - $(id(r_j), ctx_j, alg)$ if $\exists\, a \in s_j$, ξ : $\xi \not\models (act_l \wedge ctx_l)\langle\!\langle a \rangle\!\rangle_m^l$

  for each pair of rules r_j *and* r_l *such that* $r_j \rhd^{act_j \wedge\ ctx_j} s_j$ *and* $r_l \rhd^{act_l \wedge\ ctx_l} s_l$;
- $L : N \rightarrow \{p, d\}$, *i.e. the* node labelling function, *is defined as follows*

  $L(id(r_j)) = p$ *if* r_j *has decision* permit $L(alg) = p$ *if* $alg = p\text{-}unless\text{-}d$
  $L(id(r_j)) = d$ *if* r_j *has decision* deny $L(alg) = d$ *if* $alg = d\text{-}unless\text{-}p$

The graph has two types of edges: one representing a flow between two rules, the other representing a flow from a rule to the combining algorithm. In the first edge type, $\mathrm{id}(r_j)$ is connected to $\mathrm{id}(r_l)$ when there exists in the sequence s_j an action a whose induced assignment $\langle\!\langle a \rangle\!\rangle_m^l$ makes the constraint corresponding to the target of the rule r_l satisfiable, i.e. there exists ξ such that $\xi \models (act_l \wedge ctx_l)\langle\!\langle a \rangle\!\rangle_m^l$ holds. The edge is annotated with the contextual conditions ctx_j asserted by the target of r_j. In the second edge type, $\mathrm{id}(r_j)$ is connected to alg

---

[3] This splitting can always be done by appropriately applying standard boolean laws because each relational operator takes at most one variable as argument.

when there exists in the sequence s_j an action a whose induced assignment $\langle\!\langle a\rangle\!\rangle^l_m$ makes the constraint corresponding to the target of any rule r_l not satisfiable, i.e. there exists ξ such that $\xi \not\models (act_l \wedge ctx_l)\langle\!\langle a\rangle\!\rangle^l_m$ holds; the edge is annotated with ctx_j as well. If multiple edges with the same label connect a node $\mathrm{id}(r_j)$ to node alg, only one of them is retained. Notably, the same action a can cause, due to different substitutions, the creation of edges of both types. Since combining algorithms neither define controls nor obligations, alg has no outgoing edges. Notice that determining the set of edges T has a worst case complexity of $O(k^2\theta)$, where k is the number of policy rules and θ is the maximum number of actions forming the obligations of the policy rules (e.g., in the case of policy Π_S, θ has value 3 because of the obligation actions of rule S2). Indeed, the first edge type requires examining all the $k \times k$ pairs of rules, while the second edge type requires examining the k pairs formed by a rule and the combining algorithm. Each pair of both types requires examining at most θ obligation actions.

3.4   The Policy-Flow Graph at Work on the Case Study

The policies Π_S and Π_C presented in Sect. 2.1 generate the flows graphically depicted by the graphs in Fig. 1. Before commenting the construction of the graphs, we outline the constraint-based representation of some of the rule targets. For simplicity's sake, we consider a system S formed by three components: one server and two clients named $sr1$, $cl1$ and $cl2$, respectively. The set of system interfaces $\mathsf{Interf}(S)$ is defined as $\{\mathcal{I}_1, \mathcal{I}_{C_1}, \mathcal{I}_{C_2}\}$. The set of variable F_S is then straightforwardly defined, while the set A_Π depends on the policy. For example, in the case of Π_S, it is $\{id\text{-}h, arg\text{-}h, sub\text{-}h, obj\text{-}h \mid h \in \{S1, S2, S3, S4\}\}$.

Let us consider rule S1 of the policy Π_S in force at the component $sr1$. Firstly, by using functions Sbj and Obj, we get that $\mathcal{S} = \{sr1\}$, due to the control $\mathsf{equal}(\mathsf{subject/id}, sr1)^4$, and $\mathcal{O} = \{sr1, cl1, cl2\}$, i.e. it contains the names of all system components, because the occurring controls do not limit the set of names. Secondly, the function $\mathcal{T}$ translates the target of S1 to the constraint

$$(\underline{id\text{-}S1} = \mathbf{get}) \wedge (\underline{sub\text{-}S1} = sr1) \wedge (\underline{arg\text{-}S1} \text{ match } (task, \_, \_, \_)) \qquad (1)$$
$$\wedge\ (\underline{\mathsf{level}\text{-}sr1} = 1) \wedge ((\underline{\mathsf{level}\text{-}sr1} = 2) \vee (\underline{\mathsf{level}\text{-}cl1} = 2) \vee (\underline{\mathsf{level}\text{-}cl2} = 2))$$

The sub-constraints in the first row represent the target controls referring to the action; their conjunction forms the constraint act_{S1}. The sub-constraints in the second row represent the two target controls on the feature level: $(\underline{\mathsf{level}\text{-}sr1} = 1)$ is obtained from the control $\mathsf{equal}(\mathsf{subject/level}, 1)$ by exploiting the set $\mathcal{S}$, while the disjunction following the operator $\wedge$ is obtained from the control $\mathsf{equal}(\mathsf{object/level}, 2)$ by exploiting the set $\mathcal{O}$. The conjunction of the sub-constraints in the second row forms the constraint ctx_{S1}.

In case of rule S4 of the policy Π_S its target is represented by the constraint

$$(\underline{id\text{-}S4} = \mathbf{put}) \wedge (\underline{sub\text{-}S4} = sr1) \qquad (2)$$

---

[4] The name $sr1$ of the component where the policy Π_S is assumed to be in force is that referred to by the variable this occurring in the definition of rule S1.

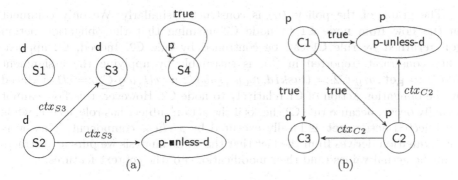

Fig. 1. Autonomic cloud case study: policy-flow graphs (some conditions ctx_h are detailed in the text): (a) policy Π_S of servers; (b) policy Π_C of clients

It forms the constraint act_{S4}, while the constraint ctx_{S4} is true since there are no contextual controls in the rule target.

Let us consider rule C2 of the policy Π_C; its target is represented as follows

$$(\underline{id\text{-}C2} = \textbf{get}) \wedge (\underline{role\text{-}sr1} = server \vee \underline{role\text{-}cl1} = server \vee \underline{role\text{-}cl2} = server) \ (3)$$

where $\mathcal{S} = \{sr1, cl1, cl2\}$ is used to define the constraints on the feature role.

The constraints just introduced can now be exploited to construct the Policy-Flow graphs of the policies Π_S and Π_C according to Definition 2. For simplicity's sake, we use the name of the rules and of the algorithm to identify the corresponding node in the graph. Since the policy rules that do not define obligations cannot trigger other rules, the corresponding nodes have no outgoing edges. As depicted in Fig. 1, this is the case, e.g., of rules S1 and S3 of policy Π_S. In the remaining cases, to determine the outgoing edges of a node, we check if any obligation action of its corresponding rule induces an assignment that makes the constraint representing a rule target satisfiable.

Let us consider the construction of the graph of the policy Π_S. Rule S4 returns the obligation action $\textbf{put}(log, \text{action}/\text{arg})$@self that, relatively to node S4, induces the assignment $[\underline{id\text{-}S4} := \textbf{put}, \underline{arg\text{-}S4} := (log, \text{action}/\text{arg}), \underline{sub\text{-}S4} := sr1, \underline{obj\text{-}S4} := sr1]$. This assignment makes the applicability constraint of S4, reported in (2), satisfiable. In fact, by applying the assignment, we get the constraint $\textbf{put} = \textbf{put} \wedge (sr1 = sr1)$ that clearly evaluates to true. Hence, there is a self loop on node S4 labelled by the contextual constraint ctx_{S4}, i.e. true. The other flows in policy Π_S are generated by the obligation actions within rule S2. By reasoning as before we can easily establish that its **fresh** and **new** actions do not match the target of any rule, therefore there is a flow from node S2 to node p-unless-d, while its **read** action can match the target of rule S3 when the subject load is higher than 60, hence there is a flow from node S2 to node S3. Notice that, when the load is less than 60, the action **read** does not match the target of rule S3, hence such an action can also cause a flow to node p-unless-d.

The graph of the policy Π_C is constructed similarly. We only comment on the flow from node C1 to node C2 meaning that the obligation action **get** returned by rule C1 can be controlled by rule C2. Indeed, C2 applicability constraint, reported in (3), is satisfiable by applying the assignment $[\underline{id\text{-}C2} := \mathbf{get}; \underline{arg\text{-}C2} := (taskId, \underline{num}); \underline{sub\text{-}C2} := cl1, \underline{obj\text{-}C2} := cl1]$ induced by the obligation action of C1 relatively to node C2. However, this flow cannot actually occur, because rule C2 checks if the action subject has role *server*, while the injected action **get** is locally executed by a *client* component. This over-approximation derives from the fact that the static analysis we pursue abstracts from the actual values (and their modifications) of the context features.

4   Progress Analysis of PSCEL Specifications

Policy evaluations may affect the progress of controlled processes. The effects on progress can be expressed in terms of the following properties

- *finite evaluation*: each action can only trigger a finite number of policy evaluations;
- *undeniable executability*: once an action is permitted, the execution of the controlled process cannot be blocked due to the injection of an action that is denied.

For example, rule S4 in the previous section shows a violation of the former property, while rules C1 and C3 show a violation of the latter one.

The properties above refer to the flows that a policy may generate and can be verified in terms of conditions on the structure of the Policy-Flow graph. Since the graph statically addresses conditions on the context, we need to assume that these conditions are somehow *stable*. We thus set the following definition.

Definition 3. (Context-Stable Policy). *A policy is* context-stable *if, along each path of its Policy-Flow graph, the features it checks do not change value.*

Intuitively, if a policy is context-stable then, given a feature n checked by (the target of a rule of) the policy, an action of the form **upd**(n, e) cannot interleave with the policy evaluations forming a path. This check could be done manually, e.g. in the case of our case study[5], or syntactically over-approximated by checking the policy specification. Indeed, a policy is context-stable if its obligations do not contain actions updating features that are checked by the enclosed rules.

The paths of Policy-Flow graphs are annotated with constraints *ctx*, which represent the context conditions holding when the corresponding policy evaluations occur. To consider them in the analysis, we introduce the following notion.

Definition 4. (Characteristic Formula of a Path). *Given a path formed by nodes* $\nu_1 \ldots \nu_k$, *its* characteristic formula *is* $\gamma \triangleq \bigwedge_{j=1}^{k} cstr(\nu_j)$, *where* $cstr(\nu_j)$ *is the constraint corresponding to the policy rule represented by the node* ν_j *(or* **true** *if the node represents the policy algorithm).*

---

[5] E.g., rule S2 of policy Π_S checks the feature load. Since S2 only generates paths of length one, possible updates of load cannot interleave with policy evaluations.

Notably, due to the context-stability assumption, it is enough to consider the context conditions occurring in a loop only once. A path is deemed *feasible* if, under the context-stability assumption, its characteristic formula is satisfiable. Unsatisfiable paths in the policy-flow graph represent sequences of flows that, due to conflictual contextual conditions, e.g. like role-*sr1* = *server* and role-*sr1* = *client*, cannot actually occur in the system.

A (context-stable) policy enjoys the finite evaluation property when each action matching the target of any rule can only trigger finite sequences of policy evaluations. It follows that the property holds when the Policy-Flow graph has no feasible infinite paths, i.e. loops, as stated by the following theorem.

Theorem 2. (Finite Evaluation). *A context-stable policy enjoys the finite evaluation property only if its Policy-Flow graph contains no feasible loops.*

A policy enjoying the finite evaluation property can anyway undermine the progress of a controlled process due to the authorisations it enforces. The undeniable executability property addresses the case of injected obligation actions that are denied. Specifically, once an action has been permitted, the denying of some of the obligations whose injection was caused by the action authorisation may prevent the execution of the controlled process. It follows that the property holds when, in the Policy-Flow graph, each path containing nodes labelled by p (i.e., enforcing permit) does not contain nodes labelled by d (i.e., enforcing deny).

Theorem 3. (Undeniable Executability). *A context-stable policy enjoys the undeniable executability property only if for each feasible path in its Policy-Flow graph, if the path contains a node labelled by p, than after this node there is no node labelled by d.*

Concerning the graphs in Fig. 1, it is easy to check that policy Π_C meets the condition of Theorem 2 while policy Π_S does not; instead, because of the path between rules C1 and C3, policy Π_C does not met the condition of Theorem 3.

The converse of Theorems 2 and 3 does not hold. This is a consequence of Theorem 1 and of the fact that the Policy-Flow graph does not take into account the evaluation of the combining algorithm, but it only considers rules separately.

5   Conclusions

In this paper, we outline the use of PSCEL to specify self-adaptive computing systems and introduce a static analysis approach based on a novel notion of Policy-Flow graph. Then, we show how this graph can be exploited to reason on the effects of policy evaluations on the progress of PSCEL systems.

Related Work. The specification approaches for developing self-adaptive computing systems are multiple and variegated. In addition to AOP, other prominent examples are component-based design and context-oriented programming (COP). Component-based approaches like, e.g., FRACTAL [2,5] and *Helena* [8] design systems in terms of components that re-organise themselves according to changes of operating conditions. Differently from PSCEL, component communications rely on rigid connectors rather than flexible predicates. The COP-based approaches exploit instead ad-hoc linguistic constructs for expressing context-dependent behaviours [16]. The most of the literature on COP is devoted to the design and implementation of concrete programming languages (a comparison can be found in [1]). Instead, PSCEL focusses on distribution, flexible communications and highly dynamic obligation-based adaptation strategies.

Declarative policies are commonly advocated [9] for regulating systems behaviour. For instance, the policy language Ponder [4] has been exploited to regulate various autonomous systems. However, differently from PSCEL, it cannot express adaptation strategies in terms of dynamically fulfilled actions. Similarly, the actor-based framework reported in [10] exploits declarative rules to adapt the configuration of computing systems managing entities. However, these rules permit defining neither authorisation controls nor dynamically fulfilled actions.

To enforce self-adaptation strategies, many proposals follow the AOP approach. Some examples are the AOP extension of FRACTAL [5] (which suffers from the same drawbacks of FRACTAL) and AspectK [7], which enriches a distributed coordination language with AOP concepts. With respect to AspectK, the AOP support offered by PSCEL is more flexible and, most of all, also provides dynamically fulfilled actions. In [17] an analysis approach of AspectK specifications aiming at discovering undesired infinite executions is introduced. Differently from our static approach that only relies on the policy-flow graph, it is there exploited an approach based on communicating pushdown systems.

Ongoing and Future Work. We are currently extending the PSCEL supporting tools [12] to deploy the proposed analysis approach. The development environment already available for PSCEL is being enriched with the rule translation procedure and the construction of the Policy-Flow graph. To this aim, rule constraints are encoded as *satisfiability modulo theories* (SMT) formulae based on multiple theories like, e.g., boolean, linear arithmetics and records. The SMT-based approach guarantees expressive specifications (e.g. pattern-matching amounts to only specify a comparison on records) and is supported by powerful automatic solvers.

To further specialise the analysis approach, we will introduce, on the one hand, abstractions for knowledge repositories, thus enabling reasoning on the execution of blocking **get** and **qry** actions, and, on the other hand, a static approximation of combining algorithms, thus addressing hierarchically structured policies. Finally, we plan to investigate the problem of infinite evaluation flows due to the mutual interplay of distributed policies and to devise techniques for distributing policies so that such situations are avoided by construction.

References

1. Appeltauer, M., Hirschfeld, R., Haupt, M., Lincke, J., Perscheid, M.: A comparison of context-oriented programming languages. In: COP, pp. 6:1–6:6 (2009)
2. Bruneton, E., Coupaye, T., Leclercq, M., Quéma, V., Stefani, J.B.: The FRACTAL component model and its support in Java. Softw.: Pract. Experience **36**, 1257–1284 (2006)
3. Charfi, A., Mezini, M.: AO4BPEL: an aspect-oriented extension to BPEL. World Wide Web **3**, 309–344 (2007)
4. Damianou, N., Dulay, N., Lupu, E.C., Sloman, M.: The ponder policy specification language. In: Sloman, M., Lobo, J., Lupu, E.C. (eds.) POLICY 2001. LNCS, vol. 1995, pp. 18–38. Springer, Heidelberg (2001)
5. David, P.-C., Ledoux, T.: An aspect-oriented approach for developing self-adaptive fractal components. In: Löwe, Welf, Südholt, Mario (eds.) SC 2006. LNCS, vol. 4089, pp. 82–97. Springer, Heidelberg (2006)
6. De Nicola, R., Loreti, M., Pugliese, R., Tiezzi, F.: A formal approach to autonomic systems programming: the SCEL language. TAAS **9**(2), 7:1–7:29 (2014)
7. Hankin, C., Nielson, F., Riis Nielson, H., Yang, F.: Advice for coordination. In: Lea, D., Zavattaro, G. (eds.) COORDINATION 2008. LNCS, vol. 5052, pp. 153–168. Springer, Heidelberg (2008)
8. Hennicker, R., Klarl, A.: Foundations for ensemble modeling – the HELENA approach. In: Iida, S., Meseguer, J., Ogata, K. (eds.) Specification, Algebra, and Software. LNCS, vol. 8373, pp. 359–381. Springer, Heidelberg (2014)
9. Huebscher, M.C., McCann, J.A.: A survey of autonomic computing-degrees, models and applications. ACM Comput. Surv. **40**(3), 7 (2008)
10. Khakpour, N., Jalili, S., Talcott, C.L., Sirjani, M., Mousavi, M.R.: Formal modeling of evolving self-adaptive systems. Sci. Comput. Program. **78**(1), 3–26 (2012)
11. Kiczales, G., Lamping, J., Mendhekar, A., Maeda, C., Lopes, C.V., Loingtier, J.M., Irwin, J.: Aspect-oriented programming. In: ECOOP, pp. 220–242 (1997)
12. Loreti, M., Margheri, A., Pugliese, R., Tiezzi, F.: On programming and policing autonomic computing systems. In: Margaria, Tiziana, Steffen, Bernhard (eds.) ISoLA 2014, Part I. LNCS, vol. 8802, pp. 164–183. Springer, Heidelberg (2014)
13. Margheri, A., Masi, M., Pugliese, R., Tiezzi, F.: A rigorous framework for specification, analysis and enforcement of access control policies. Technical Report (2016.). http://local.disia.unifi.it/wp_disia/2016/wp_disia_2016_05.pdf
14. Margheri, A., Riis Nielson, H., Nielson, F., Pugliese, R.: Design, analysis and implementation of policy-based self-adaptive computing systems. Technical report (2016). http://facpl.sf.net/research/StaticPSCEL-TR.pdf
15. Mayer, P., et al.: The autonomic cloud. In: Wirsing, M., Hölzl, M., Koch, N., Mayer, P. (eds.) Collective Autonomic Systems. LNCS, vol. 8998, pp. 495–512. Springer, Heidelberg (2015)
16. Salvaneschi, G., Ghezzi, C., Pradella, M.: Context-oriented programming: a programming paradigm for autonomic systems. CoRR, abs/1105.0069 (2011)
17. Terepeta, M., Riis Nielson, H., Nielson, F.: Recursive advice for coordination. In: Sirjani, M. (ed.) COORDINATION 2012. LNCS, vol. 7274, pp. 137–151. Springer, Heidelberg (2012)
18. Wirsing, M., Hölzl, M., Tribastone, M., Zambonelli, F.: ASCENS: engineering autonomic service-component ensembles. In: Boer, F.S., Bonsangue, M.M., Beckert, B., Damiani, F. (eds.) FMCO 2011. LNCS, vol. 7542, pp. 1–24. Springer, Heidelberg (2012). Revised Selected Papers

A Calculus for Open Ensembles
and Their Composition

Rolf Hennicker[(✉)]

Ludwig-Maximilians-Universität München, Munich, Germany
hennicker@ifi.lmu.de

Abstract. We consider specifications of dynamically evolving ensembles consisting of entities which collaborate through message exchange. Each ensemble specification defines a set of messages, a set of process type declarations and an initial ensemble state. An ensemble state is given by a set of process instances that can trigger the creation of further process instances during ensemble evolution. We distinguish between internal and external messages of an ensemble. Internal messages are exchanged between the participants of a single ensemble while the external messages can be considered as ensemble interfaces which give rise to a composition operator for open ensemble specifications. A structural operational semantics for open ensemble specifications is provided based on two levels: a process and an ensemble level. We define an equivalence relation for ensemble specifications which generalizes bisimulation to dynamic architectures. As a main result we prove that equivalence of ensemble specifications is preserved by ensemble composition. We also introduce a semantic composition operator on the level of labeled transition systems and show that it is compatible with the syntactic composition of ensemble specifications; i.e. our semantics is compositional.

1 Introduction

The formal treatment of dynamic architectures which evolve by changing their configurations and adapting behavior to changing environments is a hot topic in system engineering. Such systems are often characterized by the autonomous behavior of the individual participants of the system which collaborate to perform certain tasks. For this purpose, static component models are no more sufficient and must be appropriately adjusted and extended. In the context of the ASCENS project [13] several proposals have been investigated to provide a formal basis for the description of dynamically evolving ensembles. An overview on the contributions of this project in the area of software defined networks and reconfigurable connectors is given in [4]. Another outcome of the ASCENS project is the language SCEL [6], which is a generic, high-level language for programming autonomic systems.

This work has been partially sponsored by the European Union under the FP7-project ASCENS, 257414.

T. Margaria and B. Steffen (Eds.): ISoLA 2016, Part I, LNCS 9952, pp. 570–588, 2016.
DOI: 10.1007/978-3-319-47166-2_40

The operational semantics of SCEL is defined on two levels. The first level concerns the behavior of components and the second level the behavior of systems which are built from components and can be dynamically extended by creating new components. Also, a light version of the modeling language HELENA, which uses roles to describe different behaviors that a component can perform when participating in an ensemble, is supplied with a two level semantics, for role behaviors and for ensemble behaviors; see [8]. The two level semantics approach, goes back, at least, to the Fork Calculus of Havelund and Larsen [7] who provide a theory of communicating processes which includes a "fork"-operator for the creation of new processes in a concurrent system. The idea is to distinguish between processes and multisets of processes (called programs in [7]) such that a new process p is added to the multiset if fork(p) is executed on the process level. The two level approach differs from earlier process algebraic studies which treat process creation within the algebra, see e.g. [3]. Concerning the communication style, SCEL uses communication by knowledge exchange, HELENA uses a message passing approach and the Fork Calculus uses input and output actions (expressing reception and sending of messages) in the CCS tradition. For the analysis of components and systems it is always important to study equivalences of behaviors. While HELENA did not yet define behavioral equivalences, Havelund and Larsen have shown that the fork-operator causes difficulties for turning a straightforward equivalence notion into a congruence and they have provided a solution for this problem.

The consideration of congruences on the system level assumes that there is a composition operator for system descriptions. This means that the single constituent parts must form, in some sense, open systems which are connected by the composition. It is, however, often not clear what are the interfaces for the composition. Therefore, to get associativity of parallel composition, process calculi like CCS and the Fork Calculus use a non-blocking semantics, where a process can always execute autonomously an input or output action (even if a communication partner offering the complementary action would be ready for interaction). In SCEL the situation is similar where, e.g., so-called "willingness" actions can always be autonomously executed by a single component in a system. The semantics of a SCEL system then relies on a restriction removing undesired transitions. With this restriction it seems to be problematic to get compositionality of system semantics. The current version of HELENA considers only closed systems such that no composition of ensemble specifications is possible.

In this paper we present a basic calculus for open ensemble specifications which allows to compose ensemble specifications via explicitly defined interfaces. For this purpose, each ensemble specification is equipped with an ensemble signature, which distinguishes between the internal messages that can be exchanged inside an ensemble and the external input or output messages available for communication with an environment. For the composition of two ensemble specifications some syntactic constraints concerning the matching of input and output messages and non confusion with internal messages must be satisfied. This idea is borrowed from the composability notion used by de Alfaro and Henzinger for the composition of interface automata [1]. In our study an ensemble specification consists of an ensemble signature, a set of process type declarations, and an initial ensemble state. Process expressions include messages of the ensemble signature and actions for the creation of new process instances on the ensemble level. An ensemble state consists of a finite set of currently existing process instances each one represented by a unique process instance identifier to which a local state in the form of a process expression is assigned that shows the subsequent behavior of the instance. The consideration of process instances is a crucial difference to the Fork Calculus. The evolution of ensemble states happens by (1) exchanging internal messages between currently existing process instances according to their current local state, (2) creation of new process instances, and (3) sending or receiving external messages. In case (1) a process instance is blocked if there is no other process instance ready for communication. We use synchronous communication here but the approach could be easily adjusted to asynchronous message exchange, for instance, via message queues. In case (3) external messages are always enabled, i.e. non-blocking. However, after composition when an external message has become internal, it will be blocked as long as no other ensemble participant is ready for communication. The evolution of ensembles is formalized by an SOS semantics on the level of ensemble states which is based on an SOS semantics on the process level (since process expressions represent local states). Thus the semantics of an ensemble specification is a labeled transition system generated from the initial ensemble state by applying the SOS rules.

Due to the semantics of ensemble specifications, we consider two ensemble specifications equivalent if each step performed by one ensemble can be simulated by a step of the other ensemble and vice versa. We abstract from the concrete process instances that perform an action by using, for related ensemble states, a bijective mapping between their process instances. Therefore, we introduce a ternary bisimulation relation which involves not only ensemble states but also a mapping between their currently existing process instances. As first major result we show that the equivalence relation for ensemble specifications is preserved by ensemble composition, i.e. it is a congruence relation. Then we consider the composition of the semantic models of ensemble specifications and show, as a second major result, that our semantics is compositional, i.e. the semantics of a composed ensemble specification can be obtained by composing the semantic models of the single specifications.

We start in Sect. 2 with the definition of ensemble specifications and their composition. The semantics of ensemble specifications is defined in Sect. 3. In Sect. 4 we introduce the equivalence relation for ensemble specifications and show that it is a congruence. In Sect. 5 we present our result about semantic compositionality of ensemble specifications. Finally, we end with some concluding remarks in Sect. 6.

2   Ensemble Specifications and Their Composition

An ensemble specification defines a system of collaborating entities which communicate via message exchange. An ensemble can dynamically change its constitution by creating new members. Syntactically, an ensemble specification is built over an ensemble signature which distinguishes internal and external messages. This distinction is particularly relevant for the consideration of open ensembles and their composition. Messages are classified as output messages, denoted by $m!$, or input messages, denoted by $m?$. Output messages $m!$ and input messages $m?$ with the same message name m are complementary to each other. Internal messages are used "inside" an ensemble for communication between the current members of the ensemble. We require that for any internal message, its complementary message must also belong to the set of internal messages of the ensemble signature. This is a syntactic well-formedness condition, since an internal message which has no counterpart inside an ensemble would be useless. For external messages we require just the opposite: its complementary message should not occur in the same ensemble signature, but it may occur in the external signature of another ensemble signature when ensemble specifications are composed.

Definition 1 (Ensemble signature). *An ensemble signature is a pair $\Sigma = (\Sigma_{int}, \Sigma_{ext})$ where Σ_{int} and Σ_{ext} are two disjoint sets of internal and external messages resp., such that the following conditions are satisfied for all message names m:*

1. *$m! \in \Sigma_{int} \Leftrightarrow m? \in \Sigma_{int}$,*
2. *$(m! \in \Sigma_{ext} \Rightarrow m? \notin \Sigma_{ext})$ and $(m? \in \Sigma_{ext} \Rightarrow m! \notin \Sigma_{ext})$.*

By abuse of notation, we also use Σ to denote the disjoint union $\Sigma_{int} \cup \Sigma_{ext}$ of all messages occurring in the ensemble signature.

Besides an ensemble signature, an ensemble specification declares a set of process types, describing possible behaviors of the members of an ensemble. Different members of an ensemble can have the same process type, i.e. the same behavior. A process type declaration assigns a process expression to a process name.

Definition 2 (Process expressions). *Let Σ be an ensemble signature. A process expression over Σ is built from the following grammar, where N ranges over a set of process names and $m!$, $m?$ ranges over the messages occurring in Σ.*

$P ::=$	$\textbf{nil}$	*(null process)*
	$\mid aP$	*(action prefix)*
	$\mid P_1 + P_2$	*(nondeterministic choice)*
	$\mid N$	*(process invocation)*
$a ::=$	$m!$	*(message output)*
	$\mid m?$	*(message input)*
	$\mid \textbf{create}(P)$	*(process instance creation)*

Message outputs, message inputs and process creations are called actions.

Definition 3 (Process type declarations). *Let Σ be an ensemble signature. A set of process type declarations over Σ is a set of equations $Decls = \{N_1 = P_1, \ldots, N_k = P_k\}$ where $N_1, \ldots, N_k$ are (pairwise different) process names and*

$P_1, \ldots, P_k$ are process expressions over Σ containing only process names in $\{N_1, \ldots, N_k\}$, i.e. each process name occurring in some P_i has a declaration in Decls.

An ensemble state is characterized by the currently existing members of the ensemble. We model ensemble members by process instances each one represented by a unique process instance identifier pi to which a local state is assigned in each ensemble state. The local state of pi is a process expression P representing the subsequent behavior of pi. For the formal definitions we assume given a countably infinite set PI of process instance identifiers. An ensemble state σ is then a partial function, with finite definition domain, from PI into the set of all possible local states. The elements of the definition domain of σ represent the currently existing ensemble members.

Definition 4 (Local states and ensemble states). *Let Σ be an ensemble signature and Decls be a set of process type declarations over Σ.*

1. *A local state over $(\Sigma, Decls)$ is a process expression P over Σ containing at most process names declared in Decls. The set of all local states over $(\Sigma, Decls)$ is denoted by $LocStates(\Sigma, Decls)$.*
2. *An ensemble state over $(\Sigma, Decls)$ is a partial function $\sigma : PI \to LocStates(\Sigma, Decls)$ whose definition domain $dom(\sigma)$ is finite. The set of all ensemble states over $(\Sigma, Decls)$ is denoted by $EnsStates(\Sigma, Decls)$.*

We have now all ingredients to define ensemble specifications.

Definition 5 (Ensemble specification). *An ensemble specification is a triple $EnsSpec = (\Sigma, Decls, \sigma_0)$ where $\Sigma = (\Sigma_{int}, \Sigma_{ext})$ is an ensemble signature, Decls is a set of process type declarations over Σ and $\sigma_0 \in EnsStates(\Sigma, Decls)$ is an initial ensemble state. The ensemble specification is open if $\Sigma_{ext} \neq \emptyset$, otherwise it is closed.*

Example 1. One of the three case studies in the ASCENS project [13] is the *Science Cloud Platform (SCP)* [11]. The SCP employs a network of distributed, voluntarily provided computing nodes, in which users can deploy and execute user-defined software applications. For a full description of the SCP, we refer to [11]. The SCP is organized in several layers, the application layer, which implements the application logic, the layer for the basic networking logic, which uses the distributed peer-to-peer overlay networking substrate Pastry [12] for communication, and the infrastructure layer typically based on TCP/IP. In [10] we have developed a HELENA model for the full application logic represented by a large ensemble specification. In this paper we want to demonstrate how such a model can be developed in a modular way by composing smaller, *open* ensemble specifications. For this purpose, we consider two ensemble specifications, one focusing on the deployment and undeployment of an application and the other one on the actual execution of an application. To keep the example short, we skip here the process of finding an appropriate executor node and we omit parameters of messages and other details of our case study in [10]. In contrast to HELENA we do not consider component types and work directly with process types which correspond to the behavior of role types in [10].

Deploying and undeploying: For this subtask, we use two process types, Deployer and Storage. The Deployer provides the interface for deploying and undeploying an app and it is responsible for the selection of the node to store the app code. On this node, the Deployer creates a process of type Storage which takes care of the actual storage and deletion of the app code. The Storage also activates the initiation of the execution of the app in its environment and then it is ready to communicate with the environment by serving a request for the stored code. We formalize this subtask by an open ensemble specification, called DeploymentEnsemble, consisting of the following parts:

- The signature of DeploymentEnsemble is graphically represented in Fig. 1, left. There are four internal messages store!, store?, unstore!, unstore? indicated by the two arrows from Deployer to Storage, each arrow representing an output and a corresponding input message with the same name. And there are six external messages deploy?, undeploy?, reqCode?, sndCode!, init!, stopApp! indicated by the ingoing and outgoing arrows representing open input and output messages resp.
- DeploymentEnsemble has the following two process type declarations:
  Deployer =
  deploy?.**create**(Storage).store!.undeploy?.unstore!.Deployer,
  Storage = store?.init!.reqCode?.sndCode!.unstore?.stopApp!.**nil**
- The initial ensemble state consists of one process instance {deployer:Deployer}[1]

Executing: Execution of the app is initiated by a process of type Initiator. Once an initiator is activated (by receiving the message init), it creates an Executor process and then it takes care that the execution is kept running until the user requests to undeploy the app. We formalize this subtask by an open ensemble specification, called ExecutionEnsemble, consisting of the following parts:

- The signature of ExecutionEnsemble is graphically represented in Fig. 1, right. There are four internal messages execute!, execute?, stop!, stop? and four external messages init?, stopApp?, reqCode!, sndCode?.
- ExecutionEnsemble has the following two process type declarations:
  Initiator =
  init?.**create**(Executor).execute!.stopApp?.stop!.Initiator,
  Executor = execute?.reqCode!.sndCode?.stop?.**nil**
  We expect that an executor runs the app after having received the sndCode message which is not explicitly modeled here.[2] The execution is stopped when

---

[1] Formally, deployer is a process instance identifier which is mapped in the initial ensemble state to the process name Deployer.

[2] To model the actual execution of the app one could introduce an internal action. But this would not be a message and therefore the concept of an ensemble signature

the `Executor` receives the `stop` message from the `Initiator` which happens when the `Initiator` receives `stopApp` from the `Storage`. For simplicity, we do not model here the possibility to unstore and stop an application before the `Executor` has received the code.

– The initial ensemble state consists of one process instance {`initiator:Initiator`}.

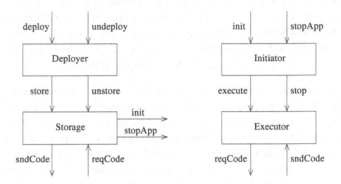

Fig. 1. Signatures of deployment and execution ensembles

In the next step, we are interested in the composition of ensemble specifications. This makes sense, since ensemble specifications may have a proper set of external messages which can be used for communication with the external messages of another ensemble specification. First we define the composition of (composable) ensemble signatures $\Sigma 1$ and $\Sigma 2$. The idea is that the message sets of the two signatures must be disjoint, but that $\Sigma 1$ and $\Sigma 2$ may have complementary external messages which are then turned into internal messages in their composition. These messages are denoted by $com(\Sigma 1, \Sigma 2)$ to indicate that their purpose is to establish communication between the members of different ensembles. Those messages of $\Sigma 1$ ($\Sigma 2$ resp.) which have no complementary message in $\Sigma 2$ ($\Sigma 1$ resp.) remain external in the composite signature.

Definition 6. (Composition of ensemble signatures). *Let $\Sigma 1 = (\Sigma 1_{int}, \Sigma 1_{ext})$ and $\Sigma 2 = (\Sigma 2_{int}, \Sigma 2_{ext})$ be two ensemble signatures. $\Sigma 1$ and $\Sigma 2$ are composable if $\Sigma 1 \cap \Sigma 2 = \emptyset$[3]. Their composition $\Sigma 1 \otimes \Sigma 2$ is defined as follows: Let $com(\Sigma 1, \Sigma 2) = \{m!, m? \mid (m! \in \Sigma 1_{ext}$ and $m? \in \Sigma 2_{ext})$ or $(m? \in \Sigma 1_{ext}$ and $m! \in \Sigma 2_{ext})\}$. Then*

$$\Sigma 1 \otimes \Sigma 2 = (\Sigma 1_{int} \cup \Sigma 2_{int} \cup com(\Sigma 1, \Sigma 2), \Sigma 1_{ext} \cup \Sigma 2_{ext} \setminus com(\Sigma 1, \Sigma 2)\}.$$

---

needs to be extended to capture internal actions as well. Such an extension would be straightforward on the syntactic and on the semantic level. It is left out here for the sake of simplicity of the presentation.

[3] Note that $m!$ and $m?$ are different messages with the same name.

Obviously, the composition $\Sigma 1 \otimes \Sigma 2$ satisfies the conditions of an ensemble signature in Definition 1. For the composition of ensemble specifications we assume that their signatures are composable, that they declare different process types, and that their initial states have no common process instances. This assumption is not really a restriction since it can always be satisfied by an appropriate renaming.

Definition 7. (Composition of ensemble specifications). *Let EnsSpec1 = $(\Sigma 1, Decls1, \sigma 1_0)$ with Decls1 = $\{N_1 = P_1, \ldots, N_k = P_k\}$ and EnsSpec2 = $(\Sigma 2, Decls2, \sigma 2_0)$ with Decls2 = $\{M_1 = Q_1, \ldots, M_r = Q_r\}$ be ensemble specifications. EnsSpec1 and EnsSpec2 are composable if $\Sigma 1$ and $\Sigma 2$ are composable, $\{N_1, \ldots, N_k\} \cap \{M_1, \ldots, M_r\} = \emptyset$, and $dom(\sigma 1_0) \cap dom(\sigma 2_0) = \emptyset$. Then their composition is defined by*

$$EnsSpec1 \otimes EnsSpec1 = (\Sigma 1 \otimes \Sigma 2, Decls1 \cup Decls2, \sigma 1_0 + \sigma 2_0)$$

where $(\sigma 1_0 + \sigma 2_0) : PI \rightarrow LocStates(\Sigma 1 \otimes \Sigma 2, Decls1 \cup Decls2)$ is defined by $(\sigma 1_0 + \sigma 2_0)(pi) = \sigma 1_0(pi)$ if $pi \in dom(\sigma 1_0)$, $(\sigma 1_0 + \sigma 2_0)(pi) = \sigma 2_0(pi)$ if $pi \in dom(\sigma 2_0)$, and $(\sigma 1_0 + \sigma 2_0)(pi)$ is undefined otherwise.[4]

Proposition 1. *The composition of ensemble specifications is commutative and associative.*

Proof. Commutativity is trivial. For associativity we have to check that the composition of ensemble signatures is associative. But this follows from the syntactic constraints for ensemble signatures and their composability. The remainder is trivial from set theory and composition of functions with disjoint definition domains. □

Example 2. The two ensemble specifications of Example 1 are composable and their composition DeploymentEnsemble $\otimes$ ExecutionEnsemble consists of the following parts:

- The composed ensemble signature is graphically represented in Fig. 2. All messages are internal except deploy? and undeploy? which are left open for communication with the user.
- The composed ensemble specification has the four process type declarations Deployer = ..., Storage = ..., Initiator = ... and Executor = ... collected from the ensemble specifications in Example 1.
- The initial ensemble state consists of two process instances {deployer:Deployer, initiator:Initiator}.

---

[4] $\sigma 1_0 + \sigma 2_0$ is well-defined, since $\sigma 1_0(pi) \in LocStates(\Sigma 1, Decls1) \subseteq LocStates(\Sigma 1 \otimes \Sigma 2, Decls1 \cup Decls2)$, and similarly for $\sigma 2_0(pi)$.

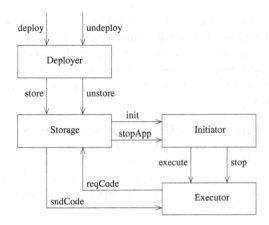

Fig. 2. Composition of deployer and executor ensembles

3   Semantics of Ensemble Specifications

The semantic domain of ensemble specifications are labeled transition systems describing the evolution of ensembles. Structural operational semantics (SOS) rules define the allowed transitions. We pursue an incremental approach, similar to the Fork Calculus in [7] and also similar to the semantics of components and autonomic systems in SCEL [6] and for components and systems with attribute-based communication in [2], by splitting the semantics into two different layers. The first layer describes how a process expression evolves according to the given constructs for process expressions. The second layer builds on the first one by defining the evolution of ensemble states.

Evolution of Processes: On the first level, we do not have any information about the global state of an ensemble. Therefore, we only formalize the progress of a single process expression. Figure 3 defines the SOS rules inductively over the structure of process expressions in Definition 2. The rule for process type invocation relies on a given process type declaration, which is always assumed to be given in an ensemble specification. We use the symbol $\hookrightarrow$ for transitions on the process level.

Evolution of Ensembles: On the next level we consider ensemble states. Transitions between ensemble states are denoted by the symbol $\rightarrow$ in Fig. 4. They are initiated in the following cases: external messages, rules (open-output) and (open-input), are propagated from the process level to the ensemble level if an ensemble member is able to perform such an action. Create actions $\mathbf{create}(Q)$ on the process level cause the creation of a new process instance in a given ensemble state σ. For this purpose the definition domain of σ is extended by a fresh process instance $fresh(\sigma) \in PI \setminus dom(\sigma)$ to which the local state $Q \in LocStates(\Sigma, Decls)$ is assigned. Such an extension is denoted by $\ldots + [fresh(\sigma) \mapsto Q]$; see rule (create). Finally we consider communication inside an ensemble by internal message

(action prefix)	$a.P \xhookrightarrow{a} P$
(choice-left)	$\dfrac{P_1 \xhookrightarrow{a} P_1'}{P_1 + P_2 \xhookrightarrow{a} P_1'}$
(choice-right)	$\dfrac{P_2 \xhookrightarrow{a} P_2'}{P_1 + P_2 \xhookrightarrow{a} P_2'}$
(process type invocation)	$\dfrac{P \xhookrightarrow{a} P'}{N \xhookrightarrow{a} P'}$ if N = P

Fig. 3. SOS rules for process expressions

exchange. In the semantics presented here we use synchronous, binary communication - rule (comm) - where message output and message input are performed simultaneously when process instances are able to communicate. If several process instances are able to communicate the choice is non-deterministic. If desired, it would be straightforward to adapt our formalism to asynchronous communication by introducing message buffers as done in [8]. Also broadcast communication could be easily defined by adjusting the rules appropriately. In rule (comm), the notation $\sigma[pi \mapsto P', qi \mapsto Q']$ expresses an update of σ where pi gets the new value P' and qi gets the new value Q'.

(open output)	$\dfrac{P \xhookrightarrow{m!} P'}{\sigma \xrightarrow{pi:m!} \sigma[pi \mapsto P']}$ $m! \in \Sigma_{ext}$ **if** $pi \in dom(\sigma), \sigma(pi) = P$.
(open input)	$\dfrac{P \xhookrightarrow{m?} P'}{\sigma \xrightarrow{pi:m?} \sigma[pi \mapsto P']}$ $m? \in \Sigma_{ext}$ **if** $pi \in dom(\sigma), \sigma(pi) = P$.
(create)	$\dfrac{P \xhookrightarrow{\textbf{create}(Q)} P'}{\sigma \xrightarrow{pi:\textbf{create}(fresh(\sigma))} \sigma[pi \mapsto P'] + [fresh(\sigma) \mapsto Q]}$ **if** $pi \in dom(\sigma), \sigma(pi) = P$.
(comm)	$\dfrac{P \xhookrightarrow{m!} P', \ Q \xhookrightarrow{m?} Q',}{\sigma \xrightarrow{(pi \rightarrow qi):m} \sigma[pi \mapsto P', qi \mapsto Q']}$ $m!, m? \in \Sigma_{int}$ **if** $pi, qi \in dom(\sigma), \sigma(pi) = P, \sigma(qi) = Q$.

Fig. 4. SOS rules for ensembles

Definition 8 (Semantics of an ensemble specification). *The semantics of an ensemble specification EnsSpec* $= (\Sigma, Decls, \sigma_0)$ *is the labeled transition system* $T = (S, \sigma_0, L, \rightarrow)$ *generated from the initial state* σ_0 *by applying the rules in Fig. 4. T is also called the* semantic model *of EnsSpec.*

4   Equivalence of Ensemble Specifications

To study the equivalence of ensemble specifications the idea is to lift the standard bisimulation notion for processes to the level of dynamically evolving ensembles. Due to the operational semantics of ensemble specifications we consider two ensemble specifications equivalent if each step performed by one ensemble can be simulated by a step of the other ensemble and vice versa. We use here a strong equivalence where all actions can be observed. We abstract, however, from the concrete process instances that perform an action by using, for related ensemble states $\sigma1$ and $\sigma2$, a bijective mapping between the currently existing instances in $\sigma1$ and $\sigma2$. Therefore, our bisimulation relation is not a binary but a ternary relation which involves not only ensemble states but also a relation between their currently existing process instances which must be propagated during ensemble executions.

Definition 9 (Bisimulation relation). *Let EnsSpec1* $= (\Sigma, Decls1, \sigma1_0)$ *and EnsSpec2* $= (\Sigma, Decls2, \sigma2_0)$ *be two ensemble specifications with the same signature* Σ*. Let* $T1 = (S1, \sigma1_0, L1, \rightarrow_1)$ *and* $T2 = (S2, \sigma2_0, L2, \rightarrow_2)$ *be the transition system semantics of EnsSpec1 and EnsSpec2 respectively. Let* $\Delta = \{(\sigma1, \sigma2, \varphi) \mid \sigma1 \in S1, \sigma2 \in S2, \varphi : dom(\sigma1) \rightarrow dom(\sigma2)$ *is bijective*$\}$*. A bisimulation relation between T1 and T2 is a relation* $R \subseteq \Delta$*, such that for all* $(\sigma1, \sigma2, \varphi) \in R$ *the following holds:*[5]

(1.1) If $\sigma1 \xrightarrow{pi:m!}_1 \sigma1'$ *then there exists* $\sigma2 \xrightarrow{\varphi(pi):m!}_2 \sigma2'$*, such that* $(\sigma1', \sigma2', \varphi) \in R$*.*[6]

(1.2) If $\sigma1 \xrightarrow{pi:m?}_1 \sigma1'$ *then there exists* $\sigma2 \xrightarrow{\varphi(pi):m?}_2 \sigma2'$*, such that* $(\sigma1', \sigma2', \varphi) \in R$*.*

(1.3) If $\sigma1 \xrightarrow{pi:\textbf{create}(fresh(\sigma1))}_1 \sigma1'$ *then there exists*
$\sigma2 \xrightarrow{\varphi(pi):\textbf{create}(fresh(\sigma2))}_2 \sigma2'$ *such that* $(\sigma1', \sigma2', \varphi') \in R$
with $\varphi'(i) = \varphi(i)$ *for all* $i \in dom(\sigma1)$ *and* $\varphi'(fresh(\sigma1)) = fresh(\sigma2)$*.*[7]

(1.4) If $\sigma1 \xrightarrow{(pi \rightarrow pi'):m}_1 \sigma1'$ *then there exists* $\sigma2 \xrightarrow{(\varphi(pi) \rightarrow \varphi(pi')):m}_2 \sigma2'$ *such that* $(\sigma1', \sigma2', \varphi) \in R$*.*

(2.1) If $\sigma2 \xrightarrow{qi:m!}_2 \sigma2'$ *then there exists* $\sigma1 \xrightarrow{\varphi^{-1}(qi):m!}_1 \sigma1'$*, such that* $(\sigma1', \sigma2', \varphi) \in R$*.*

---

[5] Note that in all cases, except (1.3) and (2.3), $dom(\sigma1) = dom(\sigma1')$ and $dom(\sigma2) = dom(\sigma2')$.

[6] Note that pi must be in $dom(\sigma1)$ and therefore $\varphi(pi) \in dom(\sigma2)$.

[7] Note that $\sigma1'$ is of the from $\sigma1_{+[fresh(\sigma1) \mapsto Q1]}$ and $\sigma2'$ is of the form $\sigma2_{+[fresh(\sigma2) \mapsto Q2]}$..

(2.2) If $\sigma2 \xrightarrow{qi:m?}_2 \sigma2'$ then there exists $\sigma1 \xrightarrow{\varphi^{-1}(qi):m?}_1 \sigma1'$, such that $(\sigma1', \sigma2', \varphi) \in R$.

(2.3) If $\sigma2 \xrightarrow{qi:create(fresh(\sigma2))}_2 \sigma2'$ then there exists $\sigma1 \xrightarrow{\varphi^{-1}(qi):create(fresh(\sigma1))}_1 \sigma1'$ such that $(\sigma1', \sigma2', \varphi') \in R$ with φ' as in case (1.3).

(2.4) If $\sigma2 \xrightarrow{(qi \to qi'):m}_2 \sigma2'$ then there exists $\sigma1 \xrightarrow{(\varphi^{-1}(qi) \to \varphi^{-1}(qi')):m}_1 \sigma1'$ such that $(\sigma1', \sigma2', \varphi) \in R$.

Definition 10 (Equivalent ensemble specifications). *Let $EnsSpec1 = (\Sigma1, Decls1, \sigma1_0)$ and $EnsSpec2 = (\Sigma2, Decls2, \sigma2_0)$ be two ensemble specifications with labeled transition system semantics $T1$, $T2$ resp. $EnsSpec1$ and $EnsSpec2$ are equivalent, denoted by $EnsSpec1 \sim EnsSpec2$, if $\Sigma1 = \Sigma2$ and if there exists a bijective function $\varphi_0 : dom(\sigma1_0) \to dom(\sigma2_0)$ and a bisimulation R between $T1$ and $T2$ such that $(\sigma1_0, \sigma2_0, \varphi_0) \in R$.*

Obviously, $\sim$ is an equivalence relation for ensemble specifications. The next theorem shows that $\sim$ is even a congruence relation w.r.t. ensemble composition.

Theorem 1. *Let $EnsSpec1, EnsSpec2$ and $EnsSpec$ be three ensemble specifications such that $EnsSpec1$ and $EnsSpec$ are composable and $EnsSpec2$ and $EnsSpec$ are composable. If $EnsSpec1 \sim EnsSpec2$ then $EnsSpec1 \otimes EnsSpec \sim EnsSpec2 \otimes EnsSpec$.*

The proof of Theorem 1 is given in the Appendix.

5   Semantic Compositionality of Ensemble Specifications

So far the semantics of composed ensemble specifications must be computed by applying the SOS rules in Fig. 4 to the whole specification. In this section we are interested in a stepwise computation of the semantics by composing the semantic models of the constituent parts of a specification.

Definition 11 (Composition of semantic models). *Let $EnsSpec1 = (\Sigma1, Decls1, \sigma1_0)$ and $EnsSpec2 = (\Sigma2, Decls2, \sigma2_0)$ be two composable ensemble specifications with semantic models $T1 = (S1, \sigma1_0, L1, \to_1)$, $T2 = (S2, \sigma2_0, L2, \to_2)$ resp. The composition of $T1$ and $T2$ is the labeled transition system $T1 \otimes T2 = (S1 \otimes S2, (\sigma1_0, \sigma2_0), L1 \otimes L2, \to_\otimes)$ generated from the initial state $(\sigma1_0, \sigma2_0)$ by applying the rules in Fig. 5.[8]*

The next theorem shows that the semantic composition is consistent with the semantics of the syntactic composition of ensemble specifications. We believe that this is an important fact which formally justifies the chosen operational semantics for open ensemble specifications.

---

[8]   W.l.o.g. the rules assume that the states in $S1$ and $S2$ have disjoint definition domains.

(open output left)	$$\dfrac{\sigma 1 \xrightarrow{pi:m!}_1 \sigma 1'}{(\sigma 1, \sigma 2) \xrightarrow{pi:m!}_\otimes (\sigma 1', \sigma 2) \ \text{for any } \sigma 2 \in S2}$$	$m! \in \Sigma 1_{ext}, m? \notin \Sigma 2_{ext}$
(open input left)	$$\dfrac{\sigma 1 \xrightarrow{pi:m?}_1 \sigma 1'}{(\sigma 1, \sigma 2) \xrightarrow{pi:m?}_\otimes (\sigma 1', \sigma 2) \ \text{for any } \sigma 2 \in S2}$$	$m? \in \Sigma 1_{ext}, m! \notin \Sigma 2_{ext}$
(open output right)	$$\dfrac{\sigma 2 \xrightarrow{qi:m!}_2 \sigma 2'}{(\sigma 1, \sigma 2) \xrightarrow{qi:m!}_\otimes (\sigma 1, \sigma 2') \ \text{for any } \sigma 1 \in S1}$$	$m! \in \Sigma 2_{ext}, m? \notin \Sigma 1_{ext}$
(open input right)	$$\dfrac{\sigma 2 \xrightarrow{qi:m?}_2 \sigma 2'}{(\sigma 1, \sigma 2) \xrightarrow{qi:m?}_\otimes (\sigma 1, \sigma 2') \ \text{for any } \sigma 1 \in S1}$$	$m? \in \Sigma 2_{ext}, m! \notin \Sigma 1_{ext}$
(create left)	$$\dfrac{\sigma 1 \xrightarrow{pi:\mathbf{create}(pi')}_1 \sigma 1'}{(\sigma 1, \sigma 2) \xrightarrow{pi:\mathbf{create}(pi')}_\otimes (\sigma 1', \sigma 2) \ \text{for any } \sigma 2 \in S2}$$	
(create right)	$$\dfrac{\sigma 2 \xrightarrow{qi:\mathbf{create}(qi')}_2 \sigma 2'}{(\sigma 1, \sigma 2) \xrightarrow{qi:\mathbf{create}(qi')}_\otimes (\sigma 1, \sigma 2') \ \text{for any } \sigma 1 \in S1}$$	
(comm left)	$$\dfrac{\sigma 1 \xrightarrow{(pi \to pi'):m}_1 \sigma 1'}{(\sigma 1, \sigma 2) \xrightarrow{(pi \to pi'):m}_\otimes (\sigma 1', \sigma 2) \ \text{for any } \sigma 2 \in S2}$$	$m!, m? \in \Sigma 1_{int}$
(comm right)	$$\dfrac{\sigma 2 \xrightarrow{(qi \to qi'):m}_2 \sigma 2'}{(\sigma 1, \sigma 2) \xrightarrow{(qi \to qi'):m}_\otimes (\sigma 1, \sigma 2') \ \text{for any } \sigma 1 \in S1}$$	$m!, m? \in \Sigma 2_{int}$
(comm left right)	$$\dfrac{\sigma 1 \xrightarrow{pi:m!}_1 \sigma 1', \sigma 2 \xrightarrow{qi:m?}_2 \sigma 2'}{(\sigma 1, \sigma 2) \xrightarrow{(pi \to qi):m}_\otimes (\sigma 1', \sigma 2')}$$	$m! \in \Sigma 1_{ext}, m? \in \Sigma 2_{ext}$
(comm right left)	$$\dfrac{\sigma 1 \xrightarrow{pi:m?}_1 \sigma 1', \sigma 2 \xrightarrow{qi:m!}_2 \sigma 2'}{(\sigma 1, \sigma 2) \xrightarrow{(qi \to pi):m}_\otimes (\sigma 1', \sigma 2')}$$	$m? \in \Sigma 1_{ext}, m! \in \Sigma 2_{ext}$

Fig. 5. Composition of semantic models

Theorem 2 (Semantic compositionality). *Let EnsSpec1 and EnsSpec2 be two composable ensemble specifications with semantic models T1 and T2 resp. Let $T^\otimes$ be the semantic model of EnsSpec1 $\otimes$ EnsSpec2. Then $T^\otimes$ and $T1 \otimes T2$ are isomorphic.*

The proof of Theorem 2 is given in the Appendix.

6   Conclusion

We have presented a basic calculus for open ensemble specifications and their composition. An equivalence relation for ensemble specifications is introduced and it is proved to be a congruence when ensemble specifications are composed.

We have also shown that our semantics is compositional. This result relies on the discrimination of external and internal messages. Our calculus focuses on openness of ensembles and can be adjusted and extended in various directions. One extension concerns the incorporation of message parameters and the extension to full HELENA (thus extending also HELENA to open ensemble specifications and their composition). Then we would use, as in HELENA, asynchronous communication based on message queues. Another direction concerns the support of multi-cast messages. A particular powerful formalization of multi-cast communication is attribute-based communication which determines communication partners dynamically by evaluating predicates over component attributes; see [2]. Component attributes storing process expressions can even be used for behavioral self-adaptation, which can be achieved in HELENA by changing the role of a component; see [9]. [2] studies also behavioral equivalences. It considers weak barbed congruences and shows that they are equivalent to weak bisimulations. A related result for distributed and mobile systems has been obtained in [5].

For the practical use of the equivalence notion for ensemble specifications we want to investigate appropriate verification methods. We claim that for proving equivalence of ensemble specifications it would be sufficient to consider process types and to prove that the initial states of two ensemble specifications contain the same number of process instances whose local states (i.e. process expressions) are pairwise bisimilar. Currently we use a strong equivalence relation with all actions being observable. It would be interesting to encapsulate open ensembles and to study an observational equivalence where internal communications inside an ensemble and creation of process instances are hidden. Finally, it would be interesting to consider behavioral compatibility of interacting ensembles, for instance in the sense that all messages sent are eventually received, and to study whether such compatibilities are preserved by ensemble equivalence.

Acknowledgement. I would like to thank the reviewers for their very careful reading of the submitted version of this paper and for their valuable remarks and suggestions.

Appendix

Proof of Theorem 1:
By assumption, *EnsSpec1* and *EnsSpec2* have the same signature. Hence, *EnsSpec1* $\otimes$ *EnsSpec* and *EnsSpec2* $\otimes$ *EnsSpec* have the same signature. In the following of the proof let *EnsSpec1* $= (\Sigma', Decls1, \sigma1_0)$, *EnsSpec2* $= (\Sigma', Decls2, \sigma2_0)$ and *EnsSpec* $= (\Sigma, Decls, \sigma_0)$. Let $T1 = (S1, \sigma1_0, L1, \rightarrow_1)$ be the semantics of *EnsSpec1*, $T2 = (S2, \sigma2_0, L2, \rightarrow_2)$ be the semantics of *EnsSpec2*, and let $T = (S, \sigma_0, L, \rightarrow)$ be the semantics of *EnsSpec*. W.l.o.g. we assume (*): For all $\sigma_1 \in S1, \sigma_2 \in S2, \sigma \in S$ we have $dom(\sigma_1) \cap dom(\sigma) = \emptyset$ and $dom(\sigma_2) \cap dom(\sigma) = \emptyset$. Let $\Delta = \{(\sigma1, \sigma2, \varphi) \mid \sigma1 \in S1, \sigma2 \in S2, \varphi : dom(\sigma1) \rightarrow dom(\sigma2) \text{ is bijective}\}$. By assumption, there exists a bijective function $\varphi_0 : dom(\sigma1_0) \rightarrow dom(\sigma2_0)$ and a bisimulation $R \subseteq \Delta$, such that

$(\sigma 1_0, \sigma 2_0, \varphi_0) \in R$. By definition,

$$EnsSpec1 \otimes EnsSpec = (\Sigma' \otimes \Sigma, Decls1 \cup Decls, \sigma 1_0 + \sigma_0), and$$
$$EnsSpec2 \otimes EnsSpec = (\Sigma' \otimes \Sigma, Decls2 \cup Decls, \sigma 2_0 + \sigma_0)$$

Obviously, φ_0 can be extended to a bijective function $(\varphi_0 + id_{dom(\sigma_0)})$: $dom(\sigma 1_0 + \sigma_0) \rightarrow dom(\sigma 2_0 + \sigma_0)$ such that $(\varphi_0 + id_{dom(\sigma_0)})(i) = \varphi_0(i)$ if $i \in dom(\sigma 1_0)$ and $(\varphi_0 + id_{dom(\sigma_0)})(i) = i$ if $i \in dom(\sigma_0)$.

Now, let $T1^{\otimes} = (S1^{\otimes}, \sigma 1_0 + \sigma_0, L1^{\otimes}, \rightarrow_1^{\otimes})$ be the semantics of $EnsSpec1 \otimes EnsSpec$ and $T2^{\otimes} = (S2^{\otimes}, \sigma 2_0 + \sigma_0, L2^{\otimes}, \rightarrow_2^{\otimes})$ be the semantics of $EnsSpec2 \otimes EnsSpec$. Let $\Delta^{\otimes} = \{(\sigma 1^{\otimes}, \sigma 2^{\otimes}, \varphi^{\otimes}) \mid \sigma 1^{\otimes} \in S1^{\otimes}, \sigma 2^{\otimes} \in S2^{\otimes}, \varphi^{\otimes} : dom(\sigma 1^{\otimes}) \rightarrow dom(\sigma 2^{\otimes})$ is bijective$\}$. We have to construct a bisimulation $R^{\otimes} \subseteq \Delta^{\otimes}$, such that $(\sigma 1_0 + \sigma_0, \sigma 2_0 + \sigma_0, \varphi_0 + id_{dom(\sigma_0)}) \in R^{\otimes}$. For this purpose, we define

$$R^{\otimes} = \{(\sigma 1^{\otimes}, \sigma 2^{\otimes}, \varphi^{\otimes}) \mid \exists (\sigma 1, \sigma 2, \varphi) \in R, \exists \sigma \in S : \sigma 1^{\otimes} = \sigma 1 + \sigma,$$
$$\sigma 2^{\otimes} = \sigma 2 + \sigma, \varphi^{\otimes} = \varphi + id_{dom(\sigma)}\}.$$

Clearly, $(\sigma 1_0 + \sigma_0, \sigma 2_0 + \sigma_0, \varphi_0 + id_{dom(\sigma_0)}) \in R^{\otimes}$. It remains to prove that $R^{\otimes}$ is a bisimulation between $T1^{\otimes}$ and $T2^{\otimes}$. We will prove the first four cases (1.1)–(1.4) of Definition 9. The other cases are symmetric. Assume $(\sigma 1^{\otimes}, \sigma 2^{\otimes}, \varphi^{\otimes}) \in R^{\otimes}$, i.e. $\sigma 1^{\otimes}$ is of the form $\sigma 1 + \sigma, \sigma 2^{\otimes} = \sigma 2 + \sigma$ and $\varphi^{\otimes} = \varphi + id_{dom(\sigma)}$ such that $(\sigma 1, \sigma 2, \varphi) \in R$.

(1.1) Let $\sigma 1^{\otimes} \xrightarrow{pi:m!}_1^{\otimes} \sigma 1'^{\otimes}$ be a transition in $T1^{\otimes}$ with an external message $m!$ of $\Sigma' \otimes \Sigma$. According to the semantics of ensemble specifications, the transition is induced by a transition on the process level of the form $P \xrightarrow{m!} P'$ such that $pi \in dom(\sigma 1^{\otimes})$ and $\sigma 1^{\otimes}(pi) = P$ and $\sigma 1'^{\otimes} = \sigma 1^{\otimes}_{[pi \mapsto P']}$. Since $m!$ is an external message of $\Sigma' \otimes \Sigma$, it is an external message of Σ' or of Σ.

If $m!$ is an external message of Σ', the transition $P \xrightarrow{m!} P'$ induces a transition $\sigma 1 \xrightarrow{pi:m!}_1 \sigma 1'$ in $T1$ with $pi \in dom(\sigma 1)$ and $\sigma 1(pi) = P$ and $\sigma 1' = \sigma 1_{[pi \mapsto P']}$. Since R is a bisimulation between $T1$ and $T2$, there exists $\sigma 2 \xrightarrow{\varphi(pi):m!}_2 \sigma 2'$, such that $(\sigma 1', \sigma 2', \varphi) \in R$. This transition is induced by a transition on the process level of the form $Q \xrightarrow{m!} Q'$ such that $\varphi(pi) \in dom(\sigma 2)$ and $\sigma 2(\varphi(pi)) = Q$ and $\sigma 2' = \sigma 2_{[\varphi(pi) \mapsto Q']}$. Taking into account that $\sigma 2^{\otimes} = \sigma 2 + \sigma$, the transition $Q \xrightarrow{m!} Q'$ induces also a transition $\sigma 2^{\otimes} \xrightarrow{\varphi(pi):m!}_2^{\otimes} \sigma 2'^{\otimes}$ in $T2^{\otimes}$ with $\sigma 2'^{\otimes} = \sigma 2' + \sigma$. Since $(\sigma 1, \sigma 2, \varphi) \in R$, $\sigma 1'^{\otimes} = \sigma 1' + \sigma$, $\sigma 2'^{\otimes} = \sigma 2' + \sigma$, we have $(\sigma 1'^{\otimes}, \sigma 2'^{\otimes}, \varphi^{\otimes}) \in R^{\otimes}$.

If $m!$ is an external message of Σ, the transition $P \xrightarrow{m!} P'$ induces a transition $\sigma \xrightarrow{pi:m!} \sigma'$ in T with $pi \in dom(\sigma)$ and $\sigma(pi) = P$ and $\sigma' = \sigma_{[pi \mapsto P']}$. Then $\sigma 1'^{\otimes} = \sigma 1 + \sigma'$. But the transition $P \xrightarrow{m!} P'$ induces also a transition $\sigma 2^{\otimes} \xrightarrow{pi:m!}_2^{\otimes} \sigma 2'^{\otimes}$ in $T2^{\otimes}$ such that $\sigma 2'^{\otimes} = \sigma 2 + \sigma'$. Since $(\sigma 1, \sigma 2, \varphi) \in R$ we then have also $(\sigma 1'^{\otimes}, \sigma 2'^{\otimes}, \varphi^{\otimes}) \in R^{\otimes}$.

(1.2) This case is proved analogously to (1.1).

(1.3) Let $\sigma1^{\otimes} \xrightarrow{\; pi:\mathbf{create}(fresh(\sigma1^{\otimes})) \;}{}^{\otimes}_1 \sigma1'^{\otimes}$ be a transition in $T1^{\otimes}$. The transition is induced by a transition on the process level of the form $P1 \xrightarrow{\; \mathbf{create}(Q1) \;} P1'$ such that $pi \in dom(\sigma1^{\otimes})$ and $\sigma1^{\otimes}(pi) = P1$ and $\sigma1'^{\otimes} = \sigma1^{\otimes}_{[pi \mapsto P1']+[fresh(\sigma1^{\otimes}) \mapsto Q1]}$. Since $\sigma1^{\otimes}$ is of the form $\sigma1 + \sigma$ with $\sigma1 \in S1$ and $\sigma \in S$, we consider two cases (a) and (b).

(a) $pi \in dom(\sigma1)$: Then $P1 \xrightarrow{\; \mathbf{create}(Q1) \;} P1'$ induces a transition $\sigma1 \xrightarrow{\; pi:\mathbf{create}(fresh(\sigma1)) \;}_1 \sigma1'$ in $T1$ such that $\sigma1' = \sigma1_{[pi \mapsto P1']+[fresh(\sigma1) \mapsto Q1]}$. Since R is a bisimulation between $T1$ and $T2$, there exists $\sigma2 \xrightarrow{\; \varphi(pi):\mathbf{create}(fresh(\sigma2)) \;}_2 \sigma2'$ in $T2$ such that $(\sigma1', \sigma2', \varphi') \in R$ with $\varphi' = \varphi + [fresh(\sigma1) \mapsto fresh(\sigma2)]$. This transition is induced by a transition on the process level of the form $P2 \xrightarrow{\; \mathbf{create}(Q2) \;} P2'$ such that $\varphi(pi) \in dom(\sigma2)$ and $\sigma2(\varphi(pi)) = P2$ and $\sigma2' = \sigma2_{[\varphi(pi) \mapsto P2']+[fresh(\sigma2) \mapsto Q2]}$.

The transition $P2 \xrightarrow{\; \mathbf{create}(Q2) \;} P2'$ induces also a transition $\sigma2^{\otimes} \xrightarrow{\; \varphi(pi):\mathbf{create}(fresh(\sigma2^{\otimes})) \;}{}^{\otimes}_2 \sigma2'^{\otimes}$ in $T2^{\otimes}$ with $\varphi(pi) \in dom(\sigma2^{\otimes})$ and $\sigma2^{\otimes}(\varphi(pi)) = P2$ and $\sigma2'^{\otimes} = \sigma2^{\otimes}_{[\varphi(pi) \mapsto P2']+[fresh(\sigma2^{\otimes}) \mapsto Q2]}$. Taking into account the assumption (*) from above on disjointness of definition domains, we have $fresh(\sigma1) \notin dom(\sigma)$ and $fresh(\sigma2) \notin dom(\sigma)$. Since $\sigma1^{\otimes} = \sigma1 + \sigma$ and $\sigma2^{\otimes} = \sigma2 + \sigma$, we can assume $fresh(\sigma1^{\otimes}) = fresh(\sigma1)$ and $fresh(\sigma2^{\otimes}) = fresh(\sigma2)$. Hence, $\sigma1'^{\otimes} = \sigma1' + \sigma$ and $\sigma2'^{\otimes} = \sigma2' + \sigma$. Since $(\sigma1', \sigma2', \varphi') \in R$, we get $(\sigma1'^{\otimes}, \sigma2'^{\otimes}, \varphi'^{\otimes}) \in R^{\otimes}$ with $\varphi'^{\otimes}$ defined as $\varphi^{\otimes} + [fresh(\sigma1^{\otimes}) \mapsto fresh(\sigma2^{\otimes})]$ which is the same as $\varphi' + id_{dom(\sigma)}$ since $\varphi^{\otimes} + [fresh(\sigma1^{\otimes}) \mapsto fresh(\sigma2^{\otimes})] = \varphi + [fresh(\sigma1) \mapsto fresh(\sigma2)] + id_{dom(\sigma)} = \varphi' + id_{dom(\sigma)}$.[9]

(b) $pi \in dom(\sigma)$: Then $P1 \xrightarrow{\; \mathbf{create}(Q1) \;} P1'$ induces a transition $\sigma \xrightarrow{\; pi:\mathbf{create}(fresh(\sigma)) \;} \sigma'$ in T such that $\sigma' = \sigma_{[pi \mapsto P1']+[fresh(\sigma) \mapsto Q1]}$.

$P1 \xrightarrow{\; \mathbf{create}(Q1) \;} P1'$ induces also a transition $\sigma2^{\otimes} \xrightarrow{\; pi:\mathbf{create}(fresh(\sigma2^{\otimes})) \;}{}^{\otimes}_2 \sigma2'^{\otimes}$ in $T2^{\otimes}$. Since $pi \in dom(\sigma), \sigma1^{\otimes} = \sigma1 + \sigma$ and $\sigma2^{\otimes} = \sigma2 + \sigma$, we assume, similarly as in case (a), $fresh(\sigma1^{\otimes}) = fresh(\sigma) = fresh(\sigma2^{\otimes})$. Hence, $\sigma1'^{\otimes} = \sigma1 + \sigma'$ and $\sigma2'^{\otimes} = \sigma2 + \sigma'$. Since $(\sigma1, \sigma2, \varphi) \in R$, we get $(\sigma1'^{\otimes}, \sigma2'^{\otimes}, \varphi'^{\otimes}) \in R^{\otimes}$ with $\varphi'^{\otimes}$ defined as $\varphi + id_{dom(\sigma')}$.

(1.4) Let $\sigma1^{\otimes} \xrightarrow{\; (pi \to qi):m \;}{}^{\otimes}_1 \sigma1'^{\otimes}$ be a transition in $T1^{\otimes}$. This transition is induced by two transitions on the process level of the form $P1 \xrightarrow{\; m! \;} P1'$, $Q1 \xrightarrow{\; m? \;} Q1'$ such that $pi, qi \in dom(\sigma1^{\otimes})$, $\sigma1^{\otimes}(pi) = P1, \sigma1^{\otimes}(qi) = Q1$ and $\sigma1'^{\otimes} = \sigma1^{\otimes}_{[pi \mapsto P1', qi \mapsto Q1']}$. Since $\sigma1^{\otimes}$ is of the form $\sigma1 + \sigma$ with

---

[9] Since $\varphi^{\otimes} = \varphi + id_{dom(\sigma)}$.

$\sigma 1 \in S1$ and $\sigma \in S$, we consider four cases (a), (b), (c) and (d) with (c) ((d) resp.) being the most interesting ones.

(a) $pi, qi \in dom(\sigma 1)$: Then $P1 \xrightarrow{m!} P1'$, $Q1 \xrightarrow{m?} Q1'$ induce a transition $\sigma 1 \xrightarrow{(pi \to qi):m}_1 \sigma 1'$ in $T1$ such that $\sigma 1' = \sigma 1_{[pi \mapsto P1', qi \mapsto Q1']}$. Hence, $\sigma 1'^\otimes = \sigma 1' + \sigma$. Since R is a bisimulation between $T1$ and $T2$, there exists $\sigma 2 \xrightarrow{(\varphi(pi) \to \varphi(qi)):m}_1 \sigma 2'$ in $T2$ such that $(\sigma 1', \sigma 2', \varphi) \in R$. This transition is induced by transitions on the process level of the form $P2 \xrightarrow{m!} P2'$, $Q2 \xrightarrow{m?} Q2'$ such that $\sigma 2' = \sigma 2_{[\varphi(pi) \mapsto P2', \varphi(qi) \mapsto Q2']}$. The transitions $P2 \xrightarrow{m!} P2'$, $Q2 \xrightarrow{m?} Q2'$ induce also a transition $\sigma 2^\otimes \xrightarrow{(\varphi(pi) \to \varphi(qi)):m}{}^\otimes_2 \sigma 2'^\otimes$ in $T2^\otimes$ such that $\sigma 2'^\otimes = \sigma 2' + \sigma$. Since $\sigma 1'^\otimes = \sigma 1 + \sigma'$ and $(\sigma 1', \sigma 2', \varphi) \in R$, we get $(\sigma 1'^\otimes, \sigma 2'^\otimes, \varphi^\otimes) \in R^\otimes$.

(b) $pi, qi \in dom(\sigma)$: Then $P1 \xrightarrow{m!} P1'$, $Q1 \xrightarrow{m?} Q1'$ induce a transition $\sigma \xrightarrow{(pi \to qi):m} \sigma'$ in T such that $\sigma' = \sigma_{[pi \mapsto P1', qi \mapsto Q1']}$. Hence, $\sigma 1'^\otimes = \sigma 1 + \sigma'$. The transitions $P1 \xrightarrow{m!} P1'$, $Q1 \xrightarrow{m?} Q1'$ induce also a transition $\sigma 2^\otimes \xrightarrow{(pi \to qi):m}{}^\otimes_2 \sigma 2'^\otimes$ in $T2^\otimes$ such that $\sigma 2'^\otimes = \sigma 2 + \sigma'$. Since $\sigma 1'^\otimes = \sigma 1 + \sigma'$ and $(\sigma 1, \sigma 2, \varphi) \in R$, we get $(\sigma 1'^\otimes, \sigma 2'^\otimes, \varphi^\otimes) \in R^\otimes$.

(c) $pi \in dom(\sigma 1)$ and $qi \in dom(\sigma)$: Then $m!$ is an external message of Σ' and $P1 \xrightarrow{m!} P1'$ induces a transition $\sigma 1 \xrightarrow{pi:m!}_1 \sigma 1'$ in $T1$ with $pi \in dom(\sigma 1)$, $\sigma 1(pi) = P1$ and $\sigma 1' = \sigma 1_{[pi \mapsto P1']}$. Moreover, $m?$ is an external message of Σ and $Q1 \xrightarrow{m!} Q1'$ induces a transition $\sigma \xrightarrow{qi:m?} \sigma'$ in T with $qi \in dom(\sigma)$, $\sigma(qi) = Q1$ and $\sigma' = \sigma_{[pi \mapsto Q1']}$. Hence, $\sigma 1'^\otimes = \sigma 1' + \sigma'$.

Since R is a bisimulation between $T1$ and $T2$, there exists $\sigma 2 \xrightarrow{\varphi(pi):m!}_2 \sigma 2'$ in $T2$, such that $(\sigma 1', \sigma 2', \varphi) \in R$. This transition is induced by a transition on the process level of the form $P2 \xrightarrow{m!} P2'$ such that $\varphi(pi) \in dom(\sigma 2)$, $\sigma 2(\varphi(pi)) = P2$ and $\sigma 2' = \sigma 2_{[\varphi(pi) \mapsto P2']}$.

Then, the transitions $P2 \xrightarrow{m!} P2'$ and $Q1 \xrightarrow{m!} Q1'$ induce also a transition $\sigma 2^\otimes \xrightarrow{(\varphi(pi) \to qi):m}{}^\otimes_2 \sigma 2'^\otimes$ in $T2^\otimes$ such that $\sigma 2'^\otimes = \sigma 2' + \sigma'$. Since $\sigma 1'^\otimes = \sigma 1' + \sigma'$ and $(\sigma 1', \sigma 2', \varphi) \in R$, we get $(\sigma 1'^\otimes, \sigma 2'^\otimes, \varphi^\otimes) \in R^\otimes$.

(d) $pi \in dom(\sigma)$ and $qi \in dom(\sigma 1)$: The proof is analogous to case (c). $\square$

Proof of Theorem 2:
Let $T1 = (S1, \sigma 1_0, L1, \to_1)$, $T2 = (S2, \sigma 2_0, L2, \to_2)$, $T1 \otimes T2 = (S1 \otimes S2, (\sigma 1, \sigma 2_0), L1 \otimes L2, \to_\otimes)$, and $T^\otimes = (S^\otimes, \sigma 1_0 + \sigma 2_0, L^\otimes, \to^\otimes)$. Since for the construction of $T1 \otimes T2$ we have assumed that the states in $S1$ and $S2$ have disjoint definition domains, we can define a bijection $\beta : S1 \otimes S2 \to S^\otimes$ such that

$\beta((\sigma 1, \sigma 2)) = \sigma 1 + \sigma 2$. To show that $\beta((\sigma 1, \sigma 2))$ is indeed in $S^{\otimes}$ and that β preserves and reflects transitions we perform an induction on the length of the derivation to reach states in $S1 \otimes S2$ and in $S^{\otimes}$. The base case holds, since $\beta((\sigma 1_0, \sigma 2_0)) = \sigma 1_0 + \sigma 2_0 \in S^{\otimes}$. For each direction we show as an example one induction step. The other cases are similar.

(open output left): Let $m! \in \Sigma 1_{ext}, m? \notin \Sigma 2_{ext}$ and $(\sigma 1, \sigma 2) \xrightarrow{pi:m!}_{\otimes} (\sigma 1', \sigma 2)$ because of $\sigma 1 \xrightarrow{pi:m!}_1 \sigma 1'$. Then $\sigma 1 \xrightarrow{pi:m!}_1 \sigma 1'$ is induced by by a transition on the process level of the form $P \xrightarrow{m!} P'$ such that $pi \in dom(\sigma 1)$, $\sigma 1(pi) = P$ and $\sigma 1' = \sigma 1[pi \mapsto P']$. By induction hypothesis, $\beta((\sigma 1, \sigma 2)) = \sigma 1 + \sigma 2 \in S^{\otimes}$. Then, the transition $P \xrightarrow{m!} P'$ induces also a transition $\sigma 1 + \sigma 2 \xrightarrow{pi:m!}^{\otimes} \sigma 1' + \sigma 2$ in $T^{\otimes}$. Hence $\beta((\sigma 1', \sigma 2)) \in S^{\otimes}$.

Conversely, let $\sigma^{\otimes} \xrightarrow{pi:m!}^{\otimes} \sigma'^{\otimes}$ be a transition in $T^{\otimes}$ with an external message $m!$ of $\Sigma 1 \otimes \Sigma 2$. The transition is induced by a transition on the process level of the form $P \xrightarrow{m!} P'$ such that $pi \in dom(\sigma^{\otimes})$, $\sigma^{\otimes}(pi) = P$ and $\sigma'^{\otimes} = \sigma^{\otimes}[pi \mapsto P']$. By induction hypothesis, $\sigma^{\otimes} = \beta((\sigma 1, \sigma 2)) = \sigma 1 + \sigma 2$ such that $\sigma 1 \in T1, \sigma 2 \in T2$ with $dom(\sigma 1) \cap dom(\sigma 2) = \emptyset$. W.l.o.g. we consider the case $m! \in \Sigma 1_{ext}$. Then, $pi \in dom(\sigma 1)$. Hence, the transition $P \xrightarrow{m!} P'$ induces also a transition $\sigma 1 \xrightarrow{pi:m!}_1 \sigma 1'$ in $T1$ such that $\sigma 1' = \sigma 1[pi \mapsto P']$. Therefore, $\sigma'^{\otimes} = \sigma 1' + \sigma 2 = \beta((\sigma 1', \sigma 2))$. Since $m!$ is external in $\Sigma 1 \otimes \Sigma 2$, we have $m? \notin \Sigma 2_{ext}$. Thus we can apply the rule (open output left) and get $(\sigma 1, \sigma 2) \xrightarrow{pi:m!}_{\otimes} (\sigma 1', \sigma 2)$. □

References

1. de Alfaro, L., Henzinger, T.A.: Interface automata. In: Proceedings of 9th ACM SIGSOFT Annual Symposium on Foundations of Software Engineering (FSE 2001), pp. 109–120 (2001)
2. Abd Alrahman, Y., De Nicola, R., Loreti, M.: On the power of attribute-based communication. In: Albert, E., Lanese, I. (eds.) FORTE 2016. LNCS, vol. 9688, pp. 1–18. Springer, Heidelberg (2016). doi:10.1007/978-3-319-39570-8_1
3. Baeten, J.C.M., Vaandrager, F.W.: An algebra for process creation. Acta Inf. **29**(4), 303–334 (1992)
4. Bruni, R., Montanari, U., Sammartino, M.: Reconfigurable and software-defined networks of connectors and components. In: Wirsing, M., et al. [13], pp. 73–106. http://dx.doi.org/10.1007/978-3-319-16310-9
5. De Nicola, R., Gorla, D., Pugliese, R.: Basic observables for a calculus for global computing. Inf. Comput. **205**(10), 1491–1525 (2007)
6. De Nicola, R., Loreti, M., Pugliese, R., Tiezzi, F.: A formal approach to autonomic systems programming: the SCEL language. TAAS **9**(2), 7:1–7:29 (2014)
7. Havelund, K., Larsen, K.G.: The fork calculus. In: Lingas, A., Karlsson, R., Carlsson, S. (eds.) ICALP 1993. LNCS, vol. 700, pp. 544–557. Springer, Heidelberg (1993). doi:10.1007/3-540-56939-1_101
8. Hennicker, R., Klarl, A., Wirsing, M.: Model-checking Helena ensembles with Spin. In: Martí-Oliet, N., Ölveczky, P.C., Talcott, C. (eds.) Meseguer Festschrift. LNCS, vol. 9200, pp. 331–360. Springer, Heidelberg (2015)

9. Klarl, A.: Engineering self-adaptive systems with the role-based architecture of Helena. In: Proceedings of 24th IEEE International Conference on Enabling Technologies: Infrastructure for Collaborative Enterprises, WETICE 2015, pp. 3–8. IEEE Computer Society (2015)
10. Klarl, A., Mayer, P., Hennicker, R.: HELENA@work: modeling the science cloud platform. In: Margaria, T., Steffen, B. (eds.) ISoLA 2014. LNCS, vol. 8802, pp. 99–116. Springer, Heidelberg (2014). doi:10.1007/978-3-662-45234-9_8
11. Mayer, P., Klarl, A., Hennicker, R., Puviani, M., Tiezzi, F., Pugliese, R., Keznikl, J., Bureš, T.: The autonomic cloud: a vision of voluntary, peer-2-peer cloud computing. In: Workshops on Challenges for Achieving Self-Awareness in Autonomic Systems, pp. 1–6. IEEE (2013)
12. Rowstron, A., Druschel, P.: Pastry: scalable, decentralized object location, and routing for large-scale peer-to-peer systems. In: Guerraoui, R. (ed.) Middleware 2001. LNCS, vol. 2218, pp. 329–350. Springer, Heidelberg (2001)
13. Wirsing, M., Hölzl, M.M., Koch, N., Mayer, P. (eds.): Software Engineering for Collective Autonomic Systems - The ASCENS Approach. LNCS, vol. 8998. Springer, Heidelberg (2015). doi:10.1007/978-3-319-16310-9

Logic Fragments: Coordinating Entities with Logic Programs

Francesco Luca De Angelis$^{(\boxtimes)}$ and Giovanna Di Marzo Serugendo

Institute of Information Services Science,
University of Geneva, Geneva, Switzerland
{francesco.deangelis,giovanna.dimarzo}@unige.ch

Abstract. Rigorous engineering of self-organising and self-adaptive systems is a challenging activity. Interactions with humans and unexpected entities, dependence on contextual information for self-organisation and adaptation represent just some of the factors complicating the coordination process among multiple entities of the system. Recently we proposed a coordination model based on logic inference named Logic Fragments Coordination Model. Logic Fragments are combinations of logic programs defining interactions among agents distributed over the nodes of the system. They are able to accommodate various types of logics, ranging from classical up to many-valued paraconsistent ones. The logical formalisation makes it possible to express coordination in a rigorous and predicle way, both at design-time and run-time. In this paper we define, under the form of an evaluation algorithm, the semantics of Logic Fragments; introducing logical predicates used to manage and reason on local and remote information. By associating specific semantics to the symbols inferred during the evaluation of logic programs it is possible to make logical inference effects unambiguous on the system; such an approach turns Logic Fragments into a coordination-oriented logic-based programming model. We conclude the paper discussing three examples showing the use of Logic Fragments to implement on-the-fly ad-hoc coordination mechanisms, as well as design-time and run-time verification of spatial properties.

1 Introduction

Chemical-based coordination models are a category of coordination models that use the chemical reaction metaphor and have proven useful to implement several types of self-organising mechanisms [17]. A well-known difficulty with self-organising systems stems from the analysis, validation and verification (at design-time or run-time) of so-called emergent properties - i.e. properties that can be observed at a global level but that none of the interacting entities exhibit on its own. Few coordination models integrate features supporting the validation of emergent properties, none of them relying on the chemical metaphor.

In previous works [5], we enriched a chemical-based coordination model with the notion of Logic Fragments, which are combination of logic programs.

© Springer International Publishing AG 2016
T. Margaria and B. Steffen (Eds.): ISoLA 2016, Part I, LNCS 9952, pp. 589–604, 2016.
DOI: 10.1007/978-3-319-47166-2_41

Our logic-based coordination model allows agents to inject logic fragments into the shared space. Those fragments actually define on-the-fly ad hoc chemical reactions that apply on matching data tuples present in the system, removing tuples and producing new tuples, possibly producing also new logic fragments. Our model is defined independently of any specific logic, an actual instantiation and implementation of the model can use its own logic(s). We also defined a spatial language to verify graph-based spatial properties of self-organising systems [6]. The language encapsulates Logic Fragments in statements that are evaluated in a distributed manner at run-time, involving several system entities at the same time.

In this paper, we present the semantics of the Logic Fragment coordination model: we express it with an evaluation algorithm, encompassing many-valued underlying logics and paving the way for the forthcoming implementation of a middleware satisfying this behaviour. We also introduce logical predicates to reason on local and remote information.

Section 2 discusses related works. Section 3 presents the Logic Fragment Coordination Model, the syntax and semantics of Logics Fragments. Section 4 highlights three features of our model: (1) creation of new coordination laws at run-time; (2) verification of emergent property at run-time; (3) verification of emergent property at design-time. Finally, Sect. 5 concludes and provides perspectives for future work.

2   Related Works

To tackle the difficulties of engineering self-organising systems, several approaches to coordination have been proposed over the past two decades [2]. Here we focus on (i) chemical-inspired approaches based on tuple spaces (e.g. [17]) and (ii) distributed logic programming (e.g. [1,13]).

Chemical-inspired models: in chemical-inspired models, coordination is expressed in terms of (distributed) virtual chemical reactions among information components, such as tuples or multisets. Such kinds of models are efficient in dynamic open systems (such as pervasive scenarios), where entities can communicate asynchronously without having global knowledge about the system and their participants.

Distributed logic programming: compared to other approaches, distributed logic programming techniques present several remarkable advantages. Following Kowalski's terminology [11], an algorithm can be decomposed in two parts: (i) logic components, i.e. formulae that determine the meaning of the algorithm and the knowledge used to solve a problem and (ii) control components, which specify the way the knowledge is used to solve the problem, i.e. the implementation activities. Distributed logic programming techniques emphasise the logic part, which finally results [13] in an important reduction of the complexity and size of code. Moreover the logic part is used to formally infer the output of the algorithm, for example through evaluation of model-theoretic semantics [9]; this means that coordination processes are inferred formally and every rule of the system has a more predicle effect on the emergent global behaviour. Loosely speaking, in distributed logic programming nodes directly execute system specifications, an important step forward for system verifiability and predicility. Nevertheless, usually there exists a trade-off between expressivity and execution performances, causing logic programs to be written for the optimization of the control part. When original specifications cannot be directly used for performance reasons, final systems can undergo light verification processes (e.g. [10,12,16]); in general, "the only difference between a complete specification and a program is one of efficiency" (Kowalski - [12]).

Most part of chemical-inspired models and distributed programming languages present several disadvantages when considered individually. In fact, designing complex system with chemical-inspired models makes it hard to avoid unpredicted interactions and to analyse and forecast the emergent global behaviour of the whole system. On the other hand, distributed programming languages tackle such a problem rigorously, but most of them (e.g. Datalog-like languages used in [1,13]) use logics unsuile for handling and reasoning on information generated in real distributed systems, which is usually: (i) implicitly affected by several levels of truthfulness and falseness (e.g. sensed contextual information); (ii) partially defined (components have only local views of the global state), thus prone to contradictions. Many-valued logics better capture such characteristics and make it possible to reason in such scenarios.

Logic fragments: the Logic Fragment model [5] is derived from SAPERE [17], a chemical-inspired coordination model for pervasive scenarios supporting the development of self-adaptive and self-organising applications. Our model aims at combining the advantages of chemical-inspired models and distributed logic programming techniques by contrasting their disadvantages. Differently from other existing chemical-inspired models, the formalism for chemical-reactions is expressed rigorously through combinations of logic programs, thus enjoying verifiability and predicility. Moreover, with respect to distributed logic programming techniques, Logic Fragments accommodate several types of non-classical logics. Also, logic programs become manipulable entities, expressed in logic languages over finite domains and associated with individual model-theoretic semantics. This aspect is important because paves the way for combining logic programs having different languages and semantics. For example, it is possible to use simultaneously classical and many-valued logics (e.g. 4QL [14]) to manipulate graded paraconsistent and partially defined information. Indeed, we have defined a family of many-valued logics [7] to be directly used in the Logic Fragment coordination model; when compared to the Datalog-like languages of [1,13], ours presents two advantages: (i) finitely many value truth-degrees, whose number can be defined according to the scenarios to model; (ii) introspection operators, a logical machinery used to realise resolution of inconsistences and to support local and global closures of the Open World Assumption (basic assumption of [7]; [1,13] are based on the Closed World Assumption instead).

Another advantage of making logic programs composable concerns modularity and reusability, hierarchically grounding complex coordination mechanisms in basic ones. Moreover, equivalent functional mechanisms can be classified and selected according to their capabilities of meeting non-functional requirements and handling environmental constraints, thus enhancing reconfigurability and robustness of the system.

3   Logic Fragment Coordination Model

3.1   General Description

The main components of our model are the following ones (Fig. 1(b)):

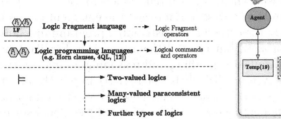 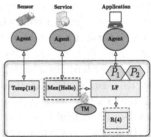

(a) Hierarchy of languages and logics.   (b) Interaction between a static tuple (Mex(Hello)) and a logic fragment LF with generation of a new tuple as output (R(4)).

Fig. 1. Logic fragment coordination model.

(I) *Agents*: active entities representing the interface between the *tuple space* and the external world including any sort of device (e.g. sensors), service and stand-alone application.

(II) *Tuple space*: shared space containing all the tuples of a node.

(III) *Tuples*: vectors of type Name($c_1, ..., c_n$) used to represent information. They are divided in two categories: static tuples containing data (e.g. Temp(19), Mex($Hello$)) and logic fragments, active tuples with name LF encapsulating combinations of logic programs (e.g. P_1, P_2) that consume and produce tuples within the *tuple space*. Logic fragments are responsible for any kind of coordination activity performed within the system, whereas tuples represent the coordinated entities; all logic fragments existing in the tuple space are evaluated in an atomic fashion. Tuples can be removed and created by logic fragment, received from remote nodes or injected by agents. In this last case, agents can receive notifications triggered by the *Tuple Space Manager* when their associated tuples are involved in coordination processes (e.g. deletion).

(IV) *Tuple Space Manager (TM)*: main component performing the evaluation of logic fragments and all the primary tasks requested by agents and logic programs (e.g. sending tuples, notifying agents, etc.).

3.2 Preliminary Definitions

Definition 1. Let *Var* be a finite set of variables (here denoted by upper-case letters), *Pred* a finite set of predicate symbols and *Cons* a finite set of constants (here denoted by lower-case letters, except for constants that refer to predicate symbols). We also assume all these sets are mutually disjoint. We define the set of terms *Ter* as the union of *Cons* and *Var*. We assume that *Pred* and *Cons* also contain model-defined predicates and constants reported in Table 1 (page 6).

Grammar 1: logic programs.

```
LP  ::= R | R R
R   ::= H ← B
B   ::= L | L LC L
LC  ::= ,
H, L ∈  ℒ
```

Grammar 2: logic fragments.

```
LF   ::= △ | LFI
LFI  ::= (LFI □ LFI) | (LFI ⊔ LFI)
      |  (LFI ⊓ LFI) | (LFI ⊓ LFI)
      |  (PSEQ, M, LF, I, A, PHI)
PSEQ ∈  𝒫_seq
M    ∈  ℳ
I    ⊆  ℐ_G
A    ⊆  𝒜_G
PHI  ∈  φ
```

Definition 2. With τ we identify a finite set of truth-degrees. In classical 2-valued logic programming $\tau = \{t, f\}$. In our model (Fig. 1(a)) we can deal with several kinds of paraconsistent many-valued logics (e.g. [7,14]), so we assume that τ can contain several truth-degrees. For instance, in [14], $\tau = \{t, f, i, u\}$, while in [7] it is parametrised by N, $\tau_N = \cup_{i=1}^{N}\{t_i, f_i\} \cup_{i,j \in \{1,...,N\}} i_{i,j} \cup \{u\}$. We use t_N and f_N to identify the truth-degrees respectively associated with the maximum grade of truthfulness and falsity.

Definition 3. Given a set of truth-degrees τ, we define the set of *literals* $\mathcal{L}$, composed of positive ($\mathcal{L}_+$) and negative ($\mathcal{L}_-$) literals:

$$\mathcal{L}_+ \overset{def}{=} \{p(t_1, ..., t_n) \mid p \in Pred, t_i \in Ter, 1 \leq i \leq n\}$$
$$\mathcal{L}_- \overset{def}{=} \{\neg p(t_1, ..., t_n) \mid p \in Pred, t_i \in Ter, 1 \leq i \leq n\}$$
$$\mathcal{L} \subset \mathcal{L}_+ \cup \mathcal{L}_- \cup \bigcup_{\tau \in \tau} \tau$$

Any literal without free variables is called *ground*. $\mathcal{L}_G$ is the set of ground literals contained in $\mathcal{L}$ and $\mathcal{L}_\tau \overset{def}{=} \mathcal{L}_G \times \tau$. With $\bar{t}$, $\bar{c}$ and $\bar{P}$ we identify sequences of terms $t_1, ..., t_n$, constants $c_1, ..., c_n$ and programs $P_1, ..., P_n$ ($|\bar{s}| \geq 0$ depicts the number of elements of a sequence $\bar{s}$), with i a numeric constant, with c_{node} a constant depicting a neighbour node's name and with c_p the constant referring to a predicate symbol (e.g. $p = sum \in Pred$, $c_p = sum \in Cons$).

Definition 4. A logic program P (see Grammar 1) is a finite set of rules of type $H \leftarrow B$, where H is named *head* of the rule and B *body* of the rule. Heads contain single literals whereas bodies are composed of literals connected with logical connectives (e.g. commas). Literals are defined over the sets of Definition 3; rules without variables are named *ground*. For space reason here we deal only with definite logic programs, having only positive literals both in heads and bodies; nonetheless, Grammar 1 can be extended depending on the logic family that one wants to use in logic fragments (e.g. [3,7]). $\mathcal{P}$ is the set of all logic programs of a given type; $\mathcal{P}_{seq}$ is the set of all finite sequences $P_1 \cdots P_n$ of elements of $\mathcal{P}$ and P_ϵ identifies the empty sequence.

Table 1. Commands and operators used in the examples.

Generic commands
remove($c_p, \bar{c}$): remove all tuples $p(\bar{c})$.
add(c_p, i, c): replace all tuples $p(c_1, ..., c_i, ..., c_n)$ with $p(c_1, ..., c_{i-1}, c_i + c, c_{i+1}, ..., c_n)$

Local verification operators (†: I-generator, ‡: A-generator)
notExists($c_p, \bar{c}$)†: t_N if there not exist any tuple in the constituent matching $p(\bar{c})$. f_N otherwise.
equal$^\ddagger(c_1, c_2)$: t_N if c_1 equals c_2. f_N otherwise. notEqual(c_1, c_2)‡: t_N if $c_1 \neq c_2$. f_N otherwise.
less(c_1, c_2)‡: t_N if c_1 and c_2 are numbers and $c_1 < c_2$. f_N otherwise.
greater$^\ddagger(c_1, c_2)$: t_N if c_1 and c_2 are numbers and $c_1 > c_2$. f_N otherwise.

Neighbourhood verification operators (A-generators)
neighNotExist($c_{node}, c_p, \bar{c}$): t_N if there are no tuples matching $p(\bar{c})$ in c_{node}. f_N otherwise.
neighIs(c_{node}): t_N ifc_{node} is the name of a neighbour. f_N otherwise.
neighIsNot(c_{node}): t_N ifc_{node} is not the name of a neighbour. f_N otherwise.
neigh($c_{node}, c_p, \bar{c}$): truth degree associated with the tuple $p(\bar{c})$ in a direct neighbour c_{node}.
In AEK semantics, f_N is the default value.

Sending commands
sendLF($c_{node}, c_{code}, c_{p_1}, ..., c_{p_n}$): sends the fragment with code c_{code} to the neighbour c_{node}.
The logic fragment is sent by adding all tuples $p_1(\bar{c}_1), ..., p_n(\bar{c}_n)$ founded in the constituent.

Logic fragments operators (A-generators)
LF_PV(c_p, c): t_N if $p(\bar{c})$ is contained in the logic fragment. f_N otherwise.

Modifiers for tuples
unique($P, \bar{c}$): $P(\bar{c})$ will be unique in the tuple space.
temp($P, \bar{c}$): creates a literal $P(\bar{c})$that will be not injected in the container.

Special constants
_nodeName: name of the node evaluating the logic fragment.
_thisLF: representation of the code of the while logic fragment evaluating the constant.

The set of rules of logic programs infer information on the basis of the knowledge introduced through *facts*, ground rules with true bodies. Facts represent local and remote knowledge affecting coordination (e.g. contextual-information, mathematical relations, etc.) and they can be automatically generated at run-time to prevent their explicit definitions in the programs (which would require to know complete knowledge of the system at design-time).

Definition 5. *I-* and *A- generators* are subsets of $\mathcal{L}_\tau$ employed to automatise the creation of facts. An I-generator p_I^S builds literals starting from a set of facts S (e.g. all the literals with a given predicate symbol existing in the tuple space) whereas an A-generator p_A is used to define relations among constants (mathematical functions or predicates, e.g. couples $(less(a, b), t)$ where a and b are two numbers such that $a < b$). Practically, I- and A- generators can be implemented in a general-purpose language function executed at run-time (e.g. a Java method).

Definition 6. The coordination model provides a set of special predicates with specific semantics; the subset used in the examples is reported in Table 1. They are divided into two categories: (i) *commands*, appearing only in the heads of the rules and used to perform actions on tuples (e.g. to manipulate local and remote tuples, to perform mathematical computations, etc.) and (ii) *operators* (I- and A- generators), used only in the bodies of rules to reason on tuples (e.g. counting tuples, retrieving truth-degrees of remote tuples, etc.). Commands are interpreted at the end of the evaluation of the semantics of logic programs.

Definition 7. Tuples within the tuple space are represented by elements of type $\langle p(\bar{c}), A, \tau \rangle$, where $p(\bar{c}) \in \mathcal{L}_G$ is a ground literal (for both static tuples and logic fragments), $A \in \mathcal{A}$ is an agent (owner) and $\tau \in \tau$ is the truth-degree. Given that our model is framed in the context of many-valued logics, for static tuples $p(\bar{c})$ can be associated simultaneously with several different τ (e.g. produced by several contextual sources). *Logic fragments*, having predicate $p \stackrel{\text{def}}{=} LF$, must be associated with exactly one truth-degree.

3.3 Logic Fragments

Definition 8. The syntax of logic fragments is defined by Grammar 2 (parenthesis enclosing logic fragments are only used to avoid ambiguity in the grammar); with $\mathcal{LF}$ we identify the set of all logic fragments generated by using such a grammar. The symbols used in the syntax are explained as follows. With $\mathcal{M}$ we identify a set of finite-domain model-theoretic semantics available for programs in $\mathcal{P}$ (e.g. AEK - Apt-van Emden-Kowalski's semantics, KK - Kripke-Kleene's semantics, 4QL for [14], NVAL for [7], etc.). We assume that any model of a logic program can be expressed as a finite subset of $\mathcal{L}_\tau$. Defining $\mathbb{P}(S)$ as the powerset of a generic set S, with Φ we identify the set of all functions $\varphi : \mathbb{P}(\mathcal{L}_\tau) \times \mathcal{L}_G \longrightarrow \{T, F\}$ ($\{T,F\}$ is independent from τ). Any φ function defines the condition to start (T) or to skip (F) the evaluation of a logic fragment; φ_T is the constant function equal to T. The first parameter passed to φ is the set of tuples generated from the evaluation of the inner logic fragments, whereas the second one is a set of predicates informing about the state of network transfers of tuples from and to neighbours. With $\mathcal{I}_G$ and $\mathcal{A}_G$ we identify respectively the set of all I-generators and A-generators. $\triangle$ is a logic fragment evaluated to the set of tuples (static and logic fragments) existing in the tuple space.

Logic fragments can be composed, i.e. the results of the evaluation of a inner one can be used as input of an outer fragment (e.g. replacing LF in (PSEQ, LF, I, A, PHI) with a new logic fragment); in that case, the I-generators of the outermost logic fragment are computed on the basis of the set of facts produced by the inner logic programs. The remaining operators combine the output of two logic fragments by considering the union ($\dot{\sqcup}$, $\sqcup$) and the intersection ($\bar{\sqcap}$, $\sqcap$) of their consequents (e.g. $LF_3 = LF_1 \sqcap LF_2$ contains only the literals inferred both by LF_1 and LF_2.) The versions with bars require both operands to be evaluated to a value different than $\bowtie$, otherwise the evaluation of the operator is $\bowtie$.

In the tuple space logic fragments are represented with literals of type $LF(c_{code}, \bar{c})$ with $|\bar{c}| \geq 0$: $c_{code} \in Cons$ represents the complete definition of the logic fragment as expressed above; the remaining constants $\bar{c}$ are chained blocks of type $c_{P_i}, c_{i1}, ..., c_{in_i}$ representing literals $P_i(c_{i1}, ..., c_{in_i})$ used as input parameter for the logic fragment; such literals can be accessed by using the predicate LF_PV of Table 1.

Example 1. Logic Fragment 1 creates a tuple of type $Sum(n)$ where $n = n_1 + \cdots + n_m$ is the sum of all the numbers stored in the tuple space under the form of tuples $N(n_1), ..., N(n_m)$. P_{sum} is a definite logic program; the head $add(Sum, 1, X)$ of the first rule is a literal with a specific meaning reported in Table 1 (i.e. adding a number X to the first component of the tuple Sum). The interpretation of the program is the so-called Apt-van Emden-Kowalski's semantics (AEK). By starting from the tuple space $(\triangle)$, all the tuples of type $N(n_i)$ (I-generator) are passed as facts to the logic program. Such a set is also called *constituent*. The set of A-generators in this case is empty. φ_T defines the condition to start the evaluation of P_{sum}; in this case, it is always evaluated to t (i.e. fragment always executed).

Logic Fragment 1: sum of numbers in the tuple space.

$LF : (P_{sum}, AEK, \triangle, \{N(X)\}, \emptyset, \varphi_T)$
Program P_{sum} :   add$(Sum, 1, X) \leftarrow$ N(X) unique$(Sum, 0) \leftarrow$

If the condition is not satisfied, the evaluation of LF is $\bowtie$; otherwise, P_{sum} is evaluated and after its execution $Sum(n)$ is inserted to the tuple space. Such tuple is associated with the modifier unique, meaning that it eventually overwrites any other tuple with the same predicate symbol. The set of tuples produced by a logic fragment is called *consequent*.

Definition 9. Let f_{const} be a function that associates sequences of logic programs and elements in $\mathcal{L}_\tau$ to the set of constants appearing in every predicate; $P_1 \cdots P_n$ a sequence of logic programs; I a set of I-generators, A a set of A-generators and $L \subseteq \mathcal{L}_\tau$. We define:

$$f_g(\bar{P}, I, A, L) \stackrel{\text{def}}{=} \bigcup_{P_I \in I} p_I^L \cup \bigcup_{P_A \in A} p_A^{C_{\bar{P}} \cup C_I}$$
$$C_{\bar{P}} \stackrel{\text{def}}{=} \bigcup_{i=1}^{|\bar{P}|} f_{const}(P_i) \quad C_I \stackrel{\text{def}}{=} \bigcup_{P_I \in I} f_{const}(p_I^L)$$

During the evaluation of logic fragments, f_g will be used to extend the programs with facts defined by I-generators and A-generators.

Definition 10. I_g and A_g are two functions identifying respectively the set of model-defined I-generators and A-generators of Table 1 contained in a generic logic program.

3.4 Semantics of Logic Fragments

Algorithms 1 and 2 report the pseudocode of the implementation of the coordination model. Every node executes a loop composed of four steps.

(I) `receiveTuples`: the tuples (and their truth-degrees) explicitly sent by neighbours (e.g. through `sendLF`) are copied from the incoming queue in the tuple space. The tuples implicitly requested through the predicates of Table 1 are temporally stored in a separate tuple space (Π). A special set of predicates (σ) is initialized with the state of tuple transfers (e.g. occurred sending errors, etc.).

(II) `evaluateLogicFragments`: all the logic fragments existing in the tuple space under the form of tuples of type $LF(c_{code}, c_1, ..., c_n)$ are converted in the form defined in Sect. 3.3. If a logic fragment contains neighbour-hood verification operators in its logic programs, the tuples specified by such predicates are requested from neighbours (notice that such tuples may become available in the next iterations; in that case σ is updated). Finally, every logic fragment is evaluated (`evaluateLF`) starting from the same content of the tuple space (Δ). The evaluation recursively evaluates all nested logic fragments starting from the innermost Δ. As first step (line 14) I- and A- generators are calculated. Later, the sequence of logic programs is evaluated from left to right: every program P receives as facts the literals generated from the evaluation of the previous program in the sequence. After computing its semantics ($\models_M$), the commands inferred by P are interpreted (`executeCommands`) and removed from the literals (along with any generator literal) and the copy of the tuple space Δ_{LF} is updated.

Algorithm 1. Main execution loop

```
1:  function MAINLOOP
2:      ; main loop
3:      while always do
4:          set (Π, σ) = receiveTuples()              ; receive tuples sent by neighbours
5:          set list = evaluateLogicFragments(Π, σ)   ; evaluate logic fragments
6:          updateTupleSpace(list)                    ; update tuple space
7:          sendMessages(list)                        ; send messages to neighbours
8:  function RECEIVETUPLES
9:      receive a set of tuples T ⊆ L_τ sent from neighbours and add them to the tuple space
10:     receive a set of tuples Π ⊆ L_τ from neighbours requested by requestNeighTuples()
11:     generate neighbourhood predicates
12:     set σ with information about incomplete/complete transfers
13:     return (Π, σ)
14: function EVALUATELOGICFRAGMENTS(Π, σ)
15:     set Δ ⊆ L_τ with the content of the tuple space
16:     for each element ⟨LF(c_code, c_1, ..., c_n), A, τ⟩ ∈ Δ do
17:         ; conversion of logic fragment and its parameters
18:         set  e ←_conversion c_code   P_i(c_{i1}, ..., c_{in_i}) ←_conversion c_i
19:         requestNeighTuples(e)                     ; requests neighbours' tuples
20:         update σ if some tuples requested in the previous point have not been received yet
21:         setR = (Δ_LF, μ) = evaluateLF(e, Δ, σ, Π)
22:         if Δ_LF ≠⋈ then add (R, A) to list
23:     return list
24: function UPDATETUPLESPACE(list)
25:     update the tuple space according to list
26:     ; notify the associated agent
27:     notify A and pass Δ_LF
28: function SENDMESSAGES(list)
29:     send messages list to neighbours according to their order of creation
30: function REQUESTNEIGHTUPLES(e)
31:     for each neighbour verification operator contained in the logic programs of e
32:         send a request to neighbours to get the tuples specified in the predicate.
```

The generated messages are stored in an outgoing queue μ. Then the next logic program in the sequence is analysed. The set of facts of the whole logic fragment is either used as input for the execution of the external one or combined with operators $\Box$, $\bar{\Box}$, $\sqcup$, $\sqcap$.

(III) **updateTupleSpace**: the tuple space is updated by considering the evaluations of logic fragments at the previous step. During the update, the agents associated with executed logic fragments are notified.

(IV) **sendMessages**: the tuples generated previously are sent to neighbours. The evaluation of logic fragments presented in the algorithm is performed to make their executions atomic: all logic fragments have the same "initial view" of the tuple space and are executed as whole entities.

4   Examples

In the following sections we use the classical two-valued logics with $\tau = \{t, f\}$ and definite logic programs evaluated with the Apt-van Emden-Kowalski's semantics. For sake of readability we hide the internal details of tuples, highlighting that, in every listing, the tuples are always associated with truth-degree t.

4.1   Creation of a Coordination Law at Run-Time

Example 2. Logic fragments can be used to create coordination laws at run-time. We reconsider the one of Example 1, evaluated on a single node (Fig. 2). Such logic fragment can be thought of as a simple coordination law synthesizing part of the data existing in the tuple space (numbers) to produce new information (their sum).

We consider the scenario of Fig. 2(a), in which the tuple space contains the following four tuples: $\Delta = \{N(1), N(2), N(3), LF(c_{code})\}$.

c_{code} is a constant representing the encoding of the logic fragment: its starting condition φ is satisfied (Algorithm 2 - line 6) and the logic fragments reacts with the current content (Fig. 2(b)). Before its evaluation, P_{sum} is enriched with the set of facts $\{N(1) \leftarrow t, N(2) \leftarrow t, N(3) \leftarrow t\}$; in this way, it is transformed into the new program:

New program P_{sum}:
add($Sum, 1, X$) $\leftarrow$ N(X)
unique($Sum, 0$) $\leftarrow$
N(1) $\leftarrow$
N(2) $\leftarrow$
N(3) $\leftarrow$

The evaluation results in the computation of the following least Herbrand's model (Algorithm 2 - line 39): $\{N(1), N(2), N(3), \text{unique}(Sum, 0),$ add($Sum, 1, 1$), add($Sum, 1, 2$), add($Sum, 1, 3$)$\}$. Every command of the model adds a specific number to $Sum(0)$, obtaining $Sum(6)$.

Algorithm 2. Evaluation of Logic Fragments

```
1: function EVALUATELF(e_LF, Δ_LF, σ_LF, Π_LF)
2:     if e_LF = Δ then
3:         return (Δ_LF, ∅)
4:     else if e_LF = (P_1 ··· P_n, e, M, I, A, φ) then
5:         set (Δ_e, μ_e) = evaluateLF(e, Δ_LF, σ_LF, Π_LF)          ; evaluation of the inner logic fragment
6:         if Δ_e =⋈ ∨φ(Δ_e, σ_LF) = F then return (⋈, ∅)          ; internal evaluation fails
7:         else                                                       ; computation of facts from generators
8:                                                                    ; and evaluation of programs
9:             set  I_e = ∪_{i=1}^n I_g(P_i)    A_e = ∪_{i=1}^n A_g(P_i)    Π_extra = f_g(P_1 ··· P_n, I ∪ I_e, A ∪ A_g, Δ_e)
10:            (Π', Δ', μ') = evalPrograms(P_1 ··· P_n, M, Π_LF ∪Π_extra, Δ_e, μ_e)  ; evaluation logic programs
11:            return (Δ', μ_e · μ')
12:        else if e_LF = (e_1 ◻ e_2) then                            ; computes e_1 ◻ e_2
13:            set  (Δ_1, μ_1) = evaluateLF(e_1, Δ_LF, σ_LF, Π_LF)    (Δ_2, μ_2) = evaluateLF(e_2, Δ_LF, σ_LF, Π_LF)
14:            if Δ_1 =⋈ ∨Δ_2 =⋈ then return (⋈, ∅)                  ; e_1 and e_2 must both succeed
15:            else return (Δ_1 ∪ Δ_2, μ_1 ∪ μ_2)
16:        else if e_LF = (e_1 ⊔ e_2) then                            ; computes e_1 ⊔ e_2
17:            set  (Δ_1, μ_1) = evaluateLF(e_1, Δ_LF, σ_LF, Π_LF)    (Δ_2, μ_2) = evaluateLF(e_2, Δ_LF, σ_LF, Π_LF)
18:            set  Δ_e = ∅  μ_e = ∅
19:            if Δ_1 ≠⋈ ∨Δ_2 ≠⋈ then                                ; at least one among e_1 and e_2 must succeed
20:                if Δ_1 ≠⋈ then  set  Δ_e = Δ_1  μ_e = μ_1
21:                if Δ_2 ≠⋈ then  set  Δ_e = Δ_e ∪ Δ_2  μ_e = μ_e ∪ μ_1
22:                return (Δ_e, μ_e)
23:            else return (⋈, ∅)                                     ; at least one among e_1 and e_2 must succeed
24:        else if e_LF = (e_1 ∩ e_2) then                            ; computes e_1 ∩ e_2
25:            set  (Δ_1, μ_1) = evaluateLF(e_1, Δ_LF, σ_LF, Π_LF)    (Δ_2, μ_2) = evaluateLF(e_2, Δ_LF, σ_LF, Π_LF)
26:            if Δ_1 =⋈ ∨Δ_2 =⋈ then return (⋈, ∅)                  ; e_1 and e_2 must both succeed
27:            else return (Δ_1 ∩ Δ_2, μ_1 ∩ μ_2)
28:        else if e_LF = (e_1 ⊓ e_2) then                            ; computes e_1 ⊓ e_2
29:            set  (Δ_1, μ_1) = evaluateLF(e_1, Δ_LF, σ_LF, Π_LF)    (Δ_2, μ_2) = evaluateLF(e_2, Δ_LF, σ_LF, Π_LF)
30:            set  Δ_e = ∅  μ_e = ∅
31:            if Δ_1 ≠⋈ ∨Δ_2 ≠⋈ then                                ; at least one among e_1 and e_2 must succeed
32:                if Δ_1 ≠⋈ then  set  Δ_e = Δ_1  μ_e = μ_1
33:                if Δ_2 ≠⋈ then  set  Δ_e = Δ_e ∩ Δ_2  μ_e = μ_e ∩ μ_2
34:                return (Δ_e, μ_e)
35:            else return (⋈, ∅)                                     ; at least one among e_1 and e_2 must succeed
36: function EVALPROGRAMS(P̄, M, Π_e, Δ_e, μ_e)
37:     P̄ = P · P̄_e
38:     replace model-defined constants of P
39:     P' =def P ∪ {p(c_1, ..., c_n) ← τ | (p(c_1, ..., c_n), τ) ∈ Π_e}    Π' ⊨_M P'
40:     set (Π', Δ', μ') = executeCommands(Π', Δ_e, μ_e)
41:     if P̄_e = P_e then  return (Π'^r, Δ', μ')                      ; if all logic programs have been evaluated
42:     else return evalPrograms(P̄_e, M, Δ', μ')                     ; recursion if there are more logic programs
43: function EXECUTECOMMANDS(Π_e, Δ_e)
44:     executes the commands in Π_e
45:     set Π' = literals of Π_e after interpreting its commands and solving inconsistences
46:     remove command and generator literals from Π'
47:     set Δ' = literals of Δ after interpreting the commands in Π_e and solving inconsistences
48:     set μ' = messages generated by the commands in Π_e
49:     return (Π', Δ', μ')
```

After the interpretation of commands (Algorithm 2 - line 40), the agent associated with the logic fragment receives a notification with a copy of the inferred literals and the final tuple space appears as follows (Fig. 2(c)): $\Delta = \{N(1), N(2), N(3), LF(c_{code}), Sum(6)\}$.

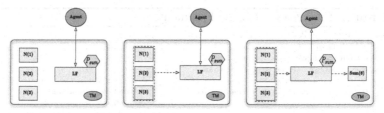

(a) Injection of the logic fragment.   (b) Evaluation of the logic fragment.   (c) Injection of the result.

Fig. 2. Creation and execution of a new coordination law

4.2 Verification of System Properties at Run-Time

Logic fragments can be easily combined and used to verify global properties of the system at run-time, as shown in the following examples.

Logic Fragment 2: distributed verification of sums of numbers.

$$LF : \quad (P_{check} \cdot P_{state} \cdot P_{send}, AEK, LF^{(1)}, \{Sum(X)\}, \emptyset, \varphi)$$
$$LF^{(1)} : (P_{sum}, AEK, \triangle, \{N(X)\}, \emptyset, \varphi_T)$$

$$\varphi(\Pi, \sigma) = t \iff trans(finished) \in \sigma$$

```
Program P_check
temp(pos) ← Sum(X), greater(X, 5)
unique(State, neg) ← neighExists(S, State, neg), neighIs(S)

Program P_state
unique(State, pos) ← notExist(State, neg), pos
unique(State, neg) ← notExist(pos)

Program P_send:
sendLF(X, _thisLF) ← neighNotExist(S, LF,_thisLF),neighIs(S)
```

Example 3. In this example we consider the following property: *the sum of numbers in every node of the network is greater than* 5. Logic Fragment 2 is used to verify such a property; it is composed of two logic fragments: the innermost one $(LF^{(1)})$ is the one presented in Example 2, whereas the outermost one resorts to the composition of P_{check}, P_{state} and P_{send}. When the system silises, every node will contain either a tuple $State(pos)$ (if the global property holds) or a tuple $State(neg)$ (if the property is not satisfied). The evaluation of the whole logic fragment on a generic node is performed as follows.

1. The innermost fragment, $LF^{(1)}$, is the first one to be evaluated. As explained in Example 2, it produces a literal of type $Sum(n)$, where n is the sum of all numbers $N(n_1), ..., N(n_m)$.
2. The execution proceeds with the evaluation of the outermost fragment, started when the current node finishes all the transfers of tuples sent by its neighbours. $Sum(n)$ is passed to P_{check}, which entails *pos* if n is greater than 5. P_{check} also verifies if one of its neighbours has detected a sum less than 5; in that case, the literal $State(neg)$ is inferred in the current node. Literals contained in the neighbourhood can be implicitly accessed by using predicates of type $\mathtt{neigh}(S, p, c_1, ..., c_n)$ and $\mathtt{neighNotExist}(S, p, c_1, ..., c_n)$:

when using such predicates inside logic programs, the platform transparently retrieves all the tuples matching $p(c_1, ... c_n)$ from neighbour S (Fig. 3(a)) and it adds such tuples as facts to the program before its evaluation. In this way, logic program can uniformly reason on remote and local information.

3. P_{state} analyses the semantics of P_{check}: if pos is produced and there are no neighbours detecting $State(neg)$, then $State(pos)$ is injected in the tuple space of the current node.

4. Finally, P_{send} sends a copy of the whole logic fragment to every neighbour that does not contain it yet.

An example of execution is reported in Fig. 3: the logic fragment is injected in S and diffuses itself across all the nodes of the network (Fig. 3(b)). During such a process, a node that locally invalidates the property is found (orange node at the right bottom corner of Fig. 3(c)); the global answer silises when all the nodes propagate $State(neg)$ to their neighbours (steady state of the system in Fig. 3(d)).

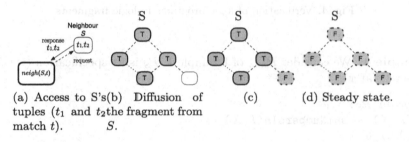

(a) Access to S's tuples (t_1 and t_2 match t). (b) Diffusion of the fragment from S. (c) (d) Steady state.

Fig. 3. Evaluation of Logic Fragment 2 on an generic network. The local property is satisfied only on nodes with T. The global answer F silises when all nodes sense tuple $State(neg)$ in their neighbours

The diffusion of the logic fragment provides nodes of the system with reasoning algorithms (in this case $P_{sum}, P_{check}, P_{state}$), performing logic inference at run-time.

The algorithm implemented by Logic Fragment 2 must silise before producing the correct answer, i.e. the value of predicate $State$ may change over time. In some cases actions must be taken only on the base of the steady state of the system: in these situations, logic fragments can implement more robust spatial structures such as evaluation-trees [6].

4.3   Verification of Logic Fragments at Design-Time

In this section we show how to verify that logic fragments meet their specifications. Leveraging such an approach, complex global (emergent) properties can decomposed and checked incrementally, reducing the difficulties of verifying them in a single step.

We adopt the Kowalski's strategy [12], which states that a program is correct if every successful goal of its semantics is inferred by its specification and vice versa; given that P_{sum} is a definite program, for its specification we use a program containing Horn clauses. In our model we must take into consideration commands that update the tuple space; for this reason (Fig. 4), given a logic program P_{LF}, we first define an equivalent (recursive) version $\hat{P}_{LF}$ containing no commands, then we compare $\hat{P}_{LF}$ against its specification P_S to verify if the program is *sound* and *complete*. All such programs are enriched with the same set of facts Π arising from I- and A- generators.

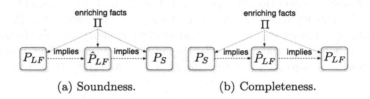

(a) Soundness.   (b) Completeness.

Fig. 4. Verification of logic programs in logic fragments

Example 4. We consider P_{sum} of Example 1; P_S is its specification (we define the set Π later):

Program P_S:
sum(L, X) $\leftarrow$ sumNumbersIn(L, X)
sum$(\emptyset, 0)$ $\leftarrow$

With abuse of notation we identify variables and constants of logic programs with the mathematical objects they refer to. L identifies a set of numbers $\{x_1, ..., x_n\}$ ($\emptyset$ is the constant referring to the empty set) and sumNumbersIn is a predicate true iff $X = \sum_{x_i \in L} x_i$.

We now consider $\hat{P}_{sum}$, an alternative declarative version of P_{sum}:

Program $\hat{P}_{sum}$:
sum(L_1, X) $\leftarrow$ N(Z), partition(L_2, Z, L_1), sum(L_2, S), add(S, Z, X)
sum$(\emptyset, 0)$ $\leftarrow$

L_1 is again a set of numbers, partition is a predicate verified iff L_2 and $\{Z\}$ form a partition of L_1 and add is true iff $X = S + Z$. We have the following Lemma:

Lemma 1. *Let L_N be the set a numbers $\{x_1, ..., x_m\}$, M be the least Herbrand's model of P_{sum} extended with the set of facts $\Pi = \{N(x_1) \leftarrow |x_i \in L_N\}$ and let be L_{com} the (finite) list of commands* add(Sum,1,x_i) *contained in M. Com is a relation such that $(L_N, n) \in Com$ iff $Sum(n)$ is the tuple obtained from $Sum(0)$ after the interpretation of all commands in L_{com}. $\hat{P}_{sum} \cup \Pi$ and $P_{sum} \cup \Pi$ are equivalent: $(L_N, n) \in Com$ iff $(\hat{P}_{sum} \cup \Pi) \models sum(L_N, n)$.* □

Theorem 1. P_{sum} *is sound and complete.*

Proof. For space reason we prove only *soundness*; the proof for *completeness* is similar. By induction on the cardinality of the set L, we prove the following statement: $(\hat{P}_{sum} \cup \Pi) \vDash sum(L, n)$ implies $(P_S \cup \Pi) \vDash sum(L, n)$.

Base: $sum(\emptyset, 0)$ is directly implied by the second rule of P_S.

Step: let be $sum(L_1, n)$ implied by $\hat{P}_{sum} \cup \Pi$ with cardinality of L_1 equal to $k + 1$. Then it exists $N(Z)$ and L_2 such that: (i) L_2 with $\{Z\}$ is a partition of L_1; (ii) $sum(L_2, S)$ is true; (iii) $n = S + Z$. For induction hypothesis, $P_S \cup \Pi \vDash sum(L_2, S)$, i.e. $S = \sum_{x_i \in L_2} x_i$. Then $n = S + Z = \sum_{x_i \in L_1} x_i$, i.e. $P_S \cup \Pi \vDash sum(L_1, n)$. After proving the *completeness*, by applying Lemma 1 we conclude that P_{sum} is sound and complete w.r.t. P_S. $\square$

Composability of logic fragments represents an important concept also for verification; in fact, through compositional verification [8] we can define a hierarchy of verified ready-to-use logic fragments that can be combined to create complex coordination mechanisms. The verification of complex logic fragments creating spatial structures can be achieved by resorting to spatial/temporal logics (e.g. [4,15]).

5   Conclusions and Future Work

In this paper we presented an extension of the Logic Fragment Coordination Model and a corresponding semantics; the coordination model is enriched with commands and operators to manipulate tuples and logic fragments inside logic programs. Such an extension confines the implementation of coordination mechanisms completely within logic fragments, making them self-contained and independent from agents. From the design viewpoint this enhances the design of complex systems, improving modularity, reusability, reconfigurability and robustness. Moreover, such an extension simplifies the verification stage by promoting the decomposition of complex interactions into basic ones, themselves provided under the form of verified ready-to-use components.

Future work will include the formalisation of the operational semantics of the coordination model and the definition of a many-valued spatial/temporal logic for design-time verification of complex spatial structures created by logic fragments.

References

1. Ashley-Rollman Meld, M.P., et al.: A declarative approach to programming ensembles. In: Proceedings of the IEEE International Conference on Intelligent Robots and Systems (IROS 2007), October 2007
2. Beal, J., Dulman, S., Usbeck, K., Viroli, M., Correll, N.: Organizing the aggregate,: Languages for spatial computing. CoRR, abs/1202.5509 (2012)
3. Belnap, N.D.: A useful four-valued logic. In: Epstein, G., Dunn, J.M. (eds.) Modern Uses of Multiple-Valued Logic, pp. 7–37. Reidel Publishing Company, Boston (1977)

4. Ciancia, V., Latella, D., Loreti, M., Massink, M.: Specifying and verifying properties of space. In: Diaz, J., Lanese, I., Sangiorgi, D. (eds.) TCS 2014. LNCS, vol. 8705, pp. 222–235. Springer, Heidelberg (2014). doi:10.1007/978-3-662-44602-7_18
5. Angelis, F.L., Marzo Serugendo, G.: Logic fragments: a coordination model based on logic inference. In: Holvoet, T., Viroli, M. (eds.) COORDINATION 2015. LNCS, vol. 9037, pp. 35–48. Springer, Heidelberg (2015). doi:10.1007/978-3-319-19282-6_3
6. De Angelis, F.L., Di Marzo Serugendo, G.: A logic language for run time assessment of spatial properties in self-organizing systems. In: 2015 IEEE International Conference on Self-Adaptive and Self-Organizing Systems Workshops, pp. 86–91 (2015)
7. De Angelis, F.L., Di Marzo Serugendo, G., Szałas, A.: Graded rule-based reasoning. Int. J. Approx. Reason. (2016). Submitted
8. De Roever, W.-P., et al.: Concurrency Verification: Introduction to Compositional and Non-compositional Methods. Cambridge University Press, Cambridge (2012)
9. Doets, K.: From Logic to Logic Programming. Foundations of Computing. MIT Press, Cambridge (1994)
10. Hogger, C.J.: Introduction to Logic Programming. A.P.I.C. Studies in Data Processing. Academic Press, Cambridge (1984)
11. Kowalski, R.: Algorithm = logic + control. Commun. ACM **22**(7), 424–436 (1979)
12. Kowalski, R.: The relation between logic programming and logic specification. In Proceedings of a Discussion Meeting of the Royal Society of London on Mathematical Logic and Programming Languages, pp. 11–27 (1985)
13. Loo, B.T., et al.: Declarative networking Language, execution and optimization. In: Proceedings of the 2006 ACM SIGMOD International Conference on Management of Data, pp. 97–108 (2006)
14. Małuszyński, J., Szałas, A.: Logical foundations and complexity of 4QL, a query language with unrestricted negation. J. Appl. Non-Class. Log. **21**(2), 211–232 (2011)
15. Nenzi, L., Bortolussi, L.: Specifying and monitoring properties of stochastic spatio-temporal systems in signal temporal logic. In: ICST 2 (2015)
16. Pedreschi, D., Ruggieri, S.: Verification of logic programs. J. Log. Program. **39**(1–3), 125–176 (1999)
17. Zambonelli, F., et al.: Developing pervasive multi-agent systems with nature-inspired coordination. Pervasive, Mob. Comput. **17**, 236–252 (2015). Special Issue "10 years of Pervasive Computing" In Honor of Chatschik Bisdikian

Mixed-Critical Systems Design
with Coarse-Grained Multi-core Interference

Peter Poplavko[✉], Rany Kahil, Dario Socci, Saddek Bensalem,
and Marius Bozga

Univ. Grenoble-Alpes, CNRS, Verimag, 38000 Grenoble, France
ppoplavko@gmail.com

Abstract. Those autonomic concurrent systems which are timing-critical and compute intensive need special resource managers in order to ensure adaptation to unexpected situations in terms of compute resources. So-called mixed-criticality managers may be required that adapt system resource usage to critical run-time situations (*e.g.,* over-heating, overload, hardware errors) by giving the highly critical subset of system functions priority over low-critical ones in emergency situations. Another challenge comes from the fact that for modern platforms – multi- and many- cores – make the scheduling problem more complicated because of their inherent parallelism and because of "parasitic" interference between the cores due to shared hardware resources (buses, FPU's, DMA's, *etc.*). In our work-in-progress design flow we provide the so-called concurrency language for expressing, at high abstraction level, new emerging custom resource management policies that can handle these challenges. We compile the application into a representation in this language and combine the result with a resource manager into a joint software design used to deploy the given system on the target platform. In this context, we discuss our work in progress on a scheduler that aims to handle the interference in mixed-critical applications by controlling it at the task level.

Keywords: Bandwidth interference · Multi-core · Embedded multi-processor · Mixed criticality

1 Introduction

In this paper we present our work-in-progress design flow for scheduling and deployment of software designs for embedded systems. Modern embedded applications constitute so-called *nodes* of *distributed systems, i.e.,* they communicate via buses and networks with other applications (nodes). We consider systems that are not only *timing-critical, i.e.,* subject to hard real-time constraints, but

Research supported by ARROWHEAD, the European ICT Collaborative Project no. 332987, and MoSaTT-CMP, European Space Agency project, Contract No. 4000111814/14/NL/MH.

© Springer International Publishing AG 2016
T. Margaria and B. Steffen (Eds.): ISoLA 2016, Part I, LNCS 9952, pp. 605–621, 2016.
DOI: 10.1007/978-3-319-47166-2_42

also *mixed-critical, i.e.,* able to sustain highly-critical functions even under harsh compute-resource shortage situations. The latter is desirable if the system has to be *autonomic* [26], *i.e.,* able to operate in open and non-deterministic environments. An example of an autonomic mixed timing-critical system is a "fleet of UAV's (unmanned air vehicles) [7]" that coordinate with the leader UAV within strict time bounds to avoid mutual collision. Such systems should not only be correctly specified but also *schedulable in real-time.* The point is that control tasks in many applications are augmented by complex computations that can load the processor significantly (*e.g.,* computer vision, trajectory/route calculation, image/video coding, graphics rendering). In such cases, to meet the high computational demands inside the nodes while keeping their energy consumption, cost and weight manageable it is important to consider multi- (2–10) or even many-core (x100's cores/'accelerators') platforms.

A major obstacle for schedulability analysis of multi-core applications is 'bandwidth interference' [2], *i.e.,* blocking due to conflicts in simultaneous accesses to shared hardware resources, such as buses, FPU's, DMA channels, IO peripherals. Next to interference, the other dimensions in the scheduling problem are (i) possible lack of preemption support in many-core systems, (ii) inter-task precedences (dependencies), commonly implied from the application's model of computation (MoC) and (iii) switching between normal and emergency mode in mixed-critical scheduling. To be able to address all these dimensions at the same time we propose simplifications which make the scheduling problem amenable for known heuristic methods with some adaptations.

We also put the proposed scheduling approach into the context of our work-in-progress design flow, which offers not only scheduling but also deployment on the platform. The deployment is ensured by a compilation tool-chain that is by construction customizable to various MoCs and online scheduling policies by mapping them to an expressive intermediate 'concurrency' language.

In Sect. 2 we introduce one-by-one the main pillars of our design flow, such as MoCs and mixed-criticality. Section 3 introduces the structure and assumptions of the proposed flow and illustrates it via a small synthetic application example. Section 4 gives a basic explanation of the scheduling algorithm and discusses the results. Section 5 concludes the paper and discusses future work.

2   Background

2.1   Models of Computation

To manage concurrency and coordination between tasks in parallel and distributed environments Models of Computations (MoCs) have been proposed in the literature. They permit the application designer to define the structure and organize the tasks and their communication channels in a way that resembles high-level specifications (functional diagrams). MoCs intend to abstract the application's behavior from any implementation detail. Figure 1 shows an example: a part of an industrial avionics application modeled in a MoC called Fixed Priority Process Network (FPPN) [18].

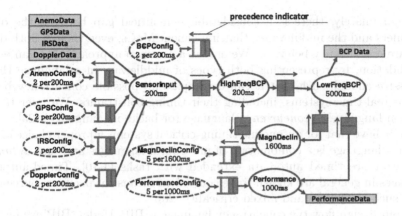

Fig. 1. Application modeled in a MoC: flight management system in FPPN

In the figure we see (1) tasks, *e.g.,* 'HighFreqBCP', *etc.,* annotated by periods, (2) inter-task channels, *e.g.,* between 'DopplerConfig' and 'SensorInput', and (3) precedence relation between tasks, *e.g.,* 'HighFreqBCP' has higher precedence than 'BCPConfig'. The application consumes data from *input buffers,* *e.g.,* 'AnemoData', and produces the results to *output buffers, e.g.,* 'BCP Data'. The buffers are supposed to keep the slots for input and output data available during the whole interval between the task arrival and the deadline. As a MoC, FPPN should define the partial ordering of execution and interaction of concurrent activities (tasks), and this is done via the precedence relation, which ensures predictable inter-task communication.

Next to FPPN, many MoCs have been proposed in the literature for embedded multi-core systems, to name just a few: MRDF (multi-rate data-flow, often named SDF – Synchronous Dataflow) [14], Prelude [8], SADF (scenario-aware data-flow) [25] and DOL-Critical [11].

2.2 Resource Managers and Concurrency Language

An important property of autonomic embedded systems is their ability to adapt themselves to unexpected phenomena [26]. When a system is compute-intensive (which should be the case when a multi-core implementation is necessary) and time-critical it has to be able to adapt itself to exceptional shortage in compute resources. In real-time systems, *'resource managers'* are software functions that monitor utilization of compute resources and ensure such adaptation. For this they apply different mechanisms, such as mixed-criticality, QoS management, DVFS (Dynamic Voltage and Frequency Scaling), *etc.*. Especially the mixed-criticality approaches are gaining more an more interest and have a high relevance for collective adaptive systems [7]. A resource manager is an integral part of an *online scheduler i.e.,* a middleware that implements a customized online scheduling policy.

Unfortunately, there is a considerable semantical gap between the online schedulers and the middlewares that implement MoCs, even though both define software concurrency behavior. We aim at a common approach that can ensure consolidation, by representing both types of middleware in a language that is expressive enough such that it can encompass all possible concurrency behaviors for real-time systems, including their timing constraints. We refer to that common language as *concurrency* language (or backbone language) [23].

We believe that for autonomic timing-critical systems a proper choice of concurrency language is a combination of procedural languages and *task automata*. The latter are timed automata extended with tasks [3,10]. Timed-automata languages in general are known to be convenient means to specify resource managers, such as QoS [1] and mixed criticality [20].

In our design flow the concurrency language is BIP. Under 'BIP' we mean in fact its 'real-time dialect' [1], designed to express networks of connected timed automata components. In [6] BIP was demonstrated relevant for distributed autonomic systems. In [11] it was extended from timed to task automata, by introducing the concept of *self-timed* (or 'continuous') automata transitions, *i.e.*, transitions that have non-zero execution time, to model task execution.

In our approach, the applications are still programmed in their appropriate high-level MoC because in many cases an automata language, though being appropriate for resource managers, may still be too low-level for direct use in application programming. Instead, we assume automatic *compilation* of higher-level MoCs into the concurrency language. Due to well-known high expressive power of automata to model concurrent systems this must be possible for most MoCs. In an ideal case, the compilation would be configured by a user-defined set of grammar rules for automatic translation of the user's preferred MoC into automata.

2.3 Concurrency Language Based Representation of System Nodes

Figure 2 gives a generic structure of a concurrency language model of a distributed-system node running an application expressed in a certain MoC. We also zoom into the BIP model of an important component.

The basic components of the model are automata, *i.e.*, finite-state machines that can interact with other components by participating in a set of interactions with other automata as they make discrete *transitions* (basic steps of execution). In our model, we have one automaton per application task and one per inter-task channel, and also an automaton to control each task – the so-called *task controller*. There is also an automaton that ensures proper task execution order according to MoC semantics, we refer to that component as MoC controller. One can also introduce an automaton that would further restrict the ordering and the timing of task executions – the online scheduler. This component would impose user-programmed scheduling policy. Note that automata can be hierarchical, *i.e.*, they can represent a composition of more primitive automata.

In Fig. 2 we zoom into a task controller for periodic tasks whose deadline is equal to the period. It consists of a cyclic sequence of states, with initial state

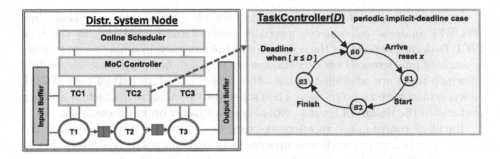

Fig. 2. Concurrency language representation of a timing-critical application

'S0' and first transition 'Arrive', which models task arrival and is followed by transition 'Start', which corresponds to starting a new iteration of task execution, called a *job*. The 'Start' transition is followed by 'Finish' transition when the job finishes. After the finish, the deadline-check transition 'Deadline' is executed. The deadline is checked as follows: upon task arrival a so-called clock variable x is reset to zero. This variable acts as a timer indicating the time elapsed since the last clock reset. After the job has finished we check whether the deadline D was respected, *i.e.,* whether $x \leq D$.

Note that in our design flow the given task controller is both time- and event-driven, as the tasks arrive periodically (in a time-driven way) but start when the MoC controller would enable the 'Start' interaction, thus indicating that the task predecessors have finished (in an event-driven way).

2.4   Multi-core Interference Aspects

When dealing with multi-core platform architectures as targets for timing critical applications a particular serious problem arises. Spontaneous unpredictable or hardly predictable 'parasitic' timing delays – *'interference'* – manifest themselves when multiple cores run in parallel. Interference appears when cores await response from resources that are in use by other cores.

The concerned resources can be either hardware or protected logical (software) resources. Shared hardware resources that can cause interference are global buses, bus bridges and switches, coprocessors, peripherals, and even FPU's (if they are shared between cores to save on-chip area). Software shared resources are, for example, mutex-lock segments in the source code and calls for mutually exclusive services in the system runtime environments.

Interference can be *coarse-grain* or *fine-grain*. In the former case the accesses to the shared resource occurs in 'coarse' blocks, called superblocks [15], which occur just once or a few times per task execution. Often a task has one superblock to read all the input data from global to local memory at the start and to write the data at the end. Fine-grain interference is sporadic and can occur a large number of times per task execution, *e.g.,* bus accesses due to loads/stores in the memory.

In a design flow for mono-core systems the 'worst-case execution time (WCET) analysis' conveniently precedes 'schedulability analysis', as the task WCETs do not depend on the schedule. On the contrary, in a multi-core system, because of interference task execution delay may significantly change depending on which tasks are scheduled on the other cores. Therefore part of task WCET analysis may have to be re-done when schedules are analysed, which is a major obstacle in the design of timing-critical systems based on multi-cores [2].

Luckily, coarse-grain interference can be *controlled* by scheduling the superblocks in a way that the resource conflicts are eliminated. To achieve this, in a 'controlled' schedule superblocks are executed sequentially. At the same time, uncontrollable fine-grained interference can be for as much as possible transformed into coarse-grained one by 'concentrating' the resource-access intensive parts of source code together into coarse-grained superblocks, which can be controlled. The controlled interference approach is well-known in the literature. For example, in [24], coarse-grained blocks of accesses to global bus are considered as special sub-tasks which are scheduled in an optimal static order.

In our scheduling algorithm we assume controlled coarse-grained interference, whereas the remaining fine-grained interference that could not be transformed into coarse-grained one is assumed to be taken into account either via extra WCET margins or, more conservatively, by modeling complete tasks as superblocks. In addition, though different resources (*e.g.*, different FPU's and different memory banks) can be accessed independently and though different superblocks can have different timing costs, we make a simplifying assumption that there is only one shared resource and the duration of all superblocks is the same, we denote it δ. In a way, we consider superblocks as instances of a special task whose WCET is δ.

A particular form of such interference that manifests itself in our design approach is called *engine interference* [11]. In our concurrency model, governed by automata, one can distinguish task-concurrency control operations which correspond to discrete transitions of the automata components that constitute the system. All discrete transitions are coordinated via a single control thread called the *engine*. Suppose that δ is the worst-case time to handle one discrete transition. Then the runtime overhead of task concurrency control operations can be conveniently modeled as interference between superblocks of size δ. In addition to the necessary accesses to the engine needed to coordinate task concurrency, each coarse-grained block of accesses to any resource can be, in principle, delegated to the engine as well. For this, the compiler would have to represent each superblock as a discrete transition or, if it is large, as a sequence of transitions. Therefore, the engine interference can be generalized to subsume other forms of coarse-grained interference.

In the present work, engine interference is the only form of interference that is automatically modelled by our tools. Compared to [11], the novelty is that in the present work we control this form of interference in the scheduling. Our scheduling algorithm assumes that there is one shared resource, and we model the engine as such. Further, it assumes that all superblocks are explicitly represented by special tasks with equal WCET δ, and we model the task-controller transitions as such.

To manage the remaining fine-grained interference we advocate the *time-triggered scheduling* approach, *i.e.*, letting the tasks start at fixed time instances even if previous tasks finish earlier. This approach does not make worst-case response-times of tasks worse, while it significantly reduces the complexity of a fine-grain interference analysis (which would compute the WCET margins) and improves its accuracy. The point is that when tasks do not shift their execution earlier upon earlier completion of previous tasks the number of task pairs that can potentially run in parallel (and hence interfere) is significantly reduced, which effectively cuts the number of analysis cases to be covered.

2.5 Mixed-Criticality Aspects

In adaptive autonomous systems one has to provide for unexpected situations. In terms of scheduling this means allocating worst-case amount of resources with a significant extra margin. To damp the high costs that such margins incur, the allocated extra resources are given, 'on an interim basis', to less-critical and less important functions in the system which can be stopped at any time to free up the resources in the case when highly-critical and highly-important functions need them. This reasoning leads to a generic resource management approach commonly referred to as mixed-criticality, see Fig. 3.

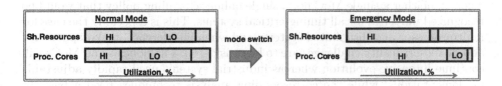

Fig. 3. Mixed-criticality resource management

We currently consider a common case of having just two levels of criticality. Less-critical functions are given low criticality level, commonly denoted 'LO'. Highly-critical functions are given high criticality level, commonly denoted 'HI'. For example, in a UAV system LO can correspond to mission critical and HI to flight-critical functions.

As shown in Fig. 3, in case of emergency the HI tasks get high resource utilization margins. However in normal mode of operation these margins are never used and are given to LO tasks. Only when emergency situation occurs where HI tasks need more resources a 'mode switch' from normal to emergency mode is performed by the resource manager whereby the extra margins are 'claimed' by HI tasks. In our approach, the respective resource management policy is implemented in concurrency language as part of the 'online scheduler' automaton component [20].

There are two distinct approaches to free up the resources from LO tasks in the case of mode switch. The first approach is *dropping* the LO tasks (*i.e.,* instantaneous aborting them with possibility to resume their execution later on). The second approach is putting the LO tasks in *degraded mode, i.e.,* signalling them to do less computations and accesses to shared resources at the cost of the lower output quality or missed deadlines. A major challenge in mixed criticality scheduling is that the mode switch may occur at any time not known in advance and that it is required to guarantee schedulability no matter whether and when the switch occurs [5].

As explained in the previous section, to better handle interference we use the time-triggered scheduling, to be more specific, we use STTM (static time triggered per mode) online policy [5,22], which is a generalization to mixed-criticality scheduling. In this policy, the normal and the emergency modes each have a time-triggered table. A switch from normal to emergency table can occur at any time instant, while it should be guaranteed that if HI critical tasks need to claim their extended resource budgets reserved for unpredictable situations then they will always get them in full amount. Though this appeared to be by far not trivial, in [22] we have proved theoretically and experimentally that this approach is as optimal in the worst case as the event-triggered approach.

3   Work-in-progress: Design Flow

3.1   Underlying Paradigm

There is neither a single MoC nor a single online scheduling policy that would be recognized universal for all timing-critical systems. This is especially the case for multiprocessor and distributed systems and when interference, task-dependency and mixed-criticality challenges are to be considered. The policies and MoCs will continue intensive evolution whereas industrial systems need rapidly adjustable implementations, while the corresponding analysis techniques need a basis to establish formal proofs for them. Therefore our target design flow is customizable, at least conceptually, to different MoCs and policies by compiling the MoC and representing the scheduling policy in a common task-automata based concurrency language, for which, in our design flow, we use BIP. Therefore, we do not create a custom middleware specialized for FPPN MoC and for STTM scheduling policy, but instead we express them in BIP [11,23]. The BIP implementation of the system on top of BIP runtime environment (RTE) should not leave the underlying platform any significant real-time scheduling decision freedom but should map the user-programmed scheduling policies to basic operating system mechanisms, like threads and dynamic priorities [11,27].

The main contribution of the present paper is handling coarse-grained interference in the context of mixed-critical systems with precedence constraints between multi-rate tasks. We address the complex problem by practically meaningful simplifications. We assume that the task system is synchronous-periodic or can be over-approximated as such by periodic servers. A synchronous system can be represented by a semantically-equivalent static task graph, [4,18], conveniently presentable to a list-scheduling heuristic, which, in turn, has reputation of reasonable performance for comparable instruction-level scheduling problems [13]. Moreover, we present a design flow where applications can be both programmed and scheduled. Other design flows that have this property, *e.g.,* [3,7,8,11,12,16], do not take into consideration all the aspects we do but in return offer other features, *e.g.,* distributed-system/network support or expressive power. We compare to [11] in the next section. Related scheduling techniques [4,5,10,15,21,22,24,25] also have some restrictions, while in return offering important theoretical properties and features. We discuss related work further in extended version of this paper [17].

3.2 Flow Structure and Assumptions

Our target design flow is shown in Fig. 4. At the input we take the application specified as a MoC instance (*i.e.,* a network of task elements connected to channel elements and annotated by parameters) and functional code for the tasks. From the MoC instance the tools derive a task-graph for offline scheduling. The task graph describes the application hyperperiod in terms of job nodes and precedence edges. The 'jobs' are task executions and the precedences are derived from the semantics of the given MoC. The application is translated into concurrency language – BIP. The schedule obtained from the offline scheduler is translated into parameters of the online-scheduler model specified in BIP.

The joint application-scheduler model (with a basic structure as previously outlined in Fig. 2) is translated by the BIP compiler into a C++ executable. The executable is linked with BIP RTE (the 'engine') and executes on a platform on top of the real-time operating system.

When running on the platform, the binary executable encounters interferences, as discussed in Sect. 2.4. Handling interference requires a feedback loop from the binary executable to the offline scheduler tool. Next to the worst-case execution times (WCET's) of tasks, the worst-case execution time δ of coarse-grained superblocks should be obtained and back-annotated at the input of the scheduler tool, and then the flow should be re-iterated (at most once, as the 'pure' WCET should not depend on the schedule).

We put the following requirements on our target design flow. We assume FPPN as application MoC. The offline scheduler should support non-preemption, precedence constraints implied from the FPPN and take into consideration coarse-grained interference. The online scheduler should support task migration and task dropping. The online scheduling should be based on STTM scheduling policy for mixed criticality.

The main reason of assuming non-preemption is lack of support of preemption in the current version of BIP language and RTE engine. Though preemption can be modeled and simulated [20], it cannot yet be executed in real-time mode. This is subject of future work. A justification for considering non-preemption is frequent lack of support of preemption in multi-core platforms that have a large number (> 8) cores (so-called many-core platforms and graphical accelerators).

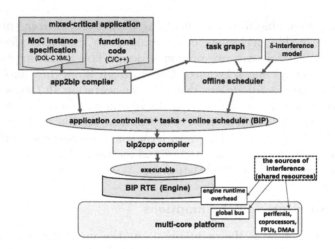

Fig. 4. Work-in-progress design flow

In our design flow we reuse certain elements from our previous 'DOL-BIP-Critical' flow [11] which was co-developed in collaboration with partners. The name of the MoC involved in that flow was DOL-Critical. It is closely related to FPPN, and the same specification language, named DOL-C, is currently used to specify instances of both FPPN and DOL-Critical models. FPPN has more general notion of task precedence than DOL-Critical, as it supports precedences between any pair of tasks, and not only between equal-rate periodic tasks.

There were essential differences in the scheduling assumptions taken in the previous flow, where the tasks were executed essentially in as-soon-as-possible (ASAP) fashion *i.e.,* immediately after the previous task mapped to the same partition. Instead we impose time-triggered start of each task, which should significantly simplify the analysis of bandwidth interference. The offline scheduler of previous flow had the advantage of supporting time partitioning, degraded mode and excluding the interference between HI and LO criticality levels.

Currently in our work-in-progress we have a version of the offline scheduler that satisfies the desired criteria, except that the interference models presented at the input of this tool are currently restricted to those for BIP engine interference of implicit-deadline periodic task controllers. Though advanced interference detection methods are known in related work [19], we still miss them in our flow. If such tools were available we could adapt or extend the δ-interference model assumed in the offline scheduler. Next to this, the online scheduler is not yet properly integrated, as it still does not support dropping and task migration, though such features are within reach, *e.g.,* we demonstrate a restrictive form of BIP-component migration in [11] and thread API's offer means for dropping.

In the remainder of the paper we discuss the currently available tools and illustrate their use by concrete examples. For multi-core experiments presented here, we use a LEON4 platform with four cores implemented on FPGA, using RTEMS OS with symmetric multiprocessing. For this platform, as measurements show, the worst-case execution time of one BIP interaction step takes: $\delta = 1$ ms.

3.3   An Example Illustrating the Flow

Figure 5 gives a synthetic application example with three tasks. The 'split' task puts two small (a few bytes) data items to the two output channels and sleeps for around 1 ms to imitate some task execution time. Tasks 'A' and 'B' read the data. Task 'A' sleeps alternately for 6 ms and 12 ms, to model 'normal' and 'emergency' workload levels. This task models a high-criticality task. Task 'B' supports two modes of execution: normal and degraded. In normal mode it sleeps for 6 ms, in degraded mode it skips all execution, even reading the input data. This task models a low-criticality task.

All tasks have the same periodic scheduling window, with period and deadline being 25 ms. In a real application, this would correspond to the time during which the two imaginary input data buffers should be read, computations should be done and the output buffers should be written.

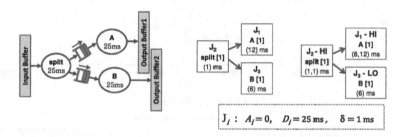

Fig. 5. Three-task example: MoC (left), Ordinary task graph (middle) and Mixed-critical task graph

The middle part of the figure gives the 'ordinary' (*i.e.*, non mixed-critical) variant of the task graph. Every task is represented by a job. The jobs are numbered: $J_i = J_1, J_2, J_3$ and annotated by their worst-case execution times. Their individual arrival times A_i and deadlines D_i are the same in this example. The right part of the figure corresponds to the 'mixed-critical' variant of the same graph. The execution times of highly-critical tasks are represented by a two-valued vector: normal-mode time and emergency-mode time.

The engine runtime overhead (as it will become clear later) constitutes 4δ = 4 ms per task (in total 12 ms). Therefore, when assuming ordinary execution times this example cannot run on a single core, as the total execution time amounts to $12 + 1 + 12 + 6 = 31$ ms, which is larger than the 25 ms deadline. The offline scheduler evaluates the load (*i.e.*, maximal demand-to-capacity ratio) of this example to $31/25 = 124$ %. Therefore it predicts that at least two cores are necessary.

On the other hand, in the mixed-criticality case we consider the two execution modes – normal and emergency – separately. In the normal mode Task 'A' has execution time 6 ms, which is 6 ms less, and we have a load $25/25 = 100$ %, for which a single-core may be sufficient. In the emergency mode the execution time of Task 'A' is again 12 ms, but we drop Task 'B', which saves us $6 + 4=10$ ms and leads to the load of $21/25=84$ %, which again may be doable on a single core. Thus, mixed criticality can help to use the cores more economically.

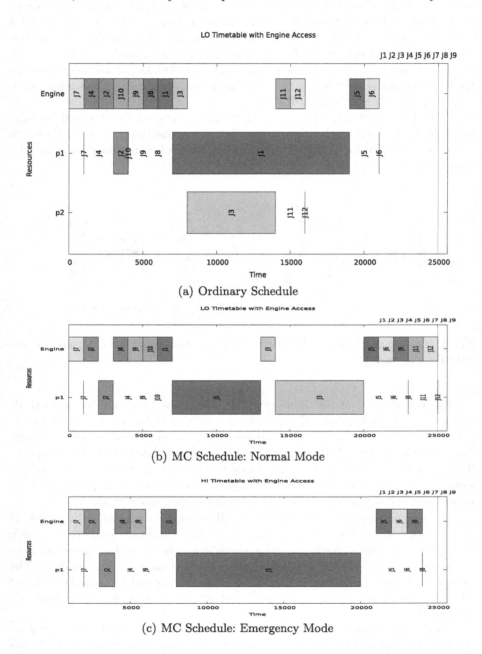

(a) Ordinary Schedule

(b) MC Schedule: Normal Mode

(c) MC Schedule: Emergency Mode

Fig. 6. Three-task example: offline-scheduler solutions

The tool generates the schedules for the ordinary graph and for the mixed-critical one, as shown in Fig. 6. Figure 7 shows the Gantt charts of executing the two variants of the schedule on the LEON4 board.

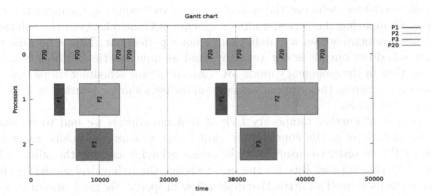

(a) Ordinary Execution Traces (No mode switch in the second period)

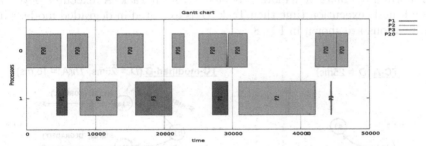

(b) Mixed-critical Execution Traces (Dropping J_3 in the second period)

Fig. 7. Three-task example: platform execution traces

In every Gantt chart the first line shows the execution of the BIP Engine on 'Core 0'. One may wonder why a whole core would have to be reserved to a runtime environment. This is due to lack of support of preemption in current BIP RTE. Moreover, it should be noted that in many-core systems (or graphical accelerators), this is justifiable, as in practice there are plenty of cores available – e.g., 16 per shared-memory cluster in [9] – and no preemption is allowed. On the contrary, a platform such as LEON4 supports preemption and does not assume one thread per core. For such platforms in future work we intend to interleave high-priority engine control thread with a lower-priority task-execution thread on Core 0. Note that the engine thread executes also the BIP components responsible for control operations, such as the task controllers, the MoC controller and the online scheduler.

Recall that the shared resource on which interference-modeling is currently supported by the tools is the engine. As we see in Fig. 6, every task execution is prefixed and suffixed by two δ-accesses to Core 0. In the ordinary schedule, Task 'split' and Task 'A' are mapped to Core 1 and Task 'B' to Core 2.

The platform-measurement charts in Fig. 7 show two periods, one in normal and one in emergency mode. The offline scheduler 'ordinary' solution assumes the overall worst-case, whereas the mixed critical (MC) solution distinguishes two modes. Comparing the corresponding segments of Gantt charts of the solutions and measurements we see a match, though not a perfect one. This is because the offline scheduler output is not yet supported as input to the online scheduler. We see that in the emergency mode MC case the offline scheduler drops task 'B' altogether, whereas the online scheduler still makes a short execution of Task 'B' in degraded mode.

Because of current temporary lack of tool integration we had to do manual modifications in the concurrency model that was automatically generated from FPPN, in order to ensure that the online behavior matches the offline solution. Note that a possibility for the user to refine the behavioral model by such modifications is itself an attractive design-flow property. We made modifications in the mixed-criticality variant of the design, in order to introduce the switch from normal to emergency mode. We ensure that if Task 'A' executes beyond its normal-mode execution time then Task 'B' is executed in degraded mode. These modifications are shown in Fig. 8.

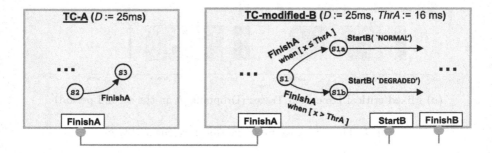

Fig. 8. Three-task example: manual modification introducing a mode switch

We have modified the structure of the TC for Task 'B', which originally was as shown in Fig. 2, by introducing a new transition between the 'Arrive' and 'Start' for Task 'B'. This transition is synchronized with 'FinishA' transition in the TC of Task 'A'. We check the value of clock 'x' which measures the time since the begin of the current period. If this value is larger than a certain threshold $ThrA$ then 'B' is executed in degraded mode.

4 Offline Scheduling Algorithm

For space reasons, here we just summarize the offline scheduling algorithm and its results, more detailed description and related work analysis can be found in extended version of this paper [17].

A scheduling problem instance consists of a DAG task graph obtained automatically from a MoC; we have seen examples in Fig. 5. The nodes, J_i are obtained from tasks and are annotated by parameters (A_i, D_i, χ_i, C_i), where $[A_i, D_i]$ give the job scheduling window (between arrival and deadline relative to the hyperperiod), χ_i gives the job criticality level ('LO' or 'HI') and C_i is a vector that gives the execution time in the normal and emergency modes. The problem instance also includes the selected number of cores (not counting the engine core) and BIP engine discrete-transition execution time δ to model interference.

The goal of the scheduling algorithm is to generate two time triggered scheduling tables: for normal mode and emergency-mode. These schedules act online as tables for time-triggered execution. For example, Figs. 6(b) and (c) are actually graphical representation of these tables for the given example.

The scheduling tool first transforms the task graph by inserting special 'satellite' jobs that model engine interference due to periodic task controller. Then the normal-mode table is generated. This is done using list scheduling. The algorithm has been adapted to take into account two types of resources: a single control core and a pool of compute cores. In order to execute, every job needs availability of one instance of both resource types to execute for δ time and immediately it continues to execute only on the compute core for WCET time. In normal mode, the *priorities* for selecting the next job to be scheduled are obtained from fixed priority table that favors jobs that have HI criticality and high difference between execution times in emergency and normal mode. Also we favor jobs that have small deadline themselves or in their successors. The results of list schedule simulation with normal job execution times are stored in normal-mode table.

The emergency mode table is calculated, again by list scheduler, but now with emergency execution times and only for HI jobs and HI-to-HI job precedences. We ensure that at any moment a switch from normal to emergency mode may take place while the HI jobs that are running at the moment of the switch may continue running on the same cores. To this end, the schedule start times in the normal mode are regarded as job arrival times in the emergency mode, whereas we enforce the same core mapping and relative job execution order as in the normal mode.

Our algorithm has the same (almost linear) algorithmic complexity as unmodified list scheduling, since it adds constant amount of additional computation for each job and precedence edge. Random benchmarks [17] confirm that for the same level of computational workload mixed critical problems are significantly harder to solve. At the same time we did not see significant sensitivity to the workload component given by interference, which possibly means that we need to improve the employed interference evaluation metric.

In future work we intend to investigate how to improve non-preemptive scheduler for better support of mixed criticality. For reference we consider to implement exact algorithm with exhaustive search. We intend to replace list scheduling by topological permutation scheduling as it is a more powerful offline global fixed-priority heuristic for the case where there is no preemption and jobs have non-zero arrival times [13]. Also, in our previous works [21] and [22] for preemptive case we realized more elaborate techniques than those in the current algorithm for optimizing for mixed-criticality, we will investigate how to port them to non-preemptive case. Integrating them directly into our design flow will be considered after we extend our BIP framework for support of preemption.

5 Conclusions and Future Work

In this paper we have proposed a scheduling algorithm and a work-in-progress design flow for timing-critical multi-core applications, taking into account coarse-grained interference, using the interference from the controlling run-time environment as an example. In our design flow we demonstrate the concept of using task automata as concurrency language, which can be used to program the custom resource managers, such as mixed-criticality ones. In future work we plan to introduce the missing features into our design flow (especially, the runtime environment to support task migration, dropping and migration). We also plan to extend our interference models to other resources (*e.g.*, buses and peripherals) and to more general task controllers and models of computation.

References

1. Abdellatif, T., Combaz, J., Sifakis, J.: Model-based implementation of real-time applications. In: Proceedings of the Tenth ACM International Conference on Embedded Software, EMSOFT 2010. ACM (2010)
2. Abel, A., Benz, F., Doerfert, J., Dörr, B., Hahn, S., Haupenthal, F., Jacobs, M., Moin, A.H., Reineke, J., Schommer, B., Wilhelm, R.: Impact of resource sharing on performance and performance prediction: a survey. In: D'Argenio, P.R., Melgratti, H. (eds.) CONCUR 2013. LNCS, vol. 8052, pp. 25–43. Springer, Heidelberg (2013). doi:10.1007/978-3-642-40184-8_3
3. Amnell, T., Fersman, E., Mokrushin, L., Pettersson, P., Yi, W.: TIMES - a tool for modelling and implementation of embedded systems. In: Katoen, J.-P., Stevens, P. (eds.) TACAS 2002. LNCS, vol. 2280, pp. 460–464. Springer, Heidelberg (2002)
4. Baruah, S.: Semantics-preserving implementation of multirate mixed-criticality synchronous programs. In: RTNS 2012, pp. 11–19. ACM (2012)
5. Baruah, S., Fohler, G.: Certification-cognizant time-triggered scheduling of mixed-criticality systems. In: RTSS 2011, pp. 3–12. IEEE (2011)
6. Bensalem, S., Bozga, M., Combaz, J., Triki, A.: Rigorous system design flow for autonomous systems. In: Margaria, T., Steffen, B. (eds.) ISoLA 2014. LNCS, vol. 8802, pp. 184–198. Springer, Heidelberg (2014). doi:10.1007/978-3-662-45234-9_13
7. Chaki, S., Kyle, D.: DMPL: programming and verifying distributed mixed-synchrony and mixed-critical software. Technical report, Carnegie Mellon University (2016). http://www.andrew.cmu.edu/user/schaki/misc/dmpl-extended.pdf
8. Cordovilla, M., Boniol, F., Forget, J., Noulard, E., Pagetti, C.: Developing critical embedded systems on multicore architectures: the Prelude-SchedMCore toolset. In: RTNS (2011)
9. de Dinechin, B.D., van Amstel, D., Poulhiès, M., Lager, G.: Time-critical computing on a single-chip massively parallel processor. In: DATE 2014. EDAA (2014)

10. Fersman, E., Krcl, P., Pettersson, P., Yi, W.: Task automata: schedulability, decidability and undecidability. Inf. Comput. **205**(8), 1149–1172 (2007)
11. Giannopoulou, G., Poplavko, P., Socci, D., Huang, P., Stoimenov, N., Bourgos, P., Thiele, L., Bozga, M., Bensalem, S., Girbal, S., Faugere, M., Soulat, R., de Dinechin, B.D.: DOL-BIP-critical: a tool chain for rigorous design and implementation of mixed-criticality multi-core systems. Technical report 363, ETH Zurich, Laboratory TIK, April 2016
12. Hansson, A., Goossens, K., Bekooij, M., Huisken, J.: CoMPSoc: a template for composable and predictable multi-processor system on chips. ACM Trans. Des. Autom. Electron. Syst. (TODAES) **14**(1), 2 (2009)
13. Heijligers, M.: The application of genetic algorithms to high-level synthesis. Ph.D. thesis, University of Eindhoven (1996)
14. Lee, E., Messerschmitt, D.: Synchronous data flow. Proc. IEEE **75**(9), 1235–1245 (1987)
15. Pellizzoni, R., Bui, B.D., Caccamo, M., Sha, L.: Coscheduling of CPU and I/O transactions in cots-based embedded systems. In: RTSS 2008, pp. 221–231 (2008)
16. Perrotin, M., Conquet, E., Dissaux, P., Tsiodras, T., Hugues, J.: The TASTE toolset: turning human designed heterogeneous systems into computer built homogeneous software. In: ERTSS 2010 (2010)
17. Poplavko, P., Kahil, R., Socci, D., Bensalem, S., Bozga, M.: Mixed-critical systems design with coarse-grained multi-core interference. Technical report, TR-2016-4, Verimag (2016)
18. Poplavko, P., Socci, D., Bourgos, P., Bensalem, S., Bozga, M.: Models for deterministic execution of real-time multiprocessor applications. In: DATE 2015 (2015)
19. Shah, H., Coombes, A., Raabe, A., Huang, K., Knoll, A.: Measurement based wcet analysis for multi-core architectures. In: RTNS 2014. ACM (2014)
20. Socci, D., Poplavko, P., Bensalem, S., Bozga, M.: Modeling mixed-critical systems in real-time BIP. In: ReTiMiCs 2013 (2013)
21. Socci, D., Poplavko, P., Bensalem, S., Bozga, M.: Multiprocessor scheduling of precedence-constrained mixed-critical jobs. In: ISORC 2015, pp. 198–207. IEEE (2015)
22. Socci, D., Poplavko, P., Bensalem, S., Bozga, M.: Time-triggered mixed-critical scheduler on single- and multi-processor platforms (revised version). Technical report, TR-2015-8, Verimag (2015)
23. Socci, D., Poplavko, P., Bensalem, S., Bozga, M.: A timed-automata based middleware for time-critical multicore applications. In: Proceedings of SEUS 2015. IEEE (2015)
24. Sriram, S., Lee, E.A.: Determining the order of processor transactions in statically scheduled multiprocessors. VLSI Signal Process. **15**(3), 207–220 (1997)
25. Stuijk, S., Geilen, M., Theelen, B.D., Basten, T.: Scenario-aware dataflow: modeling, analysis and implementation of dynamic applications. In: SAMOS 2011. IEEE (2011)
26. Wirsing, M., Hölzl, M., Tribastone, M., Zambonelli, F.: ASCENS: engineering autonomic service-component ensembles. In: Beckert, B., Damiani, F., Boer, F.S., Bonsangue, M.M. (eds.) FMCO 2011. LNCS, vol. 7542, pp. 1–24. Springer, Heidelberg (2013). doi:10.1007/978-3-642-35887-6_1
27. Zerzelidis, A., Wellings, A.J.: A framework for flexible scheduling in the RTSJ. ACM Trans. Embedded Comput. Syst. **10**(1), Article no. 3 (2010)

A Library and Scripting Language for Tool Independent Simulation Descriptions

Alexandra Mehlhase$^{(\boxtimes)}$, Stefan Jähnichen, Amir Czwink, and Robert Heinrichs

Technische Universität Berlin, Ernst-Reuter-Platz 7, 10587 Berlin, Germany
{a.mehlhase,stefan.jaehnichen,robert.heinrichs}@tu-berlin.de,
amirc@win.tu-berlin.de

Abstract. In modeling and simulation it is often necessary to simulate a model with a variety of settings and evaluate the simulation results with measured data or previously acquired results. As doing this manually is error-prone and ineffective, scripting languages are often used to automate this process. In general a simulation description is tool and model dependent. Therefore, simulating the same model with the same simulation description in different simulation tools or comparing two different models with the same settings is often not easily achieved. We propose an object-oriented, tool-independent, easy-to-use, domain-specific scripting language to describe simulations in an exchangeable and uniform manner. Through this simulation description the simulation settings and the simulation environment can easily be changed while syntax and sequence of commands remain the same. The language is Python based and is designed to be simple, well-readable and intuitive even with marginal programming experience while maintaining Pythons' strength. The language uses an in-house Python library which provides interfaces to different simulation environments (so far Dymola, OpenModelica, Simulink). This library can also be used directly in Python, enabling experienced Python users to keep describing their simulations in Python but benefiting from our efforts to achieve tool-independence.

Keywords: Scripting language · Simulation description · Python library · Model representation

1 Introduction

Models have been created by humans for a variety of purposes in various forms for millennia. Constructional drawings can be traced back to ancient Egypt where they were written on papyrus or chiseled into stone. Models also attracted intellectual curiosity of researchers of various scientific disciplines including mathematics, physics, chemistry, economy and psychology. In natural sciences, especially in engineering, models are described by mathematical equations and are used to either understand the behavior of real systems or to try to anticipate the characteristics of a not yet existent system (for instance a new type of engine) [4]. As such a model is used for inducing hypotheses for a system, usually a

© Springer International Publishing AG 2016
T. Margaria and B. Steffen (Eds.): ISoLA 2016, Part I, LNCS 9952, pp. 622–638, 2016.
DOI: 10.1007/978-3-319-47166-2_43

series of simulations with varying simulation settings are performed. Such *simulation settings* are for instance parameters of the model, start values of variables, solver settings or even the simulation environment. It is also vital to evaluate simulation results easily, while minimizing the chance of errors. More complex systems, such as collective adaptive systems, which adapt their behavior due to current circumstances [10], might also necessitate changing the model during a simulation. To achieve all this, the process of starting a simulation with different settings, post-processing the results and changing models while simulating should be automated.

Today it is often necessary to define simulation settings and start simulations manually in a specific tool, which is time consuming and error prone. Also the settings done in one tool can usually not be automatically transferred to another tool. Thus, the modeler needs to manually transfer the simulation settings if another tool is used.

To automate the simulation process and provide the means to test the simulation settings a scripting language can be used, as proposed in [5]. In such a language it should be possible to describe the pre- and post-processing of a simulation and therefore also set and test simulation settings. It should also be possible to handle the simulation of the model efficiently and if possible in different simulation environments.

In this paper we focus on simulations for models in Modelica and Simulink, which are based on differential-algebraic equations (DAEs). Other modeling variants such as Finite-Element Methods (FEM) or discrete-event simulations (DEVS) have different needs for their initialization and simulation than DAE models. Thus, a uniform way to describe simulations for all these variants is not easily done, we therefore limit our approach to DAE models for now.

Different approaches of simulation descriptions for Simulink and Modelica already exist and are used in practice.

One method is to use Matlab [17] to describe the simulation of Simulink [18] models. Matlab offers commands to describe the simulation of a Simulink model and the means to control the simulation process and all it entails.

But not all modeling environments offer such comfortable scripting methods. Modelica [16] can be simulated in different simulation environments, such as Dymola [6] and OpenModelica [13]. In Modelica simulation environments a MOS language (MOdelica Scripting language) is usually supported that allows the modeler to describe a simulation. The MOS language is not standardized and can therefore be interpreted differently in various simulation environments. It is thus not always possible to reuse a simulation description in another simulation environment. Since one of the ideas about Modelica is the exchangeability of models between different simulation environments, this is a serious drawback.

Thus, many modelers tend to program their own scripts that control the simulation environment and set the appropriate simulation settings (see Sect. 2.1).

In general any of the three indicated approaches suffer from being not interchangeable and difficult to reuse for other models or for other simulation environments. Switching to a new simulation tool would lead to having to re-implement the simulation description.

In order to provide a unified simulation description for Modelica and Simulink models, we introduce a Python library which provides interfaces to different simulation environments. Each interface to a simulation tool provides methods to set necessary data for a simulation, start a simulation and read its results thus enabling optimizing of parameters, finding start values and so forth. This library enables modelers to use the same commands for tasks, e.g. to start a simulation and plot the results, in different simulation environments. Thus, providing a uniform way of describing a simulation even when using different simulation environments. Since not all modelers are used to Python we also provide an easy to use domain-specific language, which provides important commands to describe, pre- and post-process simulations. Thus, a modeler does not need to know Python to use the library but can use the provided language to describe simulations. Our library already has interfaces to Matlab/Simulink, Dymola and OpenModelica. It is modularly designed such that new modules for communication with other simulation environments can be added. When a new simulation environment is integrated into the library, it is usable through Python or the domain-specific scripting language in the same way as the currently supported ones.

This paper starts in Sect. 2 with background information about state of the art approaches for scripting languages. We then discuss the requirements for a library and scripting language supporting different simulation environments. Section 3 introduces the design of our Python library, while Sect. 4 focuses on the design of our domain-specific language. Section 5 presents an evaluation of the scripting language and Python library through our implementation. Section 6 shows how our scripting language can be used to describe a simulation, while Sect. 7 provides the conclusion.

2   Background on Scripting Languages

2.1   State of the Art in Simulation Descriptions

Recently, tool-independent descriptions of simulations have been the subject of many research groups.

SED-ML [1] is a markup language, based on XML, that is used to describe simulation runs in a tool-independent way. Until now the language is compatible with a couple of biological and mathematical model representations. In general the concept of SED-ML is close to our work in the sense that the simulation description has a well-defined uniform format that is encapsulated from the model representation. The main difference to our work is the *type* of language used to describe simulations. The idea of markup languages is to structure information in a meaningful and logical layout. It is a static definition of data in contrast to a programming language which describes a dynamic process. In such a static definition it is easy to exchange simulation settings between different simulation environments. However, we believe that describing simulations as programs gives the user more flexibility in terms of expressiveness. A markup language is restricted to the use case it was designed for, while in a programming language the user can do what he desires. It is arguable whether a simulation description in XML form or as a program is easier readable. However, it is very cumbersome to write XML code by hand and thus, we believe, SED-ML is only useful when the simulation description is created by a GUI program in a user-friendly way.

Another paper arguing the value of unified simulation descriptions is presented in [7]. Here a domain-specific language called SESSL is introduced which is based on Scala. The key difference between their work and ours is that SESSL is declarative. Thus, a simulation is described in terms of what should be done and not *how* exactly it should be done. SESSL then chooses how to deal with the simulation descriptions. This is close to SED-ML with the difference being the type of language used, to the benefit of SESSL, which has short and easily readable and understandable simulation descriptions. However, our approach is more low-level. We offer the user the ability to describe every step in the simulation process himself. We serve the user a common communication channel, aiming at providing as little overhead as possible, to various simulation tools. The user himself decides when he wants to do what, ensuring he has full control of the whole process at any time.

In addition most simulators that SESSL is compatible with are Java libraries, so communication is established by calling native functions from dynamic modules (in the sense of calls that are not different from any other local function calls). The simulation tools that we integrated into our work can not necessarily be communicated with that easily. In general we relied so far on inter-process communication. Thus, none of the tools that our approach is compatible with is available in SESSL, as they would not fit into their design, at least not with the full feature set.

Other approaches using domain-specific languages for describing simulations include; [3] introducing APOSTLE a domain-specific language for parallel discrete event simulation, [9] introducing ML-Rules which is a language designed for systems biology models, [14] which uses SESSL for the experimentation stochastic models.

In [8] a Python interface to OpenModelica is introduced which enables a simulation description in Python while the simulation is done in OpenModelica. This approach comes closest to our approach but only supports OpenModelica, whereas our approach can support many different simulation environments.

In [11] scripting for Modelica models is used in the context of control theory. In this paper it is proposed to use Matlab or Python to describe simulations of Modelica models, whereas the Modelica models are exported as FMIs (Functional Mockup Interface) [2]. This approach is of course also feasible but the models have to be exported as FMIs first, which is not necessary in our approach.

2.2   Basics: Scripting Language

Scripting languages are a subset of imperative programming languages with a high level of abstraction. Their purpose is usually not to implement complex programs or algorithms but rather to automate a repetitive task. For instance the MOS language is designed to control operations of Modelica simulation tools, that the user normally would have to do manually. Thus, scripting languages usually have a large amount of software components and algorithms available (e.g. a simulation environment). Hence, scripting languages are sometimes also called gluing languages, as their purpose is to quickly define communications between larger software components, rather than defining new components.

Scripting languages, in contrast to programming languages like C, Java etc., are usually available only in their source form. This means when executing a script (a program that is written in a scripting language) it must first be parsed and can then be interpreted. This has the advantage that scripts are machine independent and can be changed by the user to his exact demands.

Scripting languages are typically weakly typed. Strong typing allows for error detection before starting the program. However, this makes a language inflexible and program sources get larger due to declarations. As scripts are not pre-processed anyway strong typing is usually omitted.

Since we want to create a language for describing simulations in different simulation environments and for different models a scripting language seems to be the right choice. The language should contain necessary features to describe, pre- and post-process a simulation or multiple simulations.

2.3   Requirements

In this section we look into the basic requirements for a uniform simulation description. The concept is based on the idea of separating the model from its' simulation. The model is the description of a system in some language, e.g. Modelica - in contrast the simulation is the description of an experiment on a model. To understand the significance for the distinction between a model and a simulation we will emphasize the important differences.

First of all, models are abstract descriptions of systems but still they cannot be used interchangeably among all simulation environments. One can for instance use Modelica models in different simulation environments such as Dymola or OpenModelica but none of these will accept a Simulink model simply because it does not contain Modelica code. On the other hand Matlab/Simulink will not accept anything else than Simulink models. We call the *language* or *file format* a model is described in *model representation*. As just pointed out there is a strong relation between the model representation and the simulation tool. In general a model representation can be simulated by an arbitrary number of simulation tools. It is for instance possible to simulate a Simulink model not only in Matlab/Simulink but also in Scilab/Xcos [15]. That means, it is not possible to automatically choose a tool for a model representation for it is not known which tool the user wants to use. Also the user might want to simulate the model representation in two separate tools to compare results. This decision cannot be taken away from the user, thus he has to be able to choose a desired simulation tool in the simulation description. To sum this paragraph up, the model and the simulation tool are separate things. However, from the view of the simulation tool, it is clear which model representations are accepted, thus making it possible to check whether a correct model representation was handed to the tool.

We define a tuple of the model and simulation environment. We will denote this tuple as $model_{tool}$ for the rest of the paper. One and the same model can be used in many simulation environments, each of them leading to a new tuple $model_{tool}$. A $model_{tool}$ can be simulated many times with different simulation settings (e.g. initialization). The initialization can set the start value for state variables, non-state variables and parameters. The parameters, which can be initialized, need to be parameters which do not influence the model structure, otherwise they need to be set in the model directly. Structure changing parameters are for instance array sizes in a model.

In order to achieve uniformity we need to ensure that for any simulation description S the following holds:

Let t_1, t_2 with $t_1 \neq t_2$ be two different simulation tools and $model$ be some model, then for any simulation description S for $model_{t_1}$, S can be applied to $model_{t_2}$ with minimal changes. As was already pointed out the tool a model should be simulated in, is part of the simulation description and thus S needs to be changed in regard to the tool. Other than the tool definition the simulation description S should stay the same, which would make simulating the same model in different environments and comparing results easy.

The sequence of commands and syntax describing a simulation should always be the same independent of the model representation and used simulation environment.

To provide the means of such a uniform description it is necessary to define the same methods in each interface for a simulation environment. The communication with different simulation environments is usually not uniform, for instance it is possible to communicate with Dymola through a DDE (Dynamic Data Exchange) channel, while OpenModelica can be controlled via MOS scripts. Also the commands used to start a simulation, to initialize a model and the format of simulation results is usually different. Therefore, we need to map these differences to a uniform way. The modeler thus does not need to know the different commands but can use the same commands for the same tasks in each environment.

These uniform methods can be provided in a Python library which can then be used in Python directly by experienced users. Our domain-specific language also uses this library but provides the most common commands to describe a simulation and pre- and post-process them in an easy and straightforward manner.

3 Python Library

To match our requirements, we designed a library in Python that provides interfaces to different simulation environments, allowing us to communicate with them in order to initialize and simulate models.

We chose to use Python, since it is freely available, easy to use, (mostly) platform-independent, widely used by engineers and additionally it matches our demands. Our library is built in an object-oriented way that ensures that any model or simulation tool can be accessed by common interfaces. Eventually some call to the interface will lead the library to communicate with a simulation tool. This idea is derived from the DySMo framework where different tools can be used to simulate variable-structure models [12].

Figure 1 shows the library with its two most important abstract classes *tool* and *model representation*. The class *tool* defines the method's signatures necessary for an interface to a specific simulation tool, such as Dymola or Simulink. The class *model representation* is the base class of any model representation supported by the library, e.g. Modelica or Simulink format. These two classes provide the means to define a simulation description. This description can either be in Python or in the domain-specific language defined in Sect. 4. In the simulation description only the fields and methods of the abstract classes are available, the concrete sub-classes are never present in a simulation description. Instances of these abstract classes can be requested and are provided by the library, they are never instantiated directly in a simulation description.

When requesting a model object, the library tries to deduce a model representation by checking the input files against the concrete model representation classes present in the library. This deduction can be based on the file extension (for instance .mo for Modelica files) or on the content of the files.

Tool communication classes are the heart of the library. They are programmed reusably and are instantiated only once by the library and kept in a list. They can be either requested by name or for a specific model. Every tool communicator class is able to determine which model representations it can simulate. This information is directly encoded in the class. Not only does this enable error-checking, for instance when trying to simulate a Modelica model in Simulink, but also makes the library more flexible, as the library can provide a simulator that is installed on the current local machine, which the developer of the model might not use. In addition the library includes objects for solvers. This is mainly to have unique identifiers for solvers, because they are not necessarily named interchangeably among simulation tools. A tool communication class is also requested to check whether a specific solver is supported by the tool or not. This information is also part of the program code of the communication class. As the supported model representations and solvers are usually static for a simulation tool, they can simply be kept in a list in the communication class. The compatibility check will then reduce to a simple check whether the list contains a model representation or solver.

The currently implemented communication classes for Dymola, OpenModelica and Simulink are designed not to store any state about model or simulation objects (recap that they must be reuseable). However, this is not generally required and can be integrated if needed, although this information should be kept private and not visible to the user.

After the objects have been acquired their methods can be invoked, which eventually will lead to the simulation environment being started or communicated with. If a simulation environment has special needs, which are not necessary in other environments, new methods can be added to the communication class which can also be used by the modeler in a Python script.

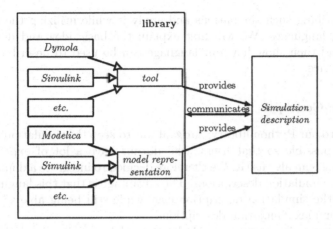

Fig. 1. Overview over Python Simulation Library communication

The advantage of our design is the encapsulation of simulation tools. Therefore, when adding support for a new simulation tool, only a communication class must be added, while the rest of the library and the way of describing simulations remains the same. Through this design it is possible to add a new simulation tool for models and only change the simulation tool in the simulation description without any further changes. The simulation is then performed exactly with the same settings only with another tool, which gives a modeler an easy opportunity to test a model in different simulation tools. In addition the communication with the simulation tool is completely transparent to the user.

The general work flow in a simulation description is the following (we will explain this flow in detail in the next section): First of all, a matching $model_{tool} =$ $(model\ representation, tool)$ object must be acquired. Parameters, that change the structure have to be set now. The model then needs to be compiled in the chosen simulation environment. Before the simulation is started initial values can be defined. Parameters, which do not change the structure of the model, can also be initialized. Then the simulation is triggered. After a simulation the simulation results can be loaded. Independent of the tool used for simulating, the results are always loaded in the same format. Thus, there is no need to consider the specific file formats of the simulation environments.

This library can be imported as a package in Python and therefore offer the modeler the possibility to communicate with all supported simulation environments in an easy and uniform fashion.

4   A Uniform Simulation Description

Our main idea for this paper is to separate the model from the simulation description. The model is therefore implemented in some modeling language and the simulation is defined in a simulation language. We define a uniform way of describing such simulations and apply it while utilizing the advantages of scripting languages. We will first explain the basic idea and design of our language and then show how our language can be used to describe simulation runs in practice.

4.1 Basic Concepts

Additional to our Python library, our goal was to keep the simulation description as easy as possible so that users, who do not have a lot of experience with programming, can also use it. We therefore decided to integrate a domain-specific language for simulation descriptions. The advantage is that this language focuses on making the simulation description easy while still being able to implement arbitrary complex simulation descriptions.

The language is oriented on Modelica models and its simulation environments, since a main idea of Modelica is to have a standard modeling language that can be used in different simulators. Therefore, it is sensible to have a scripting language which can load a Modelica model and then simulate it in different simulation environments and compare results. Thus, the models as well as the simulation descriptions are exchangeable with other modelers, even if they use different simulation environments. The danger of a model being misused by another user through wrong simulation settings is therefore reduced.

To ensure that the language is easy to use for engineers who are used to Matlab or Python we tried to use many of the known concepts for our language. The language is object-oriented so it is easy to maintain, enhance and also the description of the model and its simulation can easily be described through objects. The object-oriented approach also makes using the language convenient and it is a well known concept among many programming languages, thus learning it is straightforward. Figure 2 shows the structure of objects used in a simulation description in our language. A description contains a model, a simulation tool and a simulation object. The simulation results are also an object and have the same format for each simulation independent of the simulation environment. The simulation object and also the model object are tool independent. However, because Modelica models are usually compiled by simulation tools to a somehow executable format, models may become tool dependent until they are compiled for another tool, which again binds them to it. We will explain this in more detail later.

As most scripting languages like Python and Matlab our language is weakly typed. Classes or declarations do not exist to keep the scripts compact. Objects and functions are considered general primitive values as numbers or strings. As there are no classes, objects are more or less an extendable set of key-value pairs. A very basic script may look like the following.

```
1  a = 30;   // value 30 to a
2  b = {};   // new object to b
3  b.c = a;  // value of a to b.c
```

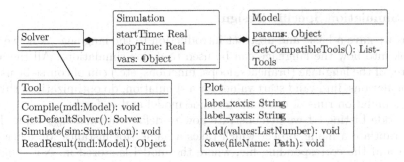

Fig. 2. Object-oriented structure

In line 1 a variable and its value are defined. An object is created in line 2 by using curly braces. In line 3 the member c with value of variable a is stored in the object referenced by variable b. Therefore, the object that b represents would look like this in mathematical set notation: $\{(c, 30)\}$.

Our language also supports common constructs like branches, loops and functions. An example of a function is shown in the following code:

```
1  i = 0;
2  f = function() // Define functionand assign to variable f
3  {
4    i++;
5  }
6  f(); // call function
```

As can be seen in this example, defining a function is quite easy. The example also shows how the scope of variables is handled. The function f is defined on the same level as i and manipulates i. So when calling the function the global variable i can be changed inside the function. If the function should only manipulate local variables a new variable i can be defined inside the function. First it is checked whether a function has a local variable and only if not the search is continued in the outer scope. When functions are defined inside of objects they serve as methods and on a call they can access the context using the keyword *this* like in many programming languages.

Functions can also have (an arbitrary number of) return values and recursion as shown in the following definition of the faculty function:

```
1  fac = function(n) // parameter n
2  {
3  if(n == 0)
4      return 1;
5    return n * fac(n-1); // recursive
6  }
7  r2 = fac(10); // r2 = 3628800
```

Therefore, our language provides basically the main feature any language usually has.

4.2 Simulation Specific Design

So far, we gave a basic and abstract introduction to the language. Now we want to look into how the language can be used to define simulations. All the above features of the language (branches, loops, functions, etc.) can of course be used to do calculations, find valid start values for a simulation, do optimizations through many simulation runs of one and the same model and so forth.

In code Listing 1.1 we demonstrate how to define the $model_{tool}$ tuple. First, we instantiate a model object which takes a name (for instance Modelica class name) and the corresponding file, where the model is stored in. Note that the second argument can also be a list of files as Modelica models may span over multiple files. For this model, parameter values can be set, as seen in line 2. As already said; structure changing parameters have to be set now, other parameters can also be set later when setting simulation configurations.

Now the second object that is needed is the tool, which can be instantiated in two different ways, which are also used in our code example. We encourage users to request tools by calling the *GetCompatibleTools* method on a model object (like in line 5) which checks the tools available for the model representation. This makes the script more flexible, as it only requires that the user has installed *some* tool compatible with the requested model representation. This way a Modelica model can be simulated in Dymola on one machine and still be simulated on another that has only installed OpenModelica. However, practical experience shows that different simulation tools often behave differently, thus the function *FindTool*, that matches a string against the available tools on the target machine, can be used to require a specific tool, which simulates the model without problems or which has been tested by the model creator. In such a case we recommend, as shown in the code example, to still fall back to the *GetCompatibleTools* method in case the *FindTool* could not provide an instance of the desired tool. In order to define the $model_{tool}$ tuple, the *Compile*-method on the tool object has to be invoked with the model. Note that although for instance a Simulink model wouldn't require this step, it is necessary in order to bind the model (here mdl) to the tool, thus define the $model_{tool}$ tuple - at least from a theoretical perspective. However, Dymola, OpenModelica or other tools will create an executable file and an initialization file, during this step. These two are later on used by the library to initialize the model and simulate it.

```
1  mdl = Model("someModelName", "somePath/someModel.someExtension");
2  mdl.params.mass = 4;
3  tool = FindTool("Dymola");
4  if(tool == null)
5    tool = mdl.GetCompatibleTools()[0];
6  tool.Compile(mdl);
```

Listing 1.1. Definition of the $model_{tool}$ tuple

Now that the *mdl* tuple is set up we still need the simulation. Listing 1.2 shows how to run a simulation. A simulation object is instantiated for the previously acquired model tuple. Having the simulation object it is possible to set start values of variables, change solver settings etc. (lines 2–6).

```
1  sim = Simulation(mdl);
2  sim.startTime = 0;
3  sim.stopTime = 10;
4  sim.solver = tool.GetDefaultSolver(); //DASSL for Dymola
5  sim.vars.velocity.start = 5;
6  sim.vars["x[2]"].start = 10000;
7  tool.Simulate(sim);
8  result = tool.ReadResult(mdl);
```

Listing 1.2. Definition of a simulation run

In line 7 the simulation of the model is started in the specified simulation environment. Because of performance reasons, simulation results are not read directly since they tend to get large and a user might not want to evaluate them right away. However, a call to *ReadResult* will read the last simulated results for a given model. The data format of the return value is always the same and the modeler therefore does not need knowledge of the structure of the simulation results from the specific tool. The reformatting to the *result* format is done by the library.

In Listing 1.3 each value in the velocity vector of the result is checked against a constant value to evaluate if the value exceeds a maximum. This of course is a rather trivial check but serves as an example of what can be done with the data after simulation. To easily handle and evaluate the simulation results the language also supports easy plotting routines. In the example below the velocity and the values of the variable $x[2]$ are plotted in the same plot and the axis titles of the plot are set appropriately.

```
1   foreach(v : result.velocity )
2   {
3   if(v > 1000)
4      {Print("VELOCITY TOO HIGH");}
5   }
6   plt = Plot();
7   plt.Add(result.velocity);
8   plt.Add(result.x[2]);
9   plt.label_xaxis = "Time";
10  plt.label_yaxis = "Velocity and x-Value";
11  plt.Save("somePictureName.someExtension");
```

Listing 1.3. Evaluating simulation results

Of course it would be possible to do more complicated post-processing routines with the language. Also it is possible to run more than one simulation with the same $model_{tool}$ (e.g. for optimizations) or create many different $model_{tool}$ tuples (e.g. to compare results). Simulating models sequentially as needed for variable-structure models is also a possibility.

With the included elements in the language it is possible to describe complicated algorithmic descriptions of simulations. We are therefore able to describe pre- and post-processing routines, do evaluations, program tests and compare models independent of the simulation environment.

For a created model the modeler could thus provide a simulation description to make sure his model is only used for specific simulations or provide a test routine so other users will use the model according to its specification.

5   Implementation

We explained the theory behind our library and our scripting language. To test if this theory works in practice we implemented the library and also the domain-specific language. In the following we give some information about the implementation.

5.1   Library

The library [1] consists basically of two abstract classes that represent a model and a simulation tool. In order to be able to deal with different model representations and tools, the library consists of a set of model and tool classes which it foreshadows from the user.

An instance of these classes is acquired by calling functions that return appropriate objects depending on the input they get. Therefore, the user always gets the same view of simulation descriptions which aids in having a uniform simulation form. In addition this approach makes the communication with the simulation tool transparent and can thus easily be extended by adding another subclass – another change in the library or in any simulation description will not be necessary. This subclass must of course fulfill the signature of the interface, but apart from that it can contain Pythons' full repertoire. For now Dymola and OpenModelica are fully supported and Simulink is at its final testing stages.

The tools are configured in a special configuration file, which allows among other settings to prioritize certain simulation tools. If the user for instance has two Modelica simulators installed on his machine, he might prefer that one specific tool should be chosen as the default one.

Tools to be integrated have to have the basic features of the already implemented tools, like setting start values, starting a simulation, having simulation results and so forth. If the simulation setup is too different a mapping to our uniform way, given in the abstract classes, will probably not be feasible. All Modelica tools should roughly have the same set up and probably most DAE simulation environments, which means they could be included in the library. But this has not been confirmed yet.

5.2   Language

Besides the *Python Simulation Library* we also implemented a prototypical script evaluator for the scripting language in Python 3.4.

---

[1] The library and language is online on github: https://gitlab.tubit.tu-berlin.de/ a.mehlhase/PySimulationLibrary. This is still a test version and is still under development.

The script evaluator basically takes a script file as input, parses it and finally interprets it. While evaluating, the special built-in functions cause the interpreter to call the library which communicates with the simulation tools. As it may be possible that users require special behavior in scripts, it is easy to add new functions or objects to the scripting language. Python-functions or Python-classes can easily be exported to variables in the scripting language. This enables programmers to benefit from Pythons' module richness and easily inject higher level code to the scripting language.

This leads to a full functioning implementation of the language with which we could test the benefits.

6 Using the Library

To evaluate the library and language we present a breaking pendulum example consisting of two Modelica models; a pendulum and a falling mass. The pendulum's length is constant, the pendulum starts hanging and the angle (*phi*) and angular velocity (*derPhi*) is calculated. We then want to find an initial velocity which leads the pendulum to become a falling mass due to the centrifugal force F falling below zero. The end values of the coordinates (x, y) and the velocities (vx, vy) are then used to initialize the ball model, which represents the free falling mass of the pendulum.

Listing 1.4 presents the script in our language for this example. In line 1 and 2 the two models are created and in line 4–6 they are paired with a compatible tool and are compiled.

In line 7 the simulation for the pendulum is created. Starting in line 12 a while loop is used which increases the initial angular velocity, simulates the pendulum with this velocity and checks whether the force F fell below zero during the simulation. If F fell below zero, we leave the loop and calculate the x and y coordinates from the angle (line 35–37), which was simulated in the pendulum model.

In line 41–42 the velocities vx and vy are calculated from the endvalues of the angle and angular velocity. These values are then used to initialize the ball model in our example (line 46–49). The ball model is then simulated.

In line 56–59 the results of both simulations are plotted as y over x to show the movement of out pendulum as shown in Fig. 3.

This example is of course a rather simple example but presents different scenarios which can be handled with our library and language:

- Optimizing or finding appropriate initial values/parameters (angular velocity of the pendulum)
- Post-Processing capabilities (calculating x, y from the angle)
- Pre-Processing capabilities (setting initial values for the ball model)
- Simulating variable-structure models (changing from pendulum to ball)

```
1    pendulum = Model("pendulum", "pendulum.mo");
2    ball = Model("ball", "ball.mo");
3
4    tool = pendulum.GetCompatibleTools()[0];
5    tool.Compile(pendulum);
6    tool.Compile(ball);
7    sim = Simulation(pendulum);
8    derPhi = 0;
9    index = null;
10
11   //simulate until negative force is found
12   while(index == null)
13   {
14       derPhi += 0.5;
15
16       sim.vars["derPhi"].start = derPhi;
17       tool.Simulate(sim);
18       result = tool.ReadResult(sim);
19
20       for(i = 0; i < result["F"].Length(); i++)
21       {
22           if(result["F"][i] < 0)
23           {
24               index = i;
25               break;
26           }
27       }
28   }
29
30   //calc x and y for pendulum
31   x = [];
32   y = [];
33   for(i = 0; i < index; i++)
34   {
35       v = result["phi"][i];
36       x.Add(sin(v) * pendulum.params["L"]);
37       y.Add(-cos(v) * pendulum.params["L"]);
38   }
39   // velocities vx, vy
40   derPhi = result["derPhi"][index];
41   vx = cos(result["phi"][index]) * derPhi * pendulum.params["L"];
42   vy = sin(result["phi"][index]) * derPhi * pendulum.params["L"];
43
44   //run ball sim
45   sim = Simulation(ball);
46   sim.vars["x"].start = sin(result["phi"][index]);
47   sim.vars["y"].start = -cos(result["phi"][index]);
48   sim.vars["vx"].start = vx;
49   sim.vars["vy"].start = vy;
50   sim.stopTime = 0.6;
51
52   tool.Simulate(sim);
53   result2 = tool.ReadResult(sim);
54
55   //plot y over x
56   p = Plot();
57   p.Add(x, y, "r");
58   p.Add(result2["x"], result2["y"], "b");
59   p.Show();
```

Listing 1.4. Pendulum simulation script

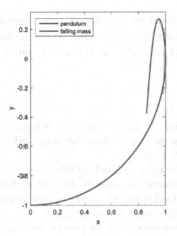

Fig. 3. Plot of the calculated values of x and y

7 Conclusion

In this paper we presented why it is beneficial to separate the model from the simulation description.

To describe a simulation we introduced our Python library which provides the means to communicate with different simulation environments. This library can be imported in a Python script and be used to initialize a model, start simulations and do a pre- and post-processing. Through the object-oriented structure of the library it is easy to add new tools to the library, which enables the modeler to use this tool in the simulation language as well as in Python directly.

In order to help modelers describe simulations with our library, we also provide a domain-specific language, which is designed for the description of simulations. The simulation language is Python based and object-oriented, which makes it easy to use and to enhance.

Using this new language or the library gives modelers a good opportunity to describe their simulation, run optimizations, simulate variable-structure models, pre- and post-process simulations and provide other users with information about how a model should be used. The language and library will soon be available as open source project.

We plan on enhancing the library to support more simulation environments. The first step will be to support other Modelica tools such as MapleSim, SimulationX and JModelica. This would enable Modelica users to test their models in different environments, which would especially be interesting for library developers who want to make sure their library works in all (or most) Modelica simulators.

It is also planned to add XCos as another possibility to simulate Simulink models.

As further steps we want to analyze if other tools based on DAEs can be added. Since the proceeding to set up simulations, simulate models and evaluate simulation results should roughly be the same, such tools should be easy to integrate in due course.

References

1. Bergmann, F.T., Cooper, J., Le Novère, N., Nickerson, D.P., Waltemath, D.: Simulation experiment description markup language (SED-ML) Level 1 Version 2. J. Integr. Bioinform. **12**(2) (2015)
2. Blochwitz, T., et al.: Functional Mockup Interface 2.0: the standard for tool independent exchange of simulation models. In: Proceedings of the 9th International Modelica Conference, Linköping Electronic Conference Proceedings, pp. 173–184. Linköping University Electronic Press (2012)
3. Bruce, D.: What makes a good domain-specific language? APOSTLE, and its approach to parallel discrete event simulation. In: Kamin, S. (ed.) DSL 1997 - First ACM SIGPLAN Workshop on Domain-Specific Languages, in Association with POPL 1997 (1997)
4. Cellier, F.E.: Continuous System Modeling. Springer Science and Business Media, New York (1991)
5. Cellier, F.E.: The complexity crisis. In: Proceedings of the 8th International Joint Conference on Software Technologies SIMULTECH 2013, pp. IS–5 (2013)
6. Dassault Systemes, A.B.: Dymola. http://www.3ds.com/products-services/catia/capabilities/systems-engineering/modelica-systems-simulation/dymola. Accessed 21 Sep 2014
7. Ewald, R., Uhrmacher, A.M.: SESSL: a domain-specific language for simulation experiments. ACM Trans. Model. Comput. Simul. **24**(2), 11: 1–11: 25 (2014)
8. Ganeson, A., Fritzson, P., Rogovchenko, O., Asghar, A., Sjlund, M., Pfeiffer, A.: An OpenModelica Python interface and its use in Pysimulator. In: 9th International Modelica Conference (2012)
9. Helms, T., Himmelspach, J., Maus, C., Rwer, O., Schtzel, J., Uhrmacher, A.M.: Toward a language for the flexible observation of simulations. In: Proceedings of the 2012 Winter Simulation Conference (WSC), pp. 1–12 (2012)
10. Hillston, J., Pitt, J., Wirsing, M., Zambonelli, F.: Collective adaptive systems: qualitative and quantitative modelling and analysis (Dagstuhl Seminar 14512). Dagstuhl Rep. **4**(12), 68–113 (2015)
11. Lie, B., Haugen, F.: Scripting Modelica models using Python. SNE - Simul. News Eur. **23**, 161–170 (2012)
12. Mehlhase, A.: A Python framework to create and simulate models with variable structure in common simulation environments. Math. Comput. Model. Dyn. Syst. **20**(6), 566–583 (2013)
13. Open Source Modelica Consortium: Open Modelica. www.openmodelica.org/. Accessed 03 Dec 2015
14. Peng, D., Warnke, T., Uhrmacher, A.M.: Domain-specific languages for flexibly experimenting with stochastic models. Simul. Notes Eur. SNE **25**(2), 17–122 (2015)
15. Scilab: http://www.scilab.org/products/scilab. Accessed Jan 2015
16. Association, T.M.: https://www.modelica.org. Accessed Jan 2015
17. TheMathWorks: MATLAB version 7.12.0 (R2011a). The MathWorks Inc., Natick, Massachusetts (2011)
18. TheMathWorks: Simulink version 7.12.0 (R2011a). The MathWorks Inc., Natick, Massachusetts (2011)

Adaptation to the Unforeseen: Do we Master our Autonomous Systems? Questions to the Panel – Panel Introduction

Stefan Jähnichen[1] and Martin Wirsing[2](✉)

[1] Technische Universität, Berlin, Germany
stefan.jaehnichen@tu-berlin.de
[2] Ludwig-Maximilians-Universität, München, Munich, Germany
wirsing@lmu.de

Abstract. This short paper gives an introduction to a panel held as part of the track on "Rigorous Engineering of Collective Adaptive Systems" at ISOLA 2016. The moderator Stefan Jähnichen (TU Berlin) and the panelists Saddek Bensalem (VERIMAG), Michele Loreti (University of Florence), Giovanna di Marzo Serugendo (University of Geneva), and Emil Vassev (LERO) discussed how to master the engineering of autonomous systems that have to cope with unforeseen events and situations. The discussion was structured along 14 questions ranging from the evolution and universality of autonomous systems to correctness, reliability, and legal issues.

Without much doubt, the construction of adaptive systems is one of the most challenging topics we currently explore in software and systems engineering. The panel discussion on "Adaptation to the Unforeseen: Do we Master our autonomous Systems?" was focussing on the prospects and the state-of-the-art in engineering autonomous systems. Stefan Jähnichen (TU Berlin) as moderator and the panelists Saddek Bensalem (VERIMAG), Michele Loreti (University of Florence), Giovanna di Marzo Serugendo (University of Geneva), and Emil Vassev (LERO) discussed this controversial topic along a list of 14 questions described in the following. Position papers of two of the panelists are contained in this volume: Di Marzo Serugendo on "Engineering Adaptivity, Universal Autonomous Systems, Ethics and Compliance Issues" [1] and of Vassev on "Safe Artificial Intelligence and Formal Methods" [2].

The term adaptive names systems that have the property to react on all situations occurring during their life time correctly and reliably; and the question comes up whether such a behavior is feasible, implementable, or even desirable.

Q1: What is your notion of adaptivity? Can you explain the term or even give a definition?

Q2: Do you consider adaptivity to be a realistic and desirable property of technical systems?

Q3: Can you give some examples of applications for which adaptivity is not just desired but essential?

© Springer International Publishing AG 2016
T. Margaria and B. Steffen (Eds.): ISoLA 2016, Part I, LNCS 9952, pp. 639–641, 2016.
DOI: 10.1007/978-3-319-47166-2_44

Our computers are commonly considered as being the most adaptive systems mankind has ever invented and, observing how computers penetrate all our life and take control in almost all applications, we have to acknowledge at least the universality of computing equipment. Obviously, the underlying reason for being adaptive and universal originates from its very simple basic mechanism to manipulate numbers in the dual system and the ongoing minimization technologies for electronic circuits. However, more important for becoming adaptive, of course, is the programmability of such machines using human intelligence and creativity, and the abilities of humans to master complexity using mathematics and computer science technologies.

Q4: Humans seem to adapt by evolution. Can we expect machines to adapt by evolution, too. What could be the meaning of evolution in a technical context?

Q5: The term machine learning is provocative as it imputes that machines can learn similar to human beings. What is your interpretation of machine learning and how does it connect to adaptivity?

Q6: What are the underlying formalisms in machine learning and how does it distinguish from human learning?

In today's technologies the term autonomous plays a major role. It denotes systems which perform its task without human intervention as e.g. automatic lawn mowers, smart home equipment, driverless train systems, or autonomous cars. The most challenging question which comes up when following the life cycle of the term autonomy is the potential to construct a system which behaves and operates similar or even better than a human being. Personally, we doubt this, but it is reasonable to discuss how far can we push the boundary towards such behavior and provide autonomous operation at least in a certain context with highest safety guarantees and finally establish trust in its innocuous operation.

Q7: Do you envision a universal autonomous system? Will robots ever be able to substitute human interaction?

Q8: What are the means to establish trust in autonomous systems

It is hard to imagine a system being constructed by a human which adapts itself to all and especially all unforeseen situations as the term unforeseen describes circumstances the human himself has not foreseen.

If we restrict ourselves to some foreseen unforeseen behaviors which we might be able to handle, we have to consider a problem of completeness. Did we cover the whole set of behaviors or did we omit some of the behaviors? This, of course, raises questions of complexity as the number of such situations might be close to infinity and thus, not foreseeable at all. In order to handle such complexity, we have to restrict the adaptability of our systems to a certain context in which we are able to capture all different behaviors or which at least enables us to classify and cluster such situations. Home environments with a few sensors only might be such a context as well as autonomous trains.

Q9: Can you imagine other contexts in which autonomy could play a dominant role?

However, autonomous systems are on their way and will definitely make it into our daily life. Autonomous cars are already seen on our streets and the first severe accidents prove that they are not as secure as we had hoped them to be. Thus, scientists vote again for more math and formalisms in their development but obviously this is much more difficult than it was to prove a non-autonomous system correct. It is not just a matter of logic and logical proofs but it has to incorporate statistical evidence, too, and, last not least, it has to integrate the physical properties of such systems, as e.g. acceleration, loss of weight or the compression of gas under pressure in order to prepare for adaptivity. We assume that in order to capture autonomy in a safe and reliable way, we will see in the near future a convergence of modeling and development techniques based on logics, statistics, and numerics.

Q10: How do we prove adaptations to be correct and reliable? Do you foresee a difference between such proofs for foreseen and unforeseen behaviors?

Q11: Do you expect autonomous systems to be more vulnerable against malicious attacks? If yes, how do you propose to handle such security issues?

Q12: Do and - if yes - how can particular modeling techniques, programming concepts and verification methods help to construct reliable autonomous systems.

Besides the mentioned technical properties, another, often neglected aspect are public laws and regulations the systems have to be conform with. Adaptation will probably make it more difficult to handle such non-functional requirements. Proving the conformance of an autonomous system with public regulations will require strict and probably new methods. For example, engineers currently argue that the most severe obstacles to drive autonomously on our streets are not of technical but of legal nature and concern warranty and guilt.

Q13: How would you propose to cover legal and warranty issues in the development and dissemination phases of systems?

Q14: Which systems do you consider being the cutting edge application to introduce adaptability as an outstanding and highly requested feature?

References

1. Di Marzo Serugendo, G.: Engineering adaptivity, universal autonomous systems, ethics and compliance issues. In: Margaria, T., Steffen, B. (eds.) ISoLA 2016. LNCS, vol. 9952, pp. 714–719. Springer, Heidelberg (2016)
2. Vassev, E.: Safe artificial intelligence and formal methods. In: Margaria, T., Steffen, B. (eds.) ISoLA 2016. LNCS, vol. 9952, pp. 704–713. Springer, Heidelberg (2016)

Smart Coordination of Autonomic Component Ensembles in the Context of Ad-Hoc Communication

Tomas Bures, Petr Hnetynka[✉], Filip Krijt, Vladimir Matena, and Frantisek Plasil

Charles University, Faculty of Mathematics and Physics,
Department of Distributed and Dependable Systems, Malostranske namesti 25,
Prague, Czech Republic
{bures,hnetynka,krijt,matena,plasil}@d3s.mff.cuni.cz

Abstract. Smart Cyber-Physical Systems (sCPS) are complex distributed decentralized systems that typically operate in an uncertain environment and thus have to be resilient to both network and individual node failures. At the same time, sCPS are commonly required to exhibit complex smart coordination while being limited in terms of resources such as network. However, optimizing network usage in a general sCPS coordination framework while maintaining the system function is complex. To better enable this, we allow incorporating key network parameters and constraints into the architecture, realized as an extension of the autonomic component ensembles paradigm. We show that when chosen well, these parameters make it possible to improve network resource usage without hampering the system utility too much. We demonstrate the parameter selection on a mobile gossip-based sCPS coordination scenario and use simulation to show the impact on overall system utility.

Keywords: Smart Cyber-Physical Systems · Autonomic components · Ensembles · Communication

1 Introduction

Smart Cyber-Physical Systems are distributed and often decentralized systems that combine sensing and actuating with distributed cooperation and coordination that allows achieving higher efficiency and reliability of the system compared to work of its individual components in isolation. From the perspective of traditional research on Cyber-Physical Systems (CPS), smart CPS (sCPS for short) are intended to have more intelligence exhibited by complex cooperation and distributed adaptation. Another important feature of sCPS is the heavy reliance on software as the means of achieving their "smart" features. This categorizes sCPS as software-intensive systems – i.e., systems where the software makes one of the most complex and most critical constituent.

Generally the development of sCPS comprises a number of research and engineering areas including mechanical, electrical, electronics, control, network, and software engineering. Even the software engineering itself requires combination of multiple disciplines spanning from real-time and embedded systems to agent-based systems and machine learning. Contrary to traditional system engineering approaches, by the

© Springer International Publishing AG 2016
T. Margaria and B. Steffen (Eds.): ISoLA 2016, Part I, LNCS 9952, pp. 642–656, 2016.
DOI: 10.1007/978-3-319-47166-2_45

opposing requirements of (i) complex and adaptive behavior and (ii) efficiency (energy, communication, etc.), sCPS exhibit much stronger intertwining among the various disciplines.

Considering sCPS as software-intensive systems, it has been observed that traditional separation of software abstractions and layers (communication middleware from application) is not satisfactory for sCPS [3]. This is because such a separation creates a knowledge gap which prevents a layer to optimize its behavior by exploiting domain knowledge of another layer. Also, in sCPS a systematic approach in addressing their complexity is required to reason at different levels of abstraction.

In accord with the concept of architecture hoisting [6], we posit in this paper that software architecture is a convenient meeting point of different disciplines. We view the architecture not only as the software structure, but also as a place where aspects of coordination and self-adaptation are captured along with domain knowledge expressed in a way which can be utilized by different interoperating layers and functions (networking, coordination, adaptation, control, etc.). To this end, we exploit the concept of autonomic component ensembles [23, 24], which are dynamically established cooperation groups of otherwise autonomic components. Ensembles provide a convenient way for describing architectures of self-adaptive systems comprised of many, typically mobile, components.

In this paper we focus specifically on the communication and coordination aspects of sCPS. We argue that since sCPS are typically comprised of mobile devices, the networking bears strong influence on the performance and functionality of the resulting sCPS system. In particular, we consider that the devices forming sCPS are primarily connected by a Mobile Ad-Hoc Network (MANET), an infrastructure-less network where devices communicate in a close range (typically max. 100 m). To extend the range, a device may relay messages by rebroadcasting. We assume this is done in a probabilistic gossip scheme, a simple yet quite effective and widespread way of building ad-hoc networks. Furthermore, we assume devices in sCPS to be fully autonomic to be able to correctly work when network connection is temporarily not available.

Goals: In the context described above, the goal of this paper is to show how the concept of autonomic component ensembles may be extended to include the communication concerns and restrictions. We do this at the architecture level, where we (i) introduce constructs to capture communication-relevant domain knowledge at an appropriate level of abstraction. Further, we (ii) show how to reflect this domain knowledge in optimizing the communication that underlies forming of autonomic ensembles.

With respect to these goals, the rest of the paper is structured as follows: Sect. 2 presents the background, mainly the concept of component ensembles, along with motivation for optimizing communication and a running example. In Sect. 3, we discuss the relationship between an ideal system and the reality, and outline our approach. In Sect. 4 we present high-level ensemble description enriched with information related to communication and explain the semantics. Section 5 details our methodology, mainly parameter selection and experiment setup, and also contains the discussion of the results. Section 6 presents a short overview of related work and the paper is concluded in Sect. 7.

2 Background and Motivation

The concept of autonomic component ensembles (ACE) has been introduced within the scope of project ASCENS[1] (EU FP7 FET). Using this paradigm, entities in a system are modeled as *components* while communication among them is realized via *ensembles*. A component features its state and activities. The state is represented by the component's data (knowledge) while the activities are either periodically or event-triggered tasks (processes) operating upon the knowledge. An ensemble is a dynamically determined group of components. To join an ensemble instance, a component has to satisfy *membership condition,* a predicate articulated upon its knowledge (e.g., to be spatially close to other components in the ensemble); communication within the established ensemble is then implicit via automated sharing of parts of component knowledge, defined in each ensemble by the *knowledge exchange* specification construct.

ACE have been already realized in several component models, e.g., JRESP[2], Helena [10] and DEECo [1] and successfully applied [24]. Ensembles prove to be an ideal design paradigm for systems of autonomous cooperating components with self-* properties. For example in [11], ACE have been employed in an e-mobility use-case, in which a number of cars cooperate in order to allocate a parking space.

Recent research showed that an ensemble concept as described above can be further extended to address the needs of future complex sCPS. In our recent work [4], we outlined an extension of ensemble semantics allowing for hierarchical ensembles with specific cardinalities of component roles and for mutual cooperation among ensembles. To illustrate this enhanced semantics of ensembles, consider a game in which a group of robots has to cooperate in order to touch as many beacons as possible, with the beacons dynamically appearing in the game area (Fig. 1). More specifically, a beacon has to be touched by a pair of robots at the same time. Additionally, the area is divided into islands and robots cannot easily move from one island to another.

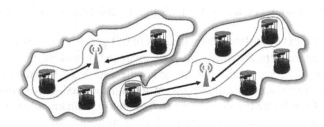

Fig. 1. A robotic example visualization

The robots in this scenario are modeled as components. A robot's data (knowledge) contain its position and the position of a targeted beacon. There are two types of ensembles in the scenario: (i) an ensemble grouping all robots on a single island (this one serves to exchange information about beacons discovered by the robots), and (ii) an ensemble

---

[1] http://ascens-ist.eu/.
[2] http://jresp.sourceforge.net/.

grouping two robots that are selected to touch a particular beacon. Obviously, the former ensemble exists in multiple instances (one per island), the latter exists in multiple instances too (up to one per beacon – there may be less if there are not enough robots to pair with all the beacons present in the area).

An ensemble is determined by the ensemble's membership condition, which is a predicate operating over the knowledge of individual components. For instance in case of ensemble (i), it expresses that all robots in the ensemble are on the same island. The ensemble coordinates robots within it and allows them to share their knowledge. For instance ensemble (i) provides each robot a union of beacons seen by each individual robot in the ensemble; ensemble (ii) tells a robot which beacon to touch.

Due to the inherently distributed nature of sCPS, communication becomes an important issue. The distributed character of sCPS, combined with the potentially limited ability to communicate, prevents a centralized management of ensemble formation and component communication – mainly due to the fact that components need to efficiently and safely operate even in cases when communication becomes unavailable.

In our robotic example, a centralized solution would simply not scale with an increasing number of robots, bringing an inherent bottle-neck and a single point of failure of the system. Thus, a decentralized solution is necessary. Not surprisingly, this is clearly in line with the fact that systems like car-to-car communications or swarms-of-robots typically rely on mobile ad-hoc networks (MANETs). In order to effectively distribute data in a decentralized and highly dynamic system, MANETs commonly use protocols that are based on proactive data distribution, i.e., gossiping [7], a rather effective style of communication for data distribution, and geographical routing [21].

The central idea in gossip protocols is iterative information exchange between network nodes. In every step, a node communicates with a selected peers and exchanges a small amount of information with them. Typically, the peers to communicate with are chosen via a randomized mechanism. Commonly, the messages are replicated by peers and thus, there is an implicit redundancy (and therefore robustness of the protocol).

In [2], we have shown an application of gossip-based decentralized communication for ACE. Nevertheless, if applied without any further restrictions/optimizations, such communication can quickly lead to very long communication latencies, or, even, can totally congest the whole network. To deal with this issue, other MANETs properties like potential data loss, varying latency, bandwidth, etc., and resulting effects like stale data, necessity to rebroadcast data, etc. have to be taken into account (MANETs are primarily intended for unreliable communication). To tackle these properties, we have proposed the *communication boundary* predicate. In short, it defines the furthermost limit where data have to be disseminated (i.e., data are not disseminated throughout the whole network), but the resulting system is functionally equivalent to a system where data would be disseminated everywhere. As shown in [2], this can lower the congestion on the network and improve other non-functional properties of the system.

The communication boundary as such provides static safe over-approximation – unfortunately, this is often not enough for complex sCPS. If we consider the robotic example above and add a further rule to the game that for pairing the robots, two robots with largest distance between them should be preferred, we essentially force the system to propagate data all over to learn about beacons that lie really far apart. The excessive communication and ensuing congestion and latencies then prevent the system from functioning as designed (the robots target beacon pairs with the largest distance apart but due to latencies, the robots are unable to coordinate in timely manner).

To remain functional in that case, the system has to adaptively modify/restrict the communication, which of course decreases its overall effectiveness, but on the other hand, it allows it to keep at least some functionality. This requires that the system has the ability to dynamically scale w.r.t. to temporarily and spatially varying properties of the communication. There are existing techniques to do this on the communication middleware layer. However, to perform such a scaling efficiently, the system has to possess a certain degree of domain knowledge. In particular, the system has to know (i) how its effectiveness and potential to reach the goals are influenced by communication (e.g., what the permissible latencies are, what of the communication parameters have positive effects on the system efficiency), and (ii) how the system can be restricted (e.g., by disregarding some mutually distant components from forming an ensemble) in order to achieve at least a sub-optimal functionality of the system. Unfortunately, there are no universal answers to the questions above since they are highly problem specific.

3   Towards Self-Optimizing Ensembles

As pointed out in the previous section, there is a clear need that designers/developers of sCPS can explicitly express the information influencing the communication in order to allow sCPS to self-optimize themselves at runtime based on the current conditions of the network. Following the architectural hoisting concept, such information has to be a part of the architectural specification. Since this is to be provided at design time, the specification of communication parameters has to be platform-independent, to reflect that decisions on a particular communication platform are typically made later than those on the architectural level.

Another strong requirement is that from the architectural description, there has to be a clear and exactly defined relationship between the views on the designed system, considering (i) an *ideal* system (i.e., a system with instant communication, without any latencies, and no congestions) and (ii) an *actual* system (i.e., a system with real latencies, limited bandwidth, etc.). The ideal system view is important since it is easy to understand it and verify (using the MDA [15] terminology, it represents a platform-independent model of the system). The actual view then reflects a reality, which should behave as the ideal system (a platform-specific model in the MDA terminology) as much as possible. From the functional point of the view, both the ideal and actual systems work correctly, however the actual system can produce sub-optimal results or behave with smaller efficiency, compared to the ideal system.

Our approach presented in the paper thus enhances ensembles with communication related information but in an underlying platform-independent way. These pieces of information are then interpreted by the deployment infrastructure keeping the goal to run the actual system to correspond to the ideal system as much as possible with regards to current conditions of network, etc.

4   Network Aware Ensembles

In this section, we demonstrate how to equip ensembles with high-level problem-specific information which allows the system to scale its functionality w.r.t. the limitations of the communication. As a particular example for illustration of the described principles we use the robotic game example defined in Sect. 2.

Figure 2 shows the example in (a simplified version of) the DSL of the DEECo [1] component model (however, almost any component model could be used to model the example). As introduced in Sect. 2, there is one type of component – Robot – and two types of ensembles – the BeaconInformationExchange ensemble and ForSingleBeacon ensemble.

The first ensemble serves for spreading information about beacon positions since the robots have just limited field of view. Simply, all robots on the same island merge their knowledge about beacons they have seen on the island. The ensemble is qualified by an island ID, which means that the system may create as many instances of the ensemble as there are islands. The second ensemble serves for both communication and coordination – it tells a pair of robots which beacon to target. The ensemble is qualified by a beacon (represented by its position), which means that the system may create as many instances of the ensemble as there are beacons.

4.1   Ideal System View

As explained above, with real-life communication in place, we distinguish between the ideal view of the system and its actual view, which comes about as the result of compromises that have to be done due to restrictions imposed by the communication. The logic of the ideal system (when communication and ensemble forming would be instantaneous) is given by the definition of membership and knowledge exchange.

The membership defines (i) types of components taking part in the ensemble along with their roles and (ii) a filtering condition over their knowledge. For instance in case of the ForSingleBeacon ensemble, it groups two robots and requires that both these robots plus the targeted beacon have to be on the same island.

The membership may further contain the fitness definition, which is a function used to rank potential ensemble instances if the membership condition allows more than one solution. This indeed happens in our case as every pair of robots on the same island satisfies the condition. Further, considering that more beacons (i.e., ensemble instances) are present on the same island and that a robot can be assigned only to one ensemble ForSingleBeacon, there ensues a large number pair combinations. Out of these, the system selects such robots-beacon pairs that yield the maximum sum of fitness (which in our example is the maximum sum of distances).

The knowledge exchange specifies what knowledge to assign to which roles in the ensemble. In case of the ForSingleBeacon ensemble it assigns the beacon position to both the robots in the pair.

To reflect the fact that the system is dynamically changing (e.g., new beacons can appear in the system), the membership (with fitness) and the knowledge exchange are

```
1   component Robot
2     knowledge
3       position          // robot's position
4       beaconPosition    // targeted beacon position
5       islandID          // island, on which the robot is located
6       beaconPositions   // positions of known beacons

7   ensemble BeaconInformationExchangen
8     id islandID
9     membership
10      roles
11        source: Robot
12        target: Robot
13      condition
14        source != target
15    knowledge exchange
16        target.beaconPositions =
      target.beaconPositions.unionWith(source.beaconPositions)
17    communication constraints
18      boundary
19        relay: RobotRelay, replica: Robot
20        relay.islandID == replica.islandID

21  ensemble ForSingleBeacon
22    id beaconPosition    // targeted beacon position
23    membership
24      roles
25        robotsAssignedForBeacon[2]: Robot
26      condition
27        robotsAssignedForBeacon[0].islandID ==
      robotsAssignedForBeacon[1].islandID == islandIDOf(beaconPosition)
28      fitness
29        max(distance(robotsAssignedForBeacon[0].position,
      beaconPosition), distance(robotsAssignedForBeacon[1].position,
      beaconPosition))
30    knowledge exchange
31        robotsAssignedForBeacon[0].beaconPosition = beaconPosition
32        robotsAssignedForBeacon[1].beaconPosition = beaconPosition
33    communication constraints
34      boundary
35        relay: RobotRelay, replica: Robot
36        relay.islandID == replica.islandID
37      optimization
38        smallestRadius > 10m
39        max staleness beaconPosition 30s
```

Fig. 2. Robotic example in the simplified DEECo DSL

continuously reevaluated and ensembles are reformed to reflect changes in the membership condition and to optimize with respect to the maximum sum of fitness.

4.2 Actual System View

The actual system is essentially a restriction of the ideal system in which no global system state is available. Technically, this boils down to limiting propagation of data between physical nodes on which components are deployed. This takes two forms: (i) communication happens only among nodes which may be together involved in forming an ensemble – i.e., there is no communication across islands because there is no ensemble needing it, (ii) ensemble instances that are hard to create and synchronize may not be considered by the system if it would lead to network congestion – i.e., very distant robots pairs on the same island which would require expensive multi-hop communication are disregarded.

The data propagation limit (i) is realized by the *communication boundary* [2] (captured in the specification as `boundary` condition under `communication constraints`). It is a predicate which tells whether to retransmit a data packet from a given node. An important feature of a communication boundary is that by design it is required to be implied by the membership. As such, the communication boundary is an over-approximation of the membership and cannot omit an ensemble instance which would normally be present in the ideal system.

The data propagation limit (ii) is realized by *dynamic communication boundary*, which is controlled by setting the communication parameters (performed by the system at runtime based on the actual network utilization). This is explained in Sect. 5 in more detail. An important feature of this is that it can omit ensemble instances that would normally be in the ideal system. As such, it makes the actual system deviate from the ideal. This tradeoff however has to be made because otherwise the system would stop functioning completely due to network congestion.

The dynamic communication boundary is continuously optimized by the system with two objectives – (a) keeping the network load below the congestion point, (b) maximizing the sum of ensemble fitness.

To prevent cases when the dynamic communication boundary would become too tight for the system to work, the ensemble specification constrains the optimization of the boundary (specified as `optimization` condition under `communication constraints`). These constraints are expressed in terms of time (`maximum staleness`) and space (`smallest radius`) rather than particular technology dependent communication parameters. This allows keeping the level of abstraction closer to the problem domain and easier to reason about on the level of the system design.

In particular the `maximum staleness` parameter defines the maximum age of data that can be still relied on. In the example, as the robots have limited range to see the beacons, the targeted bacon can become "stale", i.e., the particular robot does not see it yet and it was not "refreshed" via the `BeaconInformationExchange` ensemble. Thus, information about targeted beacon must not be too old (30 s in the DSL) as with increasing age of the beacon information, the probability that the beacon has already disappeared also increases and, regarding the overall goal of the system (maximize the number of the touched beacons), a better option might be to discard the particular ensemble instance and form a new one using more fresh data. The maximum staleness has to be defined per particular data elements as each of them can "stale" in a different pace. The `smallest radius` defines a minimum range around a component to which the data has to be disseminated. In case the radius is smaller than the neighborhood defined by the *communication boundary* specified in the ensemble, then the smallest radius is disregarded (this happens for instance if an island is very small).

Figure 3 graphically demonstrates the relation between the ideal system and the boundaries of the actual system. There are multiple components (robots and beacons) and they are deployed to physical nodes. (Note that nodes are not represented in the DSL as the particular deployment is not specified at this level of abstraction.) In order to allow formation of ensembles, the deployment infrastructure has to disseminate information between the nodes – we consider the usage of MANETs and gossiping (as outlined in Sect. 2). The *communication boundary* (CB), as described in the ensemble definition, represents a farthest limit for the data dissemination. As it is constructed as an over-approximation of the membership condition (MC), all potential sets of components which satisfy the MC are deployed on nodes within CB. Note that MC can select multiple sets, which are then ranked by fitness. This is the case in Fig. 3, where the fitness is shown as the number set in green.

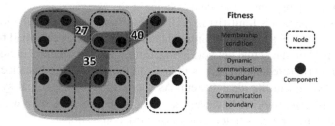

Fig. 3. Membership vs. boundary conditions in ensemble formation

The communication parameters (staleness, smallest radius) can further limit the actual dissemination, thereby establishing the *dynamic communication boundary* (DCB). In the example, there are three possible ensembles to be formed for a single particular beacon. Even though the ensemble with the fitness 40 is the best one (the best fitness) it is not considered as one of its component is beyond DCB.

5   Communication Optimization and Experiments

5.1   Communication Parameters

Assuming the communication in ensembles is realized via an optimized Gossip algorithm on top of a MANET, the dynamic communication boundary can be controlled by several communication parameters, which have positive effect on network utilization or system utility. By system utility we mean here the effectiveness of the system in reaching its goal – in our example, this can be for instance the sum of distances of the beacons which were successfully touched by two robots over the system lifetime. As such, the system utility is something which can possibly be evaluated only once the system finished its operation. However, we assume that the system is designed in such a way that maximizing the sum of ensemble fitness values at any given point in time brings the system close to its highest utility, allowing us to approximate the system utility at runtime.

Based on an initial round of experiments, we identified the following key communication parameters: (i) rebroadcast period, (ii) rebroadcast radius, (iii) max. packet age. While the semantics of the rebroadcast period is obvious, the latter two need more explanation: Together they determine when to stop propagating packets in the network based on their source location and timestamp. Rebroadcast radius is expressed as the spatial distance from the source of the packet in question, while the max. packet age limits the maximal packet age which is still considered for rebroadcasting based on its timestamp.

It should be emphasized that setting communication parameters per ensemble instance cannot be done in isolation, i.e., not considering how communication in other ensemble instances would be affected. In other words, optimizing communication in a particular instance may cause increase in network load, thus limiting communication in other ensemble instances. In order to optimize the overall system utility it is necessary to set network parameters with respect to all ensemble instances currently present in the system.

5.2   Experiment Design and Testbed

In order to exemplify the effect of the parameters on the network load and the overall systems utility, we have conducted a series of experiments on the scenario described in Sect. 2. Note that this is meant to explain the problem, not to suggest one particular setting of parameters, as the dependency between a particular parameter and network load and system utility is heavily problem specific.

The problem was modeled as a DEECo [1] application and implemented in the JDEECo framework[3] while the scenario specific environment and ensemble instantiation heuristic were implemented as reusable plugins to JDEECo.

All the experiment setups were based on the example scenario while maximizing distance from beacon to robot at ensemble instantiation time. In order to narrow down a huge number of candidate parameters influencing system utility, an initial round of experiments was conducted. In this run, parameters with the potential to optimize system utility were selected for further analysis. In the end, an experiment setup covering a range of values of the parameters (i), (ii), and (iii) mentioned in Sect. 5.1 was employed in the scenario simulation.

The simulation was conducted in a custom environment of the size 30×30 m, further determined by robot movement, beacon touching, and simple radio models. The latter featuring delivery delays between 15 ms and 35 ms in the limited range of 5 m. Even though a more precise radio model could be realized using the OMNeT++ framework[4], this option was in the end not employed given the significant slowdown in simulation runs we have experienced.

---

[3] JDEECo: http://github.com/d3scomp/JDEECo.
[4] OMNeT++: https://omnetpp.org/.

5.3 Experiment Results

The experiments were conducted in the following settings: The number of robots was 6, and the number of beacons was 4. This implied that the ensemble (specified in Fig. 2 starting at line 21) existed in at most 3 instances, even though their average number of instances was 1.4. Basically, the experiments were executed for different values of parameters (i), (ii), and (iii) described in Sect. 5.1. In detail, a series of experiments was conducted for different values of single parameter, while all the other parameters were fixed in the series. For each parameter value setting (configuration), an experiment was executed 100 times with different random seeds of robot and beacon positions. This arrangement helped determine the influence of noise in the number of underlying messages and system utility.

The actual result of the simulation runs is depicted in Fig. 4. The effect of rebroadcast period modification is depicted in Fig. 4b where there is a clear sweet spot between the rebroadcast period of 10 and 20 s. Thus setting a lower period results in producing excessive number of messages without any significant improvement in the system utility.

The impact of the rebroadcast radius modification, displayed in Fig. 4a shows that the system utility is saturated at the range of 10 m. Further extension of the range limit just implies more messages to be sent, while the system utility remains intact.

Finally, in an effect of modifying `max staleness` is presented. Essentially, removing the messages older than the desired `max staleness` may cause minor reduction in number of messages sent and even slightly improve the system utility.

Since the simulation was done for a simplified radio model, the actual position of the sweet spots and other interesting points in figures would be dynamic, depending upon the properties of the real network, such as latency, throughput, and congestion.

Furthermore, the setting of the parameters has to respect its effect on the `smallestRadius` and `max staleness` communication constraints specified in the ensemble. Here, the relation is that the rebroadcast radius has to be greater or equal to the `smallestRadius` specification. Further, the rebroadcast period and max. packet age are positively correlated with the data staleness, which has to be kept under the specified `max staleness`.

Overall, the results indicate that it is possible to optimize system utility via settings of communication parameters and, at the same time, minimize the number of messages necessary to honor the communication constraints imposed in an ensemble specification. However, it is important to keep in mind that the profit for a single ensemble instance may impact the system utility influenced by another ensemble instance.

Naturally, the exact sweet spots are specific to a particular scenario, so that the results above cannot be directly applied to a different one. Nevertheless, the simulation shows that the relationships between communication parameters and system utility can be applied in a MANET to scenarios similar in communication constraints. We envision using an optimization algorithm to continuously adjust the communication parameters at runtime while trying to stay within the communication constraints. Generally, a viable starting point for the optimization is the worst-case setting of the parameters (i.e. assuming the minimal radius and maximal staleness. From these, the optimization can

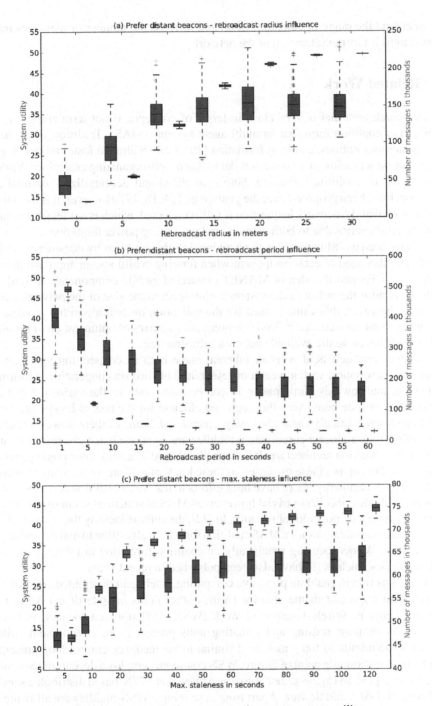

Fig. 4. Communication parameter impact on system utility

try to extend the range of communication and increase the number of messages transmitted until it hits the saturation of the network.

6 Related Work

One research area that is very close in terms of concepts, if not terminology, is the problem of coalition formation in multi-agent systems (MAS). Traditionally focusing on autonomous entities, coalition formation [20] in MAS aims to foster more complex coordination scenarios, in a manner similar to that of self-organizing ensembles. Various algorithms for coalition formation, both centralized and decentralized, optimal and heuristic, have been proposed over the years, e.g., [14, 18, 19]. However, it is a common assumption that the network in question is fully connected, which is not feasible in large distributed scenarios due to both network and processing power limitations.

Efforts such as [8] have focused on addressing this problem by considering only a small neighborhood of each component when forming coalitions, an approach that fits well with sCPS and the idea of MANET-connected mobile components. In [26], the authors monitor the utility of the system with respect to the size of the network neighborhood; however, this value is used for the validation of their algorithm (comparing the utility to an optimal, centralized solution), not as means of optimization of the algorithm itself based on the available network infrastructure.

Another research field with an inherent stake both in cooperation and network utilization is robotics, with a wealth of research published on cooperative algorithms, usually geared towards participating in competitions such as the various RoboCup[5] challenges. Despite being very thorough and efficient for the task at hand (e.g., [16]), these approaches usually cannot be easily generalized. Some of them however take the extra effort to introduce a coordination middleware layer, such as [25], resulting in an explicit coordination architecture. It is our belief that ACE abstractions could generally also be used to capture these use cases, as these kinds of systems share many properties with sCPS. Additionally, there have been efforts to use MAS coalition formation algorithms in robotics; this is not trivial however, as MAS abstractions seem to make some assumptions that do not hold for robotics. In [22], the authors identify these assumptions and propose modifications for a MAS coalition formation algorithm to make it applicable for robotics. Works focusing specifically on coalition formation in robotics and real-time scenarios, such as [9] have also been published in recent years.

Due to its role in enabling pervasive computing, intelligent distributed coordination becomes an important theme also for various other fields in spite of not being their primary concern. Wireless sensor network (WSN) [17] research focuses on having various autonomous sensing and actuating units present in an environment, with a control system built on top – making it similar to the feedback control loop present in sCPS. To avoid a single point of failure, WSN commonly employ a decentralized control scheme, e.g. [13]. In [5] the authors propose a two-layer WSN-based distributed sensing and control (DSC) middleware. Apart from describing a WSN middleware allowing for

---

[5] http://www.robocup.org/.

dynamic node removal and adaptive resource usage, the authors also recognize the need to balance application utility and network resource limitations and usage, similarly to our approach.

In the context of ACE themselves, this work further builds on the concept of self-organizing (intelligent) ensembles, as introduced in [4], and the idea that at least some high-level architecture information must be provided by the application architect to the communication layer in order to allow application-specific optimization [12].

7 Conclusions

In this paper we have presented an architectural extension of ACE that allows for declarative specification of constraints related to communication optimization, while still adhering to the principle of separation of concerns. Knowing these constraints enables the runtime to optimize data propagation to maximize the utility of the entire system – represented by the ensemble fitness functions. Moreover, a set of experiments was conducted to identify which network parameters are needed to perform such optimizations. The experimental setup consisted of MANETs and a customized gossip protocol. Finally, it is worth noting that while shown in the context of ACE, the ideas presented in this paper – elevating data quality constraints to architecture level and enabling application-specific utility optimization via network parameters – should be applicable to other approaches to collective systems that rely on gossip-like data dissemination in MANETs.

Acknowledgement. This work was partially supported by the project no. LD15051 from COST CZ (LD) programme by the Ministry of Education, Youth and Sports of the Czech Republic, partially supported by Charles University Grant Agency project No. 390615, and partially supported by Charles University institutional funding SVV-2016-260331.

References

1. Bures, T., et al.: DEECo: an ensemble-based component system. In: Proceedings of CBSE 2013, Vancouver, Canada, pp. 81–90. ACM (2013)
2. Bures, T., Gerostathopoulos, I., Hnetynka, P., Keznikl, J., Kit, M., Plasil, F.: Gossiping components for cyber-physical systems. In: Avgeriou, P., Zdun, U. (eds.) ECSA 2014. LNCS, vol. 8627, pp. 250–266. Springer, Heidelberg (2014)
3. Bures, T., et al.: Software engineering for smart cyber-physical systems – towards a research agenda: report on the first international workshop on software engineering for smart CPS. SIGSOFT Softw. Eng. Notes **40**(6), 28–32 (2015)
4. Bures, T., et al.: Towards intelligent ensembles. In: Proceedings of ECSAW 2015, Dubrovnik/Cavcat, Croatia, pp. 1–4. ACM (2015)
5. Cai, N., et al.: Application-oriented intelligent middleware for distributed sensing and control. IEEE Trans. Syst. Man Cybern. Part C (Appl. Rev.) **42**(6), 947–956 (2012)
6. Fairbanks, G., Garlan, D.: Just Enough Software Architecture: A Risk-Driven Approach. Marshall & Brainerd, Boulder (2010)

7. Friedman, R., et al.: Gossiping on MANETs: the beauty and the beast. ACM SIGOPS Oper. Syst. Rev. **41**(5), 67–74 (2007)
8. Gaston, M.E., desJardins, M.: Agent-organized networks for dynamic team formation. In: Proceedings of AAMAS 2005, Utrecht, Netherlands, pp. 230–237. ACM (2005)
9. Guerrero, J., Oliver, G.: Multi-robot coalition formation in real-time scenarios. Robot. Auton. Syst. **60**(10), 1295–1307 (2012)
10. Hennicker, R., Klarl, A.: Foundations for ensemble modeling – the Helena approach. In: Iida, S., et al. (eds.) Specification, Algebra, and Software, pp. 359–381. Springer, Heidelberg (2014)
11. Hoch, N., et al.: The E-mobility case study. In: Wirsing, M., et al. (eds.) Software Engineering for Collective Autonomic Systems. LNCS, vol. 8998, pp. 513–533. Springer, Heidelberg (2015)
12. Kit, M., et al.: Employing domain knowledge for optimizing component communication. In: Proceedings of CBSE 2015, Montreal, Canada, pp. 59–64. ACM (2015)
13. Marin-Perianu, M., et al.: Decentralized enterprise systems: a multiplatform wireless sensor network approach. IEEE Wirel. Commun. **14**(6), 57–66 (2007)
14. Michalak, T., et al.: A distributed algorithm for anytime coalition structure generation. In: Proceedings of AAMAS 2010, Toronto, Canada, pp. 1007–1014, International Foundation for Autonomous Agents and Multiagent Systems (2010)
15. OMG: MDA Guide revision 2.0 (2014). http://www.omg.org/cgi-bin/doc?ormsc/14-06-01
16. Parker, J., et al.: Exploiting spatial locality and heterogeneity of agents for search and rescue teamwork. J. Field Robot. (2015, accepted)
17. Pottie, G.J., Kaiser, W.J.: Wireless integrated network sensors. Commun. ACM **43**(5), 51–58 (2000)
18. Rahwan, T., et al.: Anytime coalition structure generation in multi-agent systems with positive or negative externalities. Artif. Intell. **186**, 95–122 (2012)
19. Sandholm, T., et al.: Coalition structure generation with worst case guarantees. Artif. Intell. **111**(1–2), 209–238 (1999)
20. Shehory, O., Kraus, S.: Methods for task allocation via agent coalition formation. Artif. Intell. **101**(1–2), 165–200 (1998)
21. Stojmenovic, I.: Position-based routing in ad hoc networks. IEEE Commun. Mag. **40**(7), 128–134 (2002)
22. Vig, L., Adams, J.A.: Multi-robot coalition formation. IEEE Trans. Rob. **22**(4), 637–649 (2006)
23. Wirsing, M., Hölzl, M., Tribastone, M., Zambonelli, F.: ASCENS: engineering autonomic service-component ensembles. In: Beckert, B., Damiani, F., Boer, F.S., Bonsangue, M.M. (eds.) FMCO 2011. LNCS, vol. 7542, pp. 1–24. Springer, Heidelberg (2012)
24. Wirsing, M., et al.: Software Engineering for Collective Autonomic Systems (The ASCENS Approach). Springer, Heidelberg (2015)
25. Witsch, A., Geihs, K.: An adaptive middleware core for a multi-agent coordination language. In: Proceedings of NetSys 2015, Cottbus, Germany, pp. 1–8. IEEE (2015)
26. Ye, D., et al.: Self-adaptation-based dynamic coalition formation in a distributed agent network: a mechanism and a brief survey. IEEE Trans. Parallel Distrib. Syst. **24**(5), 1042–1051 (2013)

A Tool-Chain for Statistical Spatio-Temporal Model Checking of Bike Sharing Systems

Vincenzo Ciancia[1]([✉]), Diego Latella[1], Mieke Massink[1], Rytis Paškauskas[1], and Andrea Vandin[2]

[1] Consiglio Nazionale delle Ricerche - Istituto di Scienza e Tecnologie dell'Informazione 'A. Faedo', CNR, Pisa, Italy
vincenzo.ciancia@isti.cnr.it
[2] IMT School for Advanced Studies Lucca, Lucca, Italy

Abstract. Prominent examples of collective systems are often encountered when analysing smart cities and smart transportation systems. We propose a novel modelling and analysis approach combining statistical model checking, spatio-temporal logics, and simulation. The proposed methodology is applied to modelling and statistical analysis of user behaviour in bike sharing systems. We present a tool-chain that integrates the statistical analysis toolkit MultiVeStA, the spatio-temporal model checker topochecker, and a bike sharing systems simulator based on Markov renewal processes. The obtained tool allows one to estimate, up to a user-specified precision, the likelihood of specific spatio-temporal formulas, such as the formation of clusters of full stations and their temporal evolution.

Keywords: Collective adaptive systems · Spatio-temporal model checking · Statistical model checking · MultiVeStA

1 Introduction

This paper studies the application of *statistical model checking* techniques to spatio-temporal verification, in the context of smart transportation systems. Statistical model checking (e.g., [28,29]) permits the quantitative estimation of the likelihood of events in a simulated system. In this paper we use a boolean model checker to evaluate qualitative properties over single runs of a probabilistic simulator, and exploit statistical model checking to estimate, via repeated simulations, the probability that such properties hold for the model. Spatio-temporal verification is a recent development in Computer Science, inspired by spatial logics for topological spaces [7]. The modal logics and model-checking perspective is enhanced with spatial information, such as proximity or reachability properties. This methodology is able to capture subtle differences in behavioural analysis, such as "the points that are *now close* to a point that will be green *tomorrow*" vs. "the points that *tomorrow* will be *close* to a point that is green *now*".

Research partially funded by the EU project QUANTICOL (nr. 600708).

T. Margaria and B. Steffen (Eds.): ISoLA 2016, Part I, LNCS 9952, pp. 657–673, 2016.
DOI: 10.1007/978-3-319-47166-2_46

In [10], the logic STLCS (Spatio-Temporal Logic for Closure Spaces) was introduced. The topological approach of spatial logics is retained, but models are generalised to *closure spaces*, in order to include *finite graphs* in the landscape of the considered models.

STLCS model checking has been explored in the context of smart cities and smart transportation, with applications in smart public bus services [12] and smart bike sharing systems (BSS) [15]. The latter have recently become a popular public transport mode in many cities [17,31] operating from a few (e.g. Pisa) up to several hundreds of docking stations (e.g. Hangzhou, Paris, or London[1]). The BSS concept is quite simple. A number of stations with docks partially filled with bicycles are placed throughout a city. Users of the service may hire any bicycle at any station at any time, and must return it at some station of their choice. The initial period of, typically, thirty minutes is free of charge, after which an hourly fee is charged. To maintain a high level of usage of the system it is important to keep the service attractive to its users. User satisfaction is difficult to evaluate quantitatively using only data obtained from real systems, as such data does not assess predictability of the service from a users point of view. A model-based approach was presented in [30] using Markov Renewal Processes (MRP) as the underlying probabilistic model. The model provides insight in the frequency and plausible causes for undesired delays in returning bikes and in the efficiency of bike sharing from a user's point of view. The model includes spatial aspects related to the presence of large groups of commuters in the morning and afternoon that go to a limited number of specific areas. Including commuters in the model turned out to be crucial to reproduce, up to a certain level of accuracy, actually observed cycling duration data for a large city such as London. In [15] we applied STLCS model checking on single simulation traces of the model. As expected, the introduction of commuter populations led to a larger number of stations being completely full in some places and empty in others. Spatio-temporal model checking also showed a number of more complex properties such as the emergence and persistence of regions in which all stations were full for some time (full clusters) and the development over time of such clusters. However, the results were only shown for individual simulation traces.

In this paper we generalise the approach of [15] to infer statistical properties of the system behaviour, rather than purely quantitative observations. We propose a methodology to quantify the likelihood of spatio-temporal properties in the system. We introduce a tool chain that integrates the simulator of [30], the spatio-temporal model checker **topochecker** [13] and MultiVeStA [35], a statistical model checker for discrete event simulators. Using MultiVeStA, *multiple* (spatio-temporal) properties can be analysed *simultaneously*, i.e. all estimators are updated at once for all points of the space during a single simulation, instead of performing one simulation for each point. In this paper this is used to obtain *separate* observations on all points of the space, using *the same* set of simulations.

---

[1] Pisa: http://www.pisamo.it, Hangzhou: http://www.publicbike.net; Paris: http://www.velib.paris.fr, London: https://tfl.gov.uk/modes/cycling/santander-cycles.

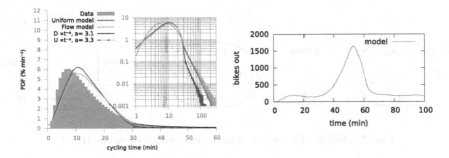

Fig. 1. Left: cycling duration histograms (Data) in London, using 831,754 trip records in October 2012, and results of simulation of the uniform model (dark lines) and the flow model (light lines). Maintenance trips are not considered. Right: total bike rentals over 100 min

The obtained performance speed-up is directly responsible for the feasibility of statistical spatio-temporal model checking.

2   Bike Sharing Simulation Model

We briefly recall the main aspects of the bike sharing model that was introduced in [30] and that forms the basis for the stochastic simulator that we use here in combination with the spatio-temporal model checker briefly described in the next section. The bike sharing model is intended to serve as an explanatory model for some of the salient aspects of the distribution of cycling times observed in real bike sharing systems. In particular, such distributions show a considerable number of surprisingly long cycling trips that cannot be attributed to maintenance events.

An illustration of such a distribution for the bike sharing systems in London is provided in Fig. 1 (Data). There, 7 % of all cycling trips are longer than thirty minutes, some extending up to two hours, which is more than the time necessary to traverse the complete service area in London (about fifteen kilometres). This range coincides with the so-called 'algebraic tail' of the distribution, the range in which the probability density function (PDF) is well approximated by $\propto t^{-a}$ with some exponent $a > 0$ (Fig. 1, inset). Such "algebraic tails" were found in data from all considered cities. Simulation results of the bike sharing model of [30] suggest that this phenomenon is a consequence of a form of risk-taking behaviour of users of bike sharing systems. Most users use bike sharing to reach a planned destination at a planned time and use an estimate of the time it will take them from their origin to their destination to know when to leave. Users risk, of course, that no parking place is found at or close to the destination in which case they would have to extend the travel itinerary to find another station where to deposit their bike. Such risk-taking behaviour can be shown to actually reduce the mean trip duration when considering the *overall system* [30]. The bike sharing model takes this risk-taking user behaviour explicitly into account, as well as other human factors such as speed of walking and biking.

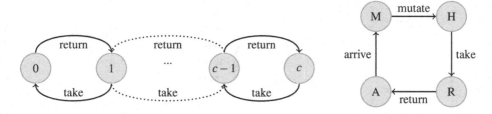

Fig. 2. Models of a bicycle station (left) and user agent (right)

The model is composed of two populations: a population of stations and a population of agents, the latter representing relevant user behaviour. Both can schematically be represented as automata as shown in Fig. 2. Users can take or return bikes from/to a station via the actions 'take' and 'return', respectively. Each station has a particular capacity c and a number of bikes parked in it n, as well as a position. To keep the model simple, stations are situated on a regular grid as shown in the left panel of Fig. 3. Users are modelled as agents that pass repeatedly through four different states as shown in Fig. 2. Each agent is parameterised by two addresses on the grid in an area at walking distance from a station which we will denote by origin and destination, respectively. Their behaviour is as follows. From the origin they walk to the nearest station where they take a bike (H), then they bike to the station close to the destination, return the bike (R) and walk to the destination. Upon arrival, the user process is re-instantiated (M).

The mathematical framework is that of Markov Renewal Processes (MRP), which are a generalisation of Continuous Time Markov Chains allowing for non-Markovian events and non-exponential distributions of inter-event times [9]. This approach was chosen in particular to reflect more accurately trip durations and agent's decisions. In particular, in MRPs the sojourn time has a distribution that depends both on the origin and the destination. In the model a user always finds a parking place, but this may not be in the preferred station if there are no places available. This then is reflected in a longer trip duration for the 'return' transition. The 'take' and 'return' transitions between users and stations are synchronised. The 'arrive' and 'mutate' transitions are not synchronised with stations but re-initialise the agent's states. For more details about the model, the Reader is invited to consult [30].

A model for station utility perception is used in which agents that want to take little risk tend to search for suitable stations in a larger area surrounding their target destination, whereas agents that take a higher risk search in a smaller area, risking not to find a parking place. Higher risk should lead to shorter trips in general when there are enough parking places available, but occasionally to much longer trips when this is not the case (see [30] for further details). The cycle time distribution obtained via simulation (Fig. 1) shows that such events affect only a small fraction of all trips if the distribution of agents' origins and destinations is *spatially homogeneously distributed*, as in Fig. 1, the 'uniform model' ($\Pr\{\text{cycling trip} > 30\,\text{min} \mid \text{uniform}\} = 0.01$) which increases sevenfold if there are larger destination concentrations as in the 'flow model' ($\Pr\{\text{cycling trip} > 30\,\text{min} \mid \text{flow}\} = 0.07$). The flow model reflects the presence of areas that attract more users than other areas at certain times of the day. This is a reasonable assumption about real cities. An obvious consequence is that also the areas of full stations will be, as a rule, larger. As shown in Fig. 1 the flow model approximates rather closely the actual distribution of cycling times in London.

Figure 3 shows a spatial simulation set-up for a grid of stations of the size of that of the London area. The panels in the middle and on the right show an artificially introduced probability distribution for the request for bikes and parking places, respectively.

Fig. 3. Spatial set-up to simulate the London data-set. Left panel: the map of randomly generated stations and a snapshot of their filling degree (circle size $\propto c$, shade $\propto n$). Middle, right: distributions of the demand origin and destination locations, respectively

The set-up of the model follows the principle that the total service area, the number and capacities of stations, the number of bicycles, and the average number of hourly trips should be close to those in London, but without pursuing a photographic accuracy of the underlying topography of the city. The result is a 7×13 km^2 area with a 19×38 array of stations with randomly perturbed locations, random capacities between 15 and 40 docks. Two groups of agents are injected into this model. The first group of 400 agents are sampled with uniformly distributed spatial and temporal demand profiles, simulating the homogeneous component of the overall demand. The second group of 2000 agents are sampled from topical spatial demand distributions that contribute to the visible peaks in Fig. 3. This group is requested to honour a kind of appointment that requires the agent to arrive at a destination by a certain epoch (time). These arrival times are sampled from $U(50, 60)$. The actual arrival time does not coincide with the appointment time, almost certainly, because the travel process is stochastic (cf. Fig. 1).

MRPs can be simulated using the methodology of 'exact stochastic simulation' of chemical reaction networks, substituting agents for 'molecules' [21], adapting it to a non-Markovian modelling framework. Among the known simulation methods, the highest efficiency was achieved by adapting a version of the 'next reaction method' [20]. Such simulations generate a stochastic trajectory $Y(\omega) = \{T_i, X_i, i \in \{0, \dots, N\}\}$ where $\{T_i\}$ is a series of epochs of events, and the state space of $X_i = \{\otimes_{a \in \mathscr{A}} \alpha_a(i), \otimes_{s \in \mathscr{S}} \sigma_s(i)\} \in \mathscr{X} = \{H, R, A, M\}^{\mathscr{A}} \times$

$\otimes_{s \in \mathscr{S}}\{0, \ldots, c_s\}$ is a product space of the agent states $\{H, R, A, M\}$ for all agents $\mathscr{A}$, and the number of parked vehicles $\sigma_s \in \{0, \ldots, c_s\}$, where c_s is the capacity of station s, for each bike-sharing station $s \in \mathscr{S}$. This trajectory is then transformed into a snapshot sequence. A snapshot sequence $\Sigma(\omega)$ is defined as a projection of $Y(\omega)$ to the station-only component, cut at regular time intervals $\Delta > 0$. Thus $\Sigma(\omega) = \{\otimes_{s \in \mathscr{S}} \hat{\sigma}_s(j), j = 0, \ldots\}$, where $\hat{\sigma}_s(j) = \{\sigma_s(i) : T_i \leq \Delta j < T_{i+1}\}$. Each sequence $(\hat{\sigma}_s(0), \hat{\sigma}_s(1), \ldots)$ is interpreted as a sequence of independent random numbers, which are integral and bounded by 0 and c_s (see Fig. 4 for a graphical illustration). The interpretation of all stations' sequences is clearly a complicated task for analysis. In the following sections, we will show the application of *statistical* spatio-temporal model checking to identify problematic stations and areas. Note that by virtue of the Hoeffding's theorem [36], such sequences are Monte Carlo-compatible [25], justifying the deployment of SMC, as described in Sect. 4.1.

3   Spatio-Temporal Model Checking

Spatio-temporal model checking is a variant of classical model checking where *spatial* logical reasoning is combined with classical temporal operators. In this work we use the *spatio-temporal logic of closure spaces* (STLCS) of [13]. The temporal fragment of the logic consists in *Computation Tree Logic* [16], whereas the spatial fragment is that of [10], comprising a spatial *near* modality, expressing topological proximity, and a binary spatial *surrounded* operator.

STLCS is interpreted over so-called *snapshot models* [27]. A snapshot model is a triple consisting of a *Kripke frame* $(S, \mathscr{R})$ with states in S, accounting for the temporal evolution of a system, a *closure space*[2] $(X, \mathscr{C})$ that represents space, and a valuation function $\mathscr{V} : X \times S \to 2^P$ assigning to each pair of a point in X, and a state in S, the boolean valuation 2^P of a finite set of atomic propositions P. Although using closure spaces for spatial logics is relevant in order to link it to the topological interpretation of [2], for the purpose of this paper, looking at so-called *quasi-discrete closure spaces* [19] is sufficient. In other words, the reader may consider X to be the nodes of a finite directed graph G, and, given $A \subseteq X$, let $\mathscr{C}(A)$ be A itself, plus the nodes b in X such that there is a node a in A, with $a \to b$ an edge of G.

The formal syntax of formulas is described by the grammar in Fig. 5, where p ranges over a finite or countable set of *atomic propositions*. The truth value of formula ϕ is defined at a point in space x and state s, written $(x, s) \models \phi$. The full semantics of the logic is provided in [13], whereas a tutorial-type introduction to spatial (and spatio-temporal) logics and their model checking can be found in [11]. We briefly comment on the spatial operators, that are less known. A pair (x, s) satisfies ϕ_1 *surrounded by* ϕ_2 (written $\phi_1 \mathscr{S} \phi_2$) whenever, in the graph

---

[2] A *closure space* is a pair $(X, \mathscr{C})$ where X is a set, and the *closure operator* $\mathscr{C} : 2^X \to 2^X$ assigns to each subset of X its *closure*, obeying to the following laws, for all $A, B \subseteq X$: 1) $\mathscr{C}(\emptyset) = \emptyset$; 2) $A \subseteq \mathscr{C}(A)$; 3) $\mathscr{C}(A \cup B) = \mathscr{C}(A) \cup \mathscr{C}(B)$. We refer to [10] for an introduction.

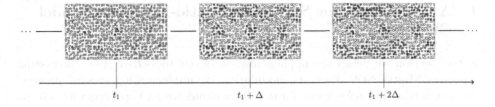

Fig. 4. Linear snapshot model based on single-simulation traces

$\Phi ::= \mathbf{TT}$ [TRUE] $\varphi ::= \mathbf{X}\, \Phi$ [NEXT]

$\quad |\ [\mathbf{p}]$ [ATOMIC PREDICATE] $\quad |\ \mathbf{F}\, \Phi$ [EVENTUALLY]

$\quad |\ !\, \Phi$ [NOT] $\quad |\ \mathbf{G}\, \Phi$ [GLOBALLY]

$\quad |\ \Phi\, |\, \Phi$ [OR] $\quad |\ \Phi\, \mathbf{U}\, \Phi$ [UNTIL]

$\quad |\ \Phi\, \&\, \Phi$ [AND]

$\quad |\ \mathbf{N}\, \Phi$ [NEAR]

$\quad |\ \Phi\, \mathbf{S}\, \Phi$ [SURROUNDED]

$\quad |\ \mathbf{A}\, \varphi$ [ALL FUTURES]

$\quad |\ \mathbf{E}\, \varphi$ [SOME FUTURE]

Fig. 5. STLCS syntax

associated to $(X, \mathscr{C})$, it is not possible to find a path p from x to a point y, with $(x, s) \nvDash \phi_1$, unless path p passes first by point z with $(z, s) \vDash \phi_2$. For interpreting the temporal operators, one uses the traditional interpretation of CTL, so that, for example, $(x, s) \vDash \mathbf{EX}\phi$ whenever there is a path p in the Kripke frame $(S, \mathscr{R})$ with $(x, p(1)) \vDash \phi$. This simple, orthogonal definition of space and time is typical of snapshot models (an example of a linear[3] snapshot model for BSS is shown in Fig. 4). However, arbitrary nesting of spatial and temporal formulas allows one to express quite complex assertions (e.g. a point x at state s being surrounded by points that *will eventually satisfy* a certain property). In STLCS, the temporal and spatial fragment can be freely nested; the computational complexity of the *global* model checking algorithm of [13] is linear in the product of the size of S, X, and the number of sub-formulas of the checked formula.

As an example, consider the STLCS formula $\mathbf{EF}\,[\mathtt{full}]\mathbf{S}\,(\mathbf{A}\,\mathbf{X}\,[!\mathtt{full}])$ where atomic proposition $[\mathtt{full}]$ is satisfied by full stations. The formula is satisfied by a point (station) x in state s if the point x possibly ($\mathbf{E}$) satisfies $[\mathtt{full}]$ in some future ($\mathbf{F}$) state s', and in that state, it is not possible to leave the area of points satisfying $[\mathtt{full}]$ unless passing by a point that will necessarily ($\mathbf{A}$) satisfy $[!\mathtt{full}]$ (not full station) in the next ($\mathbf{X}$) time step. In other words, a situation in which there is a contiguous area of full stations surrounded by stations that are not full.

---

[3] Note that snapshot models may also be branching models.

4   A Tool-Chain for Statistical Spatio-Temporal Model Checking

In this section we detail the implementation of our tool-chain. One interesting aspect of MultiVeStA [35] is its modularity. By implementing specific plugins, the tool acts as an *orchestrator* for running a simulator and observing its results. In statistical spatio-temporal model checking, MultiVeStA invokes several runs of the simulator of [30], which is deployed as a separate executable. The simulator outputs a spatio-temporal model in the format of `topochecker`. A special functionality has been added to the model-checker, permitting MultiVeStA to invoke it several times over the same model, while keeping `topochecker` running, to avoid reloading of the model and recomputation of the intermediate results. This permits one to define a large number of statistical observations in MultiVeStA, corresponding to the truth value of spatio-temporal formulas at each point of space, in an efficient way. We remark that, since the simulator is a separate executable, it is straightfoward to reuse the same tool-chain for simulations coming from other domains, as long as the simulation process formats its results using the input language of `topochecker`.

4.1   MultiVeStA

We briefly present the tool for distributed statistical model checking Multi-VeStA[4]. The tool can be easily integrated with any existing discrete event simulator, or formalism that provides probabilistic simulation. It has been successfully used in the analysis of many scenarios, including public transportation systems [22], volunteer clouds [34], crowd-steering [33], swarm robotics [6], opportunistic network protocols [3], contract-oriented middlewares [4], and software product lines [5]. Here MultiVeStA is used to estimate quantitative spatio-temporal properties of bike sharing systems. The integration is performed by instantiating a Java Interface exposing simple methods used by MultiVeStA to interact with the considered simulator (such as *reinitialize the simulator to perform a new simulation, perform one step of simulation*, or *perform a whole simulation*, depending on the specific use case).

Model specification is delegated to the integrated simulator, while Multi-VeStA offers a simple and flexible property specification language, MultiQua-TEx (which extends QuaTEx [1]). MultiQuaTEx consists of a few ingredients: (i) real-valued observations on the system states, such as the number of bikes in a bike station at a certain point in time, its current full/empty status, or the truth value of a spatio-temporal property (0 for false and 1 for true); (ii) arithmetic expressions and comparison operators; (iii) a one-step next operator (which triggers the execution of one step of a simulation); (iv) if-then-else statements; (v) recursion. MultiQuaTEx is used to define random variables, associating a real value to each simulation. Then, MultiVeStA estimates the expected value of such random variable. Note that in case we get 0 or 1 upon the occurrence of a certain

---

[4] Available at http://sysma.imtlucca.it/tools/multivesta/.

event (e.g., when considering the truth value of a spatio-temporal property), we get a Bernoulli random variable, and MultiVeStA hence estimates the probability of such an event. An in depth discussion of MultiVeStA's architecture and of MultiQuaTEx is provided in [33,35]. Estimations are computed according to a user specified confidence interval (CI) (α, δ). In particular, the mean value of n samples is computed, with n minimal but large enough to guarantee that the size of the $(1 - \alpha) \times 100\%$ CI is bounded by δ. In other words, if a MultiQuaTEx expression is estimated as $\overline{x} \in \mathbb{R}$, then its actual expected value belongs to the interval $(\overline{x} - \frac{\delta}{2}, \overline{x} + \frac{\delta}{2})$, with probability $(1 - \alpha)$. In all the experiments discussed in the next section we focus on the probabilities of bike station properties, fixing $\alpha = 0.1$ and $\delta = 0.05$. A single MultiQuaTEx query may address many different properties simultaneously, such as the number of bikes in each bike station at a certain point in time, or even at the varying of time. All such properties are analysed reusing the same simulation traces, leading to huge analysis speed ups. Note that the estimation of each property might require a different number of simulations. MultiVeStA performs only n simulations, with n the maximum number of simulations required by each individual property (see [33] for full details).

4.2   Statistical Spatio-Temporal Model Checking Using topochecker

Statistical spatio-temporal model checking assumes an underlying simulation model of a spatio-temporal system (that can be described as a snapshot model, see Sect. 3). The methodology is aimed at estimating the likelihood, at each point of space, that a given formula (with boolean valuation) is true, with a user-specified *global confidence interval* – that is, the same interval is used for all points. By this, a *heat-map* is produced that associates to each point of space a probability value. In principle, to achieve this, standard techniques from statistical model checking might be used. For each pair (x, s) to be observed and each formula ϕ, a series of simulations of a system should be executed, computing the (boolean) satisfaction value of $(x, s) \models \phi$ (see Sect. 3 for the meaning of this notation) in each specific simulation. A probability estimate can then be computed by keeping the cumulative account of the number of times the formula is satisfied, until the specified confidence interval is reached. However, such naive approach is not feasible on all but the simplest models, due to the already *cpu-hungry* simulation and model checking processes being iterated not only for the number of simulations that are necessary to achieve the required confidence, but also for each point of space. The proposed tool-chain turns the theoretical approach of statistical spatio-temporal model checking into a feasible analysis methodology. Input to the tool-chain are: (i) The parameters of the simulation, describing relevant features of a bike sharing system, such as the position and capacity of stations, and the number of users etc.; (ii) A set of qualitative or quantitative spatio-temporal formulas, characterising features of interest of the behaviour of the system, such as the formation of clusters of full stations; (iii) A set of quantitative queries whose evaluation is based on the outcome of the spatio-temporal model checking process. The approach used in this paper exploits the "multi" in MultiVeStA, by using an observation *for each point of the space*, resulting in a large number of random variables – one for each point of space and formula – being analysed at once reusing the same simulations. Since each observation in MultiVeStA corresponds to a different query in its internal language, we also adapted the spatio-temporal model checker `topochecker` to be run as a server for each bike sharing simulation. The server receives queries from MultiVeStA in the form of pairs (x, ϕ) where x is a point of space, and ϕ is a spatio-temporal formula. The value of $(x, 0) \models \phi$, where 0 is the first point of the trace obtained from the simulator, is computed and returned to MultiVeStA. The sophisticated *global* model checking algorithm of topochecker uses a cache that stores the intermediate computations of the model checker for each formula. As a result, the time required to compute the satisfaction value (x, ϕ) *for all points of space* x is just a fraction more of the time required to compute the same value on one point. Such machinery speeds up statistical model checking of a factor which is proportional to the number of points of the space. In our case, such speed-up is the key to actually be able to run our experiments. The output from MultiVeStA consists in a list of estimates of all the queries used (as we mentioned above, one for each formula and point of space). To actually produce a heat-map, the result is transformed by a simple *rendering* script, that colours the graph representing space, using the results from MultiVeStA. The resulting collaboration pattern is depicted in Fig. 6. We remark that the total execution time for all the properties we consider is in the order of around five hours on a standard laptop; this hints at the importance of observing multiple points at the same time (exploiting the specific capabilities of MultiVeStA); the size of the considered space is 722 points, and running the statistical model checking sequentially for each point would multiply our execution times accordingly, changing the approach from "feasible" to "unfeasible".

5   Properties and Results

In this section we revisit some of the spatio-temporal properties of bike sharing systems that were presented in [15]. Therein, some of the authors used spatio-temporal model checking on single traces of the BSS simulator. A regular grid representing bike sharing stations was coloured with two colours, representing the boolean satisfaction value of properties. As discussed, using statistical spatio-temporal model checking we can collect information about single simulations to assess the *probability* with which each station satisfies the property of interest in the entire system behaviour. We will visualise such probability by means of a colouring of the stations in a grid according to a sequential colour palette of 10 uniform steps ranging from light grey (denoting low probability) to dark red (denoting high probability). We use this visualisation to facilitate the quick analysis of the results. Detailed values of the probabilities, variance and size of the confidence interval δ are indeed produced by MultiVeStA. Let us first recall some basic spatio-temporal properties of bike sharing systems. Note that, throughout this section, all simulations start from an initial state in which all stations are half full.

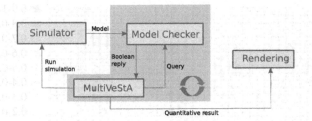

Fig. 6. Collaboration in the tool-chain used for statistical spatio-temporal model checking

Full Stations and Clusters. We characterise stations that are *full*, that is, with no vacant parking places, and *clusters* of full stations, that is, stations that are full, and are only connected to adjacent stations that are full in turn. These two (purely spatial) properties are formalised in STLCS below:

$$\texttt{full} \quad = [\texttt{vacant==0}]$$
$$\texttt{cluster} = \texttt{I}\,(\texttt{full})$$

Connectivity between stations is expressed using the derived *interior* operator $\texttt{I}\,\varPhi = !\,(\texttt{N}\,(!\,\varPhi))$. Informally speaking, in an undirected graph, points satisfying $\texttt{I}\,\varPhi$ are only connected to points satisfying $\varPhi$. The smallest possible cluster in the regular grid that was used for the simulation is therefore composed of a full station such that its direct neighbours in the north, south, east and west directions (also called its *von Neumann neighbourhood*) are also full. Note that the definition of $\texttt{cluster}$ only identifies (on purpose) these "inner" full stations and not their direct full neighbours. The abbreviation $\texttt{full}$ uses a boolean predicate (equality), applied to the quantitative value of the atomic property [$\texttt{vacant}$].

Let us now consider probability that a station will eventually be full, formalised as:

$$\texttt{eventuallyFull} = (\texttt{EF full})$$

MultiVeStA evaluates the property for all stations simultaneously, using the same set of generated simulations. As discussed in Sect. 4.1, we used $\alpha = 0.1$ and $\delta = 0.05$. The simulations cover a period of 100 min in steps of 2 min each. This includes the morning period in which there is a peak of requests for bikes and parking places due to a large group of commuters leaving from home. The results are shown in Fig. 7 that depicts the grid of stations, and for each station a colour indicating the approximate probability with which the property holds according to the colour scale shown on the right of the grid. The results clearly show that the stations that have a high probability to get full during this period of the simulation correspond to the areas in the model that have been assigned a high attractiveness for commuters as shown in Fig. 3 in a pattern that is easy to recognise.

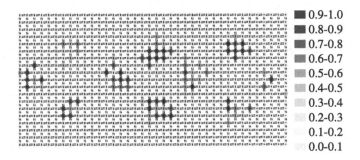

Fig. 7. Probability of stations to be eventually full within the maximal length of the simulations considered (100 min), starting from an initial situation in which all stations are 50 % full

We can identify stations belonging to clusters that *persist* for some amount of time, that is, they last for a specific number of time steps. The following formulas specify the persistence of such a situation for two and three time steps:

```
cluster2steps = cluster & (A X cluster)
cluster3steps = cluster & (A X cluster2steps)
```

By combining these formulas with the *eventually* operator, as before, we can assess the probability of stations to eventually become a cluster and remain so for 3 consecutive steps. The results are shown in Fig. 8.

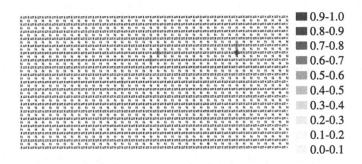

Fig. 8. Probability of stations that eventually become a cluster and remain a cluster for 3 steps

Problematic User Experience. The next property we consider is related to problematic user experience, namely not to find a parking place in a suitable station. When a user wants to leave a bike at a specific station, and such station is full, she may try to find a nearby station with available parking slots, or she may wait for some time in the same station hoping that someone is needing a bike. This behaviour may be typically sufficient to solve the problem, at the expense of a longer trip duration. One may want to check how effective this procedure is.

In the following formula, we check whether it is possible that, in three time steps of 2 min each, the user is still unable to leave the bike in the same or a nearby station because they are full when she arrives. The formula tripEnd characterises this situation. It expresses a nested spatio-temporal situation where the user arrives at a full station, and in the next step, while possibly moving to another neighbouring station, finds it full again, being unlucky this way for three consecutive attempts. In terms of the STLCS logic, this is expressed as follows:

tripEnd = full & (N (A X (full & (N (A X (full & N (A X full)))))))

Combining this formula with the *eventually* operator provides an overview of the probability that such an unlucky series of events may happen to a user at a particular station. The results are shown in Fig. 9. The resulting probabilities for the stations are very close to those for property eventuallyFull, but they are slightly lower.

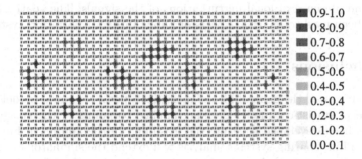

	0.9–1.0
	0.8–0.9
	0.7–0.8
	0.6–0.7
	0.5–0.6
	0.4–0.5
	0.3–0.4
	0.2–0.3
	0.1–0.2
	0.0–0.1

Fig. 9. Probability that a user willing to park her bike in a station finds it full and cannot find a parking place within three consecutive attempts in neighbouring stations

As a hint on the feasibility of the approach, we remark on the execution times. On a high-end laptop, the computations of the example of Fig. 9 take around 5 h, analysing 77 batches of 20 simulations each.

6 Related Work

The field of spatial logics is as old as modal logics itself, with early logicians such as Tarski already laying the foundations of a topological interpretation of modal operators and of the completeness of the logic $S4$ for the class of topological spaces [7]. Research efforts in spatial and spatio-temporal model checking are far more recent, and often tailored to specific applications. In [23] a linear spatial superposition logic is defined for the specification of emergent behaviour. The logic is applied to pattern recognition in the context of medical image analysis. The Mobile Stochastic Logic (MoSL) [18] has been proposed to predicate on mobile processes in models specified in StoKLAIM, a stochastic extension of KLAIM based on the tuple-space model of computation. Other variants of spatial logics concern the symbolic representation of the contents of images, and, combined with temporal logics, for sequences of images [8]. In [24], the approach of [23] has been further extended, defining the spatio-temporal logic SpaTeL, and a statistical model checking algorithm. The algorithm estimates the probability of events that relate different regions of space at different times. Regions are identified by spatial partitioning using *quad trees*. In SpaTeL, spatial formulas can only be nested below temporal formulas. In contrast, STLCS can arbitrarily nest spatial and temporal formulas, at the expenses of using simpler models that do not explicitly describe regions, but only deal with points. The spatio-temporal logic STLCS used in the current paper addresses properties of discrete, graph-based models that, in our case study, reflect the geographical position of docking stations in a city. The spatial fragment of STLCS, and related model-checking algorithms, were introduced in [10] and have also inspired the work on Spatial Signal Temporal Logics in [32], where a linear time logic is introduced to reason about properties of signals, considering both their truth values and their robustness in the presence of local perturbations of the signals. The spatial fragment has also been used to analyse aspects of public bus transportation systems [12].

7 Conclusions

We have discussed the general idea of statistical spatio-temporal model checking as a form of statistical model checking applied to points of the space. A toolchain has been developed to study the feasibility of the approach. Future work tailored to bike sharing systems analysis will extend the simulator by modelling *incentives* to analyse their usage in improving the overall performance of such systems. The effectiveness of incentives can be then captured by logic formulas and assessed statistically before their deployment.

More generally, statistical spatio-temporal model checking can be used in any kind of simulation scenario for spatio-temporal systems. As MultiVeStA can be integrated with discrete event simulators that allow for probabilistic simulation and the spatio-temporal model checker just needs spatial snapshot models in a very general format, the approach can be applied to other systems. We plan to use the approach also in modelling mitigation strategies for problems of *smart bus* networks, continuing the work of [12].

These developments are part of a more general effort in statistical spatio-temporal model checking aimed at investigating global properties of collective-adaptive systems (CAS), taking spatial aspects into account. In this light, it will be relevant to propose variants of statistical spatio-temporal model checking that operate over the semantic domains of process calculi with spatial aspects, such as [14]. A further interesting issue would be the extension of the statistical spatio-temporal model checking approach to handle rare events [26].

Acknowledgements. This work is supported by the EU project *QUANTICOL* (600708). We thank Mirco Tribastone and Daniël Reijsbergen for the usage data on the London bike sharing system.

References

1. Agha, G., Meseguer, J., Sen, K.: PMaude: rewrite- based specification language for probabilistic object systems. ENTCS **153**, 213–239 (2005)
2. Aiello, M., Pratt-Hartmann, I., van Benthem, J. (eds.): Handbook of Spatial Logics. Springer, Heidelberg (2007)
3. Arora, S., Rathor, A., Rao, M.V.P.: Statistical model checking of opportunistic network protocols. In: Proceedings of the Asian Internet Engineering Conference, pp. 62–68. AINTEC 2015. ACM (2015)
4. Bartoletti, M., Cimoli, T., Murgia, M., Podda, A.S., Pompianu, L.: A contract-oriented middleware. In: Braga, C., et al. (eds.) FACS 2015. LNCS, vol. 9539, pp. 86–104. Springer, Heidelberg (2016). doi:10.1007/978-3-319-28934-2_5
5. ter Beek, M.H., Legay, A., Lluch-Lafuente, A., Vandin, A.: Statistical analysis of probabilistic models of software product lines with quantitative constraints. In: 19th International Conference on Software Product Line, pp. 11–15. ACM (2015)
6. Belzner, L., De Nicola, R., Vandin, A., Wirsing, M.: Reasoning (on) service component ensembles in rewriting logic. In: Iida, S., Meseguer, J., Ogata, K. (eds.) Specification, Algebra, and Software. LNCS, vol. 8373, pp. 188–211. Springer, Heidelberg (2014)
7. van Benthem, J., Bezhanishvili, G.: Modal logics of space. In: Aiello, M., Pratt-Hartmann, I., Van Benthem, J. (eds.) Handbook of Spatial Logics, pp. 217–298. Springer, Heidelberg (2007)
8. Bimbo, A.D., Vicario, E., Zingoni, D.: Symbolic description and visual querying of image sequences using spatio-temporal logic. IEEE Trans. Knowl. Data Eng. **7**(4), 609–622 (1995)
9. Çinlar, E.: Introduction to Stochastic Processes. Prentice-Hall, Upper Saddle River (1975)
10. Ciancia, V., Latella, D., Loreti, M., Massink, M.: Specifying and verifying properties of space. In: Diaz, J., Lanese, I., Sangiorgi, D. (eds.) TCS 2014. LNCS, vol. 8705, pp. 222–235. Springer, Heidelberg (2014)
11. Ciancia, V., Latella, D., Loreti, M., Massink, M.: Spatial logic and spatial model checking for closure spaces. In: Bernardo, M., De Nicola, R., Hillston, J. (eds.) SFM 2016. LNCS, vol. 9700, pp. 156–201. Springer, Heidelberg (2016). doi:10.1007/978-3-319-34096-8_6
12. Ciancia, V., Gilmore, S., Latella, D., Loreti, M., Massink, M.: Data verification for collective adaptive systems: spatial model-checking of vehicle location data. In: IEEE International Conference on Self-Adaptive and Self-Organizing Systems, 2nd FoCAS Workshop (2014)
13. Ciancia, V., Grilletti, G., Latella, D., Loreti, M., Massink, M.: An experimental spatio-temporal model checker. In: Bianculli, D., et al. (eds.) SEFM 2015 Workshops. LNCS, vol. 9509, pp. 297–311. Springer, Heidelberg (2015). doi:10.1007/978-3-662-49224-6_24
14. Ciancia, V., Latella, D., Massink, M.: On-the-fly mean-field model-checking for attribute-based coordination. In: Lluch Lafuente, A., Proença, J. (eds.) COORDINATION 2016. LNCS, vol. 9686, pp. 67–83. Springer, Heidelberg (2016). doi:10.1007/978-3-319-39519-7_5

15. Ciancia, V., Latella, D., Massink, M., Paškauskas, R.: Exploring spatio-temporal properties of bike-sharing systems. In: SASO Workshops, pp. 74–79. IEEE Computer Society (2015)
16. Clarke, E.M., Emerson, E.A.: Design and synthesis of synchronization skeletons using branching time temporal logic. In: Grumberg, O., Veith, H. (eds.) 25 Years of Model Checking. LNCS, vol. 5000, pp. 196–215. Springer, Heidelberg (2008)
17. Maio, P.: Bike-sharing: its history, impacts, models of provision, and future. J. Publ. Transp. **12**(4), 41–56 (2009)
18. De Nicola, R., Katoen, J.P., Latella, D., Loreti, M., Massink, M.: Model checking mobile stochastic logic. Theor. Comput. Sci. **382**(1), 42–70 (2007)
19. Galton, A.: The mereotopology of discrete space. In: Freksa, C., Mark, D.M. (eds.) COSIT 1999. LNCS, vol. 1661, pp. 251–266. Springer, Heidelberg (1999)
20. Gibson, M.A., Bruck, J.: Efficient exact stochastic simulation of chemical systems with many species and many channels. J. Phys. Chem. A **104**(9), 1876–1889 (2000)
21. Gillespie, D.T.: Stochastic simulation of chemical kinetics. Ann. Rev. Phys. Chem. **58**, 35–55 (2007)
22. Gilmore, S., Tribastone, M., Vandin, A.: An analysis pathway for the quantitative evaluation of public transport systems. In: Albert, E., Sekerinski, E. (eds.) IFM 2014. LNCS, vol. 8739, pp. 71–86. Springer, Heidelberg (2014)
23. Grosu, R., Smolka, S.A., Corradini, F., Wasilewska, A., Entcheva, E., Bartocci, E.: Learning and detecting emergent behavior in networks of cardiac myocytes. Commun. ACM **52**(3), 97–105 (2009)
24. Haghighi, I., Jones, A., Kong, Z., Bartocci, E., Gros, R., Belta, C.: Spatel: A novel spatial-temporal logic and its applications to networked systems. In: 18th International Conference on Hybrid Systems: Computation and Control, pp. 189–198. ACM (2015)
25. Hauskrecht, M.: Monte-Carlo approximations to continuous-time semi-Markov processes. Technical report CS-03-02, University of Pittsburgh (2002)
26. Jegourel, C., Legay, A., Sedwards, S.: Importance splitting for statistical model checking rare properties. In: Sharygina, N., Veith, H. (eds.) CAV 2013. LNCS, vol. 8044, pp. 576–591. Springer, Heidelberg (2013)
27. Kontchakov, R., Kurucz, A., Wolter, F., Zakharyaschev, M.: Spatial logic + temporal logic = ? In: Aiello, M., Pratt-Hartmann, I., Van Benthem, J. (eds.) Handbook of Spatial Logics, pp. 497–564. Springer, Heidelberg (2007)
28. Larsen, K.G., Legay, A.: Statistical model checking past, present, and future. In: Margaria, T., Steffen, B. (eds.) ISoLA 2014, Part II. LNCS, vol. 8803, pp. 135–142. Springer, Heidelberg (2014)
29. Legay, A., Delahaye, B., Bensalem, S.: Statistical model checking: an overview. In: Barringer, H., et al. (eds.) RV 2010. LNCS, vol. 6418, pp. 122–135. Springer, Heidelberg (2010)
30. Massink, M., Paškauskas, R.: Model-based assessment of aspects of user-satisfaction in bicycle sharing systems. In: 18th International Conference on Intelligent Transportation Systems, pp. 1363–1370. IEEE (2015)
31. Midgley, P.: Bicycle-sharing schemes: enhancing sustainable mobility in urban areas. In: 19th session of the Commission on Sustainable Development. CSD19/2011/BP8, United Nations (2011)
32. Nenzi, L., Bortolussi, L., Ciancia, V., Loreti, M., Massink, M.: Qualitative and quantitative monitoring of spatio-temporal properties. In: Bartocci, E., Majumdar, R. (eds.) RV 2015. LNCS, vol. 9333, pp. 21–37. Springer, Heidelberg (2015). doi:10.1007/978-3-319-23820-3_2

33. Pianini, D., Sebastio, S., Vandin, A.: Distributed statistical analysis of complex systems modeled through a chemical metaphor. In: International Conference on High Performance Computing & Simulation, pp. 416–423. IEEE (2014)
34. Sebastio, S., Amoretti, M., Lluch Lafuente, A.: A computational field framework for collaborative task execution in volunteer clouds. In: ICSE workshop SEAMS, pp. 105–114. ACM (2014)
35. Sebastio, S., Vandin, A.: MultiVeStA: statistical model checking for discrete event simulators. In: ValueTools, pp. 310–315. ACM (2013)
36. Serfling, R.J.: Approximation Theorems of Mathematical Statistics, Probability and Statistics, vol. 162. Wiley, Hoboken (1980)

Rigorous Graphical Modelling of Movement in Collective Adaptive Systems

N. Zoń[✉], S. Gilmore, and J. Hillston

Laboratory for Foundations of Computer Science, School of Informatics,
University of Edinburgh, Edinburgh, Scotland
N.Zon@sms.ed.ac.uk

Abstract. Formal modelling provides valuable intellectual tools which can be applied to the problem of analysis and optimisation of systems. In this paper we present a novel software tool which provides a graphical approach to modelling of Collective Adaptive Systems (CAS) with constrained movement. The graphical description is translated into a model that can be analysed to understand the dynamic behaviour of the system. This generated model is expressed in CARMA, a modern feature-rich modelling language designed specifically for modelling CAS. We demonstrate the use of the software tool with an example scenario representing carpooling, in which travellers group together and share a car in order to reach a common destination. This can reduce their travel time and travel costs, whilst also ameliorating traffic congestion by reducing the number of vehicles on the road.

1 Introduction

Formal modelling of system dynamics makes possible the analysis and optimisation of smart city applications, many of which belong to the category of Collective Adaptive Systems (CAS). CAS are collectives of individual components acting and interacting within the context of a common environment. In contrast to systems in which all components have global and perfect knowledge of the whole system, in CAS each component has its own subset of information with the consequence that one component's knowledge might be inconsistent with the knowledge of other components.

Urban transport systems provide a good example of CAS and have been taken as a motivating context for our work. In this setting, systems often contain components whose movement in space is restricted in some way. For example, in bus systems, we can distinguish components that never change their location (bus stops), components whose movement follows a specific path (buses), as well as components that can move without additional restrictions (bus repair service cars, pedestrians). Other urban transport systems (carpooling, trams, bikesharing) also have components subject to one or more movement restrictions. Such systems with *constrained movement* are the focus of our work. In these systems the spatial locations of components can have a significant influence on the performance of the collective. A direct influence is observed when an agent

T. Margaria and B. Steffen (Eds.): ISoLA 2016, Part I, LNCS 9952, pp. 674–688, 2016.
DOI: 10.1007/978-3-319-47166-2_47

Fig. 1. A flowchart depicting CARMA code generation from graphical input.

is allowed or forbidden to perform specific actions based on the values of their location attributes. An indirect influence is, for example, a situation in which the time taken to traverse a path connecting two points is proportional to the distance between the locations of the two points in space.

CARMA is a formal modelling language designed for the purpose of representing CAS [1]. It provides a syntax for defining components, environments and systems as well as a number of tools for the exploration of the model, such as static analysis and simulation. When an underlying spatial structure also has to be captured by the model, the specification of the environment can become complex and error-prone. Moreover, the amount of CARMA code required for specifying these types of systems grows very rapidly with the complexity of the network and the number of reachable states of each component. In this paper we present an automatic tool for generating the CARMA model code from a graphical input. The tool comprises a Graphical User Interface (GUI) for defining the positions and possible movements of components, as well as a programmable API for the representation and automatic generation of CARMA code.

The GUI supports a newly-developed graphical modelling layer on top of the textual CARMA specification language. Our graphical modelling tool, consisting of a graphical editor and an implementation in the form of an Eclipse IDE plug-in, provides the user with visual ways of representing scenarios involving stationary, mobile and path-restricted agents. The graphical representation is then automatically translated into a CARMA language model template. The code generation scheme is depicted in Fig. 1.

By structuring our contribution in this way, we provide additional flexibility for CARMA users at no extra cost. If a graphical representation of the spatial aspect of the model would be helpful as a communication or documentation aid then the CARMA graphical editor is able to provide it. If, on the other hand, there is no obvious benefit in having a graphical representation for a particular model then the CARMA textual description can be produced directly instead.

The rest of the paper is structured as follows. Section 2 presents background information on CAS, CARMA, and the CARMA tools. Section 3 explains systems with constrained movement and Sect. 4 presents the graphical representation of such systems. Section 5 gives more information on the API, and Sect. 6 presents our case study. We conclude in Sect. 7.

2   Background

In this section we highlight some of the difficulties encountered when modelling CAS and give an introduction to the CARMA language. For a more formal definition the reader is referred to [1].

2.1   Modelling CAS

A major issue in faithful representation of CAS is scalability, both with respect to model expression and model analysis. By their nature CAS involve a large number of heterogeneous entities, which are subject to complex rules of interaction and communication but with limited, local knowledge. Furthermore the system is typically highly dynamic with both the entities and the environment subject to change over time. Thus communication based on addresses represented by entity identity or location will fail when entities enter and leave the system and change their location. We choose to use a process algebra-style language in which entities are represented as components and communication is *attribute-based*, meaning that communication partners are selected according to their characteristics rather than their identity or location [2]. The language concerned is CARMA (Collective Adaptive Resource-sharing Markovian Agents), a high-level language designed specifically for modelling CAS [1].

2.2   Moelling with CARMA

CARMA models consist of a *collective* of components that are situated in the context of an *environment*. Components are the dynamic entities within the model, communicating and collaborating with other components to enact the dynamic behaviour of the system. Each component has an associated *store* recording the current state of *attributes* such as location, or more general status indicators. This captures the local knowledge of the component.

These attributes form the basis of *attribute-based communication* where communication groups are dynamically-formed, making it possible to restrict the communication to sub-groups when it is appropriate to do so. These dynamically-formed communication groups are known as *ensembles* [3]. Examples of restrictions could include only co-located components, only components with adequate security permissions, or only components with sufficient battery charge. Restrictions are expressed as predicates associated with an action, and can be imposed by both the sender and the receiver.

Communication can be asynchronous, non-blocking *broadcast* communication (with many recipients) or synchronous, blocking *unicast* communication α (with only a single recipient). Broadcast communication on name α is denoted by $\alpha^\star$ whereas unicast communication is simply α. Communication occurs in a CARMA model when an output action from one component is matched with input actions of other components and both predicates are satisfied. Output predicates π place restrictions on the allowable receivers by requiring their local stores to satisfy the predicate. Input predicates similarly place restrictions on the admissible senders but can also inspect the values which are being sent, and might refuse a communication on the basis of these values if they are out-of-range or in some other way erroneous. Values which are accepted can be stored with an update σ. Additionally, process predicates can disallow certain behaviours in a component on the basis of the current state of the store; the process $[\pi]P$ will only evolve to the process P if the predicate π is satisfied.

Processes $(P, Q, \dots)$ in CARMA are thus defined by the following grammar:

$$P, Q ::= \mathbf{nil} \mid \mathbf{kill} \mid act.P \mid P + Q \mid P|Q \mid [\pi]P \mid A \quad (A \triangleq P)$$
$$act ::= \alpha^\star[\pi]\langle e \rangle \sigma \mid \alpha^\star[\pi](x)\sigma \mid \alpha[\pi]\langle e \rangle \sigma \mid \alpha[\pi](x)\sigma$$

The action prefix $\alpha^\star[\pi]\langle e \rangle \sigma$ specifies a broadcast output of the values in a vector of expressions e. The action prefix $\alpha^\star[\pi](x)\sigma$ specifies broadcast input of these values into a vector of variables x. The versions without the star are the unicast equivalents.

By convention in a CARMA model activity names begin with a lowercase letter, function and component names begin with a capital letter, and process names are written in all caps. Expressions in the CARMA language (as used in function bodies) are generated by the following grammar.

$$e_1, e_2, e_3 ::= \mathbf{return}\ e_1 \mid \mathbf{if}(e_1)\{e_2\} \mid \mathbf{if}(e_1)\{e_2\}\ \mathbf{else}\ \{e_3\} \mid e_1; e_2 \mid a_1 \mid b_1$$
$$a_1, a_2 ::= 0 \mid 1 \mid \cdots \mid -a_1 \mid a_1 + a_2 \mid a_1 - a_2 \mid a_1 * a_2 \mid a_1/a_2$$
$$b_1, b_2 ::= \mathbf{true} \mid \mathbf{false} \mid a_1 \sim a_2 \mid !b_1 \mid b_1\ \&\&\ b_2 \mid b_1||b_2$$
$$\sim ::= > \mid >= \mid == \mid != \mid <= \mid <$$

The environment in a CARMA model provides a context for the components. It imposes constraints on activities performed by components, determining the rate at which activities such as communication or movement can take place, with the option to set the rate to zero, if necessary environmental conditions are not met.

CAS are inherently spatially distributed systems and they typically involve large populations of components with the location of a component often constraining the activities that it can perform. In a CARMA model the responsibility for exerting these constraints lies with the environment. Thus the environment records the global state of the model and mediates the component interactions in the collective. Capturing complex spatial arrangements of components can mean that the environment must include functions to represent the spatial structures and the permissible placement and movement of components within those structures. For example, in a recently published CARMA model [4], ambulances travel along paths in a network, in order to reach locations at which accidents have occurred. There are two types of stationary components, hospitals and stations, and these are the locations to which ambulances can return when idle, until being activated when an accident occurs. In this scenario, even a relatively simple road network results in a large amount of CARMA code, in the form of functions in the environment, to capture the spatial layout and possible paths. This is difficult for the modeller and it is this problem which we seek to address with the CARMA graphical editor described in this paper.

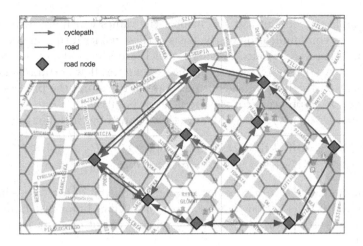

Fig. 2. An example of a system with constrained movement. The two graphs represent cyclepaths (shown in red) and roads (shown in blue). Path nodes are located on nodes of a hexagonal grid (in this case superimposed over a map of the centre of a city), and can be shared between all path types. Path-bounded components can travel along one or both of the defined paths, depending on the component type. (Color figure online)

2.3 CARMA Software and Simulation

Software support for modelling in CARMA is provided by the CARMA Eclipse plug-in [5], a toolset which supports the modelling process from model construction to execution and evaluation and analysis of results. Specifically, in this paper we will use the graphical tool for CARMA code generation and a discrete-event stochastic simulator to explore the possible behaviour of the generated CARMA models. Both of the mentioned tools are available for download from the website http://quanticol.sourceforge.net/.

3 Systems with Constrained Movement

In the current form of the graphical modelling tool we focus on systems in which the movement of components is constrained to follow certain routes in space, each route defined by a path, as seen in Fig. 2. More precisely, we consider systems which have the following properties:

1. *The environment of the system contains the definition of one or more paths (represented by graphs) which specific groups of components can traverse in order to change their location.*
2. *Components can be classified into one of three groups based on their ability to move in space:*

(a) *Stationary components* — their location attributes are constant.
(b) *Path-bounded components* — can only move along specified paths, their location attribute values belong to the set of node locations of nodes within the specified paths.
(c) *Free components* — can freely change their location attribute to any value (but are still bound by the environment's definition of space, i.e. a grid).
3. *The spatial locations of components within the system contribute either directly or indirectly to* measures *calculated during model evaluation.*
   – In other words we are interested not only in the topological arrangements of the locations of components but also in the distances between nodes.

Examples of systems with constrained movement include public/private transport networks, heterogeneous computer networks, pedestrian city networks, secure computer networks, animal migration networks, and many others.

4 Graphical Representation of Spatial Elements

In this section we outline the key elements available to the modeller in our graphical editor; essentially these are a graphical palette for specifying paths and a template of icons for representing components.

4.1 Representation of Paths

Paths are represented by graphs consisting of nodes, connected by edges. Nodes are placed on a grid which is an unbounded 2D plane, tessellated by hexagons or rectangles to define grid points. To reflect their placement on grid points every node has a location attribute which is a co-ordinate in two-dimensional space. The edges in a path graph are directed and coloured (see Fig. 3). The direction of an edge constrains movement on that edge to be in that direction. The colour of an edge constrains the types of components which can move along the edge.

The graphical palette allows the user to instantiate nodes, and the path connecting them, by laying out the nodes on the hexagonal grid. From the user's point of view, the creation of path node instances is very similar to the creation of component instances. Path nodes are distinct objects from components, and their instances are processed differently for the purpose of CARMA code generation. In contrast to component instances, path nodes are incorporated into CARMA functions. Each node can have zero or more incoming and outgoing connections of any colour, each colour representing a distinct path. All nodes have the same colour, and it is assumed that if a node has a connection of a particular colour, any component allowed to move along the route of this colour may assume the location attributes of that node.

Nodes are automatically named by the CARMA graphical editor as they are introduced. A node named nA will have integer x and y coordinates nA_x and nA_y. Nodes can later be renamed by the user to semantically-meaningful identifiers.

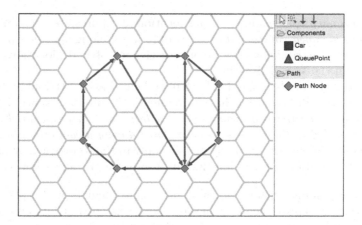

Fig. 3. A screenshot of the graphical interface for path and components layout.

4.2   Representation of Components

The user can specify a component type using structured input. The identifier and appearance of the component can be defined as well as the processes defined in the component, its allowable path and non-movement actions. Once a component type has been defined instances of that component type can then be placed within the graphical layout (by drag and drop). Component instances of the same type differ only in the values of their attributes and therefore can be represented by identical symbols. Their placement on the grid determines their location attribute. The state of a component, given by the value of one of its attributes, can determine if that instance is allowed to move on a particular path. For example, in the carpooling case study presented in Sect. 6, Car instances that are in the state PRIVILEGED can use both available lanes, while instances in the state NORMAL can only move along the slow lane.

4.3   Example Scenarios

Examples of systems that can be defined in the CARMA graphical editor include networks of paths. Each path is specified by a directed graph. The locations of the nodes of these graphs are restricted to a set of points on the plane (i.e. as nodes of a hexagonal grid). Nodes can belong to more than one graph — in this case, a component at a node may have a choice over the available paths, depending on the location, the type of the component, or the state of the instance, as explained above.

A Simple Urban Scenario. One example of a scenario with components that have movement constraints is an urban environment with four types of path-bounded components: Bikes, Cars, Pedestrians and Rollerbladers, which move within the environment using paths of the following three types: Pavement, Road, Cyclepath. Components' access to these paths is shown in the table below: In this example, the ability of a component to move along a path segment of a specific type depends only on the type of the component, not its attribute values.

Component name	Pavement	Road	Cyclepath
Bike	Allowed	Allowed	Allowed
Car	Forbidden	Allowed	Forbidden
Pedestrian	Allowed	Forbidden	Forbidden
Rollerblader	Allowed	Forbidden	Allowed

Listing 1.1 shows an example of an automatically generated function representing a two-way segment of a cyclepath. Similar functions are generated for each path type defined within the system. These functions are used within process predicates to impose the movement constraints that are appropriate for each component type. This can be seen in the subsequent listing, Listing 1.2, showing an automatically generated *Rollerblader* component.

Listing 1.1. A CARMA function to query the existence of a cycle path.

```
fun bool ExistsPath_Cyclepath(int xFrom, int yFrom,
                              int xTo, int yTo){
    if (xFrom == nAx && yFrom == nAy
        && xTo == nBx && yTo == nBy){
        return true;
    }
    if (xFrom == nBx && yFrom == nBx
        && xTo == nAx && yTo == nAy){
        return true;
    }
    return false;
}
```

Listing 1.2. The *Rollerblader* component, parameterised by its initial location (x, y), and initial process state Z.

```
component Rollerblader(int x, int y, process Z) {
    store{
        attrib x := x;
        attrib y := y;
    }
    behaviour{
        M =
          [ExistsPath_Cyclepath(my.x, my.y, nAx, nAy)]
              move_Cyclepath*[false]⟨⟩{my.x := nAx, my.y := nAy}.M
        + [ExistsPath_Cyclepath(my.x, my.y, nBx, nBy)]
              move_Cyclepath*[false]⟨⟩{my.x := nBx, my.y := nBy}.M
        + [ExistsPath_Pavement(my.x, my.y, nCx, nCy)]
              move_Pavement*[false]⟨⟩{my.x := nCx, my.y := nCy}.M;
    }
    init{ Z }
}
```

For each path node accessible from a given path type, we define an action with a predicate which ensures that there exists an incoming connection from the component's current location to the potential next location node. If the predicate is satisfied, the component may perform the action which results in an update of the values of its location attributes.

Movement actions are broadcast output actions, which means that components will perform them spontaneously without trying to synchronize with other components.

The topology-defining functions generated from the layout palette can be seen to have three roles: to store information, provide a mechanism for retrieving it, and to guard the global knowledge with respect to access rules defined for each component and location. In the modelling style implemented in CARMA, only the environment has global knowledge and components have only local knowledge. Thus the components can only access information about the paths in the system through the interface defined by the functions. These functions can be considered to be part of the environment. At the same time, the actions of any component are generated in such a way that only information concerning its current location can be requested. Thus, the restriction that components have only local knowledge is respected. Having no memory of their previous locations and no insight into future ones, components are unable to request information outside of their locality, even though a declarative specification of the network topology is always available to them through the interface.

5   Automatic Code Generation

The Java API for automatic code generation can be used as part of the Eclipse IDE plug-in as a middle layer between graphical input and the CARMA code input. This API can also be used as a standalone Java package, for users to define models directly at the level of the Java language or to provide their own GUI implementations. One reason to use the API in this way could be if we are generating CARMA code from available runtime data, instead of constructing the graphical representation manually using the graphical editor.

The Java representation of a CARMA model is a two-part specification, consisting of definitions of component types, constants, functions and measures (the template), and their use in a particular case (the instance). The CARMA code generation API reflects this structure, but constrained movement functions and component actions (which usually belong to the template part of a system), are generated with the use of information about a particular system instance (locations of path nodes and components).

Because of the need to explicitly specify location values and allowable connections for each state of each component, specification of movement constraints in CARMA is error-prone when typed by hand. The automatically generated code can be seen as a draft of a model, providing the definition of the movement policies applicable to a particular scenario. The user can later supplement the code with custom behaviour, where required.

6   Case Study: Carpooling

Carpooling is a means of improving traffic congestion in urban areas where large numbers of people move from one place to another at similar times during the day. It takes advantage of the infrastructure of High Occupancy Vehicle (HOV) road lanes, introduced on main roads in some cities. These lanes are less congested, and therefore allow faster and more comfortable travel; however only cars having at least a particular number of passengers are allowed to use them. The introduction of this infrastructure triggers the spontaneous formation of queue points, where people wait to be picked up by a car travelling in a particular direction. Both the owner of the car and passengers benefit from such an arrangement, saving time and money for journeys. The overall traffic situation in the city also improves since more people will choose to leave their cars at home and become a passenger, therefore reducing the total number of cars on the road.

Modelling carpooling can provide insights into the functioning of the system in practice and inform decisions on where to put pickup points in the network.

In our model, the Car component can change its state between NORMAL and PRIVILEGED, and its ability to move along a certain path depends on the current state of a particular instance (see Listing 1.3).

Component name	Fast lane	Slow lane
Car (NORMAL)	Forbidden	Allowed
Car (PRIVILEGED)	Allowed	Allowed

Listing 1.3. A *Car* component which has two local process states, NORMAL and PRIVILEGED. Note that here we show only the movement aspects of behaviour generated from the GUI.

```
component Car(int x, int y, process Z) {
  store{
    attrib x := x;
    attrib y := y;
  }
  behaviour{
    NORMAL =
      [ExistsPath_SlowLane(my.x, my.y, nAx, nAy)]
        move_SlowLane*[false]⟨⟩{my.x := nAx, my.y := nAy}.NORMAL
    + [ExistsPath_SlowLane(my.x, my.y, nBx, nBy)]
        move_SlowLane*[false]⟨⟩{my.x := nBx, my.y := nBy}.NORMAL;
    // Modeller-specified code to be added here.
    PRIVILEGED =
      [ExistsPath_SlowLane(my.x, my.y, nAx, nAy)]
        move_SlowLane*[false]⟨⟩{my.x := nAx, my.y := nAy}.PRIVILEGED
    + [ExistsPath_SlowLane(my.x, my.y, nBx, nBy)]
```

$move\_SlowLane^*[\textbf{false}]\langle\rangle\{\textbf{my}.x := nB_x, \textbf{my}.y := nB_y\}.PRIVILEGED$
$+ [ExistsPath\_FastLane(\textbf{my}.x, \textbf{my}.y, nA_x, nA_y)]$
$\quad move\_FastLane^*[\textbf{false}]\langle\rangle\{\textbf{my}.x := nA_x, \textbf{my}.y := nA_y\}.PRIVILEGED$
$+ [ExistsPath\_FastLane(\textbf{my}.x, \textbf{my}.y, nB_x, nB_y)]$
$\quad move\_FastLane^*[\textbf{false}]\langle\rangle\{\textbf{my}.x := nB_x, \textbf{my}.y := nB_y\}.PRIVILEGED;$
}
init{ Z }
}

Our model of carpooling is different from the one discussed by Yang and Huang in [6] in that they focus on exploring the various ways in which introducing multiple HOV lanes with toll differentiation influences the overall social welfare in a community, whereas we study the impact of lane speed differentials and the efficiency of passenger loading at queue points. Another approach to the problem was taken by Hussain *et al.* in [7] where they analysed the ways in which potential passengers can negotiate and reach agreements in order to form successful carpools with highest possible levels of satisfaction depending on their preferred start and offload location. Agent-based methods are also used by Guo *et al.* in [8] when using a genetic algorithm to solve the long-term car pooling problem efficiently with limited exploration of the search space. Simulation is the preferred computational method for car-pooling problems because the often-studied long-term car-pooling problem is a computationally hard combinatorial analysis problem best addressed by heuristics and simulation methods [9].

6.1 Specification in CARMA

In CARMA, we are able to define the Carpooling scenario, by specifying the actions available for each component state separately, and relating them to the predefined paths between nodes. In our model of the carpooling scenario, *Car* components move along path segments and can pick up passengers waiting at *QueuePoints* located at path nodes (see Fig. 4). The maximum number of passengers that can travel in a car at a time is defined as the constant *MAX_SEAT*.

A *Car* component can perform movement actions only when it is in one of the following states: *NORMAL, PRIVILEGED*. Cars in the state *NORMAL* have fewer passengers than the value of the constant *SEAT_THRESHOLD*. A car can change its state to *PRIVILEGED* by interacting with *QueuePoint* components in order to increase its number of passengers. Specifically, when a *Car* component is co-located with a *QueuePoint* component, the car and the queue can perform a sequence of actions in order to transfer a number of passengers from the queue into the car.

QueuePoint components can be in one of the following states: *EMPTY, FULL, FILLED* and *OCCUPIED*. If the queue is not *EMPTY* or *OCCUPIED*, it can synchronize with the car on the *offerPerson* output unicast action. The *offerPerson* action sends a message from the *QueuePoint* component to the *Car* component containing information about the number of people waiting in the queue, available for pickup. *Car* components try to maximize the number of new

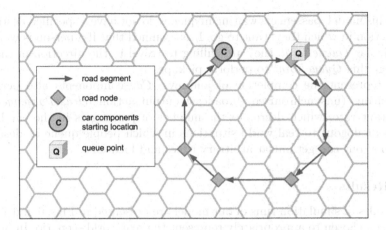

Fig. 4. A schematic view of the carpooling scenario. Path topology is the same for both the fast and the slow lane. The movement action over slow lanes has a lower rate.

passengers, while respecting the constraint that the number of uploaded passengers has to be less than or equal to the number of people available at the queue and the remaining capacity of the car. The *Car* component and the queue then perform the *carUpdate* unicast action in which the car informs the queue the number of passengers it can take, and the queue decreases its size accordingly, as shown in Fig. 5.

Fig. 5. A schematic representation of the information exchange between Car and Queue Point components during passenger pickup.

During this transfer, both the *Car* and the *QueuePoint* go into additional transition states. For a car, this state is *LOADING* and any car in this state cannot perform movement actions. For a queue, the state is *OCCUPIED*, which signifies that the component is busy performing a pickup action sequence with a car and cannot start performing pickup actions with any additional cars.

In this model, passengers waiting in queues do not have a specified destination or direction in which they want to go. It is assumed that if a person is waiting at a particular *QueuePoint*, they are willing to travel in the direction of cars that arrive at this *QueuePoint* to perform pickups.

To represent the completion of journeys, *Car* components also perform a spontaneous (unsynchronized) broadcast output action *releasePassenger*, with a constant rate, which decreases the number of passengers in the car by one. This is analogous to real world situations in which people queue at designated locations, but can get out at arbitrary times and locations.

6.2   Results

The results of simulation runs of our model are presented in Figs. 6 and 7. Rates have been chosen to appropriately represent the real world scenario. In order for the travel in the privileged lane to be beneficial, the movement action over this lane must have a higher rate than the movement action on the slow lane. The *offerPerson* action of the *QueuePoint* must also be sufficiently fast to ensure that the delay imposed by the interaction at the *QueuePoint* can be compensated by the increased speed in the priority lane. The rate at which a queue acquires new passengers is another value that can have an impact on the efficacy of the scheme. In real world scenarios, queues usually do not have a constant maximum size, but they do not grow infinitely; an approaching pedestrian will choose not to join the queue when it is sufficiently large. Similarly, a model in which the queue size is very low cannot demonstrate any benefit from carpooling.

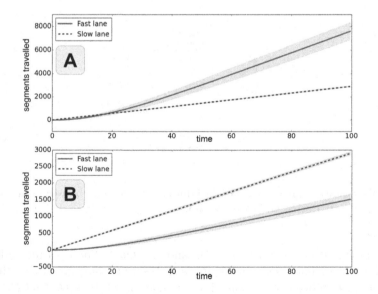

Fig. 6. Experiment showing how the movement rate in the fast lane impacts on lane usage (number of road segments traversed). Panel A: fast lane movement is 5 times faster than slow lane; Panel B: the movement rate is the same in both lanes.

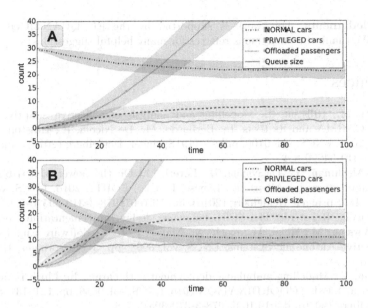

Fig. 7. Experiment showing the impact of the rate at which people are loaded as QueuePoints. Panel A: the loading rate is 1.5; Panel B: this rate is 10.0.

7   Conclusions

In this paper we have presented a newly-developed software tool which assists with the creation of CARMA models of systems in which location and movement play a significant role. CAS by their nature are large-scale systems so concepts such as location, separation, distance and movement very often have roles to play in their models.

By concentrating on location and movement, our graphical modelling tool provides a convenient separation of concerns between the spatial aspects of a model (such as location, proximity and movement) and the dynamic aspects of a model (such as attribute and state update, communication, and synchronisation). We believe that this separation can be helpful in allowing the modeller to focus their attention on particular aspects of the model in isolation.

Our graphical model-generation tool handles all of the low-level aspects of location representation such as placement on a co-ordinate system and the consistent handling of co-ordinate values throughout the model. This level of detail is often tedious and error-prone to maintain manually so we believe that the model generation approach also benefits modellers here.

We demonstrated the use of our software tool on a small CAS case study and paired our model-generation tool with the CARMA Eclipse Plug-in to take a model of a carpooling system from high-level design through compilation into Java and subsequent execution as a simulation study of the system. This gave us insights into the dynamics of carpooling, and provides some validation of the correctness of the transformation of our graphical design into running code.

Acknowledgments. This work is supported by the EU QUANTICOL project, 600708. We thank the anonymous referees for many helpful suggestions.

References

1. Loreti, M., Hillston, J.: Modelling and analysis of collective adaptive systems with CARMA and its tools. In: Bernardo, M., De Nicola, R., Hillston, J. (eds.) SFM 2016. LNCS, vol. 9700, pp. 83–119. Springer, Heidelberg (2016). doi:10.1007/978-3-319-34096-8_4
2. Abd Alrahman, Y., De Nicola, R., Loreti, M.: On the power of attribute-based communication. In: Albert, E., Lanese, I. (eds.) FORTE 2016. LNCS, vol. 9688, pp. 1–18. Springer, Heidelberg (2016). doi:10.1007/978-3-319-39570-8_1
3. De Nicola, R., et al.: The SCEL language: design, implementation, verification. In: Wirsing, M., Hölzl, M., Koch, N., Mayer, P. (eds.) Software Engineering for Collective Autonomic Systems. LNCS, vol. 8998, pp. 3–71. Springer, Heidelberg (2015)
4. Galpin, V.: Modelling ambulance deployment with carma. In: Lluch Lafuente, A., Proença, J. (eds.) COORDINATION 2016. LNCS, vol. 9686, pp. 121–137. Springer, Heidelberg (2016). doi:10.1007/978-3-319-39519-7_8
5. Hillston, J., Loreti, M.: CARMA Eclipse plug-in: a tool supporting design and analysis of Collective Adaptive Systems (2016, to appear)
6. Yang, H., Huang, H.-J.: Carpooling and congestion pricing in a multilane highway with high-occupancy-vehicle lanes. Transp. Res. Part A: Policy Pract. **33**(2), 139–155 (1999)
7. Hussain, I., Knapen, L., Galland, S., Yasar, A.-U.-H., Bellemans, T., Janssens, D., Wets, G.: Agent-based simulation model for long-term carpooling: effect of activity planning constraints. Procedia Comput. Sci. **52**, 412–419 (2015)
8. Guo, Y., Goncalves, G., Hsu, T.: A multi-agent based self-adaptive genetic algorithm for the long-term car pooling problem. J. Math. Model. Algorithms Oper. Res. **12**(1), 45–66 (2012)
9. Correia, G., Viegas, J.: A conceptual model for carpooling systems simulation. J. Simul. **3**, 61–68 (2009)

Integration and Promotion of Autonomy with the ARE Framework

Emil Vassev[(✉)] and Mike Hinchey

Lero–The Irish Software Research Centre, University of Limerick,
Limerick, Ireland
{emil.vassev,mike.hinchey}@lero.ie

Abstract. The integration and promotion of autonomy in software-intensive systems is an extremely challenging task. Among the many challenges the engineers must overcome are those related to the elicitation and expression of autonomy requirements. Striving to solve this problem, Lero the Irish Software Engineering Research Center has developed an Autonomy Requirements Engineering (ARE) approach within the mandate of a joint project with ESA, the European Space Agency. The approach is intended to help system engineers tackle the integration and promotion of autonomy in software-intensive systems, e.g., space-exploration robots. To handle autonomy requirements, ARE provides a requirements engineering baseline where despite their principle differences in application domain and functionality all autonomous and self-adaptive systems are expected to extend upstream the regular software-intensive systems with special self-managing objectives (self-* objectives). Basically, the self-* objectives provide the system's ability to automatically discover, diagnose, and cope with various problems. ARE emphasizes this ability as being driven by the system's degree of autonomicity, quality and quantity of knowledge, awareness and monitoring capabilities, and quality attributes such as adaptability, dynamicity, robustness, resilience, and mobility. As part of its successful validation, ARE was applied to capture the autonomy requirements for the ESA's BepiColombo unmanned space exploration mission.

1 Introduction

Among the most promising advantages to autonomy in software is the fact that it enables software-intensive systems to become more versatile, flexible, resilient, dependable, robust, energy-efficient, recoverable, customizable, configurable, and self-optimizing by adapting to changing operational contexts, environments or system characteristics. Although very promising, the integration and promotion of autonomy in software-intensive systems is an extremely challenging task. Among the many challenges software engineers must overcome are those related to elicitation and expression of autonomy requirements.

This paper draws upon our experience with the Autonomy Requirements Engineering (ARE) approach to present its ability to handle autonomy requirements for self-adaptive systems. The ARE approach was developed by Lero, the

T. Margaria and B. Steffen (Eds.): ISoLA 2016, Part I, LNCS 9952, pp. 689–703, 2016.
DOI: 10.1007/978-3-319-47166-2_48

Irish Software Research Center, within the mandate of a joint project with ESA, the European Space Agency. ARE combines special generic autonomy requirements with goal-oriented requirements engineering to help software engineers capture the autonomy features of a particular system as well as what artifacts that process might generate, e.g., goals models, requirements specification, etc.

The rest of this paper is organized as follows. Section 2 presents a brief introduction to the ARE approach. Then in Sect. 3, we briefly present the ESA's BepiColombo mission that was used as a case study in this research. Section 4 presents how we promote autonomy in BepiColombo through ARE. The accent is put on autonomy requirements for the mission's "transfer" objective. Finally, Sect. 5 provides some insights on related work and Sect. 6 provides brief concluding remarks and a summary of our future goals.

2   ARE - Autonomy Requirements Engineering

ARE was developed to tackle autonomous systems by extending upstream software-intensive systems with special self-managing objectives (self-* objectives). These self-* objectives provide a system's ability to autonomously and automatically discover, diagnose, and cope with various problems that need to be overcome during execution. According to ARE, this ability depends on the system's degree of *autonomicity*, quality and quantity of *knowledge*, *awareness* and *monitoring* capabilities, and quality characteristics such as *adaptability*, *dynamicity*, *robustness*, *resilience* [2], and *mobility* [19–23]. ARE defines these characteristics in special domain-specific models for *Generic Autonomy Requirements (GAR)*. The GAR models are initially developed for the domain of the system in question and then further enriched with the specifics of the system in question in the process of capturing autonomy requirements. The autonomy requirements are captured in the form of *self-* objectives* backed up by the capabilities and quality characteristics outlined by a proper GAR model.

ARE associates the *awareness autonomy requirements* with *awareness capabilities* for self-awareness and context-awareness. Moreover, *situations* (see Sect. 4.4) may introduce the basis for situational awareness. Other classes of awareness could draw attention to specific states and situations, such as operational conditions and performance (operational awareness), control processes (control awareness), interaction processes (interaction awareness), and navigation processes (navigation awareness) [18].

The requirements elicitation with ARE starts with the creation of a *goals model* that represents system objectives and their interrelationships. The Goal-Oriented Requirements Engineering (GORE) techniques assist ARE in the process of goal modeling where goals are specified with intrinsic features such as type, actor, target, etc. Further, these goals are interrelated with other goals and environmental constraints. The ARE goals models can be organized in different ways copying with the system specifics and engineers' understanding about the system purpose. Moreover, these goals models might fall in three main categories: (1) hierarchical structures where goals reside different levels of granularity;

(2) concurrent structures where goals are considered as concurrent; and (3) a structure where both hierarchical and parallel models coexist.

In the next step, the ARE approach works on each one of the captured system goals along with the elicited environmental constraints to come up with self-* objectives that provide autonomy requirements for this particular system's behavior. Here, the GAR model is applied to every system goal (objective) to derive autonomy requirements in the form of goal's supportive and alternative self-* objectives along with the necessary capabilities and quality characteristics of the appropriate GAR model.

Note that the initial recording of the autonomy requirements is in natural language and UML-like diagrams. Then, a formal notation can be used to express these requirements in a more precise way where more details about the system's autonomy can be incorporated. For example, formally-specified GAR model can be used for different analysis activities, including requirements validation and verification.

ARE is applicable to any variant of self-adaptation, as long as we can build both GORE and GAR models for the system in question. Probably, the most complex case where ARE can be used is capturing the autonomy requirements of *collective adaptive systems*, working in a self-organizing manner [26]. A self-organizing collective system consists of a large number of interacting entities that coordinate their activities often in implicit way. In such a case, we need to work on both the "collective" goals of the entire system and on the individual, yet often simple goals of the entities composing the system. Note that "intelligent swarms" often mitigate the meaning of the single individual, so in such cases we need to work on GORE and GAR models for *classes of entities* generalizing the behavior and goals of groups of entities.

3   The BepiColombo Mission

BepiColombo is an ESA mission to Mercury [3,5,9,10] (see Fig. 1) scheduled for launching in 2015. BepiColombo will perform a series of scientific experiments, tests and measures. For example, BepiColombo will make a complete map of Mercury at different wavelengths. Such a map, will chart the planet's mineralogy and elemental composition. Other experiments will be to determine whether the interior of the planet is molten or not and to investigate the extent and origin of Mercury's magnetic field.

The space segment of the BepiColombo Mission consists of two orbiters: a Mercury Planetary Orbiter (MPO) and a Mercury Magnetospheric Orbiter (MMO). Initially, these two orbiters will be packed together into a special composite module used to bring both orbiters into their proper orbits. Moreover, in order to transfer the orbiters to Mercury, the composite module is equipped with an extra electric propulsion module both forming a transfer module. The transfer module is intended to do the long cruise from Erath to Mercury by using the electric propulsion engine and the gravity assists of Moon, Venus and Mercury. The transfer module spacecraft will have a 6 year interplanetary cruise

Fig. 1. BepiColombo arriving at Mercury [5]

to Mercury using solar-electric propulsion and Moon, Venus, and Mercury gravity assists. On arrival in January 2022, the MPO and MMO will be captured into polar orbits. When approaching Mercury in 2022, the transfer module will be separated and the composite module will use rocket engines and a technique called weak stability boundary capture to bring itself into polar orbit around the planet. When the MMO orbit is reached, the MPO will separate and lower its altitude to its own operational orbit. Note that the environment around Mercury imposes strong requirements on the spacecraft design, particularly to the parts exposed to Sun and Mercury: solar array mechanisms, antennas, multilayer insulation, thermal coatings and radiators.

The Mercury Planetary Orbiter (MPO) is a three-axis-stabilized spacecraft pointing at nadir. The spacecraft shall revolve around Mercury at a relatively low altitude and will perform a series of experiments related to planet-wide remote sensing and radio science. MPO will be equipped with two rocket engines nested in two propulsion modules respectively: a solar electric propulsion module (SEPM) and a chemical propulsion module (CPM). Moreover, to perform scientific experiments, the spacecraft will carry a highly sophisticated suit of eleven instruments [3].

The Mercury Magnetospheric Orbiter (MMO) is a spin-stabilized spacecraft in a relatively eccentric orbit carrying instruments to perform scientific experiments mostly with fields (e.g., Mercury magnetic field), waves and particles. Similar to MPO, MMO is also equipped with two propulsion modules: a solar electric propulsion module (SEPM) and a chemical propulsion module (CPM). MMO has altitude control functions, but no orbit control functions. MMO's main structure consists of: two decks (upper and lower), a central cylinder (thrust tube) and four bulkheads [10]. The instruments are located on both decks. The MMO spacecraft will carry five advanced scientific experiments [3].

4   Promoting Autonomy in BepiColombo with ARE

4.1   GORE for BepiColombo

As we have seen in Sect. 2, the starting point for ARE is building a goals model for the targeted system. To do so, the first task is to establish the system's objectives.

BepiColombo's objectives are about exploring Mercury and its environment [3,10]. For example, BepiColombo will make a complete map of Mercury at different wavelengths and will chart the planet's mineralogy and elemental composition.

By applying the GORE techniques, we built a goals model for BepiColombo (see Fig. 2) that includes [3,10]: (1) the objectives of the mission that must be realized in (2) the system's operational environment (space, Mercury, proximity to the Sun, etc.), and by identifying the (3) problems that exist in this environment, as well as (4) the immediate targets supporting the mission objectives and (5) constraints the system needs to address. As shown in Fig. 2 the BepiColombo's goals model puts together all the mission goals by relating them via particular relationships such as *inheritance* and *dependency*. In this model, the low-level objectives are preliminary objectives that need to be achieved before proceeding with the middle-level objectives. Furthermore, the middle-level objectives are concrete descendants of the high-level generic objectives.

Below, we present the GORE characteristics of the Transfer objective. This objective is one of the mission's low-level, supporting objectives that provide support to the middle-level objectives (see Fig. 2) [21,23]:

- **Transfer**: Transport the BepiColombo Spacecraft to Mercury.
  - **Rationale**: Involves the long cruise phase including a combination of electric propulsion and gravity-assist maneuvers (once by Earth, twice by Venus, and four times by Mercury). During the voyage to Mercury, the two orbiters and the carrier spacecraft, consisting of electric propulsion and traditional chemical rocket units, will form one single composite spacecraft.
  - **Actors**: BepiColombo transfer module, chemical rocket engines, electric propulsion rocket engines, Earth, Venus, Mercury, the Sun, Base on Earth, BepiColombo composite module (MPO and MMO).
  - **Targets**: interplanetary trajectory.
- **Orbit-placement**: Both MPO and MMO must be placed in orbit around Mercury to fulfill the mission objectives.
  - **Rationale**: When approaching Mercury in, the carrier spacecraft will be separated and the composite spacecraft will use rocket engines and a technique called weak stability boundary capture to bring it into polar orbit around the planet. When the MMO orbit is reached, the MPO will separate and lower its altitude to its own operational orbit. Observations from orbit will be taken for at least one Earth year.
  - **Actors**: BepiColombo transfer module, electric propulsion rocket engines, chemical rocket engines, Mercury, the Sun, Base on Earth, BepiColombo composite module (MPO and MMO), MPO, MMO.
  - **Targets**: MPO orbit, MMO orbit

4.2   GAR for BepiColombo

The preliminary work in this project included building GAR (generic autonomy requirements) models for all the classes of ESA space missions [23]. Having the GAR models for the space domain completed allowed us determine the

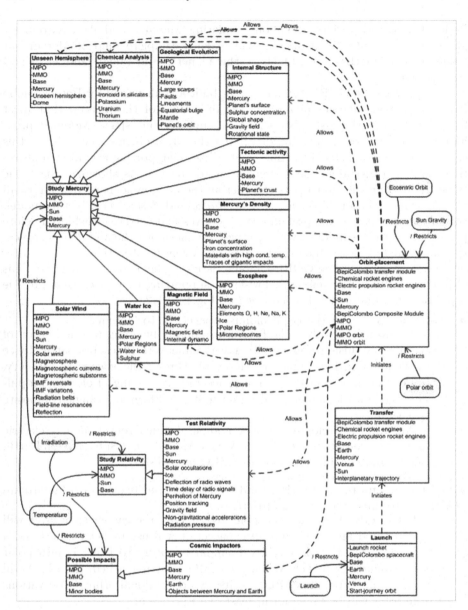

Fig. 2. GORE coals model for BepiColombo [23]

proper GAR model for the BepiColombo mission by simply categorizing the mission in the proper domain. The BepiColombo Mission falls in the category of "Interplanetary Missions" [22] and consecutively inherits the GAR model for such missions [23]. Moreover, considering that BepiColombo addresses scientific tests and exploration of the Mercury's surface, some of the relevant objectives put the mission in another category to consecutively inherit the GAR model for

"Small Object to Orbit" Missions [23]. Although, Mercury is not considered as a "small object", the BepiColombo's scientific objectives have characteristics similar to those of "Small Object to Orbit" Missions, which helped us adapt their GAR model and derive the autonomy requirements for BepiColombo's Scientific Objectives. Note that the relevant environmental constraints were also used in this process.

The following is an aspect of the GAR model for BepiColombo, which we derived by categorizing BepiColombo as an *interplanetary mission* [23]. Here, the model consider's the BepiColombo's Transfer Objective that requires the transfer trajectory to be developed with concerns about possible perturbations caused by the gravitational influence of the Sun and the near planetary bodies, e.g., the planets Earth, Venus and Mercury, and the Moon [21,23]:

- **self-* requirements (autonomicity)**:
    - *self-trajectory*:
        - autonomously acquire the most optimal trajectory to reach Mercury;
        - adapt to trajectory perturbations due to gravitational influence of the Sun, the Moon, Earth, Venus and Mercury.
    - *self-protection*:
        - autonomously detect the presence of high solar irradiation and: (1) protect the electronics on board and instruments; (2) get away if possible by using electric propulsion and/or chemical propulsion.
        - the altitude of the Transfer Module during the interplanetary cruise should be kept without solar input to the MMO's and MPO's upper surface.
    - *self-scheduling*:
        - autonomously determine the need of a gravity-assist maneuver: (1) near Earth; (2) near Venues (twice); and (3) near Mercury (4 times).
    - *self-reparation*:
        - autonomously restore broken communication links;
        - when malfunctioning, components should be fixed autonomously where possible.
- **knowledge**: mission objectives (Transfer Objective); payload operational requirements; instruments onboard together with their characteristics (acceptable levels of radiation); Base on Earth; propulsion system (electric propulsion rockets, chemical propulsion rockets); communication links; data transmission format; eclipse period; altitude; communication mechanisms onboard; gravitational forces (Earth gravity, Moon gravity, Venus gravity, Sun gravity and Mercury gravity);
- **awareness**: trajectory awareness; radiation awareness; instrument awareness; sensitive to thermal stimuli; gravitational forces awareness; data-transfer awareness; speed awareness; communication awareness.
- **monitoring**: electronic components onboard; surrounding environment (e.g., radiation level, planets, the Sun and other space objects); planned operations (status, progress, feasibility, etc.).

- **adaptability**: adaptable mission parameters concerning the Transfer Objective (e.g., what can be adapted in pursing the Transfer Objective); possibility for re-planning (adaptation) of operations; adapt to loss of energy; adapt to high radiation; adapt to weak a satellite-ground station communication link; adapt to low energy.
- **dynamicity**: dynamic communication links;
- **robustness**: robust to temperature changes; robust to cruise trajectory perturbations; robust to communication losses;
- **resilience**: loss of energy is recoverable; resilient to radiation.
- **mobility**: information goes in and out; changing trajectory.

4.3   Self-* Objectives Assisting Transfer Objective

The ultimate result "chased" by ARE is deriving the special, yet assisting self-* objectives. Recall that these self-* objectives provide system's behavior alternatives and in this particular exercise, the self-* objectives were derived from the already-built GAR model with respect to the BepiColombo Mission Objectives. The following elements describe the derived self-* objectives intended to assist the BepiColombo's Transfer Objective [21,23]:

- **Self-trajectory_1**: Autonomously acquire the most optimal trajectory to reach Mercury.
    - **Actors**: BepiColombo transfer module, chemical rocket engines, electric propulsion rocket engines, Earth, Venus, Mercury, the Sun, Base on Earth, BepiColombo composite module (MPO and MMO).
    - **Targets**: optimal interplanetary trajectory.
- **Self-trajectory_2**: Autonomously adapt to trajectory perturbations due to gravitational influence of the Sun, the Moon, Earth, Venus and Mercury.
    - **Actors**: BepiColombo transfer module, chemical rocket engines, electric propulsion rocket engines, Earth, Venus, Mercury, the Sun, Base on Earth, BepiColombo composite module (MPO and MMO), trajectory perturbations, gravitational influence.
    - **Targets**: interplanetary trajectory.
- **Self-protection_1**: Autonomously detect the presence of high solar irradiation and protect (eventually turn off or shade) the electronics and instruments on board.
    - **Actors**: BepiColombo transfer module, the Sun, Base on Earth, BepiColombo composite module (MPO and MMO), solar irradiation, shades, power system.
    - **Targets**: electronics and instruments.
- **Self-protection_2**: Autonomously detect the presence of high solar irradiation and get away if possible by using electric propulsion and/or chemical propulsion.
    - **Actors**: BepiColombo transfer module, chemical rocket engines, electric propulsion rocket engines, Earth, Venus, Mercury, the Sun, Base on Earth, solar irradiation.
    - **Targets**: safe position in space.

- **Self-protection_3**: Autonomously maintain a proper altitude of the Transfer Module during the interplanetary cruise, so no solar input will reach the MMO's and MPO's upper surface.
    - **Actors**: BepiColombo transfer module, chemical rocket engines, electric propulsion rocket engines, Earth, Venus, Mercury, the Sun, Base on Earth, solar input.
    - **Targets**: safe altitude.
- **Self-scheduling_1**: Autonomously determine when a gravity-assist maneuver is required near Earth.
    - **Actors**: BepiColombo transfer module, Earth, Earth gravitational influence.
    - **Targets**: gravity-assist maneuver, interplanetary trajectory.
- **Self-scheduling_2**: Autonomously determine when a gravity-assist maneuver is required near Venus.
    - **Actors**: BepiColombo transfer module, Venus, Venus gravitational influence.
    - **Targets**: gravity-assist maneuver, interplanetary trajectory.
- **Self-scheduling_3**: Autonomously determine when a gravity-assist maneuver is required near Mercury.
    - **Actors**: BepiColombo transfer module, Mercury, Mercury gravitational influence.
    - **Targets**: gravity-assist maneuver, interplanetary trajectory.
- **Self-reparation_1**: Autonomously restore broken communication links.
    - **Actors**: BepiColombo transfer module, BepiColombo composite module (MPO and MMO), communication link (state: broken).
    - **Targets**: communication link (state: operational).
- **Self-reparation_2**: Autonomously fix malfunctioning components if possible.
    - **Actors**: BepiColombo transfer module, BepiColombo composite module (MPO and MMO), component (state: malfunctioning).
    - **Targets**: component (state: operational).

Figure 3 depicts an enriched goals model capturing the relationships between the original Transfer Objective and the assisting self-* objectives. As shown, the self-* objectives provide behavior alternatives to Transfer Objective. Most of the assisting self-* objectives inherit the Transfer Objective, which allows them to keep the main objective's target (the mission's interplanetary trajectory). Note that the mission switches to one of the assisting objectives when alternative autonomous behavior is required, e.g., high irradiation emitted by the Sun.

4.4   Deriving the Self-* Objectives

As we have already seen, there are two milestones to be achieved before deriving the self-* objectives with ARE: (1) building a goals model and (2) deriving a GAR model for the targeted system. Once we have these two models completed, we merge them to derive the self-* objectives per system objective. The key point here is to apply the derived GAR model to each one of the system objectives

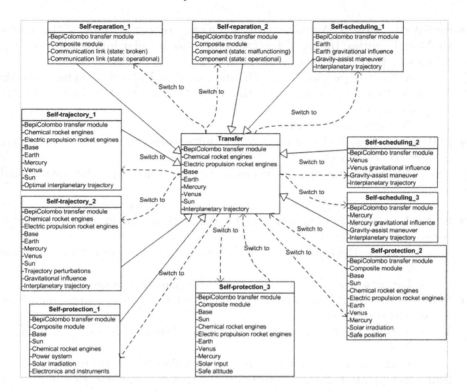

Fig. 3. Goals model for BepiColombo with self-* objectives assisting the Transfer objective [23]

(or to a class of system objectives, if the objectives can be generalized). Let's take as an example the Transfer objective and analyze how we came up with its self-* objectives.

The starting point shall be the derived GAR model. In this particular case, the GAR model is for Interplanetary Missions. Note that by definition this model defines four autonomicity requirements, which are explicitly defined as following [23]:

- self-trajectory (autonomously acquire the most optimal trajectory; adapt to trajectory perturbations);
- self-protection (autonomously detect the presence of radiation);
- self-scheduling (autonomously determine what task to perform next - equipment onboard should support the tasks execution);
- self-reparation (broken communication links must be restored autonomously; when malfunctioning, component should be fixed autonomously where possible);

The autonomicity requirements consider a generic autonomous behavior in the presence of particular circumstances, without deviation from the main objective (e.g., the Transfer objective). In general, ARE translates the autonomicity requirements into classes of self-* objectives where each class can be used to derive a few specific (not generic anymore) self-* objectives. In difference to the generic autonomicity requirements, the specific self-* objectives include a detail scenario that describes particular circumstances as a situation and a sequence of actions to be realized to move the system out of that situation. The actions are atomic actions to be realized by the system either in the operational environment (e.g., inter-planet space) or in the system itself.

To derive the sel-* objectives of the Transfer objective, we translated the autonomicity requirements of the GAR model for Interplanetary Missions into classes of self-objectives.

4.4.1 Self-trajectory Objective

The GAR model for Interplanetary Missions is based on the fact that these missions involve more than one planet or planet satellite and general trajectory information needs to be developed and understood for each mission. Moreover, the GAR model considers that interplanetary trajectories are influenced by *perturbations* caused by the gravitational influence of the Sun and planetary bodies within the solar system. ESA relies on powerful software tools to compute a large number of trajectories. Figure 4 presents possible trajectories for current Mars missions' opportunities [7].

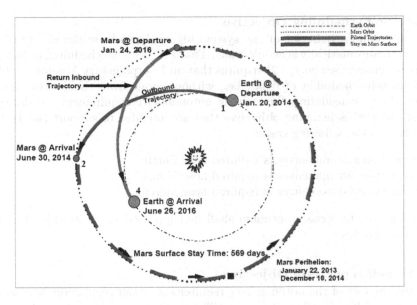

Fig. 4. Current opportunities for mars interplanetary missions [7]

Therefore, a specific self-trajectory objective needs to deal with the set of predefined trajectories and autonomously acquire the most optimal trajectory to reach Mercury. However, often, the mission shall deal with a variety of perturbations while following the currently selected optimal trajectory. This leads to another specific self-trajectory objective that shall autonomously adapt to trajectory perturbations due to the gravitational influence of the Sun, the Moon, Earth, Venus and Mercury.

4.4.2   Self-protection Objective

From another autonomicity requirement (self-protection, see Sect. 4.2), we derived a set of three specific self-protection objectives. Basically, while analyzing the possible hazards in space, we determined situations where specific circumstances may lead to the Transfer objective's fail. Then, we determined for each failure case a specific self-protection objective with a specific scenario and a sequence of actions determining the alternative behavior:

- **Self-protection_1**: this self-* objective shall help the mission keep-up with its Transfer objective in the presence of high solar radiation by protecting the vital components onboard;
- **Self-protection_2**: in the presence of high solar radiation, the spacecraft shall avoid the radiation stream by using propulsion;
- **Self-protection_3**: a proper altitude shall be maintained for the Transfer Module during the interplanetary cruise to avoid solar input to vital system parts.

4.4.3   Self-scheduling Objective

The autonomous behavior of any system highly depends on the ability of that system to automatically schedule tasks. That's it, the self-scheduling autonomicity requirement (see Sect. 4.2) requires that an Interplanetary Mission is able to perform self-scheduling of tasks, i.e., without input from the control base on Earth. Here, considering this generic autonomicity requirement we derived a set of three self-scheduling objectives that are intended to support the Transfer objective in the following cases:

- a gravity-assist maneuver is required near Earth;
- a gravity-assist maneuver is required near Venus;
- a gravity-assist maneuver is required near Mercury.

That's it, the trajectory optimum shall be supported by these objectives near planetary bodies.

4.4.4   Self-reparation Objective

Finally, the last of the autonomicity requirements - self-reparation, was used to derive two self-reparation objectives. These objectives where derived to assist the mission in keeping up with the Transfer objective even in the presence of particular system's malfunctioning, such as broken communication links and malfunctioning components. Here, to derive these self-objectives, we had to analyze all possible variants of repairing communication links along with all possible auto-repair activities that can be performed by the mission's spacecraft.

Note that these self-objectives also require a trade-off analysis. That's it. Often self-objectives need to be evaluated and re-evaluated to determine their relevance and importance. For example, repairing broken communication links may require considerable amount of energy that can be otherwise consumed for electrical propulsion, if necessary.

5   Related Work

ARE targets requirements for self-managing systems where managed systems can self-adapt with minimal human oversight. According to the closed-loop architecture, such systems are provided with a special control mechanism that monitors the system, reflects on observations for problems, and controls the system to maintain it within acceptable bounds of behavior. This mechanism is known as a feedback control mechanism in *control theory* [14].

The IBM Autonomic Computing Initiative introduced an external, feedback control approach in its Autonomic Monitor-Analyze-Plan-Execute (MAPE) Model [11]. To provide for self-management, the MAPE loop is implemented by an autonomic manager the manages the system instead of a human operator.

Requirements engineering for autonomous systems appears to be a wide open research area with only a limited number of approaches yet considered. The Autonomic System Specification Language (ASSL) [16,17] is a framework providing for a formal approach to specifying and modeling autonomous systems by emphasizing self-* requirements. Cheng and Atlee [4] report on work on specifying and verifying adaptive software. In [6,13], research on run-time monitoring of requirements conformance is described. In [15], Sutcliffe, S. Fickas and M. Sohlberg demonstrate a method called PC-RE for personal and context requirements engineering that can be applied to autonomous systems. In addition, some research approaches have successfully used goals models as a foundation for specifying the autonomic behavior [12] and requirements of adaptive systems [8].

Currently, ARE is the most advanced approach to autonomy requirements providing a complete methodology for both autonomy requirements capturing and expressing. The formal method used to express the ARE-captured requirements is KnowLang [25], developed within the mandate of the ASCENS FP7 Project [1,24].

6   Conclusion

To promote autonomy in software-intensive systems, it is very important to properly handle the autonomy requirements. In this paper, we presented an Autonomy Requirements Engineering (ARE) approach intended to solve this problem. The proposed ARE model uses the Goal-Oriented Requirements Engineering (GORE) approach to elicit and define the system goals, and then applies a special Generic Autonomy Requirements (GAR) model to derive and define assisting and often alternative goals (objectives) the system may pursue in the presence of factors threatening the achievement of the initial system goals. Once identified, the autonomy requirements might be further specified with a proper formal notation. This approach has been used in a joint project with ESA on identifying the autonomy requirements for the ESA's BepiColombo Mission. In this paper, we presented a case study where ARE was applied by putting GAR in the context of space missions to derive autonomy requirements and goals models incorporating autonomicity via self-* objectives.

Future work is mainly concerned with further development of the ARE model including a test bed based on KnowLang to verify and validate autonomy requirements.

Acknowledgments. This work was supported with the financial support of the Science Foundation Ireland grant 10/CE/I1855 to Lero - the Irish Software Research Centre (www.lero.ie).

References

1. ASCENS: ASCENS - Autonomic Service-Component Ensembles (2012). http://www.ascens-ist.eu/
2. Avizienis, A., Laprie, J., Randell, B., Landwehr, C.: Basic concepts and taxonomy of dependable and secure computing. IEEE Trans. Dependable Secure Comput. **1**(1), 11–33 (2004)
3. Benkhoff, J.: BepiColombo: overview and latest updates. In: European Planetary Science Congress. EPSC Abstracts, p. 7 (2012)
4. Cheng, B., Atlee, J.: Research directions in requirements engineering. In: Proceedings of the 2007 Conference on Future of Software Engineering (FOSE 2007), pp. 285–303. IEEE Computer Society (2007)
5. ESA: BepiColombo mercury mission to be launched in 2015 (2012). http://sci.esa.int/science-e/www/object/index.cfm?fobjectid=50105
6. Fickas, S., Feather, M.: Requirements monitoring in dynamic environments. In: Proceedings of the IEEE International Symposium on Requirements Engineering (RE 1995), pp. 140–147. IEEE Computer Society (1995)
7. George, L., Kos, L.: Interplanetary Mission Design Handbook: Earth-to-Mars Mission Opportunities and Mars-to-Earth Return Opportunities 2009–2024. National Aeronautics and Space Administration, Marshall Space Flight Center, Springfield (1998)
8. Goldsby, H., Sawyer, P., Bencomo, N., Hughes, D., Cheng, B.: Goal-based modeling of dynamically adaptive system requirements. In: Proceedings of the 15th Annual IEEE International Conference on the Engineering of Computer Based Systems (ECBS). IEEE Computer Society (2008)
9. Grard, R., Novara, M., Scoon, G.: BepiColombo - a multidisciplinary mission to a hot planet. ESA Bull. **103**, 11–19 (2000)
10. Yamakawa, H., et al.: Current status of the BepiColombo/MMO spacecraft design. Adv. Space Res. **33**(12), 2133–2141 (2004)
11. IBM: An architectural blueprint for autonomic computing (2004)
12. Lapouchnian, A., Yu, Y., Liaskos, S., Mylopoulos, J.: Requirements-driven design of autonomic application software. In: Proceedings of the 2006 Conference of the Center for Advanced Studies on Collaborative Research (CASCON 2006), p. 7. ACM (2006)

13. Savor, T., Seviora, R.: An approach to automatic detection of software failures in real-time systems. In: Proceedings of the IEEE Real-Time Technology and Applications Symposium, pp. 136–147. IEEE Computer Society (1997)

14. Seborg, D.E., Edgar, T.F., Mellichamp, D.A.: Process Dynamics and Control. Wiley Series in Chemical Engineering. Wiley, New York (1989)

15. Sutcliffe, A., Fickas, S., Sohlberg, M.: PC-RE a method for personal and context requirements engineering with some experience. Requirements Eng. J. 11, 1–17 (2006)

16. Vassev, E.: Towards a framework for specification and code generation of autonomic systems. Ph.D. thesis, Computer Science and Software Engineering Department, Concordia University, Quebec, Canada (2008)

17. Vassev, E.: ASSL: Autonomic System Specification Language - A Framework for Specification and Code Generation of Autonomic Systems. LAP Lambert Academic Publishing, Germany (2009)

18. Vassev, E., Hinchey, M.: Awareness in software-intensive systems. IEEE Comput. 45(12), 84–87 (2012)

19. Vassev, E., Hinchey, M.: Autonomy requirements engineering. IEEE Comput. 46(8), 82–84 (2013)

20. Vassev, E., Hinchey, M.: Autonomy requirements engineering. In: Proceedings of the 14th IEEE International Conference on Information Reuse and Integration (IRI 2013), pp. 175–184. IEEE Computer Society (2013)

21. Vassev, E., Hinchey, M.: Autonomy requirements engineering: a case study on the BepiColombo mission. In: Proceedings of the C* Conference on Computer Science and Software Engineering (C3S2E 2013), pp. 31–41. ACM (2013)

22. Vassev, E., Hinchey, M.: On the autonomy requirements for space missions. In: Proceedings of the 16th IEEE International Symposium on Object/Component/Service-Oriented Real-time Distributed Computing Workshops (ISCORCW 2013). IEEE Computer Society (2013)

23. Vassev, E., Hinchey, M.: Autonomy Requirements Engineering for Space Missions. NASA Monographs in Systems and Software Engineering. Springer, Heidelberg (2014). doi:10.1007/978-3-319-09816-6

24. Vassev, E., Hinchey, M.: Engineering requirements for autonomy features. In: Wirsing, M., Hölzl, M., Koch, N., Mayer, P. (eds.) Software Engineering for Collective Autonomic Systems. LNCS, vol. 8998, pp. 379–403. Springer, Heidelberg (2015)

25. Vassev, E., Hinchey, M.: Knowledge representation for adaptive and self-aware systems. In: Wirsing, M., Hölzl, M., Koch, N., Mayer, P. (eds.) Software Engineering for Collective Autonomic Systems. LNCS, vol. 8998, pp. 221–247. Springer, Heidelberg (2015)

26. Wirsing, M., Banatre, J.P., Holzl, M., Rauschmayer, A.: Software-Intensive Systems and New Computing Paradigms. LNCS, vol. 5380. Springer, Heidelberg (2008)

Safe Artificial Intelligence and Formal Methods
(Position Paper)

Emil Vassev[✉]

Lero—The Irish Software Research Centre,
University of Limerick, Limerick, Ireland
emil.vassev@lero.ie

Abstract. In one aspect of our life or another, today we all live with AI. For example, the mechanisms behind the search engines operating on the Internet do not just retrieve information, but also constantly learn how to respond more rapidly and usefully to our requests. Although framed by its human inventors, this AI is getting stronger and more powerful every day to go beyond the original human intentions in the future. One of the major questions emerging along with the propagation of AI in both technology and life is about safety in AI. This paper presents the author's view about how formal methods can assist us in building safer and reliable AI.

1 Introduction

AI depends on our ability to efficiently transfer knowledge to software-intensive systems. A computerized machine can be considered as one exhibiting AI when it has the basic capabilities to transfer data into context-relevant information and then that information into conclusions exhibiting knowledge. Going further, we can say that AI is only possible in the presence of artificial awareness [12], one by which we can transfer knowledge to machines. Artificial awareness entails much more than computerized knowledge, however. It must also incorporate means by which a computerized machine can perceive events and gather data about its external and internal worlds. Therefore, to exhibit awareness, intelligent systems must sense and analyze components as well as the environment in which they operate. Determining the state of each component and its status relative to performance standards, or service-level objectives, is therefore vital for an aware system. Such systems should be able to notice changes, understand their implications, and apply both pattern analysis and pattern recognition to determine normal and abnormal states. In other words, awareness is conceptually a product of representing, processing, and monitoring knowledge. Therefore, AI requires knowledge representation, which can be considered as a formal specification of the "brain" of an AI system. Moreover, to allow for learning, we must consider an open-world model of this "machine brain".

© Springer International Publishing AG 2016
T. Margaria and B. Steffen (Eds.): ISoLA 2016, Part I, LNCS 9952, pp. 704–713, 2016.
DOI: 10.1007/978-3-319-47166-2_49

2   Artificial Intelligence and Safety

But, how to build safe AI systems? With regard to system safety, there seem to be at least two "cultures" among the AI scientists. One culture emphasizes the limitations of systems that are amenable to formal methods (e.g., machine learning techniques), and advises that developers use traditional software development methods to build a functional system, and try to make it safe near the end of the process. The other culture mainly involves people working on safety-critical systems and it tends to think that getting strong safety guarantees is generally only possible when a system is designed "from the ground up" with safety in mind.

I believe, both research "cultures" have their niche within AI. Both cultures lean towards the use of open-world modeling of the AI by using formal methods. The difference lies mainly in the importance of the safety requirements, which justifies both approaches. Note that AI is a sort of superior control mechanism that exclusively relies on the functionality of the system to both detect safety hazards and pursue safety procedures. Therefore, in all cases AI is limited by system functionality and systems designed "from the ground up with safety in mind" are presumably designed with explicit safety-related functionality, and thus, their AI is less limited when it comes to safety.

For many NASA and ESA systems [17], safety is an especially important source of requirements. Requirements engineers can express safety requirements as a set of features and procedures that ensure predictable system performance under normal and abnormal conditions. Furthermore, AI engineers might rely on safety requirements to derive special self-* objectives controlling the consequences of unplanned events or accidents [13, 14]. You can think about the self-* objectives as AI objectives driving the system in critical situations employing self-adaptive behavior. Safety standards might be a good source of safety requirements and consecutively on safety-related self-* objectives. Such self-* objectives may provide for fault-tolerance behavior, bounding failure probability, and adhering to proven practices and standards. Explicit safety requirements provide a key way to maintain safety-related knowledge within a machine brain of what is important for safety. In typical practice, safety-related AI requirements can be derived by a four-stage process [14]:

1. Hazard identification – all the hazards exhibited by the system are identified. A hazard might be regarded as a condition – situation, event, etc., that may lead to an accident.
2. Hazard analysis – possible causes of the system's hazards are explored and recorded. Essentially, this step identifies all processes, combinations of events, and sequences that can lead from a "normal" or "safe" state to an accident. Success in this step means that we now understand how the system can get to an accident.
3. Identifying safety capabilities – a key step is to identify the capabilities (functionality) the system needs to have in order to perform its goals and remain safe. It is very likely that some of the capabilities have been already identified by for the purpose of other self-* objectives.

4. Requirements derivation – once the set of hazards is known, and their causation is understood, engineers can derive safety requirements that either prevent the hazards occurring or mitigate the resulting accidents via self-* objectives.

3   AI and Technological Singularity

But what will happen when the AI is programmed to *self-adapt* its hazard identification capabilities to improve the same or to identify new hazards that are not originally planned to be tackled. Well, we will most probably get to the next level of AI where it evolves and goes beyond its original meaning. This situation can be addressed as *technological singularity* [18]. Note that the term *singularity* has been used in math to describe an asymptote-like situation where normal rules no longer apply. For example, an originally programmed AI can stop detecting specific hazards, just because its evaluation criteria has evolved, and these hazards are not hazards anymore. From this point forward, we will be not tat far from the moment in the future when our technology's intelligence exceeds our own.

Such AI will be both powerful and dangerous. Why dangerous? The answer lays in the eventual damage - direct or indirect, that can be caused by overlooked hazards or misinterpreted human intentions. For example, your email spam filter can be loaded with intelligence about how to figure out what is spam and what is not and it will start to learn and tailor its intelligence to you as it gets experience with your particular preferences. However, you often delete emails that you want to read but do not want to keep in your email box. This can be misinterpreted by the spam filter's AI and it can start filtering these important messages for you.

4   No System Can Be 100 % Safe

Generally speaking, formal methods strive to build software right (and thus, reliable) by eliminating flaws, e.g., requirements flaws. Formal method tools allow comprehensive analysis of requirements and design and eventually near-to-complete exploration of system behavior, including fault conditions. However, good requirements formalization depends mainly on the analytical skills of the requirements engineers along with the proper use of the formal methods in hand. Hence, errors can be introduced when capturing or implementing safety requirements. This is may be the main reason why, although efficient in terms of capacity of the dedicated analysis tools such as theorem provers and model checkers, formal methods actually do not eliminate the need of testing.

In regards with safety requirements, the application of formal methods can only add on safety. Even if we assume that proper testing can capture all the safety flaws that we may capture with formal verification, with proper use of formal methods we can always improve the quality of requirements and eventually derive more efficient test cases. Moreover, formal methods can be used to create formal specifications, which subsequently can be used for automatic test case generation. Hence, in exchange for the extra work put to formally specify the safety requirements of a system, you get not only the possibility to formally verify and validate these requirements, but also to more efficiently test their implementation.

It is evident that 100 % safety cannot be guaranteed, but when properly used, formal methods can significantly contribute to safety by not replacing, but complementing testing. The quantitative measure of how much safety can be gained with formal methods may be regarded in three aspects:

1. Formal verification and validation allows for early detection of safety flaws, i.e., before implementation.
2. High quality of safety requirements improves the design and implementation of these requirements.
3. Formally specified safety requirements assist in the derivation and generation of efficient test cases.

To be more specific, although it really depends on the complexity of the system in question, my intuition is that these three aspects complement each other and together they may help us build a system with up to 99 % safety guarantee. This principle can be eventually applied to improve safety in AI by emphasizing its ability to *autonomously* tackle various hazards. Of course, this excludes the AI that is elevated to the *technological singularity* level (see Sect. 3). For such AI, some form of formal validation of "desired" technological singularity will help with the safety guarantee. Eventually, some sort of analysis and formal framing of the system's artificial awareness can help with the validation of "desired" technological singularity.

5   What Can Be Formalized?

Contemporary formal verification techniques (e.g., model checking [2]) rely on state-transition models where objects or entities are specified with states they can be in and associated with functions that are performed to change states or object characteristics. Therefore, basically every system property that can be measured or quantified, or qualified as a function can be formalized for the needs of formal verification. Usually, the traditional types of requirements – functional and non-functional (e.g., data requirements, quality requirements, time constraints, etc.), are used to provide a specific description of functions and characteristics that address the general purpose of the system. The formal verification techniques use the formal specification of such requirements to check desired safety and liveness properties. For example, to specify safety properties of a system, we need to formalize "nothing bad will happen to the system", which can be done via the formalization of non-desirable system states along with the formalization of behavior that will never lead the system to these states.

Obviously, the formalization of well-defined properties (e.g., with proper states expressed via boundaries, data range, outputs, etc.) is a straightforward task [19]. However, it is not that easy to formalize uncertainty, e.g., liveness properties (something good will eventually happen). Although, probabilistic theories such as the classical and quantum theories, help us formalize "degrees of truth" and deal with approximate conclusions rather with exact ones, the verification tools for fuzzy control systems are not efficient due to the huge state-explosion problem [2]. Moreover, testing such systems is not efficient as well, simply because, statistical evidence for their correct behavior may be not enough. Hence, any property that requires a progressive evaluation (or partial satisfaction, e.g., soft goals) is difficult and often impossible to be formalized for use in formally verified systems.

Other properties that are "intuitively desirable" (especially by AI) but still cannot be formalized today are human behavior and principles, related to cultural differences, ethics, feelings, etc. The problem is that with the formal approaches today we cannot express, for example, emotional bias as a meaningful system state.

6   Safe Self-driving Car Example

The example presented here should be regarded with the insight that "100 % safety is not possible", especially when the system in question (e.g., a self-driving car) engages in interaction with a non-deterministic and open-world environment [19] (see Fig. 1). What we should do though, to maximize the safety guarantee that "the car would never injure a pedestrian" is to determine all the critical situations involving the car itself in close proximity to pedestrians. Then we shall formalize these situations as system and environment states and formalize self-adaptive behavior (e.g., as self-* objectives [13,14]) driving the car in such situations [14,15]. For example, a situation could be defined as "all the car's systems are in operational condition and the car is passing by a school". To increase safety in this situation, we may formalize a self-adaptive behavior such as "automatically decrease the speed down to 20 mph when getting in close proximity to children or a school".

Further, we need to specify situations involving close proximity to pedestrians (e.g., crossing pedestrians) and car states emphasizing damages or malfunction of the driving system, e.g., flat tires, malfunctioning steering wheel, malfunctioning brakes, etc. For example, we may specify a self-adaptive behavior "automatically turn off the engine when the brake system is malfunctioning and the car is getting in close proximity to pedestrians".

Other important situations should involve severe weather conditions introducing hazards on the road, e.g., snow storm, ice, low visibility (formalized as environment states), and the car getting in close proximity to pedestrians. In such situations, formalized self-adaptive behavior should automatically enforce low speed, turning lights on, turning wipers on, etc.

In this example, the self-* objectives shall be driven by an AI reasoner, so different situations will be recognized and handled by an appropriate behavior.

Fig. 1. Self-driving car Interacts with the environment [7]

7   Deductive Guarantees and Probabilistic Guarantees

Many of the deductive proofs for safety properties in today's formally verified systems are already "probabilistic" in the sense that the designers have some subjective uncertainty as to whether the formal specification accurately captures the intuitively desirable safety properties, and (less likely) whether there was an error in the proof somewhere.

With deductive guarantees [11] a formal verification actually provides true statements that demonstrate that desired safety properties are held. Such a verification process is deterministic and a complete proof is required to guarantee the correctness of safety properties. For example, such a proof can be equipped with deterministic rules and expressed in the classical first-order logic (or in high-order logic if we use Isabelle to run a deductive verification). On the other hand, with the probabilistic guarantees we can accept that a complete proof is not necessary and safety properties can be verified with some degree of uncertainty. Basically, the probabilistic guarantees can be regarded as a result of quantification of uncertainty in both the verification parameters and subsequent predictions. With the Bayesian methods [3], for example, we quantify our uncertainty as prior distribution of our beliefs we have in the values of certain properties. Moreover, we also embed likelihood in the properties formalization, i.e., how likely is it that we would observe a certain value in particular conditions. You may think about it as the likelihood of holding certain safety properties in specific situations. Then, the probabilistic guarantees assert in a natural way "likely" properties over the possibilities that we envision.

Unfortunately, deductive guarantees can be provided only for simple safety properties, because their complete proof often unavoidably does not terminate. Although deductive verification may deal with infinite state systems, its automation is limited, which is mainly due to the decidability of the logical reasoning (first-order logic and its extensions such as high-order logic are not decidable, or they are rather semi-decidable [8]). If we go back to our example with the self-driving car (see Sect. 6), we may supply all the needed deterministic rules expressing our safety requirements (e.g., speed limit of 20 mph when passing by a school), but the complete proof eventually cannot be achieved, because although the desired conclusion follows from some of the premises, other premises may eventually lead to resolution refutation. That's it, two sets of premises may lead to different proof results.

The probabilistic guarantees [2] are not as complete as the deductive ones, but they may deal with more complex properties, e.g., where a larger number of states can be required. Of course, this tradeoff should be considered when evaluating the results of any probabilistic formal verification. So, if we ask ourselves how much confidence in system's safety is gained with formal methods, probabilistic guarantees bring less confidence than deductive ones, but they may bring some extra confidence to safety properties that cannot be handled otherwise.

It is important to mention that abstraction [4] is the most efficient solution to the state-explosion problem (and respectively, to the problem of deductive guarantees decidability). With abstraction the size of the state space is reduced by aggregating state transitions into coarser-grained state transitions. The technique effectively reduces the total amount of states to be considered but is likely to reduce the granularity of the system to a point where it no longer adequately represents that system. The problem is that although the abstract model (e.g., the formalization of safety properties) is relatively small it should also be precise enough to adequately represent the original system.

Therefore, in order to obtain better results, we shall consider both verification approaches and eventually apply these together. For example, we may formalize with the presumption that both deductive and probabilistic guarantees can be obtained in a sort of compositional verification where we may apply both approaches to different safety properties, and eventually combine the results under the characteristics of global safety invariants. Such invariants can be classified as: goal invariants, behavior invariants, interaction invariants and resource invariants [10].

8   Improving Our Current Verification Toolset

Maybe the most popular technique for formal verification is model checking [2] where the properties are expressed in a temporal logic and the system formalization is turned into a state machine. The model checking methods verify if the desired properties hold in all the reachable states of a system, which is basically a proof that properties will hold during the execution of that system. State explosion is the main issue model checking is facing today. This problem is getting even bigger when it comes to concurrent systems where the number of states is exponential to the number of concurrent processes. So, basically, model checking is an efficient and powerful verification method, but only when applied to finite, yet small state spaces.

Here, to improve the current verification toolset, on the one side we need to work on fully automated deductive verification based on decidable logics with both temporal and probabilistic features, and on the other side we need to work on improving the model checking ability to handle large state spaces (e.g., symbolic model-checking [9], probabilistic model checking [2], etc.).

Important work that seems neglected by the scientific community is the stabilization science, which provides a common approach to studying system stability through stability analysis [1,6,20]. In this approach, a system is linearized around its operating point to determine a small-signal linearized model of that operating point. The stability of the system is then determined using linear system stability analysis methods such as Routh-Hurwitz, Root Locus, Bode Plot, and Nyquist Criterion.

Stability analysis is the theory of validating the existence of stable states presented through differential equations that govern the system dynamics. Although, theoretically, there is no guarantee for the existence of a solution to an arbitrary set of nonlinear differential equations [5], we may use stabilization science to build small-signal linearized models for the different system components, anticipating that the linearized models of system components will yield a relatively small state space, enabling for their efficient verification [10]. Then we may apply compositional verification techniques to produce an overall system-wide verification.

Other, not that well-developed verification techniques are those related to automatic test-case generation and simulation [16], which may reduce testing costs and improve the quality of testing. For example, test cases can be generated from a formal specification of a system built with a domain-specific formal language. If combined with code generation and analysis techniques for efficient test-case generation (e.g., change-impact analysis), automatic test-case generation might be used to efficiently test system behavior under simulated conditions [16].

Moreover, high-performance computing can be used for parallelizing simulations, which will allow multiple state space explorations to occur simultaneously.

9   Conclusion

Any AI system is a subject to uncertainty due to potential evolution in execution environment, in requirements, business conditions, available technology, and the like. Thus, it is important to capture and plan for uncertainty as part of the development process. Failure to do so may result in systems that are overly rigid for their purpose, an eventuality of particular concern for domains that typically use AI, such as unmanned space flight. Contemporary formal verification techniques can be very helpful in verifying safety properties via the formalization of non-desirable system states along with the formalization of behavior that will never lead the system to these states. Although complete safety is obviously not possible, the use of both deductive and probabilistic guarantees may eventually help us cover a wide range of the uncertainty in the AI systems' behavior. The current verification toolset is not powerful enough to guarantee safety in the complex AI behavior. Further enhancement of that toolset can be achieved by developing better automated reasoning and model checking, along with development of new verification techniques based on stabilization science, test-case generation and simulation. High-performance computing can be used for parallelization of the verification process.

Acknowledgements. This work was supported with the financial support of the Science Foundation Ireland grant 10/CE/I1855 to Lero—the Irish Software Research Centre (www.lero.ie).

References

1. Arora, A.: Stabilization. In: Encyclopedia of Distributed Computing. Kluwer Academic Publishers, Dordrecht (2000)
2. Baier, C., Katoen, J.P.: Principles of Model Checking. MIT Press, Cambridge (2008)
3. Berger, J.O.: Statistical Decision Theory and Bayesian Analysis. Springer Series in Statistics, 2nd edn. Springer, Heidelberg (1985)
4. Clarke, E.M., Grumberg, O., Long, D.E.: Model checking and abstraction. ACM Trans. Program. Lang. Syst. **16**(5), 1512–1542 (1994). doi:10.1145/186025.186051. http://doi.acm.org/10.1145/186025.186051
5. Conley, M., Appleby, B., Dahleh, M., Feron, E.: Computational complexity of Lyapunov stability analysis problems for a class of non-linear systems. Soc. Ind. Appl. Math. J. Control Optim. **36**(6), 2176–2193 (1998)
6. Emadi, A., Ehsani, M.: Aircraft power systems: technology, state of the art, and future trends. Aerospace Electron. Syst. Mag. **15**(1), 28–32 (2000)
7. Keeney, T.: Autonomous vehicles will reduce the chances of dying in an auto accident by over 80 % (2015). ARK Analyst http://ark-invest.com/industrial-innovation/autonomous-vehicles-will-reduce-auto-accidents
8. Hazewinkel, M.: Logical calculus. In: Hazewinkel, M. (ed.) Encyclopedia of Mathematics. Springer, Netherlands (2001)
9. McMillan, K.L.: Symbolic Model Checking. Kluwer Academic Publishers, Norwell (1993)
10. Pullum, L., Cui, X., Vassev, E., Hinchey, M., Rouff, C., Buskens, R.: Verification of adaptive systems. In: Proceedings of (Infotech@Aerospace) Conference 2012, Garden Grove, California, USA, pp. 2012–2478. AIAA (2012)
11. Sternberg, R.J., Sternberg, K., Mio, J.: Cognitive Psychology, 6th edn. Wadsworth Publishing, Belmont (2012)
12. Vassev, E., Hinchey, M.: Awareness in software-intensive systems. IEEE Comput. **45**(12), 84–87 (2012)
13. Vassev, E., Hinchey, M.: Autonomy requirements engineering. IEEE Comput. **46**(8), 82–84 (2013)
14. Vassev, E., Hinchey, M.: Autonomy Requirements Engineering for Space Missions. NASA Monographs in Systems and Software Engineering. Springer, Switzerland (2014). doi:10.1007/978-3-319-09816-6. http://dx.doi.org/10.1007/978-3-319-09816-6
15. Vassev, E., Hinchey, M.: Knowledge representation for adaptive and self-aware systems. In: Wirsing, M., Hölzl, M., Koch, N., Mayer, P. (eds.) Software Engineering for Collective Autonomic Systems. LNCS, vol. 8998, pp. 221–247. Springer, Heidelberg (2015)

16. Vassev, E., Hinchey, M., Nixon, P.: Automated test case generation of self-managing policies for NASA prototype missions developed with ASSL. In: Proceedings of the 4th IEEE International Symposium on Theoretical Aspects of Software Engineering (TASE 2010), pp. 3–8. IEEE Computer Society (2010)

17. Vassev, E., Sterritt, R., Rouff, C., Hinchey, M.: Swarm technology at NASA: building resilient systems. IT Prof. **14**(2), 36–42 (2012)

18. Vinge, V.: The coming technological singularity: how to survive in the post-human era (1993). https://www-rohan.sdsu.edu/faculty/vinge/misc/singularity.html

19. Wirsing, M., Holzl, M., Koch, N., Mayer, P. (eds.): Software Engineering for Collective Autonomous Systems. LNCS, vol. 8998. Springer, Heidelberg (2015)

20. Yerramalla, S., Fuller, E., Mladenovski, M., Cukic, B.: Lyapunov analysis of neural network stability in an adaptive flight control system. In: Huang, S.-T., Herman, T. (eds.) SSS 2003. LNCS, vol. 2704, pp. 77–91. Springer, Heidelberg (2003)

Engineering Adaptivity, Universal Autonomous Systems Ethics and Compliance Issues
ISOLA'2016 - Panel Discussion Position Paper

Giovanna Di Marzo Serugendo[✉]

Centre Universitaire d'Informatique, Institute of Information Services Science,
University of Geneva, Geneva, Switzerland
giovanna.dimarzo@unige.ch

Abstract. This paper summarises some of the discussion held during the panel of the ISOLA'2016 conference on whether artificial systems actually adapt to unforeseen situations and whether we master autonomous adaptive systems. We focus here on three questions: (1) What is a collective adaptive system and what are the elements to consider when engineering a collective adaptive system? (2) What type of universal autonomous system can we envision and what for? and finally (3) How are we considering and integrating ethics, trust, privacy and compliance to laws and regulations in adaptive systems?

1 What is Adaptivity and how to Engineer it?

Figure 1 shows a mind-map describing the different elements participating to the engineering of (artificial) collective adaptive systems [5,6]. First it requires the use of *software agents*, autonomous in their behaviour, having a common or personal goal, able to sense and act upon their environment. They may be (among others) intelligent, reactive and/or mobile [20]. They can also be embodied into physical devices such as robots, autonomous cars, or purely sitting in electronic/computing environments, e.g. auction agents, soft-bots, or personal digital assistants.

Second, for a collective adaptive system to work as a collective of agents, we need to define an *interaction mechanism*, usually coded locally in each agent. An interaction mechanism is typically a set of rules, that the agents follow and apply according to their local perceptions. By locally applying their rules, the agents as a collective entity display some emergent behaviour. These rules allow the agents to continuously adapt their behaviour to the sensed conditions and perceived changes in their environment. Here we can identify a spectrum of rules that vary in their capability (or not) to change or adapt. Most of the engineered self-organising systems today adopt interaction mechanisms based on *fixed rules*. This is typically the case for bio-inspired systems using mechanisms such as evaporation, gradient, flocking, ant foraging, etc. For instance, agents locally apply flocking rules, and as a collective are able to move in a coherent manner as flocks of birds. A common characteristic of collective adaptive systems is their

T. Margaria and B. Steffen (Eds.): ISoLA 2016, Part I, LNCS 9952, pp. 714–719, 2016.
DOI: 10.1007/978-3-319-47166-2_50

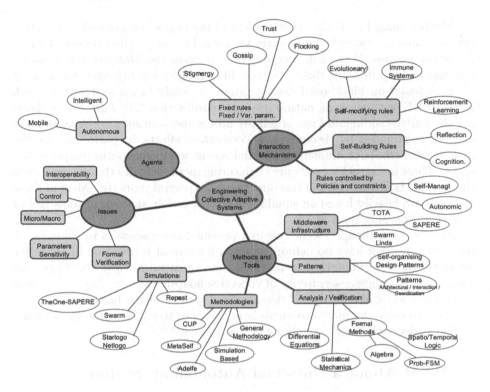

Fig. 1. Engineering Collective Adaptive Systems

sensitivity to parameters. Parameters are either set up (and fixed) in advance or may adapt on-the-fly, bringing increased adaptivity [8]. In the spectrum of adaptivity, we further distinguish interaction mechanisms that employ *self-modifying rules*: starting from a set of rules established at design-time, through evolutionary algorithms, learning and memory (e.g. immune systems), or reinforcement learning, the rules of each agents progressively change and modify themselves to better adapt to the agent's own observation and goal. If we move further along an adaptivity axis, we consider the next level, the case of interaction mechanisms provided by *self-building rules*. Here, agents are not provided with rules at design-time, but progressively build their own rules from scratch based on their own experiences [12,14]. Finally, we also consider the whole body of work on autonomic, self-managed systems involving explicit feedback loops [2,13] and revolving around four key activities: Monitor, Analyse, Plan, and Execute functions, also known as the MAPE architecture [4], decoupling the component that is adapted from the one that reasons and enforces the adaptation. Advanced versions of the MAPE architecture involve distribution and different variants supporting decentralised control [19]. Systems are generally designed in a top-down manner. This is in contrast to self-organising systems that employ multiple implicit feedback loops and decentralised control, and are generally designed in a bottom-up manner.

Moving along Fig. 1, the third element of the engineering of collective adaptive systems, necessary to make them trustworthy and possibly deployed on an industrial large-scale basis in everyday life, concerns the *Methods and Tools* we can use to help develop those systems, like *Middleware Infrastructures*, most of them based on blackboard deriving from the early Linda system [11], such as SAPERE or those using nature-inspired coordination [21]; *Patterns* facilitating the understanding and use of self-organising mechanisms [10]. A large body of work is provided by *Analysis and Verification* efforts, in particular the use of *Formal methods* of different kinds and recent works on spatio-temporal logics [3]. There are no actual software engineering methodologies that emerge, even though efforts are provided in this direction since several years [18]. Most of these methods are heavily based on simulations, either purely simulation tools [16] or hybrid prototyping tools [9,17].

Finally, even though recent research provided some answers to some pending issues, we still have no definite solution for formal verification of collective adaptive systems properties, in particular emergent ones; clear techniques for addressing parameters sensitivity of collective adaptive systems, or how to still remain in control of a fully self-* decentralised system once it has been deployed, and how to solve the macro to micro issue, i.e. how to engineer the local agents so that collectively they actually behave as intended.

2   What About a Universal Autonomous System?

There exists problems of very high complexity, such as *hyper-complex* or *wicked problems*, defined by [15] as "those that defy conventional approaches to understanding, planning, design, implementation and execution because: (1) The stakeholder interests are so diverse and divisive; (2) Interdependencies are so complex and so little understood; (3) Behaviours are so dynamic and chaotic (unpredictable)". Wicked problems have no purely algorithmic solution and need a combination of machine processing and human-based experience and heuristics to be solved. These are problems where stakeholders have different views and understanding of the problem, and the problem itself is subject to changing constraints. This is typically the case with computational or societal problems, where human intelligence, dynamically changing data, the Internet services, networks of sensors and machines need to be combined to address them. These are problems for which we often do not know if they have a good solution, or even less how to reach a reasonable solution if it exists.

A possible vision is to develop a new type of computer, a *Social Computer* [7] - a "machine-enhanced society". An instance of a Social Computer is a network of humans (individuals, groups) and machines (computers, data, services, sensors) able together and together only to assist experts in solving a specific large-scale (scientific or societal) problem that cannot be tackled by either computers or humans alone. It innately integrates human abilities based on intelligence, competences and skills with machine processing power so that they complement each other. A Social Computer is a Computer because it accepts input data, can store and process it, and can produce output results. It is, however, also Social since it is based on collaboration between humans and machines. In addition and by design, it must operate in an ethical, law-abiding, correct and trustable way.

Examples of primitive social computers encompass groups of coworkers supported by computing resources, people playing massively multiplayer online games, or a single person whose activity would be supported by a network of machines. In these cases, however, the matter at hand is often not presented under the form of a problem to be solved, or the decomposition of problems into subtasks; furthermore the links between humans and/or machines are not established in any principled, problem-solving way. A lot of burden is still placed on humans to identify problems and their solution.

The types of problems we envision a Social Computer should be able to solve, and the environments in which it should exist, are of a much higher complexity. We anticipate that people and society, by using and interacting in principled ways through a Social Computer, will be able to solve hyper-complex problems. Such issues can be computational (e.g. how to solve a scientific problem that cannot be completely formalised), consensual (e.g. how to reduce the costs of health insurance) or controversial (e.g. how to reduce our carbon footprint, more generally how to reach UN defined sustainable goals). Addressing them will require collecting partial solutions from diverse human and machine clusters, assessing opinion from experts and from the public, predicting the outcome and consequences of individual subproblems, and other similar tasks impossible to achieve by humans or machines independently. A Social Computer is an integration of humans and machines collaborating together on-demand to solve problems and answer questions. It frees users from organisational burden, helping them in breaking down problems into manageable tasks; it allows deep and exhaustive search of information and data mining in order to obtain partial solutions; and it exploits at best the different human and computational resources to obtain effective solutions. Social Computers are not fixed, pre-defined entities like today's computers, but are dynamic, evolving collaborations of humans and/or machines, adapting themselves to the problem at hand.

Social Computers can also be seen as tools supporting decisions during the process of establishing public policies. They help gather, understand and create evidence in support of policy-making processes.

3   What About Privacy, Trust, Ethics and Compliance to Laws and Regulations?

Central to Social Computers above, and central to any adaptive system are the notions of ethics, privacy, trust and legal aspects. Most of the ICT developments so far were however primarily guided by the market, leaving behind ethical, legal, and psychological considerations. Today's services offer no ethical warranty. Privacy is becoming a very fragile matter, with sensitive data often stored, used and aggregated unbeknownst to their owners, sometimes with malicious intent. For instance, people have not fully grasped the impact of the reputation of their online persona and their online actions, with undesired social or professional consequences. Society regularly define, revisit and enforces laws. Autonomous systems should not only adapt to unforeseen circumstances in their environment, but also be fully compliant with current regulations when first deployed *and* able to adapt - on their own - to any law or regulation change. The vision and proposal here is double: (1) we need to address ethical, trust, privacy and law-abiding considerations from the start, i.e. providing those consideration *by design* (ethics by design, privacy by design, compliance by design [1]); (2) we need also to develop research for engineering autonomous systems able to adapt to changes of laws and regulations *on-the-fly*. For autonomous systems, this could be provided by an ethical middleware or an ethical operating system ensuring in a built-in manner all those considerations; and/or ethical principles to be included into individual agents and global systems developed with them.

4   Conclusion

The considerations above have engineering concerns in mind. Including ethics, privacy and trust by design renders autonomous systems apparently more acceptable. Some questions still need to be considered: (1) How do we define the ethics to integrate into those systems? this shouldn't be left to individuals but thought at some universal world-wide level; (2) What about legal issues arising from situations involving autonomous systems? who is responsible when an accident, a failure or any harm happens: the user, the programmer, the designer, the company's manager? (2) To which extent is it a good thing to develop the "ultimate" adaptive system so intelligent that it may decide to question the usefulness of humans or even take over? Fortunately, ethicians, lawyers and philosophers are already busy thinking this through.

References

1. Aucher, G., Boella, G., van der Torre, L.: A dynamic logic for privacy compliance. Artif. Intell. Law **19**(2–3), 187–231 (2011)
2. Cheng, B.H.C., et al.: Software engineering for self-adaptive systems: a research roadmap. In: Cheng, B.H.C., de Lemos, R., Giese, H., Inverardi, P., Magee, J. (eds.) Software Engineering for Self-Adaptive Systems. LNCS, vol. 5525, pp. 1–26. Springer, Heidelberg (2009)
3. Ciancia, V., Latella, D., Loreti, M., Massink, M.: Specifying and verifying properties of space. In: Diaz, J., Lanese, I., Sangiorgi, D. (eds.) TCS 2014. LNCS, vol. 8705, pp. 222–235. Springer, Heidelberg (2014)
4. IBM Corporation. An architectural blueprint for autonomic computing (2006)
5. Di Marzo Serugendo, G.: Robustness and dependability of self-organizing systems - a safety engineering perspective. In: Guerraoui, R., Petit, F. (eds.) SSS 2009. LNCS, vol. 5873, pp. 254–268. Springer, Heidelberg (2009)
6. Di Marzo Serugendo, G., Gleizes, M.-P., Karageorgos, A. (eds.): Self-organising Software - From Natural to Artificial Adaptation. Natural Computing Series, 1st edn. Springer, Heidelberg (2011)

7. Di Marzo Serugendo, G., Risoldi, M., Solemayni, M.: The social computer. In: Pitt, J. (ed.) The Computer After Me, pp. 159–172. World Scientific, Singapore (2014)

8. Eiben, A.E., Michalewicz, Z., Schoenauer, M., Smith, J.E.: Parameter control in evolutionary algorithms. In: Lobo, F.G., Lima, C.F., Michalewicz, Z. (eds.) Parameter Setting in Evolutionary Algorithms, pp. 19–46. Springer, Heidelberg (2007)

9. Fernandez-Marquez, J.L., De Angelis, F., Di Marzo, G., Serugendo, G.S., Castelli, G.: The one-sapere simulator: a prototyping tool for engineering self-organisation in pervasive environments. In: SASO, pp. 201–202. IEEE Computer Society (2014)

10. Fernandez-Marquez, J.L., Di Marzo Serugendo, G., Montagna, S., Viroli, M., Arcos, J.L.: Description and composition of bio-inspired design patterns: a complete overview. Nat. Comput. **12**(1), 43–67 (2013)

11. Gelernter, D., Carriero, N.: Coordination languages and their significance. Commun. ACM **35**(2), 97–107 (1992)

12. Lana de carvalho, L., Hassas, S., Lopes, E.J., Cordier, A.: Four kinds of models of emergent representations resulting from the decomposition individual/collective and internal/external. In: Proceedings of 5th European Conference on Complex Systems (ECCS 2008) (2008)

13. de Lemos, R., et al.: Software engineering for self-adaptive systems: a second research roadmap. In: Lemos, R., Giese, H., Müller, H.A., Shaw, M. (eds.) Software Engineering for Self-Adaptive Systems. LNCS, vol. 7475, pp. 1–32. Springer, Heidelberg (2013)

14. Mazac, S., Armetta, F., Hassas, S.: Bootstrapping sensori-motor patterns for a constructivist learning system in continuous environments. In: 14th International Conference on the Synthesis and Simulation of Living Systems (Alife 2014), New York, NY, USA (2014)

15. Newman, D., Gall, N.: Gain a foundation in design thinking to apply Gartner's hybrid thinking research. Gartner Analysis (2010)

16. Pianini, D., Montagna, S., Viroli, M.: Chemical-oriented simulation of computational systems with ALCHEMIST. J. Simul. **7**(3), 202–215 (2013). doi:10.1057/jos. 2012.27

17. Pianini, D., Viroli, M., Beal, J.: Protelis: practical aggregate programming. In: Wainwright, R.L., Corchado, J.M., Bechini, A., Hong, J. (eds.), Proceedings of the 30th Annual ACM Symposium on Applied Computing, Salamanca, Spain, April 13–17, 2015, pp. 1846–1853. ACM (2015)

18. Puviani, M., Di Marzo Serugendo, G., Frei, R., Cabri, G.: A method fragments approach to methodologies for engineering self-organizing systems. ACM Trans. Auton. Adapt. Syst. **7**(3), 33:1–33:25 (2012)

19. Weyns, D., et al.: On patterns for decentralized control in self-adaptive systems. In: de Lemos, R., Giese, H., Müller, H.A., Shaw, M. (eds.) Software Engineering for Self-Adaptive Systems. LNCS, vol. 7475, pp. 76–107. Springer, Heidelberg (2013)

20. Woolridge, M., Wooldridge, M.J.: Introduction to Multiagent Systems. Wiley, New York (2001)

21. Zambonelli, F., Omicini, A., Anzengruber, B., Castelli, G., De Angelis, F.L., Di Marzo Serugendo, G., Fernandez-Marquez, J.L., Ferscha, A., Mamei, M., Mariani, S., Molesini, A., Montagna, S., Nieminen, J., Pianini, D., Risoldi, M., Rosi, A., Stevenson, G., Viroli, M., Ye, J.: Developing pervasive multi-agent systems with nature-inspired coordination. Pervasive Mobile Comput. **17**, 236–252 (2015). Special Issue "10 years of Pervasive Computing" in Honor of Chatschik Bisdikian

Correctness-by-Construction and Post-hoc Verification: Friends or Foes?

Correctness-by-Construction and Post-hoc Verification: Friends or Foes?

Maurice H. ter Beek[1]([✉]), Reiner Hähnle[2], and Ina Schaefer[3]

[1] ISTI–CNR, Pisa, Italy
maurice.terbeek@isti.cnr.it
[2] TU Darmstadt, Darmstadt, Germany
[3] TU Braunschweig, Braunschweig, Germany

Abstract. While correctness-by-construction and post-hoc verification are traditionally considered to provide two opposing views on proving software systems to be free from errors, nowadays numerous techniques and application fields witness initiatives that try to integrate elements of both ends of the spectrum. The ultimate aim is not merely to improve the correctness of software systems but also to improve their time-to-market, and to do so at a reasonable cost. This track brings together researchers and practitioners interested in the inherent 'tension' that is usually felt when trying to balance the pros and cons of correctness-by-construction versus post-hoc verification.

Motivation and Aim

Correctness-by-Construction (CbC) sees the development of software (systems) as a scientific discipline of engineering. Originally intended as a mere means of programming algorithms that are correct *by construction* [22,27], the approach found its way into commercial development processes of complex systems [24,25]. In this larger context, we can say that CbC advocates a step-wise refinement process from specification to code, ideally by CbC design tools that automatically generate error-free software implementations from rigorous and unambiguous specifications of requirements. Afterwards, testing only serves the purpose of validating the CbC process rather than to find bugs. (Of course, bugs might still be present outside the boundaries of the verified system: libraries, compilers, hardware, etc.).

In Post-hoc Verification (PhV), on the other hand, formal methods and tools are applied only after the (software) system has been constructed, not during the development process. Typically, a formal specification of (an abstraction of) the implemented system describes how it should behave, after which validation and verification techniques like testing [12,32,33], bug finding [4,26,29], model checking [3,15,17], and deductive verification [7,23,35] are used to check whether the implementation indeed satisfies the specifications and meets the user's needs.

T. Margaria and B. Steffen (Eds.): ISoLA 2016, Part I, LNCS 9952, pp. 723–729, 2016.
DOI: 10.1007/978-3-319-47166-2_51

While two independent system models that are verified against each other can provide additional assurance that the designers' intentions have been captured correctly, PhV is notoriously difficult to carry out.

Recently, numerous techniques and fields of application witness initiatives that attempt to integrate elements of both ends of the spectrum, ultimately aiming to satisfy the holy grail of improving the correctness of software systems as well as their time-to-market, and to do so at a reasonable cost. This track brings together researchers and practitioners interested in the inherent 'tension' that is usually felt when trying to balance the pros and cons of CbC vs. PhV. In particular, we invited researchers and practitioners working in the following communities to shed their light on CbC vs. PhV:

☑ People working in Software Product Line Engineering (SPLE), who try to lift successful formal methods and verification tools from single product (system) engineering to SPLE in order to say something about the correctness of all products (programs, variants) of an SPL (whose population is exponential in the number of features).

☑ People working in System-of-Systems Engineering (SoSE), who address the verification (correctness, but also issues like reliability, resilience, robustness, security, and sustainability) of networks of interacting legacy and new software (systems).

☑ People working on (system) synthesis, who aim for transforming a logical specification into a system that is guaranteed to satisfy the specification in all possible environments.

☑ People working on deductive verification, who typically require a detailed understanding of why the system works correctly before actual verification to be able to express the correctness of a program as a set of verification conditions to be discharged.

☑ People working on 'bug-finding' lightweight verification, who trade off full functional verification for being able to deal with real-world languages and large programs as well as to avoid having to write formal specifications.

☑ People working on Design for Verification (DfV), mostly in hardware design, who advocate the usage of design methodologies, languages, patterns, etc., that make PhV a realistic option.

☑ People working on Statistical Model checking (SMC), who trade off model checking's verification accuracy, which however requires the entire state space to be known upfront, for scalability by resorting to the computationally more efficient sampling of simulations of (dynamic, black-box, infinite-state) systems until sufficient statistical evidence has been found.

Contributions

Watson et al. [36] argue for the marriage of CbC with PhV in order to leverage the advantages and to mitigate the disadvantages of both approaches. CbC specifies a problem in terms of its pre- and postconditions and then develops a final algorithmic solution in small, tractable refinement steps. The paper advocates a lightweight approach to proving the correctness of each refinement step. The consequent risk of errors should then be minimised by relying on a PhV system that now obtains *for free* the pre- and postconditions, as well as loop variants and invariants that it requires for proving partial correctness as well as termination.

Beckert et al. [6] address the following important question in the specific setting of legacy code: why is it so hard to perform PhV (deductive verification in particular) and what can be done to make it any easier? They answer the first part of this question by presenting a collection of (known) insights in a systematic way, larded with examples. Subsequently, they contribute to answering the second part of the question by first discussing possible means to tackle the challenges offered by legacy code verification and then suggesting a strategy for deductive PhV, together with possible improvements to existing deductive verification methodologies and tools like KeY [2,7] and VCC [20].

Cleophas et al. [18] discuss how CbC-based development may lead to a deep comprehension of algorithm families, based on the fact that organising the refinements obtained during CbC-based design in a taxonomy leads to a classification of common and varying properties within a family of algorithms and thus to insight in the relations among its elements. They also argue that using taxonomies in the implementation of toolkits, i.e. a library of all variants, for TABASCO [19] has the additional benefit of providing a meaningful starting point for extractive and proactive SPLE. For both, a concrete methodology is presented.

Kleijn et al. [9] consider systems of systems, represented as team automata, whose components interact by the synchronised execution of common actions [8]. They study conditions for the compatibility of components, defined as being free from message loss and deadlocks, relative to notions of synchronisation other than mandatory synchronised execution. They focus on various kinds of master-slave synchronisations, which require input actions (for 'slaves') to be driven by output actions (from 'masters'). Team automata composed according to this notion of synchronisation are exemplified and studied in some detail, including an extensive discussion of (potential) applications.

Legay et al. [34] introduce DynBLTL, an extension of time-bounded LTL [16], as a new 3-valued logic specifically aimed to reason over dynamically evolving software architectures. Here dynamism is understood as allowing components to be removed, added or (re)connected differently. The third value (undefined) is used to deal with components that are absent in a system configuration being evaluated. The semantics is that of (un)timed traces of graphs seen as snapshots of the architecture at a specific moment of computation. One can quantify over all connections and components of a specific type or a specific component or connection, and the modalities allow to reasoning over a bounded number of steps or a bounded amount of time. Since the number of components is unknown upfront, SMC by means of an integration into the PLASMA statistical model checker [30] is an obvious choice. An example illustrates the approach.

Méry et al. [14] aim to show how CbC and PhV can possibly be combined in a productive way by describing a general framework that integrates the following two different approaches to software verification: program refinement as supported by Event-B [1] and program verification as supported by the Spec# programming system [5]. In particular, they describe a plug-in for Event-B's RODIN toolset that is able to automatically transform a given abstract Event-B specification into a recursive algorithm that is correct-by-construction and which can be directly translated into executable code.

Schaefer et al. [28] investigate the feasibility of generalizing the concept of proof-carrying code to proof-carrying apps as a means to verify extensible software platforms at deployment time. Rather than global safety policies, contracts are used to specify functional properties of the API of the base software platform, leaving it to the provider of the extension to verify that all API calls adhere to the contract. The resulting proof artefacts are used at deployment time to allow proof checking. After discussing the criteria that enable a verification technique for contract-based deployment-time verification, the applicability of deductive verification with KeY [2,7] and data-flow analyses with Soot [31] to the proof-carrying apps scenario is examined for a simple Java implementation.

De Vink et al. [10] illustrate the idea of supervisory controller synthesis for SPLE by applying the CIF 3 toolset [11] to an example. They show how to automatically synthesise an SPL model (in the form of an automaton for each valid product of the SPL) starting from a so-called attributed feature model, component behaviour models associated with the features, and additional behavioural requirements (like state invariants, event orderings, and guards on events). The resulting CIF 3 model then satisfies all feature-related constraints as well as all behavioural requirements, by construction. Further behavioural properties can be verified by exporting such SPL models in the input format of the mCRL2 model checker [21].

Beyer [13] outlines a few existing verification approaches that, in an attempt to try to increase the impact of formal verification, combine the advantages of automatic verification techniques and interactive verification techniques. The former, which usually expect the user to set the parameters while the prover computes the necessary invariants and the proof, work well for large systems, whereas the latter, which usually expect the user to provide invariants while the prover establishes a formal correctness proof, work well for sophisticated specifications.

References

1. Abrial, J.-R.: Modeling in Event-B: System and Software Engineering. Cambridge University Press, Cambridge (2010)
2. Ahrendt, W., et al.: The KeY platform for verification and analysis of java programs. In: Giannakopoulou, D., Kroening, D. (eds.) VSTTE 2014. LNCS, vol. 8471, pp. 55–71. Springer, Heidelberg (2014)
3. Baier, C., Katoen, J.-P.: Principles of Model Checking. MIT Press, Cambridge (2008)
4. Ball, T., Rajamani, S.K.: The SLAM project: debugging system software via static analysis. ACM SIGPLAN Not. **37**(1), 1–3 (2002)
5. Barnett, M., Leino, K.R.M., Schulte, W.: The Spec# programming system: an overview. In: Barthe, G., Burdy, L., Huisman, M., Lanet, J.-L., Muntean, T. (eds.) CASSIS 2004. LNCS, vol. 3362, pp. 49–69. Springer, Heidelberg (2005)
6. Beckert, B., Bormer, T., Grahl, D.: Deductive verification of legacy code. In: Margaria, T., Steffen, B. (eds.) ISoLA 2016, Part I, LNCS, vol. 9952, pp. 749–765. Springer, Heidelberg (2016)
7. Beckert, B., Hähnle, R., Schmitt, P.H.: Verification of Object-Oriented Software: The KeY Approach. Springer, Heidelberg (2007)
8. ter Beek, M.H., Kleijn, J.: Team automata satisfying compositionality. In: Araki, K., Gnesi, S., Mandrioli, D. (eds.) FME 2003. LNCS, vol. 2805, pp. 381–400. Springer, Heidelberg (2003)
9. ter Beek, M.H., Kleijn, J., Carmona, J.: Conditions for compatibility of components: the case of masters and slaves. In: Margaria, T., Steffen, B. (eds.) ISoLA 2016, Part I, LNCS, vol. 9952, pp. 784–805. Springer, Heidelberg (2016)
10. ter Beek, M.H., Reniers, M.A., de Vink, E.P.: Supervisory controller synthesis for product lines using CIF 3. In: Margaria, T., Steffen, B. (eds.) ISoLA 2016, Part I, LNCS, vol. 9952, pp. 856–873. Springer, Heidelberg (2016)
11. van Beek, D.A., Fokkink, W.J., Hendriks, D., Hofkamp, A., Markovski, J., van de Mortel-Fronczak, J.M., Reniers, M.A.: CIF 3: model-based engineering of supervisory controllers. In: Ábrahám, E., Havelund, K. (eds.) TACAS 2014 (ETAPS). LNCS, vol. 8413, pp. 575–580. Springer, Heidelberg (2014)
12. Bertolino, A., Inverardi, P., Muccini, H.: Software architecture-based analysis and testing: a look into achievements and future challenges. Computing **95**(8), 633–648 (2013)
13. Beyer, D.: Partial verification and intermediate results as a solution to combine automatic and interactive verification techniques. In: Margaria, T., Steffen, B. (eds.) ISoLA 2016, Part I, LNCS, vol. 9952, pp. 874–880. Springer, Heidelberg (2016)
14. Cheng, Z., Méry, D., Monahan, R.: On two friends for getting correct programs: automatically translating event-B specifications to recursive algorithms in Rodin. In: Margaria, T., Steffen, B. (eds.) ISoLA 2016, Part I, LNCS, vol. 9952, pp. 821–838. Springer, Heidelberg (2016)
15. Clarke, E.M., Emerson, E.A., Sifakis, J.: Model checking: algorithmic verification and debugging. Commun. ACM **52**(11), 74–84 (2009)
16. Clarke, E.M., Faeder, J.R., Langmead, C.J., Harris, L.A., Jha, S.K., Legay, A.: Statistical model checking in BioLab: applications to the automated analysis of T-Cell receptor signaling pathway. In: Heiner, M., Uhrmacher, A.M. (eds.) CMSB 2008. LNCS (LNBI), vol. 5307, pp. 231–250. Springer, Heidelberg (2008)

17. Clarke, E.M., Grumberg, O., Peled, D.A.: Model Checking. MIT Press, Cambridge (1999)
18. Cleophas, L., Kourie, D.G., Pieterse, V., Schaefer, I., Watson, B.W.: Correctness-by-construction ∧ taxonomies ⇒ deep comprehension of algorithm families. In: Margaria, T., Steffen, B. (eds.) ISoLA 2016, Part I, LNCS, vol. 9952, pp. 766–783. Springer, Heidelberg (2016)
19. Cleophas, L.G., Watson, B.W., Kourie, D.G., Boake, A., Obiedkov, S.A.: TABASCO: using concept-based taxonomies in domain engineering. S. Afr. Comput. J. **37**, 30–40 (2006)
20. Cohen, E., Dahlweid, M., Hillebrand, M., Leinenbach, D., Moskal, M., Santen, T., Schulte, W., Tobies, S.: VCC: a practical system for verifying concurrent C. In: Berghofer, S., Nipkow, T., Urban, C., Wenzel, M. (eds.) TPHOLs 2009. LNCS, vol. 5674, pp. 23–42. Springer, Heidelberg (2009)
21. Cranen, S., Groote, J.F., Keiren, J.J.A., Stappers, F.P.M., de Vink, E.P., Wesselink, W., Willemse, T.A.C.: An overview of the mCRL2 toolset and its recent advances. In: Piterman, N., Smolka, S.A. (eds.) TACAS 2013 (ETAPS). LNCS, vol. 7795, pp. 199–213. Springer, Heidelberg (2013)
22. Dijkstra, E.W.: A constructive approach to the problem of program correctness. BIT Numer. Math. **8**(3), 174–186 (1968)
23. Filliâtre, J.-C.: Deductive software verification. Int. J. Softw. Tools Technol. Transfer **13**(5), 397–403 (2011)
24. Hall, A.: Correctness by construction: integrating formality into a commercial development process. In: Eriksson, L.-H., Lindsay, P.A. (eds.) FME 2002. LNCS, vol. 2391, p. 224. Springer, Heidelberg (2002)
25. Hall, A., Chapman, R.: Correctness by construction: developing a commercial secure system. IEEE Softw. **19**(1), 18–25 (2002)
26. Hangal, S., Lam, M.S.: Tracking down software bugs using automatic anomaly detection. In: Proceedings of the 24th International Conference on Software Engineering (ICSE 2002), pp. 291–301. ACM (2002)
27. Hoare, C.A.R.: Proof of a program: FIND. Commun. ACM **14**(1), 39–45 (1971)
28. Holthusen, S., Nieke, M., Thüm, T., Schaefer, I.: Proof-Carrying Apps: Contract-based deployment-time verification. In: Margaria, T., Steffen, B. (eds.) ISoLA 2016, Part I, LNCS, vol. 9952, pp. 839–855. Springer, Heidelberg (2016)
29. Hovemeyer, D., Pugh, W.: Finding bugs is easy. ACM SIGPLAN Not. **39**(12), 92–106 (2004)
30. Jegourel, C., Legay, A., Sedwards, S.: A platform for high performance statistical model checking – PLASMA. In: Flanagan, C., König, B. (eds.) TACAS 2012 (ETAPS). LNCS, vol. 7214, pp. 498–503. Springer, Heidelberg (2012)
31. Lam, P., Bodden, E., Lhoták, O., Hendren, L.: The Soot framework for Java program analysis: a retrospective. In: Cetus Users and Compiler Infrastructure Workshop (CETUS 2011) (2011)
32. Mathur, A.P.: Foundations of Software Testing, 2nd edn. Addison-Wesley, Boston (2014)
33. Pezzè, M., Young, M.: Software Testing and Analysis: Process Principles and Techniques. Wiley, Hoboken (2007)
34. Quilbeuf, J., Cavalcante, E., Traonouez, L.-M., Oquendo, F., Batista, T., Legay, A.: A logic for the statistical model checking of dynamic software architectures. In: Margaria, T., Steffen, B. (eds.) ISoLA 2016, Part I, LNCS, vol. 9952, pp. 806–820. Springer, Heidelberg (2016)

35. Robinson, J.A., Voronkov, A. (eds.): Handbook of Automated Reasoning. MIT Press, Cambridge (2001)
36. Watson, B.W., Kourie, D.G., Schaefer, I., Cleophas, L.G.: Correctness-by-construction and post-hoc verification: a marriage of convenience? In: Margaria, T., Steffen, B. (eds.) ISoLA 2016, Part I, LNCS, vol. 9952, pp. 730–748. Springer, Heidelberg (2016)

Correctness-by-Construction and Post-hoc Verification: A Marriage of Convenience?

Bruce W. Watson[1,2]([⊠]), Derrick G. Kourie[1,2], Ina Schaefer[3], and Loek Cleophas[1,4]

[1] Department of Information Science, Stellenbosch University,
Stellenbosch, South Africa
{bruce,derrick,loek}@fastar.org
[2] Centre for Artificial Intelligence Research, CSIR Meraka Institute,
Pretoria, South Africa
[3] Technische Universität Braunschweig, Software Engineering Institute,
Braunschweig, Germany
i.schaefer@tu-bs.de
[4] Technische Universiteit Eindhoven, Software Engineering and Technology Group,
Eindhoven, The Netherlands

Abstract. Correctness-by-construction (CbC), traditionally based on weakest precondition semantics, and post-hoc verification (PhV) aspire to ensure functional correctness. We argue for a lightweight approach to CbC where lack of formal rigour increases productivity. In order to mitigate the risk of accidentally introducing errors during program construction, we propose to complement lightweight CbC with PhV. We introduce lightweight CbC by example and discuss strength and weaknesses of CbC and PhV and their combination, both conceptually and using a case study.

1 Introduction

In today's world, software that controls safety-, mission- and business-critical applications is pervasive. Test-first programming [1], requirements or code coverage-based testing, adherence to coding standards and reliance on software patterns are examples of common practices aimed at satisfying functional requirements. To avoid injury, loss of life or unmanageable follow-up costs resulting from such systems, much greater confidence in the functional correctness of the software is required than is demanded of more mundane software applications [2]. Hence, to complement common software engineering practices, more rigorous development approaches are needed. These may include adherence to standards such as DO178-B for avionics or ISO26262 for automotive applications. Formal methods such as formal program verification [3] may also be used.

The starting point for formal program verification, also called post-hoc verification (PhV), is an already written program. Annotations that capture the functional requirements are added to the program. These are typically in the form of a pre-/postcondition specification of each method in a class. Additionally, invariants for the class may be provided. In order to be able to prove automatically that

© Springer International Publishing AG 2016
T. Margaria and B. Steffen (Eds.): ISoLA 2016, Part I, LNCS 9952, pp. 730–748, 2016.
DOI: 10.1007/978-3-319-47166-2_52

the code adheres to these specifications, auxiliary loop annotations have to be provided, expressing loop invariants and variants. A PhV tool (such as KeY [4], VeriFast [5], Spec# [6] or Krakatoa/Why [7]) then uses a formal calculus to establish correctness of the program with respect to its pre-/postconditions and invariants. Such a tool also uses the variants of the program's loops to verify that the program terminates. However, PhV is not yet widely practiced. One reason is the limited set of program constructs supported by program verification tools (e.g. dynamic arrays and pointers are notoriously difficult to support). Another reason is that it may be very challenging to provide the annotations needed, especially if the program to be verified is poorly structured.

In pursuit of functional correctness, we propose the adoption of a *lightweight* version of the approach to software construction that was pioneered by Dijkstra, Hoare and others. They called this the "correctness-by-construction" (CbC) style of software development and based it on weakest precondition semantics [8–12]. The approach should not be confused with other concepts that carry the same name, such as the correctness-by-construction (CbyC) promoted by Hall and Chapman [2]. Their CbyC is a software development process where formal modeling techniques and analyses such as the Z-notation are used for different development phases. Their goals are *to make it difficult to introduce defects in the first place, and to detect and remove any defects that do occur as early as possible after introduction* [13]. Another approach to correctness-by-construction is the Event-B framework [14] where automata-based system specifications are refined by provably correct transformation steps until an implementable program is obtained [15, 16].

Several other approaches exist in which correct-by-construction systems are developed by synthesis or composition. Lamprecht et al. [17] present a synthesis-based approach to derive variants of a product family that are correct-by-construction by assembling existing building blocks with respect to a set of given constraints. Similarly, de Vink et al. [18] show how the CIF3 supervisory control tool allows to automatically synthesise a behavioral model of an SPL by starting from a feature model, component behaviour models associated with the features, and additional behavioural requirements in such a way that the resulting SPL model satisfies all feature-related constraints as well as all behavioral requirements. Kleijn et al. [19] study fundamental notions for the component-based development of correct-by-construction multi-component systems modeled as team automata. They provide precise conditions for the compatibility of components in systems of systems that (by construction) guarantee correct communications, free from message loss and deadlocks.

In contrast to these eponymous concepts, CbC starts by articulating a problem's pre-/postcondition specification and then derives a program from the specification in small, tractable refinement steps. Whenever a refinement step indicates that a loop structure is required, CbC requires that a suitable loop invariant and variant be stated before the body of the loop can be derived. As a result, CbC delivers not only a program that is 'correct by construction', but also the annotations required by PhV. The extent to which a CbC derived program can be guaranteed to be correct depends on the rigour with which the proof of each refinement step is undertaken. However, such rigour can be tedious and inefficient from a productivity perspective. To mitigate this problem, we argue for the lightweight application of CbC, followed by the application of PhV that can now direcly use the CbC-derived annotations that come along 'for free'. Thus CbC should not be viewed as being in opposition to traditional PhV. Rather, CbC and PhV are complementary strategies for enhancing functional correctness.

To argue this position, we outline the CbC approach in the next section, emphasizing the development of loops. Section 3 then reflects on the relationship between CbC and PhV, indicating their relative strengths and weaknesses and emphasising, *inter alia*, loop termination. Section 4 briefly outlines our experiences on a case study in which PhV was applied to a CbC solution to an algorithmic problem and then attempted on a publicly available solution. The final section recommends combining CbC and PhV for the endeavour towards correct software and finishes with an outlook to future work.

2   Correctness-by-Construction

This section provides a short and necessarily superficial introduction to CbC. Here, we focus on CbC for loops, including invariants, variants and termination. We assume the reader has read [20, Sect. 2] for a brief introduction to the Dijkstra/Hoare style of CbC, and that the reader has a basic understanding of first order predicate logic (FOPL) formulae. A thorough introduction to CbC and related topics can be found in the 'original' books [8–10] (some of which are out of print or difficult to find) as well as [11] (available as a PDF from the author) and most recently [12]. We begin with a simple sorting algorithm before moving to a simplified graph closure algorithm, both of which are chosen to illustrate aspects of loop-design and termination.

2.1   A Simple Sorting Algorithm

CbC involves constructing a program (a.k.a. algorithm) from a specification using *refinement* steps. Given an algorithmic problem, CbC, thus, requires an articulation of the problem's pre- and postcondition. For our purposes, such an articulation may be a pragmatic blend of natural language, FOPL, and diagrams. For example, if the problem is that of sorting a non-empty array A, it could be stated in a so-called pre-post formula:

$$\{A.len > 0\} \; S \; \{Sorted(A)\} \tag{1}$$

The foregoing is an assertion that states that if the length of array A is greater than 0 and some abstract command[1] S executes, then the command will terminate and the array will be sorted.

In this particular context, there is no compelling reason to provide a formal FOPL definition of what it means for an array to be sorted. Instead, we simply

---

[1] Dijkstra-speak for 'program statement'.

assert the sortedness of array A by an undefined predicate $Sorted(A)$. In a similar spirit of lightweightness (seen in more places below), we also do not formalise that A contains the same elements before and after the algorithm executes—though now sorted.

Abstractly, the notation we use for pre-post specification (known as Hoare triples) looks like

$$\{P\}\ S\ \{Q\}$$

which specifies that 'assuming precondition P holds (is true), program statement (command) S *will* terminate and Q will then hold'. Refinement rules based on weakest precondition semantics allow for stepwise refinement of this pre-post specification. By convention, Dijkstra's Guarded Command Language (GCL) [11,12] is used to specify the programming commands that are embedded in the algorithmic specification. The refinement steps yield algorithmic specifications that embed increasingly detailed programming commands until we arrive at a specification that is sufficiently detailed to be translated into a programming language for compilation. Since GCL is an *imperative* pseudo-code, it can be translated to the method bodies of most object-oriented languages.

Returning to our need for a sorting algorithm, we initially appeal to some intuition and diagrams while designing a simple algorithm[2]. Since we do not know the length of array A *a priori*, we require *at least* one loop (a.k.a. a repetition command). This loop might move left-to-right through A using an index variable i, ensuring that everything strictly to the left of i is sorted, while the elements from i to the right may be unsorted. This 'ensurance' is encapsulated in a predicate called a *loop invariant*, and is graphically presented in Fig. 1. From the figure, we also note that when i goes off the right end of A (that is, $i = A.len$), we should *stop*, and since our invariant holds, A is sorted—our postcondition is established. Of course, we also require a plausible termination argument. Intuitively, we can see that, as long as our loop increments i in steps of 1 in each iteration (and no absurdities occur such as A spontaneously growing), we will go off the end of A and terminate. This is formalised with an integer-valued expression known as a *variant*, which is initially finite, can never be less than 0 and declines in each iteration, hence, it is bounded by 0. In our case, the

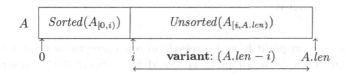

Fig. 1. Diagram of an invariant: that part of A strictly to the left of index i is sorted; subscript $[0, i)$ indicates that subrange from A strictly to the left of i. The variant is depicted as the 'distance for i to go' in A.

---

[2] We could, of course, apply ever deeper levels of intuition and arrive at the best known algorithms, but we limit our example here to the simplest sorting algorithms.

distance from i to $A.len$ fits the bill, and this is shown in the figure. In FOPL, the invariant I can be written as:

$$Sorted(A_{[0,i)}) \wedge (i \leq A.len)$$

Since it is relatively obvious, we do not bother to explicitly mention in I that $A_{[i,A.len)}$ is as yet unsorted. As mentioned before, when i goes off the right side ($i = A.len$), our invariant I implies $Sorted(A_{[0,A.len)})$, which is equivalent to our postcondition $Sorted(A)$.

We are now equipped to make two refinement steps rapidly. The first step takes us from (1) above and uses the 'sequence' (of commands) rule to give

$$\{A.len > 0\}\; S_1\; \{I\};\; S_2\; \{Sorted(A)\}$$

where we choose S_1 to do a minimal amount of work—simply set $i = 0$, which establishes I, since substituting $I[i := 0]$ gives

$$Sorted(A_{[0,0)}) \wedge (0 \leq A.len)$$

and the empty array segment $A_{[0,0)}$ is trivially sorted. We can now put the pieces together in the refinement step to introduce the loop[3], where the increment of i is already provided:

```
{ A.len > 0 }
i : = 0;
{ invariant I and variant A.len − i }
do i ≠ A.len →
     { I ∧ i ≠ A.len }
          loop guard
     S₃;
     i : = i + 1
     { I ∧ variant A.len − i has decreased and is non-negative }
od
{ I ∧ ¬(i ≠ A.len) }
       i=A.len
   Sorted(A)
```

Interestingly, at no point have we relied (in our correctness arguments) on the precondition $A.len > 0$. In fact, we could have omitted this restriction and accommodated empty arrays—the remainder of the algorithm would have been entirely correct. The precondition would then have been $\{A$ is an array$\}$ or even more simply $\{\textbf{true}\}$. The first option makes explicit the type of A, and highlights

---

[3] Here, we have written the I in many places to emphasise where it *must* hold. In most algorithm presentations, it is only mentioned in the line preceding the loop, but the other proof obligations remain (in this case for S_3 to re-establish the invariant).

that it may not be 'null', must provide $A.len$ and be homogeneous; we have left out any formal discussion of types in this paper, though GCL contains types, declarations and scoping [11,12]. Correct algorithm behaviour in corner cases such as empty arrays are often overlooked by coders, or are so 'intimidating' that the precondition is then needlessly strengthened.

Clearly, at each loop iteration (increment of i), we will need to *do some work* to ensure our invariant still holds. Command S_3 must do something to integrate element A_i into the sorted portion $A_{[0,i)}$, and for this we have some algorithmic choices:

1. We can pairwise switch A_i with its left neighbour until it is in the correct sorted position—this *bubbling* action leading to bubble sort.
2. We can search $A_{[0,i)}$ to find the appropriate place j for A_i, then bump $A_{[j,i)}$ to the right by one position so A_i can fit at position j, in this case leading to insertion sort. To find the value of j
   (a) we can use linear search;
   (b) or, thanks to $Sorted(A_{[0,i)})$, we can use binary search

With all three of these possibilities, we would then refine S_3 into another loop—a step that is omitted here as it does not yield deeper insights into CbC. Lastly, as is shown in the algorithm, we note the variant decreases by 1 with every iteration and so the algorithm's termination is assured[4].

We could have done this *algorithm derivation* much more formally, but this lightweight CbC is the essence of what we advocate, with the formalities being picked up as necessary by PhV as discussed in the coming sections.

2.2   A Simple Closure Algorithm

The previous section's refinement to a sorting algorithm involved a variant which was relatively clear from the linear data-structure (array A). In this section, we work towards an algorithm with a more complex variant, and thus termination argument. One of the simplest closure-style problems is:

> Given a finite set N, a total function $f : N \longrightarrow N$ and an element $n_0 \in N$, compute the set $f^*(n_0) = \{f^k(n_0) : 0 \le k\}$ where $f^0(n_0) = n_0$ and $f^k(n_0) = f(f^{k-1}(n_0))$ for all $k > 0$.

This can be viewed as a problem over very simple directed graphs with nodes N, where f gives the successor of a node. Despite the simplicity, the graphs can take on a variety of forms, as illustrated in Fig. 2.

The specification of an algorithm solving the simple closure problem is:

$$\{N \text{ is finite} \wedge f : N \longrightarrow N \wedge n_0 \in N\} \; S \; \{D = f^*(n_0)\}$$

Intuitively, an algorithm computing $f^*(n_0)$ will calculate all $f^k(n_0)$ for increasing k, stopping when an already-seen element of N has been reached

---

[4] Again, this is barring absurdities such as the length of A changing dynamically, which is precisely the difficulty in parallel programs, in which this may indeed happen.

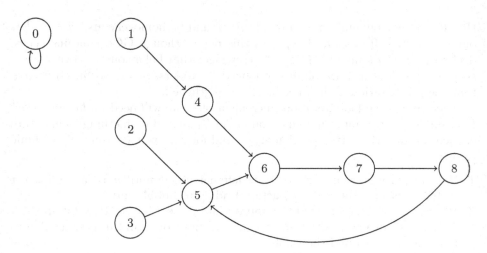

Fig. 2. Nodes representing N with arrows representing $f : N \longrightarrow N$. For example, $f^*(4) = \{4, 6, 7, 8, 5\}$

(variable D has already been presciently named for 'done'). To further refine, we introduce another set T for the 'to-do' elements; additionally, we introduce helper variable i to express the invariant J:

$$D = \{f^k(n_0) : k < i\} \wedge T = \{f^i(n_0)\}$$

We do not bother to specify trivialities such as $D \cap T \neq \emptyset$ and $D, T \subseteq N$, etc. This gives our first algorithm

$$
\begin{aligned}
&\{\ N \text{ is finite} \wedge f : N \longrightarrow N \wedge n_0 \in N \ \} \\
&D, T, i :\ = \emptyset, \{n_0\}, 0; \\
&\{\ \textbf{invariant } J \ \} \\
&\textbf{do } T \neq \emptyset \rightarrow \\
&\qquad \{\ J \wedge (T \neq \emptyset) \ \} \ S_0 \ \{\ J \ \} \\
&\textbf{od} \\
&\{\ J \wedge (T = \emptyset) \ \} \\
&\{\ D = f^*(n_0) \ \}
\end{aligned}
$$

As for our variant, we know that D cannot grow boundlessly since $D \subseteq N$ and N is finite. One possible variant is therefore $|N| - |D|$, though it is not particularly tight if we consider our example (in the caption of Fig. 2): $f^*(4) = \{4, 6, 7, 8, 5\}$ and at termination our variant is $9 - 5 = 4$, thus not reaching zero. Alternatively (as we do below), we can use the definition of f^* to give a tight variant $|f^*(n_0)| - |D|$. The latter variant of course *uses* f^* which is precisely what we are computing, and is probably therefore inappropriate for subsequent PhV; as a fall-back, the former, less tight variant may be used to still prove termination.

This gives our complete algorithm with the loop body refined to executable commands

$\{\ N$ is finite $\land f : N \longrightarrow N \land n_0 \in N\ \}$
$D, T, i : = \emptyset, \{n_0\}, 0;$
$\{\ \textbf{invariant}\ J\ \text{and}\ \textbf{variant}\ |f^*(n_0)| - |D|\ \}$
$\textbf{do}\ T \neq \emptyset \rightarrow$
$\quad \{\ J \land (T \neq \emptyset)\ \}$
$\quad \textbf{let}\ n\ \text{such that}\ n \in T;$
$\quad D, T, i : = D \cup \{n\}, T - \{n\}, i + 1;$
$\quad \{\ D = \{f^k(n_0) : k < i\}\ \}$
$\quad \textbf{if}\ f(n) \notin D \rightarrow T : = T \cup \{f(n)\}$
$\quad \rlap{[}\ \ f(n) \in D \rightarrow \textbf{skip}$
$\quad \textbf{fi}$
$\quad \{\ T = \{f^i(n_0)\}\ \}$
$\quad \{\ J \land \textbf{variant}\ |f^*(n_0)| - |D|\ \text{has decreased and is non-negative}\ \}$
$\textbf{od}$
$\{\ J \land (T = \emptyset)\ \}$
$\{\ D = f^*(n_0)\ \}$

With this last closure algorithm (and the sorting algorithms in Sect. 2.1), we have exemplified CbC's ability to use small correctness-preserving refinement steps to arrive at algorithms which are elegant and immediately understandable, while simultaneously annotating the algorithm with assertions, invariants, and variants which directly and correctly arise from the refinements. With relatively little effort, the variants can then be used to prove termination. In the next section, we will see the further use of these artifacts in connecting CbC with PhV.

3   The Relationship Between CbC and PhV

Post-hoc program verification [4–7] assumes that a program to be verified is annotated with pre-/postcondition specifications for methods, and optionally class invariants in case of object-oriented programs. Additional annotations need to be provided to give the verification tools sufficient information in order to close proofs automatically. These additional annotations are, for instance, loop invariants and variants. Those annotations are classically expressed in FOPL formulae that characterise the program's variables, data structures and operations. Post-hoc program verification tools generally build on FOPL and corresponding provers and need to provide a calculus of the program semantics, i.e., how programs change the valuation of FOPL formulae.

We distinguish two general approaches for treating programs in program verification: (1) verification condition generation and (2) dynamic logic together with symbolic execution. In verification condition generation, the postcondition is transformed backwards through the program using a weakest precondition calculus. The effect of the program—i.e. the postcondition—is used to characterise the resulting weakest precondition formulae. What then needs to be shown is that the provided precondition logically implies this derived weakest precondition with respect to the given program code and postcondition. This proof goal is a FOPL formula. In the second approach, the program and its specification is translated into a dynamic logic formula, and the program within this formula is executed symbolically, capturing the program's effects in a symbolic state. After the program is completely evaluated and, thus, removed from the proof goal, the symbolic state can be evaluated for the remaining pre/postconditions such that a first-order proof goal remains.

3.1   The Case of CbC vs. PhV

Traditionally, the relationship between CbC and PhV is considered to be one of irreconcilable difference [21]. Usually, a picture of two opposite extremes is presented: PhV means arbitrary code is proved *ex post facto* to be correct with respect to its specifications; CbC means code that is rigorously evolved in a stepwise fashion that is guaranteed to be correct. In fact, it seems that there is a space in between these two extremes. For example, when applying PhV to the code, one could insist on certain constraints about how the code should be put together. For example, one could forbid the use of certain program constructs such as `repeat..until` commands, or require that it be expressed in a very simple language, or demand compliance with certain coding standards (such as MISRA-C, used in the automotive industry[5]).

For a meaningful combination of CbC and PhV, we propose the following workflow:

– Firstly, use CbC to derive an elegant algorithmic solution to the problem at hand, simultaneously providing pre/post-specifications and variant/invariant annotations. Here one should not fall into the trap of an 'analysis paralysis', by insisting that every detail has to be rigorously defined and proved. Instead, the emphasis should be on a pragmatic *lightweight* CbC derivation, in the sense described in Sect. 2. This, of course, increases the risk of error, but the risk can then be mitigated in the next step.
– Secondly, translate the CbC-derived program into the programming language that is required by the available PhV proof tool. It will also be necessary to translate the annotations into the logical notation syntax used by the tool. It might be necessary to provide the proof tool with additional annotations. For example, a classical CbC derivation might not be as concerned as a PhV tool with the explicit ranges of variables referenced in an invariant.
– Finally, use the prover tool to apply PhV to the translated CbC-derived program.

Ideally, assuming no errors were introduced in the CbC-based derivation or during the translation to the input language of the prover and enough additional annotations were provided, the proof should go through. Otherwise, iterative

---

[5] http://www.misra.org.uk.

debugging of the program and/or its annotations as well as their addition might be necessary. In the absence of any CbC tool support that embodies an integrated proof assistant, this workflow seems like an appropriate 'marriage of convenience' between CbC and PhV.

The workflow is based on the perception that CbC and PhV actually complement one another. It is designed to leverage their respective strengths and to mitigate their respective weaknesses as discussed below:

- A decided advantage of PhV is that it constructs a machine-checked proof that is correct, subject only to the correctness of the proof calculus and the correctness of the prover. However, a PhV weakness is that articulating the predicates to verify code that was developed in an *ad hoc* fashion with poor structure or no structure is non-trivial and sometimes not even possible. In contrast, CbC generally results in well-structured code, the code being a byproduct, so to speak, of articulating the specifications and annotations needed by PhV proof tools.
- CbC is concerned with correctness at the level of intuitive meaning. It deals with specifying the algorithmic solution to a problem and can tolerate lightweight, semi-formal or informal specifications provided they pragmatically capture the intuition of the developer. For example, in CbC it might be adequate to specify that an array A is sorted by simply writing down $Sorted(A)$. However, if CbC specifications and predicates are treated too informally, one risks errors. PhV can nicely fill this gap, allowing some informality of the CbC development, and then PhV checking with the invariants, variants, pre- and postconditions already worked out by the CbC effort. Of course, PhV tools need syntactically and semantically correct program statements and annotations to successfully complete a proof. So, for the above example, a PhV tool would need a detailed formal logical description what sortedness means, if this had not been provided by the lightweight CbC exercise. Even so, the PhV exercise starts off with a well-defined framework of what needs to be done, unlike what would have been the case if the PhV exercise was undertaken *ab initio*. So things become relatively easy on both sides, as it were.
- CbC allows the taxonomisation of algorithmic families [20]: At each refinement step, there may be several possible choices about precisely how to refine the specification, each choice leading to a different variant of the algorithm. These different refinement paths can then be used to guide taxonomisation of the various algorithms for the particular problem at hand, as we have seen for the sorting algorithms in Sect. 2. In the absence of such a structured refinement process to arrive at alternative algorithms solving the same problem, it becomes very difficult to discover characteristics that fundamentally distinguish such algorithms one from another, i.e., arbitrary or insignificant differences can become confused with fundamental differences. Hence, CbC allows the deep understanding of algorithmic families.

– One of the main drawbacks of CbC and, maybe, the biggest obstacle to its adoption, is the lack of tool support. If CbC had stronger tool support from the beginning and, hence, was more widely applied, CbC might have been prescribed in the development standards for safety-critical systems, instead of PhV. However, tool support for CbC strongly relies on the advances made for PhV program verification. Essentially, tool support for CbC would build on a FOPL prover and a calculus for capturing program semantics. Indeed, it would need to extend such provers with additional functionality, such as handling uninterpreted predicates and unknown program parts while a program is refined in CbC, in addition to different interaction and editing capabilities for the developer.

3.2   Termination-by-Construction

The literature on correctness distinguishes between total and partial correctness of a program. The notation introduced in Sect. 2, $\{P\}\ S\ \{Q\}$, is an assertion of *total* correctness. It evaluates to *True* if and only if the following holds:

If P is *True* and S executes, then$S$ will terminate and Q will be *True*

By way of contrast $P\ \{S\}\ Q$ is an assertion of *partial* correctness[6]. It evaluates to *True* if and only if the following holds:

If P is *True* and S executes <u>and S</u> terminates, then Q will be *True*

The CbC approach to programming [8–12] is oriented towards deriving *totally* correct code *ab initio*. Not only does CbC require a variant, V, to be defined in lockstep with defining the loop's invariant, I. It also requires that the body of the loop, B, has to conform to the specification $\{I\}\ B\ \{I \wedge (0 \leq V < V_0)\}$ where V_0 is the value of V before B executes—i.e. it requires, by construction, that the variant strictly declines in each iteration of the loop towards a fixed lower bound (0 by convention). The CbC approach therefore seeks to avoid erroneously non-terminating code from the outset. One might say that CbC incorporates a Termination-by-Construction (TbC) approach to programming.

In contrast, PhV techniques operate on existing code. These techniques generally separate out the task of verifying that the code attains its postcondition (on condition that it terminates) from the task of verifying that the code indeed terminates. However, *partial correctness* is a weak concept in the sense that all specifications of non-terminating programs are *True* assertions[7]. This counter-intuitive observation focusses attention on the nature of non-terminating code, i.e. on whether it is intentionally or mistakenly non-terminating. There are of course, isolated instances of coded solutions to problems where the termination properties remain a matter of conjecture. One such example is the well-known

---

[6] There are alternative notational conventions in the literature for total and partial correctness.

[7] This is because both *False* $\implies$ *True* and *False* $\implies$ *False* evaluate to *True*,.

Collatz conjecture [22] that the algorithm generating the so-called hailstone sequence of numbers will always terminate.

If code is intentionally non-terminating, (e.g. an operating system that is driven by an infinite loop), then such code is *ipso facto* not focussed on attaining progressively a specific postcondition. Instead, such code typically requires that various interim postconditions should hold each time certain chunks of code within the body of the non-terminating loop complete. Of course, it might also be appropriate in such a scenario to ensure that certain globally invariant conditions are retained throughout the code—for example, the preservation of historical information in the event of an unanticipated hardware interrupt.

The point on which to focus is that postcondition semantics is only meaningful in those sections of the code that are intended to terminate. Our concern here is with such code and, in particular, with how such code should be constructed. There are a number of well-known traditional structured programming heuristics to improve the readability and maintainability of code in respect of its termination properties [8]. Examples include the avoidance of 'go to', 'break' and 'return' statements to exit loops. Such heuristics are oriented towards simplifying the task of understanding a loop's behaviour. There is a single easy-to-identify exit point of each loop. The condition for transiting through this exit point is easily located and clearly articulated, namely in the loop's condition. It goes without saying that TbC produced code complies with all these heuristics.

However, allegorical evidence suggests that these heuristics tend to be widely ignored, not only in private code, but also in industrial code and even in code intended for public inspection and use that is placed on open forums. Section 4 will give examples of such code.

It would be foolhardy to neglect tried and tested heuristics on the grounds that PhV tools are available to check for termination. We advocate, instead, for the disciplined TbC approach to code construction. A 'marriage of convenience' between CbC and PhV can be expected to benefit termination correctness in much the same way as it will enhance correctness in other areas of concern.

4   Case Study

This section reports on our experience in marrying CbC and PhV. It illustrates how PhV applied to ugly hacked-into-correctness code (often unashamedly made available on public forums) is difficult, if not impossible. This stands in contrast to applying PhV to clean, well-structured, easy-to-understand code for the same problem, as delivered by a CbC approach. As a simple example, we considered how the CbC approach would solve the *Partition* sub-algorithm used in the well-known Quicksort algorithm [23,24]. Assume that Quicksort is being applied to the array A. Recall that the purpose of *Partition* is to reorganise a sub-array $A_{[\ell,h+1)}$ into a lower section whose elements are less than or equal to a pivot element, say A_ℓ, all the elements in the remaining upper section then having elements greater than A_ℓ. *Partition* returns the boundary, say j, of these two subarrays. The upper diagram in Fig. 3 illustrates the postcondition of *Partition*,

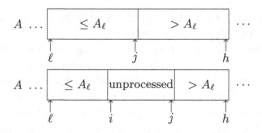

Fig. 3. Diagram of the postcondition and invariant used in *Partition*

proc *Partition*(A, ℓ, h)
    { **pre** $\equiv \ell < h$ }
    $i, j : = \ell + 1, h;$
    { **inv** $\equiv \forall k \in [\ell, i) : (A_k \leq A_\ell) \wedge \forall r : (j, h] : (A_r > A_\ell)$ }
    { **variant** : $(j + 1 - i)$ }
    do $(i \neq j + 1) \rightarrow$
        if $(A_i \leq A_\ell) \rightarrow i : = i + 1$
        ▐ $(A_j > A_\ell) \rightarrow j : = j - 1$
        ▐ $(A_i > A_\ell) \wedge (A_j \leq A_\ell) \rightarrow A_i, A_j : = A_j, A_i; \ i, j : = i + 1, j - 1$
        fi
    od;
    { $(\mathbf{inv} \wedge (i = j + 1)) \Rightarrow$ **post** }
    { **post** $\equiv \forall k \in [\ell, j] : (A_k \leq A_\ell) \wedge \forall r : (j, h] : (A_r > A_\ell)$ }
    return j
corp

Fig. 4. CbC-derived version of *Partition*

and the lower diagram shows an interim state of the algorithm that relies on variable i and j to demarcate the subscript range of unprocessed elements in $A_{[\ell, h+1)}$.

A GCL version of *Partition* is given in Fig. 4. It was derived in a lightweight CbC fashion. As is customary, the pre- and postcondition, and the loop invariant used in the derivation, were included in the algorithm as FOPL assertions embedded between the various commands. Also left in comments is the integer expression representing the loop's variant. The flow of logic and correctness of the algorithm is clear. Variables i and j are initialised to establish the invariant of the loop. The loop's body consists of a single conditional command. This command specifies the conditions under which to increment i or decrement j. If neither of these conditions apply, then the third guarded command requires that A_i and A_j should be swapped, i should be incremented and j should be decremented.

The CbC rules ensure that all paths through the conditional statement result in the loop variant decreasing in each iteration and therefore in the loop eventually terminating. Additionally, the rules ensure that the invariant holds at the

```
algorithm partition(A, lo, hi) is
    pivot := A[lo]
    i := lo - 1
    j := hi + 1
    loop forever
        do
            i := i + 1
        while A[i] < pivot
        do
            j := j - 1
        while A[j] > pivot
        if i >= j then
            return j
        swap A[i] with A[j]
```

Fig. 5. Wikipedia version of *Partition* (June 27, 2016)

end of each loop iteration. Furthermore, it can easily be shown that upon termination of the loop, the invariant and the negation of the loop's condition imply the postcondition. In this sense, the algorithm's logic is transparent and readily verified as correct.

Consider, by way of contrast, an alternative rendition of the same algorithm as given in Wikipedia's entry for Quicksort given in Fig. 5. It is significantly more difficult to follow the flow of logic in this version of the algorithm, and thus to have confidence in its correctness. Here are some of the perceived problems with this code:

- The algorithm introduces an (arguably redundant) `pivot` variable
- There is no guiding principal about why i should be one less than lo rather than the same as or one more than lo. Similarly in regard to j. By way of contrast, in the CbC version initialisation of i and j is specifically aimed at establishing the invariant.
- Use of an infinite loop unnecessarily violates good coding standards. It requires an exit point and this is found at the second last statement. This imposes an additional intellectual effort to verify whether the condition of the if-statement (i >= j) makes sense in the context.
- The infinite loop embeds two successive `do..while` loops. These are inherently difficult to reason about, since each entails a first unconditional execution of the body followed by the evaluation of a condition. Evidently the intention of the first inner loop is to increment i, while the intention of the second inner loop is to decrement j as far as possible. Clearly, the logic required to verify that there is no off-by-one error in either of these loops is much more intricate than in the case of the CbC-based algorithm.
- After these two loops, the algorithm checks whether i >= j and terminates returning j if this is the case; otherwise it swaps A[i] and A[j]. Once more, it is non-trivial to become convinced that this exit condition does not entail an off-by-one error.

There is much allegorical evidence to support the claim that poorly structured code such as this is common both in industrial software and on open forums. As another example, consider the Java function, edmondsKarp, in Wikibooks that implements the Edmonds-Karp algorithm for computing maximal flow in a network[8]. Due to space limitations, the function will not be reproduced here. It can be seen that the function also issues a return from within an if-statement that is embedded in an infinite loop—as in the Wikipedia version of the *Partition*

```
public class Partition {
/*@ normal_behavior
 @ requires l < h;
  @ requires 0 <= l;
  @ requires h < A.length;
  @ ensures (\forall int k; l <= k && k <= \result;  A[k] <= A[l]);
  @ ensures (\forall int r; r > \result && r <= h ; A[r] > A[l]);
  @ assignable A[*];
  @*/
public static int partition(int[] A, int l, int h) {
        int i = l + 1;
        int j = h;
        int temp; // for swapping
        /*@ loop_invariant l < i && i <= j+1 && j <= h;
         @ loop_invariant (\forall int r; r > j && r <= h ; A[r] > A[l]);
         @ loop_invariant(\forall int k; l <= k && k < i;  A[k] <= A[l]);
         @ assignable A[*], i, j, temp;
         @ decreasing (j + 1 - i) ;
         @*/
        while (i != j + 1 ) {
            if (A[i] <= A[l]) { i = i + 1;}
                else if (A[j] > A[l]) {j = j - 1;}
                else if (A[i] > A[l] && A[j] <= A[l]) {
                    temp = A[i];
                    A[i] = A[j];
                    A[j] = temp;
                    i = i + 1;
                    j = j - 1;
                }
        }
        return j;
    }
}
```

Fig. 6. JAVA program with JML [25] annotations for CbC-derived *Partition* function used for PhV verification with KeY [4]

---

[8] https://en.wikibooks.org/wiki/Algorithm_Implementation/Graphs/ Maximum_flow/Edmonds-Karp.

algorithm example above. Even worse, the code breaks out from a loop with the following skeletal structure:

```
LOOP: while(C1){...for(C2){...if(C3){...}else{...break LOOP}}}
```

i.e. it breaks from the else-part of an if-statement in a for-loop that is embedded in a while loop!

That code such as this is routinely found in industrial software and unashamedly presented on public platforms ought to be concerning for software professionals at many levels, not least because it erodes the professional obligation of maintaining and verifying code.

To corroborate the claims that have been made above about the benefits of marrying CbC and PhV, and the difficulties in applying PhV to arbitrary code, an attempt was made to apply PhV to the two *Partition* versions given above. The KeY [4] PhV tool was used for this purpose. In each case, the code had to be translated into Java. This was an easy exercise, the only slight variation being that an additional variable, temp, was introduced to implement the swap. In the case of the CbC version, the FOPL comments were painlessly translated into the JML [25] annotation syntax required by the tool. In addition, it was necessary to indicate a lower bound on the variable ℓ, an upper bound on h as well as to indicate that array A is assignable. The resulting input code and tool output is reproduced in Figs. 6 and 7 affirming the algorithm to be correct.

Matters were considerably more complicated in the case of the Wikipedia code. A few trial traces by hand through the code seemed to deliver the correct answer, despite an uncomfortable intuition that the condition on the first inner loop should contain <= rather than <. To explore correctness more fully, an attempt was made to annotate the KeY (Java) version of the program. Pre- and postcondition annotations were not considered a problem since they would largely correspond with those used to derive the CbC-based algorithm. Additionally, j-i seemed like a reasonable variant for the infinite loop. However, other KeY-required annotations were not at all obvious.

Fig. 7. Screenshot of KeY [4] output on proof of the CbC-derived *Partition* function

We were not able to articulate meaningful invariants for the infinite loop and the two `do B while(C)` loops. It is probable that appropriate invariants will be found if the loops are transformed into semantically equivalent standardised formats (e.g. transform `do B while(C)` to `B; while(C) B`). However, such transformations violate the principle of carrying out PhV on code as-is. We therefore decided to abandon the effort of carrying out PhV on the code.

5   Conclusions

Many contemporary software systems have stringent functional correctness requirements. This paper has proposed a *lightweight* approach to CbC as a first step to meet such demands. For example, not all annotations used in a CbC-based program derivation need to be spelt out with full formal rigour. Similarly, some latitude may be allowed in accepting the correctness of certain refinement increments without carrying out detailed correctness proofs. In doing so, it is hoped that algorithmic solutions may be achieved more efficiently. However, it is also acknowledged that this could reduce the solution's effectiveness because the risk increases of accidentally introducing errors.

Combining lightweight CbC with PhV mitigates this risk. Moreover, the burden of formulating annotations for the PhV proof checker will be lightened by the availability of CbC-produced annotations, even if they have not been formally elaborated. In addition, we have also shown that CbC tends to produce a well-structured algorithmic solution — one that is generally far more amenable to PhV than code developed in an *ad hoc* (hacked) fashion. Hence, CbC and PhV should be seen as complementary strategies for enhancing functional correctness, and brought together in a 'marriage of convenience'.

This also means that CbC should be taught more widely than is currently the case, in training professional software developers. Candidates who have been subjected to the mental discipline CbC imposes (such as rigorously defining predicates and proving refinement steps) tend to have a greater awareness of corner cases to be considered and an appreciation of the value of structure and elegance in code. Beyond formal CbC training, though, *lightweight CbC* should be widely used, even in the presence of PhV verification tools, or if PhV is mandated by development standards for safety-critical software.

For future work, we propose to consider CbC approaches for programming models and languages other than sequential programs considered in this paper. CbC approaches should be considered for deriving algorithms in targeted domain-specific languages [26] that are then used to directly generate actual implementations. Additionally, CbC approaches for parallel programs have high potential to improve application correctness and enhance provability despite the complexity of parallelism. Finally, CbC tools in the form of structured editors that directly support the CbC style of code derivation — by, for example, carrying out automated proofs of each refinement step — would greatly advance the cause of professional software development.

Acknowledgments. This work was partially supported by the DFG (German Research Foundation) under grant SCHA1635/2-2, and by the NRF (South African National Research Foundation) under grants 81606 and 93063.

References

1. Beck, K.: Extreme Programming Explained: Embrace Change. Addison-Wesley Longman Publishing Co. Inc., Boston (2000)
2. Hall, A., Chapman, R.: Correctness by construction: developing a commercial secure system. Softw. IEEE **19**(1), 18–25 (2002)
3. Beckert, B., Hähnle, R.: Reasoning and verification. IEEE Intell. Syst. **29**(1), 20–29 (2014)
4. Beckert, B., Hähnle, R., Schmitt, P.H. (eds.): Verification of Object-Oriented Software: The KeY Approach. LNCS, vol. 4334. Springer, Heidelberg (2007)
5. Jacobs, B., Smans, J., Philippaerts, P., Vogels, F., Penninckx, W., Piessens, F.: VeriFast: a powerful, sound, predictable, fast verifier for C and Java. In: Havelund, K., Holzmann, G.J., Joshi, R., Bobaru, M. (eds.) NFM 2011. LNCS, vol. 6617, pp. 41–55. Springer, Heidelberg (2011)
6. Barnett, M., M. Leino, K.R., Schulte, W.: The Spec# programming system: an overview. In: Barthe, G., Burdy, L., Huisman, M., Lanet, J.-L., Muntean, T. (eds.) CASSIS 2004. LNCS, vol. 3362, pp. 49–69. Springer, Heidelberg (2005)
7. Filliâtre, J.-C., Marché, C.: The why/krakatoa/caduceus platform for deductive program verification. In: Damm, W., Hermanns, H. (eds.) CAV 2007. LNCS, vol. 4590, pp. 173–177. Springer, Heidelberg (2007)
8. Dijkstra, E.W.: A Discipline of Programming. Prentice Hall, Upper Saddle River (1976)
9. Gries, D.: The Science of Programming. Springer, Heidelberg (1987)
10. Cohen, E.: Programming in the 1990s: An Introduction to the Calculation of Programs. Springer, Heidelberg (1990)
11. Morgan, C.: Programming from Specifications, 2nd edn. Prentice Hall, Upper Saddle River (1994)
12. Kourie, D.G., Watson, B.W.: The Correctness-by-Construction Approach to Programming. Springer, Heidelberg (2012)
13. Chapman, R.: Correctness by construction: a manifesto for high integrity software. In: Proceedings of the 10th Australian Workshop on Safety Critical Systems and Software. SCS 2005, vol. 55, pp. 43–46(2006)
14. Abrial, J.: Modeling in Event-B - System and Software Engineering. Cambridge University Press, Cambridge (2010)
15. Méry, D., Monahan, R.: Transforming event B models into verified C# implementations. In: First International Workshop on Verification and Program Transformation, VPT 2013, Saint Petersburg, Russia, 12–13 July 2013, pp. 57–73 (2013)
16. Cheng, Z., Mery, D., Monahan, R.: On two friends for getting correct programs - automatically translating event-B specifications to recursive algorithms in Rodin. In: Margaria, T., Steffen, B. (eds.) ISoLA 2016. LNCS, vol. 9953, pp. 821–838. Springer, Heidelberg (2016)
17. Lamprecht, A., Margaria, T., Schaefer, I., Steffen, B.: Synthesis-based variability control: correctness by construction. In: Formal Methods for Components and Objects, 10th International Symposium, pp. 69–88. Revised Selected Papers (2011)

18. ter Beek, M., Reniers, M., de Vink, E.: Supervisory controller synthesis for product lines using CIF 3. In: Margaria, T., Steffen, B. (eds.) ISoLA 2016. LNCS, vol. 9953, pp. 856–873. Springer, Heidelberg (2016)
19. ter Beek, M., Carmona, J., Kleijn, J.: Conditions for compatibility of components - the case of masters and slaves. In: Margaria, T., Steffen, B. (eds.) ISoLA 2016. LNCS, vol. 9953, pp. 784–805. Springer, Heidelberg (2016)
20. Cleophas, L., Kourie, D.G., Pieterse, V., Schaefer, I., Watson, B.W.: Correctness-by-construction $\wedge$ taxonomies $\Rightarrow$ deep comprehension of algorithm families. In: Margaria, T., Steffen, B. (eds.) ISoLA 2016. LNCS, vol. 9953, pp. 766–783. Springer, Heidelberg (2016)
21. ter Beek, M., Hähnle, R., Schaefer, I.: Correctness-by-construction and post-hoc verification - friends or foes? In: Margaria, T., Steffen, B. (eds.) ISoLA 2016. LNCS, vol. 9953, pp. 723–729. Springer, Heidelberg (2016)
22. Lagarias, J.C.: The 3x + 1 problem and its generalizations. IEEE Intell. Syst. **92**(1), 3–23 (1985)
23. Hoare, C.A.R.: Algorithm 64: quicksort. Commun. ACM **4**(7), 321 (1961)
24. Cormen, T.H., Leiserson, C.E., Rivest, R.L., Stein, C.: Introduction to Algorithms, 3rd edn. MIT Press, Cambridge (2009)
25. Burdy, L., Cheon, Y., Cok, D.R., Ernst, M.D., Kiniry, J.R., Leavens, G.T., Leino, K.R.M., Poll, E.: An overview of JML tools and applications. Commun. ACM **7**(3), 212–232 (2005)
26. Voelter, M., Benz, S., Dietrich, C., Engelmann, B., Helander, M., Kats, L., Visser, E., Wachsmuth, G.: DSL Engineering - Designing, Implementing and Using Domain-Specific Languages (2013). dslbook.org

Deductive Verification of Legacy Code

Bernhard Beckert[(⊠)], Thorsten Bormer, and Daniel Grahl

Karlsruhe Institute of Technology, Karlsruhe, Germany
beckert@kit.edu

Abstract. Deductive verification is about proving that a piece of code conforms to a given requirement specification. For legacy code, this task is notoriously hard for three reasons: (1) writing specifications post-hoc is much more difficult than producing code and its specification simultaneously, (2) verification does not scale as legacy code is often badly modularized, (3) legacy code may be written in a way such that verification requires frequent user interaction.

We give examples for which characteristics of (imperative) legacy code impede the specification and verification effort. We also discuss how to handle the challenges of legacy code verification and suggest a strategy for post-hoc verification, together with possible improvements to existing verification approaches. We draw our experience from two case studies for verification of imperative implementations (in Java and C) in which we verified legacy software, i.e., code that was provided by a third party and was not designed to be verified.

1 Introduction

Formal software verification is the art of proving that a given implementation conforms to a specification on all possible inputs. Here, we consider deductive program verification at source code level, which is a precise verification technique for properties given in an expressive specification language. High precision means that neither false positive nor false negatives occur; there are no bounds on the domain; and no approximations or abstractions are needed to apply the technique.

Despite the considerable advances of verification technologies and improvements in the automation of theorem proving throughout the past decade, these tools are still highly dependent on user interaction to complete proofs.

One interaction paradigm, used by 'auto-active' [28] tools, is based on the user adding the information needed by the prover to the source code: the implementation is annotated with requirement and auxiliary specifications (e.g., loop invariants). If the auxiliary annotations are sufficient, this allows the tool to find a proof automatically (provided that the program actually meets its requirements).

There is a wide range of software verification tools users may choose from, depending on, e.g., the target programming and specification language, the kind of properties to be verified and, not least, the interaction paradigm that is followed: from (mainly) manual proof interaction in tools like Isabelle [30] or HOL4 [32], to purely auto-active tools such as Dafny [27] or VCC [9]. Taking the middle ground, tools like Why3 [6] or KeY [1] can be both used in an auto-active fashion and by manual interaction during the proof process.

© Springer International Publishing AG 2016
T. Margaria and B. Steffen (Eds.): ISoLA 2016, Part I, LNCS 9952, pp. 749–765, 2016.
DOI: 10.1007/978-3-319-47166-2_53

Independently of whether an auto-active or an interactive verification style is used, the need to write formal (auxiliary) specifications has turned out to be the major bottle-neck (cf. [3]). The amount of specification typically outsizes the executable code: the ratio is reported to be 3:1 in [2] (measured in tokens), 4:1 in [7] (measured in lines of code), and almost 11:1 in [23] (measured in lines of proof script). In the light of these case studies, it becomes obvious why post-hoc verification is often unreasonably expensive: Writing specifications is a major part of the verification effort anyways, and that part is made more difficult and laborious if the program was not implemented with verification in mind.

The contribution of this paper is two-fold. Firstly, in Sect. 2, we discuss which characteristics of legacy code impede the verification effort and give examples. Secondly, we discuss how to handle the challenges of legacy code verification and suggest a strategy for post-hoc verification in Sect. 3, together with possible improvements to existing verification tools and methodologies.

Our observations are based on software written in imperative/object-oriented programming languages (C and Java). The conclusions drawn regarding the verification of legacy code are thus mainly relevant for other imperative implementations and only partially applicable to other paradigms like declarative or functional programming – e.g., while the difficulty to understand legacy systems applies to both imperative and functional programs, the need to handle shared, mutable state in specification differs between programming paradigms.

We argue that naive specification strategies that work either purely in a bottom-up or purely in a top-down fashion are ineffective: A too weak specification for some module M results in failure to prove properties about client modules invoking M; a too strong specification raises the verification effort beyond necessity.

We claim that, instead, a specification and verification process for legacy systems must be incremental and iterative. Also, using only a single verification tool and its methodology predetermines and often unnecessarily restricts the possible approaches to solve the legacy-verification problem. Instead, a good verification process supports proof exploration and construction with different tools; it lets the user apply different analysis and verification techniques for the various parts of a program and its specification. This choice is particularly important for legacy verification as the code has not been designed with a particular verification method or tool in mind.

We draw our experience from two case studies in which we verified (parts of) legacy software: the *PikeOS* microkernel [22] (using the VCC tool) and the *sElect* voting system [26] (verified with KeY). The PikeOS microkernel is part of a virtualization concept targeted at embedded real-time systems. It acts as a paravirtualizing hypervisor to support safety-critical and security-critical applications and is deployed in industry. The features of PikeOS – being part of highly safety-critical applications and having a manageable code size – made it a good choice for deductive verification.

The sElect e-voting system was developed by the group of Ralf Küsters at the University of Trier [26]. In this distributed system, a remote voter can cast one single vote for some candidate. The vote is sent through a secure channel to a tallying server. The server only publishes a result – the sum of all votes for each candidate – once all voters have cast their vote. The verification goal is to show that no confidential information (i.e., votes) is leaked to the public.

Although both systems feature concurrent computations, here, we restrict our considerations to sequential programs. Concurrency poses particular challenges that are out of the scope of this paper.

2 Why is Deductive Verification of Legacy Code Hard?

In the following we will illustrate some characteristics of legacy systems that contribute to the difficulty of post-hoc software verification, adding to the inherent complexity of any deductive verification task. We argue that coming up with the right specification is difficult already at the level of a single module. Specification is even more difficult when the right modularization (including any interface specification) has to be identified based on the legacy implementation. We also claim that current verification tools and methodologies, when each is used on its own, are often insufficient for large post-hoc verification tasks, because legacy code has not been written with a particular verification technique in mind. Thus, legacy code verification requires choosing appropriate tools and techniques on a per module basis and for individual specification parts, depending on the characteristics of the module and the property to be proven.

2.1 Legacy Code is Often Unsuitable for Verification

As part of our verification case studies we identified three causes why legacy code is hard to verify: (1) legacy code is difficult to understand; (2) the existing modularization of legacy systems is inadequate for verification and the right modules are hard to find; (3) implementations of single modules use programming language features or programming styles that are inherently difficult to verify, and the code is not written according to best practice of software development.

Both the structure of legacy systems and the implementation of single modules are often unsuitable for verification. It helps if the system was developed following best practices for software development; but that does not always lead to verifiable code. Rather, verifiability has to be considered explicitly when writing software – if not sufficiently taken into account, the following issues arise.

Legacy Code is Difficult to Understand. As a prerequisite of most of the tasks in the verification process, the verification engineer has to understand the problem that the legacy system is trying to solve – in addition to the requirements to be verified. Understanding the problem at a level of detail needed for producing a *formal* requirement specification is often non-trivial.

For both the requirement specification and the auxiliary specification (respectively the user interaction with the prover in an interactive verification tool), information has to be extracted from (1) existing documentation, which is often only informal, incomplete or imprecise, or (2) the source code.

Although the source code contains the information needed, this knowledge is implicit and has to be made explicit by the verification engineer (e.g., in form of invariants) to be of use for the prover. Determining which information is crucial for the verification task that cannot be deduced automatically by the prover and how to adequately formalize the discovered properties is non-trivial.

An example for implicit knowledge in existing, informal documentation is the description of the effects of a system call in PikeOS that changes the priority of a thread (up to a bound named MCP), taken from the kernel reference manual:

"This function sets the current thread's priority to newprio. Invalid or too high priorities are limited to the caller's task MCP. Upon success, a call to this function returns the current thread's priority before setting it to newprio."

This description keeps effects caused by concurrency implicit: the system call is preemptible and another thread may change the thread's priority before the function's return value is assigned. The "old priority" returned thus might not be what a naive observer might expect who neglects that the system is concurrent.

Establishing the Right System Modularization is Complicated. Ideally, real-world software would consist of modules that each have a single, clearly defined purpose, which would separate different concerns and lead to maintainable code. In reality, maintainability and elegance of an implementation is often not the first priority but also other quality metrics apply (e.g., efficiency). Software that is not developed according to best practices is often hard to maintain, more difficult to understand and analyze, hence also more work for formal verification.

Even if the system was developed according to best practices, the given modularization of the legacy system (given syntactically by the structure of methods, classes, etc., or described in the documentation) does often not coincide with a modularization that is optimal for verification purposes. One of the subtasks when verifying legacy systems is thus to find a better modularization for the implementation – this is a complex, iterative process.

Also, for post-hoc verification, the verification engineer can only change and optimize the modularization within boundaries given by the structure of the legacy system. Solutions of the modularisation problem are hence mostly stuck at a local optimum, which limits the suitability for verification that can be obtained.

When a reasonable division of the system into modules is found, the user still has to come up with the interface specification for each module. As a consequence of the (globally) suboptimal modularization of the system, the resulting interfaces and their specification become unnecessarily complicated in contrast to systems written for verification with a well-chosen structure.

Consider two components that together provide a single functionality to the rest of the system. If those components are treated for verification as separate modules, an additional interface is exposed that may be awkward to specify compared to the specification of a single module containing both components. In the other direction, combining two separate components that have almost no interaction on common state leads to specification overhead for describing the absence of interaction to modularize the verification task (frame problem).

Today, several approaches exist to tackle this problem, among them *dynamic frames*, *ownership* and *separation logic*. However, these approaches produce a considerable overhead in both specification and verification. In contrast, if components can be split into sub-components each operating on disjoint state, separating them already in the design and implementation phase diminishes the issue of framing overhead in the proof process.

The problem of writing interface specifications for legacy code is aggravated by interdependencies between modules. The specification and verification effort does not scale linearly with the number of modules due to interactions via shared data structures and common parts of the program states.

For example, in the PikeOS microkernel, implementations of single C functions are deliberately kept simple to facilitate maintainability and certifiability. The overall functionality of the kernel is implemented by interaction of many of these small functions, operating on common data structures (cf. [24]). More generally, all operating systems have to keep track of the system's overall state, resulting in relatively large and complex data structures on which many of the kernel functions operate conjointly. That this is not an exclusive property of system software but usual in non-trivial software projects in general is demonstrated by empirical studies on software complexity metrics (see, e.g., [5]).

As a consequence, interface specifications may have strong dependencies on each other – namely the joint data structures and their invariants. Finding the right auxiliary annotations for a single module requires the verification engineer to consider several modules at once, due to these dependencies.

For legacy systems, the (locally) optimal module structure established for post-hoc verification is more complicated and, thus, also the interface specification is more complex compared to systems written for verification. Therefore, each single attempt to find a suitable interface specification for a single module is also more complicated for legacy systems. The iterative nature of the specification process which is needed in case of highly interdependent modules acts as a multiplying factor for the disparity in specification effort at this local module level.

Single Modules are Badly Written for Verification. In the worst case, real-world code is produced with little care and low quality, resulting in buggy programs that not only fail to meet their requirements but are also difficult to analyze. Bugs in programs further increase the complexity of program verification as they introduce the uncertainty whether a proof cannot be completed due to a bug in the program or because of missing annotations or ineffective proof search.

Even if a program serves its purpose, the issue that this kind of code is often barely legible and badly maintainable remains. But even if code is well written in the sense that it is maintainable and adaptable, it is not necessarily easy to verify. A typical case is the frequent use of (standard) libraries, because the library functions may be hard to specify (e.g., string operations). Also, certain language constructs are notoriously difficult to specify and verify and should be avoided, e.g., the use of Java's reflection capabilities.

```
1    private byte [] getResult () {
2      if (! resultReady ()) return null;
3      int [] _result = new int [numberOfCandidates ];
4      for (int i=0; i<numberOfCandidates; ++i )
5          _result [i] = votesForCandidates [i];
6      return formatResult (_result );
7    }
8
9    private static byte [] formatResult (int [] _result ) {
10     String s = ''Result of the election:\n'';
11     for ( int i=0; i<_result.length; ++i )
12        s += ''Number of votes for candidate '' + i + '': '' + _result [i] + ⤸
           ↳ ''\n'';
13     return s.getBytes ();
14   }
```

Listing 1. Code example from the sElect e-voting system.

Another issue with legacy programs are overly general and flexible implementations which can be used in a broad range of scenarios – which in the real system are then actually only used for a single, well-defined purpose (e.g., software product lines). If the verification engineer is unaware of this, a complex specification for the general functionality has to be provided instead of a more specific variant that clearly communicates the intended purpose of the module.

As an example for code that is written in a way that it is hard to verify, consider the implementation from the original e-voting system [26] that retrieves the election result in the server (Listing 1). Several issues are to be noted: (a) The method **getResult()** returns a null reference in case it is called in an illegal state (Line 2). (b) The array containing the number of votes for each candidate is copied to a fresh instance (Line 5). (c) The result is embedded into a string (Line 12) and encoded into an array of bytes (Line 13). Item (a) represents a common modeling pattern, even though in good object-oriented design, it is preferable to raise an exception. Returning **null** (or any other error element) does not complicate verification, but must be reflected in the specification. Item (b) is just superfluous code – we could pass the original array reference. Both the allocation of a fresh array and copying the values invokes unnecessary complexity in verification – and also in the specification since we need an invariant for the loop. Item (c) is the most serious: The encoding in strings effectively makes verification extremely difficult, even when support for reasoning about strings is available.

2.2 Lack in Tool Support for Post-hoc Verification

We argue that the issues pointed out so far are not sufficiently mitigated by supporting measures in most deductive verification tools and methodologies.

Handling large software systems is supported by modular specification and verification. Modular verification is one of the advantages of deductive verification. But at the same time, modularity is also *essential* for deductive verification tools to scale at all. The need for auxiliary specifications that comes with modularity can be a drawback. For instance, while KeY supports inlining of method calls – which is suitable at least for smaller methods – VCC does not provide that option and the verification engineer has to provide method contracts for all methods.

There is often no good support for inspecting and understanding the interplay between different modules of a given program, as current deductive verification tools and methodologies tend to focus on specifying and verifying a single module at a time. Instead, verification tools should provide a view on dependencies of module specifications and make effects of local specification changes to the rest of the system explicit. Already the task of determining which previously completed proofs have to be re-run after a change to an auxiliary specification that is exported to other modules is often not sufficiently supported by verification tools. To assist the user, the integration of KeY into the Eclipse IDE [20] tracks dependencies between proofs for a system, automatically tries to re-run proofs affected by a change in either the program or specification and notifies the user of the proof result.

To reduce the effort needed to verify interdependent modules, techniques such as abstract operation contracts [8] or lazy behavioral subtyping [12] can be used: The former approach allows to compute and cache parts of the proofs that are independent of a given concrete specification, while the latter approach simplifies verification of object-oriented programs by reducing contracts of overriding methods to those properties actually needed at the call sites of the superclass methods.

Abstraction is another important instrument to handle verification of large systems. Good abstraction of the behavior of a system helps to focus on important details of the functionality, and allows for clear and succinct specifications. Poorly chosen abstractions may complicate verification up to making it impossible. Which abstraction is appropriate depends on both the system properties to be verified and on how well the verification tool is able to reason about the abstraction.

To find the right abstraction for a data structure, analyzing its implementation alone is often not sufficient. Rather, one has to find out which properties of the data structure are important for verifying the modules using it. While techniques exist that may help in some cases in finding the right abstractions (such as CEGAR), these methods are not sufficiently supported in current annotation-based systems.

Moreover, specification-language support for abstractions is often not flexible enough. For data abstraction, most verification systems feature some kind of user-defined abstract data types – however, there is a large amount of established formalisms, like CASL, that should be taken into further consideration when extending the specification language. For control abstraction, many established formalisms exist that could be used for one of the abstraction layers on top of the code, e.g., CSP or abstract state machines. Also, a built-in refinement mechanism is needed to connect the different abstraction levels.

3   Ways to Successful Post-hoc Verification

Given the difficulties one faces when applying deductive verification to legacy code, one may consider a re-implementation of the verification target from scratch with formal verification in mind. In particular, if full functional verification of the whole software system is required, this may well lead to less effort than a legacy code verification. In practice, re-implementation is rarely the best option, as several reasons call for verification of existing code in its original context in a legacy system: (1) To be formally verified is not the only quality the software is measured against; the newly written code has to be, e.g., as efficient or as maintainable as the legacy version. (2) Existing knowledge of the development team about the legacy implementation, and also documentation would be largely rendered worthless in case the software was written from scratch. (3) Often, full functional verification of the whole system is not necessary as either a smaller set of important parts of the system or only specific characteristics of the system is of interest (e.g., security properties such as absence of certain information flow).

Another important point is that the user's trust in a system to perform as expected, which has been developed by extensive testing or long-term use, cannot simply be replaced by the fact that the system has been formally verified.

3.1   A Verification Process Based on Separation of Concerns

To handle the challenge of verifying complex legacy software, we have to split up and simplify the specification and verification task by decomposing the verification problem into parts, which we call *verification concerns*. A concern consists of some part of the code together with part of its specification. The main goal is to arrive at a small set of simple concerns that are easy to specify and verify *in isolation* – as multiple verification attempts are often required before successfully completing a single proof and thus repeated effort in user interaction is the normal case, this isolation prevents propagation of revisions through the rest of the program and specification. As explained below, concerns are related to but not identical to the modules of the program to be verified. Moreover, concerns within one verification project may be formalised using different specification methods. And they may be intended for different validation methods, which – besides verification – may include testing or inspection for some concerns.

There are four main strategies that may be applied to handle a concern $C = (S, P)$, consisting of a (requirement) specification S and an implementation part P: decomposition, abstraction, substitution, and local verification.

Decomposition. To decompose a concern (S, P), the program P is partitioned into modules and corresponding interface specifications are added for each of the resulting modules. For example, if we have a proof sketch for the correctness of P w.r.t. specification S and have identified how different components of P contribute to its correct operation, we can use decomposition to get a new set of concerns with (possibly informal) requirements for smaller parts of P.

A special case is decomposing a program P "in situ" by marking out parts of a method body with specification constructs without affecting the actual code structure – e.g., in KeY, the user can enclose parts of a method body in a Java block and give it a contract; this allows to split large methods into more manageable pieces.

Another possibility to isolate functionality of a system is to extract and aggregate related methods of the implementation in a trait which can then be reasoned about using an incremental deductive verification approach [10].

Besides dividing the implementation, also the specification can be split up into different concerns (e.g., termination, information flow properties, functional properties) or different cases depending on the input. The different execution paths in the implementation that fit the specification parts may then also be isolated by choosing a subset of relevant or interesting statements for further analysis (resulting in a program slice).

That verifying the decomposed concerns implies validity of the original concern is either another explicit proof obligation in the verification process (i.e., is a concern itself) or is entailed by a general argument about the decomposition step.

Abstraction. Simplifying a concern by using control or data abstraction allows for hiding implementation details irrelevant for the underlying reasons of correct operation of the concern – any details removed in such a way then only appear in a separate refinement proof obligation, i.e., as additional concern in the process.

Typical examples include the abstraction of non-trivial implementation of pointer-based data structures by a suitable data type like sequences or sets, or providing an interface specification for more involved operations which is underspecified (e.g., replacing pivot selection in Quicksort by random choice). Also, producing a prototype is a special case of abstraction.

Substitution. Both the program and the specification part of a concern C can be replaced by a version C' that is optimized for further treatment in the verification process. In this case, all completed proofs that depend on C are rendered invalid and have to be reinspected and possibly redone with the new concern C'. In contrast to prototype construction, however, this approach does not need to justify the relation between C and C'. Instead, C' is the result of the process.

Local Verification. At some point, the resulting concerns cannot further decomposed, abstracted, or substituted. They then have to be verified correct in a *local* verification step with a suitable technique. Verification techniques range from interactive deductive verification, more lightweight automatic static checkers, up to testing and run-time checking – or simply adding the correctness of the concern to the set of assumptions made for correct operation of the whole system.

As a prerequisite for verification, the concern has to be prepared (e.g., by translating the specification S to another specification language – one special case is formalizing an informal requirement specification of the concern). Lastly, auxiliary specifications for the concern have to be added and a verification attempt is made.

3.2   Activities in the Concern-Centric Verification Process

The defining concepts for a concern-centric verification process are: (1) different verification and validation methods are used for different types of concerns within one project; and (2) different operations on the set of concerns are applied in an *iterative* and *incremental* fashion. How to find the right concerns and how to handle each concern depends on the program to be verified and the methodology used.

Identify and Verify Concerns by Lightweight Techniques. In many cases, program correctness (or incorrectness) can be judged by automated light-weight approaches. These approaches are very efficient (in comparison with deductive verification), but cannot be sound and complete at the same time. Combining deductive verification with one of these in a hybrid approach allows us to cut the cost of verification while maintaining soundness and completeness. Suitable technologies include bounded software verification [13], runtime checking [11] and testing, as well as program slicing [17], or invariant generation.

Not only can we make use of these techniques to *verify* particular concerns, they also allow us to *identify* components resp. concerns in the first place.

In the e-voting case study, the critical code for counting votes is interleaved with calls to a logger. Intuitively, logging does not interfere with computing the result. However, it does change the global state. Deductive verification (with the KeY tool) thus includes the concern of proving that logging does indeed not affect the election result, which is expensive. We successfully used decomposition based on a slicing to compute a (smaller) critical slice within the actual code [25], which does not include the logging concern. This allowed us to verify the original code under the assumption that logging does not change the global state, which is justified at the meta-level (correctness of the slicing technique).

Refactor the Implementation to Simplify Verification. Precise instructions on how to refactor a program to ease the verification task can only be given w.r.t. a particular verification technique and a particular target program. An easy to verify module is simple w.r.t. control flow and data flow. In general, the target modules should be implemented in a way such that they only provide functionality that is necessary for the overall system functionality.

For an example of how to improve existing code that is not written for verification, reconsider the code shown in Listing 1 and its shortcomings described in Sect. 2.1. In our prototype, we have drastically simplified the functionality:

```
private int [] getResult ()
   { return resultReady () ? votesForCandidates : null; }
```

We omit the copying and the encoding in string format, which are separate verification concerns, and return the original array. However, we retain the error reporting through returning **null** in order not to deviate too far from the original design.

Another local optimization is to decouple control flow and data flow, where possible. For example, the program fragments if (b) a = x; else a = y; and a = b? x: y; are equivalent, yet the first one combines control flow and data flow, whereas in the second one, only data flow occurs. For the latter version, in KeY's symbolic execution engine, the location a is assigned a symbolic value that depends on the value of b but the proof does not branch.

Produce Prototypes to Understand a Verification Concern. Sometimes, the measures presented so far are not enough and we need even more invasive changes to enable verifiability. With the e-voting case study, we pursued an approach in which we produced a series of gradually more complex prototypes, which were verified one after another [16, Chap. 9] – similar to a refinement-based development style to produce verified code. In this way, there is quick feedback on the validity of the more abstract specifications. While the code change between each version was rather small, the specification grew significantly. Still, we have found that it is harder to develop the complete specification for the final prototype in one step (or even the actual implementation) than to refine it on every iteration.

3.3 Where to Start the Process?

Given a software system to be verified, an important question is whether to attack the verification problem in a top-down or in a bottom-up manner.

In a top-down approach, we start with the (usually informal) high-level requirements and see how they distribute to single modules. This approach bears the advantage that we focus on the overall goal. On the other hand, it comes with a danger that the formalization of requirements is not well adapted to the modules. Typically, too weak preconditions are derived where side-conditions – in particular implementation-related – were not considered on the higher abstraction level, e.g., size restrictions of data structures. The unpleasant consequence is that we have to refine many module specifications and to repeat all affected proofs.

In a bottom-up approach, we start by specifying and verifying the most elementary modules (i.e., leaves in the call graph). Then, specifications of larger modules are derived by composing the specification of constituents. An obvious benefit of this approach is that elementary modules are of little complexity, hence it is not too difficult to develop a precise specification. We can make post-conditions strong enough that we can reuse the contracts of these components without the danger of having to repeat its correctness proof. This insight is particularly important for (helper) modules that are called often in the system under investigation. However, a bottom-up approach tends to be expensive. Firstly, there is a high human effort in exhaustively specifying the modules. Secondly, the resulting contracts may not be effectively usable, because a precise specification may consider more cases than are necessary in the given verification context. In particular, all corner case are specified, instead of excluding them from consideration through the pre-condition, e.g., it is easier to require that an array access is within bounds than to specify the effect of an illegal access.

Besides the logical strength of a contract, also its syntactic form is important for its utility in conducting a proof. Consider the two alternative postconditions for a function `sqrt` computing the integer square root of `x`:

(a) $\setminus result^2 \leq x < (\setminus result+1)^2$

(b) $(\forall y.\ 0 \leq y \leq \setminus result \Rightarrow y^2 \leq x) \land (\forall z.\ z > \setminus result \Rightarrow z^2 > x)$

While both contracts specify the same behavior of `sqrt`, one contract may be much more useful than the other, depending on the verification tool used and the properties that are needed in the verification of a caller of `sqrt`.

For these reasons, we claim that pure top-down nor pure bottom-up approaches are seldom effective. Instead, we have to start at several points simultaneously and have to refine our specification in short iterations. In this way, higher-level requirements and lower-level guarantees can converge. Choosing the concrete approach depends on the program structure. Analyzing the connectivity in the call graph first, gives a good heuristic. Strongly connected components in the call graph are recursion groups. Within them, a bottom-up approach is not possible at all, but a top-down approach can start at the node with the highest incoming connections.

For our considerations, loops behave similarly to internal nodes in the call graph with indegree and outdegree of one: while it is possible to start with the specification of a loop with invariants before writing the contract of the surrounding method, often the loop invariant is not of interest on its own as part of a requirement, but simply an auxiliary specification that enables verification of the method contract. As such, an invariant has to fit to this contract both regarding the logical strength and its syntactical structure, as shown in the `sqrt` example above. Consequently, you do not start with writing down the loop invariant, but derive it from the surrounding method's contract while abstracting.

In the e-voting case study, the modules are arranged hierarchically – without recursive method calls. This allows developing specifications, including class invariants, mostly bottom-up. However, we find it useful to have a good control over when invariants are applied within a proof. Many verification systems offer little user control over how invariants are processed. In contrast, KeY represents class invariants using a symbol in the proof obligation which can be replaced with the actual contents of the invariant only if and when needed.

This allows using the abstraction provided by invariants not only in specification, but also in the proof, since it is often enough to refer to 'the invariant' without knowing its exact contents. A similar concept exists in Dafny with *opaque* functions [18], where the user can decide when to make the body of such a function available to the prover. These mechanisms are helpful in cases where the contents of an invariant or the function body are complex, e.g., if an invariant contains existential quantification.

3.4 How to Improve Tool Support for Post-hoc Verification?

Effective verification requires good feedback to the user. In a purely interactive proof, the user has full control, but the amount of available information may be too much to handle and is sometimes not given at the right abstraction level (e.g., showing open proof goals instead of notifying the user about which specification is violated in the source code). Several techniques may improve user experience:

High-Level User Interaction. Constructing a proof interactively without any automation is infeasible for practical verification problems. In the e-voting case study, we encountered single proofs with over 200 000 proof rule applications, where single formulas in the proof goal could fill several screen pages.

Instead of fine-grained manual interaction, user input relevant for proof search and construction should be given in a way that is close to the problem description respectively the implementation. One possibility is to follow the auto-active verification paradigm, giving auxiliary annotations at source-code level.

Another approach is to provide an interaction concept that matches an abstract proof outline of the user more closely, e.g., by using proof scripts – this well-established interaction paradigm is the basis of many interactive provers, e.g., HOL4 [32] or Isabelle [30] with "tactic-based" proof interaction. One example of a more declarative interaction style compared to the procedural style is the Isar formal proof language offered in the Isabelle/Isar system [33].

Similar to these established script-based interaction approaches, proof scripts in KeY serve as a high-level interface to the proof object as the user does not apply concrete single rules, but sketches the proof structure. One use case is a long proof with only a few steps that need interaction. Scripts can often be replayed when a verification concern is modified, as they are robust against smaller changes in the code or its specification.

Better Feedback. One of the main issues in verifying large systems are the complex dependencies between verification concerns and the associated correctness proofs. To simplify the task of keeping track of the overall proof state, as well as updating this information in case a verification concern has been changed and proofs have to be redone, the KeY tool has been integrated into the Eclipse IDE [20].

Identifying errors in the specification or implementation during the verification process is another frequent issue, in particular when large proof obligations arise in interactive provers which require manual inspection or user interaction – often, only a small part of the information presented in the proof obligation is relevant for revealing the error. To automatically get quick feedback on the validity of such a proof obligation, a bounded analysis technique has been implemented for the KeY tool, giving concrete counterexamples for single KeY proof obligations [21]. Support for pinpointing the reason for incomplete proof attempts is also provided by another component of KeY's integration into the Eclipse IDE mentioned previously, by giving a view on KeY's proof goals that shows the truth status of subformulas as inferred by KeY in the current proof state [19].

For auto-active verification tools, the situation is often the opposite: too little information is available to pinpoint possible errors or missing specifications. The insight that these tools often do not produce enough feedback for failed verification attempts is not new [28,31]. To improve this situation, tools like VCC, which already show the exact annotation that could not be verified, are usually complemented with tools like the Boogie Verification Debugger (BVD) [15], presenting counterexamples for the proof obligations on the level of the original program.

Still, due to the modular verification methodology of the deductive verification tools, these counterexamples are often not sufficient to retrace the concrete program execution leading to the violated specification (if there is any). This shortcoming has been identified and is addressed by many approaches. To give early and precise feedback beyond the local module currently being verified, we proposed a combination of software bounded model checking and deductive verification [4]. Other techniques allow for generating a program reproducing a concrete trace through the original code from a failed verification attempt [29,31], allowing the user to identify mismatches between program and specification.

Regression Verification is an instance of relational program analysis [14]. Instead of asserting that a program conforms to its contract, we prove that *two programs* are functionally equivalent (or more generally, that they expose congruent behavior). While, in general, relational verification is as hard as functional verification, regression verification works well for programs that are of a similar (syntactical) shape with only minor local differences. Proof complexity does not stem from the overall program/specification complexity, but only from the difference between the two versions. This allows reducing the effort of repeating a proof for a module with only minor changes. We can use this property to verify a prototype implementation P first, and then prove that a refined version P' of the code matches the behavior of the prototype, which proves that P' conforms to the specification. This approach is particularly helpful in case where the actual legacy code must not be changed.

4 Conclusion

A pure post-hoc deductive verification approach for full functional requirement specifications is often unreasonably expensive, despite recent advancements of specification methodologies and verification tools.

It is thus crucial to identify and separate different concerns (i.e., parts of the property to be proven and portions of the implementation) to take advantage of different program analysis techniques – in the best case discharging otherwise complex deductive proof obligations automatically, e.g., by syntactic analysis such as program slicing. These analysis techniques not only play a crucial role in proving system properties, but also help with the identification of concerns as part of an iterative specification and verification process.

Any remaining concern that can only be proven correct using deductive verification tools like KeY or VCC, which often requires extensive user interaction, should be preprocessed and rewritten to ease verification: examples are property-preserving program refactorings, writing more abstract variants of the implementation and proving refinement between the different versions – or, if necessary, re-implement relevant parts of the system from scratch.

At times, also implementations that follow best practices of software engineering are needlessly complex from the point of view of software verification. Raising awareness of these issues for program verification would allow improving the state of implementations w.r.t. verifiability when legacy code is changed or new modules are implemented. In addition, verification complexity metrics or implementation and design patterns adapted to program verification could provide guidelines for how to produce code that is easier to analyze and verify using formal methods.

References

1. Ahrendt, W., et al.: The KeY platform for verification and analysis of Java programs. In: Giannakopoulou, D., Kroening, D. (eds.) VSTTE 2014. LNCS, vol. 8471, pp. 55–71. Springer, Heidelberg (2014)
2. Alkassar, E., Hillebrand, M.A., Paul, W., Petrova, E.: Automated verification of a small hypervisor. In: Leavens, G.T., O'Hearn, P., Rajamani, S.K. (eds.) VSTTE 2010. LNCS, vol. 6217, pp. 40–54. Springer, Heidelberg (2010)
3. Baumann, C., Beckert, B., Blasum, H., Bormer, T.: Lessons learned from microkernel verification: specification is the new bottleneck. In: Cassez, F., Huuck, R., Klein, G., Schlich, B. (eds.) 7th Conference on Systems Software Verification. SSV 2012, Sydney, Australia, vol. 102. Electronic Proceedings in Theoretical Computer Science (2012)
4. Beckert, B., Bormer, T., Merz, F., Sinz, C.: Integration of bounded model checking and deductive verification. In: Beckert, B., Damiani, F., Gurov, D. (eds.) FoVeOOS 2011. LNCS, vol. 7421, pp. 86–104. Springer, Heidelberg (2012)
5. Bhattacharya, P., Iliofotou, M., Neamtiu, I., Faloutsos, M.: Graph-based analysis and prediction for software evolution. In: Glinz, M., Murphy, G.C., Pezzè, M. (eds.) 34th International Conference on Software Engineering (ICSE 2012), pp. 419–429. IEEE (2012)
6. Bobot, F., Filliâtre, J.C., Marché, C., Paskevich, A.: Why3: shepherd your herd of provers. In: Boogie 2011: First International Workshop on Intermediate Verification Languages, Wroclaw, Poland, pp. 53–64 (2011)
7. Bruns, D., Mostowski, W., Ulbrich, M.: Implementation-level verification of algorithms with KeY. Softw. Tools Technol. Transf. 17(6), 729–744 (2015)
8. Bubel, R., Hähnle, R., Pelevina, M.: Fully abstract operation contracts. In: Margaria, T., Steffen, B. (eds.) ISoLA 2014, Part II. LNCS, vol. 8803, pp. 120–134. Springer, Heidelberg (2014)
9. Cohen, E., Dahlweid, M., Hillebrand, M., Leinenbach, D., Moskal, M., Santen, T., Schulte, W., Tobies, S.: VCC: a practical system for verifying concurrent C. In: Berghofer, S., Nipkow, T., Urban, C., Wenzel, M. (eds.) TPHOLs 2009. LNCS, vol. 5674, pp. 23–42. Springer, Heidelberg (2009)

10. Damiani, F., Dovland, J., Johnsen, E.B., Schaefer, I.: Verifying traits: an incremental proof system for fine-grained reuse. Formal Asp. Comput. **26**(4), 761–793 (2014)
11. Delahaye, M., Kosmatov, N., Signoles, J.: Common specification language for static and dynamic analysis of C programs. In: Shin, S.Y., Maldonado, J.C. (eds.) Proceedings of the 28th Annual ACM Symposium on Applied Computing, SAC 2013, Coimbra, Portugal, 18–22 March 2013, pp. 1230–1235. ACM (2013)
12. Dovland, J., Johnsen, E.B., Owe, O., Steffen, M.: Lazy behavioral subtyping. J. Logic Algebraic Program. **79**(7), 578–607 (2010)
13. Falke, S., Merz, F., Sinz, C.: The bounded model checker LLBMC. In: Denney, E., Bultan, T., Zeller, A. (eds.) 28th IEEE/ACM International Conference on Automated Software Engineering, ASE 2013, Silicon Valley, CA, USA. IEEE (2013)
14. Felsing, D., Grebing, S., Klebanov, V., Rümmer, P., Ulbrich, M.: Automating regression verification. In: 29th IEEE/ACM International Conference on Automated Software Engineering (ASE 2014), pp. 349–360. ACM (2014)
15. Le Goues, C., Leino, K.R.M., Moskal, M.: The Boogie verification debugger (Tool Paper). In: Barthe, G., Pardo, A., Schneider, G. (eds.) SEFM 2011. LNCS, vol. 7041, pp. 407–414. Springer, Heidelberg (2011)
16. Grahl, D.: Deductive verification of concurrent programs and its application to secure information flow for Java. Ph.D. thesis, Karlsruhe Inst. of Techn. (2015)
17. Hammer, C., Snelting, G.: Flow-sensitive, context-sensitive, and object-sensitive information flow control based on program dependence graphs. Int. J. Inf. Secur. **8**(6), 399–422 (2009)
18. Hawblitzel, C., Howell, J., Lorch, J.R., Narayan, A., Parno, B., Zhang, D., Zill, B.: Ironclad apps: end-to-end security via automated full-system verification. In: Flinn, J., Levy, H. (eds.) 11th USENIX Symposium on Operating Systems Design and Implementation, pp. 165–181. USENIX Association (2014)
19. Hentschel, M.: Integrating symbolic execution, debugging and verification. Ph.D. thesis, Technische Universität Darmstadt, January 2016
20. Hentschel, M., Käsdorf, S., Hähnle, R., Bubel, R.: An interactive verification tool meets an IDE. In: Albert, E., Sekerinski, E. (eds.) IFM 2014. LNCS, vol. 8739, pp. 55–70. Springer, Heidelberg (2014)
21. Herda, M.: Generating bounded counterexamples for KeY proof obligations. Master's thesis, KIT (2014). http://dx.doi.org/10.5445/IR/1000055929
22. Kaiser, R., Wagner, S.: Evolution of the PikeOS microkernel. In: Kuz, I., Petters, S.M. (eds.) 1st International Workshop on Microkernels for Embedded Systems (MIKES 2007). National ICT Australia (2007)
23. Klein, G., Andronick, J., Elphinstone, K., Heiser, G., Cock, D., Derrin, P., Elkaduwe, D., Engelhardt, K., Kolanski, R., Norrish, M., Sewell, T., Tuch, H., Winwood, S.: seL4: formal verification of an operating-system kernel. Commun. ACM **53**(6), 107–115 (2010). doi:10.1145/1743546.1743574
24. Klein, G., Andronick, J., Elphinstone, K., Murray, T., Sewell, T., Kolanski, R., Heiser, G.: Comprehensive formal verification of an OS microkernel. ACM Trans. Comput. Syst. **32**(1), 2: 1–2: 70 (2014)
25. Küsters, R., Truderung, T., Beckert, B., Bruns, D., Kirsten, M., Mohr, M.: A hybrid approach for proving noninterference of Java programs. In: Fournet, C., Hicks, M., Viganò, L. (eds.) 28th IEEE Computer Security Foundations Symposium (CSF) (2015)
26. Küsters, R., Truderung, T., Vogt, A.: Verifiability, privacy, and coercion-resistance: new insights from a case study. In: Proceedings of the 32nd IEEE Symposium on Security and Privacy (S&P), pp. 538–553. IEEE Computer Society (2011)

27. Leino, K.R.M.: Dafny: an automatic program verifier for functional correctness. In: Clarke, E.M., Voronkov, A. (eds.) LPAR-16 2010. LNCS, vol. 6355, pp. 348–370. Springer, Heidelberg (2010)

28. Leino, K.R.M., Moskal, M.: Usable auto-active verification. In: Usable Verification Workshop (2010). http://fm.csl.sri.com/UV10

29. Müller, P., Ruskiewicz, J.N.: Using debuggers to understand failed verification attempts. In: Butler, M., Schulte, W. (eds.) FM 2011. LNCS, vol. 6664, pp. 73–87. Springer, Heidelberg (2011)

30. Paulson, L.C.: Isabelle–A Generic Theorem Prover. LNCS, vol. 828. Springer, Heidelberg (1994)

31. Polikarpova, N., Furia, C.A., West, S.: To run what no one has run before: executing an intermediate verification language. In: Legay, A., Bensalem, S. (eds.) RV 2013. LNCS, vol. 8174, pp. 251–268. Springer, Heidelberg (2013)

32. Slind, K., Norrish, M.: A brief overview of HOL4. In: Mohamed, O.A., Muñoz, C., Tahar, S. (eds.) TPHOLs 2008. LNCS, vol. 5170, pp. 28–32. Springer, Heidelberg (2008)

33. Wenzel, M.M.: Isabelle/Isar–a versatile environment for human-readable formal proof documents. Ph.D. thesis, Technische Universität München (2002)

Correctness-by-Construction $\wedge$ Taxonomies $\Rightarrow$ Deep Comprehension of Algorithm Families

Loek Cleophas[1,2(✉)], Derrick G. Kourie[1,3], Vreda Pieterse[4], Ina Schaefer[5], and Bruce W. Watson[1,3]

[1] Department of Information Science, Stellenbosch University,
Stellenbosch, South Africa
{loek,derrick,bruce}@fastar.org
[2] Software Engineering and Technology Group,
Technische Universiteit Eindhoven, Eindhoven, The Netherlands
[3] Centre for Artificial Intelligence Research,
CSIR Meraka Institute, Pretoria, South Africa
[4] Department of Computer Science, University of Pretoria, Pretoria, South Africa
vreda@fastar.org
[5] Software Engineering Institute,
Technische Universität Braunschweig, Braunschweig, Germany
i.schaefer@tu-bs.de

Abstract. Correctness-by-construction (CbC) is an approach for developing algorithms inline with rigorous correctness arguments. A high-level specification is evolved into an implementation in a sequence of small, tractable refinement steps guaranteeing the resulting implementation to be correct. CbC facilitates the design of algorithms that are more efficient and more elegant than code that is hacked into correctness. In this paper, we discuss another benefit of CbC, i.e., that it supports the deep comprehension of algorithm families. We organise the different refinements of the algorithms carried out during CbC-based design in a taxonomy. The constructed taxonomy provides a classification of the commonality and variability of the algorithm family and, hence, provides deep insights into their structural relationships. Such taxonomies together with the implementation of the algorithms as toolkits provide an excellent starting point for extractive and proactive software product line engineering.

1 Introduction

Correctness-by-construction (CbC) is an approach for developing algorithms that was advocated by many of the founding fathers of computer science (CS) in the 60 s and 70 s. They saw it as *the scientific way* to develop software [1–3]. In CbC, an implementation of an algorithm is developed inline with the respective correctness arguments. A high-level problem specification is progressively evolved into the implementation by a sequence of small, tractable refinement steps. As all refinement steps comply with the correctness arguments, the resulting implementation is correct-by-construction. The benefits of CbC include enhanced confidence in the algorithms' correctness and improved elegance of their design.

© Springer International Publishing AG 2016
T. Margaria and B. Steffen (Eds.): ISoLA 2016, Part I, LNCS 9952, pp. 766–783, 2016.
DOI: 10.1007/978-3-319-47166-2_54

However, CbC is seldom taught in contemporary undergraduate CS programs. Rather than regarding it as a foundational approach to software development, many computer scientists regard it as an historical footnote. To misapply a GK Chesterton quote: CbC has not been tried and found wanting; it has been tried and found difficult! We contend here that the alleged difficulty of CbC can be mitigated by using discretion about when to apply it with full rigour.

In this paper, we demonstrate that CbC supports deep comprehension of algorithm families. An algorithm family is a set of solutions to an algorithmic problem. A *de facto* method to organise information—in order to create knowledge in any domain—is to classify the domain's objects or concepts. Such classification highlights their commonality and variability. This simplifies comprehension and leads to increased accessibility and usability of domain knowledge.

We provide a classification of a family of algorithms by organizing into a taxonomy different refinements obtained during CbC-based design. Such a taxonomy makes the commonalities and variabilities of the different algorithmic variants in the family explicit. Furthermore, it reveals the structural relationships of the family, hence providing deep comprehension. We argue that this approach has the additional benefit of stimulating the invention of new algorithms by filling apparent gaps in the taxonomic structure. We provide illustrative examples of algorithmic taxonomies and argue that their use in the implementation of toolkits, i.e., a library of all variants, for TABASCO [4] is beneficial. Furthermore, a taxonomy with the implementation of the algorithms in the form of a toolkit provides an excellent starting point for extractive and proactive software product line engineering [5] as described previously [6,7].

The rest of this paper is organised as follows: Sect. 2 provides necessary background on CbC and Sect. 3 an introduction to classification. Section 4 explains CbC-based algorithm classifications in taxonomies. Section 5 describes how CbC-based taxonomies can be used for toolkit implementation and extractive and proactive software product line engineering. In Sect. 6, we conclude this paper with an outlook on future work.

2   CbC Introduction and Motivation

This section motivates for using CbC and provides a short introduction to the details of CbC, focusing on notation/syntax, allowable refinement steps, and some of the variations. Readers interested in the details of CbC are referred to the classic books (some of which are no longer in print, though Morgan has made his available online) [8–11] and the most recent one [12].

CbC involves constructing a program (a.k.a. algorithm) from a specification using *refinement* steps. Since the specification is a given, and we only use correctness-preserving refinement steps, we know that the program is correct—*by construction*. Such a sequence (known as a *derivation* in CbC parlance) actually forms a complete correctness argument broken into small steps[1], which is pedagogically important for understanding the algorithm.

CbC relies crucially on the use of a single/unified notation for *specifications* (in first order predicate logic) and *programs* (in Dijkstra's guarded command language—GCL). An example of the notation (known as Hoare triples) is

$$\{P\} \ S \ \{Q\}$$

which specifies that "assuming precondition P holds (is true), program statement (command) S will terminate and Q will hold".

A more concrete example would be (for array A)

$$\{A.len > 0\} \ S \ \{Sorted(A)\}$$

Here, statement S is still *abstract*; to derive this to a concrete (executable) program, S must be some sorting algorithm. Clearly[2], a refinement may combine any of (at least) the following:

– Weaken the precondition: "expect/require less"
– Strengthen the postcondition: "provide/promise more"
– Concretize the statement: provide internal structure for the statement, perhaps leading to further Hoare triples which themselves require refinement

The first two simply require first order predicate calculus[3], whereas the last requires the GCL pseudocode. GCL is an imperative (as opposed to logic-, functional-, or object-oriented) pseudocode consisting of only three essential control structures (namely, the sequence, select and loop statements respectively) as well as variables, assignments and expressions[4].

Triple $\{P\} \ S \ \{Q\}$ may be refined using the *sequence* operator ';' into

$$\{P\} \ S_0 \ \{R\} \ ; \ S_1 \ \{Q\}$$

where R is chosen to specify a reasonable split of the 'work' between S_0 and S_1. Of course, a badly chosen R can lead us to dead-ends in attempting to refine either of the two triples $\{P\} \ S_0 \ \{R\}$ and $\{R\} \ S_1 \ \{Q\}$, and so R is usually chosen with some insight. Here, it is important to note that ';' is an *infix operator* on two statements[5], sometimes pronounced "and then."

---

[1] *Small steps* is key here: each refinement should be small enough to be immediately convincing in isolation and without extensive additional 'magic'.

[2] We say *clearly* because these notions of refinement have been known intuitively and in natural language since the 1960s, though they have been more recently properly formalised by many, including Back then Morgan [11, 13] and later for object-oriented programs by Liskov and Meyer [14, 15].

[3] We advocate *not* over-formalising this, cf. the *Sorted* predicate above, which has not been written out in detail.

[4] The latter three are all as one would expect from the Pascal family of languages and we do not further specify them.

[5] This was once well-understood by students of the Pascal family of languages, but was thoroughly bastardised by C/C++ and then Java (as a statement 'terminator'), and now forms rather arbitrary punctuation largely unneeded for parsing the language.

We can instead refine our original triple to a semi-familiar **if** statement (also called a select statement):

$$\{\ P\ \}$$
$$\textbf{if}\ \ G_0 \to \{\ P \land G_0\ \}\ S_0\ \{\ Q\ \}$$
$$[\!]\ \ \ \ G_1 \to \{\ P \land G_1\ \}\ S_1\ \{\ Q\ \}$$
$$\textbf{fi}$$
$$\{\ Q\ \}$$

Here, the two guards G_0 and G_1 take the place of the if-condition. They are carefully chosen to allow for further refinement of S_0 and S_1. There are two interesting corner cases:

– When $G_0 \land G_1$ one of the two branches is arbitrarily chosen and executed. When wanted, this symmetrical nondeterminism can allow for very elegant algorithms [16].
– When $\neg G_0 \land \neg G_1$ the statement *aborts*, making it important to cover all cases with guards and not rely on the 'silent fall through' behaviour seen in some programming languages.

In this example, we have shown two guarded statements; the only restriction is that there be at least one guarded statement in an **if**.

In a further elegance-driven stroke of genius, Dijkstra et al. introduced a **do** loop allowing for *at least* one guard, where our original triple refines to:

$$\{\ P\ \}$$
$$\{\ \textbf{invariant:}\ I\ \}$$
$$\textbf{do}\ \ G_0 \to \{\ I \land G_0\ \}\ S_0\ \{\ I\ \}$$
$$[\!]\ \ \ \ \ G_1 \to \{\ I \land G_1\ \}\ S_1\ \{\ I\ \}$$
$$\textbf{od}$$
$$\{\ I \land \neg G_0 \land \neg G_1\ \}$$
$$\{\ Q\ \}$$

Analogously to the **if** statement, the guards take the place of the while-condition in most programming languages. The **do** semantics can be summarised as:

– When $G_0 \lor G_1$, one of the true guarded statements is arbitrarily chosen and executed. Again, this allows for elegance in nondeterminism and symmetry.
– Otherwise ($\neg G_0 \land \neg G_1$, by De Morgan), the statement terminates.

Importantly, a predicate I (known as the *loop invariant*[6]) has been carefully chosen with G_0, G_1 such that $P \Rightarrow I$, $I \land \neg G_0 \land \neg G_1 \Rightarrow Q$, and of course that we

---

[6] Termination and progress arguments also require an integer function known as a *variant* — the interested reader is referred to [12].

are confident in further refining the two guarded statements S_0, S_1. Predicate I does not hold all the time: it holds before and after each iteration, though each of S_0, S_1 may be a compound statement in the middle of which I temporarily does not hold, only to be re-established by the end of the statement.

3   Classification

When the volume of information about objects in a domain grows beyond a certain limit, it becomes unmanageable and difficult to use. Classification schemes are intended to bring order to this object information, thereby increasing the ability to access, use and preserve the information. To this end, objects with similar attributes are grouped together into classes. The classes that are formed represent concepts. The classical Aristotelian view claims that a concept is a discrete object characterised by a set of attributes. Some of these attributes may be shared by other concepts in the domain of discourse. According to this view, concepts should be clearly defined, mutually exclusive, and collectively exhaustive. This way, any object of the given classification universe belongs unequivocally to one, and only one, of the proposed concepts. Such a classification scheme is called a taxonomy. The word taxonomy derives from the Greek τάξις, (*taxis*—meaning 'order') and νόμος, (*nomos*—meaning 'law' or 'science') [17]. Carl Linnaeus, the father of modern taxonomy, used the term in the first edition of his *Systema Naturae* dated 1735—a text dealing with the systematic categorisation and naming of living organisms [18].

Pieterse and Kourie [19] categorise classification schemes[7] in terms of their structure and content type. In increasing order of complexity, they distinguish between lists, taxonomies, lattices, thesauri and ontologies. A *list* is a linearly organised collection of objects and their attributes, whereas a hierarchically organised collection of objects and their attributes is a *taxonomy*. The position of every concept (i.e. an object and its associated attributes) in a taxonomy is uniquely determined and the concept may have multiple sub-concepts. If it is required that the taxonomy should be a *strict* hierarchy, then each concept may have only one super-concept. Such a taxonomy essentially forms a tree of concepts. However, in some cases this requirement may be lifted so that concepts in the taxonomy may have more than one super-concept. The taxonomy is then essentially a directed acyclic graph, generally with a single root.

Various mathematical models have been proposed to describe and reason about taxonomies. Those described in [20–22] represent some of the earliest examples. Salton's document-term matrix [23] for information retrieval results in a hierarchical taxonomy of concepts with documents as objects and terms as attributes, such that a concept may have multiple super-concepts. Other examples of taxonomies in which concepts may have multiple super-concepts are the classifications defined by Barwise and Seligman [24]. Priss [25] points out that these are essentially formal concept lattices. Formal concept analysis (FCA),

---

[7] in some contexts referred to as Knowledge Organisation Systems.

introduced in 1984 by Wille [26], studies such lattices. FCA is a mathematical formalisation of the classical Aristotelian categorisation that allows multiple super-terms per concept. FCA offers a principled way to classify objects and their properties, building on order theory and lattice theory.

A scheme that includes semantic relations beyond hierarchical ones is called a *thesaurus*. A popular term used for a classification scheme is an *ontology*. Gruber [27] introduced this term to refer to a classification scheme that supports porting knowledge between systems. The formal definition of an ontology used in artificial intelligence requires that it includes inference rules. Pieterse and Kourie [19] caution against the indiscriminate use of the term ontology in contexts where the term thesaurus would be more appropriate, and argue that the ideal representation model for a collection depends on its content and purpose.

Jonkers [28] described a method to use abstraction when classifying algorithmic problems and their solutions. He proposed the systematic ordering of problems and their solutions at various levels of abstraction through a process of "systematic generalization". Despite its clarity and rigour, this strategy has not been widely recognised. Similarly Kourie [29] formalised the notions of abstraction, refinement and enrichment of entities in terms of their properties. An entity, X, is regarded as an abstraction of entity Y if the properties of X constitute a subset of the properties of Y. If *all* of the properties of Y that are not also properties if X imply properties of X, then Y may be regarded as a refinement of X. If *none* of the properties of Y that are not also properties of X imply properties of X, then Y is regarded as an enrichment of X. This approach can be used to define partial orderings of entities based on refinement or enrichment.

Banach *et al.* [30] observe that many practitioners deem the formal program derivation using formal refinement inadequate in the face of the demands of real applications. They introduce the concept of retrenchment to accommodate practical development steps that may fail to adhere strictly to the formal definition of refinement as the sole method of passing from abstract to concrete models. These steps are typified as specification constructor tasks. Instead of weakening preconditions or strengthening postconditions, they elaborate specification details. According to Kourie's definition [29], these are indeed enrichments. Kovács [31] emphasises the importance of Kourie's work for a formal definition of refinement in the context of knowledge management.

The approaches by Jonkers [28], Kourie [29] and Morgan [11] discuss abstraction in a generic fashion, although Jonkers' work applies his approach to garbage collection algorithms as a case study. Others have independently used abstraction to classify algorithms. For example, Darlington [32], Broy [33] and Merritt [34] each offer alternative ways of classifying sorting algorithms. Following on in the footsteps of the first Eindhoven taxonomy by Jonkers in 1982, a number of taxonomies in similar style have been developed. We discuss these in Sect. 4.

Cleophas *et al.* [4] explored the use of a concept lattice for classifying algorithms. A lattice was constructed using the data in an existing taxonomy of keyword pattern matching algorithms. The resulting concept lattice is comparable to the original taxonomy. However, it combines algorithm attributes that were previously duplicated in different parts of the taxonomy, highlighting similarities that were previously less obvious. It is pointed out that attribute exploration techniques that are prescribed in formal concept analysis could potentially aid in the discovery of new algorithms or highlight previously non-obvious consequences.

4   CbC-Oriented Algorithm Classifications

While not following Jonkers' early Eindhoven approach to the letter, the taxonomisation approaches applied at Eindhoven, Pretoria, and Stellenbosch from the 1990s onwards, are similar. They have all been influenced very much by the 'Eindhoven school' of CbC algorithmics in the style of Dijkstra, Feijen, and others. In CbC, an algorithm and its correctness arguments are developed and presented hand-in-hand, using the refinement approach sketched in Sect. 2, and in contrast to post-hoc verification of an algorithm.

4.1   CbC-Based Taxonomies

An algorithm taxonomy is a hierarchical structuring of a family of algorithms in a particular domain. It may either be represented as a tree or—especially in the setting of CbC-oriented algorithm taxonomies—it may more conveniently be represented by a single-rooted directed-acyclic graphs.

Each node in the graph corresponds to an algorithm with its corresponding pre- and postcondition. In Aristotelian terms, a node may thus be regarded as a concept whose object is a sequence of commands constituting the algorithm and whose attributes are specified by the pre- and postcondition. The algorithm taxonomy has a starting point, i.e., a root algorithm corresponding to the most abstract solution to the algorithmic problem at hand—generally indicated as some unspecified command that complies with a stated pre- and postcondition.

Edges connecting any two nodes are labeled by *details*. Such details labeling taxonomy branches can be categorised into three kinds:

- Problem details, involving a restriction of algorithm input or output; e.g. restricting from multiple-keyword pattern matching to the single-keyword case.
- Algorithm details, specifying changes to algorithm structure; these change the higher-level structure of the algorithm, for example the loop structure. Such changes do not change pre- or postcondition, but merely the internal structure of the algorithm. An example could be replacing an abstract statement with a loop, (i.e. changing S to say $\mathbf{do}\,C \to S1\,\mathbf{od}$); or replacing an abstract specification such as $\{P\}\,S\,\{Q\}$ by a sequence of two abstract statements such as $\{P\}\,S1;\,\{R\}\,S2\,\{Q\}$.
- Representation details, used to indicate variance in data structures used, either internally to an algorithm or influencing input or output representation as well. In the context of automata construction algorithms, different automata types and transition functions are examples of such details.

As the case may be, the addition of a detail from either of these categories may be a *refinement* of a specification, meaning that either the precondition is weakened, the postcondition is strengthened, or both. If a detail in the taxonomy corresponds to a refinement, then we know that the child node algorithm satisfies Liskov's substitution principle [14] compared to the parent node algorithm—i.e. the child node algorithm can safely be substituted wherever the parent node algorithm is used. Problem details as mentioned above however clearly do not satisfy this property, i.e. they are not refinements in the formal sense. They have been used e.g. in the keyword pattern matching taxonomy of Watson [35], where the problem specification for most taxonomy nodes is for multiple-keyword pattern matching, yet some nodes correspond to single-keyword pattern matching algorithms; as a result, the latter involve a problem *restriction* to the single-keyword case[8]. Algorithm details do satisfy the Liskov property, while for representation details, Liskov's substitution principle holds if and only if the pre- and postcondition are unchanged.

Intermediate nodes in the taxonomy, especially those closer to the taxonomy's root, tend to correspond to abstract algorithms (though when using coarse-grained details and branches, they may still be rather concrete), while nodes closer to the leaves correspond to concrete implementations. Nodes that are closer together in the taxonomy tend to be more similar than nodes that are further away from each other, though this also depends on the granularity of the details and branches used in a particular taxonomy.

For pragmatic reasons, CbC-oriented taxonomies may not adhere to a CbC approach to the fullest, since taxonomisation typically involves many *existing* algorithms, i.e. algorithms that have been found in the literature and need to be classified. Of course the taxonomisation process may also give rise to *new* algorithms, in which cases CbC is applied to the fullest. However, even for the case of existing algorithms, the integration and eventual presentation of such algorithms as part of the eventual taxonomy does follow a CbC approach, showing how the algorithm can be obtained by step-by-step refinements on the path from taxonomy root to algorithm node, and with the respective branches along the path giving the corresponding correctness arguments.

4.2   Examples of CbC-Based Taxonomies

CbC-oriented algorithm taxonomies have been constructed for various application areas from the 1990s onwards. Marcelis [36] applied the approach to attribute evaluation algorithms, while recently Pieterse has applied the approach to transitive closure algorithms in her PhD research. Domains and algorithms dealing with symbolic data processing (e.g. sequence and tree processing) served prominently, due to the many application areas and multitude of algorithms for such processing. As a result, many CbC-oriented taxonomies developed cover this domain. In [35] Watson covered keyword pattern matching, deterministic

---

[8] An alternative taxonomy would start with a single-keyword pattern matching specification at the root, and add *refinements* to add multiple-keyword algorithms.

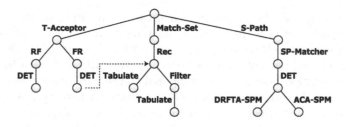

Fig. 1. ([40]) A CbC-oriented taxonomy of tree acceptance algorithms. (Branches labeled by taxonomy details).

finite automaton (DFA) construction and DFA minimisation. The keyword pattern matching taxonomy was subsequently extended in [37]. Bosman [38] and van de Rijdt [39] have addressed approximate and two-dimensional pattern matching. Cleophas [40] classified tree acceptance and pattern matching algorithms. Watson [41] later also classified algorithms that construct minimal acyclic DFAs.

The latter taxonomy will be discussed in greater detail in the next subsection; here we briefly discuss a tree algorithm taxonomy, as an additional example of our CbC-oriented algorithm taxonomies—and one that is built upon in Sect. 5. Figure 1 shows a taxonomy of acceptance algorithms [40] for determining whether a given tree is an element of a tree language. This problem is similar to the string acceptance problem of determining whether a given string is part of a language, and solutions often involve a tree automaton, a generalization of the corresponding string automaton notion. The taxonomy tree splits the tree acceptance algorithms into three main classes, i.e., using a tree acceptor, match sets, or string paths. Further details lead down the taxonomy's hierarchy in order to include both algorithms known from the literature and new ones developed during the course of the taxonomisation reported on in [40].

4.3 CbC-Based Taxonomy Case Study

The transition graph of a deterministic finite automaton (DFA) is *acyclic* if and only if its language is a finite set of words of finite length. (The abbreviation ADFA is used to denote an acyclic DFA.) In several widely used applications (e.g. spell checkers and network intrusion detection) it is of critical importance to construct from a set of words the *minimal* ADFA (MADFA) whose language is that word set. In [41] Watson provides an in-depth CbC-based study of algorithms for constructing such MADFAs. This results in an elegant classification of the studied algorithms. The purpose of this subsection is to outline the taxonomy that emerges from that study.

Let $M = (Q, \Sigma, \delta, s, F)$ denote an ADFA whose state set, alphabet, transition function, start state, and final state set are Q, Σ, δ, s and F respectively. Since M is an ADFA, $\mathcal{L}(M)$ is a finite set of words of finite length. The task of constructing a MADFA for a finite language W can be specified as finding Q, δ

and F such that:

$$\{W \subset \Sigma^*\} \, S \, \{Min \wedge \mathcal{L} = W\}$$

where Min is a suitably defined predicate that asserts M to be a MADFA and $\mathcal{L}$ represents the language of M. This specification can then be refined to

$$\{W \subset \Sigma^*\} \, add\_words \, \{\mathcal{L} = W\}; \; cleanup \, \{Min \wedge \mathcal{L} = W\} \qquad (1)$$

Specification (1) indicates that abstract code denoted by add_words "somehow" creates an ADFA whose language, $\mathcal{L}$, is W and thereafter relies on abstract code denoted by $cleanup$ to convert that ADFA into a language-equivalent MADFA. Figure 2 has add_words at the root of a small taxonomy tree. At the next level, three possible ways are enumerated in which add_words might be realised, denoted by $add\_words\_concurrent$, add_word_sets and add_single_words respectively. These entries are abstract programs that have the same pre- and postcondition as add_words. In [41] CbC was used to derive the latter abstract program as well as more concrete forms represented by its children in the tree.

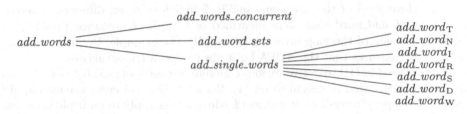

Fig. 2. A tree taxonomy of algorithms for add_words as used in MADFA construction in [41].

The abstract algorithm $add\_words\_concurrent$ builds an ADFA whose language is W by some unspecified arrangement of concurrently running processes, each process adding one or more words from W to the emerging ADFA. The abstract algorithm add_word_sets tackles the same task by an unspecified divide-and-conquer strategy that partitions W into appropriate subsets, building an ADFA for each subset and then merging them to provide an ADFA for W. To the best of our knowledge, concrete instances of these former two abstract programs have not been proposed in the literature. They exist only as ideas whose details still have to be fleshed out and that may result in interesting concrete algorithms. Of course, the ideas could arise spontaneously, but in the present case, they suggested themselves as a side-effect of the CbC derivation of add_single_words and its concrete realisations.

Figure 3 shows the CbC derived version of add_single_words. It consists of a loop whose invariant is denoted by $Struct(D)$ where D is the set of words already processed, and whose variant is the size of the set of words still to be processed, T. In each iteration $w \in W$ is selected as the minimal element of some

$$D, T : = \emptyset, W;$$
$$\{ \text{ invariant: } Struct(D) \quad \text{variant: } |T| \ \}$$
$$\textbf{do } T \neq \emptyset \rightarrow$$
$$\quad \textbf{let } w : w \text{ is any minimal element of } T \text{ under } \leq;$$
$$\quad \{ \ Struct(D) \ \}$$
$$\quad \quad Q, \delta, F : \text{add\_word}(w);$$
$$\quad \{ \ Struct(D \cup \{w\}) \ \}$$
$$\quad \quad D, T : = D \cup \{w\}, T - \{w\}$$
$$\quad \{ \ Struct(D) \ \}$$
$$\textbf{od};$$
$$\{ \ Struct(W) \ \}$$

Fig. 3. Commands excerpted from [41] corresponding to *add_single_words*.

(unspecified) partial ordering, $\leq$, on the elements of W. An abstract algorithm, *add_word*, is invoked with w as parameter. The specification of *add_word* requires that if $Struct(D)$ holds before its invocation then $Struct(D) \cup \{w\}$ should hold thereafter. Updating D and T re-establishes the invariant.

The third level of the taxonomy in Fig. 2 indicates seven different concrete instances of *add_word* that were identified in [41]. Each instance preserves a different version of the loop invariant $Struct(D)$. For example, the first of these, *add_word$_T$*, ensures that the ADFA built always has a trie-structure.

CbC is used in [41] to derive various concrete instances of the abstract *cleanup* algorithm referenced in specification (1). Some of these concrete versions apply uniquely to specific versions of *add_word*, while others apply to multiple versions. These derivations can be used to expand the tree taxonomy of *add_words* shown in Fig. 3 into a MADFA taxonomy, represented as a directed acyclic graph.

4.4   Benefits of CbC-Based Taxonomisation

In our applications of CbC and CbC-based taxonomisation, we have often seen a number of important benefits to the use of CbC—both in CbC for a single algorithm, and for CbC-based taxonomisation of a family of algorithms.

The benefits that arise from the application of CbC first and foremost include the provable correctness of the algorithms resulting from a careful application of CbC: a high-level specification with abstract statement S in between a pre- and postcondition is trivially correct, and if each of the refinement steps, applied to such a specification in sequence, is shown to be correct, then the resulting algorithm is also correct. The stepwise refinement and derivation of an algorithm tends to highlight the essence of an algorithm rather than the accidentals, borrowing from Fred Brooks' terminology [42]. For example, Hopcroft's original presentation of his DFA minimization algorithm used a list data structure, whereas a stepwise derivation showed that in essence a set was sufficient [35]. The focus on essentials often uncovers underlying symmetries and dependencies in an algorithm. The overall result tends to be a clear, aesthetically pleasing exposition of the algorithm that enhances insight, offers pedagogic benefits, and sometimes—due to the focus on essentials—enhances efficiency.

CbC thus supports the deep comprehension of derived algorithms—unlike ad hoc approaches that require verification to just prove correctness, let alone deeply understand an algorithm.

When CbC is applied to a family of algorithms instead of a single one (as when CbC is used for taxonomisation) additional benefits may arise. The development of a taxonomy of provably correct algorithms for a particular problem uncovers common structure and details (branches, root paths) between algorithms, clarifying relations and often even showing ones that were previously hidden. This was evident in e.g. the taxonomies in Watson's and Cleophas' PhD theses, as well as in Pieterse's recently submitted one. The taxonomisation thereby also provides for meta-efficiency, i.e. efficiency at the level of the algorithm derivations and proofs—common proof steps between algorithms are shared, corresponding to a shared common path in the taxonomy graph. Furthermore, the taxonomisation, especially when using fine-grained details and branches in the derivation process, exposes opportunities for *inventive algorithmics*: an intermediate node may give rise to a new, previously uninvented branch of algorithms; or to the application and re-use of an existing detail previously used in another branch of the taxonomy; etc.

By ordering and structuring the algorithms in a domain or algorithm family, taxonomisation also increases accessibility of the entire domain. This includes accessibility for non-experts in the domain, who may use the structure, commonalities and variation exposed by the taxonomy to gain an understanding of the algorithms. Combined with the association of theoretical and practical complexity and performance results to the respective algorithm nodes, this will allow them to choose among algorithms from the family.

We recognise that although we frequently experienced the above mentioned benefits, they are not guaranteed to arise. Although those who apply CbC consistently claim these benefits, there is an element of subjectivity to the claims. Those who argue against CbC generally consider that the time investment and intellectual effort required are not worthwhile. Of course, such an assessment is itself subjective and context-dependent. To mitigate such arguments, the extent of formality used in correctness arguments and proofs should be tailored to the context; e.g. to derive an algorithm used in a safety-critical context should be far more rigorous and fully elaborated than those for some trivial application.

To exploit the CbC benefits to the fullest however, a taxonomy should not be the end point, but rather form a starting point for software construction, i.e. for the design and implementation of coherent algorithm toolkits and beyond.

5   TABASCO and Beyond...

CbC-based taxonomisation of algorithm families goes beyond the mere beauty of the taxonomy structure. Software taxonomies form the starting point for the TABASCO method [4] where toolkit implementations of the taxonomised family are derived. Taxonomies and toolkits can be used for extractive software product line derivation as explained in the SPLicing TABASCO method [6]. Taxonomies can also be used for proactive software product line engineering, using a taxonomy to guide the design of the problem and solution space variability, as in the TAX-PLEASE method [7].

5.1   TABASCO: Taxonomy-Based Software Construction

TABASCO, for TAxonomy-BAsed Software COnstruction [4], is a method for domain modeling and domain engineering for algorithmic (and data structure) domains. The method relies on taxonomies such as those explained in this paper. Such taxonomies provide the starting point for the implementation of a toolkit i.e., a library comprising the family of algorithms that is captured by the taxonomy, in a way that leads to improved code structure and increased reuse.

The TABASCO process for obtaining a toolkit has the following steps:

1. **Taxonomisation**: The algorithmic domain is selected, and a literature survey is carried out in order to obtain a good understanding of the algorithmic domain. Then, a taxonomy of the algorithms is constructed based on the principles explained above.
2. **Design and Implementation of Toolkit**, based on the taxonomy: A toolkit design does not directly follow from the taxonomy, but the taxonomy does make the algorithm commonalities and variations explicit: it not only highlights groupings of algorithms but also indicates how algorithms inside such a group differ from each other. Hence, design choices are guided by this taxonomy structure, while the choice of language constructs to implement design parts can be based on standard design techniques, such as design patterns, inheritance or interface structures, template parameters etc.
3. **Usability of Toolkit:** After implementing the toolkit, the algorithms can be evaluated by benchmarking in order to provide information about their non-functional behavior for the toolkit's user. In order to assist particularly the non-expert user in instantiating and configuring algorithms from the toolkit, a Domain Specific Language (DSL) can be implemented.

Toolkits obtained by the TABASCO method differ from classical algorithm libraries in that they contain a family of algorithms designed for the same purpose or problem. The structure of the toolkit is guided by the taxonomy which leads to algorithm implementations that are correct by construction and have a high-quality code structure that systematically exploits code reuse.

5.2   SPLicing TABASCO

Software product line (SPL) engineering [43] aims at developing a family of systems with well-defined variabilities and commonalities by managed reuse in order to shorten the time to market and to improve overall system quality. Software product line engineering is a two-stage process: during domain engineering reusable artifacts are built, while during application engineering the actual product variants are derived. A product line usually consists of a problem space variability model comprising different configuration options expressed by distinguishing product features. Variable software realization artifacts capture solution space variability to realize the different product features. Configuration knowledge connects the problem space features with solution space variability. By selecting problem space features during application engineering, a specific product variant can be generated realizing the respective features from the appropriately instantiated and assembled solution space artifacts.

Toolkits designed following the TABASCO method provide a good basis for variable implementations due to the hierarchical decomposition of the program concepts along the taxonomy. However, variability is not incorporated in the monolithic implementation of a toolkit. Hence, for the application of SPL principles, the toolkit needs to be adapted to include variability and to make it configurable from a feature model.

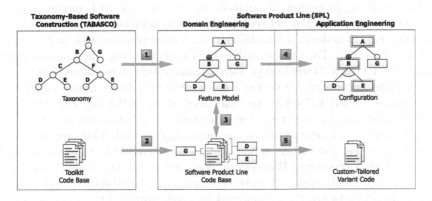

Fig. 4. SPLicing TABASCO - based on [6]

The SPLicing TABASCO method [6] transforms a taxonomy and the corresponding toolkit into an SPL in an extractive [5] manner—see Fig. 4.

1. First, we need to provide a problem space variability model representing the variability of the algorithm family on a conceptual level. A feature model [44] is derived from the taxonomy following a set of guidelines, but building on domain expertise. Figure 5 shows the feature model of the tree acceptance taxonomy as an example. We can see that the main classifications in the taxonomy are represented by top-level features while smaller refinements are captured by subfeatures.
2. Second, we need to express the variability between the different parts of the toolkit by transforming the toolkit's implementation into variable software realization artifacts.
3. Third, we need to connect problem and solution space variability by configuration knowledge in order to be able to generate specific program variants by selecting features in the problem space variability model.

4. A specific program variant of the toolkit can then be obtained by selecting the respective features in the feature model.
5. The variable realization artifacts can then be assembled according to the feature selection.

5.3 Tax-PLEASE

Traditional SPL engineering [43] starts with a domain analysis phase in which a problem space (domain) variability model is built. In this step, feature models are predominantly used. However, features in a feature model are merely labels for configuration options; they do not capture any information about the realization of a feature and, hence, about the structure of the variable realization assets.

To counter this problem, [7] proposes a taxonomy-based SPL engineering process, called Tax-PLEASE, which uses the taxonomy as the first and central artifact resulting from domain analysis in proactive [5] SPL engineering. The taxonomy bridges the gap between problem and solution space variability as a taxonomy captures domain variability from a conceptual as well as from a realization perspective. For taxonomy-based SPL engineering, the domain analysis follows the TABASCO method [4] for taxonomisation as explained above. From the resulting taxonomy, we derive a conceptual variability model (in the form of a feature model) following the guidelines of the SPLicing TABASCO approach [6]. For domain design and implementation, we obtain the structure of the reusable realization artifacts from the taxonomy as well. This step follows the general guidelines for toolkit implementation in TABASCO for obtaining the implementation structure. However, it does not result in a monolithic toolkit, but in variable realization artifacts. The conceptual variability model and the realization artifacts are then connected by configuration knowledge in order to allow generation of variants for a feature selection.

Building a software product line based on a taxonomy, as proposed in Tax-PLEASE, yields clear engineering principles for obtaining problem space variability models as well as reusable artifacts. The artifacts follow a stringent structure, which leads to improved maintainability and evolvability of the resulting SPL.

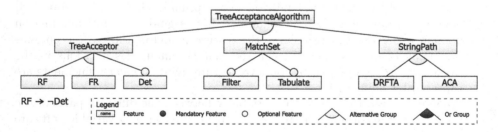

Fig. 5. Feature model for tree acceptance taxonomy (taken from [6])

6   Conclusion

Correctness-by-construction (CbC) aims at developing algorithms by refinement of a high-level specification into the algorithm's implementation. This guarantees the correctness of the resulting implementation and implies its efficiency and elegance. In this paper, we combine the use of CbC and classification. A taxonomy of a family of algorithms is constructed by organizing the correctness-preserving refinements of the algorithms in a derivation tree. This classification makes the relationship of algorithms in a family explicit, thus, supports deep comprehension of the algorithms in the family. The taxonomic classification provides an excellent starting point for transforming a family of algorithms into a software product line. For future work, we are investigating the nature of different refinements in a taxonomy and provide a formalization of the respective refinement relationships in order to support automatic reasoning. The evaluation of the Tax-PLEASE approach is currently being carried out in order to empirically validate that SPLs obtained following Tax-PLEASE indeed provide better maintainability and evolvability.

Acknowledgments. The authors thank Christoph Seidl for fruitful discussions related to this work. This work was partially supported by the DFG (German Research Foundation) under grant SCHA1635/2-2, by the NRF (South African National Research Foundation) under grants 81606 and 93063.

References

1. Dijkstra, E.W.: A constructive approach to the problem of program correctness. BIT Numer. Math. **8**(3), 174–186 (1968)
2. Hoare, C.: Proof of a program: FIND. Commun. ACM **14**(1), 39–45 (1971)
3. Wirth, N.: Program development by stepwise refinement. Commun. ACM **14**(4), 221–227 (1971)
4. Cleophas, L., Watson, B.W., Kourie, D.G., Boake, A., Obiedkov, S.: TABASCO: using concept-based taxonomies in domain engineering. S. Afr. Comput. J. **37**, 30–40 (2006)
5. Krueger, C.: Eliminating the adoption barrier. IEEE Softw. **19**(4), 29–31 (2002)
6. Schaefer, I., Seidl, C., Cleophas, L., Watson, B.W.: SPLicing TABASCO: custom-tailored software product line variants from taxonomy-based toolkits. In: SAICSIT 2015, pp. 34:1–34:10 (2015)
7. Schaefer, I., Seidl, C., Cleophas, L., Watson, B.W.: Tax-PLEASE—towards taxonomy-based software product line engineering. In: Kapitsaki, G., Santana de Almeida, E. (eds.) ICSR 2016. LNCS, vol. 9679, pp. 63–70. Springer, Heidelberg (2016). doi:10.1007/978-3-319-35122-3_5
8. Dijkstra, E.W.: A Discipline of Programming. Prentice Hall, Upper Saddle River (1976)
9. Gries, D.: The Science of Programming. Springer, Berlin (1987)
10. Cohen, E.: Programming in the 1990s: An Introduction to the Calculation of Programs. Springer, Berlin (1990)
11. Morgan, C.: Programming from Specifications, 2nd edn. Prentice Hall, Upper Saddle River (1994)

12. Kourie, D.G., Watson, B.W.: The Correctness-by-Construction Approach to Programming. Springer, Berlin (2012)
13. Back, R.J.: Refinement Calculus—A Systematic Introduction. Springer, Berlin (1998)
14. Liskov, B., Wing, J.M.: A behavioral notion of subtyping. ACM Trans. Program. Lang. Syst. **16**(6), 1811–1841 (1994)
15. Meyer, B.: Object-Oriented Software Construction, 2nd edn. Prentice Hall, Upper Saddle River (1997)
16. Feijen, W.H., van Gasteren, A., Gries, D., Misra, J. (eds.): Beauty is our Business: A Birthday Salute to Edsger W. Dijkstra. Springer, Berlin (1990)
17. Wikipedia: Taxonomy (general)–Wikipedia, The Free Encyclopedia (2016). https://en.wikipedia.org/w/index.php?title=Taxonomy_(general)&oldid=715042676. Accessed 30 Apr 2016
18. Wikipedia: Carl Linnaeus-Wikipedia, The Free Encyclopedia (2016). Accessed 30 Apr 2016
19. Pieterse, V., Kourie, D.G.: Lists, taxonomies, lattices, thesauri and ontologies: paving a pathway through a terminological jungle. Knowl. Organ. **41**(3), 217–229 (2014)
20. Brainerd, B.: Semi-lattices and taxonomic systems. Noûs **4**(2), 189–199 (1970)
21. Schock, R.: On classifications and hierarchies. J. Gen. Philos. Sci. **10**, 98–106 (1979)
22. Thomason, R.H.: Species, determinates and natural kinds. Noûs **3**(1), 95–101 (1969)
23. Salton, G.: Automatic Information Organization and Retrieval. McGraw-Hill, New York (1968)
24. Barwise, J., Seligman, J.: Information Flow: The Logic of Distributed Systems. Cambridge University Press, Cambridge (1997)
25. Priss, U.: Formal concept analysis in information science. Ann. Rev. Inf. Sci. Technol. **40**(1), 521–543 (2006)
26. Wille, R.: Liniendiagramme hierarchischer Begriffssysteme. Studien zur Klassifikation, Indeks Verlag (1984)
27. Gruber, T.R.: A translation approach to portable ontologies. Knowl. Acquisition **5**(2), 199–220 (1993)
28. Jonkers, H.: Abstraction, specification and implementation techniques: with an application to garbage collection. Ph.D. thesis, Technische Hogeschool Eindhoven (1982)
29. Kourie, D.G.: An approach to defining abstractions, refinements and enrichments. Quæstiones Informaticæ **6**(4), 174–178 (1989)
30. Banach, R., Poppleton, M., Jeske, C., Stepney, S.: Engineering and theoretical underpinnings of retrenchment. Sci. Comput. Program. **67**(2/3), 301–329 (2007)
31. Kovács, L.: Role of negative properties in knowledge modeling. In: Proceedings of the 9th International Conference on Applied Informatics, Eger, Hungary, vol. 1, pp. 67–74 (2014)
32. Darlington, J.: A synthesis of several sorting algorithms. Acta Informatica **11**(1), 1–30 (1978)
33. Broy, M.: Program construction by transformations: a family tree of sorting programs. In: Biermann, A.W., Guiho, G. (eds.) Computer Program Synthesis Methodologies, pp. 1–49. Reidel, Dordrecht (1983)
34. Merritt, S.M.: An inverted taxonomy of sorting algorithms. Commun. ACM **28**(1), 96–99 (1985)
35. Watson, B.W.: Taxonomies and toolkits of regular language algorithms. Ph.D. thesis, Technische Universiteit Eindhoven (1995)

36. Marcelis, A.: On the classification of attribute evaluation algorithms. Sci. Comput. Program. **14**(1), 1–24 (1990)
37. Cleophas, L., Watson, B.W., Zwaan, G.: A new taxonomy of sublinear right-to-left scanning keyword pattern matching algorithms. Sci. Comput. Program. **75**(11), 1095–1112 (2010)
38. Bosman, R.P.: A taxonomy of approximate pattern matching algorithms in strings. Master's thesis, Department of Mathematics and Computer Science, Technishe Universiteit Eindhoven, Eindhoven, The Netherlands, March 2005
39. van de Rijdt, M.G.: Two-dimensional pattern matching. Master's thesis, Department of Mathematics and Computer Science, Technishe Universiteit Eindhoven, Eindhoven, The Netherlands, August 2005
40. Cleophas, L.: Tree algorithms: two taxonomies and a toolkit. Ph.D. thesis, Technische Universiteit Eindhoven (2008)
41. Watson, B.W.: Constructing minimal acyclic deterministic finite automata. Ph.D. thesis, University of Pretoria (2010)
42. Brooks Jr., F.P.: The Mythical Man-month - Essays on Software Engineering, 2nd edn. Addison-Wesley, Boston (1995)
43. Pohl, K., Böckle, G., van der Linden, F.J.: Software Product Line Engineering - Foundations, Principles and Techniques. Springer, Berlin (2005)
44. Batory, D.: Feature models, grammars, and propositional formulas. In: Obbink, H., Pohl, K. (eds.) SPLC 2005. LNCS, vol. 3714, pp. 7–20. Springer, Heidelberg (2005)

Conditions for Compatibility of Components
The Case of Masters and Slaves

Maurice H. ter Beek[1], Josep Carmona[2], and Jetty Kleijn[3(✉)]

[1] ISTI–CNR, Pisa, Italy
[2] Universitat Politècnica de Catalunya, Barcelona, Spain
[3] LIACS, Leiden University, Leiden, The Netherlands
h.c.m.kleijn@liacs.leidenuniv.nl

Abstract. We consider systems composed of reactive components that collaborate through synchronised execution of common actions. These multi-component systems are formally represented as team automata, a model that allows a wide spectrum of synchronisation policies to combine components into higher-level systems. We investigate the correct-by-construction engineering of such systems of systems from the point of view of correct communications between the components (no message loss or deadlocks due to indefinite waiting). This leads to a proposal for a generic definition of compatibility of components relative to the adopted synchronisation policy. This definition appears to be particularly appropriate for so-called master-slave synchronisations by which input actions (for 'slaves') are driven by output actions (from 'masters').

1 Introduction

In an increasingly connected world in which digital communication outnumbers all other forms of communication, it is important to understand the complex underlying interconnections in the numerous systems of systems governing our daily life. In fact, modern systems are often no longer monolithic, but large-scale concurrent and distributed embedded systems whose components are again complex systems and which as a whole offer more functionality and performance than the sum of their component systems [35]. This requires a deep understanding of various communication and interaction policies (e.g. client-server, peer-to-peer, and master-slave) used in such multi-component systems and the risk of failures they entail (e.g. message loss and deadlocks can have severe repercussions on reliability, safety and security). One way to approach this challenge is to lift successful design methodologies and analysis tools from single systems engineering to systems of systems engineering. In a component-based bottom-up manner, this can be addressed through correctness by construction, where correctness is concerned with not only formal verification but also issues like reliability, resilience, safety, security and even sustainability.

Correctness by construction sees the development of (software) systems (of systems) as a true form of Engineering, with a capital 'E'. It advocates a stepwise refinement process from requirements to specification to code, ideally by

T. Margaria and B. Steffen (Eds.): ISoLA 2016, Part I, LNCS 9952, pp. 784–805, 2016.
DOI: 10.1007/978-3-319-47166-2_55

design tools that automatically generate error-free (software) implementations from rigorous and unambiguous specifications of requirements [22,27,28,36,41]. To establish that components within a system or a system and its environment always may interact correctly, a concept of compatibility can be useful. Compatibility represents an aspect of successful behaviour and as such forms a necessary ingredient for the correctness of a distributed, modular system design [25]. Compatibility failures detected in a system model may reveal important problems in the design of one or more of its components, to be repaired before implementation. Compatibility checks considering various communication and interaction policies thus significantly aid the development of techniques supporting the design, analysis and verification of systems of systems.

We are interested in studying fundamental notions for the component-based development of correct-by-construction multi-component systems. We represent multi-component systems by team automata [3–6]. Team automata are useful to specify intended behaviour of reactive systems. Their basic building blocks are component automata that can interact with each other via shared (external) actions; internal actions are never shared. External actions are input or output to the components they belong to. Components can be added in different phases of construction, allowing for hierarchically composed systems (of systems). Team automata share the distinction of output (active), input (passive) and internal (private) actions with I/O automata [38,39], Interface automata [1,19–21] and Component-Interaction Automata [10], but an important difference is that team automata impose less a priori restrictions on the role of the actions and the permitted type of interactions between the components. This particularly suits systems of systems that in practice are often composed of different models of computation that interact according to a variety of synchronisation policies.

In [16], the binary notion of I/O compatibility from [11,12] was lifted to team automata consisting of multiple reactive component automata. The aim of the ideas developed in [12] was to provide a formal framework for the synthesis of asynchronous circuits and embedded systems. The approach was restricted to two components and a closed environment, i.e. all input (output) actions of one component are output (input) actions of the other component. A characterisation was given for compatibility of two components that should engage in a dialogue free from message loss and deadlocks. Message loss occurs when one component sends a message which cannot be received by the other component as input, whereas deadlock occurs when a component is kept waiting indefinitely for a message that never arrives. Team automata proved to form a suitable formal framework for lifting the concept of compatibility to a multi-component setting in [16], in which communication and interaction may take place between more than two components at the same time (e.g. broadcasting).

In [16], emphasis was on interactions based on mandatory synchronised execution of common actions (leading to what is a.k.a. the synchronous product of the component automata). In this paper, we present an initial exploration into lifting the conditions for compatibility defined in [16] to team automata that adhere to other synchronisation strategies. We first propose a general notion of compatibility defined with respect to a given synchronisation policy. Subsequently, we focus on how to handle team automata that interact according to master-slave cooperations. In such cooperations, input (for 'slaves') is driven by output (from 'masters') under different assumptions ranging from slaves that cannot proceed on their own to masters that should always be followed by slaves. This models a well-known method of communication in which specific, more authoritative partners unidirectionally control or trigger other partners to synchronise with them. Examples include peripherals connected to a bus in a computer, master databases from which data is replicated to (synchronised) slave databases and master (precision) clocks that provide timing signals to synchronise slave clocks. The producer-consumer design pattern known from concurrency theory and programming (e.g. threading) can be seen as a simplified case of master-slave communication, where a buffer is usually used to avoid message loss.

The main contribution of this paper is thus a proposal: a generalisation of the conditions for compatibility of components defined in [16] to the context of arbitrary sets of synchronisations. After delineating some of the difficulties involved with the proposed definition, we instantiate compatibility for master-slave policies of synchronisation and illustrate how this allows to guarantee absence of deadlocks and message loss for master-slave types of team automata to which the results from [16] cannot be applied. In the future, we plan to address follow-up questions concerning these types of systems, like "how is compatibility affected when slaves are added?" and "in what way does compatibility depend on (the type of) cooperation among slaves?". Furthermore, it remains to investigate the applicability of our proposed definition to team automata composed according to still other synchronisation policies.

Outline. After introducing the team automata modelling framework in Sect. 2, we discuss and illustrate in Sect. 3 two specific synchronisation policies. Section 4 contains our main contribution: we propose a generalisation of the notion of compatibility in a multi-component environment as defined in [16] from synchronous product to arbitrary synchronisation policies. After an application in the context of master-slave synchronisations, we provide some initial observations for a restricted class of so-called master-slave systems in Sect. 5. We conclude with a list of possible applications of our approach in Sect. 6, followed by a discussion of related and future work.

2   Component and Team Automata

Notation. We use $\prod_{i=1}^{n} V_i$ to denote the Cartesian product of sets $V_1, \ldots, V_n$. If $v = (v_1, \ldots, v_n) \in \prod_{i=1}^{n} V_i$ and $i \in \{1, \ldots, n\}$, then the i-th entry of v is obtained by applying the projection function $proj_i : \prod_{i=1}^{n} V_i \to V_i$ defined by $proj_i(v_1, \ldots, v_n) = v_i$.

Component Automata. Team automata are systems composed of reactive component automata that can interact through synchronised executions of shared actions. Each such component automaton is a *labelled transition system* (LTS) in which input, output and internal actions are explicitly distinguished.

Definition 1. *A* (reactive) component automaton *is an LTS* $\mathcal{A} = (P, \Gamma, \gamma, J)$, *with set* P *of* states; *set* Γ *of* actions, *such that* $P \cap \Gamma = \varnothing$ *and* Γ *is the union of three pairwise disjoint sets* Γ_{inp}, Γ_{out} *and* Γ_{int} *of* input, output, *and* internal *actions, respectively;* $\gamma \subseteq P \times \Gamma \times P$ *is its set of (labelled)* transitions; *and* $J \subseteq P$ *its set of* initial states. □

A component automaton (P, Γ, γ, J), with input actions Γ_{inp}, output actions Γ_{out} and internal actions Γ_{int} can also be specified as $(P, (\Gamma_{inp}, \Gamma_{out}, \Gamma_{int}), \gamma, J)$. The actions $\Gamma \setminus \Gamma_{int} = \Gamma_{out} \cup \Gamma_{inp}$ are *external*. For an action $a \in \Gamma$, we define the set of *a-transitions* as $\gamma_a = \gamma \cap (P \times \{a\} \times P)$. Especially in figures, we may append input and output actions with ? and !, respectively, to indicate their roles (cf. Fig. 1).

The (dynamic) *behaviour* of a component automaton is determined by the execution of actions enabled at the current state. We say that a is *enabled* in $\mathcal{A}$ at state $p \in P$, denoted by $a \, en_{\mathcal{A}} \, p$, if there exists $p' \in P$ such that $(p, a, p') \in \gamma$. The sequential *computations* of $\mathcal{A}$, denoted by $\mathcal{C}_{\mathcal{A}}$, are now defined as those finite sequences $p_0 a_1 p_1 a_2 \cdots p_k$ and infinite sequences $p_0 a_1 p_1 a_2 \cdots$ such that $p_0 \in J$ and $(p_{i-1}, a_i, p_i) \in \gamma$ for all $i \in \{1, \ldots, k\}$ and all $i \geq 1$, respectively. A state $p \in P$ is said to be *reachable* if there exists a finite computation $p_0 a_1 p_1 a_2 \cdots p_j \in \mathcal{C}_{\mathcal{A}}$ for some $j \geq 0$ such that $p = p_j$.

Team Automata. The components forming a team automaton interact by synchronising on common actions. Their internal actions however are not meant to be externally observable and are thus unavailable for synchronisation and cannot be shared. This leads to the concept of composability.

Let $\mathcal{S} = \{ \mathcal{A}_i \mid 1 \leq i \leq n \}$ be a set of component automata specified, for each $i \in \{1, \ldots, n\}$, as $\mathcal{A}_i = (Q_i, (\Sigma_{i,inp}, \Sigma_{i,out}, \Sigma_{i,int}), \delta_i, I_i)$ with $\Sigma_i = \Sigma_{i,inp} \cup \Sigma_{i,out} \cup \Sigma_{i,int}$. Then $\mathcal{S}$ is a *composable system* if $\Sigma_{i,int} \cap \bigcup_{j=1, j \neq i}^{n} \Sigma_j = \varnothing$ for all $i \in \{1, \ldots, n\}$. Note that every subset of a composable system is again a composable system.

For the remainder of this paper, we let $\mathcal{S}$ *as just specified, be an arbitrary but fixed, composable system. We refer to* $\Sigma = \bigcup_{i=1}^{n} \Sigma_i$ *as its set of actions and to* $Q = \prod_{i=1}^{n} Q_i$ *as its state space.* The team automata we consider are defined over a composable system $\mathcal{S}$ as above and have set of actions Σ and set of states Q. Their transitions are *synchronisations* involving transitions of the automata from $\mathcal{S}$.

Synchronisations in a composable system are global transitions that combine one or more (local) transitions of different component automata; these local transitions are all labelled with the same action name. Intuitively, each component automaton that participates through a local transition in such a synchronisation changes its state accordingly. The local states of automata not taking part in the synchronisation are not affected.

Definition 2. *A transition* $(q, a, q') \in Q \times \Sigma \times Q$ *is a* synchronisation *on* a (in $\mathcal{S}$) *if* $(\text{proj}_i(q), a, \text{proj}_i(q')) \in \delta_i$, *for some* $i \in \{1, \ldots, n\}$; *moreover for all* $i \in \{1, \ldots, n\}$, *either* $(\text{proj}_i(q), a, \text{proj}_i(q')) \in \delta_i$ *or* $\text{proj}_i(q) = \text{proj}_i(q')$.

For $a \in \Sigma$, $\Delta_a(\mathcal{S})$ *is the set of all synchronisations on* a *in* $\mathcal{S}$, *while* $\Delta(\mathcal{S}) = \bigcup_{a \in \Sigma} \Delta_a(\mathcal{S})$ *is the set of all synchronisations in* $\mathcal{S}$. □

Note that the composability of $\mathcal{S}$ implies that in synchronisations on internal actions always exactly one component automaton is involved.

Team automata over a composable system are determined by their (global) transitions, i.e. a choice from the set of all synchronisations in that system under the additional condition that *all* transitions labelled with internal actions are included (combining automata into teams does not affect their ability to execute internal actions). The actions of a team automaton comprise the actions of its components. Again we distinguish between input, output, and internal actions. This division is inherited from the original roles of the actions in the component automata and is the same for all team automata over a given composable system. The internal actions of any team automaton over a composable system are the internal actions of the individual components. For the external actions, the idea is that component automata have control over their output actions whereas input actions are passive (driven by the environment). As a consequence, actions that appear as an output action in one or more of the components will be output of the team (even when they are input to some other components). Input actions that do not appear as output are input actions of the team.

Recall that $\Sigma = \bigcup_{i=1}^{n} \Sigma_i$ is the set of actions of $\mathcal{S}$. Then $\Sigma_{int} = \bigcup_{i=1}^{n} \Sigma_{i,int}$ is its set of internal actions, $\Sigma_{out} = \bigcup_{i=1}^{n} \Sigma_{i,out}$ its set of output actions and $\Sigma_{inp} = (\bigcup_{i=1}^{n} \Sigma_{i,inp}) \backslash \Sigma_{out}$ its set of input actions. All team automata over $\mathcal{S}$ will have Σ as their set of actions, with Σ_{int} as internal, Σ_{out} as output and Σ_{inp} as input actions. Moreover, $I = \prod_{i=1}^{n} I_i$ is the set of initial states of every team automaton over $\mathcal{S}$. Consequently, it is the choice of a *synchronisation policy* over $\mathcal{S}$ (i.e. a subset $\delta \subseteq \Delta(\mathcal{S})$ with $\delta_a = \Delta_a(\mathcal{S})$ for all $a \in \Sigma_{int}$) that defines a specific team automaton.

Definition 3. *The* team automaton *over* $\mathcal{S}$ *defined by the synchronisation policy* δ *over* $\mathcal{S}$ *is the reactive component automaton* $\mathcal{T} = (Q, (\Sigma_{inp}, \Sigma_{out}, \Sigma_{int}), \delta, I)$. $\square$

Since every team automaton is a reactive component automaton, they can be used to construct hierarchical systems of systems.

Subteams. Given a team automaton over a composable system, one can distinguish subteams determined by a selection of component automata from the system.

Let $\mathcal{T}$ be a team automaton over $\mathcal{S}$ and let $\delta \subseteq \Delta(\mathcal{S})$ be its set of transitions. Let $J \subseteq \{1,\ldots,n\}$ be such that $J \neq \varnothing$. The *subteam* $SUB_J(\mathcal{S},\delta)$ *of* $\mathcal{T}$ *determined by* J is the automaton specified as $(\prod_{j \in J} Q_j, (\Sigma_{J,inp}, \Sigma_{J,out}, \Sigma_{J,int}), \delta_J, \prod_{j \in J} I_j)$. Here $\Sigma_{J,int} = \bigcup_{j \in J} \Sigma_{j,int}$, $\Sigma_{J,out} = \bigcup_{j \in J} \Sigma_{j,out}$ and $\Sigma_{J,inp} = (\bigcup_{j \in J} \Sigma_{j,inp}) \backslash \Sigma_{J,out}$. It may happen that an output action of $\mathcal{T}$ is an input action in a subteam, namely when it does not have an output role in any of the component automata forming the subteam. Finally, $\delta_J = \{ (q,a,q') \in \delta \mid (proj_J(q), a, proj_J(q')) \in \Delta(\{ \mathcal{A}_j \mid j \in J \}) \}$. Hence the transitions of the subteam are restrictions of those transitions of $\mathcal{T}$ in which at least one of the components from $\{ \mathcal{A}_j \mid j \in J \}$ is actively involved. It follows that $SUB_J(\mathcal{S},\delta)$ is the team automaton over $\{ \mathcal{A}_j \mid j \in J \}$ defined by the synchronisation policy δ_J.

Input and Output Domains. The domain of an action appearing in a composable system is determined by the components in which it appears as an action. If it is an external action it may be an input action for some components and an output action for others. Thus all external actions of a composable system have a non-empty input domain or a non-empty output domain or both. A synchronisation on an action that involves components in which that action is an input action *and* components in which it is an output action, models a *communication* between the input and output subteams associated with that action.

Let $a \in \Sigma$ be an action of $\mathcal{S}$. Then $\mathrm{dom}_a(\mathcal{S}) = \{\, i \mid a \in \Sigma_i \,\}$ is the *domain* of a in $\mathcal{S}$; $\mathrm{dom}_{a,inp}(\mathcal{S}) = \{\, i \mid a \in \Sigma_{i,inp} \,\}$ is its *input domain*; and $\mathrm{dom}_{a,out}(\mathcal{S}) = \{\, i \mid a \in \Sigma_{i,out} \,\}$ is its *output domain*. Action a is *communicating* (in $\mathcal{S}$) if both its output domain and its input domain are not empty. Hence we define the communicating actions of $\mathcal{S}$ as $\Sigma_{com} = \bigcup_{i=1}^{n} \Sigma_{i,inp} \cap \bigcup_{i=1}^{n} \Sigma_{i,out}$.

For each external action $a \in \Sigma$, we write $\mathcal{S}_{a,inp} = \{\, \mathcal{A}_i \mid i \in \mathrm{dom}_{a,inp}(\mathcal{S}) \,\}$ and $\mathcal{S}_{a,out} = \{\, \mathcal{A}_i \mid i \in \mathrm{dom}_{a,out}(\mathcal{S}) \,\}$ to denote the composable subsystems of $\mathcal{S}$ comprising the *input components* and *output components of a in $\mathcal{S}$*, respectively.

Let $\delta \subseteq \Delta(\mathcal{S})$ be the set of transitions of a team automaton $\mathcal{T}$ over $\mathcal{S}$. Let a be an external action of $\mathcal{S}$. If the output domain $\mathrm{dom}_{a,out}(\mathcal{S})$ of a is not empty, then $\mathrm{SUB}_{\mathrm{dom}_{a,out}(\mathcal{S})}(\mathcal{S},\delta)$ is the *output subteam of a in $\mathcal{T}$*; it is the subteam of $\mathcal{T}$ determined by the output domain of a and thus a team automaton over the output components of a; it will be usually be denoted by $\mathrm{SUB}_{a,out}(\mathcal{S},\delta)$. Similarly, if $a \in \Sigma$ has a non-empty input domain $\mathrm{dom}_{a,inp}(\mathcal{S})$, then the *input subteam* $\mathrm{SUB}_{\mathrm{dom}_{a,inp}(\mathcal{S})}(\mathcal{S},\delta)$ *of a in $\mathcal{T}$* is denoted by $\mathrm{SUB}_{a,inp}(\mathcal{S},\delta)$; it is a team automaton over the input components of a. If no confusion arises, we may omit referencing $\mathcal{S}$ and δ, and write $SUB_{a,out}$ and $SUB_{a,inp}$, respectively.

3   Specific Synchronisation Policies

Team automata are defined through their synchronisation policies. For all (global, product) states and each (external) action enabled at a corresponding local state of at least one of the components, it has to be decided which synchronisations involving that action are to be included as a transition of the team. It will however seldom be the case that this decision is made explicitly for every candidate synchronisation separately. Rather, the designer of the system has a certain idea about the interaction between components when combining them into one system. We will discuss here two such globally defined synchronisation policies, after which we will introduce the notion of *state-sharing*. This is a relevant notion here, since as demonstrated in [16], the concept of compatibility can be transferred from synchronous products to arbitrary team automata provided that they are *not* state-sharing.

Synchronous Product. A natural and frequently used method for combining components into a team automaton, or composing automata in general, is to always and only include transitions modelling the execution of an action in which *all* components participate that have that action in common.

Let $a \in \Sigma$ be an action of $\mathcal{S}$. Then we define

$$\chi_a^{\mathcal{S}} = \{ (q, a, q') \in \Delta(\mathcal{S}) \mid \forall i \in \{1, \ldots, n\} : a \in \Sigma_i \Rightarrow (proj_i(q), a, proj_i(q')) \in \delta_i \}$$

as the set of all *product synchronisations* on a (in $\mathcal{S}$). We let $\chi^{\mathcal{S}} = \bigcup_{a \in \Sigma} \chi_a^{\mathcal{S}}$.
Note that $\chi^{\mathcal{S}}$ is a proper synchronisation policy. In particular, $\chi_a^{\mathcal{S}} = \Delta_a(\mathcal{S})$ for
every internal action a. When $\mathcal{S}$ is understood, we may omit the superscript to
write χ and χ_a.

Definition 4. *The* synchronous product (automaton) $\mathcal{X}(\mathcal{S})$ *over* $\mathcal{S}$ *is the team*
automaton over $\mathcal{S}$ *with* $\chi^{\mathcal{S}}$ *as its set of transitions.* □

Master-Slave Synchronisations. Another natural policy, relevant to automata
models that make a distinction between input and output actions, was introduced in [3,4]. It focusses on communication and thus relates input and output
domains of an external action. First, we formulate an approach based on relations between actions rather than between full components. In Sect. 5, this will
be restricted to a simpler set-up at the level of the components by assuming that
they are either output components (without input actions) or input components
(without output actions).

When input actions are seen as passive (under control of the environment)
and output actions as active (under the local control of the component), the
designer could opt for a master-slave paradigm underlying the team's definition.
Intuitively, master-slave cooperation requires that input actions ('slaves') are
driven by output actions ('masters'). This means that in a master-slave synchronisation on an external action a, always an output component of a participates.
In other words, input actions ('slaves') never proceed on their own. This does
not exclude the possibility that a is executed by one or more of its output components without simultaneous execution of a by an input component. Thus the
policy could be modified by the additional requirement that, if a is communicating, then there is always an input component of a that also participates (a master
is always accompanied by one or more slaves), or—in a weaker form—masters
are accompanied by slaves whenever possible.

Definition 5. *Let* $a \in \Sigma_{com}$, $J = dom_{a,out}(\mathcal{S})$ *and* $K = dom_{a,inp}(\mathcal{S})$.

1. *The set of all* master-slave synchronisations *on* a *in* $\mathcal{S}$ *is defined as* $MS_a^{\mathcal{S}} = \{ (q, a, q') \in \Delta(\mathcal{S}) \mid (proj_J(q), a, proj_J(q')) \in \Delta(\mathcal{S}_{a,out}) \}$;
2. *The set of all* strong master-slave synchronisations *on* a *in* $\mathcal{S}$ *is defined as* $sMS_a^{\mathcal{S}} = MS_a^{\mathcal{S}} \cap \{ (q, a, q') \in \Delta(\mathcal{S}) \mid (proj_K(q), a, proj_K(q')) \in \Delta(\mathcal{S}_{a,inp}) \}$;
3. *The set of all* weak master-slave synchronisations *on* a *in* $\mathcal{S}$ *is defined*
   as $wMS_a^{\mathcal{S}} = MS_a^{\mathcal{S}} \cap \{ (q, a, q') \in \Delta(\mathcal{S}) \mid (proj_K(q), a, proj_K(q')) \in \Delta(\mathcal{S}_{a,inp})$ *if there exists a* $k \in K$ *such that* $a \, en_{\mathcal{A}_k} \, proj_k(q)) \}$. □

In addition, we stipulate that if an action a is not communicating, then by default
all synchronisations on a are master-slave, strong master-slave and weak master-
slave. Thus $MS_a^{\mathcal{S}} = sMS_a^{\mathcal{S}} = wMS_a^{\mathcal{S}} = \Delta_a(\mathcal{S})$ for all non-communicating

actions a of $\mathcal{S}$. Note that strong master-slave synchronisations are also weak master-slave synchronisations, which again by definition, are also master-slave. Let $\mathcal{MS}^{\mathcal{S}} = \bigcup_{a\in\Sigma} \mathcal{MS}_a^{\mathcal{S}}$, $s\mathcal{MS}^{\mathcal{S}} = \bigcup_{a\in\Sigma} s\mathcal{MS}_a^{\mathcal{S}}$ and $w\mathcal{MS}^{\mathcal{S}} = \bigcup_{a\in\Sigma} w\mathcal{MS}_a^{\mathcal{S}}$. The superscript $\mathcal{S}$ may be omitted if this does not lead to confusion. Similar as for synchronous product, we can now define a unique automaton over $\mathcal{S}$ by including all and only those transitions that satisfy the requirements.

Definition 6. *The* (strong, weak) *master-slave team automaton or (s$\mathcal{MS}$-team, w$\mathcal{MS}$-team) $\mathcal{MS}$-team automaton over $\mathcal{S}$ is the team automaton over $\mathcal{S}$ with (s$\mathcal{MS}^{\mathcal{S}}$, w$\mathcal{MS}^{\mathcal{S}}$) $\mathcal{MS}^{\mathcal{S}}$, respectively, as its set of transitions.* □

Note that all synchronisations in to the synchronous product are strong master-slave: $\chi \subseteq s\mathcal{MS}$ always holds.

State-Sharing. Given a composable system, the designer chooses the team's transitions and determines which components participate in the execution of an action with which local transitions. Hence, it may happen that at some global state, an action can be executed in a certain way, while a similar synchronisation involving the same local transitions is not possible at another global state, even though it concerns the same local states for all components participating in that synchronisation. This phenomenon, by which the local states of components not actively involved in a synchronisation determine whether or not it may underlie a global transition, was coined *state-sharing* in [24] and formalised in [3].

Definition 7. *A team automaton $\mathcal{T}$, specified as in Definition 3, is state-sharing if there exist a transition $(p,a,p') \in \delta$, and a state $q \in Q$ such that $proj_i(q) = proj_i(p)$ for all i such that $(proj_i(p),a,proj_i(p')) \in \delta_i$, while there is no state $q' \in Q$ such that $(q,a,q') \in \delta$ with $proj_i(q') = proj_i(p')$ for all i such that $(proj_i(p),a,proj_i(p')) \in \delta_i$, and $proj_i(q') = proj_i(q)$ for all other i.* □

Thus in a state-sharing team automaton, there is a situation in which the possibility to synchronise on a common action by certain components depends also on the local state of one or more components not actually involved in the synchronisation. Hence, when a team automaton is not state-sharing (or *non-state-sharing*), then the possibility of executing a common action depends only on the local states of components that take part in the synchronisation. As already noted in [16], synchronous product automata are always non-state-sharing. Moreover, every (strong) master-slave team automaton is non-state-sharing. This follows from the fact that the (strong) master-slave requirement refers to participation of certain components and as a synchronisation policy includes all synchronisations that satisfy that requirement and thus does not exclude any synchronisation because non-participating components are not in a particular local state. As the next example shows, there exist however weak master-slave team automata that are state-sharing.

Example 1. Consider the component automata $\mathcal{A}_1$ and $\mathcal{A}_2$ depicted in Fig. 1.

Figure 2 depicts the $w\mathcal{MS}$-team automaton $\mathcal{T}^w$ over $\{\mathcal{A}_1,\mathcal{A}_2\}$, in which $a?!$ denotes a synchronisation of action a in its input role $a?$ and its output role $a!$.

Fig. 1. Two reactive component automata: $\mathcal{A}_1$ (left) and $\mathcal{A}_2$ (right)

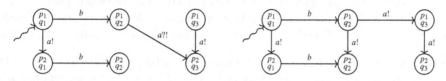

Fig. 2. Two team automata over $\{\mathcal{A}_1, \mathcal{A}_2\}$; on the left the $w\mathcal{MS}$-team automaton $\mathcal{T}^w$

We see that on the one hand $\left(\binom{p_1}{q_1}, a, \binom{p_2}{q_1}\right), \left(\binom{p_1}{q_3}, a, \binom{p_2}{q_3}\right) \in w\mathcal{MS}_a$, while on the other hand, $\left(\binom{p_1}{q_2}, a, \binom{p_2}{q_2}\right) \notin w\mathcal{MS}_a$. This implies that $\mathcal{T}^w$ is state-sharing: component $\mathcal{A}_1$ can only execute a by itself if $\mathcal{A}_2$ is *not* in state q_2.

Note that $\left(\binom{p_1}{q_1}, a, \binom{p_2}{q_1}\right)$, $\left(\binom{p_1}{q_2}, a, \binom{p_2}{q_2}\right)$ and $\left(\binom{p_1}{q_3}, a, \binom{p_2}{q_3}\right)$ are all master-slave, but none of them is a strong master-slave synchronisation on a in $\{\mathcal{A}_1, \mathcal{A}_2\}$. However, $\left(\binom{p_1}{q_2}, a, \binom{p_2}{q_3}\right)$ is both master-slave and strong-master slave.   □

As shown in [16], any team automaton $\mathcal{T}$ (over $\mathcal{S}$) can be converted into a synchronous product automaton $\chi(\mathcal{S}')$ over the new composable system $\mathcal{S}'$ derived from $\mathcal{S}$ by using synchronisations as action names. The behaviour of $\mathcal{T}$ (its sequential computations) can be obtained by a simple mapping from the behaviour of $\chi(\mathcal{S}')$. In general $\chi(\mathcal{S}')$ may exhibit too much behaviour. If, however, $\mathcal{T}$ is non-state-sharing, then each of the computations of $\chi(\mathcal{S}')$ corresponds to a computation of $\mathcal{T}$ (Theorem 13 in [16]).

4   Conditions for Compatibility

We are now ready to continue the investigation of conditions that guarantee a composable system of reactive component automata to be compatible with respect to a certain synchronisation policy, or in other words, whenever the component automata are composed according to this specific policy, they form a team automaton free from message loss and deadlocks. This approach to compatibility was originally considered in [12] for two reactive components in which all external actions are communicating and which are composed as a synchronous product. In [16], the concept was extended to systems with an arbitrary (finite) number of components and not necessarily 'complete', meaning that some of the external actions can be non-communicating. This reflects the idea that a system may be further extended by additional components (or teams). In [16], the synchronisation policy considered is the synchronous product. However, once it was demonstrated how non-state-sharing team automata policies can be encoded as synchronous products it was discussed how this might lead to a concept of compatibility for the original synchronisation policy, though no definite results could be claimed yet. Before giving the formal definition of compatibility from [16], we recall some notions.

Basic Notions. Let $\mathcal{A}$ be a component automaton specified as in Definition 1.

First we introduce a notion to reflect that components may have a (planned) option to halt: A state $p \in P$ is said to be *terminating* if no action is enabled at p and $\mathcal{A}$ is *terminating* if it has at least one reachable terminating state.

The next notion describes the—in general undesirable—situation that a component automaton may exhibit interminable internal behaviour, thus avoiding 'visible' behaviour and in particular communication: $\mathcal{A}$ exhibits a *livelock* if there exists an infinite computation $p_0 a_1 p_1 a_2 \cdots \in \mathcal{C}_{\mathcal{A}}$, such that all actions $a_1, a_2, \ldots$ are internal actions. A livelock-free component will always ultimately execute an external action or terminate.

Finally, given a composable system $\mathcal{S}$ as before, we introduce a notion to describe when an external action can be executed by its (input, output) domain.

An external action $a \in \Sigma$ is *input-domain (output-domain) enabled* at a state $q \in Q$ if $a \, \mathrm{en}_{\mathcal{A}_i} \, proj_i(q)$ for all $i \in \mathrm{dom}_{a,inp}(\mathcal{S})$ (for all $i \in \mathrm{dom}_{a,out}(\mathcal{S})$, respectively). An external action is *domain enabled* if it is both input-domain and output-domain enabled. Note that input (output) actions which are not communicating in $\mathcal{S}$ are output-domain (input-domain, respectively) enabled at all states in Q, because they have an empty output (input) domain. It should also be noted here that for an external action with non-empty input-domain, input-domain enabledness (and similarly output-domain enabledness if it has a non-empty output-domain) coincides with enabledness in its input subteam (output subteam) in the synchronous product automaton.

4.1 Compatibility and Synchronous Product

The definition of compatibility proposed in [16] applies to component automata that together form a composable system and assumes that the team will be defined by the synchronous product policy.

Definition 8. $\mathcal{R} \subseteq \Pi_{i=1}^n Q_i$ *is a* compatibility relation *for* $\mathcal{S}$ *if* $\Pi_{i=1}^n I_i \subseteq \mathcal{R}$ *and for all* $p \in \mathcal{R}$ *the following conditions are satisfied.*

Non-communicating progress: *For all* $a \in \bigcup_{i=1}^n \Sigma_i \setminus \Sigma_{com}$: *if* $a \, \mathrm{en}_{\mathcal{A}_i} \, proj_i(p)$ *for all* $i \in \mathrm{dom}_a(\mathcal{S})$, *then* $p' \in \mathcal{R}$, *whenever* $(p, a, p') \in \chi_a^{\mathcal{S}}$.

Receptiveness: *For all* $a \in \Sigma_{com}$: *if* a *is output-domain enabled at* p, *then* a *is input-domain enabled at* p, *and* $p' \in \mathcal{R}$ *whenever* $(p, a, p') \in \chi_a^{\mathcal{S}}$.

Deadlock-freeness: *If some action* $a \in \Sigma_{com}$ *is input-domain enabled at* p, *then there are* $b \in \bigcup_{i=1}^n \Sigma_i$ *and* $p' \in \Pi_{i=1}^n Q_i$ *such that* $(p, b, p') \in \chi^{\mathcal{S}}$.

$\mathcal{S}$ *is said to be* compatible *if each of its component automata* $\mathcal{A}_i$ *is livelock-free and there exists a compatibility relation for* $\mathcal{S}$. $\qquad\square$

Thus compatibility is phrased in terms of a relation over the local states (in the binary case [12] similar to a bisimulation [40]). This relation is a subset of all possible states of any team over $\mathcal{S}$ and always includes all initial states. As long as no communications take place according to the synchronisation policy, the states thus reached will all be in the relation (Non-communicating progress). Whenever the output subteam of a communicating action is enabled, its input subteam is ready for synchronisation on that action and the resulting state will still be in the relation (Receptiveness). If the input subteam of a communicating action is enabled, there is always a possibility for the system to proceed (Deadlock-freeness); as proved in [16] the new states will be again in the relation if the conditions of Non-communicating progress and Receptiveness are also fulfilled. Moreover, the absence of livelocks guarantees that the (synchronous product) team automaton proceeds visibly as long as there are pending input requests.

As said, in [16] it was shown that compatibility concepts can be transferred from synchronous product to non-state-sharing team automata. More precisely, violations of any of the three requirements for a compatibility relation in the obtained synchronous product were pre-existent in the original team automaton (Definition 6 in [16]).

To ensure deadlock-freedom, [8] uses a method based on system invariants that relate states of components to approximate global states and the method checks that the overapproximation matches an equivalent of deadlock-freeness. A difference with the set-up here is however that our composition is not formulated in terms of interactions that are added to composite systems.

4.2   Compatibility and Master-Slave Policies

Now we can formulate, as a main contribution of this paper, a proposal for a definition of compatibility between components without assumptions regarding the actual synchronisations that may take place. To do so, we lift the concept of compatibility relations to compatibility with respect to a set of team transitions.

Definition 9. *Let $\delta \subseteq \Delta(\mathcal{S})$ be a synchronisation policy over $\mathcal{S}$. Then $\mathcal{R} \subseteq \Pi_{i=1}^{n} Q_i$ is a compatibility relation with respect to δ for $\mathcal{S}$ if $\Pi_{i=1}^{n} I_i \subseteq \mathcal{R}$ and for all $p \in \mathcal{R}$ the following conditions are satisfied.*

Non-communicating progress: *For all $a \in \bigcup_{i=1}^{n} \Sigma_i \setminus \Sigma_{com}$: if $(p, a, p') \in \delta$, then $p' \in \mathcal{R}$.*

Receptiveness: *For all $a \in \Sigma_{com}$: if $a\, en_{SUB_{a,out}} proj_J(p)$ with $J = dom_{a,out}(\mathcal{S})$, then $a\, en_{SUB_{a,inp}} proj_K(p)$ with $K = dom_{a,inp}(\mathcal{S})$, and $p' \in \mathcal{R}$ whenever $(p, a, p') \in \delta$.*

Deadlock-freeness: *For all $a \in \Sigma_{com}$: if $a\, en_{SUB_{a,inp}} proj_K(p)$ with $K = dom_{a,inp}(\mathcal{S})$, then there are $b \in \bigcup_{i=1}^{n} \Sigma_i$ and $p' \in \Pi_{i=1}^{n} Q_i$ such that $(p, b, p') \in \delta$.*

$\mathcal{S}$ is said to be compatible with respect to δ if each of its component automata $\mathcal{A}_i$ is livelock-free and there exists a compatibility relation with respect to δ for $\mathcal{S}$.   □

Note that a compatibility relation with respect to an arbitrary δ relates to enabledness of actions in output and input subteams of the team automaton defined through δ, rather than enabledness of that action in simply the input or output domains as we did for χ. However, in case of the synchronous product, enabledness in all output (input) components is the same as enabledness of the subteam (at the same state). In fact, the above definition generalises the concept of compatibility defined in [16]. Thus, more precisely, $\mathcal{R}$ is a compatibility relation with respect to the synchronous product χ according to the above Definition 9, if and only if it is a compatibility relation as defined in Definition 8 (which in its turn is Definition 4 from [16]). In order to see this, one observes first that, if $\delta = \chi$, then $a \, en_{\mathcal{A}_i} \, proj_i(p)$ for all $i \in dom_a(\mathcal{S})$ and $(p, a, p') \in \chi_a^{\mathcal{S}}$ if and only if $(p, a, p') \in \delta$. Secondly, output-domain (input-domain) enabledness of an action at a global state coincides with enabledness of that action in its output (input, respectively) subteam of the synchronous product automaton at the corresponding (projected) state of the subteam.

The reason for requiring enabledness in subteams rather than enabledness in individual components (forming the output or input subteam) is the generalisation to arbitrary synchronisation policies. There is in general no reason to assume that all components that share an action have to participate in all synchronisations on that action. Hence we view subteams as 'black boxes' and treat the synchronisations that take place within them as given.

Nevertheless, there is still an implicit assumption even in this generalised definition regarding the collaboration between output and input subteams. According to the requirement of Receptiveness in Definition 9, whenever the output subteam of an action is ready to execute that action, its input subteam should be ready to participate. There is however no guarantee that the team will actually synchronise on the action from the given global state (cf. Example 2 below). It may well be the case that δ has a transition that combines the transition of the output subteam with a transition from the input subteam starting from another state of the subteam (and vice versa). Hence Receptiveness gives a necessary condition to avoid message loss, but does not impose it on δ.

Example 2 (Example 1 continued). Figure 2 (right) displays a team automaton over the component automata $\mathcal{A}_1$ and $\mathcal{A}_2$ depicted in Fig. 1.

Clearly, the output and input subteams of action a in this team automaton are basically the component automata $\mathcal{A}_1$ and $\mathcal{A}_2$. We see that both are enabled in state $\binom{p_1}{q_2}$, but the synchronisation $(\binom{p_1}{q_2}, a, \binom{p_2}{q_3})$ is not part of the team. $\square$

Therefore, we propose to investigate the case of master-slave synchronisations, because these policies express in a natural way the relation between output and input as expressed by Receptiveness, precluding message loss (reflected by masters followed by slaves) and deadlocks when the system gets blocked in a waiting state (with slaves that cannot proceed on their own).

In a preliminary exploration, we reconsider now Definition 9 with $\delta = s\mathcal{MS}^{\mathcal{S}}$, $\delta = w\mathcal{MS}^{\mathcal{S}}$ or $\delta = \mathcal{MS}^{\mathcal{S}}$. Assume that the output subteam defined by δ is currently (global state p) enabled to execute action a and that the input subteam is also ready to execute a. We then know that the corresponding transitions of the input subteam involving a occur in δ in combination with all transitions of a in its output subteam, as desired. However, $\delta = \mathcal{MS}^{\mathcal{S}}$ will also have a transition that does not involve the input subteam of a (as in the master-slave case, masters may proceed on their own). Thus even though the input subteam can oblige, messages may still get lost when its participation cannot be enforced. The weak master-slave and the strong master-slave policies however would have only transitions in which there is an (ouput-input) communication role for a. Thus, more restrictive assumptions regarding the collaboration between input and output subteams (rather than their internal workings) would support a general definition of compatibility like the one we propose here.

Before concluding this section, we recall once more that team automata composed according to non-state-sharing synchronisation policies may be encoded as synchronous product automata. Thus we can now use master-slave synchronisation policies to further our understanding of general compatibility requirements. For instance, we could apply this approach to strong master-slave team automata (as observed earlier, these are non-state-sharing) and investigate how compatibility in the encoded version relates to compatibility in the original system. Next, after encoding master-slave team automata (also these are non-state-sharing) as synchronous product automata we can investigate how compatibility in their encoded versions translates to (desirable) properties in the original system.

4.3   Applications of Compatibility

A typical example of the usefulness of a notion of compatibility in a setting of systems constructed according to synchronisation policies that differ from the policy of synchronous product may be found in the context of client-server architectures. A common solution to make such architectures more robust, i.e. resilient against server failures, is to replicate the server and thus move from a cen-

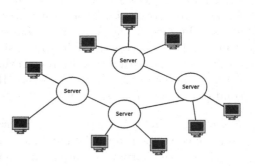

tralised architecture to a decentralised one, as depicted in the above figure. Then, when a server fails, other servers still running will continue to send messages to clients.

It might be important that these servers appear as one to the clients. This can be achieved by composing the set of servers according to so-called *(strong) output peer-to-peer synchronisations* [4]. For now, think of a scenario in which the set of servers as a whole uses so-called multicast communication to send messages to the clients (compared to broadcast communication, only clients that are within reach of the server, i.e. enabled, can receive its messages). This can be achieved by composing the set of servers (as a whole) with their clients according to weak master-slave synchronisations, upon which the definition/results of Sect. 4.2 become applicable.

We continue by describing another example, adapted from [16], inspired by the Esterel program of a ring of stations sharing a bus that was presented in [9].

Consider a system of three identical stations hooked to form a ring (cf. Fig. 3). A station's user can perform requests for accessing a common bus. User requests are granted depending on whether or not the corresponding station has the right to grant access, which is implemented by means of tokens flowing along the ring. While a station has the token, it has the right to grant access. To ensure fairness, a user is granted access for just one clock tick, after which the token is passed on. This implies we assume the presence of a global clock (not shown in the figure) whose only behaviour is producing ticks, thus synchronising all components.

The behaviour of the ith station is defined by the component automaton T_i in Fig. 3. If it has the token, then it checks whether the ith user has requested access within the current tick. If so, it grants the user bus access, after which the token is passed on upon the next tick and it returns to the initial state. If not, upon the next tick, the token is passed on and it returns to the initial state. The (simplified) behaviour of the ith user is defined by the component automaton U_i in Fig. 3. At any time, it can request access to the bus, upon which access is granted, unless a tick is received first, after which it returns to the initial state.

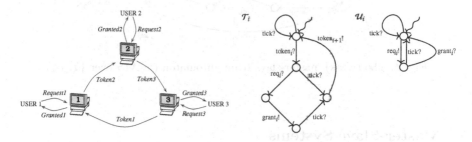

Fig. 3. A ring of stations sharing a bus, the ith station T_i and the ith user U_i

Now consider the (weak) master-slave team automata over T_i and U_i depicted in Fig. 4. Note that all occurrences of tick? actually denote synchronisations of input actions tick? as (peer-to-peer) collaborations between the station and the user.

The master-slave team automaton $\mathcal{MS}$ is the one without the dotted red req_i? transition.[1] In this case, message req_i! can obviously be lost. From the initial state, the sequence req_i! tick? leads back to the initial state with a non-granted access request, meaning that the user made a request, but the clock tick occurred before the station reacted. However, $\mathcal{MS}$ is non-state-sharing,

---

[1] We have drawn this arc as an explicit example of a non master-slave synchronisation in which the station executes input action req_i? and does not synchronise with the req_i! of the user.

which means we can apply Theorem 13 and Definition 6 from [16]: there exists a synchronous product automaton $\chi(\{\mathcal{T}_i', \mathcal{U}_i'\})$ whose every computation corresponds to a computation of $\mathcal{MS}$ and in which no compatibility problems occur that did not exist in $\mathcal{MS}$, i.e. $\mathcal{MS}$ has a Receptiveness/Non-communicating progress/Deadlock-freeness violation at state q if $\chi(\{\mathcal{T}_i', \mathcal{U}_i'\})$ does.

The weak master-slave team automaton $w\mathcal{MS}$ is $\mathcal{MS}$ without the dotted red $\mathrm{req}_i?$ transition and it also misses the dashed green $\mathrm{req}_i!$ and $\mathrm{grant}_i!$ transitions. Hence, when a token has arrived in the initial state, the request action is executed synchronously by the user and the station, after which access is granted by another synchronous execution. However, also in this case message $\mathrm{req}_i!$ can be lost, but—more importantly—this team is state-sharing, which means that we cannot apply Theorem 13 from [16]. This is where our new definition of compatibility (Definition 9) comes into play. (Cf. [16] for other team behaviour.)

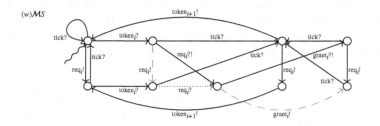

Fig. 4. The (weak) master-slave team automaton $(w)\mathcal{MS}$ over $\{\mathcal{T}_i, \mathcal{U}_i\}$

5   Master-Slave Systems

Even without explicit reference to the actual synchronisations that take place within subteams, it is quite challenging, also in case of master-slave policies, to define compatibility in terms of correct input/output behaviour. In fact, which subteams can or should communicate varies with the evolution of the system as this depends on the current state of the system (cf. [16]).

In this section, we again consider master-slave synchronisations but now with the additional assumption that all components of the system are either masters or slaves, meaning that they can have output actions or input actions, but not both. As a consequence, every component has a fixed role (master or slave) in any communication in which it is involved. This assumption leads to a simple set-up facilitating the investigation of the communication behaviour. In particular, we expect the static dichotomy of the system in masters and slaves to support an iterative (bottom-up) approach to the construction of compatible systems. After a formal definition, we will discuss some simple cases to illustrate this point.

Definition 10. *A component automaton* $(P, (\Gamma_{\mathrm{inp}}, \Gamma_{\mathrm{out}}, \Gamma_{\mathrm{int}}), \gamma, J)$ *is a* master automaton *if* $\Gamma_{\mathrm{inp}} = \varnothing$ *and it is a* slave automaton *if* $\Gamma_{\mathrm{out}} = \varnothing$.

For a set $\mathcal{A}$ of component automata, $\mu(\mathcal{A})$ denotes the subset of all master automata belonging to $\mathcal{A}$ and $\sigma(\mathcal{A})$ denotes the subset of all slave automata belonging to $\mathcal{A}$.

$\mathcal{A}$ is a master-slave system *if $\mathcal{A} = \mu(\mathcal{A}) \cup \sigma(\mathcal{A})$.*   □

Clearly, in general, $\mu(\mathcal{A}) \cup \sigma(\mathcal{A}) = \mathcal{A}$ does not hold, as $\mathcal{A}$ may contain automata with both output and input actions. Moreover, $\mu(\mathcal{A}) \cap \sigma(\mathcal{A})$ is not necessarily empty as there may be an automaton in $\mathcal{A}$ with only internal actions. A component with external actions can be either an input component or an output component, but never both.

With every component not capable of receiving input or of providing output (or both), it is clear that master-slave systems cannot be used to describe 'protocol' behaviour, i.e. chains of 'action-response' events leading to some successful computation. Instead, master-slave systems behave as 'producer-consumer' systems. The type of chain behaviour described by master-slave systems can be observed in manufacturing systems (cf. [43] and the references therein) and it is also a typical design pattern in concurrency theory and programming (e.g. threading), where a buffer is usually used to avoid message loss.

Let $\mathcal{A}$ be a master automaton and let $\mathcal{A}'$ and $\mathcal{A}''$ be two slave automata forming a composable system. Assume that both $\mathcal{S}_1 = \{\mathcal{A}, \mathcal{A}'\}$ and $\mathcal{S}_2 = \{\mathcal{A}, \mathcal{A}''\}$ are composable master-slave systems that are strong master-slave compatible (i.e. they are compatible with respect to $sMS^{\mathcal{S}_1}$ and with respect to $sMS^{\mathcal{S}_2}$, respectively). Thus in each of the team automata, the master is always followed by the slave. Moreover, it is then also guaranteed that the master will always be followed by the two slaves in a single system if the two slaves are synchronised (e.g. in a synchronous product construction) and then the resulting slave (!) automaton is combined with the master. The system that is obtained in this way, is again a master-slave system and strong master-slave compatible. Formally, $\mathcal{S}_3 = \{\mathcal{A}, \mathcal{X}(\{\mathcal{A}', \mathcal{A}''\})\}$ is a composable master-slave system compatible with respect to $sMS^{\mathcal{S}_3}$. A compatibility relation $\mathcal{R}$ for the new system $\mathcal{S}_3$ can be constructed from the compatibility relations $\mathcal{R}'$ for $\mathcal{S}_1$ and $\mathcal{R}''$ for $\mathcal{S}_2$ by letting $(q, q', q'') \in \mathcal{R}$ iff $(q, q') \in \mathcal{R}'$ and $(q, q'') \in \mathcal{R}''$.

As a second example, consider again a master automaton $\mathcal{A}$ and two slave automata $\mathcal{A}'$ and $\mathcal{A}''$. The component automaton $\mathcal{B}$ is constructed from $\mathcal{A}'$ by changing all (input) actions it shares with $\mathcal{A}''$ into output actions. Thus depending on whether $\mathcal{A}'$ shares none, all, or some of its input actions with $\mathcal{A}''$, the new $\mathcal{B}$ is a slave automaton, a master automaton, or neither. Here we assume that $\mathcal{B}$ is a master automaton. Furthermore, we suppose that the master-slave systems $\mathcal{S}_4 = \{\mathcal{A}, \mathcal{A}'\}$ and $\mathcal{S}_5 = \{\mathcal{B}, \mathcal{A}''\}$ are composable and strong master-slave compatible (i.e. they are compatible with respect to $sMS^{\mathcal{S}_4}$ and with respect to $sMS^{\mathcal{S}_5}$, respectively). Hence, $\mathcal{A}''$ is always ready to synchronise with $\mathcal{A}'$ in $\mathcal{X}(\{\mathcal{A}', \mathcal{A}''\})$. We conjecture that also the composable master-slave system $\mathcal{S}_6 = \{\mathcal{A}, \mathcal{X}(\{\mathcal{A}', \mathcal{A}''\})\}$ is compatible with respect to $sMS^{\mathcal{S}_6}$ (to be proved as above by combining the compatibility relations for $\mathcal{S}_4$ and $\mathcal{S}_5$).

6 Applications of Asynchronicity

The main characteristic of the team automata framework is that it caters for component-based modelling and composition according to a wide range of synchronisation policies. The usefulness of such a flexible framework for compatibility is witnessed by examples from both hardware and software in which synchronisation deviates from the standard synchronous product. Hence the contributions of this paper may open the door to apply correct-by-construction design techniques in unprecedented areas. We provide in this section some examples in this direction.

Swarm Intelligence. Recently, the notion of *swarm networks* has appeared as an alternative computation paradigm in the field of swarm intelligence [34]. In a swarm network, an agent communicates/cooperates through its sensors, actuators and connectors. Sensors and actuators allow the asynchronous communication through the receiving and sending of signals. Due to their limited capabilities, agents sometimes need to self-organise in communities through their connectors, in order to accomplish certain tasks. This ability resembles the hierarchical construction allowed by the team automata framework. Because of the huge number of agents a swarm network has, the simulation of such an environment may miss important facts about its correctness. Instead, the construction of swarm networks with certain compatibility guarantees may represent an important step towards their satisfactory application.

Hardware Design. The end of Moore's Law may bring in front hardware technology architectures that provide, i.a., flexible (clock) synchronisation. Hence *asynchronous circuits*, and—in a more realistic incarnation—*globally asynchronous locally synchronous* (GALS) [18] or *elastic circuits* [13], represent viable alternatives for dealing with phenomena like the problem of *clock skew*. In the late 80s, David L. Dill proposed for the first time the theory of *conformance* between an asynchronous specification and the corresponding implementation. As happened with conformance almost thirty years ago, we believe that the notion of compatibility presented in this paper, which lifts most of the restrictions the conformance notion has, may assist the safe design of future hardware architectures.

Software Engineering. Nowadays the use of the unified modeling language (UML) still dominates the field of software engineering for the design of systems. Unfortunately, due to UML's imprecise semantics, the compatibility checking of UML designs is a challenging task. Current solutions (e.g. [30]) only consider the synchronous product of UML State Charts as main composition operation, thus missing out on important constructs when modelling real systems. We believe that the work proposed in this paper can generalise previous attempts to accomplish the task of compatibility checking of UML specifications (cf. [29,30]).

Manufacturing. By focussing on particular subclasses of team automata, we have shown in Sect. 5 very interesting properties on the corresponding hierarchical construction. The systems modelled in Sect. 5 may represent a wide class of manufacturing systems, where not a protocol but (a chain of) producer-consumer behaviour is observed. In the context of manufacturing systems, incompatibility may lead to faults due to deadlocks or receptiveness violations, which may hamper the manufacturing of items.

Concurrent Asynchronous Programming. The last decade, concurrent asynchronous programming languages have reached a certain maturity, demonstrated by their widespread industrial adoption. Erlang [2] is a prominent example; its asynchronous communication mode allows for a very flexible communication architecture, but on the other hand if used incorrectly may lead to invalid/suboptimal implementations of a system. To the best of our knowledge, current approaches follow the verification principle, i.e. a *post-mortem* approach to certify certain properties (e.g. liveness, safeness) of Erlang programs [17, 26]. Instead, correct-by-construction design might become possible if the theories described in this paper are used in the specification of Erlang programs.

Web Services. Two services are *protocol compatible* if every joint execution of these services leads to a proper final state [23]. In [44], two main types of protocol mismatches were defined over a pair of service protocols: unspecified reception (lack of receptiveness in our setting) and mutual deadlock. In Fig. 2 of [23] we see a clear resemblance to our compatibility notion. Again, the limitation of using the synchronous product to verify compatibility, together with the extreme flexibility of team automata, might make the theory of this paper well-suited for the description of flexible compatibility relations also in the area of Web services.

7 Conclusions

In this paper, we continued the quest of [12,15,16] for precise conditions for the compatibility of components in systems of systems that (by construction) guarantee correct communications, free from message loss and deadlocks. We proposed a definition of compatibility for components that applies to any synchronisation policy allowed by team automata, after which we briefly discussed its application to master-slave synchronisations. While we still defined the generalised compatibility relation in terms of Non-communicating progress, Receptiveness and Deadlock-freeness, it refers to the enabledness of actions in output and input subteams rather than in their constituting components.

Related Work. Non-communicating progress prescribes that internal actions do not lead outside a compatibility relation. This extends the Internal progress condition of the I/O compatibility from [11,12] reflecting the role of silent actions in bisimulations.

Receptiveness is a weak version of the input-enabledness requirement imposed on I/O automata [38,39] by which output actions can never be blocked by components not ready to receive this communication as input because in each state, every input action has to be enabled. However, I/O automata are composed as synchronous products, meaning that one cannot distinguish different types of master-slave synchronisations, since all synchronisations on communicating actions are by definition strong master-slave (cf. Sect. 3). As the applications sketched in Sect. 6 confirm, input-enabledness is in general too strong a requirement. This was recognised also in the theory of Interface

Automata [20,21], where a form of receptiveness is achieved without imposing input-enabledness by a notion of compatibility that always guarantees at least one synchronisation that does not lead to an error state. Its extension into Sociable Interface Automata [19] moreover allows multi-way communication, while its associated tool [1] allows to check notions of composability and compatibility.

Deadlock-freeness prescribes that the system cannot terminate if an input subteam is still waiting for input, thus generalising—as in the case of Receptiveness—the notion from [12,16] in which this is required at the level of an individual component rather than a subteam. As noted in [32], interface automata compatibility does not imply deadlock-freeness.

In [31–33], an approach similar to ours considers communication-safety as a notion of compatibility in multi-component environments composed according to assembly theories to express the absence of communication errors. In this case, the modelling framework is a generalisation of both interface automata and modal I/O-transition systems [37] but the synchronous product is the only composition operator considered.

Future Work. Most importantly, we would like to investigate in depth our proposed definition of compatibility of components with respect to arbitrary synchronisation policies. This would range from explicitly taking other policies than master-slave synchronisation into account to studying the case of master-slave compatibility in more detail.

In general, we could extend Definition 9 with requirements relating to the actual synchronisations *within* the input and output subsystems. For instance, when prescribing a master-slave policy for an action a, we could require in addition that the output subteam of a is a synchronous product (masters operating as peers) or that the input subteam of a is a synchronous product, implying that all components with a as an input have to follow the master or masters (slaves operating as peers). These additional requirements could also be weakened by requiring such peer-to-peer collaborations only between enabled components. Also the obligation of slaves following masters may be formulated in a variety of ways, based on how the participation of input components (of an action's input subteam) is realised (e.g. requiring 'at least one', 'exactly one', 'all' or 'only those in which the action is enabled at the current state' to participate).

As anticipated in the Introduction, it would be interesting to study how (master-slave) compatibility is affected when (slave) components are added. Perhaps the combination of non-state-sharing and master-slave-compatible systems may lead to an incremental construction of compatible systems. For instance, assume that we have a non-state-sharing master-slave-compatible team automaton, and we add a new component to the team in a way that the new team is still non-state-sharing. Then what are the necessary conditions to also preserve the master-slave compatibility?

Finally, it would interesting to study possible cross-fertilisation with work on synthesis. In [14], the binary notion of I/O compatibility from [12] is applied to the synthesis of asynchronous circuits modelled as Petri nets. It would be interesting to see whether this can be extended to multi-component systems based on the compatibility of components with respect to synchronisation policies other than the synchronous product. In [7], supervisory control theory [42] is applied to product lines. This theory provides a means to synthesise a supervisory controller automaton from a set of components and requirements. If such a synthesised supervisory controller exists, then the resulting synchronous product of the components and the supervisory controller not only satisfies the requirements, but it is moreover non-blocking (the system can always reach an accepted stable state), controllable (only the components' external actions can be influenced, internal actions cannot) and maximally permissive (allowing as much behaviour of the components without violating the requirements). It would be interesting to see whether this mechanism can be extended to deal with components synchronised according to policies other than the synchronous product, possibly in combination with the product line theories presented in [37].

Acknowledgments. We thank the reviewers for their suggestions and additional references to related work. M.H. ter Beek was supported by the CNR through a Short-Term Mobility grant and J. Carmona was supported by funds from the Spanish Ministry for Economy and Competitiveness (MINECO) and the European Union (FEDER funds) under grant COMMAS (ref. TIN2013-46181-C2-1-R).

References

1. Adler, B.T., de Alfaro, L., da Silva, L.D., Faella, M., Legay, A., Raman, V., Roy, P.: TICC: a tool for interface compatibility and composition. In: Ball, T., Jones, R.B. (eds.) CAV 2006. LNCS, vol. 4144, pp. 59–62. Springer, Heidelberg (2006)

2. Armstrong, J.: Erlang. Commun. ACM **53**(9), 68–75 (2010)

3. ter Beek, M.H.: Team automata: a formal approach to the modeling of collaboration between system components. PhD thesis, Leiden University (2003)

4. ter Beek, M.H., Ellis, C.A., Kleijn, J., Rozenberg, G.: Synchronizations in team automata for groupware systems. Comput. Sup. Coop. Work **12**(1), 21–69 (2003)

5. ter Beek, M.H., Kleijn, J.: Team automata satisfying compositionality. In: Araki, K., Gnesi, S., Mandrioli, D. (eds.) FME 2003. LNCS, vol. 2805, pp. 381–400. Springer, Heidelberg (2003)

6. ter Beek, M.H., Kleijn, J.: Modularity for teams of I/O automata. Inf. Process. Lett. **95**(5), 487–495 (2005)

7. ter Beek, M.H., Reniers, M.A., de Vink, E.P.: Supervisory controller synthesis for product lines using CIF 3. In: Margaria, T., Steffen, B. (eds.) ISoLA 2016, Part I. LNCS, vol. 9952, pp. 856–873. Springer, Heidelberg (2016). doi:10.1007/978-3-319-47166-259

8. Bensalem, S., Bozga, M., Boyer, B., Legay, A.: Incremental generation of linear invariants for component-based systems. In: Proceedings of the 13th International Conference on Application of Concurrency to System Design (ACSD 2013), pp. 80–89. IEEE (2013)

9. Berry, G.: The Esterel v5 Language Primer. Ecole des Mines de Paris/INRIA (2000)

10. Brim, L., Cerná, I., Vareková, P., Zimmerova, B.: Component-interaction automata as a verification-oriented component-based system specification. ACM Softw. Eng. Notes **31**(2), 4:1–4:8 (2006)

11. Carmona, J.: Structural methods for the synthesis of well-formed concurrent spec-ifications. PhD thesis, Universitat Politècnica de Catalunya (2004)
12. Cortadella, J., Carmona, J.: Input/Output compatibility of reactive systems. In: Aagaard, M.D., O'Leary, J.W. (eds.) FMCAD 2002. LNCS, vol. 2517, pp. 360–377. Springer, Heidelberg (2002)
13. Carmona, J., Cortadella, J., Kishinevsky, M., Taubin, A.: Elastic circuits. IEEE Trans. Comput.-Aided Design Integr. Circuits Syst. **28**(10), 1437–1455 (2009)
14. Carmona, J.A., Cortadella, J., Pastor, E.: Synthesis of reactive systems: application to asynchronous circuit design. In: Cortadella, J., Yakovlev, A., Rozenberg, G. (eds.) Concurrency and Hardware Design. LNCS, vol. 2549, pp. 108–151. Springer, Heidelberg (2002)
15. Carmona, J., Kleijn, J.: Interactive behaviour of multi-component systems. In: Cortadella, J., Yakovlev, A. (eds.) ToBaCo 2004, pp. 27–31 (2004)
16. Carmona, J., Kleijn, J.: Compatibility in a multi-component environment. Theor. Comput. Sci. **484**, 1–15 (2013)
17. Castro, D., Gulías, V.M., Earle, C.B., Fredlund, L., Rivas, S.: A case study on verifying a supervisor component using McErlang. ENTCS **271**, 23–40 (2011)
18. Chapiro, D.M.: Globally-asynchronous locally-synchronous systems. PhD thesis, Stanford University (1984)
19. de Alfaro, L., da Silva, L.D., Faella, M., Legay, A., Roy, P., Sorea, M.: Sociable interfaces. In: Gramlich, B. (ed.) FroCos 2005. LNCS (LNAI), vol. 3717, pp. 81–105. Springer, Heidelberg (2005)
20. de Alfaro, L., Henzinger, T.A.: Interface automata. In: ESEC/FSE 2001, pp. 109–120. ACM (2001)
21. de Alfaro, L., Henzinger, T.A.: Interface-based design. In: Broy, M., Grünbauer, J., Harel, D., Hoare, T. (eds.) Engineering Theories of Software Intensive Systems. NATO Science Series, vol. 195, pp. 83–104. Springer, Dordrecht (2005)
22. Dijkstra, E.W.: A constructive approach to the problem of program correctness. BIT Numer. Math. **8**(3), 174–186 (1968)
23. Dumas, M., Benatallah, B., Nezhad, H.R.M.: Web service protocols: compatibility and adaptation. IEEE Data Eng. Bull. **31**(3), 40–44 (2008)
24. Engels, G., Groenewegen, L.: Towards team-automata-driven object-oriented collaborative work. In: Brauer, W., Ehrig, H., Karhumäki, J., Salomaa, A. (eds.) Formal and Natural Computing. LNCS, vol. 2300, p. 257. Springer, Heidelberg (2002)
25. Gössler, G., Sifakis, J.: Composition for component-based modeling. Sci. Comput. Program. **55**, 161–183 (2005)
26. Guo, Q., Derrick, J., Benac Earle, C., Fredlund, L.Å.: Model-checking Erlang – a comparison between EtomCRL2 and McErlang. In: Bottaci, L., Fraser, G. (eds.) TAIC PART 2010. LNCS, vol. 6303, pp. 23–38. Springer, Heidelberg (2010)
27. Hall, A.: Correctness by construction: integrating formality into a commercial development process. In: Eriksson, L.-H., Lindsay, P.A. (eds.) FME 2002. LNCS, vol. 2391, p. 224. Springer, Heidelberg (2002)
28. Hall, A., Chapman, R.: Correctness by construction: developing a commercial secure system. IEEE Softw. **19**(1), 18–25 (2002)
29. Hammal, Y.: A modular state exploration and compatibility checking of UML dynamic diagrams. In: AICCSA 2008, pp. 793–800. IEEE (2008)
30. Hammal, Y.: Behavioral compatibility of active components. In: SEFM 2008, pp. 372–376. IEEE (2008)

31. Hennicker, R., Knapp, A.: Modal interface theories for communication-safe component assemblies. In: Cerone, A., Pihlajasaari, P. (eds.) ICTAC 2011. LNCS, vol. 6916, pp. 135–153. Springer, Heidelberg (2011)

32. Hennicker, R., Knapp, A.: Moving from interface theories to assembly theories. Acta Inf. **52**(2–3), 235–268 (2015)

33. Hennicker, R., Knapp, A., Wirsing, M.: Assembly theories for communication-safe component systems. In: Bensalem, S., Lakhneck, Y., Legay, A. (eds.) From Programs to Systems. LNCS, vol. 8415, pp. 145–160. Springer, Heidelberg (2014)

34. Isokawa, T., Peper, F., Mitsui, M., Liu, J.-Q., Morita, K., Umeo, H., Kamiura, N., Matsui, N.: Computing by swarm networks. In: Umeo, H., Morishita, S., Nishinari, K., Komatsuzaki, T., Bandini, S. (eds.) ACRI 2008. LNCS, vol. 5191, pp. 50–59. Springer, Heidelberg (2008)

35. Jamshidi, M.: System of Systems Engineering: Innovations for the Twenty-First Century. Wiley, Hoboken (2008)

36. Kourie, D.G., Watson, B.W.: The Correctness-by-Construction Approach to Programming. Springer, Heidelberg (2012)

37. Larsen, K.G., Nyman, U., Wąsowski, A.: Modal I/O automata for interface and product line theories. In: De Nicola, R. (ed.) ESOP 2007. LNCS, vol. 4421, pp. 64–79. Springer, Heidelberg (2007)

38. Lynch, N.A., Tuttle, M.R.: Hierarchical correctness proofs for distributed algorithms. In: PODC 1987, pp. 137–151. ACM (1987)

39. Lynch, N.A., Tuttle, M.R.: An introduction to input/output automata. CWI Q. **2**(3), 219–246 (1989)

40. Milner, R.: Communication and Concurrency. Prentice Hall, Upper Saddle River (1989)

41. Morgan, C.C.: Programming from Specifications, 2nd edn. Prentice Hall, Upper Saddle River (1994)

42. Ramadge, P.J., Wonham, W.M.: Supervisory control of a class of discrete event processes. SIAM J. Control Optim. **25**(1), 206–230 (1987)

43. Silva, M., Valette, R.: Petri nets and flexible manufacturing. In: Rozenberg, G. (ed.) Advances in Petri Nets. LNCS, vol. 424, pp. 374–417. Springer, Heidelberg (1990)

44. Yellin, D.M., Strom, R.E.: Protocol specifications and component adaptors. ACM Trans. Program. Lang. Syst. **19**(2), 292–333 (1997)

A Logic for the Statistical Model Checking of Dynamic Software Architectures

Jean Quilbeuf[1,2]([✉]), Everton Cavalcante[1,3], Louis-Marie Traonouez[2], Flavio Oquendo[1], Thais Batista[3], and Axel Legay[2]

[1] IRISA-UMR CNRS/Université Bretagne Sud, Vannes, France
{jean.quilbeuf,flavio.oquendo}@irisa.fr
[2] INRIA Rennes Bretagne Atlantique, Rennes, France
{louis-marie.traonouez,axel.legay}@inria.fr
[3] DIMAp, Federal University of Rio Grande do Norte, Natal, Brazil
thais@ufrnet.br, everton@dimap.ufrn.br

Abstract. Dynamic software architectures emerge when addressing important features of contemporary systems, which often operate in dynamic environments subjected to change. Such systems are designed to be reconfigured over time while maintaining important properties, e.g., availability, correctness, etc. Verifying that reconfiguration operations make the system to meet the desired properties remains a major challenge. First, the verification process itself becomes often difficult when using exhaustive formal methods (such as model checking) due to the potentially infinite state space. Second, it is necessary to express the properties to be verified using some notation able to cope with the dynamic nature of these systems. Aiming at tackling these issues, we introduce DynBLTL, a new logic tailored to express both structural and behavioral properties in dynamic software architectures. Furthermore, we propose using statistical model checking (SMC) to support an efficient analysis of these properties by evaluating the probability of meeting them through a number of simulations. In this paper, we describe the main features of DynBLTL and how it was implemented as a plug-in for PLASMA, a statistical model checker.

1 Introduction

Dynamic software architectures are those that encompass evolution rules for a software system and its elements during runtime [20]. Their relevance is due to the fact that dynamism is an important concern for contemporary systems, which often operate on environments subjected to change. In a dynamic software architecture, constituent elements may be created, interconnected or removed, or may even undergo a complete rearrangement at runtime, ideally with minimal or no disruption. For this reason, supporting dynamism is important mainly in the case of certain safety-and mission-critical systems, such as air traffic control, energy, disaster management, environmental monitoring, and health systems. Systems in these scenarios are required to maintain a high level of availability,

© Springer International Publishing AG 2016
T. Margaria and B. Steffen (Eds.): ISoLA 2016, Part I, LNCS 9952, pp. 806–820, 2016.
DOI: 10.1007/978-3-319-47166-2_56

so that stopping and restarting them is not an option due to financial costs, physical damages, or even threats to the life and safety of people.

One of the major challenges in the design of software-intensive systems consists in verifying the correctness of their software architectures, i.e., if the envisioned architecture is able to fully realize the established requirements [26]. Ensuring correctness and other relevant system properties becomes more important mainly for evolving systems since such a verification needs to be performed before, during, and after evolution. The requirements to be verified are typically concerned with the relationship between the system behavior (e.g., a particular value is received or sent) and an architectural property, such as checking if a component is connected to or disconnected from another component. For illustrative purposes, consider a sensor-based system in which sensors measure a given value from the environment and transmit it to a base station, possibly via other sensors. A requirement of interest in this context would be that a sensor signaling its failure (a behavioral property) gets disconnected from the other sensors (an architectural property).

The automated analysis of architectural properties can be performed by means of formal verification, which determines if a software system satisfies properties capturing the system requirements. However, such a process is challenging in the context of dynamic systems. As the number of components to appear and be connected to the system is unbounded a priori, its state space is likely to be infinite. Therefore, exhaustive methods that explore the whole state space are unfeasible for dynamic software architectures unless the number of components that will be part of the system is known in advance. Nonetheless, the state space might still be quite large and hence the use of such techniques may be a prohibitive choice in terms of execution time and computational resources. This is the case of model checking [8], a formal verification technique that is among the most frequently used ones in the analysis of software architectures [30].

To face the state space explosion observed in traditional verification techniques, we propose the use of statistical model checking (SMC) to support the formal verification of architectural properties in dynamic systems. SMC is a probabilistic, simulation-based technique intended to verify, at a given confidence level, if a certain property is satisfied during the execution of a system [18]. This technique requires a stochastic executable model for the system, in which the choice of the next action to execute is done according to a probability distribution. With a stochastic system, the property to verify might be satisfied by some executions and not satisfied by some others. SMC then executes a number of stochastic simulations of the system and evaluates the approximated probability of the system to meet the property under verification. Requiring the execution to be probabilistic is not a limitation because dynamic systems can be reasonably described by assigning probabilities for new components to appear or for the existing components to fail and be disconnected, for example. Moreover, probability distributions can be used to model input values.

Besides an executable probabilistic model of the system, SMC requires a language for expressing properties to be verified and a monitor for deciding them on finite traces, which is obtained by bounding temporal operators [24]. The particular nature of dynamic software architectures is that architectural elements (components and connectors) may appear, disappear, be connected or be disconnected at runtime. Therefore, expressing behavioral and structural properties regarding a dynamic software architecture needs to take into account architectural elements that are dynamically created and removed, i.e., they may exist at a given instant in time and no longer exist at another.

To cope with these characteristics, this paper brings as main contribution DynBLTL, a new logic aimed to express properties in dynamic software architectures using bounded temporal operators. DynBLTL is designed to handle the absence of an architectural element in a given formula expressing a property by means of the *undefined* value ($\mathfrak{U}$), which is returned when reading values from components that are no longer in the system. We have implemented DynBLTL as a plug-in for PLASMA [1,13], a flexible, modular statistical model checker.

This paper is organized as follows. In Sect. 2, we provide an overview of how SMC works. Section 3 presents how to formalize a trace of a dynamic system. Section 4 defines DynBLTL and describes its semantics for execution traces. In Sect. 5, we describe how DynBLTL was implemented atop the PLASMA statistical model checker. Section 6 discusses related work. Finally, Sect. 7 contains some concluding remarks.

2   Statistical Model Checking: An Overview

SMC provides a number of advantages in comparison to traditional formal verification techniques such as model checking. First, SMC does not suffer from the exponential growth of the state space (the so-called *state space explosion problem*) as it does not build the entire representation of the state space, thus making it a promising approach for verifying complex large-scale and critical software systems [15]. Second, SMC can be applied as soon as a simulator of the system to verify is available. Third, the proliferation of parallel computer architectures allows producing multiple independent simulations, thereby speeding up the verification of large-scale systems even though it is still necessary to make the simulation procedure as efficient as possible [18]. Fourth, despite the results of SMC are approximations, the technique is more scalable and consumes less computation resources. In some cases, obtaining quickly an approximation of the result is more valuable than obtaining the exact result after a long computation [19]. As the verification accuracy parameterizes the analysis, the user can set the trade-off between verification speed and accuracy.

A statistical model checker basically consists of a simulator for running the system under verification, a checker for verifying properties on a trace, and a statistical analyzer responsible for calculating probabilities and performing statistical tests. It receives three inputs: (i) an *executable stochastic model* of the target system M; (ii) a formula φ expressing a *bounded property* to be verified, i.e., a property that can be decided over a finite execution of M; and (iii) user-defined *precision parameters* determining the accuracy of the probability estimation.

The model M is stochastic in the sense that the next state is probabilistically chosen among the states that are reachable from the current one. As a consequence, some executions of M may satisfy φ and others may not satisfy it, depending on the probabilistic choices made during these executions. We denote by p the probability that a trace satisfy φ. The goal of a statistical model checker is to approximate p. The simulator produces traces that are analyzed by the checker. For each trace, the result of the checker (i.e. whether the trace satisfies φ or not) is recorded. Based on the precision parameters and the results obtained so far, the statistical analyzer determines when enough traces have been seen to produce an accurate enough approximation of p. A more accurate approximation requires more traces.

SMC answers two types of questions. The first one is qualitative: *Is the probability p for M to satisfy φ greater or equal than a certain threshold θ?* The second question is quantitative: *What is the probability p for M to satisfy φ?* [27]. In both cases, producing a trace σ_i and checking if it satisfies φ (i.e., $\sigma_i \models \varphi$) is modeled as a random variable B_i following a Bernoulli distribution of parameter p [17]. The possible values of B_i are either 0 (if $\sigma_i \not\models \varphi$) or 1 (if $\sigma_i \models \varphi$), with probability functions $Pr[B_i = 1] = p$ and $Pr[B_i = 0] = 1 - p$. The variable B_i is associated with the i-th simulation of M.

Qualitative approach. The main existing SMC approaches for the qualitative question [28,29] rely on *hypothesis testing* as means of inferring if the simulated execution traces provide statistical evidence on the satisfaction or violation of a property [25]. To determine if $p \geq \theta$, two hypotheses can be considered, namely (i) $H : p \geq \theta$ and (ii) $K : p < \theta$. The test is parameterized by two bounds, α and β. The probability of accepting the hypothesis K when the hypothesis H holds is bounded by α, and the probability of accepting H when K holds is bounded by β. Such algorithms sequentially perform simulations until either H or K can be returned with confidence of α or β. Other sequential hypothesis testing algorithms are based on the Bayesian approach [14].

Quantitative approach. In order to compute the probability p for M to satisfy φ, Hérault et al. [11] and Laplante et al. [16] propose an estimation procedure based on the Chernoff-Hoeffding bound [12], which provides the minimum number of simulations required to ensure the desired confidence level. Given a precision ε, this procedure computes an estimate p' of p with confidence δ, thereby ensuring $Pr(|p' - p| \leq \varepsilon) \geq 1 - \delta$.

The quantitative approach is used when there is no known approximation of the probability to evaluate, i.e. when one wants to obtain a first approximation. This method is useful when the goal is to have an idea on how well the model behaves. The qualitative approach determines if the probability is above a given threshold with a high confidence and in a minimal number of simulations.

3   Representing Traces of Dynamic Systems

Typical operations performed on dynamic software architectures comprise creating, removing, attaching, and detaching components and connectors. In order to express architectural properties, we have to represent the set of components and their interconnections. Furthermore, we need to capture the behavior of the system by observing the messages exchanged between elements of the architecture.

We define a *state* of a dynamic software architecture as a directed graph $g = (V, E)$ comprising a finite set of nodes V and a finite set of edges E. Each node $v \in V$ represents an architectural element (component or connector) of the system. In turn, each edge $e \in E$ represents a communication channel between two architectural elements and is labeled by the value, if any, exchanged between the connected nodes. We represent the set of all possible values by *Val*, which contains the *undefined* value $\mathfrak{U}$ to represent the absence of value.

Definition 1 (State). A *state* of a dynamic system is a directed graph $g = (V, E)$ where:

- Each node $v \in V$ is defined by a tuple (id, T, C) in which id is a globally unique identifier for the architectural element, T is the declared type of the architectural element, and C is a finite set representing its connections. $id(v)$ returns the identifier for node, $T(v)$ returns its type, $C(v)$ denotes the set of connections of the node v, and $v.c$ denotes a connection $c \in C(v)$.
- Each edge $e \in E$ connecting two nodes in the graph is labeled by the values exchanged between them. These values are contained into *Val*, the set of all possible values that can be exchanged between two nodes. Formally, $E \subseteq \{(v_1.c_1, x, v_2.c_2) \mid x \in Val \wedge \bigwedge_{i=1}^{2} v_i \in V \wedge c_i \in C(v_i)\}$. For each connection, the set of edges connected to it contains at most one edge labeled by a value different of $\mathfrak{U}$.

Given a state graph g, $V(g)$ and $E(g)$, respectively, denote its sets of nodes and of edges. Note that we do not forbid edges between connections of the same node, because they may be allowed in the language describing dynamic architectures.

The SMC technique relies on checking multiple *execution traces* resulting from simulations of the system under verification against the specified properties. A simulation ω results in a trace σ composed of a finite sequence of state graphs.

Definition 2 (Trace). An untimed trace σ^{ut} is a sequence $g_0, g_1, \ldots, g_n$ of states. In turn, a timed trace σ is a sequence $((t_0, g_0), \ldots, (t_n, g_n))$ of states with timestamps t_i, such that $\forall i : t_i \in \mathbb{R} \wedge t_i \leq t_{i+1}$.

SMC allows verifying systems that are *stochastic processes*. For this reason, traces have to be produced by a stochastic process, i.e., each state in the trace is the restriction of a complete system state and the choice of next complete state is governed by a probability distribution. For verifying timed systems, we require that for any value $M \in \mathbb{R}$, the system eventually produces a state (t_i, g_i) with $t_i > M$ for some i. In other words, we require that the time converges towards $+\infty$ during the execution of the system.

As an example, consider a simple client-server architecture that dynamically adapts to the demand. In such a system, clients may appear and interact with a server by sending requests and receiving answers. We assume that each server can handle a limited number of clients (two in our example). If all servers have reached that limit and a new client appears, the systems spawns a new server to handle the new client. Whenever the client has completed its interaction with the server, it disconnects and disappears from the system. If a server has no client left, it is shutdown and disappears from the system. At last, if the overall utilization of the servers is low, one tries to shutdown some servers in order to save energy. This is done by reallocating clients so that some severs become unused.

Figure 1 presents an execution trace of the client-server system. Initially, only one server is present in the system and a server has four connections ($r1$, $r2$, $a1$ and $a2$). At $t = 5$, three new clients appear and two of them are directly connected to the server. At $t = 6$, a new server is spawned and is connected to the third client, while the two first clients send their requests (requests and answers are represented as numbers). At $t = 7$, the client C_2 receives the answer to its request while the client C_3 sends a request to server S_2. At $t = 9$, the client C_3 receives the answer to its request and the client C_2 has disappeared. At $t = 10$, the client C_3 is relocated to server S_1 and the server S_2 is removed.

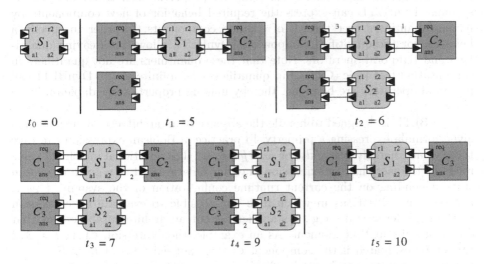

Fig. 1. An execution trace of the client-server example.

4   Expressing Properties About Dynamic Systems

Zhang et al. [30] report that linear temporal logic (LTL) [24] has been often used in the literature as underlying formalism for specifying temporal architectural properties and verifying them through model checking. LTL extends classical Boolean logic with *temporal operators* (a.k.a. modalities) that allow reasoning on the temporal dimension of the execution of the system. In this perspective, LTL expresses properties about the future of the execution (sequences of states), e.g., a condition that will be eventually true, a condition that will be true until another fact becomes true, etc.

As SMC relies on simulation, it verifies bounded properties, i.e., properties that can be decided on a finite execution of the system under verification. While LTL-based formulas aim at specifying the infinite behavior of the system, a time-bounded form of LTL called BLTL [14] considers finite sequences of execution states of the system. The bounds are specified on the temporal operators, such as for instance the *always* operator. In LTL, this operator states that a property must be verified at every step of a (potentially infinite) trace. In BLTL, it has a bound and states that the property must hold until the bound is reached.

A key characteristic of dynamic software systems is the impossibility of foreseeing the exact set of architectural elements deployed at a given point of execution. Furthermore, we may want to verify that the new components respect a particular behavior. BLTL is unable to handle this characteristic since it would require to statically know the set of components that will appear and write a dedicated formula for each of them. To tackle such a limitation, we introduce DynBLTL, a logic for expressing linear temporal properties over traces of dynamic systems. DynBLTL can express the required behavior of new components by having quantifiers over the set of existing components. In order to specify a behavior for the quantified components, DynBLTL allows interleaving quantifiers and temporal operators. Note that these quantifiers are not quantifiers in computation tree logic (CTL), but quantifiers over a finite set. In DynBLTL, all temporal operators are bounded, thereby making properties decidable on finite traces.

DynBLTL is designed to handle the absence of an architectural element in a given formula expressing a property. In practice, a Boolean expression can take three values, namely *true, false* or *undefined* ($\mathfrak{U}$). The additional undefined value refers to the fact that an expression may not be evaluated at a given execution state depending on the current runtime configuration of the system. This is necessary for situations in which it is not possible to evaluate an expression at the considered state, e.g., a statement about an architectural element that does not exist at that moment. As an example, the expression `c1.req > 3.2` cannot be evaluated if the component `c1` does not exist (as at t_0 in Fig. 1) or the connection `c1.req` is not involved in a communication at that state (as at t_1 in Fig. 1).

Figure 2 shows the concrete syntax of DynBLTL by using the Extended Backus-Naur Form (EBNF). DynBLTL is not typed, so that a property can be evaluated to any type, i.e., Boolean, integer, string or undefined. As SMC requires a Boolean value as the result of the evaluation of a property on a trace, we add a syntactical constraint on properties to enforce that the returned value is Boolean. The `until` or `isTrue` operators always return a Boolean value. Consequently, we require that the root operator of a property is either `until`, `isTrue` or a Boolean combination of them.

```
node → ID
connection → ID . ID
function → ID ( (value(,value)*)+ )
value → value OP value | − value | connection | function | node | LITERAL
predicate → value CMP value | value
bound → FLOAT time units | INT steps
property →
        exists ID : function property      | count ID : function property
    | in bound property                    | property until bound property
    | not property                         | property or property
    | isTrue property
    | predicate
```

Fig. 2. Concrete textual syntax of DynBLTL. `ID` is an identifier, `OP` is an arithmetic operator, `LITERAL` is a Boolean, float, integer or string literal, `CMP` is a comparison operator, `FLOAT` is a float-pointing number, and `INT` is an integer number.

The semantics of a property φ is a function $\llbracket \varphi \rrbracket$ that takes a trace σ as argument and returns a value in *Val*. We define the semantics for a timed trace $\sigma = (t_0, g_0), \ldots, (t_n, g_n)$. If the system is untimed, we can only evaluate temporal operators whose bound is expressed in steps. Assume that φ is a property in which all temporal operators bounds are expressed in steps. Evaluating an untimed trace $\sigma^{ut} = g_0, \ldots, g_n$ falls back to evaluating a timed trace with the same states and arbitrary timestamps. Indeed, timestamps are only relevant for temporal operators whose bound is expressed in time units.

Section 4.1 describes the main elements of DynBLTL whereas Sect. 4.2 shows some examples on how to express architectural properties in dynamic systems using our logic.

4.1   DynBLTL Elements

A property can be specified by a formula containing *literals*, *identifiers* referring to nodes and connections in the state graph, *operations* (arithmetic, logical, comparison), predefined *functions*, *quantified expressions*, and *temporal operators*. These elements are briefly described in the following.

Literals and identifiers. As basic elements, a formula expressing a property can contain (i) a literal, which can be a Boolean value, numerical value or a string, (ii) an identifier representing a node of the state graph, or (iii) a connection of a node of the state graph. The evaluation of these literals only takes into account the first state of the trace, as follows:

− if φ is a literal l, then $\llbracket \varphi \rrbracket(\sigma) = l$, i.e., the formula is evaluated to the respective value of l;
− if φ is an identifier idt representing a node, then $\llbracket \varphi \rrbracket((t_0, g_0), \ldots, (t_n, g_n))$ = true if there exists a node with that name at the current state, i.e. if $\exists v \in V(g_0)\ id(v) = idt$; otherwise, it evaluates to $\mathfrak{U}$;

- if φ is a connection c of a node v of a state graph $(v.c)$, then $[\![\varphi]\!]((t_0, g_0), \ldots, (t_n, g_n))$ is evaluated to the only non-undefined value labeling any edge of g_0 attached to the connection $v.c$, or to $\mathfrak{U}$ otherwise.

Operations and comparisons. Arithmetic operations as well as inequalities and equalities are evaluated as usual or set to $\mathfrak{U}$ if at least one argument is out of their definition domain. DynBLTL supports the usual arithmetic operators $(+,-,*,/)$, and the usual comparisons $(<,<=,>,>=,=,!=)$. Note that both $\mathfrak{U}!=\mathfrak{U}$ and $\mathfrak{U}=\mathfrak{U}$ evaluates to $\mathfrak{U}$.

Usual Boolean operators are also supported. The **not** operator acts as usual on Boolean values and returns $\mathfrak{U}$ with other values. The **or** operator returns **true** if at least one of the operands evaluates to true, **false** if both operands evaluate to false, and $\mathfrak{U}$ otherwise. Note that it may return true even if one of the operands is $\mathfrak{U}$. Other usual Boolean operators are obtained as follows: φ_1 **and** $\varphi_2 \stackrel{\text{def}}{=}$ **not** (**not** φ_1 **or not** φ_2) and φ_1 **implies** $\varphi_2 \stackrel{\text{def}}{=}$ **not** φ_1 **or** φ_2.

Functions. DynBLTL provides four predefined functions that can be used to explore the architectural configuration, i.e., the nodes of a state graph:

- **allOfType**(T) returns a collection with all nodes of type T;
- **areConnected**(v_1, v_2) returns true if nodes v_1 and v_2 are connected by an edge in the state graph, false if v_1 and v_2 exist in the state graph, but they are not connected by an edge, or $\mathfrak{U}$ otherwise;
- **areLinked**$(v_1.c_1, v_2.c_2)$ returns true if the connection c_1 of node v_1 and the connection c_2 of node v_2 are connected by an edge in the state graph, false if both $v_1.c_1$ and $v_2.c_2$ exist in the state graph, but they are not connected by an edge, or $\mathfrak{U}$ otherwise; and
- **lastValue**$(v.c)$ returns the last non-undefined value of the connection c of node v or $\mathfrak{U}$ if its value was always undefined.

Quantified expressions. In DynBLTL, three types of quantified expressions can be used to specify formulas expressing properties, namely the existential and universal quantified expressions traditionally used in predicate logic, as well as expressions involving an additional quantifier for counting elements upon the satisfaction of a predicate. These quantified expressions comprise an identifier r, a function f that returns a collection of elements, and a formula φ with free occurrences of r. In the sequel we assume that $[\![f]\!](\sigma) = e = \{e_1, \ldots, e_n\}$ and we denote by $\varphi[r \leftarrow e_i]$ the formula φ where each free occurrence of r is replaced by e_i. Quantifiers are defined as follows ($[\![\cdot]\!](\sigma)$ is omitted for readability):

- **exists** r: $f\varphi$ returns **true** if $\varphi[r \leftarrow e_i]$ evaluates to true for at least one element e_i $(1 \leq i \leq n)$ or to **false** if $\varphi[r \leftarrow e_i]$ evaluates to false for all elements e_i, or $\mathfrak{U}$ otherwise.
- **forall** r: $f\varphi$ returns **true** if $\varphi[r \leftarrow e_i]$ evaluates to **true** for all elements e_i $(1 \leq i \leq n)$ or to **false** if $\varphi[r \leftarrow e_i]$ evaluates to false for at least one element e_i, or $\mathfrak{U}$ otherwise.

- count r: $f\varphi$ returns the number of elements $e_i \in e$ such that $\varphi[r \leftarrow e_i]$ evaluates to true.

Temporal operators. Similarly to traditional BLTL, DynBLTL provides four temporal operators, namely in, until, eventually before, and always during. These operators are parametrized by a bound expressed either in steps or in time units. We provide here their definition:

- The in operator (a.k.a. *next*) evaluates its argument at a later point specified by the bound. If the bound is expressed in steps, we translate the trace by that number of steps:

$$[\![\text{in } b \text{ steps } \varphi]\!]((t_0, g_0), \ldots, (t_n, g_n)) = [\![\varphi]\!]((t_b, g_b), \ldots, (t_n, g_n))$$

We assume that n is always bigger than b. In practice, it falls back to asking the simulator to perform more steps and complete the trace. If the bound is expressed in terms of time units, we translate the trace by the amount of time units provided as argument:

$$[\![\text{in } b \text{ time units } \varphi]\!]((t_0, g_0), \ldots, (t_n, g_n)) = [\![\varphi]\!]((t_k, g_k), \ldots, (t_n, g_n))$$

where $k = min(\{0 \leq i \leq n \mid t_i - t_0 > b\})$.

- The until operator returns a Boolean value. An until expression evaluates to true if its right argument is evaluated to true within the bound and if the left argument evaluates to true or to $\mathfrak{U}$ until the right argument becomes true. We introduce new notations: $\sigma \models \varphi \equiv [\![\varphi]\!](\sigma) = \text{true}$ and $\sigma \not\models \varphi \equiv [\![\varphi]\!](\sigma) = \text{false}$[1]. If the bound is expressed in steps, we have:

$$((t_0, g_0), \ldots, (t_n, g_n)) \models \varphi_1 \text{ until } b \text{ steps } \varphi_2 \text{ iff}$$
$$\exists 0 \leq i \leq b \ . \ ((t_i, g_i), \ldots, (t_n, g_n)) \models \varphi_2 \ \wedge$$
$$\forall 0 \leq j < i . \neg ((t_j, g_j), \ldots, (t_n, g_n)) \not\models \varphi_1$$

If the bound is expressed in time units, we have:

$$((t_0, g_0), \ldots, (t_n, g_n)) \models \varphi_1 \text{ until } b \text{ time units } \varphi_2 \text{ iff}$$
$$\exists 0 \leq i \leq n \ . \ (t_i - t_0 \leq b) \ \wedge \ ((t_i, g_i), \ldots, (t_n, g_n)) \models \varphi_2 \ \wedge$$
$$\forall 0 \leq j < i \ . \ \neg ((t_j, g_j), \ldots, (t_n, g_n)) \not\models \varphi_1$$

- The eventually before operator can be defined by reusing the previous definition of the until operator as:

$$\text{eventually before } b \ \varphi \overset{\text{def}}{=} \text{true until } b \ \varphi$$

- The always during operator can be defined by reusing the previous definition of the eventually before operator as:

$$\text{always during } b \ \varphi \overset{\text{def}}{=} \text{not eventually before } b$$

---

[1] Note that if φ does not evaluate to a Boolean, then neither $\sigma \models \varphi$ nor $\sigma \not\models \varphi$ holds.

The reader may have noticed that we treat the value $\mathfrak{U}$ in a particular way when defining the `until` operator. Indeed, when $\mathfrak{U}$ appears on the left side of `until`, it is treated as `true`. However, when it appears on the right side, it is treated as `false`. We made this choice for the sake of intuitiveness. For instance, the property `c1.req < 2 until 10 steps c2.req = 5` can return true, even if `c1.req < 2` evaluates to $\mathfrak{U}$ during the 10 steps. We consider that evaluating to $\mathfrak{U}$ on the left hand side of `until` does not invalidate the formula. However, if `c1.req < 2` evaluates to false before `c2.req` evaluates to 5, then the whole expression evaluates to false.

The `isTrue` operator enforces the evaluation of a property to a Boolean value. Formally, $[\![\text{isTrue}\varphi]\!](\sigma) = \sigma \models \varphi$. This operator can be used to modify the behavior of `until`: `(isTrue c2.req < 2) until 10 steps c2.req = 5` will evaluate to false if `c2.req` evaluates to $\mathfrak{U}$ before `c2.req` evaluates to 5. We also define its dual operator `isNotFalse` $\varphi \stackrel{\text{def}}{=}$ `not isTrue not` φ.

4.2   Examples

Consider again the client-server example from Sect. 3. It is possible to express some interesting properties about such an architecture. For instance, we can express the fact that each request is treated in less than three time units:

```
always during 100 time units {
    forall c:allOfType(Client) {
        c.req > 0 implies eventually before 3 time units c.ans > 0
    }
}
```

As previously mentioned, the bound of 100 time steps on the `always during` operator is needed to ensure that the property can be decided on a finite trace. Therefore this property checks only the 100 first time units of the trace.

We can also express properties about the reconfiguration process. For instance, we can require that no client remains disconnected for more than five time units.

```
always during 100 time units {
    forall c:allOfType(Client) {
        not always during 5 time units {
            not exists s:allOfType(Server) areConnected(c,s)
        }
    }
}
```

By interleaving the `forall` quantifier between temporal operators, we require that each client meets a given property.

At last, we require that the reconfiguration effectively reduces the number of unused servers. More precisely, assuming a limit of two clients per server, if the number of servers is more than half the number of clients, then a reconfiguration is needed. We allow five time units for that reconfiguration:

```
not eventually before 100 time units {
    always during 5 time units {
        (count c:allOfType(Client) true) <
        2 * (count s:allOfType(Server) true) - 1
    }
}
```

5   Implementation

We have implemented DynBLTL as a plug-in for the PLASMA statistical model checker [1,13].[2] We have also provided a simulator plug-in that interfaces with an external simulator used to produce the traces. The simulator plug-in receives events about the architecture, such as (i) when a node v appears, (ii) when connection c_1 of node v_1 is linked to connection c_2 of node v_2, (iii) when a value x is sent from connection c_1 of node v_1 to connection c_2 of node v_2, or (iv) when a node v disappears. From this information, the simulator plug-in maintains a trace of the current execution as a sequence of states from Definition 1. If these events have a timestamp, the produced trace is also timed. The DynBLTL plug-in asks the simulator plug-in about the particular states of the trace in order to evaluate the property.

Currently, we support simulations of architectural descriptions in π-ADL [23], a formal architecture description language for specifying both structure and behavior of dynamic software architectures. Figure 3 shows an overview of our SMC-based toolchain for verifying architectural properties. An architecture description in π-ADL is first translated to source code in the Go programming language [4,5]. As π-ADL is non-deterministic, we enforce stochastic behavior by providing a probabilistic choice function that randomly chooses the next action to execute among the possible ones. Furthermore, some functions can be declared unobservable in π-ADL and implemented directly in Go. Such functions can rely on probability distributions to model inputs. Our methodology is explained in [6].

Once the probabilistic choice function and the implementation of unobservable functions are provided, the obtained Go code is compiled into an executable and run by the simulator plug-in. Whenever a new trace is required for the analysis, the simulator plug-in launches a new instance of the executable to generate a new trace. If the trace is not long enough to evaluate the property, the simulator plug-in requests more simulation steps from the executable.

6   Related Work

The idea of interleaving quantifiers and temporal logics is not new and has been used in LTL(MSO), for example [2]. In that model, the number of constituents

---

[2] The developed plug-in is available at http://plasma4pi-adl.gforge.inria.fr/.

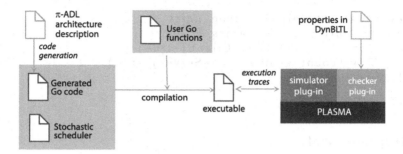

Fig. 3. Overview of our toolchain for verifying properties expressed in DynBLTL from π-ADL architecture descriptions.

is constant throughout the execution and therefore this logic is not applicable to dynamic systems.

The Bandera specification language allows model checking multi-threaded Java programs [9]. The dynamicity is handled by bounding the number of classes that can be dynamically created to be able to statically build a representation of the state space, but such an approach requires the user to annotate the Java code. Cho et al. [7] also proposed a logic for dealing with dynamic systems based on freeze quantifiers. In both cases, the logic cannot express architectural properties. The π-AAL language [21] was developed to express properties about π-ADL models, but its semantics is not suitable for performing SMC since properties are evaluated per trace, not per computation tree.

An important part of the verification of dynamic systems deals with validation of reconfiguration operations. In this context, several works have provided ways to specify what a correct reconfiguration means. In the work of Mazzara and Bhattacharyya [22], several frameworks for describing and analyzing dynamic reconfiguration are studied, but they do not handle logics similar to DynBLTL. Basso et al. [3] express architectural properties in CTL with additional predicates encoding the state of the architecture, but this logic does not allow interleaving quantifiers (over sets) and temporal operators. Finally, Dormoy et al. [10] propose a logic where architectural properties are used as predicate and expressed through quantifiers, but quantifiers and temporal operators cannot be interleaved.

7   Conclusion

In this paper, we have presented DynBLTL, a new logic tailored for the statistical model checking of dynamic software architectures. DynBLTL was implemented as a plug-in for the PLASMA statistical model checker, thus benefiting from all SMC algorithms already implemented. The developed toolchain is currently able to verify properties associated to architectural descriptions in the π-ADL language.

As future work, we first plan to improve the developed tools, especially the performance of the monitor. We also intend to identify which SMC algorithm gives the best results for verifying properties of dynamic architectures. Finally, we are interested in verifying properties for systems-of-systems and look forward to use DynBLTL in this context.

Acknowledgments. This work was partially supported by the Brazilian National Agency of Petroleum, Natural Gas and Biofuels through the PRH-22/ANP/ MCTI Program (for Everton Cavalcante) and by CNPq under grant 308725/2013-1 (for Thais Batista).

References

1. PLASMA-Lab. https://project.inria.fr/plasma-lab/
2. Abdulla, P.A., Jonsson, B., Nilsson, M., d'Orso, J., Saksena, M.: Regular model checking for LTL(MSO). Int. J. Softw. Tools Technol. Transfer **14**(2), 223–241 (2012)
3. Basso, A., Bolotov, A., Basukoski, A., Getov, V., Henrio, L., Urbanski, M.: Specification and verification of reconfiguration protocols in grid component systems. In: Proceedings of the 3rd IEEE Conference on Intelligent Systems (2006)
4. Cavalcante, E., Batista, T., Oquendo, F.: Supporting dynamic software architectures: from architectural description to implementation. In: Proceedings of the 12th Working IEEE/IFIP Conference on Software Architecture, pp. 31–40. IEEE Computer Society, Washington, D.C. (2015)
5. Cavalcante, E., Oquendo, F., Batista, T.: Architecture-based code generation: from π-ADL architecture descriptions to implementations in the go language. In: Avgeriou, P., Zdun, U. (eds.) ECSA 2014. LNCS, vol. 8627, pp. 130–145. Springer, Heidelberg (2014)
6. Cavalcante, E., Quilbeuf, J., Traonouez, L.M., Oquendo, F., Batista, T., Legay, A.: Statistical model checking of dynamic software architectures. In: Margaria, T., Steffen, B. (eds.) ISoLA 2016, Part I. LNCS, vol. 9952, pp. 806–820. Springer, Heidelberg (2016)
7. Cho, S.M., Kim, H.H., Cha, S.D., Bae, D.H.: Specification and validation of dynamic systems using temporal logic. IEE Proc. Softw. **148**(4), 135–140 (2001)
8. Clarke Jr., E.M., Grumberg, O., Peled, D.A.: Model Checking. The MIT Press, Cambridge (1999)
9. Corbett, J.C., Dwyer, M.B., Hatcliff, J.: Robby: expressing checkable properties of dynamic systems: the Bandera specification language. Int. J. Softw. Tools Technol. Transfer **4**(1), 34–56 (2002)
10. Dormoy, J., Kouchnarenko, O., Lanoix, A.: Using temporal logic for dynamic reconfigurations of components. In: Barbosa, L.S., Lumpe, M. (eds.) FACS 2010. LNCS, vol. 6921, pp. 200–217. Springer, Heidelberg (2012)
11. Hérault, T., Lassaigne, R., Magniette, F., Peyronnet, S.: Approximate probabilistic model checking. In: Steffen, B., Levi, G. (eds.) VMCAI 2004. LNCS, vol. 2937, pp. 73–84. Springer, Heidelberg (2004)
12. Hoeffding, W.: Probability inequalities for sums of bounded random variables. J. Am. Stat. Assoc. **58**(301), 13–30 (1963)

13. Jegourel, C., Legay, A., Sedwards, S.: A platform for high performance statistical model checking – PLASMA. In: Flanagan, C., König, B. (eds.) TACAS 2012. LNCS, vol. 7214, pp. 498–503. Springer, Heidelberg (2012)
14. Jha, S.K., Clarke, E.M., Langmead, C.J., Legay, A., Platzer, A., Zuliani, P.: A Bayesian approach to model checking biological systems. In: Degano, P., Gorrieri, R. (eds.) CMSB 2009. LNCS, vol. 5688, pp. 218–234. Springer, Heidelberg (2009)
15. Kim, Y., Choi, O., Kim, M., Baik, J., Kim, T.H.: Validating software reliability early through statistical model checking. IEEE Softw. **30**(3), 35–41 (2013)
16. Laplante, S., Lassaigne, R., Magniez, F., Peyronnet, S., de Rougemont, M.: Probabilistic abstraction for model checking: an approach based on property testing. ACM Trans. Comput. Logic **8**(4), 20 (2007)
17. Lefebvre, M.: Applied Probability and Statistics. Springer, New York (2006)
18. Legay, A., Delahaye, B., Bensalem, S.: Statistical model checking: an overview. In: Barringer, H., et al. (eds.) RV 2010. LNCS, vol. 6418, pp. 122–135. Springer, Heidelberg (2010)
19. Legay, A., Viswanathan, M.: Statistical model checking: challenges and perspectives. Int. J. Softw. Tools Technol. Transfer **17**(4), 369–376 (2015)
20. Magee, J., Kramer, J.: Dynamic structure in software architectures. In: Proceedings of the 4th ACM SIGSOFT Symposium on Foundations of Software Engineering, pp. 3–14. ACM, New York (1996)
21. Mateescu, R., Oquendo, F.: π-AAL: an architecture analysis language for formally specifying and verifying structural and behavioural properties of software architectures. ACM SIGSOFT Softw. Eng. Notes **31**(2), 1–19 (2006)
22. Mazzara, M., Bhattacharyya, A.: On modelling and analysis of dynamic reconfiguration of dependable real-time systems. In: Proceedings of the Third International Conference on Dependability, pp. 173–181 (2010)
23. Oquendo, F.: π-ADL: an architecture description language based on the higher-order typed π-calculus for specifying dynamic and mobile software architectures. ACM SIGSOFT Softw. Eng. Notes **29**(3), 1–14 (2004)
24. Pnueli, A.: The temporal logics of programs. In: Proceedings of the 18th Annual Symposium on Foundations of Computer Science, pp. 46–57. IEEE Computer Society, Washington, D.C. (1977)
25. Sen, K., Viswanathan, M., Agha, G.: Statistical model checking of black-box probabilistic systems. In: Alur, R., Peled, D.A. (eds.) CAV 2004. LNCS, vol. 3114, pp. 202–215. Springer, Heidelberg (2004)
26. Taylor, R.N., Medvidovic, N., Dashofy, E.M.: Software Architecture: Foundations, Theory, and Practice. Wiley, Hoboken (2010)
27. Younes, H.L.S., Kwiatkowska, M., Norman, G., Parker, D.: Numerical vs. statistical probabilistic model checking. Int. J. Softw. Tools Technol. Transfer **8**(3), 216–228 (2006)
28. Younes, H.L.S., Simmons, R.G.: Probabilistic verification of discrete event systems using acceptance sampling. In: Brinksma, E., Larsen, K.G. (eds.) CAV 2002. LNCS, vol. 2404, p. 223. Springer, Heidelberg (2002)
29. Younes, H.L.S.: Verification and planning for stochastic processes with asynchronous events. Doctoral dissertation, Carnegie Mellon University (2004)
30. Zhang, P., Muccini, H., Li, B.: A classification and comparison of model checking software architecture techniques. J. Syst. Softw. **83**(5), 723–744 (2010)

On Two Friends for Getting Correct Programs

Automatically Translating Event B Specifications to Recursive Algorithms in RODIN

Zheng Cheng[1], Dominique Méry[2(✉)], and Rosemary Monahan[1]

[1] Computer Science Department, Maynooth University, Co. Kildare, Ireland
zcheng@cs.nuim.ie, rosemary.monahan@nuim.ie
[2] LORIA, Université de Lorraine,
Campus Scientifique, BP 70239, 54506 VandœUvre-lès-nancy, France
dominique.mery@loria.fr

Abstract. We report on our progress-to-date in implementing a software development environment which integrates the efforts of two formal software engineering techniques: program refinement as supported by EVENT B and program verification as supported by the Spec# programming system. Our objective is to improve the usability of formal verification tools by providing a general framework for integrating these two approaches to software verification. We show how the two approaches Correctness-by-Construction and Post-hoc Verification can be used in a productive way. Here, we focus on the final steps in this process where the final concrete specification is transformed into an executable algorithm. We present EB2RC, a plug-in for the RODIN platform, that reads in an EVENT B model and uses the control framework introduced during its refinement to generate a graphical representation of the executable algorithm. EB2RC also generates a recursive algorithm that is easily translated into executable code. We illustrate our technique through case studies and their analysis.

1 Introduction

The problem that we address is as follows: Given a program specification how do we provide an integrated software development environment in which we can (a) refine the specification into one that is algorithmic and (b) automatically verify that the derived algorithm meets the specification?[1] Our proposed solution is to combine the efforts of two formal software engineering techniques: program refinement as supported by EVENT B [1] and program verification as supported by the Spec# Programming System [3]. Our objective is to improve the usability of formal verification tools by providing a general framework for integrating these two approaches to software verification. We focus on the strengths of each so that

---

[1] We acknowledge the Irish Research Council and Campus France for the joint funding of this research collaboration via the Ulysses scheme 2013. This work was supported by grant ANR-13-INSE-0001 (The IMPEX Project http://impex.gforge.inria.fr) from the Agence Nationale de la Recherche (ANR).

T. Margaria and B. Steffen (Eds.): ISoLA 2016, Part I, LNCS 9952, pp. 821–838, 2016.
DOI: 10.1007/978-3-319-47166-2_57

their integration makes the verification task more approachable for users. The final architecture induces a methodology which is useful for the specification, the construction and the verification of correct sequential algorithms.

Here, we report on progress in implementing our integrated software development environment. The input to our system is an abstract specification which is then refined into a more concrete specification using the EVENT B modelling language and its associated tool-set, the RODIN platform. The output from our system is a concrete Spec# program containing both the executable code and the proof obligations that are necessary for its automatic verification. Here, we focus on the later steps in this process where the final concrete specification is transformed into an executable algorithm. We present a plug-in for the RODIN platform that reads in an EVENT B model and uses the control framework introduced during its refinement to generate both a graphical representation of the executable algorithm, and a recursive algorithm that is easily translated into executable code.

In [10], we presented and verified the transformations involved in generating executable code from Event B. We verified the correctness of the transformed executable code in a static program verification environment for C# programs, namely the Spec# programming system.

In this paper, we focus on implementing one of the core transformations, which is the final concrete specification is transformed into an executable recursive algorithm. This has been implemented by the EB2RC, a plug-in for the RODIN platform. We analysis the impact of our tool through several case studies. The analysis leads us to identify and discuss on the strengths of program refinement and post-hoc program verification so that their integration makes the verification task more approachable for users.

Paper organization. We provide a brief overview of program refinement as supported by EVENT B (Sect. 2). We then give an overview of our framework for refinement based program verification (Sect. 3). The technical details of our translation procedure and its implementation as EB2RC are presented in Sect. 4. The impact of our tool is shown in Sect. 5. An analysis of more case studies that illustrate our technique and our conclusion are then presented in Sects. 6 and 7 respectively.

2   The Event B Modelling Framework

EVENT B [1] is a formal method for system-level modelling and analysis. An EVENT B model is defined via *contexts* which define the static components of the model and *machines* which define the dynamic components of the model. EVENT B *machines* are characterized by a finite list x of *state variables*, modified by a finite list of *events*, where an invariant $I(x)$ states properties that must always be satisfied by the variables x and maintained by the events. For an example see events *find* and *fail* in Sect. 5 which provides for an initial model of a binary search algorithm.

Each event has three main parts: a list of local parameters, a guard G and a relation R over values denoted *pre*-values (x) and *post*-values (x') of state variables. When the guard holds the actions in the event body modify the state variables according to the relation R. A *before–after* predicate $BA(e)(x, x')$ associated with each event describes the event as a logical predicate for expressing the relationship linking values of the state variables just before, and just after, the *execution* of event e. The most common representation of an event has the form

$$\text{ANY } t \text{ WHERE } G(t, x) \text{ THEN } x : |(R(x, x', t)) \text{ END}$$

where t is a local parameter and the event actions establish $x : |(R(x, x', t))$. The form is semantically equivalent to $\exists t \cdot (G(t, x) \land R(x, x', t))$.

2.1   Verifying Event B Models

The EVENT B modelling language is supported by the RODIN platform [12]. These both provide facilities for editing machines, refinements, contexts and projects, for generating proof obligations corresponding to a given property, for proving proof obligations in an automatic or/and interactive process and for animating models. Note that our models can only express *safety* and *invariance* properties, which are state properties. Proof obligations produced via the RODIN platform (see Listing 1) include that the initialisation event establishes the invariant I, that the event e preserves the invariant I and that the event e is feasible with respect to the invariant I. By proving feasibility, we prove that $BA(e)(x, y)$ provides an after-state whenever $grd(e)(x)$ holds. This means that the guard indeed represents the enabling condition of the event.

- (INV1) $Init(x) \Rightarrow I(x)$
- (INV2) $I(x) \land BA(e)(x, x') \Rightarrow I(x')$
- (FIS) $I(x) \land grd(e)(x) \Rightarrow \exists y.BA(e)(x, y)$
- (GLU) $I(x) \land J(x, y) \land BA(f)(y, y') \Rightarrow \exists x' \cdot (BA(e)(x, x') \land J(x', y'))$
- (SKIP) $I(x) \land J(x, y) \land BA(f)(y, y') \Rightarrow J(x, y')$

Listing 1: EVENT B proof obligations

Refinement of an EVENT B model is achieved by extending the list of state variables (and possibly suppressing some of them), by refining each abstract event to a set of possible concrete versions, and by adding new events. The abstract (x) and concrete (y) state variables are linked by means of a *glueing invariant* $J(x, y)$ which must be maintained throughout the system modelling. A number of proof obligations generated by each refinement step (see Listing 2) ensure that each abstract event is correctly refined by its corresponding concrete version, each new event refines *skip*, no new event takes control forever and relative deadlock freedom is preserved. Through refinement we can enrich our EVENT B models in a step-by-step manner and validate each decision step as we construct the final concrete model. This is the foundation of the correct-by-construction approach [7].

2.2   The Call-as-event Paradigm

The main idea of our methodology is based on the call-as-event paradigm [9]. It expresses the consequences on the correct-by-construction approach. In this section, we give a short summary of the method.

Abrial [1] shows how sequential programs can be developed by the EVENT B refinement approach. He lists rules for producing sequential programs by merging events. Kourie and Watson [6] illustrates the use of Morgan's refinement calculus for developing sequential programs without any proof assistant support. Both approaches are based on the same idea of developing invariants to prove verification conditions. However, developing invariants is generally not an easy task. The refinement-based development, which involves several steps of refinements, makes this task even more difficult (i.e. to glue/synchronize the developed invariants across refinements).

The call-as-event paradigm initiates the development of a sequential program by stating its specification (i.e. inputs-outputs behaviours through the pre/post-conditions) as abstract events in an abstract model. Then, the subsequent refinements introduce more concrete models, based on an inductive definition of the outputs with respect to the input. Each concrete model contains concrete events that aim to compute the same sequential program under development, but with more detail of the computation.

The essential idea of the call-as-event paradigm is that the concrete event can be expressed in a way to represent a procedure call (by following a straightforward syntactic naming convention for events [10]), which makes refinement proofs easier: (a) the control variables can be introduced over the events for structuring the inductive computation. (b) the invariants can be defined in a simpler way by analysing the specification of calls.

Specifically, the call-as-event paradigm has three types of events to be used in a concrete model:

- Basic events. An event e is a basic event if it represents a sequence of atomic computation steps.
- Recursive call events. An event e is a recursive call event if it corresponds to the call of the procedure under development.
- Non-recursive call events. An event e is a non-recursive call event if it corresponds to the call of another procedure.

The type of the events are distinguished by their event name. The recursive and non-recursive call events are prefixed with rec and call respectively, followed by the sub-procedure to be called. Moreover, to ensure the soundness of the program development, the sub-procedure to be called should have been defined/specified by an EVENT B machine, since the developed program should not call a miracle procedure (i.e. a procedure that does not exists). This is a incremental development strategy, where the developer can focus on developing the main-procedure, reuse of developed specifications of sub-procedures and stage their development using the same call-as-event paradigm.

In summary, the refinement process that based on the call-as-event paradigm is straightforward, and writing invariant becomes easier for following the inductive property defining the computation to program. In the next section, we show how we interact with the Spec# language.

3 An Overview of Our Integrated Development Framework

Our integrated development framework for implementing abstract EVENT B models brings together the strengths of the refinement based approaches and verification based approaches to software development. In particular, our framework supports:

1. Splitting the abstract specification to be solved into its component specifications.
2. Refining these specifications into a concrete model using EVENT B and the RODIN platform.
3. Transforming the concrete model into algorithms that can be directly implemented as real source code using graph visualisation and applying code generation transformations.
4. Verifying the iterative algorithm in the automatic program verification environment of Spec#.

In this paper we focus on the transformations involved in item number three. First we provide an overview of our integrated development framework to help set the context of our work. Figure 1 provides an overview of our framework for refinement based program verification. The problem to be solved is stated as a collection of method contracts, in the form of a Spec# program. Spec# is a formal language for API contracts (influenced by JML, AsmL, and Eiffel), which extends C# through a rich assertion language that allows the specification of objects through class invariants, field annotations, and method specifications [2,3]. Spec# comes with a sound programming methodology that allows the compiler to emit run-time checks at compile time, recording the assertions in the specification as meta-data for consumption by downstream tools. This allows the analysis of program correctness before allowing the program to be executed.

Note that in the traditional verification approach, the programmer provides both the specification and its implementation. In our integrated development framework we use model refinement in EVENT B to construct the Spec# implementation from its specification. This refinement also generates the proof obligations that must be discharged as part of the verification. We add these as invariants and assertions in the program so that its verification is completely automatic with the Spec# programming system. The result is a program, from which we can obtain a *cross-proof*, which verifies that the refinement process generates a program, which correctly implements its contract.

The EVENT B refinement square (with nodes PREPOST, CONTEXT, PROCESS and CONTROL) in Fig. 1, provides the mechanism for deriving annotations via refinement. It can be explained briefly as follows:

- The EVENT B machine PREPOST contains events, which have the same contract as that expressed in the original pre/post contract. This machine SEES the EVENT B CONTEXT, which expresses static information about the machine.
- The EVENT B machine PROCESS refines PREPOST generating a concrete specification that satisfies the contract. This machine SEES the EVENT B context CONTROL, which adds control information for the new machine.
- The labelled actions REFINES, SEES and EXTENDS, are supported by the RODIN platform and are checked *completely* using the proof assistant provided by RODIN.

The result of the refinement is the EVENT B machine PROCESS, which contains the refined events and the proof obligations that must be discharged in order to prove that the refinement is correct. The transformation of this EVENT B machine PROCESS into a concrete iterative OPTIMISED ALGORITHM is achieved via our EB2RC tool (Sect. 4) and removing recursion [10].

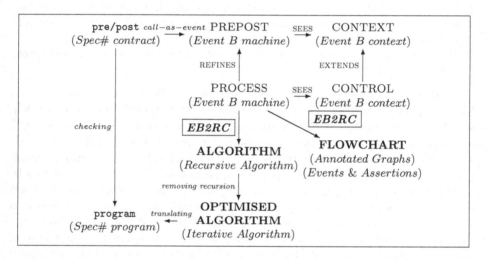

Fig. 1. An overview of our integrated development framework to combine program refinement with program verification

4   EB2RC: A Tool for Translating Event B Models to Recursive Code

We support the generation of a concrete recursive algorithm ALGORITHM from the EVENT B machine PROCESS with EB2RC, a plug-in for RODIN which we have developed. In the sections that follow we describe the generation process in detail.

4.1   Overview of Our EB2RC Plugin

As seen in Fig. 1 the result of the refinement is a concrete EVENT B machine PROCESS, which is the input of our EB2RC plugin. Then, our plugin generates a recursive algorithm (ALGORITHM) in text format, and a graphical representation of the recursive algorithm (FLOWCHART) to improve comprehensibility. The textual recursive algorithm can be easily translated into either executable code or artefacts of the post-hoc verification tools (e.g. Spec#).

Our approach for generating a recursive algorithm from a concrete machine is based on a systematic transformation using control labels: each machine has a start and an end label, and each event is characterised by a current label and a next label. The purpose of these control labels is to *simulate* the different computation steps of the developed recursive algorithm. In other words, the computation steps of the recursive algorithm are abstracted by a acyclic graph of control labels, where these labels describe the set of events used in the computation.

Specifically, our plugin first ensures the input machine is ready for recursive algorithm generation by design extra proof obligations (Sect. 4.2). Then, it extracts essential information (e.g. control labels) from the concrete machine (Sect. 4.3). This step is guided by a auxiliary configuration file provided by the user (i.e. the developer of the concrete machine). Next, based on the essential information extracted, our plugin systematically reconstructs a recursive algorithm in textual and graphical representation (Sect. 4.4).

Our EB2RC plugin is written in Java. It interacts with APIs of the RODIN platform (v2.7) to extract information from the concrete machine of interest. Then, after automatic systematic reconstruction, our plugin directly generates textual recursive algorithm, and a input file for the *Dot* tool of *GraphViz*, thereby producing its graphical representation.

4.2   Proof Obligations

A set of extra proof obligations are generated during the *generating-algorithm* stage in our Integrated Development Framework (Fig. 1). They are to ensure that the EVENT B machine can be safely translated into a recursive algorithm, for example:

- The annotated control labels in the actions and guards of each event are different (i.e. the event always progresses);
- Only one event does not have any control labels in its guards (i.e. the start event);
- Only one event does not have any control labels in its actions (i.e. the end event);
- The labels in an EVENT B machine forms an acyclic graph;

4.3   Extracting Information from Event B Machine

To guide our plugin to proceed, we require the user to define the following information into a configuration file:

- The name of the input EVENT B machine (i.e. the concrete EVENT B machine to be processed).
- The name of the control label used by the input EVENT B machine.
- The name of the start control label used by the input EVENT B machine.

Then, based on the configuration file the user provided, our EB2RC plugin extracts essential information from each event of the input machine. One of the essential information our plugin interested in is the *current* and *next* labels of each event. The control labels are used to control the order in which the events are combined to achieve a recursive algorithm. The *current* label informs us of the start state of an event, whereas the *next* label of an event determines which events will follow it. The *current* and *next* control labels are derived from the guards and actions of each event respectively.

Another essential information our plugin recorded is the type of each event. During the refinements, we distinguish three types of events by their names: (a) basic events represent a sequence of atomic computation steps, whose names are without any prefixes. (b) recursive events represent a computation step of a recursive call, whose names are prefixed with *rec*. (c) call events represent a computation step of a external function call, whose names are prefixed with *call*. By categorising events by their types, EB2RC will treat them differently while extracting information.

Our plugin also records the guards and actions of each event. To facilitate textual and graphical recursive algorithm generation, we perform some optimizations: First, for events of basic type, all the guards and deterministic actions[2] are recorded unless they reference control labels. Second, for events of recursive and call type, the guards and actions are derived from their event name. This becomes practical because of the naming convention of our approach [10], i.e. we require the guards and actions need to be explicitly referred by the name of the events of recursive and call type.

Finally, our plugin needs to store the next events of an target event. An event x is regarded as the next event of a target event y if the current label of x equals to the next label of y. In this manner, each event can be related to other events as in a transition system.

4.4 Representing Extracted Information

An intuitive diagram allows easier understanding of the algorithm, and is a prerequisite for modularizing complex algorithms. Therefore, we construct a control flow graph for the input EVENT B machine by using extracted information.

We start by consulting the configuration file for the start control label used by the input EVENT B machine. Then, we find an event of the input with this start label as its current label, printing its actions and guards (according to the grammar of the *Dot* language), and recursively apply the same printing procedure to its next events.

---

[2] In EVENT B, two types of actions (*becomes_such_that* and *becomes_in_set* actions) are non-deterministic.

Representing the developed EVENT B machine in textual format is similar to the generation of graphical format, only differs in how it is printed. We chose a general syntax that can be understand by the programmers to print, and it is straightforward to customize the printing to generate artefacts for the post-hoc verification tools (e.g. Spec#). Examples of generating textual and graphical representation for a recursive binary search algorithm is given in Sect. 5. More applications can be seen in Sect. 6.

5   Case Study: The Binary Search Problem

We detail the complete development by refinement of an algorithm which solves the problem of *searching for a value in a table*. We demonstrate concrete example of the output of our EB2RC plugin, which is a recursive algorithm and its graphical representation. Then, we discuss our experience of integrating two popular approaches to formal software development, i.e. refinement and post-hoc verification approaches.

5.1   Specifying the Binary Search Problem

The input parameters of the *binsearch* procedure are: a sorted array t; the bounds of the array within which the algorithm should search (lo and hi); and the value for which the algorithm should search (val). Output parameters are $result$ and a boolean flag ok that indicates if $t(result) = val$. The procedures pre and post conditions are presented in Algorithm 1.

Algorithm 1. *binsearch(t, val, lo, hi, ok, result)*

precondition :	$\begin{pmatrix} t \in 0..t.Length \longrightarrow \mathbb{N} \\ \forall k.k \in lo..hi - 1 \Rightarrow t(k) \leq t(k+1) \\ val \in \mathbb{N} \\ l, h \in 0..t.Length \\ lo \leq hi \end{pmatrix}$
postcondition :	$\begin{pmatrix} ok = TRUE \Rightarrow t(result) = val \\ ok = FALSE \Rightarrow (\forall i.i \in lo..hi \Rightarrow t(i) \neq val \end{pmatrix}$

The array t is sorted with respect to the ordering over integers and a simple inductive analysis is applied leading to a binary search strategy. The specification is first expressed by two events corresponding to the two possible cases (Listing 3): either a key exists in the array t containing the value val, or there is no such key. These two events correspond to the two possible resulting *calls* to the procedure *binsearch(t, val, lo, hi; ok, result)*:

- EVENT find is $binsearch(t, val, lo, hi; ok, result)$ where $ok = TRUE$
- EVENT fail is $binsearch(t, val, lo, hi; ok, result)$ where $ok = FALSE$

```
EVENT find
   ANY   j
   WHERE
      grd1 : j ∈ lo .. hi
      grd2 : t(j) = val
   THEN
      act1 : ok := TRUE
      act2 : i := j
   END
```

```
EVENT fail
   WHEN
      grd1 : ∀k·k ∈ lo .. hi ⇒ t(k) ≠ val
   THEN
      act1 : ok := FALSE
   END
```

Listing 2: The specification of the binary search algorithm in Event B

These two events form the machine called *binsearch1* which is refined to obtain *binsearch2* (corresponding to PROCESS of Fig. 1). In addition to these events, the events of this refined machine contains a new control label, l, which *simulates* how the binary search is achieved. We illustrate two of the events of *binsearch2* in Listing 3. Its complete refinement is presented in [10].

```
EVENT rightsearchOK
   REFINES find
   ANY   j
   WHERE
      grd1 : l = middle
      grd2 : val > t(mi)
      grd3 : j ∈ mi + 1 .. hi
      grd4 : t(j) = val
      grd5 : mi + 1 ≤ hi
   THEN
      act1 : i := j
      act2 : ok := TRUE
   END
```

```
EVENT rightsearchKO
   REFINES fail
   WHEN
      grd1 : l = middle
      grd2 : val > t(mi)
      grd4 : ∀j·j ∈ mi + 1 .. hi ⇒ t(j) ≠ val
      grd5 : mi + 1 ≤ hi
   THEN
      act2 : ok := FALSE
   END
```

Listing 3: Refining the specification of the binary search algorithm (shown in Listing 3) in Event B

5.2   Automatic Generation of the Algorithm

The result of our translation is two-fold. Firstly, to help people comprehend the algorithm, EB2RC reads in the EVENT B machine and visualizes it as in Fig. 2. Specifically, we draw a circular node to present each event. The guards of each event are indicated by the arrows, and the actions of the event are indicated in the text of the rectangular node belonging to each arrow. The outcome of each event is transitions to other events, which is indicated by directed edges between two circular nodes.

Secondly, a textual representation of the binary search algorithm is constructed by the EB2RC. The produced algorithm (as shown in Algorithm 2) has been compared to the algorithm produced by hand by the authors. The two algorithms are identical up to a slight reformatting.

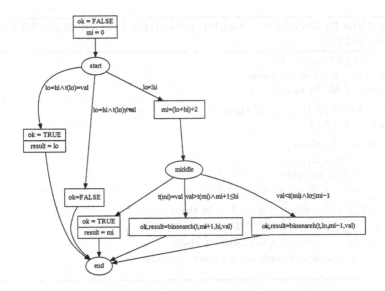

Fig. 2. Visualized representation of the binary search algorithm

Table 1. Proof effort of our refinement approach for the binary search case study

Model	Total	Auto	Manual	Reviewed	Undischarged	% auto
binsearch1	5	5	0	0	0	100 %
binsearch2	71	63	8	0	0	78 %

The proof effort of our refinement approach for the Binary Search case study is illustrated in Table 1. The first abstract model is proved automatically and the second concrete model is automatic in 78 % of its proof obligations.

5.3   Discussion

Upon this point, we have shown that our technique assists in discovering a *good* inductive process which will lead to a recursive solution. However, we do not take dynamic properties (e.g. range of array index) of general programming languages into consideration while applying our technique. As a result, it is possible to produce unreliable executable code from the recursive algorithm we generated. To our knowledge, checking dynamic properties of general programming languages is not currently supported by the EVENT B approach. It would be cumbersome to mimic this feature in EVENT B for every developed algorithm. Whereas, Spec# checks several dynamic properties of the C# language by default.

The essential idea of our integrated development framework is to bring together the strengths of the refinement based approaches and post-hoc verification based approaches to software development. This kind of interoperability between approaches allows several techniques to interact with each other

---

Algorithm 2. Recursive Algorithm binsearch(t,lo,hi,val;ok,result) generated by EB2RC

$ok := FALSE; mi := 0;$
if $lo = hi \land t(lo) = val$ **then**
 $\quad\lfloor\ ok := TRUE; result := lo;$
else if $lo = hi \land t(lo) \neq val$ **then**
 $\quad\lfloor\ ok := FALSE;$
else if $lo < hi$ **then**
 $\quad mi := (lo + hi) \div 2;$
 $\quad$**if** $t(mi) = val$ **then**
 $\quad\quad\lfloor\ ok := TRUE; result := mi;$
 $\quad$**else if** $val > t(mi) \land mi + 1 \leq hi$ **then**
 $\quad\quad\lfloor\ ok, result := binsearch(t, mi + 1, hi, val);$
 $\quad$**else if** $val < t(mi) \land lo \leq mi - 1$ **then**
 $\quad\quad\lfloor\ ok, result := binsearch(t, lo, mi - 1, val);$

(e.g. share information, chain the proof obligations) so that they can collectively prove tasks/theorems more automatically than any one of them could prove in isolation.

Kaufmann and Moore, based on their experience, suggest that what prevents interoperability between verifiers is that the time it takes to interact with another verifier is often dominated by the time it takes to convert a problem into the representation used by the "foreign" verifier [5]. In our experience, this phenomenon also applies to the interoperability between refinement based approaches and post-hoc verification based approaches.

Take the binary search algorithm we developed in this section for example. We find that the equivalent recursive program in Spec# time-out when it is verified. In fact, our experience shows that Spec# does not perform very well on recursive program (due to the two different semantics of assertion languages).

Our integrated development framework takes this into consideration. As shown in Fig. 1, we suggest to translate every recursive algorithm ALGORITHM into a partially annotated and iterative OPTIMISED ALGORITHM to be verified within the Spec# Programming System. In [10], we have proposed and proved a sound translation procedure from ALGORITHM to OPTIMISED ALGORITHM to perform this task. For example, the iterative version of the binary search algorithm in Spec# is shown in Fig. 3.

By sending this program to Spec#, Spec# reports the program as verified. No user interaction is required in this verification as all assertions required (preconditions, postconditions and loop invariants) have been generated as part of the refinement and transformation of the initial abstract specification into the final iterative algorithm. The automatic verification of the final Spec# program is available online at http://www.rise4fun.com/SpecSharp/kyKW.

```
class BS {
  int BinarySearch(int [] t, int val, int lo, int hi, bool ok)
    requires 0 <= lo && lo < t.Length && 0 <= hi && hi < t.Length;
    requires lo <= hi && 0 < t.Length;
    requires forall{int i in (0:t.Length),int j in (i:t.Length);t[i]<=t[j]};
    ensures -1 <= result && result < t.Length;
    ensures (0 <= result && result < t.Length)==> t[result] == val;
    ensures result == -1 ==> forall {int i in (lo..hi); t[i] != val};
  { int mi = (lo + hi) / 2;
    while (!(lo == hi && t[lo] == val) || ( lo == hi && t[lo] != val)
                || (lo < hi && (mi == (lo + hi) /2) && t[mi] == val))
      invariant 0 <= lo && lo < t.Length && 0 <= hi && hi < t.Length;
      invariant 0 <= mi && mi < t.Length;
      invariant (val < t[mi]) ==> forall {int i in (mi..hi); t[i] != val};
      invariant (val > t[mi]) ==> forall {int i in (lo..mi); t[i] != val};
    { mi = (lo + hi) / 2;
      if ((mi+1 <= hi) && (val > t[mi])) lo = mi +1;
      else if ((lo <= mi-1) && (val < t[mi])) hi = mi - 1;
    }
    if ((lo == hi) && (t[lo] == val)) {ok = true; return lo;}
    else{
      if ((lo == hi) && (t[lo] != val)) {ok = false; return -1;}
      else if ((lo < hi) && (t[mi] == val)) {ok = true; return mi;}
      else {ok = false; return -1;}
    }
  }
}
```

Fig. 3. Binary Search C# program corresponding to the generated iterative procedure.

6   Further Case Studies

We now summarize several case studies that have been developed using our methodology and tool-kit. We give the details of the development of an abstract Event B model into a recursive algorithm by summarizing the number of proof obligations required for each case study. Moreover, the procedures used for discharging proof obligations can help understand the automation of this process.

Insertion Sort: The effort of formalisation of the insertion sort algorithm lies in simplifying how to express inserting an element into a sorted list. Our methodology starts with a procedure *sortingspec* which is simply specified by an event *modelling* the pre/post specification of the insertion sort algorithm. As shown in Table 2, during the development, 75 % of the proof obligations is automatically discharged in both the initial specification and in the refined machine *sortingref*.

As shown in Algorithm 3, the call of the procedure **inserting** illustrates the reusability of an already developed problem within our MOdels DEveloped on the shelf (MODES) library of verified procedures. Proof obligations associated with calling these procedures must be discharged to prove the correctness of this procedure call.

Moreover, in this case study, proofs which are manually discharged relates to permutations of the input array. However, they are easier to prove than in the classical iterative algorithms for sorting, since the complexity is hidden by the recursive call.

Exponentiation: This problem is to compute the function a^b using the fact that when b is even, the value to compute is transformed into $\left(a^2\right)^{b/2}$ and when

---

Algorithm 3. Recursive Algorithm sorting(m,t;st) generated by EB2RC

$st := t$; $at := t$;

if $m = 1$ **then**
$\quad \lfloor \; st := ide; t$;

else if $m \neq 1$ **then**
$\quad \mid \; at := sorting(m - 1, t)$;
$\quad \lfloor \; st := inserting(m, at)$;

Table 2. Proof effort of our refinement approach for the insertion sort case study

Model	Total	Auto	Manual	Reviewed	Undischarged	% auto
sortingspec	4	3	1	0	0	75 %
sortingref	45	33	1	0	11	75 %

b is odd, the value to compute is $a^{b-1} \times a$. These two ways to compute the exponentiation are easy to express in the following EVENT B context:

$axm1 : a \in \mathbb{N}_1 \wedge b \in \mathbb{N} \wedge p \in \mathbb{N} \times \mathbb{N} \rightarrow \mathbb{N}$
$axm4 : \forall n \cdot n \in \mathbb{N}_1 \Rightarrow p(n \mapsto 0) = 1$
$axm5 : \forall n, m \cdot n \in \mathbb{N} \wedge m \in \mathbb{N}_1 \Rightarrow p(n \mapsto m) = p(n \mapsto m - 1) * n$
$axm6 : \forall n, m \cdot n \in \mathbb{N} \wedge m \in \mathbb{N} \wedge m/2 * 2 = m - 1 \Rightarrow p(n \mapsto m) = p((n \mapsto m - 1)) * n$
$axm7 : \forall n, m \cdot n \in \mathbb{N} \wedge m \in \mathbb{N} \wedge m/2 * 2 = m \Rightarrow p(n \mapsto m) = p((n * n \mapsto m/2))$

As shown in Table 3, our methodology leads to two refinement steps to develop the exponentiation algorithm. During the refinement, the Rodin proof system automatically *knows* which axioms to use in the context. However, in our experience, the proof obligations involves these axioms are difficult to prove automatically, which results the score of automatically discharged proof obligations to be 79 % in the refined machine. Finally, the refinement of the exponentiation algorithm generates the Algorithm 4 by the EB2RC.

Table 3. Proof effort of our refinement approach for the exponentiation case study

Model	Total	Auto	Manual	Reviewed	Undischarged	% auto
expspec	4	4	0	0	0	100 %
expref	84	66	18	0	0	79 %

Maximum of a List: The maximum of a list is quite complex for the first model which stating the specification of this algorithm. However, we find that this complexity in the specification contributes to the proof automation in the

---

Algorithm 4. Recursive Algorithm exp(u,v;r) generated by EB2RC

$r := 0; u := 0; v := 0; temp := 0;$
if $b = 0$ **then**
  $\lfloor\ r := 1;$
else if $b \neq 0$ **then**
  $\quad$ **if** $b \div 2 * 2 = b$ **then**
    $\quad \lfloor\ u := a * a; v := b \div 2; r := exp(u, v);$
  $\quad$ **else if** $b \div 2 * 2 = b - 1$ **then**
    $\quad \quad \lfloor\ u := a; v := b - 1;$
    $\quad \quad \quad temp := exp(u, v); r := temp * a;$

Table 4. Proof effort of our refinement approach for the list maximum case study

Model	Total	Auto	Manual	Reviewed	Undischarged	% auto
specmax	5	4	1	0	0	25 %
refmax	49	46	3	0	0	94 %

Algorithm 5. Recursive Algorithm max(f,n,i;m) generated by EB2RC

$m := 0; temp := 0; ftemp := 0;$
if $i = 0$ **then**
  $\lfloor\ m := f(0);$
else if $i \neq 0$ **then**
  $\quad temp := maximum(f, n, i - 1);$
  $\quad$ **if** $f(i) < temp$ **then**
    $\quad \lfloor\ ftemp := temp; m := ftemp;$
  $\quad$ **else if** $f(i) \geq temp$ **then**
    $\quad \quad \lfloor\ ftemp := f(i); m := ftemp;$

---

second model (a score of 94 % as shown in Table 4). The proof obligations that need to manually discharged in the refined model relates to prove the existence of a maximum in a list, which is proved by using a theorem of the context. Finally, Algorithm 5 is generated by EB2RC.

Shortest Paths by Floyd: Floyd's algorithm [4] computes the shortest distances in a graph and is based on an algorithmic design technique called dynamic programming, where simpler sub-problems are first solved before the full problem is solved. It computes a distance matrix from a cost matrix, where the cost of the shortest path between each pair of vertices is $O(|V|^3)$. The set of nodes N is $1..n$, where n is a constant value, and the graph is simply represented by the distance function d ($d \in N \times N \times N \nrightarrow \mathbb{N}$). When the function is not defined, it means that there is no vertex between the two nodes. The relation of the graph is defined as

---

Algorithm 6. Recursive Algorithm floyd(l,a,b,g;D,FD) generated by EB2RC

$D := D0; Fpath := FALSE; FD1 := FALSE; FD2 := FALSE; FD3 := FALSE$;

if $l = 0 \wedge a \mapsto b \in dom(D)$ **then**
  $\llcorner$ $Fpath := TRUE$;

else if $l = 0 \wedge a \mapsto b \in dom(D)$ **then**
  $\llcorner$ $Fpath := FALSE$;

else if $l > 0$ **then**
  $D1, FD1 := floyd(l - 1, a, b, g); D2, FD2 := floyd(l - 1, a, l, g); D3, FD3 := floyd(l - 1, l, b, g)$;
  if $FD1 = TRUE \wedge FD2 = TRUE \wedge FD3 = TRUE \wedge D1 \leq D2 + D3$ **then**
    $\llcorner$ $D(a \mapsto b) := D1; Fpath := TRUE$;

  else if $FD1 = TRUE \wedge FD2 = TRUE \wedge FD3 = TRUE \wedge D1 > D2 + D3$ **then**
    $\llcorner$ $D(a \mapsto b) := D2 + D3; Fpath := TRUE$;

  else if $FD1 = FALSE \wedge FD2 = TRUE \wedge FD3 = TRUE$ **then**
    $\llcorner$ $D(a \mapsto b) := D2 + D3; Fpath := TRUE$;

  else if $FD1 = TRUE \wedge (FD2 = FALSE \vee FD3 = FALSE)$ **then**
    $\llcorner$ $D(a \mapsto b) := D1; Fpath := TRUE$;

  else if $FD1 = FALSE \wedge (FD2 = FALSE \vee FD3 = FALSE)$ **then**
    $\llcorner$ $Fpath := FALSE$;

---

the domain of the function d. n is clearly greater than 1, meaning that the set of nodes is not empty. The distance function d is defined inductively from bottom to top according to the principle of dynamic programming, and axioms define this function. The optimal property is derived from the definition of d itself, because it starts by defining the bottom elements and applies an optimal principle summarized as follows: $D_{i+1}(a, b) = Min(D_i(a, b), D_i(a, i+1) + D_i(i+1, b))$. This means that the distances in D_i represent paths with intermediate vertices smaller than i. D_{i+1} is defined by comparing new paths including $i + 1$. D_i is defined by a partial function over $N \times N \times N$. The partiality of d leads to some possible problems in computing the minimum, and when at least one term is not defined, we should define a specific definition for the resulting term. Floyd's algorithm provides an algorithmic process for obtaining a matrix of all shortest possible paths with respect to a given initial matrix that represents links between nodes together with their distance. The method is applied and leads to compute the function d and to store the value into D. Algorithm 6 is generated by EB2RC.

7   Conclusions and Future Work

In this work, we illustrated the blueprint of our integrated development framework to combine the efforts of two formal software engineering techniques: program refinement as supported by EVENT B and post-hoc program verification as supported by the Spec# programming system. Our goal is to improve the usability of formal verification tools by providing a general framework for integrating these two approaches to software verification. We identified and discussed on the strengths of each so that their integration makes the verification task more approachable for users.

We detailed one of the core steps in our integrated development framework, which is the final concrete specification is transformed into an executable recursive algorithm. This has been implemented by the EB2RC, a plug-in for the RODIN platform, that reads in an Event B model and uses the control framework introduced during the models refinement, to generate both a graphical representation of the executable algorithm and a recursive algorithm that is easily translated into executable code.

This work builds on a method for code generation that is detailed by one of the authors in [8,9] and provides the foundation for an integrated development framework that brings together the world of system modelling and the world of program verification. The EB2ALL code generation tool [11] can also produce a program from the PROCESS machine. However, the control variable is not removed and the resulting code is not structured.

Our experience shows that our approach assists students in developing and understanding the tasks of software specification and verification. Moreover, we used the technique in lectures to demonstrate how the proof process can be made simpler when one uses a recursive program. A recursive program *hides* many aspects of the computations which appear to be magic. The fantasy is obtained by these events modelling recursive calls. The key idea is to use the call-as-event principle. Since the invariants are easy to discover, the proofs are also easier even if the main technical questions lie in the specialisation of prover like arithmetic.

It also makes different forms of formal software development more accessible to software engineers, helping them to build correct and reliable software systems. Future work will include the development of further plugins, which will integrate and facilitate the co-operation between Spec# tools and RODIN tools. One major component of this work is the reuse of annotations generated during the refinement of an Event B model to automatically verify iterative algorithms. Deriving loop invariants using these annotations is our particular interest here.

References

1. Abrial, J.-R.: Modeling in Event-B: System and Software Engineering. Cambridge University Press, Cambridge (2010)
2. Barnett, M., Chang, B.-Y.E., DeLine, R., Jacobs, B., M. Leino, K.R.: Boogie: a modular reusable verifier for object-oriented programs. In: de Boer, F.S., Bonsangue, M.M., Graf, S., de Roever, W.-P. (eds.) FMCO 2005. LNCS, vol. 4111, pp. 364–387. Springer, Heidelberg (2006)
3. Barnett, M., Leino, K.R.M., Schulte, W.: The Spec# programming system: an overview. In: Barthe, G., Burdy, L., Huisman, M., Lanet, J.-L., Muntean, T. (eds.) CASSIS 2004. LNCS, vol. 3362, pp. 49–69. Springer, Heidelberg (2005)
4. Floyd, R.W.: Algorithm 97: shortest path. Commun. ACM **5**(6), 345 (1962)
5. Kaufmann, M., Moore, S.J.: Some key research problems in automated theorem proving for hardware software verification. Revista de la Real Academia de Ciencias Exactas, Físicas y Naturales. Serie A. Matemâticas **98**(1), 181–195 (2004)
6. Kourie, D.G., Watson, B.W.: The Correctness-by-Construction Approach to Programming. Springer, Heidelberg (2012)
7. Leavens, G.T., Abrial, J.-R., Batory, D., Butler, M., Coglio, A., Fisler, K., Hehner, E., Jones, C., Miller, D., Peyton-Jones, S., Sitaraman, M., Smith, D.R., Stump, A.: Roadmap for enhanced languages and methods to aid verification. In: 5th International Conference on Generative Programming and Component Engineering, Portland, Oregon, pp. 221–235. ACM (2006)
8. Méry, D.: A simple refinement-based method for constructing algorithms. ACM SIGCSE Bulletin **41**(2), 51–59 (2009)
9. Méry, D.: Refinement-based guidelines for algorithmic systems. Int. J. Softw. Inform. **3**(2–3), 197–239 (2009)
10. Méry, D., Monahan, R.: Transforming Event-B models into verified C# implementations. In: 1st International Workshop on Verification and Program Transformation, Saint Petersburg, Russia, pp. 57–73. EasyChair (2013)
11. Méry, D., Singh, N.K.: The EB2ALL code generation tool (2011). http://eb2all.loria.fr/
12. Project RODIN. Rigorous open development environment for complex systems (2004). http://rodin-b-sharp.sourceforge.net/

Proof-Carrying Apps: Contract-Based Deployment-Time Verification

Sönke Holthusen, Michael Nieke, Thomas Thüm, and Ina Schaefer[⊠]

Institute of Software Engineering and Automotive Informatics,
TU Braunschweig, Braunschweig, Germany
{s.holthusen,m.nieke,t.thuem,i.schaefer}@tu-bs.de

Abstract. For extensible software platforms in safety-critical domains, it is important that deployed plug-ins work as specified. This is especially true with the prospect of allowing third parties to add plug-ins. We propose a contract-based approach for deployment-time verification. Every plug-in guarantees its functional behavior under a specific set of assumptions towards its environment. With *proof-carrying apps*, we generalize proof-carrying code from proofs to artifacts that facilitate deployment-time verification, where the expected behavior is specified by the means of design-by-contract. With proof artifacts, the conformance of apps to environment assumptions is checked during deployment, even on resource-constrained devices. This procedure prevents unsafe operation by unintended programming mistakes as well as intended malicious behavior. We discuss which criteria a formal verification technique has to fulfill to be applicable to proof-carrying apps and evaluate the verification tools KeY and Soot for proof-carrying apps.

Keywords: Deployment-time verification · Design-by-contract · Software evolution

1 Introduction

A recent development in software development is the consumers' need for customization which can be achieved by several approaches [28]. For instance, frameworks with plug-ins allow for customization and reduction of maintenance effort by code reuse. Functionality does not have to be implemented several times such that developers are able to reduce their code base. Prominent examples are mobile app platforms for smartphones and tablets running on Android and iOS, where users can extend the functionality of the operating system by installing custom apps, such as messengers or games. However, end-users installing apps and plug-ins also poses risks as additional, potentially malicious, code is added. On smartphones, misbehaving third-party apps can be mainly considered a security risk, e. g., by stealing sensitive data. If extensible platforms are also used in

This work was partially supported by the DFG (German Research Foundation) under the Researcher Unit FOR1800: Controlling Concurrent Change (CCC).

© Springer International Publishing AG 2016
T. Margaria and B. Steffen (Eds.): ISoLA 2016, Part I, LNCS 9952, pp. 839–855, 2016.
DOI: 10.1007/978-3-319-47166-2_58

other domains, such as the automotive domain, a misbehaving app might lead to physical damage and even injuries to persons. This is especially relevant when the car producers are eventually opening their platforms for third party plug-ins with access to safety-critical functions like steering or controlling the speed of the car, e. g., advanced driver assistance systems like adaptive cruise control. To support execution of apps within a car, it is mission-critical that the program logic utilizes provided safety-critical interfaces as they are intended to be used, e. g., by abiding by the contracts or by following a certain protocol.

Defensive programming [20] can catch unexpected behavior at runtime, but it cannot prevent it. For example, a car could enter a fail-safe mode, but such situations should be avoided whenever possible. Another way to ensure certain program properties is the use of formal methods, which make it possible to prove that a specific behavior will or will *not* happen. While some program properties can be verified automatically with verification techniques such as theorem proving [27] and software model checking [5,15], interaction is necessary for other properties and verification techniques. However, interaction is impractical in deployment-time verification.

To guarantee global safety properties for assembly language, Necula introduced the concept of proof-carrying code [22]. Under the assumption that the proof generation is harder than checking a proof, the verification of properties is divided into two distinct phases: In the first phase, a proof is created, possibly with user interaction. In the second phase, the proof is merely checked at the code consumer in order to speed up the verification process. Proof-carrying code can handle global safety properties, while extensible platforms call for the ability to support interface-specific specifications. Hence, proof-carrying code has to be generalized to ensure program properties in the context of extensible platforms and to allow local specifications. In this paper, our contributions are the following:

- With proof-carrying apps, we propose a generalization of proof-carrying code to deployment-time verification of apps. In particular, we generalize proof-carrying code from deductive verification to other static verification techniques and generalize proofs to any artifact that simplifies verification, whereas we specify intended behavior by means of contracts (see Sect. 2).
- We discuss criteria for verification techniques that enable their use for deployment-time verification with contracts. We discuss hard criteria, such as the need to run completely automatic, and soft criteria, such as a considerable speed-up due to proofs or other artifacts (see Sect. 3).
- We compare deductive verification, data-flow analyses, and software model checking for their advantages and limitations for proof-carrying apps. Whereas contracts are typically checked with deductive verification, we propose how to check contracts with data-flow analyses and software model checking (see Sect. 4).
- We investigate the applicability of deductive verification with KeY and data-flow analyses with Soot for proof-carrying apps (see Sect. 5).

2   Proof-Carrying Apps

Proof-carrying code was introduced to automatically ensure that a program written in assembly language complies to a specific set of safety policies [22]. This is achieved by delivering a proof with the executable and checking it before the program is executed. The principle is automated by a certifying compiler for C and Java, generating machine code and the required certificate [11,23]. The MOBIUS project applied proof-carrying code to Java and information flow properties [6]. *Proof-carrying apps* are influenced by those approaches.

2.1   Proof-Artifacts for Apps

With proof-carrying apps, we extend proof-carrying code to be used in extensible software platforms, such as black-box frameworks with plug-ins. As an abstraction from the concrete extensible system, we use plug-ins as units of extension, but the general concepts of this paper may be adapted to other approaches as well. A framework provides extension points that can be extended by plug-ins, which itself can provide further extension points to other plug-ins [3].

One way to specify what is necessary for a plug-in to work in an environment of other plug-ins is to capture its assumptions and guarantees towards this environment. We are interested in verifying a plug-in against the (observable) behavior of the other plug-ins and need an appropriate abstraction of the behavior which can be understood as guarantees towards the environment. Additionally, we want to be able to restrict the usage of an API, which is an assumption towards the environment that no plug-in uses the API otherwise. To handle assumptions and guarantees, we use contracts where assumptions are preconditions and guarantees are postconditions [20]. Contracts also allow us to express explicitly who is responsible in the case of an error. The calling plug-in is responsible to ensure the precondition of the called plug-in and therefore for possible errors due to violated preconditions. In that case, the behavior of the called plug-in can not be guaranteed. Developers may use all services provided by available plug-ins and the runtime environment. Furthermore, the contracts abstract from the implementation of a plug-in and form the basis for proof-carrying apps.

Figure 1 shows the basic concept of proof-carrying apps. The platform developers provide contracts for their API. In the first phase, developers write their plug-in, and proof artifacts are created with proof generators and possibly necessary interaction with dedicated experts. The proof artifact supports the developers' claim that their plug-in complies with the contract. Instead of the proof (i. e., certificate) in proof-carrying code, we allow every kind of *(proof) artifact* supporting the verification of a contract. Depending on the used verification technique, manual interaction with the verification tool might be required, e. g., when providing a loop invariant for the proof or applying certain tactics. In the second phase, after the proof artifact is generated, it can automatically be checked by a proof checker using the plug-in and the proof artifact. All the information provided manually in the first phase, such as loop invariants, will

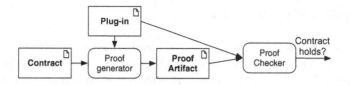

Fig. 1. The basic proof-carrying app concept.

be reused, resulting in a check without interaction being necessary. If the specification holds using the proof artifact, the plug-in can be executed safely with respect to the contract. In the case, the contract does not hold, a possible solution is that the plug-in is not allowed to be executed, and the user receives a warning.

2.2 Application Scenarios

To further motivate our concept of proof-carrying apps, we introduce two application scenarios. The first uses on-device validation, while the second involves a trusted third party for validation purposes.

Scenario 1: On-Device Validation

1. The development team writes the plug-in and creates a proof artifact to support the claim that all relevant specifications are met.
2. The plug-in and the corresponding proof artifact are deployed onto the device.
3. The device uses a trusted proof checker to check whether the provided plug-in complies with the specification using the proof artifact.

This scenario has the advantage of only requiring a very small *trusted computing base* [26]. The only component to be trusted is the proof checker on the device but as it is running on the device the checker has to be small enough and the verification on the device should be much more efficient than those in the first phase. As an extension to the first scenario, we add a trusted third party to our trusted computing base in the second scenario.

Scenario 2: Validation at a Trusted Third Party

1. The development team writes the plug-in and creates a proof artifact to support the claim that all relevant specifications are met.
2. The plug-in and the corresponding proof artifact are submitted to the trusted third party.
3. The *trusted third party* (e. g., the framework operator) checks the proof using a trusted proof checker.
4. If the check is successful, the program is marked as safe, signed cryptographically by the trusted third party, and deployed to the device.
5. On the device, only the signature has to be checked, and the plug-in is executed, if the signature was validated.

The app stores of Android or iOS for smartphones are an example where this scenario could be realized. App developers could submit their plug-in and proof artifacts to the app store where their app is checked. If the proof holds, the app is marked as safe, and it can be downloaded from the store onto the device.

3   Criteria for Deployment-Time Verification with Proof-Carrying Apps

In this section, we discuss the criteria that a verification technique has to fulfill to work with the validation scenarios introduced in Sect. 2. These criteria help to find verification techniques suitable for proof-carrying apps and give a means to compare different techniques. To be usable without user interaction, a proof-carrying app has to be checked *fully automatically* on deployment. Considering that the resources are very limited on device, the time for checking whether the contracts hold using the proof artifact should be *reasonably fast*. We do not want to trust the developers of an app and, hence, cannot trust artifacts deployed by them. In the following, we distinguish between hard criteria being mandatory and soft criteria being desirable.

Automatic Verification. The most important, hard criterion of a verification technique is its ability to check a proof fully automatically. It is not reasonable to assume that users (e. g., drivers of a car) have any knowledge of any verification techniques. While the generation process of the proof artifact may include interactions with developers, the check has to be done without requiring any input. If input is necessary for a successful verification, e. g., in the form of invariants, the technique has to provide a way to store this information for a later automatic reuse. One example are proof scripts which record every step and every decision necessary to reproduce the proof. Every formal verification technique to be considered has to be able to check proof artifacts fully automatically. Furthermore, the proof checker has to be part of the trusted computing base. Thus, has to be sound, and its footprint has to be comparably small to run on embedded devices.

Reduced Verification Effort for Deployment. In the *on-device validation* scenario, the proof checking takes place on the target device, which usually has limited resources including processing power. To reduce the verification effort on the device, we are looking for verification techniques which support a considerable speed-up for proof artifact checking, opposed to proof artifact creation. One possibility to achieve this is by generating an artifact in a first validation run to speed up a second run (in the proof artifact checker). Existing techniques exhibiting this behavior are verification techniques supporting evolution or incremental proofs. Usually the entire program is verified every time. This can be a time consuming task, even for very small changes to the source code. Verification techniques supporting evolution can reduce the necessary resources. The source code has to be verified completely once and the proof itself or an artifact helping with checking the proof is saved. The following verification run can reuse this artifact to reduce the source code which has to be verified. When the source code is modified, the differences between the two versions are calculated. It is then determined whether the changes have an impact on the validity of the proof. If it is necessary to change or redo the proof, it can be generated using the old proof artifact and the source code delta. For proof carrying apps, we assume that for this kind of verification approach, the verification effort of two *identical* programs should be minimal. The result of the first verification is saved as proof artifact and deployed with the plug-in to be used for the proof check at deployment time. Because the plug-in does not change between the two verifications, the second pass should be considerably faster. The reduction of the verification effort is a soft criterion.

Trust in Proof Artifacts. For our concept of proof-carrying apps, the developers of apps have to generate and provide the proof artifacts with their app. The proof artifacts are used in the check whether the contracts hold or not. One way to prevent a negative result of this check, could be to modify the proof artifact. Therefore, we do not want to trust the developers and the proof generator and we need verification techniques which do not need to trust generated artifacts for the check. The absence of trust towards the generated proof artifacts is a hard criterion.

4   Formal Verification Techniques

In the previous section, we introduced a set of criteria a verification technique should fulfill for deployment-time verification with proof-carrying apps. To determine whether a technique is suitable for proof-carrying apps, we give a short comparison of three verification techniques and discuss how contracts can be verified by each of them.

4.1   Data-Flow Analysis

Data-flow analysis is a method for static analysis. At the time of compilation, it calculates an approximation of how a program will behave at runtime [24]. Following the control flow of a program, data-flow analysis can give information about what values a variable at a specific statement in a program may have. The approximation allows data-flow analysis to reach a fixpoint without needing invariants for otherwise undecidable loops or recursion. Data-flow analysis can run automatically, but as a drawback it can return false positives (i.e., correct programs marked as incorrect) and false negatives (i.e., erroneous programs marked as correct). To guarantee that contracts hold, we cannot allow false negatives to occur. The analysis has to be strict enough to catch all possible false negatives. In contrast, the presence of false positives has no influence on the safety of an app, but the proof checker would mark a safe app as unsafe, and the app would not be allowed to run. Hence, we would need to reduce the number of false positives to zero, e.g., by refactoring the source code or by providing loop invariants or assertions. The Clang Static Analyzer[1] uses data-flow analyses to find errors in C/C++ programs while Soot provides data-flow analyses for Java [16].

Contracts. Data-flow analysis tools usually do not work with contracts but with data-flow problems like *reaching definitions* analysis. This analysis gives a list of variable definitions which may influence the value of variables at a specific point of the program. However, we can encode pre- and postconditions into data-flow problems, by translating them into runtime assertions. When a method with a contract is called, the calling method is responsible that the precondition is not violated. Hence, before entering the method, we have to add an explicit check for a violation using an if-statement encoding the precondition. If the precondition is violated, a *PreconditionViolationException* is thrown. The called method is responsible that the postcondition is not violated if the precondition holds. The postcondition is checked at the end of contracted method and throws a *PostconditionViolationException* if the check fails. The data-flow analysis has to verify that, for the program under verification, the statement throwing the exception cannot be reached.

4.2   Software Model Checking

A software model checker uses a combination of different verification approaches to prove properties of programs [15]. This includes abstract interpretation, predicate abstraction, and state-space exploration. A software model checker returns either that the property holds for the input model or it gives a counterexample which can help to find the error. With the right encoding of the property, a model checker can run automatically. The biggest drawback of model checking is the limited scalability, as it tends to run out of main memory. Modern model checkers have numerous parameters to improve scalability, such that good settings need to be found for verification. However, those settings could also be passed to the device for deployment-time verification. Java PathFinder[2] is a software model checker for Java [14] and CPAchecker supports model checking of programs written in C [8].

Contracts. The encoding for a software model checker can be similar to that for the data-flow analysis. If the precondition is not satisfied before the call of a contracted method, an exception is thrown. Before the contracted method returns, the postcondition is checked, and an exception is thrown if it is not satisfied. To ensure that pre- and postconditions are satisfied, the model checker has to check that none of the exceptions are thrown.

---

[1] http://clang-analyzer.llvm.org/.
[2] http://babelfish.arc.nasa.gov/trac/jpf.

4.3   Deductive Program Verification

Theorem provers use deductive reasoning to prove logical properties [27]. Techniques like symbolic execution (e. g., KeY [1]) and verification-condition generation (e. g., Dafny [19]) are also utilized. The input is processed with the help of inference rules. Due to situations in which more than one rule or different instantiations are possible, user input might be necessary. To avoid decidability problems with loops or recursion, it also might be necessary to provide invariants. Both properties make theorem proving often not a fully automatic technique. Nevertheless, once a proof is completed, it can be stored and automatically checked at deployment-time. However, it is not clear whether such proof replay is significantly faster than proof finding. Deductive program verification tools supporting proof replay are, e. g., KeY [1] or Coq [7].

Contracts. A theorem prover translates the program and contracts to a calculus. Pre- and postconditions can be transfered directly into logical expressions of that calculus. Such expressions can reference variables used in the program and can be added as an annotation to the contracted methods. Invariants can be added to loops or classes.

5   Comparison of Verification Techniques

After introducing verification techniques which support fully automatic proof checking, we investigate which tools satisfy the aforementioned criteria (cf. Sect. 3). For our comparison and the case study, we decided to focus on the Java programming language. It is a widespread language (e. g., Android) and the support for verification tools is in general quite good. The *KeY tool* [1] is a theorem prover and has the ability to load and replay proofs once they are found. The second tool, *Soot* [16], uses data-flow analysis and was extended to support incremental changes [4]. Both tools support a way to reduce the verification effort, KeY by using proof scripts and Soot by utilizing incremental analysis, which is the reason we chose them. *Java PathFinder* [14] is the most prominent example for a software model checker supporting Java. Unfortunately, we were unable to find work for supporting evolution or incremental analysis in Java PathFinder or other model checkers for Java.

5.1   Case Study

We first present the basic program to be verified before we show how it was adapted for KeY and Soot. We introduce a Java framework representing a car control with the interface shown in Listing 1.1. The interface CarControl allows setting a target speed for the car by using method setTargetSpeed. It also allows reading the current speed by using method getCurrentSpeed. The interface is annotated with contracts in JML [18] which is used for specifications in KeY. JML annotations are distinguished from normal comments by adding an @ as shown in Listing 1.1. The annotation of method `setTargetSpeed` in interface `CarControl` consists of one precondition. In this case, the value of the argument `speed` is assumed to be larger or equal to 0 and smaller or equal to 300. The interface developer has to provide the contracts for the interface.

```
1  public interface CarControl {
2  /*@
3  @ public normal_behavior
4  @ requires speed >= 0 && speed <= 300;
5  @ assignable \nothing;
6  @*/
7     public /*@ helper @*/ void setTargetSpeed(int speed);
8  /*@
9  @ public normal_behavior
10 @ requires true;
11 @ assignable \nothing;
12 @*/
13    public /*@ helper @*/ int getCurrentSpeed();
14 }
```

Listing 1.1. The interface *CarControl* and its contracts.

```
1  public class CruiseControl {
2     CarControl cc = new CarControlImpl();
3  /*@
4  @ requires true;
5  @ diverges true;
6  @*/
7     public void run(){
8        int targetSpeed = 200;
9        int currentSpeed = getNormalizedSpeed();
10 /*@ loop_invariant currentSpeed >= 0 && currentSpeed <= 300;
11 @ assignable \nothing;
12 @*/
13       while(currentSpeed != targetSpeed){
14          if(currentSpeed < targetSpeed){ cc.setTargetSpeed(currentSpeed + 1);}
15          else { cc.setTargetSpeed(currentSpeed − 1); }
16          currentSpeed = getNormalizedSpeed();
17       }}
18 /*@
19 @ requires true;
20 @ ensures \result >= 0 && \result <= 300;
21 @ assignable \nothing;
22 @*/
23    public int getNormalizedSpeed() {
24       int currentSpeed = cc.getCurrentSpeed();
25       if(currentSpeed > 300) { currentSpeed = 300; }
26       else if(currentSpeed < 0) { currentSpeed = 0; }
27       return currentSpeed;
28 }}
```

Listing 1.2. The app *CruiseControl* and its contracts.

Furthermore, we consider an app `CruiseControl`, which accesses the two methods of the platform's interface `CarControl` as shown in Listing 1.2. For the sake of simplicity, we set a fixed target speed in the `run` method, which incrementally increases the current speed and terminates once the target speed is reached.

5.2   Proof-Carrying Apps with KeY

As a first instance of proof-carrying apps, we provide an implementation utilizing the KeY tool for deductive program verification [1]. We give an introduction to the concept and determine whether KeY supports the speed-up of a proof check necessary for proof-carrying apps.

Approach. The KeY approach uses deductive reasoning as a main technology. It allows verifying Java programs using symbolic execution. At certain decisions in the proof tree, it might be necessary to manually choose a deduction rule or a specific instantiation of a rule. KeY allows storing the proof of a verification pass, which is essentially a proof script. It includes all rules (and how they were instantiated) necessary to deduce the proof and the order in which the rules have to be applied. This proof can then be reopened and used to check whether it holds for the contracts of the program. As the rules only have to be applied and not to be found, we assume that the replay is faster than finding the rules. This is especially true if the automatic mode encounters a point where manual interaction is necessary. KeY also does not need to trust the generated proof script, as all rules in the proof script are only applied if allowed. If the proof and the program are not compatible, KeY cannot finish the proof and the plug-in is rejected. KeY fulfills the three criteria *fully automatically, reduced verification effort*, and *no trust in artifacts necessary* introduced in Sect. 3.

Adapting the Case Study. To get the case study to work with KeY, we had to add some additional contracts. We assume that the implementation of the CarControl works correctly and only check whether the precondition is not violated by the new plug-in. Therefore, we use the helper modifier and tell KeY that the methods do not change the state of the object with the assignable clause. KeY only allows to verify contracted methods. To prove that methods using the interface obey the contract, app developers have to add contracts to their own source code. This can be done by simply adding a precondition which always holds, using requires true. The methods run() and getNormalizedSpeed() have a requires true precondition and can therefore be verified with KeY. In the implementation of the CruiseControl, the while loop has to be annotated by a loop invariant to allow KeY to verify the method. Without the loop invariant KeY terminates with open goals, i. e., the proof cannot be finished.

If developers want to use the interface CarControl, the contracts give preconditions they have to meet to be allowed to run. With this knowledge, developers of an app write their *plug-in* (in this case in the form of simple Java classes). It is their responsibility to ensure that the plug-in maintains the API's contracts, which may include adding necessary contracts to their source code. Developers have to find proofs for all methods with contracts by using KeY, which generates a proof script for every method. These files constitute the proof artifacts for the plug-in. The proof and the source code are then verified using KeY as the proof checker. It reads the proof script and attempts to do a proof replay. If the replay succeeds for all methods of the plug-in, the entire plug-in is verified and can be executed. After starting the KeY system and all rules are found and applied, the proof can be saved for a later replay. Developers end up with Java source-code files and a KeY proof artifact.

Results. When run fully automatically (*autopilot mode*), KeY was able to prove that the preconditions of the interface CarControl are satisfied. To detect a violation of the precondition, we modified the field `targetSpeed`, the contract of `getNormalizedSpeed` and the normalization values in `getNormalizedSpeed`. All modifications were detected and no proofs were found. The successful proof was saved and reloaded into KeY, which could correctly replay the proof. Modifying the proof or the sources resulted in an exception or remaining open proof goals.

To quantify the benefit of the proof replay, we measured the time it took for the KeY tool to find the proof and to replay it. The developers provided us with a version of KeY that allows measuring the time for parsing the source code and the proof as well as the time required to find or replay a proof. The system used for the test is an Intel Core i7-5600U @2.6GHz with 12 GB RAM running Windows 10 x64. As input, we used the code of the interface `CarControl` and the class `CruiseControl`, annotated with the contracts in JML. Table 1 shows the average times over five runs. With over five seconds, most of the time is used by parsing the source code, which is the same for finding and replaying the proof. In addition to parsing the source code, the proof replay makes it necessary to parse the proof. The time it took to find the proof is significantly larger than the time it took to replay the same proof. Considering the parsing time, the benefit decreases to only 3.4 % for the presented example. Realistic systems would be more complex and use more interfaces with preconditions. Due to this reason, we expect the impact of the parsing time for the proof to decrease. The parsing time of the sources and the proof, as well as the proof replay time, should only increase slightly, whereas the time it takes to find a proof is expected to grow faster. Thus, the benefit of replaying a proof should increase significantly.

Table 1. The results of the evaluation of our example.

Average time (5 passes)			
Proof search in autopilot mode		Proof replay	
Parsing of sources	5150 ms		Parsing of sources
		1558 ms	Parsing of proof
Proof search	2882 ms	1050 ms	Proof replay
Sum	8032 ms	7758 ms	Sum

To achieve a similar effect of detecting and handling unspecified behavior defensive programming could be used. Every method with a precondition has to check its input values whether they abide the contract. If this is not the case, the call can be ignored or error handling can be initiated. This allows detecting and handling, but not the prevention of errors. Defensive programming makes the callee responsible for error detection, although one reason to use contracts is to make the caller responsible for abiding preconditions of the callee. Especially for time critical systems handling erroneous behavior might not be possible because the handling takes time. Additionally the comfort of the driver might be affected if the car pulls over and stops due to an error in the software which could have been prevented in the first place.

5.3   Proof-Carrying Apps with Soot

As a second instance of proof-carrying apps, we use Soot, an optimization framework for Java source and byte code. Soot also allows to run static data-flow analyses. After a short introduction we show how we adapted the case study and what results we received.

Approach. Soot translates the Java code (also Android code and Java bytecode) to an internal representation, which then can be analyzed with Soot. It provides several built-in analyses, as call-graph analyses, points-to analyses, and def-use-chains. Moreover, a template driven intra-procedural data-flow analysis framework is provided that may be used to extend Soot with own analyses. Arzt et al. have introduced a tool called *Reviser* [4]. It is built on top of Soot and allows to update results of data-flow analyses due to program changes without a complete recalculation of the result. Initially, Reviser consumes about 20 % more computation time for the analyses. However, the re-computation time decreases by up to 80 %. Reviser generates an inter-procedural control-flow graph which is used for the analysis. After the first analysis is finished, the second generation does not create a new graph, but it only changes the nodes for which the source changed. If a node is changed, the change is propagated through all dependent nodes. With the changes of the control-flow graph, the analysis result of the previous pass is updated. A recalculation is only done where necessary. This means Soot/Reviser supports the two criteria to *run fully automatically* and to *reduce the verification effort* (see Sect. 3). For our experiments, we used the version of Soot provided for the *Reviser*[3].

Adapting the Case Study. While adapting the *CruiseControl* use case to be verifiable by Soot/Reviser, we encountered several issues. If Reviser does *not* find changes from one version of a program to another, it assumes the results of the first run are still valid without rechecking them. For proof-carrying apps, it means that the proof artifact delivered with the plug-in is not checked at all. Hence, Reviser does not fulfill our criterion to *not trust artifacts*. For the case that Reviser does not find changes, we can enforce an update of the analysis. To ensure we get the correct results, the analysis has to be redone completely. This would potentially increase the verification time, due to the time it takes to parse the artifacts delivered with the plug-ins. To work with our two scenarios Soot/Reviser has to be changed to not trust the provided artifacts. For our encoding of contracts as data-flow problems we rely on potentially complex conditional expressions. The implemented analyses in Reviser abstract heavily from if-else-conditions and combines different paths in the control-flow graph. Every contract would be reported as broken and we would get many false positives, essentially leading to no app being allowed to run.

   With the necessity to use trusted artifacts, Soot/Reviser is not suitable for our current use case of proof-carrying apps. Rather than using it to verify a *newly* deployed app, it might be suitable for the different use case of *updates*

---

[3] https://github.com/StevenArzt/.

of apps. In this use case a first analysis would be done without an proof artifact and the result would be saved on the device. If the app is updated, Reviser can calculate the differences between the old and the new app, and update the result of the last analysis. We will investigate this use case in future work.

5.4   Summary

Both KeY and Soot were not created for our scenario of proof-carrying apps. In particular, proof replay and parsing of KeY are not optimized for performance. For our very small use case, the verification effort with KeY could be reduced by 63.6 %. With the added time for parsing the proof, the resulting reduction is 3.4 %. The results show that making proof replays faster, e. g., by optimizing the parsing phase, needs to be addressed in future work.

The current implementation of Soot/Reviser is not suitable for proof-carrying apps, due to the fact that it trusts the provided artifacts. This might change if we extend our scenarios to include update scenarios or the implementation is changed to distrust artifacts. Java PathFinder fulfills our criterion of being able to verify fully automatically. Whereas we found approaches to reduce the verification effort of Java PathFinder [17,25], we did not find publicly available implementations to evaluate if these approaches suffice our criteria.

6   Related Work

Our approach extends on proof-carrying code and introduces contracts to specify program properties to prove.

Proof-Carrying Code. Proof-Carrying Code (PCC) was introduced by Necula to ensure that a platform running code from untrusted developers can be executed in a safe manner [22]. The focus of PCC are global safety rules and, at the beginning, the system was limited to the DEC Alpha assembly language. The source code of a program is compiled and a certificate is created which proves that the safety rules are met. After compilation, the binary and the according proof are deployed. On the platform, the proof is validated and, if it holds, the program is allowed to run. Necula et al. extended a certifying C compiler that automatically generates DEC Alpha assembly and a formal proof that the safety rules hold [23]. The idea of a certifying compiler was extended to support Java by Colby et al. [11]. The MOBIUS project also applied the idea of proof-carrying code for Java. As a target platform, mobile phones were selected which were able to run midlets, i. e., applications implemented using the MIDP profile for JavaME CLDC. The checked properties include points-to and alias information, data dependency, flow of string values, and resource-oriented analysis [6].

Contracts. Several languages exist which allow specifying permissible use of interfaces. Hatcliff et al. provide an extensive survey on different languages for behavioral interface specifications [13]. For the Java programming language, the

Java Modeling Language (JML) is commonly used. It allows specifying preconditions, postconditions, invariants, and assertions, which may be written directly into the Java source code as comments. As KeY natively works with JML and the program properties we are interested in may be expressed as preconditions, we decided to use JML for our case study.

Incremental and Evolutionary Verification. Tools and methodologies for incremental static analyses already exist. The *Java PathFinder* was intended as model checker for Java programs. It translates Java code to a *Promela* model, which may be analyzed [14]. Thus, it is possible to find all paths through the program. Moreover, it provides good traceability via backtracking. JPF is modular and, therefore, easy to extend. Brat et al. have shown that JPF is suitable for static analyses [9]. Additionally, Lauterburg et al. [17] as well as Person et al. [25] have extended JPF with incremental analyses. Lauterburg et al. could measure performance increases from 14 % up to 68 % compared to non-incremental analyses. However, the values strongly depend on the changes made to the program and the overall lines of code.

The Saturn program analysis system[4] translates programs written in C to boolean constraints [2]. These constraints can be extended by boolean expressions for custom analyses. Saturn is intended for static program analyses and provides two different analyses methods. The *whole-program* analysis translates the complete source code of the program to boolean constraints. In contrast, the *compositional-summary-based* analysis translates every function individually to boolean constraints. Afterwards, these constraints can be composed to represent the entire program or particular parts of the program. Incremental analysis could be realized by only analyzing functions which are affected by evolution. However, this is a relatively coarse-grained method. Mudduluru and Ramanathan [21] have extended Saturn to *incremental Saturn* (iSaturn). iSaturn is supposed to provide more fine-grained increments. For this, the boolean constraints are analyzed for (partial) equivalence. Thus, existing results can be reused, which results in performance increases by up to 32 %.

The tool *KeY Resources*[5] allows to automatically find proofs in the background. It is also able to reduce the effort to *find* a proof after the source code or the contracts are changed. The introduction of abstract contracts allows the reuse of parts of a proof *found* by KeY [12]. The authors extended the approach to fully abstract contracts and included abstract invariants [10]. Abstract contracts allowing a developer to reduce the effort to *find* a proof, but for the moment it is unclear how these approaches can help us with *checking* proofs.

7   Conclusion and Future Work

In this paper, we introduced proof-carrying apps as a generalization to proof-carrying code. Whereas proof-carrying code uses global safety policies, we use

---

[4] http://saturn.stanford.edu.
[5] http://www.key-project.org/eclipse/KeYResources/index.html.

contracts to specify the assumptions developers have towards apps using their API. Instead of only relying on deductive proofs, we allow the use of other proof artifacts that enable the faster verification of the contracts of a plug-in. Contracts have the additional benefit of explicitly splitting the responsibility between the calling and the called object. Furthermore, we describe three criteria a verification technique has to fulfill to work for proof-carrying apps: *fully automatic verification, generation of proof artifacts without the need of trust,* and *a decreased verification effort due to the artifact.* We determined that data-flow analysis, software-model checking, and deductive program verification are in principle suitable for proof-carrying apps. We evaluated implementations of the verification techniques, such as KeY and Soot, and found potential of reusing existing techniques for proof-carrying apps but also discuss further requirements for those tools.

For future work, it is necessary to focus on larger case studies as that discussed above and also on other languages than Java. For instance, analysis tools like FRAMA-C[6], VCC[7], or CPAchecker provide tool support for C, which could be interesting to consider for proof-carrying apps. Furthermore, we want to investigate how a speed-up in replaying proofs with KeY can be achieved.

Acknowledgments. We thank Christoph Seidl for his support in earlier phases of the paper. We gratefully acknowledge the support of Eric Bodden and Steven Arzt with Soot and Reviser.

References

1. Ahrendt, W., et al.: The KeY platform for verification and analysis of Java Programs. In: Giannakopoulou, D., Kroening, D. (eds.) VSTTE 2014. LNCS, vol. 8471, pp. 55–71. Springer, Heidelberg (2014). http://dx.doi.org/10.1007/978-3-319-12154-3_4
2. Aiken, A., Bugrara, S., Dillig, I., Dillig, T., Hackett, B., Hawkins, P.: An overview of the saturn project. In: Workshop on Program Analysis for Software Tools and Engineering, PASTE 2007, pp. 43–48. ACM, New York (2007). http://doi.acm.org/10.1145/1251535.1251543
3. Apel, S., Batory, D., Kästner, C., Saake, G.: Feature-Oriented Software Product Lines: Concepts and Implementation. Springer, Heidelberg (2013)
4. Arzt, S., Bodden, E.: Reviser: efficiently updating IDE-/IFDS-based data-flow analyses in response to incremental program changes. In: International Conference on Software Engineering, ICSE 2014, pp. 288–298. ACM, New York (2014). http://doi.acm.org/10.1145/2568225.2568243
5. Baier, C., Katoen, J.: Principles of Model Checking. MIT Press, Cambridge (2008)
6. Barthe, G., Crégut, P., Grégoire, B., Jensen, T., Pichardie, D.: The MOBIUS proof carrying code infrastructure. In: de Boer, F.S., Bonsangue, M.M., Graf, S., de Roever, W.-P. (eds.) FMCO 2007. LNCS, vol. 5382, pp. 1–24. Springer, Heidelberg (2008). http://dx.doi.org/10.1007/978-3-540-92188-2_1

---

[6] http://frama-c.com/index.html.

[7] http://vcc.codeplex.com/.

7. Bertot, Y., Castéran, P.: Interactive Theorem Proving and Program Development - Coq'Art: The Calculus of Inductive Constructions. Texts in Theoretical Computer Science. An EATCS Series. Springer, Heidelberg (2004). http://dx.doi.org/10.1007/978-3-662-07964-5

8. Beyer, D., Keremoglu, M.E.: CPACHECKER: a tool for configurable software verification. In: Qadeer, S., Gopalakrishnan, G. (eds.) CAV 2011. LNCS, vol. 6806, pp. 184–190. Springer, Heidelberg (2011). http://dx.doi.org/10.1007/978-3-642-22110-1_16

9. Brat, G., Visser, W.: Combining static analysis and model checking for software analysis. In: International Conference on Automated Software Engineering, ASE 2001, p. 262. IEEE Computer Society, Washington (2001). http://dl.acm.org/citation.cfm?id=872023.872568

10. Bubel, R., Hähnle, R., Pelevina, M.: Fully abstract operation contracts. In: Margaria, T., Steffen, B. (eds.) ISoLA 2014, Part II. LNCS, vol. 8803, pp. 120–134. Springer, Heidelberg (2014). http://dx.doi.org/10.1007/978-3-662-45231-8_9

11. Colby, C., Lee, P., Necula, G.C., Blau, F., Plesko, M., Cline, K.: A certifying compiler for Java. In: Lam, M.S. (ed.) Conference on Programming Language Design and Implementation, pp. 95–107. ACM (2000). http://doi.acm.org/10.1145/349299.349315

12. Hähnle, R., Schaefer, I., Bubel, R.: Reuse in software verification by abstract method calls. In: Bonacina, M.P. (ed.) CADE 2013. LNCS, vol. 7898, pp. 300–314. Springer, Heidelberg (2013). http://dx.doi.org/10.1007/978-3-642-38574-2_21

13. Hatcliff, J., Leavens, G.T., Leino, K.R.M., Müller, P., Parkinson, M.J.: Behavioral interface specification languages. ACM Comput. Surv. 44(3), 16 (2012). http://doi.acm.org/10.1145/2187671.2187678

14. Havelund, K., Pressburger, T.: Model checking JAVA programs using JAVA PathFinder. Int. J. Softw. Tools Technol. Transf. 2(4), 366–381 (2000). http://dx.doi.org/10.1007/s100090050043

15. Jhala, R., Majumdar, R.: Software model checking. ACM Comput. Surv. (CSUR) 41(4), 21 (2009)

16. Lam, P., Bodden, E., Lhoták, O., Hendren, L.: The Soot framework for Java program analysis: a retrospective (2011)

17. Lauterburg, S., Sobeih, A., Marinov, D., Viswanathan, M.: Incremental state-space exploration for programs with dynamically allocated data. In: International Conference on Software Engineering, ICSE 2008, pp. 291–300. ACM, New York (2008). http://doi.acm.org/10.1145/1368088.1368128

18. Leavens, G.T.: JML: expressive contracts, specification inheritance, and behavioral subtyping. In: Principles and Practices of Programming on the Java Platform, p. 1 (2015). http://doi.acm.org/10.1145/2807426.2817926

19. Leino, K.R.M.: Dafny: an automatic program verifier for functional correctness. In: Logic for Programming, Artificial Intelligence, and Reasoning, pp. 348–370 (2010). http://dx.doi.org/10.1007/978-3-642-17511-4_20

20. Meyer, B.: Applying "design by contract". IEEE Comput. 25(10), 40–51 (1992). http://doi.ieeecomputersociety.org/10.1109/2.161279

21. Mudduluru, R., Ramanathan, M.K.: Efficient incremental static analysis using path abstraction. In: Gnesi, S., Rensink, A. (eds.) FASE 2014 (ETAPS). LNCS, vol. 8411, pp. 125–139. Springer, Heidelberg (2014). http://dx.doi.org/10.1007/978-3-642-54804-8_9

22. Necula, G.C.: Proof-carrying code. In: Lee, P., Henglein, F., Jones, N.D. (eds.) Symposium on Principles of Programming Languages, pp. 106–119. ACM Press (1997). http://doi.acm.org/10.1145/263699.263712

23. Necula, G.C., Lee, P.: The design and implementation of a certifying compiler. In: Davidson, J.W., Cooper, K.D., Berman, A.M. (eds.) Conference on Programming Language Design and Implementation, pp. 333–344. ACM (1998). http://doi.acm.org/10.1145/277650.277752

24. Nielson, F., Nielson, H.R., Hankin, C.: Principles of Program Analysis. Springer, Heidelberg (1999). http://dx.doi.org/10.1007/978-3-662-03811-6

25. Person, S., Yang, G., Rungta, N., Khurshid, S.: Directed incremental symbolic execution. In: Conference on Programming Language Design and Implementation, PLDI 2011, pp. 504–515. ACM, New York (2011). http://doi.acm.org/10.1145/1993498.1993558

26. Rushby, J.M.: Design and verification of secure systems. SIGOPS Oper. Syst. Rev. 15(5), 12–21 (1981). http://doi.acm.org/10.1145/1067627.806586

27. Schumann, J.M.: Automated Theorem Proving in Software Engineering. Springer, Heidelberg (2001)

28. Thüm, T., Apel, S., Kästner, C., Schaefer, I., Saake, G.: A classification and survey of analysis strategies for software product lines. ACM Comput. Surv. 47(1), 6:1–6:45 (2014). http://doi.acm.org/10.1145/2580950

Supervisory Controller Synthesis for Product Lines Using CIF 3

Maurice H. ter Beek[1], Michel A. Reniers[2], and Erik P. de Vink[2,3(✉)]

[1] ISTI–CNR, Pisa, Italy
[2] Eindhoven University of Technology, Eindhoven, The Netherlands
evink@win.tue.nl
[3] CWI, Amsterdam, The Netherlands

Abstract. Using the CIF 3 toolset, we illustrate the general idea of controller synthesis for product line engineering for a prototypical example of a family of coffee machines. The challenge is to integrate a number of given components into a family of products such that the resulting behaviour is guaranteed to respect an attributed feature model as well as additional behavioural requirements. The proposed correctness-by-construction approach incrementally restricts the composed behaviour by subsequently incorporating feature constraints, attribute constraints and temporal constraints. The procedure as presented focusses on synthesis, but leaves ample opportunity to handle e.g. uncontrollable behaviour, dynamic reconfiguration, and product- and family-based analysis.

1 Introduction

In the current globalised economy, businesses are eager to offer a myriad of diversified products as a strategy to increase turnover. To reduce development costs and time-to-market, reuse of components (systems as well as software) is becoming common practice. The aim of Software or Systems Product Line Engineering (SPLE) is to institutionalise reuse throughout all phases of product development [37]. According to this paradigm, enterprises shift from the production, maintenance and management of single products to that of a family or product line of related products, amenable to mass customisation. This requires the identification of the core assets of the products in the domain to exploit their commonality and manage their variability, often defined in terms of features. A feature can be seen as an (increment in) functionality of a product that is visible or relevant to a customer. Consequently, to the developer feature models define the combination of features that constitute valid product configurations [13].

While the automated analysis of structural variability models (e.g. the detection of so-called dead or false optional features in feature models) has a long-standing history [13], that of behavioural variability models has received considerable attention only after the landmark paper by Classen et al. [18]. Since product lines often concern massively (re)used and critical applications (like smartphones and cars), indeed it is important to demonstrate that they are not only configured correctly, but also behave correctly.

© Springer International Publishing AG 2016
T. Margaria and B. Steffen (Eds.): ISoLA 2016, Part I, LNCS 9952, pp. 856–873, 2016.
DOI: 10.1007/978-3-319-47166-2_59

Many approaches aim to engineer systems (of systems) that are provably correct with respect to their requirements. At one side of the spectrum, (post-hoc) verification concerns the application of formal analysis techniques *after* a system (specification) has been constructed. Typically, a formal specification of the implemented system, or abstraction thereof, describes the intended behaviour, after which verification techniques like model checking or theorem proving are applied to verify whether the implementation indeed satisfies the specification [2,39]. While applications of theorem proving in SPLE have concentrated on the analysis of requirements and code [20,34,45] with tools like Coq and KeY, a number of model-checking tools have been equipped to deal with variability in their specification models for application in SPLE. These range from modal transition system [7,31] and process-algebraic models [8,24] to tools like NuSMV and mCRL2 [6,16], as well as dedicated model checkers like SNIP, VMC, and ProVeLines [10,15,19]. Research on applying model checking and theorem proving to product lines is also reflected in recent editions of ISoLA [1,4,9,14,25,32,33].

At the other end of the spectrum, the principle of correctness-by-construction has the aim of developing error-free systems from rigorous and unambiguous specifications, based on stringent correctness criteria in each refinement step. Dijkstra and Hoare focussed on the construction of provably correct *programs* based on weakest precondition semantics [21,28], whereas Hall and Chapman focussed on an effective and economical software development *process*, from user requirements to implementation, based on zero tolerance of defects [26,27]. We consider another approach to correctness-by-construction, namely synthesis seen as the development of a supervisor (or supervisory controller) in order to coordinate an assembly of (local) components into a (global) system that functions correctly. Supervisory Control Theory (SCT) [38] synthesises a supervisory control model from models of system components and a set of given requirements. Moreover, the ensemble of components controlled by the supervisor satisfies a number of desirable properties, like the possibility to reach stable local states, so-called marker states, and the impossibility to globally disable events under local control. To the best of our knowledge, we are the first to apply supervisory controller synthesis in SPLE.

At Eindhoven University of Technology, the CIF 3 toolset [11] is developed and maintained. This toolset targets model-based engineering of supervisory controllers and supports such an engineering process by offering functionality for modelling, simulation, visualisation, synthesis, and code generation. More concretely, in this paper, we show how the CIF 3 toolset [11] can automatically synthesise a single (family) model representing an automaton for each of the valid products of a product line from (i) an attributed feature model, (ii) component behaviour models associated with the features and (iii) additional behavioural requirements like state invariants, event orderings and guards on events (reminiscent of the Feature Transition Systems (FTSs) of Classen et al. [17]). *By construction*, the resulting CIF 3 model satisfies all feature-related constraints as well as all behavioural requirements that are assumed to be given beforehand.

Note that it was not needed to extend the CIF toolset for our purposes. CIF 3 moreover allows, among others, the export of such models in a format accepted by the mCRL2 model checker, which can be used to verify arbitrary behavioural properties expressed in the modal μ-calculus with data or its feature-oriented variant of [6]. An important advantage is that both CIF 3 and mCRL2 can be used off-the-shelf, meaning that no additional tools are required. Moreover, it is important to note that the explicit consideration of features as first-class citizens is a completely new way of using the CIF 3 toolset.

We thus present a unifying SCT approach to deal with structural and behavioural variability, i.e. the resulting synthesised supervisory controller not only manages feature models (product generation), but also product line behaviour (variability encoding) and further behavioural requirements (admissible scenarios). The only other integrated approach that we are aware of is a recent extension of the general-purpose modelling language Clafer [3], that was originally designed to unify (attributed) feature models with class and meta-models. Behavioural Clafer [30] provides (i) feature modelling by means of a constraint language reminiscent of Alloy [29], a light-weight class modelling language with an efficient constraint notation and an effective analyser for instance generation, (ii) behavioural variability by means of hierarchical UML state diagrams and automata (in FTS-style) and (iii) additional behavioural constraints (assertions) in the form of scenarios, allowing for (bounded) LTL model checking.

Compared to the CIF 3 toolset, Behavioural Clafer provides first-class support for architectural modelling through Clafer's rich repertoire for structural modelling, but it offers less advanced behavioural modelling facilities, little support for modularisation of feature-based variants (as in Delta-modelling [40]), and no support for controller synthesis. CIF 3 provides ample facilities to model a system's requirements and behaviour. It does so in a highly modular fashion, with a formal and compositional semantics based on (hybrid) transition systems. In fact, although not shown in this paper, CIF 3 allows to describe timed behaviour and supports the translation of timed discrete event models to UPPAAL [12], a tool for modelling, simulation and verification of real-time systems.

The remainder of the paper is organised as follows: Section 2 briefly introduces the notion of an attributed feature model and describes our running example of a family of coffee machines. Section 3 provides background on supervisory control and illustrates the modelling with CIF 3. In Sect. 4, we explain, for the product line of coffee machines, how controller synthesis with CIF 3 can be used to bring together feature constraints, component behaviour and system requirements. Section 5 discusses a number of directions for future work.

2   Product Lines

A feature model is a hierarchical and/or-tree of features [13]. A trivial root feature is considered to be present in any product, *mandatory* features must be present provided their parent is, while *optional* features may be present provided their parent is. Exactly one *alternative* feature must be present provided their parent is, and at least one *or* feature must be present whenever their parent is.

A cross-tree constraint either *requires* the presence of another feature for a feature to be present, or it *excludes* two features to be both present. In an attributed feature model, the primitive features (leaves of the tree) are moreover equipped with a non-functional attribute, like cost or weight, and complex constraints over features. Attributes further constrain the feature configuration process, in particular by limiting the cost or weight of features, or of products.

A feature model is equivalent to a propositional formula over features defined as the conjunction of the formulas obtained from the mapping on the right (adapted from [13]). As a result, deciding whether or not a product is valid according to the feature model reduces to a Boolean satisfiability problem, which implies that it can efficiently be computed with BDD or SAT solvers. However, in case of feature models displaying non-Boolean attributes and complex constraints, one needs to resort to SMT solvers, for example.

relationship		formula
root	F_0	$F_0 \iff true$
mandatory	F_1 F_2	$F_1 \iff F_2$
optional	F_1 F_2	$F_2 \implies F_1$
alternative	F F_1 F_2 F_n	$(F_1 \iff (\neg F_2 \wedge \cdots \wedge \neg F_n \wedge F))$ $\wedge \cdots \wedge$ $(F_n \iff (\neg F_1 \wedge \cdots \wedge \neg F_{n-1} \wedge F))$
or	F F_1 F_2 F_n	$F \iff (F_1 \vee F_2 \cdots \vee F_n)$
requires	$F_1 \dashrightarrow F_2$	$F_1 \implies F_2$
excludes	$F_1 \dashleftarrow\dashrightarrow F_2$	$\neg (F_1 \wedge F_2)$

As a running example, we use a family of coffee machines. This product line was used earlier too in work on the application of formal methods and tools such as VMC and mCRL2 to (software) product lines, cf. e.g. [4,5,7,10]. In short, coffee machines from our example product line are described as follows:

- A coffee machine either accepts one-euro coins (1 €), exclusively for European products, or one-dollar coins (1 $), exclusively for Canadian products.
- After inserting a coin, the user has to decide whether or not she wants sugar, by pressing one out of two buttons.
- Next, a beverage must be selected, which is either coffee (which is always available), tea or cappuccino (tea is optionally available, cappuccino is optionally available from European machines).
- After delivering a beverage, optionally a ringtone is rung. However, in case the product is offering cappuccino this must be the case.
- After the beverage is taken, the machine returns to its idle state.
- Optionally, coins of other denominations than one euro or one dollar can be inserted. Change will be returned when appropriate.

The attributed feature model depicted in Fig. 1 organises 11 features, reflecting the description of the above product family. The root feature M, mandatory features S, O, B, and C, and optional features E, D, R, P, T and X. Sibling features E and D are alternatives, whereas independent features D and P are mutually exclusive. The feature R is required by feature P. The primitive features come equipped with an attribute for costs, an integer value between 3 and 10.

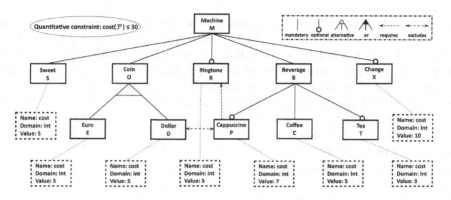

Fig. 1. Attributed feature model for the family of coffee machines [5].

More formally, the feature model yields 20 different products when ignoring the attribute constraints. Each product can be identified with a subset $\mathcal{P}$ of the set $\mathcal{F}$ of all features. For example, the subset of features $\{M, S, O, E, B, C\}$ describes a European coffee machine of a minimal number of features. The attribute function $cost: \mathcal{F} \rightarrow \mathbb{N}$ associated to the attribute cost extends to products in a straightforward manner, $cost(\mathcal{P}) = \sum \{ cost(f) \mid f \in \mathcal{P} \}$, by assigning cost 0 to non-primitive features. If we consider the attributes and their overall quantitative constraint requiring $cost(\mathcal{P}) \leqslant 30$ for all $\mathcal{P} \subseteq \mathcal{F}$, then the attributed feature model only defines 16 valid products. For instance, the product $\{M, S, O, E, R, B, C, T, X\}$ meets the feature requirements of the feature model, but has a cost of 33, exceeding the bound of 30.

3   Supervisory Control Synthesis

SCT provides a mechanism to obtain a model, an automaton, of a supervisory controller from given (component) models of the uncontrolled system and its requirements. The synthesised supervisory controller, if successfully produced, is such that the controlled system, which is the synchronous product of the uncontrolled system and the supervisory controller, satisfies the requirements and is additionally non-blocking, controllable and maximally permissive [38]. In the context of supervisory control, an automaton is called *non-blocking* in case from each state at least one of the so-called *marker states* can be reached. This indicates that the system always has the capability to return to an accepted rest state or stable state. The user has to indicate for each of the component models which are such marker locations.

In SCT, one distinguishes *controllable* and *uncontrollable* events. *Controllability* means that the supervisory controller is not permitted to block uncontrollable events from happening. The controller is only allowed to disable behaviour of the uncontrolled system indirectly by preventing controllable events from happening. Intuitively, controllable events correspond to stimulating or actuating the system, while the uncontrollable events correspond to messages provided by the sensors (which may be neglected, but cannot be denied from existing). However, in the application of SCT demonstrated in this paper, all events are assumed to be controllable for simplicity. The resulting supervisory controller is *maximally permissive* (or least restrictive). This means that as much behaviour of the uncontrolled system as possible is still present in the controlled system without violating neither the requirements, nor the controllability nor the non-blocking condition on the reachability of marker states.

In earlier work, both the components and the requirements were expressed by means of finite automata. Thus the complete model of the system is a network or composition of automata. These automata may share certain events, and it is assumed that shared events will only occur at the system level if all automata that share that event execute it simultaneously. It is this form of *multi-party synchronisation* that allows a compact and modular specification [11,42]. More recently, in order to increase modelling comfort, finite state machines were replaced by extended finite automata, which allow the use of variables in the automata [41]. In addition, the original algorithm for synthesis was strengthened to be able to deal with these as well [36]. Requirements for the controlled system to hold may be specified in various ways. First of all, allowed event sequences may be specified using automata. Also, state invariants and event conditions are typically used [35]. Invariants are predicates evaluating the overall state of the system. An event condition restricts the occurrence of an event to states that satisfy a specific state predicate.

As mentioned above, component models and (part of) the requirements are provided by means of extended finite automata. More specifically, a (component or requirement) automaton has a name. Refer to Listings 1 and 2 for examples of the concepts introduced here. Its name is used in other automata and requirements to refer to concepts that are defined inside the automaton, such as its events, variables and locations. In the automaton, local events may be declared (together with the indication that these are controllable). Similarly, local variables may be declared with their type and initial value (Listing 2). Furthermore, locations are declared together with the transitions emitting from them. Transitions are described using the keyword edge. A transition may have an event name, a condition or guard (following the keyword when), and an update or assignment (following the keyword do). The guard is a Boolean expression in terms of the values of variables and the current location of other automata. The update is an assignment of new values (by using an expression over variables and locations) to local variables. In CIF 3, a variable may only be assigned in the automaton it is declared in, but may be read/used in all other automata and requirements. CIF 3 distinguishes algebraic variables, like cost in Listing 3, and discrete variables, like cnt in Listing 2. An algebraic variable is a variable for which the value is at all times defined as the result of an expression in the right-hand side of the declaration of that variable.

In Listing 1, the textual description of the component automaton COFFEE is given. It declares controllable events done, coffee, cappuccino, pour_coffee and pour_milk. Other automata may refer to these events by prefixing the name of the defining automaton, e.g. COFFEE.cappuccino.

Listing 1. Automaton COFFEE

```
controllable
    done, coffee, cappuccino, pour_coffee, pour_milk;
location NoChoice: initial, marked;
    edge coffee goto Coffee;
    edge cappuccino goto Cappuccino;
location Coffee: marked;
    edge pour_coffee;
    edge done goto NoChoice;
    edge cappuccino goto Cappuccino;
location Cappuccino: marked;
    edge pour_coffee;
    edge pour_milk;
    edge done goto NoChoice;
    edge coffee goto Coffee;
```

The automaton of the COFFEE component model has three locations, of which the location NoChoice is the initial location. Note that all locations are marked. From the location NoChoice with the event coffee the automaton may transit to location Coffee. Note that in the automaton there are no variables and, therefore, no conditions and updates are specified for the transitions. If the description of a transition does not reveal a target location explicitly (using the keyword goto) then a loop is implied.

As another example, consider the requirement SWEETNESS specified in Listing 2. In this automaton a discrete variable with name cnt is introduced of type int[0..2], which means it can only take one of the values 0, 1, or 2. Initially, it has value 0. In this automaton, the use of conditions and updates is illustrated. For the transition labeled by event pour_sugar (from automaton SWEET, introduced later) it is required that the value of variable cnt is at most 1. Taking this transition results in adding 1 to the value of the variable by means of the assignment described after do. Observe that the order of transitions as described does *not* imply any priority among them.

Listing 2. Requirement SWEETNESS

```
disc int[0..2] cnt:=0;
location Idle: initial, marked;
    edge SWEET.sugar goto SugarNeeded;
    edge SWEET.done when SWEET.NoSugar;
location SugarNeeded: marked;
    edge SWEET.pour_sugar when cnt⩽1 do cnt:=cnt+1;
    edge SWEET.done when cnt=2 do cnt:=0 goto Idle;
```

Note how the requirement forces the sweet component to provide two portions of sugar when sugar is requested.

CIF 3 has ample features for defining templates with parameters and for reusing those. Please refer to http://cif.se.wtb.tue.nl for more information. We only make limited use of these mechanisms in this paper. CIF 3 has been applied to several industrial size case studies, cf. e.g. [22,44].

4 Modelling Product Lines with CIF 3

In this section, we demonstrate several aspects involving the modelling of product lines with CIF 3. First, we consider the modelling of the set of acceptable products as defined by a feature model. Then we add to this model the uncontrolled behaviour of components, with the behaviour of the components as is. Furthermore, we show how behavioural requirements can easily be incorporated in the CIF 3 model, and we describe how these may be used to obtain a supervisory controller for the family of valid products, satisfying both the feature-related and the behavioural requirements.

4.1 Valid Products

In this section, we propose a simple way of obtaining all valid products from a feature model. In line with Sect. 2, we introduce Boolean variables for the presence and absence of features. We demonstrate how the restrictions imposed by a feature model can be described by invariants on these Boolean variables.

We introduce a generic definition FEATURE for features, shown in Listing 3. The definition may have multiple instances (cf. e.g. FM and FS representing an automaton for the features M and S, respectively). Here, the cost of each feature is taken as a so-called algebraic parameter. In this declaration an if-then-else expression is used to provide different values for the variable depending on a condition (present in this case). In CIF 3, every automaton needs to have at least one location, hence the dummy location (with name Dummy) defined in Listing 3.

Listing 3. Generic feature definition FEATURE

```
def FEATURE(alg int cost):
    alg int cost = if present : cost else 0 end;
    disc bool present in any;
    location Dummy: initial, marked;
end

FM: FEATURE(0); FS: FEATURE(5); ... ; FX: FEATURE(10);
```

We next discuss how in-tree, cross-tree and attribute constraints, as given by an attributed feature model, can be represented as CIF 3 requirements.

An example of a mandatory feature is the link between the beverage feature B and the coffee feature C in Fig. 1. In CIF 3, we define a requirement that states that, invariantly, presence of the beverage feature B, represented by the Boolean variable present of automaton FB, coincides with presence of the coffee feature, i.e. the Boolean variable present of automaton FC (cf. the mapping in Sect. 2).

```
requirement invariant FB.present ⇔ FC.present;
```

An example of an optional feature is the connection between features B for beverage and T for tea in Fig. 1. As an optional feature is allowed to be present when the parent feature is present, but it is not allowed to be present when the parent feature is absent, we have the following invariance requirement in CIF 3.

```
requirement invariant FT.present ⇒ FB.present;
```

Selection from alternative features occurs in Fig. 1 concerning the features O, E and D. The intended meaning of the alternative features E and D is that presence of the parent feature O implies presence of exactly one of these alternative features, and the other way around: presence of E or D requires presence of O. The requirement generalises straightforwardly to more than two alternatives.

```
requirement invariant
    FO.present ⇔ ( FE.present ⇔ not FD.present );
```

An example of a 'requires' cross-tree constraint occurs in Fig. 1 between the requiring cappuccino feature P and the required ringtone feature R. We define the following invariant as CIF 3 requirement.

```
requirement invariant FP.present ⇒ FR.present;
```

Figure 1 shows an 'excludes' cross-tree constraint between the dollar feature D and the cappuccino feature P. The meaning is that these features are not allowed to be both present in the same product, i.e. dollar machines do not offer cappuccino. Therefore, in CIF 3 we define the following requirement.

```
requirement invariant not (FD.present and FP.present);
```

The example feature model of Fig. 1 includes one (global) attribute constraint. It states that the total cost of the selected features may not exceed the threshold of 30 units. We have modelled the cost associated with each feature as a parameter (cf. Listing 3). The total cost can therefore be modelled in CIF 3 as the sum of the costs of the features that are present. Note that in the generic feature definition the cost of a non-present feature is defined to be 0.

```
requirement invariant FM.cost + FS.cost + ··· + FT.cost ⩽
    30;
```

Apart from the five categories of constraints mentioned above, for feature models it is often assumed that a product contains at least one non-trivial feature, i.e. a feature which is not the root feature. The requirement below encodes a disjunction over all non-trivial features.

```
requirement invariant
    (FS.present or FO.present or ··· or FT.present);
```

Observe that the in-tree and cross-tree requirements arising from a feature model have been modelled in CIF 3 in such a way that the transformation from a feature model to a CIF 3 model can easily be automated. Translation of the attribute constraints requires some attribute constraint specific modelling; this can be automated too with a modest effort dependent on the expressiveness of the constraints allowed.

Synthesis with CIF 3 of a supervisory controller capturing the constraints of Fig. 1 yields a product automaton of all features together with a supervisor which has 16 initial states, each corresponding to a valid product. This is the same number as reported in [4,5].

4.2   Component Behaviour

The CIF 3 toolset is very much suited to describe the dynamic behaviour of components. With CIF 3 we initially define the *potential* behaviour of each individual component. It follows that the combined potential behaviour of the components together may contain undesired behaviour. In a later stage, we impose the additional behavioural requirements that are needed to obtain meaningful and acceptable behaviour (cf. Sect. 4.3).

For the coffee machine example we identified seven components in [4]: COIN, CANCEL, SWEET, RINGTONE, COFFEE, TEA and MACHINE. We will specify the potential behaviour of each of these in isolation by means of CIF 3 automata. In principle this needs to be described textually, but for presentation purposes we provide it in a graphical way as illustrated in Fig. 2. The textual description of automaton COFFEE has been given in Listing 1 in Sect. 3.

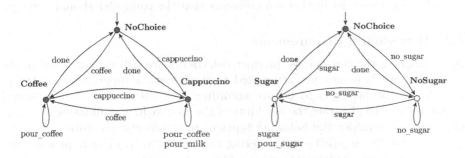

Fig. 2. Graphical representation of CIF 3 automata for components COFFEE and SWEET. Initial states indicated by an incoming arrow, marker states indicated by a filled state.

Using the CIF 3 toolset one can easily obtain the uncontrolled behaviour of the seven components together, an automaton with 18 states and 207 transitions. It contains all possible behaviour for the case in which all components are included (which may very well be prohibited by the feature constraints when imposed). More interestingly, based on the attributed feature model defined in

CIF 3 and the component automata we can synthesise a state space that contains 16 initial states, one for each valid product, and display the behaviour for each of them. The state space has 147 states and 1254 transitions. It is obtained in less than 2 seconds of user time on a standard laptop. In the composed system at hand we have included the requirement PRESENCE_CHECK below, which couples features and components, i.e. it states for each event of the components which features need to be present for it to be available. This is similar to the notion of an FTS [17] mentioned in the introduction, where transitions are not labelled with action names only but by a Boolean expression of features as well. Note that here we choose to give global conditions for events. However, if we instead require these conditions locally in the component automata, different occurrences of the same event can be made subject to different conditions (as in FTSs).

Listing 4. Requirement PRESENCE_CHECK

```
location Dummy:  initial, marked;
   edge CANCEL.cancel when FX.present;
   edge COFFEE.coffee when FB.present and FC.present;
   edge TEA.tea when FB.present and FT.present;
   ...
```

With the model presented so far we have achieved to describe the behaviour of all 16 valid products of the running example, as specified by the feature model and the component models. Note that so far the products are not supervised yet, we have only achieved to enforce behaviour that is consistent with the feature model. This means that we may still be allowing unacceptable behaviour, such as pouring coffee while no coin has been inserted. In the next subsection, we describe how to model further requirements that the controller should enforce.

4.3   Behavioural Requirements

As mentioned, the constructed product behaviours are still uncontrolled, in the sense that we have not yet attempted to implement a supervisory controller that forces the products to behave according to a list of desired behavioural requirements. To illustrate the flexibility of the approach, we will introduce some of these. We consider the following types of requirements: (i) state invariants, (ii) event conditions, (iii) event ordering requirements, (iv) requirements using observers and (v) requirements using additional variables.

State Invariants. In many applications of supervisory controller synthesis one uses so-called state invariants to express that certain combinations of states of components should not occur at the same time. In the case study of this paper, for instance, one may desire to require that it is impossible to be ready for pouring coffee and tea at the same time. In CIF 3 this can be expressed as follows.

```
requirement invariant not (COFFEE.Coffee and TEA.Tea);
```

Event Conditions. An event condition is a requirement in which a state predicate must be satisfied before an event may be executed. In CIF 3, the following notation is used for such event conditions: `requirement <event> needs <pred>`, where `<event>` is an event name and `<pred>` is a state predicate. The meaning of this requirement is that the event may only be executed in case the predicate holds. For instance, we may want to impose that it is not allowed to change the choice of a beverage (coffee, cappuccino or tea) once the choice has been made. This means that a choice may only be made if no choice has been made yet. Observe that reference is made to events and locations of component automata in such requirements.

Listing 5. Example event conditions

```
requirement
    COFFEE.coffee needs COFFEE.NoChoice and TEA.NoChoice;
requirement
    COFFEE.cappuccino needs COFFEE.NoChoice and TEA.NoChoice
      ;
requirement
    TEA.tea needs COFFEE.NoChoice and TEA.NoChoice;
```

Event Ordering Requirements. Another type of requirement is used to express that certain events may only occur in specific orderings. For instance, one may have the requirement that a ringtone may only occur after a drink has been delivered. We can use automata to model such requirements, as in Listing 6.

Listing 6. Requirement RING_AFTER_BEVERAGE_COMPLETION

```
location NotCompleted: initial, marked;
    edge COFFEE.done when FR.present goto Completed;
    edge TEA.done when FR.present goto Completed;
    edge COFFEE.done, TEA.done when not FR.present;
location Completed:
    edge RINGTONE.ring goto NotCompleted;
```

Requirements Using Observers. Many of the events that can be performed by the components of the coffee machine should only occur if a coin is in the machine. For such a requirement, we define an additional automaton, commonly called an observer, which establishes whether or not a coin is in the machine. It is depicted in Listing 7. It uses the events from the component automata to observe their occurrences and then uses these to decide on the logical state of the system. Note that we have taken care to develop this observer in such a way that all its events are possible from any of its states. Thus, the automaton itself does not restrict the behaviour of the components.

Listing 7. Observer automaton COIN_PRESENCE

```
location NoCoinPresent: initial , marked;
    edge COIN.insert goto CoinPresent;
    edge CANCEL.cancel, Machine.take_cup;
location CoinPresent:
    edge CANCEL.cancel goto NoCoinPresent;
    edge MACHINE.take_cup goto NoCoinPresent;
    edge Coin.insert;
```

Next, this observer automaton may be used in requirements. For example, coffee may only be poured if a coin is in the system.

```
requirement COFFEE.coffee needs COIN_PRESENCE.CoinPresent;
```

Using Additional Variables. An exemplary quantitative requirement to restrict the behaviour of products in such a way that if sugar is chosen, then always two portions are used, was provided in Listing 2 in Sect. 3.

4.4 Synthesis

Above we have illustrated how various types of requirements regarding the behaviour of the components may be modelled in CIF 3. With this in place, we can obtain a supervisor for each of the valid products by simply combining the feature model, the component behaviour models and all of the requirements into one model. The synthesis algorithm then constructs the synchronous product of the component and requirement automata and starts an iterative process of removing states that do not satisfy the invariants and the nonblocking property until a proper supervisor is obtained, or an empty supervisor results indicating that no supervisor may exist at all. The synthesis algorithm suffers from the same state space explosion problem as for model checking [23].

In this case, application of the supervisory controller synthesis options offered by CIF 3 then results in a single CIF 3 model that represents an automaton for each of the valid products. The state space of the 16 valid products together contains 503 states an 868 transitions. Again, it was obtained within 2 seconds user time on a standard laptop.

Among others, the resulting CIF 3 model describes for each event the additional conditions that need to be satisfied in terms of the locations and values of variables for the presence of features, component, observer and requirement automata. Listing 8 provides part of this. Note that in these conditions several automata, such as X, Y, Z, RESTRICTED_CANCEL and NO_FREE_LUNCH are referenced that have not been shown in this paper.

Listing 8. Supervisor automaton

```
edge COFFEE.cappuccino when not FD.present and (FP.present
    and X.Idle) and (TEA.NoChoice and (RESTRICTED_CANCEL.
    CancelAllowed and NO_FREE_LUNCH.Full));

edge COFFEE.pour_milk when not X.OneUnitNeeded and
            Z.OneUnitNeeded or (X.OneUnitNeeded and (Z.
    OneUnitNeeded and SWEET.NoSugar) or X.OneUnitNeeded and
    (Z.OneUnitNeeded and SWEET.Sugar));

edge SWEET.pour_sugar when X.Idle and FT.present and
            (TEA.Tea and SWEETNESS.cnt≠2) or (X.
    OneUnitPoured and SWEETNESS.cnt≠2 or X.OneUnitNeeded
    and SWEETNESS.cnt≠2);

edge TEA.pour_tea when Y.OneUnitNeeded and
                    (not Y.OneUnitNeeded or not SWEET.
    NoChoice);

edge TEA.tea when X.Idle and FT.present and
                    (RESTRICTED_CANCEL.CancelAllowed and
    NO_FREE_LUNCH.Full);
...
```

It must be mentioned that these conditions are not simplified in any way. For example the condition of event pour_tea may be simplified to Y.OneUnitNeeded and not SWEET.NoChoice.

5   Concluding Remarks

We have shown how CIF 3 can be put to work for feature-guided integration of components. Given (i) an attributed feature model capturing in-tree, cross-tree and attribute constraints, (ii) a description of the potential behaviour of a number of components and (iii) additional static, dynamic and quantitative requirements, the CIF 3 machinery synthesises a composition of the components that is consistent with the attributed feature model and adheres to the additional requirements, if possible at all. Otherwise CIF 3 reports that a composition is non-existent. Each initial state of the overall system corresponds to a unique valid product from the product line as defined by the feature model. All products are sound *by construction* and the set of products is complete with respect to the combined feature model and behavioural requirements, because of the maximal permissiveness guaranteed by CIF 3 [36,38].

Since we focussed on supervisory controller synthesis for product lines as supported by CIF 3, many notions from SCT that are useful to SPLE have been left unspoken here. For instance, one can imagine a coffee machine to come equipped with a sensor to monitor whenever one of the ingredients, say sugar, has become depleted. By its nature, the sensor's messaging that the machine is out of sugar is an *uncontrollable* event. From the perspective of model-based engineering such a distinction is relevant; the modelling formalism of CIF 3 is sufficiently expressive to take this into account. Incorporation of uncontrollable events may be useful to detect feature interaction as failure of synthesis may reveal unexpected dependencies. For this to work the synthesis algorithm needs to be refined.

In the present case study, it is assumed that presence/absence of features is statically organised. However, many systems, including the coffee machine, may be reconfigured while operating. For instance, one may wish to remove or add the tea feature dynamically (possibly dependent on the ingredients that are available). This can easily be achieved by adding a self-loop transition in the FT automaton labelled with a reconfigure event which switches presence of the feature. More complicatedly, a reconfiguration modifying a specific feature may immediately result in a violation of some of the constraints imposed by the feature model because of the interplay of the feature with other features. It is possible to also model this type of reconfigurations in CIF 3 by introducing events that represent the simultaneous reconfiguration of several features, temporarily lifting the constraints stemming from the feature model.

Often, especially in earlier design phases, the set of requirements that are to be enforced has not become clear yet. As a consequence, supervisory control synthesis may result in the impossibility to produce a supervisor, or lead to a controlled system that omits states of which the designer would not expect their omission. In recent work [43], the synthesis algorithm has been adapted to retrieve the reason why the controlled system is blocked from reaching specific states. This information can then be used for understanding which requirements (under which conditions) are conflicting, whereupon the model of the components and/or the requirement may be refined. For future work, we plan to consider adaptations to the synthesis algorithm that may reveal conflicts among features and/or their attributes. Such conflicts may be used to discover that changes in the components interfere with the feature model in force, excluding products that were valid before.

Acknowledgments. Ter Beek is supported by EU project QUANTICOL, 600708. We are thankful to the ISOLA reviewers for their constructive comments.

References

1. Asirelli, P., ter Beek, M.H., Fantechi, A., Gnesi, S.: A compositional framework to derive product line behavioural descriptions. In: Margaria, T., Steffen, B. (eds.) ISoLA 2012, Part I. LNCS, vol. 7609, pp. 146–161. Springer, Heidelberg (2012)
2. Baier, C., Katoen, J.-P.: Principles of Model Checking. MIT Press, Cambridge (2008)
3. Bąk, K., Diskin, Z., Antkiewicz, M., Czarnecki, K., Wąsowski, A.: Clafer: unifying class and feature modeling. Softw. Syst. Model. **15**, 811–845 (2015)
4. ter Beek, M.H., de Vink, E.P.: Towards modular verification of software product lines with mCRL2. In: Margaria, T., Steffen, B. (eds.) ISoLA 2014, Part I. LNCS, vol. 8802, pp. 368–385. Springer, Heidelberg (2014)

5. ter Beek, M.H., de Vink, E.P.: Using mCRL2 for the analysis of software product lines. In: FormaliSE 2014, pp. 31–37. IEEE (2014)
6. ter Beek, M.H., de Vink, E.P., Willemse, T.A.C.: Towards a feature mu-Calculus targeting SPL verification. In: FMSPLE 2016, EPTCS, vol. 206, pp. 61–75 (2016)
7. ter Beek, M.H., Fantechi, A., Gnesi, S., Mazzanti, F.: Modelling and analysing variability in product families: model checking of modal transition systems with variability constraints. J. Log. Algebr. Methods Program. 85(2), 287–315 (2016)
8. ter Beek, M.H., Legay, A., Lafuente, A.L., Vandin, A.: Statistical analysis of probabilistic models of software product lines with quantitative constraints. In: SPLC 2015, pp. 11–15. ACM (2015)
9. ter Beek, M.H., Legay, A., Lafuente, A.L., Vandin, A.: Statistical model checking for product lines. In: Margaria, T., Steffen, B. (eds.) ISoLA 2016. LNCS, vol. 9952, pp. 114–133. Springer, Heidelberg (2016)
10. ter Beek, M.H., Mazzanti, F., Sulova, A.: VMC: a tool for product variability analysis. In: Giannakopoulou, D., Méry, D. (eds.) FM 2012. LNCS, vol. 7436, pp. 450–454. Springer, Heidelberg (2012)
11. van Beek, D.A., Fokkink, W.J., Hendriks, D., Hofkamp, A., Markovski, J., van de Mortel-Fronczak, J.M., Reniers, M.A.: CIF 3: model-based engineering of supervisory controllers. In: Ábrahám, E., Havelund, K. (eds.) TACAS 2014 (ETAPS). LNCS, vol. 8413, pp. 575–580. Springer, Heidelberg (2014)
12. Behrmann, G., David, A., Larsen, K.G., Håkansson, J., Pettersson, P., Yi, W., Hendriks, M.: UPPAAL 4.0. In: QEST 2006, pp. 125–126. IEEE (2006)
13. Benavides, D., Segura, S., Ruiz-Cortés, A.: Automated analysis of feature models 20 years later: a literature review. Inf. Syst. 35(6), 615–636 (2010)
14. Bubel, R., Hähnle, R., Pelevina, M.: Fully abstract operation contracts. In: Margaria, T., Steffen, B. (eds.) ISoLA 2014, Part II. LNCS, vol. 8803, pp. 120–134. Springer, Heidelberg (2014)
15. Classen, A., Cordy, M., Heymans, P., Legay, A., Schobbens, P.-Y.: Model checking software product lines with SNIP. Int. J. Softw. Tools Technol. Transfer 14(5), 589–612 (2012)
16. Classen, A., Cordy, M., Heymans, P., Legay, A., Schobbens, P.-Y.: Formal semantics, modular specification, and symbolic verification of product-line behaviour. Sci. Comput. Program. 80, 416–439 (2014)
17. Classen, A., Cordy, M., Schobbens, P.-Y., Heymans, P., Legay, A., Raskin, J.-F.: Featured transition systems: foundations for verifying variability-intensive systems and their application to LTL model checking. IEEE Trans. Software Eng. 39(8), 1069–1089 (2013)
18. Classen, A., Heymans, P., Schobbens, P.-Y., Legay, A., Raskin, J.-F.: Model checking lots of systems: efficient verification of temporal properties in software product lines. In: ICSE 2010, pp. 335–344. ACM (2010)
19. Cordy, M., Classen, A., Heymans, P., Schobbens, P.-Y., Legay, A.: ProVeLines: a product line of verifiers for software product lines. In: SPLC 2013, vol. 2, pp. 141–146. ACM (2013)
20. Delaware, B., Cook, W.R., Batory, D.S.: Product lines of theorems. In: Lopes, C.V., Fisher, K., (eds.) OOPSLA 2011, pp. 595–608. ACM (2011)
21. Dijkstra, E.W.: A constructive approach to the problem of program correctness. BIT Numer. Math. 8(3), 174–186 (1968)
22. Forschelen, S.T.J., van de Mortel-Fronczak, J.M., Su, R., Rooda, J.E.: Application of supervisory control theory to theme park vehicles. Discrete Event Dyn. Syst. 22(4), 511–540 (2012)

23. Gohari, P., Wonham, W.M.: On the complexity of supervisory control design in the RW framework. IEEE Trans. Syst. Man Cybern. **30**(5), 643–652 (2000). Part B
24. Gruler, A., Leucker, M., Scheidemann, K.: Modeling and model checking software product lines. In: Barthe, G., Boer, F.S. (eds.) FMOODS 2008. LNCS, vol. 5051, pp. 113–131. Springer, Heidelberg (2008)
25. Hähnle, R., Schaefer, I.: A Liskov principle for delta-oriented programming. In: Margaria, T., Steffen, B. (eds.) ISoLA 2012, Part I. LNCS, vol. 7609, pp. 32–46. Springer, Heidelberg (2012)
26. Hall, A.: Correctness by construction: integrating formality into a commercial development process. In: Eriksson, L.-H., Lindsay, P.A. (eds.) FME 2002. LNCS, vol. 2391, pp. 224–233. Springer, Heidelberg (2002)
27. Hall, A., Chapman, R.: Correctness by construction: developing a commercial secure system. IEEE Softw. **19**(1), 18–25 (2002)
28. Hoare, C.A.R.: Proof of a program: FIND. Commun. ACM **14**(1), 39–45 (1971)
29. Jackson, D., Abstractions, S.: Logic, Language, and Analysis. MIT Press, Cambridge (2006)
30. Juodisius, P., Sarkar, A., Mukkamala, R.R., Antkiewicz, M., Czarnecki, K., Wąsowski, A.: Clafer: lightweight modeling of structure and behavior with variability. Unpublished manuscript
31. Lauenroth, K., Pohl, K., Töhning, S.: Model checking of domain artifacts in product line engineering. In: ASE 2009, pp. 269–280. IEEE (2009)
32. Leucker, M., Thoma, D.: A formal approach to software product families. In: Margaria, T., Steffen, B. (eds.) ISoLA 2012, Part I. LNCS, vol. 7609, pp. 131–145. Springer, Heidelberg (2012)
33. Lochau, M., Mennicke, S., Baller, H., Ribbeck, L.: DeltaCCS: a core calculus for behavioral change. In: Margaria, T., Steffen, B. (eds.) ISoLA 2014, Part I. LNCS, vol. 8802, pp. 320–335. Springer, Heidelberg (2014)
34. Mannion, M., Camara, J.: Theorem proving for product line model verification. In: van der Linden, F.J. (ed.) PFE 2003. LNCS, vol. 3014, pp. 211–224. Springer, Heidelberg (2004)
35. Markovski, J., Jacobs, K.G.M., van Beek, D.A., Somers, L.J.A.M., Rooda, J.E.: Coordination of resources using generalized state-based requirements. In: Raisch, J., Giua, A., Lafortune, S., Moor, T. (eds.) WODES 2010, pp. 287–292. International Federation of Automatic Control (2010)
36. Ouedraogo, L., Kumar, R., Malik, R., Åkesson, K.: Nonblocking and safe control of discrete-event systems modeled as extended finite automata. IEEE Trans. Autom. Sci. Eng. **8**(3), 560–569 (2011)
37. Pohl, K., Böckle, G., van der Linden, F.J.: Software Product Line Engineering: Foundations, Principles, and Techniques. Springer, Heidelberg (2005)
38. Ramadge, P.J., Wonham, W.M.: Supervisory control of a class of discrete event processes. SIAM J. Control Optim. **25**(1), 206–230 (1987)
39. Robinson, J.A., Voronkov, A. (eds.): Handbook of Automated Reasoning. MIT Press, Cambridge (2001)
40. Schaefer, I.: Variability modelling for model-driven development of software product lines. In: Benavides, D., Batory, D.S., Grünbacher, P. (eds.) VaMoS 2010, ICB-Research report, vol. 37, pp. 85–92. Universität Duisburg-Essen (2010)
41. Skoldstam, M., Åkesson, K., Fabian, M.: Modeling of discrete event systems using finite automata with variables. In: CDC 2007, pp. 3387–3392 (2007)
42. van der Sanden, B., Reniers, M.A., Geilen, M., Basten, T., Jacobs, J., Voeten, J., Schiffelers, R.R.H.: Modular model-based supervisory controller design for wafer logistics in lithography machines. In: MoDELS 2015, pp. 416–425. IEEE (2015)

43. Swartjes, L., Reniers, M.A., van Beek, D., Fokkink, W.: Why is my supervisor empty? Finding causes for the unreachability of states in synthesized supervisors. In: Cassandras, C.G., Giua, A., Li, Z. (eds.) WODES 2016, pp. 14–21. IEEE (2016)
44. Theunissen, R.J.M., van Beek, D.A., Rooda, J.E.: Improving evolvability of a patient communication control system using state-based supervisory control synthesis. Adv. Eng. Inform. **26**(3), 502–515 (2012)
45. Thüm, T., Schaefer, I., Hentschel, M., Apel, S.: Family-based deductive verification of software product lines. In: GPCE 2012, pp. 11–20. ACM (2012)

Partial Verification and Intermediate Results as a Solution to Combine Automatic and Interactive Verification Techniques

Dirk Beyer

LMU Munich, Munich, Germany

Abstract. Many of the current verification approaches can be classified into automatic and interactive techniques, each having different strengths and weaknesses. Thus, one of the current open problems is to design solutions to combine the two approaches and accelerate technology transfer. We outline four existing techniques that might be able to contribute to combination solutions: (1) Conditional model checking is a technique that gives detailed information (in form of a condition) about the verified state space, i.e., informs the user (or tools later in a tool chain) of the outcome. Also, it accepts as input detailed information (again as condition) about what the conditional model checker has to do. (2) Correctness witnesses, stored in a machine-readable exchange format, contain (partial) invariants that can be used to prove the correctness of a system. For example, tools that usually expect invariants from the user can read the invariants from such correctness witnesses and ask the user only for the remaining invariants. (3) Abstraction-refinement based approaches that use a dynamically adjustable precision (such as in lazy CEGAR approaches) can be provided with invariants from the user or from other tools, e.g., from deductive methods. This way, the approach can succeed in constructing a proof even if it was not able to come up with the required invariant. (4) The technique of path invariants extracts (in a CEGAR method) a path program that represents an interesting part of the program for which an invariant is needed. Such a path program can be given to an expensive (or interactive) method for computing invariants that can then be fed back to a CEGAR method to continue verifying the large program. While the existing techniques originate from software verification, we believe that the new combination ideas are useful for verifying general systems.

1 Introduction

Automatic verification techniques usually expect the user to set parameters, and the prover computes the necessary invariants and the proof — the strength of this technique is that it works for large systems. Interactive verification techniques usually expect the user to provide invariants and the prover establishes a formal correctness proof — the strength of this technology is that it works for sophisticated specifications. In order to increase the impact of formal verification, we need approaches that combine the advantages of both. The organizers

© Springer International Publishing AG 2016
T. Margaria and B. Steffen (Eds.): ISoLA 2016, Part I, LNCS 9952, pp. 874–880, 2016.
DOI: 10.1007/978-3-319-47166-2_60

of the ISoLA 2016 track on "Correctness-by-Construction and Post-hoc Verification" [36] emphasize the importance of bringing together researchers from different verification communities, in order to exchange ideas and discuss ways to combine techniques and improve the overall verification process. Bringing together different communities and develop verification tools that integrate solutions from various viewpoints takes time and requires a long series of such meetings (for example, a similar event with the same objective took place at Dagstuhl a few years ago [15]). A similar "joining effort" of two communities took place in the past: the research areas of data-flow analysis and software model checking were originally using separate concepts, techniques, and algorithms, but were unified in the past two decades [9,33]. Today, tools for automatic software verification usually combine techniques from data-flow analysis with techniques from software model checking (e.g., [11,16,19,22–24,29,34,35,38]).

Maturity Level of Research Areas. Both automatic and interactive verification are mature research areas. This is not only witnessed by the many valuable publications (cf. surveys [4,28] for an overview), but in particular by the large set of available tools that make it possible to actually verify real software with the help of new technology [2,30]. There are several well-maintained software projects that reflect the state of the art in the area of automatic verification, for example, BLAST [11], CBMC [19], CPACHECKER [16], SLAM [3], and ULTIMATE [24]; a large list of recent tool implementations can be found in the SV-COMP competition report [5]. Also in interactive verification, the state of the art is available in well-maintained software projects, for example, AUTO-PROOF [37], DAFNY [31], KEY [1], KIV [20], and VERIFAST [27]; a larger list can be found in the VERIFYTHIS competition report [26].

There are four international competitions in the area of software verification, which all have the goal to showcase the strengths and abilities of the latest technology, and at the same time identify the limits of the existing approaches. RERS [25] is a competition on verification of generated event-condition-action programs. This allows to control the features that are used in the program and for which support is needed during the verification process. The goal is to identify the overall current abilities of software verifiers, without any restriction of the process or of the resources. SV-COMP [5] is a controlled experiment to measure effectiveness and efficiency of fully-automatic software verification. Verifiers are executed without interaction on a dedicated computing environment and with limited, controlled computing resources (CPU time, memory). TERMCOMP [21] focuses on the particular specification of termination. VERIFYTHIS [26] concentrates on evaluating different verification approaches and ideas to formalize a given problem, i.e., develop a model and a specification and then prove correctness.

Outline. This article presents a position statement that was prepared for the ISoLA 2016 meeting. We use a few existing approaches from the viewpoint of automatic verification which might be able to contribute to combination approaches. We outline four solutions to combine automatic verification with interactive verification by exchanging partial and intermediate verification results using well-defined interfaces.

2   Exchanging Partial and Intermediate Results

Conditional Model Checking. In classical model checking, the outcome of a model checker is either TRUE or FALSE. In practice, however, executions of classical model checkers often end without delivering any useful result (tool gives up, component or tool crashes, tool runs out of resources), which means that the resources that the user spent on the verification task are lost without any benefit for the user. *Conditional model checking* [12] is a technique that gives detailed information (in form of a condition) about the verified state space, i.e., informs the user or tools later in the tool chain of the outcome. Also, it accepts as input detailed information (again as condition) about what the conditional model checker has to do, i.e., which parts of the state space to verify.

The idea to use a sequential combination of different approaches is not new, for example, a combination of CCURED [32] with BLAST [11] was explored more than ten years ago: in a first phase, CCURED added run-time checks to the program in order to make sure that no memory-safety violation happens without run-time notification of the user; in a second phase, BLAST removed all run-time checks that it was able to verify statically [10]. All run-time checks that could not be verified remained in the reduced "cured" program. Conditional model checking formalized the approach and emphasizes the flow of information about what is still to be verified between different checkers.

If developers of automatic and interactive verification tools agree on an exchange format for conditions that describe the state-space that is to be verified, then many verifiers (both automatic and interactive) can be turned into conditional model checkers.

Correctness Witnesses. Until recently, model checkers reported counterexample traces in proprietary formats, mostly in formats that were difficult to read, not only for users but also for machines, i.e., the reported counterexamples were sometimes difficult to inspect and thus of limited use. *Error witnesses* [8], stored in an exchangeable standard format, overcome this problem. Witnesses can now be inspected by users and tools without knowledge about the implementation of the verifier that produced the witness, and the trust in the verification result can be increased by independent witness validators. The witnesses can also be visualized and used for debugging [6]. Further extending this concept, *correctness witnesses* [7] store hints for establishing a correctness proof. Program invariants (perhaps partial invariants) are stored in a machine-readable exchange format.

In a combination scenario, tools that usually expect invariants from the user can be provided with invariants from correctness witnesses. This way, automatic tools can compute as many invariants as possible automatically, the resulting invariants are provided to the interactive tool as input, and the interactive tool needs to ask only for the remaining invariants. While interactive tools already compute some invariants automatically, the exchange with automatic verifiers accelerates technology transfer and adoption of implementations with less effort.

Precisions. One of the key challenges in automatic software verification is to algorithmically compute an abstract model that is precise enough to be able to prove that the specification holds and that is at the same time coarse enough to make the verification process efficient. The level of abstraction of the abstract model can be expressed as a *precision* [14]. The precision is often computed using counterexample-guided abstraction refinement (CEGAR) [18]. An *infeasible error path* is an error path through the to-be-verified program that is possible in the abstract model, but not in the concrete program, i.e., the precision of the abstract model is too coarse. CEGAR uses infeasible error paths to derive useful information for refining the abstract model, i.e., to increase the precision. For many abstract domains that are used with dynamic abstraction refinement (predicates, variable assignments, shape graphs, intervals), the precision can be stored for later reuse [17], for example, for regression verification.

In case of an incomplete verification run, an automatic verifier was perhaps identifying the correct variables that the invariant should talk about, but the constructed precision was not correctly establishing the relation of the variables. For example, consider the code snippet in Fig. 1 (meant as a part of a very large program) and assume that CEGAR with predicate abstraction brought up an infeasible error path that goes once through the body of the loop and then violates the assertion (due to not yet tracking any variables). For a human it might be easy to see that the invariant $x = y$ is needed at the loop head in order

```
1  x = 0;
2  y = 0;
3  while (x < n) {
4      x++;
5      y++;
6  }
7  assert(x==y);
```

Fig. 1. Code snippet that requires loop invariant $x = y$

to prove the correctness of the program, while the value of the unknown constant n is irrelevant for the safety property and can be abstracted away. But an interpolation-based refinement procedure might unluckily come up with interpolants that contain predicates like $x = 0$, $y = 0$, $x = 1$, $y = 1$, which are sufficient to eliminate the current infeasible error path, but in the next CEGAR iteration, an infeasible error path that goes twice through the loop body will be brought up, and so on. This (rather simple) automatic approach would fail because it is not able to generalize the information from the path to the loop invariant $x = y$.

So it would be an interesting approach to interactively tell the user (or a different tool) that an invariant is needed that talks about variables x and y. Then, either an interactive prover is fed with the invariants that were computed by the automatic verifier together with the additional invariants from the user, or the automatic verifier is restarted with the additional invariants. Together, the different approaches might be able to completely solve the verification task.

Path Invariants. Sometimes, adding a certain information about the path to the precision is sufficient to eliminate the infeasible error path from further exploration, but not other error paths that are infeasible for a similar reason (cf. explanation of the example of Fig. 1 above). The approach of *path invariants* [13] constructs a *path program* (hopefully much smaller than the original program) that contains the infeasible error path, and in addition many similar error paths. Now, such a path program for which an invariant is needed can be given to an expensive method for computing invariants, and the invariants can then be fed back to a CEGAR method to refine the precision and continue verifying the large original program. The loop invariants for the path program will eliminate a whole series of infeasible error paths, instead of only one single infeasible error path.

If an automatic verifier is not able to derive an invariant and would have to abort the verification process, it could instead ask the user for an appropriate invariant. Since the path program is small and focuses on the reason for which the automatic verifier was not able to construct an invariant, a user can perhaps use an interactive verifier to construct an invariant for the path program and feed this back to the automatic verifier. The advantage over the precision-based solution above is that the user (or interactive tool) is given the isolated, but full context of a complete (path) program.

3   Conclusion

Currently, automatic techniques can verify large systems, but with rather simple specifications, while interactive techniques can verify complicated specifications, but only for systems of rather limited size. To further improve the verification technology, we need solutions to combine the techniques from automatic and interactive verification. We have outlined a few new ideas for combining very different verification approaches using existing techniques that support partial verification and the exchange of intermediate verification results. To further stimulate the discussion and develop new combination ideas, it is necessary to implement the above-mentioned combination ideas and report experimental results.

References

1. Ahrendt, W., Beckert, B., Bruns, D., Bubel, R., Gladisch, C., Grebing, S., Hähnle, R., Hentschel, M., Herda, M., Klebanov, V., Mostowski, W., Scheben, C., Schmitt, P.H., Ulbrich, M.: The KEY platform for verification and analysis of Java programs. In: Giannakopoulou, D., Kröning, D. (eds.) VSTTE 2014. LNCS, vol. 8471, pp. 55–71. Springer, Heidelberg (2014)
2. Ball, T., Levin, V., Rajamani, S.K.: A decade of software model checking with SLAM. Commun. ACM **54**(7), 68–76 (2011)
3. Ball, T., Rajamani, S.K.: The SLAM project: Debugging system software via static analysis. In: POPL 2002, pp. 1–3. ACM (2002)
4. Beckert, B., Hähnle, R.: Reasoning and verification: State of the art and current trends. IEEE Intell. Syst. **29**(1), 20–29 (2014)
5. Beyer, D.: Reliable and reproducible competition results with BenchExec and witnesses (Report on SV-COMP 2016). In: Chechik, M., Raskin, J.-F. (eds.) TACAS 2016. LNCS, vol. 9636, pp. 887–904. Springer, Heidelberg (2016)
6. Beyer, D., Dangl, M.: Verification-aided debugging: An interactive web-service for exploring error witnesses. In: Chaudhuri, S., Farzan, A. (eds.) CAV 2016. LNCS, vol. 9780, pp. 502–509. Springer, Heidelberg (2016)

7. Beyer, D., Dangl, M., Dietsch, D., Heizmann, M.: Correctness witnesses: Exchanging verification results between verifiers. In: FSE 2016. ACM (2016)
8. Beyer, D., Dangl, M., Dietsch, D., Heizmann, M., Stahlbauer, A.: Witness validation and stepwise testification across software verifiers. In: FSE 2015, pp. 721–733. ACM (2015)
9. Beyer, D., Gulwani, S., Schmidt, D.: Combining model checking and data-flow analysis. In: Clarke, E.M., Henzinger, T.A., Veith, H. (eds.) Handbook on Model Checking. Springer (to appear, 2017)
10. Beyer, D., Henzinger, T.A., Jhala, R., Majumdar, R.: Checking memory safety with BLAST. In: Cerioli, M. (ed.) FASE 2005. LNCS, vol. 3442, pp. 2–18. Springer, Heidelberg (2005)
11. Beyer, D., Henzinger, T.A., Jhala, R., Majumdar, R.: The software model checker BLAST. Int. J. Softw. Tools Technol. Transfer 9(5–6), 505–525 (2007)
12. Beyer, D., Henzinger, T.A., Keremoglu, M.E., Wendler, P.: Conditional model checking: A technique to pass information between verifiers. In: FSE 2012. ACM (2012)
13. Beyer, D., Henzinger, T.A., Majumdar, R., Rybalchenko, A.: Path invariants. In: PLDI 2007, pp. 300–309. ACM (2007)
14. Beyer, D., Henzinger, T.A., Théoduloz, G.: Program analysis with dynamic precision adjustment. In: ASE 2008, pp. 29–38. IEEE (2008)
15. Beyer, D., Huisman, M., Klebanov, V., Monahan, R.: Evaluating software verification systems: Benchmarks and competitions (Dagstuhl reports 14171). Dagstuhl Rep. 4(4), 1–19 (2014)
16. Beyer, D., Keremoglu, M.E.: CPACHECKER: A tool for configurable software verification. In: Gopalakrishnan, G., Qadeer, S. (eds.) CAV 2011. LNCS, vol. 6806, pp. 184–190. Springer, Heidelberg (2011)
17. Beyer, D., Löwe, S., Novikov, E., Stahlbauer, A., Wendler, P.: Precision reuse for efficient regression verification. In: ESEC/FSE 2013, pp. 389–399. ACM (2013)
18. Clarke, E.M., Grumberg, O., Jha, S., Lu, Y., Veith, H.: Counterexample-guided abstraction refinement for symbolic model checking. J. ACM 50(5), 752–794 (2003)
19. Clarke, E., Kröning, D., Lerda, F.: A tool for checking ANSI-C programs. In: Jensen, K., Podelski, A. (eds.) TACAS 2004. LNCS, vol. 2988, pp. 168–176. Springer, Heidelberg (2004)
20. Ernst, G., Pfähler, J., Schellhorn, G., Haneberg, D., Reif, W.: KIV: Overview and VERIFYTHIS competition. Int. J. Softw. Tools Technol. Transfer 17(6), 677–694 (2015)
21. Giesl, J., Mesnard, F., Rubio, A., Thiemann, R., Waldmann, J.: Termination competition. In: Felty, A.P., Middeldorp, A. (eds.) CADE-25. LNCS, vol. 9195, pp. 105–108. Springer, Heidelberg (2015)
22. Albarghouthi, A., Gurfinkel, A., Li, Y., Chaki, S., Chechik, M.: UFO: Verification with interpolants and abstract interpretation (Competition Contribution). In: Piterman, N., Smolka, S.A. (eds.) TACAS 2013. LNCS, vol. 7795, pp. 637–640. Springer, Heidelberg (2013)
23. Gurfinkel, A., Kahsai, T., Navas, J.A.: SEAHORN: A framework for verifying C programs (Competition Contribution). In: Baier, C., Tinelli, C. (eds.) TACAS 2015. LNCS, vol. 9035, pp. 447–450. Springer, Heidelberg (2015)
24. Heizmann, M., Dietsch, D., Greitschus, M., Leike, J., Musa, B., Schätzle, C., Podelski, A.: ULTIMATE automizer with two-track proofs (Competition Contribution). In: Chechik, M., Raskin, J.-F. (eds.) TACAS 2016. LNCS, vol. 9636, pp. 950–953. Springer, Heidelberg (2016)

880   D. Beyer

25. Howar, F., Isberner, M., Merten, M., Steffen, B., Beyer, D., Păsăreanu, C.S.: Rigorous examination of reactive systems. The RERS challenges 2012 and 2013. Int. J. Softw. Tools Technol. Transfer **16**(5), 457–464 (2014)
26. Huisman, M., Klebanov, V., Monahan, R., Tautschnig, M.: VERIFYTHIS 2015: A program verification competition. Int. J. Softw. Tools Technol. Transfer (2016)
27. Jacobs, B., Smans, J., Philippaerts, P., Vogels, F., Penninckx, W., Piessens, F.: VERIFAST: A powerful, sound, predictable, fast verifier for C and Java. In: Bobaru, M., Havelund, K., Holzmann, G.J., Joshi, R. (eds.) NFM 2011. LNCS, vol. 6617, pp. 41–55. Springer, Heidelberg (2011)
28. Jhala, R., Majumdar, R.: Software model checking. ACM Comput. Surv. **41**(4), Article No. 21 (2009)
29. Karpenkov, E.G.: LPI: Software verification with local policy iteration (Competition Contribution). In: Chechik, M., Raskin, J.-F. (eds.) TACAS 2016. LNCS, vol. 9636, pp. 930–933. Springer, Heidelberg (2016)
30. Khoroshilov, A., Mutilin, V., Petrenko, A., Zakharov, V.: Establishing Linux driver verification process. In: Pnueli, A., Virbitskaite, I., Voronkov, A. (eds.) PSI 2009. LNCS, vol. 5947, pp. 165–176. Springer, Heidelberg (2010)
31. Leino, K.R.M.: DAFNY: An automatic program verifier for functional correctness. In: Clarke, E.M., Voronkov, A. (eds.) LPAR-16 2010. LNCS, vol. 6355, pp. 348–370. Springer, Heidelberg (2010)
32. Necula, G.C., McPeak, S., Weimer, W.: CCURED: Type-safe retrofitting of legacy code. In: POPL 2002, pp. 128–139. ACM (2002)
33. Schmidt, D.A., Steffen, B.: Program analysis as model checking of abstract interpretations. In: Levi, G. (ed.) SAS 1998. LNCS, vol. 1503, pp. 351–380. Springer, Heidelberg (1998)
34. Schrammel, P., Kröning, D.: 2LS for program analysis (Competition Contribution). In: Chechik, M., Raskin, J.-F. (eds.) TACAS 2016. LNCS, vol. 9636, pp. 905–907. Springer, Heidelberg (2016)
35. Ströder, T., Aschermann, C., Frohn, F., Hensel, J., Giesl, J.: APROVE: Termination and memory safety of C programs (Competition Contribution). In: Baier, C., Tinelli, C. (eds.) TACAS 2015. LNCS, vol. 9035, pp. 417–419. Springer, Heidelberg (2015)
36. ter Beek, M., Hähnle, R., Schaefer, I.: Correctness-by-construction and post-hoc verification. In: Margaria, T., Steffen, B. (eds.) ISoLA 2016 Part I. LNCS, vol. 9952, pp. 723–729. Springer, Heidelberg (2016)
37. Tschannen, J., Furia, C.A., Nordio, M., Polikarpova, N.: AUTOPROOF: Auto-active functional verification of object-oriented programs. In: Baier, C., Tinelli, C. (eds.) TACAS 2015. LNCS, vol. 9035, pp. 566–580. Springer, Heidelberg (2015)
38. Zheng, M., Edenhofner, J.G., Luo, Z., Gerrard, M.J., Rogers, M.S., Dwyer, M.B., Siegel, S.F.: CIVL: Applying a general concurrency verification framework to C/Pthreads programs (Competition Contribution). In: Chechik, M., Raskin, J.-F. (eds.) TACAS 2016. LNCS, vol. 9636, pp. 908–911. Springer, Heidelberg (2016)

Privacy and Security Issues
in Information Systems

Security and Privacy of Protocols and Software with Formal Methods

Fabrizio Biondi$^{(\boxtimes)}$ and Axel Legay

Inria, Rennes, France
`fabrizio.biondi@inria.fr`

Abstract. The protection of users' data conforming to best practice and legislation is one of the main challenges in computer science. Very often, large-scale data leaks remind us that the state of the art in data privacy and anonymity is severely lacking. The complexity of modern systems make it impossible for software architect to create secure software that correctly implements privacy policies without the help of automated tools. The academic community needs to invest more effort in the formal modelization of security and anonymity properties, providing a deeper understanding of the underlying concepts and challenges and allowing the creation of automated tools to help software architects and developers. This track provides numerous contributions to the formal modeling of security and anonymity properties and the creation of tools to verify them on large-scale software projects.

1 Introduction

Security and Anonymity Properties. Security and privacy are fundamental interests of computer science research. Security refers to the guarantee that the computer system being used does not act against the interest of the user, either maliciously or accidentally. The security of a system is usually associated with the following properties [33, 41, 47]:

Confidentiality. Sensitive information about the user that is handled by the system cannot be accessed by unauthorized third parties;

Integrity. Information handled by the system cannot be deleted, altered or modified by unauthorized third parties; and

Authentication. Each agent interacting with the system is who they claim to be.

However, these basic properties are not defining which potentially sensitive information about the user is the system handling, or whether the system should have access to such information to start with [6, 11, 35]. This is the reason why we add the following property:

Anonymity. The user has control on what information about them is collected by the system, and can decide how it is collected and used, by whom, and for what purpose.

© Springer International Publishing AG 2016
T. Margaria and B. Steffen (Eds.): ISoLA 2016, Part I, LNCS 9952, pp. 883–892, 2016.
DOI: 10.1007/978-3-319-47166-2_61

While other interesting properties (e.g. availability) are considered in computer science research, this track focuses on the four properties listed above, as they allow the user to trust that their data is properly handled by the system and not used against them by third parties.

Problem: Large Attack Surface. [3,21,24,44] The complexity of modern systems means that the attack surface for a malicious agent is huge. The system can be compromised at any level and leak information in hundred of possible ways, like improperly handling access rights to databases, or leaking kernel memory through improperly written implementations, or even allowing private keys to be recovered by analyzing the system's energy consumption. Complex protocol interaction means that different agents are executing their parts of the protocol on machines with different environment and operative systems.

Solution: Formal Models and Automated Tools. [15,27,34] The approach to secure such a complex system is the modelization of security protocols with formal languages, and of the security properties to be preserved with formal logics. This formalization effort allows us to produce automated techniques and tools that verify whether the protocols and their implementations respect the security requirements.

The formal models of systems, protocols and properties are simpler and more intuitive than their implementations, since they abstract away irrelevant details. This allows users and developers to examine the properties themselves and determine if they satisfy their needs, thus making it easier for the user to trust that the system is doing what they expect it to do and does not have any harmful behavior, either intentional or accidental.

We will discuss the use of formal methods and tools to improve the security at both the software implementation and the protocol level.

1.1 The Software Level

Attacks at the software level exploit vulnerabilities in the implementation of a secure system that are not present in the system specification. It is common for software developers and engineers to introduce bugs in an implementation, particularly when using non-strongly-typed languages [38]. Bugs that can be used to compromise the security and privacy properties of the system are known as vulnerabilities. It is common for an attacker targeting a specific system to start analyzing the system for such vulnerabilities, then writing an exploit leveraging on some vulnerabilities to steal information from or take control of the system [17].

Vulnerabilities are categorized by cause and by severity [2,42]. Categories by cause include input and access validation errors, race conditions, secret information leaks, and many more. In particular, information leaks endanger both security and privacy properties, leaking confidential user data or even private cryptographic keys, like in the case of the Heartbleed bug.

Severity is normally categorized in High, Medium and Low, where High severity means that the vulnerability makes it possible for an attacker to violate the security properties of the system, Low severity means that the vulnerability only provides the attacker with more information to look for more severe vulnerabilities, and Medium severity is anything that is not High or Low severity.

Helping software developers writing bug-free code is a large field of computer science and software engineering. However, from the security and privacy perspective we have a slightly different view of the problem, since we are only interested in finding and reducing vulnerabilities.

For instance, considering the handling of private and confidential information, we can develop tools that track how a given implementation of a protocol handles such information. Taint analysis [32,45] and information leakage computation techniques [9,10,22,46] can trace the flow of information in a particular system given its source code, thus detecting vulnerabilities that would allow private information to be inferred by unauthorized users. The track presents a new state of the art in the automated detection of information leaks in large projects.

Additionally, protocol implementations can leverage the formal specifications of the protocols. Automated tools [8,23,25,48] can be used to verify whether an implementation respects the formal protocol implementation it is supposed to implement, or even automatically produce code from the protocol specifications that is guaranteed to correctly implement them, avoiding vulnerabilities caused by design errors. The track presents a new formal framework to help software developers validate their software for the complex case of cyber-physical systems.

1.2   The Protocol Level

Protocols model the exchange of communications and data between agents to obtain a common goal. The formalization of protocols is necessary to determine univocally what each agent is supposed to do, and to be able to prove that their behavior contributes to achieving the goal of the protocol. Many formal languages for protocols exist, capturing different primitives and granularity of the communications. One of the classical approaches is Burrows-Abadi-Needham (BAN) logic [13], used to model authentication systems since it allows to model what agents know and believe on each other during the protocol, and it assumes that the network itself is vulnerable to tampering and information leakage.

More recently, model checking techniques and properties have been shown to be more effective than BAN logic to model protocols and automatically verify whether they respect security properties.

Information-theoretical properties like non-interference [20,39] can be used to prove that the communications of an agent do not leak information about the agent's secret information in any way, allowing to automatically verify whether a protocols guarantees confidentiality and anonymity. When this strong property is impossible to guarantee while achieving the protocol's goal, quantitative leakage computation [12,16,28,43] can prove that the amount of secret information leaked is too small to significantly hinder the confidentiality and anonymity properties, or at worst to exactly quantify the loss of anonymity allowing the agent to decide if it is an acceptable price to pay to run the protocol.

Temporal properties [5,14,36] are concerned with the sequence of operations performed by the protocol, and can be used to prove that the required steps to achieve the protocol's goal are always executed correctly and in the correct order. This enables formally verifying that if the protocol succeeds all the proper steps have been executed, and if it fails it does so graciously and properly notifying the agents of the cause of the failure. Temporal properties are very close to the protocol's flow of operations, and mature tools exist [8,23,25,48] to automatically verify that they are respected even by complex system interactions.

Cryptographic properties [1,7,19,30] are used to guarantee security properties of the protocol, and are often based on complexity results of problems that are hard to treat at the current state of the art. Cryptographic properties can be used to guarantee the hardness of retrieving private keys in shared-key and public-key cryptosystems, verify agents' identities in authentication schemes, provide secure key exchange protocols and multiparty computation over unsecured channels, and be used to express most security properties. While some of the hardness results they are based on are currently unproven, and sometimes technological advancements may cripple protocols previously considered secure, cryptographic properties and primitives are the building blocks of most of the successful secure protocols currently used in any computer system.

The definition of secure and anonymous protocols in terms of formal models and properties allows automated verification of the protocols' correctness. This is a fundamental requirement for a user to be able to trust that the protocol is correctly designed to defend their interests and the security of their data. While many authentication and confidentiality properties can be defined as cryptographic trace properties and analyzed with temporal logics, anonymity properties depend on the data flow and interaction between different agents and are hard to define in terms of traces. The track presents contributions to model systems with process calculi and model transformations, allowing the expression and formal verification of anonymity properties.

Privacy and anonymity policies are often defined by legislative bodies in natural language. The duty of translating these policies into formal properties falls on computer scientists. Due to the inherent ambiguity of natural language, the formalization of policies may not correspond with the legislator's intent. Also, since protocols can be distributed among different legislative jurisdictions, it is not clear that all agents involved conform to the same rules and enforce the required policies. The track presents contributions to validate whether formal security protocols correctly implement legislative policies, and to automatically negotiate security policies between agents to guarantee that data owners and consumers agree on the policies for the treatment of the data.

2   Contribution to the Track

This track provides several contributions to apply formal methods to improve the security and privacy of system at the software and protocol levels. A summary is given here.

2.1 On Building Secure Software

The track offers two major contributions on using information flow and formal models to find vulnerabilities in software implementations:

- Information leaks in software may have devastating consequences, as demonstrated for instance by the Heartbleed bug. Academic work focuses on information theory to compute the amount of information leaked by a software implementation, but tools able to perform an automated analysis of real-world complex C code are still lacking. On the other hand, effective working solutions rely on ad-hoc principles that have little theoretical justification. In [29], the authors bridge this chasm between advanced theoretical work and concrete practical needs of programmers developing real world software. They present an analysis, based on clear security principles and verification tools, which is largely automatic and effective in detecting information leaks in complex C code running everyday on millions of systems worldwide.
- Cyber-physical systems are computer systems that interact with physical objects. Such systems are composed of several software components executed on different processors and interconnected through physical buses. These complex systems collocate functions operating at different security levels, which can introduce unexpected interactions that affect system security. The security policy for these systems is realized through various complex physical or logical mechanisms. The security policy, as a stakeholder goal, is then refined into system requirements and implementation constraints that guarantee security objectives. Unfortunately, verifying the correct decomposition and its enforcement in the system architecture is an overwhelming task. Because requirements are often written manually, they can be contradictory and inconsistent, which can lead to incorrect implementations. To overcome these issues, requirements must be specified using a formal and unambiguous language, traced through the system architecture, and automatically verified throughout the development process.

    In [31], the authors introduce a modeling framework for the design and validation of requirements from a security perspective. The framework is composed of a new language for requirements specification, an extension of the Architecture Analysis & Design Language, for specifying security and a set of theorems to check the requirements against the architecture. The framework provides the capability to validate the requirements of several candidate architectures and analyze the impact of changes to requirements and architecture during development. This model-based approach helps software architects and developers detect requirements and architecture issues early in the development life cycle and avoid the propagation of their effects during integration.

2.2 On Designing Privacy-Preserving Protocols

The track offers approaches to formalize the transmission of private and confidential information in protocols, guaranteeing that user privacy is respected:

- Formal, symbolic techniques for modeling and automatically analyzing security protocols are extremely successful and were able to discover many security flaws. Initially, these techniques were mainly developed to analyze authentication and confidentiality properties. Both these properties are trace properties and efficient tools for their verification exist. In more recent years anonymity-like properties have received increasing interest. Many flavors of anonymity properties are naturally expressed in terms of indistinguishability and modeled as an observational equivalence in process calculi.

  In [26], the authors present recent advances in the verification of such indistinguishability properties.

- Within distributed systems with completely distributed interactions between parties with mutual distrust, it is hard to control the (illicit) flowing of private information to unintended parties.

  In [40], the authors propose a novel model-based approach based on model transformations to build a secure-by-construction multiparty distributed system. First, starting from a component-based model of the system, the designer annotates different parts of it in order to define the security policy. Then, the security is checked and when valid, a secure distributed model, consistent with the desired security policy, is automatically generated. To illustrate the approach, the authors present a framework that implements our method and use it to secure an online social network application.

- The users of location-based services (LBSs) are always vulnerable to privacy risks since they need to disclose, at least partially, their locations in order to receive personalized services.

  In [18], the authors discuss the adaptation of differential privacy to the context of LBSs. More precisely, assuming that the LBS provider is queried with a perturbed version of the position of the user instead of his exact one, differential privacy is used to quantify the level of indistinguishability (privacy) provided for the user's position by such a perturbation. In this setting, the adaptation of differential privacy can lead to various models depending on the precise form of indistinguishability required. The authors describe an example of these models, the (D,e)-location privacy, which is directly inspired from the standard differential privacy model. In this model, they present the characterization of (D,e)-location privacy for a mechanism and also measure the utility of this mechanism with respect to an arbitrary loss function. Afterwards, they present a special class of mechanisms, called symmetric mechanisms in which all locations are perturbed in a unified manner through a noise function, focusing in particular on circular noise functions. They show that under certain assumptions, the circular functions are rich enough to provide the same privacy and utility levels as other more complex (non-circular) noise functions, while being easier to implement. Finally, the authors describe the extension of the above model to a generalized notion for location privacy, called l-privacy capturing both (D,e)-location privacy and also the recent notion of geo-indistinguishability.

2.3   On Automated Policy Enforcement

The track contributes formal approaches to policy enforcement, allowing the design of systems that respect legal bounds by design and guarantee that the other entities are treating private data properly:

- Handling personal data adequately is one of the biggest challenges of our era. Consequently, law and regulations are in the process of being released, like the European General Data Protection Regulation (GDPR), which attempt to deal with these challenging issue early on. The core question motivating this work is how software developers can validate their technical design vis-a-vis the prescriptions of the privacy legislation.

  In [4], the authors outline the technical concepts related to privacy that need to be taken into consideration in a software design. Also, the authors extend a popular design notation in order to support the privacy concepts illustrated in the previous point. Finally, they show how some of the prescriptions of the privacy legislation and standards may be related to a technical design that employs our enriched notation, which would facilitate reasoning about compliance.
- Privacy is a major concern in large of parts of the world when exchanging information. Ideally, we would like to be able to have fine-grained control about how information that we deem sensitive can be propagated and used. While privacy policy languages exist, it is not possible to control whether the entity that receives data is living up to its own policy specification.

  In [37], the authors present our initial work on an approach that empowers data owners to specify their privacy preferences and data consumers to specify their data needs. Using a static analysis of the two specifications, they find a communication scheme that complies with these preferences and needs. While applicable to online transactions, the same techniques can be used in development of IT systems dealing with sensitive data. To the best of our knowledge, no existing privacy policy languages supports negotiation of policies, but only yes/no answers.

References

1. Abadi, M., Gordon, A.D.: A calculus for cryptographic protocols: the spi calculus. In: Proceedings of the 4th ACM Conference on Computer and Communications Security, pp. 36–47. ACM (1997)
2. Alhazmi, O.H., Woo, S., Malaiya, Y.K.: Security vulnerability categories in major software systems. In: Rajasekaran, S. (ed.) Proceedings of the Third IASTED International Conference on Communication, Network, and Information Security, 9–11 October 2006, Cambridge, MA, USA, pp. 138–143. IASTED/ACTA Press (2006)
3. Anderson, R.: Why information security is hard-an economic perspective. In: ACSAC 2001 Proceedings of the 17th Annual Computer Security Applications Conference, pp. 358–365. IEEE (2001)

4. Antignac, T., Scandariato, R., Schneider, G.: A privacy-aware conceptual model for handling personal data. In: Margaria, T., Steffen, B. (eds.) ISoLA 2016. LNCS, vol. 9952, pp. 942–957. Springer, Heidelberg (2016)
5. Baier, C., Katoen, J.-P., Larsen, K.G.: Principles of Model Checking. MIT Press, Cambridge (2008)
6. Bailey, M.: Complete Guide to Internet Privacy, Anonymity & Security. Nerel (2011)
7. Barthe, G., Grégoire, B., Zanella Béguelin, S.: Formal certification of code-based cryptographic proofs. ACM SIGPLAN Notices 44(1), 90–101 (2009)
8. Bengtsson, J., Larsen, K.G., Larsson, F., Pettersson, P., Yi, W.: Uppaal - a tool suite for automatic verification of real-time systems. In: Alur, R., Henzinger, T.A., Sontag, E.D. (eds.) Hybrid Systems III. LNCS, vol. 1066, pp. 232–243. Springer, Heidelberg (1995)
9. Biondi, F., Legay, A., Malacaria, P., Wasowski, A.: Quantifying information leakage of randomized protocols. Theor. Comput. Sci. 597, 62–87 (2015)
10. Biondi, F., Legay, A., Traonouez, L.-M., Wąsowski, A.: QUAIL: a quantitative security analyzer for imperative code. In: Sharygina, N., Veith, H. (eds.) CAV 2013. LNCS, vol. 8044, pp. 702–707. Springer, Heidelberg (2013)
11. Bosworth, S.: Computer Security Handbook, 4th edn. Wiley, New York (2002)
12. Braun, C., Chatzikokolakis, K., Palamidessi, C.: Quantitative notions of leakage for one-try attacks. Electr. Notes Theor. Comput. Sci. 249, 75–91 (2009)
13. Burrows, M., Abadi, M., Needham, R.M.: A logic of authentication. In: Proceedings of the Royal Society of London A: Mathematical, Physical and Engineering Sciences, vol. 426, pp. 233–271. The Royal Society (1989)
14. Clarke, E.M., Emerson, E.A., Sistla, A.P.: Automatic verification of finite-state concurrent systems using temporal logic specifications. ACM Trans. Program. Lang. Syst. (TOPLAS) 8(2), 244–263 (1986)
15. Cortier, V., Kremer, S. (eds.): Formal Models and Techniques for Analyzing Security Protocols. Cryptology and Information Security Series, vol. 5. IOS Press, Amsterdam (2011)
16. Denning, D.E.: A lattice model of secure information flow. Commun. ACM 19(5), 236–243 (1976)
17. Dowd, M., McDonald, J., Schuh, J.: The Art of Software Security Assessment: Identifying and Preventing Software Vulnerabilities. Addison-Wesley Professional, Boston (2006)
18. ElSalamouny, E., Gambs, S.: Differential privacy models for location-based services. Trans. Data Priv. 9, 15–48 (2016)
19. Ferguson, N., Schneier, B., Kohno, T.: Cryptography Engineering: Design Principles and Practical Applications. Wiley, Hoboken (2010)
20. Focardi, R., Gorrieri, R., Martinelli, F.: Non interference for the analysis of cryptographic protocols. In: Welzl, E., Montanari, U., Rolim, J.D.P. (eds.) ICALP 2000. LNCS, vol. 1853, pp. 354–372. Springer, Heidelberg (2000)
21. Gruschka, N., Jensen, M.: Attack surfaces: a taxonomy for attacks on cloud services. In: IEEE CLOUD, pp. 276–279 (2010)
22. Heusser, J., Malacaria, P.: Quantifying information leaks in software. In: Proceedings of the 26th Annual Computer Security Applications Conference, pp. 261–269. ACM (2010)
23. Holzmann, G.: Spin Model Checker, the: Primer and Reference Manual, 1st edn. Addison-Wesley Professional, Boston (2003)
24. Howard, M.: Attack surface: mitigate security risks by minimizing the code you expose to untrusted users. MSDN Magazine, November 2004

25. Jegourel, C., Legay, A., Sedwards, S.: A platform for high performance statistical model checking – PLASMA. In: Flanagan, C., König, B. (eds.) TACAS 2012. LNCS, vol. 7214, pp. 498–503. Springer, Heidelberg (2012)

26. Kremer, S., Künnemann, R.: Automated analysis of security protocols with global state. CoRR (2014). http://arxiv.org/abs/1403.1142

27. Landwehr, C.E.: Formal models for computer security. ACM Comput. Surv. 13(3), 247–278 (1981)

28. Malacaria, P.: Algebraic foundations for quantitative information flow. Math. Struct. Comput. Sci. 25(2), 404–428 (2015)

29. Malacaria, P., Tautchning, M., DiStefano, D.: Information leakage analysis of complex C code and its application to OpenSSL. In: Margaria, T., Steffen, B. (eds.) ISoLA 2016. LNCS, vol. 9952, pp. 909–925. Springer, Heidelberg (2016)

30. Meadows, C.: Formal methods for cryptographic protocol analysis: Emerging issues and trends. IEEE J. Sel. Areas Commun. 21(1), 44–54 (2003)

31. Nam, M.-Y., Delange, J., Feiler, P.: Integrated modeling workflow for security assurance. In: Margaria, T., Steffen, B. (eds.) ISoLA 2016. LNCS, vol. 9952, pp. 926–941. Springer, Heidelberg (2016)

32. Newsome, J., Song, D.: Dynamic taint analysis for automatic detection, analysis, and signature generation of exploits on commodity software (2005)

33. Olovsson, T.: A structured approach to computer security. Technical report, 33 (1992)

34. Patel, R., Borisaniya, B., Patel, A., Patel, D., Rajarajan, M., Zisman, A.: Comparative analysis of formal model checking tools for security protocol verification. In: Meghanathan, N., Boumerdassi, S., Chaki, N., Nagamalai, D. (eds.) CNSA 2010. CCIS, vol. 89, pp. 152–163. Springer, Heidelberg (2010)

35. Peng, K.: Anonymous Communication Networks: Protecting Privacy on the Web, 1st edn. Auerbach Publications, Boston (2014)

36. Pnueli, A.: The temporal logic of programs. In: 18th Annual Symposium on Foundations of Computer Science, pp. 46–57. IEEE (1977)

37. Probst, C.W.: Guaranteeing privacy-observing data exchange. In: Margaria, T., Steffen, B. (eds.) ISoLA 2016. LNCS, vol. 9952, pp. 958–969. Springer, Heidelberg (2016)

38. Ray, B., Posnett, D., Filkov, V., Devanbu, P.: A large scale study of programming languages and code quality in github. In: Proceedings of the 22nd ACM SIGSOFT International Symposium on Foundations of Software Engineering, FSE 2014, pp. 155–165. ACM (2014)

39. Ryan, P.Y., Schneider, S.A.: Process algebra and non-interference. J. Comput. Secur. 9(1–2), 75–103 (2001)

40. Said, N.B., Abdellatif, T., Bensalem, S., Bozga, M.: A model-based approach to secure multiparty distributed systems. In: Margaria, T., Steffen, B. (eds.) ISoLA 2016. LNCS, vol. 9952, pp. 893–908. Springer, Heidelberg (2016)

41. Scarfone, K.A., Jansen, W., Tracy, M.: SP 800-123. Guide to general server security. Technical report, Gaithersburg, MD, United States (2008)

42. Seacord, R., Householder, A.: A structured approach to classifying security vulnerabilities. Technical report CMU/SEI-2005-TN-003, Software Engineering Institute, Carnegie Mellon University, Pittsburgh, PA (2005)

43. Smith, G.: On the foundations of quantitative information flow. In: de Alfaro, L. (ed.) FOSSACS 2009. LNCS, vol. 5504, pp. 288–302. Springer, Heidelberg (2009)

44. So, K.: Cloud computing security issues and challenges. Int. J. Comput. Netw. 3(5) (2011)

45. Song, D., Brumley, D., Yin, H., Caballero, J., Jager, I., Kang, M.G., Liang, Z., Newsome, J., Poosankam, P., Saxena, P.: BitBlaze: a new approach to computer security via binary analysis. In: Sekar, R., Pujari, A.K. (eds.) ICISS 2008. LNCS, vol. 5352, pp. 1–25. Springer, Heidelberg (2008)
46. Val, C.G., Enescu, M.A., Bayless, S., Aiello, W., Hu, A.J.: Precisely measuring quantitative information flow: 10k lines of code and beyond. In: IEEE European Symposium on Security and Privacy, EuroS&P. 2016, Saarbrücken, Germany, 21–24 March 2016, pp. 31–46. IEEE (2016)
47. Venter, H., Eloff, J.: A taxonomy for information security technologies. Comput. Secur. **22**(4), 299–307 (2003)
48. Visser, W., Havelund, K., Brat, G., Park, S., Lerda, F.: Model checking programs. Autom. Softw. Eng. **10**(2), 203–232 (2003)

A Model-Based Approach to Secure Multiparty Distributed Systems

Najah Ben Said[1,2], Takoua Abdellatif[3], Saddek Bensalem[1,2], and Marius Bozga[1,2(✉)]

[1] Univ. Grenoble Alpes, VERIMAG, F-38000 Grenoble, France
marius.bozga@imag.fr
[2] CNRS, VERIMAG, F-38000 Grenoble, France
[3] Tunisia Polytechnic School, University of Carthage, Tunis, Tunisia

Abstract. Within distributed systems with completely distributed interactions between parties with mutual distrust, it is hard to control the (illicit) flowing of private information to unintended parties. Unlike existing methods dealing with verification of low-level cryptographic protocols, we propose a novel model-based approach based on model transformations to build a secure-by-construction multiparty distributed system. First, starting from a component-based model of the system, the designer annotates different parts of it in order to define the security policy. Then, the security is checked and when valid, a secure distributed model, consistent with the desired security policy, is automatically generated. To illustrate the approach, we present a framework that implements our method and use it to secure an online social network application.

1 Introduction

Model-based development aims at both reducing development costs and increasing the integrity of system implementations by using explicit models employed in clearly defined transformation steps leading to correct-by-construction implementation artifacts. This approach is beneficial, as one can first ensure system requirements by dealing with a high-level formally specified model that abstracts implementation details and then derive a correct implementation through a series of transformations that terminates when an actual executable code is obtained.

Nonetheless, ensuring end-to-end security requirements in distributed systems remains a difficult and error-prone task. In many situations, security reduces to access control to prevent sensitive information from being read or modified by unauthorized users. However, access control is insufficient to regulate the propagation of information once released for processing by a program especially with non-trivial interactions and computations. Thus access control

---

The research leading to these results has received funding from the European Community's Seventh Framework Programme [FP7/2007-2013] under grant agreement ICT-318772 (D-MILS).

T. Margaria and B. Steffen (Eds.): ISoLA 2016, Part I, LNCS 9952, pp. 893–908, 2016.
DOI: 10.1007/978-3-319-47166-2_62

offers no guarantees about whether an information is subsequently protected and deciding how to set access control permissions in complex systems is a difficult problem in itself. Equally, using cryptographic primitives that provides strong confidentiality and integrity guarantees, is also less helpful to ensure that the system obeys an overall security policy.

Information flow control is a much robust alternative which tracks information propagation in the entire system and prevent secret or confidential information from being publicly released. Information flow control relies on annotating system data and/or actions with specific levels of security and use specific methods for checking non-interference, that is, absence of leakage, between different security levels. Nonetheless, providing annotations and establishing their correctness is equally difficult especially for distributed implementations, where only code is available and no higher-level abstractions.

In this paper we introduce a model-based development approach for dealing with information flow control in distributed systems. Our contribution can be summarized as follows. First, we provide a high-level component-based model and associated security annotations to allow system designers to configure the system security in an intuitive way. They do not need to be experts in security or cryptographic protocols. Second, we provide a security checker that applies information flow techniques and verifies formally the correctness of the provided configuration. Third, a distributed model is automatically generated and respects the designer configured security policy. The mapping between the high-level policy and the distributed model is formally proven.

In the paper, we use the *secureBIP* framework [1] as underlying component-based modeling framework. *secureBIP* is an extension of the *BIP* framework [2] with information flow security. Given security annotations for data and interactions, *secureBIP* captures two types of non-interference, respectively *event* and *data non-interference*. For events (that is, occurrences of interactions), non-interference states that the observation of public events does not reveal any information about the occurrence of secret events. For data, it states that there is no leakage of secret data into public ones.

We provide model transformations allowing to transform high-level *secureBIP* models into a distributed models while preserving event and data non-interference. In this way, information flow security needs to be verified once, for the high-level model, and then it holds *by construction* on the distributed model and later on the final implementation. The proposed transformation extends previous work [3,4] on distributed implementation of *BIP* components models, which essentially addressed functional and performance aspects, while being totally agnostic about security-related issues.

The paper is structured as follows. Section 2 presents a running example to be used along the paper. Section 3 recalls the main concepts of the *secureBIP* framework, associated non-interference definitions and security conditions. Next, Sect. 4 contains the new automated distribution approach to derive secure distributed models. Finally, Sect. 5 discusses related work and Sect. 6 concludes and presents some perspectives for future research. Proofs of technical results are given in a technical report[1].

2   Running Example

Throughout the paper, we consider a simplified social network application, called Whens-App, and illustrated in Fig. 1. The application is intended for organizing virtual events where participants can meet and exchange data.

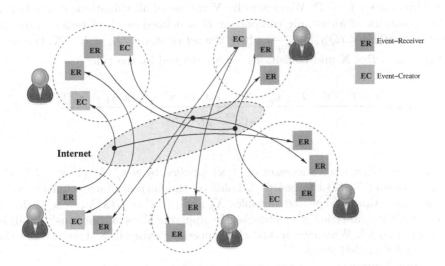

Fig. 1. Overview of the Whens-App application

As social network application, Whens-App entails several of security requirements. In this paper we focus on requirements related to information flow security: assuming that components are trustful and the network is unsecure, *(1)* the interception and observation of exchanged data messages must not reveal any information about event organization and *(2)* confidentiality of classified data is always preserved and kept secret inter- and intra-components. We will show that both requirements are ensured by using security annotations for tracking events and data in the system. Then, we show how the annotated model can be automatically and systematically transformed towards a distributed implementation while preserving the security properties.

3   Secure Component Model

Systems are constructed from atomic components, that is, finite state automata or 1-safe Petri nets, extended with data and ports. Communication between components is achieved using multi-party interactions with data transfer.

---

[1] no. TR-2014-6 on http://www-verimag.imag.fr/Rapports-Techniques,28.html.

Definition 1 (atomic component). *An atomic component B is a tuple $(L,$ X, P, $T)$ where L is a set of locations, X is a set of variables, P is a set of ports and $T \subseteq L \times P \times L$ is a set of port labelled transitions. For every port $p \in P$, we denote by X_p the subset of variables exported and available for interaction through p. For every transition $\tau \in T$, we denote by g_τ its guard, that is, a Boolean expression defined on X and by f_τ its update function, that is, a parallel assignment $\{x := e_\tau^x\}_{x \in X}$ to variables of X.*

Let $\mathcal{D}$ be an universal data domain, fixed. A valuation of a set of variables Y is a function $\mathbf{y} : Y \to \mathcal{D}$. We denote by $\mathbf{Y}$ the set of all valuations defined on Y. The semantics of an atomic component B is defined as the labelled transition system $\mathrm{SEM}(B) = (Q_B, \Sigma_B, \underset{B}{\longrightarrow})$ where the set of states $Q_B = L \times \mathbf{X}$, the set of labels $\Sigma_B = P \times \mathbf{X}$ and transitions $\underset{B}{\longrightarrow}$ are defined by the rule:

$$\text{ATOM} \quad \frac{\tau = \ell \xrightarrow{p} \ell' \in T \quad \mathbf{x}_p'' \in \mathbf{X}_p \quad g_\tau(\mathbf{x}) \quad \mathbf{x}' = f_\tau(\mathbf{x}[X_p \leftarrow \mathbf{x}_p''])}{(\ell, \mathbf{x}) \xrightarrow[B]{p(\mathbf{x}_p'')} (\ell', \mathbf{x}')}$$

That is, $(\ell', \mathbf{x}')$ is a successor of $(\ell, \mathbf{x})$ labelled by $p(\mathbf{x}_p'')$ iff (1) $\tau = \ell \xrightarrow{p} \ell'$ is a transition of T, (2) the guard g_τ holds on the current state valuation $\mathbf{x}$, (3) $\mathbf{x}_p''$ is a valuation of exported variables X_p and (4) $\mathbf{x}' = f_\tau(\mathbf{x}[X_p \leftarrow \mathbf{x}_p''])$ that is, the next-state valuation $\mathbf{x}'$ is obtained by applying f_τ on $\mathbf{x}$ previously modified according to $\mathbf{x}_p''$. Whenever a p-labelled successor exists in a state, we say that p is *enabled* in that state.

Figure 2 presents the atomic components used in the Whens-App application model. The Event Creator (left) coordinates an event lifetime (invite, open and cancel transitions), get raw information from participants (store) and

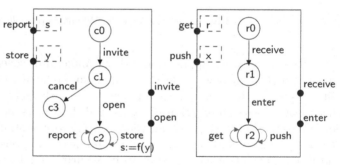

Fig. 2. Example of atomic components

delivers some information digests (report). The Event Receiver (right) enters an event (receive, enter), share information (push) and receive event digests (get). [Colors are explained later]

Composite components are obtained by composing atomic components $B_i = (L_i, X_i, P_i, T_i)_{i=1,n}$ through multiparty interactions. We consider that atomic components have pairwise disjoint sets of locations, ports, and variables i.e., for any two $i \neq j$ from $\{1..n\}$, we have $L_i \cap L_j = \emptyset$, $P_i \cap P_j = \emptyset$, and $X_i \cap X_j = \emptyset$.

A multiparty *interaction* a is a triple (P_a, G_a, F_a), where $P_a \subseteq \bigcup_{i=1}^n P_i$ is a set of ports, G_a is a guard, and F_a is a data transfer function. By definition, P_a

uses at most one port of every component, that is, $|P_i \cap P_a| \le 1$ for all $i \in \{1..n\}$. Therefore, we simply denote $P_a = \{p_i\}_{i \in I}$, where $I \subseteq \{1..n\}$ contains the indices of the components involved in a and for all $i \in I, p_i \in P_i$. G_a and F_a are both defined on the variables exported by the ports in P_a (i.e., $\bigcup_{p \in P_a} X_p$).

Definition 2 (composite component). *A composite component* $C = \gamma(B_1, \ldots, B_n)$ *consists of the composition of* $B_1, \ldots, B_n$ *by a set of interactions* γ.

Given $\text{SEM}(B_i) = (Q_i, \Sigma_i, \xrightarrow[B_i]{})_{i=1,n}$, the semantics of C is defined as the labelled transition system $\text{SEM}(C) = (Q_C, \Sigma_C, \xrightarrow[C]{})$ where the set of states $Q_C = \otimes_{i=1}^{n} Q_i$, the set of labels $\Sigma_C = \gamma$ and transitions $\xrightarrow[C]{}$ are defined by the rule:

$$a = (\{p_i\}_{i \in I}, G_a, F_a) \in \gamma \quad G_a(\{\mathbf{x}_{p_i}\}_{i \in I}) \quad \{\mathbf{x}''_{p_i}\}_{i \in I} = F_a(\{\mathbf{x}_{p_i}\}_{i \in I})$$

$$\text{COMP} \quad \frac{\forall i \in I. (\ell_i, \mathbf{x}_i) \xrightarrow[B_i]{p_i(\mathbf{x}''_{p_i})} (\ell'_i, \mathbf{x}'_i) \forall i \notin I. (\ell_i, \mathbf{x}_i) = (\ell'_i, \mathbf{x}'_i)}{((\ell_1, \mathbf{x}_1), \ldots, (\ell_n, \mathbf{x}_n)) \xrightarrow[C]{a} ((\ell'_1, \mathbf{x}'_1), \ldots, (\ell'_n, \mathbf{x}'_n))}$$

For each $i \in I$, $\mathbf{x}_{p_i}$ above denotes the valuation $\mathbf{x}_i$ restricted to variables of X_{p_i}. The rule expresses that C can execute an interaction $a \in \gamma$ *enabled* in state $((\ell_1, \mathbf{x}_1), \ldots, (\ell_n, \mathbf{x}_n))$, iff (1) for each $p_i \in P_a$, the corresponding atomic component B_i can execute a transition labelled by p_i, and (2) the guard G_a of the interaction holds on the current valuation $\mathbf{x}_{p_i}$ of exported variables on ports in a. Execution of a triggers first the data transfer function F_a which modifies exported variables X_{p_i}. The new values obtained, encoded in the valuation $\mathbf{x}''_{p_i}$, are then used by the components' transitions. The states of components that do not participate in the interaction remain unchanged.

We call a trace any finite sequence of interactions $w = a_1 a_2 \cdots \in \gamma^*$ executable from a given initial state q_0. The set of all traces w from state q_0 is denoted by $\text{TRACES}(C, q_0)$.

Figure 3 presents a simplified composite component for an instance of the *Whens-App* application with two event creators and three event receivers. Interactions are represented using connecting lines between the interacting ports.

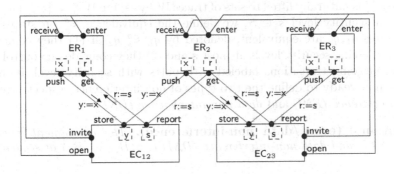

Fig. 3. Example of composite component

Binary interactions (push store) and (report get) include data transfers between components, that is, assignments of data across interacting components.

3.1 Information Flow Security

We consider transitive information flow policies expressed on system variables and we focus on the non-interference properties. We restrict ourselves to confidentiality and we ensure that no illegal flow of information exists between variables having incompatible security levels.

Formally, we represent security domains as finite lattices $\langle \mathbb{S}, \sqsubseteq \rangle$ where $\mathbb{S}$ denotes the security levels and $\sqsubseteq$ the *flows to* relation. For example, a security domain with two levels *High* (H), *Low* (L) and where information is allowed to flow from *Low* to *High* is $\langle \{L, H\}, \{(L, L), (L, H), (H, H)\} \rangle$.

Let $C = \gamma(B_1, \dots B_n)$ be a composite component, fixed. Let X (resp. P) be the set of all variables (resp. ports) defined in all atomic components $(B_i)_{i=1,n}$. Let $\langle \mathbb{S}, \sqsubseteq \rangle$ be a security domain, fixed.

Definition 3 (security assignment σ). *A security assignment for component C is a mapping $\sigma : X \cup P \cup \gamma \to \mathbb{S}$ that associates security levels to variables, ports and interactions such that, moreover, the levels of ports and interactions match, that is, for all $a \in \gamma$ and for all $p \in P$ it holds $\sigma(p) = \sigma(a)$.*

The security levels for ports and variables track the flow of information along computation steps within atomic components. The security levels for interactions track the flow of information along inter-component communication. We consider that deducing event-related information represent a risk that should be handled while controlling the system's information flow in addition to data flows. End-to-end security is defined according to transitive non-interference.

Let σ be a security assignment for C, fixed. For a security level $s \in \mathbb{S}$, we define $\gamma \downarrow_s^\sigma$ the restriction of γ to interactions with security level at most s that is formally, $\gamma \downarrow_s^\sigma = \{a \in \gamma \mid \sigma(a) \sqsubseteq s\}$. For a security level $s \in \mathbb{S}$, we define $w|_s^\sigma$ the projection of a trace $w \in \gamma^*$ to interactions with security level lower or equal to s. Formally, the projection is recursively defined on traces as $\epsilon|_s^\sigma = \epsilon$, $(aw)|_s^\sigma = a(w|_s^\sigma)$ if $\sigma(a) \sqsubseteq s$ and $(aw)|_s^\sigma = w|_s^\sigma$ if $\sigma(a) \not\sqsubseteq s$. The projection operator $|_s^\sigma$ is naturally lifted to sets of traces W by taking $W|_s^\sigma = \{w|_s^\sigma \mid w \in W\}$.

For a security level $s \in S$, we define the equivalence $\approx_s^\sigma$ on states of C. Two states q_1, q_2 are equivalent, denoted by $q_1 \approx_s^\sigma q_2$ iff (1) they coincide on variables having security levels at most s and (2) they coincide on control states having outgoing transitions labeled with ports with security level at most s. We are now ready to define the two types of non-interference respectively *event non-interference (ENI)* and *data non-interference (DNI)*.

Definition 4 (event/data non-interference). *The assignment σ ensures event (ENI) and data non-interference (DNI) of $\gamma(B_1, \dots, B_n)$ at security level s iff,*

(ENI) $\forall q_0 \in Q_C^0 : \text{TRACES}(\gamma(B_1,\ldots,B_n),q_0)|_s^\sigma = \text{TRACES}((\gamma \downarrow_s^\sigma)(B_1,\ldots,B_n),q_0)$

(DNI) $\forall q_1, q_2 \in Q_C^0,\ \forall w_1 \in \text{TRACES}(C,q_1), w_2 \in \text{TRACES}(C,q_2),\ \forall q_1', q_2' \in Q_C :$

$$q_1 \approx_s^\sigma q_2\ \wedge\ w_1|_s^\sigma = w_2|_s^\sigma\ \wedge\ q_1 \xrightarrow[C]{w_1} q_1' \wedge q_2 \xrightarrow[C]{w_2} q_2' \Rightarrow q_1' \approx_s^\sigma q_2'$$

Moreover, σ is said secure *for a component $\gamma(B_1,\ldots,B_n)$ iff it ensures both event and data non-interference, at all security levels $s \in \mathbb{S}$.*

Both variants of non-interference express some form of indistinguishability between several states and traces of the system. For instance, an attacker that can observe the system's variables and occurences of interactions at security level s_1 must not be able to distinguish neither changes on variables or occurrence of interactions having higher or incomparable security level s_2.

The running example presented in Figs. 2 and 3 is annotated with two levels of security *Low* (in black) and *High* (in red). With this assignement, the exchange of information during the event and some related data are *High* whereas the event initiation is *Low*.

3.2 Noninterference Checking

In our previous work [1], we established sufficient syntactic conditions that reduce the verification of non-interference to local constrains checking on transitions (intra-component) and interactions (inter-components). We recall these conditions hereafter as they are going to be used later in Sect. 4 for establishing security correctness of the decentralized component model. Indeed, these conditions offer a syntactic way to ensure both event and data non-interfrence and therefore to obtain preservation proofs for along decentralization.

Definition 5 (security conditions). *Let $C = \gamma(B_1,\ldots,B_n)$ be a composite component and let σ be a security assignment. We say that C satisfies the security conditions for security assignment σ iff:*

(i) *the security assignment of ports, in every atomic component B_i is locally consistent, that is, for every pair of causal transitions:*
$\forall \tau_1, \tau_2 \in T_i\ :\ \tau_1 = \ell_1 \xrightarrow{p_1} \ell_2,\ \tau_2 = \ell_2 \xrightarrow{p_2} \ell_3 \Rightarrow (\ell_1 \neq \ell_2 \Rightarrow \sigma(p_1) \sqsubseteq \sigma(p_2))$
and for every pair of conflicting transitions:
$\forall \tau_1, \tau_2 \in T_i\ :\ \tau_1 = \ell_1 \xrightarrow{p_1} \ell_2,\ \tau_2 = \ell_1 \xrightarrow{p_2} \ell_3 \Rightarrow \sigma(p_1) = \sigma(p_2)$

(ii) *all assignments $x := e$ occurring in transitions within atomic components and interactions are sequential consistent, in the classical sense:*
$\forall y \in use(e)\ :\ \sigma(y) \sqsubseteq \sigma(x)$

(iii) *variables are consistently used and assigned in transitions and interactions:*
$\forall \tau \in \cup_{i=1}^n T_i,\ \forall x,y \in X : x \in def(f_\tau), y \in use(g_\tau) \Rightarrow\ \sigma(y) \sqsubseteq \sigma(p_\tau) \sqsubseteq \sigma(x)$
$\forall a \in \gamma,\ \forall x,y \in X\ :\ x \in def(F_a), y \in use(G_a) \Rightarrow \sigma(y) \sqsubseteq \sigma(a) \sqsubseteq \sigma(x)$

(iv) *all atomic components B_i are port deterministic:*
$\forall \tau_1, \tau_2 \in T_i\ :\ \tau_1 = \ell_1 \xrightarrow{p} \ell_2,\ \tau_2 = \ell_1 \xrightarrow{p} \ell_3 \Rightarrow (g_{\tau_1} \wedge g_{\tau_2})$ *is unsatisfiable*

The first family of conditions (i) is similar to Accorsi's conditions [5] for excluding causal and conflicting places for Petri net transitions having different security levels. Similar conditions have been considered in [6,7] and lead to more specific definitions of non-interferences and bisimulations on annotated Petri nets. The second condition (*ii*) represents the classical condition needed to avoid information leakage in sequential assignments. The third condition (*iii*) tackles covert channels issues. Indeed, (*iii*) enforces the security levels of the data flows which have to be consistent with security levels of the ports or interactions (e.g., no low level data has to be updated on a high level port or interaction). Such that, observations of public data would not reveal any secret information. Finally, condition (*iv*) enforces deterministic behavior on atomic components.

The following result, proven in [1], states that the security conditions are sufficient to ensure both event and data non-interference.

Theorem 1. *Whenever the security conditions hold, the security assignment σ is secure for the composite component C.*

For example, the security conditions hold for the security assignment considered for the running example in Figs. 2 and 3. Notice that local consistency is ensured in both atomic components: the security level can only increase from *Low* to *High* along causal transitions and no choices exist between *Low* and *High* transitions. Equally, notice that no *High* data is assigned on *Low* interactions.

4   Automatic Decentralization Method

In this section, we describe the decentralization method for our component-based model and provide formal proofs for information-flow security preservation. The decentralization method extends the method for decentralization of BIP models [3,4]. The existing method transforms BIP models with multiparty interactions (and priorities) into functionally equivalent BIP models using only send/receive (S/R) interactions. S/R interactions are binary, point-to-point, directed interactions from one sender component (port), to one receiver component (port) implementing asynchronous message passing.

From a functional viewpoint, the main challenge when transforming a BIP model into a decentralized S/R BIP model is to enable parallelism for execution of atomic components and concurrently enabled interactions. That is, in a distributed setting, every atomic component executes independently and communication is restricted to asynchronous message passing. The existing method for decentralizing BIP relies on structuring the distributed components according to a hierarchical architecture with two[2] layers:

- the *atomic components* layer includes transformed atomic components. Whenever an atomic component needs to interact, it publish an offer, that is the list of its enabled ports, then wait for a notification indicating which interaction has been chosen, and then resume its execution.

---

[2] In general, a third *conflict resolution* layer is used, however, it has a confined impact on information flow and is ommited here for the sake of simplicity of the presentation.

– the *interaction protocols (IP)* layer deals with distributed execution of interactions by implementing specific protocols. Every IP component handles a
subset of interactions, that is, check them for enabledness and schedule them
for execution accordingly. The interface between this layer and the component layer provides ports for receiving offers and notifying the ports selected
for execution.

The existing methods in [3,4] have been designed without taking into account
security concerns. In the following, we will show that they can be extended such
that to preserve information flow security. Roughly speaking, this is achieved
by using a slightly different transformation for atomic components as well as by
imposing few additional restrictions on the structure of the interaction protocol
layer. We show that the security assignment from the original model is naturally
lifted to the decentralized model and consequently, non-interference is preserved
along the transformation.

Let $C = \gamma(B_1, \cdots B_n)$ be a composite component and σ be a secure assignment for C which satisfies the security conditions for non-interference.

4.1   Atomic Components Layer

The transformation of atomic components consists in breaking atomicity of transitions. Precisely, each transition is split into two consecutive steps: (1) an offer
that publishes the current state of the component, and (2) a notification that
triggers an update function and resume local computation. The intuition behind
this transformation is that the offer transition correspond to sending information
about component's intention to interact to some IP component and the notification transition corresponds to receiving the answer from an IP component,
once an interaction has been completed. Update functions can be then executed
concurrently and independently by components upon notification reception.

In constrast to the transformation proposed in [3], several changes are needed
to protect information flow. Distinct offer ports o_s and interaction counters n_s are
introduced for every security level. Thus, offers and corresponding notifications
have the same security level, and moreover, no information about execution of
interactions is revealed through the observation of interaction counters.

Definition 6 (transformed atomic component). *Let $B = (L, X, P, T)$ be
an atomic component within C. The corresponding transformed S/R component
is $B^{SR} = (L^{SR}, X^{SR}, P^{SR}, T^{SR})$:*

– *$L^{SR} = L \cup L^{\perp}$, where $L^{\perp} = \{\perp_{\ell} \mid \ell \in L\}$*
– *$X^{SR} = X \cup \{e_p\}_{p \in P} \cup \{n_s | s \in \mathbb{S}\}$ where e_p is a fresh boolean variable indicating
whether port p is enabled, and n_s is a fresh integer variable called interaction
counter for security level s.*
– *$P^{SR} = P \cup \{o_s \mid s \in S\}$. The offer ports o_s export the variables $X_{o_s} =
\{n_s\} \bigcup \{\{e_p\} \cup X_p \mid \sigma(p) = s\}$ that is the interaction counter n_s, the newly
added variable e_p and the variables X_p associated to ports p with security level
s. For other ports, the set of variables exported remains unchanged.*

- *For each state $\ell \in L$, let S_ℓ be the set of security levels assigned to ports labeling all outgoing transitions of ℓ. For each security level $s \in S_\ell$, we include the offer transition $\tau_{o_s} = (\perp_\ell \xrightarrow{o_s} \ell) \in T^{SR}$, where the guard g_{o_s} is true and f_{o_s} resets variables e_p to false, for all ports p with security level s.*
- *For each transition $\tau = \ell \xrightarrow{p} \ell' \in T$ we include a notification transition $\tau_p = (\ell \xrightarrow{p} \perp_{\ell'})$ where the guard g_p is true and the function f_p applies the original update function f_τ on X, sets e_r variables to g_{τ_r} for every port $r \in P$ such that $\tau_r = \ell' \xrightarrow{r} \ell'' \in T$ and increments n_s.*

We introduce now the extended security assignment for transformed atomic components B^{SR}. Intuitively, all existing variables and ports from B keep their original security level, whereas the newly introduced ones are assigned such that to preserve the security conditions of the trasformed component.

Definition 7 (security assignement σ^{SR} for B^{SR}). *The security assignment σ^{SR} is the extension of the original security assignment σ to variables X^{SR} and ports P^{SR} from B^{SR} as follows:*

$$\sigma^{SR}(x) = \begin{cases} \sigma(p) & \text{if } x = e_p \text{ and } p \in P \\ s & \text{if } x = n_s \text{ and } s \in S \\ \sigma(x) & \text{otherwise, for } x \in X^{SR} \end{cases} \qquad \sigma^{SR}(p) = \begin{cases} s & \text{if } p = o_s \text{ and } s \in \mathbb{S} \\ \sigma(p) & \text{otherwise, for } p \in P^{SR} \end{cases}$$

As example, the component transformation and the extended security assignement for the Event Receiver are depicted in Fig. 4. Variables $n_L, e_{invite}, e_{open}$ and the offer port o_L are assigned to *Low*. Variables n_H, e_{push}, e_{get} and the port o_H are assigned to *High*. Ones can check that this assignement obeys all the (local) security conditions related to B^{SR}.

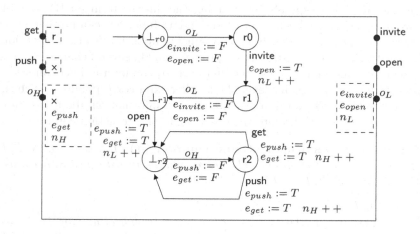

Fig. 4. Transformation of atomic components illustrated on the Event Receiver

Actually, security conditions are preserved along the proposed transformation of atomic components with respect to extended security assignement. The following lemma formalizes this result.

Lemma 1. B^{SR} *satisfies the security conditions with security assignment* σ^{SR}.

Proof. easy check, security conditions hold by definition of B^{SR} and σ^{SR}.

4.2 Interaction Protocol Layer

This layer consists of a set of components, each in charge of execution of a subset of interactions from the original component model. Every such IP component is a controller that, iteratively, receives offers from the transformed atomic components, computes enabled interactions and schedule them for execution.

In this paper, we consider IP components handling a conflict-free partitioning of interactions, as in [3]. Two interactions a_1 and a_2 are in conflict iff either (i) they share a common port p (i.e. $p \in a_1 \cap a_2$) or (ii) there exist two conflicting transitions at a local state ℓ of a component B_i that are labeled with ports p_1 and p_2, where $p_1 \in a_1$ and $p_2 \in a_2$. Conflict-free partitioning allows IP components to run fully independently of each other, that is, local decisions taken on every IP component about executing one of its interactions do not interfere with others.

Moreover, in order to ensure information flow security, we impose an additional restriction on partitioning, that is, the subset of interactions handled within every IP component must have the same security level. Intuitively, this restriction allows us to enforce by construction the security conditions for all IP components and later, for the system composition.

Bearing this in mind, let us observe that if the original system satisfies the security conditions then the partitioning of interactions according to their security level is conflict-free. That is, no conflict exists between interactions with different security levels - this simply follows from the condition (i) on the labeling of conflicting transitions. Therefore, for the sake of simplicity of presentation, we restrict hereafter our construction to the partitioning according to security levels. For every security level s we consider one IP component IP_s handling the subset of interactions $\gamma_s = \{a \in \gamma \mid \sigma(a) = s\}$ with security level s.

Definition 8 (IP_s **component for** γ_s). *Interaction protocol component* IP_s *handling interactions* γ_s *is defined according to [3], Definition 7.*

The extended security assignement σ^{SR} for IP_s variables and ports is defined as follows. All ports are annotated with security level s. Regarding variables, σ^{SR} maintains the same security level for all variables having their level greater than s in the original model and *upgrades* the others to s. That is, all variables within the IP_s component will have security level at least s. This change is mandatory to ensure consistent transfer of data in offers (resp. notifications) between atomic components and IP_s.

Definition 9 (security assignment σ^{SR} **for** IP_s**).** *The security assignment* σ^{SR} *is built from the original security assignment* σ. *For variables* X^{IP} *and ports* P^{IP} *of the* IP_s *component that handles* γ_s, *we define*

$$\sigma^{SR}(x) = \begin{cases} \sigma(x) & \text{if } x \in X_p \text{ and } s \sqsubseteq \sigma(x) \\ s & \text{otherwise} \end{cases} \qquad \sigma^{SR}(p) = s \text{ if } p \in P^{IP}$$

The above definition enforces the security conditions for IP_s.

Lemma 2. *IP_s satisfies the security conditions with security assignment σ^{SR}.*

Proof. Trivial check for conditions (i, iv). The condition (ii) on sequential consistency is also valid, even if some (replicated) variables within IP_s are upgraded to level s. On one hand, these variables, if any, were exclusively *used* (e.g., within guards, or left-hand sides of assignments) and never *defined* in interactions from γ_s. On the other hand, all defined variables have the security level greater than s. Same reasoning applies for the condition (iii) with respect to ports.

4.3 System Composition

As a final step, the decentralized model C^{SR} is obtained as the composition $\gamma^{SR}(B_1^{SR}, ..., B_n^{SR}, (IP_s)_{s \in \mathbb{S}})$ involving the transformed components B_i^{SR} and components IP_s. The set γ^{SR} contains S/R interactions and is defined as follows:

- for every component B_i^{SR} participating in interactions having security level s, include in γ^{SR} the *offer* interaction $(B_i^{SR}.o_s, IP_s.o_i)$ associated with the transfer of data from the component port o_s to the IP component port o_i.
- for every port p in component B_i^{SR} with security level s, include in γ^{SR} the *notification* interaction $(IP_s.p, B_i.p)$ associated with the transfer of the subset of X_p variables having security level at least s from the IP component port p to the component port p. Actually, these are the only variables that could have been modified by an interaction having level s.

The security assignment σ^{SR} is naturally lifted from offer/notification ports to the interactions of γ^{SR}. Intuitively, every S/R interaction involving component IP_s has security level s. The construction is illustrated for the running example in Fig. 5. We omitted the representation of ports and depict only the interactions and their associated data flow. In particular, consider the x variable of Event Receiver which is upgraded to H when sent to IP_H and not sent back on the notification of the push interaction.

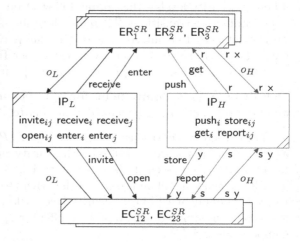

Fig. 5. Decentralized model for the WhensApp example

The following theorem states our main result, that is, the constructed two-layer S/R model satisfies the security conditions by construction.

Theorem 2. *The decentralized component* $C^{SR} = \gamma^{SR}(B_1^{SR}, ..., B_n^{SR}, (IP_s)_{s \in S})$ *satisfies security conditions for the security assignment* σ^{SR}.

Proof. From lemmas 1 and 2 all security conditions related to transformed components and IP components are satisfied. The only remaining condition (iii) concerns the assignement of data along S/R interactions. As all the variables in IP_s have been eventually upgraded to level s, the assignment within offer interactions is consistent. Similar for notifications at level s, their assignement is restricted by construction to variables having security level at least s.

5   Related Work

Model-based security aims at simplifying security configuration and coding. The work in [8] considers modeling security policies in UML and targets automating security code generation for business applications using JEE and .net. The work of [9] uses a model-based approach to simplify secure code deployment on heterogeneous platforms. Compared to these, our work is not restricted to point-to-point access control and deals with information flow security. The work on designing web services from [10] relies on Petri-nets for modeling composed services and annotations for the flow of interactions. Our component model is more general and deals with both data and event- non-interference.

Information flow control for programming languages dates back to Denning who originally proposed a language for static information flow checking [11]. Since then, information-flow control based on type systems and associated compilation tools has widely developed [12–14]. Recently, it extends to provably-secure languages including cryptographic functions [15–19]. With few exceptions, all these approaches are restricted to sequential imperative languages and ignore distribution/communication aspects. Among the exceptions, JifSplit [20] takes as input a security-annotated program, and splits it into threads by assuming that the communication through the network is secure. Furthermore, in [21] the communication's security is enforced by adding cryptographic mechanisms. The drawback of these is that the security aspect guides the system distribution. In practice, a separation of concerns is required and the system architecture must be independent of security constraints. Our approach is different since our starting point is a component-based model and the security constraints are expressed with annotations at the architecture level.

Operating systems like Flume [22], HiStar [23] and Asbestos [24] ensure information flow control between processes by associating security labels to processes and messages. DStar [25] extends HiStar to distributed applications. These approaches may appear attractive since transparent to the developer. Nevertheless, the granularity of processes may be too coarse to establish end-to-end security for distributed applications with complex interactions.

Component-based design is appealing for verification of security since the system structure and communications are explicitly represented. However, existing work focus merely on point-yo-point access control. The work of [26] considers dependencies between service components but not advanced properties like implicit information flow. In [27], authors provide APIs to configure the security of component connectors. The work in [28] deals with non-interference on component-based models using annotation propagation inside component code. In our work, we achieve complete separation between the abstract high-level component model on which non-interference is verified, and the low-level platform-dependent model where security is enforced by construction.

6   Conclusion and Future Work

We introduced a tool-supported approach to automatically secure information flow in distributed systems. Starting from an abstract component-based model with multiparty interactions, we verify security policy preservation, that is, non-interference property at both event and data levels. Then, we generate a distributed model where multiparty interactions are replaced with protocols based on asynchronous message passing. The distributed model is proved "secure-by-construction". This work is being extended towards code generation and deployment on distributed platforms. More specifically, we envisage to use web services as a target for the S/R distributed model and to rely on web services security standards to ensure the required protection of the information flow, following idea from [29]. On longer term, we plan to extend both the security model and the associated transformations for relaxed versions of non-interference i.e., allowing runtime re-labelling, declassification, intransitive.

References

1. Ben Said, N., Abdellatif, T., Bensalem, S., Bozga, M.: Model-driven information flow security for component-based systems. In: Bensalem, S., Lakhneck, Y., Legay, A. (eds.) From Programs to Systems. LNCS, vol. 8415, pp. 1–20. Springer, Heidelberg (2014)
2. Basu, A., Bozga, M., Sifakis, J.: Modeling heterogeneous real-time systems in BIP. In: Proceedings of the SEFM 2006, pp. 3–12. IEEE Computer Society Press (2006)
3. Bonakdarpour, B., Bozga, M., Jaber, M., Quilbeuf, J., Sifakis, J.: Automated conflict-free distributed implementation of component-based models. In: Proceedings of the SIES 2010, pp. 108–117. IEEE (2010)
4. Bonakdarpour, B., Bozga, M., Jaber, M., Quilbeuf, J., Sifakis, J.: A framework for automated distributed implementation of component-based models. Distrib. Comput. 25(5), 383–409 (2012)
5. Accorsi, R., Lehmann, A.: Automatic information flow analysis of business process models. In: Barros, A., Gal, A., Kindler, E. (eds.) BPM 2012. LNCS, vol. 7481, pp. 172–187. Springer, Heidelberg (2012)
6. Focardi, R., Rossi, S., Sabelfeld, A.: Bridging language-based and process calculi security. In: Sassone, V. (ed.) FOSSACS 2005. LNCS, vol. 3441, pp. 299–315. Springer, Heidelberg (2005)
7. Frau, S., Gorrieri, R., Ferigato, C.: Petri net security checker: structural non-interference at work. In: Degano, P., Guttman, J., Martinelli, F. (eds.) FAST 2008. LNCS, vol. 5491, pp. 210–225. Springer, Heidelberg (2009)

8. Basin, D.A., Doser, J., Lodderstedt, T.: Model driven security: from UML models to access control infrastructures. ACM Trans. Softw. Eng. Methodol. **15**(1), 39–91 (2006)

9. Chollet, S., Lalanda, P.: Security specification at process level. In: Proceedings of the SCC 2008, pp. 165–172. IEEE Computer Society (2008)

10. Accorsi, R., Wonnemann, C.: Static information flow analysis of workflow models. In: Proceedings of the ISSS and BPSC 2010, LNI, vol. 177, pp. 194–205 (2010)

11. Denning, D.E., Denning, P.J.: Certification of programs for secure information flow. Commun. ACM **20**, 504–513 (1977)

12. Goguen, J.A., Meseguer, J.: Security policies and security models. In: 1982 IEEE Symposium on Security and Privacy, pp. 11–20. IEEE Computer Society (1982)

13. Heintze, N., Riecke, J.G.: The slam calculus: programming with secrecy and integrity. In: Proceedings of the POPL 1998, pp. 365–377. ACM (1998)

14. Volpano, D.M., Irvine, C.E., Smith, G.: A sound type system for secure flow analysis. J. Comput. Secur. **4**(2/3), 167–188 (1996)

15. Laud, Peeter: Semantics and program analysis of computationally secure information flow. In: Sands, David (ed.) ESOP 2001. LNCS, vol. 2028, pp. 77–91. Springer, Heidelberg (2001)

16. Adão, P., Fournet, C.: Cryptographically sound implementations for communicating processes. In: Bugliesi, M., Preneel, B., Sassone, V., Wegener, I. (eds.) ICALP 2006. LNCS, vol. 4052, pp. 83–94. Springer, Heidelberg (2006)

17. Courant, J., Ene, C., Lakhnech, Y.: Computationally sound typing for non-interference: the case of deterministic encryption. In: Arvind, V., Prasad, S. (eds.) FSTTCS 2007. LNCS, vol. 4855, pp. 364–375. Springer, Heidelberg (2007)

18. Laud, P.: On the computational soundness of cryptographically masked flows. In: Proceedings of the POPL 2008, pp. 337–348. ACM (2008)

19. Fournet, C., Rezk, T.: Cryptographically sound implementations for typed information-flow security. In: Proceedings of the POPL 2008, pp. 323–335. ACM (2008)

20. Zdancewic, S., Zheng, L., Nystrom, N., Myers, A.C.: Secure program partitioning. ACM Trans. Comput. Syst. **20**, 283–328 (2002)

21. Fournet, C., Le Guernic, G., Rezk, T.: A security-preserving compiler for distributed programs: from information-flow policies to cryptographic mechanisms. In: Proceedings of the CCS 2009, pp. 432–441. ACM (2009)

22. Krohn, M.N., Yip, A., Brodsky, M.Z., Cliffer, N., Kaashoek, M.F., Kohler, E., Morris, R.: Information flow control for standard OS abstractions. In: Proceedings of the SOSP 2007, pp. 321–334. ACM (2007)

23. Zeldovich, N., Boyd-Wickizer, S., Kohler, E., Mazières, D.: Making information flow explicit in HiStar. In: Proceedings of the OSDI 2006, pp. 263–278. Usenix Assoc. (2006)

24. Vandebogart, S., Efstathopoulos, P., Kohler, E., Krohn, M.N., Frey, C., Ziegler, D., Kaashoek, M.F., Morris, R., Mazières, D.: Labels and event processes in the Asbestos operating system. ACM Trans. Comput. Syst. **25**(4), 1–11 (2007)

25. Zeldovich, N., Boyd-Wickizer, S., Mazières, D.: Securing distributed systems with information flow control. In: Proceedings of the NSDI 2008, pp. 293–308. Usenix Assoc. (2008)

26. Parrend, P., Frénot, S.: Security benchmarks of OSGi platforms: toward hardened OSGi. Softw. Pract. Exper. **39**(5), 471–499 (2009)

27. Kuz, I., Liu, Y., Gorton, I., Heiser, G.: Camkes: a component model for secure microkernel-based embedded systems. J. Syst. Softw. **80**(5), 687–699 (2007)

28. Abdellatif, T., Sfaxi, L., Robbana, R., Lakhnech, Y.: Automating information flow control in component-based distributed systems. In: Proceedings of the CBSE 2011, pp. 73–82. ACM (2011)
29. Ben Said, N., Abdellatif, T., Bensalem, S., Bozga, M.: A robust framework for securing composed web services. In: Braga, C., et al. (eds.) FACS 2015. LNCS, vol. 9539, pp. 105–122. Springer, Heidelberg (2016). doi:10.1007/978-3-319-28934-2_6

Information Leakage Analysis of Complex C Code and Its application to OpenSSL

Pasquale Malacaria[✉], Michael Tautchning, and Dino DiStefano

School of Electronic Engineering and Computer Science,
Queen Mary University of London, London, UK
{p.malacaria,michael.tautschnig,d.distefano}@qmul.ac.uk

Abstract. The worldwide attention generated by the Heartbleed bug has demonstrated even to the general public the potential devastating consequences of information leaks.

While substantial academic work has been done in the past on information leaks, these works have so far not satisfactorily addressed the challenges of automated analysis of real-world complex C code. On the other hand, effective working solutions rely on ad-hoc principles that have little or no theoretical justification.

The foremost contribution of this paper is to bridge this chasm between advanced theoretical work and concrete practical needs of programmers developing real world software. We present an analysis, based on clear security principles and verification tools, which is largely automatic and effective in detecting information leaks in complex C code running everyday on millions of systems worldwide.

1 Introduction

The OpenSSL Heartbleed vulnerability (CVE-2014-0160)[1] has attracted international attention both from media and security experts. It is difficult to imagine a more serious security flaw: devastating (clear-text passwords are leaked), widespread (running on millions of systems), untraceable, and repeatable while leaking up to 64 KB of memory at a time.

Automated security analysis of code have so far proven to be of limited help: Heartbleed seemingly demonstrated the limitations of current static analysis tools for this kind of leaks. As noted by Kupsch and Miller [14], static analysis tools struggle detecting Heartbleed due to the use of pointers, and the complexity of the execution path from the buffer allocation to its misuse.

Static analyses capable of scrutinising large code bases are effective at detecting bugs that may bring undefined behaviour (e.g., a crash), but they are less effective at detecting deep intricate bugs which represent functional misbehaviour in code of any size.

The code analysis technique used in this paper, while being static in the sense of being applied at compile time and considering all (bounded) execution paths,

---

[1] cve.mitre.org/cgi-bin/cvename.cgi?name=CVE-2014-0160 and heartbleed.com.

© Springer International Publishing AG 2016
T. Margaria and B. Steffen (Eds.): ISoLA 2016, Part I, LNCS 9952, pp. 909–925, 2016.
DOI: 10.1007/978-3-319-47166-2_63

is an ideal complement to classical static analysis. Our analysis aims at detecting deep, intricate confidentiality violations. While our methodology allows for abstractions and sometimes may need them, it is largely a precise analysis down to the bit level. As such, all aspects of the code and the security requirements are translated into logic formulae and then checked by SAT or SMT solvers. Our technique would be a valuable tool for both developers and for code reviewers. The manual effort required is a labelling of confidential information and to write appropriate drivers. In this context, it is worth noting that Heartbleed was originally discovered as part of a code review, described as "laborious auditing of OpenSSL" [16].

Our methodology is not about detecting undefined behaviour in the code, such as generic memory errors, but rather detecting confidentiality violations.

The principles underpinning this work go back to the fundamental definition of security. To the best of our knowledge, however, it was unknown how to implement such principles for large and complex C code. As such, the first and foremost contribution of this work is in enabling such real-world, complex security analysis.

Related Work. There are several commercial static analysers for C such as Grammatech's CodeSonar [9], Coverity [7], Klokwork [12], HP/Fortify [11]. None of these tools detected Heartbleed ahead-of-time. Some of the vendors of these tools are now extending their heuristics for being able to catch similar bugs [1,4]. Their approach is based on the general idea of *taint analysis*. All these tools are very effective at detecting implementation bugs (which may or may not necessarily be security vulnerabilities) violating certain patterns. OpenSSL code is extremely complex; it includes multiple levels of indirection and other issues that can easily prevent these tools from finding vulnerabilities. Heartbleed is not an exception. Most importantly, these tools are not confidentiality checkers and so may not be able to find leaks not originating from undefined behaviour. Our technique instead is aimed at detecting subtle information leaks.

Dynamic analysis used in tools like Valgrind [22] is very effective in finding code defects and improving the security of code. While extremely useful, dynamic analysis techniques can only check for a limited number of inputs and, therefore, do not provide the same strong security guarantees as our approach does. Similar to dynamic analyses symbolic execution tools are very scalable and our approach can be implemented in KLEE and similarly in other such platforms.

There is a large body of literature on non-interference [17,20] with related type systems, abstract domains, and data-flow and dynamic analysis. As already mentioned these approaches have had limited success on complex C code. Our work builds on the security literature of self-composition and its implementation [2,21]. Previously, none of these works was able to deal with complex C code. CBMC has been used to implement self-composition also in [10]. Comparing their work with the proposed methodology, they neither use quantifiers, hence are limited to bounded analysis. Also they didn't attack the engineering challenges of an automated analysis of a large code basis like OpenSSL.

2   Background

Our confidentiality analysis is based on the definition of non-interference [8]. Informally:

> A program is *non-interfering* (i.e., doesn't leak confidential information) if and only if two runs of the program that only differ in some confidential value do not yield different behaviours that can be observed by an attacker.

In other words a non-leaking program behaves, from the point of view of an attacker, as a constant function once its non-confidential arguments are fixed. More formally noting $\langle P, \mu \rangle \downarrow \nu$ for "the program P starting from memory configuration (contents) μ terminates with a resulting memory ν" then (termination insensitive) non-interference is defined as: for all memory configurations $\mu_1, \mu_2, \nu_1, \nu_2$:

$$[\langle P, \mu_1 \rangle \downarrow \nu_1 \wedge \langle P, \mu_2 \rangle \downarrow \nu_2 \wedge \mu_1 =_L \mu_2] \rightarrow \nu_1 =_L \nu_2$$

where $\mu_1 =_L \mu_2$ means the memory configurations agree on the non-confidential values (also called the public values or *low* values; public values are assumed to be observable).

We refer the interested reader to the literature [17] for a more extensive background on non-interference and confidentiality.

2.1   An Introductory Example

To illustrate non-interference, consider an authentication system testing whether a user-provided string is a valid password:

```
int authenticate(int passwd, int guess)
{
int authenticated;
if(passwd==guess)
authenticated=1;
else authenticated=0;
return authentic;
}
```

The authenticate function above is not secure because we can find two different confidential values for the variable passwd resulting in two observables by an attacker. The first one is the value of passwd being equal to the value of guess. The second can be chosen as any different value. In this case the program will return two different values for authenticated, which is observable by an attacker.

More specifically, by observing authenticated==1 the attacker will know the password is the value of guess, and by observing authenticated==0 the attacker will know the password is not the value of guess. In both cases the attacker will learn something about the password, hence some information is being leaked.

Handling Randomness. The classic definition of confidentiality fails to account for programs the behaviour of which depends on sources of randomness. Consider the following variation of the above program:

if (random_value) authenticated=1; **else** authenticated=0;

This program would be deemed non secure following the definition of non-interference. Assuming `random_value` doesn't use any confidential values in its computation then the above program is, however, secure. One way to understanding this in the context of non-interference is to think that a `random_value` in a deterministic systems is in fact the result of a deterministic function on some possibly difficult-to-guess non-confidential inputs, e.g. the seed used in the function generating random numbers in standard programming languages. A full discussion of this topic is beyond the scope of this work. For the purposes of our analysis hence when allowing random values we need to check whether the source of randomness is non confidential and if that is the case then not count that as a security violation. If fact we will deal with random values using CBMC in the same way as we deal with missing code, which is explained in Sect. 4.4. Handling randomness is crucial when analysing some OpenSSL functions, such as `dtls1_heartbeat` or `tls1_heartbeat` (see Sect. 4.5). To correctly label the source of randomness is usually the task of the developer.

3   Confidentiality Analysis Using CBMC

The workflow of the analysis implemented using CBMC is summarised in Fig. 1. We first expand on how the driver is defined, its relation to non-interference and self-composition and how C code is handled by CBMC. We explain pre-processing in Sect. 4.2, i.e., how to prepare the source code for the analysis, and in Sects. 4.3 and 4.4 we will discuss how to deal with missing code and unbounded analysis using quantifiers.

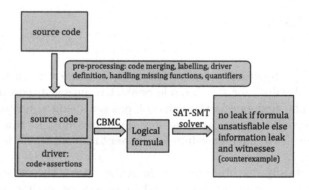

Fig. 1. Workflow of the analysis using CBMC

To start with let's explain how we check non-interference using the bounded model checker CBMC [5, 13]. To illustrate the use of CBMC in this context, let us consider the program of Fig. 2, taken from [6]. The first listing on the left contains the program with an assertion describing the desired postcondition. That is, for all possible executions of the program it holds that $x \leq 3$ at the end. As first step, CBMC transforms the program into Static Single Assignment (SSA) form, which introduces the new variables x_1, x_2, x_3 corresponding to the different definitions of the variable x in the program, and similarly y_1 for variable y. The code in SSA form induces a system of equations which is then translated to a propositional formula $\mathcal{C}$ the atoms of which are bit vector equations. $\mathcal{C}$ represents the program as equation system and a model of $\mathcal{C}$ can be interpreted as an input and its execution trace. Finally the assertion is translated to the formula $\mathcal{P}$.

```
x=2; y=1;          x₁=2; y₁=1;
if(x!=1)           if(x₁!=1)
{                  {
  x=2;               x₂=2;
  if(y) x++;         if(y₁!=0) x₃=x₂+1;
}                  }
assert(x<=3);      assert(x₃<=3);
```

$$\mathcal{C} := x_1 = 2 \wedge y_1 = 1 \wedge$$

$$x_2 = ((x_1 \neq 1)?2 : x_1) \wedge$$

$$x_3 = ((x_1 \neq 1 \wedge y_1 \neq 0)?x_2 + 1 : x_2)$$

$$\mathcal{P} := x_3 \leq 3$$

Fig. 2. Example of renaming and transformation in CBMC

Following the rules of Hoare Logic, the postcondition $\mathcal{P} \equiv x_3 \leq 3$ holds if and only if $\mathcal{C} \Rightarrow \mathcal{P}$ is valid. Equivalently, the original assertion is valid in the original program if only if the propositional formula $\mathcal{C} \wedge \neg \mathcal{P}$ is unsatisfiable.

To see that the above statement is true reason as follows: if $\mathcal{C} \wedge \neg \mathcal{P}$ is satisfiable then the satisfying assignment will provide a counterexample for the property $\mathcal{P}$, i.e., a trace showing why the program doesn't satisfy $\mathcal{P}$. If, however, $\mathcal{C} \wedge \neg \mathcal{P}$ is unsatisfiable then the property $\mathcal{P}$ holds for all execution traces.

CBMC is a bounded model checker, hence only a bounded version of a program, where the loops are unwound up to a user-defined bound, can be analysed. Consequently it is first and foremost a bug-finding approach, unless the program under scrutiny only exhibits bounded loops or bounded recursion.

While unbounded verification is thus beyond the scope of CBMC, the user has options that may, in certain cases, provide unbounded verification results (i.e., proofs of correctness): an example is mentioned in Sect. 4.3 where we replace loops with universally quantified expressions.

Self-composition. The definition of non-interference is a semantic one. A translation of this definition to verification terms, called *self-composition*, has been introduced in [2, 21]. In self-composition we consider a program P and a copy P' of P. The copy P' consists of P with all variables renamed (public variables

$\overrightarrow{x}$ renamed as $\overrightarrow{x'}$). Let $\uplus$ be disjoint union. Then non-interference is defined as: for all memory configurations μ, μ', ν, ν':

$$[\langle P; P', \mu \uplus \mu' \rangle \downarrow \nu \uplus \nu' \wedge \mu' =_L \mu[\overrightarrow{x'} := \overrightarrow{x}]] \rightarrow \nu' =_L \nu[\overrightarrow{x'} := \overrightarrow{x}]$$

In words: the program $P; P'$, i.e., the sequential composition of P and P', starting from the memory $\mu \uplus \mu'$ (where μ' is the same memory as μ on the public variables $\overrightarrow{x}$, except for renaming of $\overrightarrow{x}$ to $\overrightarrow{x'}$) will terminate resulting in memory $\nu \uplus \nu'$ (where ν' is the same memory as ν on the public variables $\overrightarrow{x}$, except for renaming of $\overrightarrow{x}$ to $\overrightarrow{x'}$).

Our implementation of self-composition using CBMC follows the approach in [10]. Here we only give an intuition about the approach and refer the interested reader to the literature for a more formal definition and relationship between self-composition and non-interference [2,10,21]. Recall that by definition of non-interference to find a violation of confidentiality we need to find two runs of the function under analysis that only differ in some confidential value and result in two different observables. To implement this using CBMC we add a driver to the program where we assert that *any two runs of the function which differ on only the confidential values will result in the same observable.* A violation to this assertion (i.e., a counterexample) will hence be an assignment describing two confidential values for which the function will return two different observables.

Going back to the simple password program in Sect. 2.1, its security analysis using CBMC is realised using the following code:

```
int authenticate(int passwd, int guess)
{
  int authenticated;
  if(passwd==guess)
  authenticated=1;
  else authenticated=0;
  return authentic;
}
```

```
void driver()
{
  int pwd1, pwd2, guess;
  int res1=authenticate(pwd1, guess);
  int res2=authenticate(pwd2, guess);
  assert(res1==res2);
}
```

We have inserted a driver method with the declaration of three variables of type `int`. These variables will be used as arguments to the function `authenticate` in the two calls and finally an assertion is made about the equality of the results of the calls. CBMC will translate the above code into a formula and will look for an assignment satisfying that formula. As the variables are not initialised their values will be determined by the SAT solver. By running CBMC on the above code we will get a counterexample, and thus values v, v', u for `pwd1`, `pwd2`, `guess`, respectively, have been found by the SAT solver. As those result in the assertion to fail, this means that the program is leaking confidential information. In the terminology of self-composition

$$\mu = \{\text{pwd1} \mapsto v, \ \text{guess} \mapsto u\}, \ \mu' = \{\text{pwd2} \mapsto v', \ \text{guess} \mapsto u\}$$

and the renaming[2] of μ to μ' is

$$\{\{\texttt{pwd1} \mapsto v\} := \{\texttt{pwd2} \mapsto v'\},\ \{\texttt{guess} \mapsto \texttt{u}\} := \{\texttt{guess} \mapsto \texttt{u}\}\}.$$

To sum up there are three key ingredients to identify and label when performing a non-interference analysis when using a model checker like CBMC:

1. *Confidential inputs*: the secret we don't want the code to leak (in the above example, the values of password in function authenticate).
2. *Public inputs*: the inputs that do not contain confidential information (in the above example the argument guess).
3. *Observables*: what we assume an attacker can observe when the function is run (in the above example is the return value of function authenticate).

4   Analysis of OpenSSL

4.1   Labelling and Drivers for OpenSSL

A key aspect of the analysis is the labelling of confidential, public, and observable data. This step cannot be fully automated because it is easy to imagine how the same code may be used for different purposes and hence the meaning of confidential, public, and observable data may be application dependent.

We assume that this process of labelling is in general a simple task for the code developer (and the code reviewer): by writing the code they should know easily what the confidential, non confidential, and observable components in the code are.

Of course the labelling is more challenging for a third party not familiar with the code and, in that case, may require some non-trivial reverse engineering.

In the case of OpenSSL our labelling is determined by reverse engineering what confidential, public and observable are in the functions where Heartbleed originated (i.e. functions: dtls1_process_heartbeat and tls1_process_heartbeat). Once this labelling is determined we can proceed to analyse all of OpenSSL for leaks from similar inputs to similar observables. The labelling is the following:

1. *Confidential data*: this is the process memory. It is confidential because it holds confidential data, such as passwords or private keys [23]. Notice that this is not an input to a function.
2. *Public data*: these are the ssl_st structures containing the payload from the sender or any argument that are provided by the user as arguments to OpenSSL functions. The attacker can control these inputs, which is how Heartbleed is triggered. In security jargon we are considering an active attacker because the attacker can control the public inputs.

---

[2] Here we map guess on the same name whereas we should use different names; it is easy to see this is harmless in this context.

```
void driver(){
        declare a_1,  ...,  a_n, b_1,  ...,  b_n;
        a_1 = ...;   // optional  initialisation  argument a_1
          :
          :
        a_n = ...;   // optional  initialisation  argument a_n
        b_1 = ...;   // optional  initialisation  argument b_1
          :
          :
        b_n = ...;   // optional  initialisation  argument b_n
        assert(observable(f(a_1,  ...,  a_n))==observable(f(b_1,  ...,  b_n)));
}
```

Fig. 3. Driver template for checking function f(i1,..., in).

3. *Observables*: this is the structure used for communicating between the client
   and server. They use (part of) the structures of type ssl_st for communication and the medium is (the function pointer) msg_callback. The third
   and fourth arguments of msg_callback consists of the data buffer of communication and its length. We hence select the third and fourth arguments of
   msg_callback as the observables.

We stress that, while this labelling originated from the Heartbleed bug functions, it is not specific to the Heartbleed bug: labelling the process memory
as confidential is natural and general because the process memory, no matter
what OpenSSL function we consider, contains data like passwords. Labelling
msg_callback as observable is natural and general because this is the main
communication medium between client and server for all OpenSSL functions,
and is also the medium by which data is transferred and so it could be leaked.
Labelling the structure ssl_st as public is natural and general because this is a
structure, argument to most OpenSSL functions, that both parties have access
to and can manipulate.

To check a function, say f(i1,..., in), for information leaks, we write a
driver function defined according to the template in Fig. 3. This driver declares
and possibly initialises the arguments (ensuring $a_i = b_i$ if that argument is public) and then checks that the results for the observables are the same. Given
the OpenSSL labelling above described it is easy to instantiate such schema for
a particular function that needs to be checked. In the case of these OpenSSL
functions the driver asserts that given two calls to the function which have the
same public inputs the resulting msg_callback observables are the same. For two
of these functions, namely the ones with the Heartbleed bug we were able, by
using quantifiers, to perform an unbounded security analysis. For the remaining
functions the security analysis is bounded. Bounded means we can only assert
that the observables in the resulting msg_callback are the same for the first n
elements. The OpenSSL functions using msg_callback are shown in Fig. 4.

int dtls1_process_heartbeat(**struct** ssl_st ∗)
int dtls1_heartbeat(**struct** ssl_st ∗)
int dtls1_do_write(**struct** ssl_st ∗, **int**)
long int dtls1_get_message(**struct** ssl_st ∗, **int**, **int**, **int**, **long int**, **int** ∗)
long int dtls1_get_message_fragment(**struct** ssl_st ∗, **int**, **int**, **long int**, **int** ∗)
int dtls1_read_bytes(**struct** ssl_st ∗, **int**, **unsigned char** ∗, **int**, **int**)
int dtls1_dispatch_alert(**struct** ssl_st ∗)
int ssl23_client_hello(**struct** ssl_st ∗)
int ssl23_get_server_hello(**struct** ssl_st ∗)
int ssl23_get_client_hello(**struct** ssl_st ∗)
int ssl3_do_write(**struct** ssl_st ∗, **int**)
long int ssl3_get_message(**struct** ssl_st ∗, **int**, **int**, **int**, **long int**, **int** ∗)
int ssl3_read_bytes(**struct** ssl_st ∗, **int**, **unsigned char** ∗, **int**, **signed int**)
int ssl3_dispatch_alert(**struct** ssl_st ∗)
int tls1_process_heartbeat(**struct** ssl_st ∗)
int tls1_heartbeat(**struct** ssl_st ∗)

Fig. 4. OpenSSL functions analysed

Most OpenSSL are of the form f(x) where x is public, however if f uses process memory say by a call to `malloc` then it may well be that the two calls with the same public input result in different observables. This is automatically detected by CBMC thanks to its memory model.

We stress that while we check for information leakage on individual functions, our analysis is an information leakage analysis of the whole OpenSSL and not just a "unit testing" of a subset of OpenSSL. OpenSSL is essentially a library whose functions are called by server and client. By considering all functions affecting the observable `msg_callback` we are considering the whole of OpenSSL involving the data communication medium `msg_callback`.

4.2 Preparing for Analysis

Software projects of the scale of OpenSSL cannot be analysed at source-code level by picking up a single C file: numerous header files and configuration parameters contribute to each compilation unit. To employ CBMC in such a context, we use `goto-cc`, which can be used as drop-in replacement of various common compilers, including GCC. Running OpenSSL's standard build process, `goto-cc` builds an intermediate representation, called "goto programs" – a control-flow graph like representation – rather than executable binaries. The compiled files could be used directly with CBMC; for our experiments, however, we took the additional step of decompiling to C source code using `goto-instrument` (which is also part of CBMC's distribution). The resulting C code has all preprocessor macros and typedefs expanded, and adheres to any compile-time command-line options affecting the semantics of the program. A key benefit of this decompilation step is that our analysis could potentially be performed using any software analysis tool for C programs – such as KLEE.

4.3   Using Quantifiers for Unbounded Verification

Bounded model checkers unfold loops up to user-defined bounds. In certain cases, however, it is possible to use CBMC in a more powerful way. If we can replace a loop with a *quantified formula characterising the loop* then we can achieve unbounded verification.

The OpenSSL functions which suffered from Heatbleed allowed for this transformation. These functions call the standard library function memcpy in the following way:

memcpy((**void** *)bp, (**const void** *)pl, (**unsigned long**)payload)

The semantics of the function memcpy is to copy payload bytes of memory from the area pointed-to by pl to the memory area pointed-to by bp (we assume the memory regions involved do not overlap). Therefore the effect of this call can be summarised by the following quantified formula:

$$\forall\ (0 \leq i < \text{payload})\colon \text{bp}[i] == \text{pl}[i]$$

When loops are replaced by quantifiers, we can then use CBMC to translate the program and the assertions into a first-order formula over the theory of bitvectors. The obtained formulae are then passed to the SMT-solver Z3 [15] for satisfiability checking.

4.4   Missing Source Code and Compositionality Principle

When CBMC encounters a function call like v=g(b) and has no source code for the function g then a non-deterministically chosen value of the appropriate type is given to v. The implication for our analysis is that if there are some calls to missing functions and the analysis is successful, then the verification would be successful also if the source code were not missing[3].

On the other hand if the verification is unsuccessful then the failure may be spurious and originate from the non-deterministic choice of the missing function return value, because in each of the two runs different values may be non-deterministically chosen. A way to determine whether this is indeed the case is to make sure that the non-deterministically chosen return value for g is the same for the two calls of the function under analysis. This is easily achieved by defining this symbolic value as a non-deterministic global variable. Because of scalability issues we have excluded from the analysis the code of a few functions which we believe are safe to exclude, e.g., dtls1_write_bytes.

Compositionality Principle: If a function f(a) calls a function g(b) and the analysis reports f(a) to be secure while the source code for g(b) is missing (where the missing code is handled as explained above), and in an independent analysis g(b) is reported to be secure, then f(a) is secure[4].

---

[3] Provided these functions don't leak and return deterministic values. Also if these functions have side-effects these should be deterministic.

[4] A soundness proof of this principle for a complex language like C is arguably infeasible and surely beyond the scope of this work.

To verify confidentiality we can thus split the code base in several fragments. This compositionality principle is helpful when dealing with a large code base.

Notice that the converse direction is not valid, i.e., it is possible that the analysis returns that f(a) is not secure in the analysis where the source code for g(b) is missing, and the analysis returns g(b) is not secure but in fact the function f *is* secure. A simple example is the following program:

```
int f(int a) {
    int b=1;                int g(int b) {
    int v=g(b);                if(b) return 0;
    if(v) leak ...             else leak ...
    else non−leak ...       }
}
```

The function f leaks only if the value of v is 1 and v is set by the call to g. The function, g leaks only when b is 0. As b is set to 1 in f before calling g then g will not leak and return 0. This in turn will prevent f from leaking.

The analysis will return that f and g both leak when analysed in isolation. However, f is secure as v is never 1 inside f which is the only case when f leaks.

4.5   Analysis of OpenSSL Functions

For the analysis of the OpenSSL functions we use the basic driver pattern of Fig. 3. An example of initialisation of arguments for dtls1_process_heartbeat and tls1_process_heartbeat is reported in Fig. 5. The data size used is 37, because the size of payload and padding of a non-malicious heartbeat sent by the client is 34 bytes plus 2 bytes for the length and 1 byte for the type. Pointer rrec.data points to a structure for which we provide an unspecified values: this can be achieved in CBMC by giving to the element of the structure a non-initialised value.

Other functions analysed in OpenSSL use the pointer init_buf.data instead of rrec.data; however, the initialisation is similar. For init_buf.data we used the value 12, 24, and 48 as possible lengths. These values are simple guessworks on possible sizes and are just meant to prove that our methodology provides us with the ability to perform the analysis. An OpenSSL developer would be able to assign appropriate range of sizes for init_buf.data allowing therefore a more complete security analysis of the OpenSSL functions unrelated to Heartbleed.

Table 1 summarises the experimental results of the automated analysis using CBMC version 5.0. The tests were performed on Linux systems with 64-core AMD Opteron processors running at 2.5 GHz, equipped with 256 GB of memory.

In the table we write fun_N_OPTION meaning that the function fun was analysed by unrolling its loops N times and OPTION is one of the following:

– C_NO_OBSERVATION_IS_LEAK: with this option the assertion used is precisely the one from non-interference, i.e. it states that the observables are equal.

```
struct ssl_st s_1,s_2;
int i;
s_1.msg_callback=fobservable_1;
s_2.msg_callback=fobservable_2;
struct ssl3_state_st s3_1,s3_2;
unsigned char r_data_1[37], r_data_2[37];
for(i=0; i<37; i++) {
  r_data_2[i]=r_data_1[i];
}
s3_1.rrec.data=r_data_1;
s3_2.rrec.data=r_data_2;
s3_1.rrec.length=37;
s3_2.rrec.length=37;
s_1.s3=&s3_1;
s_2.s3=&s3_2;
```

Fig. 5. Initialisation of data structures for `dtls1_process_heartbeat` and `tls1_process_heartbeat`. These structures are the public inputs for those functions

If this option is not selected we use a weaker assertion, i.e. the assertion states that either the observables are equal or one of the observables is null, i.e. with the option not selected we accept a possible 1 bit leakage because, depending on the value of the secret, the function may produce a null observable or a specific non-null observable. The combination of these two assertions has shown to be helpful to detect spurious 1 bit leakage (details below).

- C_INIT_BUF_LENGTH__M: this option sets `init_buf.data` to size M.
- C_HB_SEQ_HIGH: this option sets `tlsext_hb_seq` field as high (i.e., confidential). This option only applies to `dtls1_heartbeat` and `tls1_heartbeat`.
- C_HB_ART_LEAK: this option adds an artificial information-flow leak (described later on) inside the function `(d)tls1_process_heartbeat`.
- C_HB_BUG: this option disables the Heartbleed patch.
- C_FORALL: this option introduces quantifiers.
- C_HB_CORR_SIZE: configures the heartbeat payload to the correct size.
- C_RANDOM_LOW__M: set M random bytes in the heartbeat payload to be public.
- C_CLIENT_HELLO_CONSTRAINED: forbid `ssl23_write_bytes` return value between 2 and 5.

Notice that a few functions with no option selected verify successfully and with option C_NO_OBSERVATION_IS_LEAK yield a counterexample. This indicates a possible maximal one-bit leak. A quick code inspection following the CBMC error trace suggests this small leak is spurious and caused by some missing initialisation or missing functions called by the analysed functions.

Functions `dtls1_process_heartbeat`, `dtls1_heartbeat`, `tls1_heartbeat`, `tls1_process_heartbeat`, and `ssl23_client_hello` show more serious failures: from a security perspective they are the most interesting and we now comment more in details on our findings.

Functions dtls1_process_heartbeat and tls1_process_heartbeat. The verification fails when there is no patch and rrec.data[1], rrec.data[2] are left unspecified (i.e., option C_HB_BUG). This is the Heartbleed bug. In fact rrec.data[1] and rrec.data[2] together define the payload size. By not initialising these variables CBMC will find values mismatching the real payload size and so triggering Heartbleed. Notice that we are not only able to detect the leak but CBMC's counterexample tells us precise inputs triggering Heartbleed.

An important point is that our analysis require absolutely no knowledge or suspect of the existence of the Heartbleed in order to detect it. We stress that by leaving the size of the buffers rrec.data[1], rrec.data[2] unspecified we are eliminating the guesswork on the buffer size. That is we leave to CBMC to determine if there exist buffer sizes for which there is an information leak. CBMC is able to find the buffer sizes triggering the bug. This is an important feature of our analysis because if it were to rely on this guess work it would require the developer already to suspect the leak and where it could arise.

Once the patch is applied (i.e., removing option C_HB_BUG), the verification becomes successful. We add option C_FORALL to perform an unbounded verification by using quantifiers. As such our result provides the first formal verification that the patch actually fixes the Heartbleed bug.

Another case where the verification is successful is when the code is unpatched but rrec.data[1] and rrec.data[2] are given as values the correct payload size (option C_HB_CORR_SIZE). Since rrec.data is 37 bytes (the first byte is the type; the following two bytes are the length description and 16 bytes are padding) this is achieved by setting rrec.data[1]=0;rrec.data[2]=18;. As expected the verification is in this case successful.

To test the power of our approach we then inserted in hearbeat functions a leak originating from an indirect flow modelling the reading of one byte of process memory (option C_HB_ART_LEAK). Figure 6 reports a snippet of the modified function once C_HB_ART_LEAK is used. The added lines test whether some byte from the process memory has a specific value (say 1). In that case the function assigns to the 6th element of bp the value 0 otherwise 1. Because bp is in fact a name for the buffer becoming later observable via msg_callback that bit of information about the process memory is leaked. Given this setting we get a verification failure. This case shows our ability to detect all possible leaks, i.e., not only leaks due to the bugs as in Heartbleed, but also those originating from direct and indirect flows of confidential information in code without bugs.

Functions dtls1_heartbeat and tls1_heartbeat. The verification fails. On code inspection following the counterexample we notice that the reason is that the payload is randomly generated (see Sect. 2.1 for discussion). Once we assume that the payload is not confidential we can eliminate this leak from our analysis (option C_RANDOM_LOW). Consistently with the handling of random data described in the introduction, to implement the assumption that payload is not confidential we initialise all elements in the payload buffer to arbitrary yet identical values for the two runs. Under these conditions the verification succeeds.

```
bp = bp + (signed long int)2;
memcpy((void *)bp, (const void *)pl, (unsigned long int)payload);
char process_memory_byte;                    //ADDED CODE
if(process_memory_byte) bp[5]=0; else bp[5]=1; //ADDED CODE
bp = bp + (signed long int)payload;
RAND_pseudo_bytes(bp, (signed int)padding);
```

Fig. 6. Modified (d)tls1_process_heartbeat code with artificial leak.

We detected another potential leak (option C_HB_SEQ_HIGH) which could lead an eavesdropper to estimate how many heartbeats are exchanged. The leak originates from the tlsext_hb_seq field of the structure argument to the functions dtls1_heartbeat and tls1_heartbeat. This field stores a heartbeat sequence number and this information is leaked in the observable. Our default assumption

Table 1. Benchmarks results obtained using CBMC 5.0; ✓ is successful (bounded) verification, ✗ denotes a counterexample

Benchmark	Result	Time [s]	RAM [GB]
dtls1_dispatch_alert__104__	✓	267.6	3.0
dtls1_dispatch_alert__104__C_NO_OBSERVATION_IS_LEAK	✗	222.5	3.0
dtls1_do_write__58__	✓	305.3	0.8
dtls1_do_write__58__C_INIT_BUF_LENGTH__24	✓	234.1	0.9
dtls1_do_write__58__C_INIT_BUF_LENGTH__48	✓	202.3	1.0
dtls1_do_write__58__C_NO_OBSERVATION_IS_LEAK	✓	243.2	0.8
dtls1_get_message__7__	✓	32842.6	16.8
dtls1_get_message__7__C_INIT_BUF_LENGTH__24	✓	26933.5	16.9
dtls1_get_message__7__C_INIT_BUF_LENGTH__48	✓	27528.4	17.2
dtls1_get_message__7__C_NO_OBSERVATION_IS_LEAK	✓	30636.2	16.8
dtls1_get_message_fragment__18__	✓	5655.1	8.7
dtls1_get_message_fragment__18__C_INIT_BUF_LENGTH__24	✓	5493.6	8.8
dtls1_get_message_fragment__18__C_INIT_BUF_LENGTH__48	✓	3397.5	9.0
dtls1_get_message_fragment__18__C_NO_OBSERVATION_IS_LEAK	✓	5649.6	8.7
dtls1_heartbeat__20000__	✗	3.5	0.1
dtls1_heartbeat__20000__C_HB_SEQ_HIGH__C_RANDOM_LOW__32	✗	3.5	0.1
dtls1_heartbeat__20000__C_RANDOM_LOW__32	✓	3.3	0.1
dtls1_process_heartbeat__102__	✓	13.6	0.3
dtls1_process_heartbeat__102__C_FORALL	✓	3.1	0.0
dtls1_process_heartbeat__102__C_HB_ART_LEAK	✗	8.3	0.3
dtls1_process_heartbeat__102__C_HB_ART_LEAK__C_FORALL	✗	2.4	0.0
dtls1_process_heartbeat__102__C_HB_BUG	✗	8.3	0.3
dtls1_process_heartbeat__102__C_HB_BUG__C_FORALL	✗	636.3	0.2
dtls1_process_heartbeat__102__C_HB_BUG__C_HB_CORR_SIZE	✓	5.2	0.2
dtls1_process_heartbeat__102__C_NO_OBSERVATION_IS_LEAK	✓	10.8	0.3
dtls1_process_heartbeat__102__C_HB_ART_LEAK__C_FORALL__C_HB_CORR_SIZE	✗	2.6	0.0
dtls1_process_heartbeat__102__C_HB_ART_LEAK__C_HB_CORR_SIZE	✗	5.5	0.2
dtls1_read_bytes__	✓	247.2	4.0
dtls1_read_bytes__C_NO_OBSERVATION_IS_LEAK	✓	211.4	4.0
ssl23_client_hello__100__	✗	108.9	2.0
ssl23_client_hello__100__C_INIT_BUF_LENGTH__24	✗	96.5	2.1
ssl23_client_hello__100__C_INIT_BUF_LENGTH__48	✗	99.7	2.1
ssl23_client_hello__100__C_NO_OBSERVATION_IS_LEAK	✗	95.8	2.0
ssl23_client_hello__100__C_CLIENT__HELLO__CONSTRAINED	✓	83.8	2.0

Table 1. *(Continued)*

Benchmark	Result	Time [s]	RAM [GB]
ssl23_get_client_hello__1040__	✓	1026.1	10.4
ssl23_get_client_hello__1040__C_NO_OBSERVATION_IS_LEAK	X	933.0	10.3
ssl23_get_server_hello__1040__	✓	600.2	7.0
ssl23_get_server_hello__1040__C_NO_OBSERVATION_IS_LEAK	X	552.4	7.0
ssl3_dispatch_alert__18__	✓	1603.7	11.3
ssl3_dispatch_alert__18__C_NO_OBSERVATION_IS_LEAK	✓	1465.1	11.3
ssl3_do_write__58__	✓	1.1	0.0
ssl3_do_write__58__C_INIT_BUF_LENGTH__24	✓	1.4	0.1
ssl3_do_write__58__C_INIT_BUF_LENGTH__48	✓	1.6	0.1
ssl3_do_write__58__C_NO_OBSERVATION_IS_LEAK	X	1.4	0.1
ssl3_get_message__6__	✓	21.5	0.1
ssl3_get_message__6__C_INIT_BUF_LENGTH__24	✓	14.9	0.1
ssl3_get_message__6__C_INIT_BUF_LENGTH__48	✓	15.3	0.1
ssl3_get_message__6__C_NO_OBSERVATION_IS_LEAK	✓	20.0	0.1
ssl3_read_bytes__	✓	158.1	4.1
ssl3_read_bytes__C_NO_OBSERVATION_IS_LEAK	✓	222.7	4.1
tls1_heartbeat__102__	X	3.0	0.1
tls1_heartbeat__102__C_HB_SEQ_HIGH__C_RANDOM_LOW__32	X	3.7	0.1
tls1_heartbeat__102__C_RANDOM_LOW__32	✓	2.8	0.1
tls1_process_heartbeat__102__	✓	10.1	0.2
tls1_process_heartbeat__102__C_FORALL	✓	3.2	0.0
tls1_process_heartbeat__102__C_HB_ART_LEAK	X	8.8	0.2
tls1_process_heartbeat__102__C_HB_ART_LEAK__C_FORALL	X	1.7	0.0
tls1_process_heartbeat__102__C_HB_BUG	X	8.1	0.2
tls1_process_heartbeat__102__C_HB_BUG__C_FORALL	X	4.7	0.0
tls1_process_heartbeat__102__C_HB_BUG__C_HB_CORR_SIZE	✓	5.5	0.2
tls1_process_heartbeat__102__C_NO_OBSERVATION_IS_LEAK	✓	11.8	0.2
tls1_process_heartbeat__102__C_HB_ART_LEAK__C_FORALL__C_HB_CORR_SIZE	X	1.4	0.0
tls1_process_heartbeat__102__C_HB_ART_LEAK__C_HB_CORR_SIZE	X	5.1	0.2

is that the argument is public. However, our methodology is flexible enough to consider arguments that have both confidential and public components.

Function ssl23_client_hello. The verification fails. On code inspection following the error trace provided by CBMC we discovered a possible (very large) information leak depending on the return value of ssl23_write_bytes which is called by ssl23_client_hello. With option C_CLIENT_HELLO_CONSTRAINED this return value is assumed not to be between 2 and 5 and we then succeed to verify the absence of leaks. The bound 5 comes from the packet header and should guarantee no abnormal behaviour is triggered. It would be possibly better to add a fail-safe feature to enforce these bounds, e.g., an if-then-else making sure the return value of ssl23_write_bytes is within those safe bounds and exit otherwise. This case illustrates how our analysis can help to determine possible conditions triggering a leak.

5 Conclusion

We presented a general technique for the analysis of confidentiality in complex C code. We applied our analysis to OpenSSL and showed that it correctly detects Heartbleed as a form of information leak. Moreover we verified that the patched code does not leak information. We verified the whole of OpenSSL for similar leaks. The analysis returned interesting findings and where CBMC failed to verify the absence of leaks, by using error traces we have found some possible security problems with the functions `dtls1_heartbeat`, `tls1_heartbeat` and `ssl23_client_hello`. In doing so we didn't have to modify the analysed code, but our approach, except for labelling, and writing the driver, works out of the box. The only annotation required is to label the confidential and non confidential data and what data and structures are observables to an attacker.

As any program analysis, our approach presents limitations. The main are:

- As it is based on the bounded model checker CBMC, the approach is in general bounded. In some simple, yet crucial, case we were able to overcome this limitation by encoding loops with quantified formulae. However a general automated translation from loops to quantified formulae is a challenging problem and a topic left for further research.
- The analysis is not completely automatic but it requires some simple annotations by the user: *public*, *secret*, and *observable* data. The driver also requires some user effort, but it follows a simple pattern easy to implement. Also for a given specific software contexts the driver can be automated.
- While the methodology is completely general there may be some limitation introduced by the implementation platform. For example CBMC provides limited support for string manipulation functions. Hence it may return false positive when analyzing leakage from string formatting attacks involving uninterpreted functions in CBMC.

Acknowledgments. This research was supported by EPSRC grant EP/K032011/1.

References

1. Anderson, P.: Finding heartbleed with codesonar. www.grammatech.com/blog/finding-heartbleed-with-codesonar
2. Barthe, G., D'Argenio, P.R., Rezk, T.: Secure information flow by self-composition. In: 17th IEEE Computer Security Foundations Workshop, (CSFW-17 2004), pp. 100–114. IEEE Computer Society (2004)
3. Cadar, C., Dunbar, D., Engler, D.R.: KLEE: unassisted and automatic generation of high-coverage tests for complex systems programs. In: 8th USENIX Symposium on Operating Systems Design and Implementation, OSDI 2008, pp. 209–224. USENIX Association (2008)
4. Chou, A.: On detecting heartbleed with static analysis. security.coverity.com/blog/2014/Apr/on-detecting-heartbleed-with-static-analysis.html
5. Clarke, E., Kroning, D., Lerda, F.: A tool for checking ANSI-C programs. In: Jensen, K., Podelski, A. (eds.) TACAS 2004. LNCS, vol. 2988, pp. 168–176. Springer, Heidelberg (2004)
6. Clarke, E.M., Kroening, D., Yorav, K.: Behavioral consistency of C and verilog programs using bounded model checking. In: DAC 2003, pp. 368–371. ACM (2003)
7. Coverity. www.coverity.com
8. Goguen, J.A., Meseguer, J.: Security policies and security models. In: 1982 IEEE Symposium on Security and Privacy, pp. 11–20. IEEE Computer Society (1982)

9. Grammatech. www.grammatech.com/codesonar
10. Heusser, J., Malacaria, P.: Quantifying information leaks in software. In: Twenty-Sixth Annual Computer Security Applications Conference, pp. 261–269. ACM (2010)
11. HP/Fortify. saas.hp.com/software/fortify-on-demand
12. Klokwork. www.klokwork.com
13. Kroening, D., Tautschnig, M.: CBMC – C bounded model checker. In: Ábrahám, E., Havelund, K. (eds.) TACAS 2014 (ETAPS). LNCS, vol. 8413, pp. 389–391. Springer, Heidelberg (2014)
14. Kupsch, J.A., Miller, B.P.: Why do software assurance tools have problems finding bugs like heartbleed? April 2014. continuousassurance.org/swamp/SWAMP-Heartbleed-White-Paper-22Apr2014-current.pdf
15. de Moura, L., Bjørner, N.S.: Z3: an efficient SMT solver. In: Ramakrishnan, C.R., Rehof, J. (eds.) TACAS 2008. LNCS, vol. 4963, pp. 337–340. Springer, Heidelberg (2008)
16. Business, R.: #339 - Neel Mehta on Heartbleed, Shellshock, October 2014. media.risky.biz/RB339.mp.3
17. Sabelfeld, A., Myers, A.C.: Language-based information-flow security. IEEE J. Sel. Areas Commun. 21(1), 5–19 (2003)
18. Schneier, B.: Heartbleed, April 2014. www.schneier.com/blog/archives/2014/04/heartbleed.html
19. Seggelmann, R., Tuexen, M., Williams, M.: Transport layer security (TLS) and datagram transport layer security (DTLS) heartbeat extension. RFC 6520, RFC Editor, February 2012. www.rfc-editor.org/rfc/rfc6520.txt
20. Smith, G.: Principles of secure information flow analysis. In: Christodorescu, M., Jha, S., Maughan, D., Song, D., Wang, C. (eds.) Malware Detection. Advances in Information Security, vol. 27, pp. 291–307. Springer, Heidelberg (2007)
21. Terauchi, T., Aiken, A.: Secure information flow as a safety problem. In: Hankin, C., Siveroni, I. (eds.) SAS 2005. LNCS, vol. 3672, pp. 352–367. Springer, Heidelberg (2005)
22. Valgrind. valgrind.org
23. Zhang, L., Choffnes, D.R., Levin, D., Dumitras, T., Mislove, A., Schulman, A., Wilson, C.: Analysis of SSL certificate reissues and revocations in the wake of heartbleed. In: Internet Measurement Conference, pp. 489–502. ACM (2014)

Integrated Modeling Workflow
for Security Assurance

Min-Young Nam, Julien Delange(✉), and Peter Feiler

Carnegie Mellon Software Engineering Institute,
4500 Fifth Avenue, Pittsburgh, PA 15213, USA
{mnam,jdelange,phf}@sei.cmu.edu

Abstract. Cyber-physical systems are generally composed of several software components executing on different processors that are interconnected through entities that can be represented as buses. These complex systems collocate functions operating at different security levels, which can introduce unexpected interactions that affect system security. The security policy for these systems is realized through various complex physical or logical mechanisms. The security policy, as a stakeholder goal, is then refined into system requirements and implementation constraints that are used to guarantee security objectives. Unfortunately, verifying the correct decomposition and its enforcement in the system architecture is an overwhelming task. To overcome these issues, requirements must be clearly specified and traced through the system architecture, and automatically verified throughout the development process.

In this report, we introduce a modeling framework for the design and validation of requirements from a security perspective. It is composed of a new language for requirements specification, an extension of the Architecture Analysis & Design Language, for specifying security and a set of theorems to check the requirements against the architecture. The framework provides the capability to validate the requirements of several candidate architectures and reiterate models to cope with the impact of changes to requirements and architecture during development. This model-based approach helps software architects and developers detect requirements and architecture issues early in the development life cycle and avoid the propagation of their effects during integration.

1 Introduction

For more than two decades, the viruses and malware that infect our computers have proliferated, resulting in higher attention to cyber security. The usual approach to addressing security threats has been reactive—through anti-virus and malware detection software. Yet every month, the news media report on security issues in systems that affect our everyday lives, from medical devices to cars, as one after another they prove vulnerable to intrusion. The trend toward the connected world of the Internet of Things is accelerating, and the increased interaction complexity and emergent behavior of the resulting systems have inadvertently created richer attack surfaces.

© Springer International Publishing AG 2016
T. Margaria and B. Steffen (Eds.): ISoLA 2016, Part I, LNCS 9952, pp. 926–941, 2016.
DOI: 10.1007/978-3-319-47166-2_64

These challenges have led to more proactive approaches to assuring cyber security. First, security policies must be specified not just for individual systems but also for interconnected systems. System specifications, along with their security characteristics, must be analyzable in order to assure that they are consistent and that they enforce compliance with the security policies. Requirements of such policies in an operational system must be specified. Enforcement policies identify runtime protection of security domains for information and commands in motion, during processing, and at rest through appropriate encryption, authorization, and authentication mechanisms.

Software-reliant systems, especially interconnected systems, continuously evolve to provide new functionalities that affect security requirements. At the same time, the mechanisms in the infrastructure that enforce security policies continuously evolve. As the system design evolves, these specifications are refined into requirements and assumptions on the subsystems. Requirements become more detailed regarding how they are realized in the system. As we move to such implementation-specific requirements, the likelihood grows that requirements will change, especially security requirements. Inconsistencies that were not noticeable in high-level requirements may be discovered as the design evolves. Similarly, with the ever-changing techniques of cyber attacks and the increasing connectedness of security features and systems, assuring security on a continuous basis is critical. These various causes for software changes challenge architects and developers to define security requirements in a manner that will reap the greatest benefits from automated verification.

In this report, we present a workflow for incremental security assurance of cyber-physical systems. This workflow adapts the incremental life-cycle assurance approach to security and supports it through a workbench framework that enables virtual system integration and automated verification. By using an architecture model that is annotated with both security policy information and specification of the mechanisms that enforce those policies, we are able to assure security in multiple steps. We assure that the specified security enforcement mechanisms are consistently applied to cover all aspects of the security policy. For example, the model allows an analysis tool to verify that a secure virtual channel is correctly used throughout the control loop of a control system. In a second step, we verify that the mechanisms are correctly used. For example, the secure channel may be realized through encryption, which requires appropriate key management and application of encryption and decryption in the correct places. Such security specification are applied by auto generated code and configuration files which are not the scope of this paper.

2   Related Work

Since the 1990s, the aerospace industry has experienced exponentially increasing development costs in safety-critical systems [1] due to their increased dependence on software systems. Rapidly growing interaction complexity and mismatched assumptions as they migrated to the new Integrated Modular Avionics architecture have created a context in which 70 % of defects are introduced during the requirements and architecture design phases and 80 % are discovered post-unit test [2]. To address these problems, the industry has embraced virtual system integration, a model-based engineering approach based on SAE AADL [3] that addresses integration issues early in the life cycle through analysis of semantically rich architecture models [4]. Such models reduce ambiguity and allow tools to utilize static analysis techniques ranging from scheduling and latency analysis to behavior verification through model checking, resulting in cost savings from early discovery of defects and reduction of rework. In addition, a contract-based compositional verification approach, which uses AADL models to incrementally verify one architecture layer at a time as the architectural design evolves, has been applied to realistic flight control systems [5].

Assurance case technology has its roots in safety cases [6] as a structured argument supported by evidence to assess residual risks in safety-critical systems of the space, transportation, and medical device industries [7]. Recent research has focused on applying assurance cases to security [8], extending virtual system integration to support automated verification and assurance case generation [9], and integrating systems with an architecture-led requirement specification [10] to achieve incremental assurance of critical systems throughout the development life cycle [11].

In [12], the authors used an extension to the SAE AADL standard to support verification of information flow policies and their realization through security protocols. In [13], the authors investigated an approach to modeling and verification of network and system security configurations.

Information security is well established to address confidentiality and integrity through the Bell-LaPadula [14] and Biba [15] approaches and is reflected in the Orange Book [16]. More recently, the Multiple Independent Levels of Security (MILS) approach [17] has allowed designers of software-intensive systems to specify security levels and requirements for access to protected data.

The cyber-security community has maintained a repository of Common Weakness Enumerations (CWE), or weaknesses found in software CWE. The purpose of CWE is to facilitate the effective use of tools that can identify, find, and resolve bugs, vulnerabilities, and exposures in computer software. The IEEE Center for Secure Design shifts some of the focus in security from finding bugs to identifying common design flaws [18] in the hope that software architects can use this information to design more secure systems.

3   Integrated Modeling Environment

Our framework relies on several domain-specific languages (DSLs) to specify the requirements, design the architecture, and define the verification activities that produce the assurance cases. The following paragraphs introduce these different notations.

3.1   Requirement Specification: ReqSpec

ReqSpec (for requirement specification) is a language to define stakeholder and system requirements. Stakeholder requirements are the goals (i.e., *what* the system should do) while the system requirements define their technical realization (i.e., *how* the system implements the goals). In ReqSpec, requirement specifications contain attributes (such as description, category, and rationale) and define values that can be reused by other requirements (e.g., a system requirement can reuse values defined by stakeholder requirements). The language also connects requirements: a requirement is related to a goal (stakeholder requirements) but can have subrequirements that refine the actual requirement.

3.2   System Architecture: AADL with Security Extensions

The Architecture Analysis & Design Language (AADL) is an architecture description language standardized by SAE International [3]. It defines a notation for describing embedded software and system concerns with implementation details (e.g., task scheduling, communication protocols) and their interactions with their environment (e.g., use of devices, sensors, or actuators). The language has been used to design and analyze embedded systems in several domains, including the avionics [4], aerospace [19], medical device [20], and automotive [21] industries.

The AADL core language specifies several categories of components—hardware, software, and hybrid—with well-defined semantics that are stated in the standard for the users to agree upon. For example, it states that every **process** has its own virtual address space and **threads** contained in a process execute within the virtual address space of the process. Hardware components include **device**, **processor**, **memory**, and **bus**. Software components include **thread**, **process**, **data**, **subprogram**, **virtual processor**, and **virtual bus**. Hybrid components include **system** and **abstract**. For each component, the modeler defines a component type to represent its external interface, and one or more component implementations to represent a blueprint of subcomponents.

We extended AADL with the following additional AADL property definitions:

- **security_levels** of a component or a communication port (e.g., top secret, secret).
- **security_domains** of a component. These distinguish the domains of each component, which helps the modeler analyze how information is shared across domains. For example, in a car, some components are related to the cruise control system while others are related to the entertainment functions.
- **trust** specifies how confident the component has been validated or verified against security vulnerability.
- **exposure** specifies the degree of physical exposure of a component to the environment. The value is an integer between 0 (no exposure, the component is physically isolated) and 100 (high exposure). This property characterizes the likelihood of a physical attack on a component.

- **authentication_method** specifies the authentication mechanism on a connection between two components. The annex includes a list of predefined mechanisms (e.g., shared password, IP address of incoming network traffic), but it can be extended or replaced by the user.
- **encryption** specifies the encryption mechanism used to protect a shared data or a memory (either physical, such as a USB key, or logical, such as a memory segment).

These additional properties, used in conjunction with the AADL model and its execution semantics, provide the basis for doing security analysis on a system. An AADL model extended with this security notation can be analyzed to check that the software architecture correctly reflects the security mechanisms.

3.3   Requirements Verification: Verify

The system architecture (specified using AADL) should be compliant with the requirements (specified using ReqSpec) defined previously. To do so, a specific DSL (called verify) defines verification methods (what to analyze and how to analyze) and verification plans (what verification methods should be used to check the architecture). This language is based on concepts from SVM [22], JUnit [23], and Resolute [9].

A `verification method` defines how to process the system architecture to check a particular characteristic (i.e., does the system contain a component of type X?) or retrieve a specific value from the model (i.e., how many speed sensors are in the car?). It can be written using executable code (e.g., Java) or a constraint language such as OCL [24] and Resolute [9]. The modeling environment includes a verification methods registry (or library) that can be reused among different models.

A `verification plan` is composed of several `claims` that define how requirements are correctly implemented in the architecture. A claim is associated with a system requirement and defines the methods for verifying it. The claim also defines the **execution logic**: all activities must be completed, or just some of them are sufficient. For example, to check that a connection is secure (a system requirement), the associated claim can be specified to require validation through one of these verification activities: check whether the connection is physically isolated, OR check that it is using a strong enough encryption mechanism. This signifies that the system was designed to handle such requirements in these manners.

3.4   Assurance Case: Alisa and Assure

The last part of our integrated modeling tool set is the assurance case, defined with two DSLs: Alisa and Assure. The Alisa language specifies the list of all verification plans used to analyze the system and check the correctness of the architecture with regard to its associated system requirements. The Assure language is the result of executing all the assurance plans. It is automatically generated when executing the assurance plans specified by the related Alisa file.

In this framework, the assurance case is executable and repeatable: because its associated verification plan uses executable code to check the model, it can be executed to automatically verify the model. The results of this execution provide metrics for the architecture about how many requirements are verified and the requirements coverage of the system. The results also provide information about requirements that are not validated, why a requirement is not verified, and how to fix it.

In addition to these metrics, the execution generates a graphical version of the assurance case (using D-CASE [25]). The graphical version shows relationships among the requirements, the verification plan, and the system architecture. This user-friendly notation can help system designers analyze a system and find the cause of unverified requirements.

3.5   Traceability Among Models

This environment interconnects all modeling elements, from requirements to assurance cases:

1. The stakeholder requirements are referenced by the system requirements.
2. System requirements are associated with components of the system architecture.
3. A verification plan contains claims that are associated with system requirements (and their associated architectural elements) and defines how to verify them.
4. The assurance case lists all verification plans necessary to validate a system.

These links among the modeling elements have several benefits. First, they provide a convenient way to trace elements of the development process from both top to bottom (i.e., how a stakeholder goal is finally verified) or bottom to top (i.e., what requirements are related to an architecture element). In addition, they also provide a way to get requirements metrics (i.e., how many architecture elements are missing requirements) and detect requirements inconsistencies (i.e., the same requirement is defined twice with different objectives).

4   Workflow and Tool Support

4.1   Rationale

It can be very difficult for system architects and model developers to complete all the modeling elements (requirements, architectural model, verification) when the models are tightly integrated. It becomes even more challenging to maintain models because one change can have multiple side effects. But if the models are not kept up to date, a development effort forfeits the benefits of verification. The inconsistencies of out-of-date models can quickly accumulate in a development process of continuously reiterating integration, thinking each next one will be the last. Even if the next integration is successful, it is unlikely to represent the best choices that the architects and developers could have made if they had used all the available analysis tools. Postponing the recording or modeling until later in the development effort can also cause new requirements to be forgotten or neglected.

In the following section, we will formalize a set of workflows to build each modeling element and help users acquire the skill of understanding the different modeling stages as one. It is then easier to maintain each model and fix discrepancies as they are discovered. This method will also save time later during assurance, verification, and integration because, just as for physical systems, it is less costly to fix models as early as possible.

4.2 Workflow Descriptions

Figure 1 shows the workflow for adding a new requirement, and Table 1 shows the list of abbreviations that are used in the workflows. One may add a new requirement whether or not the modeling elements, including the AADL model and verification methods, are available. The workflow should be executed once for each requirement added. After some elements, such as stakeholders or goals, are defined, they will be reused and the whole process will become shorter. Time-consuming activities such as implementing the verifica-

Table 1. Abbreviations

Abbreviation	Term
req	Requirement
s-req	System requirement
g-req	Global requirement
ver	Verification
ver-m	Verification method
ver-p	Verification plan
assu	Assurance
assu-p	Assurance plan
ext	Extension

tion method or updating the AADL model can be done in parallel for concurrent engineering as long as they follow the steps in the workflow. It is common to work on adding the next requirement while waiting for the AADL model to be updated for the previous requirement.

The process defines the following steps:

- **D.3** The requirement set is represented by a ReqSpec file. The user decides how to organize all the requirements that a system will support.
- **D.4** Global requirements can be imported into system requirements for reuse.
- **D.6** There can be only one system requirement linked to any AADL type.
- **D.7** Initial thoughts of how to assure the requirement using verification methods should be recorded at this stage for a successful integration. Implementation of the verification method can be done in parallel while requirement specification continues.
- **D.8** This step could require the workflow to continue in the workflow of Fig. 2 and return. The AADL model should be updated to support the verification methods required for assurance.

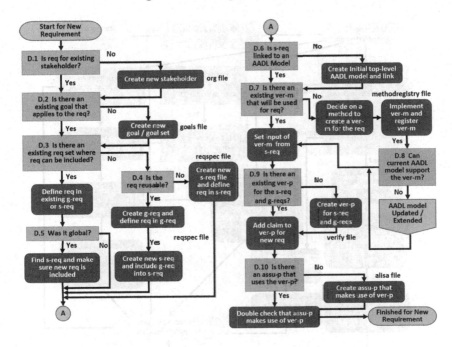

Fig. 1. New requirement workflow

- **D.9** Separate verification plans should exist for each reqspec file.
- **D.10** The assurance plan can implicitly include verification plans by default, depending on the AADL model it targets.

Another workflow is specific to refining or extending an AADL model. AADL models will be updated frequently during their life cycles due to changes in requirement specifications, in verification methods, or in the actual system. Users can take the necessary steps to make sure everything else is valid, especially when the AADL model is already linked to requirements and has accompanying verification methods by following the AADL update/extension workflow (Fig. 2). Users need to follow each path (D.11, D.12, D.13, and D.14) to handle the AADL changes.

- **D.11** In an updated model, new requirements can appear with the inclusion of new elements, such as detailed implementation properties or added components.
- **D.12** With more detail in the AADL model, verification methods can also be improved. A verification method may no longer function correctly due to unexpected inputs that now exist in the extended AADL model.
- **D.14** While any existing verification method can be revised in accordance with small changes in AADL, in the case of AADL model extensions, it would be best to replace the old verification method with a new method.

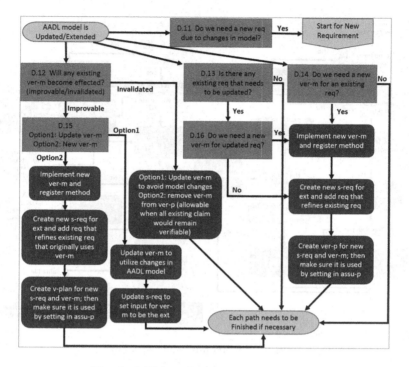

Fig. 2. AADL update/extension workflow

Finally, the last workflow is for updating an existing requirement for a reason other than changes in the AADL model (Fig. 3). This workflow is partially similar to the AADL update/extension workflow from Step D.16 onward. But since this workflow does not start due to a change in the AADL model, it requires a check in the middle to see whether the AADL model should be updated, extended, or both as a result of the requirement change.

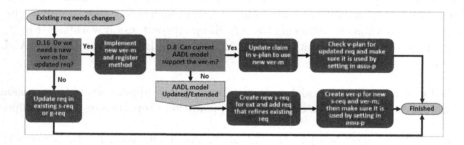

Fig. 3. Requirement update workflow

We did not define a workflow for other cases where we believe the procedure is trivial or the workflow would quickly begin to follow one of the three workflows that we defined. For example, to correct a verification method, one would first update the AADL model to support the verification method, which would require using the AADL update/extension workflow. If a verification method is newly added, the architect should wonder why the system needs the new verification method and start with adding a new requirement (New Requirement Workflow). It is also worth noting that the workflows do not cover some aspects, design directions, and steps to prevent them from becoming too complex to follow.

4.3   Tool Support

As explained in Sect. 3, the workflow for incremental security assurance involves multiple DSLs. The support for DSLs is newly integrated into OSATE, which is an open-source tool platform to support AADL that is built on top of Eclipse. Since the languages are implemented in the same environment, it is possible to make sure that elements in the languages are linked and referenced correctly. Scope providers and validators take the roles of checking numerous rules to make sure that the modeling elements are semantically correct. If not, an error or warning message appears with the content-assist features of Eclipse. Workflows are interconnected so that one can jump from one workflow to another and return but it is still a process that needs to be followed manually.

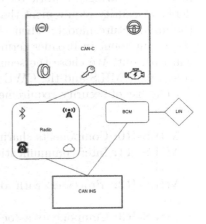

Fig. 4. 2014 Jeep Cherokee Network Architecture (Extracted with Permission [26])

Additionally, OSATE now has special views for running assurance tests. Requirement coverage and progress views show how many requirements are verified correctly and how longer types of verification activities are proceeding. When not successful, verification activities can result in failure, errors, or time-out. After verification, our code generation tool creates configuration files related to security settings.

5   Case Study

We will use a case study to demonstrate how the workflow that we introduced in Sect. 4 can be used. For the architectural model, we created an initial AADL model of a Jeep Cherokee based on the networking architecture from [26] (Fig. 4). Such an architecture is fairly simple to specify during the early stages of development. For deeper understanding of all the subsystems in the Cherokee, the reader should refer to [26].

We first define and add a set of initial security requirements to the integrated modeling environment. We then show how security requirements that are linked to models and verification methods can require updates due to policy changes or expansion in the coverage of AADL models. These are only two of many reasons why changes to modeling elements can occur and why every possible side effect must be dealt correctly to maintain a consistent integrated model of requirements, architecture, and verification methods.

5.1   Requirement Modeling

For requirements specification, one would initially start modeling each require-ment by following the workflow depicted in Fig. 1. At this step, it is difficult to define a security requirement that will be compatible with all future updates to the architecture model. When we first add a security requirement, we specify the requirement in broader terms by speculating about how the AADL model will turn out. We chose the security requirements that we model from general rules of the MILS and the CWE repository, which is available online.

The list of security requirements that we want to assure in the model is as follows:

- **MILS-R0:** Components sharing a bus should have the same security level.
- **MILS-R1:** Inter-communicating components should have the same security level.
- **MILS-R2:** Processes with different security levels use isolated memory regions.
- **MILS-R3:** Components associated with identical processing resources share the same security level.
- **MILS-R4:** Threads inside the same process share the same security level.
- **CWE-131:** Incorrect calculation of buffer size (should not happen).
- **CWE-311:** Missing encryption of sensitive data (should not happen).
- **CWE-805:** Buffer access with incorrect length value (should not happen).

Using the new requirement workflow from Fig. 1, we add each requirement while the AADL is updated in support of the verification method that assures the requirement. In our example, all the verification methods are implemented using a constraint language (Resolute [9]), which allows us to specify what must be calculated for the assurance analysis. In the following subsections, we will continue to work on the overall model to demonstrate using the workflows that we defined in Sect. 4.

5.2   Adding a New Requirement

We will add the following new requirement, "**MILS-R5:** All non-verified com-ponents should have a security level assigned for in/out ports," to the model that we previously made. Such a requirement could be additionally needed for upgrading the code generation tool to consider the assignment of security levels to all ports for the purpose of configuring security features. This demonstrates a good reason to add a new security requirement later in the modeling process due to necessary requirements from different domains (code generation) of system development.

Listing 1. Verification Method for MILS-R5

```
check_mls_components_definition () <=
**"MILS-R5: Check that all non-verified components should have a security
        level assigned for in/out ports" **
forall (comp : component) .
   (length (property (comp, security_properties::security_levels)) > 1) and
   (is_verified (comp) = false)
   => check_mls_components_definition_comp (comp)

check_mls_components_definition_comp (comp : component) <=
** "R6: Check component:" comp **
forall (f : features (comp)) . is_port (f)
   => check_security_level (f, comp)
```

```
requirement MILS_R3 : "R3: Components associated with identical
    processing resources share the same security level"
    for processor virtual processor[
        see goal Security_goals.MILS_goal
]

requirement MILS_R4 : "R4: Threads inside the same process
        share the same security levels"
    for process [
    see goal Security_goals.MILS_goal
]

//For Adding a New Requirement
requirement MILS_R5 : "MILS_R5: All non-verified components
        should have a security level assigned for in/out ports"[
    see goal Security_goals.Secure_comm
]
```

```
system requirements securityReqISOLA for
    case_study::automotive::jeep::integration [

    include securityForMILS.MILS_R0
    include securityForMILS.MILS_R1
    include securityForMILS.MILS_R2
    include securityForMILS.MILS_R3
    include securityForMILS.MILS_R4

    //Added for new requirement
    include securityForMILS.MILS_R5

    include CWEsecurity.CWE131
    include CWEsecurity.CWE311
    include CWEsecurity.CWE805
]
```

Fig. 5. Adding Req to Global Req

Fig. 6. Including Global Req in Sys Req

While following the workflow depicted in Fig. 1, we assume that the requirement MILS-R5 is for an existing stakeholder (D.1). We have a goal that describes secure communication, and we decide that this requirement serves the same goal of secure communication (D.2). When determining whether the requirement relates to an existing requirement set (D.3), we note that the purpose of this new requirement is to address a new feature in the code generation process. We expect that we will reuse this requirement in the future for other secure systems that would use the same feature during code generation. Thus, we include this requirement in the global requirement set named securityForMILS (Fig. 5), which already exists (D.5). So we update the system requirement to include the new requirement, as shown in Fig. 6. The system requirement should already be linked to an AADL model that is the AADL top-level system type `case_study::automotive::jeep::integration`. Next, we define and register a new verification method (Listing 1) to be used (D.7). The AADL model is updated to include the property values that the new verification method checks. If the verification method is executed, it would point out what property values are missing, which is of course the purpose of the requirement.

We then update the existing verification plan to include a claim for MILS-R5, as in Listing 2. In the verification plan, we specify how requirements will be assured using the registered verification methods. The claim for MILS-R3 shows that it relies on two verification methods which are related to analyzing the processors and the virtual processors in the AADL model (`assert all`).

Listing 2. Adding Claim in Verification Plan for MILS-R5

```
verification plan securityForMILSvplan for securityForMILS
[ ...
claim securityForMILS.MILS_R3 [
  activities
  //for processor
    va3_1 : Resolute.check_processor_separation_same_security_level()

  //for virtual processor
    va3_2 : Resolute.check_virtual_processor_separation_same_security_level()
assert all [va3_1, va3_2]
]
...
//Added for new requirement
claim securityForMILS.MILS_R5 [
  activities
    va5 : Resolute.check_mls_components_definition()
  assert va5
]
]
```

Listing 3. Updating Claim in Verification Plan for MILS-R1

```
verification plan securityForMILSvplan for securityForMILS
[ ...
claim securityForMILS.MILS_R1 [
  activities
    //Old verification method
    //va1 : Resolute.check_ports_connections_same_security_level()

    //New verification method
    va1 : Resolute.check_bouncer()
  assert va1
]
...
]
```

5.3 Updating Existing Requirements

In this example, we will follow the steps to update an existing requirement (MILS-R1). For the purpose of secure communication, we learn that it is not enough to check only that inter-communication occurs between components at the same security level. It is actually too restrictive to say that only components with the same security level can communicate. Thus, we update the requirement to specify that "**MILS-R1:** Components with different security levels should not be able to communicate through non-verified components." To follow the requirement update workflow (Fig. 3), we need to implement a new verification method that checks any middle components in connections (D.16). The only update we need to make in the model is to ensure that verified and non-verified components are identifiable by the security properties. Such changes are small enough that they do not extend the AADL model (D.8). We then update the verification plan to use the new verification method, as shown in Listing 3. The call to Resolute.check_ports_connections_same_security_level() is changed to Resolute.check_bouncer().

5.4 Handling an AADL Update/Extension

In this example, we extend the AADL model to include cellular access to the vehicle. One of the security vulnerabilities that Valasek and Miller [26] discovered was that attackers could gain access to a vehicle through the cellular network. If this problem had been known during system development, a software architect would have modeled the cellular network to record the kinds of security issues

that the system must handle. After extending the AADL model, we use the
AADL update/extension workflow (Fig. 2).

To verify the model for the vulnerability of the cellular network, we add another
requirement (D.11), "**MILS-R6:** All communication that is bound to an exposed bus must
have encryption." We define a new verification method that would identify the cellular
network as an exposed bus and check that
all communication that goes over the bus is
encrypted. One interesting issue is that unless
a logical connection from a possible attacker
exists in the model, it is not possible to show
that the logical connection can be a security
risk. In fact, once a modeler considers security
problems in modeling, he or she should consider modeling not only the existing system
but also the possible malicious attacks that
are expected and how the system will defend
against them.

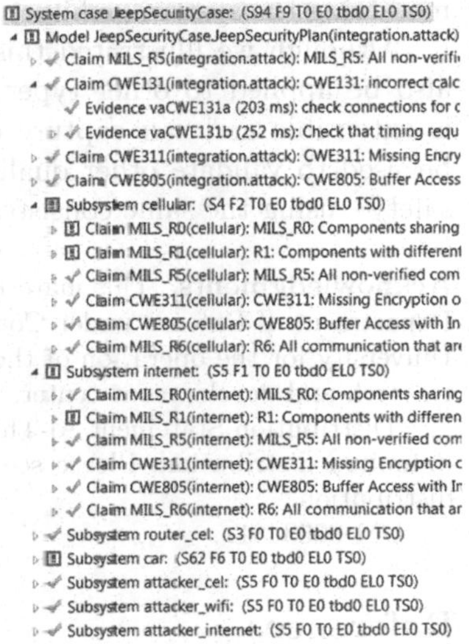

Figure 7 shows a result of verifying the
security requirements with the final model.

Fig. 7. Verification result

The execution environment decides which verification method to execute for
each AADL component, based on the input required by the verification method
linked to each requirement. Claims that have failed are marked with red excla-
mation icons and should be investigated by the user.

6   Conclusion

Cyber-physical systems are becoming extremely software-reliant and exhibit a
complex structure that hardens the validation of a security policy. Security objectives can be implemented using many different mechanisms, but the complex
structure of these systems can bypass some mechanisms, introduce covert channels, and ultimately expose the system to a vulnerability. Requirements design
is typically done manually using ambiguous and informal notation (natural languages). Requirements verification usually relies on manual efforts, which are
expensive, error-prone, and time-consuming and ultimately do not guarantee
system correctness.

In this report, we introduced a modeling framework with workflows to specify
and verify requirements from a security perspective. It relies on new languages
(Reqspec, verify) to specify the requirements and on AADL to design the system architecture with its quality attributes (e.g., security). Stakeholder goals
are refined into system requirements, associated with verification methods, and
verified against an architecture. Requirements verification is automated so that
designers can have a measure of requirements enforcement: as the requirements

or system design evolves, requirements are being validated or invalidated. We show how this approach can highlight problems when refining requirements or modifying the system architecture.

Although we illustrated this framework from a security perspective, it can also be applied to other types of requirements. Because the AADL language is extensible and can capture different system attributes, the framework can be used to validate other quality attributes—such as scheduling, latency, and safety—using the same consistent model.

Acknowledgments. This material is based upon work funded and supported by the Department of Defense under Contract No. FA8721-05-C-0003 with Carnegie Mellon University for the operation of the Software Engineering Institute, a federally funded research and development center.

[Distribution Statement A] This material has been approved for public release and unlimited distribution. Please see Copyright notice for non-US Government use and distribution.

DM-0003481.

References

1. Dvorak, D.L.: NASA Study on Flight Software Complexity (2009)
2. National Institute of Standards and Technology: The Economic Impacts of Inadequate Infrastructure for Software Testing. Technical report, NIST (2002)
3. SAE International: AS5506 - Architecture Analysis and Design Language (AADL) (2012)
4. Redman, D., Ward, D., Chilenski, J., Pollari, G.: Virtual Integration for Improved System Design: The AVSI System Architecture Virtual Integration (SAVI) Program. Analytic Virtual Integration of Cyber-Physical Systems Workshopp, 31st IEEE Real-Time Systems Symposium (RTSS 2010) (2010)
5. Backes, J., Cofer, D., Miller, S., Whalen, M.W.: Requirements analysis of a quad-redundant flight control system. In: Havelund, K., Holzmann, G., Joshi, R. (eds.) NFM 2015. LNCS, vol. 9058, pp. 82–96. Springer, Heidelberg (2015)
6. Kelly, T.: A systematic approach to safety case management. In: Proceedings of SAE 2004 World Congress, Detroit, MI (2004)
7. Kobayashi, N., Yamamoto, S.: The effectiveness of D-case application knowledge on a safety process. Procedia Comput. Sci. **60**, 908–917 (2015). 19th Annual Conference on Knowledge-Based and Intelligent Information and Engineering Systems, KES-2015, Singapore, Proceedings, September 2015
8. Hawkins, R., Kelly, T., Habli, I.: Developing assurance cases for D-MILS systems. In: International Workshop on MILS: Architecture and Assurance for Secure Systems, Amsterdam, The Netherlands, January 2015
9. Gacek, A., Backes, J., Cofer, D., Slind, K., Whalen, M.: Resolute: an assurance case language for architecture models. In: Proceedings of the 2014 ACM SIGAda Annual Conference on High Integrity Language Technology. HILT 2014. ACM, New York (2014)
10. Blouin, D., Senn, E., Turki, S.: Defining an annex language to the architecture analysis and design language for requirements engineering activities support. In: Model-Driven Requirements Engineering Workshop (MoDRE), 2011, pp. 11–20, August 2011

11. Delange, J., Feiler, P., Ernst, N.: Incremental life cycle assurance of safety-critical systems. In: 8th European Congress ERTS, Toulouse (2016)

12. Van der Pol, K., Noll, T.: Security type checking for MILS-AADL specifications. In: International Workshop on MILS: Architecture and Assurance for Secure Systems, Amsterdam, The Netherlands, January 2015

13. Alsaleh, M.N., Al-Shaer, E., El-Atawy, A.: Towards a unified modeling and verification of network and system security configurations. In: Al-Shaer, E., Ou, X., Xie, G. (eds.) Automated Security Management, pp. 3–19. Springer, Cham (2013)

14. Bell, D.E., LaPadula, L.J.: Secure computer system: unified exposition and MULTICS interpretation. Technical report, The MITRE Corporation, Bedford, MA (1976)

15. Biba, K.J.: Integrity considerations for secure computer systems. Technical report, The MITRE Corporation, Bedford, MA (1977)

16. Lipner, S.B.: The birth and death of the orange book. IEEE Ann. Hist. Comput. **37**(2), 19–31 (2015)

17. Alves-Foss, J., Harrison, W.S., Oman, P., Taylor, C.: The MILS architecture for high-assurance embedded systems. Intl. J. Embed. Syst. **2**(3/4), 239–247 (2005)

18. IEEE Center of Secure Design: Avoiding the TOP 10 Software Security Design Flaws. Technical report, IEEE (2014)

19. Zalila, B., Hamid, I., Hugues, J., Pautet, L.: Generating distributed high integrity applications from their architectural description. In: Abdennadher, N., Kordon, F. (eds.) Ada-Europe 2007. LNCS, vol. 4498, pp. 155–167. Springer, Heidelberg (2007)

20. Larson, B., Hatcliff, J., Fowler, K., Delange, J.: Illustrating the AADL error modeling annex (V.2) using a simple safety-critical medical device. In: Proceedings of the 2013 ACM SIGAda Annual Conference on High Integrity Language Technology, HILT 2013, pp. 65–84. ACM, New York (2013)

21. Shiraishi, S.: An AADL-based approach to variability modeling of automotive control systems. In: Petriu, D.C., Rouquette, N., Haugen, Ø. (eds.) MODELS 2010, Part I. LNCS, vol. 6394, pp. 346–360. Springer, Heidelberg (2010)

22. Aldrich, B., Fehnker, A., Feiler, P.H., Han, Z., Krogh, B.H., Lim, E., Sivashankar, S.: Managing verification activities using SVM. In: Davies, J., Schulte, W., Barnett, M. (eds.) ICFEM 2004. LNCS, vol. 3308, pp. 61–75. Springer, Heidelberg (2004)

23. Massol, V., Husted, T.: JUnit in Action. Manning, Stamford (2003)

24. Warmer, J.B., Kleppe, A.G.: The Object Constraint Language: Getting Your Models Ready for MDA. Addison-Wesley Professional, Boston (2003)

25. Matsuno, Y., Takamura, H., Ishikawa, Y.: A dependability case editor with pattern library. In: 2010 IEEE 12th International Symposium on High-Assurance Systems Engineering (HASE), pp. 170–171, November 2010

26. Miller, C., Valasek, C.: Remote Exploitation of an Unaltered Passenger Vehicle. Black Hat USA (2015)

A Privacy-Aware Conceptual Model
for Handling Personal Data

Thibaud Antignac[✉], Riccardo Scandariato, and Gerardo Schneider

Department of Computer Science and Engineering,
Chalmers | University of Gothenburg, Gothenburg, Sweden
thibaud.antignac@chalmers.se, {riccardo.scandariato,gerardo}@cse.gu.se

Abstract. Handling personal data adequately is one of the biggest challenges of our era. Consequently, law and regulations are in the process of being released, like the European General Data Protection Regulation (GDPR), which attempt to deal with these challenging issue early on. The core question motivating this work is how software developers can validate their technical design vis-a-vis the prescriptions of the privacy legislation. In this paper, we outline the technical concepts related to privacy that need to be taken into consideration in a software design. Second, we extend a popular design notation in order to support the privacy concepts illustrated in the previous point. Third, we show how some of the prescriptions of the privacy legislation and standards may be related to a technical design that employs our enriched notation, which would facilitate reasoning about compliance.

Keywords: Privacy · Conceptual model · Data flow diagrams

1 Introduction

Handling personal data adequately is one of the biggest challenges of our era. As smart objects equipped with sensors and network connectivity begin to populate our daily life and collect more and more data about our life style, opinions and preferences, we perceive an increased discomfort for the potential of privacy violations that are hanging over us. Therefore, law and regulations are in the process of being released, like the European General Data Protection Regulation (GDPR) [10], which attempt to deal with these shifting circumstances early on. At the same time, one of the commendable concepts that have emerged from the privacy research community is known as the *Privacy by Design* (PbD) principle [3], which is based on the idea that any personal data processing environment should be designed so that privacy is taken into account since the very beginning of the development process. In particular, PbD implies that privacy concerns should be addressed as early as the requirement elicitation phase as well as when designing the software architecture.

However, there is a big disconnect between the technical concepts handled by software architects and the prescriptions stated by laws and regulations, including the upcoming ones. For instance, architects use boxes-and-arrows diagrams

T. Margaria and B. Steffen (Eds.): ISoLA 2016, Part I, LNCS 9952, pp. 942–957, 2016.
DOI: 10.1007/978-3-319-47166-2_65

to conceptualise and describe how a software system is structured. Boxes represent high-level computational entities (like software component or sub-systems) while arrows symbolise the exchange of information between them. From a notation perspective, *Data Flow Diagrams* (or DFDs) represent a very popular option used to draw such architectural diagrams. DFDs are also a convenient representation should an architect choose to validate their software design, as popular threat analysis techniques (e.g., STRIDE [15]) make use of such diagrams as their starting point.

The law is generally written as normative texts stating citizens rights and obligations for legal entities with respect to information processing. Granted that the PbD principle is applied, the core question motivating this work is how an architect can validate their technical design vis-a-vis the prescriptions of the privacy legislation.

In this context, the present paper provides the following *contributions*. First, we outline the technical concepts related to privacy that need to be taken into consideration in a software design. In particular, we show that three complementary angles need to be addressed: data processing, data management and data accounting. Second, we extend the DFD notation in order to support the privacy concepts illustrated in the previous point. Such enriched models directly reduce the semantic gap between the design world and the privacy law. Third, and related to the previous statement, we show how many of the prescriptions of the legislation (like the GDPR) and standards (like ISO 29100) can be related to a technical design that employs our enriched notation. Therefore, we argue that the augmented models we propose in this paper serve as a stepping stone to (formally) reason about the compliance of a technical design with respect to the privacy legislation and standards. Clearly, the PbD approach requires a holistic re-thinking of the software development lifecycle. This has happened for software security to a large extent, which is a comparably more mature discipline than privacy[1]. Therefore, this paper has also the ambition to outline a roadmap for future research in order to actualise the tenets of the PbD principle.

The rest of this paper is organised as follows. Section 2 discusses how taking into account privacy impacts the software design. Section 3 proposes an extension to classical DFD making it possible to deal with the notions derives previously. Section 4 shows how this extension allows to address most of the commonly acknowledged privacy principles. Finally, Sect. 5 proposes new directions of research to improve further the state of privacy awareness and personal data protection in information systems before concluding by Sect. 6.

2 Privacy in Software Design

Beyond functional requirements, software designers are used to deal with non-functional ones for a long time, be them security, performance, or maintainability just to name a few. Compliance with personal data regulations and standards is another kind of non-functional requirement which strongly emerged in the recent

---

[1] See the "Building Security in Maturity Model" (https://www.bsimm.com/).

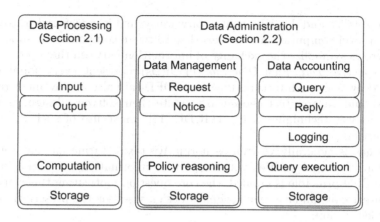

Fig. 1. Architectural view of an information system

past few years. As a result, designers have to take privacy into account from the beginning when they build information systems; a practice known as PbD. This calls for modelling techniques and tools equipped with privacy-related concepts in order to support these practitioners.

As shown in Fig. 1, we propose to distinguish three different high-level facets of personal data processing, which are data processing (concerned with the actual data being manipulated), data management (concerned with the policy management of the system), and data accounting (aiming at logging and treating events occurring in the system). In what follows we describe how the handling of personal data can be viewed as lying on these three pillars.

2.1 Data Processing

Standards and regulations in general, and thus the personal data protection legislation in particular, do not rely on rigorous models. However, formally modelling the concepts at hand along with their properties is a necessary step to define what it means to *computationally* conform to a standard or to a regulation. This also helps to detect ambiguities that may come from informal reasoning[2]. We choose a model for such computations and show how it can be used in the context of personal data handling in the following paragraphs.

Generic Data. Many levels could be chosen to represent computation, ranging from very low-level (such as transistors in the processor) to very high-level (such as application level abstract state machines). There is no such a thing as a one-level-fits-all model and we have to choose our level of abstraction as the simplest one allowing to represent the properties we are interested in.

---

[2] Law makers use techniques such as *legal drafting* which include a set of techniques and patterns to improve law consistency and clarity. However, they should be best regarded as best practices than as full-fledged analysis tools.

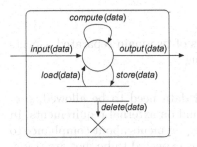

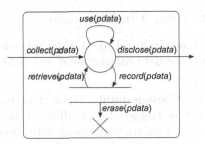

Fig. 2. Generic data processing.　　　**Fig. 3.** Personal data processing.

Figure 2 shows a high-level conceptual model for generic data processing. It models generic computations and is independent of personal data. In the figure, the circle represents a computational component while the element with two parallel lines represents a storage component. There are three kinds of activities a data processing system may perform on some *data*: communication, computation, and storage. The performance of these activities is modelled as the occurrence of events. Communications are modelled as *input* and *output* events. Computations are represented by *compute* events, and storage by *store* and *load* events. The *delete* event models data disposal.

We observe that computation cannot happen on stored data without it being loaded. Similarly, only stored data may be erased. This choice gives some freedom for the operation modes that can be modelled. For instance, it is possible to model on-the-fly data stream processing by not involving any *store* event.

Personal Data. As outlined in the GDPR, personal data processing generally implies the following kinds of computations: collection, disclosure, usage, record, retrieval, and erasure. As shown in Fig. 3, these privacy-sensitive events mirror the events in Fig. 2, although they deal with personal data instead (*pdata*).

The definition of these notions with respect to a processing model allows us to make the link with normative prescriptions as they are stated in standards and regulatory texts. Indeed, personal data is subject to more obligations and duties for data controllers and data processors than generic data is (although what we consider as generic data here may actually be classified information, which may be subject to other kinds of sensitive data protection frameworks).

There is one more event related to personal data, not shown in the figure, which denotes (irreversible) anonymisation of personal data: *anonymise*. This event transforms some personal data *pdata* into generic (non-personal) *data*. When used, the data can be considered as free from any constraint deriving from personal data regulation.

The abstractions in Figs. 2 and 3 enable us to specifically target personal data events in a model to check their conformance to specific provisions. For instance, it is generally considered, as a basic requirement, that personal data should be processed for a specific *purpose* to which the data subject has given his or her *consent*. Taking into account such constraints is the topic of the next section about data administration.

2.2   Data Administration

As shown in Fig. 1, data administration consists of two main separated aspects which are data management and data accounting.

Data Management. Operations on personal data need to be allowed, prevented, or triggered depending on their nature and on external requirements. In this paper we are particularly interested in the requirements about compliance to personal data regulations. The privacy provisions expected to be met are translated into *policies* allowing to manage data processing as defined above. These policies themselves are considered as generic or as personal data depending on their generality or whether or not they embed references to individuals. Thus they can also be matched to the data processing as defined in Figs. 2 and 3. The *request* and *notice* components of the architecture in Fig. 1 reflect the communication capabilities at the data management level, the *policy reasoning* component stands for the computation capabilities, and the *storage* component links to the storage capabilities. However, they have an additional power compared to the simple data considered in the previous section: they have effect on simple data with the purpose of enforcing policies. The enforcement of these policies is treated through reference enforcement mechanisms, similar to their security homologues.

Data Accounting. Beyond data processing and data management, which constitutes the core of the activities of a data processing system, accountability is another recommended aspect to be taken into account. Data accounting is decomposed into two main activities consisting in: (i) logging some or all the events occurring during data processing, and (ii) allowing queries on the set logged events and providing replies accordingly. These communication capabilities are reflected by the *logging* and the *query* and *reply* components in Fig. 1. Data accounting is also equipped with computation capabilities (offered by the *query execution* component) and storage capabilities (cf. the *storage* component).

3   Enabling Privacy in Software Design

In the previous section we introduced some of the basic concepts needed to model an information system while having privacy in mind, so that software designers are enabled to put PbD into practice. In this section, we show how to integrate these notions with a specific notation, namely DFDs [16]. We start by giving some preliminaries about DFDs before showing how they can be extended to become privacy-aware.

3.1   Data Flow Diagrams (DFDs)

DFDs are a graphical notation which allows to model data flows in information systems. Their generality and modularity make them suitable for a large span

Fig. 4. Standard DFD notation.

of contexts and this is the main reason why they are widely used by practitioners to represent information systems architectures. As shown in Fig. 4, the basic elements in a DFD are *external entities* (like users or third-party systems), *processes* (representing units of functionality), *data stores* (like data bases) and *data flows*. Complex processes can be refined into sub-processes and, in this case, are marked with a double edged circle. All data flows need to start from or to lead to a process (or to a complex process) for the data flow to be valid. For example, there cannot be a data flow directly from one data store to another.

Why Data Flow Diagrams? DFDs are already widely used in information security techniques. For example, the STRIDE threat modelling method developed at Microsoft [15] relies on a model of the software system expressed as a DFD. STRIDE is a risk-based security methodology aiming at eliciting controls and counter-measures when potential security flaws are discovered in a design. Another method, inspired by STRIDE and called LINDDUN [7], proposes a similar approach targeted at privacy threat modelling. The threats addressed by LINDDUN are linkability, identifiability, non-repudiation, detectability, disclosure of information, unawareness, and non-compliance. In this paper, we focus our attention on this last category of threats (i.e., non-compliance), which is only partially addressed by LINDDUN and largely delegated to the advise of a legal counselor. This work shows how the provisions dictated by standards or regulations can be handled on a technical level.

Example 1. Let us consider a Slippery Road Alert (SRA) system such as the ones proposed by car manufacturers[3]. A very simple DFD illustrating the main function of this system is presented in Fig. 5. A car, modelled as an external entity, sends an SRA which is stored in an SRA database. These alerts are composed of the identifier of the car, a timestamp, a location, and a status. The alerts are then broadcast to all other cars. In practice, this broadcast should be limited to cars potentially impacted by the alert (i.e., in the same geographical area for instance). In this example, we keep it as simple as possible to focus on the privacy aspects as will be detailed later.

3.2 Privacy-Aware Data Flow Diagrams (PA-DFDs)

In order to enable designers to take privacy principles into account we extend standards DFDs with privacy-aware annotations. The new elements of a *Privacy-*

---

[3] https://www.media.volvocars.com/global/en-gb/media/videos/159534/
slippery-road-alert-technology-by-volvo-cars5.

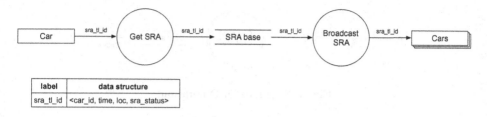

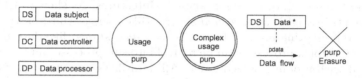

Fig. 5. DFD of a slippery road alert system.

Fig. 6. Privacy-Aware DFD notation.

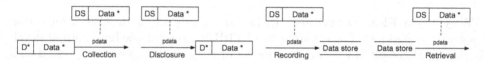

Fig. 7. Element interactions in privacy-aware DFDs.

Aware DFD (PA-DFD) are presented in Fig. 6. We introduce three different kinds of external entities which are *data subjects*, *data controllers*, and *data processors* as these are the three main kinds of natural and legal persons discussed in regulatory texts. We also add the *usage* and *complex usage* process elements, which are annotated with a purpose *purp*. The element modelling a *data flow* of personal data is labeled with *pdata* and linked through a dotted line to the corresponding data subject the personal data refers to. We should note here that *pdata* embeds some useful metadata, as for instance the *purposes* to which the data subject has *consented*. More metadata may be added, such as the allowed *retention time* or the *age* of the data subject (specific provisions happen when the data subject is minor). Finally, we add a process element to model *erasure*. Such an element is also associated with a purpose *purp*. Adding a purpose to limit the erasure of data may seem useless, as deleting data could be considered a general good practice with respect to privacy. However, this may not be the case when data has to be stored without the consent of the data subject (for penal purposes for instance) or when the erasure could lead to a weakening of the rights of the data subject (a service provider could delete a contract to escape his obligations for example). Regulations expect all kinds of personal data processing to be associated with a purpose, which is reflected here in this choice.

The addition of these elements to DFDs allows to represent all the personal data processing events shown previously in Fig. 3. Indeed, usage, storage, and erasure are first-class citizens of PA-DFDs, while the other events (collection,

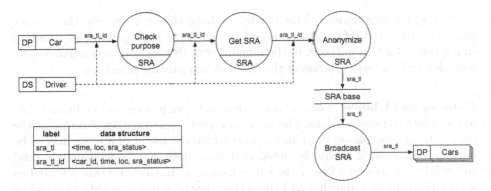

Fig. 8. PA-DFD of the slippery road alert system from Fig. 5.

disclosure, recording and retrieval) can be represented as interactions of atomic events, as shown in Fig. 7. A collection of data happens when some personal data (and its associated metadata) flows from an external entity. This personal data is linked to the corresponding data subject through the dotted line. Rules about valid PA-DFDs require the data flow to lead to a (complex) usage element (not shown here due to space consideration). The same applies for other kinds of personal data processing.

Example 2. We exemplify now how the extensions presented previously prove to be useful in the SRA system introduced in Example 1. Two processes are added as shown in Fig. 8: (i) to check whether the purpose of use satisfies the consent given by the data subject (i.e., the driver), and (ii) to anonymise the data by pruning the car identifier. After anonymisation, the data is no longer considered as personal data, hence not linked to the data subject (and free from personal data regulations). More privacy aspects have to be taken into account for a full-fledged analysis. This example only illustrates how the notation is used.

Thanks to the privacy-aware extension, the designer's choices vis-à-vis privacy can be made explicit in the design model and analysed in a rigorous way. In next section we review several privacy principles and hint to how they fit the PA-DFD model.

4   Privacy Principles and Privacy-Aware DFDs

The definition of privacy is not unique, depends on cultures and contexts, and has varied in time since its first mention by Warren and Brandeis in 1890 [19]. Today, companies follow mainly two regulatory sources: (i) legal frameworks, which are defined by the law maker and thus vary among jurisdictions, and (ii) standards, which are defined by the industry through consensus procedures and thus contain commonly agreed good practices. Though not imperative, standards have the two advantages of being closer to the views of industry and not to vary depending on jurisdictions. This is why we have chosen to review the privacy principles from the ISO 29100 standard, which is the most prominent standard in use today for this purpose. In the remainder of this section, we systematically consider and discuss each one of the ISO's eleven privacy principles.

Consent and Choice. The consent to personal data processing can be attached as metadata to personal data. The metadata should contain a set of purposes the data subject has consented to and against which the intent of a usage has to be checked. However, it should be noted that some data may be legitimately (and so lawfully) processed without the subject consent. In this case this is stated as a specific metadata allowing to bypass the consent/purpose satisfaction. Some aspects may be more challenging to model such as the fact that a consent has been given in a specific way (for it to be considered as freely chosen) for instance. This constraint, and others of the same kind, may be represented as boolean metadata, set to `true` by authorised parties such as a legal counsellor.

Purpose Legitimacy and Specification. Ensuring that the purpose complies with applicable laws or whether a piece of data is particularly sensitive is also out of the scope of the PA-DFD-based modelling. We will then also rely on boolean metadata attached to the personal data. On the other hand, by relying on the PA-DFD notation it is possible to model that the purpose of a processing element has been communicated to the data subject before collection by adding a notice in the data management part of the architecture.

Collection Limitation. The limitation of the collection can be divided into two aspects: one is legal and the other is technical. On the legal side, we model the lawfulness of the collection under relevant regulations as a boolean metadata which then has to be checked. The technical limitation ensures that only the data technically needed to fulfil the purpose is collected. This would require the analysis of the information system to check as follows: for each piece of personal data collected, there should be a usage element (or complex usage) in the PA-DFD diagram that takes it as an input. Note that this can be done syntactically or semantically, depending on the precision desired and the tools available[4].

Data Minimisation. Data minimisation is divided into four different concerns:

- The first is about minimising the quantity of data processed and the number of people having access to it. In the PA-DFD model, disclosures and retrievals are clearly identified and each of them should be questioned about its necessity by an expert. This may be instantiated through a set of questions for which the replies given by the designer (or an expert) are traced.

---

[4] Many dependency analysis rely on syntactic dependence, which is weak from a security standpoint, but reasonable for debugging cases to support the designer when it is assumed there is no voluntary attack.

- The need-to-know principle also has to be checked by an expert. This is because it is linked with the semantics of the data itself, and the PA-DFD model only addresses the information system architecture. Such principles could also be addressed by having a validated semantic ontology linking data to purposes which the analysis could rely on.
- Privacy by default has to be ensured at the application level, and thus it is defined as a boolean metadata attached to the data (also validated by an external expert or by the use of an approved library or collection of patterns).
- Erasure of personal data, as soon as the retention period expires, is a requirement that can be modelled relying on the time dimension of the model.

Use, Retention, and Disclosure Limitation. Limitations are also divided into four different concerns according to the ISO standard:

- Data minimisation applied to the whole data lifecycle is similar to Collection Limitation, as described above. Thus the same way to proceed is chosen.
- Limiting the use of personal data to purposes specified by the controller is done as for the Consent and Choice principle described above.
- Retaining data as long as needed is a global property. We should check whether the data could (legally) be processed in the future. If we model future potential usages it would be possible to determine whether the data should be retained. However, this is difficult to determine. Also, the choice between deleting and anonymising data could be based on whether there is a need to anonymise part of the data. For example, if aggregated statistics are expected then date should be retained and anonymised.
- Legal obligations to archive personal data can be taken into account by preventing an erasure of these data (and so should be globally verified for the modelled system). Moreover, the data accounting part of the architecture may play a role here through the logging of personal data processing.

Accuracy and Quality. Accuracy and quality is mainly treated as a boolean metadata as it calls other subtasks, such as verifying the semantic quality of the data before processing it. However, an implicit implication is the consistency of the data in the model. If some personal data is stored at different locations, the data itself should be consistent. This can be tracked by verifying that modifications on data retrieved from a data store are propagated to other data stores where this data may also reside (as a global property of the information system).

Openness, Transparency, and Notice. These principles are subdivided into four different facets as follows:

- A mechanism to release policies to data subjects is implemented at the data management layer through the request/notice mechanism. This mechanism allows communication about data processing between the data controller and the data subject. We assume all policies are public (maximum transparency)

though it would not be difficult to add some guards to restrict the communication of the policy and thus restrict the transparency in case of a trade's
secret (as it is an allowed exception in some regulations for instance).

- Notifications to the data subject when her data is being processed, detailed
  data such as the purpose, the stakeholders involved, and the identity of the
  controller, are also addressed by the data management part of the architecture
  which should systematically send notifications before data is processed.
- The data controller also has to inform the data subject about the actions she
  may have taken concerning her data, and about the means to actually exercise
  her control. This is somehow similar to an interface notification. We assume
  this is standardised, and addressed by the data management layer.
- Notification of major changes in procedures, however, is hard to model as it
  would imply being able to dynamically detect evolutions in the data processing
  layer of the information system. This is clearly out of reach of the notation we
  are defining. Here, PA-DFDs only model static architectures.

Individual Participation and Access. Four points to be taken into account:

- Access and reviews of personal data by the data subjects are handled by the
  request and notice parts of the data management component. Authentication is assumed to be performed by a suitable additional component, and the
  absence of any prohibition to access such data by the data controller should
  be attested by a boolean metadata.
- The right to modify the data handled by the data controller is also enforced by
  the data manager. Through requests, the data subject may express requirements for changes on her data. These have to be forwarded and enforced
  adequately by triggering the relevant events in the data processing layer.
- The preceding item should also be notified to third-parties through their
  request/notice interface to ensure the required changes are applied.
- Procedures should be created to enable data subjects to exercise their rights
  in an easy way.

Accountability. Modelling the information system with a PA-DFD is a major
advance in term of accountability as it shows demonstrably that many decisions
have been taken along with their motivations (provided it has then been implemented correctly). One important point is the presence of ways to complain for
the data subjects and to redress issues if needed. This can be modelled through
dedicated usage elements in the data management part of the architecture and
triggered through the request/notice interface. Similarly, privacy breaches in the
system should be notified to the data subject by an appropriate mean.

Information Security. Our modelling assumes the events are performed
as they should (meaning securely). Security issues should be part of a security analysis (such as STRIDE) and are not modelled here. However, security
breaches may be notified by the notification mechanism as mentioned earlier.

Moreover, if we want to model security attacks, we could add an event *corrupt* for integrity, and *reveal* for confidentiality attacks, to the data processing in Fig. 3.

Privacy Compliance. Modelling an information system with PA-DFD will help to improve privacy compliance. Note that the ISO standard contains many more aspects also covered by regulations and that are not easy to be directly addressed by technical means. The most conservative approach is to add boolean metadata and associated guards for each event that should be reviewed before being performed. Some of these verifications could be automated and integrated into the model at a later stage. An important part of privacy compliance focuses on *accountability* through the data accounting layer, as described earlier.

Example 3. We now discuss how the privacy-aware entities introduced in Example 2 improve the privacy compliance along the privacy principles just described. The purposes added to the processes consists in the purpose specification of the personal data processing. They are used to guarantee consent respect. Use of anonymisation allows to minimise the amount of personal data stored and processed. Though not complete w.r.t. the ISO standard, these aspects improve privacy compliance and illustrate how PA-DFD help designers to adopt PbD.

5 Roadmap for Research

Modelling a system while relying on the approach presented here calls for research in two orthogonal dimensions: (i) Methodologies to build a PbD architecture; (ii) Tools and techniques used during the data lifecycle, including both foundational as well as practical aspects, in order to mitigate attacks and non-compliance. We describe below a non-exhaustive list of research directions along these two different axes.

Privacy by Design

PbD is still a promise to be fulfilled and challenges abound (see for instance [18] and the recent ENISA[5] reports [5,6]). To address the privacy principles detailed in Sect. 4, we have argued for the need of a more rigorous model allowing to describe the different facets of personal data handling as shown in Fig. 1. The need for formal models for privacy has already been discussed in the literature (e.g., [1,17]). We have here proposed to rely on enriched DFDs (cf. Figs. 6 and 7), due to their acceptance in industry. One clear research direction is to enhance these privacy-aware DFDs with formal semantics. Different approaches may be envisaged for this purpose depending on the kind of analysis one might be interested on. One possibility would be to use *Petri nets* [14], in particular the *Timed-Colored* variant [11]. Indeed, data flowing in the information system can

---

[5] *European Union Agency for Network and Information Security.*

be encoded as (colored) tokens, while conditions (including timing constraints) to be fulfilled may be modelled by guards on transitions. Such tokens can hold any arbitrary data, including time, allowing for extended policy reasoning.

The advantages of giving a formal semantic will not only make more precise to software engineers about the meaning of what they write, but also will give the possibility to reduce the number of design errors taking advantage of formal verification. Some properties might be enforced by construction while editing. For instance, while designing the architecture, the tool could warn the engineer on a missing check for a data containing a retention time constraint, or when deleting data on that these should be done on every component if the data is being forwarded somewhere else. Other properties could be verified *a posteriori*. For instance, the enforcement of data retention policies implies that there should not be any reachable state in which the data is still stored after expiration of the retention time (a *safety* property). A *liveness* property would be checking that a data subject should always be able to access or rectify the data about herself.

The model presented in this paper allows to model personal data processing and how it interacts with privacy principles prescribed by industrial good practices. However, these prescriptions give very few indications to the designer about how to actually build a model such that they are met. So, another research direction concerns the need of a methodology to guide the designer through the multiple steps leading to a satisfactory architecture. The model presented here makes it easier for the designer as each data processing and data management unit is self-sufficient with regard to the satisfaction of some privacy principles. However, some other principles are global and cannot be achieved by a simple composition of conformant sub-components, such as data minimisation for instance. To this aim, a computer-aided design tool should help and guide the software designer not to include specific privacy issues in relevant places of the design. This diagram-based formalism could be enriched with automatic pop-up windows while editing the architecture to remind the designer that the data minimisation should be checked.

Attacks and Non-compliance

We look here at where improper personal data processing may occur during the data life cycle. Before describing some concrete research directions let us clarify why we split the possible issues into two kinds, *attacks* and *non-compliance*. This distinction relies on the activity or passivity of the parties, corresponding to two complementary dimensions: security and privacy, respectively.

Non-compliance captures the cases when a flaw happen without any active behaviour targeting the flaw. On the other hand, *attacks* are intentional actions. With regard to attacker models frequently encountered in the computer security literature, even passive attackers (also called honest-but-curious), are considered to belong to the attacks category because the unexpected computations themselves are positive actions taken by the attacker. Another difference is that in the case of attacks, there is always an attacker (or a group of attackers) while this is not the case for non-compliance. In general, a security attack involving personal data implies some form of personal data non-compliance. Moreover, information security is considered as one of the privacy principles to meet. Some security attacks do not involve personal data and are addressed elsewhere in the literature and will thus not be described here.

Issues from privacy non-compliance come from technical policies and implementation which do not conform to provisions (stated in regulations, laws, terms, contracts or binding corporate rules). Such non-compliances may occur at any step of the lifecycle. They can be defined by any violation of the regulatory prescription. Some of them apply to any computation on personal data (known as processing) while others apply only to some parts of the data life cycle.

When collecting data an important issue is that of *data minimisation*, i.e. that a program does not use more data than needed for the intended purpose. To the best of our knowledge not much research has been done in what concerns how to guarantee that a program satisfies this principle. To start with, there is a need to do some foundational research concerning minimisation: What does it mean, formally? The idea would be to determine what are exactly the needed input to compute each possible output. This notion seems to be related to other concepts in information-flow security like *non-interference* [4]. It would be interesting to spell out the connection, if any. How to build programs satisfying data minimisation by construction? Or at least to find out how to check whether a program satisfies the principle. To find suitable answers to these questions is an interesting research direction.

Accountability is another important issue mostly now when third-party software is everywhere and finding liabilities is not easy. In the presence of a privacy breach, who is to be held responsible? How to find the component causing the breach, and thus the ultimate responsible? Keeping a log of all the system events seem an attractive solution, and might somehow help here. That said, keeping a log file could by itself be the cause of a privacy breach. A challenge here is to find good ways to log all the events of a system while protecting the log file, developing strong authentication techniques to control who may access it.

Cross-cutting the different phases in the personal data life cycle is that of ensuring that private data is well managed across multiple parties. Though our approach does try to help designing software that takes this into account, there still is the possibility that data is misused. One way to complement the PbD approach is to consider different kinds of runtime checking. In particular, one concrete interesting approach is *sticky policies*: attaching policies to data in order to constrain their use so the policies are respected. Some work has been done in this direction, notably in the context of the EnCoRe project [13], but more research is needed in order to make the approach part of the PbD process.

A different aspect of privacy is that of making queries to multiple databases and making inferences by aggregating information. One recent promising technique to guarantee that (some quantity of) privacy is preserved is *differential privacy* [8]. The theory establishes that by adding the right amount of noise to statistical queries, it is possible to get useful results at the same time as providing a quantifiable notion of privacy. Adding noise raises the issue of usability vs. privacy. Though there are few prototypical tools based on differential privacy, e.g. PINQ implementing the original idea [12], and the tool ProPer refining PINQ to individual records [9], there still is a gap between theory and practice [2]. More research is needed to make differential privacy practical.

6   Conclusion

In this paper we have outlined PA-DFD, a conceptual model based on an extension of DFDs with privacy concepts taken from the GDPR and the ISO 29100 standard. As discussed in Sect. 4, not all the privacy principles of the ISO standard are captured by our model, but it is encouraging to see that we do capture most of them in a direct way, while other principles can be captured by using added metadata. We are aware that our proposal does not solve all privacy issues related to design. However, our aim is to provide a first step towards a systematic precise methodology (supported by tools) to help software engineers to design software having privacy in mind. We envisage a tool where the engineer writes a DFD focusing only on the functional aspects, and the tool would automatically generate the PA-DFD. As discussed in Sect. 5, a lot remains to be done. We hope that more researchers and practitioners continue to address those (and other) issues to help towards suitable solutions to the privacy problem.

Acknowledgements. This research has been supported by the Swedish funding agency SSF under the grant *DataBIn: Data Driven Secure Business Intelligence*.

References

1. Abe, A., Simpson, A.: Formal models for privacy. In: EDBT/ICDT Workshops. CEUR Workshop Proceedings, vol. 1558 (2016). CEUR-WS.org
2. Bambauer, J., Muralidhar, K., Sarathy, R.: Fool's gold: an illustrated critique of differential privacy. Vanderbilt J. Entert. Tech. Law **16**(4), 701–755 (2014)
3. Cavoukian, A.: Privacy by design: origins, meaning, and prospects. In: Privacy Protection Measures and Technologies in Business Organisation: Aspects and Standards, p. 170 (2011)
4. Cohen, E.: Information transmission in computational systems. SIGOPS Oper. Syst. Rev. **11**(5), 133–139 (1977)
5. D'Acquisto, G., Domingo-Ferrer, J., Kikiras, P., Torra, V., de Montjoye, Y.A., Bourka, A.: Privacy by design in big data. ENISA report, December 2015
6. Danezis, G., Domingo-Ferrer, J., Hansen, M., Hoepman, J.H., Le Métayer, D., Tirtea, R., Schiffner, S.: Privacy and data protection by design. ENISA report, January 2015
7. Deng, M., Wuyts, K., Scandariato, R., Preneel, B., Joosen, W.: A privacy threat analysis framework: supporting the elicitation and fulfillment of privacy requirements. Requirements Eng. **16**(1), 3–32 (2010)
8. Dwork, C.: Differential privacy. In: Bugliesi, M., Preneel, B., Sassone, V., Wegener, I. (eds.) ICALP 2006. LNCS, vol. 4052, pp. 1–12. Springer, Heidelberg (2006)
9. Ebadi, H., Sands, D., Schneider, G.: Differential Privacy: Now it's Getting Personal. In: POPL 2015, pp. 69–81. ACM (2015)

10. European Commission: Proposal for a general data protection regulation. In: Codecision Legislative Procedure for a Regulation 2012/0011 (COD). European Commission, Brussels, Belgium, January 2012
11. Jensen, K., Kristensen, L.M.: Coloured Petri Nets: Modelling and Validation of Concurrent Systems. Springer Science & Business Media, Heidelberg (2009)
12. McSherry, F.D.: Privacy integrated queries: an extensible platform for privacy-preserving data analysis. In: ACM SIGMOD 2009, pp. 19–30. ACM (2009)
13. Pearson, S., Mont, M.C.: Sticky policies: an approach for managing privacy across multiple parties. IEEE Comput. 44(9), 60–68 (2011)
14. Petri, C.A.: Kommunikation mit automaten. Ph.D. thesis, Institut für instrumentelle Mathematik, Bonn (1962)
15. Shostack, A.: Threat Modeling: Designing for Security. Wiley, Hoboken (2014)
16. Stevens, W.P., Myers, G.J., Constantine, L.L.: Structured design. IBM Syst. J. 13(2), 115–139 (1974)
17. Tschantz, M.C., Wing, J.M.: Formal methods for privacy. In: Cavalcanti, A., Dams, D.R. (eds.) FM 2009. LNCS, vol. 5850, pp. 1–15. Springer, Heidelberg (2009)
18. Tsormpatzoudi, P., Berendt, B., Coudert, F.: Privacy by design: from research and policy to practice– the challenge of multi-disciplinarity. In: Berendt, B., et al. (eds.) APF 2015. LNCS, vol. 9484, pp. 199–212. Springer, Heidelberg (2016). doi:10.1007/978-3-319-31456-3_12
19. Warren, S.D., Brandeis, L.D.: The right to privacy. In: Harvard Law Review, pp. 193–220 (1890)

Guaranteeing Privacy-Observing Data Exchange

Christian W. Probst[✉]

Technical University of Denmark, Kongens Lyngby, Denmark
cwpr@dtu.dk

Abstract. Privacy is a major concern in large of parts of the world when exchanging information. Ideally, we would like to be able to have fine-grained control about how information that we deem sensitive can be propagated and used. While privacy policy languages exist, it is not possible to control whether the entity that receives data is living up to its own policy specification. In this work we present our initial work on an approach that empowers data owners to specify their privacy preferences, and data consumers to specify their data needs. Using a static analysis of the two specifications, our approach then finds a communication scheme that complies with these preferences and needs. While applicable to online transactions, the same techniques can be used in development of IT systems dealing with sensitive data. To the best of our knowledge, no existing privacy policy languages supports negotiation of policies, but only yes/no answers. We also discuss how the same approach can be used to identify a qualitative level of sharing, where data may be shared according to, *e.g.*, the level of trust to another entity.

1 Introduction

Privacy is a major concern in large of parts of the world when exchanging information. While we do not have control over, how our data is used in the real world, we would ideally like to be able to have that kind of fine-grained control about how information that we deem sensitive can be propagated and used in the cyber world. Privacy policy languages have been developed to this end, but it is not possible to control whether the entity that receives data is living up to its own policy specification. Techniques such as proof-carrying code enable servers to assure of properties of client code, but not the other way around.

In this work we present an approach that empowers data owners to specify their privacy preferences, and data consumers to specify their data needs. Our approach then finds a communication scheme that complies with these preferences and needs. Instead of relying on the data consumer to obey the data owner's preferences, this approach does only enable interactions that guarantee that the data is treated accordingly.

Using our approach, data owners specify whom they trust, and which items they want to share, with whom, and at which quality. If no sharing is specified for a specific entity, the trust hierarchy is queried, otherwise, sharing is prohibited. Data consumers specify their own trust hierarchy and the data they

© Springer International Publishing AG 2016
T. Margaria and B. Steffen (Eds.): ISoLA 2016, Part I, LNCS 9952, pp. 958–969, 2016.
DOI: 10.1007/978-3-319-47166-2_66

request at which quality. The quality of data is an important feature of our approach; it describes not only sharing/not sharing, but also shades in between these extremes. A picture, for example, can be shared in many different shades of quality, making it more or less useful to the recipient.

Based on the specifications, a resolution engine tries to identify a series of interactions that result in the exchange of the requested data, either directly, or at least as "functional" sharing. Functional sharing results in the data consumer obtaining the same information, just not the underlying data. For a credit card, for example, it would be possible to verify payments, but not to obtain the actual card number.

To the best of our knowledge, no existing privacy policy languages (PPLs) support this kind of negotiation of policies. Policy matching usually only checks that the data consumer's intentions of data usage and obligations are compliant with the data owner's preferences. While most PPLs are very powerful, we believe that our approach can be added to most of them to introduce policy negotiations; we are currently working on developing such an extension.

The remainder of this article is structured as follows. After a brief discussion of privacy policy languages in the next section, we present an overview of our framework in Sect. 3, followed by our approach to specifying data sharing preferences and data needs in (Sect. 4). These specifications are the input to the generation of joint strategies described in Sect. 5, followed in Sect. 5.2 by some considerations about the quality of shared data. Finally, we discuss the application of our approach to software system development in Sect. 6 and conclude the paper in Sect. 7 with an outlook on future work.

2   Privacy Policy Languages

Privacy policy languages (PPLs) [1] aim at representing an entity's policies in a computer-readable format, especially to make them available for policy enforcement. These languages exist both for data owners and data consumers, so that they can be employed to check whether a given web site lives up to a users privacy preferences or not. PPLs come in many different formats and with differing features, which makes them hard to compare [2].

The World Wide Web Consortium's (W3C) Platform for Privacy Preferences (P3P) aimed at representing websites' privacy policies in machine-readable format [3,4] in the P3P Preference Exchange Language (APPEL) [5]. Similar approaches exist for business-to-business communication [6], organisations' privacy concerns [7], and more generally access control languages [8]. Recent developments include the PrimeLife Privacy Language [1,9] and the Accountability Policy Language (A-PPL) [10].

To the best of our knowledge, neither of these languages supports negotiation of policies, but only yes/no answers. The PrimeLife Privacy Language [1,9], e.g., supports policy matching, but this matching does only check that the data consumer's intentions of data usage and obligations are compliant with the data owner's preferences. While most PPLs are very powerful, we believe that our approach can be added to most of them; we are currently working on developing such an extension.

3   Guaranteeing Observance of Privacy Specifications

In this section we describe the overall framework for our approach. The individual components will be described in more detail in the next sections.

The goal of the framework (Fig. 1) is to ensure that data owner and data consumer agree on a communication protocol that guarantees that the data owner's privacy preferences are observed, and that the data consumer's need for data is fulfilled. The main observation is that in many scenarios data consumers require a functional property of the data, not necessarily the data itself. For credit cards, for example, the essential information is not the credit card number, but the authorization for a payment.

Our framework consists of the data owner, the data consumer, and potentially a number of other components that are used, *e.g.*, for replacing data exchange with authorization exchange as in the example described above. Figure 1 shows the overall structure and the involved phases in our framework:

1. The data owner starts with requesting a service from a data consumer.
2. The data consumer requests in turn some data from the data owner, *e.g.*, credit card data or address.
3. The data owner replies with a privacy policy specification for the data requested. The data consumer combines its data needs with the data owner's privacy policy specification to compute a least upper bound, which observes the privacy specification and the data needs.
4. The data consumer sends back the protocol identified by the policy engine. The data owner checks that the protocol observes the privacy policy specification and initiates the protocol.

In each step any of the two parties can either cancel the communication if the step fails, *e.g.*, if the data owner does not want to share the requested data or if no acceptable protocol can be found, or can shortcut the framework, *e.g.*, if the data owner has no restrictions on sharing the requested data.

The essential component in our framework is the resolution engine, which takes the privacy policy specification from the data owner and the data needs specification from the data consumer, and generates a protocol that guarantees that the data owner's privacy preferences are observed, and that the data consumer's need for data is fulfilled. For credit card data this could result in using a trusted third party such as the credit card issuer.

The resolution engine is obviously part of the trusted code base; both the data owner and the data consumer, as well as other entities participating in the communication, must trust the engine. However, just as with proof-carrying code, each entity can check that the protocol identified by the resolution engine obeys the entity's preferences.

Another possibility in our approach is to allow *shaded* sharing of information, where data is shared fully with certain data consumers, not shared with other data consumers, and possibly in shades with others. An example application of shaded sharing are pictures, which a data owner might want to share in high

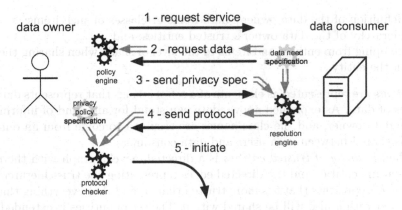

Fig. 1. Framework for guaranteeing observance of privacy specifications. The dark arrows show the flow of control, the gray arrows the flow of information.

resolution with family members, not at all with unknown entities, and in a low resolution with not so close acquaintances.

Before initiating the protocol from the resolution engine, the all entities can check whether the protocol proposed by the resolution engine actually complies with its privacy policy specification. Similar to proof carrying code [11], checking compliance of a protocol with preferences is easy. This step guarantees that data is only shared with parties approved by the data consumer, in a shading according to the privacy policy.

4   Specifying Preferences and Needs

In this section we describe the specification of privacy preferences and data needs by the data owner and the data consumer, respectively. These specifications are the input to the resolution engine, which generates a joint strategy that guarantees that the data owner's privacy preferences are observed, and that the data consumer's need for data is fulfilled.

In our current work, the specification of the data owner's privacy preferences consists of the user's data items, a hierarchy of the user's trusted entities, and a mapping from entities and items to shade of sharing. The data consumer's data needs are currently a pair of required data item and minimum level of shading, and a hierarchy of trusted entities. In all cases specific items and users can be abstracted by classes, e.g., a specific image could be replaced by the class "jpg file" or "image".

4.1   Data Owners' Privacy Preferences

In its privacy preferences, the data owner can specify, whom to share which data with in which quality. This specification is split up in three parts:

- A definition of the data owner's data items or classes of such items;
- A hierarchy of the data owner's trusted entities; and
- A mapping from entities and items to the level of shade when sharing the item with the entity.

The *items* are represented as elements of a set of strings that represents data and classes of data. As explained above, data can stand for any kind of information at the data owner, and the class names are assumed to come from an ontology that is shared between data users and data consumers.

The *hierarchy of trusted entities* is a directed, acyclic graph with the nodes representing entities and the directed edges representing the trust hierarchy. An edge (a, b) represents that b is more trusted than a, and that everything that will be shared with a also will be shared with b. The set of entities is extended with two special elements $\bot, \top \notin$ *Entities* that represent the untrusted or unknown entity ($\bot$) or the completely trusted entity ($\top$) (Table 1).

Finally, for each item and entity, the mapping *share* returns the shade of sharing for this item with this entity as a number between 0 and 1, with the extremes represent no sharing or unconstrained sharing, respectively. The semantics of the values in between depends on the kind of item; for images it might represent the quality of the file shared, for credit card data it may be undefined or require rounding, assuming that this data is shared or not Table 2.

Table 1. Specification of data owners' privacy preferences. The trust component is a directed acyclic graph between nodes representing entities or the untrusted ($\bot$) or completely trusted ($\top$) entities. The sharing level is specified as a number between 0 and 1, with the extremes representing no sharing (0) or unconstrained sharing (1), respectively. The semantics of the values in between depends on the kind of item; for images it might represent the quality of the file shared.

$$Items \quad \subseteq Data \cup Classes$$

$$Trust \quad := (N = Entities \cup \{\bot, \top\}, E = \{(s, t) \in N \cup \{\bot\} \times N \cup \{\top\}|s \neq t\}\wedge$$

$$\nexists 0 \leq k : \{(s_i, t_i) \in E, 1 \leq i \leq k | \forall 1 \leq j \leq k : s_j = t_{j-1} \wedge s_0 = t_k\}$$

$$share : Items \times Entities \rightarrow [0, 1]$$

$$share(i, e) := \begin{cases} 1 & \text{, if item } i \text{ is shared with } e \text{ without restrictions} \\ 0 < x < 1 & \text{, if item } i \text{ is shared with } e \text{ at level } x \\ 0 & \text{, if item } i \text{ is not shared with } e \end{cases}$$

4.2   Data Consumers' Data Needs

The data consumer specifies in its data needs, which data in which quality it requires to perform an operation. Like the privacy policy specification of the data owner, this specification is split up in three parts:

- A definition of the data consumer's data items or classes of such items;
- A hierarchy of the data consumer's trusted entities; and
- A mapping from items to the required minium level of shade when the item is shared by an entity.

The specifications of *items* and *trust* are identical for the data consumers' and data owners' specifications.

Finally, for each item, the mapping *need* returns the minium required shade of sharing for this item as a number between 0 and 1. The meaning of the extremal values are optional element (0) and mandatory element (1). As discussed for the sharing specification, the semantics of the values in between depends on the kind of item; all values represent a minimum quality of the shared data.

The specification of *need* can easily be extended to take other factors into account, *e.g.*, the entity sharing the data to enable personalized requirements, or a time factor to make the required quality dependent on the time since, *e.g.*, the last authentification of the entity.

Table 2. Specification of data consumers' data needs. The items and trust components are shared with data owners. The *need* component specifies the required level of sharing as a number between 0 and 1, with the extremes representing optional and required elements. As before, the semantics of the values in between depends on the kind of item.

$$Items \quad \subseteq Data \cup Classes$$

$$Trust \quad := (N = Entities \cup \{\bot, \top\}, E = \{(s,t) \in N \cup \{\bot\} \times N \cup \{\top\} | s \neq t\} \wedge$$

$$\not\exists 0 \leq k : \{(s_i, t_i) \in E, 1 \leq i \leq k | \forall 1 \leq j \leq k : s_j = t_{j-1} \wedge s_0 = t_k\}$$

$$need : Items \rightarrow [0..1]$$

$$need(i) := \begin{cases} 1 & \text{, if item } i \text{ is required} \\ 0 < x < 1 & \text{, if item } i \text{ is only required at level } x \\ 0 & \text{, if item } i \text{ is optional} \end{cases}$$

Table 3. Example specification for sharing of credit card information. Since the data owner is willing to share the information with the data consumer, this will result in direct communication.

data consumer	data owner
$need = \{(creditcard, 1)\}$	$share(shop, creditcard) = 1$

Table 4. Example specification for sharing of credit card information. In this case, the data owner is not willing to share the information with the data consumer, but with the bank, which is trusted by both parties.

data consumer	data owner
$need = \{(creditcard, 1)\}$	$share(shop, creditcard) = 0$
$trust = \{(\bot, bank), (bank, \top)\}$	$share(bank, creditcard) = 1$
	$trust = \{(\bot, bank), (bank, \top)\}$

5   Generating a Joint Strategy

As mentioned in the previous section, the resolution engine is at the centre of our approach (Fig. 1), as it guarantees the consolidation of the data owner's privacy policy specification and the data consumer's data needs. The main goal of the resolution engine is to map direct data sharing that is not permitted by the data owner's privacy policy to indirect data sharing, e.g., with a third party. In general, any entity participating in a data exchange can trigger the protocol negotiation, e.g., this could also be the data consumer.

The resolution engine takes a data consumer's data need specification and a data provider's privacy policy specification, and translates them into a constraint graph that contains entities as nodes and items as data. Tables 3 and 4 illustrate this in two cases for the credit card example. The data need specification states that the shop requires the credit card data from the customer. In the first specification, the data owner is explicitly mentioning the shop and is willing to share the credit card information. However, the privacy policy in the second case denies this sharing.

The resolution engine works lazily from the node representing the data consumer. Based on the data need, the entity from which the data is requested is added together with an edge. The resolution engine then searches for direct or indirect edges from the data owner to the data consumer. In the resulting graph, the resolution engine identifies all cycles, and computes their sharing sum, where edges from the data consumer count positive as obligations for the data owner, and edges from the data owner count negative as fulfillments of obligations.

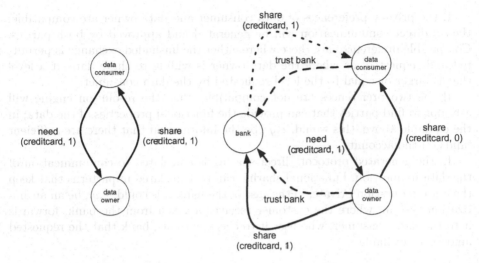

Fig. 2. Resulting graphs for the example specifications from Tables 3 and 4. In the left hand graph, the data owner shares the credit card data, so the resolution engine finds a circle that fulfils the data consumer's data need. In the right hand graph, the data owner does not share the credit card data. As a result, the resolution engine adds the bank node, since it is trusted by both the data consumer and owner, the edge of sharing the credit card, and eventually the edge back to the data consumer, indicating that here, only "functional" sharing is possible. The labels on the arrows indicate, which part of the privacy preference specification caused this edge to be added.

Figure 2 shows the two graphs resulting from the example specifications in Tables 3 and 4. The left hand graph represents the example where the data owner is willing to share the credit card information, while the right hand graph represents the result of several iterations. In the first iteration, the sum of the circle is not 0, since the data owner does not want to share the credit card information with the data consumer. As a result, the resolution engine adds the bank node, which is trusted by both parties. In the general case, this step may add several nodes, that lead to a node that transitively is shared by both parties. Since the data owner is willing to share the credit card data with the bank, this edge is added, leading to a situation where an edge is missing from the bank to the data consumer. Since the data consumer trusts the bank, the resolution engine adds a "functional" sharing edge from the bank to the data consumer, completing the circle and the sharing.

5.1   Properties of the Generated Protocols

The generated protocol is by construction acceptable by the data consumer and data owner (if a protocol is found). This fact is easily established by the translation mechanism from specifications to graph, and easily checked by the two parties once the protocol is shared.

If the privacy preferences of data consumer and data owner are compatible, then a direct communication will be generated and approved by both parties. Compatible preferences are those where either the unshaded exchange is permitted and requested, or where the data owner is willing to share data at a level that is larger or equal to the level requested by the data consumer.

If the two preferences are not compatible, then the resolution engine will attempt to find parties that can provide the functional properties of the data; in the example above, this would, *e.g.*, be the information that there are sufficient funds on the account.

In the generated protocol, direct sharing is translated to communication of the data in question. Functional sharing can be translated in patterns that keep the data in question private, in the case of the bank this could, *e.g.*, be an authorization system, where the customer receives a token from the bank, forwards it to the data consumer, who uses it to check with the bank that the requested amount is available.

5.2   Quality of Data Sharing

An important property of our approach is the ability to specify the quality of the data shared, or the shade of sharing. As discussed above, possible values are from $[0, 1]$, and range from no sharing, represented by 0, to complete or untampered sharing, represented by 1. The values between 0 and 1 do not have a predefined meaning beyond that an increase in sharing is represented by an increased value.

The meaning of values is first defined in relation to the kind of item being shared. For images, it might be the quality or the size of the shared picture, such that high shades result in close to perfect pictures, and low shades result in distorted versions of the picture. For data, often only 0 and 1 may make sense, even though values in between might represent that only part of the data is shared or requested, like for example in the case of credit card numbers, where only the last 4 numbers may be requested. The usefulness of this information depends again on the kind of data shared.

6   Guaranteeing Privacy in Software Systems

While our approach considers items and communicating parties in, *e.g.*, e-commerce systems, the approach fits equally well the development of software systems and guaranteeing privacy in the resulting system. When considering privacy in software systems, the data items in the discussion above are translated to the data the system is working on. The data consumer and data owner are, *e.g.*, translated to caller and callee, or data store and computation method.

Consider, for example, a robust versus a fragile implementation of a queue [12]. The fragile version would share a direct pointer to the information stored in the queue, giving the consumer of the pointer direct access to the data. The robust version, on the other hand, would select a token from a large token space, and would internally map the token to the real address of the data item in question. In principle, this is exactly the same situation as the credit card scenario described above: the pointer to the information is the credit card, the data owner is the queue algorithm, and the data consumer is a method that creates a queue. Since the pointer gives direct access to the information stored, the data owner should not want to share this information; instead, a hash map can be used to hide the concret information.

The same holds for limitting the risk that parts of an application pose towards properties of data such as availability or consistency. The data designer attaches negated criticality values to the data, and data sinks are annotated with the maximally acceptable level of criticality at each sink. If in the application there is a data flow from a highly critical piece of data, *e.g.*, of .9 translated to .1, to a sink with a lower level, *e.g.*, .5, then flow would trigger an alert.

By specifying, which level of such properties is required by parts of an application, we are currently working on identifying several such analogies between data privacy and ensuring privacy in software systems. Patterns such as the token that hides the concrete information can be generated automatically just like the functional sharing of credit card data. Also here we do not really require the concrete address of the data, but only a handle to obtain the information stored at the address.

7   Conclusion

In a world that increasingly depends on automated software systems that handle large parts of our sensitive data, we would like to have fine-grained control about how our sensitive information is handled, and where it might end up. Privacy policy languages cannot enforce that data recipients actually use the data in the way they have specified.

We have presented an approach that does not overcome this limitation, but that empowers data consumers and data owners to specify what they need and what they want to share; our framework then finds a protocol for exchange of this information that obeys the data owner's privacy policy specification, and fulfils the data consumer's data needs.

Using our approach, data owners specify whom they trust, and which items they want to share, with whom, and at which quality. If no sharing is specified for a specific entity, the trust hierarchy is queried, otherwise, sharing is prohibited. Data consumers specify their own trust hierarchy and the data they request at which quality. A resolution engine uses these specifications to compute a protocol that filfils all specified requirements and constraints. Currently, the generated protocol exchanges data either correctly (or in some shade), or as functional equivalent, where the data consumer does not get access to the data but only to its functionality – functional sharing results in the data consumer obtaining the same information, just not the underlying data. For a credit card, for example, it would be possible to verify payments, but not to obtain the actual card number. For email addresses, it would be possible to send the email through a relay server, but not directly.

7.1 Future Work

We have started to explore the quality of shared data. Instead of sharing/not sharing, parties in our approach can specify more fine grained how the want to share data with whom. We are currently working on modelling more systems for shades of sharing, also to develop a hierarchy of different shades to be applied. We also look at extending the specification of needs, for example, to add situational dependencies based on time or actor, and to add functional properties to share, not just the data itself. Last but not least we are currently looking at a re-implementation of our system in JIF [13], to compare our approach with information flow.

Acknowledgment. Part of the research leading to these results has received funding from the European Union Seventh Framework Programme (FP7/2007-2013) under grant agreement no. 318003 (TRE$_S$PASS). This publication reflects only the authors' views and the Union is not liable for any use that may be made of the information contained herein.

References

1. The PrimeLife Consortium: Policy Languages (2011). http://primelife.ercim.eu/images/stories/primer/policylanguage-plb.pdf. Accessed May 2016
2. Kumaraguru, P., Cranor, L., Lobo, J., Calo, S.: A survey of privacy policy languages. In: Proceedings of the Workshop on Usable IT Security Management (USM 2007) at Symposium on Usable Privacy and Security 2007 (2007)
3. Cranor, L.F.: Web Privacy with P3P. O'Reilly, Sebastopol (2002)
4. Cranor, L.F., Langheinrich, M., Marchiori, M., Presler-Marshall, M., Reagle, J.: The platform for privacy preferences 1.0 (2002). http://www.w3.org/TR/P3P. Accessed May 2016
5. Cranor, L.F., Langheinrich, M., Marchiori, M.: A p3p preference exchange language 1.0 (2002). http://www.w3.org/TR/P3P-preferences. Accessed May 2016
6. Bohrer, K., Holland, B.: Customer profile exchange (cpexchange) specification, v1.0. Technical report, International Digital Enterprise Alliance, Inc. (2000). http://xml.coverpages.org/cpexchangev1_0F.pdf. Accessed May 2016
7. Ashley, P., Hada, S., Karjoth, G., Powers, C., Schunter, M.: Enterprise privacy authorization language, v1.2. Technical report, IBM (2003). http://www.zurich.ibm.com/security/enterprise-privacy/epal. Accessed May 2016
8. Rissanen, E.: eXtensible Access Control Markup Language (XACML), v3.0. Technical report, OASIS standard (2013). http://docs.oasis-open.org/xacml/3.0/xacml-3.0-core-spec-os-en.html. Accessed May 2016
9. Trabelsi, S., Neven, G., Raggett, D.: Primelife privacy policy langauge (PPL) and engine - report on design and implementation. Technical report D5.3.4, The PrimeLife Consortium (2011). http://primelife.ercim.eu/images/stories/deliverables/d5.3.4-report_on_design_and_implementation-public.pdf. Accessed May 2016
10. Azraou, M., Elkhiyaoui, K., Önen, M., Bernsmed, K., de Oliveira, A.S., Sendor, J.: A-PPL: an accountability policy language. Technical report RR-14-294, EURECOM (2014)

11. Necula, G.C.: Proof-carrying code. In: Proceedings of the 24th ACM SIGPLAN-SIGACT Symposium on Principles of Programming Languages, POPL 1997, pp. 106–119. ACM, New York (1997)
12. Bishop, M.: Robust programming. http://nob.cs.ucdavis.edu/bishop/secprog/robust.html. Accessed May 2016
13. Myers, A.C., Liskov, B.: A decentralized model for information flow control. In: Proceedings of the Sixteenth ACM Symposium on Operating Systems Principles, SOSP 1997, pp. 129–142. ACM, New York (1997)

Erratum to: Leveraging Applications of Formal Methods, Verification and Validation (Part I)

Tiziana Margaria[1]([⊠]) and Bernhard Steffen[2]

[1] Lero, Limerick, Ireland
tiziana.margaria@lero.ie
[2] TU Dortmund, Dortmund, Germany

Erratum to:
T. Margaria and B. Steffen (Eds.)
Leveraging Applications of Formal Methods,
Verification and Validation (Part I)
DOI: 10.1007/978-3-319-47166-2

In the initially published version of chapter 61 of Part II (Leveraging Applications of Formal Methods, Verification and Validation), two author names were erroneously omitted. This has been updated. Consequently, the Table of Contents and the Author Index have also been updated in this volume (LNCS 9952), Part I (Leveraging Applications of Formal Methods, Verification and Validation).

The updated original online version for this Book can be found at 10.1007/978-3-319-47166-2

T. Margaria and B. Steffen (Eds.): ISoLA 2016, Part I, LNCS 9952, p. E1, 2016.
DOI: 10.1007/978-3-319-47166-2_67

Author Index

à Tellinghusen, Danilo   II-380
Abd Alrahman, Yehia   I-539
Abdellatif, Takoua   I-893
Abdelzad, Vahdat   II-187
Ábrahám, Erika   I-496
Adami, Kristian Zarb   II-400
Adesina, Opeyemi   II-187
Ahmad, Abbas   II-727
Ahmad, Waheed   I-94
Ahrendt, Wolfgang   I-402
Ait-Ameur, Yamine   I-340
Aït-Sadoune, Idir   I-321
Amme, Wolfram   I-227
Antignac, Thibaud   I-942
Antkiewicz, Michał   II-447
Aotani, Tomoyuki   II-80
Arora, Shiraj   I-62
Azzopardi, Shaun   I-416

Badreddin, Omar   II-50
Bagge, Anya Helene   I-517
Baier, Christel   II-598
Bainczyk, Alexander   II-655
Barthe, Gilles   II-601
Bartocci, Ezio   I-46, II-333, II-371
Basile, Davide   II-315
Batista, Thais   I-806
Baum, Kevin   II-633
Beckert, Bernhard   I-749
Bellatreche, Ladjel   I-358
Bensalem, Saddek   I-605, I-893
Berkani, Nabila   I-358
Berry, G.   II-134
Bessai, Jan   I-266, I-303
Beyer, Dirk   I-191, I-195, I-874
Binder, Walter   II-531
Biondi, Fabrizio   I-883
Bodden, Eric   I-431
Bonakdarpour, Borzoo   II-363
Bormer, Thorsten   I-749
Bos, Herbert   II-609
Boßelmann, Steve   II-757, II-809
Bouquet, Fabrice   II-727
Bozga, Marius   I-605, I-893

Brinkkemper, Sjaak   II-609
Broy, Manfred   II-3, II-238
Bueno, Marcos L.P.   I-134
Bures, Tomas   I-642
Butterfield, Andrew   I-374

Camilleri, Luke   II-400
Carmona, Josep   I-784
Cavalcante, Everton   I-806
Cheng, Zheng   I-821
Chesta, Cristina   II-497
Ciancia, Vincenzo   I-657
Cleophas, Loek   I-730, I-766
Colombo, Christian   I-416, II-400
Czarnecki, Krzysztof   II-447
Czwink, Amir   I-622

D'Argenio, Pedro R.   II-601
Damiani, Ferruccio   II-423, II-497, II-579
De Angelis, Francesco Luca   I-589
de Boer, Pieter-Tjerk   I-16
De Nicola, Rocco   I-539
de Vink, Erik P.   I-856
Delange, Julien   I-926
Di Giandomenico, Felicita   II-315
Di Marzo Serugendo, Giovanna   I-589, I-714
Dimech, Claire   II-400
DiStefano, Dino   I-909
Djilani, Zouhir   I-358
Dobriakova, Liudmila   II-497
Düdder, Boris   I-261, I-266, I-303
Dudenhefner, Andrej   I-266

Eilertsen, Anna Maria   I-517
Elaasar, Maged   II-50
Elmqvist, Hilding   II-198

Falcone, Ylies   II-333
Fantechi, Alessandro   II-261, II-279, II-465
Farrugia, Reuben   II-400
Feiler, Peter   I-926
Felderer, Michael   II-704, II-707
Ferrari, Alessio   II-261, II-297

Fetzer, Christof II-626
Finkbeiner, Bernd II-601
Fischer, Joachim II-119
Fitzgerald, John II-171
Foidl, Harald II-707
Foster, Simon I-374, II-171
Fourneret, Elizabeta II-727
Fraigniaud, Pierre II-363
Frohme, Markus II-809

Gamble, Carl II-171
Geske, Maren II-787
Gibson, J. Paul I-321
Gilmore, S. I-674
Gnesi, Stefania II-261, II-315, II-465
Goodloe, Alwyn I-446
Grahl, Daniel I-749
Grech, Jean Paul II-400
Groote, Jan Friso II-609
Grosu, Radu I-46, II-371
Guernieri, Marco II-497
Gurov, Dilian I-397

Hacid, Kahina I-340, II-747
Hähnle, Reiner I-723, II-433
Hallé, Sylvain II-356
Havelund, Klaus I-397, II-3, II-238, II-339,
    II-394
Haxthausen, Anne E. II-32, II-266, II-279
Heineman, George T. I-261, I-303
Heinrichs, Robert I-622
Heinze, Thomas S. I-227
Hennicker, Rolf I-570
Henningsson, Toivo II-198
Hermanns, Holger II-598, II-601
Hessenkämper, Axel II-754, II-757
Hillston, J. I-674
Hinchey, Mike I-689
Hnetynka, Petr I-642
Holthusen, Sönke I-839
Howar, Falk II-651, II-672, II-787
Huisman, Marieke I-397, II-609
Husseini Orabi, Ahmed II-187
Husseini Orabi, Mahmoud II-187

Iftikhar, M. Usman I-243
Isberner, Malte II-655

Jähnichen, Stefan I-535, I-622, I-639
Jaksic, Stefan II-371

James, Phillip II-294
Jansen, Nils I-496
Jasper, Marc I-212, II-787
Javed, Omar II-531
Jegourel, C. I-46
Johnsen, Einar Broch II-482
Jörges, Sven I-282
Joshi, Rajeev II-394

Kahil, Rany I-605
Kalajdzic, K. I-46
Karsai, Gábor II-68
Kauffman, Sean II-394
Kecskés, Tamás II-68
Khalilov, Eldar II-447
Khoury, Raphaël II-356
Kleijn, Jetty I-784
Kopetzki, Dawid II-809
Kosmatov, Nikolai I-461
Kourie, Derrick G. I-730, I-766
Křetínský, Jan I-27
Krijt, Filip I-642
Küçükay, Ferit II-688
Kugler, Hillel II-131
Kumar, Rahul II-3, II-238

Lago, Patricia II-609
Lal, Ratan II-833
Laleau, Régine I-325
Lamprecht, Anna-Lena I-282, II-744
Larsen, Kim G. I-3, II-843
Larsen, Peter Gorm II-171
Latella, Diego I-657
Lattmann, Zsolt II-68
Le Gall, Franck II-727
Leavens, Gary T. II-80
Lédeczi, Ákos II-68
Legay, Axel I-3, I-46, I-77, I-114, I-806,
    I-883, II-843
Legeard, Bruno II-727
Lemberger, Thomas I-195
Leofante, Francesco I-496
Lethbridge, Timothy C. II-187
Leucker, Martin I-515, II-380
Lienhardt, Michael II-579
Lin, Jia-Chun II-482
Linard, Alexis I-134
Lluch Lafuente, Alberto I-114
Loreti, Michele I-539

Lukina, A. I-46
Lundberg, Jonas I-191, I-243
Lybecait, Michael II-809

Macedo, Hugo D. II-279
Magro, Alessio II-400
Malacaria, Pasquale I-909
Mammar, Amel I-325
Marché, Claude I-461
Margaria, Tiziana I-282, II-218, II-655
Margheri, Andrea I-554
Mariani, Leonardo II-388
Martens, Moritz I-266
Martini, Simone II-497
Massink, Mieke I-657
Matena, Vladimir I-642
Mauritz, Malte II-672
Mauro, Jacopo II-563
Mazzanti, Franco II-297
Mehlhase, Alexandra I-622
Meijer, Patrik II-68
Meinke, Karl II-651
Méry, Dominique I-821
Michel, Malte II-774
Moller, Faron II-294
Møller-Pedersen, Birger II-119
Monahan, Rosemary I-397, I-821
Motika, Christian II-150
Moy, Yannick I-461
Muschevici, Radu II-433

Nam, Min-Young I-926
Naujokat, Stefan I-282, II-218, II-774,
    II-809
Naumann, David II-80
Neubauer, Johannes II-218, II-655, II-809
Nguyen, Hoang Nga II-294
Nguyen, Thang II-371
Ničković, Dejan II-371
Nieke, Michael I-839, II-497, II-563
Nielson, Flemming I-554
Nielson, Hanne Riis I-554
Nilsson, René II-171

Oquendo, Flavio I-806
Østergaard, Peter H. II-266
Otter, Martin II-198

Pace, Gordon J. I-402, I-416, II-400, II-407
Pantel, Marc I-321

Pardo, Raúl II-407
Paškauskas, Rytis I-657
Pastore, Fabrizio II-388
Peled, Doron I-182
Peleska, Jan II-32
Pieterse, Vreda I-766
Plasil, Frantisek I-642
Poplavko, Peter I-605
Prabhakar, Pavithra II-833
Prinz, Andreas II-119
Probst, Christian W. I-958
Pugliese, Rosario I-554
Pun, Ka I. I-431

Qi, Xiaofei II-688
Quilbeuf, Jean I-806

Rabiser, Daniela II-512
Rajan, Hridesh II-80
Rajsbaum, Sergio II-363
Rao, M.V. Panduranga I-62
Rausch, Andreas II-651, II-672, II-688
Reger, Giles I-479, II-339
Rehof, Jakob I-261, I-266, I-303
Reijsbergen, Daniël I-16
Reniers, Michel A. I-856
Rodrigues, Vítor II-497
Roggenbach, Markus II-294
Rosà, Andrea II-531
Ross, Jordan II-447
Rouquette, Nicolas F. II-97
Ruijters, Enno I-151
Rybicki, Francesca II-150

Said, Najah Ben I-893
Sammut, Andrew C. II-400
Scandariato, Riccardo I-942
Schaefer, Ina I-723, I-730, I-766, I-839,
    II-547
Scheinhardt, Werner I-16
Schieferdecker, Ina II-704
Schieweck, Alexander II-655
Schmitz, Malte II-380
Schneider, Gerardo I-402, I-942, II-407,
    II-413
Schordan, Markus I-191, I-212, II-787
Schudeleit, Mark II-688
Schulze, Sandro II-547
Schulz-Rosengarten, Alexander II-150
Schuster, Sven II-497

Sedwards, Sean   I-77
Seidewitz, Ed   II-27
Seidl, Christoph   II-423, II-512, II-547,
     II-563
Selić, Bran   II-11
Selyunin, Konstantin   II-371
Semini, Laura   II-465
Signoles, Julien   I-461
Smolka, S.A.   I-46
Smyth, Steven   II-150
Socci, Dario   I-605
Soto, Miriam Garcia   II-833
Spagnolo, Giorgio O.   II-297
Stănciulescu, Ştefan   II-512
Steffen, Barbara   II-757
Steffen, Bernhard   I-282, II-3, II-218, II-655,
     II-787, II-809
Steffen, Martin   I-431
Stoelinga, Mariëlle   I-151
Stolz, Volker   I-431, I-517
Strnadel, Josef   I-166
Sun, Haiyang   II-531

Tacchella, Armando   I-496
Tautchning, Michael   I-909
ter Beek, Maurice H.   I-114, I-723, I-784,
     I-856, II-465
Thüm, Thomas   I-839
Tiede, Michael   II-547
Traonouez, Louis-Marie   I-77, I-806

Travers, Corentin   II-363
Treharne, Helen   II-294

van de Pol, Jaco   I-94, II-609, II-787
van Deursen, Arie   II-609
Vandin, Andrea   I-114, I-657
Vassev, Emil   I-689, I-704
Visser, Eelco   II-609
Völgyesi, Péter   II-68
Völter, Markus   II-447
von Hanxleden, Reinhard   II-150
Vuotto, Simone   I-496

Waldmann, Omar   II-356
Wang, Xu   II-294
Watson, Bruce W.   I-730, I-766
Weidenbach, Christoph   II-626
Weyns, Danny   I-243
Wickert, Anna-Katharina   I-431
Wille, David   II-547
Wirkner, Dominic   II-809
Wirsing, Martin   I-535, I-639
Wischnewski, Patrick   II-626
Woodcock, Jim   I-374, II-171
Wortmann, Nils   II-774

Yu, Ingrid Chieh   II-423, II-482, II-563

Zhang, Meng   II-688
Zheng, Yudi   II-531
Zoń, N.   I-674
Zweihoff, Philip   II-809

Printed in the United States
By Bookmasters